CONQUER YOUR FEARS

GO WHERE YOU WANT TO GO, DO WHAT YOU WANT TO DO... WITH COMFORT AND CONFIDENCE

E. Wayne Hart, Ph.D.

With Diane Craver, M.S.

Lisa Armstrong, M.A.

**CONQUER YOUR FEARS
SELF-IMPROVEMENT MATERIALS**

SKILLS FOR REDUCING WORRY, STRESS, FEAR, & ANXIETY

Accelerated Development Inc., Publishers
Muncie, Indiana

CONQUER YOUR FEARS

Go Where You Want to Go, Do What You Want to Do...

with Comfort and Confidence

Technical Development: Cynthia Long

Marguerite Mader

Sheila Sheward

Library of Congress Cataloging-in-Publication Data

Hart, E. Wayne, 1945-
   Conquer your fears : go where you want to go, do what you want to do— with comfort and confidence / E. Wayne Hart with Diane Craver, Lisa Armstrong.
        p.   cm.
   Includes index.
   ISBN 1-55959-061-0
   1. Fear. 2. Anxiety. 3. Worry. 4. Stress (Psychology)
5. Stress management. I. Craver, Diane. II. Armstrong, Lisa.
III. Title.
BF575.F2H247 1994   94-400
152.4' 6—dc20   CIP

LCN: 94-400
ISBN: 1-55959-061-0

Order additional copies from

ACCELERATED DEVELOPMENT INC., Publishers
3808 West Kilgore Avenue
Muncie, Indiana 47304-4896
Toll Free Order Number 1-800-222-1166

Dedications

♦ To my patients, who wanted my help. Thanks for trying new things. Keep doing the Steps!

♦ To my mother, Darlene Hart, who wanted me to be a teacher. You encouraged me to have confidence in myself and concern for the welfare of others. Bless you.

♦ To my father, Dr. Edward Hart, who wanted me to be a doctor. You taught that if a job is worth doing, it is worth doing right, and that good treatment means enabling the body to heal itself. Thank you.

♦ And to Melody, who wanted a family. You made a good home for me.
I apologize for the time you sacrificed while I worked. I wish you well.

Acknowledgements

Many of the ideas presented have their roots in the work of fine clinicians and researchers who have come before me. I am grateful to them for their pioneering work. Notable among them is Eric Berne, M.D., who developed the concepts of Transactional Analysis. These underlie the content of many chapters as well as the learning philosophy of the entire workbook. Also, from the same school of thought, the work of Taibi Kahler, Ph.D., on Drivers, contributed to the chapters on People-pleasing, Perfection-seeking, and Being-strong.

Diane Craver, M.S., assisted with extensive literature review, field testing, problem solving, and editing. Her contribution was very significant, and distinguished her as a scientist and clinician.

Lisa Armstrong, M.A., helped with editing and development of "Comments on the Exercises." Her loyalty and diligence got us across the finish line. Her clinical sensitivity brought clarity to many points.

TABLE OF CONTENTS

Introduction

HOW IT ALL STARTED

TREATMENT

On a warm and sunny afternoon in the last month of my psychology internship, I entered the clinic lobby to meet a new patient. I was about to meet two patients who would launch my 15-year quest to learn how to teach people to reduce worry, stress, fear, and anxiety.

Sitting on the lobby sofa was a young girl. To estimate her age, at first, was hard, because her face was buried in a paper bag. She looked about 14 years old.

At first I wasn't sure what to make of the bag. My first impression was based on having seen people do something like that on airplanes.

I could see that she was not heaving or nauseous. Instead, she was breathing heavily into the bag. She was frenzied and almost hysterical as she intently collapsed and then inflated the bag. What could account for the girl's rapid breathing? Why was she using a sack? What do I do with this?

Sitting next to her was Mother, who stood up as I introduced myself. She offered her name and pointed to the young girl, indicating her daughter's name. Mother seemed frazzled, tensely held together, and worn down. Her face looked weary and worried; she was forming bags under her eyes. Nevertheless, she was poised and well dressed and groomed. She just looked frazzled around the edges, like a new car that needed a wash.

Mother behaved in an intense and preoccupied manner. She was wringing her hands from the moment she stood up. It was not a dramatic or exaggerated gesture; it was more like her hands needed something to do. Maybe they were holding things together. I had compassion for her. I thought, "I'd be worried too if my daughter was breathing into a paper bag."

After introductions, I invited them into my office. Daughter pulled the bag down from her face to follow her mother into the office. She seemed to be fighting back tears. She held her breath against convulsions in her chest and then desperately gasped for air several times. Then she held her breath again.

I invited them to sit. There was a long silence. No one took initiative for what happened next. Mother became noticeably uncomfortable with the lack of structure. Daughter's face soon was buried in the paper bag again. I suggested Mother tell me why they had come to the clinic.

With relief, Mother began to tell the story. She explained that her daughter had started the ninth grade and a new high school six months ago. She was exposed to many new friends. Daughter had started worrying what other kids were thinking about her, and how she was doing on assignments and tests. The worry seemed to erupt into these "anxiety attacks," as Mother's doctor had called them.

When the attacks hit, Daughter suddenly became terrified as if she were going to die. From a baseline of mild anxiety or even a relaxed state, she would skyrocket into full-blown fear with all the autonomic nervous system responses to go with it, like pounding heart, rapid breathing, sweaty palms, and a dry mouth.

Mother was afraid that something was wrong with her daughter. I tried to relieve her concern by telling her that I would evaluate the situation and help her understand the problem. That helped some, but not much.

Mother went on to tell about the girl's father. He was gone a great deal on business and had expressed considerable concern that this condition had gone on for three months and was getting worse instead of better. Mother was worried that it would interfere with his concentration at work.

Seeing that Mother was distressed about the welfare of yet another person, I tried once again to reduce her misery. I explained that I would be glad to speak with her husband about the situation in person or over the phone at his convenience. I told her we could schedule an appointment to do so. I encouraged her not to take on responsibility for relaying information unless she wanted to. This helped too, but just a little.

Mother changed the subject again, this time to her worry that she must have done something wrong as a mother. I could see that she was prone to blaming herself, probably for everything.

Again, I tried to be give her relief. I said it was likely that these problems were unrelated to flaws in parenting and that I would be able to give her concrete information on that when I had finished an evaluation.

During the session, Daughter's rapid breathing slowed. She never surrendered the paper sack, but she occasionally lowered it from her face for short periods. She looked more relaxed as time passed but not the least bit happy about being in my office.

I tried, with little success, to draw Daughter out. "How are things at school?" "How are things at home?" "Tell me about your friends." I got short, vague, empty answers. She held onto the bag, and that was it. I hoped she would open up next time.

I scheduled an initial series of five private sessions with the young girl. She looked apprehensive about coming to the office alone. So, I reassured her she could bring her paper bag. She seemed to like that.

In the next session, Daughter and I began by exploring how she felt. Clearly she was aware only of worrying, which I explained is really a thought process and not a feeling at all. She indicated little experience of an emotion except when she had her panic attacks and she felt like she was going to die. She reported no other feelings. We returned to this topic each session. I probed and explored at deeper levels. In time she began to recognize that in addition to her fears, she was actually quite frustrated and angry.

We also explored what her life had been like. In time she revealed that she had spent her whole life trying to please her mother and father, and trying to take care of everything in the family. She had two younger brothers, and she tried to "keep them in line" while Mother and Father were at work. She worried about her performance at school a great deal because she wanted to go to college, and she feared that her grades would be too low. She thought none of the other kids liked her, although she tried everything she could think of to fit in. She felt trapped and overwhelmed about all this. "I can't get control of it," she blurted out in tears.

Daughter thought there was no place for emotions. She thought she should be strong and not let all the pressure get to her. She began to see that she just bottled her emotions inside of herself.

From Mother I learned Daughter was never a problem at home or school. School confirmed that her attendance, her social functioning, and her academic performance were all at above average levels. Daughter didn't complain about being restricted by her parents, or unfairly punished, or having too much expected of her. She only complained that she never did anything for herself. In time she described feeling deprived and isolated because of this.

Yet, this young lady was angry because it seemed to her that she was doing all those things because she had no choice. She wasn't living her own life. She didn't know how to channel her anger into asserting herself.

By the end of the first five private sessions, I understood what caused Daughter's anxiety. There were three factors. One was control. She didn't feel like she had enough, and she stressed herself out trying to get it. She did this by pleasing people, being strong, trying to do everything right, and trying to make everything and everybody the way they should be. It was as though if she did everything right and met everybody else's needs, she wouldn't have to worry about anything going wrong.

But she did worry, and she pushed; thus, she neglected her own desires and interests as she catered to what she thought others wanted. This created stress. The second factor was the tension she held inside because of all this control behavior. She had no way to release it.

Feeling out of control and tense caused Daughter to lose confidence in herself. And she began to see others as demanding and intolerant. This was the third factor, a negative attitude about herself, others, and life in general. We concluded that these forces combined to erupt periodically like a volcano in the form of her anxiety attacks, which were actually "panic attacks."

As Daughter came to understand these factors, she felt hope and became more calm. We agreed that by continuing treatment, she could learn more and master skills for reducing her distress. We continued meeting for another 15 sessions.

Armed with new understanding, treatment continued with teaching new ways to think and act. From the start I had taught her a variety of relaxation techniques, including slow, steady breathing. These efforts were not as helpful as hoped. We began to focus on the first factor- - control.

She learned the limits of what she should try to control. She learned to accept that she couldn't control things that fell beyond those limits. And, she learned to set limits to her control-seeking behavior so that she wouldn't try to control those things that couldn't be controlled. She also learned to limit her efforts to please others, be strong, and do things perfectly.

Setting limits to control-seeking reduced some tension, but not enough. We began working on ways to channel tension and emotions into problem solving. She learned to take full responsibility for doing what she could do. She began taking control of the things that she could, in fact, control. These had to do with her own thoughts, feelings, and actions.

One helpful subject was channeling emotions into problem solving through identifying what she really valued and taking action to achieve her values. She also learned to channel her emotions, especially anger, into assertiveness and self-discipline. I recommended experiments that helped her get in touch with her anger and express it through practice exercises. Soon she was able to experience her emotions with relative ease. I then helped her understand what her emotions meant. I helped her recognize how they pointed toward her values, and that these were important parts of her to recognize and to validate.

We found that she could prevent panic attacks by being angry and releasing tension through aggressive breathing out. First I taught her to express her anger directly through things like telling off an imaginary someone or pounding with a towel. This helped some. Then we discovered that she could prevent or stop the rapid breathing attacks if she just breathed out hard, the way she would if she were angry. I never saw the paper bag again.

Gradually, while working on these issues, Daughter's attitude improved. She began to feel better about herself and others. She was happier about life.

About midway through Daughter's treatment, Mother came in to see me for a private session. She looked about the same as before. She was still worried. She began by expressing her concerns that her daughter seemed to be getting more emotional lately. She seemed to get upset easily, and on a few occasions she had raised her voice. She never had called names or used foul language, but she had complained angrily about too much being expected of her and that it was her turn for a change.

I tried to relieve Mother. First I asked about the frequency of panic attacks. Mother conceded that there had been none lately. I explained to her that her daughter's behavior was a predictable and positive development in the treatment process. I explained to her that if her daughter learned to feel and express her emotions in productive ways, she would develop a sense of personal control in life and release a lot of tension. The combination of these things ultimately would make her feel better about herself and better about other people as well.

Mother looked confused. There was a definite change in her demeanor. She sat up and back. She stopped wringing her hands. Her state of mind improved as she began to deal with her confusion about what I had said. She began to reveal her conflicts about letting Daughter be herself and needing Daughter to be okay.

As we explored the issues in various ways, I noticed that she sustained this confused state for about five minutes. Then she again changed the subject to concern about her husband's distress over Daughter's emotional behavior. She again leaned forward and began wringing her hands. She was worried again.

I had an interesting opportunity to compare two behavioral states--one of worry and one of confusion rooted in conflict. I encouraged her to face her mixed thoughts and feelings rather than trying to make others OK. This took mother by surprise. She was accustomed to avoiding her conflicts by worrying about family. "Let go," I insisted.

Mother relaxed some, or was she surrendering? She was confused about this letting go stuff. I recommended we see each other two or three times so that I could help her with her confusion. She must have liked being confused better than being worried, because she agreed to meet with me a few times.

In talking together, we discovered that while Mother was conscious of being worried all the time, she, like Daughter, rarely experienced her fear as an emotion. Further, she rarely experienced other emotions in a real and concrete way. She began talking about how her parents had been alcoholics. She had to take care of them. She devised rigid rules for living as a means of feeling in control, like never talking about how she felt. This sheltered her from feeling like any love or approval she got was conditional upon her performing well in the caretaker role. We also discovered that except for alcoholism, Mother had created the same family atmosphere for Daughter.

As I probed, we discovered that she really felt sad and disappointed that her life had not been fulfilling in other ways. She insisted there was no one else to blame, but complained of a sense of emptiness and grief that it hadn't been different. She gave all kinds of reasons why she had to follow the course in life that she followed, which she described as "part-time homemaker and overtime real estate agent."

It seems that Mother had been strong, responsible, and loyal. She looked out for the welfare of others, and she paid little attention to what she really wanted. She wasn't even clear what she really wanted. As a result, she wasn't sure that she had accomplished anything of true value in life, and this caused her a great deal of distress and tension.

Further, it caused her to feel poorly about herself and, at a deeper level, to resent other people for having taken so much and given so little. We worked to identify what these emotions meant, and as she discovered the values of self-expression that lay behind, she began channeling those emotions into identifying pursuits where she could express herself in constructive and meaningful ways.

In order to pursue this course of action, she had to take personal control by setting limits to what she did on behalf of others and disciplining herself to take measures on her own behalf. As she began implementing behaviors of this type, she felt a great release of tension, and it was replaced by enthusiasm for life.

Seeing herself as more successful, she began to like herself better and have less complaints about the ingratitude of others. She was still confused from time to time, but mostly she was enthusiastic. Rarely did she worry, and when she did I let her languish in the misery until she got herself out of it. She reached a point where she changed gears rather quickly when worry started setting in.

DISCUSSION

Both Mother and Daughter presented elements of background and behavior that I have since found to cause worry, stress, fear, and anxiety for many people. Certain family themes create certain personality traits. Together, these cause behavior that leads to "feeling out of control," holding tension inside until the point of overload, and sinking into a negative attitude about self, others, and life in general.

At the root of these conditions is a negative attitude toward life. This includes bad feelings about one's own adequacy and worth, and these are experienced as "I am Not Okay." Then there are negative feelings about how others let them down, expect too much, and mistreat them. This constitutes "They are Not Okay." There are also complaints about how circumstances have taken unwanted turns. This takes the form of "It's Not Okay."

These "Not Okay" emotions have their roots in a sense of isolation and helplessness. This isolation and helplessness comes from the tension that creates a barrier between us and others. This tension builds when we are preoccupied with things outside of ourselves that we can't control. Feeling out of control provokes various kinds of worrying, which in turn creates stress. As the person behaves artificially in order to try to regain a sense of control, further deterioration occurs in self-esteem because of more perceived failure and inadequacy.

These forces combine to create various forms of fear, whether the emotion is experienced or not. They also promote loss of awareness of self in such forms as our values and emotions, goals and priorities, and achievement consistent with these factors.

Treatment involves the mobilization of emotions in the form of self-clarification and problem solving. This problem solving usually involves setting limits to personal control of one's own perfection-seeking, being strong, and people-pleasing behaviors, and asserting themselves in productive ways, pursuing goals based on personal values.

From these efforts comes a heightened sense of personal control and with that, a release of tension in the direction of these constructive efforts. The effect of all of this is an improved sense of self-esteem and improved attitude toward others and external events. As a result, we end up with a positive attitude. The combination of a positive attitude, a sense of Personal Control and outlets for tension go together to create an overall sense of peace of mind.

WHERE IT ALL LED

GENERALLY, WHAT'S THE CYF WORKBOOK LIKE?

OVERVIEW

The workbook consists of learning exercises. Psychological, social, and life-style issues are dealt with to help the participant alter attitudes and behaviors that have been contributing to worry, stress, fear, and anxiety.

The workbook was designed so that you may start the lessons anywhere in the series and complete the lessons in any order. But remember, all the lessons reinforce each other. So, be sure you do them all, and that you review each lesson regularly over the course of time. Keep repeating your cycle.

A key feature built into the workbook is carefully designed and researched homework assignments that keep your learning process active and productive over time. Do the homework exercises in between reviews of lessons.

GOALS OF THE WORKBOOK

The mission of the *Conquer Your Fears* workbook is teaching participants to reduce worry, stress, fear, and anxiety. We believe this is possible if people take control of their own behavior (thoughts, feelings, and actions). Participants learn to have Personal Control, release tension, and develop positive attitudes through developing an understanding of

1.   the nature of worry, stress, fear, and anxiety;

2.   the causes of worry, stress, fear, and anxiety;

3.   how our family background and personality traits can predispose us to (set us up for) worry, stress, fear, and anxiety;

4. how to reduce or relax worry, stress, fear, and anxiety when they start; and

5. how to prevent worry, stress, and fear from starting.

WHO BENEFITS FROM THE WORKBOOK?

The workbook has been successful with teenagers over the age of 14 and adults up to the age of 60. It has helped people with uncomfortable, distressing, and disabling worry, stress, fear, and anxiety. Many people with depression have found the lessons helpful. The chapters present lessons that have universal appeal.

HOW DOES THE WORKBOOK HELP PEOPLE?

The *Conquer Your Fears* workbook helps people reduce and eliminate worry, stress, fear, and unnatural levels of anxiety. It helps people overcome panic attacks and phobias (especially agoraphobia). It also helps people overcome other anxiety related symptoms like flashbacks, nightmares, sleep disruptions, and obsessive compulsive behavior.

The benefits of this workbook are very personal. They differ from person to person. Participants who have completed the entire workbook describe benefits such as the following:

1. "I feel liberated. I like being free from the limitations imposed by my fears. I go where I want to go and do what I want to do...with comfort and confidence."

2. "I feel better about myself. I experience a sense of personal achievement that comes from doing what I want, when I want."

3. "I am relieved. The frequency and intensity of my anxiety are both down. I've learned to keep my anxiety at normal levels."

4. "I enjoy the stimulation and usefulness of normal anxiety. I don't have discomfort."

WHAT IS THE LEARNING PHILOSOPHY?

People learn best by doing. That means 1) learning new ways to behave that produce new and better experiences, and 2) practicing the new behaviors so that attitudes and habits change for the better.

1.   Participants learn different methods of behaving:

   a.   new attitudes and ways of thinking about things and
   b.   new behaviors or actions to take (methods, skills, or techniques to use in various situations).

2.   Participants can learn and practice these new behaviors in a classroom-like group setting, in learning labs, in the privacy of their own home and family life, at work, and in all the situations that formerly aroused worry, stress, and fear.

3.   Participants practice the techniques until they can apply them easily when needed.

HOW SHOULD THE WORKBOOK BE USED?

The workbook is designed as a self-improvement tool. Virtually anyone can use it, on their own, to reduce their worry, stress, fear, and anxiety.

People are likely to benefit most from the workbook if they progress through the lessons with a group. (You are encouraged to contact a clinician in your area who has been trained   by Dr. Hart to conduct a *Conquer Your Fears* program.)

HOW IS THE WORKBOOK STRUCTURED?

The workbook is a series of 12 lessons. After studying Chapter 1, *What We're Up Against*, and Chapter 2, *Why Me?*, you will understand what causes worry, stress, fear, and anxiety. You also will know which chapters are most likely to help you. Work hardest on these. Remember, though, that all the chapters benefit from each other. Be sure you do each one.

GETTING STARTED

Chapter 1.   *What We're Up Against* This section describes the problem that the skills taught by this workbook will help you solve, who is most likely to benefit from the workbook, and different ways to use the workbook.

Chapter 2.   *Why Me?* This chapter helps you identify elements of your history and personality that contribute to your worry, stress, fear, and anxiety. It also helps you plan the order in which to study each of the other chapters.

THE BASICS OF PERSONAL CONTROL--SETTING PERSONAL LIMITS

Chapter 3. **Take Control of Your Life.** A method for focussing on what you can control and Letting Go of the rest.

Chapter 4. **How Good Does It Have to Be?** A method for setting healthy limits to Perfection-seeking.

Chapter 5. **Tired of Pleasing Everybody Else?** A method for setting healthy limits to People-pleasing.

Chapter 6. **Have You Taken Enough?** A method for setting healthy limits to Being Strong.

THE BASICS OF RELEASING TENSION--CHANNELING YOUR ENERGY

Chapter 7. **Make Feelings Work for You!** A method for understanding and properly using emotions.

Chapter 8. **Turn Conflict into Action!** A method for reducing internal conflict.

Chapter 9. **Get the Most From Relationships!** A method for avoiding destructive roles with others.

Chapter 10. **Action without Anger.** A method for successfully asserting yourself.

Chapter 11. **Be Realistic!** A method for changing thoughts that cause stress.

Chapter 12. **Set Your Sights on Relief.** A method for reducing life-style stress.

Chapter 13. **Releasing Tension.** A method for reducing mental, physical, and emotional stress.

To get the most from these chapters, remember that each one presents a lesson that teaches a complete skill. On many occasions you will need to use the entire skill. That is, you will need to go through all the steps when you apply the skill.

At other times you will use only part of the skill. Those are cases when you reach a decision on a second, third, or fourth step, which tells you that you need not apply the skill further. These will be the occasions when you discover that you are not engaged in a problem behavior. You won't need to go on to final steps when you conclude that your actions fall within acceptable limits.

Therefore, the skills are to be used in a large variety of situations. Only some of the time will the steps of each skill uncover behavior that causes worry, stress, fear, and anxiety. In those occasions where the early steps help you uncover problematic behavior, the final steps give you a tool for changing that behavior.

Being able to employ these tools increases our sense of Personal Control, releases tension, and builds a more positive attitude about ourselves, others, and life in general.

HOW TO GET THE MOST FROM THE WORKBOOK

Complete Each Chapter in One Setting.

The lessons are most effective if you reserve 60 uninterrupted minutes to savor each chapter. The most popular pace for progressing through the lessons is one per week. Some people prefer two weeks per lesson.

Review the Chapter.

If you have given the chapter full attention during your initial setting, you can maintain maximum benefits from the lesson by reviewing the chapter for 5 to 10 minutes on two or three sessions during the next week or two.

Do the Homework Assignments.

We learn through practice. The homework offered through this workbook provides learning experiences that have proven successful for others. If you do the exercises, you will gain relief from the frequency and intensity of your worry, stress, fear, and anxiety. Without enough practice, you will likely not improve or even get worse.

But there's more! Every lesson you study teaches skills that are helpful for everybody whether they are troubled by worry, stress, fear, and anxiety or not. If you study and practice the lessons in this workbook, your whole life will begin running more smoothly and providing more satisfaction to you.

A critical learning procedure is for you to complete the homework and practice the First Aid Steps, even when you are not really worrying or feeling threatened. Each tool must become a habit that helps you day in and day out.

Work Sheets. The work sheets take from one to two minutes to complete. Repetition helps us identify with the steps and begin to see the benefits of using them. The work sheets over-teach the lesson. By over-learning the steps in full detail and as separate actions in sequence, you develop a total familiarity that will make it easier to use the steps quickly when you need them. Do at least one a day for one or two weeks. One work sheet a day is a small commitment; that's two minutes of time and effort.

There are eight work sheets at the end of each lesson. The idea is to do one a day for a week. By then you will have mastered the technique. In the middle of the lesson, make as many copies of the unused work sheet as you need for additional practice.

Apply each work sheet to a different event in your daily life so that you practice using the steps in different real-life situations. Each time you apply the steps to a new and different situation, you increase your understanding and confidence.

First Aid Steps. Go over the steps in your mind several times a day during the period of time when you are working on the work sheets. Clip out and make copies of the First Aid Steps. Put them in various places to remind yourself to think through the steps. Practice in your mind.

Tell A Friend; Tell Everybody!

Discuss the First Aid Steps and your personal experiences with others as much as possible. Spread the word. Teach friends and loved ones how to help themselves using the same skills you are learning. Research* has shown that this will help you benefit from the workbook. Each time you tell someone else about what you are learning, you increase your understanding and commitment. (* The social psychology research on cognitive dissonance referenced here is very plentiful.)

Be Patient with Yourself.

Habits of thought, feeling, and action change slowly. Resistance is normal. Give yourself time. Practice. Believe in yourself and the lessons. Just keep practicing.

Validate Yourself.

Give yourself deliberate, positive strokes for doing the assignments. That will help keep you practicing, increase your sense of Personal Control, relieve tension, and boost your self-esteem and your outlook on others and life in general.

Commit Yourself to Study Time.

Set aside a regular time each day to work on your homework assignments and review notes of experiences. Usually 15 minutes each day is enough to make good progress over the course of a week. Don't let anything distract you from doing your *Conquer Your Fears* workbook study time.

HOW WAS THE WORKBOOK DEVELOPED?

IN THE BEGINNING

The workbook was developed by E. Wayne Hart, Ph.D., with research assistance from Diane Craver, M.S. While working with dozens of anxious patients over a span of 15 years, Dr. Hart reviewed the research on causes and cures of anxiety and studied workbooks and materials developed by researchers and other professionals.

Dr. Hart pooled all this information and reached three important conclusions:

1. No one workbook combined the best information and learning methods known to be helpful. Nor did any single theory seem to explain all aspects of anxiety disorders.

2. Some information and methods that promised to be helpful were not present in any workbook.

3. Each person has special needs from any self-improvement book or program. Those needs can best be met if the material is used in the sequence that attends to a person's greatest needs first.

FEATURES DESIGNED INTO THE WORKBOOK

After concluding that basic education was the most cost-effective way to begin to help most people, Dr. Hart then began developing the *Conquer Your Fears* workbook so that it

1. combines the information and methods that have proven helpful before;

2. adds new, promising information and methods;

3. uses learning processes based on proven educational principles;

4. reflects a comprehensive and systematic theory; and

5. permits you to master skills beginning with the most needed first.

Chapter 1

WHAT WE'RE UP AGAINST

WHAT IS ANXIETY?

Worry, stress, and fear are all natural reactions to threat. Everyone reacts in this way to some degree.

- ♦ Worry is a thought process: you go over and over something in your mind. This is an attempt to gain control.

- ♦ Stress is a reaction of the body to the build-up of internal and external pressure.

- ♦ Fear is a natural emotional reaction to a threat.

Most people describe anxiety as a combination of worry, stress, and fear. It is a complex mental and emotional reaction of troubled thoughts, negative expectations, fear, dread, apprehension, physical tension, and/or uneasiness.

We consider anxiety a problem condition when worry, stress, and/or fear

- ♦ linger because of a prolonged threat,
- ♦ exist in prolonged anticipation of a threat,
- ♦ continue after a threat has passed,
- ♦ are inappropriate to a threat, and
- ♦ exist without an identifiable threat.

Anxiety is relatively normal, just like worry, stress, and fear. Everyone experiences it, to some degree, at some time.

Worry, stress, fear, and anxiety get worse the more we feel out of control, feel tense, and have negative attitudes about ourselves, others, and life in general.

WHAT ARE THE SYMPTOMS OF ANXIETY?

Anxiety takes different forms in different people. These can be divided into four categories:

BODY   muscle tension and nervous energy,

THOUGHTS   excessive mental activity and impaired cognitive functions,

EMOTIONS   uncomfortable feelings and emotional thoughts, and

ACTIONS   behaviors that are an expression of anxiety or a defense against it.

THE BODY--PHYSICAL SYMPTOMS

Muscle Tension
- Trembling, twitching, or feeling shaky
- Knots or cramps in the stomach
- Muscle tension, aches, or soreness
- Agitation or restlessness

Nervous Energy--Arousal of the Autonomic Nervous System
- Shortness of breath or smothering sensations
- Trouble swallowing or a "lump in the throat"
- Pounding heart (palpitations) or speeded heart (tachycardia)
- Sweating or cold, clammy hands
- Dry mouth
- Dizziness or light-headed
- Nausea and/or diarrhea
- Flushes (hot flashes) or chills
- Frequent urination

THE THOUGHTS--MENTAL SYMPTOMS

Excessive Mental Activity
- Exaggerated startle responses
- Trouble sleeping due to racing, obsessive, or ruminating thoughts
- Difficulty paying attention and concentrating; easy distractibility
- Excessive worrying, mulling, and dwelling
- Obsessing

Impaired Cognitive Functions
- Difficulty making basic or simple decisions
- Difficulty with familiar calculating, organizing, and planning skills

THE EMOTIONS--FEELING SYMPTOMS

Uncomfortable Feelings
- Fear, panic, apprehension
- Dread
- Irritability
- Feeling keyed up or on edge

Emotional Thoughts
- Insecurity
- Helplessness and isolation

ACTIONS--BEHAVIORS

- Compulsive behavior like checking, double checking, and rechecking to be sure that things are turned off, doors are locked, and that things are in their proper places
- Restlessness, fidgeting, keeping busy
- Social isolation
- Irritability and impatience with others and life situations

HOW SEVERE CAN THE SYMPTOMS GET?

Anxiety can be weak or strong; it can fall anywhere in between. When worry, stress, fear and anxiety get bad enough, you can begin to experience depression, sleep difficulties, trouble concentrating, forgetfulness, and difficulty making basic decisions.

An important procedure is to monitor the intensity of your worry, stress, fear, and anxiety. That way you can use a tool to reduce it when it gets too strong or it goes on too long. To think of a range of severity from discomfort, to distress, to disability is helpful.

DISCOMFORT

Weak anxiety is short-term and mild: apprehension, worry, or distress. It is a natural reaction when we face risk, a threatening situation, or uncertainty. We think of this strength of anxiety as predictable and expectable. We need to adjust to it, but not cure it. For instance, two examples are

- butterflies in your stomach when your work performance is being reviewed, or

- fear or "stage fright" about giving a speech.

DISTRESS

Mid-range anxiety is long lasting mild anxiety or anxiety that is stronger than just being "uncomfortable." It includes prolonged anxiety about identified threats (phobia), episodic anxiety (panic disorder), and general or free-floating anxiety. Generalized anxiety is a more persistent feeling that varies in strength and does not stem from concerns about a specific event; it also can develop from a long-term concern over specific events. For instance, two examples are

- being in a constant state of feeling tense or troubled for no apparent reason, or

- apprehension about the outcome of a prolonged legal battle.

DISABILITY

Disabling anxiety is so severe or intense that we can't do normal things like concentrate at work or drive a car. For example, phobia is a strong fear of a specific object, activity, or situation.

Phobic people try to avoid that particular experience, making themselves unable to function normally. For instance, three examples are

♦ avoiding the snake exhibit at the zoo,

♦ not going up past a certain floor in the elevator of a tall building, or

♦ avoiding travel in an airplane.

SEVERITY SCALE

Use a 10-point scale to keep track of your discomfort. Think of this scale as an internal yardstick for measuring the severity of your worry, stress, fear, and anxiety. Use the scale several times a day. Note the measurements at different times and in different situations. Take action when you get high scores. The workbook teaches tools you use at those times and in those situations.

1 - 2 - 3 - 4 - 5 - 6 - 7 - 8 - 9 - 10
Discomfort　　　　*Distress*　　　　*Disability*

WHAT FORMS DOES ANXIETY TAKE?

GENERALIZED ANXIETY

This involves prolonged, intense levels of tension. The tension is almost constant and overwhelming. People have both physical and psychological symptoms.

PANIC DISORDER

This involves sudden attacks of intense anxiety associated with physical symptoms. Body symptoms include racing heartbeat, dizziness, shortness of breath, abdominal cramps, and sweating. The panic attacks occur for no apparent reason. This fact often makes it worse. It leads people to think they are becoming out of control, going crazy, embarrassing themselves, having a heart attack, or dying. Those threatening thoughts cause more fear and panic.

AGORAPHOBIA

This involves fear of becoming overly anxious or having a panic attack in a "bad" place or situation. A bad place or situation is one in which help is not available, or one in which a person will feel trapped or think escape is difficult. It is a learned condition in which one has begun avoiding places due to a fear of being in a particular place or situation and having an attack there. It is not a fear of something out in the world. It is fearing the threat that something may happen while being out there in the world.

PHOBIC DISORDER

This involves deliberate avoidance of specific objects or situations that bring on an intense anxiety. People with phobic disorder are afraid to do things that other people do without significant discomfort.

POST-TRAUMATIC STRESS DISORDER

This involves anxiety symptoms caused by an unusually distressing event. It includes three components:

1. *Reliving* includes symptoms like distressing: flashbacks (being there again) or acting or feeling as if the event were happening again; nightmares; memories; and strong distress when exposed to events that are symbolic of the original event, like anniversaries.

2. *Avoidance* includes symptoms like efforts to block out or distract ourselves from thoughts or emotions, avoiding activities and situations, having lowered interest in familiar activities, detachment, and the sense of "no future."

3. *Arousal* involves symptoms like irritability and angry outbursts, trouble concentrating, being too alert and on guard and being easily startled, body reactions when reminded of the event, and sleep disruptions.

OBSESSIVE COMPULSIVE DISORDER

This involves thoughts and behaviors. The person feels forced by something inside of self to think or act a certain way. The obsessive compulsive person recognizes that the thoughts and behaviors are inappropriate.

1. *Obsessions* involve recurring and persistent ideas, thoughts, impulses, or images. They seem intrusive and senseless. The person tries to ignore them, neutralize them, or distract self from them.

2.   *Compulsions* involve recurring, purposeful, and intentional behaviors performed in response to an obsession. The behaviors are ritualistic; they are performed according to certain rules, or they are stereotyped. The behavior is intended to neutralize obsessions or relieve the discomfort caused by obsessions, or the behavior is clearly excessive. The person recognizes that the behavior is excessive or unrealistic.

WHO IS LIKELY TO HAVE TROUBLE WITH ANXIETY?

Except when some physical condition is the sole cause of anxiety, it is more common among people who are intelligent and who value such things as

- ◆   neatness, orderliness, and organization;
- ◆   competence and productivity;
- ◆   dependability, reliability, and responsibility;
- ◆   keeping peace and satisfying the needs of others;
- ◆   sensitivity to others' needs and feelings;
- ◆   eagerness to be helpful and do things for others; and/or
- ◆   getting lots of things done (jobs, projects).

WHAT PARTS CAN BE TREATED?

The experience of anxiety involves 5 parts or components. A component is a part of the experience that can be treated to improve the overall quality of life.

COGNITIVE COMPONENT

Two groups of thoughts are associated with worry, stress, fear, anxiety. There are thoughts that cause or aggravate worry, stress, fear and anxiety. These are mostly of two varieties:

1.   *Exaggerating*. This involves making things worse than they are. "The sky is falling...the sky is falling."

2.   *Forecasting*. This involves anticipating problems in the future. "What if this...what if that?"

Also thoughts occur about being anxious. The person thinks about the sensations, thoughts, emotions, and actions associated with anxiety. Many people have learned wrong information or too little information about anxiety. They misinterpret and overreact or under-react. People usually don't know what tools to use to deal with worry, stress, fear, and anxiety. Often they have learned the ineffective or self-destructive methods of coping.

All these thoughts cause us to feel more out of control, build up tension, and form negative attitudes.

STRESS COMPONENT

This includes our internal reaction to stressors (stressors are stress-producing factors in the environment). Often elements of our life-style are more threatening or stressful than we realize. We often overlook ways to reduce stress.

The more we feel stressed out, the more out of control we feel and the worse our attitude becomes.

INTERPERSONAL COMPONENT

This includes our habits of interacting with other people: what we do and how we end up feeling.

We often act in ways that put us out of control, build stress, or cause us to collect bad feelings that turn our attitude negative.

PSYCHOLOGICAL COMPONENT

This includes our habits of behavior (thinking, feeling, and acting) and the forces that drive them. It involves how we interpret things and how we react to them. And, it includes all our beliefs and attitudes about ourselves (self-image and self-esteem), other people and institutions, and life events and situations.

If we behave in automatic and ineffective ways, we feel more out of control, we become tense about the problems, and we reinforce a negative outlook.

BIOLOGICAL AND PHYSIOLOGICAL COMPONENT

Biological and physiological processes are involved. Illnesses and injuries play a role. Each of us differs in how we function at this level; much of that individuality is related to genetics. Alcohol and drug use often contribute to anxiety as well.

Biological processes seem beyond our control, create tension directly or create problems that cause tension, and turn our attitude negative.

WHAT IF ANXIETY IS CAUSED BY THE BODY?

Sometimes our physical condition or body chemistry can cause us to experience anxiety. The chemical processes that create anxiety can be triggered by a number of medical conditions. Also, physical disorders are known to "mimic" or appear like anxiety, for example

- endocrine disorders,
- central nervous system disorders,
- infectious diseases,
- metabolic diseases,
- tumors and cancer,
- cardiovascular disorders,
- respiratory disorders,
- reactions to environmental toxins,
- alcohol and drug abuse, and/or
- adverse reactions to prescription medications and over-the-counter drugs.

Also, imbalances of chemistry in the brain can cause anxiety. These issues can be evaluated and treated by your medical doctor or a biological psychiatrist, often in collaboration with your family physician or internist.

WHAT IS THE THEORY?

LEARNING THEORY

Most often, anxiety reactions result from learned thoughts, feelings, and actions. Anything learned can be relearned or unlearned. It can be replaced by a new behavior. New learning must include

     1.   new *understanding* about what's going on inside us (internal events) and what's happening to us (external events), and

     2.   new *behavioral responses* to internal and external events.

The single most important element to developing new understandings and behavioral responses is practice. That's how people learn, through repetition. As we practice and change how we think and feel about things, and how we act or react, we regain a sense of Personal Control, which includes releasing tension and developing positive attitudes about ourselves, others, and life in general.

ANXIETY THEORY

     Personal Control. Control is the central issue in our struggles with anxiety. When people "think" they are in control, they don't feel anxious. When people "think" they are facing a threat and are out of control, they become worried or tense, feel afraid, or get anxious.

Feeling safe involves an "I'm in control" state of mind. When there are no threats, or when we think we can handle the threats, we feel in charge and secure.

Feeling unsafe, on the other hand, involves an "I'm out of control" state of mind. We usually experience the threat of potential harm as a loss of control and security. The change from feeling safe to feeling threatened is easier to understand if we think of it as a three-step process.

STEP 1	*STEP 2*	*STEP 3*
Start with a safe Attitude: "I'm in control," or "It's OK."	Recognize an external threat, or fear losing control of yourself.	Your attitude changes to "I'm out of control," or "It's not OK."

People can control what they think, feel, and do. Nothing else. There are four benefits from learning to control just those three things that we can control:

1. efficient coping with stressful events;

2. less build-up of tension that comes from frustration, failure, and fear;

3. improved self-acceptance, self-confidence, and self-esteem; and

4. letting go of bad thoughts and feelings about other people and events of life.

Personal Control is Dr. Hart's term for the state of mind in which we take full responsibility for the functions of our thoughts, emotions, and body and let go of efforts to control that which is beyond our power to control. Every lesson in the workbook helps develop Personal Control.

Releasing Tension. Life is stressful, and that builds tension. A number of ways exist to release tension. We can all benefit from learning to release our tension through actions that solve social, vocational, family, and personal problems.

Developing Positive Attitudes. Controlling the right things and letting go of the rest, and channeling our tension toward problem solving combine to make us more effective and competent.

Chapter 2

WHY ME?

<u>INTRODUCTION</u>

Things that happen over and over again become a way of life. This is especially true for children, who don't see any other options. "If it happens again and again, that's how things are." Childhood Themes are behavior and relationship patterns that we learned when we were kids. Sometimes they resurface in our adult lives. When they do, we end up acting the same way or relating to other people in the same way as when we were children.

We all develop ways of thinking, feeling, and acting in order to deal with people and situations. We call these, "personality traits." Personality traits determine how we deal with events.

Resurfacing Childhood Themes and personality traits can be good or bad for us. Certain ones are known to cause worry, stress, fear, and anxiety. If you recognize these themes and traits, then you can plan new actions to increase your sense of Personal Control, release tension, and develop positive attitudes toward yourself, others, and life in general.

<u>GOALS</u>

1.   Learn to identify childhood themes that keep resurfacing and causing you worry, stress, fear, and anxiety.

2.   Learn to identify your personality traits that cause worry, stress, fear, and anxiety.

3.   Learn what *Conquer Your Fears* methods you could use to help you deal with your resurfacing childhood themes and personality traits.

<u>REMEMBER</u>

The secret to overcoming worry, stress, fear, and anxiety is learning and practicing the things that will help you increase your sense of Personal Control, release tension, and develop positive attitudes toward yourself, others, and life in general. This starts with understanding yourself better.

*

<u>FIRST AID STEPS FOR UNDERSTANDING WHY YOU ARE</u>

<u>BOTHERED BY WORRY, STRESS, FEAR, and ANXIETY.</u>

Step 1:   **Always...Breathe Out! Release Tension.**

Step 2:   **Is This a Resurfacing Childhood Theme?**

Step 3:   **Is This One of My Personality Traits?**

Step 4:   **Study the Index of *Conquer Your Fears* Methods.**

Step 5:   **Complete Your Self-improvement Planner.**

* Permission is given to reproduce First Aid Steps for your personal use.

STEP 1

ALWAYS...BREATHE OUT!

We recommend Release Breathing for reducing the tension that builds up as we deal with life stressors. Release Breathing is different from methods taught in other programs. It is not intended to relax us. Its purpose is releasing tension.

Stress management and anxiety recovery programs often teach some form of controlled breathing. This is very helpful for relaxing and calming down. This technique involves pacing our breathing. The method usually involves counting to measure the time of breathing in and out. This is a valuable skill to learn and it can be used at times when relaxing is more important than releasing tension.

But, sometimes we need to stay alert (like when we are in a meeting, driving our cars, or discussing sensitive issues). Most people find Release Breathing to be better for releasing tension and reducing anxiety at these times.

More important, relaxation breathing involves fighting ourselves. In relaxation breathing we are trying to get ourselves to resist the excitement and energy that make up our stress. Release Breathing channels our energy rather than resisting it. Breathing out forcefully is a physical symbol of taking action rather than resisting it. Release Breathing sends an important "I'm in control" message to our brain. It involves 3 steps.

RELEASE BREATHING STEPS:

1.   Breathe in deeply, using *medium force*. Use your diaphragm. Take in a full breath. Feel your chest expand.

2.   Breathe out through your mouth, using *medium strong force*. Let your shoulders fall and your chest collapse. Notice, you breathe out harder than you breathe in. Release air and tension at the same time.

3.   Pause for a moment at the end of the breath. Relax. Feel the release of tension.

STEP 2

<u>IS THIS A RESURFACING CHILDHOOD THEME?</u>

Childhood experiences that happen many times can have an effect on how we think, feel, and act throughout our life. Even small things can make their mark if they are repeated many times. Their effect can be positive or negative.

A Childhood Theme is behavior or events that occurred frequently when we were children. Often our Childhood Themes continue to occur throughout our lives, although they change their form as we get older. We act in about the same way, we are treated in about the same way, or we find ourselves in a similar situation. We call this a Resurfacing Childhood Theme.

> **FOR EXAMPLE:** One *Conquer Your Fears* participant told her group how when she was a child, she would feel worthless when her father criticized her. Before learning *Conquer Your Fears* methods, she had always felt worthless whenever her husband was even the least bit critical, even when he was being fair about it.

Resurfacing Childhood Themes can be positive or negative. Negative ones are involved with worry, stress, fear, and/or anxiety. The eight key Childhood Themes that commonly resurface in adult life of people troubled by worry, stress, fear and anxiety are

- ◆ Acting Like a Parent
- ◆ Living by Many Rules
- ◆ Being from an Unstable Family
- ◆ Fearing Separation

- ◆ Feeling Love and Approval Are Conditional
- ◆ Having Trouble Pleasing Others
- ◆ Avoiding Talk about Feelings
- ◆ Pretending Things Didn't Happen

EXERCISE

A

IDENTIFYING RESURFACING CHILDHOOD THEMES

DIRECTIONS: For Exercise A... Each theme is presented in the following pages. There are eight Resurfacing Childhood Themes. Each presentation is a carefully structured learning process. The process will teach you how to recognize each theme. Complete all eight learning steps listed here for each Resurfacing Childhood Theme.

FOLLOW THESE LEARNING STEPS

1. Think about the descriptive *NAME OF EACH THEME*.

2. Learn the nature of the theme by studying examples. Read and rate the *COMMON EXAMPLES OF THIS THEME DURING CHILDHOOD*. Think about each example and compare it to your own life. Circle one number to show how much you agree with each statement.

3. Then, read the *DISCUSSION OF THIS THEME*. It will help you understand ways the theme can be good or bad in your life.

4. Next, consider ways the theme could resurface in your life today. To do this, read and rate *COMMON EXAMPLES OF THIS THEME RESURFACING DURING ADULTHOOD*. Think about each example and compare it to your own life. Circle one number to show how much you agree with each statement.

5. Then, think about your life and this theme. How has this theme played out in your life? Use the space provided to add *OTHER EXAMPLES* of that childhood theme resurfacing in your adult life.

6. Now, you have studied the theme and thought about its role in your life. Think about it some more and then indicate how much *INFLUENCE* that childhood theme has in your current life. To do this, circle one number to show how much that theme has resurfaced in recent years.

7.	Stop for a moment. Pay attention to what you are thinking about, what emotions you are feeling, and what sensations are in your body. Then, jot down a description of your experience. Use the space reserved for *PERSONAL REACTIONS AND IMPRESSIONS.*

8.	Your understanding will be complete if you think about alternatives to the theme running your life. To do this, study the list of *CONQUER YOUR FEARS LESSONS* (Chapters) that will help you deal with that Resurfacing Theme. Think about the names and descriptions of these lessons.

CHILDHOOD THEME

ACTING LIKE A PARENT

COMMON EXAMPLES OF THIS THEME DURING CHILDHOOD:

How Much Do You Agree?

1. I cooked meals regularly for my brothers and sisters.

1 - 2 - 3 - 4 - 5
A Little...A Lot

2. I took care of one of my parents.

1 - 2 - 3 - 4 - 5
A Little...A Lot

3. I made sure my younger siblings got to school okay.

1 - 2 - 3 - 4 - 5
A Little...A Lot

4. I had to do things for the family that a parent usually does.

1 - 2 - 3 - 4 - 5
A Little...A Lot

5. I bought my own clothes.

1 - 2 - 3 - 4 - 5
A Little...A Lot

6. A parent got sick and I took over.

1 - 2 - 3 - 4 - 5
A Little...A Lot

7. I learned to accept responsibility very young.

1 - 2 - 3 - 4 - 5
A Little...A Lot

8. I cooked meals for my parents.

1 - 2 - 3 - 4 - 5
A Little...A Lot

DISCUSSION OF THIS THEME:

Acting Like a Parent may be helpful now if you accept responsibility in ways that make life successful. *Acting Like a Parent* may be a problem for you now if you too often act in a serious "adult" manner.

COMMON EXAMPLES OF THIS THEME RESURFACING DURING ADULTHOOD:

How Much Do You Agree?

9.   I have a hard time "letting go."

1 - 2 - 3 - 4 - 5
A Little...A Lot

10.   It is hard for me to play.

1 - 2 - 3 - 4 - 5
A Little...A Lot

11.   I'm uncomfortable when I'm supposed to be having fun.

1 - 2 - 3 - 4 - 5
A Little...A Lot

OTHER EXAMPLES: List ways *Acting Like a Parent* resurfaces in your life now:

....

....

INFLUENCE:

How much does *Acting Like a Parent* resurface in your current life?

1 - 2 - 3 - 4 - 5
A Little...A Lot

WHAT DO I DO WITH MY RATINGS?...You will rate items throughout this workbook. Often, like in this lesson, you will rate an item by indicating how much you agree with a statement. There are two reasons to rate things. First, in order to rate you have to analyze the item and compare it to your experiences. That process helps learning and increases your sense of Personal Control. Second, the issues and items you rate higher are the most important for you. They deserve special attention. If your rating is a 1, this item is not relevant for you. You will benefit from learning how to deal with any item that is rated higher.

PERSONAL REACTIONS AND IMPRESSIONS:

....

....

CONQUER YOUR FEARS LESSONS that help us deal with *Acting Like a Parent:* For more information about each lesson, read the Index of *Conquer Your Fears* Methods in Step 4.

CONQUER YOUR FEARS LESSONS
THAT HELP YOU DEAL WITH THIS THEME

Take Control of Your Life. A method for Focussing on what you can control and Letting Go of the rest.

How Good Does It Have to Be? A method for setting healthy limits to Perfection-seeking.

Tired of Pleasing Everybody Else? A method for setting healthy limits to People-pleasing.

Have You Taken Enough? A method for setting healthy limits to Being Strong.

Get the Most from Relationships! A method for avoiding destructive roles with others.

Be Realistic! A method for changing thoughts that cause stress.

Set Your Sights on Relief. A method for reducing life-style stress.

Releasing Tension. A method for reducing mental, physical, and emotional stress.

CHILDHOOD THEME

LIVING BY MANY RULES

COMMON EXAMPLES OF THIS THEME DURING CHILDHOOD:

How Much Do You Agree?

1. I had to be very careful about what subjects I brought up.

    1 - 2 - 3 - 4 - 5
    A Little...A Lot

2. I was to be "seen and not heard."

    1 - 2 - 3 - 4 - 5
    A Little...A Lot

3. I couldn't have friends over on the weekends.

    1 - 2 - 3 - 4 - 5
    A Little...A Lot

4. There were strict rules about how to act.

    1 - 2 - 3 - 4 - 5
    A Little...A Lot

5. There were many rules about what kinds of things to say.

    1 - 2 - 3 - 4 - 5
    A Little...A Lot

6. There were many rules about cleanliness.

    1 - 2 - 3 - 4 - 5
    A Little...A Lot

7. My room had to be maintained in a certain condition.

    1 - 2 - 3 - 4 - 5
    A Little...A Lot

8. I was expected to be on my "best" behavior around others.

    1 - 2 - 3 - 4 - 5
    A Little...A Lot

9. I was scolded when I was just having fun.

    1 - 2 - 3 - 4 - 5
    A Little...A Lot

DISCUSSION OF THIS THEME:

Living by Many Rules may be helpful now if rules give your family structure, direction, and order. ***Living by Many Rules*** may be a problem now if you always try to be in control.

COMMON EXAMPLES OF THIS THEME RESURFACING DURING ADULTHOOD:

How Much Do You Agree?

10. I am content only when things
go as I have planned.

1 - 2 - 3 - 4 - 5
A Little...A Lot

11. I have a hard time being
spontaneous.

1 - 2 - 3 - 4 - 5
A Little...A Lot

OTHER EXAMPLES: List ways *Living by Many Rules* resurfaces in your life now:

....

....

INFLUENCE:

How much does *Living by Many Rules*
resurface in your current life?

1 - 2 - 3 - 4 - 5
A Little...A Lot

PERSONAL REACTIONS AND IMPRESSIONS:

....

....

CONQUER YOUR FEARS LESSONS that help us deal with *Living by Many Rules:* For more information about each lesson, read the Index of *Conquer Your Fears* Methods in Step 4.

CONQUER YOUR FEARS LESSONS
THAT HELP YOU DEAL WITH THIS THEME

Take Control of Your Life. A method for focussing on what you can control and Letting Go of the rest.

How Good Does It Have to Be? A method for setting healthy limits to Perfection-seeking.

Tired of Pleasing Everybody Else? A method for setting healthy limits to People-pleasing.

Have You Taken Enough? A method for setting healthy limits to Being Strong.

Make Feelings Work for You! A method for understanding and properly using emotions.

Get the Most from Relationships! A method for avoiding destructive roles with others.

Action without Anger. A method for successfully asserting yourself.

Be Realistic! A method for changing thoughts that cause stress.

Set Your Sights on Relief. A method for reducing life-style stress.

CHILDHOOD THEME

BEING FROM AN UNSTABLE FAMILY

COMMON EXAMPLES OF THIS THEME DURING CHILDHOOD:

How Much Do You Agree?

1. My parents argued a lot.

1 - 2 - 3 - 4 - 5
A Little...A Lot

2. I never knew if a parent would be home when I got there.

1 - 2 - 3 - 4 - 5
A Little...A Lot

3. There was abuse in my home.

1 - 2 - 3 - 4 - 5
A Little...A Lot

4. My family split up and got back together again.

1 - 2 - 3 - 4 - 5
A Little...A Lot

5. My home life was chaotic, unpredictable, and unstable.

1 - 2 - 3 - 4 - 5
A Little...A Lot

6. The family atmosphere was tense.

1 - 2 - 3 - 4 - 5
A Little...A Lot

7. I was often afraid.

1 - 2 - 3 - 4 - 5
A Little...A Lot

8. Someone in my family was always getting upset.

1 - 2 - 3 - 4 - 5
A Little...A Lot

DISCUSSION OF THIS THEME:

Being from an Unstable Family may be helpful now if you learned how to handle variety and change. *Being from an Unstable Family* may be a problem now in your relationships with others if you are always on guard.

COMMON EXAMPLES OF THIS THEME RESURFACING DURING ADULTHOOD:

How Much Do You Agree?

9. I never know what kinds of behavior to expect from others.

1 - 2 - 3 - 4 - 5
A Little...A Lot

10. I am unsure how to act around others.

1 - 2 - 3 - 4 - 5
A Little...A Lot

11. It is hard for me to trust others.

1 - 2 - 3 - 4 - 5
A Little...A Lot

OTHER EXAMPLES: List ways *Being from an Unstable Family* resurfaces in your life now:

....

....

INFLUENCE:

How much does *Being from an Unstable Family* resurface in your current life?

1 - 2 - 3 - 4 - 5
A Little...A Lot

PERSONAL REACTIONS AND IMPRESSIONS:

....

....

CONQUER YOUR FEARS LESSONS that help us deal with *Being from an Unstable Family:*
For more information about each lesson, read the Index of *Conquer Your Fears* Methods in Step 4.

CONQUER YOUR FEARS LESSONS
THAT HELP YOU DEAL WITH THIS THEME

Take Control of Your Life. A method for Focussing on what you can control and Letting Go of the rest.

Make Feelings Work for You! A method for understanding and properly using emotions.

Get the Most from Relationships! A method for avoiding destructive roles with others.

CHILDHOOD THEME

FEELING LOVE AND APPROVAL ARE CONDITIONAL

COMMON EXAMPLES OF THIS THEME DURING CHILDHOOD:

How Much Do You Agree?

1. I felt inadequate because I didn't learn as quickly as others.

1 - 2 - 3 - 4 - 5
A Little...A Lot

2. I felt my parents were only proud of me when I did well in sports.

1 - 2 - 3 - 4 - 5
A Little...A Lot

3. I got approval for what I did instead of for who I was.

1 - 2 - 3 - 4 - 5
A Little...A Lot

4. I thought my parents wouldn't approve of me unless I did housework.

1 - 2 - 3 - 4 - 5
A Little...A Lot

5. My parents didn't care about what I thought or felt.

1 - 2 - 3 - 4 - 5
A Little...A Lot

6. I was put down when I failed or performed badly.

1 - 2 - 3 - 4 - 5
A Little...A Lot

7. I thought the only way to win my parents' approval was to do well in school.

1 - 2 - 3 - 4 - 5
A Little...A Lot

8. I thought my parents didn't love me when they were upset.

1 - 2 - 3 - 4 - 5
A Little...A Lot

DISCUSSION OF THIS THEME:

Feeling Love and Approval Are Conditional may be a problem now if you still believe that your performance is what determines if others accept you or like you.

COMMON EXAMPLES OF THIS THEME RESURFACING DURING ADULTHOOD:

How Much Do You Agree?

9.　I feel I must perform well to gain approval from others.

1 - 2 - 3 - 4 - 5
A Little...A Lot

10.　I won't be appreciated unless I live up to certain standards.

1 - 2 - 3 - 4 - 5
A Little...A Lot

OTHER EXAMPLES:　List ways *Feeling Love and Approval Are Conditional* resurfaces in your life now:

....

....

INFLUENCE:

How much does *Feeling Love and Approval Are Conditional* resurface in your current life?

1 - 2 - 3 - 4 - 5
A Little...A Lot

PERSONAL REACTIONS AND IMPRESSIONS:

....

....

CONQUER YOUR FEARS LESSONS that help us deal with *Feeling Love and Approval Are Conditional:* For more information about each lesson, read the Index of *Conquer Your Fears* Methods in Step 4.

CONQUER YOUR FEARS LESSONS
THAT HELP YOU DEAL WITH THIS THEME

Take Control of Your Life. A method for Focussing on what you can control and Letting Go of the rest.

How Good Does It Have to Be? A method for setting healthy limits to Perfection-seeking.

Tired of Pleasing Everybody Else? A method for setting healthy limits to People-pleasing.

Have You Taken Enough? A method for setting healthy limits to Being Strong.

Make Feelings Work for You! A method for understanding and properly using emotions.

Turn Conflict into Action! A method for reducing internal conflict.

Get the Most from Relationships! A method for avoiding destructive roles with others.

Action without Anger. A method for successfully asserting yourself.

Be Realistic! A method for changing thoughts that cause stress.

Set Your Sights on Relief. A method for reducing life-style stress.

Releasing Tension. A method for reducing mental, physical, and emotional stress.

CHILDHOOD THEME

FEARING SEPARATION

COMMON EXAMPLES OF THIS THEME DURING CHILDHOOD:

How Much Do You Agree?

1. I threw temper tantrums
when I had to go to school.

1 - 2 - 3 - 4 - 5
A Little…A Lot

2. Someone I felt close to died
or went away, and it really
upset me.

1 - 2 - 3 - 4 - 5
A Little…A Lot

3. I cried a lot when my parents
left me with someone else
to care for me.

1 - 2 - 3 - 4 - 5
A Little…A Lot

4. A parent worried a lot about
my welfare.

1 - 2 - 3 - 4 - 5
A Little…A Lot

5. I became very frightened or
upset when my parents went away.

1 - 2 - 3 - 4 - 5
A Little…A Lot

6. I become very frightened or upset
when I had to leave my parents.

1 - 2 - 3 - 4 - 5
A Little…A Lot

DISCUSSION OF THIS THEME:

Fearing Separation may be helpful now if it helps you realize how important your relationships are to you. **Fearing Separation** can be a problem now if you fear abandonment.

COMMON EXAMPLES OF THIS THEME RESURFACING DURING ADULTHOOD:

How Much Do You Agree?

6.   I often "hold too tightly"   1 - 2 - 3 - 4 - 5
       to the people I love.   A Little...A Lot

7.   I am often afraid the people I   1 - 2 - 3 - 4 - 5
       love will leave me.   A Little...A Lot

8.   I have scared people away by   1 - 2 - 3 - 4 - 5
       wanting too much from them.   A Little...A Lot

OTHER EXAMPLES: List ways *Fearing Separation* resurfaces in your life now:

....

....

INFLUENCE:

How much does *Fearing Separation*   1 - 2 - 3 - 4 - 5
resurface in your current life?   A Little...A Lot

PERSONAL REACTIONS AND IMPRESSIONS:

....

....

CONQUER YOUR FEARS LESSONS that help us deal with *Fearing Separation:* For more information about each lesson, read the Index of *Conquer Your Fears* Methods in Step 4.

CONQUER YOUR FEARS LESSONS
THAT HELP YOU DEAL WITH THIS THEME

Take Control of Your Life. A method for focussing on what you can control and Letting Go of the rest.

Tired of Pleasing Everybody Else? A method for setting healthy limits to People-pleasing.

Have You Taken Enough? A method for setting healthy limits to Being Strong.

Make Feelings Work for You! A method for understanding and properly using emotions.

Turn Conflict into Action! A method for reducing internal conflict.

Get the Most from Relationships! A method for avoiding destructive roles with others.

Be Realistic! A method for changing thoughts that cause stress.

Releasing Tension. A method for reducing mental, physical, and emotional stress.

CHILDHOOD THEME

HAVING TROUBLE PLEASING OTHERS

COMMON EXAMPLES OF THIS THEME DURING CHILDHOOD:

How Much Do You Agree?

1. I heard things like, "You can do better than that."

    1 - 2 - 3 - 4 - 5
    A Little...A Lot

2. I heard things like, "Why can't you be like so-and-so?"

    1 - 2 - 3 - 4 - 5
    A Little...A Lot

3. I felt ignored while a brother or sister got lots of attention.

    1 - 2 - 3 - 4 - 5
    A Little...A Lot

4. One or more grown-ups seemed critical or judgmental of me.

    1 - 2 - 3 - 4 - 5
    A Little...A Lot

5. I was ridiculed for not measuring up.

    1 - 2 - 3 - 4 - 5
    A Little...A Lot

6. I was jealous of the attention a sibling got.

    1 - 2 - 3 - 4 - 5
    A Little...A Lot

DISCUSSION OF THIS THEME:

Having Trouble Pleasing Others may be helpful now if it helps you perform to the best of your abilities. *Having Trouble Pleasing Others* may be a problem now if you try very hard and are never satisfied with yourself.

COMMON EXAMPLES OF THIS THEME RESURFACING DURING ADULTHOOD:

How Much Do You Agree?

7. I often feel like I never do things well enough.

    1 - 2 - 3 - 4 - 5
    A Little...A Lot

8. I am unsure if doing my best is good enough for others.

    1 - 2 - 3 - 4 - 5
    A Little...A Lot

9. I am unsure if doing my best is good enough for me.

    1 - 2 - 3 - 4 - 5
    A Little...A Lot

OTHER EXAMPLES: List ways *Having Trouble Pleasing Others* resurfaces in your life now:

....

....

INFLUENCE:

How much does *Having Trouble Pleasing Others* resurface in your current life?

1 - 2 - 3 - 4 - 5
A Little...A Lot

PERSONAL REACTIONS AND IMPRESSIONS:

....

....

CONQUER YOUR FEARS LESSONS that help us deal with *Having Trouble Pleasing Others:*
For more information about each lesson, read the Index of *Conquer Your Fears* Methods in Step
4.

CONQUER YOUR FEARS LESSONS
THAT HELP YOU DEAL WITH THIS THEME

Take Control of Your Life. A method for focussing on what you can control and Letting
Go of the rest.

How Good Does It Have to Be? A method for setting healthy limits to Perfection-
seeking.

Tired of Pleasing Everybody Else? A method for setting healthy limits to People-
pleasing.

Make Feelings Work for You! A method for understanding and properly using emotions.

Get the Most from Relationships! A method for avoiding destructive roles with others.

CHILDHOOD THEME   AVOIDING TALK ABOUT FEELINGS

COMMON EXAMPLES OF THIS THEME DURING CHILDHOOD:

How Much Do You Agree?

1. It didn't feel safe to show
    anger or any "negative" emotions.

    1 - 2 - 3 - 4 - 5
    A Little...A Lot

2. I was put down if I
    cried when my feelings
    were hurt.

    1 - 2 - 3 - 4 - 5
    A Little...A Lot

3. I didn't feel like I could
    talk about certain emotions,
    like anger.

    1 - 2 - 3 - 4 - 5
    A Little...A Lot

4. My family avoided topics such
    as emotions and feelings.

    1 - 2 - 3 - 4 - 5
    A Little...A Lot

DISCUSSION OF THIS THEME:

Avoiding Talk about Feelings may be helpful now when it is appropriate to keep personal things to yourself. *Avoiding Talk about Feelings* can be a problem now if you bottle up your emotions.

COMMON EXAMPLES OF THIS THEME RESURFACING DURING ADULTHOOD:

How Much Do You Agree?

5. I have a hard time being in touch with my feelings.
1 - 2 - 3 - 4 - 5
A Little...A Lot

6. I feel as if my emotions are out of control.
1 - 2 - 3 - 4 - 5
A Little...A Lot

7. I am unsure of how to express my feelings.
1 - 2 - 3 - 4 - 5
A Little...A Lot

OTHER EXAMPLES: List ways *Avoiding Talk about Feelings* resurfaces in your life now:

....

....

INFLUENCE:

How much does *Avoiding Talk about Feelings* resurface in your current life?
1 - 2 - 3 - 4 - 5
A Little...A Lot

PERSONAL REACTIONS AND IMPRESSIONS:

....

....

CONQUER YOUR FEARS LESSONS that help us deal with *Avoiding Talk about Feelings:*
For more information about each lesson, read the Index of *Conquer Your Fears* Methods in Step
4.

CONQUER YOUR FEARS LESSONS
THAT HELP YOU DEAL WITH THIS THEME

Have You Taken Enough? A method for setting healthy limits to Being Strong.

Make Feelings Work for You! A method for understanding and properly using emotions.

Turn Conflict into Action! A method for reducing internal conflict.

Get the Most from Relationships! A method for avoiding destructive roles with others.

Action without Anger. A method for successfully asserting yourself.

Be Realistic! A method for changing thoughts that cause stress.

Set Your Sights on Relief. A method for reducing life-style stress.

Releasing Tension. A method for reducing mental, physical, and emotional stress.

CHILDHOOD THEME

PRETENDING THINGS DIDN'T HAPPEN

COMMON EXAMPLES OF THIS THEME DURING CHILDHOOD:

How Much Do You Agree?

1. Someone's pregnancy was kept secret.

   1 - 2 - 3 - 4 - 5
   A Little...A Lot

2. A family member's behavior or problem wasn't talked about.

   1 - 2 - 3 - 4 - 5
   A Little...A Lot

3. The subject of someone's background was avoided.

   1 - 2 - 3 - 4 - 5
   A Little...A Lot

4. My family had a big secret that no one was supposed to talk about.

   1 - 2 - 3 - 4 - 5
   A Little...A Lot

DISCUSSION OF THIS THEME:

Pretending Things Didn't Happen may be helpful now because you sometimes leave well enough alone. *Pretending Things Didn't Happen* can be a problem now if you feel like you shouldn't open up to other people about anything "bad."

COMMON EXAMPLES OF THIS THEME RESURFACING DURING ADULTHOOD:

How Much Do You Agree?

5.   I feel I shouldn't think "bad"   1 - 2 - 3 - 4 - 5
        thoughts.   A Little...A Lot

6.   I often pretend I have no "bad"   1 - 2 - 3 - 4 - 5
        feelings.   A Little...A Lot

7.   I should keep my "bad" feelings   1 - 2 - 3 - 4 - 5
        to myself.   A Little...A Lot

8.   I don't let things others do   1 - 2 - 3 - 4 - 5
        get to me.   A Little...A Lot

OTHER EXAMPLES: List ways *Pretending Things Didn't Happen* resurfaces in your life now:

....

....

INFLUENCE:

How much does *Pretending Things Didn't Happen*   1 - 2 - 3 - 4 - 5
resurface in your current life?   A Little...A Lot

PERSONAL REACTIONS AND IMPRESSIONS:

....

....

CONQUER YOUR FEARS LESSONS that help us deal with *Pretending Things Didn't Happen:* For more information about each lesson, read the Index of *Conquer Your Fears* Methods in Step 4.

CONQUER YOUR FEARS LESSONS
THAT HELP YOU DEAL WITH THIS THEME

Take Control of Your Life. A method for focussing on what you can control and Letting Go of the rest.

How Good Does It Have To Be? A method for setting healthy limits to Perfection-seeking.

Have You Taken Enough? A method for setting healthy limits to Being Strong.

Make Feelings Work for You! A method for understanding and properly using emotions.

Turn Conflict into Action! A method for reducing internal conflict.

Get the Most from Relationships! A method for avoiding destructive roles with others.

Action without Anger. A method for successfully asserting yourself.

Set Your Sights on Relief. A method for reducing life-style stress.

Releasing Tension. A method for reducing mental, physical, and emotional stress.

STEP 3

<u>IS THIS ONE OF MY PERSONALITY TRAITS?</u>

Our personalities are made up of several elements. These personality traits consist of the thoughts, feelings and actions that determine how you experience life and react to it. Our traits even contribute to whether or not we experience worry, stress, fear, and anxiety.

Some traits can be either helpful or harmful. Other traits are only harmful. Certain traits increase our chances of worrying or feeling stress, fear, and anxiety. By identifying our personality traits, we can gain Personal Control over them and reduce our worry, stress, fear, and anxiety.

> ***FOR EXAMPLE*...One *Conquer Your Fears* participant told his group how before learning *Conquer Your Fears* methods, he felt up tight and restless whenever a task or project was incomplete or anything short of perfect. He used to drive himself to exhaustion reorganizing and improving things.**

There are a lot of personality traits. Certain key traits are associated with worry, stress, fear, and anxiety more than others. The fourteen key traits are

- ◆ Being Alert
- ◆ Trying to Hide Flaws
- ◆ Being Calm
- ◆ Feelings Hurt Easily
- ◆ Having Low Self-esteem
- ◆ Having Trouble Trusting
- ◆ Feeling Guilt

- ◆ Being in Control
- ◆ Having Many Shoulds
- ◆ Seeking Perfection
- ◆ Thinking Black-and-White
- ◆ Fearing Rejection
- ◆ Changing Focus
- ◆ Having Few Friends

EXERCISE

B

PERSONALITY TRAIT CHECKLIST

DIRECTIONS: For Exercise B...Each of the personality traits is presented in the following pages. There are 14 key traits. Each presentation is a carefully structured learning process. The process will teach you how to recognize each trait. Complete all seven learning steps listed here for each Personality Trait.

FOLLOW THESE LEARNING STEPS

1. Think about the descriptive *NAME OF EACH TRAIT*.

2. Learn the nature of the theme by studying examples. Read and rate the *COMMON EXAMPLES OF THIS TRAIT*. Think about each example and compare it to your own life. Circle one number to show how much you agree with each statement.

3. Then, read the *DISCUSSION OF THIS TRAIT*. It will help you understand ways the trait can be good or bad in your life.

4. Then, think about your life and this trait. How have you used this trait? Use the space provided to add *OTHER EXAMPLES* of you behaving with that trait.

5. Now, you have studied the theme and thought about its role in your life. Think about it some more and then indicate how much *INFLUENCE* that personality trait has over your behavior. Circle one number to show how much you have behaved with that trait in recent years.

6. Stop for a moment. Pay attention to what you are thinking about, what emotions you are feeling, and what sensations are in your body. Then, jot down a description of your experience. Use the space reserved for *PERSONAL REACTIONS AND IMPRESSIONS*.

7. Study the list of *CONQUER YOUR FEARS LESSONS* that would help you deal with that trait.

TRAIT

BEING ALERT

COMMON EXAMPLES OF THIS TRAIT:

How Much Do You Agree?

1. I notice things that others don't, like lights, sounds, and smells.

1 - 2 - 3 - 4 - 5
A Little...A Lot

2. I have very quick responses, like stopping my car quickly.

1 - 2 - 3 - 4 - 5
A Little...A Lot

3. I wake up easily, like when there is a noise outside my room while I am sleeping.

1 - 2 - 3 - 4 - 5
A Little...A Lot

4. I am pretty observant of things around me.

1 - 2 - 3 - 4 - 5
A Little...A Lot

5. I am constantly alert.

1 - 2 - 3 - 4 - 5
A Little...A Lot

6. I feel constantly watchful.

1 - 2 - 3 - 4 - 5
A Little...A Lot

7. I am jumpy most of the time.

1 - 2 - 3 - 4 - 5
A Little...A Lot

8. I feel on edge most of the time.

1 - 2 - 3 - 4 - 5
A Little...A Lot

DISCUSSION OF THIS TRAIT:

Being Alert may be helpful in avoiding accidents or in reading body language. *Being Alert* can be a problem if you are easily distracted.

OTHER EXAMPLES: List ways *Being Alert* may be a problem in your life now:

....

....

INFLUENCE:

How much is *Being Alert* one of your
personality traits?

1 - 2 - 3 - 4 - 5
A Little...A Lot

PERSONAL REACTIONS AND IMPRESSIONS:

....

....

CONQUER YOUR FEARS LESSONS that help us deal with *Being Alert:* For more information about each lesson, read the Index of *Conquer Your Fears* Methods in Step 4.

CONQUER YOUR FEARS LESSONS
THAT HELP YOU DEAL WITH THIS TRAIT

Take Control of Your Life. A method for focussing on what you can control and Letting Go of the rest.

Set Your Sights on Relief. A method for reducing life-style stress.

Releasing Tension. A method for reducing mental, physical, and emotional stress.

TRAIT

BEING IN CONTROL

COMMON EXAMPLES OF THIS TRAIT:

How Much Do You Agree?

1. I have very specific standards for the way certain things should be done.

    1 - 2 - 3 - 4 - 5
    A Little…A Lot

2. I have strong beliefs about how people (especially myself and those close to me) should act.

    1 - 2 - 3 - 4 - 5
    A Little…A Lot

3. I worry or think "what if" a lot.

    1 - 2 - 3 - 4 - 5
    A Little…A Lot

4. I need to be in control of myself.

    1 - 2 - 3 - 4 - 5
    A Little…A Lot

5. I need things to go my way.

    1 - 2 - 3 - 4 - 5
    A Little…A Lot

6. I need to be in control of my family.

    1 - 2 - 3 - 4 - 5
    A Little…A Lot

DISCUSSION OF THIS TRAIT:

Being in Control may be helpful in creating a sense of security.   *Being in Control* can be a problem if what you are trying to control is not in your power to control, so you end up feeling frustrated.

OTHER EXAMPLES: List ways *Being in Control* may be a problem in your life now:

....

....

INFLUENCE:

How much is *Being in Control* one of your   1 - 2 - 3 - 4 - 5
personality traits?   A Little...A Lot

PERSONAL REACTIONS AND IMPRESSIONS:

....

....

CONQUER YOUR FEARS LESSONS that help us deal with *Being in Control:* For more information about each lesson, read the Index of *Conquer Your Fears* Methods in Step 4.

CONQUER YOUR FEARS LESSONS
THAT HELP YOU DEAL WITH THIS TRAIT

Take Control of Your Life. A method for focussing on what you can control and Letting Go of the rest.

How Good Does It Have to Be? A method for setting healthy limits to Perfection-seeking.

Have You Taken Enough? A method for setting healthy limits to Being Strong.

Get the Most from Relationships! A method for avoiding destructive roles with others.

Be Realistic! A method for changing thoughts that cause stress.

Set Your Sights on Relief. A method for reducing life-style stress.

Releasing Tension. A method for reducing mental, physical, and emotional stress.

TRAIT

TRYING TO HIDE FLAWS

COMMON EXAMPLES OF THIS TRAIT:

How Much Do You Agree?

1. I am well-known for always being able to "get the job done."

1 - 2 - 3 - 4 - 5
A Little...A Lot

2. I want others to know I am competent.

1 - 2 - 3 - 4 - 5
A Little...A Lot

3. I want others to know I am dependable.

1 - 2 - 3 - 4 - 5
A Little...A Lot

4. I agree to do more work when I'm already swamped.

1 - 2 - 3 - 4 - 5
A Little...A Lot

5. I try to prove to others that I am trustworthy.

1 - 2 - 3 - 4 - 5
A Little...A Lot

6. I should be able to handle anything that comes my way.

1 - 2 - 3 - 4 - 5
A Little...A Lot

7. People rely on me.

1 - 2 - 3 - 4 - 5
A Little...A Lot

8. I often end up doing more work than my co-workers.

1 - 2 - 3 - 4 - 5
A Little...A Lot

DISCUSSION OF THIS TRAIT:

Trying to Hide Flaws may be helpful because it feels good to know others depend on you. *Trying to Hide Flaws* can be a problem if you strive to deal with too much and get overwhelmed.

OTHER EXAMPLES: List ways *Trying to Hide Flaws* may be a problem in your life now:

....

....

INFLUENCE:

How much is *Trying to Hide Flaws*
one of your personality traits?

1 - 2 - 3 - 4 - 5
A Little...A Lot

PERSONAL REACTIONS AND IMPRESSIONS:

....

....

CONQUER YOUR FEARS LESSONS that help us deal with *Trying to Hide Flaws:* For more information about each lesson, read the Index of *Conquer Your Fears* Methods in Step 4.

CONQUER YOUR FEARS LESSONS
THAT HELP YOU DEAL WITH THIS TRAIT

Take Control of Your Life. A method for focussing on what you can control and Letting Go of the rest.

How Good Does It Have to Be? A method for setting healthy limits to Perfection-seeking.

Have You Taken Enough? A method for setting healthy limits to Being Strong.

Turn Conflict into Action! A method for reducing internal conflict.

Get the Most from Relationships! A method for avoiding destructive roles with others.

Action without Anger. A method for successfully asserting yourself.

Be Realistic! A method for changing thoughts that cause stress.

Set Your Sights on Relief. A method for reducing life-style stress.

Releasing Tension. A method for reducing mental, physical, and emotional stress.

TRAIT

HAVING MANY SHOULDS

COMMON EXAMPLES OF THIS TRAIT:

How Much Do You Agree?

1. I feel I should accomplish everything I set out to accomplish.

1 - 2 - 3 - 4 - 5
A Little...A Lot

2. I believe my house should always be clean.

1 - 2 - 3 - 4 - 5
A Little...A Lot

3. I believe my house should always be neat.

1 - 2 - 3 - 4 - 5
A Little...A Lot

4. I think I should always look as if I know what I am doing.

1 - 2 - 3 - 4 - 5
A Little...A Lot

5. I have a large mental list of things I feel I should do.

1 - 2 - 3 - 4 - 5
A Little...A Lot

6. I place a high priority on getting lots done.

1 - 2 - 3 - 4 - 5
A Little...A Lot

DISCUSSION OF THIS TRAIT:

Having Many Shoulds may be helpful because it makes you a productive person. *Having Many Shoulds* can be a problem if trying to live up to your rules is impossible. This leads to failure and feeling bad about yourself.

OTHER EXAMPLES: List ways *Having Many Shoulds* may be a problem in your life now:

....

....

INFLUENCE:

How much is *Having Many Shoulds*
one of your personality traits?

1 - 2 - 3 - 4 - 5
A Little...A Lot

PERSONAL REACTIONS AND IMPRESSIONS:

....

....

CONQUER YOUR FEARS LESSONS that help us deal with *Having Many Shoulds:* For more information about each lesson, read the Index of *Conquer Your Fears* Methods in Step 4.

CONQUER YOUR FEARS LESSONS
THAT HELP YOU DEAL WITH THIS TRAIT

Take Control of Your Life. A method for focussing on what you can control and Letting Go of the rest.

How Good Does It Have to Be? A method for setting healthy limits to Perfection-seeking.

Tired of Pleasing Everybody Else? A method for setting healthy limits to People-pleasing.

Have You Taken Enough? A method for setting healthy limits to Being Strong.

Make Feelings Work for You! A method for understanding and properly using emotions.

Get the Most from Relationships! A method for avoiding destructive roles with others.

Action without Anger. A method for successfully asserting yourself.

Be Realistic! A method for changing thoughts that cause stress.

Set Your Sights on Relief. A method for reducing life-style stress.

Releasing Tension. A method for reducing mental, physical, and emotional stress.

TRAIT

BEING CALM

COMMON EXAMPLES OF THIS TRAIT:

How Much Do You Agree?

1. I get upset if I think
I have come across looking
flustered.

1 - 2 - 3 - 4 - 5
A Little...A Lot

2. I want to leave public places if
I think others can tell I am
feeling nervous.

1 - 2 - 3 - 4 - 5
A Little...A Lot

3. I try hard to remain calm or
at least appear calm in most
situations.

1 - 2 - 3 - 4 - 5
A Little...A Lot

4. I try to keep my emotions
under control.

1 - 2 - 3 - 4 - 5
A Little...A Lot

5. People probably think I handle
all types of situations very well.

1 - 2 - 3 - 4 - 5
A Little...A Lot

6. I avoid doing things that are
unfamiliar.

1 - 2 - 3 - 4 - 5
A Little...A Lot

DISCUSSION OF THIS TRAIT:

Being Calm may be helpful in many situations because you can focus on solving problems or keep others from getting upset. *Being Calm* can be a problem if you bottle up or block off upset feelings. This can cause worry, stress, fear, and anxiety.

OTHER EXAMPLES: List ways *Being Calm* may be a problem in your life now:

....

....

INFLUENCE:

How much is *Being Calm*   1 - 2 - 3 - 4 - 5
one of your personality traits?   A Little...A Lot

PERSONAL REACTIONS AND IMPRESSIONS:

....

....

CONQUER YOUR FEARS LESSONS that help us deal with *Being Calm:* For more information about each lesson, read the Index of *Conquer Your Fears* Methods in Step 4.

CONQUER YOUR FEARS LESSONS
THAT HELP YOU DEAL WITH THIS TRAIT

Take Control of Your Life. A method for focussing on what you can control and Letting Go of the rest.

How Good Does It Have to Be? A method for setting healthy limits to Perfection-seeking.

Have You Taken Enough? A method for setting healthy limits to Being Strong.

Make Feelings Work for You! A method for understanding and properly using emotions.

Be Realistic! A method for changing thoughts that cause stress.

Set Your Sights on Relief. A method for reducing life-style stress.

Releasing Tension. A method for reducing mental, physical, and emotional stress.

TRAIT

SEEKING PERFECTION

COMMON EXAMPLES OF THIS TRAIT:

How Much Do You Agree?

1. I feel I should not make
    mistakes.

    1 - 2 - 3 - 4 - 5
    A Little...A Lot

2. I feel I should always
    be on time.

    1 - 2 - 3 - 4 - 5
    A Little...A Lot

3. I should always follow through
    with commitments.

    1 - 2 - 3 - 4 - 5
    A Little...A Lot

4. I feel I should live up to
    extremely high standards
    and expectations.

    1 - 2 - 3 - 4 - 5
    A Little...A Lot

5. I try to be the best I can be.

    1 - 2 - 3 - 4 - 5
    A Little...A Lot

6. I try to be helpful.

    1 - 2 - 3 - 4 - 5
    A Little...A Lot

7. I try to be nice.

    1 - 2 - 3 - 4 - 5
    A Little...A Lot

DISCUSSION OF THIS TRAIT:

Seeking Perfection may be helpful because trying to be your best helps your self-esteem and benefits society. *Seeking Perfection* can be a problem if your rules and expectations are unrealistic, so you can't live up to all of them. You end up feeling bad about yourself.

OTHER EXAMPLES: List ways *Seeking Perfection* may be a problem in your life now:

....

....

INFLUENCE:

How much is *Seeking Perfection*
one of your personality traits?

1 - 2 - 3 - 4 - 5
A Little...A Lot

PERSONAL REACTIONS AND IMPRESSIONS:

....

....

CONQUER YOUR FEARS LESSONS that help us deal with *Seeking Perfection:* For more information about each lesson, read the Index of *Conquer Your Fears* Methods in Step 4.

CONQUER YOUR FEARS LESSONS THAT HELP YOU DEAL WITH THIS TRAIT

Take Control of Your Life. A method for focussing on what you can control and Letting Go of the rest.

How Good Does It Have to Be? A method for setting healthy limits to Perfection-seeking.

Tired of Pleasing Everybody Else? A method for setting healthy limits to People-pleasing.

Have You Taken Enough? A method for setting healthy limits to Being Strong.

Get the Most from Relationships! A method for avoiding destructive roles with others.

Action without Anger. A method for successfully asserting yourself.

Be Realistic! A method for changing thoughts that cause stress.

Set Your Sights on Relief. A method for reducing life-style stress.

Releasing Tension. A method for reducing mental, physical, and emotional stress.

TRAIT

FEELINGS HURT EASILY

COMMON EXAMPLES OF THIS TRAIT:

How Much Do You Agree?

1. I become upset when a complete stranger is rude to me.

1 - 2 - 3 - 4 - 5
A Little...A Lot

2. I feel upset or put down for a long time after being criticized.

1 - 2 - 3 - 4 - 5
A Little...A Lot

3. Work performance reviews make me nervous.

1 - 2 - 3 - 4 - 5
A Little...A Lot

4. I am very sensitive to criticism, whether it is constructive or not.

1 - 2 - 3 - 4 - 5
A Little...A Lot

5. I tend to take things personally.

1 - 2 - 3 - 4 - 5
A Little...A Lot

6. I have difficulty telling the difference between constructive criticism and abusive or destructive criticism.

1 - 2 - 3 - 4 - 5
A Little...A Lot

DISCUSSION OF THIS TRAIT:

Feelings Hurt Easily may be helpful if it leads to your having compassion and understanding toward others. *Feelings Hurt Easily* can be a problem if you upset yourself over things that needn't affect you so strongly.

OTHER EXAMPLES: List ways *Feelings Hurt Easily* may be a problem in your life now:

....

....

INFLUENCE:

How much is *Feelings Hurt Easily*
one of your personality traits?

1 - 2 - 3 - 4 - 5
A Little...A Lot

PERSONAL REACTIONS AND IMPRESSIONS:

....

....

CONQUER YOUR FEARS LESSONS that help us deal with *Feelings Hurt Easily:* For more information about each lesson, read the Index of *Conquer Your Fears* Methods in Step 4.

CONQUER YOUR FEARS LESSONS
THAT HELP YOU DEAL WITH THIS TRAIT

Tired of Pleasing Everybody Else? A method for setting healthy limits to People-pleasing.

Have You Taken Enough? A method for setting healthy limits to Being Strong.

Make Feelings Work for You! A method for understanding and properly using emotions.

Get the Most from Relationships! A method for avoiding destructive roles with others.

Action without Anger. A method for successfully asserting yourself.

Set Your Sights on Relief. A method for reducing life-style stress.

Releasing Tension. A method for reducing mental, physical, and emotional stress.

TRAIT

THINKING BLACK-AND-WHITE

COMMON EXAMPLES OF THIS TRAIT:

How Much Do You Agree?

1.   If I go off my diet by eating the wrong thing, I stay off the diet for the rest of the day because I "blew it."

1 - 2 - 3 - 4 - 5
A Little...A Lot

2.   Things are good or bad.

1 - 2 - 3 - 4 - 5
A Little...A Lot

3.   I get very involved in the "fairness" of things.

1 - 2 - 3 - 4 - 5
A Little...A Lot

4.   I get very angry at injustices.

1 - 2 - 3 - 4 - 5
A Little...A Lot

5.   Things are right or wrong.

1 - 2 - 3 - 4 - 5
A Little...A Lot

6.   I only work on a project in my spare time if I have enough time to complete it.

1 - 2 - 3 - 4 - 5
A Little...A Lot

7.   Things are "either-or."

1 - 2 - 3 - 4 - 5
A Little...A Lot

8.   If something is not perfect, it is useless or worthless.

1 - 2 - 3 - 4 - 5
A Little...A Lot

9.   Things should be a certain way only.

1 - 2 - 3 - 4 - 5
A Little...A Lot

DISCUSSION OF THIS TRAIT:

Thinking Black-and-White may be helpful if it makes things concrete and simple. *Thinking Black-and-White* can be a problem if looking at life in such extremes leads to disappointment and hurt.

OTHER EXAMPLES: List ways *Thinking Black-and-White* may be a problem in your life now:

....

....

INFLUENCE:

How much is *Thinking Black-and-White*
one of your personality traits?

1 - 2 - 3 - 4 - 5
A Little...A Lot

PERSONAL REACTIONS AND IMPRESSIONS:

....

....

CONQUER YOUR FEARS LESSONS that help us deal with *Thinking Black-and-White:* For more information about each lesson, read the Index of *Conquer Your Fears* Methods in Step 4.

CONQUER YOUR FEARS LESSONS THAT HELP YOU DEAL WITH THIS TRAIT

Take Control of Your Life. A method for focussing on what you can control and Letting Go of the rest.

How Good Does It Have to Be? A method for setting healthy limits to Perfection-seeking.

Have You Taken Enough? A method for setting healthy limits to Being Strong.

Action without Anger. A method for successfully asserting yourself.

Be Realistic! A method for changing thoughts that cause stress.

Set Your Sights on Relief. A method for reducing life-style stress.

Releasing Tension. A method for Reducing mental, physical, and emotional stress.

TRAIT

HAVING LOW SELF-ESTEEM

COMMON EXAMPLES OF THIS TRAIT:

How Much Do You Agree?

1. I am really hard on myself.

1 - 2 - 3 - 4 - 5
A Little...A Lot

2. Other people do things better than I do.

1 - 2 - 3 - 4 - 5
A Little...A Lot

3. I feel inferior to others.

1 - 2 - 3 - 4 - 5
A Little...A Lot

4. I think I am not worth much.

1 - 2 - 3 - 4 - 5
A Little...A Lot

5. I feel bad about myself.

1 - 2 - 3 - 4 - 5
A Little...A Lot

6. I often feel unsure of myself or like I have done something wrong.

1 - 2 - 3 - 4 - 5
A Little...A Lot

7. I lack confidence in myself.

1 - 2 - 3 - 4 - 5
A Little...A Lot

8. I often feel insecure.

1 - 2 - 3 - 4 - 5
A Little...A Lot

9. I often feel like a failure.

1 - 2 - 3 - 4 - 5
A Little...A Lot

DISCUSSION OF THIS TRAIT:

Having Low Self-esteem causes worry, stress, fear and anxiety by its very nature, since it involves being very hard on yourself in your thinking and in how you feel about yourself.

OTHER EXAMPLES: List ways *Having Low Self-esteem* may be a problem in your life now:

....

....

INFLUENCE:

How much is *Having Low Self-esteem*   1 - 2 - 3 - 4 - 5
one of your personality traits?   A Little...A Lot

PERSONAL REACTIONS AND IMPRESSIONS:

....

....

CONQUER YOUR FEARS LESSONS that help us deal with *Having Low Self-esteem:* For more information about each lesson, read the Index of *Conquer Your Fears* Methods in Step 4.

CONQUER YOUR FEARS LESSONS THAT HELP YOU DEAL WITH THIS TRAIT

Tired of Pleasing Everybody Else? A method for setting healthy limits to People-pleasing.

Make Feelings Work for You! A method for understanding and properly using emotions.

Turn Conflict into Action! A method for reducing internal conflict.

Get the Most from Relationships! A method for avoiding destructive roles with others.

Action without Anger. A method for successfully asserting yourself.

Set Your Sights on Relief. A method for reducing life-style stress.

Releasing Tension. A method for reducing mental, physical, and emotional stress.

TRAIT

FEARING REJECTION

COMMON EXAMPLES OF THIS TRAIT:

How Much Do You Agree?

1. I want to please others,
    especially those I
    depend upon.

    1 - 2 - 3 - 4 - 5
    A Little...A Lot

2. I am uncomfortable taking risks
    in public.

    1 - 2 - 3 - 4 - 5
    A Little...A Lot

3. I avoid new or
    unfamiliar situations.

    1 - 2 - 3 - 4 - 5
    A Little...A Lot

4. I think people won't
    accept me.

    1 - 2 - 3 - 4 - 5
    A Little...A Lot

5. I'm afraid people will reject me.

    1 - 2 - 3 - 4 - 5
    A Little...A Lot

DISCUSSION OF THIS TRAIT:

This is a very natural feeling. *Fearing Rejection* may be helpful in getting you to act in socially appropriate ways. *Fearing Rejection* can be a problem if it takes away your peace of mind, because peace of mind comes from feeling good about yourself.

OTHER EXAMPLES: List ways *Fearing Rejection* may be a problem in your life now:

....

....

INFLUENCE:

How much is *Fearing Rejection*
one of your personality traits?

1 - 2 - 3 - 4 - 5
A Little...A Lot

PERSONAL REACTIONS AND IMPRESSIONS:

....

....

CONQUER YOUR FEARS LESSONS that help us deal with *Fearing Rejection:* For more information about each lesson, read the Index of *Conquer Your Fears* Methods in Step 4.

CONQUER YOUR FEARS LESSONS THAT HELP YOU DEAL WITH THIS TRAIT

How Good Does It Have to Be? A method for setting healthy limits to Perfection-seeking.

Tired of Pleasing Everybody Else? A method for setting healthy limits to People-pleasing.

Have You Taken Enough? A method for setting healthy limits to Being Strong.

Make Feelings Work for You! A method for understanding and properly using emotions.

Turn Conflict into Action! A method for reducing internal conflict.

Get the Most from Relationships! A method for avoiding destructive roles with others.

Action without Anger. A method for successfully asserting yourself.

Be Realistic! A method for changing thoughts that cause stress.

Set Your Sights on Relief. A method for reducing life-style stress.

Releasing Tension. A method for reducing mental, physical, and emotional stress.

TRAIT

HAVING TROUBLE TRUSTING

COMMON EXAMPLES OF THIS TRAIT:

How Much Do You Agree?

1. I wonder why some people are nice to me.

1 - 2 - 3 - 4 - 5
A Little...A Lot

2. I become annoyed when people act superior to me.

1 - 2 - 3 - 4 - 5
A Little...A Lot

3. I often suspect people are doing things for reasons they are not disclosing.

1 - 2 - 3 - 4 - 5
A Little...A Lot

4. I have little patience for people who do not live up to their potential.

1 - 2 - 3 - 4 - 5
A Little...A Lot

5. I'm afraid people will reject me.

1 - 2 - 3 - 4 - 5
A Little...A Lot

6. I have a hard time accepting compliments.

1 - 2 - 3 - 4 - 5
A Little...A Lot

7. When things are going well, I expect something bad to happen.

1 - 2 - 3 - 4 - 5
A Little...A Lot

DISCUSSION OF THIS TRAIT:

Having Trouble Trusting may be helpful in that it keeps people from taking advantage of you. *Having Trouble Trusting* can be a problem if you don't trust anyone at all. When that happens, you are not able to develop intimate relationships.

OTHER EXAMPLES: List ways *Having Trouble Trusting* may be a problem in your life now:

....

....

INFLUENCE:

How much is *Having Trouble Trusting*
one of your personality traits?

1 - 2 - 3 - 4 - 5
A Little...A Lot

PERSONAL REACTIONS AND IMPRESSIONS:

....

....

CONQUER YOUR FEARS LESSONS that help us deal with *Having Trouble Trusting:* For more information about each lesson, read the Index of *Conquer Your Fears* Methods in Step 4.

CONQUER YOUR FEARS LESSONS THAT HELP YOU DEAL WITH THIS TRAIT

Take Control of Your Life. A method for focussing on what you can control and Letting Go of the rest.

Have You Taken Enough? A method for setting healthy limits to Being Strong.

Make Feelings Work for You! A method for understanding and properly using emotions.

Turn Conflict into Action! A method for reducing internal conflict.

Get the Most from Relationships! A method for avoiding destructive roles with others.

Be Realistic! A method for changing thoughts that cause stress.

Set Your Sights on Relief. A method for reducing life-style stress.

Releasing Tension. A method for reducing mental, physical, and emotional stress.

TRAIT

CHANGING FOCUS

COMMON EXAMPLES OF THIS TRAIT:

How Much Do You Agree?

1.   I often switch from one
     activity to another.

1 - 2 - 3 - 4 - 5
A Little...A Lot

2.   I can be very interested in
     something one minute then
     quickly lose interest.

1 - 2 - 3 - 4 - 5
A Little...A Lot

3.   My thoughts are often very fast.

1 - 2 - 3 - 4 - 5
A Little...A Lot

4.   I get bored with things easily.

1 - 2 - 3 - 4 - 5
A Little...A Lot

DISCUSSION OF THIS TRAIT:

Changing Focus may be helpful by keeping you active and interested in many things. *Changing Focus* can be a problem if you have trouble finishing things.

OTHER EXAMPLES: List ways *Changing Focus* may be a problem in your life now:

....

....

INFLUENCE:

How much is *Changing Focus*   1 - 2 - 3 - 4 - 5
one of your personality traits?   A Little...A Lot

PERSONAL REACTIONS AND IMPRESSIONS:

....

....

CONQUER YOUR FEARS LESSONS that help us deal with *Changing Focus:* For more information about each lesson, read the Index of *Conquer Your Fears* Methods in Step 4.

CONQUER YOUR FEARS LESSONS
THAT HELP YOU DEAL WITH THIS TRAIT

Make Feelings Work for You! A method for understanding and properly using emotions.

Turn Conflict into Action! A method for reducing internal conflict.

Get the Most from Relationships! A method for avoiding destructive roles with others.

Set Your Sights on Relief. A method for reducing life-style stress.

Releasing Tension. A method for reducing mental, physical, and emotional stress.

TRAIT

FEELING GUILT

COMMON EXAMPLES OF THIS TRAIT:

How Much Do You Agree?

1.   I often feel guilty for
something I did.

1 - 2 - 3 - 4 - 5
A Little...A Lot

2.   I often feel remorse about
something I said.

1 - 2 - 3 - 4 - 5
A Little...A Lot

3.   I often feel bad about
something I thought.

1 - 2 - 3 - 4 - 5
A Little...A Lot

4.   I get depressed easily.

1 - 2 - 3 - 4 - 5
A Little...A Lot

5.   I feel guilty when others feel
hurt, upset, or disappointed.

1 - 2 - 3 - 4 - 5
A Little...A Lot

DISCUSSION OF THIS TRAIT:

Feeling Guilt may be helpful if it keeps you from doing things that you feel are unproductive or damaging. *Feeling Guilt* can be a problem if you restrict your life to an excessive degree.

OTHER EXAMPLES: List ways *Feeling Guilt* may be a problem in your life now:

....

....

INFLUENCE:

How much is *Feeling Guilt*
one of your personality traits?

1 - 2 - 3 - 4 - 5
A Little...A Lot

PERSONAL REACTIONS AND IMPRESSIONS:

....

....

CONQUER YOUR FEARS LESSONS that help us deal with *Feeling Guilt:* For more information about each lesson, read the Index of *Conquer Your Fears* Methods in Step 4.

CONQUER YOUR FEARS LESSONS
THAT HELP YOU DEAL WITH THIS TRAIT

Take Control of Your Life. A method of focussing on what you can control and Letting Go of the rest.

How Good Does It Have to Be? A method for setting healthy limits to Perfection-seeking.

Tired of Pleasing Everybody Else? A method for setting healthy limits to People-pleasing.

Have You Taken Enough? A method for setting healthy limits to Being Strong.

Make Feelings Work for You! A method for understanding and properly using emotions.

Turn Conflict into Action! A method for reducing internal conflict.

Get the Most from Relationships! A method for avoiding destructive roles with others.

Action without Anger. A method for successfully asserting yourself.

Be Realistic! A method for changing thoughts that cause stress.

Set Your Sights on Relief. A method for reducing life-style stress.

Releasing Tension. A method for reducing mental, physical, and emotional stress.

TRAIT

HAVING FEW FRIENDS

COMMON EXAMPLES OF THIS TRAIT:

How Much Do You Agree?

1. Most of my friends are older than I am.

1 - 2 - 3 - 4 - 5
A Little...A Lot

2. Most of my friends are younger than I am.

1 - 2 - 3 - 4 - 5
A Little...A Lot

3. I have few friends from work.

1 - 2 - 3 - 4 - 5
A Little...A Lot

4. I have few friends from my neighborhood.

1 - 2 - 3 - 4 - 5
A Little...A Lot

DISCUSSION OF THIS TRAIT:

Having Few Friends may be helpful if it keeps you from doing things that you feel are unproductive or damaging. *Having Few Friends* can be a problem if you restrict your life to an excessive degree.

OTHER EXAMPLES: List ways *Having Few Friends* may be a problem in your life now:

....

....

INFLUENCE:

How much is *Having Few Friends*
one of your personality traits?

1 - 2 - 3 - 4 - 5
A Little...A Lot

PERSONAL REACTIONS AND IMPRESSIONS:

....

....

CONQUER YOUR FEARS LESSONS that help us deal with *Having Few Friends:* For more information about each lesson, read the Index of *Conquer Your Fears* Methods in Step 4.

CONQUER YOUR FEARS LESSONS THAT HELP YOU DEAL WITH THIS TRAIT

Take Control of Your Life. A method for focussing on what you can control and Letting Go of the rest.

Have You Taken Enough? A method for setting healthy limits to Being Strong.

Get the Most from Relationships! A method for avoiding destructive roles with others.

Action without Anger. A method for successfully asserting yourself.

STEP 4 STUDY THE INDEX OF CONQUER YOUR FEARS METHODS

Each *Conquer Your Fears* lesson teaches a method. Each method provides us with skills for dealing with most or all of our Resurfacing Childhood Themes and Personality Traits.

Each *Conquer Your Fears* method is listed below. Below each method is a definition of the method. Following the definition is a list of examples that show how themes and traits can be managed, reduced, or eliminated by using that method.

FOLLOW THESE LEARNING STEPS

1. Read and think about the name and definition of the method.

2. Read each example of how that method would be helpful with a theme or a trait.

3. Place a check mark in the box beside examples that sound beneficial to you.

4. Then count the total number of examples you checked and enter that number in the space provided.

INDEX OF CONQUER YOUR FEARS METHODS

TAKE CONTROL OF YOUR LIFE (Chapter 3)

A method for focussing on what you can control and letting go of the rest so that

☐ You take responsibility only for what is in your power to control, rather than *Acting Like a Parent* by controlling others.

☐ You loosen your code of conduct, rather than *Living by Many Rules*.

☐ You learn to go with the flow, rather than feeling unsettled from *Being from an Unstable Family*.

☐   You trust that others will react to you based on a number of factors--many of which you have no control over--rather than ***Feeling Love and Approval Are Conditional***.

☐   You trust that healthy relationships will work out for the best, rather than ***Fearing Separation***.

☐   You gain control by pleasing yourself, rather than ***Having Trouble Pleasing Others***.

☐   You admit and deal with total reality rather than ***Pretending Things Didn't Happen***.

☐   You reduce your vigilance, rather than ***Being Alert***.

☐   You take control (to the best of your ability) of that which is in your power to control and let go of the rest, rather than ***Being in Control***.

☐   You allow some of your flaws to be acknowledged, rather than ***Trying to Hide Flaws***.

☐   You gain control by limiting the rules you impose on yourself, rather than ***Having Many Shoulds***.

☐   You allow yourself to let your feelings out at times, rather than ***Being Calm***.

☐   You accept that no one--including yourself--is flawless, rather than ***Seeking Perfection***.

☐   You gain more control when you allow yourself to see the grey, rather than ***Thinking Black-and-White***.

☐   You open yourself to the possibility of believing in another person, rather than ***Having Trouble Trusting***.

☐   You release yourself from the burden of an overactive conscience, rather than ***Feeling Guilt***.

☐   You open yourself up to new possibilities, rather than controlling your social life by ***Having Few Friends***.

> *Enter the number of examples you checked. Now, or later, you can do part of Step 5 by circling that same number in the row beside this lesson's name on the Self-improvement Planner. See the last page of this chapter.*

HOW GOOD DOES IT HAVE TO BE? (Chapter 4)

A method for setting healthy limits to Perfection-seeking so that

☐ You take responsibility only for what is in your power to control, rather than *Acting Like a Parent* by trying to get others to be perfect.

☐ You loosen your code of conduct for yourself, rather than *Living by Many Rules*.

☐ You realize that others do not (or should not) expect you to be perfect, rather than *Feeling Love and Approval Are Conditional*.

☐ You set limits for yourself so you are not trying to prove your perfection, rather than *Having Trouble Pleasing Others*.

☐ You admit errors and admit when things go wrong, rather than *Pretending Things Didn't Happen*.

☐ You take responsibility only for what is in your power to control, rather than trying to be perfect by *Being in Control*.

☐ You allow some of your flaws to be acknowledged, rather than trying to be perfect by *Trying to Hide Flaws*.

☐ You limit the rules you impose on yourself, rather than *Having Many Shoulds*.

☐ You allow yourself to let your feelings out at times, rather than *Being Calm*.

☐ You reduce the pressure you place on yourself to be perfect by letting up on *Thinking Black-and-White*.

☐ You allow others to see that you are imperfect (human), rather than *Fearing Rejection*.

☐ You work out mistakes and then forgive yourself for not being perfect, rather than *Feeling Guilt*.

Enter the number of examples you checked. Now, or later, you can do part of Step 5 by circling that same number in the row beside this lesson's name on the Self-improvement Planner. See the last page of this chapter.

TIRED OF PLEASING EVERYBODY ELSE? (Chapter 5)

A method for setting healthy limits to People-pleasing so that

☐ You take responsibility only for what is in your power to control, rather than *Acting Like a Parent* by trying to be responsible for too much.

☐ You loosen your code of conduct, rather than *Living by Many Rules* about what you should do for others.

☐ You let go of worrying whether others like you, rather than *Feeling Love and Approval Are Conditional*.

☐ You trust that healthy relationships will work out for the best, rather than letting your actions be governed by *Fearing Separation*.

☐ You set limits to your People-Pleasing rather than feeling as if you are *Having Trouble Pleasing Others*.

☐ You limit the rules you have regarding how you ought to act toward others, rather than *Having Many Shoulds*.

☐ You accept that no one--including yourself--is flawless, rather than *Seeking Perfection* in your relationships with others.

☐ You develop boundaries around your emotions rather than having your *Feelings Hurt Easily*.

☐ You validate and appreciate yourself regardless of what others think of you, rather than *Having Low Self-esteem*.

☐ You learn that rejection is a natural part of life that everyone must deal with, rather than *Fearing Rejection*.

☐ You give your feelings priority when dealing with other people, rather than *Feeling Guilt*.

> *Enter the number of examples you checked. Now, or later, you can do part of Step 5 by circling that same number in the row beside this lesson's name on the Self-improvement Planner. See the last page of this chapter.*

___

HAVE YOU TAKEN ENOUGH? (Chapter 6)

A method for setting healthy limits to Being Strong so that

☐ You don't take on more responsibility than you should, rather than *Acting Like a Parent* by taking on too much.

☐ You loosen your code of conduct, rather than *Living by Many Rules* to be strong.

☐ You learn to say no, rather than basing your behavior on *Feeling Love and Approval Are Conditional*.

☐ You work at having healthy relationships, rather than *Fearing Separation*.

☐ You have courage to acknowledge your positive and negative feelings and open up with them, rather than *Avoiding Talk about Feelings*.

☐ You admit errors and admit when things go wrong, rather than *Pretending Things Didn't Happen*.

☐ You take control (to the best of your ability) of that which is in your power to control and let go of the rest, rather than *Being in Control*.

☐ You allow some of your flaws to be acknowledged, rather than *Trying to Hide Flaws*.

☐ You limit the rules you impose on yourself, rather than trying to be strong by *Having Many Shoulds*.

☐ You allow yourself to let your feelings out sometimes, rather than *Being Calm*.

☐ You accept that no one--including yourself--is flawless, rather than trying to be strong by *Seeking Perfection*.

☐ You develop boundaries around your emotions rather than having your *Feelings Hurt Easily*.

☐ You reduce the pressure on yourself to be strong by allowing yourself to see the grey, rather than *Thinking Black-and-White*.

☐ You learn that rejection is a natural part of life that everyone must deal with, rather than *Fearing Rejection*.

☐ You open yourself up to the possibility that other people will accept your feelings and your flaws, rather than *Having Trouble Trusting*.

☐ You give your feelings priority when dealing with other people, rather than *Feeling Guilt*.

☐ You open yourself up to new possibilities, rather than controlling your social life by *Having Few Friends*.

_____

Enter the number of examples you checked. Now, or later, you can do part of Step 5 by circling that same number in the row beside this lesson's name on the Self-improvement Planner. See the last page of this chapter.

MAKE FEELINGS WORK FOR YOU! (Chapter 7)

A method for understanding and properly using emotions so that

☐ You listen to your feelings before making decisions, rather than *Living by Many Rules*.

☐ You learn how to deal with emotions, rather than be affected by *Being from an Unstable Family*.

☐ You let go of worrying whether others like you, rather than *Feeling Love and Approval Are Conditional*.

☐ You trust that healthy relationships will work out for the best, rather than *Fearing Separation*.

☐ You set limits for yourself rather than *Having Trouble Pleasing Others*.

☐ You have courage to acknowledge your feelings and open up with them, rather than *Avoiding Talk about Feelings*.

☐ You admit errors and admit when things go wrong, rather than *Pretending Things Didn't Happen*.

☐ You limit the rules you have regarding how you ought to act toward others, rather than *Having Many Shoulds*.

☐ You allow yourself to let your feelings out at times, rather than *Being Calm*.

☐ You develop boundaries around your emotions rather than having your *Feelings Hurt Easily*.

☐ You validate and appreciate yourself, rather than *Having Low Self-esteem*.

☐ You learn that rejection is a natural part of life that everyone must deal with, rather than *Fearing Rejection*.

☐ You learn to let your feelings properly indicate who you can trust, rather than *Having Trouble Trusting*.

☐ You learn how to stick with an interest or activity when it is appropriate to do so, rather than *Changing Focus*.

☐ You release yourself from the burden of an overactive conscience, rather than *Feeling Guilt*.

Enter the number of examples you checked. Now, or later, you can do part of Step 5 by circling that same number in the row beside this lesson's name on the Self-improvement Planner. See the last page of this chapter.

TURN CONFLICT INTO ACTION! (Chapter 8)

A method for reducing internal conflict so that

☐　　　You learn to deal with your conflicts on the basis of your beliefs and needs, rather than your fears that *Feeling Love and Approval Are Conditional.*

☐　　　You deal with your conflicts, rather than avoiding them based on *Fearing Separation.*

☐　　　You deal with your conflicts over showing or hiding your feelings by having the courage to acknowledge your feelings and open up with them, rather than *Avoiding Talk about Feelings.*

☐　　　You deal with your conflicts over honesty and looking good to others by admitting errors and admitting when things go wrong, rather than *Pretending Things Didn't Happen.*

☐　　　You deal with your conflicts over being yourself and risking ridicule or rejection by being open rather than *Trying to Hide Flaws* and *Fearing Rejection.*

☐　　　You deal with conflicts over acting upon your feelings or holding them back through learning to validate and appreciate yourself and to direct your energy toward solving problems, rather than doing too little because of *Having Low Self-esteem.*

☐　　　You learn to overcome mixed emotions about people, rather than *Having Trouble Trusting.*

☐　　　You learn how to stick with an interest or activity when it is appropriate to do so, rather than being distracted by other interests or priorities and *Changing Focus.*

☐　　　You release yourself from the burden of an overactive conscience, rather than *Feeling Guilt.*

Enter the number of examples you checked. Now, or later, you can do part of Step 5 by circling that same number in the row beside this lesson's name on the Self-improvement Planner. See the last page of this chapter.

GET THE MOST FROM RELATIONSHIPS! (Chapter 9)

A method for avoiding destructive roles with others so that

☐   You take responsibility only for what is in your power to control, rather than *Acting Like a Parent*.

☐   You loosen your code of conduct for yourself and others, rather than *Living by Many Rules*.

☐   You develop positive relationships, rather than being affected by *Being from an Unstable Family*.

☐   You trust that others will react to you based on a number of factors--many of which you have no control over--rather than *Feeling Love and Approval Are Conditional*.

☐   You trust that healthy relationships will work out for the best, rather than *Fearing Separation*.

☐   You set limits for yourself rather than being held back by *Having Trouble Pleasing Others*.

☐   You have courage to acknowledge your feelings and open up with them, rather than *Avoiding Talk about Feelings*.

☐   You admit errors and admit when things go wrong, rather than *Pretending Things Didn't Happen*.

☐   You take control (to the best of your ability) of that which is in your power to control and let go of the rest, rather than *Being in Control*.

☐   You limit the rules you impose on yourself and others, rather than *Having Many Shoulds*.

☐   You allow some of your flaws to be acknowledged, rather than *Trying to Hide Flaws*.

☐   You accept that no one--including yourself--is flawless, rather than *Seeking Perfection*.

☐   You develop boundaries around your emotions, rather than having your *Feelings Hurt Easily*.

☐   You validate and appreciate yourself, rather than *Having Low Self-esteem*.

☐ You learn that rejection is a natural part of life that everyone must deal with, rather than *Fearing Rejection*.

☐ You increase the level of intimacy in your relationships, rather than ***Having Trouble Trusting***.

☐ You decrease the level of frustration in your relationships, rather than ***Changing Focus***.

☐ You learn from interpersonal mistakes then let them go, rather than ***Feeling Guilt***.

☐ You learn to let peers into your circle of friends, rather than ***Having Few Friends***.

> *Enter the number of examples you checked. Now, or later, you can do part of Step 5 by circling that same number in the row beside this lesson's name on the Self-improvement Planner. See the last page of this chapter.*

ACTION WITHOUT ANGER (Chapter 10)

A method for successfully asserting yourself so that

☐ You relax your code of conduct about how you should act, rather than ***Living by Many Rules***.

☐ You have courage to acknowledge and productively use and share your feelings, rather than ***Avoiding Talk about Feelings***.

☐ You admit making errors and when things go wrong, rather than emotional defensiveness and ***Pretending Things Didn't Happen***.

☐ You act based on your feelings, needs, and beliefs, rather than ***Trying to Hide Flaws***.

☐ You become more effective by limiting the rules you have regarding how you ought to act toward others, rather than ***Having Many Shoulds***.

☐ You accept that no one--including yourself--acts perfectly, rather than ***Seeking Perfection***.

☐ You develop boundaries around your emotions so you don't have to hold back, rather than having your *Feelings Hurt Easily*.

☐ You allow yourself to see many different aspects of events and situations so you can act accordingly, rather than *Thinking Black-and-White*.

☐ You validate and appreciate yourself and take meaningful action, rather than *Having Low Self-esteem*.

☐ You learn that rejection is a natural part of life that everyone must deal with, rather than hiding because you are *Fearing Rejection*.

☐ You avoid over-blaming yourself so you can be free to be assertive, rather than *Feeling Guilt*.

☐ You learn how to express yourself so you can expand your circle of friends, rather than *Having Few Friends*.

> *Enter the number of examples you checked. Now, or later, you can do part of Step 5 by circling that same number in the row beside this lesson's name on the Self-improvement Planner. See the last page of this chapter.*

BE REALISTIC! (Chapter 11)

A method for changing thoughts that cause stress so that

☐ You take responsibility only for what is in your power to control, rather than thinking you need to be *Acting Like a Parent*.

☐ You loosen your thoughts about how you should act, rather than *Living by Many Rules*.

☐ You let go of worrying whether others like you, rather than *Feeling Love and Approval Are Conditional*.

☐ You trust that healthy relationships will work out for the best, rather than *Fearing Separation*.

☐   You learn to have confidence that your feelings are valid. This makes it OK to talk about them, rather than *Avoiding Talk about Feelings*.

☐   You stop thinking you can control that which is not in your power to control, rather than *Being in Control*.

☐   You realize it is okay to acknowledge flaws, rather than *Trying to Hide Flaws*.

☐   You limit the rules you impose on yourself, rather than *Having Many Shoulds*.

☐   You allow yourself to let your feelings out at times, rather than *Being Calm*.

☐   You accept that no one--including yourself--is flawless, rather than *Seeking Perfection*.

☐   You allow yourself to see the grey, rather than *Thinking Black-and-White*.

☐   You realize that rejection is a natural part of life that everyone must deal with, rather than *Fearing Rejection*.

☐   You let go of suspicion toward others, rather than *Having Trouble Trusting*.

☐   You relax blaming yourself, rather than *Feeling Guilt*.

> *Enter the number of examples you checked. Now, or later, you can do part of Step 5 by circling that same number in the row beside this lesson's name on the Self-improvement Planner. See the last page of this chapter.*

SET YOUR SIGHTS ON RELIEF (Chapter 12)

A method for reducing life-style stress so that

☐   You take responsibility only for what is in your power to control, rather than *Acting Like a Parent*.

☐   You loosen your code of conduct, rather than *Living by Many Rules*.

☐   You have courage to acknowledge your feelings and open up with them, rather than *Avoiding Talk about Feelings*.

☐ You admit errors and admit when things go wrong, rather than *Pretending Things Didn't Happen*.

☐ You reduce your vigilance, rather than *Being Alert*.

☐ You take responsibility only for what is in your power to control, rather than *Being in Control*.

☐ You allow some of your flaws to be acknowledged, rather than *Trying to Hide Flaws*.

☐ You limit the rules you impose on yourself, rather than *Having Many Shoulds*.

☐ You allow yourself to let your feelings out at times, rather than *Being Calm*.

☐ You accept that no one--including yourself--is flawless, rather than *Seeking Perfection*.

☐ You develop boundaries around your emotions rather than having your *Feelings Hurt Easily*.

☐ You allow yourself to see the grey, rather than *Thinking Black-and-White*.

☐ You validate and appreciate yourself, rather than *Having Low Self-esteem*.

☐ You learn that rejection is a natural part of life that everyone must deal with, rather than *Fearing Rejection*.

☐ You let go of the tension of constantly being on guard, rather than *Having Trouble Trusting*.

☐ You reduce frustration from uncompleted projects, rather than *Changing Focus*.

☐ You reduce the stress caused by an overactive conscience, rather than *Feeling Guilt*.

Enter the number of examples you checked. Now, or later, you can do part of Step 5 by circling that same number in the row beside this lesson's name on the Self-improvement Planner. See the last page of this chapter.

RELEASING TENSION (Chapter 13)

A method for reducing mental, physical, and emotional stress so that

- ☐ You take responsibility only for what is in your power to control, rather than *Acting Like a Parent*.

- ☐ You trust that others will react to you based on a number of factors--many of which you have no control over--rather than *Feeling Love and Approval Are Conditional*.

- ☐ You trust that healthy relationships will work out for the best, rather than *Fearing Separation*.

- ☐ You have courage to acknowledge your feelings and open up with them, rather than *Avoiding Talk about Feelings*.

- ☐ You admit errors and admit when things go wrong, rather than *Pretending Things Didn't Happen*.

- ☐ You reduce your vigilance, rather than *Being Alert*.

- ☐ You take responsibility only for what is in your power to control, rather than *Being in Control*.

- ☐ You allow some of your flaws to be acknowledged, rather than *Trying to Hide Flaws*.

- ☐ You limit the rules you impose on yourself, rather than *Having Many Shoulds*.

- ☐ You allow yourself to let your feelings out sometimes, rather than *Being Calm*.

- ☐ You accept that no one--including yourself--is flawless, rather than *Seeking Perfection*.

- ☐ You develop boundaries around your emotions rather than having your *Feelings Hurt Easily*.

- ☐ You allow yourself to see the grey, rather than *Thinking Black-and-White*.

- ☐ You validate and appreciate yourself, rather than *Having Low Self-esteem*.

- ☐ You learn that rejection is a natural part of life that everyone must deal with, rather than *Fearing Rejection*.

- ☐ You let go of the tension of constantly being on guard, rather than *Having Trouble Trusting*.

☐ You reduce frustration from uncompleted projects, rather than *Changing Focus*.

☐ You reduce the stress caused by an overactive conscience, rather than *Feeling Guilt*.

> *Enter the number of examples you checked. Now, or later, you can do part of Step 5 by circling that same number in the row beside this lesson's name on the Self-improvement Planner. See the last page of this chapter.*

STEP 5

<u>COMPLETE YOUR SELF-IMPROVEMENT PLANNER.</u>

Each *Conquer Your Fears* lesson is listed below. Beside each lesson name is a counting scale. Use that scale to show how many examples of themes and traits you checked for each CYF lesson in the Index of Conquer Your Fears Methods in Step 4.

On the page, the length of each counting scale is the same, even though the number of examples is different for each method list in Step 4. This way you can compare the relative importance of each method for you.

FOLLOW THESE PLANNING STEPS

1. For each lesson, circle the number that is the same as your count of checked examples.

2. Draw a line to connect the circles. The lessons with circles farthest to the right are most likely to be helpful to you now.

3. Plan to do these lessons first if you are using the workbook alone.

   Pay special attention to these lessons if you do them with a group.

4. Plan to review these lessons more often after you have completed the entire CYF workbook.

SELF–IMPROVEMENT PLANNER

Take Control of Your Life. 1 2 3 4 5 6 7 8 9 10 11 12 13 14 15 16 17

How Good Does It Have to Be? 1 2 3 4 5 6 7 8 9 10 11 12

Tired of Pleasing Everybody Else? 1 2 3 4 5 6 7 8 9 10 11

Have You Taken Enough? 1 2 3 4 5 6 7 8 9 10 11 12 13 14 15 16 17

Make Feelings Work for You! 1 2 3 4 5 6 7 8 9 10 11 12 13 14 15

Turn Conflict into Action! 1 2 3 4 5 6 7 8 9

Get the Most from Relationships! 1 2 3 4 5 6 7 8 9 10 11 12 13 14 15 16 17 18 19

Action without Anger. 1 2 3 4 5 6 7 8 9 10 11 12

Be Realistic! 1 2 3 4 5 6 7 8 9 10 11 12 13 14

Set Your Sights on Relief. 1 2 3 4 5 6 7 8 9 10 11 12 13 14 15 16 17

Releasing Tension. 1 2 3 4 5 6 7 8 9 10 11 12 13 14 15 16 17 18 19

Chapter 3

TAKE CONTROL OF YOUR LIFE

INTRODUCTION

Controlling is directing, regulating, or governing something. It's natural to try to control what happens in our lives. In fact, most of what we do can be interpreted as some form of attempt to control, even when we don't mean it that way.

However, trying to control can be overdone or go out-of-bounds. This is the case when we try to control things that are actually beyond our power. It usually leads to frustration and failure. When it does, we end up with a negative attitude.

Trying to control things that you can't control causes worry, stress, fear, and anxiety. But, if you set proper limits to what you try to control, you increase your sense of Personal Control, release tension, and develop a positive attitude toward yourself, others, and life in general.

GOALS

1.   You will learn how to identify what you are trying to control.

2.   You will learn how to decide which of those things you should stop trying to control.

3.   You will learn how to focus your attention on those things you should try to control.

<u>REMEMBER</u>

Don't miss another opportunity to build your peace of mind. When worry, stress, fear, or anxiety strike this week...Conquer Your Fears! Use...

*

<u>FIRST AID for...WORRY, STRESS, FEAR, AND ANXIETY</u>

Step 1: Always...Breathe Out!

Step 2: What Am I Trying to Control?

Step 3: Let Go of What's Out-of-bounds.

Step 4: Control What's In-bounds.

* Permission is given to reproduce the First Aid Steps for your personal use.

STEP 1

<u>ALWAYS...BREATHE OUT!</u>

Much of our tension comes from holding on to things. This takes different forms. Several chapters in the workbook will help you let go of something. By learning to let go, we learn to release tension.

Release Breathing is an excellent way to practice letting go. The way we breathe is basic and concrete. If we learn to let go when we breathe, we master a fundamental model of this important tension reducing skill. The method of Release Breathing will help you learn to let go.

Let's take a closer look at holding on. When we hold on, we try to make things a certain way. We are holding on when we try to make ourselves think, feel, or act a certain way. We are holding on when we try to make or keep something in our life unchanged. We are holding on when we don't throw things away or we want someone else to act differently.

You can see from these examples that holding on is a form of control. This lesson teaches you how to decide what not to control or hold on to. It teaches of what to let go.

The Release Breathing method is excellent practice at giving up control and letting go. In this case, you let go of the air in your lungs and tension in your body. Don't force it out, because that is control. Don't regulate the release of air. Don't cut it short. Let it flow.

Release Breathing sends an important "Let go" message to our brain. It involves 3 steps:

1. Breathe in deeply, using *medium force*. Use your diaphragm.

2. Breathe out through your mouth, using *medium strong force*. Let your shoulders, chest, and diaphragm sag or fall downward.

    Think "Let go of control" as you release the air in your lungs. Let go of the air and all the tension in your body.

3. Pause for a moment at the end of the breath. Feel the release of tension.

    Think about having "Let go" of the air and tension in your body.

STEP 2

WHAT AM I TRYING TO CONTROL?

Controlling is making things the way we want them or the way we think they should be. Everyone tries to control a number of things. We do it all the time. This is normal.

Two Forms of Control. Trying to control takes two forms:

■ Gaining Control. Trying to get control involves efforts to make things a certain way.

■ Maintaining Control. Trying to avoid losing control involves efforts to prevent things from getting out of hand, becoming unpredictable, or becoming undesirable.

When Efforts Fail. We feel threatened or frustrated when we fail in our efforts to gain or maintain control. Worry, stress, fear, and anxiety often set in when we "think" we are out of control or when we "think" we may lose control.

When Efforts Succeed. We feel secure and adequate when we succeed in our efforts to gain or maintain control. We can be successful if we limit ourselves to controlling the right things. We experience more Personal Control when we do the following:

 Try to Control What's In-Bounds. Our own behavior is in-bounds. We can control our own behavior. We end up feeling good more often if we try to control only the things that we actually can control. This creates a sense of Personal Control.

 Don't Try to Control What's Out-of-Bounds. External things are out-of-bounds. We can't control external things. We end up feeling frustrated or inadequate when we try to control things that are impossible for us to control. This takes away our sense of Personal Control.

Things We Try to Control. There are seven categories of things we try to control. Three are *in-bounds* because they involve our own behavior, which we can control. Four are *out-of-bounds* because they involve external things that we can't control.

In-Bounds	Out-of-Bounds
■ What you think.	■ What others think.
■ How you feel.	■ How others feel.
■ How you act.	■ How others act.
	■ Circumstances.

Influence Is Not Control. Our behavior may influence things that are out-of-bounds, but that doesn't mean we have control. Our actions play a part in most events and situations in our lives. We do things that provoke reactions in others or shape events. Still, we can only control our own behavior. What we do is a part of the big picture, but not the whole picture. The rest is out of our control.

We Do It Constantly. Thoughts about being in control or out of control can be conscious or unconscious. In fact, most of the time we automatically interpret situations and react to them without consciously thinking about the issue of control. But we are always aware of control at least unconsciously. Whether we know it or not, we are always trying to gain or maintain control of what's happening. And we develop worry, stress, fear, and anxiety when we interpret ourselves, the situation, or the event as being out of control. This happens whether our interpretation is conscious or unconscious.

Be Aware and Analyze. This lesson teaches you how to limit your controlling efforts to those things that are in-bounds, the ones with which you can succeed. You must be conscious of what you are trying to control in order to focus on the right things. So, you must start with being aware. And, you must recognize whether the thing you are trying to control is in-bounds or out-of-bounds. To analyze this, you need to ask yourself the right questions.

EXERCISE

A

RECOGNIZING BOUNDARIES AND WHAT YOU TRY TO CONTROL

This exercise will help you learn to think about your reactions, figure out WHAT YOU ARE TRYING TO CONTROL, and decide if it is in-bounds or out-of-bounds.

DIRECTIONS FOR EXERCISE A:

◆   Imagine yourself in each sample situation below. Ask yourself what things you might have been trying to control if you reacted that way.

◆   Use a check mark to indicate which general types of things (categories) you might have been trying to control in each sample situation.

◆   Some of your selections may be "in-bounds." But most people recognize that, probably, they would be trying to gain or maintain control of things that are "out-of-bounds."

◆   Compare your selections with the Comments On The Exercise. Remember, your answers are neither right nor wrong, because everyone approaches this exercise in his/her own way. This is not a test. The exercise teaches you a thinking process.

BEGIN EXERCISE A:

A1.   Ask yourself what things you might be trying to control if...
you get angry at a waiter who ignores you.

In-Bounds

☐ What I think.
☐ How I feel.
☐ How I act.

Out-of-Bounds

☐ What the waiter or others think.
☐ How the waiter or others feel.
☐ How the waiter or others act.
☐ Circumstances there in the restaurant.

A2.   Ask yourself what things you might be trying to control if...
       you worry about how someone will react if you do what you want.

   In-Bounds   Out-of-Bounds

   ☐ What I think.   ☐ What the other person will think.
   ☐ How I feel.   ☐ How the other person will feel.
   ☐ How I act.   ☐ How the other person will act.
                                    ☐ Circumstances related to the other person's reaction.

A3.   Ask yourself what things you might be trying to control if...
       you are scared about how your boss will evaluate you.

   In-Bounds   Out-of-Bounds

   ☐ What I think.   ☐ What my boss or others think or will think.
   ☐ How I feel.   ☐ How my boss or others feel or will feel.
   ☐ How I act.   ☐ How my boss or others act or will act.
                                    ☐ Circumstances related to my evaluation and job.

A4.   Ask yourself what things you might be trying to control if...
       you try to stop someone from drinking.

   In-Bounds   Out-of-Bounds

   ☐ What I think.   ☐ What the drinker or someone else thinks.
   ☐ How I feel.   ☐ How the drinker or someone else feels.
   ☐ How I act.   ☐ How the drinker or someone else acts.
                                    ☐ Circumstances related to the drinking behavior.

A5.   Ask yourself what things you might be trying to control if...
       you want to introduce yourself to someone, but you "chicken out."

   In-Bounds   Out-of-Bounds

   ☐ What I think.   ☐ What others think.
   ☐ How I feel.   ☐ How others feel.
   ☐ How I act.   ☐ How others act.
                                    ☐ Circumstances.

COMMENTS ON THE EXERCISE

A1.   People often select

a.   *How I feel.* For example, not losing control of your temper. In this your attention is drawn in-bounds to your emotional reactions, which you can control.

b.   *How the waiter or others act and think.* For example, you want him to pay attention to you. In this case you are focussing your attention out-of-bounds, on behavior of another person, which you cannot control.

A2.   People often select

a.   *How I act.* For example, should you do something or not? In this case you are trying to control your own behavior, which is in-bounds.

b.   *What others think and how they feel and act.* For example, are they going to be upset, hurt, or angry? Will they try to get even? Will they overreact? In this case you are focussing your attention on the out-of-bounds reaction of another person, which you cannot control.

A3.   People often select

a.   *How I feel or act.* For example, you don't want to feel as afraid as you do, nor do you want to "freeze up." How can you be more confident? Haven't you been doing the job to the best of your ability? In this case attention is directed in-bounds to your own emotional reactions, which you can control.

b.   *How your boss will think and act.* For example, what if he thinks you're not doing a good enough job and fires you? In this case your attention is drawn to the out-of-bounds reaction of another person, which you cannot control.

A4.   People often select

   a.   *How I act*. For example, whether or not you throw liquor out of the house. In this case your attention is focussed in-bounds, on your own behavior, which you can control.

   b.   *How the other person acts*. For example, whether or not the person goes to a bar. Trying to control where another person goes is out-of-bounds. You cannot control it.

A5.   People often select

   a.   *How I act*. For example, will you feel good about what you say and how you say it? Your behavior is in-bounds; you can control it.

   b.   *How the other person thinks or acts*. For example, will s/he think you are too forward or act insulted? The other person's reaction is out-of-bounds and beyond your control.

STEP 3

LET GO OF WHAT'S OUT-OF-BOUNDS

Letting go involves letting something be its own way. We must let go of things we cannot control. First we must recognize that we are trying to gain or maintain control of something that is out-of-bounds, as you practiced in Step 2. Then we should let go of it.

Letting go takes self-discipline for most of us. We have to practice in order to learn how and to stick with it. One method that works for most people is simply to tell ourselves what to do.

We can use four basic "Letting Go Statements" to remind ourselves to set limits to our efforts at gaining and maintaining control of things that are out-of-bounds.

- ■   I can't control how s/he thinks. That's out-of-bounds.

- ■   I can't control how s/he feels. That's out-of-bounds.

- ■   I can't control how s/he acts. That's out-of-bounds.

- ■   I can't control circumstances. They're out-of-bounds.

EXERCISE

B

TELLING YOURSELF TO LET GO

This exercise will help you learn to LET GO OF WHAT'S OUT-OF-BOUNDS.

DIRECTIONS FOR EXERCISE B:

- ◆   The sample items from Exercise A are used again. Like before, imagine yourself in each sample situation. Select the Letting Go Statement that would best fit any out-of-bounds things you might have been trying to control.

- ◆   Use a check mark to indicate which Letting Go Statements you could use to remind yourself to limit your efforts to gain or maintain control.

BEGIN EXERCISE B:

B1.   Select the best Letting Go Statement to tell yourself if...
       you get angry at a waiter who ignores you.

       ☐ I can't control how s/he thinks. That's out-of-bounds.
       ☐ I can't control how s/he feels. That's out-of-bounds.
       ☐ I can't control how s/he acts. That's out-of-bounds.
       ☐ I can't control circumstances. They're out-of-bounds.

B2.   Select the best Letting Go Statement to tell yourself if...
       you worry about how someone will react to what you do.

       ☐ I can't control how s/he thinks. That's out-of-bounds.
       ☐ I can't control how s/he feels. That's out-of-bounds.
       ☐ I can't control how s/he acts. That's out-of-bounds.
       ☐ I can't control circumstances. They're out-of-bounds.

B3.   Select the best Letting Go Statement to tell yourself if...
       you are scared about how your boss will evaluate you.

       ☐ I can't control how s/he thinks. That's out-of-bounds.
       ☐ I can't control how s/he feels. That's out-of-bounds.
       ☐ I can't control how s/he acts. That's out-of-bounds.
       ☐ I can't control circumstances. They're out-of-bounds.

B4.   Select the best Letting Go Statement to tell yourself if...
       you try to stop someone from drinking.

       ☐ I can't control how s/he thinks. That's out-of-bounds.
       ☐ I can't control how s/he feels. That's out-of-bounds.
       ☐ I can't control how s/he acts. That's out-of-bounds.
       ☐ I can't control circumstances. They're out-of-bounds.

B5.   Select the best Letting Go Statement to tell yourself if...
       you want to introduce yourself to someone, but you "chicken out."

       ☐ I can't control how s/he thinks. That's out-of-bounds.
       ☐ I can't control how s/he feels. That's out-of-bounds.
       ☐ I can't control how s/he acts. That's out-of-bounds.
       ☐ I can't control circumstances. They're out-of-bounds.

STEP 4 CONTROL WHAT'S IN-BOUNDS

Sometimes just Letting Go of out-of-bounds things is a big relief. Other times we need to do more. Once we let go of things we can't control, we can tell ourselves how to control things over which we have real power. Our own thoughts, feelings, and actions are in-bounds. We can control them.

Controlling the things that are in-bounds takes self-discipline just like letting go of what's out-of-bounds. The key is focussing on what actions to take. There are 10 basic actions we can take to gain or maintain control over our own behavior.

- <u>Limiting Perfection-seeking.</u> Stop insisting on things being "better" or "the right way" if it leads to feeling out of control, building tension, or a negative attitude.

- <u>Limiting People-pleasing.</u> Stop doing things to please other people if it leads to feeling out of control, building tension, or a negative attitude.

- <u>Limiting Being Strong.</u> Stop taking on more and bottling up your feelings if it leads to feeling out of control, building tension, or a negative attitude.

- <u>Using Your Feelings.</u> Recognize, understand, and channel your feelings into problem solving if they start building up or confusing you in ways that lead to feeling out of control, building tension, or forming a negative attitude.

- <u>Deciding and Acting.</u> Make a decision and take action when you are in conflict. Stop holding back when mixed feelings or conflicting thoughts lead to feeling out of control, building tension, or a negative attitude.

- <u>Treating Someone Differently.</u> Change a relationship by altering the old patterns that have happened over and over again if they lead to feeling out of control, building tension, or a negative attitude.

- <u>Being Assertive.</u> Stop holding yourself back when it leads to feeling out of control, building tension, or a negative attitude.

- <u>Practicing Realistic Thoughts.</u> Analyze situations rather than automatically reacting to your own exaggerations and unrealistic interpretations and expectations of events when they lead to feeling out of control, building tension, or a negative attitude.

- Reacting Differently to a Stressor. Work on one reaction to something that causes you stress. Stop feeling powerless over stressors that overwhelm you if it leads to feeling out of control, building tension, or a negative attitude.

- Releasing Tension. Do things to reduce or release tension. Let go of stress that builds up inside if it leads to feeling out of control, building tension, or a negative attitude.

Each of these 10 basic actions can be stated in a self-directive way. We call these "Self-control Statements."

- I only have to do well enough.

- I can please myself.

- I can do less or let down.

- I feel this way for a good reason. What can I do about it?

- I can decide and act; or let go, do nothing, and not worry about it.

- I can treat someone differently.

- I can be assertive.

- I can be realistic.

- I can react differently to one stressor.

- I can do things to reduce tension.

EXERCISE

C

USING SELF-CONTROL STATEMENTS

This exercise will help you learn to CONTROL WHAT'S IN-BOUNDS.

DIRECTIONS FOR EXERCISE C:

♦   The items from Exercises A & B are used again below. Like before, imagine yourself in each sample situation. Select the Self-control Statement that would remind you of the best action you can take to gain or maintain control of an in-bounds element of the situation.

♦   Use a check mark to indicate which Self-control Statements you could use to remind yourself to keep your controlling efforts in-bounds.

BEGIN EXERCISE C:

C1.   Select the best Self-control Statement for you to tell yourself if...
you get angry at a waiter who ignores you.

<u>What I Think</u>
☐ I only have to do well enough.
☐ I can please myself.
☐ I can do less or let down.
☐ I can be realistic.

<u>How I Feel</u>
☐ I feel this way for a good reason. What can I do about it?

<u>How I Act</u>
☐ I can treat someone differently.
☐ I can be assertive.
☐ I can decide and act; or let go, do nothing, and not worry about it.
☐ I can react differently to one stressor.
☐ I can do things to reduce tension.

C2.   Select the best Self-control Statement for you to tell yourself if...
      you worry about how someone will react if you do what you want.

      What I Think
      ☐ I only have to do well enough.
      ☐ I can please myself.
      ☐ I can do less or let down.
      ☐ I can be realistic.

      How I Feel
      ☐ I feel this way for a good reason. What can I do about it?

      How I Act
      ☐ I can treat someone differently.
      ☐ I can be assertive.
      ☐ I can decide and act; or let go, do nothing, and not worry about it.
      ☐ I can react differently to one stressor.
      ☐ I can do things to reduce tension.

C3.   Select the best Self-control Statement for you to tell yourself if...
      you are scared about how your boss will evaluate you.

      What I Think
      ☐ I only have to do well enough.
      ☐ I can please myself.
      ☐ I can do less or let down.
      ☐ I can be realistic.

      How I Feel
      ☐ I feel this way for a good reason. What can I do about it?

      How I Act
      ☐ I can treat someone differently.
      ☐ I can be assertive.
      ☐ I can decide and act; or let go, do nothing, and not worry about it.
      ☐ I can react differently to one stressor.
      ☐ I can do things to reduce tension.

C4.   Select the best Self-control Statement for you to tell yourself if...
you try to stop someone from drinking.

<u>What I Think</u>
☐ I only have to do well enough.
☐ I can please myself.
☐ I can do less or let down.
☐ I can be realistic.

<u>How I Feel</u>
☐ I feel this way for a good reason. What can I do about it?

<u>How I Act</u>
☐ I can treat someone differently.
☐ I can be assertive.
☐ I can decide and act; or let go, do nothing, and not worry about it.
☐ I can react differently to one stressor.
☐ I can do things to reduce tension.

C5.   Select the best Self-control Statement for you to tell yourself if...
you want to introduce yourself to someone, but you "chicken out."

<u>What I Think</u>
☐ I only have to do well enough.
☐ I can please myself.
☐ I can do less or let down.
☐ I can be realistic.

<u>How I Feel</u>
☐ I feel this way for a good reason. What can I do about it?

<u>How I Act</u>
☐ I can treat someone differently.
☐ I can be assertive.
☐ I can decide and act; or let go, do nothing, and not worry about it.
☐ I can react differently to one stressor.
☐ I can do things to reduce tension.

PRACTICE YOUR WORK SHEETS

<u>DIRECTIONS:</u>   The more you study the steps in this lesson, the more effective your new skills will become. Work Sheets are designed to help you master these skills. So, read the story below. We will use it as an example to help you learn to use the Work Sheets successfully.

Billy was throwing another one of his tantrums. He was whining and angry, stomping around the house, and throwing himself on the furniture--all this drama because Betty wouldn't let him eat cookies for breakfast! "You never let me eat what I want." "You don't love me."

Betty tried ignoring him.   But she couldn't force the questions out of her mind. "How could he say such things?" "Did he really believe them?" "Why does he get so upset?" "What makes him act that way?"

The longer it went on, the more inadequate, helpless, and desperate she felt. "I should be more patient." "I'm a terrible mother." "I'm gonna kill him!"

What could she do? Thoughts raced through her mind. "Spank him?" "Send him to his room?" "Run off to Tahiti with that cute shoe salesman?"

<u>DIRECTIONS:</u>   For your practice homework exercise...Imagine that you are Betty in this situation. Complete the "Practice Self-control Work Sheet" on the next page.

NEXT PAGE

PRACTICE SELF-CONTROL WORK SHEET

Step 1: <u>Breathe out, relaxing your diaphragm.</u> *Practice Release Breathing while you are completing each of the other steps...*

Step 2: <u>What Am I Trying to Control?</u> *Identify what you would have been trying to control if you were Betty...*

<u>In-Bounds</u>
- ☐ What I think.
- ☐ How I feel.
- ☐ How I act.

<u>Out-of-Bounds</u>
- ☐ What others think.
- ☐ How others feel.
- ☐ How others act.
- ☐ Circumstances.

Step 3: <u>Let Go of What's Out-of-bounds.</u> *What external things should you stop trying to control if you were Betty?*

- ☐ I can't control how s/he thinks. That's out-of-bounds.
- ☐ I can't control how s/he feels. That's out-of-bounds.
- ☐ I can't control how s/he acts. That's out-of-bounds.
- ☐ I can't control circumstances. They're out-of-bounds.

Step 4: <u>Control What's In-Bounds.</u> *What could you control if you were Betty?*

<u>What I Think</u>
- ☐ I only have to do well enough.
- ☐ I can please myself.
- ☐ I can do less or let down.
- ☐ I can be realistic.

<u>How I Feel</u>
- ☐ I feel this way for a good reason. What can I do about it?

<u>How I Act</u>
- ☐ I can treat someone differently.
- ☐ I can be assertive.
- ☐ I can decide and act; or let go, do nothing, and not worry about it.
- ☐ I can react differently to one stressor.
- ☐ I can do things to reduce tension.

<u>Step 1: Breathe out, relaxing your diaphragm.</u> *Practice Release Breathing while you are completing each of the other steps...*

<u>Step 2: What Am I Trying to Control?</u> *Identify what you would have been trying to control if you were Betty... (Darkened boxes are responses chosen for this sample.)*

In-Bounds	Out-of-Bounds
☐ What I think.	■ What others think.
☐ How I feel.	■ How others feel.
☐ How I act.	■ How others act.
	☐ Circumstances.

<u>Step 3: Let Go of What's Out-of-bounds.</u> *What external things should you stop trying to control if you were Betty?*

■ I can't control how s/he thinks. That's out-of-bounds.
■ I can't control how s/he feels. That's out-of-bounds.
■ I can't control how s/he acts. That's out-of-bounds.
☐ I can't control circumstances. They're out-of-bounds.

<u>Step 4: Control What's In-Bounds.</u> *What could you control if you were Betty?*

<u>What I Think</u>
☐ I only have to do well enough.
■ I can please myself.
☐ I can do less or let down.
■ I can be realistic.

<u>How I Feel</u>
☐ I feel this way for a good reason. What can I do about it?

<u>How I Act</u>
■ I can treat someone differently.
☐ I can be assertive.
☐ I can decide and act; or let go, do nothing, and not worry about it.
■ I can react differently to one stressor.
☐ I can do things to reduce tension.

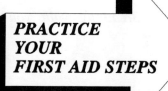

PRACTICE YOUR FIRST AID STEPS

<u>DIRECTIONS:</u> The more you practice your First Aid Steps, the better you will feel. Practice your First Aid Steps now. Imagine you are in a situation used in this lesson, or think about your life in general.

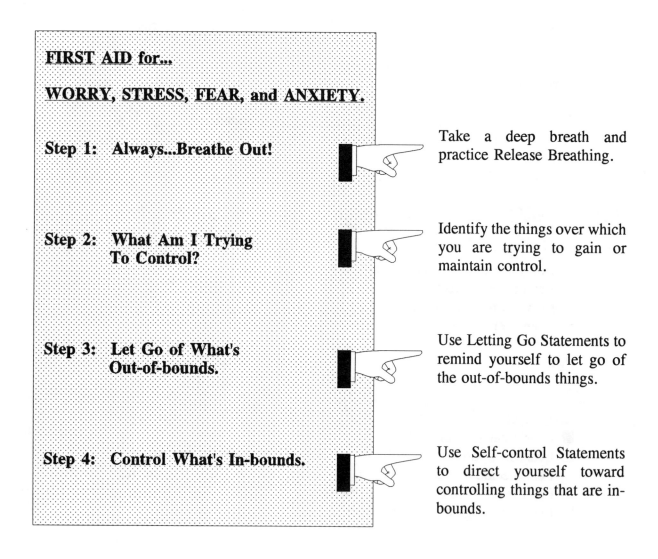

<u>FIRST AID for...</u>

<u>WORRY, STRESS, FEAR, and ANXIETY.</u>

Step 1: Always...Breathe Out! — Take a deep breath and practice Release Breathing.

Step 2: What Am I Trying To Control? — Identify the things over which you are trying to gain or maintain control.

Step 3: Let Go of What's Out-of-bounds. — Use Letting Go Statements to remind yourself to let go of the out-of-bounds things.

Step 4: Control What's In-bounds. — Use Self-control Statements to direct yourself toward controlling things that are in-bounds.

HOMEWORK

<u>THE METHODS...</u>

Use each of the methods below to learn and successfully use this skill to TAKE CONTROL OF YOUR LIFE.

<u>Work Sheets.</u> Complete at least one Self-Control Work Sheet each day. Do the Work Sheets for situations in which you worry or feel stress, fear, or anxiety. Complete the Work Sheets at the time of these events or very soon thereafter.

<u>First Aid Steps.</u> Practice your First Aid Steps as often as possible, even when you are not really worrying or feeling threatened.

*

<u>FIRST AID for...WORRY, STRESS, FEAR, AND ANXIETY</u>

Step 1: Always...Breathe Out!

Step 2: What Am I Trying to Control?

Step 3: Let Go of What's Out-of-bounds.

Step 4: Control What's In-bounds.

<u>Clip-outs:</u> Make copies of the First Aid Steps. Place them in spots where you will see them and remember to practice. Give some to a friend, and tell him or her how to use them.

<u>Teach Others.</u> Share the lesson with others. Teach them how to help themselves by using the same skills you are learning.

* Permission is given to reproduce the First Aid Steps for your personal use.

Step 1: Breathe out, relaxing your diaphragm. *Practice Release Breathing while you are completing each of the other steps...*

Step 2: What Am I Trying to Control? *Identify what you have been trying to control...*

In-Bounds
☐ What I think.
☐ How I feel.
☐ How I act.

Out-of-Bounds
☐ What others think.
☐ How others feel.
☐ How others act.
☐ Circumstances.

Step 3: Let Go of What's Out-of-bounds. *What external things should you stop trying to control?*

☐ I can't control how s/he thinks. That's out-of-bounds.
☐ I can't control how s/he feels. That's out-of-bounds.
☐ I can't control how s/he acts. That's out-of-bounds.
☐ I can't control circumstances. They're out-of-bounds.

Step 4: Control What's In-Bounds. *What can you control?*

What I Think
☐ I only have to do well enough.
☐ I can please myself.
☐ I can do less or let down.
☐ I can be realistic.

How I Feel
☐ I feel this way for a good reason. What can I do about it?

How I Act
☐ I can treat someone differently.
☐ I can be assertive.
☐ I can decide and act; or let go, do nothing, and not worry about it.
☐ I can react differently to one stressor.
☐ I can do things to reduce tension.

Step 1: Breathe out, relaxing your diaphragm. *Practice Release Breathing while you are completing each of the other steps...*

Step 2: What Am I Trying to Control? *Identify what you have been trying to control...*

In-Bounds	Out-of-Bounds
☐ What I think.	☐ What others think.
☐ How I feel.	☐ How others feel.
☐ How I act.	☐ How others act.
	☐ Circumstances.

Step 3: Let Go of What's Out-of-bounds. *What external things should you stop trying to control?*

☐ I can't control how s/he thinks. That's out-of-bounds.
☐ I can't control how s/he feels. That's out-of-bounds.
☐ I can't control how s/he acts. That's out-of-bounds.
☐ I can't control circumstances. They're out-of-bounds.

Step 4: Control What's In-Bounds. *What can you control?*

<u>What I Think</u>
☐ I only have to do well enough.
☐ I can please myself.
☐ I can do less or let down.
☐ I can be realistic.

<u>How I Feel</u>
☐ I feel this way for a good reason. What can I do about it?

<u>How I Act</u>
☐ I can treat someone differently.
☐ I can be assertive.
☐ I can decide and act; or let go, do nothing, and not worry about it.
☐ I can react differently to one stressor.
☐ I can do things to reduce tension.

Step 1: Breathe out, relaxing your diaphragm. *Practice Release Breathing while you are completing each of the other steps...*

Step 2: What Am I Trying to Control? *Identify what you have been trying to control...*

<u>In-Bounds</u>
- ☐ What I think.
- ☐ How I feel.
- ☐ How I act.

<u>Out-of-Bounds</u>
- ☐ What others think.
- ☐ How others feel.
- ☐ How others act.
- ☐ Circumstances.

Step 3: Let Go of What's Out-of-bounds. *What external things should you stop trying to control?*

- ☐ I can't control how s/he thinks. That's out-of-bounds.
- ☐ I can't control how s/he feels. That's out-of-bounds.
- ☐ I can't control how s/he acts. That's out-of-bounds.
- ☐ I can't control circumstances. They're out-of-bounds.

Step 4: Control What's In-Bounds. *What can you control?*

<u>What I Think</u>
- ☐ I only have to do well enough.
- ☐ I can please myself.
- ☐ I can do less or let down.
- ☐ I can be realistic.

<u>How I Feel</u>
- ☐ I feel this way for a good reason. What can I do about it?

<u>How I Act</u>
- ☐ I can treat someone differently.
- ☐ I can be assertive.
- ☐ I can decide and act; or let go, do nothing, and not worry about it.
- ☐ I can react differently to one stressor.
- ☐ I can do things to reduce tension.

Step 1: Breathe out, relaxing your diaphragm. *Practice Release Breathing while you are completing each of the other steps...*

Step 2: What Am I Trying to Control? *Identify what you have been trying to control...*

<table>
<tr><td>

In-Bounds
☐ What I think.
☐ How I feel.
☐ How I act.
</td><td>

Out-of-Bounds
☐ What others think.
☐ How others feel.
☐ How others act.
☐ Circumstances.
</td></tr>
</table>

Step 3: Let Go of What's Out-of-bounds. *What external things should you stop trying to control?*

    ☐ I can't control how s/he thinks. That's out-of-bounds.
    ☐ I can't control how s/he feels. That's out-of-bounds.
    ☐ I can't control how s/he acts. That's out-of-bounds.
    ☐ I can't control circumstances. They're out-of-bounds.

Step 4: Control What's In-Bounds. *What can you control?*

What I Think
☐ I only have to do well enough.
☐ I can please myself.
☐ I can do less or let down.
☐ I can be realistic.

How I Feel
☐ I feel this way for a good reason. What can I do about it?

How I Act
☐ I can treat someone differently.
☐ I can be assertive.
☐ I can decide and act; or let go, do nothing, and not worry about it.
☐ I can react differently to one stressor.
☐ I can do things to reduce tension.

Step 1: Breathe out, relaxing your diaphragm. *Practice Release Breathing while you are completing each of the other steps...*

Step 2: What Am I Trying to Control? *Identify what you have been trying to control...*

In-Bounds	Out-of-Bounds
☐ What I think.	☐ What others think.
☐ How I feel.	☐ How others feel.
☐ How I act.	☐ How others act.
	☐ Circumstances.

Step 3: Let Go of What's Out-of-bounds. *What external things should you stop trying to control?*

☐ I can't control how s/he thinks. That's out-of-bounds.
☐ I can't control how s/he feels. That's out-of-bounds.
☐ I can't control how s/he acts. That's out-of-bounds.
☐ I can't control circumstances. They're out-of-bounds.

Step 4: Control What's In-Bounds. *What can you control?*

What I Think
☐ I only have to do well enough.
☐ I can please myself.
☐ I can do less or let down.
☐ I can be realistic.

How I Feel
☐ I feel this way for a good reason. What can I do about it?

How I Act
☐ I can treat someone differently.
☐ I can be assertive.
☐ I can decide and act; or let go, do nothing, and not worry about it.
☐ I can react differently to one stressor.
☐ I can do things to reduce tension.

Step 1: Breathe out, relaxing your diaphragm. *Practice Release Breathing while you are completing each of the other steps...*

Step 2: What Am I Trying to Control? *Identify what you have been trying to control...*

<table>
<tr><td>

In-Bounds
☐ What I think.
☐ How I feel.
☐ How I act.

</td><td>

Out-of-Bounds
☐ What others think.
☐ How others feel.
☐ How others act.
☐ Circumstances.

</td></tr>
</table>

Step 3: Let Go of What's Out-of-bounds. *What external things should you stop trying to control?*

☐ I can't control how s/he thinks. That's out-of-bounds.
☐ I can't control how s/he feels. That's out-of-bounds.
☐ I can't control how s/he acts. That's out-of-bounds.
☐ I can't control circumstances. They're out-of-bounds.

Step 4: Control What's In-Bounds. *What can you control?*

What I Think
☐ I only have to do well enough.
☐ I can please myself.
☐ I can do less or let down.
☐ I can be realistic.

How I Feel
☐ I feel this way for a good reason. What can I do about it?

How I Act
☐ I can treat someone differently.
☐ I can be assertive.
☐ I can decide and act; or let go, do nothing, and not worry about it.
☐ I can react differently to one stressor.
☐ I can do things to reduce tension.

<u>Step 1: Breathe out, relaxing your diaphragm.</u> *Practice Release Breathing while you are completing each of the other steps...*

<u>Step 2: What Am I Trying to Control?</u> *Identify what you have been trying to control...*

<u>In-Bounds</u>
☐ What I think.
☐ How I feel.
☐ How I act.

<u>Out-of-Bounds</u>
☐ What others think.
☐ How others feel.
☐ How others act.
☐ Circumstances.

<u>Step 3: Let Go of What's Out-of-bounds.</u> *What external things should you stop trying to control?*

☐ I can't control how s/he thinks. That's out-of-bounds.
☐ I can't control how s/he feels. That's out-of-bounds.
☐ I can't control how s/he acts. That's out-of-bounds.
☐ I can't control circumstances. They're out-of-bounds.

<u>Step 4: Control What's In-Bounds.</u> *What can you control?*

<u>What I Think</u>
☐ I only have to do well enough.
☐ I can please myself.
☐ I can do less or let down.
☐ I can be realistic.

<u>How I Feel</u>
☐ I feel this way for a good reason. What can I do about it?

<u>How I Act</u>
☐ I can treat someone differently.
☐ I can be assertive.
☐ I can decide and act; or let go, do nothing, and not worry about it.
☐ I can react differently to one stressor.
☐ I can do things to reduce tension.

Step 1: <u>Breathe out, relaxing your diaphragm.</u> *Practice Release Breathing while you are completing each of the other steps...*

Step 2: <u>What Am I Trying to Control?</u> *Identify what you have been trying to control...*

<u>In-Bounds</u>
- ☐ What I think.
- ☐ How I feel.
- ☐ How I act.

<u>Out-of-Bounds</u>
- ☐ What others think.
- ☐ How others feel.
- ☐ How others act.
- ☐ Circumstances.

Step 3: <u>Let Go of What's Out-of-bounds.</u> *What external things should you stop trying to control?*

- ☐ I can't control how s/he thinks. That's out-of-bounds.
- ☐ I can't control how s/he feels. That's out-of-bounds.
- ☐ I can't control how s/he acts. That's out-of-bounds.
- ☐ I can't control circumstances. They're out-of-bounds.

Step 4: <u>Control What's In-Bounds.</u> *What can you control?*

<u>What I Think</u>
- ☐ I only have to do well enough.
- ☐ I can please myself.
- ☐ I can do less or let down.
- ☐ I can be realistic.

<u>How I Feel</u>
- ☐ I feel this way for a good reason. What can I do about it?

<u>How I Act</u>
- ☐ I can treat someone differently.
- ☐ I can be assertive.
- ☐ I can decide and act; or let go, do nothing, and not worry about it.
- ☐ I can react differently to one stressor.
- ☐ I can do things to reduce tension.

Chapter 4

HOW GOOD DOES IT HAVE TO BE?

INTRODUCTION

One of the ways we try to control our lives is making things the way we think they "should" be. We call this Perfection-seeking. It's natural and healthy to try to do things well. It makes things better. Sometimes, Perfection-seeking is OK.

However, Perfection-seeking can be overdone or go out-of-bounds. This is when we try to make the impossible happen, when we can't let up, or when we can't feel satisfied. We call this *negative Perfection-seeking*.

Negative Perfection-seeking can cause worry, stress, fear, and anxiety. But if you set proper limits to your Perfection-seeking, you increase your sense of Personal Control, release tension, and develop a positive attitude toward yourself, others, and life in general.

GOALS

1. You will identify some of your own Perfection-seeking behavior and learn how to recognize it when it starts.

2. You will learn how to decide if it is positive (healthy) or negative (self-destructive) Perfection-seeking.

3. You will learn how to set limits to your Perfection-seeking behavior.

Don't miss another opportunity to build your peace of mind. When worry, stress, fear, or anxiety strike this week...Conquer Your Fears! Use...

*

FIRST AID for...WORRY, STRESS, FEAR, AND ANXIETY

Step 1:   **Always...Breathe Out!**

Step 2:   **Am I Perfection-seeking?**

Step 3:   **Does It Involve a Negative Attitude?**

Step 4:   **Let Go of Negative Perfection-seeking.**

* Permission is given to reproduce the First Aid Steps for your personal use.

STEP 1

ALWAYS...BREATHE OUT!

We can increase internal tension by trying too hard to do things well. We recommend Release Breathing for briefly reducing the tension that builds up from this Perfection-seeking behavior.

Release Breathing enables us to let go of the tension we build up through being dissatisfied and pressuring ourselves to make things better. And we can use this skill on the spot, in the middle of any activity, as often as we wish, especially when we realize that we are trying too hard to do things well.

Let's take a closer look at Perfection-seeking. When we seek perfection, we are being dissatisfied with how things are. That is a negative attitude. Our negative attitude of dissatisfaction is active when we think we aren't getting something done fast enough, aren't trying hard enough, aren't doing enough, and should be doing better.

Perfection-seeking is a form of control rooted in our negative attitude. This lesson teaches how to decide when to let go of Perfection-seeking methods of maintaining control. It teaches you to be satisfied when appropriate.

The negative attitude of dissatisfaction causes tension to build in our bodies. That tension often takes the form of restricting our breathing as the muscles of our chest tighten. The Release Breathing technique is an excellent way to practice giving up both your physical tension and your dissatisfied, negative attitude.

Release Breathing sends an important "let go" message to the brain. It involves 3 steps:

1.   breathe in deeply, using *medium force*. Using your diaphragm,

2.   breathe out through your mouth, using *medium strong force*. Let your shoulders, chest, and diaphragm sag or fall downward.

      Think "let go of being perfect" as you release air from your lungs. Let go of the air and all the tension in your body, and

3.   pause for a moment at the end of the breath. Feel the release of tension.

      Think of having "let go" of both the tightness in your chest and the need to make things better.

STEP 2

Perfection-seeking is trying to make things better. The need to improve things is usually based on dissatisfaction, the belief that if things are better life will be better, or insecurity. Often beliefs and feelings like these are unconscious.

There are two aspects to Perfection-seeking: 1) what we do; and 2) why we do it. We are Perfection-seeking when we put effort into making things different or improving them. We do this so that we will be more satisfied and/or more secure.

Perfection-seeking consists of living up to your own standards, values, wishes, and expectations about how life should be. This results in one of 4 basic Perfection-seeking behaviors:

    Hurrying Up.

    Trying Hard.

    Doing More.

    Doing Better.

RECOGNIZING WHEN YOU ARE PERFECTION-SEEKING

EXERCISE A

<u>DIRECTIONS:</u> For Exercise A...Circle a number to show how much you agree with each statement. Use the space provided to add other examples of ways you do each type of Perfection-seeking behavior.

BEGIN EXERCISE A:

HURRYING UP:

How Much Do You Agree?

1. I often find myself running late.

1 - 2 - 3 - 4 - 5
A Little....A Lot

2. I often seem to be concerned about catching up with someone else or thinking of someone else as slowing me down.

1 - 2 - 3 - 4 - 5
A Little....A Lot

3. I find it hard to slow my pace and take things in stride.

1 - 2 - 3 - 4 - 5
A Little....A Lot

4. I tend to be impatient.

1 - 2 - 3 - 4 - 5
A Little....A Lot

5. I often get ahead of myself, doing something first that should have waited until I had completed some other task.

1 - 2 - 3 - 4 - 5
A Little....A Lot

Other examples of my Hurrying Up:

....

....

TRYING HARD: How Much Do You Agree?

1.   I often make a big effort   1 - 2 - 3 - 4 - 5
      but don't fully succeed.   A Little....A Lot

2.   I often feel overwhelmed   1 - 2 - 3 - 4 - 5
      and/or frustrated.   A Little....A Lot

3.   I find it hard to be content that I have tried hard enough   1 - 2 - 3 - 4 - 5
      or put enough effort into making things right.   A Little....A Lot

Other examples of my Trying Hard:

....

....

DOING MORE:
                                                            How Much Do You Agree?

1.   I often have a lot   1 - 2 - 3 - 4 - 5
      on my mind.   A Little....A Lot

2.   I usually take on   1 - 2 - 3 - 4 - 5
      more than one thing at a time.   A Little....A Lot

3.   I find it hard to limit the number   1 - 2 - 3 - 4 - 5
      of things I try to get done.   A Little....A Lot

Other examples of my Doing More:

....

....

DOING BETTER:

How Much Do You Agree?

1.   I find it hard to be content with things that are   1 - 2 - 3 - 4 - 5
unfinished, disorganized, or flawed.   A Little....A Lot

2.   I try very hard to be sure   1 - 2 - 3 - 4 - 5
I get things right.   A Little....A Lot

3.   I usually notice how something   1 - 2 - 3 - 4 - 5
could be improved or done better.   A Little....A Lot

4.   I find it natural to rearrange   1 - 2 - 3 - 4 - 5
or redo things.   A Little....A Lot

5.   I tend to put things off   1 - 2 - 3 - 4 - 5
when I don't know where to start.   A Little....A Lot

6.   I often find fault with things;   1 - 2 - 3 - 4 - 5
I can be pretty critical.   A Little....A Lot

Other examples of my Doing Better:

....

....

PICK A REAL EXAMPLE FROM YOUR OWN LIFE.

SAMPLE SITUATION

Learning Steps 3 and 4 will be easier if you can refer to a personal example of Perfection-seeking. Use the space below to describe one event or situation where you did, or have done, or still do, a lot of Perfection-seeking.

Write a description of your event or sample situation here.

....

....

....

Check-off "YES" or "NO" to show which basic Perfection-seeking behavior(s) you were using.

Hurrying Up	☐ YES	☐ NO
Trying Hard	☐ YES	☐ NO
Doing More	☐ YES	☐ NO
Doing Better	☐ YES	☐ NO

DOES IT INVOLVE A NEGATIVE ATTITUDE?

Many of us have been taught that Perfection-seeking is a good thing to do. There's nothing wrong with working to make things better. Perfection-seeking is OK as long as our attitude stays positive. But we can go too far. In that case, we need to think a new way.

Perfection-seeking is self-destructive when it goes beyond healthy limits. It's out-of-bounds when a negative attitude is involved in one of two ways: 1) if Perfection-seeking is **driven** by a negative attitude; or 2) if Perfection-seeking **leads us to form** a negative attitude. Four Key Questions help us recognize when our Perfection-seeking is out-of-bounds.

- ◆ Am I Doing It Because I'm Not OK?

- ◆ Am I Doing It Because S/he or It Is Not OK?

- ◆ Do I End Up Feeling Not OK after Doing It?

- ◆ Do I End Up Thinking S/he or It Is Not OK after Doing It?

Why ask the Key Questions? Usually, we are unconscious of our Not OK attitude about ourselves, others, or the situation. If we ask the question, we have a chance to identify the attitude and make a change for the better. If we are aware of it, and we know what to do differently, we can take Personal Control.

Remember, the Key Questions are designed to help make you aware of the unconscious role played by negative attitudes about yourself, others, and life in general.

Awareness and options equal Personal Control!

<u>**Driven:**</u> "Driven" means allowing a force to make you do something. Perfection-seeking is self-destructive when the force driving it is a negative attitude about yourself, someone else, or life in general:

     Am I Doing It Because I'm Not OK?

     Am I Doing It Because S/he or It Is Not OK?

Am I driven to Perfection-seeking because I'm Not OK?

This question asks if you are striving for perfection because of some defect in yourself. Because you are not better in some way, you have to always do things better to make up for it.

BECAUSE... I'm not good enough... I'm not worth enough... I'm not wanted enough...

I HAVE TO DO THINGS BETTER

Am I driven to Perfection-seeking because something else is Not OK?

This question asks if you are striving for perfection because you think someone or something else is defective.   Because that person, those people, or the situation is not better in some way, you have to try to do things better to make up the difference or keep things OK.

BECAUSE... Someone isn't good enough... Someone isn't worth enough... Someone isn't wanted enough...

I HAVE TO DO THINGS BETTER

Leads to: "Leads to" means how things end up. Usually, Perfection-seeking leads to some kind of outcome or result. Perfection-seeking is self-destructive when it leads to a result that includes you having a negative attitude about yourself, someone else, or life in general:

 Do I End Up Feeling Not OK after Doing It?

 Do I End Up Thinking S/he or It Is Not OK after Doing It?

Do I end up feeling Not OK after Perfection-seeking?

This question asks if you end up feeling bad or defective after you have been trying to do things better. Even though you covered all the bases, things didn't go as you hoped.

WHEN I'M PERFECTION-SEEKING		*I END UP...* Feeling unappreciated or exploited... Doing too much and burning out... Feeling frustrated...

Do I end up thinking something else is Not OK after Perfection-seeking?

This question asks if you end up thinking that someone or something else is defective after you have been trying to do things better. It is Not OK because your Perfection-seeking didn't work.

WHEN I'M PERFECTION-SEEKING		*I END UP...* Thinking someone isn't good enough... Thinking something isn't worth enough... Thinking someone isn't wanted enough...

EXERCISE

B

DECIDING IF YOUR PERFECTION-SEEKING INVOLVES A NEGATIVE ATTITUDE

<u>DIRECTIONS:</u> For Exercise B...Continue using the Sample Situation you described at the end of Exercise A or refer to your life in general.

◆ Check off "Yes" or "No" to show if each typical, negative attitude below is/was involved with your Sample Situation or with Perfection-seeking events in your life in general.

◆ Use the space provided to add other negative attitudes involved with your Sample Situation or Perfection-seeking events in your life in general.

BEGIN EXERCISE B:

FIND OUT IF PERFECTION-SEEKING IS DRIVEN BY A NEGATIVE ATTITUDE ABOUT YOURSELF BY ASKING: *Am I doing it because I'm Not OK? If I do it better, then I will be adequate, worthwhile, or desirable.*

Do You Agree?

1. I get into Perfection-seeking because
I'm not good, smart, or capable enough. ☐ YES ☐ NO

2. I get into Perfection-seeking because
I'm not important, popular, or likeable enough. ☐ YES ☐ NO

3. I get into Perfection-seeking because
if I do something wrong, I don't deserve to have what I want. ☐ YES ☐ NO

Other ways I feel Not OK that drive me toward Perfection-seeking:

....

....

FIND OUT IF PERFECTION-SEEKING IS DRIVEN BY A NEGATIVE ATTITUDE
ABOUT SOMEONE ELSE OR LIFE IN GENERAL BY ASKING: *Am I doing it because
s/he or it is Not OK? Do I do it because s/he is critical or inadequate?*

Do You Agree?

1. I get into Perfection-seeking because
    someone is hard to please.   ☐ YES   ☐ NO

2. I get into Perfection-seeking because
    if I make a mistake, someone will put me down or be upset.   ☐ YES   ☐ NO

3. I get into Perfection-seeking because
    I can't stand it if things are half done or disorganized.   ☐ YES   ☐ NO

Other ways of thinking s/he or it is Not OK that drive me toward Perfection-seeking:

....

FIND OUT IF PERFECTION-SEEKING LEADS TO A NEGATIVE ATTITUDE ABOUT
YOURSELF BY ASKING: *Do I end up feeling not OK after doing it? If I do it better, do I
end up feeling exploited, un-appreciated, or "taken-advantage-of?"*

Do You Agree?

1. Through Perfection-seeking I end up
    getting the bad end of deals.   ☐ YES   ☐ NO

2. Through Perfection-seeking I end up
    exhausting or over-extending myself.   ☐ YES   ☐ NO

3. Through Perfection-seeking I end up
    thinking that I don't get enough done.   ☐ YES   ☐ NO

4. Through Perfection-seeking I end up
    thinking that what I do is never good enough.   ☐ YES   ☐ NO

Other ways I end up feeling Not OK because of my Perfection-seeking:

....

FIND OUT IF PERFECTION-SEEKING LEADS TO A NEGATIVE ATTITUDE ABOUT SOMEONE ELSE OR LIFE IN GENERAL BY ASKING: *Do I end up thinking s/he or it is Not OK after I do it? If I do it better, do I end up thinking s/he is inadequate, worthless, or undesirable?*

		Do You Agree?	
1.	Through Perfection-seeking I end up thinking they cheated or took advantage of me.	☐ YES	☐ NO
2.	Through Perfection-seeking I end up thinking that what happened to me wasn't fair.	☐ YES	☐ NO
3.	Through Perfection-seeking I end up thinking that nothing is good enough for him/her.	☐ YES	☐ NO

Other ways I end up thinking s/he or it is Not OK because of my Perfection-seeking:

....

....

STEP 4 — LET GO OF NEGATIVE PERFECTION-SEEKING

We feel better if we release or avoid the tension that builds up through negative Perfection-seeking. To do this, we must give ourselves permission to let go of our Perfection-seeking standards, values, wishes, expectations, and behaviors when they involve a negative attitude.

Letting go involves setting limits to how much Perfection-seeking we do. Letting go does not mean giving up all Perfection-seeking. It only involves giving up Perfection-seeking that is out-of-bounds because it is driven by or leads to a negative attitude. It also involves leaving other things and people as they are. Four Limit Setting Statements will help you do this:

 When you need to let go of negative hurrying up, tell yourself, *"It's OK if I take my time."*

 When you need to let go of negative trying hard, tell yourself, *"It's OK if I focus only on what I do accomplish."*

 When you need to let go of negative trying to do more, tell yourself, *"It's OK if I don't take on any more."*

 When you need to let go of negative trying to do better, tell yourself, *"It's OK if I leave it as it is."*

EXERCISE

C

PRACTICE LETTING GO OF PERFECTION-
SEEKING

DIRECTIONS: For Exercise C, Part 1...Continue using the Sample Situation you described at the end of Exercise A.

♦   Check off one or more Limit Setting Statements that would remind you to let go of Perfection-seeking in your Sample Situation.

BEGIN EXERCISE C, PART 1:

☐   It's OK if I take my time.

☐   It's OK if I focus only on what I do accomplish.

☐   It's OK if I don't take on any more.

☐   It's OK if I leave it as it is.

DIRECTIONS: For Exercise C, Part 2...Think about your life overall.

♦   Check off one or more Limit Setting Statements that are likely to remind you to let go of Perfection-seeking behavior in your life in general.

BEGIN EXERCISE C, PART 2:

☐   It's OK if I take my time.

☐   It's OK if I focus only on what I do accomplish.

☐   It's OK if I don't take on any more.

☐   It's OK if I leave it as it is.

PRACTICE YOUR WORK SHEETS

<u>DIRECTIONS:</u> The more you study the steps in this lesson, the more effective your new skills will become. Your Work Sheets are designed to help you master these skills. So, read the story below. We will use it as an example to help you learn to use the Work Sheets successfully.

Bill was exhausted. It was well past 8:00 pm and he still hadn't finished that report. He'd been at it most of the day at work and every minute since he got home. He even ate dinner at his desk while going over figures and editing text.

He just knew he could make the report better. There was always room for making things more clear and convincing. Maybe he should add more data or a new section on other plans that failed. He felt insecure about his job, and he wanted to create a really good impression. If only he could finish before Bill Jr.'s bedtime so he could read him a story.

Betty had been a good sport about it. But Bill Jr. was unhappy. He missed his father. Bill felt guilty. He was so wrapped up in work that he wasn't being a very good father and husband.

<u>DIRECTIONS:</u> Practice your homework exercises. Imagine that you are Bill in this situation. Complete the "Practice Limiting Perfection-seeking Work Sheet" on the next page.

NEXT PAGE

PRACTICE LIMITING PERFECTION-SEEKING WORK SHEET

Step 1: Breathe out, relaxing your diaphragm. *Practice Release Breathing while you are completing each of the other steps.*

Step 2: Am I Perfection-Seeking? *Check off "YES" or "NO" to show which Perfection-seeking behaviors Bill was probably using...*

Hurrying Up ☐YES   ☐NO   Trying Hard ☐YES   ☐NO
Doing More   ☐YES   ☐NO   Doing Better ☐YES   ☐NO

Step 3: Does It Involve a Negative Attitude? *Check off "YES" or "NO" to show whether or not each of the negative attitudes probably was involved for Bill. Use the space provided to add details...*

Am I Doing It Because I'm Not OK?   ☐YES   ☐NO.   How?

....

Do I End Up Feeling Not OK after Doing It?   ☐YES   ☐NO.   How?

....

Am I Doing It Because S/he or It Is Not OK?   ☐YES   ☐NO.   How?

....

Do I End Up Thinking S/he or It Is Not OK after I Do It?   ☐YES   ☐NO.   How?

....

Step 4: Let Go of Negative Perfection-seeking. *Check off one or more Limit Setting Statements that would remind Bill to let go of Perfection-seeking...*

☐   It's OK if I take my time.
☐   It's OK if I focus only on what I do accomplish.
☐   It's OK if I don't take on any more.
☐   It's OK if I leave it as it is.

SAMPLE! PRACTICE LIMITING PERFECTION-SEEKING WORK SHEET

<u>Step 1: Breathe out, relaxing your diaphragm.</u> *Practice Release Breathing while you are completing each of the other steps.*

<u>Step 2: Am I Perfection-Seeking?</u> *Check off "YES" or "NO" to show which Perfection-seeking behaviors Bill was probably using...*

Hurrying Up	■YES	☐NO	Trying Hard	☐YES	■NO
Doing More	■YES	☐NO	Doing Better	■YES	☐NO

<u>Step 3: Does It Involve a Negative Attitude?</u> *Check off "YES" or "NO" to show whether or not each of the negative attitudes probably was involved for Bill. Use the space provided to add details...*

Am I Doing It Because I'm Not OK?　　　　　　　　■YES　☐NO.　How?

....My work isn't good enough..

Do I End Up Feeling Not OK after Doing It?　　　■YES　☐NO.　How?

....Exhausted and guilty...

Am I Doing It Because S/he or It Is Not OK?　　　☐YES　■NO.　How?

....

Do I End Up Thinking S/he or It Is Not OK after I Do It?　　☐YES　■NO.　How?

....

<u>Step 4: Let Go of Negative Perfection-seeking.</u> *Check off one or more Limit Setting Statements that would remind Bill to let go of Perfection-seeking...*

- ■　It's OK if I take my time.
- ☐　It's OK if I focus only on what I do accomplish.
- ■　It's OK if I don't take on any more.
- ■　It's OK if I leave it as it is.

Chapter 4: How Good Does It Have to Be?   *Page 169*

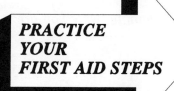

PRACTICE YOUR FIRST AID STEPS

<u>DIRECTIONS:</u> The more you practice your First Aid Steps, the better you will feel. Practice your First Aid Steps now. Imagine you are in a situation used in this lesson, or think about your life in general.

<u>FIRST AID for...</u>

<u>WORRY, STRESS, FEAR, and ANXIETY.</u>

Step 1: Always...Breathe Out!   Take a deep breath and practice Release Breathing.

Step 2: Am I Perfection-seeking?   Recognize whether or not you are Perfection-seeking.

Step 3: Does It involve a Negative Attitude?   Decide if your Perfection seeking is out-of-bounds because it involves a negative attitude.

Step 4: Let Go of Negative Perfection-seeking.   Use Limit Setting Statements to help you let go of negative Perfection-seeking.

THE METHODS...

Work Sheets. This week complete 8 Limiting Perfection-seeking Work Sheets. Do the Work Sheets for situations in which you worry or feel stress, fear, or anxiety. Complete the Work Sheets at the time of these events or very soon thereafter.

First Aid Steps. Practice your First Aid Steps as often as possible, even when you are not really worrying or feeling threatened.

*

FIRST AID for...WORRY, STRESS, FEAR, AND ANXIETY

Step 1:   Always...Breathe Out!

Step 2:   Am I Perfection-seeking?

Step 3:   Does It Involve a Negative Attitude?

Step 4:   Let Go of Negative Perfection-seeking.

Use your Clip-outs: Cut out the First Aid Steps reminders. Place them in spots where you will see them and remember to practice. Give some to a friend, and tell him or her how to use them.

Teach Others. Share the lesson with others. Teach them how to help themselves using the same skills you are learning.

* Permission is given to reproduce the First Aid Steps for your personal use.

Step 1: Breathe out, relaxing your diaphragm. *Practice Release Breathing while you are completing each of the other steps.*

Step 2: Am I Perfection-Seeking? *Check off "YES" or "NO" to show which Perfection-seeking behaviors you were using...*

Hurrying Up	☐YES	☐NO	Trying Hard	☐YES	☐NO
Doing More	☐YES	☐NO	Doing Better	☐YES	☐NO

Step 3: Does It Involve a Negative Attitude? *Check off "YES" or "NO" to show whether or not each of the negative attitudes was involved for you. Use the space provided to add details...*

Am I Doing It Because I'm Not OK?   ☐YES   ☐NO.   How?

....

Do I End Up Feeling Not OK after Doing It?   ☐YES   ☐NO.   How?

....

Am I Doing It Because S/he or It Is Not OK?   ☐YES   ☐NO.   How?

....

Do I End Up Thinking S/he or It Is Not OK after I Do It?   ☐YES   ☐NO.   How?

....

Step 4: Let Go of Negative Perfection-seeking. *Check off one or more Limit Setting Statements that would remind you to let go of Perfection-seeking...*

- ☐ It's OK if I take my time.
- ☐ It's OK if I focus only on what I do accomplish.
- ☐ It's OK if I don't take on any more.
- ☐ It's OK if I leave it as it is.

Step 1: Breathe out, relaxing your diaphragm. *Practice Release Breathing while you are completing each of the other steps.*

Step 2: Am I Perfection-Seeking? *Check off "YES" or "NO" to show which Perfection-seeking behaviors you were using...*

Hurrying Up ☐YES ☐NO   Trying Hard ☐YES ☐NO
Doing More ☐YES ☐NO   Doing Better ☐YES ☐NO

Step 3: Does It Involve a Negative Attitude? *Check off "YES" or "NO" to show whether or not each of the negative attitudes was involved for you. Use the space provided to add details...*

Am I Doing It Because I'm Not OK?   ☐YES ☐NO. How?

....

Do I End Up Feeling Not OK after Doing It?   ☐YES ☐NO. How?

....

Am I Doing It Because S/he or It Is Not OK?   ☐YES ☐NO. How?

....

Do I End Up Thinking S/he or It Is Not OK after I Do It?   ☐YES ☐NO. How?

....

Step 4: Let Go of Negative Perfection-seeking. *Check off one or more Limit Setting Statements that would remind you to let go of Perfection-seeking...*

☐   It's OK if I take my time.
☐   It's OK if I focus only on what I do accomplish.
☐   It's OK if I don't take on any more.
☐   It's OK if I leave it as it is.

Step 1: Breathe out, relaxing your diaphragm. *Practice Release Breathing while you are completing each of the other steps.*

Step 2: Am I Perfection-Seeking? *Check off "YES" or "NO" to show which Perfection-seeking behaviors you were using...*

Hurrying Up	☐YES	☐NO	Trying Hard	☐YES	☐NO
Doing More	☐YES	☐NO	Doing Better	☐YES	☐NO

Step 3: Does It Involve a Negative Attitude? *Check off "YES" or "NO" to show whether or not each of the negative attitudes was involved for you. Use the space provided to add details...*

Am I Doing It Because I'm Not OK? ☐YES ☐NO. How?

....

Do I End Up Feeling Not OK after Doing It? ☐YES ☐NO. How?

....

Am I Doing It Because S/he or It Is Not OK? ☐YES ☐NO. How?

....

Do I End Up Thinking S/he or It Is Not OK after I Do It? ☐YES ☐NO. How?

....

Step 4: Let Go of Negative Perfection-seeking. *Check off one or more Limit Setting Statements that would remind you to let go of Perfection-seeking...*

☐   It's OK if I take my time.
☐   It's OK if I focus only on what I do accomplish.
☐   It's OK if I don't take on any more.
☐   It's OK if I leave it as it is.

Step 1: Breathe out, relaxing your diaphragm. *Practice Release Breathing while you are completing each of the other steps.*

Step 2: Am I Perfection-Seeking? *Check off "YES" or "NO" to show which Perfection-seeking behaviors you were using...*

Hurrying Up	☐YES	☐NO	Trying Hard	☐YES	☐NO
Doing More	☐YES	☐NO	Doing Better	☐YES	☐NO

Step 3: Does It Involve a Negative Attitude? *Check off "YES" or "NO" to show whether or not each of the negative attitudes was involved for you. Use the space provided to add details...*

Am I Doing It Because I'm Not OK? ☐YES ☐NO. How?

....

Do I End Up Feeling Not OK after Doing It? ☐YES ☐NO. How?

....

Am I Doing It Because S/he or It Is Not OK? ☐YES ☐NO. How?

....

Do I End Up Thinking S/he or It Is Not OK after I Do It? ☐YES ☐NO. How?

....

Step 4: Let Go of Negative Perfection-seeking. *Check off one or more Limit Setting Statements that would remind you to let go of Perfection-seeking...*

      ☐   It's OK if I take my time.
      ☐   It's OK if I focus only on what I do accomplish.
      ☐   It's OK if I don't take on any more.
      ☐   It's OK if I leave it as it is.

Step 1: Breathe out, relaxing your diaphragm. *Practice Release Breathing while you are completing each of the other steps.*

Step 2: Am I Perfection-Seeking? *Check off "YES" or "NO" to show which Perfection-seeking behaviors you were using...*

      Hurrying Up ☐YES   ☐NO   Trying Hard ☐YES   ☐NO

      Doing More ☐YES   ☐NO   Doing Better ☐YES   ☐NO

Step 3: Does It Involve a Negative Attitude? *Check off "YES" or "NO" to show whether or not each of the negative attitudes was involved for you. Use the space provided to add details...*

Am I Doing It Because I'm Not OK?   ☐YES   ☐NO.   How?

....

Do I End Up Feeling Not OK after Doing It?   ☐YES   ☐NO.   How?

....

Am I Doing It Because S/he or It Is Not OK?   ☐YES   ☐NO.   How?

....

Do I End Up Thinking S/he or It Is Not OK after I Do It? ☐YES   ☐NO.   How?

....

Step 4: Let Go of Negative Perfection-seeking. *Check off one or more Limit Setting Statements that would remind you to let go of Perfection-seeking...*

      ☐   It's OK if I take my time.

      ☐   It's OK if I focus only on what I do accomplish.

      ☐   It's OK if I don't take on any more.

      ☐   It's OK if I leave it as it is.

Step 1: Breathe out, relaxing your diaphragm. *Practice Release Breathing while you are completing each of the other steps.*

Step 2: Am I Perfection-Seeking? *Check off "YES" or "NO" to show which Perfection-seeking behaviors you were using...*

Hurrying Up	☐YES	☐NO	Trying Hard	☐YES	☐NO
Doing More	☐YES	☐NO	Doing Better	☐YES	☐NO

Step 3: Does It Involve a Negative Attitude? *Check off "YES" or "NO" to show whether or not each of the negative attitudes was involved for you. Use the space provided to add details...*

Am I Doing It Because I'm Not OK?　　　　　　☐YES　☐NO.　How?

....

Do I End Up Feeling Not OK after Doing It?　　☐YES　☐NO.　How?

....

Am I Doing It Because S/he or It Is Not OK?　☐YES　☐NO.　How?

....

Do I End Up Thinking S/he or It Is Not OK after I Do It?　☐YES　☐NO.　How?

....

Step 4: Let Go of Negative Perfection-seeking. *Check off one or more Limit Setting Statements that would remind you to let go of Perfection-seeking...*

☐　　It's OK if I take my time.
☐　　It's OK if I focus only on what I do accomplish.
☐　　It's OK if I don't take on any more.
☐　　It's OK if I leave it as it is.

<u>Step 1: Breathe out, relaxing your diaphragm.</u> *Practice Release Breathing while you are completing each of the other steps.*

<u>Step 2: Am I Perfection-Seeking?</u> *Check off "YES" or "NO" to show which Perfection-seeking behaviors you were using...*

Hurrying Up ☐YES ☐NO   Trying Hard ☐YES ☐NO
Doing More ☐YES ☐NO   Doing Better ☐YES ☐NO

<u>Step 3: Does It Involve a Negative Attitude?</u> *Check off "YES" or "NO" to show whether or not each of the negative attitudes was involved for you. Use the space provided to add details...*

Am I Doing It Because I'm Not OK?   ☐YES   ☐NO.   How?

....

Do I End Up Feeling Not OK after Doing It?   ☐YES   ☐NO.   How?

....

Am I Doing It Because S/he or It Is Not OK?   ☐YES   ☐NO.   How?

....

Do I End Up Thinking S/he or It Is Not OK after I Do It?   ☐YES   ☐NO.   How?

....

<u>Step 4: Let Go of Negative Perfection-seeking.</u> *Check off one or more Limit Setting Statements that would remind you to let go of Perfection-seeking...*

☐   It's OK if I take my time.
☐   It's OK if I focus only on what I do accomplish.
☐   It's OK if I don't take on any more.
☐   It's OK if I leave it as it is.

Step 1: Breathe out, relaxing your diaphragm. *Practice Release Breathing while you are completing each of the other steps.*

Step 2: Am I Perfection-Seeking? *Check off "YES" or "NO" to show which Perfection-seeking behaviors you were using...*

Hurrying Up	☐YES	☐NO	Trying Hard	☐YES	☐NO
Doing More	☐YES	☐NO	Doing Better	☐YES	☐NO

Step 3: Does It Involve a Negative Attitude? *Check off "YES" or "NO" to show whether or not each of the negative attitudes was involved for you. Use the space provided to add details...*

Am I Doing It Because I'm Not OK?   ☐YES   ☐NO.   How?

....

Do I End Up Feeling Not OK after Doing It?   ☐YES   ☐NO.   How?

....

Am I Doing It Because S/he or It Is Not OK?   ☐YES   ☐NO.   How?

....

Do I End Up Thinking S/he or It Is Not OK after I Do It?   ☐YES   ☐NO.   How?

....

Step 4: Let Go of Negative Perfection-seeking. *Check off one or more Limit Setting Statements that would remind you to let go of Perfection-seeking...*

☐   It's OK if I take my time.
☐   It's OK if I focus only on what I do accomplish.
☐   It's OK if I don't take on any more.
☐   It's OK if I leave it as it is.

Chapter 5

TIRED OF PLEASING EVERYBODY ELSE?

<u>INTRODUCTION</u>

One of the ways we try to control our lives is doing things that satisfy other people. We call this People-pleasing.

It's natural and healthy to try to make other people happy. It makes things go better. Sometimes People-pleasing is OK.

However, People-pleasing can be overdone or go out-of-bounds.   This is when we hurt ourselves in the process, or we struggle with someone who won't be satisfied. We call this **negative People-pleasing.**

Negative People-pleasing can cause worry, stress, fear, and anxiety. But if you set proper limits to your People-pleasing, you increase your sense of Personal Control, release tension, and develop a positive attitude toward yourself, others, and life in general.

GOALS

1.   You will identify some of your own People-pleasing behavior and learn how to recognize it when it starts.

2.   You will learn how to decide if it is positive (healthy) or negative (self-destructive) People-pleasing.

3.   You will learn how to set limits to your People-pleasing behavior.

REMEMBER

Don't miss another opportunity to build your peace of mind. When worry, stress, fear, or anxiety strike this week...Conquer Your Fears! Use...

*

FIRST AID for...WORRY, STRESS, FEAR, AND ANXIETY

Step 1:   **Always...Breathe Out!**

Step 2:   **Am I People-pleasing?**

Step 3:   **Does It Involve a Negative Attitude?**

Step 4:   **Let Go of Negative People-pleasing.**

* Permission is given to reproduce the First Aid Steps for your personal use.

STEP 1

We can build up stress and tension within ourselves by trying too hard to please other people. We recommend Release Breathing for briefly reducing the tension that builds up from this People-pleasing behavior.

Release Breathing enables us to let go of the tension we build up through worrying about the thoughts, opinions, well- being, and feelings of others. And we can practice Release Breathing on the spot, in the middle of any activity, as often as we wish, especially whenever we are trying too hard to please others.

Let's take a closer look at People-pleasing. When we go too far in pleasing others, we are being disloyal to ourselves. We are not trusting ourselves and we are making other people a more important source of guidance. That is a negative attitude; it is negative about ourselves. We are betraying ourselves when we go too far in doing what others want, agreeing with others, giving in to keep the peace, and taking care of others.

People-pleasing is a form of control rooted in our negative attitude. This lesson teaches you how to decide when to let go of People-pleasing methods of maintaining control. It teaches you to set limits when appropriate.

The negative attitude of discounting ourselves and striving to meet the needs and expectations of others causes tension to build in our bodies. That tension often causes us to tighten up or shut down. The result is restricted breathing. The Release Breathing technique is an excellent way to practice giving up both the stress in your body and this self-devaluing, negative attitude.

Release Breathing sends an important "let go" message to the brain. It involves 3 steps:

1. breathe in deeply, using *medium force*. Using your diaphragm,

2. breathe out through your mouth, using *medium strong force*. Let your shoulders, chest, and diaphragm sag or fall downward. Note that you breathe out harder than you breathe in.

   Think "let go of pleasing people" as you release air from your lungs. Let go of the air and all the tension in your body, and

3. pause for a moment at the end of the breath. Feel the release of tension.

   Think of having "let go" of both the pressure in your chest and the need to please others.

STEP 2

People-pleasing is trying to make other people happy. The need to satisfy others is usually based on insecurity or the belief that if others are happy, life will be better. Often beliefs and feelings like these are unconscious.

There are two elements to People-pleasing--what we do and why we do it. People-pleasing is acting the way we think others want us to act, or acting in ways that will make others happy. The reason we do this is to make ourselves feel more secure or to make life go better.

People-pleasing consists of satisfying the standards, values, wishes, and expectations of other people. These may be directly expressed by the other person. Or, they may be implied by how the other person acts. There are 4 basic People-pleasing behaviors:

Complying.

Agreeing.

Peacemaking.

Caretaking.

EXERCISE

A

<u>RECOGNIZING WHEN YOU ARE PEOPLE-PLEASING</u>

<u>DIRECTIONS:</u> For Exercise A...Circle a number to show how much you agree with each statement. Use the space provided to add other examples of ways you do each type of People-pleasing behavior.

BEGIN EXERCISE A:

COMPLYING:

How Much Do You Agree?

1. I do what others demand, want, or expect me to do.

1 - 2 - 3 - 4 - 5
A Little....A Lot

2. I try to keep up appearances by pretending things are fine when they are not.

1 - 2 - 3 - 4 - 5
A Little....A Lot

Other examples of my Complying:

....

....

AGREEING:

How Much Do You Agree?

1. I lead others to think I agree with them when I really don't.

1 - 2 - 3 - 4 - 5
A Little....A Lot

2. I actually change my thinking to be more like others think.

1 - 2 - 3 - 4 - 5
A Little....A Lot

Other examples of my Agreeing:

....

....

PEACEMAKING:

How Much Do You Agree?

1. I keep my true thoughts to myself to avoid confrontation or upsetting others.

1 - 2 - 3 - 4 - 5
A Little....A Lot

2. I tolerate, ignore, or make excuses for other people's disturbing behavior to avoid confrontation or upsetting others.

1 - 2 - 3 - 4 - 5
A Little....A Lot

3. I feel I have to make it up to others when even the smallest deed is done for me.

1 - 2 - 3 - 4 - 5
A Little....A Lot

4. I do things for others because I think I should, even when others do too little in return.

1 - 2 - 3 - 4 - 5
A Little....A Lot

5. I don't take advantage of opportunities or go after things I want if it might make someone else upset.

1 - 2 - 3 - 4 - 5
A Little....A Lot

Other examples of my Peacemaking:

....

....

CARETAKING:

How Much Do You Agree?

1. I meet the needs of others.

1 - 2 - 3 - 4 - 5
A Little....A Lot

2. I try to tell others what they want to hear.

1 - 2 - 3 - 4 - 5
A Little....A Lot

3. I do things that I don't want to do for others.

1 - 2 - 3 - 4 - 5
A Little....A Lot

Other examples of my Caretaking:

....

....

COMMENTS ON THE EXERCISE

Exercise A:

Complying: People have written examples like:

      A.   Doing things at work that I really don't like doing.
      B.   Doing chores at home that I don't want to do.
      C.   Paying taxes.

Agreeing: People have written examples like:

      A.   Agreeing with others to keep the peace.
      B.   Agreeing with others at work so I don't lose my job.
      C.   Agreeing with my spouse when I actually don't agree just to keep from arguing.

Peacemaking: People have written examples like:

      A.   Trying to stop arguments in my family by trying to solve others' problems.
      B.   Putting up with a boss being a jerk but not saying anything even though I want to.

Caretaking: People have written examples like:

      A.   Thinking of others needs before I take care of myself.
      B.   Helping out friends with moving or other projects when I really don't want to help them.
      C.   Not always being honest with others about how I feel because the truth would upset them.

PICK A REAL EXAMPLE FROM YOUR OWN LIFE.

<u>SAMPLE SITUATION</u>

Learning Steps 3 and 4 will be easier if you can refer to a personal example of People-pleasing. Use the space below to describe one event or situation where you did, or have done, or still do, a lot of People-pleasing.

Write a description of your event or sample situation here...

....

....

....

Check off "YES" or "NO" to show which basic People-pleasing behavior(s) you were doing.

Complying   ☐ YES   ☐ NO

Agreeing   ☐ YES   ☐ NO

Peacemaking   ☐ YES   ☐ NO

Caretaking   ☐ YES   ☐ NO

STEP 3

DOES IT INVOLVE A NEGATIVE ATTITUDE?

Many of us have been taught that People-pleasing is a good thing to do. There's nothing wrong with satisfying the needs and wants of other people. People-pleasing is OK as long as our attitude stays positive. But we can go too far. In that case, we need to act a new way.

People-pleasing is self-destructive when it goes beyond healthy limits. It's out-of-bounds when a negative attitude is involved in one of two ways: 1) if People-pleasing is *driven* by a negative attitude; or 2) if People-pleasing *leads us to form* a negative attitude. Four Key Questions help us recognize when this is the case.

- ◆ Am I Doing It Because I'm Not OK?

- ◆ Am I Doing It Because S/he or It Is Not OK?

- ◆ Do I End Up Feeling Not OK after Doing It?

- ◆ Do I End Up Thinking S/he or It Is Not OK after Doing It?

Why ask the Key Questions? Usually, we are unconscious of our Not OK attitude about ourselves, others, or the situation. If we ask the question, we have a chance to identify the attitude and make a change for the better. If we are aware of it, and we know what to do differently, we can take Personal Control.

Remember, the Key Questions are designed to help make you aware of the unconscious role played by negative attitudes about yourself, others, and life in general.

> **Awareness and options equal Personal Control!**

Driven: "Driven" means allowing a force to make you do something. People-pleasing is self-destructive when the force driving it is a negative attitude about yourself, someone else, or life in general:

 Am I Doing It Because I'm Not OK?

 Am I Doing It Because S/he or It Is Not OK?

Am I driven to People-pleasing because I'm Not OK?

This question asks if you are living up to other people's expectations because you believe you are defective. Since you're not better in some way, you have to make people like what you do.

BECAUSE... I'm not good enough... I'm not worth enough... I'm not wanted enough...

I HAVE TO PLEASE OTHERS

Am I driven to People-pleasing because something else is Not OK?

This question asks if you are pleasing people because you think someone or something else is defective. Because that person, those people, or the situation is not better in some way, you have to try to do things better to make up the difference or keep things OK.

BECAUSE... Someone isn't good enough... Someone isn't worth enough... Someone isn't wanted enough...

I HAVE TO PLEASE OTHERS

<u>Leads to:</u> "Leads to" means how things end up. Usually, People-pleasing leads to some kind of outcome or result. People-pleasing is self-destructive when it "leads to" you having a negative attitude about yourself, someone else, or life in general:

   Do I End Up Feeling Not OK after Doing It?

   Do I End Up Thinking S/he or It Is Not OK after Doing It?

Do I end up feeling Not OK after People-pleasing?

This question asks if you end up feeling bad after you have been trying to meet the expectations of others. Even though you tried not to disappoint them, things didn't go as you hoped.

WHEN I'M PEOPLE-PLEASING		**I END UP...** Feeling unappreciated or exploited... Feeling like a failure... Feeling frustrated...

Do I end up thinking something else is Not OK after People-pleasing?

This question asks if you end up thinking that someone or something else is defective after you have been trying to do things better. It is Not OK because your Perfection-seeking didn't work.

WHEN I'M PEOPLE-PLEASING		**I END UP...** Thinking someone isn't good enough... Thinking something isn't important... Thinking someone is too hard to satisfy...

EXERCISE

B

<u>DECIDING IF YOUR PEOPLE-PLEASING INVOLVES A NEGATIVE ATTITUDE.</u>

<u>DIRECTIONS:</u> For Exercise B...Continue using the Sample Situation you described at the end of Exercise A.

♦ Check off "Yes" or "No" to show if each typical, negative attitude below is/was involved with your Sample Situation or with People-pleasing events in your life in general.

♦ Use the space provided to add other negative attitudes involved with your Sample Situation or People-pleasing events in your life in general.

BEGIN EXERCISE B:

FIND OUT IF PEOPLE-PLEASING IS DRIVEN BY A NEGATIVE ATTITUDE ABOUT YOURSELF BY ASKING: *Am I doing it because I'm Not OK?*

Do You Agree?

1.   I get into People-pleasing because
     I'm not good, smart, likeable, or loveable enough.   ☐YES   ☐NO

2.   I get into People-pleasing because
     I'm not sure just how to fit in.   ☐YES   ☐NO

3.   I get into People-pleasing because
     I will feel guilty if I don't.   ☐YES   ☐NO

Other ways I feel Not OK that drive me toward People-pleasing:

....

....

FIND OUT IF PEOPLE-PLEASING IS DRIVEN BY A NEGATIVE ATTITUDE ABOUT SOMEONE ELSE OR LIFE IN GENERAL BY ASKING: *Am I doing it because s/he or it is Not OK?*

Do You Agree?

1. I get into People-pleasing because they disapprove a lot. ☐ YES   ☐ NO

2. I get into People-pleasing because they get upset easily. ☐ YES   ☐ NO

3. I get into People-pleasing because I'll get in trouble if I don't. ☐ YES   ☐ NO

Other ways of thinking s/he or it is Not OK that drive me toward People-pleasing:

....

....

FIND OUT IF PEOPLE-PLEASING LEADS TO A NEGATIVE ATTITUDE ABOUT YOURSELF BY ASKING: *Do I end up feeling Not OK?*

Do You Agree?

1. Through People-pleasing I end up getting a bad deal. ☐ YES   ☐ NO

2. Through People-pleasing I end up selling myself out. ☐ YES   ☐ NO

3. Through People-pleasing I end up exhausting or over-extending myself. ☐ YES   ☐ NO

Other ways I end up feeling Not OK because of my People-pleasing:

....

....

FIND OUT IF PEOPLE-PLEASING LEADS TO A NEGATIVE ATTITUDE ABOUT
SOMEONE ELSE OR LIFE IN GENERAL BY ASKING: *Do I end up thinking s/he or it is
Not OK?*

		Do You Agree?	
1.	Through People-pleasing I end up thinking they're too hard to please.	☐ YES	☐ NO
2.	Through People-pleasing I end up thinking they cheated or took advantage of me.	☐ YES	☐ NO
3.	Through People-pleasing I end up thinking they don't care how hard I tried.	☐ YES	☐ NO

Other ways I end up thinking s/he or it is Not OK because of my People-pleasing:

....

....

COMMENTS ON THE EXERCISE

Exercise B:

Other ways of being driven toward people-pleasing when feeling Not OK about self.

    A.   Because I am not right in how I perceive others.
    B.   Because I don't feel accepted by others.
    C.   Because I don't feel comfortable being assertive with others.

Other ways of being driven toward people-pleasing when thinking that s/he or it is Not OK.

    A.   I get into people-pleasing because people get angry with me.
    B.   I get into people-pleasing because my spouse will reject me if I don't.

Other ways of ending up thinking that s/he or it is Not OK after people-pleasing.

    A.   Through people-pleasing I feel that I haven't been honest with how I feel.
    B.   Through people-pleasing I have to take care of things at work because my co-worker is incompetent and then I feel taken advantage of.
    C.   Through people-pleasing I feel I have to do something because my spouse won't help out and I feel manipulated.

Other ways of ending up thinking s/he or it is Not OK because of people-pleasing.

    A.   Through people-pleasing I end up thinking that people cannot be trusted and that people are going to let me do all of the work instead of helping out.

    B.   Through people-pleasing I will end up thinking that people will never be satisfied with what I do for them.

STEP 4

LET GO OF NEGATIVE PEOPLE-PLEASING

We feel better if we release or avoid the tension that builds up through negative People-pleasing. To do this, we must give ourselves permission to let go of our People-pleasing standards, values, wishes, expectations, and behaviors when they involve a negative attitude.

Letting go involves setting limits to how much People-pleasing we do. Letting go does not mean giving up all People-pleasing. It only involves giving up People-pleasing that is out-of-bounds because it is driven by or leads to a negative attitude. It also involves leaving other things and people as they are. Four Limit Setting Statements will help you do this:

 When you need to let go of negative complying with someone else, tell yourself, *"It's OK if I do it my own way."*

 When you need to let go of negative agreeing with someone else, tell yourself, *"It's OK if I think and express myself differently."*

 When you need to let go of negative peacemaking with someone else, tell yourself, *"It's OK if my actions stir up a conflict."*

 When you need to let go of negative caretaking, tell yourself, *"It's OK if I don't take care of him/her."*

EXERCISE

C

<u>PRACTICE LETTING GO OF PEOPLE-PLEASING</u>

<u>DIRECTIONS:</u> For Exercise C, Part 1...Continue using the Sample Situation you described at the end of Exercise A. Check off one or more Limit Setting Statements that would remind you to let go of People-pleasing in that situation.

BEGIN EXERCISE C, PART 1:

- ☐ It's OK if I do it my own way.
- ☐ It's OK if I think and express myself differently.
- ☐ It's OK if my actions stir up a conflict.
- ☐ It's OK if I don't take care of him/her.

<u>DIRECTIONS:</u> For Exercise C, Part 2...Think about your life overall. Check off one or more Limit Setting Statements that are likely to remind you to let go of People-pleasing behavior in your life in general.

BEGIN EXERCISE C, PART 2:

- ☐ It's OK if I do it my own way.
- ☐ It's OK if I think and express myself differently.
- ☐ It's OK if my actions stir up a conflict.
- ☐ It's OK if I don't take care of him/her.

PRACTICE YOUR WORK SHEETS

DIRECTIONS: The more you study the steps in this lesson, the more effective your new skills will become. Your Work Sheets are designed to help you master these skills. So, read the story below. We will use it as an example to help you learn to use the Work Sheets successfully.

It was crowded at the market, like a typical Friday afternoon. Betty had found everything she needed, but the check-out line was half a mile long. It was a holiday weekend, too, so the traffic would be extra heavy. She was bound to be so late that dinner wouldn't be ready by the time Bill got home from work. He got irritable when dinner was late.

She didn't think there should be so much pressure about dinner time. It should be more flexible. But Bill would never consider that. She was afraid that if she brought it up they would argue, or he'd pout and she'd feel guilty.

Then 3-year-old Bill Jr. started demanding that she buy him a toy. He wouldn't let up! "I want it." "Can we get it now?" "When are we gonna get it?" "I've been good." And finally, "You don't love me anymore."

She couldn't get him a toy now without giving up her place in line, and that would make her even later. She couldn't keep them both happy. Bill Jr. was getting louder and more upset. But he had plenty of toys. This went on every time they went shopping, and she was fed up with it. She felt bad about disappointing him, but she wasn't going to give in.

DIRECTIONS: For your practice homework exercise...Imagine that you are Betty in this situation. Complete the "Practice Limiting People-pleasing Work Sheet" on the next page.

NEXT PAGE

Step 1: Breathe out, relaxing your diaphragm. *Practice Release Breathing while you are completing each of the other steps.*

Step 2: Am I People-pleasing? *Check off "YES" or "NO" to show which People-pleasing behaviors Betty probably was using...*

Complying	☐YES	☐NO	Agreeing	☐YES	☐NO
Peacemaking	☐YES	☐NO	Caretaking	☐YES	☐NO

Step 3: Does It Involve a Negative Attitude? *Check off "YES" or "NO" to show whether or not each of the negative attitudes probably was involved for Betty. Use the space provided to add details...*

Am I Doing It Because I'm Not OK?   ☐YES   ☐NO.   How?

....

Do I End Up Feeling Not OK?   ☐YES   ☐NO.   How?

....

Am I Doing It Because S/he or It Is Not OK?   ☐YES   ☐NO.   How?

....

Do I End Up Thinking S/he or It Is Not OK?   ☐YES   ☐NO.   How?

....

Step 4: Let Go of Negative People-pleasing. *Check off one or more Limit Setting Statements that would remind Betty to let go of People-pleasing...*

☐   It's OK if I do it my own way.
☐   It's OK if I think and express myself differently.
☐   It's OK if my actions stir up a conflict.
☐   It's OK if I don't take care of him/her.

<u>Step 1: Breathe out, relaxing your diaphragm.</u> *Practice Release Breathing while you are completing each of the other steps.*

<u>Step 2: Am I People-pleasing?</u> *Check off "YES" or "NO" to show which People-pleasing behaviors Betty probably was using...*

Complying	☐YES	☐NO	Agreeing	☐YES	☐NO
Peacemaking	■YES	☐NO	Caretaking	■YES	☐NO

<u>Step 3: Does It Involve a Negative Attitude?</u> *Check off "YES" or "NO" to show whether or not each of the negative attitudes probably was involved for Betty. Use the space provided to add details...*

Am I Doing It Because I'm Not OK?   ☐YES   ■NO.   How?

....

Do I End Up Feeling Not OK?   ■YES   ☐NO.   How?

....*Overwhelmed*..

Am I Doing It Because S/he or It Is Not OK?   ■YES   ☐NO.   How?

....*Demanding, inflexible people*...

Do I End Up Thinking S/he or It Is Not OK?   ■YES   ☐NO.   How?

....*Demanding, inflexible, unreasonable*..

<u>Step 4: Let Go of Negative People-pleasing.</u> *Check off one or more Limit Setting Statements that would remind Betty to let go of People-pleasing...*

☐   It's OK if I do it my own way.
☐   It's OK if I think and express myself differently.
■   It's OK if my actions stir up a conflict.
■   It's OK if I don't take care of him/her.

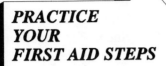

PRACTICE YOUR FIRST AID STEPS

DIRECTIONS: The more you practice your First Aid Steps, the better you will feel. Practice your First Aid Steps now. Imagine you are in a situation used in this lesson, or think about your life in general.

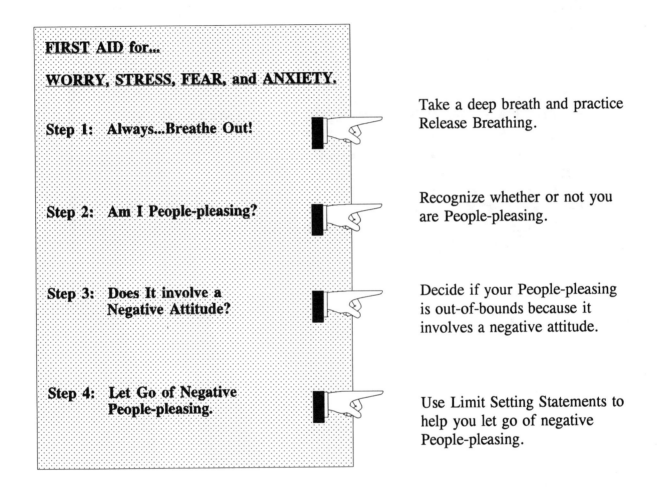

FIRST AID for...

WORRY, STRESS, FEAR, and ANXIETY.

Step 1: Always...Breathe Out!

Take a deep breath and practice Release Breathing.

Step 2: Am I People-pleasing?

Recognize whether or not you are People-pleasing.

Step 3: Does It involve a Negative Attitude?

Decide if your People-pleasing is out-of-bounds because it involves a negative attitude.

Step 4: Let Go of Negative People-pleasing.

Use Limit Setting Statements to help you let go of negative People-pleasing.

HOMEWORK

THE METHODS...

Work Sheets. This week complete 8 Limiting People-pleasing Work Sheets. Do the Work Sheets for situations in which you worry or feel stress, fear, or anxiety. Complete the Work Sheets at the time of these events or very soon thereafter.

First Aid Steps. Practice your First Aid Steps as often as possible, even when you are not really worrying or feeling threatened.

*

FIRST AID for...WORRY, STRESS, FEAR, AND ANXIETY

Step 1:   **Always...Breathe Out!**

Step 2:   **Am I People-pleasing?**

Step 3:   **Does It Involve a Negative Attitude?**

Step 4:   **Let Go of Negative People-pleasing.**

Use your Clip-outs: Cut out the First Aid Steps reminders. Place them in spots where you will see them and remember to practice. Give some to a friend, and tell him or her how to use them.

Teach Others. Share the lesson with others. Teach them how to help themselves using the same skills you are learning.

* Permission is given to reproduce the First Aid Steps for your personal use.

Step 1: Breathe out, relaxing your diaphragm. *Practice Release Breathing while you are completing each of the other steps.*

Step 2: Am I People-pleasing? *Check off "YES" or "NO" to show which People-pleasing behaviors you used...*

Complying	☐YES	☐NO	Agreeing	☐YES	☐NO
Peacemaking	☐YES	☐NO	Caretaking	☐YES	☐NO

Step 3: Does It Involve a Negative Attitude? *Check off "YES" or "NO" to show whether or not each of the negative attitudes was involved for you. Use the space provided to add details...*

Am I Doing It Because I'm Not OK?　　　　　☐YES　☐NO.　How?

....

Do I End Up Feeling Not OK?　　　　　　☐YES　☐NO.　How?

....

Am I Doing It Because S/he or It Is Not OK?　　☐YES　☐NO.　How?

....

Do I End Up Thinking S/he or It Is Not OK?　　☐YES　☐NO.　How?

....

Step 4: Let Go of Negative People-pleasing. *Check off one or more Limit Setting Statements that would remind you to let go of People-pleasing...*

- ☐ It's OK if I do it my own way.
- ☐ It's OK if I think and express myself differently.
- ☐ It's OK if my actions stir up a conflict.
- ☐ It's OK if I don't take care of him/her.

Step 1: Breathe out, relaxing your diaphragm. *Practice Release Breathing while you are completing each of the other steps.*

Step 2: Am I People-pleasing? *Check off "YES" or "NO" to show which People-pleasing behaviors you used...*

Complying	☐YES	☐NO		Agreeing	☐YES	☐NO
Peacemaking	☐YES	☐NO		Caretaking	☐YES	☐NO

Step 3: Does It Involve a Negative Attitude? *Check off "YES" or "NO" to show whether or not each of the negative attitudes was involved for you. Use the space provided to add details...*

Am I Doing It Because I'm Not OK?   ☐YES   ☐NO.   How?

....

Do I End Up Feeling Not OK?   ☐YES   ☐NO.   How?

....

Am I Doing It Because S/he or It Is Not OK?   ☐YES   ☐NO.   How?

....

Do I End Up Thinking S/he or It Is Not OK?   ☐YES   ☐NO.   How?

....

Step 4: Let Go of Negative People-pleasing. *Check off one or more Limit Setting Statements that would remind you to let go of People-pleasing...*

- ☐ It's OK if I do it my own way.
- ☐ It's OK if I think and express myself differently.
- ☐ It's OK if my actions stir up a conflict.
- ☐ It's OK if I don't take care of him/her.

LIMITING PEOPLE-PLEASING WORK SHEET # 3

Step 1: Breathe out, relaxing your diaphragm. *Practice Release Breathing while you are completing each of the other steps.*

Step 2: Am I People-pleasing? *Check off "YES" or "NO" to show which People-pleasing behaviors you used...*

Complying ☐YES ☐NO   Agreeing ☐YES ☐NO
Peacemaking ☐YES ☐NO   Caretaking ☐YES ☐NO

Step 3: Does It Involve a Negative Attitude? *Check off "YES" or "NO" to show whether or not each of the negative attitudes was involved for you. Use the space provided to add details...*

Am I Doing It Because I'm Not OK?   ☐YES   ☐NO.   How?

....

Do I End Up Feeling Not OK?   ☐YES   ☐NO.   How?

....

Am I Doing It Because S/he or It Is Not OK?   ☐YES   ☐NO.   How?

....

Do I End Up Thinking S/he or It Is Not OK?   ☐YES   ☐NO.   How?

....

Step 4: Let Go of Negative People-pleasing. *Check off one or more Limit Setting Statements that would remind you to let go of People-pleasing...*

☐   It's OK if I do it my own way.
☐   It's OK if I think and express myself differently.
☐   It's OK if my actions stir up a conflict.
☐   It's OK if I don't take care of him/her.

Step 1: Breathe out, relaxing your diaphragm. *Practice Release Breathing while you are completing each of the other steps.*

Step 2: Am I People-pleasing? *Check off "YES" or "NO" to show which People-pleasing behaviors you used...*

Complying	☐YES	☐NO	Agreeing	☐YES	☐NO
Peacemaking	☐YES	☐NO	Caretaking	☐YES	☐NO

Step 3: Does It Involve a Negative Attitude? *Check off "YES" or "NO" to show whether or not each of the negative attitudes was involved for you. Use the space provided to add details...*

Am I Doing It Because I'm Not OK?   ☐YES   ☐NO.   How?

....

Do I End Up Feeling Not OK?   ☐YES   ☐NO.   How?

....

Am I Doing It Because S/he or It Is Not OK?   ☐YES   ☐NO.   How?

....

Do I End Up Thinking S/he or It Is Not OK?   ☐YES   ☐NO.   How?

....

Step 4: Let Go of Negative People-pleasing. *Check off one or more Limit Setting Statements that would remind you to let go of People-pleasing...*

- ☐ It's OK if I do it my own way.
- ☐ It's OK if I think and express myself differently.
- ☐ It's OK if my actions stir up a conflict.
- ☐ It's OK if I don't take care of him/her.

Step 1: Breathe out, relaxing your diaphragm. *Practice Release Breathing while you are completing each of the other steps.*

Step 2: Am I People-pleasing? *Check off "YES" or "NO" to show which People-pleasing behaviors you used...*

Complying	☐YES	☐NO	Agreeing	☐YES	☐NO
Peacemaking	☐YES	☐NO	Caretaking	☐YES	☐NO

Step 3: Does It Involve a Negative Attitude? *Check off "YES" or "NO" to show whether or not each of the negative attitudes was involved for you. Use the space provided to add details...*

Am I Doing It Because I'm Not OK?   ☐YES   ☐NO.   How?

....

Do I End Up Feeling Not OK?   ☐YES   ☐NO.   How?

....

Am I Doing It Because S/he or It Is Not OK?   ☐YES   ☐NO.   How?

....

Do I End Up Thinking S/he or It Is Not OK?   ☐YES   ☐NO.   How?

....

Step 4: Let Go of Negative People-pleasing. *Check off one or more Limit Setting Statements that would remind you to let go of People-pleasing...*

- ☐   It's OK if I do it my own way.
- ☐   It's OK if I think and express myself differently.
- ☐   It's OK if my actions stir up a conflict.
- ☐   It's OK if I don't take care of him/her.

Step 1: Breathe out, relaxing your diaphragm. *Practice Release Breathing while you are completing each of the other steps.*

Step 2: Am I People-pleasing? *Check off "YES" or "NO" to show which People-pleasing behaviors you used...*

Complying	☐YES	☐NO		Agreeing	☐YES	☐NO
Peacemaking	☐YES	☐NO		Caretaking	☐YES	☐NO

Step 3: Does It Involve a Negative Attitude? *Check off "YES" or "NO" to show whether or not each of the negative attitudes was involved for you. Use the space provided to add details...*

Am I Doing It Because I'm Not OK? ☐YES ☐NO. How?

....

Do I End Up Feeling Not OK? ☐YES ☐NO. How?

....

Am I Doing It Because S/he or It Is Not OK? ☐YES ☐NO. How?

....

Do I End Up Thinking S/he or It Is Not OK? ☐YES ☐NO. How?

....

Step 4: Let Go of Negative People-pleasing. *Check off one or more Limit Setting Statements that would remind you to let go of People-pleasing...*

☐ It's OK if I do it my own way.
☐ It's OK if I think and express myself differently.
☐ It's OK if my actions stir up a conflict.
☐ It's OK if I don't take care of him/her.

Step 1: Breathe out, relaxing your diaphragm. *Practice Release Breathing while you are completing each of the other steps.*

Step 2: Am I People-pleasing? *Check off "YES" or "NO" to show which People-pleasing behaviors you used...*

Complying	☐ YES	☐ NO	Agreeing	☐ YES	☐ NO
Peacemaking	☐ YES	☐ NO	Caretaking	☐ YES	☐ NO

Step 3: Does It Involve a Negative Attitude? *Check off "YES" or "NO" to show whether or not each of the negative attitudes was involved for you. Use the space provided to add details...*

Am I Doing It Because I'm Not OK?   ☐ YES   ☐ NO.   How?

....

Do I End Up Feeling Not OK?   ☐ YES   ☐ NO.   How?

....

Am I Doing It Because S/he or It Is Not OK?   ☐ YES   ☐ NO.   How?

....

Do I End Up Thinking S/he or It Is Not OK?   ☐ YES   ☐ NO.   How?

....

Step 4: Let Go of Negative People-pleasing. *Check off one or more Limit Setting Statements that would remind you to let go of People-pleasing...*

☐   It's OK if I do it my own way.
☐   It's OK if I think and express myself differently.
☐   It's OK if my actions stir up a conflict.
☐   It's OK if I don't take care of him/her.

Step 1: Breathe out, relaxing your diaphragm. *Practice Release Breathing while you are completing each of the other steps.*

Step 2: Am I People-pleasing? *Check off "YES" or "NO" to show which People-pleasing behaviors you used...*

Complying	☐YES	☐NO		Agreeing	☐YES	☐NO
Peacemaking	☐YES	☐NO		Caretaking	☐YES	☐NO

Step 3: Does It Involve a Negative Attitude? *Check off "YES" or "NO" to show whether or not each of the negative attitudes was involved for you. Use the space provided to add details...*

Am I Doing It Because I'm Not OK?   ☐YES   ☐NO.   How?

....

Do I End Up Feeling Not OK?   ☐YES   ☐NO.   How?

....

Am I Doing It Because S/he or It Is Not OK?   ☐YES   ☐NO.   How?

....

Do I End Up Thinking S/he or It Is Not OK?   ☐YES   ☐NO.   How?

....

Step 4: Let Go of Negative People-pleasing. *Check off one or more Limit Setting Statements that would remind you to let go of People-pleasing...*

☐   It's OK if I do it my own way.
☐   It's OK if I think and express myself differently.
☐   It's OK if my actions stir up a conflict.
☐   It's OK if I don't take care of him/her.

Chapter 6

HAVE YOU TAKEN ENOUGH?

INTRODUCTION

One of the ways we try to control our lives is trying not to think about, feel, or show our needs, wants, and emotions. We call this Being Strong.

It's natural and healthy to restrict or manage our needs, wants, and emotions. It helps us stay rational, solve problems, and pay attention to the job at hand. Sometimes Being Strong is OK.

However, Being Strong can be overdone or go out-of-bounds. This is when we hurt ourselves in the process. We call this *negative Being Strong* because it is self-destructive.

Negative Being Strong can cause worry, stress, fear, and anxiety. But if you set proper limits to your Being Strong, you increase your sense of Personal Control, reduce tension, and develop a positive attitude toward yourself, others, and life in general.

GOALS

1.	You will identify some of your own Being Strong behaviors and learn how to recognize them when you start.

2.	You will learn how to decide if it is positive (healthy) or negative (self-destructive) Being Strong.

3.	You will learn how to set limits to your Being Strong behavior.

REMEMBER

Don't miss another opportunity to build your peace of mind. When worry, stress, fear, or anxiety strike this week...Conquer Your Fears! Use...

*

FIRST AID for...WORRY, STRESS, FEAR, AND ANXIETY

Step 1:   **Always...Breathe Out!**

Step 2:   **Am I Being Strong?**

Step 3:   **Does It Involve a Negative Attitude?**

Step 4:   **Let go of Negative Being Strong.**

* Permission is given to reproduce the First Aid Steps for your personal use.

We can increase internal stress by trying too hard to push aside our thoughts, feelings, needs, wants, and emotions. We recommend Release Breathing for reducing the tension that builds up from this Being Strong behavior. Relief from this technique may last from a few seconds to hours.

Release Breathing enables us to let go of the tension we build up through Being Strong in order to cope with a situation. And we can practice Release Breathing on the spot, in the middle of any activity, as often as we wish, especially whenever we are trying too hard to be strong.

Let's take a closer look at Being Strong. When we ignore the importance of our thoughts, feelings, needs, wants, and emotions, we are being disloyal to ourselves. We are not trusting ourselves and are making handling some external situation more important than tending to ourselves. That is a negative attitude; it is negative about ourselves. We are betraying ourselves when we go too far in staying or looking calm and in control, being or looking reasonable, taking on whatever comes, enduring and persevering, or self-sacrificing.

Being Strong is a form of control rooted in that negative attitude. This lesson teaches you how to decide when to let go of Being Strong methods. It teaches you to set limits when appropriate.

The negative attitude of devaluing our thoughts, feelings, needs, wants, and emotions and striving to be strong causes tension to build in our bodies. That tension often causes our breathing to become shallow. The Release Breathing technique is an excellent way to expand your breathing and practice giving up this self-devaluing and driven, negative attitude.

Release Breathing sends an important "let go" message to the brain. It involves 3 steps:

1.   breathe in deeply, using *medium force*. Using your diaphragm,

2.   breathe out harder, through your mouth, using *medium strong force*. Let your shoulders, chest, and diaphragm sag or fall downward.

    Think "let go of Being Strong" as you release air from your lungs. Let go of the air and all the tension in your body, and

3.   pause for a moment at the end of the breath. Feel the release of tension.

    Think of having "let go" of both the tightness in your chest and the need to be strong.

AM I BEING STRONG?

Being Strong is "carrying on" in spite of personal discomfort. We set aside our own needs, wants, and emotions. We act a certain way because we "should," while we really "feel" like doing something else.

We use Being Strong as a way to live up to our own standards, values, wishes, and expectations about how we should be taking care of other people or tasks, or about what impression we should create in others. We usually do this because we believe that our needs, wants, and emotions just get in the way or serve no purpose. Often this belief is unconscious.

Being Strong is not all bad. It is self-destructive only when it involves a negative attitude. Before we study how to decide if it involves a negative attitude, let's take a closer look at different ways we use Being Strong. There are 5 basic Being Strong behaviors:

 Staying or Looking Calm and In Control.

 Being or Looking Reasonable.

 Taking On Whatever Comes.

 Enduring and Persevering.

 Self-sacrificing.

EXERCISE

A

RECOGNIZING WHEN YOU ARE BEING STRONG

DIRECTIONS: For Exercise A...Circle a number to show how much you agree with each statement. Use the space provided to add other examples of ways you do each type of Being Strong behavior.

BEGIN EXERCISE A:

STAYING or LOOKING CALM and IN CONTROL:

How Much Do You Agree?

1. I try to appear composed in most situations instead of showing fear, hurt, sadness, or anger.

1 - 2 - 3 - 4 - 5
A Little...A Lot

2. I hide how excited I get.

1 - 2 - 3 - 4 - 5
A Little...A Lot

3. I hide how upset I get.

1 - 2 - 3 - 4 - 5
A Little...A Lot

4. I hide how irritable I feel.

1 - 2 - 3 - 4 - 5
A Little...A Lot

Other examples of my Staying or Looking Calm and In Control:

....

....

BEING or LOOKING REASONABLE:

How Much Do You Agree?

1. I try to be reasonable about things rather than getting emotional.

    1 - 2 - 3 - 4 - 5
    A Little...A Lot

2. I tend to think about things rather than react to them emotionally.

    1 - 2 - 3 - 4 - 5
    A Little...A Lot

Other examples of your Being or Looking Reasonable:

....

....

TAKING ON WHATEVER COMES:

How Much Do You Agree?

1. I have difficulty saying "No" when someone wants me to take on a project.

    1 - 2 - 3 - 4 - 5
    A Little...A Lot

2. I tend to pick up the slack when someone else is having a tough time.

    1 - 2 - 3 - 4 - 5
    A Little...A Lot

3. I tend to fill in or take over for others when they are overloaded.

    1 - 2 - 3 - 4 - 5
    A Little...A Lot

4. I find it hard to lose, give in, give up, surrender, or concede.

    1 - 2 - 3 - 4 - 5
    A Little...A Lot

Other examples of your Taking on Whatever Comes:

....

....

ENDURING and PERSEVERING:

How Much Do You Agree?

1.   I try to carry on and get the job done no matter
     how many problems or obstacles stand in the way.

1 - 2 - 3 - 4 - 5
A Little...A Lot

2.   I tend to continue working toward
     goals in spite of how I feel.

1 - 2 - 3 - 4 - 5
A Little...A Lot

3.   I never let my emotional upsets
     get in the way of work.

1 - 2 - 3 - 4 - 5
A Little...A Lot

Other examples of your Enduring and Persevering:

....

....

SELF-SACRIFICING:

How Much Do You Agree?

1.   I tend to put off taking care of myself and end up
     taking care of others.

1 - 2 - 3 - 4 - 5
A Little...A Lot

2.   I tend to set my own needs, wants, or emotions aside
     and think about someone else's welfare instead.

1 - 2 - 3 - 4 - 5
A Little...A Lot

Other examples of your Self-sacrificing:

....

....

COMMENTS ON THE EXERCISE

Exercise A:

Other examples of Staying or Looking Calm and In Control responses are:

    1.   I hide my anger for fear of losing control.

    2.   I hide my hurt so others won't know that they have hurt me emotionally.

Other examples of Being or Looking Reasonable responses might be:

    1.   I try to be reasonable when I have embarrassed myself or made a mistake.

    2.   I tend to be analytical when I don't understand how I feel.

Other examples of your Taking on Whatever Comes responses might be:

    1.   I tend to take on responsibilities other than my own at work when no one else will do the work.

    2.   I find it impossible to say "No" when someone asks me to do something and I really do not have the time to do it.

Other examples of Enduring or Perservering:

    1.   I will strive to complete a project even though I really want to stop and rest.

    2.   I will put overtime in at work when others have gone home so that I can finish the work that needs to be done.

Other examples of Self-sacrificing:

    1.   I tend to take care of other people's needs first and mine last.

    2.   I will try to do what is best for the situation but not what is always best for my interests.

PICK A REAL EXAMPLE FROM YOUR OWN LIFE.

SAMPLE SITUATION

Learning Steps 3 and 4 will be easier if you can refer to a personal example of Being Strong. Use the space below to describe one event or situation where you did, or have done, or still do, a lot of Being Strong.

Write a description of your event or sample situation here...

....

....

....

Check off "YES" or "NO" to show which basic Being Strong behavior(s) you were using.

Staying or Looking Calm & In Control	☐ YES	☐ NO
Being or Looking Reasonable	☐ YES	☐ NO
Taking On Whatever Comes	☐ YES	☐ NO
Enduring and Persevering	☐ YES	☐ NO
Self-sacrificing	☐ YES	☐ NO

STEP 3

DOES IT INVOLVE A NEGATIVE ATTITUDE?

Many of us have been taught that Being Strong is a good thing to do. There's nothing wrong with setting our feelings aside and being tough. Being Strong is OK as long as our attitude stays positive. But we can go too far. In that case, we need to learn to act a new way.

Being Strong is self-destructive when it goes beyond healthy limits. It's out-of-bounds when a negative attitude is involved in one of two ways: 1) if Being Strong is *driven* by a negative attitude; or 2) if Being Strong *leads us to form* a negative attitude. Four Key Questions help us recognize when this is the case.

- ◆ Am I Doing It Because I'm Not OK?

- ◆ Am I Doing It Because S/he or It Is Not OK?

- ◆ Do I End Up Feeling Not OK after Doing It?

- ◆ Do I End Up Thinking S/he or It Is Not OK after Doing It?

Why ask the Key Questions? Usually, we are unconscious of our Not OK attitude about ourselves, others, or the situation. If we ask the question, we have a chance to identify the attitude and make a change for the better. If we are aware of it, and we know what to do differently, we can take Personal Control.

Remember, the Key Questions are designed to help make you aware of the unconscious role played by negative attitudes about yourself, others, and life in general.

> **Awareness and options equal Personal Control!**

<u>Driven</u>: "Driven" means allowing a force to make you do something. Being Strong is self-destructive when the force driving it is a negative attitude about yourself, someone else, or life in general:

 Am I Doing It Because I'm Not OK?

 Am I Doing It Because S/he or It Is Not OK?

Am I driven to Being Strong because I'm Not OK?

This question asks if you are Being Strong because of some defect in yourself. Because you are not better in some way, you have to be strong to make up for it or cover it up.

BECAUSE...		I HAVE TO
I'm too emotional... I don't do enough... I'm inadequate...		BE STRONG

Am I driven to Being Strong because someone or something else is Not OK?

This question asks if you are Being Strong because you think someone or something else is defective. Because that person, those people, or the situation is not better in some way, you have to be strong to make up the difference or keep things OK.

BECAUSE...		I HAVE TO
Someone is critical... Someone is unreliable... Someone is too weak...		BE STRONG

Leads to: "Leads to" means how things end up. Usually, Being Strong leads to some kind of outcome or result. Being Strong is self-destructive when it leads you to have a negative attitude about yourself, someone else, or life in general:

 Do I End Up Feeling Not OK after Doing It?

 Do I End Up Thinking S/he or It Is Not OK after Doing It?

Do I end up feeling Not OK after Being Strong?

This question asks if you end up feeling bad or defective after you have been Being Strong. Even though you were strong, things didn't go as you hoped.

WHEN I'M BEING STRONG		**I END UP...** Feeling taken-advantage-of... Doing too much and burning out... Feeling hollow or dead inside...

Do I end up thinking someone or something else is Not OK after Being Strong?

This question asks if you end up thinking that someone or something else is defective after you have been Being Strong. S/he or it is Not OK because your Being Strong did not work.

WHEN I'M BEING STRONG		**I END UP...** Thinking someone is unfair... Thinking someone is unappreciative... Thinking life is a drag...

EXERCISE

B

DECIDING IF YOUR BEING STRONG INVOLVES A NEGATIVE ATTITUDE

DIRECTIONS: For Exercise B...Refer to the Sample Situation you described at the end of Exercise A or think about your life in general.

♦ Below, typical negative attitude statements are grouped with each Key Question. Check off "Yes" or "No" to show if each statement describes your negative attitude in your Sample Situation or with Being Strong events in your life in general.

♦ Use the space provided to add other negative attitudes involved with your Sample Situation or in your life in general.

BEGIN EXERCISE B:

FIND OUT IF BEING STRONG IS DRIVEN BY A NEGATIVE ATTITUDE ABOUT YOURSELF BY ASKING: *Am I doing it because I'm Not OK?*

Do You Agree?

1. I get into Being Strong because
    I shouldn't feel needy, weak, or empty.　　□YES　□NO

2. I get into Being Strong because
    my emotions only get in the way.　　□YES　□NO

3. I get into Being Strong because
    I'd be Not OK if I gave into my feelings.　　□YES　□NO

Other ways I feel Not OK that drive me toward Being Strong:

....

....

FIND OUT IF BEING STRONG IS DRIVEN BY A NEGATIVE ATTITUDE ABOUT SOMEONE ELSE OR LIFE IN GENERAL BY ASKING: *Am I doing it because s/he or it is Not OK?*

Do You Agree?

1.   I get into Being Strong because
     they don't care what I feel.   ☐YES   ☐NO

2.   I get into Being Strong because
     they won't appreciate me unless I take more on.   ☐YES   ☐NO

3.   I get into Being Strong because
     they aren't doing their share.   ☐YES   ☐NO

Other ways of thinking s/he or it is Not OK that drive me toward Being Strong:

....

....

FIND OUT IF Being Strong LEADS TO A NEGATIVE ATTITUDE ABOUT YOURSELF BY ASKING: *Do I end up feeling Not OK?*

Do You Agree?

1.   Through Being Strong I end up
     feeling cheated or let down.   ☐YES   ☐NO

2.   Through Being Strong I end up
     exhausting or over-extending myself.   ☐YES   ☐NO

3.   Through Being Strong I end up
     feeling disappointed or unsatisfied.   ☐YES   ☐NO

Other ways I end up feeling Not OK because of my Being Strong:

....

....

FIND OUT IF Being Strong LEADS TO A NEGATIVE ATTITUDE ABOUT SOMEONE
ELSE OR LIFE IN GENERAL BY ASKING: *Do I end up thinking s/he or it Is Not OK?*

Do You Agree?

1. Through Being Strong I end up
    thinking they cheated or took advantage of me.   ☐ YES   ☐ NO

2. Through Being Strong I end up
    thinking they don't care how hard I tried.   ☐ YES   ☐ NO

3. Through Being Strong I end up thinking
    life is a drag, no fun, or too much effort.   ☐ YES   ☐ NO

Other ways I end up thinking s/he or it is Not OK because of my Being Strong:

....

....

COMMENTS ON THE EXERCISE

Exercise B:

Other ways I feel Not OK that drive me toward Being Strong:

A.   I get into Being Strong because if I gave into my feeling I might be seen as weak.

B.   I get into Being Strong because I should be able to take care of things by myself.

Other ways of thinking that s/he or it is Not OK that drive me toward Being Strong:

A.   I get into Being Strong because they won't do things correctly so I have to do everything.

B.   I get into Being Strong because the people at work just don't care about the quailty of their work so I have to take care of things.

Other ways I end up feeling Not OK because of my Being Strong:

A.   Through Being Strong I end up feeling taken advantage of by others.

B.   Through Being Strong I end up feeling like a fool for doing so much.

LET GO OF NEGATIVE BEING STRONG

STEP 4

We feel better if we release or avoid the tension that builds up through negative Being Strong. To do this we must give ourselves permission to let go of our Being Strong standards, values, wishes, expectations, and behaviors when they involve a negative attitude.

Letting go involves setting limits to how much Being Strong we do. Letting go does not mean giving up all Being Strong. It only involves giving up Being Strong that is out-of-bounds because it is driven by or leads to a negative attitude. It also involves leaving other things and people as they are. Often we need permission to let go. Five Limit Setting Statements help us do this:

 When you need to let go of negative being calm and in control, tell yourself, *"There are OK ways to express my needs and wants, and release my emotions."*

 When you need to let go of negative being reasonable, tell yourself, *"My needs, wants, and emotions are important too."*

 When you need to let go of negative taking on whatever comes, tell yourself, *"It's OK to stop when I'm doing too much."*

 When you need to let go of negative enduring and persevering, tell yourself, *"It's OK to put myself first."*

 When you need to let go of negative self-sacrificing, tell yourself, *"Other people can handle it from here."*

EXERCISE

C

<u>PRACTICE LETTING GO OF NEGATIVE BEING STRONG</u>

<u>DIRECTIONS:</u> For Exercise C, Part 1...Continue using the Sample Situation you described at the end of Exercise A. Check off one or more Limit Setting Statements that would remind you to let go of Being Strong in that situation.

BEGIN EXERCISE C, PART 1:

- ☐ There are OK ways to express my needs and wants, and release my emotions.
- ☐ My needs, wants, and emotions are important too.
- ☐ It's OK to stop when I'm doing too much.
- ☐ It's OK to put myself first.
- ☐ Other people can handle it.

<u>DIRECTIONS:</u> For Exercise C, Part 2...Think about your life overall. Check off one or more Limit Setting Statements that are likely to remind you to let go of Being Strong behavior in your life in general.

BEGIN EXERCISE C, PART 2:

- ☐ There are OK ways to express my needs and wants, and release my emotions.
- ☐ My needs, wants, and emotions are important too.
- ☐ It's OK to stop when I'm doing too much.
- ☐ It's OK to put myself first.
- ☐ Other people can handle it.

PRACTICE YOUR WORK SHEETS

<u>DIRECTIONS:</u> The more you study the steps in this lesson, the more effective your new skills will become. Your Work Sheets are designed to help you master these skills. So, read the story below. We will use it as an example to help you learn to use the Work Sheets successfully.

Shipments were late. Orders were piling up. His assistant was still out with the flu. The freeway was a mess all the way home. The car was still overheating.

Bill walked in the door ready to collapse on the sofa. But Betty was there first, and she was sobbing. Something about long lines at the market and Billy throwing a tantrum over a toy.

He really wanted to rest a few minutes and eat dinner. But how could he ignore Betty's suffering? He should have known. "No rest for the wicked," his mother had always said.

This happened over and over. He ended up stuffing his feelings and reassuring Betty every time. He'd feel guilty if he didn't, yet he felt like a chump for always being the one that she could lean on. When would it be his turn to let down?

<u>DIRECTIONS:</u> Practice your homework exercises. Imagine that you are Bill in this situation. Complete the "Practice Limiting Being Strong Work Sheet" on the next page.

NEXT PAGE

PRACTICE LIMITING BEING STRONG WORK SHEET

Step 1: Breathe out, relaxing your diaphragm. *Practice Release Breathing while you are completing each of the other steps.*

Step 2: Am I Being Strong? *Check off "YES" or "NO" to show which Being Strong behaviors Bill probably was using...*

Staying or Looking Calm & In Control	☐ YES	☐ NO
Being or Looking Reasonable	☐ YES	☐ NO
Taking On Whatever Comes	☐ YES	☐ NO
Enduring and Persevering	☐ YES	☐ NO
Self-sacrificing	☐ YES	☐ NO

Step 3: Does It Involve a Negative Attitude? *Check off "YES" or "NO" to show whether or not you think each of the negative attitudes was involved for Bill. Use the space provided to add details...*

Am I Doing It Because I'm Not OK?   ☐ YES   ☐ NO.   How?

....

Am I Doing It Because S/he or It Is Not OK?   ☐ YES   ☐ NO.   How?

....

Do I End Up Feeling Not OK?   ☐ YES   ☐ NO.   How?

....

Do I End Up Thinking S/he or It Is Not OK?   ☐ YES   ☐ NO.   How?

....

Step 4: Let Go of Negative Being Strong. *Check off the Limit Setting Statements that would remind Bill to let go of Being Strong...*

☐ There are OK ways to express my needs and wants, and release my emotions.
☐ My needs, wants, and emotions are important too.
☐ It's OK to stop when I'm doing too much.
☐ It's OK to put myself first.
☐ Other people can handle it.

SAMPLE! PRACTICE LIMITING BEING STRONG WORK SHEET

Step 1: Breathe out, relaxing your diaphragm. *Practice Release Breathing while you are completing each of the other steps.*

Step 2: Am I Being Strong? *Check off "YES" or "NO" to show which Being Strong behaviors Bill probably was using...*

Staying or Looking Calm & In Control	■YES	□NO
Being or Looking Reasonable	□YES	■NO
Taking On Whatever Comes	■YES	□NO
Enduring and Persevering	■YES	□NO
Self-sacrificing	■YES	□NO

Step 3: Does It Involve a Negative Attitude? *Check off "YES" or "NO" to show whether or not you think each of the negative attitudes was involved for Bill. Use the space provided to add details...*

Am I Doing It Because I'm Not OK? □YES ■NO. How?

....

Am I Doing It Because S/he or It Is Not OK? ■YES □NO. How?

....Betty can't take care of herself...

Do I End Up Feeling Not OK? ■YES □NO. How?

....Poor me..

Do I End Up Thinking S/he or It Is Not OK? ■YES □NO. How?

....Betty's a drag...

Step 4: Let Go of Negative Being Strong. *Check off the Limit Setting Statements that would remind Bill to let go of Being Strong...*

■ There are OK ways to express my needs and wants, and release my emotions.
□ My needs, wants, and emotions are important too.
■ It's OK to stop when I'm doing too much.
■ It's OK to put myself first.
■ Other people can handle it.

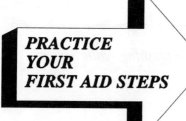

PRACTICE YOUR FIRST AID STEPS

<u>DIRECTIONS:</u> The more you practice your First Aid Steps the better you will feel. Practice your First Aid Steps now. Imagine you are in a situation used in this lesson, or think about your life in general.

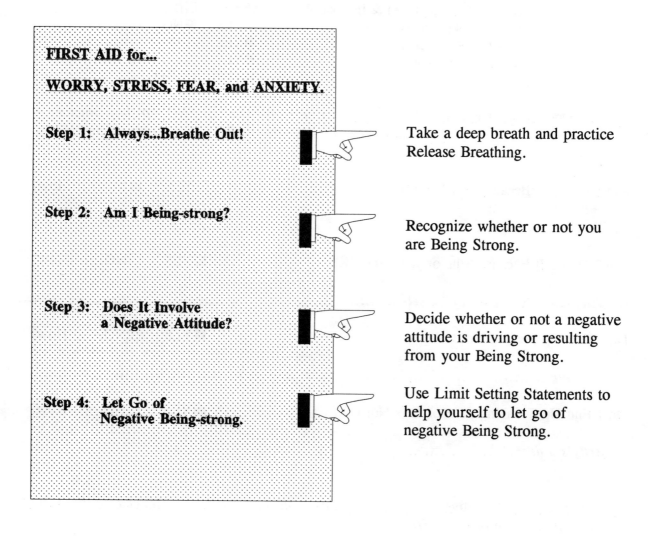

FIRST AID for...

WORRY, STRESS, FEAR, and ANXIETY.

Step 1: Always...Breathe Out!
Take a deep breath and practice Release Breathing.

Step 2: Am I Being-strong?
Recognize whether or not you are Being Strong.

Step 3: Does It Involve a Negative Attitude?
Decide whether or not a negative attitude is driving or resulting from your Being Strong.

Step 4: Let Go of Negative Being-strong.
Use Limit Setting Statements to help yourself to let go of negative Being Strong.

HOMEWORK

THE METHODS...

Work Sheets. This week complete 8 Limiting Being Strong Work Sheets. Do the Work Sheets for situations in which you worry or feel stress, fear, or anxiety. Complete the Work Sheets at the time of these events or very soon thereafter.

First Aid Steps. Practice your First Aid Steps as often as possible, even when you are not really worrying or feeling threatened.

*

FIRST AID for...WORRY, STRESS, FEAR, AND ANXIETY

Step 1: **Always...Breathe Out!**

Step 2: **Am I Being Strong?**

Step 3: **Does It Involve a Negative Attitude?**

Step 4: **Let go of Negative Being Strong.**

Use your Clip-outs: Cut out the First Aid Steps reminders. Place them in spots where you will see them and remember to practice. Give some to a friend, and tell him or her how to use them.

Teach Others. Share the lesson with others. Teach them how to help themselves using the same skills you are learning.

* Permission is given to reproduce the First Aid Steps for your personal use.

Step 1: Breathe out, relaxing your diaphragm. *Practice Release Breathing while you are completing each of the other steps.*

Step 2: Am I Being Strong? *Check off "YES" or "NO" to show which Being Strong behaviors you used...*

Staying or Looking Calm & In Control	☐YES	☐NO
Being or Looking Reasonable	☐YES	☐NO
Taking On Whatever Comes	☐YES	☐NO
Enduring and Persevering	☐YES	☐NO
Self-sacrificing	☐YES	☐NO

Step 3: Does It Involve a Negative Attitude? *Check off "YES" or "NO" to show whether or not you think each of the negative attitudes was involved for you. Use the space provided to add details...*

Am I Doing It Because I'm Not OK?   ☐YES   ☐NO.   How?

....

Am I Doing It Because S/he or It Is Not OK?   ☐YES   ☐NO.   How?

....

Do I End Up Feeling Not OK?   ☐YES   ☐NO.   How?

....

Do I End Up Thinking S/he or It Is Not OK?   ☐YES   ☐NO.   How?

....

Step 4: Let Go of Negative Being Strong. *Check off the Limit Setting Statements that would remind you to let go of Being Strong...*

☐ There are OK ways to express my needs and wants, and release my emotions.
☐ My needs, wants, and emotions are important too.
☐ It's OK to stop when I'm doing too much.
☐ It's OK to put myself first.
☐ Other people can handle it.

Step 1: Breathe out, relaxing your diaphragm. *Practice Release Breathing while you are completing each of the other steps.*

Step 2: Am I Being Strong? *Check off "YES" or "NO" to show which Being Strong behaviors you used...*

Staying or Looking Calm & In Control	☐YES	☐NO
Being or Looking Reasonable	☐YES	☐NO
Taking On Whatever Comes	☐YES	☐NO
Enduring and Persevering	☐YES	☐NO
Self-sacrificing	☐YES	☐NO

Step 3: Does It Involve a Negative Attitude? *Check off "YES" or "NO" to show whether or not you think each of the negative attitudes was involved for you. Use the space provided to add details...*

Am I Doing It Because I'm Not OK?　　　　☐YES　☐NO.　How?

....

Am I Doing It Because S/he or It Is Not OK?　　☐YES　☐NO.　How?

....

Do I End Up Feeling Not OK?　　　　　　☐YES　☐NO.　How?

....

Do I End Up Thinking S/he or It Is Not OK?　　☐YES　☐NO.　How?

....

Step 4: Let Go of Negative Being Strong. *Check off the Limit Setting Statements that would* **remind** *you to let go of Being Strong...*

☐　There are OK ways to express my needs and wants, and release my emotions.
☐　My needs, wants, and emotions are important too.
☐　It's OK to stop when I'm doing too much.
☐　It's OK to put myself first.
☐　Other people can handle it.

Step 1: Breathe out, relaxing your diaphragm. *Practice Release Breathing while you are completing each of the other steps.*

Step 2: Am I Being Strong? *Check off "YES" or "NO" to show which Being Strong behaviors you used...*

Staying or Looking Calm & In Control	☐ YES	☐ NO
Being or Looking Reasonable	☐ YES	☐ NO
Taking On Whatever Comes	☐ YES	☐ NO
Enduring and Persevering	☐ YES	☐ NO
Self-sacrificing	☐ YES	☐ NO

Step 3: Does It Involve a Negative Attitude? *Check off "YES" or "NO" to show whether or not you think each of the negative attitudes was involved for you. Use the space provided to add details...*

Am I Doing It Because I'm Not OK?   ☐ YES   ☐ NO.   How?

....

Am I Doing It Because S/he or It Is Not OK?   ☐ YES   ☐ NO.   How?

....

Do I End Up Feeling Not OK?   ☐ YES   ☐ NO.   How?

....

Do I End Up Thinking S/he or It Is Not OK?   ☐ YES   ☐ NO.   How?

....

Step 4: Let Go of Negative Being Strong. *Check off the Limit Setting Statements that would remind you to let go of Being Strong...*

☐ There are OK ways to express my needs and wants, and release my emotions.
☐ My needs, wants, and emotions are important too.
☐ It's OK to stop when I'm doing too much.
☐ It's OK to put myself first.
☐ Other people can handle it.

Step 1: Breathe out, relaxing your diaphragm. *Practice Release Breathing while you are completing each of the other steps.*

Step 2: Am I Being Strong? *Check off "YES" or "NO" to show which Being Strong behaviors you used...*

Staying or Looking Calm & In Control	☐YES	☐NO
Being or Looking Reasonable	☐YES	☐NO
Taking On Whatever Comes	☐YES	☐NO
Enduring and Persevering	☐YES	☐NO
Self-sacrificing	☐YES	☐NO

Step 3: Does It Involve a Negative Attitude? *Check off "YES" or "NO" to show whether or not you think each of the negative attitudes was involved for you. Use the space provided to add details...*

Am I Doing It Because I'm Not OK? ☐YES ☐NO. How?

....

Am I Doing It Because S/he or It Is Not OK? ☐YES ☐NO. How?

....

Do I End Up Feeling Not OK? ☐YES ☐NO. How?

....

Do I End Up Thinking S/he or It Is Not OK? ☐YES ☐NO. How?

....

Step 4: Let Go of Negative Being Strong. *Check off the Limit Setting Statements that would remind you to let go of Being Strong...*

☐ There are OK ways to express my needs and wants, and release my emotions.
☐ My needs, wants, and emotions are important too.
☐ It's OK to stop when I'm doing too much.
☐ It's OK to put myself first.
☐ Other people can handle it.

Step 1: Breathe out, relaxing your diaphragm. *Practice Release Breathing while you are completing each of the other steps.*

Step 2: Am I Being Strong? *Check off "YES" or "NO" to show which Being Strong behaviors you used...*

Staying or Looking Calm & In Control	☐YES	☐NO
Being or Looking Reasonable	☐YES	☐NO
Taking On Whatever Comes	☐YES	☐NO
Enduring and Persevering	☐YES	☐NO
Self-sacrificing	☐YES	☐NO

Step 3: Does It Involve a Negative Attitude? *Check off "YES" or "NO" to show whether or not you think each of the negative attitudes was involved for you. Use the space provided to add details...*

Am I Doing It Because I'm Not OK? ☐YES ☐NO. How?

....

Am I Doing It Because S/he or It Is Not OK? ☐YES ☐NO. How?

....

Do I End Up Feeling Not OK? ☐YES ☐NO. How?

....

Do I End Up Thinking S/he or It Is Not OK? ☐YES ☐NO. How?

....

Step 4: Let Go of Negative Being Strong. *Check off the Limit Setting Statements that would remind you to let go of Being Strong...*

☐ There are OK ways to express my needs and wants, and release my emotions.
☐ My needs, wants, and emotions are important too.
☐ It's OK to stop when I'm doing too much.
☐ It's OK to put myself first.
☐ Other people can handle it.

Step 1: Breathe out, relaxing your diaphragm. *Practice Release Breathing while you are completing each of the other steps.*

Step 2: Am I Being Strong? *Check off "YES" or "NO" to show which Being Strong behaviors you used...*

Staying or Looking Calm & In Control	☐YES	☐NO
Being or Looking Reasonable	☐YES	☐NO
Taking On Whatever Comes	☐YES	☐NO
Enduring and Persevering	☐YES	☐NO
Self-sacrificing	☐YES	☐NO

Step 3: Does It Involve a Negative Attitude? *Check off "YES" or "NO" to show whether or not you think each of the negative attitudes was involved for you. Use the space provided to add details...*

Am I Doing It Because I'm Not OK?   ☐YES   ☐NO.   How?

....

Am I Doing It Because S/he or It Is Not OK?   ☐YES   ☐NO.   How?

....

Do I End Up Feeling Not OK?   ☐YES   ☐NO.   How?

....

Do I End Up Thinking S/he or It Is Not OK?   ☐YES   ☐NO.   How?

....

Step 4: Let Go of Negative Being Strong. *Check off the Limit Setting Statements that would remind you to let go of Being Strong...*

☐ There are OK ways to express my needs and wants, and release my emotions.
☐ My needs, wants, and emotions are important too.
☐ It's OK to stop when I'm doing too much.
☐ It's OK to put myself first.
☐ Other people can handle it.

Step 1: Breathe out, relaxing your diaphragm. *Practice Release Breathing while you are completing each of the other steps.*

Step 2: Am I Being Strong? *Check off "YES" or "NO" to show which Being Strong behaviors you used...*

Staying or Looking Calm & In Control	☐YES	☐NO
Being or Looking Reasonable	☐YES	☐NO
Taking On Whatever Comes	☐YES	☐NO
Enduring and Persevering	☐YES	☐NO
Self-sacrificing	☐YES	☐NO

Step 3: Does It Involve a Negative Attitude? *Check off "YES" or "NO" to show whether or not you think each of the negative attitudes was involved for you. Use the space provided to add details...*

Am I Doing It Because I'm Not OK?   ☐YES   ☐NO.   How?

....

Am I Doing It Because S/he or It Is Not OK?   ☐YES   ☐NO.   How?

....

Do I End Up Feeling Not OK?   ☐YES   ☐NO.   How?

....

Do I End Up Thinking S/he or It Is Not OK?   ☐YES   ☐NO.   How?

....

Step 4: Let Go of Negative Being Strong. *Check off the Limit Setting Statements that would remind you to let go of Being Strong...*

☐ There are OK ways to express my needs and wants, and release my emotions.
☐ My needs, wants, and emotions are important too.
☐ It's OK to stop when I'm doing too much.
☐ It's OK to put myself first.
☐ Other people can handle it.

Step 1: Breathe out, relaxing your diaphragm. *Practice Release Breathing while you are completing each of the other steps.*

Step 2: Am I Being Strong? *Check off "YES" or "NO" to show which Being Strong behaviors you used...*

Staying or Looking Calm & In Control	☐ YES	☐ NO
Being or Looking Reasonable	☐ YES	☐ NO
Taking On Whatever Comes	☐ YES	☐ NO
Enduring and Persevering	☐ YES	☐ NO
Self-sacrificing	☐ YES	☐ NO

Step 3: Does It Involve a Negative Attitude? *Check off "YES" or "NO" to show whether or not you think each of the negative attitudes was involved for you. Use the space provided to add details...*

Am I Doing It Because I'm Not OK?   ☐ YES   ☐ NO.   How?

....

Am I Doing It Because S/he or It Is Not OK?   ☐ YES   ☐ NO.   How?

....

Do I End Up Feeling Not OK?   ☐ YES   ☐ NO.   How?

....

Do I End Up Thinking S/he or It Is Not OK?   ☐ YES   ☐ NO.   How?

....

Step 4: Let Go of Negative Being Strong. *Check off the Limit Setting Statements that would remind you to let go of Being Strong...*

☐ There are OK ways to express my needs and wants, and release my emotions.
☐ My needs, wants, and emotions are important too.
☐ It's OK to stop when I'm doing too much.
☐ It's OK to put myself first.
☐ Other people can handle it.

Chapter 7

MAKE FEELINGS WORK FOR YOU!

INTRODUCTION

Feelings are a natural and important part of ourselves. They make life rich and rewarding.

However, there are three unhealthy ways of handling our feelings. *Denial*, *inaction*, and *losing control* lead to loss of Personal Control, stress, and negative attitudes:

 Denial. We can hold in or bottle up our feelings without even knowing we are doing so. This usually causes emotional shutting down or deadness, irritability, or restlessness.

 Inaction. We can hold in or bottle up our feelings and be aware of it. This causes a sense of emotions building up inside or "eating away" at us. In this case, we are aware of our feelings but unsure what to do with them.

 Losing Control. We can "lose control" of our feelings and do something we regret. While losing control temporarily reduces stress and tension, it usually causes social problems or physical harm.

Denial, inaction, and losing control can cause worry, stress, fear, and anxiety. But by using feelings to understand and validate yourself, and to solve problems, you increase your sense of Personal Control, reduce tension, and develop a positive attitude toward yourself, others, and life in general.

GOALS

1. You will learn how to use your feelings to understand yourself. You will learn how this involves identifying your values.

2. You will learn how to use your feelings to like and respect yourself.

3. You will learn how to use your feelings productively to solve problems and reach goals.

REMEMBER

Don't miss another opportunity to build your peace of mind. When worry, stress, fear, or anxiety strike this week...Conquer Your Fears! Use...

*

FIRST AID for..WORRY, STRESS, FEAR, AND ANXIETY

Step 1:   Always...Breathe Out!

Step 2:   How Am I Feeling?

Step 3:   What Do I Value?

Step 4:   Validate Myself!

Step 5:   Channel My Feelings into Action!

* Permission is given to reproduce the First Aid Steps for your personal use.

STEP 1

We create or increase the tension within ourselves when we resist or misunderstand our feelings. We recommend Release Breathing for briefly reducing the tension that builds from bottling up our feelings. It helps us allow our emotions to flow naturally and be used in a healthy way.

Release Breathing enables us to let go of the tension we build up through resisting our feelings in order to cope with a situation. And we can practice Release Breathing on the spot, in the middle of any activity, as often as we wish, especially when we have been over-controlling our emotions.

Let's take a closer look at working with our feelings. We are disowning a part of ourselves when we deny our feelings, take no action with them, or lose control of them. We are not trusting ourselves and we are making thoughts and external things more important than respecting the value of our emotions and using the energy contained in them. That is a negative attitude; it is negative about ourselves.

Resisting our feelings is a form of control rooted in that negative attitude. This lesson teaches you how to recognize, interpret, react to, and use your feelings in productive ways.

The negative attitude of misunderstanding and devaluing our feelings causes tension to build in our bodies. That tension shuts down our breathing as well. The Release Breathing technique is an excellent way to practice breaking free of this shutting down, to open up your breathing and your emotions.

Release Breathing sends an important "let go" message to the brain. It involves 3 steps:

1. breathe in deeply, using *medium force*. Using your diaphragm,

2. firmly breathe out through your mouth, using *medium strong force*. Let your shoulders, chest, and diaphragm sag or fall downward.

    Think "how do I feel?" as you release air from your lungs. Let go of the air and all the tension in your body, and

3. pause for a moment at the end of the breath. Feel the release of tension.

    Think of having "let go" of the tightness in your chest and "experienced" your feelings.

STEP 2

<u>HOW AM I FEELING?</u>

Feelings are an emotional reaction to something. They are more physical than mental. Feelings involve sensations in our body more than thinking.

There are 11 basic feelings that we have to deal with in a healthy way to avoid worry, stress, fear, and anxiety. Some of these feelings are pure emotion. Others involve a combination of an emotion and a thought or interpretation. We have to recognize these feelings before we can put them to good use.

<u>Pure Emotion</u>	<u>Combined Thought and Emotion</u>
■ Fear	■ Helpless/Hopeless
■ Anger	■ Confused/Undecided
■ Boredom	■ Humiliated/Embarrassed
■ Sadness/Hurt	■ Inadequate/Worthless
■ Guilt/Shame	■ Isolated
■ Frustration	

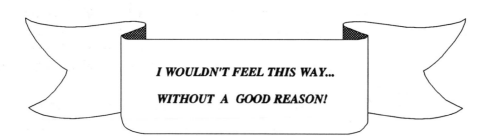

I WOULDN'T FEEL THIS WAY...

WITHOUT A GOOD REASON!

EXERCISE A

IDENTIFYING YOUR FEELINGS

DIRECTIONS: For Exercise A...Four situations are described below. Imagine you are in each one. Check off the feelings that situation might arouse in you. Use the space provided to add other feelings you might have.

BEGIN EXERCISE A:

Situation # 1, Audit. You get a letter from the IRS. You open it and learn that your accountant made errors on one of your returns. The IRS says you will be audited for that year.

☐ Fear ☐ Sadness/Hurt ☐ Helpless/Hopeless
☐ Anger ☐ Guilt/Shame ☐ Confused/Undecided
☐ Boredom ☐ Frustration ☐ Humiliated/Embarrassed
  ☐ Isolated ☐ Inadequate/Worthless

Other feelings you might have:..

....

Situation # 2, Inefficiency. You buy a telephone answering machine. It breaks down almost immediately after you get it home. You end up sending it to the manufacturer three times for repairs. It still doesn't work after each time they return it.

☐ Fear ☐ Sadness/Hurt ☐ Helpless/Hopeless
☐ Anger ☐ Guilt/Shame ☐ Confused/Undecided
☐ Boredom ☐ Frustration ☐ Humiliated/Embarrassed
  ☐ Isolated ☐ Inadequate/Worthless

Other feelings you might have:..

....

<u>Situation # 3, Criticism.</u> You are at work or in a public place. Someone you know well (a boss, co-worker, friend, or a member of your family) starts to criticize you in the worst way: loud, dramatic, and putting you down.

☐ Fear   ☐ Sadness/Hurt   ☐ Helpless/Hopeless
☐ Anger   ☐ Guilt/Shame   ☐ Confused/Undecided
☐ Boredom   ☐ Frustration   ☐ Humiliated/Embarrassed
                  ☐ Isolated   ☐ Inadequate/Worthless

Other feelings you might have:..

....

<u>Situation # 4, Rejection.</u> You are trying very hard to join a group or organization because you really want to be part of it. You get a letter rejecting your application; it explains that you don't have the qualities for which the group or organization is looking.

☐ Fear   ☐ Sadness/Hurt   ☐ Helpless/Hopeless
☐ Anger   ☐ Guilt/Shame   ☐ Confused/Undecided
☐ Boredom   ☐ Frustration   ☐ Humiliated/Embarrassed
                  ☐ Isolated   ☐ Inadequate/Worthless

Other feelings you might have:..

....

STEP 3

<u>WHAT DO I VALUE?</u>

Situations arouse feelings. Once you identify your feelings you can use them to identify your values. Once you identify your values you can validate yourself. This process will increase your sense of Personal Control, reduce tension, and develop positive attitudes.

<u>WHAT ARE VALUES?</u> Your values are the things that are important to you. Therefore, your values are part of who you are. They are part of your identity. And they are part of what is worthwhile about you. Recognizing your values helps in two ways:

■ Using feelings to identify your values builds your identity. Step 3 helps you do this.

■ Consciously, deliberately validating yourself for having those values builds your self-esteem. Step 4 helps you do this.

 <u>HOW ARE VALUES AND FEELINGS RELATED?</u> You have to value something in order to feel an emotion. The best way to understand your feelings is to identify the values that stand behind them. There are 4 basic things we value (or classifications of things that we value):

■ <u>Security:</u> Protection, safety, strength, certainty, confidence, guarantee, and assurance.

■ <u>Esteem:</u> (Self and Others) Honor, admiration, appreciation, and respect.

■ <u>Pleasure:</u> Enjoyment, serenity, comfort, fun, excitement, joy, satisfaction, and gratification.

■ <u>Profit:</u> Improvement, advancement, benefit, returns, gains, accumulation, and earnings.

USING YOUR FEELINGS TO IDENTIFY YOUR VALUES

DIRECTIONS: For Exercise B...Use your responses to Exercise A to do this exercise.

♦ Select <u>one</u> feeling you identified in each Situation of Exercise A.

♦ Check off the general value(s) with which that feeling is connected. Use the space provided to add other, more specific values.

BEGIN EXERCISE B:

<u>Situation # 1, Audit.</u> Feeling:...

General Values: ☐ Security   ☐ Esteem   ☐ Pleasure   ☐ Profit

Other more specific values:..

....

<u>Situation # 2, Inefficiency.</u> Feeling:...

General Values: ☐ Security   ☐ Esteem   ☐ Pleasure   ☐ Profit

Other more specific values:..

....

<u>Situation # 3, Criticism.</u> Feeling:...

General Values: □ Security   □ Esteem   □ Pleasure   □ Profit

Other more specific values:...

....

<u>Situation # 4, Rejection.</u> Feeling:...

General Values: □ Security   □ Esteem   □ Pleasure   □ Profit

Other more specific values:...

....

VALIDATE MYSELF!

Self-validation involves reminding yourself who you are (your basic identity) and telling yourself that you are worthwhile. Self-validation consists of deliberately thinking two things:

■ How part of your identity is what you value.

■ How you are worthwhile because of what you value.

Exercise C will help you create self-validating statements that declare your identity and your worth based on your values.

SELF-VALIDATION THROUGH YOUR VALUES

DIRECTIONS: For Exercise C...Use your responses to Exercise B to complete the self-validating statements below. You will enter the same values to complete each statement. Repetition contributes to the success of this exercise.

BEGIN EXERCISE C:

Situation # 1, Audit.

I'm the kind of person who values:...

I'm worthwhile as a person because I value:...

Situation # 2, Inefficiency.

I'm the kind of person who values:...

I'm worthwhile as a person because I value:...

Situation # 3, Criticism.

I'm the kind of person who values:...

I'm worthwhile as a person because I value:...

Situation # 4, Rejection.

I'm the kind of person who values:...

I'm worthwhile as a person because I value:...

CHANNEL MY FEELINGS INTO ACTION!

Channel your feelings by directing them into productive action. This is much more healthy than bottling them up by denial or inaction or losing control of them. Productive actions help you achieve what you value.

There are 6 basic productive actions:

- ■ Study the Situation
- ■ Set Limits/Let Go
- ■ Confront Something

- ■ Show Compassion
- ■ Be Careful/Thorough
- ■ Be Determined

EXERCISE

D

IDENTIFYING ACTIONS YOU CAN TAKE

DIRECTIONS: For Exercise D...Use your responses to the Situations in Exercises A, B, and C. Check one or more of the feeling channeling statements below for <u>one</u> feeling & value you identified in each Situation. Use the space provided to add other, more specific actions.

BEGIN EXERCISE D:

<u>Situation # 1, Audit.</u> Because of what I value I will use my feelings to motivate me to:

- ☐ Study the Situation
- ☐ Set Limits/Let Go
- ☐ Confront Something

- ☐ Show Compassion
- ☐ Be Careful/Thorough
- ☐ Be Determined

Other actions I can take:...

....

Situation # 2, Inefficiency. Because of what I value I will use my feelings to motivate me to:

- ☐ Study the Situation
- ☐ Set Limits/Let Go
- ☐ Confront Something
- ☐ Show Compassion
- ☐ Be Careful/Thorough
- ☐ Be Determined

Other actions I can take:..

....

Situation # 3, Criticism. Because of what I value I will use my feelings to motivate me to:

- ☐ Study the Situation
- ☐ Set Limits/Let Go
- ☐ Confront Something
- ☐ Show Compassion
- ☐ Be Careful/Thorough
- ☐ Be Determined

Other actions I can take:..

....

Situation # 4, Rejection. Because of what I value I will use my feelings to motivate me to:

- ☐ Study the Situation
- ☐ Set Limits/Let Go
- ☐ Confront Something
- ☐ Show Compassion
- ☐ Be Careful/Thorough
- ☐ Be Determined

Other actions I can take:..

....

PRACTICE YOUR WORK SHEETS

DIRECTIONS: The more you study the steps in this lesson, the more effective your new skills will become. Your Work Sheets are designed to help you master these skills. So, read the story below. We will use it as an example to help you learn to use the Work Sheets successfully.

Bill thought about the situation for a moment. Sure, he was frustrated with Betty. She really should be able to handle a three-year-old.

It also worried him. He knew Betty was sending mixed messages to Bill Jr. How might that affect him in later life? He might never learn to accept that there were things he can not have. That reminded Bill of is own father.

Bill wouldn't have been so upset if he didn't care about both of them. He decided to take action. He resolved to get Betty to read that book on parenting that Bill's mother gave Betty for Christmas.

DIRECTIONS: Practice your homework exercises. Imagine that you are Bill in this situation. Complete the "Practice Feelings Work Sheet" on the next page.

NEXT PAGE

PRACTICE FEELINGS WORK SHEET

Step 1: Breathe out, relaxing your diaphragm. *Practice Release Breathing while you are completing the other steps.*

Step 2: How Am I Feeling? *Identify what Bill was probably feeling...*

☐ Fear	☐ Sadness/Hurt	☐ Helpless/Hopeless
☐ Anger	☐ Guilt/Shame	☐ Confused/Undecided
☐ Boredom	☐ Frustration	☐ Humiliated/Embarrassed
	☐ Isolated	☐ Inadequate/Worthless

Other feelings I might have:...

Step 3: What Do I Value? *Identify what values Bill must have in order to feel that way...*

General Values: ☐ Security   ☐ Esteem   ☐ Pleasure   ☐ Profit

Other more specific values:..

Step 4: Validate Myself! *Complete the self-validating statements below as if you were Bill...*

I'm the kind of person who values:...

I'm worthwhile as a person because I value:...

Step 5: Channel My Feelings into Action! *Identify actions Bill could use to release his feelings in a way that achieves what he values...*

☐ Study the Situation	☐ Show Compassion
☐ Set Limits/Let Go	☐ Be Careful/Thorough
☐ Confront Something	☐ Be Determined

Other actions I can take:...

....

Step 1: Breathe out, relaxing your diaphragm. *Practice Release Breathing while you are completing the other steps.*

Step 2: How Am I Feeling? *Identify what Bill was probably feeling...*

■ Fear	☐ Sadness/Hurt	■ Helpless/Hopeless
☐ Anger	☐ Guilt/Shame	☐ Confused/Undecided
☐ Boredom	■ Frustration	☐ Humiliated/Embarrassed
	☐ Isolated	☐ Inadequate/Worthless

Other feelings I might have:..

Step 3: What Do I Value? *Identify what values Bill must have in order to feel that way...*

General Values: ■ Security   ☐ Esteem   ☐ Pleasure   ☐ Profit

Other more specific values:....*Family welfare*................................

Step 4: Validate Myself! *Complete the self-validating statements below as if you were Bill...*

I'm the kind of person who values:....*The security of my family*.........................

I'm worthwhile as a person because I value:....*Family security*...........................

Step 5: Channel My Feelings into Action! *Identify actions Bill could use to release his feelings in a way that achieves what he values...*

■ Study the Situation	☐ Show Compassion
☐ Set Limits/Let Go	☐ Be Careful/Thorough
■ Confront Something	■ Be Determined

Other actions I can take:....*Get Betty to read the book*....................................

....

....

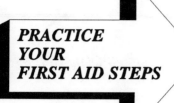

PRACTICE YOUR FIRST AID STEPS

<u>DIRECTIONS:</u> The more you practice your First Aid Steps, the better you will feel. Practice your First Aid Steps now. Imagine you are in a situation used in this lesson, or think about your life in general.

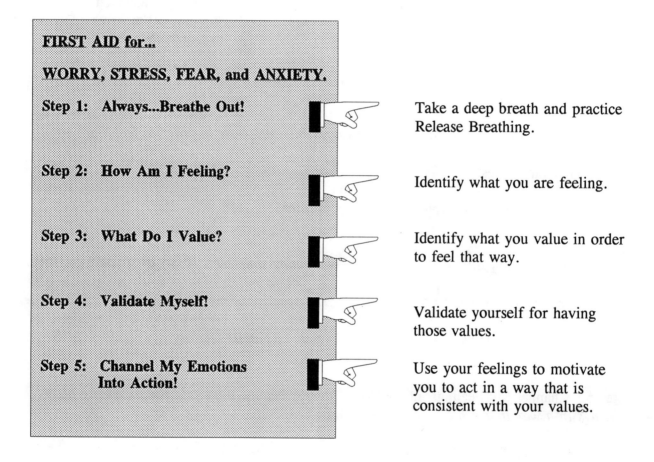

FIRST AID for...

WORRY, STRESS, FEAR, and ANXIETY.

Step 1: Always...Breathe Out! — Take a deep breath and practice Release Breathing.

Step 2: How Am I Feeling? — Identify what you are feeling.

Step 3: What Do I Value? — Identify what you value in order to feel that way.

Step 4: Validate Myself! — Validate yourself for having those values.

Step 5: Channel My Emotions Into Action! — Use your feelings to motivate you to act in a way that is consistent with your values.

HOMEWORK

<u>THE METHODS...</u>

<u>Work Sheets.</u> This week complete 8 Feelings Work Sheets. Do the Work Sheets for situations in which you worry or feel stress, fear, or anxiety. Complete the Work Sheets at the time of these events or very soon thereafter.

<u>First Aid Steps.</u> Practice your First Aid Steps as often as possible, even when you are not really worrying or feeling threatened.

*

FIRST AID for... WORRY, STRESS, FEAR, AND ANXIETY

Step 1:   **Always...Breathe Out!**

Step 2:   **How Am I Feeling?**

Step 3:   **What Do I Value?**

Step 4:   **Validate Myself!**

Step 5:   **Channel My Feelings into Action!**

<u>Use your Clip-outs:</u> Cut out the First Aid Steps reminders. Place them in spots where you will see them and remember to practice. Give some to a friend, and tell him or her how to use them.

<u>Teach Others.</u> Share the lesson with others. Teach them how to help themselves using the same skills you are learning.

* Permission is given to reproduce the First Aid Steps for your personal use.

Step 1: Breathe out, relaxing your diaphragm. *Practice Release Breathing while you are completing the other steps. Describe the situation in which you worried or felt stress, fear, or anxiety...*

Step 2: How Am I Feeling? *Identify your feelings..*

☐ Fear   ☐ Sadness/Hurt   ☐ Helpless/Hopeless
☐ Anger   ☐ Guilt/Shame   ☐ Confused/Undecided
☐ Boredom   ☐ Frustration   ☐ Humiliated/Embarrassed
                ☐ Isolated   ☐ Inadequate/Worthless

Other feelings I might have:..

Step 3: What Do I Value? *Identify what values you must have in order to feel those feelings...*

General Values: ☐ Security   ☐ Esteem   ☐ Pleasure   ☐ Profit

Other more specific values:..

Step 4: Validate Myself! *Complete the self-validating statements below...*

I'm the kind of person who values:......................................

I'm worthwhile as a person because I value:..

Step 5: Channel My Feelings into Action! *Identify actions you could use to release your feelings in a way that achieves what you value...*

☐ Study the Situation   ☐ Show Compassion
☐ Set Limits/Let Go   ☐ Be Careful/Thorough
☐ Confront Something   ☐ Be Determined

Other actions I can take:..

....

Step 1: Breathe out, relaxing your diaphragm. *Practice Release Breathing while you are completing the other steps. Describe the situation in which you worried or felt stress, fear, or anxiety...*

Step 2: How Am I Feeling? *Identify your feelings..*

      □ Fear   □ Sadness/Hurt   □ Helpless/Hopeless
      □ Anger   □ Guilt/Shame   □ Confused/Undecided
      □ Boredom   □ Frustration   □ Humiliated/Embarrassed
                     □ Isolated   □ Inadequate/Worthless

Other feelings I might have:...

Step 3: What Do I Value? *Identify what values you must have in order to feel those feelings...*

General Values: □ Security   □ Esteem   □ Pleasure   □ Profit

Other more specific values:...

Step 4: Validate Myself! *Complete the self-validating statements below...*

I'm the kind of person who values:...

I'm worthwhile as a person because I value:...

Step 5: Channel My Feelings into Action! *Identify actions you could use to release your feelings in a way that achieves what you value...*

      □ Study the Situation   □ Show Compassion
      □ Set Limits/Let Go   □ Be Careful/Thorough
      □ Confront Something   □ Be Determined

Other actions I can take:..

....

Step 1: Breathe out, relaxing your diaphragm. *Practice Release Breathing while you are completing the other steps. Describe the situation in which you worried or felt stress, fear, or anxiety...*

Step 2: How Am I Feeling? *Identify your feelings..*

☐ Fear   ☐ Sadness/Hurt   ☐ Helpless/Hopeless
☐ Anger   ☐ Guilt/Shame   ☐ Confused/Undecided
☐ Boredom   ☐ Frustration   ☐ Humiliated/Embarrassed
                      ☐ Isolated   ☐ Inadequate/Worthless

Other feelings I might have:...

Step 3: What Do I Value? *Identify what values you must have in order to feel those feelings...*

General Values: ☐ Security   ☐ Esteem   ☐ Pleasure   ☐ Profit

Other more specific values:...

Step 4: Validate Myself! *Complete the self-validating statements below...*

I'm the kind of person who values:...

I'm worthwhile as a person because I value:..

Step 5: Channel My Feelings into Action! *Identify actions you could use to release your feelings in a way that achieves what you value...*

☐ Study the Situation   ☐ Show Compassion
☐ Set Limits/Let Go   ☐ Be Careful/Thorough
☐ Confront Something   ☐ Be Determined

Other actions I can take:..

....

Step 1: Breathe out, relaxing your diaphragm. *Practice Release Breathing while you are completing the other steps. Describe the situation in which you worried or felt stress, fear, or anxiety...*

Step 2: How Am I Feeling? *Identify your feelings..*

- ☐ Fear
- ☐ Anger
- ☐ Boredom

- ☐ Sadness/Hurt
- ☐ Guilt/Shame
- ☐ Frustration
- ☐ Isolated

- ☐ Helpless/Hopeless
- ☐ Confused/Undecided
- ☐ Humiliated/Embarrassed
- ☐ Inadequate/Worthless

Other feelings I might have:..

Step 3: What Do I Value? *Identify what values you must have in order to feel those feelings...*

General Values: ☐ Security   ☐ Esteem   ☐ Pleasure   ☐ Profit

Other more specific values:...

Step 4: Validate Myself! *Complete the self-validating statements below...*

I'm the kind of person who values:...

I'm worthwhile as a person because I value:...

Step 5: Channel My Feelings into Action! *Identify actions you could use to release your feelings in a way that achieves what you value...*

- ☐ Study the Situation
- ☐ Set Limits/Let Go
- ☐ Confront Something

- ☐ Show Compassion
- ☐ Be Careful/Thorough
- ☐ Be Determined

Other actions I can take:...

....

Step 1: Breathe out, relaxing your diaphragm. *Practice Release Breathing while you are completing the other steps. Describe the situation in which you worried or felt stress, fear, or anxiety...*

Step 2: How Am I Feeling? *Identify your feelings..*

- ☐ Fear
- ☐ Anger
- ☐ Boredom
- ☐ Sadness/Hurt
- ☐ Guilt/Shame
- ☐ Frustration
- ☐ Isolated
- ☐ Helpless/Hopeless
- ☐ Confused/Undecided
- ☐ Humiliated/Embarrassed
- ☐ Inadequate/Worthless

Other feelings I might have:...

Step 3: What Do I Value? *Identify what values you must have in order to feel those feelings...*

General Values: ☐ Security ☐ Esteem ☐ Pleasure ☐ Profit

Other more specific
values:..

Step 4: Validate Myself! *Complete the self-validating statements below...*

I'm the kind of person who values:..

I'm worthwhile as a person because I value:..

Step 5: Channel My Feelings into Action! *Identify actions you could use to release your feelings in a way that achieves what you value...*

- ☐ Study the Situation
- ☐ Set Limits/Let Go
- ☐ Confront Something
- ☐ Show Compassion
- ☐ Be Careful/Thorough
- ☐ Be Determined

Other actions I can take:..

....

Step 1: Breathe out, relaxing your diaphragm. *Practice Release Breathing while you are completing the other steps. Describe the situation in which you worried or felt stress, fear, or anxiety...*

Step 2: How Am I Feeling? *Identify your feelings..*

☐ Fear	☐ Sadness/Hurt	☐ Helpless/Hopeless
☐ Anger	☐ Guilt/Shame	☐ Confused/Undecided
☐ Boredom	☐ Frustration	☐ Humiliated/Embarrassed
	☐ Isolated	☐ Inadequate/Worthless

Other feelings I might have:..

Step 3: What Do I Value? *Identify what values you must have in order to feel those feelings...*

General Values: ☐ Security   ☐ Esteem   ☐ Pleasure   ☐ Profit

Other more specific values:..

Step 4: Validate Myself! *Complete the self-validating statements below...*

I'm the kind of person who values:..

I'm worthwhile as a person because I value:...

Step 5: Channel My Feelings into Action! *Identify actions you could use to release your feelings in a way that achieves what you value...*

☐ Study the Situation	☐ Show Compassion
☐ Set Limits/Let Go	☐ Be Careful/Thorough
☐ Confront Something	☐ Be Determined

Other actions I can take:...

....

Step 1: Breathe out, relaxing your diaphragm. *Practice Release Breathing while you are completing the other steps. Describe the situation in which you worried or felt stress, fear, or anxiety...*

Step 2: How Am I Feeling? *Identify your feelings..*

- ☐ Fear
- ☐ Anger
- ☐ Boredom

- ☐ Sadness/Hurt
- ☐ Guilt/Shame
- ☐ Frustration
- ☐ Isolated

- ☐ Helpless/Hopeless
- ☐ Confused/Undecided
- ☐ Humiliated/Embarrassed
- ☐ Inadequate/Worthless

Other feelings I might have:..

Step 3: What Do I Value? *Identify what values you must have in order to feel those feelings...*

General Values: ☐ Security   ☐ Esteem   ☐ Pleasure   ☐ Profit

Other more specific values:..

Step 4: Validate Myself! *Complete the self-validating statements below...*

I'm the kind of person who values:..

I'm worthwhile as a person because I value:..

Step 5: Channel My Feelings into Action! *Identify actions you could use to release your feelings in a way that achieves what you value...*

- ☐ Study the Situation
- ☐ Set Limits/Let Go
- ☐ Confront Something

- ☐ Show Compassion
- ☐ Be Careful/Thorough
- ☐ Be Determined

Other actions I can take:..

....

Step 1: Breathe out, relaxing your diaphragm. *Practice Release Breathing while you are completing the other steps. Describe the situation in which you worried or felt stress, fear, or anxiety...*

Step 2: How Am I Feeling? *Identify your feelings..*

☐ Fear   ☐ Sadness/Hurt   ☐ Helpless/Hopeless
☐ Anger   ☐ Guilt/Shame   ☐ Confused/Undecided
☐ Boredom   ☐ Frustration   ☐ Humiliated/Embarrassed
              ☐ Isolated   ☐ Inadequate/Worthless

Other feelings I might have:...

Step 3: What Do I Value? *Identify what values you must have in order to feel those feelings...*

General Values: ☐ Security   ☐ Esteem   ☐ Pleasure   ☐ Profit

Other more specific values:...

Step 4: Validate Myself! *Complete the self-validating statements below...*

I'm the kind of person who values:..

I'm worthwhile as a person because I value:..

Step 5: Channel My Feelings into Action! *Identify actions you could use to release your feelings in a way that achieves what you value...*

☐ Study the Situation   ☐ Show Compassion
☐ Set Limits/Let Go   ☐ Be Careful/Thorough
☐ Confront Something   ☐ Be Determined

Other actions I can take:...

....

Chapter 8

TURN CONFLICT INTO ACTION!

<u>INTRODUCTION</u>

Conflict is the opposition of two or more forces. When it happens within us, we have internal conflict.

Internal conflict is a natural condition because people can see things from two or more points of view. Different points of view often conflict with each other.

However, conflict prevents action and blocks energy. Blocked energy causes stress.

The way you handle conflict may contribute to your worry, stress, fear, and anxiety. But if you reduce internal conflict and release the blocked energy, you increase your sense of Personal Control, release tension, and develop a positive attitude toward yourself, others, and life in general.

<u>GOALS</u>

1.   You will identify some of your conflicts and learn to recognize when you are in conflict.

2.   You will learn a basic method for analyzing your conflict.

3.   You will learn a basic method for reducing conflict.

<u>REMEMBER</u>

Don't miss another opportunity to build your peace of mind. When worry, stress, fear, or anxiety strike this week...Conquer Your Fears. Use...

*

<u>FIRST AID for...WORRY, STRESS, FEAR, AND ANXIETY</u>

Step 1:   **Always...Breathe Out!**

Step 2:   **Am I in Conflict?**

Step 3:   **What Are the Sides?**

Step 4:   **Decide and Act!**

* Permission is given to reproduce the First Aid Steps for your personal use.

STEP 1

Internal conflict can build tension. We recommend Release Breathing for briefly reducing this tension.

Release Breathing enables us to let go of the tension we build up when mixed emotions and conflicting thoughts compete within us. And we can practice Release Breathing any time we are in conflict, in the middle of any activity, as often as we wish.

Let's take a closer look at internal conflict, which is when we have mixed and contradictory thoughts and feelings. The more conflict we experience, the less we feel in control. That promotes a negative attitude; it is negative about ourselves because we can't take action and negative about the situation because it goes unresolved.

This lesson teaches you how to recognize and analyze your conflicts, and then how to take action to break free from them.

The tension of conflict causes our chest muscles to become tight, and this shuts down our breathing as well. The Release Breathing technique is an excellent way to relax your chest, clear your mind, and work through your conflicts.

Release Breathing sends an important "let go" message to the brain. It involves 3 steps:

1.   breathe in deeply, using *medium force*. Using your diaphragm,

2.   breathe out through your mouth, using *medium strong force*. Let your shoulders, chest, and diaphragm sag or fall downward.

     Think "I can resolve the conflict" as you release air from your lungs. Let go of the air and all the tension in your body, and

3.   pause for a moment at the end of the breath. Feel the release of tension.

     Think of having "let go" of both the tightness in your chest and "being stuck" in your conflict.

STEP 2

AM I IN CONFLICT?

Conflict is the opposition of two forces. It can happen inside of us or between us and someone else.

Often we don't know it's happening. We can even experience symptoms of conflict without knowing what causes them. That prevents us from taking charge of the conflict.

Whether we are aware of an internal conflict or not, it can do us harm. In order to take care of ourselves, we need to recognize our internal conflicts whether they take the form of thoughts, emotions, or physical sensations and restlessness.

In order to recognize when we are in conflict, we need to be aware of three things:

 The Nature of Conflict.

 The Difference Between Internal Conflict and External Conflict.

 Symptoms of Internal Conflict.

EXERCISE

A

In order to understand conflict, you must be able to recognize *opposing forces*.

<u>DIRECTIONS:</u> For Exercise A...There is a list of pairs below. Each part of a pair is separated by three dots (...).

◆ Check off "Yes" if the parts of the pair seem to be in conflict with each other.

◆ Check off "No" if the parts of the pair do not seem to be in conflict with each other.

◆ <u>Note:</u> This exercise isn't about your personal conflicts. It isn't asking which pairs create conflict for you personally. This exercise asks, "In which pairs do the forces seem to be in conflict with each other?" Just indicate whether or not the pair represents opposing forces.

BEGIN EXERCISE A:

Are They in Conflict?

1. Democrats...Republicans. ☐ YES ☐ NO

2. A person wants to eat the desert...the person knows s/he should stay on a diet. ☐ YES ☐ NO

3. A person spends money...the person gets something s/he wants. ☐ YES ☐ NO

4. A person stays up late...the person feels tired all the next day. ☐ YES ☐ NO

5. A person considers sticking his/her neck out by saying something someone might not want to hear...the person doesn't like taking risks. ☐ YES ☐ NO

6. A person wants to buy a gift...the person is short of cash. ☐ YES ☐ NO

7. A person's friend has a birthday
   coming up...the person buys a gift. □ YES □ NO

8. A person sees something interesting...the
   person buys it and takes it home. □ YES □ NO

9. A person expects someone else to change how
   s/he acts...the other person doesn't want to change. □ YES □ NO

COMMENTS ON THE EXERCISE

Exercise A:

People usually select:

1. Yes	2. Yes	3. No
4. No	5. Yes	6. Yes
7. No	8. No	9. Yes

EXERCISE

B

THE DIFFERENCE BETWEEN INTERNAL CONFLICT AND EXTERNAL CONFLICT

Both internal and external conflict cause worry, stress, fear, and anxiety. But internal conflict causes a build-up of blocked energy that makes stress much worse. Exercise B will help you recognize the difference between internal and external conflict.

Diagram 1 describes a person in conflict within himself. The person has opposing thoughts or emotions about something. Diagram 2 describes a person in conflict with another person. The conflict is external because it involves opposition from an outside source.

One Person
Internal Conflict
Diagram 1.

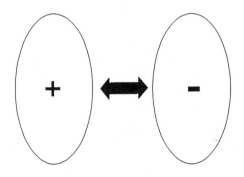

Person A   Person B
External Conflict
Diagram 2.

DIRECTIONS: For Exercise B...There is a list of conflicts below. All of them are presented as pairs, with each part of the pair separated by three dots (...). Some pairs suggest internal conflict. Some pairs suggest external conflict.

♦ Check off "INT" if the pair suggests internal conflict to you.

♦ Check off "EXT" if the pair suggests external conflict to you.

BEGIN EXERCISE B:

Is the Conflict
*Int*ernal or *Ext*ernal?

1. A person wants more freedom...the government wants more control over people's lives.   ☐ INT   ☐ EXT

2. One person wants to go north...the other person wants to go south.   ☐ INT   ☐ EXT

3. A person wants to take a vacation...s/he is also aware s/he can't afford to take a vacation.   ☐ INT   ☐ EXT

4. A person thinks s/he should confront someone... the person is afraid the relationship will end if s/he confronts the other person.   ☐ INT   ☐ EXT

5. The boss assigns things to do...the employee refuses to do the assigned things.   ☐ INT   ☐ EXT

6. A person wants to get quick compensation or revenge for how s/he was injured by someone's negligence...the legal system moves slowly, through a series of steps.   ☐ INT   ☐ EXT

7. A person wants to tell someone off for treating him/her badly...the person is afraid of hurting the other person's feelings or making him/her angry.   ☐ INT   ☐ EXT

8. A person needs to express what s/he really feels about something going on between him/her and someone else...the person dreads being criticized, rejected, humiliated, or abandoned.   ☐ INT   ☐ EXT

9.   A person tells someone off...the other
      person gets defensive.   ☐ INT   ☐ EXT

10.   A person says what s/he really thinks...the
      other person rejects or abandons him/her.   ☐ INT   ☐ EXT

11.   A person asks for what s/he wants...
      the other person doesn't care what
      the person wants.   ☐ INT   ☐ EXT

12.   A person has the impulse to ask for what s/he
      wants...the person worries about receiving
      ridicule or judgment.   ☐ INT   ☐ EXT

COMMENTS ON THE EXERCISE

Exercise B:

People usually select:

1. EXT	2. EXT	3. INT
4. INT	5. EXT	6. EXT
7. INT	8. INT	9. EXT
10. EXT	11. EXT	12. INT

EXERCISE

C

SYMPTOMS OF INTERNAL CONFLICT

Many symptoms are commonly caused by internal conflict. Exercise C will help you identify which ones you experience.

DIRECTIONS: For Exercise C...Circle a number to show how much you experience each symptom. Use the space provided to add other examples of ways you experience internal conflict.

BEGIN EXERCISE C:

How Much Do You
Experience It?

1. Changing your mind
    back and forth.

    1 - 2 - 3 - 4 - 5
    A Little....A Lot

2. Your wants fighting
    with your shoulds.

    1 - 2 - 3 - 4 - 5
    A Little....A Lot

3. Some of your wants fighting
    with your other wants.

    1 - 2 - 3 - 4 - 5
    A Little....A Lot

4. Some of your shoulds fighting
    with your other shoulds.

    1 - 2 - 3 - 4 - 5
    A Little....A Lot

5. Having difficulty making decisions
    about certain things.

    1 - 2 - 3 - 4 - 5
    A Little....A Lot

6. Feeling mixed emotions
    about something or someone.

    1 - 2 - 3 - 4 - 5
    A Little....A Lot

7. Feeling like doing something
    that you don't let yourself do.

    1 - 2 - 3 - 4 - 5
    A Little....A Lot

8. Putting things off,
    procrastinating.

    1 - 2 - 3 - 4 - 5
    A Little....A Lot

9. Avoiding or ignoring things
    that you need to deal with.

    1 - 2 - 3 - 4 - 5
    A Little....A Lot

10.   Acting nervous or fidgety, being agitated or restless,   1 - 2 - 3 - 4 - 5
nail biting, or being overly active.   A Little....A Lot

11.   Feeling overwhelmed.   1 - 2 - 3 - 4 - 5
A Little....A Lot

12.   "Veging-out," loss of interest or motivation,   1 - 2 - 3 - 4 - 5
loss of energy, drive, or desire.   A Little....A Lot

13.   Trouble sleeping.   1 - 2 - 3 - 4 - 5
A Little....A Lot

Other examples of ways you experience internal conflict:.....................................

....

STEP 3

WHAT ARE THE SIDES?

To reduce internal conflict, we first need to explore both sides of the issue. This builds a sense of Personal Control and adds clarity to the picture.

EXERCISE

D

EXPLORING BOTH SIDES OF YOUR INTERNAL CONFLICTS

DIRECTIONS: For Exercise D, Part 1...Describe each side of your internal conflicts or mixed feelings about the subjects listed below:

BEGIN EXERCISE D:

Subject: Having and Spending Money

One side of your thoughts and feelings about money:

....

....

....

....

The other side of your thoughts and feelings about money:

....

....

....

....

Subject: Getting and Not Getting Exercise

*One side of your thoughts
and feelings about exercise:*

....

....

....

....

*The other side of your thoughts
and feelings about exercise:*

....

....

....

....

Subject: Eating Tasty, Fattening Foods

*One side of your thoughts
and feelings about eating:*

....

....

....

....

*The other side of your thoughts
and feelings about eating:*

....

....

....

....

COMMENTS ON THE EXERCISE

Exercise D:

Consider this example for "Having and Spending Money":

I want to hold on to whatever I make so I can invest and have a cushion for the future.

I want to feel the freedom of spending whenever I want to.

PICK A REAL EXAMPLE FROM YOUR OWN LIFE.

<u>SAMPLE SITUATION</u>

Learning Steps 3 and 4 will be easier if you can refer to a personal example of internal conflict. Use the space below to describe one subject or situation about which you experience internal conflict.

Write a description of your internal conflict here...

....

....

<u>DIRECTIONS:</u> For Exercise D, Part 2...Describe each side of your Sample Situation internal conflict.

*One side of your thoughts
and feelings about the Sample Situation:*

*The other side of your thoughts
and feelings about the Sample Situation:*

....

....

....

....

....

....

....

....

STEP 4

<u>DECIDE AND ACT!</u>

People with internal conflict often divide their energy between the options, making only a partial commitment to each one. This is always inefficient. Sometimes it is paralyzing.

Taking action releases the energy tied up in your conflict. Action also increases your sense of Personal Control and builds your Self-esteem. You have a better attitude about yourself, others, and life in general.

You can use the 51/100 rule to release your energy in the form of action. The rule states:

When it's time to decide...
If your thoughts and feelings lean 51% one way...
Put 100% of your energy in that direction.

The diagram below illustrates this rule.

♦   The top arrow represents the stronger side of your opposing thoughts and/or feelings about the issue. Decide in favor of that option.

♦   The bottom arrow represents putting all of your energy and effort into doing the stronger option. That means doing the stronger option with 100% of your effort.

EXERCISE

E

PRACTICING THE 51/100 RULE
DIRECTIONS: For Exercise E...Remembering the Sample Situation you described at the end of Step 3, answer the action questions below.

Which way do you lean 51% or more?

....

....

What action will/can you take?

....

....

PRACTICE YOUR WORK SHEETS

DIRECTIONS: The more you study the steps in this lesson, the more effective your new skills will become. Your Work Sheets are designed to help you master these skills. So, read the story below. We will use it as an example to help you learn to use the Work Sheets successfully.

Betty appreciated Bill being so patient with her when she complained about Billy. But she knew she should be able to handle this herself.

She didn't understand why she got so emotional over struggles with Billy. He was just a little kid. Of course he wanted things he should not have. Come to think of it, he was just like his father!

She knew it was better to be patient and firm. But Billy acted so crazy when he didn't get his way. She wanted to make him happy, but she didn't want to spoil him either.

Betty agonized over whether to give in or stand her ground in situations like this. Finally it would get to her. She would end up yelling at Billy and then breaking down as soon as her husband got home. It was starting to disrupt her sleep. She just didn't know how to be consistent.

DIRECTIONS: For your homework practice exercise...Imagine that you are Betty in this situation. Complete the "Practice Conflict Reduction Work Sheet" on the next page.

NEXT PAGE

PRACTICE CONFLICT REDUCTION WORK SHEET

Step 1: Breathe out, relaxing your diaphragm. *Practice Release Breathing while you are completing each of the other steps.*

Step 2: Am I in Conflict. *Check off "YES" or "NO" to show which symptoms of internal conflict you had.*

1. Changing your mind   ☐YES ☐NO
2. Wants versus shoulds   ☐YES ☐NO
3. Wants versus wants   ☐YES ☐NO
4. Shoulds versus shoulds   ☐YES ☐NO
5. Feeling mixed emotions   ☐YES ☐NO
6. Feeling nervous, agitating, being overactive, nail biting   ☐YES ☐NO
7. Avoiding/ignoring things   ☐YES ☐NO
8. Not doing what you feel like doing   ☐YES ☐NO
9. Difficulty making decisions   ☐YES ☐NO

10. Overwhelmed   ☐YES ☐NO
11. Trouble sleeping   ☐YES ☐NO
12. Low energy, veging   ☐YES ☐NO
13. Putting things off   ☐YES ☐NO

Other symptoms of internal conflict:...

Step 3: What Are the Sides?

One side of your thoughts and feelings:

....

....

Other side of your thoughts and feelings:

....

....

Step 4: Decide and Act! *Decide what action you could take...*

Which way do you lean 51% or more?

....

....

What action will/can you take?

....

....

Step 1: Breathe out, relaxing your diaphragm. *Practice Release Breathing while you are completing each of the other steps.*

Step 2: Am I in Conflict. *Check off "YES" or "NO" to show which symptoms of internal conflict you had.*

1. Changing your mind	■YES ☐NO	10. Overwhelmed	■YES ☐NO
2. Wants versus shoulds	☐YES ■NO	11. Trouble sleeping	■YES ☐NO
3. Wants versus wants	■YES ☐NO	12. Low energy, veging	☐YES ■NO
4. Shoulds versus shoulds	■YES ☐NO	13. Putting things off	☐YES ■NO
5. Feeling mixed emotions	■YES ☐NO		

6. Feeling nervous, agitating, being over active, nail biting   ■YES ☐NO
7. Avoiding/ignoring things   ☐YES ■NO
8. Not doing what you feel like doing   ■YES ☐NO
9. Difficulty making decisions   ■YES ☐NO

Other symptoms of internal conflict:..

Step 3: What Are the Sides?

One side of Betty's thoughts and feelings:	*Other side of Betty's thoughts and feelings:*
....*Make him happy by giving in*............	....*Be firm, stand my ground*...............
....	....

Step 4: Decide and Act! *Decide what action Betty could take...*

Which way does Betty lean 51% or more?

....*Be firm*..

....

What action will/can Betty take?

....*Say No*...

....

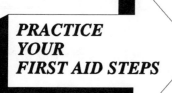

PRACTICE YOUR FIRST AID STEPS

<u>DIRECTIONS:</u> The more you practice your First Aid Steps, the better you will feel. Practice your First Aid Steps now. Imagine you are in a situation used in this lesson, or think about your life in general.

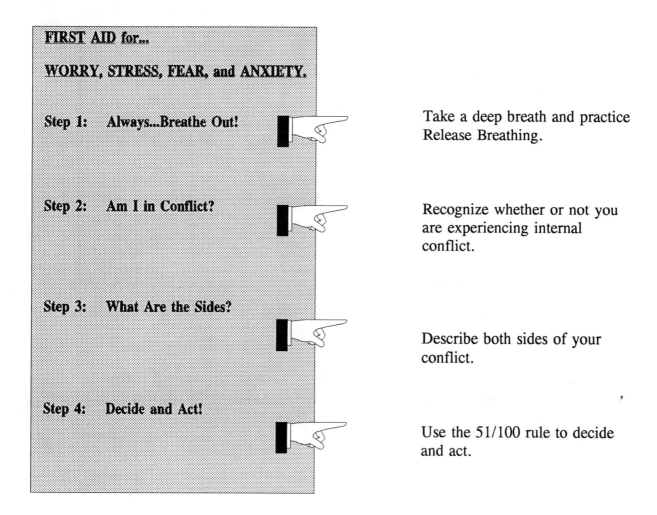

<u>FIRST AID for...</u>

<u>WORRY, STRESS, FEAR, and ANXIETY.</u>

Step 1: Always...Breathe Out!

Take a deep breath and practice Release Breathing.

Step 2: Am I in Conflict?

Recognize whether or not you are experiencing internal conflict.

Step 3: What Are the Sides?

Describe both sides of your conflict.

Step 4: Decide and Act!

Use the 51/100 rule to decide and act.

HOMEWORK

THE METHODS...

Work Sheets. This week complete 8 Conflict Reduction Work Sheets. Do the work sheets for situations in which you worry or feel stress, fear, or anxiety. Complete the Work Sheets at the time of these events or very soon thereafter.

First Aid Steps. Practice your First Aid Steps as often as possible, even when you are not really worrying or feeling threatened.

*

FIRST AID for...WORRY, STRESS, FEAR, AND ANXIETY

Step 1:   Always...Breathe Out!

Step 2:   Am I in Conflict?

Step 3:   What Are the Sides?

Step 4:   Decide and Act!

Use your Clip-outs: Cut out the First Aid Steps reminders. Place them in spots where you will see them and remember to practice. Give some to a friend, and tell him or her how to use them.

Teach Others. Share the lesson with others. Teach them how to help themselves using the same skills you are learning.

* Permission is given to reproduce the First Aid Steps for your personal use.

Step 1: Breathe out, relaxing your diaphragm. *Practice Release Breathing while you are completing each of the other steps.*

Step 2: Am I in Conflict. *Check off "YES" or "NO" to show which symptoms of internal conflict you had.*

1. Changing your mind   ☐YES ☐NO   10. Overwhelmed   ☐YES ☐NO
2. Wants versus shoulds   ☐YES ☐NO   11. Trouble sleeping   ☐YES ☐NO
3. Wants versus wants   ☐YES ☐NO   12. Low energy, veging   ☐YES ☐NO
4. Shoulds versus shoulds   ☐YES ☐NO   13. Putting things off   ☐YES ☐NO
5. Feeling mixed emotions   ☐YES ☐NO
6. Feeling nervous, agitating, being overactive, nail biting   ☐YES ☐NO
7. Avoiding/ignoring things   ☐YES ☐NO
8. Not doing what you feel like doing   ☐YES ☐NO
9. Difficulty making decisions   ☐YES ☐NO

Other symptoms of internal conflict:..

Step 3: What Are the Sides?

One side of your thoughts and feelings: *Other side of your thoughts and feelings:*

....

....

Step 4: Decide and Act! *Decide what action you could take...*

Which way do you lean 51% or more?

....

....

What action will/can you take?

....

....

Step 1: Breathe out, relaxing your diaphragm. *Practice Release Breathing while you are completing each of the other steps.*

Step 2: Am I in Conflict. *Check off "YES" or "NO" to show which symptoms of internal conflict you had.*

1. Changing your mind ☐YES ☐NO	10. Overwhelmed ☐YES ☐NO	
2. Wants versus shoulds ☐YES ☐NO	11. Trouble sleeping ☐YES ☐NO	
3. Wants versus wants ☐YES ☐NO	12. Low energy, veging ☐YES ☐NO	
4. Shoulds versus shoulds ☐YES ☐NO	13. Putting things off ☐YES ☐NO	
5. Feeling mixed emotions ☐YES ☐NO		

6. Feeling nervous, agitating, being overactive, nail biting ☐YES ☐NO
7. Avoiding/ignoring things ☐YES ☐NO
8. Not doing what you feel like doing ☐YES ☐NO
9. Difficulty making decisions ☐YES ☐NO

Other symptoms of internal conflict:..

Step 3: What Are the Sides?

One side of your thoughts and feelings: *Other side of your thoughts and feelings:*

....

....

Step 4: Decide and Act! *Decide what action you could take...*

Which way do you lean 51% or more?

....

....

What action will/can you take?

....

....

Step 1: Breathe out, relaxing your diaphragm. *Practice Release Breathing while you are completing each of the other steps.*

Step 2: Am I in Conflict. *Check off "YES" or "NO" to show which symptoms of internal conflict you had.*

1. Changing your mind   ☐YES ☐NO   10. Overwhelmed   ☐YES ☐NO
2. Wants versus shoulds   ☐YES ☐NO   11. Trouble sleeping   ☐YES ☐NO
3. Wants versus wants   ☐YES ☐NO   12. Low energy, veging   ☐YES ☐NO
4. Shoulds versus shoulds   ☐YES ☐NO   13. Putting things off   ☐YES ☐NO
5. Feeling mixed emotions ☐YES ☐NO
6. Feeling nervous, agitating, being overactive, nail biting   ☐YES ☐NO
7. Avoiding/ignoring things   ☐YES ☐NO
8. Not doing what you feel like doing   ☐YES ☐NO
9. Difficulty making decisions   ☐YES ☐NO

Other symptoms of internal conflict:...

Step 3: What Are the Sides?

One side of your thoughts and feelings: *Other side of your thoughts and feelings:*

....

....

Step 4: Decide and Act! *Decide what action you could take...*

Which way do you lean 51% or more?

....

....

What action will/can you take?

....

....

Step 1: Breathe out, relaxing your diaphragm. *Practice Release Breathing while you are completing each of the other steps.*

Step 2: Am I in Conflict. *Check off "YES" or "NO" to show which symptoms of internal conflict you had.*

1. Changing your mind	☐YES ☐NO	10. Overwhelmed	☐YES ☐NO
2. Wants versus shoulds	☐YES ☐NO	11. Trouble sleeping	☐YES ☐NO
3. Wants versus wants	☐YES ☐NO	12. Low energy, veging	☐YES ☐NO
4. Shoulds versus shoulds	☐YES ☐NO	13. Putting things off	☐YES ☐NO

5. Feeling mixed emotions ☐YES ☐NO
6. Feeling nervous, agitating, being overactive, nail biting ☐YES ☐NO
7. Avoiding/ignoring things ☐YES ☐NO
8. Not doing what you feel like doing ☐YES ☐NO
9. Difficulty making decisions ☐YES ☐NO

Other symptoms of internal conflict:...

Step 3: What Are the Sides?

One side of your thoughts and feelings: *Other side of your thoughts and feelings:*

....

....

Step 4: Decide and Act! *Decide what action you could take...*

Which way do you lean 51% or more?

....

....

What action will/can you take?

....

....

Step 1: Breathe out, relaxing your diaphragm. *Practice Release Breathing while you are completing each of the other steps.*

Step 2: Am I in Conflict. *Check off "YES" or "NO" to show which symptoms of internal conflict you had.*

1. Changing your mind	☐YES ☐NO	10. Overwhelmed	☐YES ☐NO
2. Wants versus shoulds	☐YES ☐NO	11. Trouble sleeping	☐YES ☐NO
3. Wants versus wants	☐YES ☐NO	12. Low energy, veging	☐YES ☐NO
4. Shoulds versus shoulds	☐YES ☐NO	13. Putting things off	☐YES ☐NO
5. Feeling mixed emotions	☐YES ☐NO		

6. Feeling nervous, agitating, being overactive, nail biting   ☐YES ☐NO
7. Avoiding/ignoring things   ☐YES ☐NO
8. Not doing what you feel like doing   ☐YES ☐NO
9. Difficulty making decisions   ☐YES ☐NO

Other symptoms of internal conflict:...

Step 3: What Are the Sides?

One side of your thoughts and feelings: *Other side of your thoughts and feelings:*

....

....

Step 4: Decide and Act! *Decide what action you could take...*

Which way do you lean 51% or more?

....

....

What action will/can you take?

....

....

Step 1: Breathe out, relaxing your diaphragm. *Practice Release Breathing while you are completing each of the other steps.*

Step 2: Am I in Conflict. *Check off "YES" or "NO" to show which symptoms of internal conflict you had.*

1. Changing your mind ☐YES ☐NO
2. Wants versus shoulds ☐YES ☐NO
3. Wants versus wants ☐YES ☐NO
4. Shoulds versus shoulds ☐YES ☐NO
5. Feeling mixed emotions ☐YES ☐NO
6. Feeling nervous, agitating, being overactive, nail biting ☐YES ☐NO
7. Avoiding/ignoring things ☐YES ☐NO
8. Not doing what you feel like doing ☐YES ☐NO
9. Difficulty making decisions ☐YES ☐NO

10. Overwhelmed ☐YES ☐NO
11. Trouble sleeping ☐YES ☐NO
12. Low energy, veging ☐YES ☐NO
13. Putting things off ☐YES ☐NO

Other symptoms of internal conflict:...

Step 3: What Are the Sides?

One side of your thoughts and feelings:

....

....

Other side of your thoughts and feelings:

....

....

Step 4: Decide and Act! *Decide what action you could take...*

Which way do you lean 51% or more?

....

....

What action will/can you take?

....

....

Step 1: Breathe out, relaxing your diaphragm. *Practice Release Breathing while you are completing each of the other steps.*

Step 2: Am I in Conflict. *Check off "YES" or "NO" to show which symptoms of internal conflict you had.*

1. Changing your mind ☐YES ☐NO	10. Overwhelmed	☐YES ☐NO
2. Wants versus shoulds ☐YES ☐NO	11. Trouble sleeping	☐YES ☐NO
3. Wants versus wants ☐YES ☐NO	12. Low energy, veging	☐YES ☐NO
4. Shoulds versus shoulds ☐YES ☐NO	13. Putting things off	☐YES ☐NO
5. Feeling mixed emotions ☐YES ☐NO		

6. Feeling nervous, agitating, being overactive, nail biting ☐YES ☐NO
7. Avoiding/ignoring things ☐YES ☐NO
8. Not doing what you feel like doing ☐YES ☐NO
9. Difficulty making decisions ☐YES ☐NO

Other symptoms of internal conflict:...

Step 3: What Are the Sides?

One side of your thoughts and feelings: *Other side of your thoughts and feelings:*

....

....

Step 4: Decide and Act! *Decide what action you could take…*

Which way do you lean 51% or more?

....

....

What action will/can you take?

....

....

Step 1: Breathe out, relaxing your diaphragm. *Practice Release Breathing while you are completing each of the other steps.*

Step 2: Am I in Conflict. *Check off "YES" or "NO" to show which symptoms of internal conflict you had.*

1. Changing your mind	☐YES ☐NO	10. Overwhelmed ☐YES ☐NO
2. Wants versus shoulds	☐YES ☐NO	11. Trouble sleeping ☐YES ☐NO
3. Wants versus wants	☐YES ☐NO	12. Low energy, veging ☐YES ☐NO
4. Shoulds versus shoulds	☐YES ☐NO	13. Putting things off ☐YES ☐NO
5. Feeling mixed emotions	☐YES ☐NO	

6. Feeling nervous, agitating, being overactive, nail biting   ☐YES ☐NO
7. Avoiding/ignoring things   ☐YES ☐NO
8. Not doing what you feel like doing   ☐YES ☐NO
9. Difficulty making decisions   ☐YES ☐NO

Other symptoms of internal conflict:...

Step 3: What Are the Sides?

One side of your thoughts and feelings: *Other side of your thoughts and feelings:*

....

....

Step 4: Decide and Act! *Decide what action you could take...*

Which way do you lean 51% or more?

....

....

What action will/can you take?

....

....

Chapter 9

GET THE MOST FROM RELATIONSHIPS!

INTRODUCTION

Every relationship develops patterns. A pattern is behavior that happens over and over. Some relationship patterns are good; some do us harm.

One way to understand relationship patterns is to study the roles people play in them. A role consists of thinking, feeling, and acting in certain ways.

The roles you play in a relationship can cause worry, stress, fear, and anxiety. You will feel better if you change your roles so that you increase your sense of Personal Control, release tension, and develop positive attitudes toward yourself, others, and life in general.

GOALS

1.   You will learn to identify the relationship roles you play that cause you worry, stress, fear, and anxiety.

2.   You will learn to practice new behaviors that change your roles and break the old patterns.

<u>REMEMBER</u>

Don't miss another opportunity to build peace of mind. When worry, stress, fear, or anxiety strike this week...Conquer Your Fears! Use...

*

<u>FIRST AID for...WORRY, STRESS, FEAR, AND ANXIETY</u>

Step 1:   **Always...Breathe Out!**

Step 2:   **What's My Role?**

Step 3:   **Practice Role-free Behavior!**

* Permission is given to reproduce the First Aid Steps for your personal use.

STEP 1

ALWAYS...BREATHE OUT!

When relationships are going well, they make us feel good and in control. This tends to release our tension. When relationships go badly, tension builds within us. We recommend Release Breathing for briefly reducing this tension.

Release Breathing enables us to let go of the tension we build up when dealing with problem relationships. And we can practice Release Breathing any time we are facing a relationship problem, as often as we wish.

Let's take a closer look at problematic relationships. We feel less in control the more we become trapped in roles of being the heavy (the persecutor), trying to make others feel OK (the rescuer), or feeling mistreated (the victim). That promotes a negative attitude; it is negative about ourselves and others because we can't get our needs met and negative about the situation because it seems to cause our unhappiness.

This lesson teaches you how to break free from unrewarding relationship roles.

The tension of relationship problems causes our breathing to shut down and become restricted. The Release Breathing technique is an excellent way to expand your breathing and free your mind for identifying role-free behaviors.

Release Breathing sends an important "let go" message to the brain. It involves 3 steps:

1.   breathe in deeply, using *medium force*. Using your diaphragm,

2.   breathe out through your mouth, using *medium strong force*. Let your shoulders, chest, and diaphragm sag or fall downward.

       Think "I can stay out of unhealthy roles" as you release air from your lungs. Let go of the air and all the tension in your body, and

3.   pause for a moment at the end of the breath. Feel the release of tension.

       Think of having "let go" of both the tightness in your chest and "being stuck" in your old roles.

WHAT'S MY ROLE?

There are three roles people play that promote worry, stress, fear, and anxiety. The better you understand the roles you and others play, the easier it will be to change your Relationship Patterns.

<u>Persecutor.</u> The Persecutor (or villain) makes a Victim feel bad by criticism, domination, abuse, exploitation, or neglect.

<u>Rescuer.</u> The Rescuer (or hero) makes a Victim feel good by doing things for the Victim that the Victim can and should do for him/herself; this enables the Victim to remain dependent in some way.

<u>Victim.</u> The Victim (or casualty) sees a Persecutor as the source of all his/her troubles and usually waits for a Rescuer to fix things.

We can play out two roles at the same time, like when we Rescue someone and then s/he lets us down. And, we play different roles with different people, like being a Victim in reaction to our boss who Persecutes, while being a Rescuer to our spouse, who can't take care of him/herself in some way.

EXERCISE

A

RECOGNIZING THE ROLES

Exercise A will help you recognize when you are taking on one of the roles that cause worry, stress, fear, and anxiety.

<u>DIRECTIONS:</u> For Exercise A...Read each description of behavior given below. Then show which role you think it is by making a check mark.

♦ Depending on how you interpret some items, they can suggest more than one role. If you see two or more possibilities, pick the role that fits your strongest interpretation.

BEGIN EXERCISE A:

A1. A person criticizing, finding fault with, or putting down someone else.

    ☐ Persecutor
    ☐ Rescuer
    ☐ Victim

A2. A person feeling worthwhile only when someone else needs him/her.

    ☐ Persecutor
    ☐ Rescuer
    ☐ Victim

A3. A person helping someone else in a way that prevents the person's own needs from being met.

    ☐ Persecutor
    ☐ Rescuer
    ☐ Victim

A4. A person taking care of someone else in ways that the other should be taking care of him/herself, encouraging the other's dependency.

    ☐ Persecutor
    ☐ Rescuer
    ☐ Victim

A5.   A person seeing him/herself as helpless or powerless.

         ☐   Persecutor
         ☐   Rescuer
         ☐   Victim

A6.   A person letting someone else down by not doing something that s/he made a commitment to do.

         ☐   Persecutor
         ☐   Rescuer
         ☐   Victim

A7.   A person dominating, controlling, or insisting on getting his/her own way.

         ☐   Persecutor
         ☐   Rescuer
         ☐   Victim

A8.   A person expecting someone else to solve problems for him/her.

         ☐   Persecutor
         ☐   Rescuer
         ☐   Victim

A9.   A person abusing, beating, or harming someone else.

         ☐   Persecutor
         ☐   Rescuer
         ☐   Victim

A10.   A person making it easier for (enabling) someone else to act in a way that leads to self-harm or self-defeat.

         ☐   Persecutor
         ☐   Rescuer
         ☐   Victim

A11.   A person feeling worthwhile only when someone else is taking care of him/her.

         ☐   Persecutor
         ☐   Rescuer
         ☐   Victim

A12. A person exploiting or taking advantage of someone else's weakness or vulnerability.

☐ Persecutor
☐ Rescuer
☐ Victim

A13. A person neglecting, abandoning, or rejecting someone else.

☐ Persecutor
☐ Rescuer
☐ Victim

A14. A person doing something that leads to self-harm or self-defeat.

☐ Persecutor
☐ Rescuer
☐ Victim

A15. A person blaming someone else for his/her own problems or making excuses for his/her own problems.

☐ Persecutor
☐ Rescuer
☐ Victim

A16. A person feeling worthwhile only when someone else is less worthwhile.

☐ Persecutor
☐ Rescuer
☐ Victim

A17. A person complaining, suffering, and feeling self-pity.

☐ Persecutor
☐ Rescuer
☐ Victim

A18. A person feeling guilt, shame, or inadequacy.

☐ Persecutor
☐ Rescuer
☐ Victim

A19. A person avoiding making waves.

    ☐   Persecutor
    ☐   Rescuer
    ☐   Victim

A20. A person feeling like his/her hands are tied.

    ☐   Persecutor
    ☐   Rescuer
    ☐   Victim

STEP 3

PRACTICE ROLE-FREE BEHAVIOR!

One good way to break out of unhealthy roles is to practice different behavior. There are several behaviors you can use to stay out of each unhealthy role. We call these Role-free behaviors.

<u>For the Persecutor.</u> Role-free behaviors that help you stay out of Persecuting involve letting other people be OK, adequate, and autonomous. These behaviors include

♦ Supporting & validating the other person's ways of thinking, feeling, and acting.
♦ Allowing & accepting how others are different.
♦ Keeping agreements and commitments.
♦ Limiting what you try to control.
♦ Being sensitive to the welfare of others.

<u>For the Rescuer.</u> Role-free behaviors that help you stay out of Rescuing involve leaving it up to the other person to learn to solve his/her own problems when s/he is capable of doing so.

♦ Taking care of your own needs and self-esteem.
♦ Allowing someone else to solve his/her own problems.
♦ Withholding support that contributes to someone else's self-harm or self-defeat.

<u>For the Victim.</u> Role-free behaviors that help you stay out of being a Victim involve taking responsibility for events in your life and staying emotionally independent from others.

♦ Taking responsibility for what happens to you.
♦ Taking charge of your own problem solving and well-being.
♦ Not taking the attitudes or actions of others personally.

EXERCISE

B

IDENTIFYING ROLE-FREE BEHAVIOR

Exercise B will help you learn to think of and then practice Role-free behaviors.

DIRECTIONS: For Exercise B...The first 5 items from Exercise A are revised for Exercise B. They are rewritten as if you are the actor.

◆ Following each item is the list of Role-free behaviors. Place a check mark beside the Role-free behaviors you could use instead of the behavior described in the item.

◆ More than one Role-free behavior will fit many items.

BEGIN EXERCISE B:

B1. You find yourself criticizing, finding fault with, or putting down someone else.

- ☐ Supporting & validating the other person's ways of thinking, feeling, and acting.
- ☐ Allowing & accepting how others are different.
- ☐ Keeping agreements and commitments.
- ☐ Limiting what you try to control.
- ☐ Being sensitive to the welfare of others.
- ☐ Taking care of your own needs and self-esteem.
- ☐ Allowing someone else to solve his/her own problems.
- ☐ Withholding support that contributes to someone else's self-harm or self-defeat.
- ☐ Taking responsibility for what happens to you.
- ☐ Taking charge of your own problem solving and well-being.
- ☐ Not taking the attitudes or actions of others personally.

B2.	You only feel worthwhile when someone else needs you.

☐	Supporting & validating the other person's ways of thinking, feeling, and acting.
☐	Allowing & accepting how others are different.
☐	Keeping agreements and commitments.
☐	Limiting what you try to control.
☐	Being sensitive to the welfare of others.
☐	Taking care of your own needs and self-esteem.
☐	Allowing someone else to solve his/her own problems.
☐	Withholding support that contributes to someone else's self-harm or self-defeat.
☐	Taking responsibility for what happens to you.
☐	Taking charge of your own problem solving and well-being.
☐	Not taking the attitudes or actions of others personally.

B3.	You find yourself helping someone else in a way that prevents you from meeting your own needs.

☐	Supporting & validating the other person's ways of thinking, feeling, and acting.
☐	Allowing & accepting how others are different.
☐	Keeping agreements and commitments.
☐	Limiting what you try to control.
☐	Being sensitive to the welfare of others.
☐	Taking care of your own needs and self-esteem.
☐	Allowing someone else to solve his/her own problems.
☐	Withholding support that contributes to someone else's self-harm or self-defeat.
☐	Taking responsibility for what happens to you.
☐	Taking charge of your own problem solving and well-being.
☐	Not taking the attitudes or actions of others personally.

B4. You find yourself taking care of someone else in ways that the other should be taking care of him/herself.

- ☐ Supporting & validating the other person's ways of thinking, feeling, and acting.
- ☐ Allowing & accepting how others are different.
- ☐ Keeping agreements and commitments.
- ☐ Limiting what you try to control.
- ☐ Being sensitive to the welfare of others.
- ☐ Taking care of your own needs and self-esteem.
- ☐ Allowing someone else to solve his/her own problems.
- ☐ Withholding support that contributes to someone else's self-harm or self-defeat.
- ☐ Taking responsibility for what happens to you.
- ☐ Taking charge of your own problem solving and well-being.
- ☐ Not taking the attitudes or actions of others personally.

B5. You find yourself feeling helpless or powerless.

- ☐ Supporting & validating the other person's ways of thinking, feeling, and acting.
- ☐ Allowing & accepting how others are different.
- ☐ Keeping agreements and commitments.
- ☐ Limiting what you try to control.
- ☐ Being sensitive to the welfare of others.
- ☐ Taking care of your own needs and self-esteem.
- ☐ Allowing someone else to solve his/her own problems.
- ☐ Withholding support that contributes to someone else's self-harm or self-defeat.
- ☐ Taking responsibility for what happens to you.
- ☐ Taking charge of your own problem solving and well-being.
- ☐ Not taking the attitudes or actions of others personally.

COMMENTS ON THE EXERCISE

B1.   Frequently selected role-free behaviors are:

    A.   Supporting and validating the other person's ways of thinking, feeling, and acting.
    B.   Allowing and accepting how others are different.
    C.   Keeping agreements and commitments.
    D.   Limiting what you try to control.
    E.   Being sensitive to the welfare of others.

B2.   Frequently selected role-free behaviors are:

    A.   Taking care of your own needs and self-esteem.
    B.   Taking responsibility for what happens to you.

B3.   Frequently selected role-free behaviors are:

    A.   Allowing someone else to solve his/her own problems.
    B.   Taking responsibility for what happens to you.
    C.   Taking care of your own needs and self-esteem.
    D.   Withholding support that contributes to someone else's self-harm or self-defeat.

B4.   Frequently selected role-free behaviors are:

    A.   Allowing someone else to solve his/her own problems.
    B.   Withholding support that contributes to someone else's self-harm or self-defeat.
    C.   Taking charge of your own problem solving and well-being.

B5.   Frequently selected role-free behaviors are:

    A.   Taking responsibility for what happens to you.
    B.   Taking charge of your own problem solving and well-being.
    C.   Not taking the attitudes or actions of others personally.

PRACTICE YOUR WORK SHEETS

<u>DIRECTIONS:</u> The more you study the steps in this lesson, the more effective your new skills will become. Your Work Sheets are designed to help you master these skills. So, read the story below. We will use it as an example to help you learn to use the Work Sheets successfully.

Anne was very troubled by events with her friends Betty and Bill. It was on her mind a lot of the time. They were both good people; she hated seeing them in such a mess. Anne had tried everything she could think of to help.

For example, there was that time Anne stayed home from her class to watch Billy so that Betty could have "a morning off." Nothing changed after that. And Anne ended up missing a great guest lecturer at her class.

Betty often called to talk about the problems with Billy. Anne would just drop everything and concentrate on Betty. Sometimes the calls would go on for an hour or more. Anne just couldn't cut Betty off.

And then there was the time she spent a whole afternoon at the book store looking for something that might help Betty with the boy. She had felt pretty satisfied with herself when she found Betty that great sounding book, <u>Perfect Children through Brute Force.</u> How could she have known that Bill Sr.'s mother had sent Betty the same book? Not only did Anne end up wasting the whole afternoon, but she was late getting dinner ready. Anne's husband got upset with her for that. He wasn't very understanding about Betty, Billy, and Bill.

<u>DIRECTIONS:</u> Practice your homework exercise. Imagine that you are Anne in this situation. Complete the " Practice Relationship Patterns Work Sheet" on the next page.

NEXT PAGE

Step 1: Breathe out, relaxing your diaphragm. *Practice Release Breathing while you are completing each of the other steps.*

Step 2: What's My Role? *Identify the role(s) Anne is playing...*

☐ Persecutor   ☐ Rescuer   ☐ Victim

Step 3: Practice Role-free Behavior! *Select Role-free behaviors from the list that Anne could practice to stay out of unhealthy relationship patterns...*

☐ Supporting & validating the other person's ways of thinking, feeling, and acting.
☐ Allowing & accepting how others are different.
☐ Keeping agreements and commitments.
☐ Limiting what you try to control.
☐ Being sensitive to the welfare of others.
☐ Taking care of your own needs and self-esteem.
☐ Allowing someone else to solve his/her own problems.
☐ Withholding support that contributes to someone else's self-harm or self-defeat.
☐ Taking responsibility for what happens to you.
☐ Taking charge of your own problem solving and well-being.
☐ Not taking the attitudes or actions of others personally.

Step 1: Breathe out, relaxing your diaphragm.   *Practice Release Breathing while you are completing each of the other steps.*

Step 2: What's My Role? *Identify the role(s) Anne is playing...*

    ☐ Persecutor   ■ Rescuer   ☐ Victim

Step 3: Practice Role-free Behavior! *Select Role-free behaviors from the list that Anne could practice to stay out of unhealthy relationship patterns...*

    ■   Supporting & validating the other person's ways of thinking, feeling, and acting.
    ☐   Allowing & accepting how others are different.
    ☐   Keeping agreements and commitments.
    ■   Limiting what you try to control.
    ☐   Being sensitive to the welfare of others.
    ■   Taking care of your own needs and self-esteem.
    ■   Allowing someone else to solve his/her own problems.
    ☐   Withholding support that contributes to someone else's self-harm or self-defeat.
    ☐   Taking responsibility for what happens to you.
    ☐   Taking charge of your own problem solving and well-being.
    ☐   Not taking the attitudes or actions of others personally.

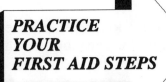

PRACTICE YOUR FIRST AID STEPS

<u>DIRECTIONS:</u> The more you practice your First Aid Steps, the better you will feel. Practice your First Aid Steps now. Imagine you are in a situation used in this lesson, or think about your life in general.

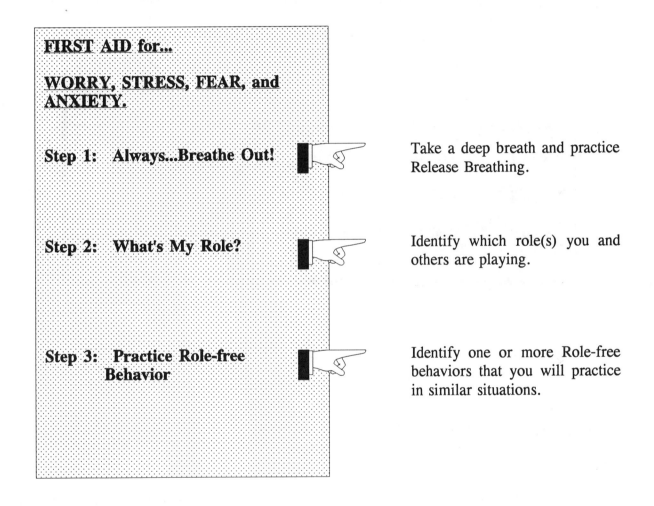

<u>**FIRST AID for...**</u>

<u>**WORRY, STRESS, FEAR, and ANXIETY.**</u>

Step 1:   Always...Breathe Out!

Take a deep breath and practice Release Breathing.

Step 2:   What's My Role?

Identify which role(s) you and others are playing.

Step 3:   Practice Role-free Behavior

Identify one or more Role-free behaviors that you will practice in similar situations.

HOMEWORK

<u>THE METHODS...</u>

<u>Work Sheets.</u> This week complete 8 Relationship Patterns Work Sheets. Do the Work Sheets for situations in which you worry or feel stress, fear, or anxiety. Complete the Work Sheets at the time of these events or very soon thereafter.

<u>First Aid Steps.</u> Practice your First Aid Steps as often as possible, even when you are not really worrying or feeling threatened.

*

FIRST AID for...WORRY, STRESS, FEAR, AND ANXIETY

Step 1:   **Always...Breathe Out!**

Step 2:   **What's My Role?**

Step 3:   **Practice Role-free Behavior!**

<u>Use your Clip-outs:</u> Cut out the First Aid Steps reminders. Place them in spots where you will see them and remember to practice. Give some to a friend, and tell him or her how to use them.

<u>Teach Others.</u> Share the lesson with others. Teach them how to help themselves using the same skills you are learning.

* Permission is given to reproduce the First Aid Steps for your personal use.

Step 1: Breathe out, relaxing your diaphragm. *Practice Release Breathing while you are completing each of the other steps.*

Step 2: What's My Role? *Identify the role(s) you play or almost play...*

☐ Persecutor   ☐ Rescuer   ☐ Victim

Step 3: Practice Role-free Behavior! *Select Role-free behaviors from the list that you could practice to stay out of unhealthy relationship patterns...*

☐ Supporting & validating the other person's ways of thinking, feeling, and acting.
☐ Allowing & accepting how others are different.
☐ Keeping agreements and commitments.
☐ Limiting what you try to control.
☐ Being sensitive to the welfare of others.
☐ Taking care of your own needs and self-esteem.
☐ Allowing someone else to solve his/her own problems.
☐ Withholding support that contributes to someone else's self-harm or self-defeat.
☐ Taking responsibility for what happens to you.
☐ Taking charge of your own problem solving and well-being.
☐ Not taking the attitudes or actions of others personally.

Step 1: Breathe out, relaxing your diaphragm. *Practice Release Breathing while you are completing each of the other steps.*

Step 2: What's My Role? *Identify the role(s) you play or almost play...*

☐ Persecutor   ☐ Rescuer   ☐ Victim

Step 3: Practice Role-free Behavior! *Select Role-free behaviors from the list that you could practice to stay out of unhealthy relationship patterns...*

☐ Supporting & validating the other person's ways of thinking, feeling, and acting.
☐ Allowing & accepting how others are different.
☐ Keeping agreements and commitments.
☐ Limiting what you try to control.
☐ Being sensitive to the welfare of others.
☐ Taking care of your own needs and self-esteem.
☐ Allowing someone else to solve his/her own problems.
☐ Withholding support that contributes to someone else's self-harm or self-defeat.
☐ Taking responsibility for what happens to you.
☐ Taking charge of your own problem solving and well-being.
☐ Not taking the attitudes or actions of others personally.

Step 1: Breathe out, relaxing your diaphragm. *Practice Release Breathing while you are completing each of the other steps.*

Step 2: What's My Role? *Identify the role(s) you play or almost play…*

☐ Persecutor   ☐ Rescuer   ☐ Victim

Step 3: Practice Role-free Behavior! *Select Role-free behaviors from the list that you could practice to stay out of unhealthy relationship patterns…*

☐   Supporting & validating the other person's ways of thinking, feeling, and acting.
☐   Allowing & accepting how others are different.
☐   Keeping agreements and commitments.
☐   Limiting what you try to control.
☐   Being sensitive to the welfare of others.
☐   Taking care of your own needs and self-esteem.
☐   Allowing someone else to solve his/her own problems.
☐   Withholding support that contributes to someone else's self-harm or self-defeat.
☐   Taking responsibility for what happens to you.
☐   Taking charge of your own problem solving and well-being.
☐   Not taking the attitudes or actions of others personally.

Step 1: Breathe out, relaxing your diaphragm. *Practice Release Breathing while you are completing each of the other steps.*

Step 2: What's My Role? *Identify the role(s) you play or almost play...*

☐ Persecutor   ☐ Rescuer   ☐ Victim

Step 3: Practice Role-free Behavior! *Select Role-free behaviors from the list that you could practice to stay out of unhealthy relationship patterns...*

☐   Supporting & validating the other person's ways of thinking, feeling, and acting.
☐   Allowing & accepting how others are different.
☐   Keeping agreements and commitments.
☐   Limiting what you try to control.
☐   Being sensitive to the welfare of others.
☐   Taking care of your own needs and self-esteem.
☐   Allowing someone else to solve his/her own problems.
☐   Withholding support that contributes to someone else's self-harm or self-defeat.
☐   Taking responsibility for what happens to you.
☐   Taking charge of your own problem solving and well-being.
☐   Not taking the attitudes or actions of others personally.

Step 1: Breathe out, relaxing your diaphragm. *Practice Release Breathing while you are completing each of the other steps.*

Step 2: What's My Role? *Identify the role(s) you play or almost play...*

    ☐ Persecutor   ☐ Rescuer   ☐ Victim

Step 3: Practice Role-free Behavior! *Select Role-free behaviors from the list that you could practice to stay out of unhealthy relationship patterns...*

- ☐ Supporting & validating the other person's ways of thinking, feeling, and acting.
- ☐ Allowing & accepting how others are different.
- ☐ Keeping agreements and commitments.
- ☐ Limiting what you try to control.
- ☐ Being sensitive to the welfare of others.
- ☐ Taking care of your own needs and self-esteem.
- ☐ Allowing someone else to solve his/her own problems.
- ☐ Withholding support that contributes to someone else's self-harm or self-defeat.
- ☐ Taking responsibility for what happens to you.
- ☐ Taking charge of your own problem solving and well-being.
- ☐ Not taking the attitudes or actions of others personally.

<u>Step 1: Breathe out, relaxing your diaphragm.</u> *Practice Release Breathing while you are completing each of the other steps.*

<u>Step 2: What's My Role?</u> *Identify the role(s) you play or almost play...*

☐ Persecutor ☐ Rescuer ☐ Victim

<u>Step 3: Practice Role-free Behavior!</u> *Select Role-free behaviors from the list that you could practice to stay out of unhealthy relationship patterns...*

☐ Supporting & validating the other person's ways of thinking, feeling, and acting.
☐ Allowing & accepting how others are different.
☐ Keeping agreements and commitments.
☐ Limiting what you try to control.
☐ Being sensitive to the welfare of others.
☐ Taking care of your own needs and self-esteem.
☐ Allowing someone else to solve his/her own problems.
☐ Withholding support that contributes to someone else's self-harm or self-defeat.
☐ Taking responsibility for what happens to you.
☐ Taking charge of your own problem solving and well-being.
☐ Not taking the attitudes or actions of others personally.

Step 1: Breathe out, relaxing your diaphragm. *Practice Release Breathing while you are completing each of the other steps.*

Step 2: What's My Role? *Identify the role(s) you play or almost play...*

☐ Persecutor   ☐ Rescuer   ☐ Victim

Step 3: Practice Role-free Behavior! *Select Role-free behaviors from the list that you could practice to stay out of unhealthy relationship patterns...*

☐ Supporting & validating the other person's ways of thinking, feeling, and acting.
☐ Allowing & accepting how others are different.
☐ Keeping agreements and commitments.
☐ Limiting what you try to control.
☐ Being sensitive to the welfare of others.
☐ Taking care of your own needs and self-esteem.
☐ Allowing someone else to solve his/her own problems.
☐ Withholding support that contributes to someone else's self-harm or self-defeat.
☐ Taking responsibility for what happens to you.
☐ Taking charge of your own problem solving and well-being.
☐ Not taking the attitudes or actions of others personally.

Step 1: Breathe out, relaxing your diaphragm. *Practice Release Breathing while you are completing each of the other steps.*

Step 2: What's My Role? *Identify the role(s) you play or almost play...*

☐ Persecutor   ☐ Rescuer   ☐ Victim

Step 3: Practice Role-free Behavior! *Select Role-free behaviors from the list that you could practice to stay out of unhealthy relationship patterns...*

☐ Supporting & validating the other person's ways of thinking, feeling, and acting.
☐ Allowing & accepting how others are different.
☐ Keeping agreements and commitments.
☐ Limiting what you try to control.
☐ Being sensitive to the welfare of others.
☐ Taking care of your own needs and self-esteem.
☐ Allowing someone else to solve his/her own problems.
☐ Withholding support that contributes to someone else's self-harm or self-defeat.
☐ Taking responsibility for what happens to you.
☐ Taking charge of your own problem solving and well-being.
☐ Not taking the attitudes or actions of others personally.

Chapter 10

ACTION WITHOUT ANGER

INTRODUCTION

There are three general types of behavior through which we channel our energy. Assertive and aggressive behaviors involve channeling our energy as action. Holding back or withholding energy, on the other hand, is called passive behavior.

As a rule, the best alternative is to channel our thoughts and feelings into action that is consistent with our values. And there are times when our values are best served by holding back. It allows others to initiate action or be responsible for themselves.

However, passive behavior usually causes us to be ineffective because we aren't taking charge of our lives. The frustration of not meeting our own needs causes a sense of losing control of our lives and builds tension. It weakens our self-esteem and causes us to resent others. This leads to negative attitudes.

Passivity causes worry, stress, fear, and anxiety. But being assertive channels your emotional energy into productive actions. If you are assertive, you increase your sense of Personal Control, release tension, and develop a positive attitude toward yourself, others, and life in general.

GOALS

1. You will learn to recognize the difference between passive, aggressive, and assertive behavior.

2. You will learn to identify options for assertive action so that you can select ones that are consistent with your values.

3. You will learn to channel your energy into assertive actions that are consistent with your values.

REMEMBER

Don't miss another opportunity to build your peace of mind. When worry, stress, fear, or anxiety strike this week...Conquer Your Fears. Use...

*

FIRST AID for..WORRY, STRESS, FEAR, AND ANXIETY

Step 1: **Always...Breathe Out!**

Step 2: **Am I Being Passive?**

Step 3: **What Are My Assertive Options?**

Step 4: **Plan Assertive Action!**

* Permission is given to reproduce the First Aid Steps for your personal use.

STEP 1

<u>ALWAYS...BREATHE OUT!</u>

Tension builds up inside of us when we need to take action but we are holding back. We recommend Release Breathing for briefly reducing this tension.

Release Breathing enables us to let go of the tension we build up when we hold back assertive action. And we can practice Release Breathing any time we are facing a situation that calls for assertion or in which we are preparing to act, but we are reluctant to "make waves."

Let's take a closer look at these situations. Holding back is passive. When we are passive, we are not taking action, and often dissatisfaction sets in. We are dissatisfied with others or ourselves. That dissatisfaction promotes a negative attitude; it is negative about ourselves because we aren't taking action to meet our own needs, and negative about others and the situation because they seem to cause our unhappiness.

This lesson teaches you how to be assertive without losing control of your anger and doing damage.

The tension of passive inaction causes our breathing to shut down and become restricted. The Release Breathing technique is an excellent way to release this tension and start action.

Release Breathing sends an important "let go" message to the brain. It involves 3 steps:

1. breathe in deeply, using *medium force*. Using your diaphragm,

2. mobilize yourself by breathing out through your mouth, using *medium strong force*. Let your shoulders, chest, and diaphragm sag or fall downward.

    Think "I can act" as you release air from your lungs. Let go of the air and all the tension in your body, and

3. pause for a moment at the end of the breath. Feel the release of tension.

    Think of having "let go" of both the tightness in your chest and "holding back."

STEP 2

Passivity is not taking action. It involves waiting for someone else to act.

In order to improve our skills at acting assertively, we need to recognize which type of behavior we are using to channel our energy. The first step is to develop our understanding of the difference between passive, aggressive, and assertive behavior.

 Passivity. Passivity is indirect or inactive. You are being passive when you wait for others to take the initiative in satisfying your needs or solving your problems. Passivity takes such forms as hinting, procrastinating, withdrawing, holding back, and being indirect. Behavior is passive when it lacks problem solving action.

 Aggression. Aggression is destructive. You are being aggressive when you impose your will upon others as a way of satisfying your own needs or solving your own problems. Aggression takes such forms as intimidating, bullying, belittling, and physical abuse. Behavior is aggressive when it is harmful or destructive. Aggression releases tension and stress, so being aggressive does not cause anxiety. It may cause social problems, though, so assertion is a better way to take action.

 Assertiveness. Assertion is constructive. You are being assertive when you take the initiative in the service of satisfying your own needs or solving your own problems. Assertion takes such forms as asking for what you want, setting limits, and ethical competition. Behavior is assertive when it accomplishes these things without being harmful or destructive.

EXERCISE

A

RECOGNIZING THE DIFFERENCE BETWEEN
THE BEHAVIORS

<u>DIRECTIONS:</u> For Exercise A...Read the statements below and think about yourself in general. Think about your overall life. Consider different situations with different people. Think about your different states of mind. Circle a number to show how much you agree with each statement. Use the space provided to add other examples of each type of behavior.

ACTING PASSIVELY:

How Much Do You Agree?

1. I have trouble asking for help.

1 - 2 - 3 - 4 - 5
A Little....A Lot

2. I avoid disagreements and conflicts.

1 - 2 - 3 - 4 - 5
A Little....A Lot

3. In the face of disagreements and conflicts, I tend to let others have their way.

1 - 2 - 3 - 4 - 5
A Little....A Lot

4. I am uncomfortable talking in a group.

1 - 2 - 3 - 4 - 5
A Little....A Lot

5. I am reluctant to bring up a subject if I think it will upset someone.

1 - 2 - 3 - 4 - 5
A Little....A Lot

6. I don't complain when something goes wrong.

1 - 2 - 3 - 4 - 5
A Little....A Lot

7. I am reluctant to ask questions. 1 - 2 - 3 - 4 - 5
A Little....A Lot

8. When somebody wants me to do
something I don't want to do, 1 - 2 - 3 - 4 - 5
I stall, forget, or shine them on. A Little....A Lot

9. I hold back when I think others 1 - 2 - 3 - 4 - 5
will be hurt or angry by what I do. A Little....A Lot

Other examples of your acting passively:...

....

<u>ACTING AGGRESSIVELY:</u>

1.   I find it easy to demand the help I want or to feel entitled to the help I want.

      1 - 2 - 3 - 4 - 5
      A Little....A Lot

2.   I welcome or look forward to confrontations, conflicts, and disagreements.

      1 - 2 - 3 - 4 - 5
      A Little....A Lot

3.   In the face of disagreements and conflicts, I get irritated with others if they don't see things my way.

      1 - 2 - 3 - 4 - 5
      A Little....A Lot

4.   I am outspoken in a group.

      1 - 2 - 3 - 4 - 5
      A Little....A Lot

5.   I don't hesitate to bring up a subject if I think it will upset someone, and if it does, it's their problem.

      1 - 2 - 3 - 4 - 5
      A Little....A Lot

6.   I complain when something goes wrong, and if someone else has a problem with that, I don't care.

      1 - 2 - 3 - 4 - 5
      A Little....A Lot

7.   I ask questions without worrying if someone else will disapprove or be troubled or harmed by it.

      1 - 2 - 3 - 4 - 5
      A Little....A Lot

8.   When somebody wants me to do something I don't want to do, I tell them to "get lost."

      1 - 2 - 3 - 4 - 5
      A Little....A Lot

9.   I do what I want, even when I think others will be hurt or angry by what I do.

      1 - 2 - 3 - 4 - 5
      A Little....A Lot

Other examples of your acting aggressively:...

....

ACTING ASSERTIVELY:

How Much Do You Agree?

1.   I feel comfortable asking for help   1 - 2 - 3 - 4 - 5
      when I need it.   A Little....A Lot

2.   I face conflicts or disagreements   1 - 2 - 3 - 4 - 5
      when they come up.   A Little....A Lot

3.   In the face of disagreements and conflicts, I tend to   1 - 2 - 3 - 4 - 5
      look for solutions that respect all points of view.   A Little....A Lot

3.   I'm comfortable talking in a group.   1 - 2 - 3 - 4 - 5
                                       A Little....A Lot

4.   I'm fairly comfortable bringing up a subject even if   1 - 2 - 3 - 4 - 5
      I think it will upset someone.   A Little....A Lot

5.   I am fairly comfortable and willing to complain when 1 - 2 - 3 - 4 - 5
      something goes wrong.   A Little....A Lot

6.   I'm fairly comfortable asking   1 - 2 - 3 - 4 - 5
      questions.   A Little....A Lot

7.   If somebody wants me to do something I don't want to 1 - 2 - 3 - 4 - 5
      do, I explore options and try to meet both our needs. A Little....A Lot

8.   I do what I judge to be best even when I think others 1 - 2 - 3 - 4 - 5
      will be hurt or angry about what I do.   A Little....A Lot

Other examples of your acting assertively:...

....

STEP 3

WHAT ARE MY ASSERTIVE OPTIONS?

In order to be more assertive, we need to be able to figure out how to act assertively. We need to be able to think of assertive options.

Assertive options are alternative behaviors. They are different ways to behave in situations where we normally would be passive. For most of us, the easiest way to identify assertive options is by contrasting them with passive and aggressive options.

EXERCISE

B

IDENTIFYING OPTIONS

DIRECTIONS: For Exercise B... Fill in optional behaviors for each situation below. Don't limit yourself to things you would actually do. Be creative, have fun, exaggerate. For ideas, review the lists in Exercise A.

Situation 1, Restaurant. You and a companion are seated at a nice restaurant. The waiter is very abrupt. He takes only your beverage orders and leaves. He doesn't come back. A long time goes by and you get tired of waiting.

What passive things <u>could</u> you do?

....

....

What aggressive things <u>could</u> you do?

....

....

What assertive things <u>could</u> you do?

....

....

Situation 2, Rental Property. Property you rent needs repair. The landlord has not returned your two calls about the problem.

What passive things <u>could</u> you do?

....

....

What aggressive things <u>could</u> you do?

....

....

What assertive things <u>could</u> you do?

....

....

Situation 3, Guest. A guest stays at your home longer than you wanted. S/he is nice enough, but you are tired of having someone else in your house.

What passive things <u>could</u> you do?

....

....

What aggressive things <u>could</u> you do?

....

....

What assertive things <u>could</u> you do?

....

....

STEP 4

PLAN ASSERTIVE ACTION!

It is usually hard to get yourself to be assertive in situations where you have been passive before. Once you identify assertive options, you have to pick one that is consistent with your values and channel your emotions into doing it.

One way to get yourself to change your old behaviors is by writing commitment statements. An Assertive Action Statement is a positive statement of what assertive action you will take. The statement has 4 parts:

Your Values. Your values are a part of your Assertive Action Statement because if you do what you believe is right, you will have more respect for yourself. What's the most important ethical, humanitarian, moral, or spiritual issue involved with the situation?

Your Feelings. Your feelings are a part of your Assertive Action Statement because they motivate you. The idea is to channel your feelings into action.

Your Action. Action is part of your Assertive Action Statement so that your thinking is clear and focussed. Your statement should be very specific and concrete about what you will do. Say exactly what you will do. This makes you more efficient and makes it more likely that you will succeed.

Your Appointment. Your appointment is the time or situation when you will take your assertive action. Commitment to a time or situation helps you focus your energy and makes it more likely that you will succeed.

Examples of Assertive Action Statements:

■   I value *my son becoming responsible and self-sufficient*,
     so I will channel my *anger*
     into *telling my son 'No'*
     ...the next time he asks for money.

■   I value *doing a good job and preserving my peace of mind*,
     so I will channel my *insecurity*
     into *insisting that my supervisor set priorities for work*
     ...the next time she gives me too much to do.

■   I value *relationships and attachment*,
     so I will channel my *loneliness*
     into *inviting that good-looking sales rep to lunch*
     ...the next time he is in the office.

EXERCISE

C

COMMITTING YOURSELF TO ASSERTIVE ACTION

DIRECTIONS: For Exercise C...Build on your responses to Exercise B to do this exercise. Write an Assertive Action Statement for each situation.

Situation 1, Restaurant.   You and a companion are seated at a nice restaurant and getting bad service.

I value:...

So I will channel my (what feeling):...

Into (name an action):..

(State When, the Appointment):...

Situation 2, Rental Property.   Property you rent needs repair.

I value:...

So I will channel my (what feeling):...

Into (name an action):..

(State When, the Appointment):...

Situation 3, Guest   A guest stays at your home longer than you wanted.

I value:...

So I will channel my (what feeling):...

Into (name an action):..

(State When, the Appointment):...

PRACTICE YOUR WORK SHEETS

DIRECTIONS: The more you study the steps in this lesson, the more effective your new skills will become. Your Work Sheets are designed to help you master these skills. So, read the story below. We will use it as an example to help you learn to use the Work Sheets successfully.

Betty was tired of Bill's reactions to how she and Billy get along. Bill Sr. gets frustrated with the arguments and tries to talk her into reading that stupid book his mother gave them. Betty disliked the book from the first moment she laid eyes on it. First of all, there was the title, Perfect Children through Brute Force. What kind of a book is that? Then there was that statement on the cover, "What every wishy-washy woman should know about parenting." Bad enough Billy had a temperament just like his father. Now Betty's mother-in-law had her pegged as a wimp!

Betty tried to ignore the book for months. That was hard because Bill kept leaving it out where Betty was sure to stumble upon it--on the coffee table, on the nightstand, in the refrigerator. So, she hid it under the bed. She said it was lost. Ultimately Bill found it. Too bad he didn't run the vacuum while he was under there!

For a while Betty made promises to read the book. When Bill asked, she said she had forgotten or that she'd been busy. He was getting fed up with these tactics; those puffy veins started showing on his forehead again. Whenever Betty tried to figure out what to do about that book and her husband's attitude, Billy started whining about wanting candy or something else. Betty just couldn't concentrate.

DIRECTIONS: Practice your homework exercise. Imagine that you are Betty in this situation. Complete the "Practice Asserting Yourself Work Sheet" on the next page.

NEXT PAGE

Step 1: Breathe out, relaxing your diaphragm. *Practice Release Breathing while you are completing each of the other steps. Describe the situation as if you were Betty...*

Step 2: Am I Being Passive? *Describe Betty's actions...*

....

....

....

Classify Betty's behavior: Check one... ☐ *Passive* ☐ *Aggressive* ☐ *Assertive*

Step 3: What Are My Assertive Options? *Describe two or more assertive options that Betty could use...*

....

....

....

Step 4: Plan Assertive Action! *Write an Assertive Action Statement for Betty...*

I value:..

So I will channel my:...

Into:..

(When):..

<u>Step 1:   Breathe out, relaxing your diaphragm.</u>   *Practice Release Breathing while you are completing each of the other steps.   Describe the situation as if you were Betty...*

<u>Step 2:   Am I Being Passive?</u>   *Describe Betty's actions...*

....Not being honest about the book.   Avoiding a confrontation.................................

....

....

Classify Betty's behavior: Check one...   ■ *Passive*   ☐ *Aggressive*   ☐ *Assertive*

<u>Step 3:   What Are My Assertive Options?</u>   *Describe two or more assertive options that Betty could use...*

....Tell Bill her true feelings about the book.   Find a better sounding book.   Talk to a

....counselor..

....

....

<u>Step 4:   Plan Assertive Action!</u>   *Write an Assertive Action Statement for Betty...*

I value:....*Being a good parent*..

So I will channel my:....*Anger*..

Into:....*Confronting Bill and calling a doctor*..

(When):.....*Tonight, or tomorrow at the latest*...

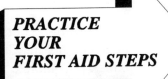

PRACTICE YOUR FIRST AID STEPS

DIRECTIONS: The more you practice your First Aid Steps, the better you will feel. Practice your First Aid Steps now. Imagine you are in a situation used in this lesson, or think about your life in general.

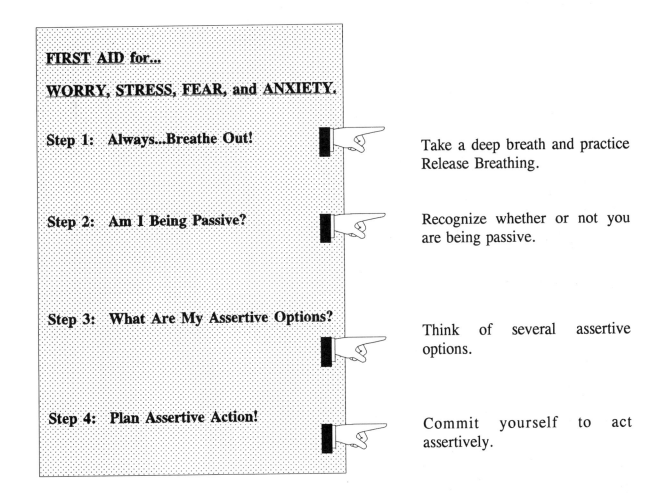

FIRST AID for...

WORRY, STRESS, FEAR, and ANXIETY.

Step 1:   Always...Breathe Out!

Take a deep breath and practice Release Breathing.

Step 2:   Am I Being Passive?

Recognize whether or not you are being passive.

Step 3:   What Are My Assertive Options?

Think of several assertive options.

Step 4:   Plan Assertive Action!

Commit yourself to act assertively.

HOMEWORK

THE METHODS...

<u>Work Sheets.</u> This week complete 8 Asserting Yourself Work Sheets. Do the Work Sheets for situations in which you worry or feel stress, fear, or anxiety. Complete the Work Sheets at the time of these events or very soon thereafter.

<u>First Aid Steps.</u> Practice your First Aid Steps as often as possible, even when you are not really worrying or feeling threatened.

*

> ## FIRST AID for...WORRY, STRESS, FEAR, AND ANXIETY
>
> **Step 1:**   **Always...Breathe Out!**
>
> **Step 2:**   **Am I Being Passive?**
>
> **Step 3:**   **What Are My Assertive Options?**
>
> **Step 4:**   **Plan Assertive Action!**

<u>Use your Clip-outs:</u> Cut out the First Aid Steps reminders. Place them in spots where you will see them and remember to practice. Give some to a friend, and tell him or her how to use them.

<u>Teach Others.</u> Share the First Aid Steps with others. Teach them how to help themselves using the same skills you are learning.

* Permission is given to reproduce the First Aid Steps for your personal use.

Step 1:   Breathe out, relaxing your diaphragm.   *Practice Release Breathing while you are completing each of the other steps.   Describe the situation in which you worried or felt stress, fear, or anxiety...*

Step 2:   Am I Being Passive?   *Describe your actions...*

....

....

....

Classify your behavior: Check one...   ☐ *Passive*   ☐ *Aggressive*   ☐ *Assertive*

Step 3:   What Are My Assertive Options?   *Describe two or more assertive options that you could use...*

....

....

....

Step 4:   Plan Assertive Action!   *Write an Assertive Action Statement...*

I value:..

So I will channel my:..

Into:..

(When):..

ASSERTING YOURSELF WORK SHEET # 2

Step 1: Breathe out, relaxing your diaphragm. *Practice Release Breathing while you are completing each of the other steps. Describe the situation in which you worried or felt stress, fear, or anxiety...*

Step 2: Am I Being Passive? *Describe your actions...*

....

....

....

Classify your behavior: Check one... ☐ *Passive*   ☐ *Aggressive*   ☐ *Assertive*

Step 3: What Are My Assertive Options? *Describe two or more assertive options that you could use...*

....

....

....

Step 4: Plan Assertive Action! *Write an Assertive Action Statement...*

I value:...

So I will channel my:..

Into:...

(When):..

Step 1: Breathe out, relaxing your diaphragm. *Practice Release Breathing while you are completing each of the other steps. Describe the situation in which you worried or felt stress, fear, or anxiety...*

Step 2: Am I Being Passive? *Describe your actions...*

....

....

....

Classify your behavior: Check one...   ☐ *Passive*   ☐ *Aggressive*   ☐ *Assertive*

Step 3: What Are My Assertive Options? *Describe two or more assertive options that you could use...*

....

....

....

Step 4: Plan Assertive Action! *Write an Assertive Action Statement...*

I value:..

So I will channel my:..

Into:...

(When):...

Step 1: Breathe out, relaxing your diaphragm. *Practice Release Breathing while you are completing each of the other steps. Describe the situation in which you worried or felt stress, fear, or anxiety...*

Step 2: Am I Being Passive? *Describe your actions...*

....

....

....

Classify your behavior: Check one...   ☐ *Passive*   ☐ *Aggressive*   ☐ *Assertive*

Step 3: What Are My Assertive Options? *Describe two or more assertive options that you could use...*

....

....

....

Step 4: Plan Assertive Action! *Write an Assertive Action Statement...*

I value:..

So I will channel my:...

Into:...

(When):..

<u>Step 1:</u> <u>Breathe out, relaxing your diaphragm.</u> *Practice Release Breathing while you are completing each of the other steps. Describe the situation in which you worried or felt stress, fear, or anxiety...*

<u>Step 2:</u> <u>Am I Being Passive?</u> *Describe your actions...*

....

....

....

Classify your behavior: Check one... ☐ *Passive* ☐ *Aggressive* ☐ *Assertive*

<u>Step 3:</u> <u>What Are My Assertive Options?</u> *Describe two or more assertive options that you could use...*

....

....

....

<u>Step 4:</u> <u>Plan Assertive Action!</u> *Write an Assertive Action Statement...*

I value:...

So I will channel my:..

Into:...

(When):...

Step 1: Breathe out, relaxing your diaphragm. *Practice Release Breathing while you are completing each of the other steps. Describe the situation in which you worried or felt stress, fear, or anxiety...*

Step 2: Am I Being Passive? *Describe your actions...*

....

....

....

Classify your behavior: Check one... ☐ *Passive*   ☐ *Aggressive*   ☐ *Assertive*

Step 3: What Are My Assertive Options? *Describe two or more assertive options that you could use...*

....

....

....

Step 4: Plan Assertive Action! *Write an Assertive Action Statement...*

I value:...

So I will channel my:...

Into:...

(When):...

Step 1: Breathe out, relaxing your diaphragm. *Practice Release Breathing while you are completing each of the other steps. Describe the situation in which you worried or felt stress, fear, or anxiety...*

Step 2: Am I Being Passive? *Describe your actions...*

....

....

....

Classify your behavior: Check one... ☐ *Passive*   ☐ *Aggressive*   ☐ *Assertive*

Step 3: What Are My Assertive Options? *Describe two or more assertive options that you could use...*

....

....

....

Step 4: Plan Assertive Action! *Write an Assertive Action Statement...*

I value:...

So I will channel my:..

Into:...

(When):..

ASSERTING YOURSELF WORK SHEET # 8

Step 1: Breathe out, relaxing your diaphragm. *Practice Release Breathing while you are completing each of the other steps. Describe the situation in which you worried or felt stress, fear, or anxiety...*

Step 2: Am I Being Passive? *Describe your actions...*

....

....

....

Classify your behavior: Check one...   ☐ *Passive*   ☐ *Aggressive*   ☐ *Assertive*

Step 3: What Are My Assertive Options? *Describe two or more assertive options that you could use...*

....

....

....

Step 4: Plan Assertive Action! *Write an Assertive Action Statement...*

I value:..

So I will channel my:...

Into:...

(When):...

Chapter 11

BE REALISTIC!

<u>INTRODUCTION</u>

When we believe we are in danger, we worry or develop stress, fear, and anxiety. This is normal. These are natural reactions to danger; they prepare us to take action.

But believing we are in danger does not mean we actually are in danger. What if we misjudge the situation? What if our interpretations and expectations are unrealistic? Then we get upset needlessly or we get more upset than is appropriate for our situation.

You can reduce the severity and frequency of your stress and anxiety if you learn to "test reality" and think alternative, realistic thoughts. If you reduce stress-causing thoughts you increase your sense of Personal Control, release tension, and develop a positive attitude toward yourself, others, and life in general.

<u>GOALS</u>

1. Learn to identify the threats to which you react.

2. Learn to evaluate how realistic the threats actually are.

3. Learn to think thoughts that are more realistic and less stressful.

<u>REMEMBER</u>

Don't miss another opportunity to build peace of mind. When worry, stress, fear, or anxiety strike this week...Conquer Your Fears. Use...

*

<u>FIRST AID for...WORRY, STRESS, FEAR, AND ANXIETY</u>

Step 1:   Always...Breathe Out!

Step 2:   What Am I Thinking?

Step 3:   How Realistic Is It?

Step 4:   Think a More Realistic Thought!

* Permission is given to reproduce the First Aid Steps for your personal use.

STEP 1

Internal stress and tension mounts when we think we are being threatened. We recommend Release Breathing for briefly reducing this tension caused when we sense danger.

Release Breathing enables us to let go of the tension we build up when we become afraid of a perceived threat. And we can practice Release Breathing any time we think we are threatened, as often as we need to.

Seeing life situations as threatening promotes a negative attitude; it is negative about ourselves because we feel helpless to defend ourselves and negative about the situation because it represents harm to us.

This lesson teaches you how to assess the threat that is actually present and how to think about it in a realistic manner.

Feeling threatened causes our breathing to shut down and become restricted. The Release Breathing technique is an excellent way to release this tension and clear your mind for effective reality testing and thought changing.

Release Breathing sends an important "let go" message to the brain. It involves 3 steps:

1. breathe in deeply, using *medium force*. Using your diaphragm,

2. breathe out through your mouth, using *medium strong force*. Let your shoulders, chest, and diaphragm sag or fall downward.

    Think "it's not really that bad" as you release air from your lungs. Let go of the air and all the tension in your body, and

3. pause for a moment at the end of the breath. Feel the release of tension.

    Think of having "let go" of both the tightness in your chest and catastrophic thoughts.

WHAT AM I THINKING?

Our reactions come from what we think, not from the reality of the situation. Our worry, stress, fear and anxiety get worse if we think we are threatened. There are two types of thoughts that can trigger a threatened reaction:

 EXPECTATIONS. When we expect something harmful or dangerous to happen or when we expect a loss.

 INTERPRETATIONS. When we interpret something that is happening or has happened as harmful or dangerous, or when we interpret something as a loss.

A situation is threatening to us only if we form scary thoughts about it. If we don't think a situation is threatening, we don't feel threatened. Even when we are in mortal danger, if we don't recognize the threat, we don't react with worry, stress, fear, and anxiety.

On the other hand, if we think we're threatened with danger or a loss we react. Even when we are not in real danger, if we think we are threatened, we react with worry, stress, fear, and anxiety.

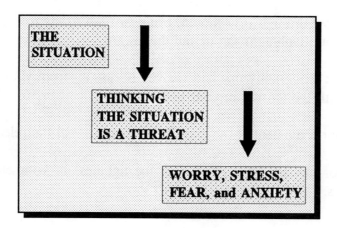

We often react to situations as if they are threatening without being aware of the scary thoughts that trigger our reaction. Because our thoughts tend to be automatic, we take them for granted. We rarely examine them to determine how realistic they are.

If we recognize our scary thoughts, we can examine them to be sure they are realistic or adjust them when necessary. If our thoughts are realistic, we won't needlessly react with worry, stress, fear, and anxiety.

EXERCISE

A

IDENTIFYING YOUR AUTOMATIC, SCARY THOUGHTS

The first step in dealing with automatic, scary thoughts is noticing them. Exercise A will help you learn to identify the upsetting expectations and interpretations of threat you form when you are reacting to situations.

<u>DIRECTIONS:</u> For Exercise A...Write the expectation or interpretation you automatically form for each situation below. Then circle one number to show how much worry, stress, fear or anxiety your scary thoughts cause.

Situation #1: IRS Letter.

You receive a letter from the IRS. Before you open it, what thoughts do you have?

....

....

....

How much worry, stress, fear, or
anxiety do your scary thoughts cause?

1 - 2 - 3 - 4 - 5
A Little...A Lot

Chapter 11: Be Realistic!

Situation #2: The Message.

A friend leaves a message on your answering machine: "I won't be seeing you for a while. Don't call me, I'll call you." What thoughts do you have?

....

....

....

How much worry, stress, fear, or   1 - 2 - 3 - 4 - 5
anxiety do your scary thoughts cause?   A Little...A Lot

Situation #3: The Elevator.

You get in an elevator. The doors close but the elevator doesn't move. What thoughts do you have?

....

....

....

How much worry, stress, fear, or   1 - 2 - 3 - 4 - 5
anxiety do your scary thoughts cause?   A Little...A Lot

HOW REALISTIC IS IT?

We react to our scary thoughts as if they are reality. But what if our scary thoughts aren't realistic? Then we get worried, stressed, or fearful for nothing! We can avoid this needless distress by asking how realistic our interpretations and expectations are. We call this "reality testing."

Reality testing is a process of comparing our automatic, scary thoughts with other possibilities-- additional facts, different interpretations, and reasoning. Reality testing exposes our exaggerations of how threatening the situation actually is.

COMPARING SCARY THOUGHTS WITH OTHER POSSIBILITIES

You can reduce the stress caused by automatic, scary thoughts by comparing them with other possibilities. Exercise B will help you develop this skill.

DIRECTIONS: For Exercise B...Continue using the thoughts you wrote for Exercise A.

1. Think about other possibilities. Write down some of them. Compare your original thoughts with the other possibilities.

2. Circle one number to rate how realistic your automatic, scary thought was.

3. Circle one number to rate how much worry, stress, or fear you have after comparing your automatic thoughts with other possibilities.

Situation #1: The IRS Letter.

Write down and compare some other possibilities.

....

....

....

Now that you have compared, how certain
or realistic was your automatic, scary   1 - 2 - 3 - 4 - 5
thought about the situation?   Not Very...Very

How much worry, stress, fear, or   1 - 2 - 3 - 4 - 5
anxiety do you have after comparing?   A Little...A Lot

Situation #2: The Message.

Write down and compare some other possibilities.

....

....

....

Now that you have compared, how certain
or realistic was your automatic, scary   1 - 2 - 3 - 4 - 5
thought about the situation?   Not Very...Very

How much worry, stress, fear, or   1 - 2 - 3 - 4 - 5
anxiety do you have after comparing?   A Little...A Lot

Situation #3: The Elevator.

Write down and compare some other possibilities.

....

....

....

Now that you have compared, how certain   1 - 2 - 3 - 4 - 5
or realistic was your automatic, scary   Not Very...Very
thought about the situation?

How much worry, stress, fear, or   1 - 2 - 3 - 4 - 5
anxiety do you have after comparing?   A Little...A Lot

COMMENTS ON THE EXERCISE

Exercise B: Some people find it hard to think up other possibilities at first. This gets
               easier with time. Keep practicing. By the way, just trying to think of
               other possibilities shifts the mind from an "out of control" attitude to an
               "in control" attitude.

STEP 4 ▷ <u>THINK A MORE REALISTIC THOUGHT!</u>

Reality-tested thoughts almost always cause less worry, stress, fear, and anxiety than our automatic thoughts, which tend to be *negative or negativistic*. Step 3 demonstrated this. So, if we practice thinking realistic expectations and interpretations, we will feel better and see life more accurately.

<u>Reality-tested Thoughts vs. Positive Thinking.</u> Practicing reality-tested thoughts is different than practicing "positive thinking." Positive thinking involves looking on the bright side of things without regard for objective reality. We just interpret or expect the best. That isn't bad, but it is *idealistic*.

Positive thinking is helpful to many people, and it can be used along with practicing reality-tested thoughts. Reality-tested thoughts, however, have an advantage. They are based on three active, rational processes that are rooted in objective reality:

- Analysis

- Reason

- Judgment

Using these active processes produces the benefits of increasing our sense of Personal Control, releasing tension, and developing healthy attitudes regardless of how we define reality as a result of using them. When we practice reality-tested thoughts, we strengthen these processes and gain the benefits they create. Don't be negativistic or idealistic: be *realistic*.

EXERCISE

C

<u>DIRECTIONS:</u> For Exercise C...Continue using the thoughts you wrote for Exercise A. Write a reality tested statement of your expectations or interpretations of what each situation actually is.

<u>Situation #1:</u> <u>The IRS Letter.</u> Write a realistic thought.

....

....

....

<u>Situation #2:</u> <u>The Message.</u> Write a realistic thought.

....

....

....

<u>Situation #3:</u> <u>The Elevator.</u> Write a realistic thought.

....

....

....

COMMENTS ON THE EXERCISE

Exercise C: Most people see that realistic thoughts can be developed if we first recognize the scary thoughts and then we work to think about other possibilities. The first two steps open our mind to several possibilities, and this makes it easier to abandon initial, impulsive, scary thoughts and settle on a realistic alternative.

PRACTICE YOUR WORK SHEETS

<u>DIRECTIONS:</u> The more you study the steps in this lesson, the more effective your new skills will become. Your Work Sheets are designed to help you master these skills. So, read the story below. We will use it as an example to help you learn to use the Work Sheets successfully.

All the message said was, "Your wife phoned. Call home ASAP." Bill had been trying to return the call for over an hour. The line was busy. He'd even had the operator check to see if it was out of order. It wasn't! Maybe the answering machine was messing up again?

Bill kept trying to figure out what was wrong. He knew Betty had been upset with Billy lately. Maybe they got into a fight with each other. What if one of them was injured or sick? Maybe they were in a car accident. What if the house was on fire? Why couldn't he get through? What should he do?

The whole thing was getting him uptight. He couldn't concentrate on work and he was getting irritable. Other people in the office were starting to avoid him again. They had that "run for cover" look in their eyes.

<u>DIRECTIONS:</u> Practice your homework exercises. Imagine that you are Bill in this situation. Complete the "Practice Reality Testing Work Sheet" on the next page.

NEXT PAGE

PRACTICE REALITY TESTING WORK SHEET

<u>Step 1:</u> <u>Breathe out firmly, relaxing your diaphragm.</u> *Practice Release Breathing while you are completing each of the other steps...*

<u>Step 2:</u>   <u>What Am I Thinking?</u>   *Describe Bill's likely automatic expectations and interpretations...*

> ....
>
> ....

How much worry, stress, fear, or anxiety would these scary thoughts cause you if you were Bill?	1 - 2 - 3 - 4 - 5 A Little...A Lot

<u>Step 3: How Realistic Is It?</u> *Write down and compare some other possibilities...*

> ....
>
> ....

How realistic was your (Bill's) automatic, scary thought about the situation?	1 - 2 - 3 - 4 - 5 Not Very...Very
How much worry, stress, fear, or anxiety do you have after comparing?	1 - 2 - 3 - 4 - 5 A Little...A Lot

<u>Step 4: Think a More Realistic Thought!</u> *Write one reality-tested statement of more realistic expectations or interpretations...*

> ....
>
> ....

<u>PRACTICE REALITY TESTING WORK SHEET</u>

<u>Step 1:</u> <u>Breathe out firmly, relaxing your diaphragm.</u> *Practice Release Breathing while you are completing each of the other steps...*

<u>Step 2:</u> <u>What Am I Thinking?</u> *Describe Bill's likely automatic expectations and interpretations...*

...***Something bad has happened***...

....

| How much worry, stress, fear, or anxiety would these scary thoughts cause you if you were Bill? | 1 - 2 - 3 - <u>4 - 5</u>
A Little...A Lot |

<u>Step 3:</u> <u>How Realistic Is It?</u> *Write down and compare some other possibilities...*

...***Phone off the hook. Betty over-reacting***..

....

| How realistic was your (Bill's) automatic, scary thought about the situation? | <u>1</u> - 2 - 3 - 4 - 5
Not Very...Very |
| How much worry, stress, fear, or anxiety do you have after comparing? | 1 - <u>2</u> - 3 - 4 - 5
A Little...A Lot |

<u>Step 4:</u> <u>Think a More Realistic Thought!</u> *Write one reality-tested statement of more realistic expectations or interpretations...*

...***Betty can handle it. I'll get through in good time***....................................

....

PRACTICE YOUR FIRST AID STEPS

<u>DIRECTIONS:</u> The more you practice your First Aid Steps, the better you will feel. Practice your First Aid Steps now. Imagine you are in a situation used in this lesson, or think about your life in general.

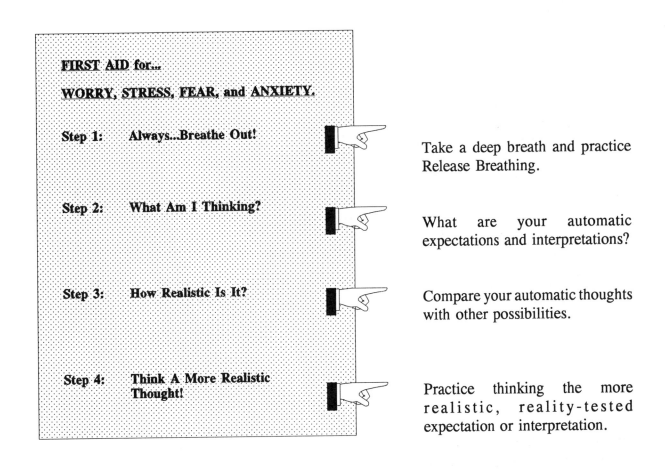

<u>FIRST AID for...</u>

<u>WORRY, STRESS, FEAR, and ANXIETY.</u>

Step 1: Always...Breathe Out!

Take a deep breath and practice Release Breathing.

Step 2: What Am I Thinking?

What are your automatic expectations and interpretations?

Step 3: How Realistic Is It?

Compare your automatic thoughts with other possibilities.

Step 4: Think A More Realistic Thought!

Practice thinking the more realistic, reality-tested expectation or interpretation.

HOMEWORK

<u>THE METHODS...</u>

<u>Work Sheets.</u> This week complete 8 Reality Testing Work Sheets. Do the Work Sheets for situations in which you worry or feel stress, fear, or anxiety. Complete the Work Sheets at the time of these events or very soon thereafter.

<u>First Aid Steps.</u> Practice your First Aid Steps as often as possible, even when you are not really worrying or feeling threatened.

*

<u>FIRST AID for...WORRY, STRESS, FEAR, AND ANXIETY</u>

Step 1:   **Always...Breathe Out!**

Step 2:   **What Am I Thinking?**

Step 3:   **How Realistic Is It?**

Step 4:   **Think A More Realistic Thought!**

<u>Use your Clip-outs:</u> Cut out the First Aid Steps reminders. Place them in spots where you will see them and remember to practice. Give some to a friend, and tell him or her how to use them.

<u>Teach Others.</u> Share the lesson with others. Teach them how to help themselves using the same skills you are learning.

* Permission is given to reproduce the First Aid Steps for your personal use.

<u>Step 1:</u> <u>Breathe out firmly, relaxing your diaphragm.</u>   *Practice Release Breathing while you are completing each of the other steps...*

<u>Step 2:</u> <u>What Am I Thinking?</u>   *Describe your automatic expectations and interpretations...*

....

....

How much worry, stress, fear, or anxiety do these scary thoughts cause you?	1 - 2 - 3 - 4 - 5 A Little...A Lot

<u>Step 3:</u> <u>How Realistic Is It?</u>   *Write down and compare some other possibilities...*

....

....

How realistic was your automatic, scary thought about the situation?	1 - 2 - 3 - 4 - 5 Not Very...Very
How much worry, stress, fear, or anxiety do you have after comparing?	1 - 2 - 3 - 4 - 5 A Little...A Lot

<u>Step 4:</u> <u>Think a More Realistic Thought!</u>   *Write one reality-tested statement of more realistic expectations or interpretations...*

....

....

Step 1:   Breathe out firmly, relaxing your diaphragm.   *Practice Release Breathing while you are completing each of the other steps...*

Step 2: What Am I Thinking?   *Describe your automatic expectations and interpretations...*

....

....

How much worry, stress, fear, or anxiety do these scary thoughts cause you?	1 - 2 - 3 - 4 - 5 A Little...A Lot

Step 3: How Realistic Is It?   *Write down and compare some other possibilities...*

....

....

How realistic was your automatic, scary thought about the situation?	1 - 2 - 3 - 4 - 5 Not Very...Very
How much worry, stress, fear, or anxiety do you have after comparing?	1 - 2 - 3 - 4 - 5 A Little...A Lot

Step 4: Think a More Realistic Thought!   *Write one reality-tested statement of more realistic expectations or interpretations...*

....

....

Step 1: Breathe out firmly, relaxing your diaphragm. *Practice Release Breathing while you are completing each of the other steps...*

Step 2: What Am I Thinking? *Describe your automatic expectations and interpretations...*

....

....

How much worry, stress, fear, or anxiety do these scary thoughts cause you?	1 - 2 - 3 - 4 - 5 A Little...A Lot

Step 3: How Realistic Is It? *Write down and compare some other possibilities...*

....

....

How realistic was your automatic, scary thought about the situation?	1 - 2 - 3 - 4 - 5 Not Very...Very
How much worry, stress, fear, or anxiety do you have after comparing?	1 - 2 - 3 - 4 - 5 A Little...A Lot

Step 4: Think a More Realistic Thought! *Write one reality-tested statement of more realistic expectations or interpretations...*

....

....

Step 1:   Breathe out firmly, relaxing your diaphragm.   *Practice Release Breathing while you are completing each of the other steps...*

Step 2: What Am I Thinking?   *Describe your automatic expectations and interpretations...*

....

....

How much worry, stress, fear, or anxiety do   1 - 2 - 3 - 4 - 5
these scary thoughts cause you?   A Little...A Lot

Step 3: How Realistic Is It?   *Write down and compare some other possibilities...*

....

....

How realistic was your automatic, scary   1 - 2 - 3 - 4 - 5
thought about the situation?   Not Very...Very

How much worry, stress, fear, or   1 - 2 - 3 - 4 - 5
anxiety do you have after comparing?   A Little...A Lot

Step 4: Think a More Realistic Thought!   *Write one reality–tested statement of more realistic expectations or interpretations...*

....

....

Step 1: <u>Breathe out firmly, relaxing your diaphragm.</u> *Practice Release Breathing while you are completing each of the other steps...*

Step 2: <u>What Am I Thinking?</u> *Describe your automatic expectations and interpretations...*

....

....

How much worry, stress, fear, or anxiety do these scary thoughts cause you?	1 - 2 - 3 - 4 - 5 A Little...A Lot

Step 3: <u>How Realistic Is It?</u> *Write down and compare some other possibilities...*

....

....

How realistic was your automatic, scary thought about the situation?	1 - 2 - 3 - 4 - 5 Not Very...Very
How much worry, stress, fear, or anxiety do you have after comparing?	1 - 2 - 3 - 4 - 5 A Little...A Lot

Step 4: <u>Think a More Realistic Thought!</u> *Write one reality-tested statement of more realistic expectations or interpretations...*

....

....

Step 1: Breathe out firmly, relaxing your diaphragm. *Practice Release Breathing while you are completing each of the other steps...*

Step 2: What Am I Thinking? *Describe your automatic expectations and interpretations...*

....

....

How much worry, stress, fear, or anxiety do these scary thoughts cause you?	1 - 2 - 3 - 4 - 5 A Little...A Lot

Step 3: How Realistic Is It? *Write down and compare some other possibilities...*

....

....

How realistic was your automatic, scary thought about the situation?	1 - 2 - 3 - 4 - 5 Not Very...Very
How much worry, stress, fear, or anxiety do you have after comparing?	1 - 2 - 3 - 4 - 5 A Little...A Lot

Step 4: Think a More Realistic Thought! *Write one reality-tested statement of more realistic expectations or interpretations...*

....

....

Step 1:   Breathe out firmly, relaxing your diaphragm.   *Practice Release Breathing while you are completing each of the other steps...*

Step 2:   What Am I Thinking?   *Describe your automatic expectations and interpretations...*

....

....

How much worry, stress, fear, or anxiety do
these scary thoughts cause you?

1 - 2 - 3 - 4 - 5
A Little...A Lot

Step 3:   How Realistic Is It?   *Write down and compare some other possibilities...*

....

....

How realistic was your automatic, scary
thought about the situation?

1 - 2 - 3 - 4 - 5
Not Very...Very

How much worry, stress, fear, or
anxiety do you have after comparing?

1 - 2 - 3 - 4 - 5
A Little...A Lot

Step 4:   Think a More Realistic Thought!   *Write one reality-tested statement of more realistic expectations or interpretations...*

....

....

Step 1: Breathe out firmly, relaxing your diaphragm. *Practice Release Breathing while you are completing each of the other steps...*

Step 2: What Am I Thinking? *Describe your automatic expectations and interpretations...*

....

....

How much worry, stress, fear, or anxiety do these scary thoughts cause you?   1 - 2 - 3 - 4 - 5   A Little...A Lot

Step 3: How Realistic Is It? *Write down and compare some other possibilities...*

....

....

How realistic was your automatic, scary thought about the situation?   1 - 2 - 3 - 4 - 5   Not Very...Very

How much worry, stress, fear, or anxiety do you have after comparing?   1 - 2 - 3 - 4 - 5   A Little...A Lot

Step 4: Think a More Realistic Thought! *Write one reality-tested statement of more realistic expectations or interpretations...*

....

....

Chapter 12

SET YOUR SIGHTS ON RELIEF

INTRODUCTION

Our life-style is what we do and where we do it. Our life-style can have a lot of stressful things in it. They are called stressors. If stressors get bad enough, we can build up tension that can turn into worry, stress, fear, and anxiety.

The amount of stress we feel often has to do with the sense that the stressors are everywhere or coming from all sides. This can make us feel overwhelmed or disorganized. We want to make it better, but it's hard to know where to start.

There is a way to sort this out and get control. The key idea is to pick one stressor and make it the target of our efforts. First, we clearly define our stressors by classifying them in two ways. Through this process, we identify Target Stressors. Next, we plan new ways of dealing with the stressors we have targeted for change.

Feeling overwhelmed by stressors in your life can cause worry, stress, fear, and anxiety. But, if you target your stressors and plan new actions, you will increase your sense of Personal Control, release tension, and develop a positive attitude toward yourself, others, and life in general.

GOALS

1. Learn to identify your Target Stressors by classifying

    a. the type of stressor that bothers you, and

    b. the areas of your life-style where that stressor bothers you.

2. Learn to develop plans through which you will act differently as you deal with your Target Stressors.

REMEMBER

Don't miss another opportunity to build peace of mind. When worry, stress, fear, or anxiety strike this week...Conquer Your Fears! Use...

*

FIRST AID for...WORRY, STRESS, FEAR, AND ANXIETY

Step 1:   Always...Breathe Out!

Step 2:   What's Stressing Me?

Step 3:   Where's It Coming From?

Step 4:   Schedule Planning Time!

* Permission is given to reproduce the First Aid Steps for your personal use.

STEP 1

Our overall life-style can cause tension to build within us. We recommend Release Breathing for temporarily reducing the tension caused by life-style stress.

Release Breathing enables us to let go of the tension we build up when our life-style overloads us or pulls us in too many directions. And, we can practice Release Breathing any time we feel overwhelmed, as often as we wish, regardless of what we are doing at the time.

When life has too many negative stressors, we develop a negative attitude; it is negative about ourselves because we feel helpless to cope with it all and negative about the situation because it demands too much of us.

This lesson teaches you how to identify what is stressing you, identify the source of that stress, and plan life-style changes that will reduce stress over time.

The tension of an overwhelming life-style causes our breathing to become restricted and shallow. The Release Breathing technique is an excellent way to release this tension and clear your mind for effective problem solving.

Release Breathing sends an important "let go" message to the brain. It involves 3 steps:

1. breathe in deeply, using *medium force*. Using your diaphragm,

2. breathe out through your mouth, using *medium strong force*. Let your shoulders, chest, and diaphragm sag or fall downward.

    Think "I can lighten the load" as you release air from your lungs. Let go of the air and all the tension in your body, and

3. pause for a moment at the end of the breath. Feel the release of tension.

    Think of having "let go" of both the tightness in your chest and feeling helpless.

STEP 2

<u>WHAT'S STRESSING ME?</u>

In order to target a stressor for change effectively, you need to define it clearly in your mind.

One part of clearly defining a stressor is describing it in your own words and classifying it by type. Describing the stressor in your own words makes it feel concrete rather than vague. Classifying it by type makes it feel manageable rather than overwhelming.

There are 8 general types of stressors. Often a specific stressor can be classified as more than one type. The types are:

- How someone treats you.

- How someone acts around you.

- How someone reacts to you.

- What someone does when s/he is not around you.

- Things you have to get done.

- Obstacles and complications.

- Interruptions and distractions.

- Losses.

EXERCISE

A

CLASSIFYING STRESSORS BY TYPE

<u>DIRECTIONS:</u> For Exercise A, Part 1... Several common stressors are described below. Even if you have never had to face one of the sample stressors, place a check mark beside the stressor type(s) that best classifies each stressor. Then circle one number to show how much that stressor bothers you.

1.   **Someone expects you to do too much for them.**
  ☐   How someone treats you.
  ☐   How someone acts around you.
  ☐   How someone reacts to you.
  ☐   What someone does when s/he is not around you.
  ☐   Things you have to get done.
  ☐   Obstacles and complications.
  ☐   Interruptions and distractions.
  ☐   Losses.
How much does this stressor   1 - 2 - 3 - 4 - 5
bother you?   A Little....A Lot

2.   **Someone acts disappointed by what you do.**
  ☐   How someone treats you.
  ☐   How someone acts around you.
  ☐   How someone reacts to you.
  ☐   What someone does when s/he is not around you.
  ☐   Things you have to get done.
  ☐   Obstacles and complications.
  ☐   Interruptions and distractions.
  ☐   Losses.
How much does this stressor   1 - 2 - 3 - 4 - 5
bother you?   A Little....A Lot

3. **There's too much work to do.**
   - ☐ How someone treats you.
   - ☐ How someone acts around you.
   - ☐ How someone reacts to you.
   - ☐ What someone does when s/he is not around you.
   - ☐ Things you have to get done.
   - ☐ Obstacles and complications.
   - ☐ Interruptions and distractions.
   - ☐ Losses.

   How much does this stressor   1 - 2 - 3 - 4 - 5
   bother you?   A Little....A Lot

4. **Someone is slow or inefficient.**
   - ☐ How someone treats you.
   - ☐ How someone acts around you.
   - ☐ How someone reacts to you.
   - ☐ What someone does when s/he is not around you.
   - ☐ Things you have to get done.
   - ☐ Obstacles and complications.
   - ☐ Interruptions and distractions.
   - ☐ Losses.

   How much does this stressor   1 - 2 - 3 - 4 - 5
   bother you?   A Little....A Lot

5. **The phone keeps ringing.**
   - ☐ How someone treats you.
   - ☐ How someone acts around you.
   - ☐ How someone reacts to you.
   - ☐ What someone does when s/he is not around you.
   - ☐ Things you have to get done.
   - ☐ Obstacles and complications.
   - ☐ Interruptions and distractions.
   - ☐ Losses.

   How much does this stressor   1 - 2 - 3 - 4 - 5
   bother you?   A Little....A Lot

6. **Someone argues with you too much.**
   - ☐ How someone treats you.
   - ☐ How someone acts around you.
   - ☐ How someone reacts to you.
   - ☐ What someone does when s/he is not around you.
   - ☐ Things you have to get done.
   - ☐ Obstacles and complications.
   - ☐ Interruptions and distractions.
   - ☐ Losses.

   How much does this stressor   1 - 2 - 3 - 4 - 5
   bother you?   A Little....A Lot

7. **Someone criticizes you and/or finds fault with you too much.**
   - ☐ How someone treats you.
   - ☐ How someone acts around you.
   - ☐ How someone reacts to you.
   - ☐ What someone does when s/he is not around you.
   - ☐ Things you have to get done.
   - ☐ Obstacles and complications.
   - ☐ Interruptions and distractions.
   - ☐ Losses.

   How much does this stressor   1 - 2 - 3 - 4 - 5
   bother you?   A Little....A Lot

8. **Someone demands too much of you.**
   - ☐ How someone treats you.
   - ☐ How someone acts around you.
   - ☐ How someone reacts to you.
   - ☐ What someone does when s/he is not around you.
   - ☐ Things you have to get done.
   - ☐ Obstacles and complications.
   - ☐ Interruptions and distractions.
   - ☐ Losses.

   How much does this stressor   1 - 2 - 3 - 4 - 5
   bother you?   A Little....A Lot

9. **You can't make enough money.**
    ☐   How someone treats you.
    ☐   How someone acts around you.
    ☐   How someone reacts to you.
    ☐   What someone does when s/he is not around you.
    ☐   Things you have to get done.
    ☐   Obstacles and complications.
    ☐   Interruptions and distractions.
    ☐   Losses.
    How much does this stressor   1 - 2 - 3 - 4 - 5
    bother you?   A Little....A Lot

10. **A legal problem goes on and on.**
    ☐   How someone treats you.
    ☐   How someone acts around you.
    ☐   How someone reacts to you.
    ☐   What someone does when s/he is not around you.
    ☐   Things you have to get done.
    ☐   Obstacles and complications.
    ☐   Interruptions and distractions.
    ☐   Losses.
    How much does this stressor   1 - 2 - 3 - 4 - 5
    bother you?   A Little....A Lot

11. **Someone does self-destructive things.**
    ☐   How someone treats you.
    ☐   How someone acts around you.
    ☐   How someone reacts to you.
    ☐   What someone does when s/he is not around you.
    ☐   Things you have to get done.
    ☐   Obstacles and complications.
    ☐   Interruptions and distractions.
    ☐   Losses.
    How much does this stressor   1 - 2 - 3 - 4 - 5
    bother you?   A Little....A Lot

12. **Someone does stupid things.**
   - ☐ How someone treats you.
   - ☐ How someone acts around you.
   - ☐ How someone reacts to you.
   - ☐ What someone does when s/he is not around you.
   - ☐ Things you have to get done.
   - ☐ Obstacles and complications.
   - ☐ Interruptions and distractions.
   - ☐ Losses.

   How much does this stressor
   bother you?

   1 - 2 - 3 - 4 - 5
   A Little....A Lot

13. **Things you have need maintenance and repair.**
   - ☐ How someone treats you.
   - ☐ How someone acts around you.
   - ☐ How someone reacts to you.
   - ☐ What someone does when s/he is not around you.
   - ☐ Things you have to get done.
   - ☐ Obstacles and complications.
   - ☐ Interruptions and distractions.
   - ☐ Losses.

   How much does this stressor
   bother you?

   1 - 2 - 3 - 4 - 5
   A Little....A Lot

14. **You can't get things organized.**
   - ☐ How someone treats you.
   - ☐ How someone acts around you.
   - ☐ How someone reacts to you.
   - ☐ What someone does when s/he is not around you.
   - ☐ Things you have to get done.
   - ☐ Obstacles and complications.
   - ☐ Interruptions and distractions.
   - ☐ Losses.

   How much does this stressor
   bother you?

   1 - 2 - 3 - 4 - 5
   A Little....A Lot

15. **Someone is ill or injured.**
    - ☐ How someone treats you.
    - ☐ How someone acts around you.
    - ☐ How someone reacts to you.
    - ☐ What someone does when s/he is not around you.
    - ☐ Things you have to get done.
    - ☐ Obstacles and complications.
    - ☐ Interruptions and distractions.
    - ☐ Losses.

    How much does this stressor   1 - 2 - 3 - 4 - 5
    bother you?   A Little....A Lot

16. **Someone has problems.**
    - ☐ How someone treats you.
    - ☐ How someone acts around you.
    - ☐ How someone reacts to you.
    - ☐ What someone does when s/he is not around you.
    - ☐ Things you have to get done.
    - ☐ Obstacles and complications.
    - ☐ Interruptions and distractions.
    - ☐ Losses.

    How much does this stressor   1 - 2 - 3 - 4 - 5
    bother you?   A Little....A Lot

17. **Someone gets upset by what you do.**
    - ☐ How someone treats you.
    - ☐ How someone acts around you.
    - ☐ How someone reacts to you.
    - ☐ What someone does when s/he is not around you.
    - ☐ Things you have to get done.
    - ☐ Obstacles and complications.
    - ☐ Interruptions and distractions.
    - ☐ Losses.

    How much does this stressor   1 - 2 - 3 - 4 - 5
    bother you?   A Little....A Lot

18. **You try to help someone out, but nothing works.**
    - ☐ How someone treats you.
    - ☐ How someone acts around you.
    - ☐ How someone reacts to you.
    - ☐ What someone does when s/he is not around you.
    - ☐ Things you have to get done.
    - ☐ Obstacles and complications.
    - ☐ Interruptions and distractions.
    - ☐ Losses.

    How much does this stressor   1 - 2 - 3 - 4 - 5
    bother you?   A Little....A Lot

19. **Someone worries about what you do.**
    - ☐ How someone treats you.
    - ☐ How someone acts around you.
    - ☐ How someone reacts to you.
    - ☐ What someone does when s/he is not around you.
    - ☐ Things you have to get done.
    - ☐ Obstacles and complications.
    - ☐ Interruptions and distractions.
    - ☐ Losses.

    How much does this stressor   1 - 2 - 3 - 4 - 5
    bother you?   A Little....A Lot

20. **Someone acts rude to other people.**
    - ☐ How someone treats you.
    - ☐ How someone acts around you.
    - ☐ How someone reacts to you.
    - ☐ What someone does when s/he is not around you.
    - ☐ Things you have to get done.
    - ☐ Obstacles and complications.
    - ☐ Interruptions and distractions.
    - ☐ Losses.

    How much does this stressor   1 - 2 - 3 - 4 - 5
    bother you?   A Little....A Lot

DIRECTIONS: For Exercise A, Part 2... Use the space provided to add descriptions of some of your own stressors. Place a check mark beside the stressor type that best classifies each stressor. Then circle one number to show how much that stressor bothers you.

Other stressors in your life:..

....

- ☐ How someone treats you.
- ☐ How someone acts around you.
- ☐ How someone reacts to you.
- ☐ What someone does when s/he is not around you.
- ☐ Things you have to get done.
- ☐ Obstacles and complications.
- ☐ Interruptions and distractions.
- ☐ Losses.

How much does this stressor   1 - 2 - 3 - 4 - 5
bother you?   A Little....A Lot

Other stressors in your life:..

....

- ☐ How someone treats you.
- ☐ How someone acts around you.
- ☐ How someone reacts to you.
- ☐ What someone does when s/he is not around you.
- ☐ Things you have to get done.
- ☐ Obstacles and complications.
- ☐ Interruptions and distractions.
- ☐ Losses.

How much does this stressor   1 - 2 - 3 - 4 - 5
bother you?   A Little....A Lot

STEP 3

<u>WHERE'S IT COMING FROM?</u>

The second part of clearly defining a stressor is classifying it in terms of the lifestyle area in which it bothers you. There are 7 life-style areas where stressors can occur.

- ■   Job, career, or work life.

- ■   Home life, marriage, or family.

- ■   Social life, close and casual friends.

- ■   Financial and legal affairs.

- ■   Personal health--mental and physical.

- ■   Recreation life and leisure time.

- ■   Spiritual life, religious doctrine, religious community.

Some people have no stressors in several areas. Others have stressors in several or all the life-style areas. Often a single stressor can bother us in more than one life-style area. Finally, for some people the absence of activity in a life-style area, like recreation or spirituality, is a stressor.

EXERCISE

B

CLASSIFY STRESSORS BY LIFE-STYLE AREA

Exercise B will help you classify stressors according to the areas of your life-style in which they bother you.

DIRECTIONS: For Exercise B... Refer to Exercise A and the sample stressors and "Other" stressors you added.

♦ Select the 3 stressors that are most relevant for you. Describe them in the space provided.

♦ Make a check mark beside your life-style areas in which that stressor bothers you.

1. Describe the stressor:...
....

☐ Job, career, or work life.
☐ Home life, marriage, or family.
☐ Social life, close and casual friends.
☐ Financial and legal affairs.
☐ Personal health--mental and physical.
☐ Recreation life and leisure time.
☐ Spiritual life, religious doctrine, religious community.

2.   Describe the stressor:...

....
        ☐   Job, career, or work life.
        ☐   Home life, marriage, or family.
        ☐   Social life, close and casual friends.
        ☐   Financial and legal affairs.
        ☐   Personal health--mental and physical.
        ☐   Recreation life and leisure time.
        ☐   Spiritual life, religious doctrine, religious community.

3.   Describe the stressor:...

....
        ☐   Job, career, or work life.
        ☐   Home life, marriage, or family.
        ☐   Social life, close and casual friends.
        ☐   Financial and legal affairs.
        ☐   Personal health--mental and physical.
        ☐   Recreation life and leisure time.
        ☐   Spiritual life, religious doctrine, religious community.

STEP 4

SCHEDULE PLANNING TIME!

You have learned how to target stressors for change by being clear about their description, type, and life-style area. The next step is planning different behavior in response to that stressor.

The keys to learning new behaviors are:

 Scheduling time to plan new behavior. Scheduling planning time is First Aid Step #4 to reduce worry, stress, fear, and anxiety. You benefit from committing yourself to a specific time when you will plan new responses to your stressors.

 Planning new behavior. When that time arrives, you will complete a Stress Reduction Planner that defines the new behavior you will practice and when you will practice it.

 Practicing new behavior. The only way to learn to behave differently is through practice. The more you practice the sooner you will enjoy a reduction of stress.

EXERCISE

C

Exercise C will help you commit yourself to a specific time to plan new responses to your stressors.

<u>DIRECTIONS:</u> For Exercise C, Part 1... Three sets of sample planning times are listed below. Place a check mark beside the most specific time in each set.

Set # 1:   Select the most specific time.

☐   Later.
☐   Later today.
☐   As soon as I get home.

Set # 2:   Select the most specific time.

☐   Saturday morning over coffee.
☐   This weekend.
☐   Saturday at 8:00 a.m.

Set # 3:   Select the most specific time.

☐   When I can get a spare minute at work.
☐   During my lunch break tomorrow.
☐   During lunch break at work.

COMMENTS ON THE EXERCISE

C1, Set #1.   People usually select: "As soon as I get home."

C1, Set #2.   People usually select: "Saturday at 8:00 a.m." Sunday morning coffee time could vary.

C1, Set #3.   People usually select: "During my lunch break tomorrow." This states a time and a day.

<u>DIRECTIONS:</u> For Exercise C, Part 2... Identify a specific planning time you can schedule during the next week. During that time you will complete a Stress Reduction Planner that defines what new behavior you will practice and when you will practice it.

I will complete a Stress Reduction Planner...

....

COMMENTS ON THE EXERCISE

C2.   For example: I will complete a Stress Reduction Planner *tomorrow evening as soon as dinner is over.*

PRACTICE YOUR WORK SHEETS

<u>DIRECTIONS:</u> The more you study the steps in this lesson, the more effective your new skills will become. Your Work Sheets are designed to help you master these skills. So, read the story below. We will use it as an example to help you learn to use the Work Sheets successfully.

The freeway was backed up as usual with homeward bound commuters. Bill thought it wasn't so bad. At least there wasn't much to do. It gave him a chance to think about the day.

He was relieved that Betty's call wasn't an emergency after all. But he was fed up with his secretary. She was forever distorting messages. Bill never knew what he was up against. Half the time she wouldn't ask what the caller wanted, and the other half she got it wrong.

Bill had been over and over this with her. She didn't get it, no matter how many examples he gave her. He just couldn't take it anymore. Something had to be done.

<u>DIRECTIONS:</u> Practice your homework exercises. Imagine that you are Bill in this situation. Complete the "Practice Target Stressor Work Sheet" on the next page.

NEXT PAGE

PRACTICE TARGET STRESSOR WORK SHEET

Step 1: Breathe out, relaxing your diaphragm. *Practice Release Breathing while you are completing each of the other steps on the Work Sheet.*

Step 2: What's Stressing Me? *Describe the stressor as if you were Bill...*

....

....

What type of stressor is it?
- ☐ How someone treats you.
- ☐ How someone acts around you.
- ☐ How someone reacts to you.
- ☐ What someone does when s/he is not around you.
- ☐ Things you have to get done.
- ☐ Obstacles and complications.
- ☐ Interruptions and distractions.
- ☐ Losses.

How much does this stressor
bother you?

1 - 2 - 3 - 4 - 5
A Little....A Lot

Step 3: Where's It Coming From? *In which area(s) of Bill's life-style does the stressor bother him?*
- ☐ Job, career, or work life.
- ☐ Home life, marriage, or family.
- ☐ Social life, close and casual friends.
- ☐ Financial and legal affairs.
- ☐ Personal health--mental and physical.
- ☐ Recreation life and leisure time.
- ☐ Spiritual life, religious doctrine, religious community.

Step 4: Schedule Planning Time! *Define an appointment time when Bill could complete a Stress Reduction Planner...*

....

<u>Step 1: Breathe out, relaxing your diaphragm.</u> *Practice Release Breathing while you are completing each of the other steps on the Work Sheet.*

<u>Step 2: What's Stressing Me?</u> *Describe the stressor as if you were Bill...*

....*Freeway. Bad secretary*...

....

What type of stressor is it?

- ☐ How someone treats you.
- ■ How someone acts around you.
- ☐ How someone reacts to you.
- ■ What someone does when s/he is not around you.
- ☐ Things you have to get done.
- ■ Obstacles and complications.
- ☐ Interruptions and distractions.
- ☐ Losses.

How much does this stressor   1 - 2 - 3 - <u>4</u> - 5
bother you?   A Little....A Lot

<u>Step 3: Where's It Coming From?</u> *In which area(s) of Bill's life-style does the stressor bother him?*

- ■ Job, career, or work life.
- ☐ Home life, marriage, or family.
- ☐ Social life, close and casual friends.
- ☐ Financial and legal affairs.
- ☐ Personal health--mental and physical.
- ☐ Recreation life and leisure time.
- ☐ Spiritual life, religious doctrine, religious community.

<u>Step 4: Schedule Planning Time!</u> *Define an appointment time when Bill could complete a Stress Reduction Planner...*

....*Tomorrow morning over coffee*...

STEP 5

USING YOUR STRESS REDUCTION PLANNER

The Stress Reduction Planner has been developed to help you plan specific new behaviors that, practiced one at a time, will gradually and systematically reduce your stress.

When your planing time arrives, review your Target Stressor Work Sheets and other notes. Then answer the questions on a Stress Reduction Planner.

EXERCISE

D

USING THE STRESS REDUCTION PLANNER

Planning and doing gives you a sense of Personal Control, releases tension, and builds a positive attitude. Exercise C will help you learn to do this.

DIRECTIONS: For Exercise D...Reflect on the stressors you classified for Exercise B. Select one. Then, complete the "Practice Stress Reduction Planner."

Planning Step #1: Assessment. *Briefly describe your Target Stressor in specific terms...*

....

....

Which single type of stressor is it?	Life-style area where you will reduce stress?
☐ How someone treats you.	☐ Job, career, or work life.
☐ How someone acts around you.	☐ Home life, marriage, or family.
☐ How someone reacts to you.	☐ Social life, close and casual friends.
☐ What someone does when s/he is not around you.	☐ Financial and legal affairs.
☐ Things you have to get done.	☐ Personal health--mental and physical.
☐ Obstacles and complications.	☐ Recreation life and leisure time.
☐ Interruptions and distractions.	☐ Spiritual life, religion, religious community.
☐ Losses.	

Planning Step #2: Options: *Check off or list other options for dealing with the Target Stressor...*

☐ Limiting what you try to control.	☐ Reducing internal conflict.
☐ Limiting Perfection-seeking.	☐ Improving relationship patterns.
☐ Limiting People-pleasing.	☐ Asserting yourself.
☐ Limiting Being Strong.	☐ Releasing tension.
☐ Understanding and properly using feelings.	☐ Changing thoughts that cause stress.

Other behaviors you can use to react differently to stressors:

....

....

Planning Step # 3: Describe a Strategy. *Select one option from the list above. Restate it below and then list specific thoughts and actions you will practice...*

....

....

Planning Step #1: Assessment. *Briefly describe your Target Stressor in specific terms...*

....

....

Which single type of stressor is it? | Life-style area where you will reduce stress?

☐ How someone treats you.
☐ How someone acts around you.
☐ How someone reacts to you.
■ What someone does when s/he is not around you.
☐ Things you have to get done.
☐ Obstacles and complications.
☐ Interruptions and distractions.
☐ Losses.

■ Job, career, or work life.
☐ Home life, marriage, or family.
☐ Social life, close and casual friends.
☐ Financial and legal affairs.
☐ Personal health--mental and physical.
☐ Recreation life and leisure time.
☐ Spiritual life, religion, religious community.

Planning Step #2: Options: *Check off or list other options for dealing with the Target Stressor...*

☐ Limiting what you try to control.
☐ Limiting Perfection-seeking.
■ Limiting People-pleasing.
☐ Limiting Being Strong.
■ Understanding and properly using feelings.

■ Reducing internal conflict.
■ Improving relationship patterns.
■ Asserting yourself.
☐ Releasing tension.
☐ Changing thoughts that cause stress.

Other behaviors you can use to react differently to stressors:

....

....

Planning Step # 3: Describe a Strategy. *Select one option from the list above. Restate it below and then list specific thoughts and actions you will practice...*

....Fire her Monday...

....

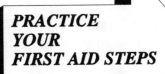

PRACTICE YOUR FIRST AID STEPS

<u>DIRECTIONS:</u> The more you practice your First Aid Steps, the better you will feel. Practice your First Aid Steps now. Imagine you are in a situation used in this lesson, or think about your life in general.

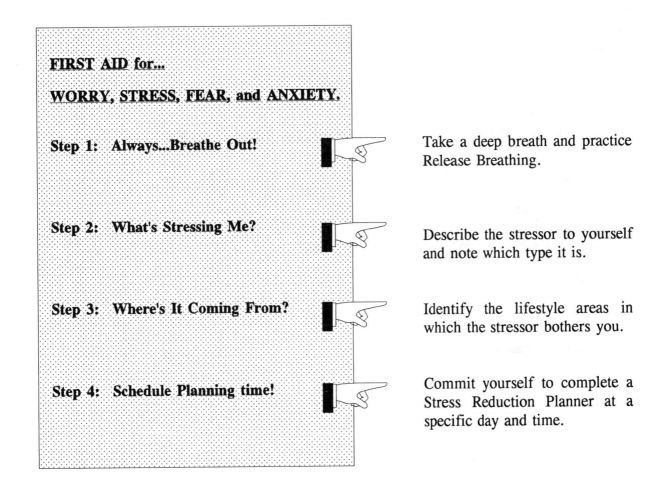

<u>**FIRST AID for...**</u>

<u>**WORRY**</u>, <u>**STRESS**</u>, <u>**FEAR**</u>, **and** <u>**ANXIETY.**</u>

Step 1: Always...Breathe Out! — Take a deep breath and practice Release Breathing.

Step 2: What's Stressing Me? — Describe the stressor to yourself and note which type it is.

Step 3: Where's It Coming From? — Identify the lifestyle areas in which the stressor bothers you.

Step 4: Schedule Planning time! — Commit yourself to complete a Stress Reduction Planner at a specific day and time.

HOMEWORK

THE METHODS...

Work Sheets. This week complete 10 Target Stressors Work Sheets. Do the Work Sheets for situations in which you worry or feel stress, fear, or anxiety. Complete the Work Sheets at the time of these events or very soon thereafter.

Stress Reduction Planners. Complete two Stress Reduction Planners. Do them a few days apart.

First Aid Steps. Practice your First Aid Steps as often as possible, even when you are not really worrying or feeling threatened.

*

FIRST AID for...WORRY, STRESS, FEAR, AND ANXIETY

Step 1:   **Always...Breathe Out!**

Step 2:   **What's Stressing Me?**

Step 3:   **Where's It Coming From?**

Step 4:   **Schedule Planning Time!**

Use your Clip-outs: Cut out the First Aid Steps reminders. Place them in spots where you will see them and remember to practice. Give some to a friend, and tell him or her how to use them.

Teach Others. Share the lesson with others. Teach them how to help themselves using the same skills you are learning.

* Permission is given to reproduce the First Aid Steps for your personal use.

TARGET STRESSOR WORK SHEET # 1

Step 1: Breathe out, relaxing your diaphragm. *Practice Release Breathing while you are completing each of the other steps on the Work Sheet.*

Step 2: What's Stressing Me? *Describe the stressor...*

....

....

What type of stressor is it?
- ☐   How someone treats you.
- ☐   How someone acts around you.
- ☐   How someone reacts to you.
- ☐   What someone does when s/he is not around you.
- ☐   Things you have to get done.
- ☐   Obstacles and complications.
- ☐   Interruptions and distractions.
- ☐   Losses.

How much does this stressor
bother you?

1 - 2 - 3 - 4 - 5
A Little....A Lot

Step 3: Where's It Coming From? *In which area(s) of your life-style does the stressor bother you?*
- ☐   Job, career, or work life.
- ☐   Home life, marriage, or family.
- ☐   Social life, close and casual friends.
- ☐   Financial and legal affairs.
- ☐   Personal health--mental and physical.
- ☐   Recreation life and leisure time.
- ☐   Spiritual life, religious doctrine, religious community.

Step 4: Schedule Planning Time! *Define an appointment time when you will complete a Stress Reduction Planner...*

....

Step 1: Breathe out, relaxing your diaphragm. *Practice Release Breathing while you are completing each of the other steps on the Work Sheet.*

Step 2: What's Stressing Me? *Describe the stressor...*

....

....

What type of stressor is it?
- ☐ How someone treats you.
- ☐ How someone acts around you.
- ☐ How someone reacts to you.
- ☐ What someone does when s/he is not around you.
- ☐ Things you have to get done.
- ☐ Obstacles and complications.
- ☐ Interruptions and distractions.
- ☐ Losses.

How much does this stressor bother you?

1 - 2 - 3 - 4 - 5
A Little....A Lot

Step 3: Where's It Coming From? *In which area(s) of your life-style does the stressor bother you?*
- ☐ Job, career, or work life.
- ☐ Home life, marriage, or family.
- ☐ Social life, close and casual friends.
- ☐ Financial and legal affairs.
- ☐ Personal health--mental and physical.
- ☐ Recreation life and leisure time.
- ☐ Spiritual life, religious doctrine, religious community.

Step 4: Schedule Planning Time! *Define an appointment time when you will complete a Stress Reduction Planner...*

....

TARGET STRESSOR WORK SHEET # 3

<u>Step 1: Breathe out, relaxing your diaphragm.</u> *Practice Release Breathing while you are completing each of the other steps on the Work Sheet.*

<u>Step 2: What's Stressing Me?</u> *Describe the stressor...*

....

....

What type of stressor is it?
- ☐ How someone treats you.
- ☐ How someone acts around you.
- ☐ How someone reacts to you.
- ☐ What someone does when s/he is not around you.
- ☐ Things you have to get done.
- ☐ Obstacles and complications.
- ☐ Interruptions and distractions.
- ☐ Losses.

How much does this stressor bother you?

1 - 2 - 3 - 4 - 5
A Little....A Lot

<u>Step 3: Where's It Coming From?</u> *In which area(s) of your life-style does the stressor bother you?*
- ☐ Job, career, or work life.
- ☐ Home life, marriage, or family.
- ☐ Social life, close and casual friends.
- ☐ Financial and legal affairs.
- ☐ Personal health--mental and physical.
- ☐ Recreation life and leisure time.
- ☐ Spiritual life, religious doctrine, religious community.

<u>Step 4: Schedule Planning Time!</u> *Define an appointment time when you will complete a Stress Reduction Planner...*

....

Step 1: Breathe out, relaxing your diaphragm. *Practice Release Breathing while you are completing each of the other steps on the Work Sheet.*

Step 2: What's Stressing Me? *Describe the stressor...*

....

....

What type of stressor is it?
- ☐ How someone treats you.
- ☐ How someone acts around you.
- ☐ How someone reacts to you.
- ☐ What someone does when s/he is not around you.
- ☐ Things you have to get done.
- ☐ Obstacles and complications.
- ☐ Interruptions and distractions.
- ☐ Losses.

How much does this stressor   1 - 2 - 3 - 4 - 5
bother you?   A Little....A Lot

Step 3: Where's It Coming From? *In which area(s) of your life-style does the stressor bother you?*
- ☐ Job, career, or work life.
- ☐ Home life, marriage, or family.
- ☐ Social life, close and casual friends.
- ☐ Financial and legal affairs.
- ☐ Personal health--mental and physical.
- ☐ Recreation life and leisure time.
- ☐ Spiritual life, religious doctrine, religious community.

Step 4: Schedule Planning Time! *Define an appointment time when you will complete a Stress Reduction Planner...*

....

Step 1: Breathe out, relaxing your diaphragm. *Practice Release Breathing while you are completing each of the other steps on the Work Sheet.*

Step 2: What's Stressing Me? *Describe the stressor...*

....

....

What type of stressor is it?
- ☐   How someone treats you.
- ☐   How someone acts around you.
- ☐   How someone reacts to you.
- ☐   What someone does when s/he is not around you.
- ☐   Things you have to get done.
- ☐   Obstacles and complications.
- ☐   Interruptions and distractions.
- ☐   Losses.

How much does this stressor
bother you?

1 - 2 - 3 - 4 - 5
A Little....A Lot

Step 3: Where's It Coming From? *In which area(s) of your life-style does the stressor bother you?*
- ☐   Job, career, or work life.
- ☐   Home life, marriage, or family.
- ☐   Social life, close and casual friends.
- ☐   Financial and legal affairs.
- ☐   Personal health--mental and physical.
- ☐   Recreation life and leisure time.
- ☐   Spiritual life, religious doctrine, religious community.

Step 4: Schedule Planning Time! *Define an appointment time when you will complete a Stress Reduction Planner...*

....

Step 1: Breathe out, relaxing your diaphragm. *Practice Release Breathing while you are completing each of the other steps on the Work Sheet.*

Step 2: What's Stressing Me? *Describe the stressor...*

....

....

What type of stressor is it?

- ☐ How someone treats you.
- ☐ How someone acts around you.
- ☐ How someone reacts to you.
- ☐ What someone does when s/he is not around you.
- ☐ Things you have to get done.
- ☐ Obstacles and complications.
- ☐ Interruptions and distractions.
- ☐ Losses.

How much does this stressor bother you?

1 - 2 - 3 - 4 - 5
A Little....A Lot

Step 3: Where's It Coming From? *In which area(s) of your life-style does the stressor bother you?*

- ☐ Job, career, or work life.
- ☐ Home life, marriage, or family.
- ☐ Social life, close and casual friends.
- ☐ Financial and legal affairs.
- ☐ Personal health--mental and physical.
- ☐ Recreation life and leisure time.
- ☐ Spiritual life, religious doctrine, religious community.

Step 4: Schedule Planning Time! *Define an appointment time when you will complete a Stress Reduction Planner...*

....

<u>Step 1:</u> <u>Breathe out, relaxing your diaphragm.</u> *Practice Release Breathing while you are completing each of the other steps on the Work Sheet.*

<u>Step 2:</u> <u>What's Stressing Me?</u> *Describe the stressor...*

....

....

What type of stressor is it?
- ☐ How someone treats you.
- ☐ How someone acts around you.
- ☐ How someone reacts to you.
- ☐ What someone does when s/he is not around you.
- ☐ Things you have to get done.
- ☐ Obstacles and complications.
- ☐ Interruptions and distractions.
- ☐ Losses.

How much does this stressor   1 - 2 - 3 - 4 - 5
bother you?   A Little....A Lot

<u>Step 3:</u> <u>Where's It Coming From?</u> *In which area(s) of your life-style does the stressor bother you?*
- ☐ Job, career, or work life.
- ☐ Home life, marriage, or family.
- ☐ Social life, close and casual friends.
- ☐ Financial and legal affairs.
- ☐ Personal health--mental and physical.
- ☐ Recreation life and leisure time.
- ☐ Spiritual life, religious doctrine, religious community.

<u>Step 4:</u> <u>Schedule Planning Time!</u> *Define an appointment time when you will complete a Stress Reduction Planner...*

....

Step 1: Breathe out, relaxing your diaphragm. *Practice Release Breathing while you are completing each of the other steps on the Work Sheet.*

Step 2: What's Stressing Me? *Describe the stressor...*

....

....

What type of stressor is it?
- ☐ How someone treats you.
- ☐ How someone acts around you.
- ☐ How someone reacts to you.
- ☐ What someone does when s/he is not around you.
- ☐ Things you have to get done.
- ☐ Obstacles and complications.
- ☐ Interruptions and distractions.
- ☐ Losses.

How much does this stressor   1 - 2 - 3 - 4 - 5
bother you?   A Little....A Lot

Step 3: Where's It Coming From? *In which area(s) of your life-style does the stressor bother you?*
- ☐ Job, career, or work life.
- ☐ Home life, marriage, or family.
- ☐ Social life, close and casual friends.
- ☐ Financial and legal affairs.
- ☐ Personal health--mental and physical.
- ☐ Recreation life and leisure time.
- ☐ Spiritual life, religious doctrine, religious community.

Step 4: Schedule Planning Time! *Define an appointment time when you will complete a Stress Reduction Planner...*

....

<u>Step 1:</u> <u>Breathe out, relaxing your diaphragm.</u> *Practice Release Breathing while you are completing each of the other steps on the Work Sheet.*

<u>Step 2:</u> <u>What's Stressing Me?</u> *Describe the stressor...*

....

....

What type of stressor is it?
- ☐ How someone treats you.
- ☐ How someone acts around you.
- ☐ How someone reacts to you.
- ☐ What someone does when s/he is not around you.
- ☐ Things you have to get done.
- ☐ Obstacles and complications.
- ☐ Interruptions and distractions.
- ☐ Losses.

How much does this stressor   1 - 2 - 3 - 4 - 5
bother you?   A Little....A Lot

<u>Step 3:</u> <u>Where's It Coming From?</u> *In which area(s) of your life-style does the stressor bother you?*
- ☐ Job, career, or work life.
- ☐ Home life, marriage, or family.
- ☐ Social life, close and casual friends.
- ☐ Financial and legal affairs.
- ☐ Personal health--mental and physical.
- ☐ Recreation life and leisure time.
- ☐ Spiritual life, religious doctrine, religious community.

<u>Step 4:</u> <u>Schedule Planning Time!</u> *Define an appointment time when you will complete a Stress Reduction Planner...*

....

Step 1: Breathe out, relaxing your diaphragm. *Practice Release Breathing while you are completing each of the other steps on the Work Sheet.*

Step 2: What's Stressing Me? *Describe the stressor...*

....

....

What type of stressor is it?
- ☐ How someone treats you.
- ☐ How someone acts around you.
- ☐ How someone reacts to you.
- ☐ What someone does when s/he is not around you.
- ☐ Things you have to get done.
- ☐ Obstacles and complications.
- ☐ Interruptions and distractions.
- ☐ Losses.

How much does this stressor
bother you?

1 - 2 - 3 - 4 - 5
A Little....A Lot

Step 3: Where's It Coming From? *In which area(s) of your life-style does the stressor bother you?*
- ☐ Job, career, or work life.
- ☐ Home life, marriage, or family.
- ☐ Social life, close and casual friends.
- ☐ Financial and legal affairs.
- ☐ Personal health--mental and physical.
- ☐ Recreation life and leisure time.
- ☐ Spiritual life, religious doctrine, religious community.

Step 4: Schedule Planning Time! *Define an appointment time when you will complete a Stress Reduction Planner...*

....

Planning Step #1: Assessment. *Briefly describe your Target Stressor in specific terms...*

....

....

Which single type of stressor is it?

- ☐ How someone treats you.
- ☐ How someone acts around you.
- ☐ How someone reacts to you.
- ☐ What someone does when s/he is not around you.
- ☐ Things you have to get done.
- ☐ Obstacles and complications.
- ☐ Interruptions and distractions.
- ☐ Losses.

Life-style area where you will reduce stress?

- ☐ Job, career, or work life.
- ☐ Home life, marriage, or family.
- ☐ Social life, close and casual friends.
- ☐ Financial and legal affairs.
- ☐ Personal health--mental and physical.
- ☐ Recreation life and leisure time.
- ☐ Spiritual life, religion, religious community.

Planning Step #2: Options: *Check off or list other options for dealing with the Target Stressor...*

- ☐ Limiting what you try to control.
- ☐ Limiting Perfection-seeking.
- ☐ Limiting People-pleasing.
- ☐ Limiting Being Strong.
- ☐ Understanding and properly using feelings.

- ☐ Reducing internal conflict.
- ☐ Improving relationship patterns.
- ☐ Asserting yourself.
- ☐ Releasing tension.
- ☐ Changing thoughts that cause stress.

Other behaviors you can use to react differently to stressors:

....

....

Planning Step # 3: Describe a Strategy. *Select one option from the list above. Restate it below and then list specific thoughts and actions you will practice...*

....

....

Planning Step #1:   Assessment. *Briefly describe your Target Stressor in specific terms...*

....

....

Which single type of stressor is it?	Life-style area where you will reduce stress?
☐ How someone treats you.	☐ Job, career, or work life.
☐ How someone acts around you.	☐ Home life, marriage, or family.
☐ How someone reacts to you.	☐ Social life, close and casual friends.
☐ What someone does when s/he is not around you.	☐ Financial and legal affairs.
☐ Things you have to get done.	☐ Personal health--mental and physical.
☐ Obstacles and complications.	☐ Recreation life and leisure time.
☐ Interruptions and distractions.	☐ Spiritual life, religion, religious community.
☐ Losses.	

Planning Step #2:   Options: *Check off or list other options for dealing with the Target Stressor...*

☐ Limiting what you try to control.	☐ Reducing internal conflict.
☐ Limiting Perfection-seeking.	☐ Improving relationship patterns.
☐ Limiting People-pleasing.	☐ Asserting yourself.
☐ Limiting Being Strong.	☐ Releasing tension.
☐ Understanding and properly using feelings.	☐ Changing thoughts that cause stress.

Other behaviors you can use to react differently to stressors:

....

....

Planning Step # 3: Describe a Strategy. *Select one option from the list above. Restate it below and then list specific thoughts and actions you will practice...*

....

....

Chapter 13

RELEASING TENSION

<u>INTRODUCTION</u>

Most of us experience stress as tension. That tension can take three forms.

Sometimes we notice muscle tension. This can take forms like stiff or sore muscles, restricted breathing, knots in the stomach, or headaches.

Other times we experience mental tension. This can take forms like having a lot on our mind, confusion and indecision, or worrying.

Events often trigger feelings that we bottle up as emotional tension. This is especially true for anger and fear.

When tension builds up inside we often become irritable, depressed, or anxious. You can reduce stress by releasing muscular, mental, and emotional tension. Releasing tension can increase your sense of Personal Control and help you develop a positive attitude toward yourself, others, and life in general.

<u>GOALS</u>

1.   Learn basic ways to reduce muscle tension.

2.   Learn basic ways to reduce mental tension.

3.   Learn basic ways to reduce emotional tension.

REMEMBER

Don't miss another opportunity to build your peace of mind. When worry, stress, fear, or anxiety strike this week...Conquer Your Fears! Use...

*

FIRST AID for...WORRY, STRESS, FEAR, AND ANXIETY

Step 1:   Always...Breathe Out!

Step 2:   Relax My Muscles!

Step 3:   Relax My Mind!

Step 4:   Get Angry!

* Permission is given to reproduce the First Aid Steps for your personal use.

STEP 1

This book presents lessons on many sources of tension. In all cases, that tension can be relieved, at least a little bit, for at least short periods of time, through Release Breathing.

Release Breathing is the most fundamental method of letting go of the tension we build in so many ways. And we can practice Release Breathing any time we feel that tension, in a virtually endless series of situations.

This lesson teaches you many different physical ways to reduce tension. Release Breathing is the most basic technique in this group of methods.

Release Breathing sends an important "let go" message to the brain. It involves 3 steps:

1. breathe in deeply, using *medium force*. Using your diaphragm,

2. breathe out through your mouth, using *medium strong force*. Let your shoulders, chest, and diaphragm sag or fall downward.

   Think "I can release tension" as you release air from your lungs. Let go of the air and all the tension in your body, and

3. pause for a moment at the end of the breath. Feel the release of tension.

   Think of having "let go" of the tightness in your body.

RELAX MY MUSCLES!

Our muscles become tight or tense when we are under stress. The tension that builds up in our muscles needs to be released. But it is difficult to just relax our muscles. So, a number of techniques have been developed.

Stretching, a casual stroll, a brisk walk, heavy exercise, self-hypnosis, and progressive muscle relaxation can all help. But these take some time or special circumstances.

There is a quick technique we can use in almost any situation. First, you tense your muscles, and then you relax them. This works because it is more natural to move our muscles by contracting them.

People hold tension in different muscle groups. The most common three groups are:

 Shoulders and Neck. Tension in this area usually involves the muscles in the back of the neck. It can include the muscles that go from the bottom, sides, and back of the neck across the top of the shoulders and the top of the back.

 Chest. Tension in this area usually involves the muscles around the front and back of the rib cage. It may include the diaphragm, causing a restriction of breathing. Sometimes the upper arms are involved.

 Stomach. Tension in this area usually involves the muscles in the upper and lower abdomen and the lower back. It may include the diaphragm, causing a restriction of breathing. Sometimes it spreads down into the groin and inner thighs.

EXERCISE

A

<u>TENSE AND RELAX YOUR MUSCLES</u>

<u>DIRECTIONS:</u> For Exercise A...Practice tensing and relaxing your muscles in each of the three common tension-collecting muscle groups. Practice each group two ways, once with exaggerated tensing and once with subtle tensing.

1. Take a deep breath, and tense the muscle group.
2. Hold the tension and your breath for 2 - 5 seconds.
3. At the same time, release your muscle tension and your breath (using medium strong force, like Release Breathing). Let your muscles fully relax.

<u>Muscle Group 1:</u> Tense and Relax Your Shoulders and Neck Muscles.

    <u>Trial One: Exaggerated Tensing.</u>

    How much tension   1 - 2 - 3 - 4 - 5
    did you release?   A Little....A Lot

    <u>Trial Two: Subtle Tensing.</u>

    How much tension   1 - 2 - 3 - 4 - 5
    did you release?   A Little....A Lot

<u>Muscle Group 2:</u> Tense and Relax Your Chest Muscles.

    <u>Trial One: Exaggerated Tensing.</u>

    How much tension   1 - 2 - 3 - 4 - 5
    did you release?   A Little....A Lot

    <u>Trial Two: Subtle Tensing.</u>

    How much tension   1 - 2 - 3 - 4 - 5
    did you release?   A Little....A Lot

Muscle Group 3: Tense and Relax Your Stomach Muscles.

    Trial One: Exaggerated Tensing.

    How much tension   1 - 2 - 3 - 4 - 5
    did you release?   A Little....A Lot

    Trial Two: Subtle Tensing.

    How much tension   1 - 2 - 3 - 4 - 5
    did you release?   A Little....A Lot

Other Muscle Groups: Describe any other muscle groups where you collect tension:

....

....

Practice tensing and relaxing with these other muscle groups the same way you did with the three common tension-collecting muscle groups.

    Trial One: Exaggerated Tensing.

    How much tension   1 - 2 - 3 - 4 - 5
    did you release?   A Little....A Lot

    Trial Two: Subtle Tensing.

    How much tension   1 - 2 - 3 - 4 - 5
    did you release?   A Little....A Lot

STEP 3

<u>RELAX MY MIND!</u>

Sometimes your mind will race, worry, or dwell. This builds tension. You will release mental tension if you briefly focus your mind on something peaceful or serene, or on an "in control" fantasy about a situation.

<u>Favorite-Place Visualization.</u> This is a retreat to a soothing, peaceful situation. Imagine yourself in a relaxing place. This is like taking a mini-vacation. For example:

■ A meadow.

■ The beach.

■ High in the mountains.

<u>Revise-the-Situation Visualization.</u> This is a revision of a stressful or threatening situation. Imagine the situation being different in a way that puts you back in control, releases your tension, and relieves your discomfort. For example:

■ Telling someone off.

■ Someone doing just what you want them to do.

■ Winning the lottery.

PRACTICE A FAVORITE-PLACE VISUALIZATION

DIRECTIONS: For Exercise B...Identify a soothing scene that you can use for a brief escape. Select a scene that is safe, predictable, relaxing, and peaceful.

1.   Describe your scene:

....

....

....

....

....

2.   Imagine yourself in the scene. Enjoy being there. Do this for a few seconds while you practice your Release Breathing.

3.   How much tension   1 - 2 - 3 - 4 - 5
      did you release?   A Little....A Lot

EXERCISE

C

PRACTICE   A   REVISE-THE-SITUATION VISUALIZATION

<u>DIRECTIONS:</u> For Exercise C...Identify a situation where you need to have more control.

1. Describe your situation:

    ....

    ....

    ....

2. Describe the scene as you would like it to go so that you were in control:

    ....

    ....

    ....

3. Imagine yourself in the scene, with events going as you want. Do this for a few seconds while you practice your Release Breathing.

4. How much tension   1 - 2 - 3 - 4 - 5
    did you release?   A Little....A Lot

STEP 4

<u>GET ANGRY!</u>

Worry, stress, and anxiety always have fear at their root. You can replace some or all your fear if you get angry. This works even if you have to make up your anger. Even when you deliberately manufacture anger, it triggers body chemistry that replaces fear chemistry. There are many exercises you can use to release anger. They can be used individually or in combinations. Some of them are:

 <u>Pounding.</u> You can pound with things like your fists, a tennis racket, a hammer, or a bat. Be sure you don't hurt yourself or damage a valuable object.

 <u>Twisting.</u> You can twist things like paper, or a towel or washcloth.

 <u>Telling Someone Off.</u> You can imagine that someone is there, and give them a piece of your mind. You can be brief, for example saying "No" or "Stop it." You can go on and on, giving all the details. Feel free to rant and rave.

 <u>Pacing.</u> You can walk aggressively back and forth or in a circular pattern. You might like telling someone off as you pace.

 <u>Throwing.</u> You can throw wads of paper, soft objects, or even old china. Be sure you don't aim at a valuable object.

EXERCISE

D

POUNDING

Pounding is a very basic, fundamental, or primitive expression of anger. Exercise D will show you how to pound to release tension and anger without harming yourself or anyone else.

DIRECTIONS: For Exercise D...Roll a towel into a tube, like a baseball bat. Strike a chair, the bed, or a table top. Practice Release Breathing as you pound.

Be careful not to hit your hand! Pound from 1 to 3 times and then pause to be aware of how you feel. Ask yourself if you connected with anger. If not, try again. Don't pound over and over. Try to connect with and express your anger a few, isolated times.

Trial 1: Channel Your Anger into Pounding with a Towel.

How much tension   1 - 2 - 3 - 4 - 5
did you release?   A Little....A Lot

Trial 2: Channel Your Anger into Pounding with a Towel.

How much tension   1 - 2 - 3 - 4 - 5
did you release?   A Little....A Lot

Trial 3: Channel Your Anger into Pounding with a Towel.

How much tension   1 - 2 - 3 - 4 - 5
did you release?   A Little....A Lot

EXERCISE

E

TWISTING

Twisting is another very basic, fundamental, or primitive expression of anger. Exercise E will show you how to twist to release tension and anger without harming yourself or someone else.

DIRECTIONS: For Exercise E...Roll a towel into a tube, like a baseball bat. Twist it like you want to wring the life out of it. Practice Release Breathing as you twist.

Ask yourself if you connected with anger. If not, try again. Don't twist over and over. Try to connect with and express your anger a few, isolated times.

Trial 1: Channel Your Anger into Twisting with a Towel.

How much tension
did you release?

1 - 2 - 3 - 4 - 5
A Little....A Lot

Trial 2: Channel Your Anger into Twisting with a Towel.

How much tension
did you release?

1 - 2 - 3 - 4 - 5
A Little....A Lot

Trial 3: Channel Your Anger into Twisting with a Towel.

How much tension
did you release?

1 - 2 - 3 - 4 - 5
A Little....A Lot

TELLING SOMEONE OFF

EXERCISE F

Sometimes you need to direct your anger verbally. Exercise F will show you how to do this without actually involving someone else. This exercise works best if you pretend someone you're angry at is there. Try to be as angry as you can. You then tell them what's on your mind without being careful or deliberate. Just let it all come out.

<u>DIRECTIONS:</u> For Exercise F...Practice saying two different things. These are very basic-- "No" and "Stop it." When you are practicing on your own, you can say anything that comes to mind.

<u>Trial 1, "No.":</u> Think of someone who asks or demands things of you that you don't want to give. Say "No" to that person in a loud, angry voice.

How much tension
did you release?

1 - 2 - 3 - 4 - 5
A Little....A Lot

<u>Trial 2, "No.":</u> Think of someone who asks or demands things of you that you don't want to give. Say "No" to that person in a loud, angry voice.

How much tension
did you release?

1 - 2 - 3 - 4 - 5
A Little....A Lot

<u>Trial 3, "Stop it.":</u> Think of someone who does something upsetting, irritating, or destructive to you. Say "Stop it" to that person in a loud, angry voice.

How much tension
did you release?

1 - 2 - 3 - 4 - 5
A Little....A Lot

<u>Trial 4, "Stop it.":</u> Think of someone who does something upsetting, irritating, or destructive to you. Say "Stop it" to that person in a loud, angry voice.

How much tension
did you release?

1 - 2 - 3 - 4 - 5
A Little....A Lot

PRACTICE YOUR WORK SHEETS

<u>DIRECTIONS:</u> The more you study the steps in this lesson, the more effective your new skills will become. Your Work Sheets are designed to help you master these skills. So, read the story below. We will use it as an example to help you learn to use the Work Sheets successfully.

"Billy is driving me nuts," Betty thought. "He gives me a pain in the neck." Betty was at the end of her rope. Her 3-year-old had gotten into two fights the previous morning at pre-school. He'd hassled the dog and cat from the time he'd gotten home. He refused to take a nap in the afternoon or a bath at bedtime. And he whined about something new every 5 minutes. She was tense and uptight.

"Bill thinks you should discipline children with an iron fist," she grumbled to herself. "He believes in raising them by the book. But Billy just clams up when his dad's around. That can't be good."

Betty thought Bill must get it from his mother. She just sent Betty that stupid book about using brute force to get kids to behave. That was the last straw.

Betty knew she got angry and just bottled it up inside. She was about ready to explode. "I just need some time to relax or blow off a little steam," she thought. Betty tried so hard to be the perfect super-mom that Billy was spoiled rotten. And Bill just seemed to criticize without giving much help.

<u>DIRECTIONS:</u> Practice your homework exercises. Imagine that you are Betty in this situation. Complete the "Practice Releasing Tension Work Sheet" on the next page.

NEXT PAGE

Step 1: Breathe out, relaxing my diaphragm. *Practice Release Breathing while imagining you are Betty in this situation.*

How much tension
did you release?

1 - 2 - 3 - 4 - 5
A Little....A Lot

Step 2: Relax My Muscles! *Practice tensing and relaxing a group of muscles while you imagine you are Betty in this situation.*
Check off which muscle group(s) you tensed/relaxed:
☐ Shoulders and Neck   ☐ Chest   ☐ Stomach

Other muscle group:..
How much tension
did you release?

1 - 2 - 3 - 4 - 5
A Little....A Lot

Step 3: Relax My Mind! *Practice a visualization while you imagine you are Betty in this situation.*
Check off which type of visualization(s) you used:
☐ Favorite-Place Visualization   ☐ Revise-The-Situation Visualization

Describe the visualization:...

....
How much tension
did you release?

1 - 2 - 3 - 4 - 5
A Little....A Lot

Step 4: Get Angry! *Practice one or more of the anger expression exercises while you imagine you are Betty in this situation.*
Check off which type of anger expression exercise(s) you used:
☐ Pounding   ☐ Twisting   ☐ Telling Someone Off   ☐ Pacing   ☐ Throwing

How much tension
did you release?

1 - 2 - 3 - 4 - 5
A Little....A Lot

SAMPLE!   <u>PRACTICE RELEASING TENSION WORK SHEET</u>

<u>Step 1: Breathe out, relaxing my diaphragm.</u> *Practice Release Breathing while imagining you are Betty in this situation.*

       How much tension did you release?   1 - <u>2</u> - 3 - 4 - 5
                                            A Little....A Lot

<u>Step 2: Relax My Muscles!</u> *Practice tensing and relaxing a group of muscles while you imagine you are Betty in this situation.*
Check off which muscle group(s) you tensed/relaxed:
■ Shoulders and Neck   ☐ Chest   ☐ Stomach

Other muscle group:..
How much tension did you release?   1 - 2 - <u>3</u> - 4 - 5
                                 A Little....A Lot

<u>Step 3: Relax My Mind!</u> *Practice a visualization while you imagine you are Betty in this situation.*
Check off which type of visualization(s) you used:
■ Favorite-Place Visualization   ☐ Revise-The-Situation Visualization

Describe the visualization:....***Beach in Hawaii***...

How much tension did you release?   1 - 2 - <u>3</u> - 4 - 5
                                 A Little....A Lot

<u>Step 4: Get Angry!</u> *Practice one or more of the anger expression exercises while you imagine you are Betty in this situation.*
Check off which type of anger expression exercise(s) you used:
☐ Pounding ■ Twisting ☐ Telling Someone Off ☐ Pacing ☐ Throwing

How much tension did you release?   1 - 2 - 3 - <u>4</u> - 5
                                 A Little....A Lot

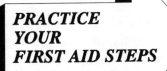

PRACTICE YOUR FIRST AID STEPS

<u>DIRECTIONS:</u> The more you practice your First Aid Steps, the better you will feel. Practice your First Aid Steps now. Imagine you are in a situation used in this lesson, or think about your life in general.

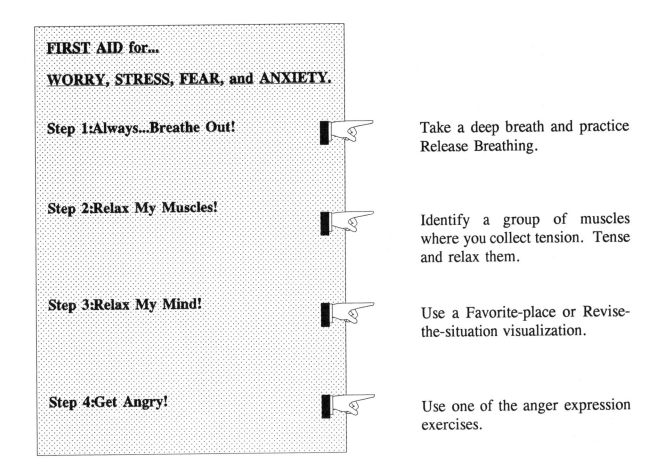

<u>FIRST AID for...</u>

<u>WORRY, STRESS, FEAR, and ANXIETY.</u>

Step 1:Always...Breathe Out!

Take a deep breath and practice Release Breathing.

Step 2:Relax My Muscles!

Identify a group of muscles where you collect tension. Tense and relax them.

Step 3:Relax My Mind!

Use a Favorite-place or Revise-the-situation visualization.

Step 4:Get Angry!

Use one of the anger expression exercises.

HOMEWORK

<u>THE METHODS...</u>

<u>Work Sheets.</u> This week complete 8 Releasing Tension Work Sheets. Do the Work Sheets for situations in which you worry or feel stress, fear, or anxiety. Complete the Work Sheets at the time of these events or very soon thereafter.

<u>First Aid Steps.</u> Practice your First Aid Steps as often as possible, even when you are not really worrying or feeling threatened.

*

<u>FIRST AID for...WORRY, STRESS, FEAR, AND ANXIETY</u>

Step 1: **Always...Breathe Out!**

Step 2: **Relax My Muscles!**

Step 3: **Relax My Mind!**

Step 4: **Get Angry!**

<u>Use your Clip-outs:</u> Cut out the First Aid Steps reminders. Place them in spots where you will see them and remember to practice. Give some to a friend, and tell him or her how to use them.

<u>Teach Others.</u> Share the lesson with others. Teach them how to help themselves using the same skills you are learning.

* Permission is given to reproduce the First Aid Steps for your personal use.

Step 1: Breathe out, relaxing my diaphragm. *Practice Release Breathing while imagining you are a situation in which you worried or felt stress, fear, or anxiety...*

How much tension   1 - 2 - 3 - 4 - 5
did you release?   A Little....A Lot

Step 2: Relax My Muscles! *Practice tensing and relaxing a group of muscles while you imagine you are in this situation.*
Check off which muscle group(s) you tensed/relaxed:
☐ Shoulders and Neck   ☐ Chest   ☐ Stomach

Other muscle group:..
How much tension   1 - 2 - 3 - 4 - 5
did you release?   A Little....A Lot

Step 3: Relax My Mind! *Practice a visualization while you imagine you are in this situation.*
Check off which type of visualization(s) you used:
☐ Favorite-Place Visualization   ☐ Revise-The-Situation Visualization

Describe the visualization:..

....
How much tension   1 - 2 - 3 - 4 - 5
did you release?   A Little....A Lot

Step 4: Get Angry! *Practice one or more of the anger expression exercises while you imagine you are in this situation.*
Check off which type of anger expression exercise(s) you used:
☐ Pounding   ☐ Twisting   ☐ Telling Someone Off   ☐ Pacing   ☐ Throwing

How much tension   1 - 2 - 3 - 4 - 5
did you release?   A Little....A Lot

Step 1: Breathe out, relaxing my diaphragm. *Practice Release Breathing while imagining you are a situation in which you worried or felt stress, fear, or anxiety...*

How much tension
did you release?

1 - 2 - 3 - 4 - 5
A Little....A Lot

Step 2: Relax My Muscles! *Practice tensing and relaxing a group of muscles while you imagine you are in this situation.*
Check off which muscle group(s) you tensed/relaxed:
☐ Shoulders and Neck   ☐ Chest   ☐ Stomach

Other muscle group:...
How much tension
did you release?

1 - 2 - 3 - 4 - 5
A Little....A Lot

Step 3: Relax My Mind! *Practice a visualization while you imagine you are in this situation.*
Check off which type of visualization(s) you used:
☐ Favorite-Place Visualization   ☐ Revise-The-Situation Visualization

Describe the visualization:...
....
How much tension
did you release?

1 - 2 - 3 - 4 - 5
A Little....A Lot

Step 4: Get Angry! *Practice one or more of the anger expression exercises while you imagine you are in this situation.*
Check off which type of anger expression exercise(s) you used:
☐ Pounding   ☐ Twisting   ☐ Telling Someone Off   ☐ Pacing   ☐ Throwing

How much tension
did you release?

1 - 2 - 3 - 4 - 5
A Little....A Lot

Step 1: Breathe out, relaxing my diaphragm. *Practice Release Breathing while imagining you are a situation in which you worried or felt stress, fear, or anxiety...*

> How much tension
> did you release?

1 - 2 - 3 - 4 - 5
A Little....A Lot

Step 2: Relax My Muscles! *Practice tensing and relaxing a group of muscles while you imagine you are in this situation.*
> Check off which muscle group(s) you tensed/relaxed:
> ☐ Shoulders and Neck   ☐ Chest   ☐ Stomach
>
> Other muscle group:...
> How much tension
> did you release?

1 - 2 - 3 - 4 - 5
A Little....A Lot

Step 3: Relax My Mind! *Practice a visualization while you imagine you are in this situation.*
> Check off which type of visualization(s) you used:
> ☐ Favorite-Place Visualization   ☐ Revise-The-Situation Visualization
>
> Describe the visualization:...
> ....
> How much tension
> did you release?

1 - 2 - 3 - 4 - 5
A Little....A Lot

Step 4: Get Angry! *Practice one or more of the anger expression exercises while you imagine you are in this situation.*
> Check off which type of anger expression exercise(s) you used:
> ☐ Pounding   ☐ Twisting   ☐ Telling Someone Off   ☐ Pacing   ☐ Throwing
>
> How much tension
> did you release?

1 - 2 - 3 - 4 - 5
A Little....A Lot

Step 1: Breathe out, relaxing my diaphragm. *Practice Release Breathing while imagining you are a situation in which you worried or felt stress, fear, or anxiety...*

How much tension   1 - 2 - 3 - 4 - 5
did you release?   A Little....A Lot

Step 2:   Relax My Muscles! *Practice tensing and relaxing a group of muscles while you imagine you are in this situation.*

Check off which muscle group(s) you tensed/relaxed:

☐ Shoulders and Neck   ☐ Chest   ☐ Stomach

Other muscle group:...
How much tension   1 - 2 - 3 - 4 - 5
did you release?   A Little....A Lot

Step 3: Relax My Mind! *Practice a visualization while you imagine you are in this situation.*

Check off which type of visualization(s) you used:

☐ Favorite-Place Visualization   ☐ Revise-The-Situation Visualization

Describe the visualization:..

....

How much tension   1 - 2 - 3 - 4 - 5
did you release?   A Little....A Lot

Step 4: Get Angry! *Practice one or more of the anger expression exercises while you imagine you are in this situation.*

Check off which type of anger expression exercise(s) you used:

☐ Pounding   ☐ Twisting   ☐ Telling Someone Off   ☐ Pacing   ☐ Throwing

How much tension   1 - 2 - 3 - 4 - 5
did you release?   A Little....A Lot

Step 1: Breathe out, relaxing my diaphragm. *Practice Release Breathing while imagining you are a situation in which you worried or felt stress, fear, or anxiety...*

How much tension
did you release?

1 - 2 - 3 - 4 - 5
A Little....A Lot

Step 2: Relax My Muscles! *Practice tensing and relaxing a group of muscles while you imagine you are in this situation.*
Check off which muscle group(s) you tensed/relaxed:
☐ Shoulders and Neck   ☐ Chest   ☐ Stomach

Other muscle group:..
How much tension
did you release?

1 - 2 - 3 - 4 - 5
A Little....A Lot

Step 3: Relax My Mind! *Practice a visualization while you imagine you are in this situation.*
Check off which type of visualization(s) you used:
☐ Favorite-Place Visualization   ☐ Revise-The-Situation Visualization

Describe the visualization:..

....
How much tension
did you release?

1 - 2 - 3 - 4 - 5
A Little....A Lot

Step 4: Get Angry! *Practice one or more of the anger expression exercises while you imagine you are in this situation.*
Check off which type of anger expression exercise(s) you used:
☐ Pounding   ☐ Twisting   ☐ Telling Someone Off   ☐ Pacing   ☐ Throwing

How much tension
did you release?

1 - 2 - 3 - 4 - 5
A Little....A Lot

Step 1: Breathe out, relaxing my diaphragm. *Practice Release Breathing while imagining you are a situation in which you worried or felt stress, fear, or anxiety...*

How much tension   1 - 2 - 3 - 4 - 5
did you release?   A Little....A Lot

Step 2: Relax My Muscles! *Practice tensing and relaxing a group of muscles while you imagine you are in this situation.*
Check off which muscle group(s) you tensed/relaxed:
☐ Shoulders and Neck   ☐ Chest   ☐ Stomach

Other muscle group:...
How much tension   1 - 2 - 3 - 4 - 5
did you release?   A Little....A Lot

Step 3: Relax My Mind! *Practice a visualization while you imagine you are in this situation.*
Check off which type of visualization(s) you used:
☐ Favorite-Place Visualization   ☐ Revise-The-Situation Visualization

Describe the visualization:..

....
How much tension   1 - 2 - 3 - 4 - 5
did you release?   A Little....A Lot

Step 4: Get Angry! *Practice one or more of the anger expression exercises while you imagine you are in this situation.*
Check off which type of anger expression exercise(s) you used:
☐ Pounding   ☐ Twisting   ☐ Telling Someone Off   ☐ Pacing   ☐ Throwing

How much tension   1 - 2 - 3 - 4 - 5
did you release?   A Little....A Lot

Step 1: Breathe out, relaxing my diaphragm. *Practice Release Breathing while imagining you are a situation in which you worried or felt stress, fear, or anxiety...*

How much tension   1 - 2 - 3 - 4 - 5
did you release?   A Little....A Lot

Step 2:   Relax My Muscles! *Practice tensing and relaxing a group of muscles while you imagine you are in this situation.*
Check off which muscle group(s) you tensed/relaxed:
☐ Shoulders and Neck   ☐ Chest   ☐ Stomach

Other muscle group:...
How much tension   1 - 2 - 3 - 4 - 5
did you release?   A Little....A Lot

Step 3:   Relax My Mind! *Practice a visualization while you imagine you are in this situation.*
Check off which type of visualization(s) you used:
☐ Favorite-Place Visualization   ☐ Revise-The-Situation Visualization

Describe the visualization:...
....
How much tension   1 - 2 - 3 - 4 - 5
did you release?   A Little....A Lot

Step 4: Get Angry! *Practice one or more of the anger expression exercises while you imagine you are in this situation.*
Check off which type of anger expression exercise(s) you used:
☐ Pounding   ☐ Twisting   ☐ Telling Someone Off   ☐ Pacing   ☐ Throwing

How much tension   1 - 2 - 3 - 4 - 5
did you release?   A Little....A Lot

Step 1: Breathe out, relaxing my diaphragm. *Practice Release Breathing while imagining you are a situation in which you worried or felt stress, fear, or anxiety...*

How much tension   1 - 2 - 3 - 4 - 5
did you release?   A Little....A Lot

Step 2:   Relax My Muscles! *Practice tensing and relaxing a group of muscles while you imagine you are in this situation.*
Check off which muscle group(s) you tensed/relaxed:
☐ Shoulders and Neck   ☐ Chest   ☐ Stomach

Other muscle group:..
How much tension   1 - 2 - 3 - 4 - 5
did you release?   A Little....A Lot

Step 3:   Relax My Mind! *Practice a visualization while you imagine you are in this situation.*
Check off which type of visualization(s) you used:
☐ Favorite-Place Visualization   ☐ Revise-The-Situation Visualization

Describe the visualization:...
....
How much tension   1 - 2 - 3 - 4 - 5
did you release?   A Little....A Lot

Step 4: Get Angry! *Practice one or more of the anger expression exercises while you imagine you are in this situation.*
Check off which type of anger expression exercise(s) you used:
☐ Pounding   ☐ Twisting   ☐ Telling Someone Off   ☐ Pacing   ☐ Throwing

How much tension   1 - 2 - 3 - 4 - 5
did you release?   A Little....A Lot

INDEX

LIST OF EXERCISES

E. Wayne Hart

Dr. Hart is a licensed psychologist and a licensed Marriage, Family, Child Counselor. In the early 1980s, a member of his family was stricken with anxiety, panic attacks, and depression. His interest in anxiety, stress disorders, and mood disorders, grew from the search to find help for someone he loved. After several years of treating anxiety and mood disorders, Dr. Hart began developing the Conquer Your Fears Self-improvement Materials in 1987. His mission was to speed recovery.

Dr. Hart earned a Baccalaureate in English, a Teaching Credential, and a Master of Education from California State University at Long Beach. After teaching in the public schools for six years, he earned a second Master's and Ph.D. in Clinical Psychology from The Fielding Institute in Santa Barbara. He completed internships in marriage, family and child counseling, chemical dependency rehabilitation, and a two-year psychology internship at Metropolitan State Hospital. His additional advanced training in transactional analysis included accreditation by the International T. A. Association as a clinical trainer.

Dr. Hart has maintained a private practice in Orange County, since 1975. His office is in Newport Beach at Fashion Island. His clinical practice now emphasizes anxiety disorders and issues related to singles and relationships. He has published and lectured extensively, and has continuously trained fellow clinicians. He is a recognized practice consultant and expert witness, now specializing in educating and supervising licensed mental health practitioners in the area of clinical, ethical, and business standards of practice. Dr. Hart has continuously served as a leader in professional organizations and is Past President of Orange County Chapter, California Association of Marriage, Family Therapists.

Last, but not least, Dr. Hart has created *Thought Concerts*, which he presents to large audiences. These are entertaining, enjoyable, and informative programs that combine popular music with psychological tips, self-examination, and social interaction.

The District of Columbia, and the suburban corridor to Baltimore, as viewed from an American satellite. *(National Aeronautics and Space Administration.)*

AMERICAN POLITICS
AND GOVERNMENT

AMERICAN POLITICS AND GOVERNMENT

RICHARD M. PIOUS

BARNARD COLLEGE
AND THE GRADUATE FACULTIES
OF COLUMBIA UNIVERSITY

McGRAW-HILL BOOK COMPANY

NEW YORK ST. LOUIS SAN FRANCISCO AUCKLAND BOGOTÁ
HAMBURG JOHANNESBURG LONDON MADRID MEXICO
MONTREAL NEW DELHI PANAMA PARIS SÃO PAULO
SINGAPORE SYDNEY TOKYO TORONTO

AMERICAN POLITICS AND GOVERNMENT

1 2 3 4 5 6 7 8 9 0   VNHVNH   8 9 8 7 6

ISBN 0-07-050121-1

This book was set in Zapf Book Light by York Graphic Services, Inc.
The editors were David V. Serbun and Susan Gamer;
the designer was Hermann Strohbach;
the production supervisor was Leroy A. Young.
The photo editor was Ellen Horan.
The drawings were done by Fine Line Illustrations, Inc.
Von Hoffmann Press, Inc., was printer and binder.
Cover photograph by Mike Mitchell: Photo Researchers.

Library of Congress Cataloging-in-Publication Data

Pious, Richard M., date
    American politics and government.
    Includes bibliographies and index.
    1. United States—Politics and government.   I. Title.
JK274.P56   1986   320.973   85-14079
ISBN 0-07-050121-1

Richard M. Pious graduated from Colby College, where he was editor in chief of the student newspaper and president of the senior honor society, Blue Key. While in college he demonstrated his political talent by losing the election for student body president. Pious received his M.A. and Ph.D degrees from the Department of Public Law and Government of Columbia University, where he was a Harriman Fellow. He began teaching the introductory course in American politics in 1968 at Colby College, then taught at Columbia College and York University (Toronto). He has been the course director for Dynamics of American Politics at Barnard College in New York City since 1973. He is the editor of *Civil Rights and Liberties in the 1970s* (1972); a ten-volume reprint series of classic nineteenth-century books on constitutional, comparative, and international public law (1981); and the centennial volume of the Academy of Political Science, *The Power to Govern* (1983). He is the author of *The American Presidency* (1979) and coauthor (with Christopher Pyle) of *The President, Congress and the Constitution* (1984). He has contributed articles to *Political Science Quarterly*, *Journal of International Affairs*, and *Wisconsin Law Review* and has lectured at many colleges and universities, including Columbia University, Mount Holyoke, New York University, the University of Wisconsin, and the Washington, D.C., program of the Claremont Colleges. He has been a commentator for the Voice of America, several public and network radio and television stations, *Newsday*, and the *Wall Street Journal*; and his op-ed pieces have appeared on the editorial pages of several newspapers. His consulting work has recently included Public Affairs and Research Communications (Washington, D.C.) and the Sloan Foundation. When not teaching or writing, the author enjoys trail bicycling, photography, and tennis.

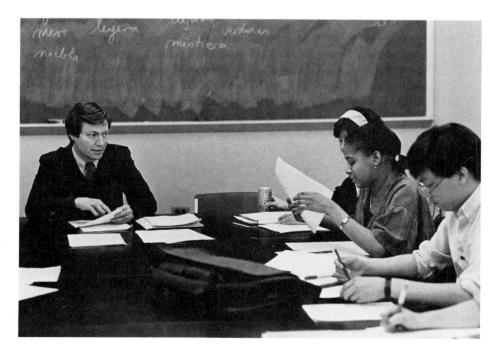

CONTENTS

PREFACE

In the midst of the American Civil War, President Lincoln called on the American people at Gettysburg to prove to the world not only that our nation could endure, but also that "government of the people, by the people, and for the people, shall not perish from the earth." Today we face the same problems as did those who created our nation in 1787 and forged a stronger union out of the Civil War. How should we provide for our security and prosperity? How can we create a government strong enough to defend us without posing a threat to our freedoms?

If you are a typical reader of this book, you were born in the late 1960s, in years of racial unrest, campus disorders, and political assassinations; and you have grown up with economic uncertainty, political scandals, and increasing skepticism about the ability of government to solve social and economic problems. You began to study civics or social studies just as the Iranian hostage crisis and the Marine casualties in Lebanon were making clear how difficult it is to project American power in the world. You have seen one politician after another campaign on television against the "mess in Washington."

But it is nonsense to say that government causes all our problems and solves none. Politics, in the best sense, is the art of bringing people together to solve problems. Those who would change the way the world works (and I count myself among them) can do no better than to change the way government works or change the leaders of government. In a democracy we have that opportunity. Before making changes, however, it is sensible to learn how the system works, to assess its effectiveness, and to think seriously about how it can be improved.

APPROACH

I wrote this book because I wanted to learn more about American politics and government and then convey my ideas to the generation of Americans who will meet the challenges of our third century of democracy. I followed Paul Samuelson's approach in writing his best-selling economics textbook: give students "nothing unnecessarily hard, but omit nothing essential as being beyond the grasp of the serious student; and above all, present nothing that later must be unlearned as wrong." I hope I have raised the most important political issues that face our nation and provided a comprehensive and balanced discussion to help students draw their own conclusions.

Instead of providing a narrow framework in which to view politics, I offer a broad, eclectic view, which allows instructors to use this book as a teaching tool or supplement that extends their own approach to politics. I take neither a liberal nor a conservative slant; rather, I present several aspects of each issue, hoping that my own iconoclastic stance will encourage readers to question conventional wisdom or their own preconceived notions and to develop skepticism about political rhetoric along with a deeper awareness of the way the game of politics is played.

FEATURES

Special sections in each chapter will help you learn about American politics. Some chapters have an *issue and debate* section which presents the pros and cons of an important issue, such as industrial planning. Many have *close-ups*, short analytical biographies of leaders such as Jeane Kirkpatrick, Martin Luther King, Jr., Sandra Day O'Connor, and Daniel P. Moynihan, to show the diversity of experiences and viewpoints in American politics. Key topics are examined in *focus* sections. Each chapter closes with a section called *in conclusion*. At the end of each chapter there are references for *further reading*, as well as a *study break*—a guide to films, biographies, and novels about politics which you might enjoy. There are also lists of *organizations* and *useful sources* of information. Near the end of the book there is a *glossary* of important terms (these are set in ***bold italic*** throughout the text). Finally, the Constitution of the United States is given with explanatory notes.

Your instructor may also assign the *study guide* which accompanies this text. It not only will help you review the material but also provides a self-test section on key concepts, data, and terms. The research exercises can also be used to apply some of the concepts and information to practical problems of the kind that political scientists, pollsters, journalists, lobbyists, and government officials routinely deal with.

ORGANIZATION AND CONTENT

Now to specifics. The book is organized in four parts, each with a specific objective. In Part One, Chapter 1 defines politics and government and provides you with key concepts. Chapter 2 applies these concepts to a case study: the writing of the Constitution and the creation of our government in 1787. Chapters 3 and 4 discuss two of the key characteristics of our system: its federal structure, making us a nation of diverse states; and its limited powers and guarantees of civil liberties.

Part Two is concerned with the pursuit of power. Chapter 5 discusses voting and nonvoting, because differences in participation help explain who gets elected to office and what those elected do once they get into power. Chapter 6 examines the structure and functions of the Democratic and Republican parties from the local level to the national level. It describes how interest groups and their political action committees (PACS) increased their influence while parties became weaker, and how parties are trying to stage a comeback in the 1980s. Chapters 7 through 9 discuss congressional and presidential nominations and elections and describe campaign finance and organization, the impact of the media and advertisements, voting behavior, and how election results influence both the two-party system and the way the government subsequently works.

Part Three deals with governmental powers and processes. Chapters 10 and 11 deal with the presidency and Congress. They examine the formal and informal "checks and balances" of the Constitution and party system, focusing on the circumstances in which each branch collaborates with or confronts the other. Each chapter also deals with a "power problem": how the President must try to lead Congress without adequate constitutional or political resources; how Congress must represent diverse interests which tend to fragment it, while producing laws which require a majority. Chapter 12 deals with the Supreme Court and other federal courts—the "least dangerous branch"— and shows how the judiciary has expanded its powers while at the same time

remaining strongly influenced by the other two branches. It also discusses the "power problem" of the federal courts: how to balance their responsibility to interpret the law against the reactions of the other branches when they stake out politically unpopular positions. Chapter 13 discusses the "fourth branch," the bureaucracy, and describes how the other three try to control it. The bureaucracy, however, is strongly influenced by interest groups, which are analyzed in terms of "iron triangles" and "issue networks," two concepts which have great implications for the way government really works. Chapter 14, on the budget process, ties much of the preceding analysis together, by showing how the four branches interact with each other to answer one of the fundamental political questions: who gets what, when, and how?

Finally, Part Four is concerned with governmental policies. Chapters 15 through 19 take up economic, social welfare, civil rights, foreign, and defense policies. Each chapter describes the coalitions which compete for influence in formulating and implementing proposals, the impact of public opinion and organized interest groups on policymakers, the policies which have been adopted in the past half century, and the options being considered today.

THE FIRST STEP

In his inaugural address to the nation more than twenty-five years ago, President John F. Kennedy set forth his program and then observed, "All this will not be finished in the first hundred days. Nor will it be finished in the first thousand days, nor in the life of this administration, nor even perhaps in our lifetime on this planet. But let us begin." The Chinese philosophers say that every journey, no matter how long, begins with a single step. So it is with the study and practice of politics. I took my first step the month and year President Kennedy gave that inaugural address, when I enrolled in an introductory course in American politics at Colby College. Since then I have taught this course in four different colleges for almost twenty years, as a teaching assistant and professor. Your steps begin today, and I hope that this book helps you in the hundred days of your semester as much as the textbook I used helped me.

ACKNOWLEDGMENTS

I wish to thank the following scholars for their help and advice in reviewing the manuscript of this book: Kristi Andersen, Ohio State University; Gottlieb J. Baer, American River College; Lawrence Baum, Ohio State University; A.M. Burns, III, University of Florida; George F. Cole, University of Connecticut; Howard T. East, Jr., Menlo College; Paul L. Hain, University of New Mexico; Murray C. Havens, Texas Technical University; Richard P. Hiskes, University of Connecticut; Jerome M. Mileur, University of Massachusetts, Amherst; Robert E. Murphy, Florissant Valley Community College; Michael Nelson, Vanderbilt University; Benjamin I. Page, University of Texas; Mark P. Petracca, University of California, Irvine; Palmer C. Pilcher, University of Arkansas; Mavis Mann Reeves, University of Maryland; Donald L. Robinson, Smith College; Robert C. Sahr, Oregon State University; Richard K. Scher, University of Florida; James Sheffield, Wichita State University; Edward I. Sidlow, Miami University; Steven S. Smith, Northwestern University.

I also wish to thank my editors at McGraw-Hill, Eric Munson, David V. Serbun, Stephen Wagley, and Susan Gamer; the production supervisor, Leroy Young; the designer, Hermann Strohbach; and the copy editor, Pamela Haskins.

I am grateful for the help of research assistants Sharon Epstein, Susan Kaye, and Cindy Gordon, all Barnard College students; and several Barnard and Columbia College students acknowledged in the footnotes. Melissa Mulliken of Barnard College public relations arranged for my photograph. The librarians at Barnard and Columbia University were, as always, indispensable sources of advice. My colleague Tom Gais provided me with updated data for several tables. Michael Goldstein of Public Affairs Research and Communications gave me access to his extensive files on civil rights politics.

I have benefited from the roundtable discussions of ongoing research conducted by the Political Science Department at Barnard and the Center for the Social Sciences at Columbia University, chaired by Jonathan Cole. The Montauk Seminar on presidential nominating politics, funded by the Sloan Foundation and chaired by Alexander Heard, enabled me to exchange ideas with many of the leading scholars of party and electoral politics. I benefited from the ideas of guest speakers at the YMHA series on the imperial presidency which I chaired in 1984: James MacGregor Burns, William Leuchtenburg, Fred Greenstein, Doris Kearns Goodwin, Robert Caro, and James David Barber.

Friends, colleagues, and acquaintances whose conversations with me involved topics which appear in this book include: Susan Bales, Gerald Benjamin, Richard Brifault, Andre Burgstaller, Demetrios Caraley, John Chambers, Henry S. F. Cooper, Jr., Flora Davidson, Jerry Davis, Louis Fisher, Thomas Franck, Julian Franklin, Ester Fuchs, David Garth, George Gilder, Charles V. Hamilton, Peter Hart, Roger Hilsman, Robert Hirschfield, Dorothy James, Peter Juviler, Ethel Klein, Louis Koenig, Robert Lamb, William McNeil, Lawrence Mead, Robert Mutch, Amy Piro, John Prados, Chris Pyle, Nicholas Rango, Katherine Roome, Hugh Roome, Richard Rubin, Robert Shapiro, Allan Silver, Hilary Silver, Steven Singer, Stephen Solarz, Daniel Traister, Gary Wasserman, Kathryn Yatrakis, and my colleagues at the Barnard Roundtable.

I want to acknowledge the enormous support given to this effort by my mother, Edith Pious; and my mother-in-law, Susan F. C. Weil. Above all else, I acknowledge the help of my wife, Sacha Weil, whose career in high technology gives me insights into the politics of the future.

FINALLY . . .

I welcome any comments students or instructors wish to make about this textbook. Please write to the author at the following address: Department of Political Science, Barnard College, 606 West 120 Street, New York, New York 10027.

Richard M. Pious

CHAPTER 1
POLITICS:
WHO GETS WHAT?

From the election of Andrew Jackson as president in 1828 to Martha Lane Collins's victory in the 1982 Kentucky gubernatorial election, increased democratization has affected the pursuit of power. (*Granger Collection; Pat Pfister: Picture Group.*)

In the *Devil's Dictionary* the journalist Ambrose Bierce defines politics as "a strife of interests masquerading as a contest of principles. The conduct of public affairs for private advantage." To call people *politicians* or to charge them with "playing politics" on an issue is a serious insult. But politics in the best sense is also, as Ralph Waldo Emerson once said, "the greatest science and service of mankind." This book will explore both aspects of politics: the conduct of public affairs for personal advantage and the effort to solve problems democratically and in the public interest.

Four issues will be considered: the pursuit of power, the uses and abuses of power, the accountability of those who exercise power, and the ends of power. In Part One we will study the formation of the union in 1787 and the ways in which federalism and the Bill of Rights limit governmental power. Part Two discusses how politicians are elected to Congress and the White House and how the parties and interest groups influence the voters' choices. In Part Three we will look at the governing institutions and processes: the three branches of national government (the presidency, Congress, and the judiciary), the bureaucracy (sometimes considered the fourth branch), and the budget process. The book concludes with a section devoted to economic, social, foreign, and military policies.

WHAT IS POLITICS?

To begin, we will consider some definitions and concepts: about politics and government in general and about constitutional and democratic politics and government in particular.

Politics as power and influence

Politics involves ***power:*** a relationship between people in which some get others to obey them, even if they would rather not do so, by means of subtle or overt pressure and even by the use of force. And it involves influence: the ability of people to get others to do what they want them to do by convincing them that it is in their own best interests. Thus politics exists in the classroom, where the college can compel students to take examinations if they wish to pass a course; in the military, where officers can give orders to their subordinates; and in business, where executives can convince the head of a company to make a certain decision.

Politics as the pursuit of position

Politics is about getting power and influence as well as about exercising it. It is about running for public office, becoming an adviser, and getting an appointment to an important government agency. Jockeying for position happens everywhere: academic politics determines who gets to be dean or department chair; corporate politics is played to see who becomes president or chairman of the board; religious politics occurs when a new spiritual leader is elected.

Who gets what is often worked out in the corridors of Congress. Lyndon Johnson (then Senate majority leader) makes a point to Senator Theodore Green of Rhode Island. *(George E. Tames: New York Times.)*

The wear and tear of campaigning is evident in Senator Gary Hart's shoe leather—and this was only the first primary of the 1984 season. *(G. Peress: Magnum.)*

Politics as conflict management

"Civilization," as José Ortega y Gasset once wrote, "is nothing else but the attempt to reduce force to being the last resort." Politics is the art of managing conflicts between different individuals or groups by substituting peaceful decision making for brute force. Instead of equating might with right and allowing the strongest to decide, politics settles disputes by means of bargaining, negotiation, and compromise between the parties; through appeals to the customs and laws of the community; by voting on the issues; or by transferring disputes to government agencies or courts. In this sense politics is a *game*, and its rules must be understood by both spectators and participants.

Politics as who gets what, when, and how

Yet another way of thinking about politics is to focus on the score of the game: who wins and who loses, and by how much? Politics sometimes substitutes for other ways of allocating goods and services, such as the marketplace. Samuel Johnson once defined politics as "nothing more than a means of rising in the world," and this is true when politics involves redistributing income and services from the haves to the have-nots, or vice versa, depending on who controls the government.

When a nation makes a decision to establish a system of old-age pensions or public universities, for example, usually the costs are borne by one group

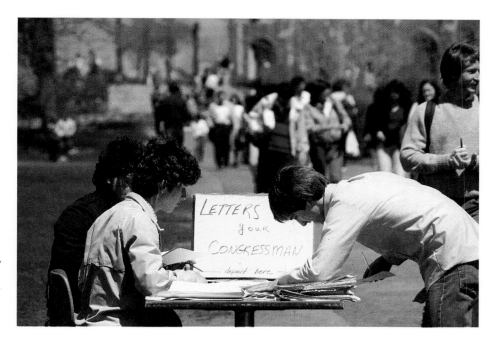

Students are a constituency, too, and at Boston College and elsewhere many sign petitions against proposed cuts in student aid. *(Bruce Flynn: Picture Group.)*

(taxpayers), while the benefits accrue to others (the elderly or students, neither of whom pay much in taxes at the time). This may result in a massive redistribution of wealth from people who work to those who do not. When tariffs are raised or lowered, when defense budgets are increased or cut, and when public works projects are planned or abandoned, different regions win or lose. There is nothing new in these observations. "The art of government consists in taking as much money as possible from one class of citizens to give to the other," Voltaire wrote in the eighteenth century; however cynical, sometimes this statement seems to be true.

Politics as continuity and change

The history, traditions, and customs of a nation—its past political practices and ideas—have a profound impact on its politics. Our separation of church and state, our mistrust of big government and bureaucracy, our reliance on state and local governments for many functions, and our emphasis on individual rights and liberties—these are rooted in hundreds of years of our history. Other nations, just as democratic as our own, like England, France, and Canada, have entirely different traditions of church-state relations, different ways of balancing the responsibilities of central government and local governments, and different ways of safeguarding the civil rights and liberties of their peoples. How a nation conducts its politics today is always based in large measure on how it has acted in the past.

To understand politics fully one must observe how political practices change from one decade to the next and from one century to the next. The rate of political change in a nation is important: in some countries changes occur slowly; other countries have a strong reformist streak and are constantly improvising; and still others alternate between reactionary governments that are unwilling to make needed reforms and revolutionary regimes that make fundamental breaks with the past. Our own tradition is a mixture of institutional

reform and dramatic, often violent, revolutionary developments that include our independence from Britain, our expansion across a continent by force of arms against Mexico and the Indians, our consolidation of the union through civil war between the north and the south, and our emergence as a great power through two world wars and several smaller conflicts. In the twentieth century our politics has been transformed by the impact of the industrial and communications revolutions. Our system of party competition is always in flux, our federal-state arrangements have gone through at least five transformations, and the balance of power between the president and Congress constantly changes.

Politics as future shock

Politics is about the future and about how to manage the accelerating pace of economic, scientific, social, and cultural change. Our role in the world economy, for example, has shifted enormously in the past quarter-century; government, working with industry, must devise a strategy to enable the United States to compete in the world marketplace. Scientific changes have enabled people to live longer (requiring changes in social security and medical care programs) but in greater peril (requiring new diplomatic initiatives and defense policies).

"No government can remain stable in an unstable society and unstable world," argued the French prime minister Léon Blum. The world seems more unstable today than at any other time since the end of the Second World War. Does this mean that we are destined to live with unstable government? Can our democracy cope with the crises that we face? How can we best transform it to meet modern challenges?

Politics as ends

"If the people want religion," the British prime minister Harold Macmillan once said, "they should look to their archbishops." But people also look to their politicians, if not for answers to ultimate questions about the meaning of life, then at least for answers to fundamental questions about the larger purposes of civilization. Politics is concerned with more than power and problem solving; it deals with the culture and values of the community and becomes

President Reagan visits a job retraining center in Pittsburgh. What the government should do to combat unemployment remains a divisive issue in American politics. (*Associated Press.*)

the secular equivalent of religion in nations in which church and state are formally separated, as they are in our own. And in much of the world it becomes much more; where it is formally entwined with an established religion, politicians use religion to maintain their power. How a democratic nation manages its religious and cultural politics can ultimately determine whether the people remain united or divide along sectarian lines—whether they remain a community or dissolve into warring tribes.

WHAT IS GOVERNMENT?

A definition

Politics takes place everywhere, but the focus of this text is on politics in government. We have so many governments in our own country—thousands of municipal and county governments—that the Census Bureau had to come up with a definition when counting them so that it would know what to include and what to leave out. Its definition: If an organization can make law or collect a tax, it is a government. Some other characteristics of a government are discussed below.

Government and the monopoly of force

A *government* is the organization that has a monopoly of force over the people in a particular territory. It has armed forces which can put down civil disturbances or attempts to secede from or overthrow the government. It can collect taxes to finance its operations and can compel compliance with its laws.

In reality, no government has a monopoly on force. Organized crime syndicates, guerrilla movements, and terrorists can employ force and can sometimes coerce people into complying with their wishes. But a government has a monopoly over the *lawful* use of force. Only the force it uses (or permits others to use) is lawful, by definition, and the government can regulate or forbid the use of force by others. Those who have power call themselves *the government* and call their force *lawful;* eventually the test of this claim is experiential— either they maintain themselves in power, or they are overthrown and others form a government which makes the same claims.

The "nightwatchman" state

Why should people in any territory allow the government a monopoly on the lawful use of force? Would the people not be better off if they refused to give anyone such a monopoly and kept arms themselves? Historically, many conquered peoples have allowed a government to rule them because it promised to maintain order. It protected them from groups that might tax or coerce them: crime syndicates, religious sects, terrorists, neighboring tribes, warrior hordes, or other countries. Without government, the English philosopher Thomas Hobbes argued, life would be "nasty, brutish and short." People turn to government for protection, from both external and internal threats. The first duty of any government is to act as a *nightwatchman state*—a term derived from the guards who patrolled city streets in the evening centuries ago. Many nations spend more of their money for armaments than for anything else, while local governments usually spend heavily on police protection.

The positive state

In the United States we expect government to do much more than simply take our money by taxing us and provide us with protection in return. We assume that it will take some responsibility for the welfare of the people and for the management of the economy and that it will promote education, the arts, and the sciences. But how much responsibility should government take? How

Liberals have generally favored public housing to replace slums. Conservatives generally prefer free-market solutions or government rent subsidies. *(Burt Glinn: Magnum.)*

much government do we want? Some people, like Tom Paine, argue that government, "even in its best state, is but a necessary evil; in its worst state, an intolerable one." Others, like Andrew Jackson, say that "there are no necessary evils in government. Its evils exist only in its abuses."

Reasonable people disagree about the *role* of government. **Liberals** see government positively, arguing that regulations, services, and benefits free those who are disadvantaged and discriminated against from social and economic burdens and enable them to join the mainstream of economic life. They believe that government must take decisive action to mobilize the resources of society to deal with the complex issues of the modern world. They see danger in weak, indecisive, or ineffective government, for as Franklin Roosevelt warned, "History proves that dictatorships do not grow out of strong and successful governments, but out of weak and helpless ones." **Conservatives** argue that the government has a more limited role, because its programs do not work well and because a government large enough to provide benefits is also a government large enough to take away rights and liberties. They believe that confiding power in the people is dangerous because, as Lord Acton warned, "Power tends to corrupt, and absolute power corrupts absolutely." They believe that people equate government's power with wisdom—a dangerous mistake. "The less government we have, the better," Ralph Waldo Emerson said; "the fewer laws, and the less confided power."

We will be looking at the way in which these disputes have influenced the size, the structure, and the processes of government. Is there a trade-off between the powers of government and the rights and liberties of the people? Do we have to give up some of our freedom to get a more efficient government, or is this a false issue? Does stronger and more effective government, equipped with greater powers, actually increase our freedom? Would weaker government actually lessen it?

CONSTITUTIONAL
AND DEMOCRATIC
POLITICS:
FIRST PRINCIPLES

The ancient Greek philosopher Aristotle argued in *Politics* that to be a good person, one had to be a good citizen—one had to participate in politics or else lead an incomplete life. In a democratic government the people are guaranteed the right to participate. That guarantee can be ensured only when the power of government itself is limited—when there is constitutional politics.

Constitutional politics

Characteristics of constitutional government. When people create a government, they usually specify and limit its powers at the outset. To do so they sometimes write a ***constitution***, which establishes the governmental structure, provides the governing institutions with their formal powers, sets limits on the uses of these powers, and guarantees the people certain specific rights and liberties. Constitutional politics involves the *consent of the governed*, and when the people find the constitution unsatisfactory, they can amend its provisions and change it to their liking—as we have done with our own Constitution many times—or create a new one if necessary.

In many nations rulers exercise virtually unlimited powers, and their constitutions are merely a facade, providing paper guarantees that no one believes will be respected. Having a constitution means nothing unless the political leaders and the people are willing to abide by it, defend it, and fight to preserve it, if necessary.

Limited government and the rule of law. Our Constitution was formed partly to increase the powers and efficiency of government, but also partly to limit these powers and confine them to certain purposes. The Constitution, laws passed by Congress, regulations framed by the bureaucracy, and decisions handed down by federal courts all retain this dual quality: they empower officials to take action, but they also limit them in what they can do. Our government must operate according to the Constitution, laws, and formal procedures, and officials can be challenged in court and often prevented from exceeding their authority. We value the means by which government acts as much as the ends for which it acts.

Geraldine Ferraro, the Democratic vice-presidential nominee, courts black delegates at the Democratic national convention in San Francisco in 1984. *(Gilles Peress: Magnum.)*

Democratic politics are defined by free elections. The Progressive Conservative party leader, Brian Mulroney, votes in his home district in Quebec in the 1984 election that made him prime minister of Canada. *(CP Laserphoto.)*

Democratic politics

Democratic politics involves three principles: (1) that governments are established by and with the consent of the people, almost always by a constitution; (2) that the people choose their leaders in free and fair elections; and (3) that the government and its leaders must ultimately obey the will of a majority of those elected to make laws, except in the case of matters that are specifically exempted from this rule by the constitution. "Democracy is the recurrent suspicion," E. B. White said, "that more than half of the people are right more than half of the time."

Characteristics of democracies. Almost every nation in the world has a written constitution, holds elections, and claims to be a democracy in which the will of the people prevails. Yet few nations are real democracies. How can we distinguish those which are democracies from those in which democratic forms are a sham?

COMPETITIVE ELECTIONS. In a democracy there are regularly scheduled elections in which people can compete for office; they have the following characteristics:

- Each citizen votes for each elective office.
- Two or more candidates run for each office.
- Elections are scheduled at or within regular intervals.
- The government does not interfere with the campaigns of opposition candidates.
- The government does not coerce the voters into making a specific choice (though in some nations it requires people to vote).
- The person with the greatest number of votes (the **_plurality_**) or more than half the votes (the **_majority_**) wins.
- Those who win the elections are not prevented by the government or the military from assuming office.

Most of the time such elections are held in the United States, Canada, western European nations, some nations in Latin America, Australia, New Zealand, Japan, India, and Israel. But few nations in Africa, the middle east, or Asia— and no communist states—hold competitive elections.

MAJORITY RULE. In a democracy the will of the majority ultimately determines government policy. But the people do not resolve every issue. They may have no opinions or may prefer to have elected officials and "experts" make the decisions. When a majority holds a strong opinion, however, this often is translated into public policy. The people may have to wait several years until they can elect new leaders, but they can get their way.

MINORITY RIGHTS. There are some exceptions to the principle of majority rule. The constitution itself may specify certain limitations so that the rights of minorities can be guaranteed against the rule of the majority. Suppose, for example, that the majority wanted to make its own religion the official religion of the nation; the constitution might specifically prohibit the establishment of an official religion.

CONSTITUTIONAL LIMITS. The rules of the game embodied in the constitution may limit the will of the majority. Even if the majority wished to end elections, abolish guarantees of minority rights, or limit freedom of speech, for example, the constitution would prevent it from doing so. Certain rules are necessary for a functioning democracy (each nation determining its own unique set) and may not be changed by rulers who represent transitory majorities.

Direct and indirect democracy. According to our definition of democratic politics, the people must adopt a constitution, elect leaders, and allow the leaders to make policy by majority vote. This is sometimes referred to as ***indirect democracy*** because policies are made only indirectly by the people, who must entrust most decisions to their elected officials. (We also call this *representative democracy,* and the government that is established a **republic.**)

There is another type of democratic politics, however, in which the people vote directly on decisions without entrusting them to representatives. This is called ***direct democracy:*** people assemble, discuss the issues and the alternatives, and eventually decide by majority vote what to do about them. They may elect permanent officials to carry out all their decisions, or they may elect

Direct democracy still exists in town meetings like this one in Vermont. *(Magnum.)*

Representative democracy should mean responsive democracy. Edward Brooke, then senator of Massachusetts, discusses problems with a constituent. *(AP Photocolor.)*

temporary officials to implement particular decisions and report back to the assembly.

ADVANTAGES OF DIRECT DEMOCRACY. At first glance direct democracy seems to be a simple and attractive way to conduct politics. Everyone gets to participate and speak his or her mind. It is an educational experience, in which everyone learns more about problems. A consensus may emerge, or at least a compromise position that brings people together. All those involved, even the losers, have the feeling that they made the decisions that affect their lives.

DISADVANTAGES OF DIRECT DEMOCRACY. Direct democracy might work for a college fraternity or sorority, for a faculty meeting, or for a small New England town, but it is impracticable for a large territory containing many people because it would be impossible to get everyone together at one time and in one place. In a small community people know one another, and when they discuss issues, it is not only *what* is said, but also *who* says it, that helps them make up their minds. They listen to people they trust, and they discount the views of others. But in the case of a large community, a meeting would involve hundreds of thousands, or even millions, of people. No nation could pack all its citizens together and expect real deliberation and debate.

SOLVING THE SIZE PROBLEM. Indirect democracy solves the size problem. The people vote for representatives of their choice, who then meet in a much smaller assembly. Indirect democracy allows the people to *recreate* the advantages of direct democracy: the assembly which they elect conducts face-to-face meetings, debates the issues, and reaches a consensus or a compromise so that a majority can decide. Yet when representative institutions are created, they may not truly mirror the views or interests of the people who elected them. They may instead prefer to exercise their own judgment or to substitute their own values for those of their constituents, which may or may not be a bad thing. Special interests may distort the outcomes of elections and reduce the accountability of elected leaders to the people. Representative governments are "more or less" rather than fully democratic.

Nondemocratic governments

A nation is not democratic simply because it holds elections for a president, congress, or parliament. Hitler's Germany had a parliament, but Hitler wrote that the leaders would be free "from the parliamentary principle of decision by the majority" and that decisions would be made only by "responsible persons," which in practice meant himself. In communist countries which call themselves *people's democracies* there are elections to representative bodies, but in almost every case only the Communist Party nominates candidates for office, and the only choice the voter has is to deposit the ballot with the name of the communist nominee or to go into a voting booth and cross off the name in protest. Few people enter a voting booth under such circumstances. A one-party government does not satisfy the conditions for democracy, nor does it provide adequate representation or accountability. "It has been said that democracy is the worst form of government," said Winston Churchill, "except for all those other forms that have been tried from time to time."

Authoritarian government. Some political scientists distinguish two types of nondemocratic government: authoritarian and totalitarian. *Authoritarian* governments base their power solely on brute force rather than the consent of the governed. Their leaders usually come from the ranks of the military or from internal security agencies. They take power in a coup d'état and maintain themselves with rigged elections. Their governments arrest, torture, and kill their political opponents. They tolerate or encourage "goon squads" and "death squads" which support the government by killing or mutilating opponents. Often these regimes justify such use of force in the name of "fighting communism" or "preserving western values" and seek to win public support from democracies by arguing that free elections and a multiparty system are luxuries which they cannot afford while they are putting down their opponents. Their arguments would be more convincing if they did not crush democratic movements and parties that have no connections to communists. They still have no effective answer to Lincoln's question: "Why should there not be a patient confidence in the ultimate justice of the people? Is there any better or equal hope in the world?"

Some authoritarian rulers are little more than thugs, hardly distinguishable from the organized crime figures who prosper under their rule. They may traffic in drugs, smuggle arms, manipulate the currency, divert foreign aid for their own use, and loot the treasury. They run *gangster states;* their leaders take power just for the payoffs, and not only can they be bought, but they can also be rented by anyone with a money-making proposition likely to exploit their own people. Recent examples include Cuba under Fulgencio Batista, Haiti under "Papa Doc" Duvalier and his son "Baby Doc," and Uganda under Idi Amin.

Totalitarian governments. As bad, if not worse, are the *totalitarian* governments. A governing party, either the communists of the left or the fascists of the right, assumes power from a weak democracy—sometimes by winning an election and sometimes by using force. Imbued with its vision of remolding the people and creating a perfect society, its idealism leads it to excesses. Totalitarians must dominate all groups—religious, social, economic, cultural, and political—and subordinate them to the government. The individual must bow to the will of "the people" (as determined by the ruling party) in

all matters. The totalitarian government wishes to control the population in mind and spirit as well as in body.

Totalitarian governments have liquidated millions of people: Nazi Germany sent 12 million people (including 6 million Jews) to death in concentration camps; the Soviet Union under Stalin killed, imprisoned, or exiled millions in its Gulag prisons. For those who live in such countries, there is very little difference between totalitarian and authoritarian regimes.

POLITICAL AUTHORITY AND LEGITIMACY

"Political power," Mao Tse-tung said, "grows out of the barrel of a gun." But people are ruled by more than force, and power is not the only basis of a relationship between rulers and the ruled. *Authority,* which rests on the people's belief in the ruler's capability, and *legitimacy,* which rests on their acceptance of the leader's right to rule, are two important aspects of politics.

Political authority

What is authority? In everyday speech we might say that a professor is an authority in a field or that a sportscaster is an authority on football; we also put someone down by asking, "What are you, some kind of authority?" Both these examples involve someone who is communicating to other people about a subject. Authority is a relationship which exits when someone sets forth a reasoned elaboration of his or her ideas and this reasoning is accepted by others.

Not all authority is rational. *Traditional* authority depends on magic, superstition, customs, and ritual and might be exercised by a tribal leader, headman, or shaman (witch doctor). *Charismatic* authority involves faith that the personal qualities of the ruler will result in the best policies; the "man on horse-

The authority of government rests in large part on the success and credibility of the laws it makes. Bill-signing ceremonies in the Rose Garden give presidents publicity which helps them lead public opinion. *(Wide World Photos.)*

back" in Latin America is typical, and Indira Gandhi in India, Mao Tse-tung in China, Vladimir Lenin in Russia, and Adolph Hitler in Germany are other examples.

Governments must maintain their authority; people are more likely to obey laws and regulations and to cooperate with the government when they believe that their leaders know what they are doing and are acting in the people's best interests. The politician who loses authority in a democracy is likely to lose the next election.

Authority in the United States.   American leaders often find it difficult to maintain their authority. "The Constitution provides for every accidental contingency," Senator Sherman once said about President Buchanan's administration, "except for a vacancy in the mind of the president." In the 1920s Will Rogers made a career out of ridiculing politicians, deadpanning to his audiences, "I don't make jokes, I just watch the government and report the facts." The novelist Saul Bellow says, "Take our politicians, they're a bunch of yo-yos," a sentiment which many Americans share. President Hoover became a laughingstock during the ***depression*** because of his promises that "prosperity is just around the corner," and Nixon had to tell the American people that "your president is not a crook." Jimmy Carter's authority eroded as a result of the Iranian hostage crisis and the energy crisis, and Reagan lost some public support over the Bitburg incident.

When American politicians lose authority—because they lack the expertise necessary to solve problems, because their forecasts turn out to be incorrect, because their subordinates abuse power, or for any other reason—public support for their programs drops sharply, even when they remain personally popular. It becomes more difficult for them to exert power or influence at home and abroad. Allies reassess their support, while enemies probe for weaknesses. Their party splits into factions and may even challenge the president for renomination, as happened in 1952, 1968, 1976, and 1980. The opposition party keeps up its strong criticism, confident of winning the next election.

It is not always the case that our leaders and our government have little authority. George Washington and his supporters had the confidence of most Americans. Abraham Lincoln actually gained authority during the Civil War. When he entered office, even his own Cabinet and Republican Party leaders, who viewed him as a hopeless frontier politician incapable of leading the nation during a crisis, had little respect for him; at his death he was a major figure, "Father Abraham" to the nation. Franklin Roosevelt's ability as a communicator sustained the authority of the government in the midst of the depression and during the Second World War. "The only thing we have to fear is fear itself," he told the American people at his first inaugural, and they believed him. More recently, presidents Kennedy and Johnson used their authority to preside over a revolution in race relations that secured civil rights for racial minorities. One of the most important tasks in the United States today is that of restoring the government's authority with the people. Ultimately this must involve more effective government, which institutes policies that command wide public support—something easier said than done.

Legitimacy

"The strongest is never strong enough to be always the master," argued the French philosopher Jean-Jacques Rousseau, "unless he transforms strength

into right, and obedience into duty." People obey their leaders because they believe that they ought to.

What is legitimacy? By what right does a government exist? By what right do politicians rule? Why should they be obeyed? Each of these questions involves legitimacy. In the most practical sense a government is *legitimate* when other governments concede that it has a right to exercise a monopoly of force over the people in a particular territory and when most of the people it rules concede that it has a right to do so.

To delegitimize an existing government is to raise questions about its right to rule, usually by arguing that, by its very nature, it is unjust or evil. As the philosopher Blaise Pascal said, "Force without justice is tyrannical." When enough people believe that they are living in a society which is fundamentally unjust to them, in which the rulers may abuse their trust without penalty, or in which the rules of the game are rigged against them, that government faces a legitimacy crisis.

Throughout history, rulers have had to legitimize their governments. European kings in the seventeenth century relied on *divine right:* the monarch upheld the authority of an established church (and exempted it from taxation and civil law), and in return the church presided over the coronation and invested the reign with divine sanction. It was a useful arrangement for both church and crown. Other legitimizing principles include **aristocracy** (rule by those suited by birth to govern), **plutocracy** (rule by those who have made money and presumably have demonstrated ability), **technocracy** (rule by those who are scientifically and technically trained to deal with complex problems), and **democracy** (rule by the people, or at least a majority of the people).

Legitimacy in American politics. The American independence movement involved an attack on the right of the British king, George III, to rule over the colonies: the Declaration of Independence is a long list of complaints against the king for his alleged misrule. "The history of the present King of Great Britain," the Declaration says, "is a history of repeated injuries and usurpations, all having in direct object the establishment of an absolute Tyranny over these states." There follow twenty-seven paragraphs, listing in detail all the crimes, abuses of power, and tyrannical acts committed by the king. The Declaration of Independence tried to delegitimize George III so that the rebellion of American subjects against their sovereign could be justified at home and abroad.

We have had other legitimacy crises. In the 1830s, a sectional crisis involving tariffs almost led to the secession of South Carolina. That state argued that any state had a right to *nullify* (that is, to refuse to enforce within its borders) laws passed by Congress. In the 1850s we had a legitimacy crisis between the north and the south over slavery: the north wanted to confine slavery to those states in which it already existed; the south wanted to extend it across the west. Southerners argued that restrictions would be unjust and that if they were imposed, the union was no longer worth maintaining. President Lincoln, in his 1861 inaugural address, pointed out that the Constitution contained no provision for its termination or for the secession of any state. It was a contract between the people of all the states, and it would be illegitimate for a state to

All governments maintain a monopoly of force within the territory they control. Army troops, acting under orders of President Franklin Roosevelt, disperse the "Bonus Army" of unemployed World War I veterans, camped out in the Capital District, during the depression. (*National Archives.*)

leave the union without the consent of all the other states. The south remained unpersuaded, and the Civil War was the result.

We have not had a full-blown legitimacy crisis since the Civil War. The fundamental principles of our government and the right of our elected leaders to govern have not come under sustained attack by a significant part of the nation since 1861. But we have had some close calls. During the great depression of the 1930s, some of the millions of unemployed and desperate men and women turned to communist or fascist movements and parties. But because the New Deal government of President Roosevelt successfully maintained its authority and gave most suffering Americans hope for the future by establishing new government agencies to provide aid, the crisis of legitimacy was confined to only a small minority of the people. In the 1960s, white student radicals and black nationalists also challenged the legitimacy of the system, but their critiques never commanded the support of more than a small fraction of the people, even though many of their specific proposals were incorporated into the reform agenda of the decade.

Legitimacy crises may involve *usurpation* or *abuse* of power. To usurp power is to take the rightful place of another, as when a military strongman institutes a coup and replaces an elected official, suspends civil liberties, and scraps the constitution. To abuse power is to refuse to enforce or follow the laws, to enforce them arbitrarily, or to act completely outside the law. "Nobody has a more sacred obligation to obey the law than those who make the law," the Greek playwright Sophocles wrote, but many politicians cannot seem to get the idea straight. The Watergate crisis of the early 1970s, for example, involved not usurpation of power (Richard Nixon had been reelected president by an overwhelming majority in 1972), but rather abuse of power, since the president conspired not only to ignore certain laws but also to disobey others.

18

Some respected political scientists (such as James MacGregor Burns, a Pulitzer prizewinning presidential biographer) and government practitioners (such as Lloyd Cutler, a former White House counsel) believe that our constitutional arrangements are so antiquated and inefficient that only a complete overhaul will suffice to provide a constitution suited for the third century of democracy in the United States. Other people think that some sort of *world government* should replace nation-states like our own.

Is our Constitution suited to modern conditions? Can it be adapted with minor modifications, or does it need a complete overhaul? Should we try to strengthen our democracy, relying further on the principle of majority rule? Or should we turn over government to a technocracy, to the "experts," and limit the role of the people and their elected representatives? If we still believe, as Churchill did, that although democracy may not be very efficient, it is better than any other form of government, how can we improve our democracy to keep it that way?

PREVIEW

POWER, AUTHORITY, AND LEGITIMACY IN A NEW NATION. Chapter 2 will discuss the pursuit, uses, and ends of power, as well as the accountability of those in power, by examining the politics of the Constitutional Convention of 1787. The events of that year involved politics in the best sense of the word. Crises which threatened the independence and prosperity of the American people reached a climax and were resolved. Analyzing what the convention delegates accomplished

Members of the Continental Congress sign the Declaration of Independence in Philadelphia in 1776. *("Declaration of Independence," John Trumbull; Yale University Art Gallery.)*

is no sterile exercise in "history," nor does it provide merely "background" knowledge, a preface one must endure before getting to the subject of politics today. Far from it. Chapter 2 is a case study which describes the skills and techniques of professional politicians. You will learn a great deal about practical politics, and you will also gain a useful perspective on some of the problems we face two centuries later, as we continue our experiment in democratic government. For if our system now seems antiquated, there is nothing to stop us from using the same techniques used by the convention delegates to modernize our politics if we choose to do so. That too is what democratic politics is all about.

FURTHER READING

Barnes, James F., Marshall Carter, and Max J. Skidmore: *The World of Politics*, 2d ed., St. Martin's, New York, 1984. The important concepts of politics are summarized and explained, with excellent examples given throughout.

de Tocqueville, Alexis: *Democracy in America*, Vintage Books, New York (first published in 1839). This account by a young French nobleman who was impressed by American society and politics remains one of the most accurate and influential discussions of American politics.

Huntington, Samuel P.: *American Politics: The Promise of Disharmony*, Belknap Press, Harvard University Press, Cambridge, Mass., 1981. A study of the differences between political theory and rhetoric and political practice in American politics.

Lasswell, Harold: *Politics: Who Gets What, When, How*, Meridian Books, New York, 1958. A classic discussion of political power.

Perlmutter, Amos: *Modern Authoritarianism*, Yale University Press, New Haven, Conn., 1984. A discussion of totalitarian and authoritarian states and leaders, from Hitler to Idi Amin.

Rosenau, James M.: *The Dramas of Politics: An Introduction to the Joys of Inquiry*, Little, Brown, Boston, 1973. A highly recommended discussion of ways of approaching political studies, written by a noted political scientist.

Schatschneider, E. E.: *The Semi-Sovereign People*, Holt, New York, 1975. A critique of American politics from the point of view of a political scientist who would like to see greater democratization.

Wolfe, Alan: *The Limits of Legitimacy: Political Contradictions of Contemporary Capitalism*, Free Press, New York, 1977. A radical critique from the point of view of a democratic socialist who believes that this country's class-based and liberal politics is not democratic.

THE STUDY BREAK

Doonesbury. A syndicated comic strip by Garry Trudeau, dealing with students of the 1960s who are now grown-up professionals adapting to the 1980s.

Feiffer, Jules: *Jules Feiffer's America.* A collection of cartoons by a leading liberal, from the 1950s to the present.

Trudeau, Garry: *In Search of Reagan's Brain.* A collection of comic strips by the creator of *Doonesbury,* covering the 1980 election and the early days of the Reagan administration.

1984. A movie based on George Orwell's vision of a totalitarian society, starring Richard Burton.

USEFUL SOURCES

ABC POL-SCI. A monthly compendium (published by ABC-CLIO, in Santa Barbara, California) of the tables of contents of more than 300 journals in political science, international affairs, law, and public policy.

Blum, John N., Edmund S. Morgan, Willie Lee Rose, Arthur M. Schlesinger, Jr., Kenneth M. Stampp, and C. Vann Woodward: *The National Experience: A History of the United States,* Harcourt Brace Jovanovich, New York, 1981. A one-volume history which discusses many of the events mentioned in this textbook.

Degenhardt, Henry W.: *Political Dissent: An International Guide to Dissident, Extra-Parliamentary, Guerilla and Illegal Political Movements,* Gale Research, Detroit, 1983. A discussion of the opponents of sovereign nations in the 1980s.

Handbook of the Nations, 1981, Gale Research, Detroit, 1981. A guide to the economy, government, and defense establishments of 188 nations and other entities.

Holler, Frederick L.: *Information Sources of Political Science,* ABC-CLIO, Santa Barbara, Calif., 1981. A compendium of periodicals, newspapers, and radio and television broadcasts on political topics.

Plano, Jack, Robert E. Riggs, and Helen S. Robin (eds.): *The Dictionary of Political Analysis,* ABC-CLIO, Santa Barbara, Calif., 1982. A useful political dictionary.

Worldwide Government Directory with Inter-Governmental Organizations, 1983, Lambert Publications, Washington, D.C., 1982. A guide to sovereign governments.

CHAPTER 2
CONSTITUTIONAL DEMOCRACY

The ratification of the Constitution was celebrated in New York in 1788. Ever since, it has been amended and adapted to meet new circumstances. One amendment proposed in the 1980s would outlaw abortions. *(Granger Collection; Paul Hosefros: New York Times.)*

They called themselves *regulators*. They were farmers in Massachusetts, many of them veterans of the Revolution, and in the summer of 1786 they faced hard times. Taxes were high, and prices for their crops were low. The lawyers circled around their farms like buzzards, obtaining writs from the courts to take their crops, their livestock, and even their ancestral land in payment for debts.

In the hills of western Massachusetts they held popular conventions and drafted petitions to the state legislature in which they told of their suffering. In Bristol they called for paper money. In Hatfield they asked that the Court of Common Pleas be abolished and that the state stop sending money to Congress. But the state legislature adjourned without heeding the petitions or passing a law which would stay foreclosures.

On August 31 armed men prevented a court from sitting in Northampton, and on September 5 a court meeting in Worcester was disrupted. Crowds would not let cases be tried, and in many places they freed farmers from debtors' prisons. When the state supreme court tried to meet in Springfield, 600 farmers, led by Daniel Shays, who had been a captain in the Revolutionary War, squared off against an equal number of militiamen sent by Governor James Bowdoin, and the judges withdrew to Boston. Mobs prevented courts from sitting in Great Barrington, and judges had to sign pledges that they would not act until the grievances of the people were redressed.

Governor Bowdoin took a hard line. He suspended habeas corpus (which meant that he could hold people without trial), raised a militia with pledges of contributions from the financiers and merchants of Boston who were opposed to paper money, and sent his forces out to crush the farmers. On January 25 Daniel Shays and 1200 followers confronted General William Shepherd and an equal force at the federal arsenal at Springfield. The militia's cannon routed Shays and his men. Some returned home. Others fled through the Berkshires, in deep winter snows over frozen ground, but 4400 fresh militiamen, commanded by General Lincoln, overtook them by surprise at Petersham on February 4, dispersing them and capturing Shays and 150 of his followers.

On March 14 Shays and a dozen other leaders were tried, convicted, and sentenced to death. But Governor Bowdoin, soon to leave office, granted a reprieve, and his successor, John Hancock, pardoned all of them. The legislature, realizing that the farmers had legitimate grievances, decided not to impose a direct tax, lowered court fees, and exempted clothing, household goods, and workers' tools from court judgments.

Shays's rebellion profoundly shocked American political leaders. "For God's sake tell me what is the cause of all these commotions," George Washington said. "Do they proceed from licentiousness, British influence disseminated by the Tories, or real grievances which admit of redress?" To conservatives, like Abigail Adams, wife of John Adams, the American ambassador to London, the

rebels were simply "ignorant, wrestless desperadoes, without conscience or principles," acting on "grievances which have no existence but in their imaginations." To Thomas Jefferson, the ambassador to Paris, they were a necessary stimulus to reform. "I like a little rebellion now and then," he wrote to Abigail Adams. "It is like a storm in the atmosphere." Yet everyone knew that Shays's rebellion was not the first of the debtors' rebellions, nor would it be the last, unless some drastic changes were made in the way Americans went about the business of self-government. The troubles in Massachusetts had far more impact than the farmers fleeing in the Berkshire woods could have known. Even then, George Washington and other American political leaders were making plans for a constitutional convention in Philadelphia, one that might be the last chance to preserve democratic government in the states and the nation.

There were strong doubts about the survival of the thirteen state governments and of the Articles of Confederation, which loosely united them. Washington, at his Virginia plantation, feared "the worst consequences from a half-starved, limping government, always moving on crutches and tottering at every step." James Madison received a letter from a friend serving in Congress warning that "if it remains much longer in its present state of imbecility, we shall be one of the most contemptible nations on the face of the earth." In the spring of 1787 Madison himself wrote to Edmund Randolph, the governor of Virginia, saying, "No money comes into the federal treasury, no respect is paid to the federal authority; and people of reflection unanimously agree that the existing confederacy is tottering to its foundation." At the Harvard College commencement of 1787, John Quincy Adams (who later served as the sixth president of the United States) delivered the valedictory address, in which he complained of a people "groaning under the intolerable burden of . . . accumulated evils."[1]

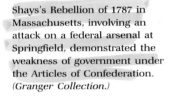

Shays's Rebellion of 1787 in Massachusetts, involving an attack on a federal arsenal at Springfield, demonstrated the weakness of government under the Articles of Confederation. *(Granger Collection.)*

Yet one year later the national mood had changed completely. A constitution, replacing the Articles of Confederation, had created a union of the thirteen states. At the parades held in New York City, Philadelphia, Boston, Charleston, Baltimore, and elsewhere, floats expressed the new optimism: coopers put thirteen staves, each representing a state, into a tremendous barrel symbolizing the union; ship carpenters built huge models of the "ship of state," *Constitution;* chairmakers hung a banner that read, "The Federal States in Union bound, O'er all the world our chairs are found"; and blacksmiths paraded under the slogan, "While industry prevails, We need no foreign nails."[2]

Why had the American spirit changed so completely? And what could a written constitution possibly have contained that would have made Americans so confident about the future of their nation? To answer these questions about the creation of our Constitution is to take up the central problems of politics: authority, legitimacy, and power.

THE BREAKDOWN OF THE OLD POLITICS: THE ARTICLES OF CONFEDERATION

The thirteen colonies declared themselves free and independent from England in 1776 and then won their freedom in the Revolutionary War, which was fought between 1775 and 1781 and was ended by the Treaty of Paris, signed in 1783. Initially, each state was an independent government represented in the ***Continental Congress.***

Government under the Articles

The thirteen states were allied under the ***Articles of Confederation.*** Drafted in 1777 during the Revolutionary War by the Continental Congress (representatives of each state authorized to fight the war and handle diplomatic relations) and put into effect in 1781, the Articles created a league of friendship rather than a government.

Most Americans mistrusted a strong central government, equating it with the excesses of British rule. They believed that such a government would dominate the states and threaten their individual liberties, as they believed that

Figure 2-1. Claims of states to lands in the west were a source of potential conflict with European powers and with each other. The British maneuvered against New York and Massachusetts for control of Vermont. The Northern border of Maine remained in dispute. Connecticut and Pennsylvania almost went to war when Connecticut settlers were blocked by the Pennsylvania militia from farming western lands. By 1786 most states had renounced claims to the Northwest Territory, and Congress passed the law providing for its regulation at the same time the Constitutional Convention was meeting in Philadelphia. But unless the states had created a strong central government, other claims would undoubtedly have caused friction in the future.

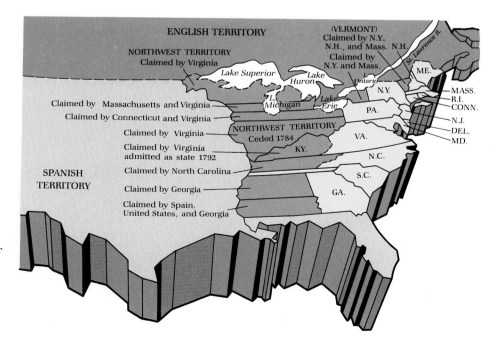

THE ARTICLES OF CONFEDERATION: HOW THINGS LOOKED IN THE 1780S

Features of the government. The state governments have most of the powers. They control commerce with one another and with foreign nations, and they impose duties on imports and taxes on exports. They issue currency and determine which bank notes, coins, and bills from other states are legal tender. They have police and judicial power and their own militia.

Congress has few powers. It decides on matters of war and peace and requisitions funds from the states, but only by unanimous vote. It conducts diplomatic relations and enters into treaties and alliances with other nations. (The states may also enter into treaties with the approval of Congress.) By the vote of seven states, it may issue currency and coins, manage the public debt, run a post office, and arbitrate disputes between states.

Congress has no power to tax. It has no power to raise armed forces directly. It cannot take action against the citizens of the states. It has no police powers and no courts to enforce national law.

National security and foreign relations (Figure 2-1). The British demand payment of their merchants' claims from the Revolutionary War. They use this as a pretext to refuse to evacuate their garrisons in New York and the west. They incite Indian raids against American settlers, encourage Vermont to become a province of Canada, and discriminate against American shipbuilders and merchants. Congress cannot agree on a commerce act to retaliate against the British.

The Spanish close the Mississippi River to American commerce in 1784, putting western settlers at their mercy for trade. They incite Indian raids and claim territory belonging to Georgia—what later became Alabama, Mississippi, Tennessee, and Kentucky.

Indian tribes raid settlements in the Ohio valley in 1786. Congress cannot raise the money to provide protection for western settlers.

Barbary pirates seize American ships in the Mediterranean. Most nations pay a tribute to the pirates to protect their ships, but Congress cannot raise the money for a tribute, and thus American ships and cargoes are put at risk.

Territorial and sectional issues. Settlers in the Northwest Territories threaten to secede. They might ally themselves with the Spanish, who control the Mississippi, their lifeline to the world.

The states have conflicting claims in the Northwest Territories. Some claim lands that belong to others, and there is armed conflict between Connecticut settlers on disputed land (the Wyoming valley) in Pennsylvania. New York and New Hampshire feud over the Green Mountains (later Vermont).

Foreign observers and many Americans believe that the confederation will dissolve into three regional groups, each allied with a different European power.

Economic issues. The states refuse to give the unanimous agreement necessary to pass financial plans drawn up by Congress. Many revenue plans are defeated.

The states refuse to pay their assessments, even though Congress has passed them unanimously.

The states place burdens on interstate commerce by levying duties or erecting trade barriers. They burden foreign commerce with export taxes and import duties.

Congress is unable to raise foreign loans except by borrowing from private bankers at very high rates of interest.

Congress is unable to give soldiers the pensions and bonuses they were promised during the war.

Foreign investors have no confidence in the financial solvency of the government or in its stability, and they hold off on plans to invest in the American economy.

King George and Parliament had done. The states would be the guardians of the "right to life, liberty, and the pursuit of happiness," which Americans had claimed for themselves in the Declaration of Independence.

The Articles guaranteed the sovereignty and independence of the states, which retained vast powers. Congress was limited in what it could do, as "The Articles of Confederation: How Things Looked in the 1780s" indicates. Because it could act only on important matters with extraordinary majorities, it could not solve the most pressing problems: threats to security from foreign powers and Indians, disputes over settlement of western territories, and the payment of debts, the regulation of currencies, and the promotion of commerce.

There was no executive branch. A president of Congress, elected by its members, was the presiding officer and represented the "dignity" of the nation on ceremonial occasions. The powerlessness of this office can best be understood by noting that in the president's absence, a *clerk* was designated to perform his duties. Congress used boards and commissions to transact public business until 1781, when it began to establish departments, each run by a single executive and loosely supervised by congressional committees.

The failure of the Articles

By 1787 most people believed that the Continental Congress had worked better in the 1770s than the Articles of Confederation were working in the 1780s. Americans were of two minds about the Articles. They did not want a strong government, but neither did they respect a weak one. Thus Congress, under the Articles, was intentionally ineffective; it was not given enough power to manage national affairs. Because it had little power, it did not attract the most important politicians, who preferred to serve in state government. There was a high rate of turnover in delegations to Congress, partly because of a provision that prevented anyone from serving for more than three years in any six-year period. Often members did not attend sessions, and it was difficult to keep a quorum of seven states to transact business, much less obtain the approval of nine for important matters.

The drift toward anarchy. The small army was a volatile factor in domestic politics. Peace brought the soldiers and veterans neither the pay nor the pensions they had been promised. In December 1782, a petition from army units in Newburgh, New York, warned Congress that "any further experiments on their patience might have fatal effects." Since Congress refused to bow to pressure, Alexander Hamilton (a former aide of George Washington) encouraged the commanding officer at Newburgh, Thomas Gates, to call a camp meeting, presumably to have the troops march on Philadelphia and pressure Congress. Washington raced to the encampment and called his own meeting. In this tense atmosphere, he took out a speech he had prepared and, fumbling with his spectacles, remarked that "he had grown old and grey in the service of his country, and now he had grown blind as well."[3] Washington called on the men to disavow mutiny, have patience with Congress, and support his own peaceful efforts to secure them their due. The mutiny collapsed. Washington rebuked Hamilton and warned him against conspiracies, though he observed that "no man in the United States is, or can be, more deeply impressed with the necessity of reform in our present Confederation than myself."[4]

Two years later a group of eighty drunken soldiers from a camp near Philadelphia marched into the city, ransacked an arsenal for weapons, took up

Alexander Hamilton, the future Federalist and Secretary of the Treasury, serving as an aide to General Washington during the Revolutionary War. *(Culver Pictures, Inc.)*

positions near Congress, and, after firing some rounds, forced the legislators to flee to Princeton, New Jersey. The Pennsylvania state militia refused to help Congress, and only after the mutineers threatened to break into the Bank of North America did the state militia chase them out of the city. Between 1784 and 1787 Congress wandered from one town to another, settling temporarily in Princeton, then in Trenton, then in Annapolis, and then in Trenton again, finally coming to rest in New York City, where Benjamin Rush observed that it was "abused, laughed at, pitied, and cursed in every company." The confederation seemed to be drifting toward **anarchy.**

The reaction to Shays's rebellion. Americans were deeply divided, with the most intense conflicts involving debtors against creditors. The latter insisted that the former pay loans off with hard currency, and they foreclosed on property when payments were not made. Enraged debtors, primarily small farmers, won control of the legislatures in some states, and when they did they enacted laws which made paper money legal tender to pay debts, even though such currency quickly depreciated and was almost worthless. Seven states issued such currency in 1786. They also passed "stay laws" that prevented lenders from foreclosing on property.

The situation got out of hand in Rhode Island. The paper money was worth so little that merchants finally decided to close up shop rather than accept it for their goods. Farmers forcibly opened stores and looted them to obtain needed supplies, and they threatened to stop bringing food into towns if merchants stuck to their policy.

The events in Rhode Island, Massachusetts, and other states frightened everyone. The smell of class warfare and revolution was in the air. John Jay, a prominent New York politician (and later the first chief justice of the Supreme Court), wrote to Washington, predicting that "if faction should long bear down Law and Government, Tyranny may raise its head, or the more sober parts of the people may even think of a King." Jay hinted to Washington that the general should consider becoming the American monarch, but Washington responded negatively. It seemed clear to American leaders that if class antagonisms could not be controlled, the fabric of American society, and of the state governments, would be torn to shreds. Disorder, as Jay observed, leads to calls for order, and the choice would then be between tyranny of the masses and a monarchy, with Washington wearing the crown.

It seemed clearer than ever that Congress under the Articles could not maintain order. In the midst of Shays's rebellion, Henry Knox, the secretary of war, informed Congress that the confederation did not have funds to raise and pay troops to put down the insurrection and could not even guard its own arsenal at Springfield, which had almost been captured by Shays's followers.[5]

The crisis and political response

Almost as soon as independence had been won, a few statesmen with vision recognized the need for strong government. Alexander Hamilton in 1781 and James Madison in 1783 proposed that the Articles be amended to strengthen Congress and allow it to regulate commerce and raise taxes. George Washington released a letter in 1783 calling for a stronger government; to avoid any misunderstanding, he pledged that he would "never take any share in public business." But in 1784 and 1786 proposed amendments to the Articles dealing with commerce were rejected.

Alexander Hamilton (a founder of the Bank of New York), Robert Morris, and James Wilson (both cofounders of the Bank of North America in Philadelphia) proposed a national bank which could issue its own currency and manage the national debt for Congress. They thought that a national bank would restore the confidence of property holders and foreign investors in the government. Congress gave a national charter to the Bank of North America in 1781, but its charter to do business in its home state was revoked in 1786 by the Pennsylvania legislature; this put an end to their efforts at commercial and financial reform.

Hamilton and Madison next called for a convention to revise the Articles with regard to commerce. Delegates from only five states showed up at the meeting in Annapolis in 1786 (delegates from several other states were delayed), and so nothing could be done at that meeting, but Hamilton had the group call for a national convention to be held in Philadelphia the following spring. Madison convinced Washington to attend, and twelve states agreed to send delegates.

Such a convention would do more than amend the Articles: leading politicians, especially those in Washington's circle, were upset about events in Massachusetts. If debtors acquired political power, then the prospects of "legal Shaysism" would ensue. Washington was now convinced that only bold steps could end the crisis.

But most Americans continued to mistrust strong government and did not want a national government. They also were opposed to monarchy in any form. There were rumors that the Society of the Cincinnati, a group of former officers who had served with Washington, planned to obtain land grants in the west and fill them with German peasant farmers, thus establishing a feudal system in America. Give Congress the power to tax, some thought, and it would create a monarchy and an aristocracy with an extravagant court life and a large capital city at the expense of country folk.

Prospects for change. Weighed against these difficulties were certain favorable circumstances. Washington was a delegate to the convention. He remained popular with the military—officers and enlisted men alike. He was close to financiers and merchants, was himself a plantation owner and a speculator in western lands, and had ties to northern financial interests. He understood the interests of all regions and of important economic groups. Exasperated by the disorders in Massachusetts, he pressed for fundamental change, not minor reforms.

Above all, Washington reflected the optimism, confidence, and love of experimentation with political forms that spurred Americans to act boldly in crises. The historian David Ramsey caught the spirit of the times in his account of the Revolution, written in 1789, when he observed that the war "gave a spring to the active powers of the inhabitants and set them on thinking, speaking and acting in a line far beyond that to which they had been accustomed. . . . It seemed as if the war not only required but created talents."[6] The same could be said of the crisis that followed.

Limits to change. In hindsight it is obvious that by 1787 a new form of government was needed to replace the Articles. But it was not so obvious at the time to most Americans, who were weary from the war and uninterested in

Within two years of presiding over the Constitutional Convention at Philadelphia in 1784, George Washington became the first president of the United States of America. *(Granger Collection.)*

politics. Most felt that the disturbances in the states would eventually be sorted out and that the economy would improve in the postwar reconstruction.

Most state politicians were willing to support modification of the Articles to improve commerce, but they did not want radical change—especially not change that would reduce their own powers. The convention delegates would be forcing change on a people reluctant to accept it. They would have to convince their colleagues in the states that it was necessary for them to yield power, and always their proposals would be tempered by calculations of what state politicians would accept.

IN CONVENTION ASSEMBLED

From up and down the eastern seaboard delegates chosen by state legislatures to attend the ***Constitutional Convention of 1787*** converged on Philadelphia in the spring of that year. Traveling by coach on muddy turnpikes and post roads or by coastal packets, they were to meet in late May at Independence Hall, where just eleven years earlier another group had signed the Declaration of Independence.

The state delegations

Rhode Island alone among the states refused to send a delegation, realizing that this convention would try to clip the powers of state legislatures. Virginia sent the most prestigious delegation: George Washington, James Madison, Edmund Randolph, and George Mason, all of whom played a major part in the deliberations. Pennsylvania sent a group of eight, six of whom had opposed the state constitution adopted in 1777 because they thought that it was too

31

democratic. They included James Wilson and Robert Morris, cofounders of the Bank of North America, and Gouverneur Morris, a founder of the Bank of New York, as well as Benjamin Franklin, the grand old man of the Revolution and former ambassador to France.

Massachusetts sent a group of seasoned politicians, including the governor, Elbridge Gerry, for whom the **gerrymander** (the drawing of political boundaries to favor one party over another) would later be named. Connecticut and New Jersey sent moderates such as Roger Sherman and William Paterson, who were intent on protecting the rights of the small states. New York sent a curious delegation. Hamilton, who favored a strong national government, was counterbalanced by two delegates, John Lansing and Robert Yates—known as his "chaperones," since they opposed major changes in the Articles and could outvote him.

Overall, the fifty-five delegates represented the cream of American leadership. Over half had received a university education, including nine from Princeton, four each from William and Mary and Yale, and three each from Harvard and Columbia. There were two college presidents, three professors, and several teachers. A dozen were planters or farmers, a dozen were lawyers, and a dozen, including seven governors, held high state office. Forty-six had served in either colonial or state legislatures. Thirty-nine had served in Congress. Twenty had served in, and several had played important roles in, the Revolutionary War. They were young; the average age was the early forties, but five were under 30, and Alexander Hamilton, James Madison, and Gouverneur Morris were all under 36. George Washington himself was only 55. They were, in the words of James MacGregor Burns, "the well read, well fed, well bred, and well wed."[7]

The delegates did not represent a cross section of American political thinking. Most were conservative or moderate. Radicals like Sam Adams of Massachusetts and Tom Paine of Pennsylvania had not been chosen by their states to attend, and Patrick Henry of Virginia refused to serve. Thomas Jefferson and John Adams were abroad serving as ambassadors, and few of the signers of the Declaration of Independence had been chosen as delegates. There were no representatives of debtors, small farmers, western settlers, or societies of mechanics and artisans. Blacks and women had no place. Indians were considered members of sovereign tribes with whom the states had concluded treaties or truces, not citizens who could participate in politics.

We sometimes think of the men who created the Constitution as demigods blessed with infinitely superior wisdom and vision, far removed from the politicians who occupy office today. Nothing could be further from the truth. The Constitution was created by flesh-and-blood politicians. They were first and foremost practical men of affairs. They had founded banks, engaged in commerce, speculated in western lands, and cultivated great plantations and estates. They came together in 1787 as pragmatic experimenters, determined to improve the machinery of government only because the existing machinery had failed them.

Political ideas at the convention

The delegates to the convention were eager to try out some of the new political theories which were being developed both in Europe and in the American states at the end of the eighteenth century.[8] Many corresponded with one another and with Washington in the months before the convention, testing out

their ideas. A few belonged to the newly formed Society for Political Inquiry, founded by Madison and Franklin. The delegates—at least the most influential ones—were widely read in history, philosophy, and law, and their ideas informed the convention debates.

Constitutionalism: Limited government by consent. American politicians were familiar with the principles of constitutional government: that a formal compact existed between the people establishing the government; that government rested on the *consent of the people;* that government could exercise only powers delegated to it by the people; and that powers not delegated by the people remained with them and could not be exercised by the government. The first settlers in America established such an agreement—the Mayflower Compact of 1620—even before they set foot on land in America, and American settlers had always claimed the "rights of Englishmen," stemming all the way back to documents such as the Magna Carta of the thirteenth century and the various settlements between Parliament and the crown through the seventeenth century.

The Declaration of Independence embodied these theories of limited government resting on the consent of the people. Now in place of the "rights of Englishmen," the signers had proclaimed: "We hold these truths to be self-evident: That all men are created equal, that they are endowed by their Creator with certain unalienable Rights, that among these are Life, Liberty, and the Pursuit of Happiness. That to secure these rights, Governments are instituted among Men, deriving their just powers from the consent of the governed." Governments were instituted to secure these rights, and "whenever any Form of Government becomes destructive of these ends," the Declaration concluded, "it is the Right of the People to alter or abolish it, and to institute new Government."

After independence each state had written a constitution, most of them providing for strong, popularly elected legislatures, weak executives, and an independent judiciary and most of them recognizing the rights of the people and the limited delegation of power to the government. It was only natural that in establishing a national government, they would also draft a written constitution.

Representative government. Americans agreed that the new government would be based on popular consent. There would be no monarch. Most agreed with Tom Paine's observation that "a thirst for absolute power is the natural disease of monarchy" and his conclusion that "in England a King hath little more to do than to make war and give away places; which in plain terms is to impoverish the nation and set it together by the ears."[9] But direct democracy could not take the place of monarchy: the nation was much too large for that. Some form of indirect democracy or representative government would be required. The convention delegates did *not* believe that any system of representation should simply reflect the social structure: that would allow debtors, the poor, tradespeople and mechanics, and small farmers to dominate the new government. Representative institutions were to operate *for* the people but not consist *of* the people. They would "elevate" the government by creating electoral systems that would keep Congress in the hands of "men of intelligence and uprightness," as James Wilson put it.[10]

The great advantage of a national government, according to James Madison, was that it could be only a representative democracy, and therefore "the public voice, pronounced by the representatives of the people, will be more consonant of the public good than if pronounced by the people themselves, convened for the purpose."[11] Instead of raucous town meetings that might degenerate into more Shays's rebellions, representative government would provide, according to Madison, "the cool and deliberate sense of the community." In a large republic, moreover, there would be many men of talent and virtue, and so it would not be difficult, he reasoned, to fill up political offices with them, thus ensuring that the new government would be off to a good start. In similar words Alexander Hamilton argued that "the Republican principle demands that the deliberate sense of the community should govern the conduct of those to whom they intrust the management of their affairs."[12] There would be regular elections, of course, for as John Adams remarked, "Where the annual elections end, there slavery begins."

Pluralism. What the delegates to the convention worried about most was the possibility of class warfare in America: the have-nots against the haves, the debtors against the creditors, the poor without property against the rich with property. Madison sought to discover a principle that might prevent such conflict and provide for social stability; he believed that he found it in the relationship between federalism and popular government. Madison knew that people would pursue their own interests by combining into *factions*, and he knew that these factions would come into conflict with one another. If the majority-rule principle applies, then the majority with little or no property presumably can band together and govern in their own interest, which will be the antithesis of the interest of the minority with property. Such conflict was occuring in 1787.

One possible solution was to eliminate the cause of factions, which Madison identified as the unequal distribution of property. But to divide up property equally would require so much coercion against the wealthy that it could not be done except by force—and that would mean the end of liberty. If liberty could not be maintained without allowing factions to exist, then the solution would have to involve control, rather than elimination, of factions.

Madison came up with the idea that if the *size* of the republic were extended, so that it comprised all thirteen states, none of the various economic interests would be a majority. People would divide along religious lines (each of the Protestant sects, Catholics, and Jews), occupational interests (small farmers, plantation owners, tradespeople and mechanics, merchants, and professionals), and nationality (for example, those of English, Scotch, German, or Dutch ancestry)—but no one group would have a majority. Factions could not be *eliminated* from politics, Madison argued, but they could be *controlled* by setting one faction against another so that none could establish "the tyranny of the majority." Groups and sects would still clash with one another, but each would be zealous about safeguarding its own liberties and preventing others from transgressing them. The national government, according to Madison, could remain a "disinterested and dispassionate umpire in disputes" between different groups.[13] The result would be **pluralism** in place of majority rule.

Federalism. But how could the size of the republic be extended? At the time of the convention only two kinds of political associations were known: strong, centralized states, with a single government exercising all power and delegating functions to local governments, and leagues and confederacies of states, which allowed councils or congresses to exercise limited authority. The Articles of Confederation had followed the second model and had failed. But no one believed that it would be possible simply to scrap the state governments and replace them with a single national government—even though at various times during the convention both Hamilton and Madison argued for such a course. Neither the state politicians nor the people would support such a change. Americans would have to devise a governmental system that would provide stronger central government while retaining strong state governments. Such a system would have to rest on popular consent and embody democratic principles, and yet up to that time democracy had never been tried on so large a scale. At the time, no model for such a hybrid form of government existed; the delegates would be improvising and experimenting as they went along.

Avoiding tyranny: Separation of powers. "Where might is right there is no right," the playwright Sophocles had his chorus intone in ancient Greece. How to avoid the excesses of unrestrained power had always been a central concern of political theory, and no American government that did not address the problem could be legitimate. Seventeenth- and eighteenth-century political theorists developed the doctrine of *separation of powers* to ensure the rights of people against despotic government. John Locke, the English philosopher, wrote *Two Treatises on Government* after the Glorious Revolution of 1688 had limited the powers of the British monarch; in it he argued that there were three powers of government—legislative, executive, and federative (foreign affairs)—and that free government was best maintained when these powers were entrusted to different institutions. Baron de Montesquieu, in *The Spirit of the Laws*, written a half-century later, held that only when government was separated into executive, legislative, and judicial branches could liberty be ensured. "When the legislative and executive powers are united in the same person, or in the same body of magistracy," he wrote, "there can then be no liberty, because apprehensions may arise, lest the same monarch or senate should enact tyrannical laws, to execute them in a tyrannical manner." Similarly, "if the prince were to have a share in the legislature by the power of enacting, liberty would be lost."[14] William Blackstone's *Commentaries on the Laws of England* also emphasized the doctrine of separation of powers in its analysis of the British constitution. Most state constitutions written after American independence followed the maxim of separation of powers, and many contained clauses that forbade the executive from exercising legislative and judicial power, the judiciary from exercising legislative and executive power, and the legislature from exercising executive and judicial power. By the 1780s both John Adams[15] and Thomas Jefferson[16] had written tracts which defended the state constitutions to skeptical Europeans.

The convention at work: The politics of change

Not only would the delegates to the convention have to create a new form of government, but they would also have to create one that could solve concrete problems and resolve tensions between various sections. How should com-

merce be regulated? What should be done about the slave trade? How should taxes be collected? What could be done about navigation on the Mississippi? How should large and small states be represented so that all would feel secure in a new union? Political practice, not theory, would solve these problems at the convention.

Preconvention politics.   ESTABLISHING AUTHORITY.   In the 1780s many Americans thought that economic problems stemmed from postwar conditions and would soon work themselves out. Others thought that debtors were simply shiftless rabble-rousers who would be best dealt with by force. But people like Washington, Hamilton, and Madison recognized the true nature of the economic problems: that they were due in large part to the weakness of political arrangements. From the instability of government came the instability of the currency and the uncertainties about the debt.

The convention called for in 1786 attracted little attention until the Virginia legislature, at Madison's urging, named Washington a delegate. Seven other states then agreed to send delegates, and Congress sanctioned the plan. Washington's prospective participation attracted a roster of other distinguished leaders, twelve of whom had served with him during the war. Twelve others knew him through service in Congress. People like Benjamin Franklin (the president, or governor, of Pennsylvania) and William Johnson (the president-elect of Columbia College) agreed to attend. The presence of such a distinguished group of delegates guaranteed that the convention would have authority.

ENSURING LEGITIMACY.   Those who planned on scrapping the Articles of Confederation were proposing a bloodless transfer of power from the states to a new national government. They had to ensure the legitimacy of their efforts, or else they would be accused of usurping power. Washington understood (far

The new Constitution did not gain immediate universal respect. To a pamphleteer of 1792, a national government was a convention of asses. *(Historical Pictures Service.)*

Convention of Asses
or Spirit of Democracy.

better than Hamilton) that the people would never accept a military takeover, and he understood (far better than Jay) that they would not accept him as their king. Any new plan would have to have popular support.

This did not mean that the people had to be consulted about the Constitution as it was being drafted, or even that the plans had to conform to the wishes of the people. Some delegates argued that the people would never accept a strong central government. Those proposing one argued that it was the duty of the convention to convince the people that such a government was needed.

Madison and Hamilton called for the convention, which was similar to the state constitutional conventions, and arranged to have its meeting endorsed by Congress. Each state would send a delegation, chosen by its state legislature, and would cast a single vote at the convention, arrangements which accorded with the system of representation in Congress. By organizing the convention in terms familiar to the people, the delegates hoped to establish its legitimacy.

CONVENTION ARRANGEMENTS. "Secrecy is the first essential in affairs of state," Cardinal Richelieu pointed out in seventeenth-century France. Politicians must debate candidly, find areas of compromise, and make deals. All this requires frank discussion. To encourage candor, the convention closed its deliberations to the public and the press. Only delegates could attend, and only they could examine the daily journal of proceedings, kept under lock and key by the convention secretary. The delegates agreed that the proceedings would not be made available to the public for fifty years. Thus they could express their opinions without fear of public reaction. They could talk frankly about popular government, sectional disputes, and economic and class interests. Although the deliberations remained secret, the Constitution itself was to be presented to the people as soon as the convention was over. At that time full debate was encouraged by its supporters. Secrecy was a means to obtain consensus on a plan, not a way to thwart the ultimate right of the people to give or withhold their consent to it.

George Washington was elected the presiding officer on the first day. His very presence at the front of the hall was a reminder that the enterprise had a good chance to succeed—especially since most delegates assumed that he would probably head the new government. In fact, during the debates, many of the seemingly abstract discussions about the power of the government (and of the presidency in particular) took place with the realization that those involved were actually discussing powers that *Washington* would exercise.

The art of the possible. "A system must be suited to the habits & genius of the people it is to govern," argued Charles Pinckney, "and must grow out of them."[17] The convention delegates knew their political theories, but they relied primarily on practical experience with colonial government and state governments. "Experience must be our only guide," John Dickinson warned them. "Reason may mislead us."[18] The art of politics is the art of the possible. Pierce Butler reminded the delegates that they "must follow the example of Solon, who gave Athenians not the best Government he could devise, but the best they would receive."[19]

Every provision of the Constitution that was considered or adopted was known from experience with either colonial government or state governments

or from observation of English government. For the most part the framers adapted already-existing mechanisms to their own particular circumstances; there were few inventions. Separation of powers was derived from the states. The powers of the president were modeled after those of the governors of New York and Massachusetts. Impeachment was adapted from English practices. Popular elections owed much to the experience of the Virginia House of Burgesses—the state legislature—in which every male Virginian over the age of 21 could vote, but the plantation gentry provided the candidates.[20] This was *deferential politics:* the leading citizens of the nation would run for office and submit themselves to the verdict of their countrymen; this was what most delegates had in mind when they thought of popular government.

Bargaining and compromises. The convention delegates represented large and small states, northern and southern states, slave and free states, and agricultural and commercial interests. To draft a constitution that would appeal to the entire nation, they would have to compromise.

CONGRESSIONAL REPRESENTATION. The most important compromise, on which all else turned, was between the large states, which favored the *Virginia Plan,* and the small states, which favored the *New Jersey Plan.* The Virginia Plan, drawn up by Madison with Washington's concurrence and presented early to the convention by Edmund Randolph, the governor of Virginia, conceived of a strong central government with veto power over state actions. The New Jersey Plan, presented by William Paterson of New Jersey, was a modification of the Articles of Confederation that would have added a judiciary, a weak executive, and some new congressional powers. The convention voted to use the Virginia Plan as the basis for its deliberations.

But the convention soon became deadlocked on the most important problem: the apportioning of seats in Congress. "If proportional representation takes place," Ben Franklin wryly observed, "the small States contend that their liberties will be in danger. If an equality of votes is to be put in its place, the large States say their money will be in danger."[21] Madison warned that if the large and the small states had equal representation in Congress, the convention would dissolve, and he hinted that the large states might then form a government by themselves—a veiled threat to the survival of the small states. "The large states dare not dissolve the Confederation," Gunning Bedford responded; "if they do the small ones will find some foreign ally of more honor and good faith, who will take them by the hand and do them justice."[22]

With tempers rising, the large states did not force the issue. Massachusetts, large in population and influence and also a leader of the smaller New England states, supported the equal representation plan. North Carolina, a large state, also shifted to equal representation. The result was the *Connecticut Compromise,* which was adopted on July 16 and which saved the convention from dissolution. Oliver Ellsworth of Connecticut, author of the plan, observed that "we were partly national, partly federal; . . . on this middle ground a compromise would take place."[23] The House of Representatives was to be apportioned on the basis of state population, while each state would have equal representation in the Senate. The members of the House would be chosen by direct elections, while senators would be selected by their state legislatures.

COMPROMISES BETWEEN NORTH AND SOUTH. As an inducement to the south, approval of treaties would require a two-thirds vote; thus the north could not make a treaty with Spain about commerce on the Mississippi River that would harm southern and western interests. The small states also offered a deal involving the Northwest Territories. Congress, at that moment meeting in New York City, was stalled on a plan offered by the south to create states from the territories. The north wanted to hold off on forming states. At the Philadelphia convention, the small states agreed that they would end opposition to the southern plan regarding the territories if the large states agreed to support the Connecticut Compromise. Congress agreed to create three new states from the territories. Three days later the convention agreed to the Connecticut Compromise.[24]

The convention concluded other sectional agreements. The north wanted to end the slave trade. The south opposed any ban. The north wanted Congress to have greater powers over trade and navigation. Again, there was the basis for a deal: the slave trade was permitted to continue for twenty years, fugitive slaves would be returned from the north, and a slave would be counted as three-fifths of a free person for the purposes of apportioning seats in the House of Representatives and levying taxes. Congress was given the power to regulate foreign commerce. Another agreement provided for a national capital district, with the understanding that it would be located between the north and the south, rather than in Philadelphia or New York, the obvious choices.

Techniques for compromise. COMMITTEES. Politicians identify the important issues and refer them to committees. In open debate tempers flare, positions harden, and the temptation is to score points against the opposition rather than to discuss the issues calmly. Committees are small groups, and so conversation rather than posturing is the norm. The setting is conducive to courtesy and cooperation. Committees have the time to think through a problem, to experiment with proposals and language, and to listen to arguments—none of which is easy in large deliberative assemblies. It is easier for people to change their minds and to persuade others to do so in committees. And it is easier to strike complicated agreements and think them through in the relative calm of a small group.

At the convention the Committee of States came up with the Connecticut Compromise; the Committee on Detail expanded the powers of Congress and the president beyond what was proposed in the original draft; the Committee on Postponed Matters adopted a plan for election of the president by an electoral college rather than Congress; the Committee on Style included ambiguous language about the presidency that would later allow for its expanded powers in the final draft. All these committees were dominated by those wanting a strong central government, but they were also skilled in the art of compromise, and so they could develop proposals that the convention would accept. In each case, the committees came up with something more than compromise—they developed new proposals, sometimes departing drastically from plans that the convention had referred to them.

BARGAINING. There are several different ways to bargain. In the *compromise*, each side modifies its position to reach a middle ground. This can usually be done in connection with any issue which can be framed as a "more or less"

issue, especially if it involves money or some other quantity. Thus the convention compromised on the requirements to override a presidential veto between those who wanted no override at all and those who wanted an override by a majority: the result was a two-thirds vote. Making a slave equivalent to three-fifths of a free person was a compromise between those who wanted to make a slave fully equivalent (the south) for the purpose of apportioning seats in Congress and those who did not want to count slaves at all (the north). *Logrolling* involves giving up something to get something else, a technique used by the south to preserve the slave trade and by the north to get congressional powers over foreign commerce. The *package deal* is used to consider several related issues at the same time so that the "big picture" can be voted up or down. The delegates did not consider the president's election, term of office, and reeligibility for election as separate matters. Instead, they considered two alternative packages: the weak-president model (election by Congress for a six-year term with no eligibility for reelection) and the strong-president model (election by an electoral college for a four-year term with indefinite eligibility for reelection).[25]

EFFICIENCY NEGOTIATIONS. An agreement in which everyone gains is called an *efficiency negotiation*, and it can be distinguished from a negotiation in which whatever one person gains must come at the expense of another (sometimes called a *zero-sum game*). The convention itself was a gigantic efficiency negotiation conducted between the various regions and different economic interests. More protection against Indian attacks would be good for western settlers, as well as for eastern speculators who had invested in western lands. A navy would be good for southern planters who had crops on ships, as well as for northern boat owners and merchants. A government capable of attracting foreign investment would provide funds for industry in the north and for internal improvements in the south and west. If the states could not pass laws impairing contracts, propertied people everywhere would be more secure and the economy would improve with foreign investment.

POSTPONING CONFLICT. When agreement cannot be reached, a final decision may be postponed. The convention could not decide whether the Supreme Court should have the power to strike down laws passed by Congress. Similarly, no one wished to define precisely what was meant by *direct taxation*. And the question of the land claims of various states was left for the government to determine once the Constitution was adopted. By allowing the slave trade to continue for twenty years but refusing to outlaw slavery, the convention only postponed serious sectional conflicts for a later day.

PURPOSIVE USE OF AMBIGUITY. Sometimes in a negotiation each side agrees to a particular wording, even though the words have no plain meaning and the parties understand them differently. Disagreements can be camouflaged until after the accord has been signed and other provisions have been put into effect. This technique was used at the convention in dealing with the presidency. Those favoring a strong presidency gave the president the "executive power," and made the president commander-in-chief of the armed forces. Because these words lacked precision, they did not engender great controversy at the convention, and the delegates did not take seriously Madison's warning that they should consider ways to "define and confine" the presidency more precisely.

CLOSE-UP

**MADISON, WILSON, AND HAMILTON—
WHAT THE CONVENTION REJECTED.** *James Madison* is considered the father of the Constitution. Yet by the time the convention adjourned, Madison had been defeated on all the following proposals:

- Give Congress the power to veto state laws.
- Base Senate representation on population.
- Increase the size of the House of Representatives.
- Let Congress set suffrage requirements for the states, tax exports, create a national university, incorporate companies and a national bank, and have the power to pardon.
- Give the Senate a share in the presidential power to pardon.
- Give the Supreme Court the power to impeach and a share in the president's veto power.
- Establish a council of state to supervise departments.
- Outlaw the slave trade immediately (rather than in twenty years).
- Provide for ratification of the Constitution by seven states.

James Wilson was one of the most influential of the delegates. He was a strong supporter of popular government. Yet most of his specific proposals were also defeated:

- Treaties to be approved by majority vote.
- The House as well as the Senate to vote on treaties.
- Congress not to be able to override a presidential veto.
- The president to be elected directly by the people.

Alexander Hamilton delivered a speech at the convention which called for the strongest possible central government—a plan, as delegate William Johnson put it, which was "praised by everybody [and] supported by none." Some specifics:

- A supreme governor to be elected for life.
- The governor to have a veto over all laws passed by Congress and the states.
- The governor to have many enumerated powers in a strong central government.
- The governor to appoint the state governors.

Each of these men had strong convictions about his ideal form of government. Each had his most treasured ideas defeated or watered down at the convention. Each had grave reservations about whether the new Constitution, as finally drafted, would work. Yet each strongly supported the plan and fought hard for its ratification, on the premise that half a good constitution is better than none.

James Madison, leading theorist of the Constitution, cofounder (with Thomas Jefferson) of the Anti-Federalist party, and fourth president of the United States. *(Culver Pictures, Inc.)*

RESULTS OF POLITICS: THE CONSTITUTION OF 1787

The triumph of federalism

Our Constitution has four main features, each a uniquely American approach to the art and science of government: federalism, popular government, separation of powers, and checks and balances.

The convention delegates divided into two camps at the outset: a majority believed that they should simply revise the Articles of Confederation to improve commercial relations between the states and that the existing confederacy should be preserved, with its principle that state governments were sovereign. They would strictly define any new powers to be granted to the national Congress. But a minority had other ideas. Madison, Hamilton, Wilson, and others argued that in 1776, when independence had been declared, the American people had transferred their allegiance from King George III to the United States in Congress assembled. Sovereignty, they believed, always had resided in a single American nation, and never completely in the states. Consequently, the convention could act on behalf of the American people to establish a stronger national government with full *sovereign* powers—a government strong enough to solve the existing crisis of authority, and yet legitimate enough to be accepted by the people.

The supremacy clause. Perhaps the most important decision which the convention made early in its work was to accept three principles, proposed jointly by Edmund Randolph and Gouverneur Morris, which stated:

1. That a Union of the States merely federal[26] will not accomplish the objects proposed by the articles of Confederation, namely common defence, security of liberty, & general welfare.
2. That no treaty or treaties among the whole or part of the States, as individual Sovereignties, would be sufficient.
3. That a *national* Government ought to be established consisting of a *supreme* Legislative, Executive, and Judiciary.[27]

These resolutions required the convention to establish a national government whose institutions would be supreme over the states—a common sover-

The Supremacy clause allows the president to use federal troops to uphold laws passed by Congress or enforce judicial orders. *(Danny Lyon: Magnum.)*

To enforce a court order against striking Pullman Company employees, President Grover Cleveland nationalized the Illinois National Guard in 1894. The Guards fired into the strikers. Governor Altgeld of Illinois protested Cleveland's actions. *(Granger Collection.)*

eignty for all Americans. The convention adopted the ***supremacy clause***—the most important single provision of the Constitution—which appears as Article VI, Section 2:

> This Constitution, and the Laws of the United States which shall be made in Pursuance thereof; and all Treaties made, or which shall be made, under the Authority of the United States, shall be the Supreme Law of the Land; and the Judges in every State shall be bound thereby, any Thing in the Constitution or Laws of any State to the Contrary notwithstanding.

The supremacy clause established that the national Constitution and laws were supreme over state constitutions and laws. It required state judges to enforce the national Constitution and laws over state constitutions and laws, just as judges of the national government would do. The new Constitution set limits on state governments: neither the national government nor the state governments could take any actions that would violate the Constitution. The supremacy clause established the principle that all actions of the national government and the state governments must be constitutionally sound, for, as Madison argued, "A law violating a constitution established by the people themselves would be considered by the Judges as null and void."[28]

Enforcement of national laws. Under the Articles of Confederation, laws passed by Congress could be enforced only with the consent of the states. If a dispute broke out between Congress and the citizens of a state, Congress had to ask the state government for help. If a state sided with its own citizens, it would weaken the confederacy, and, as Madison argued, such conflicts between Congress and individuals "would look more like a declaration of war, than an infliction of punishment" on a citizen who had violated a law.[29]

Under the new Constitution the national government could enforce laws without asking for cooperation from the states. Disputes between the national

43

government and citizens of states could be settled by state or national judges. State legislatures and governors would not be dragged into these cases. Gouverneur Morris explained that the new government would have "a compleat and *compulsive* operation"—the definition of a sovereign government.[30]

Some delegates could not accept this. Elbridge Gerry, who ultimately refused to sign the Constitution, "warned the Convention against pushing the experiment too far. Some people will support a plan of vigorous Government at every risk. Others of a more democratic cast will oppose it with equal determination, and a Civil War may be produced by the conflict."[31] But others saw things differently. As John Langdon of New Hampshire argued:

> The General & State Governments were not enemies to each other, but different institutions for the good of the people of America. As one of the people he could say, the National Government is mine, the State Government is mine. In transferring power from one to the other, I only take out of my left hand what it can not so well use, and put it into my right hand where it can be better used.[32]

Limitations on state power. The powers of the states were limited in the new Constitution. The states were prohibited from issuing paper money and from passing laws that would impair contracts, two provisions which would benefit creditors and investors. They were required to give "full Faith and Credit to the Acts, Records, and Judicial Proceedings" of other states, another provision favored by lenders who might want to enforce judgments against debtors who had fled out of state. The states could no longer levy imposts or duties on interstate or foreign commerce. They could make no interstate compacts without the consent of Congress. They could make no treaties and form no alliances with foreign nations.

Maintaining domestic order. The Constitution guaranteed the people in each state a republican form of government. Then national government was required to give military assistance to a state in the event of "domestic violence" (such as another Shays's rebellion) if the state legislature requested such aid (or on application of the governor if the legislature was unable to meet as a result of insurrection). The national government was given the power to call the state militia into its service to "suppress insurrections," in which case it would be directed by national officials rather than by the state governor. If absolutely necessary the national government could suspend the privilege of the ***writ of habeas corpus***—a document issued by a judge ordering that anyone holding a person in custody bring that person before the court; it is used by prisoners and their lawyers to question the legality of arrest and detention.

Promoting national security. By locating sovereign powers in the national government, the convention delegates hoped to convince Europeans that they were serious about maintaining independence. Congress could raise and maintain a navy without asking the states for contributions or personnel. It now had the power to declare war by majority vote, rather than with the unanimity required under the Articles. No longer would European powers be permitted to send ministers to state governments or conclude agreements with them. Henceforth, only the national government could make war and peace, recognize foreign nations, conclude alliances and treaties, and determine trade policy with foreign nations.

With improved commerce and transportation, typified by the Erie Canal (opened by Governor DeWitt Clinton of New York in 1825), the west was opened to development. *(Culver Pictures, Inc.)*

Expanding the powers of Congress. The Constitution added vast new powers to those already granted to Congress by the Articles. In Article I of the Constitution, Congress was given seventeen specific new powers over the economy and the diplomacy of the nation.

Congress was granted, in paragraph 18 of Article I, Section 8, the power "to make all laws which shall be Necessary and Proper for carrying into Execution the foregoing powers, and all other powers vested by this Constitution in the Government of the United States, or in any Department or Officer thereof." This ***necessary and proper clause*** stretched the power of Congress (and for that reason it is also known as the ***elastic clause***). Congress could legislate on any topic involving its own powers or those given to other branches. It could legislate on the means needed to achieve the ends set forth in the Constitution— even if there was no specific language in the Constitution referring to these means. Madison, in arguing for the clause, told the convention delegates that "he should shrink from nothing which should be found essential to such a form of Government as would provide for the safety, liberty, and happiness of the community."[33] To the extent that political leaders could convince the American people that new powers would be needed to deal with problems (that is, if the government could expand its authority), this clause would allow the Constitution to adapt to meet changing conditions.

Majority rule. Under the Articles extraordinary majorities of state delegations were required for important legislation. The Constitution provided instead that each member of the House of Representatives and the Senate would cast an individual vote, with no provision for voting by states. Simple majorities in each chamber (that is, a majority of those present) would be sufficient to pass any bills, including taxes and the declaration of war. Simple rather than extraordinary majorities would decide.

Creation of an executive branch. The convention met to create a more efficient government. Most delegates started by favoring a plural executive, elected by Congress and subject to a recall by a majority of state governors or state legislatures. But some delegates, such as Hamilton, went to the other

extreme, calling for a single "supreme governor," elected by the people (or their delegates) and chosen either for life or for a term which could be extended by reelection. The presidential office created by the convention represented a compromise, but one which leaned in the direction of a strong executive.

There was to be a president, elected indirectly by the people through the mechanism of an electoral college (discussed further in Chapter 9) and serving for a fixed term of four years, but eligible for reelection. The president could not be removed from office by state officials, but could be removed only after impeachment by the House and a trial by the Senate in which two-thirds of those present voted for removal.

The president was to have the "executive power of the United States." No council of state or cabinet would share the presidential powers. The president alone would nominate the important civil and military officials, who would assume office if the Senate consented by majority vote. The president was to receive the opinions, in writing, of the principal officers of the departments on matters of presidential interest and was charged with the duty to "see that the laws be faithfully executed" by all government officials. The president was to recommend to Congress such measures as might be deemed expedient and was to report to Congress annually on the state of the union.

The president was to be commander in chief of the armed forces of the United States and of the state militias when called into national service. Other presidential responsibilities were the enforcement of provisions of the supremacy clause against individuals or states and the use of military force if necessary to guarantee the states a republican form of government or to carry out orders of the national courts. The president was given the power to pardon offenses against the Constitution or laws, a useful technique that made it possible to end insurrections and rebellions by offering clemency.

Creation of an independent judiciary. In Article III the Constitution assigned the judicial power of the United States to a Supreme Court and to the lower federal (that is, national) courts that Congress by law would create. Certain original jurisdiction was given to the Supreme Court. Its remaining original and appellate jurisdiction (that is, cases reviewed by higher courts after a trial) was to be determined by law after the Constitution was put into effect.

The supremacy clause provided that national laws, treaties, and the Constitution would be supreme over state laws and state constitutions. Federal or state judges could declare state laws or actions null and void on the grounds that they violated the national Constitution. They could also issue decrees and judgments directly affecting citizens, declaring that their action violated national laws, treaties, or the Constitution.

Justices of the Supreme Court and other federal judges would be nominated by the president and would assume office if approved by a majority of the Senate. They would serve on "good behavior" (that is, for life) and could not be removed by the president; this made the judiciary independent of the executive branch. They could be impeached by the House and removed by the Senate after a trial.

Popular government

The convention delegates rested the legitimacy of the new government on the principle of *popular consent* (Figure 2-2). The preamble to the Constitution expresses the idea.

WE THE PEOPLE of the United States, in Order to form a more perfect Union, establish justice, insure domestic tranquility, provide for the common defence, promote the general welfare, and secure the blessings of Liberty to ourselves and our posterity, do ordain and establish this Constitution for the United States of America.

But some delegates mistrusted popular government (see Figure 2-3). Sherman argued that "the people immediately should have as little to do as may be about the Government. They want [lack] information and are constantly liable to be misled."[34] Gerry, alluding to Massachusetts, argued that "the evils we experience flow from the excess of democracy. The people do not want [lack] virtue, but are the dupes of pretended patriots."[35]

Other delegates insisted that the government be made accountable to the people. George Mason of Virginia, no friend of the common people, was willing to admit that "we had been too democratic, but was afraid we should incautiously run into the opposite extreme. We ought to attend to the rights of every class of the people."[36] James Wilson spoke of "raising the federal pyramid to a

Figure 2-2. In a system of popular government the executives, legislators, and judges are all elected by the people to serve limited terms in office.

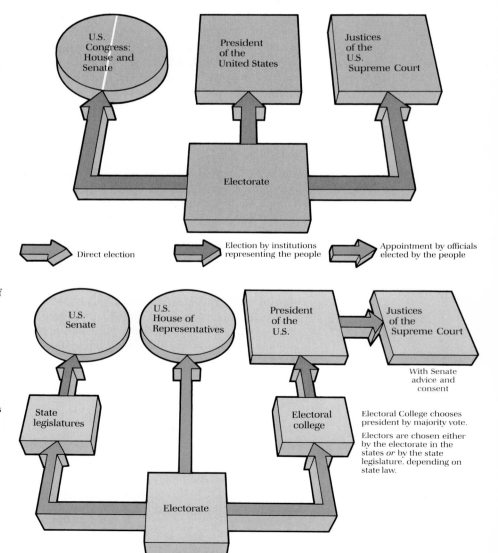

Figure 2-3. The Constitution of 1787 provided for limited popular government. Only members of the House of Representatives were to be elected directly by the people. Senators were to be elected by the legislatures of the state. The president was to be elected by an electoral college. The justices of the Supreme Court were to be nominated by the president and appointed with the advice and consent of the Senate. While the president and members of Congress would serve for fixed terms, the justices would serve for life.

considerable altitude, and for that reason wished to give it as broad a basis as possible. No government could long subsist without the confidence of the people."[37]

It remained for James Madison to fashion the essential compromise shown in Figure 2-3. Direct elections were to be limited to the House of Representatives, which would be the "popular assembly" likely to represent all social classes and interests. Senators would be chosen by state legislatures, and since

THE ELECTORAL COLLEGE IN THE CONSTITUTION

Several times a majority of the delegates to the convention voted in favor of having Congress select the president. At first only a few delegates opposed the plan. James Madison, considering it a question of separation of powers, argued that "the appointment of the Executive should either be drawn from some source, or held by some tenure, that will give him a free agency with regard to the Legislature. This could not be done if he was to be appointable from time to time by the Legislature." It would be better, thought James Wilson, to create a mechanism that would bring the people into the decision and keep Congress out. But how could this be done without giving the people the power to elect, which a majority of the delegates opposed?

The answer was an *electoral college.* State legislatures would determine, by state law, how their *electors* (equal in number to their congressional delegation) would be chosen—either by the state legislature itself or by popular vote. Then, in each state capitol, the electors would meet on a date fixed by law to cast two ballots each for president. The results would be sent to Congress, where the outgoing vice president, in the presence of the members of Congress, would count the ballots and announce the name of the next president. The person who received the largest number of votes would be president, and the person who received the next largest number would be vice president.[a]

The electoral college would make it virtually impossible for anyone to fix an election, since there would be so many electors and they would meet in their own states. The electors would be the leading people of character in their states, and they would canvass the states and the nation to choose the best person for the office. At least that was how the delegates hoped the system would work.

The delegates thought that the electoral college would be dominated by electors from the large states. They would vote for someone from their own state, which would result in five leading candidates, none of whom could win the necessary majority. The election for president would then be thrown into the House of Representatives, where each state delegation would cast a single vote for one of the top five contenders.[b] The convention delegates assumed that the electoral college would do the nominating for the presidency, while the House, voting by state delegation, would make the actual selection, thereby giving the states—especially the small states—equal weight in the selection process. Thus, the cumbersome system of a contingency election by the electoral college was actually a compromise between the large and the small states, which is why the convention delegates eventually decided to accept it.

a. The Eleventh Amendment (adopted in 1801) provides for separate ballots to be cast for the president and the vice president; this prevents a tie vote between candidates for the two offices, as occurred in the election of 1800, which had to be decided by the House of Representatives.

b. The Eleventh Amendment restricts the choice of the House to the top three candidates. In the event no candidate for vice president obtains a majority in the electoral college, the vice president is chosen by the Senate, from among the top two candidates, with each senator casting one vote.

there would be only two from each state, they would probably represent the interests of property holders as well as the interests of the state governments. Federal judges would be appointed by the president, not elected by the people. And the president would be chosen by an electoral college, consisting of electors who could be chosen either by the people or by state governments, according to the wishes of each state legislature.

The convention delegates decided that eligibility to vote in national elections would be determined by the states, with only such exceptions or regulations as Congress might provide by law. At the time, all states restricted the vote to white males over the age of 21. Some included further qualifications based on property or instituted voting fees to cut down on eligibility. The Constitution provided that citizens of a state who were eligible to vote for the lower house of the state legislature would also be eligible to vote for members of the House of Representatives. Thus, the extent to which the government would rest on a broad popular base, and therefore the extent to which the national government would be democratic, was left to the individual state governments.

Separation of powers

The convention delegates, like all Americans, were mistrustful of governmental power. Because they were expanding the powers of the national government, especially Congress, and because they were creating a more powerful and efficient government, they concentrated on preventing the abuse of power. There would be what Madison referred to as "auxiliary precautions": governmental mechanisms which would check tyranny. One of these precautions was the separation of powers.

Partial separation of powers. Although Montesquieu, Locke, and other political theorists had argued that separation of powers was necessary to guard against abuse of power, Madison and the convention delegates hit upon an even better approach: the *partial* rather than the *complete* separation of powers. The three branches of government—Congress, the president, and the Supreme Court—would *not* correspond exactly with the legislative, executive, and judicial powers. The Constitution would not provide for a Congress that could exercise all legislative powers and nothing but legislative powers; for a president who functioned as an executive and as nothing but an executive; or for a Supreme Court that operated only with judicial power. It is more accurate to say that the Constitution created separate branches of government which would share in, and compete fiercely for, the various powers. The president could recommend measures to Congress or veto its bills and therefore would share in legislative power. Congress would create and fund the agencies of government, and so it would share in executive power. The courts, in deciding cases, would interpret the law and thus would share in legislative power.

Constitutional ambiguities. The Constitution, by deliberate design of the framers, is silent on some important points, or else ambiguous in its meanings. Often it assigns a duty to a branch without providing expressly for the powers to perform that duty.

The president, for example, is assigned the executive power, and yet nowhere does the Constitution give the president the explicit power to issue orders to department officials or remove them from office. The Supreme Court

has the judicial power, but nowhere does the Constitution explicitly give it the power to declare a law of Congress or an action of the president unconstitutional. Congress has all legislative powers, but nowhere does the Constitution specify at what point its powers must give way to executive actions or judicial decisions.

Overlapping grants of power. The new Constitution provided for overlapping grants of power. Congress was given the power to declare war and regulate and fund the armed forces, but the president was commander in chief. The Constitution did not sort out the president's authority to order troops abroad when Congress provided by law that they were to remain at home. It did not specify whether Congress could issue instructions—by law—to military commanders which were at variance with presidential orders. It did not say whether, in the absence of a declaration of war, the president could make war.

Boundary disputes. Ambiguity, overlapping grants of power, and the partial rather than the complete separation of powers all lead to boundary disputes. Either the branches must cooperate and accommodate these claims, or else they must fight constitutional battles. The Constitution is not a blueprint with detailed plans for the workings of government, but rather an arena for conflict. Madison believed that the friction which would inevitably result would be the best safeguard against tyranny, because with branch fighting branch, powers would be limited.

The separation clause. Under the provisions of this clause, members of one branch could not serve simultaneously in another. Members of Congress could not serve in the executive branch, and "no Person holding any Office under the United States, shall be a member of either House during his continuance in office." The *separation clause* distinguished our government from *cabinet government*, which Europeans were just beginning to adopt at the end of the eighteenth century; in a cabinet government, the prime minister and other department heads also hold seats in the legislature. Under the American Constitution, neither the president nor Cabinet officials are members of Congress, and they may not debate or vote. Because the president cannot offer members of Congress any executive office (unless they resign from the legislature), presidential influence with them is lessened.

Checks and balances

To preserve the independence of each branch, the convention delegates relied on **checks and balances.** As Madison explained to them:

> Instead therefore of contenting ourselves with laying down the Theory in the Constitution that each department ought to be separate and distinct, it was proposed to add a defensive power to each which should maintain the theory in practice. In so doing we did not blend the departments together. We erected effectual barriers for keeping them separate.[38]

To preserve the three-branch system and prevent tyranny, it would be necessary to give each branch a means to defend itself against the others. In particular, the delegates believed that it would be necessary to prevent encroachment by the legislature, which they viewed as the strongest branch.

Checks on the president. The president could make neither treaties nor appointments to office without the advice and consent of the Senate. The president needed Congress to pass laws to establish, fund, and empower the departments. Presidential choices for Supreme Court justices and for lower court judges had to be approved by the Senate. According to the provision for *impeachment,* the president could be removed from office by Congress for "treason, bribery, and other High Crimes and Misdemeanors."

Checks on Congress. Most of the convention delegates agreed with Madison that "experience had proved a tendency in our governments to throw all power into the Legislative vortex."[39] Madison believed that Congress must be checked by the president. The president was given the responsibility to "faithfully execute the laws" and thus was allowed a certain amount of discretion. All laws and appropriations (funding bills) were subject to a presidential veto, which itself could be nullified by a two-thirds vote of each chamber of Congress. But if the president held the support of just over one-third of the members of either the House or the Senate, the veto attempt would fail.

The Supreme Court could check Congress by interpreting laws in ways which might not gibe exactly with congressional intent. It could strike down laws passed by Congress which it believed were inconsistent with the Constitution itself. (This power, while not specified in the Constitution, was claimed by the Court in the 1790s.)

Checks within Congress. Congress was *bicameral,* or organized into two independent chambers: the House of Representatives and the Senate. Each chamber had a check on the other. Bills, written in identical language, had to pass each chamber before being sent to the president. The House had the sole power to originate revenue bills, but the Senate would have to concur for a measure to become law. The House could vote to impeach officials, but the Senate had the exclusive power to try them. The Senate had the power to consent to presidential treaties and appointments, but often treaty commitments could be carried out only if the House agreed to pass implementing laws or appropriations.

Checks on the judiciary. Supreme Court justices and federal judges were to be appointed by the president with the advice and consent of the Senate. They could be impeached by the House and removed from office after trial by the Senate. Congress was to establish, fund, and determine the jurisdiction of the federal courts, including some of the jurisdiction of the Supreme Court. The courts would not be able to enforce their own decisions in most instances, but would have to rely on national and state officials.

The ultimate check: Constitutional amendments. The convention delegates knew that they could not provide for all circumstances and that periodically the Constitution would have to be modified. They created an amending process (Figure 2-4) which involved Congress, the state legislatures, and the people. According to Article V, amendments could be proposed either by a two-thirds vote of each chamber of Congress or by a national amending convention called by Congress on the application of two-thirds of the states. Amendments were to be ratified either by a vote of three-fourths of the state

Amendments are suggested | Amendments are proposed | Amendments are ratified

By the president in a message to Congress.

or

By members of Congress who introduce an amendment.

or

Through resolutions passed by two-thirds of the state legislatures.

By two-thirds vote of the House and Senate after hearings on the pros and cons, and appropriate revisions. (Most amendments are defeated.)

or

By a national amending convention

If they are approved by resolutions passed by legislatures in three-fourths of all the states.

or

If they are approved by ratifying conventions called for the purpose in three-fourths of all the states.

Figure 2-4. There are two ways amendments may be proposed and two ways they may be ratified. No amendment has ever been proposed by a national amending convention as of 1985. Only the Prohibition Amendment has been approved by ratifying conventions called by the states; all others have been approved by state legislatures.

legislatures or by a vote of three-fourths of special conventions called in the states, whose delegates would be elected directly by the people.

The amendment process could be used to make changes in the federal system, modify separation of powers and checks and balances, further democratize the electoral process, and guarantee the liberties of the people, even against the government itself.

THE RATIFICATION CONTROVERSY

When the convention finished its work at the end of a long, hot Philadelphia summer, thirty-nine delegates signed the document. Thirteen were not present or refused to sign, including Edmund Randolph (who had sponsored the original Virginia Plan) and such influential members as Elbridge Gerry and George Mason. Their refusals were based in part on the omission of a bill of rights and on their fears that the president and the Senate would together constitute a monarchy and an aristocracy that would throttle popular government. Their opposition foreshadowed the problems the signers would have in convincing state leaders to accept their plan.

The ratification procedure

The original mandate from Congress provided that the convention was to report back to it and propose a set of amendments to the existing Articles of Confederation, which would have required a unanimous vote in Congress. According to the Constitution, the people would choose delegates to state conventions, which would either ratify or reject the document. The Constitution would go into effect if only nine state conventions ratified it. The very legitimacy of the new government might be put in doubt by this procedure.

Madison argued that the convention could not establish a "firm national government" which would be "adequate to the exigencies of government and the preservation of the Union" (its mandate from Congress in its resolution approving the convention) unless it *disregarded* the procedures of that resolution. To meet the goals of the resolution, he argued, it was necessary to ignore the means. This could be done by recourse to the people. The Constitution was to be considered by more than 1200 popularly elected delegates at state ratifying conventions. "The people were, in fact, the fountain of all power," Madison reassured the delegates in Philadelphia, and "by resorting to them, all difficulties were got over. They could alter constitutions as they pleased."[40]

Bowing to pressure from the convention, which appealed to the people at the expense of Congress and the state legislatures, Congress itself unanimously passed a resolution agreeing to the procedures set forth in the Constitution. The legitimacy crisis had been surmounted.

The Anti-Federalists attack

Supporters of the Constitution took the name ***Federalists***—a brilliant strategy, since it implied that their plan was simply an improvement on the existing confederation, rather than a radically different form of government. Opponents let themselves be known as ***Anti-Federalists***—an unfortunate decision, since it put them in the position of being against rather than for something.

The distinguishing characteristic of the Anti-Federalists was neither social class nor regional interest—most of their leaders were as distinguished and successful in business and society as the Federalists, and they included such powerful politicians as George Clinton, the governor of New York—but rather an honest doubt that the plan would do what its supporters claimed, coupled with a desire to retain power at the state level. They were "men of little faith," in Cecilia Kenyon's apt phrase.[41] Patrick Henry spoke for many of them at the Virginia convention when he derided the intricate mechanisms that Madison had created to prevent abuses of power. "There will be no checks, no real balances, in this government," he thundered, adding: "What can avail your specious, imaginary balances, your rope-dancing, chain-rattling, ridiculous ideal checks and contrivances?"[42] Instead, Henry and others believed that the national government would soon act to destroy the states. James Monroe argued that the president, at the head of the army, would combine with the Senate and establish a monarchy, leading to a civil war. Tom Paine argued that the proposed Constitution was undemocratic because only the House was directly elected.

The Federalists respond

The Federalists downplayed the vast new powers granted to the national government, and instead they pointed to the similarities between the proposed national government and the existing state governments. They pointed out that Washington, who was sure to become president, had already demonstrated that he had no desire to be a king. They denied that the Senate and the president would combine to create an aristocratic government, pointing out that the Senate was to guarantee the rights of the small states.

The Federalists and the Anti-Federalists sparred in the newspapers. ***The Federalist,*** a series of newspaper essays by Alexander Hamilton, John Jay, and James Madison, was written to sway public opinion toward the Constitution in New York. It discussed the failures of the existing confederacy, showed how a large republic could end the "tyranny of faction" (an allusion to Shays's rebel-

lion), analyzed the proposed powers of the national government and the state governments and the advantages of a system of separation of powers and checks and balances, and concluded by reassuring the people that the proposed president would not have the power of a British monarch (but would be much more like the governor of New York!) and that the judiciary would not be a threat to the liberties of the people.

The Federalist is the first major commentary on the new Constitution. Although many people consider it an authority on specific provisions, it should be approached with caution. It was primarily a work of political propaganda. Hamilton, in particular, was not above providing interpretations of the Constitution which were at odds with his own understanding of the powers which the president would exercise if the Constitution were adopted. Nevertheless, as a work of American political thought, it ranks among the few classics that this nation has produced. Madison's contributions in *The Federalist*, numbers 10 and 47 to 51 (on pluralism, separation of powers, and checks and balances), and Hamilton's discussion of the presidency in *The Federalist*, numbers 67 to

Figure 2-5. The map shows the counties in each state which supported or opposed ratification of the Constitution through their votes for delegates to the state ratifying conventions. The pie charts offshore show the final votes for and against ratification in these conventions.

77 (describing its expanded powers), deserve reading by every student of politics.

But when the issue remained in doubt in New York after the *Federalist* papers appeared, Hamilton resorted to extreme tactics. He spread the rumor that if New York's convention voted the plan down, New York City would secede and take some downstate counties with it, creating a new state that would join the union. In spite of the opposition of Governor George Clinton and many of the upstate politicians, the Constitution was narrowly approved. In one state after another, a similar combination of argument and maneuver won the day for the Federalists (Figure 2-5).

The call for a bill of rights

The feature of the Constitution that most worried the delegates at the state conventions was the fact that it would enable the new national government to operate directly on the citizens of the states. If Congress could pass laws, to be enforced by federal courts, then the people must have further protections against the possibility of abuse of power.

The Constitution placed few limitations on the power of the national government. Congress could not pass a bill of attainder (a law naming a particular person a criminal and providing punishment) or an ex post facto bill (a law which declares that an action already taken is illegal and which provides punishment for those who have taken it). No religious test could be applied to prospective officeholders. The privilege of the writ of habeas corpus would apply in federal courts unless suspended during a state of emergency. No title of nobility could be granted by the national government. All trials in federal courts would be by jury. Congress, by law, could punish those guilty of treason, but the courts could not convict anyone without the testimony of at least two witnesses to an overt act or without a confession in open court.

Omissions in the Constitution. The Constitution did not provide for freedom of religion, the press, assembly, or speech. It had little to say about judicial procedures. George Mason and Elbridge Gerry wanted the Constitution to provide the same kinds of guarantees of rights and liberties that most state constitutions already provided. Mason observed that "he would sooner chop off his right hand than put it to the Constitution as it now stands." But Gerry's motion for a committee to draft a bill of rights at the convention was handily defeated.

George Washington, James Madison, Alexander Hamilton, and Gouverneur Morris opposed a bill of rights because they believed that it would weaken the new national government. But John Adams in London and Thomas Jefferson in Paris, when they read the provisions of the new Constitution after the convention adjourned, immediately noticed the omission and wrote letters across the Atlantic to their colleagues in protest. Jefferson suggested that the states ratify the Constitution and then use the amending procedures to create a bill of rights. The Federalists realized that they would be defeated in the two states that mattered most—New York and Virginia—unless they agreed to Jefferson's idea.

The Bill of Rights. After the Constitution was adopted, the first Congress passed ten amendments in 1789 which were approved by the necessary number of states in 1791. The ***Bill of Rights*** was based on the theory of the *reserved*

Frederick Kemmelmeyer's "Washington Reviewing the Western Army at Fort Cumberland, Maryland." Washington resigned his commission, establishing a principle of civilian leadership in government. *(Metropolitan Museum of Art.)*

rights of the people: in their compact establishing a national government, the people retained certain rights, some of which were now enumerated in the ten amendments, and others of which remained with the people or the states. The Bill of Rights was to protect people from arbitrary and coercive action by the national government, particularly Congress, just as state declarations or bills of rights protected them from actions of the state governments. (Later the Bill of Rights would also be interpreted by the courts as applying to state governments, but that would not occur until the twentieth century.)

FROM RATIFICATION TO IMPLEMENTATION

By July 1788, almost one year after the convention finished its work, the requisite nine states had agreed to the plan, and soon thereafter Virginia and New York also ratified it. Crucial to the success of the Federalists was the support of artisans and mechanics in the cities and of some of the small farmers in the west, all of whom decided that the economic gains they might reap under a strong national government were more important than safeguarding their power in strong state governments.

After ratification, Congress passed a measure providing for a transition from the old to the new form of government. By law it fixed dates on which electors would be chosen in the states and assemble at the state capitols to choose a president, and it fixed dates on which congressional elections would be held. By the winter of 1788 electors had been chosen, and early in 1789 they chose George Washington as the first president and John Adams as the first vice president. The state legislatures convened and selected members of the Senate. The people voted in elections for the House of Representatives.

According to procedures adopted by the outgoing Congress, the new government assembled in New York City, which was the temporary capital until a new federal district could be established. In March, George Washington entered the city in triumph at the head of a parade of exuberant citizens to take up his duties. In April the new Congress convened. "Our Constitution is in actual operation," Ben Franklin reported to his friends abroad. "Everything appears to promise that it will last; but in this world nothing is certain but death and taxes." The American experiment in constitutional democracy had begun.

FOCUS

PROJECT '87—CELEBRATING THE CONSTITUTION. Project '87, a joint undertaking of the American Historical Association and the American Political Science Association, commemorates the bicentennial of the adoption of the Constitution by promoting public understanding and scholarly appraisal. The project is chaired by the historian Richard B. Morris of Columbia University and by the political scientist James MacGregor Burns of Williams College; Chief Justice Warren Burger serves as honorary chairman of the advisory board.

Research and conferences have been under way for the past several years, and the project has awarded numerous research grants and fellowships and has provided support for five scholarly meetings. It has also funded programs for more effective teaching about the Constitution at the high school and college levels.

Support for Project '87 comes from the William and Flora Hewlett Foundation, with grants for specific programs provided by the National Endowment for the Humanities, the Lilly Endowment, and the Rockefeller, Ford, and Mellon foundations.

Project '87 puts out a quarterly magazine containing articles about its funding programs and research results. For further information, write to: Project '87, 1527 New Hampshire Avenue, N.W., Washington, D.C. 20036.

As part of its efforts to promote the bicentennial of the adoption of the Constitution, Project '87 has made planning and production grants for the following television programs, many of which will be broadcast in 1987 and 1988:

The Living Constitution. National Video Communications, Inc., San Diego, California. Four programs on contemporary issues and how the founders viewed them.

A More Perfect Union. Yale University Media Design Studio. A three-hour television film on the drafting of the Constitution and the Bill of Rights.

To Form a More Perfect Union. WTIF, Philadelphia, Pennsylvania. The history of the Constitution, the Bill of Rights, and the American political party system.

The U.S. Constitution Project. WGBH-TV, Boston, Massachusetts, and the Institute of Politics, Harvard University. An evaluation of the usefulness and the continued vitality of our constitutional system.

Visions of the Constitution. WQED, Pittsburgh, Pennsylvania. Eight half-hour profiles of scholars of the Constitution and their interpretations of it.

We, the People. KQED-TV, San Francisco, California. Seven half-hour documentaries on current issues such as judicial review, federalism, and the First Amendment.

Witnesses at the Creation. Capitol Cities Communication and Lou Reda Productions. Biographies of the writers of the *Federalist* papers.

IN CONCLUSION

The Constitution created in 1787 came about as a result of the failure of the Articles of Confederation to provide for security and prosperity after the Revolutionary War. Calls for reform went unheeded between 1781 and 1786, and Congress was unable to raise taxes to pay its war debts and veterans' pensions, which contributed to instability. Shays's rebellion in 1786–1787 was merely the culmination of several years of disorders between debtors and creditors in many states. It spurred leading state politicians to agree to calls by Washington, Hamilton, Madison, and others for a national convention.

The Philadelphia convention established a new government based on three principles: federalism, popular government, and partial separation of powers. The federal system divided power between a national government and the state governments: a unique American experiment, it was a hybrid of the existing national and confederal models. Popular government meant periodic elections for the House of Representatives. Senators were to be chosen by the state legislators, the president was to be chosen by an electoral college, and the federal judiciary was to be appointed. Partial separation of powers involved three branches—the legislative, the executive, and the judicial—with overlapping jurisdictions and with a system of checks and balances designed to preserve the independence of each branch. The federal principle would promote stability by preventing any single interest or faction from dominating the government. Popular government would keep rulers accountable to the ruled. Partial separation of powers would prevent abuse of power and legislative encroachment on the other branches.

Just as important as the provisions of the Constitution was the politics of the convention. Compromises between the large states and the small states, between the north and the south, and between proponents of different political principles were the key to its success. The convention itself was an efficiency negotiation, in which the compromises and logrolling provided advantages for all participants.

Although the Constitution and its novel ratification arrangements were criticized by the Anti-Federalists, the political skills of the Federalists, combined with a pledge to support a bill of rights, won ratification in the necessary number of states. The new government was instituted in 1789, with George Washington as president, and the Bill of Rights was ratified in 1791.

NOTES

1. Gordon Wood, *The Creation of the American Republic, 1776–1787.* Norton, New York, 1972, p. 393.
2. Robert A. Goldwin and William A. Schambra (eds.), *How Democratic Is the Constitution?* American Enterprise Institute, Washington, D.C., 1980; Alfred F. Young, "Conservatives, the Constitution, and the 'Spirit of Accommodation,'" pp. 145–146.
3. Paul Ford (ed.), *The Writings of George Washington*, Putnam, New York, 1890, vol. 10, p. 170.
4. Richard H. Kohn, "Inside History of the Newburgh Conspiracy," *William and Mary Quarterly*, vol. 28, no. 2, April 1970, pp. 187–220.
5. *Journals of the Continental Congress*, Sept. 28, 1786, pp. 698–699; Oct. 21, 1786, p. 896.
6. Goldwin and Schambra, op. cit.; Young, op. cit., p. 122. See also Daniel Boorstin, "The American Revolution: Revolution without Dogma," in *The Genius of American Politics*, University of Chicago Press, Chicago, 1953, pp. 35–50; and Richard Hofstadter, "The Founding Fathers: An Age of Realism," in *The American Political Tradition*, Knopf, New York, 1948.

7. James MacGregor Burns, *The Vineyard of Liberty*, Knopf, New York, 1982, p. 33.
8. W. B. Gwynn, *The Meaning of the Separation of Powers: An Analysis of the Doctrine from Its Origin to the Adoption of the United States Constitution*, Tulane University Press, New Orleans, 1965. See also Stanley N. Katz, "The Origins of American Constitutional Thought," *Perspectives in American History*, vol. 3, 1969, pp. 474–490; and Edward Corwin, "The Progress of Constitutional Thought between the Declaration of Independence and the Meeting of the Philadelphia Convention," *American Historical Review*, vol. 30, no. 4, 1923, pp. 511–536.
9. Thomas Paine, *Common Sense*, in Moncure D. Conway (ed.), *The Writings of Thomas Paine*, vol. 1, AMS Press, New York, 1894, pp. 67–84.
10. Goldwin and Schambra, op. cit.; Wood, op. cit., p. 13.
11. Joseph M. Bessette, "Deliberative Democracy: The Majority Principle in Republican Government," in Goldwin and Schambra, op. cit., p. 105.
12. Ibid., p. 107.
13. Wood, op. cit., p. 12.
14. Baron de Montesquieu, *The Spirit of the Laws*, 1748.
15. John Adams, *A Defence of the Constitution of the United States of America*, Dilly, London, 1787.
16. Thomas Jefferson, *Notes on the State of Virginia*, in Paul Ford (ed.), *The Writings of Thomas Jefferson*, Putnam, New York, 1892–1899.
17. James Madison, *Notes of Debates in the Federal Convention of 1787*, Ohio University Press, Athens, 1966, p. 185.
18. Ibid., p. 447.
19. Goldwin and Schambra, op. cit.; Young, op. cit., p. 134.
20. Charles S. Sydnor, *American Revolutionaries in the Making*, Free Press, New York, 1965, pp. 60–73.
21. Madison, op. cit., p. 126.
22. Ibid., p. 230.
23. Max Farrand, *The Framing of the Constitution of the United States*, vol. 1, Yale University Press, New Haven, Conn., 1913, pp. 461–462, 468.
24. Calvin Jillson and Thornton Anderson, "Voting Bloc Analysis in the Constitutional Convention," *Western Political Quarterly*, vol. 31, no. 4, December 1978, pp. 535–547.
25. Calvin Jillson, "The Executive in Republican Government: The Case for American Founding," *Presidential Studies Quarterly*, vol. 9, no. 4, fall 1979, pp. 386–401.
26. The word *federal* as it appears in this resolution signifies the existing arrangements under the Articles of Confederation.
27. Madison, op. cit., p. 34.
28. Ibid., p. 353.
29. Ibid., p. 45.
30. Ibid., p. 35.
31. Ibid., p. 516.
32. Ibid., p. 514.
33. Ibid., p. 44.
34. Ibid., p. 39.
35. Ibid.
36. Ibid., p. 40.
37. Ibid.
38. Ibid., p. 340.
39. *The Federalist*, no. 40.
40. Madison, op. cit., p. 564.
41. Cecilia Kenyon, "Men of Little Faith," *William and Mary Quarterly*, 3d Series, no. 12, 1955, pp. 3–43.
42. Jonathan Elliot (ed.), *The Debates of the Several State Conventions*, vol. 2, 2d ed., Franklin, Burt, New York, 1876, p. 54.

FURTHER READING

Beard, Charles A.: *An Economic Interpretation of the Constitution of the United States,* Macmillan, New York, 1913. A study of the framers, emphasizing their desire for personal gain through financial speculation in government debts, which could be secured by a stronger national government.

Becker, Carl: *The Declaration of Independence,* Random House, New York, 1958. A study of the political theory and politics involved in drafting the Declaration.

Burns, James MacGregor: *The Vineyard of Liberty,* Knopf, New York, 1982. A vivid description of the social and economic conditions in early America and of the political leaders of the time.

Farrand, Max: *The Framing of the Constitution of the United States,* Yale University Press, New Haven, Conn., 1913. A narrative account of the work of the convention.

Goldwin, Robert A., and William A. Schambra (eds.): *How Democratic Is the Constitution?* American Enterprise Institute, Washington, D.C., 1980. Essays assessing the motives of those who called for the Constitutional Convention.

————: *How Does the Constitution Secure Rights?* American Enterprise Institute, Washington, D.C., 1985. Essays on the Bill of Rights.

Jensen, Merrill: *The New Nation,* Knopf, New York, 1950. A history of the confederation from 1781 to 1789, written by a historian who is sympathetic to its purposes and generous in his estimation of its success.

Koch, Adrienne: *Power, Morals and the Founding Fathers,* Cornell University Press, Ithaca, N.Y., 1961. Essays on the political thought of Adams, Franklin, Hamilton, Jefferson and Madison.

McDonald, Forrest: *We the People: Economic Origins of the Constitution,* University of Chicago Press, Chicago, 1958. A reexamination of Beard's thesis and a fresh interpretation of the motivations of the framers.

Main, Jackson Turner: *The Anti-Federalists: Critics of the Constitution, 1781–1788,* University of North Carolina Press, Chapel Hill, 1961. An examination of the factions in each state that opposed the Constitution, arguing that they were primarily small farmers and others with no need to promote interstate and foreign commerce.

Rakove, Jack N.: *The Beginnings of National Politics,* Knopf, New York, 1979. An account of the successes and failures of the Continental Congress and of events leading up to the convention of 1787.

Rossiter, Clinton: *1787: The Grand Convention,* Macmillan, New York, 1966. Still the most readable account of the convention and the men who made it.

Rutland, Robert A.: *The Birth of the Bill of Rights, 1776–1791,* Collier, New York, 1962. How the Bill of Rights was framed, proposed, and adopted.

Storing, Herbert J.: *What the Anti-Federalists Were For,* University of Chicago Press, Chicago, 1981. A study of the political principles and programs of those who opposed ratification.

Wood, Gordon S.: *The Creation of the American Republic, 1776–1787,* University of North Carolina Press, Chapel Hill, 1969. A study of the politics of the confederation, emphasizing the weakness of the state governments, and an interpretation of the work of the delegates to the Constitutional Convention.

THE STUDY BREAK

Alexander Hamilton. A movie biography (1931).

The Rebels. In this television movie, a fictional character, Philip Kent, fights in the American Revolution and meets up with some of the founding fathers (1984).

1776. Originally a Broadway musical and later (1972) a movie, starring Howard Da Silva as Ben Franklin.

Vidal, Gore: *Burr.* Random House, New York, 1973. A witty and irreverent view of the founding fathers, written as a novel with a point of view (Aaron Burr's) rather than as objective history.

Washington. A six-part made-for-television series produced by CBS in 1984, emphasizing Washington's love for Martha (his wife) and for Sally Fairfax (his neighbor's wife!).

USEFUL SOURCES

Congressional Research Service, *The Constitution of the United States of America: Analysis and Interpretation,* GPO, Washington, D.C., 1972 (with later supplements). A study of the provisions of the Constitution in the light of 200 years of experience and adaptation.

Elliot, Jonathan (ed.): *The Debates of the Several State Conventions,* 2d ed., Franklin, Burt, New York, 1888–1896. A compilation of debates in the ratifying conventions, shedding light on the interpretations given to particular provisions of the Constitution by key figures.

Farrand, Max (ed.): *The Records of the Federal Convention of 1787,* Yale University Press, New Haven, Conn., 1937 (reprinted in 1966). A four-volume set, including an extensive index, containing notes of Madison, Yates, King, Paterson, Pierce, and Brearley and of the official journal. The most useful source on the debates and reports of the committees at the convention.

Hamilton, Alexander, James Madison, and John Jay: *The Federalist* (first published in 1788 in *The New York Packet* and reprinted in many editions). An interpretation of the Constitution by three prominent supporters.

Levy, Leonard W. (ed.): *The Encyclopedia of the American Constitution,* 4 vols., Macmillan, New York, forthcoming in 1987. Will contain 2000 articles on the history and present state of American constitutional law.

Storing, Herbert J. (ed.): *The Complete Anti-Federalist,* University of Chicago Press, Chicago, 1984. A seven-volume compilation, with commentary and notes, of the essential writings of Anti-Federalist politicians.

This Constitution: A Bicentennial Chronicle. A quarterly magazine published by Project '87 containing articles and documents relating to the Constitution and to proposed constitutional reforms.

ORGANIZATIONS

Federal Bicentennial Commission. 736 Jackson Place, Washington, D.C. A commission created in 1983 to promote and coordinate activities for the commemoration of the adoption of the Constitution. For more information phone 202-456-1414.

Project '87. 1527 New Hampshire Avenue, N.W., Washington, D.C. 20036. An organization of historians, political scientists, constitutional lawyers, and politicians who are conducting research on the Constitution and its relevance to American politics. For more information phone 202-483-2512.

FEDERALISM: A NATION OF STATES

Federal-state and state-to-state governmental relations are both parts of federalism. The twin towers of Manhattan's World Trade Center were built by the Port Authority of New York and New Jersey. State governors are very sensitive to federal budget cuts, such as those proposed by President Reagan. (*Mike Yamashita; Larry Downing.*)

The American system, Justice Samuel Chase decided at the end of the Civil War, "looks to an indestructible Union composed of indestructible states."[1] But neither the Constitution nor the war provided a definitive answer to the question of what *form* the union would take. Every issue in American politics becomes bound up with the question of federalism. The "when," "why," and "how" of the question, "Who gets what?" are determined in part by federalism, and changing the relations between the national government and the state governments can change the outcomes; thus our federal arrangements are always controversial, always in flux.

Federalism involves the issues of legitimacy and authority. Which government—the national government or a state government—may constitutionally do what? And which would be more effective, more responsive, and more innovative? Some critics say that federalism is an outmoded, inefficient, and cumbersome way to organize American politics—useful in 1787, but not today. Its defenders claim, as Madison did two centuries ago, that federalism offers numerous advantages and that what seem to be complex and inefficient mechanisms are actually the safeguards that make our democracy work.

WHAT IS FEDERALISM?

A federal system divides powers between a national government and smaller territorial units located within the nation's boundaries. (These smaller units are called *provinces*, *republics*, *cantons*, or, in the United States, *states*.) The national government is sovereign over the entire territory and its population, and it conducts foreign affairs and is responsible for national defense. But the states have their own powers, usually guaranteed by a national constitution. Some powers are exercised solely by the national government, some are exercised by the states, and some are exercised concurrently.

Federation versus confederation

In a ***federation*** the national government is fully sovereign; the states may not withdraw without the consent of the national authorities; and the people create both the national government and the state governments, delegate powers to both, and may restrict both through the written constitution. The national government may act directly on the people: it can tax and draft them. In contrast, in a ***confederation*** the states are sovereign: they may join the nation or withdraw from it at will. They delegate specified powers to national institutions and reserve all others to themselves. The national "government" is a creature of the states and can deal only with the states, not directly with their citizens.

Confederation is an ancient form of government; it has bound people together throughout history, from the time of the alliances of the Israelite tribes to the Renaissance and the confederacies which flourished in what is today

64

POWERS OF THE NATIONAL GOVERNMENT AND THE STATE GOVERNMENTS AS SPECIFIED IN THE CONSTITUTION

The national supremacy clause. The Constitution, treaties, and laws of the United States are the supreme law of the land. Anything to the contrary in state constitutions or laws is null and void. State officials must enforce national law at the expense of contradictory state laws.

Republican form of government. The states are guaranteed a republican form of government. No state may have any other type of government.

Powers granted exclusively to the national government. The national government has power over foreign affairs, military affairs, interstate commerce, commerce with foreign nations, and currency.

Powers which the states may not exercise without congressional assent. Without the agreement of Congress, the states may not tax imports or exports or foreign shipping, keep armed forces other than a state militia, enter into agreements with other states or foreign nations, or engage in warfare.

Powers denied to the states. The states may not impair obligations of contracts; deprive anyone of life, liberty, or property without due process of law; or deny anyone equal protection of the law.

Obligations of the states to one another. The states must give full faith and credit to the judicial proceedings of other states and must grant the citizens of other states the privileges and immunities of their own citizens.

Powers exercised concurrently by the national government and the state governments. The national government and the state governments concurrently regulate elections, taxation, commerce, spending for the general welfare, and judicial functions.

Powers exercised solely by the state governments. The Tenth Amendment reserves powers not granted to the national government by the Constitution to the states or the people. Since 1937 that has become a truism: what the national government does not do remains reserved. It is a boundary rather than a limitation on the national government in most instances.

Territories can be admitted to the union by Congress. Once admitted, states can secede only with the consent of Congress. Alaska and Hawaii were the last admitted, in 1959. (*Bettmann Archive.*)

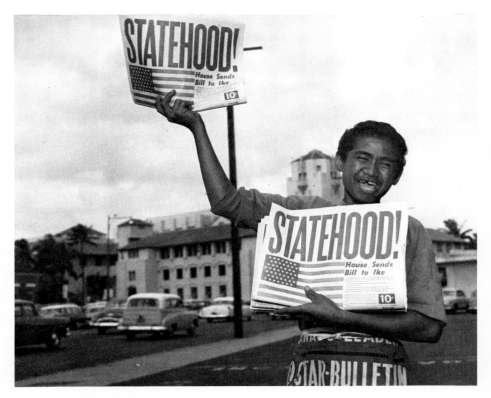

Germany, Italy, the Netherlands, and Switzerland. Federalism is more modern; it was developed first in the United States and later was adopted by one-third of the countries of the world, including the Soviet Union, Brazil, India, Nigeria, Mexico, Switzerland, Yugoslavia, West Germany, Canada, and Australia.

Federal versus unitary government

In a *unitary* system (such as that of the British or the French) the national government develops policies and implements them locally in regions and districts, using its own officials. Today, even nations with unitary systems have modified their constitutions to provide for political autonomy for regions. Great Britain and Spain now have regional legislatures. The Sudan has experimented with autonomy for its religious minorities.

Federalism versus decentralization

In our federal system the powers reserved to the states are specified and guaranteed by the Constitution. State officials are elected by the people, not appointed by the national government, and elected officials run the 3000 counties (smaller territorial units within the states), the 16,700 townships and 19,000 municipalities, and the 28,000 special districts and 15,000 school districts. Only when the states can make their own policies *independently* of the national government—especially their own decisions on taxing and spending and their own economic and social regulations—and only when the right to make these policies is *guaranteed* by the national constitution is there a federal system.

In a unitary system the substantial autonomy that local officials enjoy can be taken away by central authorities. None of their powers are guaranteed by the constitution. They can be removed from office if they do not carry out the instructions of the central government. Occasionally even our national government and our state governments operate as if they were parts of a unitary system. The White House has designated the states as planners for the operations of federal programs and has made the governors "chief federal planning officers" to oversee their implementation. It also has made localities into districts for nationally funded programs, or, in the words of President Carter, into "the delivery mechanisms for most of the actual services the federal government provides."[2] What seems to be federalism, involving cooperation between federal and state officials, is actually decentralization: policies are made at the national level, and the states play an administrative role, however flexible.[3]

THE CHANGING NATURE OF AMERICAN FEDERALISM

American federalism has gone through four distinct phases and in the 1980s is going through a fifth.[4] Each has represented an attempt by politicians to adjust the original constitutional understandings to their own needs.

Phase 1: 1789–1867

The first phase, *classic federalism*, began in 1789 and lasted until the adoption of the Fourteenth Amendment at the end of the Civil War. Members of Congress wanted the national government to serve the states. While some strict constructionists tried to limit the activities of the national government, there was no strict separation between its functions and those of the states.

Administrative collaboration. As a practical matter national officials cooperated closely with their state counterparts: they organized joint stock companies to construct turnpikes and canals and to finance the national bank, with stock held by the United States Treasury, the state governments, and private

investors. The national government gave the states land grants, which they used at the end of the Civil War to build the great public universities.[5]

Conflicts over sovereignty. At the level of constitutional theory the issue of sovereignty remained unsettled until the end of the Civil War. The Constitution did not explicitly create a national government with full sovereign powers. It did not claim that the powers of the states were delegated from the national government. And it did not make the states into creatures of the national government by giving Congress a veto power over their laws. Instead, the Constitution granted some powers to the national government, recognized that others were exercised by the state governments, and then forbade the national government to take certain actions and the state governments to take others (and allowed the states to act in some matters only with the permission of Congress). The result was a hybrid government, as Madison suggested in *Federalist* 39, neither fully national nor fully confederal, but partaking of both forms.

The doctrine of national supremacy. The Supreme Court took the first controversial steps toward establishing the supremacy of national law over state law. In *McCulloch v. Maryland* (1819), Chief Justice John Marshall declared that the Constitution was established by the people, not the states, and denied that the states retained any sovereignty. Marshall upheld the power of Congress both to establish a national bank and to prevent the states from taxing the operations of national agencies. He denied that the Tenth Amendment, which reserves all powers not mentioned in the Constitution to the states and the people, could limit the powers of Congress as to the means it could use to implement powers granted to the government by the Constitution.[6] In *Dartmouth College v. Woodward* (1819) the Court upheld a clause in the Constitution forbidding the states to make laws that would impair the validity of contracts.[7] Later, in *Gibbons v. Ogden* (1824), Marshall struck down a New York law giving a company a monopoly on steamboat operations, and in doing so he argued against the notion that a state law and a national law, if in conflict with each other, involved two opposed sovereignties. Instead, he pointed out that Article VI gave supremacy to Congress. The national government was superior and the state governments were subordinate, with the federal courts serving as instruments to implement the policies of Congress.[8]

The doctrine of dual federalism. Counterpoised against the notion of national supremacy was the idea that the Constitution remained a compact of sovereign states which had ceded only limited powers to the national government. State and national authorities faced each other as equals, across a dividing line demarcating their respective powers. In some areas, only the states could act. In others, both the states and the national government could act. Both, for example, had *concurrent power* to control interstate commerce, although the power of the states was limited to matters of local concern.[9] Chief Justice Taney resurrected the Tenth Amendment, arguing that the states were sovereign in certain matters and that the final determination was to be made by the courts—now a neutral arbiter between Congress and the states— "deciding in the peaceful forms of judicial proceeding the angry and irritating controversies between sovereignties, which in other countries have been determined by the arbitrament of force."[10]

The doctrine of nullification. Dual federalism left the issue of sovereignty unsettled. When the Federalists took the nation to war against France in 1798, its majorities in Congress also passed a sedition law, which restricted freedom of speech and of the press. The Anti-Federalists, who were opposed to the conflict, struck back with the Kentucky Resolution and the Virginia Resolution (passed by the legislatures of those states), which declared the law null and void in the two states. This doctrine of *nullification* was later used by the Federalists themselves: during the War of 1812 they refused to heed a call from the Republican-dominated Congress to put the New England state militias into the service of the federal government.

In 1832, when Congress imposed a high tariff, South Carolina declared the law null and void and threatened to secede from the union if the tariff was collected in the port of Charleston by federal officials. President Andrew Jackson issued a proclamation warning the citizens of the state not to violate federal law. He urged antisecessionists to arm themselves and prepare to assist national authorities, and then he warned South Carolina that he would use the army to put down its resistance. Eventually, after Jackson promised to work for a lower tariff law, the state backed down and repealed its ordinance of nullification.

CLOSE-UP

JOHN C. CALHOUN. No other nineteenth-century politician exemplifies the unresolved tensions of American federalism as well as John C. Calhoun. Born in 1782, Calhoun graduated from Yale in 1804 and returned south to practice law. In 1810, after serving a term in the South Carolina legislature (1808), he became a member of Congress. At that time he was a strong nationalist, one of the "war hawks" who pushed the nation into the War of 1812. Later, in 1817, he became secretary of war, and in 1824 he was elected vice president.

In 1828 he was reelected, even though the presidency had shifted from John Quincy Adams to Andrew Jackson. Calhoun and Jackson soon found themselves on opposite sides of the "states' rights" issue. Calhoun believed that the sectional compromises of the 1820s were unfavorable to the south. He thought that the southern minority needed protection against unfavorable laws (having to do with tariffs, banking, and slavery) which might be passed by Congress. In 1832, in pro-

John C. Calhoun. (*New York Public Library.*)

test against a tariff law, Calhoun resigned from the vice presidency, and the South Carolina legislature promptly elected him a United States senator. He was a leader in the attempt by that state to "nullify" the tariff law, an effort which failed when President Jackson made it clear that he would use military force if necessary to collect the duties in southern ports.

While in the Senate, Calhoun proposed to revise the federal system radically. He argued, in his *Disquisition on government*, that the states should be allowed to nullify laws passed by Congress—an argument that had previously been made by the Jeffersonians in the 1790s (during a naval war with France) and by the Federalists in 1812. The states' right not to enforce federal law should be final, he said, except in cases where a new constitutional amendment had been passed. He also proposed a system of concurrent regional majorities to pass laws: only when a majority of northern, southern, and western representatives all voted aye would a bill become a law. If a majority from any region dissented, that would be enough to "veto" the bill.

Calhoun's ideas were not accepted, even in the south. Unionists saw no reason to change the existing system. Moderates believed that threats of secession would induce the north to agree to new compromises on their substantive demands, thus avoiding the need to make changes in the system. Hard-liners were ready to secede if the north did not give in. By 1850 Calhoun was predicting that there would be a civil war within twelve years.[11]

The federal crisis resolved.   The Civil War settled the issue of sovereignty. The national government was supreme over the states; Congress, by simple majorities, could make laws which the states were bound to enforce; no state or region could nullify a national law once it was enacted; none could secede from the union to protest policies it opposed; and the president had the power to execute the law, if necessary by the use of armed forces. The north's victory over the south ended any lingering conceptions that the union involved dual sovereignty or should operate according to doctrines of nullification or concurrent majorities; by 1865 there was only one sovereign—the national government.

Phase 2: 1867–1913

Ironically, during the postwar period, when the issue of the union's sovereign *constitutional* powers was settled, the doctrine of ***dual federalism*** flourished: the national government had its responsibilities, the states had theirs, and the national government should stay clear of the business of the states, and vice versa. The courts would make sure that the national government did not overstep its bounds.

Industrial regulation.   Dual federalism was a response to the growing industrialization of the nation. A conservative business community and a federal judiciary drawn from the ranks of lawyers that served business wished to limit national regulation of the economy. The courts made a sharp distinction between commerce between the states, which Congress could regulate, and all other commercial, financial, and industrial matters, which they argued were left to the states.[12] The boundaries were far sharper and more restrictive than they had been before the Civil War period, when Congress had used the general welfare clause and the necessary and proper clause for economic regula-

The Supreme Court long struck down federal child labor laws on the ground that they infringed upon states' rights. A 1941 reversal eventually upheld the federal government's regulation of child labor under the interstate commerce clause. (*Lewis Hine: Bettmann Archive.*)

tion. The postwar courts struck down national laws on the grounds that the states had jurisdiction. Antitrust laws were interpreted in such a way as to prevent the national government from interfering with manufacturing combinations.[13]

Substantive due process. The federal courts used the Fourteenth Amendment guarantee of due process of law—a provision enacted at the end of the Civil War primarily to protect the freed slaves in the south—and interpreted it to mean that corporations were "persons" within the meaning of the amendment.[14] Therefore, corporations could not be denied due process of law by the states. The federal courts created a set of protections for corporations known as *substantive due process*, the effect of which was to strike down much (though not all) state regulation of minimum wages, maximum hours, health and safety in the workplace, and the like.[15]

The states were limited in regulating the economy because of substantive due process guarantees to corporations, while Congress was limited in this respect because the courts said that these matters did not involve interstate commerce. Thus neither level of government could act.

The "state" versus the "government." The most noted constitutional lawyers and professors of the day, most of them northerners who had supported a strong union during the Civil War, interpreted the Constitution in a way that reconciled the need for national supremacy with this handcuffing of Congress. They argued that the function of the *union* was equivalent to that of the European state: it was to have all sovereign powers; handle matters of diplomacy, war, and internal security; and remain supreme over the state governments. Meanwhile, the national *government* (which they distinguished from the sov-

ereign state) was to function in limited spheres, with its powers divided among separate, mutually antagonistic branches and with its operations monitored by the judiciary, which would be ever vigilant in protecting the rights of individuals and corporations.[16]

Phase 3: 1913–1941

But the American people wanted more national regulation of the economy. They supported Teddy Roosevelt's "trust-busting" campaign and Woodrow Wilson's "new freedom" program in the presidential election of 1912. Later the depression forced the national government to aid state governments in the relief, welfare, public housing, public employment, and unemployment insurance programs of the New Deal. Funds were provided by the national government, but the programs were also partly funded and fully administered by state and county agencies. Many of these programs were passed by Congress in response to pleas by state officials for help.

The courts at first tried to reaffirm their laissez-faire decisions. They struck down federal laws prohibiting or taxing child labor.[17] Between 1865 and 1937 the Supreme Court struck down seventy-six laws passed by Congress and hundreds passed by states, most regulating the economy. More than 130 state laws were struck down in the 1920s alone. But the Court limited the reach of the due process clause, first by establishing certain exceptions (such as "protective legislation" involving women and children) and then by repudiating substantive due process and allowing the states to regulate corporations.[18] It also expanded the conceptions of the general welfare clause and the necessary and proper clause so that Congress could once again legislate on a large number of social matters, including wages and hours, child labor, social security, and unemployment insurance. It expanded the interpretation of commerce between the states to include manufacturing. It also broadened the definition of interstate commerce to include commerce *within* states that has an effect on commerce *between* states.[19]

Phase 4: 1941–1969

In the next period the focus shifted from the economy to race and poverty. Blacks moved off the land in the south and into the factories of the north during the Second World War. In the postwar period their demands for racial justice profoundly affected the federal system. When the Supreme Court ruled

Federal-state cooperation during the depression led to public housing such as the Whitman Park Project in Philadelphia. (*Department of Housing and Urban Development.*)

in 1954 that public schools must be desegregated because "separate but equal" facilities were inherently unconstitutional, southerners responded with a policy of "massive resistance" and refused to obey court orders to desegregate schools. In some instances this required federal officials to use federal marshals, the FBI, and even federal troops to enforce judicial orders and uphold the Constitution.

Race. Southern politicians responded with claims that their states' rights were at stake and that the southern voters had a right to pass laws and ordinances maintaining racial segregation in public facilities to preserve their "way of life." Meanwhile, blacks and northern liberals argued that only national law could protect the civil rights of minorities and that Congress had the right to pass laws that overrode state and local practices. At times federal troops had to be used to uphold court orders for desegregation involving public schools and state universities. Congress passed the Civil Rights Act of 1964, which desegregated public accommodations involved in interstate commerce; this included most restaurants, hotels, and commercial establishments. The Voting Rights Act of 1965 overrode state election practices such as literacy tests and even provided for federal registrars to take over local functions in certain cases. The Fair Housing Act of 1968 prohibited racial discrimination in the sale or rental of housing, although in practice much discrimination remained.

The national-local relationship. In the 1960s, unlike earlier periods, there was a direct link between national bureaucrats and local officials, especially in the new urban renewal and antipoverty programs. Often the states were bypassed. At times it seemed as if federal and local officials were in alliance against state legislators and governors, who seemed more cautious, more conservative, and even hostile in their attitude toward the new urban-oriented antipoverty, housing, and community development programs. The states felt that they were whipsawed: that they were required to implement national laws and regulations and to fund part of the costs of national programs but were denied adequate input into policy-making and at times were bypassed by the new national-local alliances.

Criticism no longer focused on the right of the national government to act, but rather on how effectively the complex and increasingly costly intergovernmental system was working. Questions of authority had replaced those of legitimacy.

Phase 5: 1969 to the present

Today we are in a fifth phase of American federalism, one which has not yet run its course. It is marked by an increased mistrust of centralized government and by skepticism that "the feds" can solve domestic problems. State governments have become better at solving problems, and many have modernized their antiquated bureaucratic methods. State governments are eager to make policy in areas that have long been controlled by national officials. Meanwhile, the national government, faced with monstrous deficits, has no appetite for new programs and is cutting back or eliminating many old ones. Polls show that more than two-thirds of the public favor granting the states more power and that an overwhelming majority of Americans think that the states understand the needs of the people better than the national government, will administer programs more efficiently, and are less likely to operate corruptly.[20] (See Figure 3-1.)

Figure 3-1. "Which level of government—federal, state, or local—is most effective?" The ACIR poll shows a large increase in percentage of respondents who believe that state and local governments, rather than the national government, is most effective in dealing with problems. (Source: Advisory Commission on Intergovernmental Relations, *Significant Features of Fiscal Federalism*, p. 122. *The Washington Post National Weekly Edition,* July 23, 1984, p. 38.)

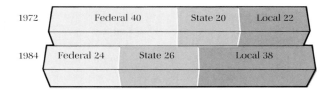

| 1972 | Federal 40 | State 20 | Local 22 |
| 1984 | Federal 24 | State 26 | Local 38 |

Unwinding the federal system. The result has been some extreme rhetoric about reviving "state sovereignty" and "unwinding the federal system" so that most functions now handled cooperatively would be assigned exclusively either to the states or to the national government. For example, the states now handle low-level radioactive-waste disposal, and the national government has the exclusive responsibility for high-level radioactive wastes. In part this represents principle, but it is also good politics. Let the states handle difficult or even intractable problems, and let them raise taxes to do so. Meanwhile, national politicians can take the credit for lowering national taxes and reducing the burden of federal regulation.

The reality has been more complex. The existing cooperative mechanisms remain, and state officials fight to keep them rather than unwind the system. But there have been significant cutbacks in funding to the states and attempts to give them greater responsibility.

The new regional issues. Racial and social issues have been displaced in importance by other controversies, often centered on energy, natural resources, and industrial policy. In the west, the so-called sagebrush rebellion involves conflicts between locals and feds over the management of federal lands—parks, forests, grazing lands, and military tracts. The west also challenges federal power to deal with water management and coastal management.[21] In some states there has been intense opposition to plans for basing the MX missile and other strategic nuclear weapons systems. Throughout the nation there have been conflicts over policy involving the construction and operation of nuclear plants, the transportation of nuclear fuel, and the disposal of nuclear wastes. Environmental regulations, toxic-waste disposal,

At times of natural disaster the states move in first. Jim Hunt, then the governor of North Carolina, took charge of relief after a tornado at Faison. The federal government provides disaster relief if the state has difficulty coping. (*AP Laser photo.*)

transportation regulations, and even the issue of speed limits on interstate highways have all become issues in the federal system.

The states continue to resist the power of the national government. Federal civil defense planners call for the evacuation of cities in the event of a nuclear crisis, but local officials refuse to make such plans in Marin County, California; Boulder, Colorado; and Cambridge, Massachusetts. In Connecticut, local officials for a while refused to allow on their interstate highways trucks which exceeded their own standards for weight and bulk, even though federal law permits trucks to travel on such highways.

HOW FEDERALISM WORKS

With all the conflicts over sovereign powers, jurisdictions, and the administration of programs, one might wonder whether federalism is worth it. Why should any nation experiment with such a complicated form of government when a unitary system would be simpler? As it turns out, federalism has some significant advantages; some were understood in 1787, and others have been discovered only in practice.

Checking and balancing power

The framers believed that a federal system would allow national officials to check state officials, and vice versa. The Constitution requires the national government to guarantee each state a republican form of government, which prevents local despotism.

State governments led by the opposition party served to check the excesses of the party in power in Washington in our early history. The first transfer of power between parties, for example, came about in part because the state militia in Virginia served notice in 1800 that it expected the Federalists to turn over the government to the Anti-Federalists or face armed conflict.

Today federalism serves to improve the authority of the government with the public. If national policies are unwise or inadequate, state politicians can be expected to call for a different approach or to demand more power to deal with issues. Likewise, if the states fail to solve their problems, the public may demand that Congress and the president act, and national legislation and programs will supplant those of the states.

Diversity and accountability

A federal system allows different regions and states to pursue different social and economic policies. Voters can compare the programs in their states and regions with those adopted elsewhere and see which are more viable. Since voters elect state officials (and the officials of county and other local governments established by the state), they can make the government responsive to the wishes of local people, even as they change their views about what constitutes intelligent social and economic policy. Some may be permissive, and others restrictive, on issues such as the drinking age, grounds for divorce, gambling, prostitution, use of drugs, the sale of pornography, and punishment for crime. Sometimes allowing states to make social policy can reduce national tensions over an issue and can keep issues out of national politics, especially divisive social issues: drugs, gun control, and child abuse, for example.

Experimentation. A state can experiment, and if an experiment is not successful, others need not adopt the idea. "A mistake in Washington is a mistake for all 50 states," according to Richard Williamson, a Reagan aide, while a

States are often ahead of the national government in social policy. Women voted in the presidential elections in Wyoming in 1888 under state suffrage laws; the federal government did not guarantee women the right to vote until 1920. (*Granger Collection.*)

mistake in one state "only affects that state and they can learn from each other."[22] The states are laboratories which can diffuse innovations to other states or the national government. Wisconsin created unemployment insurance in 1931, and the national government soon followed suit. During the depression other states experimented with legislation for welfare, public works, and collective bargaining before such legislation was adopted by Washington. In the 1940s and 1950s northern states passed fair housing and fair employment laws and established enforcement commissions; the federal government did so in the 1960s. Some western states allowed women to vote in state elections two decades before the suffrage amendment was put in the Constitution. The sun belt tax revolt in the late 1970s was followed by federal tax reductions in 1981.

Constraints on experimentation. But federalism also inhibits experimentation. States compete with one another for business investment, and a state must offer a better "business climate" than other states. If personal and corporate taxes are too high and if services are less than adequate, industries and the most productive people will pull up stakes and go elsewhere. States give incentives to industry by reducing taxes and offering credits and exemptions and special depreciation schedules. They spend money on services needed by industry, including convenient transportation, health care, schooling, and job retraining, thus skewing their policies.

A state may not spend as much money as it would like on facilities or services because some will be used by out-of-state citizens who do not pay their share of the costs. States that benefit from the services offered by another state are *free riders*—or, more accurately, *freeloaders.*

One solution to this problem is to have the national government make grants to a state to cover part of the cost of building or operating a facility. The state pays an amount which is proportional to the benefits that will accrue to its own citizens, while the national government pays an amount which is proportional to the benefits that will accrue to citizens of other states.

Since air pollution does not stop at state lines, national standards and joint federal-state enforcement efforts are necessary to reduce air pollution and clean up toxic waste dumps. (*Bruce Flynn; George Hall.*)

A state that provides well for its disadvantaged citizens may find that it draws migrants from other states (or foreign nations) who are attracted by the services—the *magnet effect.* If other states do not increase their own services, such a state will wind up with a higher tax burden, a greater level of public expenditure, and inadequate services, because the clientele will have increased enormously. As more poor people move in, the quality of life deteriorates for others, and as their taxes rise, they "vote with their feet" and move elsewhere.

National problem, national action. States and cities may regulate industry in the absence of national regulation, but sometimes they are inhibited by threats that companies will relocate to a more hospitable state. And a state has no incentive to regulate an industry if the benefits (such as maintaining air or water quality) are received by citizens of neighboring states. Nor does a state have any such incentive if regulation would not work unless many other states also acted. It makes little sense for New England states to control their own smokestack emissions if most of the acid rain which pollutes their lakes is caused by smokestacks in the middle west and in Canada. Sometimes the only way to solve a problem is through national action; experimentation by states can be worse than useless because it may delay meaningful efforts.

Going overboard with national action. But the national government, prodded by interest groups and legislators who want to help out financially hard-pressed state and local governments, often takes on more than it needs to: it shares with state governments the responsibility for school security, pothole repair, noise control, arson prevention, snow removal, rat and pest control, jellyfish control, bikeway construction, and car-pool formation. One may wonder what is the point of having state and local officials if they cannot somehow contrive to deal with these issues without involving the national government. Aaron Wildavsky has accurately characterized the present system as *fruitcake*

federalism: state and local officials compete for grants that they do not need, and they expect the national government to deal with problems and provide funding for all sorts of programs—all without rhyme, reason, or rationale, but simply because it has become a habit to look to Washington for help and to blame Washington for problems that should have been solved locally.[23]

Liberals, conservatives, and states' rights

The standard textbook generalization has it that conservatives favor **state action** because **states' rights** prevent federal regulation of industry and because states and cities are more likely to promote the interests of corporations and to provide a "favorable business climate" through lower taxes and antiunion legislation. Liberals, on the other hand, favor national regulation of industry because it is likely to be stiffer, and they favor national social programs because they are likely to be better funded.

But whether one favors regulation by the national government or by the states depends on the issue. Liberals call for national action on welfare, civil rights, urban reconstruction, and pollution—unless a conservative is in the White House, in which case they look to state governments for innovative programs and more funding.

Conservatives often oppose national programs in principle, but in practice conservative business leaders often prefer a single national law or regulation instead of fifty state laws with which they must comply. They often support national services such as collection of economic statistics, postal services, highway and airport construction, mass transit, freight-rail service, and the bailout of depressed regions. They favor national licensing and regulation of nuclear power plants, while environmentalists and antinuke groups favor state licensing. (The Supreme Court, in a compromise, gave the federal government the exclusive power to regulate safety and environmental issues, and it gave the states the power to regulate the economic aspects of nuclear power.) Conservative politicians in the mountain states line up for national funding for public works, reclamation, and water resource projects; conservatives in the south welcome national funding for canals, power stations, highways, and crop support programs. In sum, whether politicians favor or oppose national action depends less on ideology than on the answer to the question, "Who gets what, when, and how?"

Fiscal federalism

State taxation. In a federal system both the national government and the state governments impose taxes on individuals and corporations. The national government relies primarily on personal income taxes, corporate income taxes, customs duties, alcohol excises, and estate and gift taxes. The states take in most of their revenue from general sales taxes, income taxes (all but nine now have them), automobile registration fees, and excises (taxes on particular goods). Local governments receive most of their revenue from the property tax. Excises on tobacco products and utilities are shared evenly by the national government and the state governments.

The national government accommodates the states' needs for revenue in several ways. Taxpayers who itemize their deductions on federal income tax returns deduct $31 billion worth of state and local income taxes and $6 billion worth of sales taxes and thus reduce their tax liability to the national government. Therefore, state and local governments have leeway to raise these taxes without triggering a taxpayers' revolt.

The interest which the national government pays on **bonds** is not taxable by state and local governments, and the $19 billion in interest which state and local governments pay on their bonds is not taxed by the national government. This means that states and cities can offer bonds at lower interest rates than corporations, since the after-tax income that a person receives is the important consideration; in effect, this is a Treasury subsidy to states and cities.

Fiscal crises in the cities. *Fiscal federalism* can help cities whose own resources are insufficient to deal with urban decay and poverty, although national tax policies have hurt the cities. Tax codes have favored new construction, not rehabilitation, which has led industries to build new facilities in the suburbs rather than fix up existing sites. New owner-occupied suburban tract housing was favored over the rehabilitation of rental housing in cities by making the interest on home mortgages and on federally insured mortgages tax-deductible. The interstate highway systems, financed with federal funds, allowed people to move to the country, while urban mass transit fell into disrepair.

The cities' populations are declining, but their elderly, minorities, and immigrants are increasing in number, and most of these people require government services, while few can afford high taxes to pay for them. Municipal unions often escalate wage demands without corresponding increases in productivity. The rehabilitation of bridges, tunnels, harbors, roads, hospitals, and schools requires massive funding. Yet the tax base of many cities has eroded.

Between 1970 and 1980 cities received injections of new money from the national government as direct federal aid to large cities increased by 1500 percent. This money came from urban programs passed by Democrats in Congress. In some large cities up to half the local budgets consisted of federal funds.[24] By 1978, however, federal aid to cities (adjusted for inflation) had begun to decline.

Republican presidents and candidates do not favor direct aid to cities. Reagan did away with job programs and ended a program of antirecessionary fiscal assistance. He also slashed funding for public works and community development. To the extent that funds were made available, they were given to state governments rather than to the big cities. The Reagan administration did propose to use the tax code to target some aid to disadvantaged areas in the big cities. Under this plan, certain depressed areas would have been designated as "urban enterprise zones." Tax breaks for companies locating in these zones would have included credits for capital investment in plant and machinery, no **capital gains taxes** on property sales, a twenty-year period during which business losses could be offset against later profits, and tax credits if young unemployed workers were hired. The Treasury estimated that the cost of these tax breaks would have amounted to $900 million, which is a small commitment, considering the total amount of aid to urban areas, but the program stalled in Congress.

Meanwhile, nineteen states passed their own legislation for enterprise zones. In Camden and Newark, New Jersey, for example, the zones allowed corporations to pay lower state taxes and reduced their taxes by $1500 for each new employee hired who lived in the city and had been jobless for more than ninety days. Sales taxes were also cut or eliminated on goods and services that corporations bought and on any new building or plant expansion in the zone.

BAILING OUT THE BIG APPLE: FEDERAL LOAN GUARANTEES

In 1975 New York City nearly defaulted on loans which a group of banks had made to it. The banks refused to roll over the loans because they did not believe that the city could ever pay the money back. New York came close to declaring bankruptcy. No one could say for certain what that would have meant, but it might have affected the stability of the entire national banking system.

The New York State legislature devised a plan to meet the crisis. City finances were placed under the supervision of an emergency financial control board. It would require the city to balance its budget within three years, and it could reject the city's plans. To refinance existing loans and pay off the banks, the Municipal Assistance Corporation (Big MAC) was created; it had the authority to issue long-term bonds to investors to replace the short-term city notes issued to the banks.

Big MAC found that investors would not buy its bonds, and so Congress, after much lobbying by city officials and the New York State congressional delegation, bailed out the city. It provided $2.3 billion for three years in the form of seasonal loans which the city could draw upon when it needed cash to pay its expenses. Later, in 1978, with its budget not yet balanced, the city returned to Congress to ask for $1.65 billion in loan guarantees for four years. With these guarantees Big MAC was able to market its bonds. By 1985 the city once again could market bonds without federal loans or guarantees.

Those opposing the bailout argued that the city was in trouble because it had lived beyond its means. It provided large welfare and Medicaid benefits, ran a free city university system, broadcast over a municipal radio station, maintained a large free public library system, and so forth. Supporters claimed that the city was in trouble because of the way federalism works: New York City was expected to take care of immigrants who made it their first port of call before moving inland; it had costs associated with the United Nations; and its libraries and cultural facilities were used by visitors but were paid for primarily by residents. They argued that the federal government should increase its aid to the city rather than require it to pay for what were actually national programs to solve national problems.

By the mid-1980s the cities were in greater trouble than ever before. A Joint Economic Committee report revealed that most of the fifty largest cities had raised taxes, cut services, reduced the number of employees, and postponed capital improvements. A survey by the National League of Cities showed that most could not prevent serious deterioration of their facilities.

Fiscal equalization. One of the most important functions of federalism in many countries is to redistribute national income from wealthier regions to poorer ones—*fiscal equalization.* The United States, unlike most other countries with a federal system (such as Australia and Canada), has no explicit goals for fiscal equalization, either in the Constitution or in its laws. Grants made by the federal government to states and cities provide virtually no fiscal equalization because the wealthier states are also those with large concentrations of poor people and with crumbling facilities in need of replacement. Also, the higher-income states in the north spend more on their poor citizens than the low-income states in the south, and so fiscal equalization might actually hurt the poor in the north.[25]

But if one considers *all* federal expenditures in states—such as for defense contracts, military bases, federal offices, and purchases of goods and services—the poorer parts of the country do benefit from federalism. The New England,

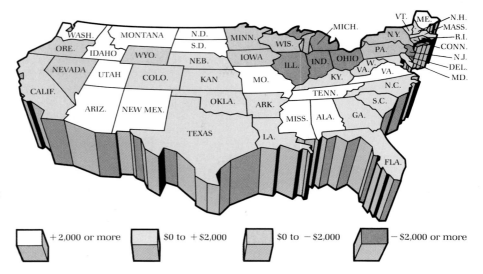

Figure 3-2. The industrial states of the northeast and midwest pay more in taxes per capita than they receive back in federal grants and services. Most southern and western states receive more per capita than their residents pay out. (Source: Advisory Commission on Intergovernmental Relations.)

mid-Atlantic, plains, and Great Lakes states pay more in taxes per capita than their citizens receive back in federal expenditures in their states, while theL south Atlantic, south central, mountain, and Pacific states receive more in expenditures than their citizens pay in per capita taxes.[26] (See Figure 3-2.)

Redundancy

A simplistic approach to government organization argues that if one unit of government can do something, having two or three different units involved will lead to duplication and waste. There is no reason to have state governments, some critics charge, because the national government at this point has so many duties that keeping the states involved only confuses things.

Paradoxical as it may seem, duplication may lead to more efficient government. This involves the ***redundancy principle:*** the idea that one should have a "backup" which can take over if something goes wrong. In the *Columbia* space shuttle there are five different computers. When a power cell in the shuttle failed in a 1981 mission, two others provided power, allowing the mission to continue. Having *system redundancy* improves the odds in any operation: if a unit will fail 1 in 10 times, having two units means that the odds are that both will fail only 1 in 100 times.

Load sharing versus system failure. These principles apply to government. Having two or three different units of government means that if one is not equal to the job, another can take over and carry the load. It also means that if the national government is not carrying out its functions properly, pressure from the states or cities may force it to take a more active role, and vice versa.[27]

During the 1973 energy crisis the national government was supposed to allocate oil supplies. Because it did the job poorly, state energy offices proposed better allocations, which resulted in more efficient distributions. Congress then delegated power to the state governors to allocate fuel, establish conservation measures, and monitor consumption. During the 1979 energy crisis the Department of Energy could not develop efficient rationing plans. Congress refused to pass most of President Carter's energy program. The governors stepped in again; using a combination of national power delegated to

them by Congress and their own powers, they installed state rationing systems, provided funds so that the elderly and the poor could pay their oil bills, and allocated fuel to industry. Congress then passed the Emergency Energy Conservation Act of 1979, which allowed the governors to set goals, choose measures to achieve the goals, and implement their own plans rather than those of the Department of Energy.[28]

Taking up the slack. If one level of government reduces its services, another level may increase its commitments. When the states could no longer provide welfare and food to the poor during the depression, the national government stepped in with welfare, job, and housing programs. In the 1980s, as the national government cut back on its commitment to the hungry and the homeless, the cities and states took on a greater role. When President Reagan cut student aid, the states increased their need-based tuition scholarship programs, took over some of the work-study reimbursements, expanded loan programs, and allowed students to transfer to state universities.

Buck-passing. Unfortunately, redundancy systems have their disadvantages. When everyone is responsible for something, sometimes no one is responsible—and nothing happens. Mayors and governors campaign on promises to increase services and cut costs, and then they blame their deteriorating services and facilities on Washington.[29] The feds want the locals to raise taxes and solve problems, while the locals expect Washington to take the political heat for tax increases and to send more money their way. Voters find it increasingly difficult to sort out who is to blame.

INTERGOVERNMENTAL POLITICS

Much of the work of American government is carried out intergovernmentally. Rather than have each level of government run its own programs, a system sometimes called *layer cake federalism*, the modern **intergovernmental system** involves each unit in the work of the others. The administration of such programs has been likened to a *marble cake*, characterized by "an inseparable mingling of differently colored ingredients, the colors appearing in vertical and diagonal strands and unexpected whirls."[30] There are no separate levels and there is no hierarchy; instead, there are matrices where clusters of federal, state, and local officials jointly administer programs with the cooperation of private organizations. The marble cake seems complex, with no neat boundaries separating the national government and the state and local governments—and it is.

Intergovernmental cooperation often involves federal funding for part or all of state programs. This may take several forms: categorical grants, project grants, block grants, formula grants, and revenue sharing.

Intergovernmental administration: The grant-in-aid

The federal **grant-in-aid** is extremely important to state and local governments; at their peak in 1977, grants-in-aid accounted for more than one-fourth of all state and local expenditures (up from one-tenth in 1950), and in 1985 they accounted for 22 percent, more than 3.4 percent of the gross national product.

Categorical grants. The traditional way to administer programs involves the **categorical grant.** The national government grants funds to state and local

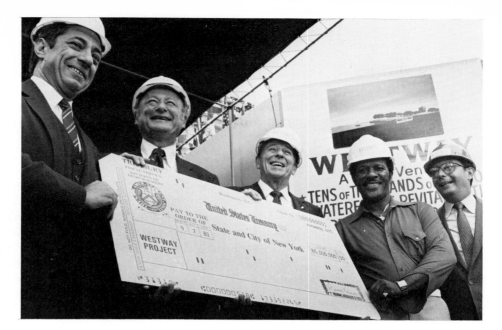

President Reagan, along with Governor Mario Cuomo of New York State, Mayor Edward Koch of New York City, Senator Alphonse D'Amato of New York, and a construction worker, dramatizes the joint federal-state interest in developing interstate highways. (*AP Laserphoto.*)

governments for particular services or facilities. States are not required to participate. The federal government may require states to put up *matching funds*—usually between one-tenth and one-half of the federal contribution—and most states do so because participation brings in federal money which otherwise would go elsewhere. In 1862, under one of the first such grants, states were given federal land, which they could sell to get the money to build their public university systems, the great land-grant universities. In 1879 grants were begun to aid the blind, in 1887 to construct agricultural experimentation stations, in 1916 to build state highways, in 1917 to provide vocational education, and in 1920 to aid veterans.

During the depression the national government created the welfare and unemployment insurance systems through categorical grants. Payments were made to individuals by state agencies, with some of the funding coming from the national government.

The peak years for categorical grants were the 1960s and 1970s, when the "new frontier" and "great society" programs established by Democratic presidents Kennedy and Johnson expanded under Republican presidents Nixon and Ford. By 1980 there were close to 600 such programs, transferring about $90 billion from the national government to state and local governments. The Reagan administration cut back these programs sharply: the total amount of funds was reduced by almost half between 1980 and 1984, and many programs were eliminated. (Figure 3-3 shows trends in grant outlays.)

Categorical grants are created by Congress, often as a result of lobbying by governors and mayors who want more aid and by program specialists and interest groups. But sometimes programs are created as a result of presidential, congressional, or departmental insistence that national priorities or standards be imposed on the states—even over the opposition of state and local officials. The federal government created a food stamp program for the poor, even though many of the counties with the largest proportions of malnourished people opposed it.

Project grants. Often money is given by the federal government to help states

or cities construct particular facilities. Local officials apply to regional federal offices. In ranking the applications, economists favor the *cost-benefit* approach: costs are divided into the anticipated benefits, and projects with the highest ratios of benefits to costs are funded first. But state politicians and their allies in Congress are not impressed with this approach, especially when their pet projects would cost a great deal and would confer benefits only on particular farmers or business people. In such cases they do not want cost-benefit ranking. They view federal government funds not as part of their costs, but rather as "free goods" for their state.

Politicians rely on *community mobilization:* they get local businesses, labor leaders, bankers, contractors, newspapers, and others who would benefit from a project to support their efforts, and then they get their entire state's congressional delegation to back them.[31] Legislators bargain with other state delegations in Congress and with the White House and department secretaries to win approval for the funding. Thirty states and a number of large cities maintain full-time lobbying offices in Washington to expedite these efforts.

Congressional committees are influential in determining who gets these allocations, although studies have shown that most committee members do not receive a disproportionate share of funds in programs over which they have jurisdiction.[32]

Formula grants. Funds may also be distributed by automatic formula, a system preferred by states and cities. This system, which is designed to end political influence, is used for about one-third of categorical grants. But politics remains: instead of trying to get a particular project grant by changing the rankings, legislators try to change the weighting of the factors in the distribution of the formula. A typical formula for distributing housing funds, for example, might take into account the following: overall population, the percentage

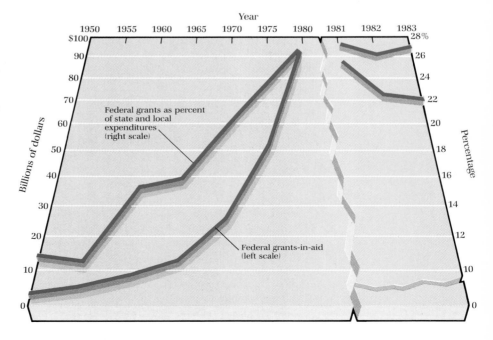

Figure 3-3. Dotted line shows amount of money spent by the national government for intergovernmental grants. Note the cutbacks which occurred in 1982. Solid line shows these amounts as the percentage of all state and local expenditures, and it too begins to decline in the 1980s. (Source: Advisory Commission on Intergovernmental Relations.)

of the population below the poverty level, the tax effort the state makes in funding its own programs, the fiscal capacity of the state to increase its funding by raising taxes, and the number of people in need of the program.

Members of Congress use computer programs to tell exactly how much money their district or state will receive under various versions of the formula. They can then propose a change in the formula which will increase their allocation. Usually a coalition forms, along regional lines, which can impose the formula it wants.

Grants: The view from the states. Governors are not interested in conforming to national standards or meeting national goals. They want the federal government to give them lots of money with very little interference. They want vetoes over any projects in their states that will be funded by the feds. They insist that program funds be routed through state budgets rather than going directly to counties and cities. State legislatures sometimes insist that funds not be spent unless and until they authorize and appropriate the projects or services.

Although state officials consider money from the federal government to be free goods, there is a *diversionary cost*, since state matching funds expended according to national priorities are no longer available for other purposes. In addition, when Congress requires the states to participate in open-ended reimbursement programs like welfare, Medicaid, and unemployment compensation, the states have to pay out funds to all who are eligible, which means that they no longer control their budgets. State officials are subject to federal laws and regulations and to federal court orders interpreting them.

There are at least thirty-seven legal mandates—involving discrimination based on race, sex, or age; access for the handicapped to public places; environmental protection; preservation of historic sites; citizen participation; long-range planning; individual privacy; freedom of information; and the like—which apply to intergovernmental programs. Compliance increases the expenses of states and localities, and the mandates do not take local conditions into account. Sometimes officials refuse to comply, and a case winds up in the federal courts, which are likely to rule for these mandates if issues concerning civil rights or liberties are involved, if the requirement is reasonably related to a

THE FEDS VERSUS THE LOCALS: TWO SUPREME COURT CASES

Must a state always comply with federal regulations? In *National League of Cities v. Usury* (1976), the Supreme Court reviewed a law passed by Congress—the Fair Labor Standards Amendments of 1974—which would have applied maximum wage and hour laws to state and local government employees. The Supreme Court struck down the law, ruling that because the states remained a coordinate and not a subordinate part of the constitutional system, they could apply their own wage and hour rules, even in programs partly funded by the national government.

In 1985 the Supreme Court reversed itself. In *Garcia v. San Antonio Metropolitan Transit Authority*, it ruled that the Labor Department could order local transit authorities to abide by national wage and hour regulations. A majority of the Court held that the 1976 approach was unworkable, that national standards could be applied by Congress to state and local employees, and that the states had sufficient influence with their congressional delegations to protect their workers' interests when Congress considered laws to regulate workers.

Congress requires states and cities to provide access to federally funded programs to the handicapped. Peter Axelson, a veteran, demonstrates a new bicycle for the handicapped to Representative Bob Edgar (left) near the Capitol. (*AP Laserphoto.*)

program, and if state participation in the program is voluntary and the state is free to leave. But in several decisions the courts have warned that if national officials *coerce* a state into remaining in a program, they might strike down some of the requirements that interfered with the constitutional powers of the state.

Controls are not as onerous in practice as in theory. Departments do not have enough enforcement personnel. They need more auditors to review financial records and more special investigators to fight corruption. They are lax in holding state and local officials to account in upholding national standards. Members of Congress often pressure department officials to ease up on the local officials. National officials are lax where they should be tough and tough where they should be lax: they insist on compliance with routine paperwork requirements, even though the red tape serves no useful purpose. Yet they rarely cut off funds, even when the local officials are not complying with constitutional or legal guarantees. There is an incentive on both sides to compromise and cooperate.

Grants: The local view. County and city officials want to be free of both national and state controls. "We are sick to death of being an administrative province of the federal government," said Margaret Hance, the mayor of Phoenix, "and we want to avoid becoming administrative provinces of state governments."[33] Local officials want to pick and choose the exact combination of national and state grant programs that suits their needs. They do not want federal aid channeled through, or coordinated by, the states. They think about these grants the way students think about taking courses: while a college tries to impose various requirements concerning majors, distribution of courses, and a core curriculum, students try to fashion programs that suit their own individual needs. If the national government demands lengthy applications or other paperwork from the local officials, they will comply, but like a bored student who wants the credit but thinks that the course requirement (or the teacher) is idiotic, they will produce the paperwork but not make any use of it. This often happens when a local government is supposed to produce a comprehensive plan in order to get a grant.

85

In the 1970s local officials could shop around because there were so many grants available: seven for highways, twenty-three for pollution control, thirty-six for social services, and seventy-eight for education.[34] Aid was fungible: one program could be substituted for another, and money from a categorical program received by a local government enabled it to transfer its own funds to other programs. Some analysts approved of this, arguing that it enabled localities to create the most flexible mix of programs for their citizens, who in turn would (ideally) have more choices about what kinds of services (public or private, local or national) to accept.[35]

The conversion to block grants

A *block grant* provides funds for a state or local government for a broad functional area (such as education or law enforcement) to be used according to the goals and priorities of the recipient. State officials have long been in favor of converting most categorical grants into block grants.

Lyndon Johnson won congressional approval of two block grants involving health (1966) and law enforcement (1968). Richard Nixon converted thirty-one categorical grants into block grants for health, employment and job training, and community development. They all involved an overall increase in funding to buy congressional support. During the Carter administration, however, no new block grants were created, and block grants accounted for only 10 percent of federal aid.

The Reagan administration proposed another round of consolidations, and Congress responded by converting seventy-three programs into nine block grants in the Omnibus Reconciliation Act of 1981. The following year Congress took other job-training and education programs and created two new block grants: the total number of categorical grants declined from more than 600 to only 441.

Block grants in operation. Congress creates these programs only under presidential pressure, because it prefers categorical grants and the opportunities these grants give it to exert political pressure for the benefit of friends. When Congress creates block grants, it tries to retain some of its influence. Some are really the old categorical grants dressed in new wrappings: four of the block grants created in 1981 consisted of a single former categorical grant. Even when consolidation occurs, Congress may earmark funds for specific purposes or restrict the transfer of funds by the states from one category to another. In some cases, such as the Maternal Health and Childcare grant, there are more restrictions in the block grant than there were in the categorical grant.[36] In some cases block grants may be "recategorized" by administrative regulations to ensure that the money goes for designated purposes.

Once a block grant is in operation, the states pay less attention to national regulations and priorities, and after the funds are received and put into state budgets, it becomes difficult to trace their impact on specific programs and hard to prove or disprove *maintenance of effort:* the requirement that federal funds not be used simply to replace state money which can be diverted to something else. For some grants that requirement has been eliminated, as have rules concerning accounting, auditing, and management by the federal government. Congress has provided that the national government may not establish burdensome reporting requirements.

Conflict over block grants. Conflict occurs between the specialists, who

operate the categorical programs, and the generalists—governors, mayors, and state legislators—who want maximum discretion in using federal funds. The generalists win when Republican presidents pressure Congress into transforming categorical grants into block grants. The specialists who operate these programs then pass regulations that have the effect of converting some of them back into categorical programs, in practice if not in form. The generalists then counter with White House pressure to abolish the new regulations or see that exceptions are made.

Conflict also occurs between mayors, county officials, and governors, all of whom want to control federal funds. The governors want the money transferred to their budgets. The county officials and the mayors want *pass-through provisions,* which automatically transfer some of the funds to their jurisdictions. In a 1982 study by the U.S. Conference of Mayors, 70 percent of the city officials surveyed said that they were not fully represented in state decisions on distributing federal money. They wanted advisory committees that would give them input at the state level.

Retrenchment and block grants. In the 1980s the Reagan administration used consolidation as a budget-cutting strategy. Reagan proposed in 1981 to cut intergovernmental expenditures for the programs being converted to block grants by 25 percent, from $8.15 to $6.1 billion. Congress went along with cuts equaling 13 percent. "Block grants are now a tactical budget to cut the federal budget while deputizing governors to hand out the bad news," observed the Democratic governor of Arizona, Bruce Babbit.[37] The Reagan administration argued that the states could make up the difference with savings from less paperwork. In fact, most states reduced services or used their own funds to make up for the cuts.

Reagan's ultimate goal seemed to be to unwind the intergovernmental system and replace it with a traditional conception of federalism that would have each level of government assume the exclusive responsibility for different programs and would give each level the resources to do so. In his 1982 State of the Union address the president put restructuring of the federal system at the top of his agenda. He called for the national government to take over funding for the $18 billion Medicaid health program and for the states to take the sole responsibility for food stamps and welfare, at an estimated cost of $16.5 billion. The national government would transfer $30 billion worth of domestic programs to the states, along with federal tax sources to pay for them. "I dream of a day," Reagan told the National Association of Counties in 1981, "when the federal government can substitute for these, the turning back to local and state governments of the tax sources that we ourselves had preempted here at the federal level, so that you would have the resources."[38] His proposals were undercut by departments, members of Congress from both parties, and many state governors, and they were quickly buried. As Jack Brooks, a Democratic representative from Texas, noted, "New Federalism, New Federalism. What it means is, let's dump our expenses on somebody else and run."

General revenue sharing

Since 1972 the categorical grants and block grants have been supplemented by ***general revenue sharing***—a direct sharing of national revenues with states and cities. First proposed in the 1960s as a means of increasing state funding for social programs, the State and Local Fiscal Assistance Act was passed in 1972 to enable states and cities to substitute national funds for their own funds

President Nixon chose Independence Hall in Philadelphia as the site for signing the "new federalism" revenue-sharing legislation of 1972. (*Wide World Photos.*)

in an effort to keep taxes down while maintaining services. (Most states and cities, as it turned out, preferred to increase operating budgets for new programs, and only one-sixth of the revenues went toward tax reductions.) By the 1980s general revenue sharing was viewed as a form of emergency fiscal relief for hard-pressed local governments reeling under the impact of cuts in categorical and block grants and the impact of a **recession** on their revenues. It accounted for only 8.3 percent of federal grants by 1980.

Revenue sharing has gone through several phases. Between 1972 and 1977 Congress appropriated a total of $30.2 billion to the states, which were required to pass through two-thirds of the funds to local governments. For the period 1977–1980 the program was renewed at the same funding level, but in 1980 Congress provided that all funds would go directly to local governments. In 1982 the states could receive $2.3. billion, but only if they gave up an equivalent amount of categorical aid. Since then, all aid has gone to local governments.

Congress has never been enthusiastic about the program. Support comes from Republicans who are antagonistic to particular categorical grants and responsive to governors and mayors who need operating funds. The attitudes of Democrats are best expressed by John Brademas (a former representative and now the president of New York University), who argued that revenue sharing was "an essential part of a general attempt to diminish the role of Congress" while "increasing the central power of a handful of decision-makers in the executive branch."[39] In 1985 President Reagan asked Congress to eliminate the program entirely.

Retrenchment politics

Until recently the amount of funds available for intergovernmental programs, in absolute terms and as a proportion of the federal budget and the GNP, has

increased annually. Even conservative Republican administrations, committed to cutting back on the functions of the federal government in domestic affairs, did not stop this growth. But by 1978 the ravages of inflation had done what no politician had dared to do: effect the first real cutbacks in many programs. With high inflation and low percentage increases in available funds, intergovernmental funding was reduced—in inflation-adjusted dollars—by 2.7 percent in 1979, by 2.9 percent in 1980, and by 8.3 percent in 1981.[40] (See Figure 3-4.)

To reduce the large deficits, Reagan has called for highly visible and controversial cutbacks. In 1981 he proposed cuts of $13.4 billion from Carter's recommendations, or $8 billion from the existing 1981 program levels. He also proposed additional cuts totaling 32 percent for his first term. Although Reagan did not get all he asked for, his policies did produce some visible results. In 1978 federal aid to state and local governments amounted to $231 for every American; by 1982 that figure had been slashed to $174.

These cuts were aimed at programs benefiting traditionally Democratic constituencies: the poor, minorities, low-income women, and unemployed. Antirecessionary public works programs were eliminated. Urban development grants were frozen. Attempts were made to cut back on social services in the welfare system and to cap expenses for food stamps and medical aid to the poor.

State and local officials, Democrats and Republicans alike, raised strong protests. "This so-called new federalism is a sham and a shame," proclaimed Ed Koch, the mayor of New York. John Gunther, the executive director of the U.S. Conference of Mayors, charged that Reagan had "made it clear that it's his real goal to get rid of federal aid to state and local government." Richard Snelling, the Republican governor of Vermont and the chairman of the National Governors Association, proposed a "summit meeting" between Reagan, the gover-

Figure 3-4. Intergovernmental expenditures, 1972–1982. Expenditures adjusted for the high inflation rates of the late 1970s (constant dollars) show a drop in 1978, although the totals continued to climb until 1982. (Source: Advisory Commission on Intergovernmental Relations.)

nors, and big-city mayors. The vice chairman of the Republican Governors Association, James Thompson of Illinois, said that the states could not take any more cuts and asked Reagan to cut the defense budget instead. "You cut 'em with a scalpel, you don't use a meataxe" on these programs, advised George Voinovich, the Republican mayor of Cleveland; another Republican, William Hudnut, the mayor of Indianapolis, argued that at some point "cutting becomes gutting."[41]

ISSUE AND DEBATE

MEAT-AX FEDERALISM. Faced with huge and rising budget deficits, President Reagan began his second term by proposing more than $34 billion in spending cuts for the next year. The Reagan meat-ax would cut sharply into domestic programs, especially into grants to state and local governments, which made up more than one-fifth of their budgets. Would such drastic cuts damage the federal system?

The background. Reagan's proposals came in the wake of previous 15 percent cuts in projected spending in 1981 and a reduction from 26 to 22 percent in the percentage which federal funds constitute of state and local budgets. The proposals for 1985 included education; highways; Medicare and Medicaid; food stamps; housing subsidies; welfare for the aged, blind, and disabled; legal services; and block grants. Sewer grants, urban development grants, and federal revenue sharing would be terminated completely.

The revenue proposals offered by the Treasury Department also would affect the states. Ending the deductibility of state and local tax payments from federal income taxes would put pressure on states and cities to reduce their income and sales taxes. Other changes in the federal tax system would depress the real estate market and possibly lower the value of homes and commercial properties, thus reducing the yield from real estate taxes.

As a result, the states seemed to be caught in a double bind: cuts in federal spending would require the states to use their own funds to maintain services, but they would find it impossible to raise or even maintain their current taxes.

The pros. Those in favor of these cuts, like David Stockman, the budget director, and Donald Regan, the secretary of the Treasury, argued that the runaway deficits simply must be brought under control and that necessary sacrifices must be made now, or else the situation will get worse later. They claim that the states will be able to make up the difference with increased revenues coming from the economic prosperity that they foresee in the next decade. Even during the 1982–1983 recession, they say, the states found the money to lessen the impact of the previous rounds of cuts by the federal government. They argue that the most important programs will be maintained, that others will be only frozen rather than increased, and that if all goes well and the deficits are brought under control, it will be possible to restore some programs in the 1990s.

Others, ideologically more conservative, believe that the current deficit crisis provides the opportunity to end or reduce the federal government's participation in domestic programs and give the states back their preeminent role in developing, funding, and administering these programs. Some even argue that if the states cannot fund these programs, it will be no great loss anyway.

The cons. Most state and local officials strongly oppose these cuts. Mayor Voinovich calls them "bad public policy." Democratic mayors and governors have also joined in the criticism. They argue that defense spending should be cut proportionately as well. They believe that the states and cities will not have the huge

revenues forecast by the Treasury, especially if parts of Reagan's tax plan pass. They claim that the states have not been able to absorb the last set of cuts. "We've already been pressed to the wall," claims William Bechtel, the director of Wisconsin's lobbying office in Washington, arguing that his state is "reeling and staggering."[42] Democratic mayors and governors believe that these cuts are unfair because they would have the greatest effect on programs aiding the poor and would hurt the northeast and the midwest more than the sun belt states. One official of the National Governors Association says that the governors believe that there should be "no added cuts in basic safety-net programs, such as aid to families with dependent children, food stamps, the social services block grant, child nutrition and Medicaid."[43]

The outlook. President Reagan did not get his 1983 "new federalism" program, and he will get only some of his 1985 meat-ax initiatives. But he has shifted the terms of the debate: no longer is the issue the way in which the federal government will provide more funds and tax assistance to hard-pressed states; instead, it has become how many sacrifices the states can make to help the hard-pressed national government.

IN CONCLUSION

Our federal system was created in 1787 under the Constitution. It involves a sovereign national government, which may act directly on the people and was created by them, and the states, which may exercise powers recognized by the Constitution. Our system has evolved from early attempts at cooperative federalism; to nineteenth-century dual federalism, which protected states' rights and retarded efforts to regulate the economy; into the modern structure of intergovernmental administration of domestic programs.

The advantages of federalism are that it allows diversity, promotes experimentation, checks the power of the national government, and provides redundant safeguards against poor policies. Its disadvantages involve buck-passing, unwieldy administration, and a tendency to provide local solutions to what are actually national problems.

The federal system remains in a state of flux. The important issues no longer involve the legitimacy of regulation by the national government versus regulation by the states, but rather the efficacy of intergovernmental programs. The American people believe that state and local governments are better able to serve them and that they understand their problems better.

In the 1980s, the efforts to unwind the federal system stalled during President Reagan's first term, but his second-term budget-cutting and tax reform proposals would, if adopted by Congress, dramatically reshape the federal system.

NOTES

1. *Texas v. White*, 74 U.S. 700 (1869).
2. Memorandum to the heads of executive departments and agencies, Feb. 25, 1977; see also OMB Circular 95-a, which makes governors the chief executive officers for federal programs.
3. Lewis Kaden, "State Sovereignty," *The Columbia University Law Review*, vol. 79, no. 4, 1979, pp. 869–870; Jane Perry Clark, *The Rise of a New Federalism*, Russell Sage, New York, 1938.
4. Daniel Elazar, "The Evolving Federal System," in Richard M. Pious (ed.), *The Power to Govern*, Academy of Political Science, New York, 1981, pp. 5–19.

5. Daniel Elazar, *The American Partnership*, University of Chicago Press, Chicago, 1962, pp. 297–341.
6. 4 Wheat. 816 (1819).
7. *Dartmouth College v. Woodward*, 4 Wheat. 518 (1819).
8. 9 Wheat. 1 (1824).
9. *Cooley v. Board of Wardens*, 12 How. 299 (1851).
10. *Ableman v. Booth*, 21 How. 506 (1859).
11. Researched by Stacy Burnham.
12. *Wabash R.R. v. Illinois*, 118 U.S. 557 (1886).
13. *U.S. v. E. C. Knight*, 156 U.S. 1 (1895).
14. *The Slaughterhouse Cases*, 16 Wall 36 (1873).
15. *Lochner v. New York*, 198 U.S. 45 (1905).
16. These theories are discussed in Thomas M. Cooley, *The General Principles of Constitutional Law in the United States of America*, Little, Brown, Boston, 1880, pp. 3–54; and Woodrow Wilson, *The State*, Heath, London, 1888, pp. 177–194.
17. *Hammer v. Dagenhart*, 247 U.S. 251 (1918); *Massachusetts v. Mellon, Frothingham v. Mellon*, 262 U.S. 447 (1920).
18. *West Coast Hotel v. Parrish*, 300 U.S. 379 (1936).
19. *NLRB v. Jones and Loughlin*, 301 U.S. 1 (1937); *Seward Machine Co. v. Davis, Helvering v. Davis*, 301 U.S. 548 (1937); *U.S. v. Darby*, 312 U.S. 100 (1941).
20. Advisory Commission on Intergovernmental Relations, *Significant Features of Fiscal Federalism*, GPO, Washington, D.C., 1983, p. 122.
21. Richard Lamm and Michael McCarthy, *The Angry West*, Houghton Mifflin, Boston, 1982.
22. *The New York Times*, Dec. 2, 1981.
23. Aaron Wildavsky, "Birthday Cake Federalism," in Robert B. Hawkins, Jr. (ed.), *American Federalism: A New Partnership for the Republic*, Institute for Contemporary Studies, Berkeley, Calif., 1982, pp. 181–193.
24. Richard Musgrave and Peggy Musgrave, *Public Finance in Theory and Practice*, McGraw-Hill, New York, 1981, pp. 570–571.
25. Ibid., p. 564.
26. Ibid., pp. 576–577; see also Janet R. Pack, "The States Scramble for Federal Funds," *Journal of Policy Analysis and Management*, vol. 1, no. 2, 1982, pp. 175–195.
27. Martin Landau, "Federalism, Redundancy and System Reliability," *Publius*, vol. 3, no. 2, 1970, pp. 173–196; and "Redundancy, Rationality and the Problem of Duplication and Overlap," *Public Administration Review*, vol. 29, no. 4, July–August 1969, pp. 346–357.
28. Alfred R. Light, "Federalism and the Energy Crisis: A View from the States," *Publius*, vol. 9, no. 4, winter 1976, pp. 81–96; and "The Governors Push for Emergency Power," *Publius*, vol. 13, no. 4, winter 1980, pp. 57–67.
29. David Walker, "A New Intergovernmental System in 1977," *Publius*, winter 1978, p. 114.
30. President's Commission on National Goals, *Goals for Americans: Programs for Action in the Sixties*, American Assembly, New York, 1960, p. 265.
31. Morton Grodzins, *The American System*, Rand McNally, Chicago, 1966, especially chap. 9, "Local Mobilization of Public-Private Influence."
32. R. Douglas Arnold, *Congress and the Bureaucracy*, Yale University Press, New Haven, Conn., 1979, pp. 15, 139.
33. *The New York Times*, Sept. 27, 1981.
34. ACIR Information Bulletin 77-2, September 1977, p. 2.
35. Wildavsky, op. cit., pp. 181–193.
36. Richard P. Nathan, "Clearing Up the Confusion over Block Grants," *The Wall Street Journal*, Nov. 3, 1981.
37. Rochelle Stanfield, "For the States, It's Time to Put Up or Shut Up on Federal Block Grants," *The National Journal*, Oct. 10, 1981.

38. ACIR, *Intergovernmental Perspective*, vol. 7, no. 2, spring 1981, p. 4.

39. John Brademas, "Revenue Sharing," *Publius*, vol. 9, no. 3, fall 1976, p. 159.

40. Joseph Pechman, *Setting National Priorities: The 1982 Budget*, Brookings, Washington, D.C., 1981, p. 108.

41. *The New York Times*, Dec. 2, 1981; *Congressional Quarterly Weekly Reports*, Oct. 24, 1981, p. 2047.

42. "Reagan's Proposed Cuts Would Strike Hard at States and Cities," *Washington Post National Weekly Edition*, Dec. 24, 1984, p. 31.

43. Ibid.

FURTHER READING

Elazar, Daniel: *American Federalism: A View from the States*, Crowell, New York, 3d ed., 1984. A comprehensive textbook on the workings of the federal system.

———: *The American Partnership*, University of Chicago Press, Chicago, 1962. A fresh interpretation of the origins and operations of federalism in the nineteenth century, emphasizing the degree of cooperation that existed rather than the separation of functions described by other writers.

Glendening, Parris and Mavis Reeves: *Pragmatic Federalism: An Intergovernmental Review of American Government*, 2d ed., Palisades Publishers, Pacific Palisades, Calif., 1984. An analysis of our intergovernmental system works in theory and in practice.

Goldwin, Robert A. (ed.): *A Nation of States*, 2d ed., Rand McNally, Chicago, 1974. A collection of essays.

Grodzins, Morton: *The American System*, Rand McNally, Chicago, 1966. A collection of articles and case studies which look at all units of government as a single governing system.

Haider, Donald: *When Governments Come to Washington*, Free Press, New York, 1974. A study of the lobbying activities of big-city officials as they fight to obtain federal funds.

Hale, George, and Marian Palley: *The Politics of Federal Grants*, Congressional Quarterly Press, Washington, D.C., 1981. A study of how local officials obtain grants and try to expand the intergovernmental system.

Hamilton, Alexander, James Madison, and John Jay: *The Federalist* (first published in 1788 in *The New York Packet* and reprinted in many editions). Consult numbers 1 to 9, 21 to 23, and 25 on the advantages of a federal republic over a confederacy; see number 39 for a discussion of the federal system. Specific interpretations of the constitutional allocation of power are contained in numbers 32, 41 to 46, and 82. The advantages of a federal system in maintaining social stability are discussed in number 10, a classic of political science.

Hawkins, Robert B., Jr.: *American Federalism: A New Partnership for the Republic*, Institute for Contemporary Studies, Berkeley, Calif., 1982. A presentation of the pros and cons of the new federalism and other recent proposals.

Howitt, Arnold: *Managing Federalism*, Congressional Quarterly Press, Washington, D.C., 1984. An up-to-date account of the intergovernmental system.

Reagan, Michael D., and John F. Stanzone: *The New Federalism*, 2d ed., Oxford University Press, New York, 1981. A comprehensive treatment of developments during the Carter administration.

Walker, David B.: *Toward a Functioning Federalism*, Winthrop, Cambridge, Mass., 1981. The former assistant director of the Advisory Commission on Intergovernmental Relations argues that our intergovernmental system needs some unwinding.

Wright, Deil S.: *Understanding Intergovernmental Relations*, 2d ed., Brooks/Cole, Belmont, Calif., 1982. A comprehensive textbook.

THE STUDY BREAK

Caro, Robert: *The Power Broker: Robert Moses and New York*, Vintage Books, New York, 1975. A biography of the city's master planner and builder, describing how he used the intergovernmental grant system to accomplish his goals. A fascinating account of politics at its best and its worst.

USEFUL SOURCES

The Budget of the United States, GPO, Washington, D.C., annually. Each budget submitted by the president contains statistical information on intergovernmental programs and often recommendations for changes in the system.

Congressional Quarterly Weekly Reports. Reports on new developments in the intergovernmental system, emphasizing congressional politics.

The National Journal. A journal reporting on new developments in the intergovernmental system and emphasizing the politics of the executive branch.

Public Administration Review. A journal containing articles on how intergovernmental programs are funded, implemented, and evaluated.

Publius: The Journal of Federalism. A journal devoted exclusively to issues of federalism.

ORGANIZATIONS

Advisory Commission on Intergovernmental Relations. Suite 2000, Vanguard Bldg., 1111 Twentieth Street, N.W., Washington, D.C. 20006. A government commission that publishes journals, newsletters, special studies, and formal reports on the state of the federal system. For more information phone 202-653-5540.

National Association of Counties. 1735 New York Avenue, N.W., Washington, D.C. 20006. For more information phone 202-783-5113.

National Association of Towns and Townships. 1522 K Street, N.W., Washington, D.C. 20005. For more information phone 202-737-5200.

National Governors Association. 444 North Capitol Street, N.W., Suite 250, Washington, D.C. 20001. For more information phone 202-624-5300.

National League of Cites. 1301 Pennsylvania Avenue, N.W., Washington, D.C. 20004. For more information phone 202-626-3000.

U.S. Conference of Mayors. 1620 I Street, N.W., Washington, D.C. 20006. For more information phone 202-293-7330.

CIVIL LIBERTIES: LIMITED GOVERNMENT AND THE RULE OF LAW

College students (opposite) at a peaceful demonstration against construction of the Shoreham nuclear power plant being removed from the highway leading to the site by state police; June 4, 1983. Right, Senator Jesse Helms (R–N.C.) empties a mailbag which contains some of the more than 500,000 petitions received by Congress in September 1982, supporting voluntary prayer in the public schools. With Helms are Representative Gerald Solomon (R–N.Y.) and Martha Rountree, president of Leadership Action, a group lobbying for a prayer amendment to the Constitution. (*Tannenbaum-Sygma; AP Laserphoto.*)

All people are endowed, says the Declaration of Independence, with "certain inalienable rights," among them "Life, Liberty, and the Pursuit of Happiness." The Constitution and the Bill of Rights establish two fundamental principles: (1) that the government must not infringe on the liberties of the people and (2) that the government has an affirmative duty to secure these liberties.

This chapter will define and describe our civil liberties, especially the First Amendment freedoms of religion and conscience, speech and expression, and petition and assembly and the Fifth Amendment guarantees of due process of law. We will look at some struggles between different groups over the role of government in regulating individual behavior, and we will see how judges decide cases involving civil liberties claims.

WHAT ARE CIVIL LIBERTIES?

Civil liberties are those freedoms which allow people to think and speak freely and participate fully in politics without fear of repression. The most important of these liberties are guaranteed by the First Amendment to the Constitution:

> Congress shall make no law respecting an establishment of religion, or prohibiting the free exercise thereof; or abridging the freedom of speech, or of the press; or the right of the people peaceably to assemble, and to petition the Government for a redress of grievances.

Civil liberties also include protections against arbitrary government action. No one may be deprived of life, liberty, or property without due process of law, a protection guaranteed by the Fifth and Fourteenth Amendments.

The establishment clause

The prohibition against an established (that is, state) religion—the ***establishment clause***—means that government officials are subject to no religious law and are not accountable to religious authorities. Laws and policies are based on the will of the majority, expressed by representative institutions, not on the will of a priesthood expounding divine intent. It is neither the right nor the duty of the government to state by law or regulation what the clergy cannot obtain from the people through their consent. "Congress shall never meddle with religion," John Adams predicted, "other than to say their own prayers and to give thanks once a year." Combined with Article VI—"No religious Test shall ever be required as a Qualification to any Office or public Trust under the United States"—the First Amendment creates a wall of separation between church and state. Whatever many Americans think of themselves culturally and historically, *constitutionally* we are not, in spite of the claims of the fundamentalists, a "Christian nation," but a secular one.

But this separation is not absolute. The government puts "In God We Trust" on its currency. Chaplains, paid for by the government, serve the armed forces and Congress, and members of the clergy participate in presidential inaugurations. The courts have upheld the rights of cities to pay for holiday

decorations such as a municipal crèche, arguing that the intent is commercial (to bring shoppers to the downtown area during the Christmas season) and that such decorations include cultural and not solely religious symbols. (Thus in New York City the Catholic League for Religious and Civil Rights puts up depictions of the nativity scene in public parks, and the orthodox Jewish Lubavitch Youth Organization displays a menorah on Fifth Avenue.) The White House puts a nativity scene in its Christmas pageant.

The government provides funds to churches and religious schools for textbooks, lunches, teacher training, student testing, and remedial classes. Some states allow taxpayers whose children attend private schools—some of which are religious—to deduct the cost of tuition, textbooks, and transportation. The

Right: There has never been a rigid separation of church and state. National and local politicians greet Archbishop John J. O'Connor on the steps of Saint Patrick's cathedral in New York City during a Columbus Day parade up Fifth Avenue. Ethnic celebrations always bring church and political leaders to the same reviewing stands and podiums. (*AP Laserphoto.*)

Below, left: Recent Supreme Court decisions have made it constitutionally permissible for cities and towns to permit religious symbols—such as the nativity scene at Christmas—on public property. Each December, an Orthodox Jewish organization erects a Hanukkah menorah in Grand Army Plaza in New York. (*Fred R. Conrand: New York Times.*)

By Meyer for San Francisco Chronicle; New York Times Special Features.

A NATION OF WORSHIPERS?
• Forty percent of the public attend a church or synagogue in a typical week. • Fifty-one percent of Catholics attend mass, compared with thirty-nine percent of Protestants and twenty-two percent of Jews who attend services. Source: Gallup poll, December 1984.

courts, however, insist that such funding must have a completely secular purpose and not promote any particular religion and that it must not involve the government in "excessive entanglements" in religious affairs.[1] But the standard is not rigid. "Not every law that confers an 'indirect,' 'remote,' 'or incidental' benefit upon religious institutions," Justice Lewis Powell decided, "is, for that reason alone, constitutionally invalid."[2]

For many people public morality, as well as private conscience, has its underpinnings in religious belief. The clergy has always played a significant role in public affairs. The abolition of slavery and the underground railroad before the Civil War; the temperance movement, which led to Prohibition; the social gospel movement, which underlay much of the progressive movement's efforts to regulate wages and working conditions in the early 1900s; the civil rights movement of the 1960s; the new right campaigns against abortion and pornography in the 1970s; and the nuclear freeze movement of the 1980s—these were spurred in large measure by members of the clergy and their congregations. While no particular religion has an established place in our government or a particular claim to government support, the combined weight of all religions has a profound influence on our notion of public morality—and on our laws, bureaucratic regulations, and court decisions. It is *religiosity* rather than any particular religion that animates our politicians.

Freedom of religion

The government may not suppress religious freedom or freedom of conscience. "From the beginning," Walter Mondale reminded members of an audience who were quizzing him about religious issues during his 1984 campaign for the presidency, "we told government and the politicians keep your nose out of my own private religion and let me practice my faith."[3] This principle has prevented the violent religious strife that wracked England, France, and Germany in the century before our nation was formed. We have escaped the violence between Protestants and Catholics that still afflicts Ireland, the persecution and mass murder of Jews that stained Germany, and the sectarian conflict that destroyed Lebanon. "I protect my right to be a Catholic by preserving your right to be a Jew, or a Protestant, or a nonbeliever, or anything else you choose," said Mario Cuomo, the governor of New York.[4]

Disputes over the "true word of God" do not dominate our political agenda, though coalitions of religious groups, representing various faiths, often line up against one another on such highly charged issues as abortion, prayer in schools, and aid to parochial schools. These conflicts have not polarized American society along religious lines. Conflicts cross religious boundaries, with some Protestants, Catholics, and Jews in coalition against others.

Regulating religion. Government regulation sometimes infringes on religious beliefs and practices. Mormons may not legally practice polygamy. Old

Order Amish must pay social security taxes. Christian Scientists must obey court orders to hospitalize their sick children. Orthodox Jews in the military must remove their yarmulkes (hats). The Reverend Sun Myung Moon, head of the Unification Church, must pay his taxes as everyone else does or go to jail (which he did). As Chief Justice Warren Burger argued, "The State may justify a limitation on religious liberty by showing that it is essential to accomplish an overriding governmental interest."[5] Thus state laws license church schools, certify their teachers, and require them to follow the state curriculum. All religions must obey the civil and criminal laws. The First Amendment cannot, according to the Supreme Court, "be invoked as protection for the punishment of acts inimical to the peace, good order, and morals of society."[6]

Prayer in schools. In 1962 and 1963 the Supreme Court held that starting the school day with prayer was unconstitutional. The Court banned both prayer and Bible reading as violations of the establishment clause. Polls have shown that an overwhelming majority, about two-thirds of the public, favor voluntary prayer in schools: this includes majorities of liberals and conservatives, Democrats and Republicans, and people in the north, south, and west. President Reagan, recognizing a good political issue, announced during a "national day of prayer" in 1982 that he would introduce a constitutional amendment to permit voluntary prayer in schools. Several versions have been introduced; some would have school officials create a nonsectarian prayer, others would allow students to say any prayer they wished on a voluntary basis, and still others would simply prevent school officials from interfering with the right of students to pray in schools.

In some school districts the Supreme Court's decision has been defied. Some allow spoken prayer, and others permit silent prayer or meditation. The West Virginia state constitution provides for one minute of "contemplation, meditation or prayer." Students, according to state guidelines, may kneel, stand, sit, "or engage in other acts symbolic of their faith," provided they do so silently and without moving around the room. Teachers may not tell students how to pray or meditate "or to whom prayer should be directed," nor may they

Students at the Wilson school in Sayerville, New Jersey, stand for a moment of silence at the beginning of the school day, following provisions of a law enacted by their state legislature. (*James Pozerik: Picture Group.*)

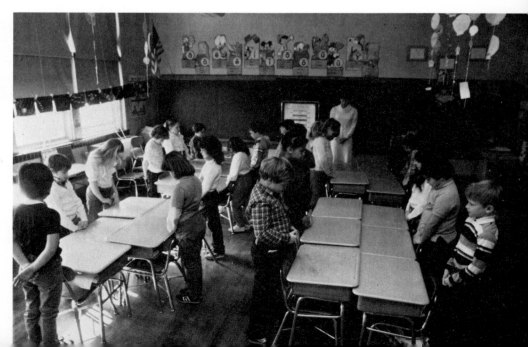

suggest the content of the meditation or prayer. In some school districts another approach is to encourage voluntary prayer groups to form in the classroom just before the start of the "official" school day. Another idea is to have students form a club, such as Students for Voluntary Prayer, and allow the club to use classrooms for a period of voluntary prayer or Bible discussion.

Some parents believe that the issue involves simply the right of their children to pray wherever they wish to: an issue of religious freedom. Other parents believe that their children might be coerced into saying the prayers of the majority or else suffer religious discrimination by their classmates. Some members of the clergy believe that the state should foster a religious attitude in schools by permitting prayer. Others see a great danger if school officials write nonsectarian prayers.

Thus far the proposed constitutional amendments have been defeated in Congress. But in 1984 Congress passed an "equal access" amendment to a federal aid-to-education bill which sanctioned the use of schools for student-initiated religious, political, or philosophical meetings during noninstructional periods. The law cuts off federal aid to schools which do not allow such activities or which allow students to meet for other extracurricular activities but not for religious prayer and discussion. While the Supreme Court has not (as of 1985) ruled on such after-school activities, several federal courts of appeals have barred them in high schools, viewing them as involving a "sponsorship" of religion by the government.

Some religious groups, adamantly opposed to a constitutional amendment permitting or requiring prayer in schools, are just as strongly in favor of permitting extracurricular student-initiated religious activities outside the classroom and after the instructional day.

Freedom of expression   The initial provisions of the First Amendment guarantee freedom of conscience and belief, and the remainder guarantee the freedom to communicate one's beliefs—freedoms without which no democratic society can function. They are essential for free elections. They guarantee a free press and permit interest groups to function independently rather than as quasi-official instruments of the authorities (like trade unions in Poland or the Soviet Union). They guarantee that people can meet, speak their minds, and take political action without being subjected to surveillance, harassment, intimidation, or violence.

The market of ideas. We believe that freedom of expression in a democratic society involves the clash of ideas. "The best test of truth," Justice Oliver Wendell Holmes observed, "is the power of the thought to get itself accepted in the competition of the market."[7] No barriers to this competition can be permitted to obstruct the free workings of the political marketplace. No idea, in and of itself, can be too obnoxious or dangerous to express. We must, said Holmes, grant "freedom for the thoughts we hate."

The democratic creed. A democracy assumes that people can discover the truth by themselves. There is no need for the state to "protect" its citizens by censoring ideas, even if they might be nonsensical. The truth emerges through discussion and debate. Justice Louis Brandeis observed that the framers of the Constitution believed that

An American Nazi standing next to his party's symbol, the swastika. In the United States this symbolic expression of free speech is protected by the First Amendment. In West Germany, Italy, and the Soviet Union, the display of a swastika is a criminal act. (*Jim Anderson: Woodfin Camp.*)

. . . freedom to think as you will and speak as you think are means indispensable to the discovery and spread of political truth; that without free speech and assembly, discussion would be futile; that with them, discussion affords ordinarily adequate protection against the dissemination of noxious doctrine; that the greatest menace to freedom is an inert people; that public discussion is a political duty; and that this should be a fundamental principle of the American government. . . .[8]

Advantages of free expression. Leaders in some developing nations insist that the people are not ready for freedom of expression or that it is a luxury which must wait until economic development has reached higher levels. But societies which guarantee these liberties also provide the best conditions for development. The media can report fully on the activities of government; interest groups can press their demands; and the people can make their grievances known. Incompetent officials are less likely to flourish in such a climate. As Thomas Emerson of Yale Law School argues: "Freedom of expression, far from causing upheaval, is more properly viewed as a leavening process, facilitating necessary social and political change and keeping a society from stultification and decay."[9]

Freedom of expression. The government may not interfere with our thoughts, our conscience, or our personal lives without demonstrating a convincing necessity to the courts. "No official, high or petty, can prescribe what shall be orthodox in politics, nationalism, religion, or other matters of opinion, or force citizens to confess by word or act their faith therein," says Justice Robert Jackson.[10] Freedom of expression, guaranteed by the First Amendment, implies the right *not* to have to say what one *does not* believe. Those who do not wish to recite the pledge of allegiance or salute the flag need not do so.

Symbolic speech. The courts protect *symbolic speech:* actions intended to communicate ideas. These include gesturing or miming, wearing buttons or armbands, holding placards, handing out leaflets, and even burning the American flag or draft registration cards. In a case involving junior high school students in Iowa who wore armbands to protest the Vietnamese war, the Supreme Court held that the students had engaged in symbolic speech, which could not be forbidden by school authorities.[11] When a California college student entered a state courthouse with the words "F____k the draft" (completely spelled out) emblazoned on his jacket, a state judge held him in contempt of

court, but the Supreme Court overruled this decision, for, as Justice John Harlan wrote, "While the particular four-letter word being litigated here is perhaps more distasteful than most others of its genre, it is nevertheless often true that one man's vulgarity is another's lyric."[12]

Judicial protection of obscene language or symbolic speech has its limits. If a person addresses "fighting words" to a police officer, the courts will let the resulting arrest stand, and they also uphold convictions for incitement to riot, disturbing the peace, and disorderly conduct based on loud and abusive language. And the courts have little patience with the arguments concerning freedom of speech put forth by proprietors of "head shops" that sell drug paraphernalia such as pipes, clips, and cigarette papers.[13]

Access to the marketplace of ideas

The Constitution and laws guarantee that individuals and groups can present their ideas to the public.

Mails. The government may not censor the mails, and propaganda and pornography are protected along with everything else.[14] But the use of the mails to commit an illegal action (such as securities, bank, or consumer fraud) or to conspire to act illegally (espionage or terrorism) is not free speech and is punishable by the government.

Malls. Groups may assemble and solicit passersby and give them material. But there is no constitutional right to do so on private property, including malls and shopping centers. On the other hand, property owners have no constitutional right to prohibit the actions of such groups. Whether groups can solicit and how they may do so are matters subject to state and city regulations.[15]

Meetings. People may gather in streets and in parks and other public places. But the police may lawfully order unruly crowds to disperse to keep the peace, and they may detain a speaker who incites a crowd to violence.[16] The courts insist that where the state can protect a speaker from a hostile crowd, it must do so, and they often strike down laws giving the police authority to disperse crowds if the laws are too broadly drawn. The government can make reasonable regulations as to when, where, and how speeches are made, but it may not regulate or discriminate against people because of the content of their speeches or ideas.[17]

Media. People have no constitutional right to use the radio or television airwaves or cables or satellite transmission facilities. Since the transmission bands are limited, access is granted by the Federal Communications Commission (FCC), an independent regulatory agency, when it licenses broadcasters and by local authorities who award cable franchises. The FCC's fairness doctrine requires broadcasters to present all significant viewpoints on public issues and a wide variety of spokespersons, but who appears on the air is up to the broadcasters. The FCC has ruled, and the courts have upheld, the principle that no one has a constitutional right to buy airtime, even for political commercials during a campaign.[18]

Freedom of the press

The First Amendment states that Congress shall make no law abridging free-

---

FREEDOM OF ASSOCIATION: THE AMERICAN COMMUNIST PARTY

Should a democratic society permit the operation of political parties which vow to overthrow the government by violent means? Or should it outlaw movements or parties which themselves are nondemocratic? The courts have not formulated consistent answers to these questions.

In 1940 Congress passed the Smith Act, which made it unlawful for anyone knowingly or willingly to "advocate, abet, advise, or teach the duty, necessity, desirability, or propriety of overthrowing or destroying any government in the United States by force or violence" and which made an attempt to commit or conspire to commit such acts a federal crime. The Department of Justice brought indictments against leaders of the American Communist Party. In *Dennis v. U.S.*, 341 U.S. 494 (1951), the Supreme Court affirmed convictions of members of the party. It agreed with the prosecution that the group advocated violent overthrow of the government, and it did not consider the probabilities of their success.

Later the Supreme Court took a different tack. In *Yates v. U.S.*, 354 U.S. 298 (1957), the Court overturned convictions of several party leaders in California. It distinguished between "advocacy" and "action," freeing these leaders because the government had not proved that any actions were about to take place. The Court read *Dennis* to mean that such actions as indoctrination for action or exhortation to immediate action must have taken place to find a conspiracy under the Smith Act. Merely to show that people had advocated, as an abstract proposition, the overthrow of the government (even if by violent action) was not enough for a conviction.

In *Noto v. U.S.*, 367 U.S. 290 (1961), the Supreme Court held that membership in the Communist Party was not in itself evidence of a conspiracy to overthrow the government. In *Scales v. U.S.*, 367 U.S. 203 (1961), the Court interpreted the Internal Security Act of 1950 as requiring not only membership in the party but also "active and purposeful membership, purposive that is as to the organization's criminal ends," in order to convict under the Smith Act. The Court did require the party and other "communist action or front" groups to register with the Department of Justice.

The Communist Party cannot be outlawed under the provisions of the Smith Act, and membership in the party does not in itself constitute evidence of subversive activity. The party need not comply with election laws requiring political parties to disclose the names of campaign contributors because a federal appeals court ruled in 1982 that such disclosure requirements for an "unpopular minority party" might have a chilling effect on potential contributors. The party is constitutionally protected in the rights of association, speech, and privacy, but it remains subject to FBI surveillance and infiltration. To the extent that it acts within the democratic rules of the game, it is given an opportunity to influence electoral politics. But if it steps out of line and conspires to overthrow the government, its members can be prosecuted.

---

dom of the press. People may write and publish what they choose. But these freedoms are not absolute.

Sedition. An early test of the First Amendment occurred during the undeclared naval war with France in 1798. Congress, controlled by the Federalists, passed a **sedition** law, which made it illegal to publish "fake, scandalous and malicious writing" that would "bring the government into disrepute" or would "incite against them the hatred of the good people of the United States." The law was directed at the Anti-Federalist faction, and it prompted the state legislatures in Kentucky and Virginia to pass resolutions of nullification, declaring these laws unconstitutional and unenforceable. Public opinion turned against

the law, just as it turned against the war, and in 1800, when their opponents won the elections, the Federalists got their comeuppance.

Libel. Newspaper owners have the freedom to publish what they choose, but they are subject to *libel* suits by people who claim that they have been damaged by untruths. *Time* magazine, for example, was sued by the Israeli general Ariel Sharon after it claimed in a report that he had ordered the massacre of Palestinians in Beirut. CBS was sued by General William Westmoreland for a *Sixty Minutes* documentary which claimed that he falsely inflated "body counts" of enemy soldiers during the Vietnamese war. Neither general won damages from the courts. Public figures are given less protection by the courts on the assumption that by entering the public arena, they have exposed themselves voluntarily to accounts that may be inaccurate. The plaintiff must prove not only that the statements were incorrect, but that they showed malice and a reckless disregard for the truth.[19] Nevertheless, some civil libertarians believe that expensive libel suits can serve as a deterrent to a free press, and they urge Congress to pass legislation preventing public officials from suing for damages.

Temporary injunctions; restraining orders. The federal courts do not consider freedom of the press to be absolute. They balance this freedom against compelling national interests. In 1971 *The New York Times* published excerpts from a classified multivolume history of the Vietnamese war prepared by Pentagon historians. The history had been copied (without the permission of the government) by Dr. Daniel Ellsberg, a civilian analyst who had worked on them, and given to the *Times*. After publication of the first article, the government went into federal court and obtained an injunction against further publication, the first time in American history that a prepublication injunction had been imposed by a court. The *Times* argued that the government's request for a permanent injunction violated the First Amendment. The government argued that the papers had been stolen, that they involved classified documents and information, and that national security was involved. The Supreme Court ruled in favor of the *Times*, allowing it to print other articles from the Pentagon papers. Six justices held that the government had not shown any compelling justification for prior restraint by the courts.[20]

In 1979 *The Progressive* magazine was ready to print an article entitled "The H-Bomb Secret: How We Got It, Why We're Telling It," which showed how anyone could build a hydrogen bomb using nonclassified sources. The purpose of the article was to demonstrate just how lax government secrecy is and how such secrecy cannot prevent the proliferation of nuclear weapons. The government obtained a temporary order preventing publication from a federal judge alleging that publication would "result in grave, direct, immediate and irreparable harm to the security of the United States and its people." The government based its argument on a loophole which the Supreme Court left in the Pentagon papers case: courts could prevent publication if the government showed "immediate and irreparable damage." The government also claimed that the Atomic Energy Act of 1954 had made it a crime to "communicate, transmit or disclose" certain "restricted data" about the design or manufacture of nuclear weapons. But the statute did not include the word *publish*, leaving it unclear whether it covered this situation. While *The Progressive* argued its case before the court of appeals, several newspapers printed a letter

Myron Farber, a reporter for the *New York Times*, in a Bergen County, New Jersey, jail after being sentenced for contempt of court for failing to provide evidence in a state criminal case on which he had reported. Farber unsuccessfully claimed journalistic privilege to keep his sources confidential. (Eventually he was released by the judge.) (*Wide World.*)

which disclosed most of the "restricted data" that would have appeared in the article. Having failed to prevent publication of the information, the government moved to have the courts dismiss the case. The article appeared in the magazine a few months later.

Enforcing contractual agreements. Frank Snepp, a former CIA agent, published a book entitled *Decent Interval*, which recounts the agency's activities in Saigon just before the communists took over in 1975. While an employee of the CIA, Snepp had signed an agreement with the agency which permitted it to review and censor, before publication, any manuscript dealing with its activities. Snepp did not submit his book to the CIA, as required by the terms of the agreement, arguing that he did not have to because he had not used any secret information. The CIA sued in federal court to enforce its agreement with Snepp. It asked the court to uphold the agreement and require Snepp to submit future writings, and it sued for damages because the agreement had been violated. The Supreme Court affirmed lower court decisions that required Snepp to turn over all his royalties ($170,000 at the time of the decision) to the government, and it allowed the CIA prepublication clearance and censorship of all his future work.[21]

Reporters and sources. The courts guarantee everyone a fair trial. Sometimes the right of defendants to cross-examine witnesses and obtain all evidence relevant to their guilt or innocence conflicts with claims made by doctors, lawyers, members of the clergy, and reporters that what people tell them in connection with their professional duties must remain confidential and cannot be revealed, even in a court of law. Journalists argue that they must protect their sources and that they cannot obtain confidential information unless they assure their sources anonymity. But the Supreme Court in 1972 ruled that reporters do not have any right to withhold information about a crime from a grand jury.[22]

Some journalists go to jail for contempt rather than comply with court orders (they are usually let out after sixty days or so). Others comply under protest. Journalists want Congress and the states to pass "shield laws" that would allow them to protect their sources—even people who have committed crimes. Here the balance of competing claims is excruciatingly difficult. What happens if a reporter finds out a fact that has a bearing on the guilt or innocence of someone accused of a serious crime? Which is more important: the right of the accused to everyone's testimony or the right of a reporter trying to protect sources?

Due process of law

The Fifth Amendment (applicable to national officials) and the Fourteenth Amendment (applicable to state officials) require the government to act with ***due process of law*** in depriving people of their lives, liberties, or property. ***Substantive due process*** focuses on the reasonableness of government actions and requires that they be least burdensome to other constitutional rights and liberties. ***Procedural due process*** examines the methods used by officials and requires that these conform to the Constitution and laws and be conducted with fundamental fairness. Due process guarantees are closely related to First Amendment freedoms. Without them, anyone who opposed government policies could be arrested and imprisoned after rigged trials. People would be afraid to exercise their freedoms of speech and association.

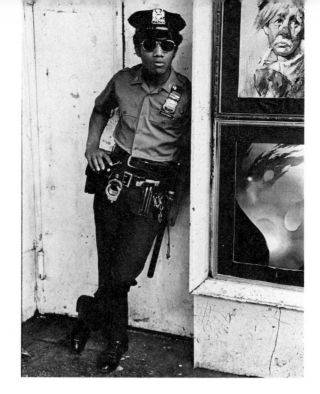

A New York City police officer on patrol in Times Square, Manhattan. (*Bernard Pierre Wolff: Magnum.*)

Police patrol. Traditionally the police have emphasized crime control in patrolling neighborhoods: an aggressive search for information that might lead to arrests. People may be stopped and frisked on general suspicion or questioned at length about their presence in a neighborhood (especially if they seem out of place), and those who are considered potential troublemakers may be told to move on. The police control public spaces, threatening to arrest people for vagrancy, loitering, disorderly conduct, failure to move on, and failure to obey a lawful order. They stop people in high-crime areas and make systematic searches or vehicle checks. They search people and cars without warrants, looking for weapons, criminal tools, or stolen property.

What seem to the police to be reasonable efforts at deterrence may be considered harassment by minorities, teenagers, ex-convicts, and others who think that they are being unfairly singled out. Many law-abiding people resent being stopped for no reason at all and asked to give an account of themselves and their presence in a neighborhood. (One Yale Law School professor who was stopped by the New Haven police one evening while jogging even went so far as to write an article for a law review defending his right to refuse to answer such inquiries!)

Civil libertarians try to get the police to institute a due process approach to patrol: the police could not bother anyone unless they had a *reasonable suspicion* that a crime had been, was being, or was about to be committed. People could not be questioned without being advised of their right to remain silent or obtain legal assistance. They could be questioned only if the police suspected them of having committed or witnessed a crime. Anyone who was being investigated for a crime would have to be taken to a station house for questioning and advised of the right to have a lawyer present.[23] Arrests could take place only with *probable cause:* when the facts and circumstances were such that a reasonable person would be justified in believing that a crime had been committed and that the person arrested had committed it. People would

not have to identify themselves or account for their presence unless they were being investigated for a crime. They would not have to move on command from the police, and arrests for loitering would not be permitted except where criminal violations were involved. Warrants would be required to search cars unless the search was incidental to an arrest for a crime in progress. Even then, the trunk and the glove compartment could be searched only after a warrant was obtained.

In the past two decades the crime control approach has been challenged in federal and state courts, and many due process elements have been introduced into police practices. Today there is conflict between judges who would extend due process protections even further and those who would cut back on them.

The due process approach is politically unpopular. The aggressive patrol approach and the function of the police in maintaining control of public spaces have the support of the majority, even in many poor neighborhoods that are overrun with drunks, pimps and prostitutes, drug pushers, petty criminals, and "street people." A majority of the public believe that the police have the right to question people and make them account for themselves.[24]

With community support the police sometime evade the decisions of the federal courts. Since it is impossible for a judge to be present in every patrol car, the courts cannot supervise the police and must rely on good-faith implementation. Unconstitutional searches and seizures and questioning still occur.[25] Civil liberties and civil rights groups sometimes sue police departments, alleging brutality or abuse of suspects such as the use of "stun guns" to extract confessions. Civil damages are occasionally awarded. Where police brutality is directed against minorities, the Justice Department has occasionally won decisions on the basis of civil rights statutes (which provide for prison sentences as well as fines).

Criminal procedure. The Federal courts have extended due process guarantees to defendants in state criminal trials. These include the following rights: to be brought before a judicial officer for arraignment within a reasonable time after arrest; to have counsel present after arrest and during police interrogation, at police lineups, and at court-ordered psychiatric examinations; to be furnished with counsel if the defendant cannot afford to pay for it; to present evidence, question friendly witnesses, and cross-examine witnesses for the prosecution; to be tried by a jury of at least six persons who have been selected in a racially nondiscriminatory way; to have a speedy trial; to be furnished a written transcript of the trial for appeals; and to be free of double jeopardy.

In recent years the Supreme Court has cut back on its supervision of the practices of state courts. After being convicted in such courts, prisoners often seek *collateral review* of the procedures by federal courts and a new trial if their constitutional rights have been violated. In 1976 the Supreme Court ruled that state prisoners could not sue in federal courts if they had been given the opportunity to challenge their violation of rights in state courts and had lost.[26] In a 1982 decision, the Court indicated that it would review state cases only if there might be a "miscarriage of justice," not merely technical violations of constitutionally mandated state criminal procedures.[27]

CASE STUDY: THE EXCLUSIONARY RULE. Recent Supreme Court decisions have focused attention on the *exclusionary rule:* the judicial practice of excluding from trials evidence which has been obtained in an unconstitutional or illegal

manner; the purpose is to give an incentive to the police and to prosecutors to carry out their functions lawfully. No other rule of law is as controversial. The victims of a crime, the police, prosecutors, and the public are all outraged when courts set aside convictions on the grounds that the evidence was illegally obtained. It seems like a mere technicality and a gross violation of justice. "It just doesn't make sense that just because a police officer made a technical error for the accused to go free [sic]," said Ed Meese, then a White House aide and later attorney general in the Reagan administration.[28] Although a new trial may be ordered, it is often difficult to convict without the "tainted" evidence or to get witnesses to testify a second time. But in spite of complaints by the police, the exclusionary rule has not hampered most prosecutions. In slightly more than 1 percent of federal prosecutions evidence is excluded, and in half of these cases the defendants are convicted anyway.

The courts need the rule to uphold judicial power: it is a procedural instrument which regulates access to the courts, and it is a way to compel the police and prosecutors to comply with judicial supervision. It is the only practical sanction that the courts can impose on law enforcement personnel who act illegally. Other remedies, such as private lawsuits for violation of a defendant's rights, are ineffective: juries are reluctant to award damages against the police or prosecutors. In any event, state or local governments could indemnify these officials and protect them against suits.

As the crime rate soared, law enforcement officials pressed their attack against the exclusionary rule. The courts have backed away from a broad application (1) by limiting its application to give the police and prosecutors more latitude in introducing illegally obtained evidence if the violation was inadvertent and the search was conducted "in good faith" by police officers who believed that their actions were legal (that their search warrant was not defective); (2) by allowing evidence if it would have been inevitably obtained in the course of the arrest, even if it was obtained illegally or with a defective warrant; (3) by refusing to overturn convictions when the evidence was not central to the issue of guilt or innocence; and (4) by limiting the collateral review of the federal courts and relying on state courts instead. While the exclusionary rule remains in reserve for serious abused of due process rights, it has become less of an inhibition to the police and prosecutors, reflecting the hardening of public attitudes toward crime control.

CIVIL LIBERTIES: THE POLITICAL CONTEXT

Most Americans strongly support the freedoms of religion, conscience, and expression and the due process guarantees of the Constitution. But one person's pursuit of happiness may be an affront to someone else. The due process rights of a defendant may seem excessive to victims of crime. Free speech may shade into political activity, such as street demonstrations, which must be regulated. Often civil liberties conflicts involve not the good guys against the bad guys, but competing claims involving important social values.

Group conflicts

Most civil liberties conflicts involve interest groups, which try to educate the public, lobby Congress and state legislatures to pass laws, and negotiate with executive officials about government actions. They try to elect candidates who favor their cause, and they fund research institutes, lobbying offices in Washington and state capitals, and litigating units to try to score judicial victories.

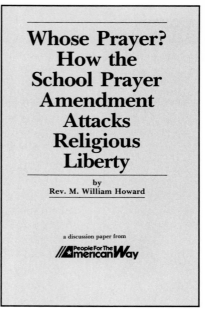

Pamphlets published by People for the American Way, a civil liberties group which strongly opposes any prayer in public schools. Two members of its board of directors are Protestant ministers.

The litigating units are sometimes referred to as *private attorneys general* because they act on behalf of individuals who believe that they have been wronged by a state action, much as a state attorney general brings cases on behalf of persons who have been wronged by criminals.

The oldest and most important group is the American Civil Liberties Union (ACLU), founded in the 1920s. It has a national staff of more than 400 located in New York City, and it has fifty state chapters with more than 275,000 members and 5000 volunteer attorneys; it handles over 7000 cases annually. The ACLU litigates on behalf of every conceivable group, including the poor, minorities, women, the handicapped, mental patients, and politically unpopular groups such as the American Nazi Party, defending freedom of expression for all.

Another important group is People for the American Way, organized by Norman Lear (the television producer responsible for such programs as *All in the Family*). It was formed in 1980 to educate the American public about its First Amendment freedoms. It sponsors and produces television specials, and it combats efforts at book censorship in schools and libraries, especially by right-wing political and religious organizations.

Many other groups are concerned about separation of church and state, abortion, prayer in schools, gun control, pornography, censorship, and other issues, and they litigate in cases involving their interests. Below we consider three examples of groups that are trying to define the permissible limits of government regulation.

Gun control and the National Rifle Association (NRA). The NRA has over 2 million members in more than 11,000 clubs. It sponsors programs aimed at the safety of hunters and the safe use of firearms. It lobbies states for laws making it easy to own handguns and rifles, and it opposes all efforts at gun control sponsored by the National Coalition to Ban Handguns and by police departments. According to the NRA, polls show that 80 percent of the public oppose bans on handguns, although Gallup polls in the early 1980s showed a narrower margin against handgun control, more like 54 against to 41 in favor—

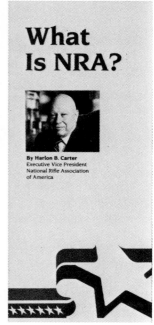

The National Rifle Association runs an extensive public relations and education program, which includes the distribution of these and other pamphlets.

with those in favor of regulation getting more and more support—compared with polls in the 1970s, which showed that fewer than one-third favored gun control. The NRA claims that possession of a gun is a right guaranteed by the Second Amendment, which states that "a well regulated Militia, being necessary to the security of a free State, the right of the people to keep and bear arms, shall not be infringed." Gun control groups argue that the Second Amendment prevents only Congress, not the states, from regulating and prohibiting arms and that it protects only militias and does not grant individuals the right to bear arms.

These issues are far from settled. The federal courts have allowed the states to regulate weapons, and the Supreme Court has allowed Congress to ban sawed-off shotguns.[29] Some states and cities have passed strict gun control measures and have banned handguns altogether; in Massachusetts, for example, possession of a handgun means a mandatory year in jail. Meanwhile, the NRA litigates against these measures in court. It brings cases against the federal government's Bureau of Alcohol, Tobacco, and Firearms (BATF), which enforces bans on cheap handguns, claiming that BATF agents beat, abuse, and harass gun dealers and obtain evidence for prosecutions by violating due process guarantees. The NRA's Institute for Legislative Action lobbies states to head off new laws. In spite of polls showing public support for new measures, it manages a successful rearguard action.

Book banners. Many schools and libraries are pressured by community organizations to remove certain books from their shelves or not use them in courses. In the 1960s most such cases involved charges that the books were racist or sexist, but in the 1980s most of the action has come from religious and "profamily" groups on the political right, which claim that some books are unpatriotic, immoral, or antifamily. In this decade more than 250 book titles have been challenged in more than 400 public schools, while the American

Norma Gabler, a Texas homemaker, brings her battle against textbooks that depart from "traditional values" to the Texas Textbook Committee hearings in August 1982. Mrs. Gabler and her husband Mel have influenced school boards throughout the nation. (*AP Laserphoto.*)

THE BOOK BANNERS AND THEIR NONREADING LISTS

Book banners on the right include the Moral Majority, Mel and Norma Gabler's Educational Research Analysts (which distributes lists of books that should be removed from school library shelves), and Phyllis Schlafly's Eagle Forum. Other groups (liberal and left) protest against books on the grounds that they portray religious or racial groups unfairly.

Some of the titles banned by various schools and libraries around the nation include the following: *The American Heritage Dictionary*, John Steinbeck's *Grapes of Wrath*, Mario Puzo's *Godfather*, Ernest Hemingway's *Farewell to Arms*, F. Scott Fitzgerald's *Great Gatsby*, J. D. Salinger's *Catcher in the Rye*, and William Shakespeare's *Merchant of Venice*.

But the book-banning prize goes to the Mark Twain Middle School in Virginia, whose principal banned *Huckleberry Finn*, written by Mark Twain, on the grounds that it portrays blacks unfavorably—which isn't even true.

Book Banners are opposed by the National Coalition against Censorship, which includes the American Library Association's Office for Intellectual Freedom, the National Council of Teachers of English, the National Education Association, the Writers Guild of America, the Association of American Publishers (Freedom to Read Committee), and People for the American Way (Schools and Libraries Project and National Resource Center on Censorship).

Library Association reports more than 1000 complaints involving public libraries each year.[30]

Conflicts between book banners and anticensorship groups sometimes wind up in court. The Supreme Court decided *Pico v. Island Trees School District*, which involved a school board's 1976 decision to remove nine books from its library.[31] The board called the books "anti-American, anti-Christian, anti-Semitic, and just plain filthy." The ACLU represented five students who objected to the removal of books such as *Slaughterhouse Five*, by Kurt Vonnegut; *The Fixer*, by Bernard Malamud; and *Best Short Stories of Negro Writers*, edited by Langston Hughes. The Supreme Court ordered a federal district court to conduct a trial and consider the motives of the school board, ruling that the lower court could limit the discretion of the school board if it had intended to limit "access to ideas," although the Supreme Court indicated that it would uphold the school board if it was removing books merely because they were vulgar or lacked educational content. In 1983, the school board decided to allow the books back on the shelves.

"Censorship in a Free Society" poster. An advertisement from People for the American Way attacking library and textbook censorship.

THE FBI AND MARTIN LUTHER KING

The national government and the state governments have the constitutional and legal power to thwart conspiracies which involve treason, bombing, kidnapping, assassination, or other criminal actions. But agencies responsible for counterespionage and counterintelligence may themselves commit excesses. What prevents the government from using these security organizations to stifle legitimate dissent? How do we prevent police agencies from creating a *police state*—a government in which the police influence partisan politics? The relationship between the Federal Bureau of Investigation (FBI) and Dr. Martin Luther King, Jr., the most influential black civil rights leader of the 1960s, demonstrates some of the problems involved in political surveillance.

The FBI became interested in Dr. King as a result of an operation known as COMINFIL (aimed at infiltration of communist organizations). An FBI informant in the Communist Party claimed that one of King's closest associates, Stanley Levison, had been a member of the party in the 1950s. The FBI put Levison under surveillance to see whether he was still a member and found nothing. But the FBI leaked documents to Congress showing Levison's influence on King and, by inference, the influence of communists on the civil rights movement. J. Edgar Hoover, the chief of the FBI, did this because he opposed civil rights bills being considered by Congress.

Because King believed that Levison had severed his connection with the communists, he kept him on as an adviser. Because Levison remained an adviser, Attorney General Robert Kennedy thought that King might be a communist dupe or sympathizer. Hoover convinced Kennedy to allow the FBI to place wiretaps in King's Atlanta and New York City offices and in his hotel rooms when he led civil rights demonstrations.

These FBI taps indicated that King and his associates often made negative (and sometimes graphically explicit) remarks about various government leaders. By invading King's privacy, the FBI obtained information which had no bearing on his possible connection with communists. It chose to use this information to damage King. The FBI provided President Lyndon Johnson with some of the tapes, and Johnson asked the agency to find out what King's plans for the presidential contest of 1964 were, particularly his attitude toward an attempt by blacks in Mississippi to unseat the regular state delegation to the Democratic convention and replace it with a black group. Johnson asked for the wiretapping to obtain political intelligence involving his party, not for reasons of national security.

Meanwhile, William Sullivan, director of the FBI Division Five (domestic intelligence), used the tapes for his own "dirty tricks." He was outraged that King might have been in the company of women other than his wife when he was on the road. He sent King's wife copies of some of the FBI tapes, together with a letter in which he threatened to release them publicly if King accepted the Nobel peace prize that he had just been awarded. And he hinted that King should consider committing suicide! The FBI even tried to get the local police to raid an apartment in Atlanta to catch King with a woman companion.

These tactics did not destroy King's marriage or dampen his resolve to continue his civil rights efforts. King accepted the Nobel prize, and the FBI did not release any tapes. But until his assassination in 1968, King remained under surveillance by the FBI, which developed political intelligence on his "poor people's campaign" and his activities in opposition to the Vietnamese war. The FBI never found any information confirming that King or his movement was controlled or influenced by communists or that the movement represented any threat to national security.

The FBI's conduct in this matter raises the most serious questions about the uses of surveillance. Hoover used tapes to try to sidetrack a congressional bill; his deputy tried to destroy King's marriage and lead him to suicide; and President Johnson used the surveillance to keep himself informed about domestic politics. Each of them violated King's civil rights as well as his own public trust.

Source: Based on David J. Garrow, *The FBI and Martin Luther King, Jr.*, Norton, New York, 1981 .

Political surveillance. How to keep the police effective in their mission against terrorism and subversion, and yet safe for a democracy, is a problem that defies easy solution. It may be necessary to place individuals or groups under surveillance, but once surveillance begins, it almost inevitably leads to abuses. Civil liberties groups propose that surveillance be strictly limited by Congress and the courts. They claim that it violates the First Amendment rights of free speech and association, the Fourth Amendment ban on unreasonable searches and seizures, the Fifth Amendment ban on self-incrimination, and the Ninth Amendment guarantee of the right to privacy. They say that surveillance constitutes a *general warrant*, which is banned by the Constitution—a fishing license for investigators who hope that "something will turn up—rather than a specific warrant that says exactly what crime is being investigated and what evidence is being searched for.

Civil libertarians would restrict surveillance to circumstances in which there is probable cause to believe that someone is planning or engaging in serious illegal acts, for which ordinary after-the-fact criminal prosecution would be insufficient to protect the public interest. The police would have to obtain a judicial warrant, and the courts would supervise the operation by granting warrants only for a limited time and for specific criminal investigations.

The courts have decided many surveillance cases against the FBI and against the state and local police. *U.S. v. U.S. District Court* held that domestic organizations cannot be put under surveillance without a warrant if criminal prosecution is to be sustained by the courts. The case also decided that in national security investigations of organizations involving foreign agents or funding, warrants are not required to sustain a later prosecution.[32]

An important consideration for the courts is the **chilling effect** of government surveillance: are people inhibited from joining a group and speaking their minds if they know that the organization is likely to be watched by the

The Reverend Martin Luther King and his wife, Coretta Scott King, leading a voting rights demonstration in Selma Alabama in 1965. Marches like these were directly responsible for passage of the Voting Rights Act of 1965. (*Bruce Davidson: Magnum Photos, Inc.*)

police? The leading case is *Dombroski v. Pfister*, in which Louisiana's law deal-ing with subversive activities was found to be unconstitutional because it might have a chilling effect on freedom of association.[33] Later the Court sought to strike a balance, indicating that the good or bad faith of the government would determine the constitutionality of surveillance.

Public opinion and civil liberties

Through the 1920s a restrictive view of civil liberties, rather than an expansive view, commanded public support. Severe restrictions on political expression were upheld, especially against unorthodox fringe groups. Prosecutors in criminal cases were heavily advantaged over defendants. But since 1937 the Supreme Court and the lower federal courts have turned their attention to civil liberties issues, especially those dealing with claims against state governments. Their decisions upholding the rights of defendants in criminal cases and of unpopular political groups have run ahead of public opinion, leaving the courts vulnerable to political counterattack. Yet as the pace of such attacks increased in the 1980s, public opinion surveys demonstrated greater support than in earlier decades for civil liberties claims, possibly indicating that the Court had successfully educated the public.

Tolerance for unpopular groups has increased. As Figure 4-1 shows, support for the rights of atheists and communists to speak and teach has increased. Surveys have shown that 71 percent of the public in the 1980s were proudest of the "freedom and liberty" enjoyed in the United States. They believed that they "fully and completely" enjoyed freedom of religion (97 percent), the freedom to travel anywhere (95 percent), a free press (90 percent), the freedom to vote for a candidate of their choice (84 percent), the freedom to lead their lives as they saw fit (78 percent), and privacy in their personal lives (63 percent).

Support for civil liberties claims is weakest under the following circum-stances: when the group itself is controversial, such as Nazis, the Ku Klux Klan, or communists; when the action to be protected offends most of the commu-nity, such as flag burning, homosexual activity, or the sale of pornography; and when the action to be prohibited is strongly supported by the community, such as prayer in schools.

A Ku Klux Klan rally held in Danbury, Connecticut, in August 1982. Even hate groups that espouse racial or religious discrimination are protected by the First Amendment freedoms of speech and assembly. (*Steve Silk: Picture Group.*)

Figure 4-1. Civil liberties for unpopular groups. Between 1954 and 1977 support (blue) for the civil liberties of unpopular groups increased sharply. (Source: *Public Opinion*, December-January, 1980, using data from National Opinion Research Center.)

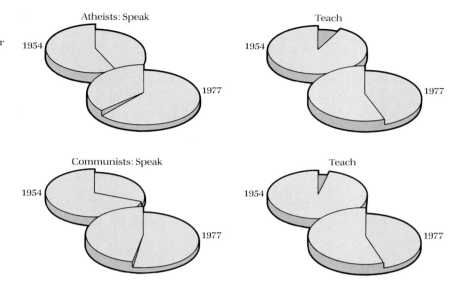

The problem for the courts

It is precisely when the majority wants to suppress the liberties of an unpopular group that the courts become vulnerable. People may agree with the local official, faced with an invasion of cultists, who remarked: "When the Founding Fathers gave us religious freedom, they didn't have these people in mind." But the courts cannot permit an abridgment of freedom based on the popularity of the group involved. As Justice Frankfurter says, "The safeguards of liberty have been forged in controversies involving not very nice people."[34]

The validity of a judicial decision never rests on its popularity with the public. In civil liberties cases the courts are required to act as instruments of constitutional government rather than of democratic rule. Judges are granted life tenure so that they will have the backbone to stand up to community pressure. As Justice Robert Jackson points out, "One's right to life, liberty and property, to free speech, a free press, freedom of worship and assembly, and other fundamental rights, may not be submitted to vote; they depend on the outcome of no election."[35]

Public disapproval of court decisions may even be taken as evidence that the courts are doing their job. Yet such decisions may weaken the authority of the courts with the majority and ultimately weaken the legitimacy of judges cho-

sen for life (and not even elected to federal courts), leading to charges of "government by the judiciary."

The courts balance competing claims, and sometimes they extend and sometimes retreat from civil libertarian positions. In the late 1930s they extended liberties, but in the late 1950s, faced with congressional opposition to several decisions involving members of the Communist Party, the courts began to rule in favor of the government on some free-speech regulations. In the 1960s the rights of criminal defendants were extended, but by the late 1970s a Supreme Court with a majority of the justices committed to "law and order" had begun to cut back on some of these rights, a situation which continued in the 1980s, as the Justice Department argued that some civil liberties decisions were unwise intrusions on the powers of the legislative and executive branches.

In the 1980s right-wing groups—spearheaded by the Moral Majority, Citizens for the Republic, the Committee for the Survival of a Free Congress, the National Conservative PAC, and the Congressional Club—have used the media to defeat members of Congress who do not agree with their positions on social issues. After the 1980 elections, when seven liberal senators were replaced by conservatives as a result of such media campaigns, the civil liberties groups counterattacked. People for the American Way presented a two-hour television special, *I Love Liberty*, broadcast in 1982, with former president Ford, Walter Cronkite, and Lady Bird Johnson as hosts and with such media stars as Jane Fonda, Burt Lancaster, Mary Tyler Moore, and Christopher Reeves. The fundamentalists and the civil libertarians had taken their disagreements from the nation's courtrooms and put them into the nation's living rooms.

CIVIL LIBERTIES CASES: HOW FEDERAL COURTS DECIDE

The federal judges and the Supreme Court justices must consider two issues in most civil liberties cases. One involves *federalism:* the power of the national courts to issue orders to state and local officials. The other is the role of the judiciary when dealing with elected executives and legislators: to what extent should judges be activists, and to what extent should they accept the authority of these officials?

The federal issue

The Bill of Rights was originally intended to safeguard the people against actions of the national government, particularly Congress. The First Amendment refers to Congress, while other amendments deal with the federal courts, the military, and the executive branch—but none mention or seem to apply to the state governments. Yet most civil liberties cases decided by the federal courts involve actions of state officials or laws passed by state legislatures. How can the federal courts apply the Bill of Rights to the states? How far should protections originally intended to apply to the national government be applied to the states?

Dual citizenship. During the nineteenth century the Supreme Court embraced the doctrine of dual citizenship. Chief Justice John Marshall, in *Barron v. Baltimore*, restricted the application of the Bill of Rights to the national government. "These amendments contain no expression indicating an intention to apply them to state governments," he observed, concluding that "this

court cannot so apply them."[36] In a post-Civil War case Justice Samuel Miller held that "there is a citizenship of the United States, and a citizenship of the state, which are distinct from each other, and which depend on different characteristics or circumstances in the individual."[37] By the turn of the century the prevailing doctrine was summarized by Justice Brewer, who concluded that the first ten amendments "contain no restrictions on the powers of the state, but were intended to operate solely on the federal government."[38]

Applying the Bill of Rights to the states. In this century the Bill of Rights has been applied to state governments, and therefore the federal courts can hold unconstitutional the actions of state officials and private individuals.[39]

The change began when the Fourteenth Amendment was adopted in 1868; it provided in part that no state could deprive anyone of life, liberty, or property without due process of law. This language echoed the due process clause of the Fifth Amendment, which applied to the national government; now the states were under the same restrictions. But what is due process of law? According to *strict-constructionist* judges, it refers to the rules designed to ensure a fair trial. The federal courts could review state trials only if, in the words of Justice Frankfurter, their proceedings would "shock the conscience." Torture, extreme forms of interrogation, intimidation of witnesses, and other methods of gaining an unfair advantage for the prosecution during a trial would be held unconstitutional by the federal courts, but otherwise the federal judges would stand aside.

Other judges argued that the Fourteenth Amendment incorporated some of the fundamental guarantees of the original Bill of Rights—not only the right to a fair trial—which could now be applied to the states. Justice Sanford began the process of incorporating the Bill of Rights into the Fourteenth Amendment in *Gitlow v. New York*, a 1925 case, in which he decided:

> For present purposes we may and do assume that freedom of speech and of the press which are protected by the First Amendment from abridgment by Congress are among the fundamental personal rights and liberties protected by the due process clause of the Fourteenth Amendment from impairment by the States.[40]

Six years later, in *Near v. Minnesota*, freedom of the press was protected against state laws. *DeJonge v. Oregon* incorporated freedom to assemble six years after that. In *Hamilton v. Board of Regents*, freedom of religion was incorporated.[41]

FULL VERSUS PARTIAL INCORPORATION. Some justices argued that the judiciary should complete the *incorporation* of all ten amendments. As Justice Hugo Black argued, the purpose of the Fourteenth Amendment was "to extend to all the people of the nation the complete protection of the Bill of Rights. To hold that this court can determine what, if any, provisions of the Bill of Rights will be enforced [against the states] and if so, to what degree, is to frustrate the great design of a written Constitution."[42]

With few exceptions the full-incorporationist view has prevailed. Just about everything in the Bill of Rights now applies to the states, with the following minor exceptions: the right to bear arms, which the states may regulate through gun control laws; the protection against quartering troops in houses in peacetime; indictment by jury in major criminal cases (the states may use other methods to indict); and the right to a jury trial in civil cases involving

amounts over $20 (the states may hold nonjury civil trials in cases involving larger amounts).

INCORPORATION PLUS. The due process clause of the Fourteenth Amendment not only incorporates most of the Bill of Rights but also may include liberties not mentioned in the first ten amendments, through the "incorporation-plus" doctrine. Justice Benjamin Cardozo argued that certain liberties are "the very essence of a scheme of ordered liberty" because they involve "those fundamental principles of liberty and justice which lie at the base of all our civil and political institutions."[43] As Justice Murphy noted, "Occasions may arise where a [state] proceeding falls so far short of conforming to fundamental standards of procedure as to warrant constitutional condemnation in terms of lack of due process despite the absence of a specific provision in the Bill of Rights."[44] Or as Justice Goldberg put it, "The Framers of the Constitution believed there are additional fundamental rights, protected from governmental infringements, which exist alongside those fundamental rights mentioned in the first eight constitutional amendments."[45]

CIVIL LIBERTIES AND STATE JUDICIARIES. In recent decades the state judiciaries have developed their own civil liberties protections, based on the state constitutions and laws, and often these go beyond the rights and liberties recognized by the federal courts. At least thirty-nine state constitutions provide greater protection of freedom of speech than the Bill of Rights.[46] A state court decision based on the state's own constitution is insulated from review by the federal courts, which lack jurisdiction over decisions made on grounds independent of the national Constitution. In the 1980s, as the federal courts have allowed the police and prosecutors more leeway, civil liberties groups and defense attorneys have looked to the state courts for safeguards for defendants. The state courts also have pioneered in extending rights to privacy, especially rights involving sexual behavior, the "right to die" for the severely ill, and freedom of speech and of the press.

Some state courts have rejected the reasoning of the Supreme Court in interpreting language in state constitutions which is similar to that in the national Constitution, such as due process of law and equal protection of the laws. Some have ruled that women have a right to public funding for abortions, which is opposite to the ruling of the Supreme Court. Justice William Brennan approvingly noted that the supreme court of Hawaii went beyond the United States Supreme Court in one case, and he claimed that "while this results in a divergence of meaning between words which are the same in both federal and state constitutions, the system of federalism envisaged by the United States Constitution tolerates such divergence where the result is greater protection of individual rights under state law. . . ."[47]

Most experts in constitutional law see state civil liberties protections as part of a redundant system of judicial power. As Laurence Tribe explains, "There is a reciprocal relationship between the U.S. Supreme Court and the state courts. As the Supreme Court's own energy flags or it reaches the limits of appropriate federal judicial activity, it may nonetheless have marked the path that creative state jurists will want to follow." He adds that "in the long view of history, most of the truly creative developments in American law have come from the states."[48] As the Supreme Court has backtracked on civil liberties protections, some states have moved forward in response.

The role of the judiciary

The extent to which the federal courts will decide cases that have civil liberties dimensions involves not only issues of federalism but also conceptions of the proper role of the judiciary in dealing with other branches and levels of government.

Self-restraint versus close scrutiny. In many kinds of cases judges prefer to assume that legislators and executives have acted rationally, lawfully, and constitutionally, putting the burden of proof on those with complaints who must demonstrate otherwise. But this principle of *self-restraint*, applied to such matters as presidential powers in foreign affairs or laws regulating the economy passed by Congress, is not the principle by which justices operate in civil liberties cases. Instead, they rely on *close scrutiny:* actions of officials are considered suspect, and the burden of proof is on the government, which must demonstrate that limitations or restraints serve a public purpose. This principle was articulated in the most famous footnote ever to appear in a Supreme Court case, written by Justice Harlan Fiske Stone in *United States v. Carolene Products Co.*, in which he argued that there was little or no presumption of constitutionality for any law "which restricts those political processes which can ordinarily be expected to bring about repeal of undesirable legislation."[49] Justice Benjamin Cardozo similarly identified for close scrutiny anything that infringed upon First Amendment rights, which he said were "the matrix, the indispensable condition, of nearly every form of freedom."[50] The courts must protect these freedoms and give them the benefit of the doubt against any form of government regulation precisely because these freedoms are at the core of the workings of the entire system of government.

Preferred freedoms. The courts have developed a set of **preferred freedoms** (First Amendment freedoms) to which they apply the rule of close scrutiny. They will not uphold regulations which define or limit in any way the type of person or group which is protected by the First Amendment, but they may uphold a law or regulation, applied to everyone, which reasonably regulates when, how, and where speech or assembly may occur. The courts uphold laws punishing people who joke about planting bombs on airplanes or who shout "Fire!" in a crowded theater. They allow bans on the sale of pornography involving children. They permit communities to establish regulations governing the use of loudspeakers.

Ruling for the government. The courts do not always rule against the government in case involving freedom of expression; indeed, many of the ringing defenses of civil liberties quoted thus far were written as part of dissenting opinions or were majority opinions upholding a government prosecution.

CLEAR AND PRESENT DANGER. The toughest test is that of demonstrating a *clear and present danger* to public order. The government must prove that a regulation or law which it passed or that an action which it took was necessary to eliminate or prevent such a danger. As formulated by Justice Holmes in a World War I case involving the conviction of an antiwar protestor who passed out leaflets, "The question in every case is whether the words used are in such circumstances and are of such a nature as to create a clear and present danger that they will bring about the substantive evils that Congress has a right to

prevent."[51] Holmes insisted that a danger had to be clear and imminent because he thought that in most circumstances, even if the danger was great, a democratic society could tolerate speech. As justices Brandeis and Holmes argued in their dissent in another case:

> No danger flowing from speech can be deemed clear and present, unless the incidence of the evil apprehended is so imminent that it may befall before there is opportunity for full discussion. If there be time to expose through discussion the falsehood and fallacies, to avert the evil by the processes of education, the remedy to be applied is more speech, not enforced silence.[52]

In more recent cases the courts have extended this argument to consider the likelihood that an action will succeed. Even if a danger is imminent, there must be a substantial probability that it will occur before the government is justified in intervening.[53]

CLOSE-UP

JUSTICE OLIVER WENDELL HOLMES, JR. One of the greatest Supreme Court justices, Oliver Wendell Holmes, Jr., played an important role in strengthening the First Amendment guarantees of freedom of expression. Holmes went to Harvard College and became acquainted with Henry Wadsworth Longfellow, William James, and Ralph Waldo Emerson. The same year in which he received the honor of class poet, Holmes enlisted in Company G to fight in the Civil War, reaching the rank of captain after being wounded three times.

Holmes attended Harvard Law School, taught at Harvard, and was appointed to the Supreme Judicial Court of Massachusetts in 1882. He became chief justice of that court in 1899. His legal scholarship put him in the first rank of American jurists. He took a sociological rather than narrowly legalistic approach to the law. "The life of the law has not been logic," he wrote in his book *The Common Law*, "it has been experience." He tried to adjust legal doctrines to the realities of life, believing that the law was meant to adapt.

President Theodore Roosevelt appointed Holmes to the Supreme Court in 1902. Holmes's decisions and dissents often followed the principles of the progressive movement. He favored state regulation of working hours and a minimum wage for women and children, he opposed child labor ("If there is any matter upon

Associate Justice Oliver Wendell Holmes, Jr. (*Bettmann Archive.*)

which civilized countries have agreed," he wrote in a dissent, "it is the evil of premature and excessive child labor"), and he wanted to hold employers responsible for injuries sustained in the workplace. Holmes did not always vote the White House line, however. When Roosevelt had the Northern Securities Company prosecuted for alleged restraint of trade, Holmes dissented, along with the chief justice and two other judges, against the president's policy (beginning his opinion with the words, "Great cases like hard cases make bad law,"), arguing that the size of the company did not make it illegal. His opinion outraged Roosevelt, who told his friends, "I could carve out of a banana a judge with more backbone than that!"

Holmes was a defender of personal freedom and consistently dissented against a conservative-dominated court, often in tandem with Justice Louis Brandeis. True, he wrote the majority opinion which sent the socialist Eugene Debs to prison, but he did that because Debs had taken illegal actions—he had tried to obstruct military recruitment for the war. But in 1919 the Court upheld convictions under the Espionage Act of men who had distributed pro-Soviet pamphlets. Holmes dissented, arguing that they were being prosecuted solely for their beliefs. "Congress," Holmes said, "certainly cannot forbid all effort to change the mind of the country." In 1925 the Court upheld the conviction of Benjamin Gitlow for publishing a manifesto that was illegal under the Criminal Anarchy act. Holmes dissented because in his view Gitlow had not incited anarchy, but had simply put forth his ideas. In 1928 the Court held that wiretapping did not violate the Fourth Amendment guarantees against unreasonable search because there had been "only listening" and no search, seizure, or entry. Holmes again dissented, calling wiretapping a "dirty business" and arguing that it was "less an evil that some criminals should escape than that the Government should play an ignoble part."

Holmes was called "the great dissenter" because of these and other opinions (he dissented in about one-tenth of the cases brought before him). In his time he was respected more for the grace and clarity of his opinions than for his influence on the law. But today we recognize his immense influence on civil liberties: his "clear and present danger" test, his distinction between thought and action, and his insistence that wiretapping must require a judicial warrant are all ideas which have been accepted by the courts and Congress.[54]

LEAST-MEANS TEST. Any restriction on First Amendment freedom has to pass the least-means test: the government must limit its infringement as much as possible, doing only that which is necessary to prevent danger. It must not take advantage of any situation to substantially weaken freedom of expression. The courts will strike down laws or regulations for *vagueness* and *overbreadth* if they go beyond a particular situation and could be applied to other situations. Thus an ordinance that prevents people from marching in uniforms, designed to discourage the Nazi Party, for example, will be struck down because it could also apply to members of high school marching bands.

SPARK THEORY. The courts also have doctrines which favor the government. One focuses on the content of free speech. If people advocate the violent overthrow of the government, there is no need, according to this doctrine, to prove that the danger is clear, imminent, or likely to occur. Justice Sanford argued instead that "a single revolutionary spark may kindle a fire that, smoldering for a time, may burst into a sweeping and destructive conflagration." Therefore, he

continued, the state may "extinguish the spark" at the outset.[55] Along with this doctrine there is the *bad-tendency test*, which has to do with speech that is "inimical to the public welfare" as well as incitement to crime, disturbing the peace, and threatening to overthrow the government. For some justices, speech is a form of action because it incites criminal conduct. The government does not regulate speech, but rather *illegal actions taking the form of speech*.

The courts are more likely to distinguish between the advocacy of ideas and a conspiracy to act. Justice Brandeis, for example, would not uphold a lower court conviction unless the government could show "either that immediate serious violence was to be expected or was advocated, or that the past conduct furnished reason to believe that such advocacy was then contemplated."[56]

BALANCING TESTS. Many justices prefer neither restrictive nor permissive doctrines. They take the approach of Chief Justice Vinson, who argued that the balance would involve "whether the gravity of the 'evil' discounted by its improbability, justifies such invasion of free speech as is necessary to avoid the danger." Similarly, justices Frankfurter and Harlan were great balancers; Frankfurter claimed that he approached each case with a "candid and informed weighing of the competing interests involved."

This balancing approach infuriated Justice Black, a constitutional absolutist who thought that no conceivable government interference with free speech could be justified. "I do not believe that any federal agencies, including Congress and this Court, have power or authority to subordinate speech and press to what they think are 'more important interests,'" Black said in a dissent.[57] Yet even Black, faced with a case in which civil rights demonstrators marched around and around a state courthouse while a trial was pending, reacted sharply to what he viewed as attempts to pressure the courts, and he upheld convictions of the demonstrators for violating a statute prohibiting such demonstrations.

ISSUE AND DEBATE

RIGHT TO LIFE VERSUS FREEDOM OF CHOICE. *The background.* Until a century ago neither the state governments nor the national government legislated about abortion. Between the 1870s and the turn of the century doctors convinced the states to outlaw most abortions. Most states prohibited abortion unless the life of the mother was at stake; this resulted in many illegal abortions and consequent injury to, and death of, mothers as well as fetuses. In 1973 the Supreme Court ruled, in *Roe v. Wade,* 410 U.S. 113 (1973), that state laws prohibiting abortion in the first trimester of pregnancy were unconstitutional violations of the Ninth Amendment guarantee of the right to privacy. No other civil liberties decision of the Court has evoked so much controversy. A coalition of Roman Catholic and Protestant fundamentalist clergymen and clergywomen bitterly attacked it, and the pro-life movement was born. The Republican Party platforms of 1980 and 1984 opposed the decision, while the Democrats remained deeply divided. Conservative organizations have embraced the "right-to-life" cause, and it is the top priority on the new right's social agenda. Congress has responded to pressure from antiabortion groups and has prohibited the expenditure of federal health care funds for abortions. This provision was upheld by the Supreme Court in *Harris v. McRae,* 100 S. Ct. 2671 (1980).

Pro-life groups in state legislatures have proposed or passed laws which would cut off state funding for abortions for the poor, disallow abortions after the first

trimester, and make them difficult to obtain. The Justice Department, in several cases that reached the Supreme Court in 1983 and 1984, asked the justices to give "heavy deference" to these laws, arguing that it is for the states and not federal judges to make policy.

Many politicians are caught in the middle. The Catholic church and many Protestant fundamentalist groups, believe that abortion is murder. Yet most politicians wish to maintain a distinction between their personal beliefs and morality and their obligations to the entire community. Geraldine Ferrarro, the democratic vice presidential nominee, and the governor of New York, Mario Cuomo (a potential presidential candidate), have both tangled with New York's Cardinal O'Connor, who has called on Catholic politicians to heed the teachings of the church. Vice President Bush, in the 1984 debates, embraced the pro-life position of his party's conservative wing, but other moderate Republicans have not done so.

Public opinion. Public opinion polls show that the nation is sharply divided on the issue of abortion; a 56 to 44 majority agreed with the statement in a 1982 Gallup poll that "every woman who wants an abortion should be able to have one." An October 1984 survey by the National Opinion Research Center indicated that 90 percent of those surveyed believed in abortion if the woman's health was endangered, 80 percent if the baby would have birth defects or if the woman had been raped, 46 percent if she could not afford more children, 44 percent if she was unmarried and did not want to marry the father, and 43 percent if she did not want more children. There is little difference between Protestants and Catholics in such surveys, which do show a stronger pro-life position among blacks than among whites.

The proposed constitutional amendment. Several different versions of antiabortion amendments to the Constitution have been proposed. One would simply ban all abortions, while others would make exceptions if the life of the mother was in danger. None has been seriously considered by Congress. Instead, the Life Amendment Political Action Committee, the Right to Life Committee, and the Ad Hoc Committee in Defense of Life have proposed a constitutional amendment (the Hatch Amendment, named for its sponsor in the senate) which would declare the fetus a human being endowed with constitutional liberties and would permit states to ban abortion, making such laws unreviewable by the Supreme Court. Policy would then be made at the state level rather than by the national government. The amendment passed the Senate Judiciary Committee in 1982. Prochoice groups such as Planned Parenthood, the National Organization of Women, the National Abortion Rights Action League, and Friends of Family Planning joined in a coalition to defeat the amendment in the House. Three-fourths of respondents in Gallup polls taken at the time opposed amending the Constitution to outlaw abortion.

The pros. Supporters of the Hatch Amendment believe that it is a sensible compromise. By returning the issue to the states, it would allow diverse social policy. Given the mobility of the American people, most pregnant women who wished to have abortions would still be able to obtain them in states that permitted them. Meanwhile, in states with large antiabortion majorities, the will of the state legislature would not be obstructed by the courts.

Supporters of amendments banning some or all types of abortion believe that all abortion is murder, that it violates divine law, and that it must be outlawed. Given the Supreme Court decision upholding the right to an abortion, the only way to prevent abortion, they believe, is through a constitutional amendment.

The cons. Opponents of the Hatch Amendment believe that returning the issue to the states would allow abortions to continue but would unfairly discriminate against women who did not have the money to travel to states where abortions were legal. The back-alley practitioners who perform illegal abortions would endanger the lives of these women.

Opponents of a constitutional amendment banning abortion argue that it would embed social policy (and an unenforceable one at that) in the Constitution. It would be similar to Prohibition: it would not prevent abortions from taking place, just as prohibition did not prevent the sale and consumption of alcoholic beverages, and it would create a disrespect for the Constitution among the millions of women who would obtain abortions. Opponents believe that the opinion of the Supreme Court should be respected and that no other burdens should be placed by Congress or the states on the right of women to make their own choices. Those who believe that abortions are morally wrong, they argue, should work privately to prevent them, through counseling expectant mothers to give birth voluntarily, rather than relying on the coercive power of the state to force childbirth on them.

IN CONCLUSION

Civil liberties are guaranteed by the Bill of Rights, the first ten amendments to the Constitution. Almost all have been incorporated into the due process clause of the Fourteenth Amendment and also apply to the states. The most important First Amendment rights involve a ban on establishing a state religion and a guarantee of freedom of religion, making the United States a secular nation (albeit with a religious dimension to its public morality), as well as freedoms of speech, petition, assembly, and the press. The other important provisions guarantee that the government cannot take life, liberty, or property without due process of law, and they specify certain police and criminal procedures. These prevent the United States from becoming a police state.

Since 1937, federal judges have given greater weight to the protection of civil liberties than to other actions of the national government and the state governments. They have elevated civil liberties to a preferred position and have given state action closer scrutiny in these matters than in others. Nevertheless, no liberties are absolute: judges often weigh and balance competing claims, and many decisions favor the government. In recent years freedom of speech and freedom of religious practice have been extended, while the police have, in the past decade, won a number of cases that have restored some of their "crime control" model of patrol and arrest. The outlook is for most civil liberties protections to remain intact, mirroring recent developments in public opinion, but for the courts to reconsider and possibly modify their positions on abortion and prayer in schools.

NOTES

1. *Walz v. Tax Commission*, 397 U.S. 664 (1970); *Lemon v. Kurtzman*, 403 U.S. 602 (1971).
2. *Committee for Public Education and Religious Liberty v. Nyquist*, 413 U.S. 756 (1973).
3. *The New York Times*, Sept. 14, 1984.
4. Ibid.
5. *Lee v. United States*, 457 U.S. 1122 (1982).
6. *Reynolds v. United States*, 98 U.S. 145 (1879).
7. *Abrams v. United States*, 250 U.S. 616 (1919), p. 630.
8. *Whitney v. California*, 274 U.S. 357 (1927), p. 375.
9. Thomas Emerson, *The System of Freedom of Expression*, Random House, New York, 1970, p. 7.

10. *West Virginia Board of Education v. Barnette*, 319 U.S. 629 (1943), p. 638.
11. *Tinker v. Des Moines School District*, 393 U.S. 503 (1969).
12. *Cohen v. California*, 403 U.S. 15 (1971).
13. *Hoffman Estates v. Flipside*, 456 U.S. 950 (1982).
14. *Bolger v. Youngs Drug Product Corp.*, 77 L. Ed. 2d, 469 (1983).
15. *Pruneyard Shopping Center v. Robins*, 447 U.S. 74 (1980).
16. *Feiner v. New York*, 340 U.S. 315 (1951).
17. *United States v. Marty T. Grace*, 75 L. Ed. 2d, 736 (1983).
18. *Red Lion Broadcasting Co. v. FCC*, 395 U.S. 367 (1969).
19. *New York Times v. Sullivan*, 376 U.S. 255 (1964).
20. *New York Times v. United States*, 403 U.S. 713 (1971).
21. *Snepp v. United States*, 444 U.S. 507 (1980).
22. *Branzburg v. Hayes*, 408 U.S. 665 (1972).
23. *Miranda v. Arizona*, 384 U.S. 436 (1966).
24. James Q. Wilson, and George L. Kelling, "Broken Windows" *The Atlantic Monthly*, March, 1982, pp. 29–38.
25. Lawrence Baum, *The Supreme Court*, Congressional Quarterly Press, Washington, D.C., 1981, pp. 187–188.
26. *Stone v. Powell*, 428 U.S. 465 (1976).
27. *Rose v. Lundy*, 455 U.S. 509 (1981).
28. *The New York Times*, June 14, 1982.
29. *United States v. Miller*, 307 U.S. 174 (1939).
30. *The New York Times*, Apr. 5, 1982.
31. *Pico v. Island Trees School District*, 455 U.S. 903 (1982).
32. *United States v. U.S. District Court*, 407 U.S. 297 (1972).
33. *Dombrowski v. Pfister*, 380 U.S. 479 (1965).
34. *United States v. Rabinowitz*, 339 U.S. 56 (1950), p. 69.
35. *West Virginia Board of Education v. Barnette*, 319 U.S. 629 (1943), p. 642.
36. *Barron v. Baltimore*, 32 U.S. 243 (1833), p. 250.
37. *The Slaughterhouse Cases*, 16 Wallace 36 (1873), p. 74.
38. *Brown v. New Jersey*, 175 U.S. 1972, p. 174.
39. Richard C. Cortner, *The Supreme Court and the Second Bill Rights*, University of Wisconsin Press, Madison, 1981.
40. *Gitlow v. New York*, 268 U.S. 652 (1925).
41. *Near v. Minnesota*, 283 U.S. 679 (1931); *DeJonge v. Oregon*, 299 U.S. 353 (1937); *Hamilton v. Board of Regents*, 293 U.S. 245 (1934).
42. *Adamson v. California*, 332 U.S. 46 (1947), p. 89.
43. *Palko v. Connecticut*, 302 U.S. 319 (1937), p. 325; also *Hebert v. Louisiana*, 272 U.S. 312 (1926).
44. *Adamson v. California*, 332 U.S. 46 (1947), p. 124.
45. *Griswold v. Connecticut*, 381 U.S. 479 (1965), p. 488
46. David Margolick, "State Judiciaries Are Shaping Law That Goes Far Beyond Supreme Court," *The New York Times*, May 19, 1982, pp. 1, B-8.
47. William J. Brennan, Jr., "State Constitutions and the Protection of Individual Rights," *Harvard Law Review*, vol. 90, no. 489, 1977, p. 500.
48. Margolick, op. cit.
49. *United States v. Carolene Products Co.*, 304 U.S. 144 (1938), p. 152.
50. *Palko v. Connecticut*, 302 U.S. 319 (1937), p. 327.
51. *Schenck v. United States*, 249 U.S. 47 (1919).
52. *Whitney v. California*, 274 U.S. 357 (1927), p. 377.
53. *Brandenberg v. Ohio*, 395 U.S. 444 (1969).
54. Researched by Maurice Suh, Columbia College.
55. *Gitlow v. New York*, 268 U.S. 652 (1925), p. 669.
56. *Whitney v. California*, 274 U.S. 357 (1927), p. 376.
57. *Dennis v. United States*, 341 U.S. 494 (1951).

FURTHER READING

Abraham, Henry J.: *Freedom and the Court*, 3d ed., Oxford University Press, New York, 1977. A comprehensive textbook on civil liberties.

Barker, Lucius J., and Twiley W. Barker: *Civil Liberties and the Constitution*, Prentice-Hall, Englewood Cliffs, N.J., 1981. A study of leading civil liberties cases.

Berns, Walter: *The First Amendment and the Future of American Democracy*, Basic Books, New York, 1976. A conservative view of the reach and limits of First Amendment freedoms.

Brant, Irving: *The Bill of Rights*, Bobb-Merrill, Indianapolis, 1965. A treatment of the adoption and subsequent application of the Bill of Rights, including incorporation into the Fourteenth Amendment.

Chaffee, Zechariah, Jr.: *Free Speech in the United States*, Harvard University Press, Cambridge, Mass., 1941. A classic treatise on First Amendment freedoms.

Cox, Archibald J.: *Freedom of Expression*, Harvard University Press, Cambridge, Mass., 1981. An update on civil liberties decisions of the Burger Court.

Emerson, Thomas: *The System of Freedom of Expression*, Random House, New York, 1970. A comprehensive discussion of First Amendment freedoms.

Friendly, Fred: *The Good Guys, the Bad Guys, and the First Amendment*, Random House, New York, 1977. An account of the news media and the government.

Garrow, David: *The FBI and Martin Luther King, Jr.*, Norton, New York, 1982. A vivid account of FBI harassment of this civil rights leader.

Hayes, Arthur G.: *Let Freedom Ring*, Boni and Liveright, New York, 1928. Accounts of some of the most controversial cases involving freedom of expression in the early twentieth century, including the Scopes "monkey trial" in Tennessee and the Sacco and Vanzetti trial in Massachusetts.

Hentoff, Nat: *The First Freedom*, Delacorte Press, New York, 1980. A discussion of some of the important post-World-War II First Amendment cases.

Levy, Leonard: *Legacy of Suppression*, Harvard University Press, Cambridge, Mass., 1960. An account of the early struggles for civil liberties.

Lewis, Anthony: *Gideon's Trumpet*, Random House, New York, 1964. A case study of a landmark Supreme Court criminal justice decision.

Markham, Charles L.: *The Noblest Cry*, St. Martin's, New York, 1965. An account of the history and accomplishments of the American Civil Liberties Union.

Morgan, Richard: *The Supreme Court and Religion*, Free Press, New York, 1973. A survey of church-state issues as decided by the Supreme Court.

Schwartz, Bernard: *The Great Rights of Mankind: A History of the American Bill of Rights*, Oxford University Press, New York, 1977. A study of the historical evolution of civil liberties and rights.

Shapiro, Martin: *The Pentagon Papers and the Courts*, Chandler, San Francisco, 1972. A study of a case involving freedom of the press decided by the Supreme Court.

THE STUDY BREAK

Lenny. Stars Dustin Hoffman. A movie about Lenny Bruce, a comedian who ran afoul of local antiobscenity ordinances, and the events that eventually led to his suicide (1974).

Roth, Philip. *Our Gang*, Random House, New York, 1971. A fictionalized satire of President Nixon's commitment to civil liberties.

USEFUL SOURCES

Brownlie, Ian (ed.): *Basic Documents on Human Rights, 2d ed.*, Oxford University Press, New York, 1981.

Emerson, Thomas, David Haber, and Norman Dorsen: *Political and Civil Rights in the United States*, 2 vols., 3d. ed., Boston, Little, Brown, 1967. Leading court cases and commentary.

Kelly, Alfred H. (ed.): *Foundations of Freedom in the American Constitution*, Harper & Row, New York, 1958. Articles on civil liberties.

ORGANIZATIONS

American Civil Liberties Union. 132 West 43d Street, New York, N.Y. 10036. For more information phone 212-944-9800.

American Enterprise Institute. 1150 17th Street, N.W. Washington, D.C. 20036. Useful polls from many sources on public support for civil liberties protections are reprinted in its magazine, *Public Opinion*. For more information phone 202-862-5800.

Moral Majority. 499 South Capitol Street, Washington, D.C. 20003. Publishes *Moral Majority Report*. For more information phone 202-484-7511.

People for the American Way. 1424 16th St., N.W., Suite 601, Washington, D.C. 20036. Publishes *Quarterly Report*. For more information phone 202-462-4777.

PART TWO
THE PURSUIT OF POWER

POLITICAL PARTICIPATION: WHO VOTES?

Legal barriers against women, minorities, and the poor restricted the suffrage for much of American history. Today these restrictions have been abolished, but turnout rates have fallen. (*Bettmann Archive; Shepard Sherbell: Picture Group.*)

It was to be the biggest mobilization of voters in the twentieth century, and it would bring about a fundamental change in American politics—at least that was the feeling during the spring and summer before the 1984 presidential election. Close to 60 million eligible Americans were not registered to vote, and if past practices were any indication, close to half the total of 174 million eligible voters would not show up at the polls. But what would happen if large numbers of people did register and vote? That was the joker in the electoral deck, the wild card that could upset all the pundits' calculations.

The Democrats announced a drive to register more than 10 million new voters; then the Republicans countered with a goal of 2 million. Jesse Jackson's Rainbow Coalition coordinated voter registration drives in the black churches of the nation and urged the congregations to register and vote in the Democratic primaries. The National Organization of Women sponsored a drive which it said resulted in the registration of 250,000 new voters; the Southwest Voter Registration Project, active among Hispanics and Indians, claimed more than 200,000 new registrants in Texas. The Voter Education Project spurred the effort in the south, while the NAACP organized "overground railroad" marches to publicize its campaign among black voters in the midwest. The U.S. Students Association and the National Student Educational Fund sponsored Freedom Summer '84, the purpose of which was to register black voters in Mississippi. The American Coalition for Traditional Values, a group of 100,000 conservative ministers, sponsored a drive to register 2 million fundamentalist Christians.

Other drives were nonpartisan. The National NonPartisan Voter Registration Campaign encouraged officials to set up telephone numbers so that people could dial VOTER-84, leave their names and addresses on an answering machine, and receive voter registration forms by mail. Nineteen foundations donated money to the Advertising Council of America, which sponsored a "get out the vote" series of print and television commercials. The Ad Hoc Funders Committee for Voter Registration and Education coordinated more than $4 million in foundation donations to nonpartisan voter registration groups. The National Student Campaign on Voter Registration helped campus "get out the vote" groups, and their activities reached a peak on October 1, which was proclaimed National Student Voter Registration Day.

Did all this effort change the course of American politics? Not really. In 1980, 115 million people were registered—69.8 percent of those eligible. In 1984, the number rose to 125 million, but since the population had also increased, the percent of those eligible rose to only 71.8 percent. And there was just a 1 percent increase in voting in the 1984 elections—almost half the eligible voters stayed away from the polls, just as they have done in every presidential election year since 1972.

Each party wants to increase voter registration and turnout. Neither seems able to make the breakthrough that would reshape the political map. Each has

experimented with new ways to mobilize nonvoters; thus far these efforts have amounted to treading water. Ways to increase registration would be the super-weapon of American politics; the inability to do so remains its great mystery.

CITIZEN OR SUBJECT?

"If liberty and equality, as is thought by some, are chiefly to be found in democracy," the Greek philosopher Aristotle argued thousands of years ago, "they will be best attained when all persons alike share in the government to the utmost."[1] But not all American citizens share in the government. Those who vote for Democratic and Republican candidates are far outnumbered by those who vote for no one; the "nonvoter" party attracts almost half of all those eligible to vote in presidential elections; and each of the two major parties manages to win the votes of slightly more than one-fourth of the people.

Does democratic government require that most of the people vote most of the time? Would it make any difference if they did? Some people believe that low rates of voting enhance the stability of democracies. They think that most nonvoters are satisfied with their leaders and that nonvoting is a rational response for citizens when the costs of voting (that is, the inconvenience of registering, learning about issues and candidates, and going to the polls) are not justified by any conceivable benefits which they could obtain by choosing new leaders. The political scientist Everett Ladd argues that the overall record of western democracies fits this linkage of "low turnout to relative voter satisfaction."[2] Sam Ervin, a former senator, recalled the nineteenth-century tradition which restricted voting to those who deserved the privilege when he said, "I don't believe in making it easy for lazy, apathetic people. I'd be extremely happy if nobody in the United States voted except for the people who thought about the issues and made up their own minds and wanted to vote."[3]

But others believe that nonvoting is a symptom of deep-seated problems. "The legitimacy of a democratic leadership and the health of the democratic process depend squarely on the informed and active participation of the electorate," argues Curtis Gans, the director of the Committee for the Study of the American Electorate, a group which monitors low turnouts.[4] In ancient democracies a distinction was made between the good person and the good citizen. To be merely the former, personally honest and obedient to the government, was to be a good subject—but that was not good enough. "We regard the man who takes no part in public affairs not as easygoing and sensible," the Athenian leader Pericles observed, "but as worthless and foul."[5]

Voter turnout is the key to political power. Candidates for office devote most of their campaign efforts to bringing their supporters to the polls. Anyone who wants to influence politics—by helping in a campaign, running for office, or lobbying politicians for change—learns that getting out the vote is the way to do it.

In this chapter we begin our study of campaigns and elections by studying *registration* and *turnout rates.* Who are the voters, and how do they differ from nonvoters? How might turnout rates be increased? We will consider the American experience in historical and comparative perspective, and we will look for an explanation of the central paradox in Americans' voting behavior: as the constitutional and legal requirements for voting have been eased and as the people have become better educated about, and more interested in, politics, the percentage of the eligible population that votes has declined.

Direct democracy

In a *direct democracy* the majority of the people decide on the policies of the government. At a ***town meeting*** the whole community meets in one place, discusses matters, and then votes. But such meetings are limited to communities in which all citizens can gather in one place at one time.

On a larger scale, direct democracy relies on the ***plebiscite,*** or issue election.[6] The community need not meet in one place at one time, and the election does not follow right after any particular meeting or discussion.

In the United States there are two types of plebiscites: the ***initiative,*** which allows anyone to put a proposal on the ballot if enough people sign petitions to do so (usually 1 to 2 percent of the voters), and the ***referendum,*** which is a proposal submitted to the people by the state legislature. Twenty-three states now use initiatives, and all provide for the referendum. As yet there is no form of direct democracy for the national government, making the United States one of the few democratic nations that do not use such procedures.

Indirect democracy

The main problem with any plebiscite is that there is no way to improve a proposal by discussing and amending it, as could be done at a town meeting. The public has to accept or reject it and cannot shape it once it has been put on the ballot. Effective democracy requires indirect methods: a way for representatives of the people to recreate the advantages of the town meeting—its discussion, and debate.

In representative democracies the people choose the representatives who decide the issues. There is only an indirect relationship between candidates and issues: candidates make pledges during a campaign and, if elected, hold themselves most accountable to those who voted for them and try to translate these voters' preferences into public policy. Elections provide clues as to the wishes of the voters, and politicians "read the returns" accordingly.

**WHO VOTES?
TURNOUT RATES**

In our ***political culture*** (our beliefs about what should and what should not be done and about what is and what is not legitimate) we think that the good citizen is one who votes. Perhaps this is why, when people are asked whether they vote in elections, there is significant overreporting—as if people were ashamed to tell pollsters that they do not bother to go to the polls. In 1984 the Census Bureau found that its national sample of 66,000 households overreported their rate of voting by almost 10 percent, and a sample of voters questioned by the Survey Researcher Center of the University of Michigan (the leading academic center studying voting behavior) overreported by up to 15 percent.[7] When the Gallup poll asked people in 1984 whether they were registered, about 4 percent falsely reported yes. In spite of our political culture, what we say is quite different from what we do.

Calculating turnouts

To determine voting rates in any election, we need to know two things: the number of adults who are eligible to vote (the voting-age population, or VAP) and the number of people who actually voted (the turnout). The voting-age population consists of American citizens age 18 and older who are not in prison or mental institutions. We can obtain reasonably good estimates of the VAP from the Census Bureau, which two years after the end of every decade (for example, in 1972 and 1982), publishes a report on the size of the VAP, as well as the number of people who registered and who voted for president and

TURNOUTS AND DIRECT DEMOCRACY

Would turnouts be higher if there were more direct votes on the issues? In a Gallup poll 48 percent of the respondents who had not voted in the 1980 presidential election said that they would be more likely to vote, and only 2 percent said that they would be less likely to vote, in issue elections. In another Gallup survey 52 percent favored and 23 percent opposed national referendums.

Before we decide that such elections would increase turnouts, we should examine the experience of states in which they are held. In 1978 the average turnout rate was only 40 percent, and in 1980 it rose to 52.1 percent—slightly less than the turnout rate for candidate elections.[a]

Even intensely debated issues do not bring majorities to the polls. Consider Proposition 13, a 1978 California initiative to cut property taxes and state spending and a battle which began the great tax revolt of the past decade. The turnout rate was only 43 percent. Turnout rates in the 1982 nuclear freeze referendums held in nine states ranged from 32 percent in Arizona to 49 percent in Oregon.

Issue elections of the past decade have not attracted more voters to the polls than candidate elections. They have not stimulated interest in voting or prevented the decline in turnout rates.[b] In fact, in nonsouthern states in 1980 the turnouts were lower in states that held issue elections than in states that did not.

a. *Public Opinion*, vol. 42, no. 4, November–December 1978, pp. 26–28; *Public Opinion*, vol. 45, no. 1, February–March 1981, p. 40.
b. David Everson, "The Effects of Initiatives on Voter Turnout," *Western Political Quarterly*, vol. 34, no. 3, 1981, pp. 415–425.

for representatives in each state. For the 1984 elections there were 174 million people in the voting-age population. By dividing the turnout in each presidential and congressional election by the voting-age population for that election, we can calculate past turnouts (Figure 5-1).

Figure 5-1. Turnout rates, 1856–1984. There is higher turnout in presidential election years than in midterm election years (shown here since 1922). (Sources: *Historical Statistics of the United States*, Washington, D.C., Government Printing Office, 1975; U.S. Bureau of the Census, *Statistical Abstract of the United States*, Washington, D.C., Government Printing Office, 1984.)

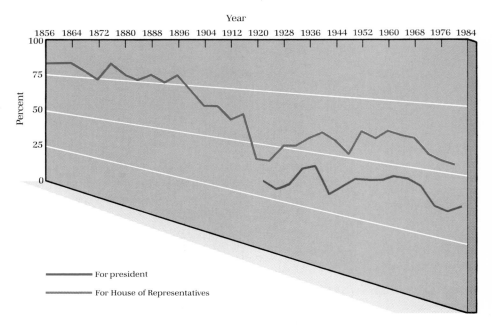

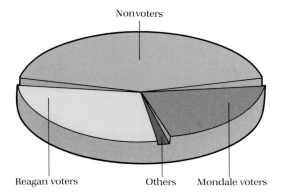

Figure 5-2. Turnout and choice in the presidential election of 1984. Of approximately 178 million Americans eligible to vote in 1984, 96 million did so, giving Ronald Reagan a landslide reelection share of 31.5 percent of the electorate.

Nonvoters

Reagan voters   Others   Mondale voters

National turnouts. Turnout rates vary for different kinds of elections. In presidential elections recent rates have varied from 63 to 53 percent. Of the voting-age population, the largest number, almost a majority, choose not to vote at all. The winning presidential candidate receives votes from only 26 to 35 percent of the VAP (Figure 5-2).

If all these nonvoters suddenly turned up at the polls, would it change the results? Most nonvoters have weak ties to the major parties (although the Democrats have a small lead in this regard), and many are independents. If they voted, they would probably support the presidential candidate who was going to win anyway, simply adding to the margin of victory. In 1956, for example, 72 percent of the nonvoters favored the winning candidate, Dwight Eisenhower; in 1960 John Kennedy had the support of 57 percent of the nonvoters; and in 1964 Lyndon Johnson was favored by 77 percent of those who did not vote. In 1972, 1976, and 1984 the margins of victory of Nixon, Carter, and Reagan also would have been increased if nonvoters had gone to the polls. The only election in which nonvoters would have made a difference was that held in 1968: the nonvoters favored Humphrey over Nixon by a small margin, but their support could have been crucial in the close race.[8]

Turnouts for congressional elections vary enormously. In presidential election years (for example, 1980 and 1984) slightly fewer votes are cast for senators and representatives than for president, while in off years (for example, 1978 and 1982) considerably fewer votes are cast. In the 1982 congressional elections only 38 percent of the VAP chose to vote. On the average, the winners in these elections received the support of slightly more than one-fifth of those eligible to vote.

State and local turnouts. The turnout rates are even lower in most state and local contests. In part this is a matter of timing, since most of these elections are not held in presidential election years. Turnout rates vary; in some states they approach 60 percent, and in others they plunge to 20 percent or lower, but usually they range between 30 and 50 percent of the VAP in elections for state legislators, governors, mayors, and city council members. The typical state officeholder is elected with the support of only one-fifth of the VAP.

Turnouts in historical perspective

Turnouts today are neither the highest nor the lowest in our history. Between 1856 (the first year for which accurate statistics are available) and 1896, a period which was marked by extensive corruption and mediocre leadership and

during which neither major party focused on the issues, turnout rates were the highest they have ever been. This was due in part to the close two-party competition for the presidency, in part to relaxed registration requirements (that is, all white males over the age of 21 were eligible to vote), and in part to massive vote fraud, which inflated the totals. Between 1900 and 1916 the progressive movement encouraged measures such as issue elections, petitions to recall public officials, and party primaries that gave voters a chance to participate in nominations, and elections were fought on the issues. Yet the turnout rates slumped as more stringent registration requirements were introduced and as the Democrats dominated the south and the Republicans dominated the north, thus lessening two-party competition: they declined by an average of 2.9 percent in each election. Although more people voted after 1920, when women were given the right to vote, the rate of voting declined sharply.

In the 1930s, when the economy was in dire straits and the very survival of our economic and political institutions seemed at stake, voting rates began to climb dramatically, breaking the previous pattern of low interest–high turnout and high interest–low turnout: the Democrats mobilized new constituencies, while the Republican Party fought to maintain its status as a major party. Between 1960 and 1980, as it became easier for the young, the poor, and minorities to register and vote, we went back to the old pattern, and turnout rates dropped 10 percent in those two decades.[9] In the 1980s turnout rates began once again to increase: there was a 3 percent rise between the 1978 and the 1982 midterm congressional elections, followed by a 1 percent rise between the 1980 and the 1984 presidential elections.

Turnouts in comparative perspective

Besides electing candidates to office, voters are frequently asked to pass on referendums as well. No nation gives its voters as many issues to decide or candidates to elect as the United States. (*Tony Karody: Sygma.*)

In most nations with democratic governments the turnout rates are higher than they are in the United States. In western European democracies 85 to 95

Figure 5-3. Turnout in selected democratic nations.

percent of the eligible adults register, compared with our rate of 72 percent in 1984 (Figure 5-3).

Do these turnout rates mean that the United States is less democratic than other nations? Not necessarily. Most other countries hold only a national election (every four to seven years) to choose the members of parliament and local elections for mayors and city council members. In the United States there are dozens of elections every year: in presidential election years for president, senators, and representatives; in off years for senators and representatives; and in odd or off years for state governors, state senators, and state representatives (and in some states for judges). There are also county elections for sheriffs, judges, and executives and local elections for mayors, city council members, judges, school board members, etc. In addition, we have a large number of ***primary elections*** (in which voters choose the nominees of their party to run in the general elections—a practice almost unknown in other countries) and referendums and initiatives. In no other nation are voters kept so busy or called upon to make up their minds on so many candidates and issues: the United States has more than 450,000 elected officials, far more per capita than any other nation in the world.

LEGAL FACTORS: REGISTERING TO VOTE

Explanations for the fluctuations in turnouts focus on the constitutional and legal factors which encourage or inhibit voting, on the characteristics of the population, and on the political environment. This section considers legal factors involving registration.

Voter registration was introduced in many states at the turn of the century as a progressive measure designed to improve the quality of the electorate and prevent vote fraud. In the nineteenth century, any male, even a noncitizen, could go to the polls on election day and vote; but the new registration laws required that local officials record the names and addresses of people who intended to vote, often well in advance of an election. State laws also required that in order to be accepted by the registrars, one had to be a citizen, to have resided in the community for a specified period of time, and to meet certain other requirements, such as literacy in English. By enforcing such requirements in an unfair or discriminatory manner, local political leaders could use them to encourage some people to vote and discourage others. To keep immigrants from voting, for example, a law might require residency of one year and proof of an eighth grade reading knowledge of English. Some states required periodic reregistration and purged the rolls of those who had not voted in previous elections (almost all still do so).

Registration and racial discrimination

Millions of blacks were disenfranchised in eleven southern states between 1890 and 1910, when registration procedures were introduced. At the time, poor blacks and whites, represented by the Populist movement, were challenging entrenched interests for control of state governments. Conservative whites, who controlled local newspapers, tried to turn whites against blacks by describing in lurid detail crimes supposedly committed by black men against white women. They called for the separation of the races in all public facilities. Race politics, based on mutual suspicion, soon supplanted class politics, and the white Populists embraced white supremacy. In state after state, constitutional conventions or the state legislatures used the following means to purge blacks from the registration lists:

1. *Literacy tests,* administered unfairly by local registrars, which kept even black college graduates from voting.
2. *Poll taxes,* payment of which was required in order to register and vote; these also discouraged poor whites from voting.
3. *Good-character tests,* which required prospective registrants to get two people already on the rolls to vouch for them. Once blacks were removed from the rolls, no white voter would help them get back on.

Because many low-income and poorly educated whites could not meet the stringent new requirements, some states adopted *grandfather clauses:* anyone whose grandfather had been eligible to vote would not have to meet these new requirements. Since only the grandfathers of whites had voted (the grandfathers of blacks had all been slaves), this satisfied whites. But in 1915 the Supreme Court, in *Guinn v. United States,* ruled that this provision was unconstitutional and struck it down; as a result, many uneducated whites were eliminated from the rolls.[10] Through the 1920s, it was not uncommon in parts of the south for turnout rates to remain as low as 10 percent.

The civil rights movement in the 1960s completely transformed the registration systems of the southern states. Before 1965 fewer than one-third of eligible blacks had managed to register in the region. As a result of the efforts of civil

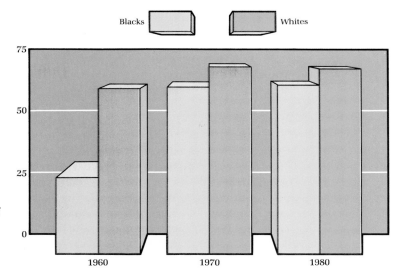

Figure 5-4. Registration rates in the south, 1960–1980. The registration rate for blacks increased markedly after passage of the Civil Rights Act of 1965. Rates for whites also increased as state literacy tests were suspended. (Source: U.S. Commission on Civil Rights.)

rights groups and of a coalition of liberal Democrats, labor unionists, religious groups, and moderate Republicans, Congress passed the Voting Rights Act (VRA) of 1965, which provided that in counties in which the turnout rate in presidential elections was less than 50 percent, literacy tests would be suspended. Federal registrars would register blacks who encountered serious obstacles from local registrars. Discrimination based on race or color was made a federal crime. The Justice Department was given the right to review any changes in state or local election laws to make sure that they did not discriminate against blacks. In 1970 an amendment to the VRA suspended the application of literacy tests throughout the nation. Registration rates for blacks and uneducated whites rose dramatically in the south, as Figure 5-4 indicates.

Although much has been done to end discrimination, as late as 1982 the United States Commission on Civil Rights reported that in some parts of the south discrimination and even threats of violence still affected registration and voter turnout among blacks.[11] And in 1984 the House Judiciary Subcommittee on Civil and Constitutional Rights reported that artificial and arbitrary barriers to registration were still being used against minorities, including inconvenient locations and hours to register, failure to appoint minority registrars, bans on door-to-door registration, and the requirement that mail registration forms be notarized. But today racists must violate national and state laws to actually keep minorities from registering, even though they can still make it inconvenient for them to do so.

Registration and language barriers

In the north and west, barriers were put up against newly arrived immigrants by groups that were already in control of state politics. Under the *Americanization doctrine*, developed between 1910 and 1920, immigrants would not be able to register until they assimilated the language and political values of Americans. They would have to prove that they had done so by becoming citizens and then demonstrating their literacy in English, according to the provisions of some state constitutions (like New York's constitution of 1915) or election laws. There is something to be said for assimilating people into the culture of the majority and having them learn the language, since this promotes national

unity, facilitates communication, and speeds the social and economic progress of immigrants. But the politicians who instituted these requirements did so to disenfranchise their opponents; when immigrants supported the party in power, the laws were disregarded.

Most of the requirements for literacy in the English language have been eliminated. The VRA provided in 1965 that Puerto Rican citizens could vote if they had attended an "American flag" school through the sixth grade in Puerto Rico, even though their education might have been in Spanish. The 1970 amendment, which suspended all literacy tests, eased voting for millions of Hispanics in the southwest and in Florida as well. Amendments to the VRA in 1975 and 1982 provided for bilingual registration materials and ballots and for interpreters for many different groups—including Hispanics, Asians, American Indians, and native Alaskans—in counties in which the Census Bureau determines that these groups make up more than 5 percent of the population and in which their illiteracy rates are above the national average.

Easing registration

Poll taxes for national elections imposed by the states were abolished by the Twenty-Fourth Amendment, ratified in 1964. Two years later the Supreme Court, in *Harper v. Virginia State Board of Elections*, abolished poll taxes for state elections as well.[12] The 1970 amendments to the VRA lowered the voting age for national and state elections from 21 to 18, but the Supreme Court ruled that the law could apply only to national elections. In 1971 the Twenty-Sixth Amendment lowered the voting age for both national and state elections to 18. The 1970 VRA amendments provided that people who live in a state for thirty days before a federal election may vote in that election, no matter what the state residency requirements are.

Almost all states have now dropped periodic reregistration in favor of permanent registration. Most states now allow people to vote in state as well as national elections if they have lived in the state for thirty days, and some states allow registration on election day. Hours for registration have been lengthened, offices are kept open on weekends and are in convenient locations, and many states allow candidates, parties, and grass-roots organizations to provide deputy registrars who can register people in their homes as well as in shopping malls, banks, and other, similar locations. Some states also permit registration by mail.

Local *registrars* still discriminate against college students. Some election boards claim that students who live in dormitories do not have a legal residence and refuse to register them. Students have won cases against such decisions in the federal courts; for example, a 1984 decision in New York allowed hundreds of thousands of students to register for the election. But in other states they still find it difficult to vote. Nevertheless, more than a quarter of a million college students registered to vote from their campuses in 1984.

Some changes in registration laws have had a enormous impact on registration and voter turnout, as the data for the south between 1960 and 1980 indicate. But political scientists disagree on whether further easing of requirements—which makes fraud easier and increases costs—would increase turnouts. Raymond Wolfinger and Steven Rosenstone speak for those who think that easing requirements would bring more people to the polls when they argue that "if every state had had registration laws in 1972 as permissive as those in the most permissive states, turnout would have been about 9 per-

centage points higher in the presidential election."[13] Reformers believe that states could eliminate the thirty-day residency requirement and permit (as a few states do) election-day registration; simplify absentee registration and voting for the sick, the disabled, the handicapped, and those who are away from home; and institute a nationally funded system of postcard registration.[14] They also suggest that election day be made a national holiday and that states end the practice of purging the rolls of nonvoters after two or four years, as most of them do. Congress has refused to enact postcard registration (proposed by President Carter in 1977) or any of the other suggested reforms.

More skeptical political scientists argue that further easing of registration is not likely to increase turnouts. They point out that while many states did change their laws in the 1970s, their turnouts diminished or remained the same, and often there was no difference in turnout in adjoining states, one of which had eased requirements, while the other had not.

More could be done to ensure that the 2 million Americans who live overseas can register and vote in their home states. Many states require them to file early in an election year and then mail ballots to them too late, failing to process the forms or even count the ballots which are sent back. The Defense Department could encourage voting in the military, where the rates are 15 percent lower than the rates in the civilian population in presidential elections and as much as 25 percent lower in off-year congressional elections.

ISSUE AND DEBATE

SHOULD VOTERS BE REGISTERED IN GOVERNMENT OFFICES? *The background.* For the 1984 elections a number of states—including Texas, Ohio, Michigan, and New York—allowed their residents to obtain voter registration forms or assistance at state agencies, either from state workers or from volunteer "get out the vote" groups. In Michigan, people who are renewing a boat, car, or driver's license are asked whether they are registered, and more than 4.6 million voters have filled out voter registration forms in government offices. In New York State, five agencies (labor, motor vehicles, social services, and workers' compensation) were ordered to conduct voter registration projects and help citizens fill out mail registration forms. Drivers who were renewing their licenses were routinely invited to register to vote by clerks at the counters. In Ohio, state laws require that government officials ask citizens whether they would like to register and that each high school have a designated registrar so that 18-year-old students can sign up. In West Virginia and New Mexico, on the other hand, people must ask for registration forms before assistance can be given to them, although signs are posted announcing that aid is available. Various private organizations, such as Project Vote and Human SERVE, set up shop in government buildings and register low-income citizens who are waiting in agencies that handle welfare, unemployment insurance, food stamps, disability payments, and day care.

In 1982, after Project Vote's first major effort resulted in the registration of more than 100,000 people in nine states, four Republican governors barred registrations in unemployment offices. Project Vote sued in federal court, and these bans were overturned as violations of the First Amendment guarantees of freedom of speech and freedom to petition the government. But whether state employees could be directed to conduct such registration drives remained a separate issue. Was it a proper activity for state employees?

The arguments for. Those in favor, such as the League of Women Voters, the

AFL-CIO, the nonpartisan registration groups, and the Democratic Party, argue that making it easier for prospective voters to register is the most important factor in increasing the turnout rate. They believe that most state election laws can be interpreted to require that registration forms be distributed as widely and freely as possible, including at state agencies. They believe that state employees can be trusted to conduct such drives in a fair and nonpartisan manner, and they point to Governor Cuomo's order which requires that state officials in New York "shall maintain a position of strict neutrality with respect to a person's party enrollment."

The arguments against.   Republican politicians have argued that in most states registration is already easy, that state election laws should be interpreted strictly and do not now permit state officials to conduct registration drives, and that state employees, especially those affiliated with the human services employees' unions, are likely to conduct such drives to benefit the Democrats.

Critics also point out that regulations prohibit federal employees from using their official authority for the purpose of interfering with, or affecting the results of, an election. The White House Office of Personnel Management threatened three Democratic governors with cutoffs of some federal funds unless they could demonstrate that their orders did not violate these federal regulations. In response, the Democrats charged that the administration was using blackmail and pressure tactics.

Resolving the issues.   The state and federal courts will eventually resolve this dispute. After Governor Cuomo issued his Executive Order 43 in New York, the Republican Party filed suit in the state court to block its implementation. A lower court judge agreed, arguing that "it is a use of state funds for purposes not authorized by law," and that it violated a provision of the state constitution requiring bipartisan control of registration. The court insisted that such actions must be authorized by the legislature before being put into effect by the governor, and the state's high court extended the ban for a year while the case was being considered.

THE NONVOTERS: WHO ARE THEY?

In modern times it has become easier to register and vote than at any other time in our history, and yet the percentage of eligible adults who choose to register has declined from approximately 85 percent in the 1950s to around 70 percent in the 1980s, while the percentage of people who vote has declined from about 63 percent to about 53 percent.

The image of the nonvoter, Arthur Hadley points out, is that of "Boobus Americanus," whom he describes as a "young lunkhead, bombed on beer or stoned on pot, a high school dropout, perhaps a motorcycle-revving white or jiving black, living in the rural South or Northern city slum, dirty, poor, alienated, undereducated, and alone."[15] While some nonvoters fit this description, the fact is that most do not.

Nonregistrants

Younger, poorer, less well educated, more mobile, and single people are more likely not to register. Members of racial and linguistic minority groups are less likely to register than white English-speaking Americans, as Figure 5-5 shows.

These figures must be approached with caution. It is not true that all minorities and all poor, young, and uneducated people do not register, but it is true that they are less likely to register than wealthier, older, better-educated people. High *rates* should not be confused with large *numbers of voters:* Jews, who

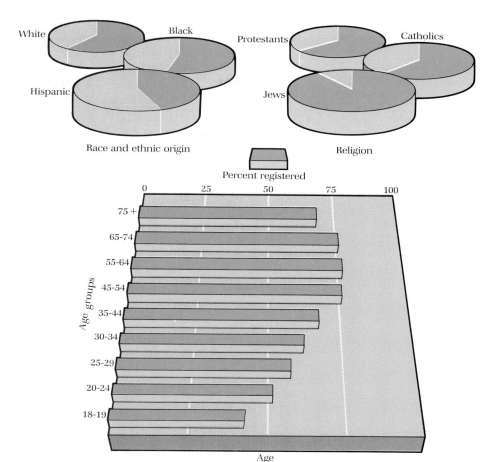

Figure 5-5. Registration rates for selected categories: race and ethnic origin, age, and religion. Whites have the highest voting rates, followed by blacks and Hispanics. Young voters, 18–29, have the lowest rates of any age group. (Sources: For race and ethnic origin and age: U.S. Bureau of the Census, *Voting and Registration in the Election of November 1980*, Current Population Reports, Series P-20, no. 370; for religion: *Gallup Opinion Index*, September 1979, p. 271.)

have high rates, constitute less than 3 percent of the population, and the number of Jewish voters is far smaller than the number of Hispanic or black voters—even though Hispanics and blacks have much lower registration rates.

Registrants: Core and peripheral voters

The decision to register or not to register is the major determinant of voting or not voting. But even among those who register, approximately one-fifth will not vote in presidential elections, and almost half will not vote in off-year congressional elections. Between one-half and three-fourths of those who are registered will not vote in off-year state and local elections.

How do we explain the dropouts? The *core-peripheral* explanation argues that most registrants vote most of the time but that some vote very little; thus there are significant differences between the core and the peripheral electorate.[16] A core, consisting of about 40 percent of the VAP—60 percent of the registered voters—vote in most elections. A group of peripheral voters vote occasionally; they constitute about 20 percent of the VAP and about 30 percent of the registered voters. Those who have voted in the past are likely to vote in future elections, while those who have voted only occasionally in the past (or not at all) are likely not to vote in forthcoming elections.[17] The key in any election is to get larger numbers of peripheral voters into the voting booths.

DO COLLEGE STUDENTS VOTE IN CAMPUS ELECTIONS?

The turnout rates in student elections on most college campuses are quite low. At the University of Texas the students abolished their students' association in 1978, and in a vote to reestablish it in 1982, only 3905 students voted out of a total enrollment of 45,825. At the University of Kentucky only 2112 of the 23,000 students voted for a president of the student body in 1982. At Columbia College the 1983 elections for class president produced a turnout of less than 7 percent, while at Barnard College in 1984 a similar percentage voted for president of the freshman class.

How does your college compare?

Socioeconomic and demographic factors influencing participation

The most important *socioeconomic factors* influencing political participation are education, income, and occupation. The most important *demographic factors* are age, gender, race, ethnicity and language, and class.

Education. The key factor is education. Figure 5-6 shows the relationship between years of school completed and turnout rates in the 1980 presidential election. Note that as the number of years of school completed increases, the voting rates rise. Schools emphasize a citizen's obligation to vote, and they impart information which makes people feel more confident about participating in public affairs.

But an increase in the educational levels of the entire population has not led to an increase in turnouts; in fact, just the reverse occurred in the 1960s and 1970s. As the educational levels rose, turnouts fell. Clearly, other factors must have worked to drive turnouts down.

Figure 5-6. Education and turnout, 1980. Turnouts are higher among people who have completed more years of schooling. (Source: U.S. Bureau of the Census, *Current Population Reports*, Series P-20, no. 370.)

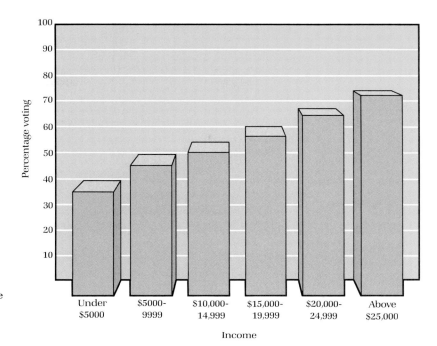

Figure 5-7. Income and turnout, 1980. Turnouts are higher among people with more income. (Source: U.S. Bureau of the Census, *Current Population Reports*, Series P-20, no. 370.)

Income. Higher income levels are associated with sharply increased rates of voting, as Figure 5-7 shows. This is due in part to the fact that more years of school completed are associated with higher income, and it is the schooling, rather than the income level, that is the important factor. People who have finished college vote at high rates no matter what their income.

Yet just as with education, increased income does not lead to larger turnouts. As the per capita wealth of the population increased in the past two decades, turnouts fell. And although real income had fallen for several years, turnouts in the 1982 congressional elections increased. This mirrors the dramatic rise in turnouts in the 1930s, when economic misery rather than prosperity brought people to the polls.

Occupation. Professionals and executives have the highest rates; managers and white-collar workers come next. They are followed by farmers; clerical, skilled, and service workers; unskilled workers; and farm laborers. The lower the occupation, the less education completed and the lower the income, all of which reinforces nonvoting.

Turnouts are especially low among those who have recently been laid off from work, a result of the blow to their self-esteem. The higher the short-term unemployment rate, the lower the turnout. In the 1980 elections only 50 percent of those who were unemployed reported registering, and only 41 percent reported voting—and it is likely that the actual voting rates were lower. Sometimes those who are most affected by worsening economic conditions are least likely to make their presence felt in elections.[18] At other times, such as during the great depression and in the 1982 congressional elections, the jobless have a respectable turnout (only 3 percent less than the employed in 1982).

Unionized workers vote at higher rates than nonunionized workers. Since the early 1970s union members have made up a declining proportion of the

labor force, now constituting less than one-fifth. This could account for millions of dropouts in the past decade, since formerly unionized workers and new unionized entrants into the labor force are not mobilized to vote by union shop stewards.

Recent transformations in the American economy may also affect turnout. Workers in thriving industries in the 1960s had a sense of job security and relative affluence. But in the 1970s, as their industries declined, many of these workers became insecure. New entrants to the work force could not obtain these good industrial jobs. Many found nonunion, lower-paying, seasonal, service employment, which requires lower levels of skill but involves higher levels of stress. Lower-paid workers who are seasonally unemployed are less likely to vote than higher-paid workers with steady jobs.

Age. Turnouts are much lower among younger people than among older people. In 1972, when those between the ages of 18 and 21 were given the vote, 11 million people entered the electorate. Their initial registration and voting rates were the lowest of any age group; only 48 percent voted in 1972, and in every subsequent election a lower percentage of people in this age group have registered and voted. In 1980 only 35 percent voted, and in 1984 only half even bothered to register. The young are less likely to vote because they are highly mobile; three-fifths of them move every two years, and they have few ties to their communities. But in the near future voting rates may increase: between 1987 and 1993 the number of people between ages of 18 and 31 will decline from 57 million to 53.5 million, and meanwhile the number between the ages of 32 and 38 will increase from 26.5 million to 29.5 million—which means that the population is aging and, other things being equal, older people are more likely to vote.

Gender. Turnouts were lower among women than among men until recently. Women were socialized to believe that politics was "men's business" or were discouraged from voting by their husbands or fathers. Times have changed, and gradually the turnout rates of men and women have converged. As Figure 5-8 shows, by 1972 women had just about ended the gender gap, and by 1980

Figure 5-8. Age and sex and turnout, 1980. Turnout rates are higher for women than men. The only exception is among women over 60, some of whom may not vote because they were brought up to believe that politics is "for men only." In another decade it is likely that women of all age groups will have higher turnout rates than men. (Source: U.S. Bureau of the Census, *Current Population Reports*, Series P-20, no. 370.)

women under 45 were voting at higher rates than men, giving women a higher overall turnout rate than men for the first time in American history. Since there are approximately 6 million more women than men in the eligible electorate, for the foreseeable future women will constitute a majority of those voting.

Still, many women do not vote, especially women who are members of minority groups, poor women, and working women (although the rates of women under 45 are higher than those of men under 45); only 30.4 percent of Hispanic women and 52 percent of black women voted in 1980. In the 1984 elections, the Women's Vote Project was organized by sixty-five national women's organizations to conduct a nonpartisan drive to register 1.5 million women and concentrate on lower-income working women and minorities.

Race. Because of the constitutional and legal barriers erected by southern states against blacks, until the 1970s their registration and turnout rates were far lower than those of the white majority. Since then the gap has narrowed, especially in the south, where participation of blacks equals or exceeds that of whites. In the remainder of the nation it is a different story. Turnouts among blacks decreased after 1968, to a low of 43.5 percent in 1980. But the increase in numbers is impressive: from 4 million registered in 1966 to 8 million in 1980. The successful mayoral candidacies of blacks in Chicago, Philadelphia, and other big cities in the 1980s—including Los Angeles, Detroit, New Orleans, Atlanta, Oakland, Newark, Birmingham, Richmond, and the District of Columbia—and the presidential primary campaign of Reverend Jesse Jackson in 1984 reversed the decade-long trend. Black registration increased by 573,000 between 1980 and 1982, by 600,000 in 1983, and by another 2 million in 1984.[19]

Turnouts have also increased because the Voting Rights Act, as amended in 1982 and subsequently interpreted by the courts, voided certain ways of organizing elections that made it unlikely that black candidates could win. These included at-large, multiple-slate, and other winner-take-all systems which allowed white majorities to shut out black minorities from political power. Instead, systems which created districts that black candidates could win in local and congressional elections (drawn to maximize the number of black voters) encouraged large turnouts among blacks, and these systems were increasingly in use in the 1980s.

Ethnicity and language. Studies have shown that among people whose native language is not English, a greater facility in reading and understanding English is associated with a greater likelihood of voting.[20] There are more than 15 million Hispanics in the United States, which makes them the second largest, and the fastest-growing, minority group in the nation. About 60 percent are of Mexican origin and are concentrated in the southwest; the remainder consist of Cubans in Florida, Central Americans in California and Texas, and Puerto Ricans in the northeast.

Hispanics have a median age of 23, compared with a median age of 25 for blacks and of 30 for whites. Their median family income in 1982 was $16,401, compared with $23,517 for whites and $13,266 for blacks. They have fewer years of schooling, and some have less facility in English. Many have chosen not to become citizens. Not surprisingly, these socioeconomic and demographic characteristics are associated with low rates of voting. Only 44 percent of Hispanics, or 6.6 million, are even eligible to vote.

Immediately following their naturalization at Miami's Orange Bowl in 1984, 10,000 new citizens register to vote. (*AP Worldwide Photos.*)

For the 1984 elections Hispanic organizations mounted registration drives in Texas, Florida, and California. The Republicans registered Cuban Americans in Dade County, Florida, where surveys show that 57 percent are Republicans and that only 16 percent are Democrats. Mexican-American mayors in Denver and San Antonio and a Cuban-American mayor in Miami spurred voter registration drives. The Southwest Voter Education Project and the Midwest Voter Registration Project conducted a $2 million drive to register Hispanics in the west, hoping to increase the total to 4.4 million registered and more than 3.6 million voting. As the proportion of Hispanics who are citizens, speak English well, are married and settled, and have completed high school increases greatly in this decade, the number of Hispanics who vote will also increase markedly. By the year 2000 there will be 30 million Hispanics in the United States, about 12 percent of the total population, and as they show up at the polls in larger numbers, they will transform the politics of the southwest, just as voting by blacks has changed the politics of the south and of the cities of the north.

Class. Between 1960 and 1980 as many as 15 million white middle-class and working-class people dropped out of the electorate or decided to vote only occasionally; thus a new group of peripheral voters emerged. Most of these voters are concentrated in the large northern industrial states.[21] This shift from the core to the periphery of the electorate increased *class polarization* among white voters: the tendency to divide along *class* lines. Increasingly, voters were the affluent and well educated, and nonvoters were the less affluent and less well educated. In 1980 people who described themselves as "working-class" voted at a 40 percent rate, while self-identified members of the "upper middle class" voted at a 70 percent rate.[22]

151

Some observers have pointed out that class polarization in the 1970s was no greater than it was in the 1950s and that it was sharply reduced in the mid-1980s; thus these changes from one decade to the next should be put in perspective. Also, as some working-class whites dropped out of the core electorate, their places were taken by blacks and Hispanics.

Socioeconomic and demographic factors: A caution. The data presented thus far show that people with different characteristics—race, income, education, occupation, and age—have different rates of registration and voting. There is nothing inevitable about these rates. There is no natural or sociological "law" which says that some kinds of people will always participate less than others. In New York City, two-thirds of the Puerto Ricans are unregistered, while in Puerto Rico the turnout rates among all groups exceed those on the mainland. In Miami when a Cuban-American mayor ran for reelection in 1981, the turnout of Hispanics exceeded that of whites. In Atlanta in 1981 the turnout of blacks was equal to that of whites when Andrew Young, a black candidate, ran successfully for mayor. Black turnout rates in primaries exceeded those of whites in many states in 1984, when Jesse Jackson ran for president. Socioeconomic correlations can describe rates of voting among different people, but they cannot tell us why rates differ or when rates will change.

Political factors influencing participation

Deciding to vote or not to vote, to register or not to register, is political behavior, and it is shaped by attitudes toward politics. Nonvoters have somewhat different political attitudes from those of voters; these include party identification and conservative versus liberal attitudes toward government policies.

Party identification. The stronger a person's identification with a major political party, the more likely that person is to vote. The people who are most likely to vote are strong Republicans, followed by weak Republicans and independents who lean toward the Republican Party. Strong, weak, and independent Democrats are less likely to vote. People who claim to be independent of the parties and have no identification with them are least likely to vote. The data are summarized in Figure 5-9.

Figure 5-9. Party identification and turnout, 1980. Strong Republicans and Democrats have the highest turnout rates, followed by weak and independent Republicans, then by weak and independent Democrats. Pure independents have the lowest turnout rates. (Source: Center for Political Studies of the Institute for Social Research, University of Michigan.)

Of those who vote, Republicans are more likely than Democrats to remain in the core electorate. A 1976 survey indicated that 68 percent of the Democrats, compared with 79 percent of the Republicans, reported voting in all or most presidential elections, while 18 percent of the Democrats reported voting in some elections, compared with 14 percent of the Republicans.[23]

A common misconception is that most nonvoters are Democrats. Democrats hold a slight margin among unregistered men (38 to 43 percent) and a greater margin among unregistered women (31 to 48 percent), but the lead is not overwhelming, and it decreased shortly before the 1984 elections. Most youthful voters, again contrary to popular belief, are not Democrats: among the 14 million unregistered people between the ages of 18 and 24, Republicans hold a slight edge (42 to 41 percent). Again, among the 4 million unregistered college graduates, Republicans hold their own against Democrats (44 to 44 percent). Republicans therefore concentrate their voter registration drives on young men, especially those with good jobs and a college education. Democrats are more likely to gain among women, minorities, and those without a college education.

Liberalism versus conservatism. Most voters consider themselves liberal (favoring a large role for government and innovation in policy-making), conservative (favoring a smaller role for government and more traditional policies), or moderate. Self-described liberals and conservatives have the same voting rate, which is somewhat higher than that of moderates or of those who describe themselves as "very conservative." From a sample of unregistered people who were asked to describe their orientation, we can project that, among all the unregistered, 9 million are liberals, 16 million are moderates, and 13 million are conservatives.[24]

Conservatives have often argued that if the millions of nonvoters could be mobilized for a cause, their side would benefit. Liberals have made the same argument for their side. But the data indicate that if all the nonvoters did register and vote, there would be little change in the moderate to conservative politics of American life. Polls have shown little difference between voters and nonvoters on the issues of abortion, taxes, defense spending, and the Equal Rights Amendment. Major change would occur, however, if a party or cause registered its supporters, while other nonvoters remained unregistered.

EXPLAINING THE TURNOUT RATES

Thus far this chapter has discussed registration and turnout rates in historical and comparative perspective and has described in socioeconomic and political terms the characteristics of voters and nonvoters. But such *descriptions* are not *analysis:* we know who votes and who does not vote, but not why; and we do not know why rates rise and fall. To analyze voting and nonvoting, we need to isolate differences in attitudes between voters and nonvoters. For anyone interested in political office or power, an explanation of these differences offers the possibility of new strategies and tactics to mobilize supporters.

Is the electorate disillusioned?

People may feel negatively about politics: they may believe that "the system" is rigged and corrupt and benefits other people or groups at their expense, and if they decide that the system is no longer legitimate, they become alienated from it. Or they may lose trust in politicians, considering them corrupt, incom-

A casual observer at this New York polling place might conclude that turnout is heavy, but antiquated procedures can snarl even a short line. (*Richard Hackett.*)

petent, or evil, which erodes the authority relationship. They may believe in the system and in their leaders, but oppose some of the policies of the government. They may lose interest in politics and become apathetic.

The alienated: Mistrust of government. Mistrust of government and politicians has increased in the past two decades.[25] Figure 5-10 shows that this mistrust has been paralleled by a loss of confidence in most other institutions.

It would be misleading to assume from these data that such attitudes directly affect registration and turnouts. Studies conducted by the National Opinion Research Center in 1977 and 1978 found few differences between voters and nonvoters (Figure 5-11). Nonvoters were more likely than voters to agree that "people running the country do not care what happens to you" (60

Figure 5-10. The decline of confidence in institutions, 1966, 1971–1981. In 1966 and from 1971 to 1981, the Harris survey used the following question to poll opinion about major institutions of American society: "As far as people in charge of running _____ are concerned, would you say you have a great deal of confidence, only some confidence, or hardly any confidence at all in them?" Results for four of the institutions are shown here. (Source: Data from Harris survey, 22 October 1981, no. 85; used with permission of Chicago Tribune-New York News Syndicate.)

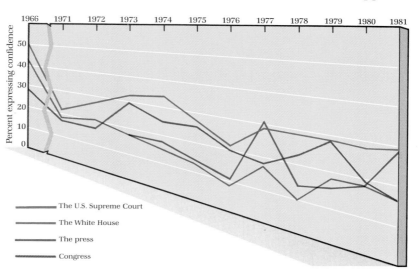

The U.S. Supreme Court

The White House

The press

Congress

Figure 5-11. Increase in suspicion of government, 1964–1980. People were polled in election year on the following questions: (1) "Would you say the government is pretty much run by a few big interests looking out for themselves or that it is run for the benefit of all the people?" (2) "How much of the time do you think you can trust the government in Washington to do what is right—just about always, most of the time, or only some of the time?" (3) "Do you feel that almost all of the people running the government are smart people, or do you think that quite a few of them don't seem to know what they are doing?" (Source: Surveys by Center for Political Studies of the Institute for Social Research, University of Michigan Election Studies, latest that of April 1980; graph adapted from *Public Opinion*, June/July 1981.)

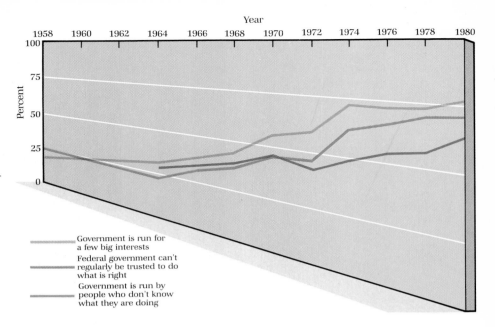

to 50 percent), and they were more likely to agree that "public officials are not interested in problems facing the average person" (72 to 62 percent). But on most other questions, such as "people in Washington are out of touch with the rest of the country," there were hardly any differences between the two groups. Similarly, Louis Harris Associates found virtually no difference between voters and nonvoters in levels of confidence or in the leaders of major institutions.

The apathetic: No enthusiasm for candidates. Low turnouts might be due to lack of enthusiasm for the candidates. The 1980 Census Bureau survey of nonvoters, for example, found that 47 percent did not prefer a candidate or were not interested in the election and that 27 percent of those who were registered but did not vote also felt that way. Such apathy could account for as many as 21 million nonvoters.[26] Since 1952 the Gallup organization has polled voters in the summer of each presidential election year. Its interviewers hand respondents a "scalometer" card with ten boxes, numbered from +5 on the top to 0 in the middle and down to −5 at the bottom. The respondent marks +5 to indicate the highest opinion of a candidate and −5 to indicate the lowest opinion. For every election between 1952 and 1980, with the exception of that in 1976, the trend has been downward, as Figure 5-12 makes clear.

Again, we should not conclude that apathy about candidates causes low turnouts. The Census Bureau survey shows that only one-ninth of the registered nonvoters had no preference among candidates. Some studies have shown that there is little or no difference between voters and nonvoters in terms of their feelings about candidates.[27]

The dissatisfied: Disagreement with policies. Some people may leave the core electorate or become nonvoters because they disagree with government policies. Minorities and the poor may think that government favors the white working class and middle class; the white working class and middle class may

Figure 5-12. Perceptions of presidential candidates, 1952–1980: percentage of respondents to the Gallup Poll giving highly favorable ratings to presidential candidates. (Source: *The New York Times*, 31 October 1980.)

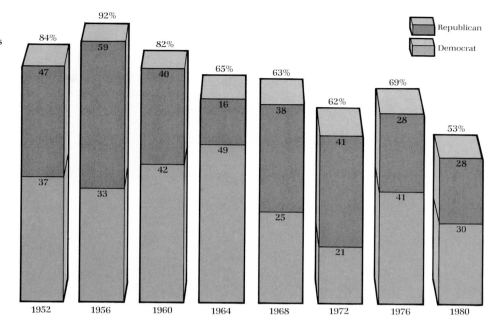

think that government is oriented toward minorities and the poor. Hawks may want the government to take a stronger stand against communism; doves may oppose any American interventions in foreign countries. Profamily groups and religious fundamentalists may believe that the government's policies favor the side of those whose views are more humanist and secular, and vice versa.

But again, there seems to be little difference between voters and nonvoters here. And there is little difference between the poor and minorities who choose to vote and those who do not or between white core voters who have dropped out of the electorate and those who have not. One could also argue that dissatisfaction with government policies can just as easily lead to larger turnouts and a protest vote as to smaller turnouts—something that seemed true in the 1984 presidential election.

Mobilizing large numbers of nonvoters around dissatisfaction with issues seems to be the Holy Grail of presidential politics. Conservatives like Barry Goldwater in 1964 argued that there were millions of disaffected people just waiting for a conservative presidential candidate; he expected them to come out of the woodwork and propel him to victory, but they never appeared and he was crushed in the election. George McGovern in 1972 thought that there were millions of disaffected liberals who were eagerly awaiting his candidacy to come back to the polls; he expected to get 60 percent of the young people (who he thought were antiwar liberals and radicals) to vote and to get at least 60 percent of their vote. Instead, only 40 percent turned out, and of these, only 40 percent voted for him. In the 1980s the religious and conservative groups of the new right argued that millions of religious fundamentalists could be mobilized to vote for right-wing candidates for the presidency and Congress, while social welfare activists on the liberal and left radical end of the political spectrum believed that millions of the poor would go to the polls in protest against

Reaganomics and completely reshape public priorities, from the military to social welfare. Both groups were disappointed.

Social scientists find little evidence to support such assumptions. On most issues, either nonvoters hold opinions that are virtually identical to those of voters, or they have weak opinions or no opinions at all.[28] Sometimes voters are more liberal than nonvoters and sometimes they are more conservative, depending on the issue. On most issues voters represent the attitudes of the entire population. Surveys taken in the 1970s, when participation was declining, show that there was little difference of opinion between voters and nonvoters. Yet it may well be that in the 1980s, after years of cutbacks, retrenchment, and conservative domestic and foreign policies, the poor and minority nonvoters have a quite different political agenda from that of the majority of voters.

The cynical: Voting does not matter. Some people believe that voting is meaningless. Arthur Hadley labels these people *refrainers* and argues that they are disgusted with politics and politicians because they believe that their own values and ethics are not reflected in a corrupt system. Most of these people are white, are middle-class, and have strong ethical or religious values.[29] In 1984 many of them were mobilized by fundamentalist religious leaders, and more than 2 million registered to vote for the first time—most in the Republican Party.

The powerless: Loss of efficacy. Some voters and nonvoters differ significantly in their feelings of *efficacy:* their belief that they can successfully influence politicians. The Survey Research Center asked a national sample questions which measured feelings of efficacy, and it found that since 1960 the trend has been downward for the entire population.

The greatest declines in feelings of efficacy are associated with the movement from core to peripheral voting and with dropping out of the electorate. One study showed that a decrease in feelings of efficacy accounts for 30 percent of the drop in turnout since 1960.[30] The way to get more people to the polls is to convince them that they can make a difference and that politicians will have to respond to their needs. An increase in feelings of efficacy can be promoted by candidates for office, as Franklin Roosevelt managed to do with his coalition of religious minorities, the poor, and the unemployed in the 1930s and as Jesse Jackson did with racial and ethnic minorities in 1984, with his "I am somebody" slogan.

The mass media: Impact on participation

The two-way flow of political communication—between leaders and the electorate—may also offer a partial explanation for fluctuations in turnouts.

Communicating to voters. The American people have changed their reading and viewing habits in the past two decades. Surveys have shown that people who rely on newspapers or news magazines obtain more factual information than those who rely on thirty minutes of televised network or local news. A front-page article in a serious newspaper contains 10 to 20 times as much information as a one-minute feature on the nightly news.

The print and the broadcast media present political events differently: the print media emphasize issues and try to put events into context and give them

Computerized direct-mail techniques can reach millions of voters, as shown by Richard Viguerie, who handles conservative candidates and causes. (*David Burnett: Contact.*)

larger meaning. They offer editorial opinion and comment by columnists. The better papers have op-ed pages that feature contributions from politicians, civic leaders, and academics. Broadcasts give a brief summary of the day's events, often without providing any context, background, or comparative perspective. They emphasize visual excitement and personalities, but often they leave the viewer with an emotional rather than a reasoned response to a story and with the impression that politics involves a series of random, disconnected, and violent events with little meaning.

More than two-thirds of the public rely primarily on news broadcasts for information or politics. Studies indicate that as much as 20 percent of the decline in voter turnout can be attributed to the changeover from reading to viewing, presumably because the broadcast media provide less information than the print media and leave people more confused.[31]

Communicating with politicians. Campaigning has always been a form of entertainment. Once it involved face-to-face contact between voters and candidates. Parades, marches, ballgames, and picnics were organized by parties. Local party workers passed around ribbons, buttons, and leaflets to people in their neighborhoods. They asked people to vote for candidates, and they were in the neighborhoods on election day to make sure that their friends went to the polls. Today candidates use political commercials, phone banks, and direct mail to communicate with voters; face-to-face communication has disappeared. It is easier to drop out of the electorate when there is no one to answer to. It is easier to believe that "no one cares" when politicians are just images on the screen—when their messages are no different from advertisements for soap or sodas.

Studies have shown that turnouts in poorer neighborhoods in the early twentieth century were high because these neighborhoods were organized by strong local parties. At the Joint Center for Political Studies, researchers have found that registration campaigns among black voters were most effective when they were controlled by party groups which could follow up with election-day efforts to pull voters to the polls.

Chloroforming the electorate. Some efforts at communication involve at-

tempts to keep voters away from the polls. "Some of the tactics we use in political campaigns do very much suppress the vote," admitted Robert Squier, a consultant for the Democratic Party.[32] Commercials may try to play on voters' apathy, alienation, or feelings of inefficacy in an effort to reduce turnout in opposition strongholds. The key to such efforts at communication is to use commercials which cast doubt on the character and integrity of opposition candidates or which try to weaken the party loyalty of opposition voters.

THINGS TO COME

COMPUTER DEMOCRACY. Turnouts are once again increasing, as we saw in the congressional elections of 1982 and the presidential election of 1984. The development of new campaign technologies should maintain this trend.

Media "narrowcasting." The proliferation of radio and cable and of low-power and satellite television stations means that more stations appeal to narrow segments of the community. There are stations for minorities (known as *urban contemporary* or *inner-city* stations), for suburbanites, for immigrants, and for non-English-speaking minorities. Often these stations put on "get out the vote" drives, and increasingly these are being sponsored by major corporations. Modern advertising techniques applied to voter registration have the potential to increase turnouts among young voters.

"Merge and purge" computerized drives. Many organizations that are interested in issues have sponsored voter registration drives. The traditional "shoe leather" approach involves canvassing neighborhoods or setting up booths where pedestrian traffic is heavy; the Republican Party's "Reagan roundups" of potential voters in 1984 are an example. New computerized technology is aiding these efforts. A local group can obtain lists of registered voters. It can match these lists against car registrations, magazine subscription lists, new utility hookups in suburban developments, and census tracts. The various lists are "merged and purged," and everyone who is already registered is removed. The remaining nonvoters can be sorted by neighborhood, income, race, religion, ethnicity, occupation, and social class; this enables each party to concentrate on those who are most likely to support its candidates. The computer can then automatically dial a number and connect a party worker with one of these nonvoters, simultaneously displaying information about the person on the monitor. Or it can play a recorded "get out the vote" pitch or even a recorded message from a prominent politician. In 1984 computerized drives worked very effectively for the Republican Party, which dominated new registrations in important sun belt states.[33]

Interactive media. In the next two decades other technological changes in the area of ***interactive media*** have the potential to transform our electoral processes dramatically. From the ballot box of the past to the modern voting machine, we have relied on primitive mechanical methods of registering voters and counting votes. In the future it will be possible to register voters by using telephone links to central computers or by using a home computer or a "two-way" cable television hookup (which permits a viewer to send a message to a central computer).

Interactive communication. A crucial change will come when interactive television becomes a familiar household amenity. By pushing buttons, viewers can shop, bank, make plane or theater reservations, and even take college courses—all in their own homes. The implications of interactive television were noted as early as 1961, when Buckminster Fuller (an inventor best known for the geodesic dome) argued that "with two-way TV, constant referendum of democracy will be

The next century may well see "push-button voting." Already Warner Communications' QUBE system conducts public opinion polls for local cablecasters. (*Michael Abramson: © Warner Amex Cable Communications.*)

manifest, and democracy will become the most practical form of industrial and space-age government by all people, for all people."

Warner Communications has developed the QUBE system for cable television. Viewers press buttons on their hand-held consoles, and their opinions on any subject are recorded by the studio's central computer. Within minutes, the results of an opinion poll can be flashed onto the television screen, and viewers can see how everyone else responded—and so can pollsters and politicians. In Columbus, Ohio, local officials used the station to conduct a poll that determined the city's snow-removal plans; the viewers told the mayor that they did not want to pay higher city taxes just to get the streets cleared sooner.

Push-button voting? Interactive systems could be used for election-day voting. The ballot could appear on television, and the votes could be transmitted over telephone or cable lines to a central computer. People could use special identifying codes (much as they safeguard themselves when using a bank money machine or a long-distance telephone service), which they would be given when they registered to vote.

Before we assume that electronic registration and voting are just around the corner, we should recognize some of the problems. First, the cable technologies are expensive—the push-button mechanisms and cable boxes cost as much as $300, and two-way cable services cost $50 or more per month. Unless the government decided to give them to everyone (which could cost as much as $1000 per household, or $70 billion), access would be limited to those who could afford them. We would then have a two-tier system: home voting by the affluent and voting at the polls by the poor. Other problems include fraud by people voting at home, stealing elections by tampering with the central computers, and ways to preserve privacy and prevent any pressuring of voters at home. If these problems can be surmounted, interactive media could transform registration and voting, leading to much higher rates of voting (especially among the elderly and disabled and those who are away from home). But these changes are not likely to occur before the year 2000, and a national system of home voting is probably least likely. It is more likely that politicians will use nonbinding public opinion polls on a regular basis to gather information; yet if such systems are instituted in the next two decades, they will in effect become "votes" that influence politics just as much as the real votes that elect people to office.[34]

IN CONCLUSION

A small majority of eligible Americans vote for president, and the percentage of eligible voters who vote for candidates for other offices is even lower. Of all the western democracies, the United States holds the most elections, asks the most of its voters—and has the lowest rates of registration and turnout.

Those who register and vote often differ significantly from those who vote infrequently or have dropped out of the electorate. Better-educated, wealthier, older people have higher voting rates, as do women, whites, and those who are strongly identified with a party (especially Republicans). Minorities, the young, the unemployed, and nonunionized workers have the lowest rates of voting. Alienation and apathy, although widespread, do not distinguish voters from nonvoters; voters, however, believe that they can act effectively in politics and nonvoters do not.

The outlook for mass participation by the electorate in the near future is improving. Massive voter registration drives, aided by computer technologies, the aging of the electorate, and the elimination of remaining discriminatory practices, led to the increases in turnout in the 1982 and 1984 national elections. In the more distant future, new technological developments may dramatically transform the entire election process and lead to much higher rates of participation and a renewed emphasis on direct democracy.

NOTES

1. Aristotle, *Politics*, Clarendon Press, Oxford, 1948, book 4, chap. 2, pp. 262–267.
2. *Public Opinion*, vol. 44, April–May 1980, p. 32; see also Seymour Martin Lipset, *Political Man*, Doubleday, Garden City, N.Y., 1960, part 2.
3. Arthur T. Hadley, *The Empty Polling Booth*, Prentice-Hall, Englewood Cliffs, N.J., 1978, p. 106; see also E. E. Schattschneider, *The Semi-Sovereign People*, Holt, New York, 1960.
4. Curtis B. Gans, "The Empty Ballot Box," *Public Opinion*, September–October 1978, p. 34.
5. Pericles, "Funeral Oration," in Thucydides, *The Peloponnesian Wars*.
6. David B. Magleby, *Direct Legislation: Voting on Ballot Propositions in the United States*, Johns Hopkins, Baltimore, 1984.
7. Lee Sigelman, "The Nonvoting Voter in Voting Research," *American Journal of Political Science*, vol. 26, no. 1, February 1982, pp. 47–55.
8. *Public Opinion*, vol. 44, April–May 1980, p. 33; see also John R. Petrocik, "Voter Turnout and Electoral Oscillation," *American Politics Quarterly*, vol. 9, no. 2, April 1981, pp. 161–180.
9. Richard W. Boyd, "Decline of U.S. Voter Turnout," *American Politics Quarterly*, vol. 9, no. 2, April 1981, pp. 133–136.
10. *Guinn v. United States*, 238 U.S. 347 (1915).
11. U.S. Commission on Civil Rights, *The Voting Rights Act: Unfinished Goals*, GPO, Washington, D.C., 1982, pp. 22–37.
12. *Harper v. Virginia State Board of Elections*, 383 U.S. 663 (1966).
13. Raymond Wolfinger and Steven Rosenstone, *Who Votes?* Yale University Press, New Haven, Conn., 1980, p. 88.
14. Steven Rosenstone and Raymond Wolfinger, "The Effect of Registration Laws on Voter Turnouts," *American Political Science Review*, vol. 72, March 1978, p. 33.
15. Hadley, op. cit., p. 17.
16. This concept was developed in Boyd, op. cit.
17. Michael W. Traugott and Clyde Tucker, "Strategies for Predicting whether a Citizen Will Vote and Estimation of Electoral Outcomes," *Public Opinion Quarterly*, vol. 48, no. 1, spring 1984, pp. 332–334.
18. Steven J. Rosenstone, "Economic Adversity and Voter Turnout," *American Journal of Political Science*, vol. 26, no. 1, February 1982, p. 438.

19. Data from Joint Center for Political Studies.
20. Carlos Arce, *Language Proficiency and Other Correlates of Voting by Mexican Origin Citizens*, University of Michigan, Survey Research Center, Ann Arbor, 1982.
21. Howard L. Reiter, "Why Is Turnout Down?" *Public Opinion Quarterly*, vol. 43, no. 3, fall 1979, pp. 297–311.
22. Data from William A. Crotty, *American Parties in Decline*, 2d ed., Little, Brown, Boston, 1984, table 1.4, p. 14.
23. Data from University of Michigan, Survey Research Center, Ann Arbor.
24. Data from Crotty, op. cit., and New York Times/CBS polls, 1983–1984.
25. Seymour Martin Lipset, *The Confidence Gap*, Free Press, New York, 1984, p. 15.
26. Bureau of the Census, "Voting and Registration in the Election of 1980," ser. P-20, no. 359, p. 113.
27. William Maddox, "Candidate Images among Voters and Non-Voters in 1976," *American Politics Quarterly*, vol. 18, no. 2, April 1980, pp. 209–220.
28. Wolfinger and Rosenstone, op. cit., p. 109.
29. Hadley, op. cit.
30. Stephen D. Shaeffer, "A Multivariate Explanation of Decreasing Turnout in Presidential Elections, 1960–1976," *American Journal of Political Science*, vol. 25, no. 1, February 1981, pp. 68–93.
31. Ibid.
32. Thomas Edsall, "How to Keep Voters Away from the Polls," *Washington Post National Weekly Edition*, May 14, 1984.
33. Thomas Edsall, "The GOP's Registration Coup," *Washington Post National Weekly Edition*, Oct. 1, 1984.
34. Susan D. Weil and Richard M. Pious, "Emerging New Technologies: Political Applications," report to the Sloan Foundation Commission on the Presidential Selection Process, Sept. 30, 1983.

FURTHER READING

Amundsen, Kirsten: *A New Look at the Silenced Majority*, Prentice-Hall, Englewood Cliffs, N.J., 1977. A study of nonvoting.
Hadley, Arthur T.: *The Empty Polling Booth*, Prentice-Hall, Englewood Cliffs, N.J., 1978. Ideas on what makes nonvoters tick.
Kimball, Penn: *The Disconnected*, Columbia University Press, New York, 1972. A pioneering study of nonvoters in urban centers.
Lane, Robert E.: *Political Life*, Free Press, New York, 1959. A historical analysis of turnouts in the United States and other democracies, with useful comments on the role of the media.

Lipset, Seymour Martin: *Political Man*, Doubleday, Garden City, N.Y., 1960. A consideration of political behavior. Part 2 compares the United States with other democracies and argues that larger turnouts might lead to political instability.

Scott, Anne F., and Andrew M. Scott (eds.): *One-Half the People*, University of Illinois Press, Urbana, 1983. A study of the fight for women's suffrage.

U.S. Commission on Civil Rights: *The Voting Rights Act: Unfinished Goals*, GPO, Washington, D.C., 1982. A discussion of racial discrimination and its effects on turnouts in the 1980s.

Wolfinger, Raymond, and Steven Rosenstone: *Who Votes?* Yale University Press, New Haven, Conn., 1980. A consideration of voting behavior, debunking many social science theories about the causes of low turnouts and describing the impact of changes in registration laws in the 1970s.

USEFUL SOURCES

Burnham, Walter Dean: *Presidential Ballots, 1836–1892*, Johns Hopkins, Baltimore, 1955. Statistics on the popular vote and the electoral vote.

Kinnell, Susan, et al.: *The American Electorate: A Historical Bibliography*, ABC-CLIO Information Services, Santa Barbara, Calif., 1984. Lists sources on suffrage and turnout.

Robinson, E. E.: *The Presidential Vote: 1896–1932*, Stanford University Press, Stanford, Calif., 1947. Statistics on the popular vote and the electoral vote.

Scammon, Richard: *America at the Polls*, Governmental Affairs Institute, Washington, D.C., 1920–1964. Election statistics.

———et al. (eds.): *America Votes: A Handbook of Contemporary American Election Statistics*, Congressional Quarterly Press, Washington, D.C., biannually. Statistics on national elections, useful for calculating turnouts.

U.S. Bureau of the Census: *Voting and Registration in the Election of November 1984*, issued after each presidential election.

ORGANIZATIONS

Committee for the Study of the American Electorate. 421 New Jersey Avenue, S.E., Washington, D.C. 20003. For more information phone 202-471-1539.

Project Vote. 1200 Fifteenth Street, N.W., Suite 201, Washington, D.C. 20005. A coalition of groups that conduct nonpartisan voter registration drives. For more information phone 202-293-3933.

Southwest Voter Registration and Education Project. 201 N. St. Mary, Suite 501, San Antonio, Texas 78205. Reports on minority voting in the southwest. For more information phone 512-222-0224.

Voter Education Project. 52 Fairlie St., N.W., Atlanta, Georgia 30303. Reports on minority voting in the south. For more information telephone 404-522-7495.

From Cook County's Democratic organization
to the Republican National convention of
1984, there are many ways to participate in
party politics. (*D. Goldberg: Sygma; Kevin
Horan: Picture Group.*)

PARTIES AND PACS: FROM OLD POLITICS TO NEW

Americans have always been ambivalent about political parties. "A good party is better than the best man that ever lived," said Thomas Reed, the Speaker of the House, at the end of the nineteenth century; but George Washington, in his farewell address to the nation, had warned of "the baneful effect of the spirit of party," and an antiparty spirit has been with us ever since.[1]

The Constitution makes no mention of parties. But the constitutional arrangements which preclude parties in theory almost require them in fact. Without them, how could a majority form in the electoral college to choose a president? How could Congress form majorities to pass legislation? Washington himself did nothing to discourage his followers from creating the Federalist Party, and James Madison, who in the Federal papers had written so eloquently of "curing the mischief of faction" (that is, party spirit), was one of the founders of the Anti-Federalist Party. Even those who have opposed parties in theory have found them indispensable in practice.

PARTIES: DEFINITIONS AND CHARACTERISTICS

A *political party* is an organization whose goal is to elect its members to public office. In the United States it is a private association, although it performs public functions. It differs from an *interest group* (which is also a private association) in that the goal of the latter is to affect policy, and to do this it elects its friends to office. The goal of a party is to win elections, and its means of accomplishing this involve policy.

Parties differ from *campaign organizations*, such as polling or advertising agencies: parties are organized to contest elections in a particular area—a city, a county, or a state—while professional campaign organizations go anywhere they are hired to go in order to help candidates win elections.

The people in parties

A party consists of three parts: the party-in-government, the party-in-the-electorate, and the party organization.

The *party-in-government* is made up of the elected or appointed officials who hold public office and belong to the party—the president and the Cabinet, other top administration appointees, members of Congress, state governors, state legislators, mayors, members of city councils, and the like. There are about 3000 elected and appointed officials in the national government and 600,000 or so in the state and local governments.

The *party-in-the-electorate* consists of voters who are identified with the party and (depending on state law) who are registered as party members. Of the 174 million people who were eligible to vote in 1984, about 125 million registered, and most identified themselves as Democrats or Republicans. Parties have open membership: the voter decides whether to join when registering to vote and cannot be kept out by party officials. The party cannot drop anyone from membership. It does not limit participation in party affairs or votes in party elections to an elite group, and in this respect American parties differ from most foreign parties, which set stiff membership requirements and can "purge" members who do not follow the party line.

Table 6-1. Activity of the electorate, 1980

Voted	53.2%
Attended political meetings, rallies, etc.	7%
Worked for a party or a candidate	4%
Gave money to a presidential candidate	6%

Source: Center for Political Studies.

The *party organization* consists of people who campaign and help candidates win elections but who usually do *not* themselves hold public office. As of 1980 only 3 percent of the public had ever belonged to a political party organization.[2] Table 6-1 summarizes other party activities.

We are a nation of joiners, but not when it comes to parties. Fewer than 1 percent of us currently belong to a party organization, compared with the 30 to 40 percent of voters who join community and civic organizations.

Functions of parties

Parties recruit people to run for public office. They limit the number of serious candidates to those nominated by the two major parties, which simplifies the choice for voters. They set priorities in elections by emphasizing some issues and ignoring others. The party in power holds itself accountable to voters for its conduct in office, while the opposition party gives voters an alternative: they can replace the incumbents with the challengers.

Parties provide a link between voters and the government by giving people the opportunity to voice their discontent to party workers. They mobilize voters and help increase turnouts. They organize the government to bridge the formal separation of powers, making it possible for party members to work together even though they are in different branches.

Responsible parties. There are two ways in which parties can perform these functions. One is for each party to be organized around a set of principles, develop its program from them, and offer a clear alternative to voters. The party should be prepared to implement the program in its entirety if it wins.[3]

Coalition parties. American parties rarely organize around consistent principles. Instead, they create coalitions from a variety of racial, religious, ethnic, sectional, cultural, and occupational constituencies. Coalition parties often embrace groups with competing interests, which requires them to put principles in second place. The New Deal coalition, organized by the Democrats in the 1930s, contained white racists and blacks, antiunion businesspeople and union members, conservatives opposing and liberals favoring regulation of business and greater expenditures for social welfare, and those favoring and those opposing a greater role for the national government. Republicans since the 1930s have included Main Street businesspeople who want low interest rates and Wall Street bankers who accept higher rates; sun belt and snow belt politicians who are competing for the same defense contracts and public works; and supply-siders who want tax cuts and fiscal conservatives who want tax increases.

CONVERGENCE. To keep a coalition intact, principles must be compromised, extreme positions moderated, and divisive issues submerged. Our parties span a continent and must appeal to a majority coalition fashioned from more than 180 million people of voting age. They usually win by appealing to a broad middle ground, although the Republicans move toward the center from a con-

servative position, and the Democrats move toward the center from a liberal one. Even when parties make appeals to principles, once they are in office, they are likely to depart from them. In the last two decades, supposedly liberal Democratic administrations increased defense spending, became involved in foreign wars, cut taxes for businesses and increased their subsidies, and by 1978 called for retrenchment in spending for social welfare. Supposedly conservative Republican administrations in the 1970s ended the Vietnamese war, cut the size of the military, negotiated arms agreements with the Soviets, made diplomatic overtures to communist China, and imposed wage-price controls on the economy, while presiding over a massive increase in spending for social welfare. In the 1980s the most conservative Republican administration in modern times ran up the largest deficits in history and got Congress to enact major tax cuts.[4]

DIVERGENCE. But convergence has its limits. The Republicans remain positioned to the right of center, and the Democrats to the left of center, and since 1980 they have diverged rather than converged. Thirty years ago the Democratic party-in-the-electorate was spread equally among all income groups; in the 1980s it has become increasingly the party of lower-income people, families with a female head of household, minorities, and liberals. In the same period the Republican party-in-the-electorate has gone from being only slightly skewed to upper-income families to a situation in which more than half of its membership consists of families whose income puts them in the top third. The changes in the parties' constituencies give them incentives to propose different economic and social policies.

Party structure: Key principles

American parties mirror the formal structure of government: they are federalized, decentralized, and split into legislative, executive, and judicial wings. These structural arrangements prevent the party organization from controlling the party-in-government.

Federal structure. The national parties are coalitions of fifty state parties, which in turn are coalitions of county and local parties.[5] Historically, the national party, as one local leader put it, "meets as infrequently as possible, decides as little as possible, establishes no public policy whatsoever, but does manage to hold a convention every four years."[6] Parties are organized horizontally rather than vertically: there are no "higher" or "lower" units. On most matters the national party cannot give orders to state parties, and state parties cannot give orders to county and local parties. All units of the party are autonomous and can deal with other units as equals—and so can their leaders.[7]

Executive, legislative, and judicial parties. The parties are organized around the major institutions of the national government and the state governments. The president, governors, and mayors—and their key appointees—form the "executive party," the members of Congress and state legislatures form the "legislative party," and candidates for state and local judgeships form the "judicial party."[8]

State and local party organization

The two national parties are organized from the bottom up rather than from the top down, in **party committees** which compete for public office. Those in villages, towns, townships, and cities compete for mayoral and city council

posts. The members of county committees compete for county executive and legislative posts, for state judgeships, and for positions as prosecutors and sheriffs. The members of state committees compete for the offices of governor, lieutenant governor, attorney general, treasurer, and other statewide positions (including United States senator). The members of congressional district committees compete for seats in the House.

Choosing candidates for the party-in-government. There are three ways in which a ***candidate*** is chosen, depending on the state election laws: *designation* by a party committee, nomination by a *convention* to which registered party voters have chosen delegates, and nomination by a *primary* in which registered party voters (and sometimes independents) have participated.

Selecting the party organization. The members of these party committees are chosen in party elections, at conventions, or by the designation of other party committees. Party elections are organized in precincts (known in some states as *election districts*); a ***precinct*** is a small geographic area containing close to 1000 voters (nationwide there are 188,432 precincts). Each holds elections for party and public office, and each has a ballot box or voting machine, a list of registered voters, and election officials. The party's registered voters in each precinct choose a precinct committeeman and a precinct committeewoman (depending on state law, the names of these positions may differ) to represent the precinct on the party's county committee. (Nationwide there are 3041 counties, about sixty in each state.) That committee, in turn, elects a county leader. Either the precincts or the county committee selects members to serve on other party committees (unless state law requires a primary).

MACHINES AND RINGS

Between 1840 and 1960 machines and rings dominated party politics. They were controlled by party bosses, without formal education, who went into politics because they had few other opportunities. They were neighborhood leaders with followings in the streets. They gained control of one or more precincts and formed alliances with others like them to dominate city and county party committees.

The machine had precinct workers and a ***precinct captain,*** who could bring out the vote. In rural areas they would report directly to the county leader; in urban areas the district leader or ward leader (whose area comprised about ten to thirty precincts that elected a member of the state legislature or city council) controlled the precinct captains. Together the leaders and the precinct captains constituted the ***urban machine*** or ***county courthouse ring:*** they were interested as much in the gain from politics as in the game of politics—in living off politics rather than for it.

The machine nominated candidates for public office, or if conventions did the nominating, it made sure that its people were elected to the convention. If a primary was used, the machine would bring its supporters to the polls. Machines rigged party and general elections in the nineteenth century. They paid "venal voters," and, as James Michael Curley, the mayor of Boston, observed, "Some of the bosses also made sure that the men exercised their voting prerogative as frequently as possible. Men who were in jail, in hospitals, out of town or peacefully reposing in a cemetery often swung elections."[a]

The machine offered voters benefits in exchange for their support. It helped them

a. As quoted in *The New York Times,* Dec. 26, 1982.

(*Continued.*)

The death of Richard Daley, Chicago's mayor and Cook County Democratic chairman for nearly two decades, was the beginning of the end for the strongest of the big-city political machines. (*Cornell Capa: Magnum.*)

Daley's successor as mayor, Michael Bilandic, never achieved control of the organization. (*UPI; Bettmann Archive.*)

Defeating Bilandic, Jane Byrne served a term as mayor, only to be defeated in an election that polarized black and white voters, ending the black alliance with the county organization. (*Jeff Lowenthal: Woodfin Camp.*)

get jobs, brought them food baskets and coal in hard times, and clothed and housed them after fires. It could fix traffic tickets, get people out of jury duty, and arrange for the release of people who had been arrested by the police for assault or drunkenness. It gave free legal advice and made bail for its supporters.

Precinct captains were rewarded with lower-level government jobs: as street sweepers, sanitation workers, police officers, fire fighters, transit workers, water workers, inspectors, and clerks. This does not sound like much today, but for youngsters in poor neighborhoods at the time, these jobs were hard to get, and they offered opportunities for payoffs. Ward and district leaders got jobs as sheriffs and city marshalls, performing duties for the courts in return for high fees. They became law secretaries to judges—powerful positions in which they influenced the courts to benefit their friends in return for other favors or money. They became commissioners or deputy commissioners in city or county agencies. Anyone who received such a job was expected to contribute between 1 and 2 percent of his or her salary to the party each year, usually by buying tickets to picnics, dances, or party banquets. Those nominated to high public office, such as judges, were expected to contribute the equivalent of one year's salary to the party.

Machines thrived on corruption, permitting party and public officials to misuse their offices for personal gain. Members could be *bribed* to make decisions. They might grant delays, exemptions, or variances from local laws or administrative codes, especially those involving health, safety, sanitation, zoning, waste disposal, construction, and fire hazards. They could propose special-situation laws to benefit particular companies. Or they might *extort* funds by threatening to withhold city services or permits, proposing ordinances or laws that would harm businesspeople unless they paid up, or threatening to enforce existing laws in ways that would

Harold Washington, Chicago's first black mayor, presides over a factionalized city government. (*John Picara: Woodfin Camp.*)

Alderman Edward Vrdolyak squares off against Mayor Washington in a struggle for control of the city council. (*AP Laserphoto/John Swart.*)

impose extra costs on local businesses. The machine could receive *kickbacks:* contributions from companies that had been awarded government contracts. When a party organization held its annual dinner, those who had been given government contracts would buy blocks of tickets and also put paid "advertisements" in the party's yearbook.

Party workers set up businesses which received government contracts: companies involved in construction, maintenance, painting, building supplies, janitorial services, furniture and fixtures, cafeteria services, security services, and insurance. Their contracts, negotiated with people they had put into office, ensured them excessive profits. The employees of these businesses could be counted on to back the machine in elections, since their jobs depended on the machine's control of government.

Machines and rings were not an unalloyed evil. They helped immigrants assimilate, become citizens, and then voters. They helped the poor, the uneducated, and the unconnected. They gave the natural leaders of the community a chance to advance. As Richard Daley, the mayor of Chicago, argued: "The party permits ordinary people to get ahead. Without the party I couldn't be Mayor. The rich guys can get elected on their money, but somebody like me, an ordinary person, needs the party. Without the party only the rich would be elected to office."[b]

But many activities of machines and rings were indefensible. While some stayed within the letter of the law, most did not. They put the government up for auction to the highest bidders. They lined their own pockets with bribes and kickbacks. They rigged elections. They corrupted the police, prosecutors, and judges. The worst of them cooperated with organized crime.

b. Mike Royko, *Boss!* New American Library, New York, 1971, p. 84.

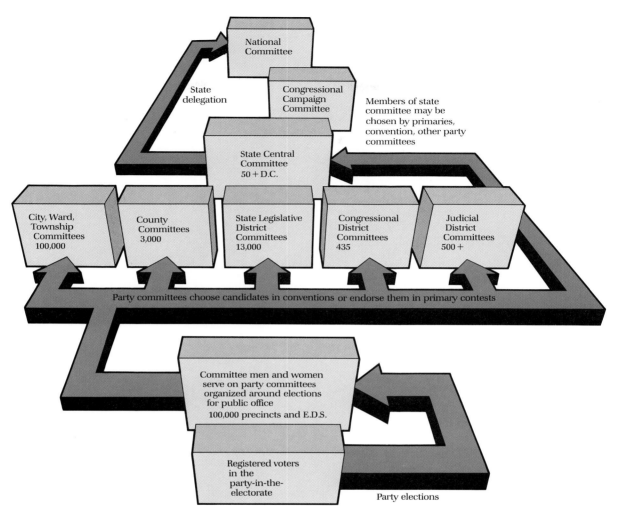

Figure 6-1. Party structure. There are thousands of party committees at the local level and fifty state parties. Each unit is autonomous, and its relationships with others depends on influence, persuasion, bargaining, and negotiation. The party structure is not hierarchical. In a hierarchy, commands are issued at the top and carried out by subordinate units. But the national committee does not control the state parties, and the state parties do not control the county or local parties. There are only a limited number of national party rules, designed to regulate the presidential nominating contest.

The state committees are usually composed of all the county committeemen and committeewomen (Figure 6-1).

Most voters know nothing about these organizations, and they do not turn out for elections to choose members of party committees (unless these elections are held at the same time as high-turnout presidential contests). Otherwise, only about 5 percent might turn out, and so a small number of voters can control the party committees. Even in general elections few voters have any idea whom to choose for such strange jobs as "state committeewoman" or "delegate to the nominating convention for the state committee," and often voters decide not to cast ballots for them. The party organization gets its own

supporters to the polls and instructs them whom to vote for, which ensures its control of these positions.

National party organization

The national party consists of representatives of each of the state parties, organized into a *national committee* with the following functions:

- Prepare for the national convention (which meets every four years to nominate a presidential candidate) by deciding on the place and date and handling arrangements for thousands of delegates and reporters.
- Ensure compliance of the state party with the rules of the presidential nominating contest agreed to at the previous national convention.
- Ensure compliance of the state party with all rules of the national party.
- Recommend new party rules to the national convention.
- Raise funds for presidential and congressional elections.
- Give campaign assistance to state and local parties and their candidates.
- Fill any vacancies that might arise on the presidential ticket between the end of the convention and the election.

The national committee has very little power. It cannot tell state and local parties what to do, determine their candidates for office (including candidates for seats in the House and Senate), or establish candidates' positions on the issues. It cannot nominate candidates or determine the party platform or rules (this is done by the national convention). It does not manage election campaigns (the candidates themselves do this). It does not speak or act authoritatively for the party-in-government or set its policies.

Each national party has congressional and senatorial campaign committees which provide services (and funds) for the legislative party. These are discussed in Chapter 7.

MEDIA POLITICS

For more than a century—from 1830 to 1960—political power was exercised by strong party organizations at the local and state levels. They chose the party-in-government and influenced what it did. But power has shifted in modern times to the party-in-government, which no longer needs the state or local party to get nominated or elected to public office. Parties no longer have a monopoly on recruiting potential candidates for office, on financing and running their campaigns, on mobilizing voters, or on providing a link between the party-in-government and the party-in-the-electorate. All these functions are now shared with the candidates' own campaign organizations and political action committees.

Candidate-centered politics

Since the early 1960s *party* organizations have been displaced by *candidate* organizations. Candidates who run for office can communicate directly with voters. As Pat Caddell, a campaign consultant who helped Jimmy Carter win the presidency in 1976, explained:

> What we've done with media, what we've done with polling, and what we've done with direct organizational techniques is that we've provided candidates who have the resources (and that's the important thing, the resources), the ability to reach the voters and have a direct contact with the electorate without regard to party or party organization.[9]

Traditional party politics has given way to some extent to ***media politics.***

Candidates communicate directly with voters without using the party organization. They use radio and television (because the average American watches more than three hours of television daily); in the era of new politics the amounts spent on advertising have skyrocketed: from $24.6 million in 1972 to more than $150 million in 1984. Direct mailings and phone banks cost an equal amount.

Candidates who can afford this advertising can run for office without the support of the party leaders, and sometimes against their wishes. The consultant Bob Goodman, who has helped elect a number of Republican senators, says, "We have enabled people to come into a party or call themselves independent Democrats or Republicans and run for office without having to pay the dues of being a party member in a feudal way."[10] The loser of a Democratic primary for governor of Pennsylvania says, "You can't rely any more on political organizations. They don't work anymore."[11]

People who want to enter politics figure that the easy way to get to the top is to start there. Wealthy businesspeople, athletes, and movie celebrities can run for Congress or the Senate or for governorships without serving apprenticeships, provided they can put together their own campaign organization (Figure 6-2).

The new campaign organization

To run a media politics campaign, the candidate must raise money, create an image, communicate this image to potential voters, and then mobilize the electorate.

Fund-raising. The campaign techniques of media politics are expensive. The candidate must raise money and cannot rely on the party for funds. This restricts the field to the wealthy and to those who are adept at fund-raising. The initial funds come from the candidate's family and friends. This campaign chest allows the candidate to open an office, hire a manager, and poll voters. It also permits the candidate to hire a direct-mail fund-raising firm, which prepares a letter (on the basis of poll results), designs the envelope (there is an art involved in getting recipients to open a letter rather than toss it away), and sends the letter to likely contributors.

Getting a good mailing list of potential contributors is the key to fund-raising. There are several kinds of lists:

- House lists, owned by the firm, which may generate a positive reply of as high as 20 percent
- Past-contributor lists—lists of people who have donated to previous campaigns
- Borrow lists, owned by other politicians, who give them to newcomers they like
- Membership lists—lists of people who belong to organizations or who subscribe to magazines which make it likely that they will agree with the candidate's stance on the issues

The funds collected, minus the considerable expenses involved in raising them, are used to enlarge the campaign organization. The candidate hires a consulting firm, which manages the campaign and creates the media image, subcontracting out much of the work of actually making commercials to specialists.

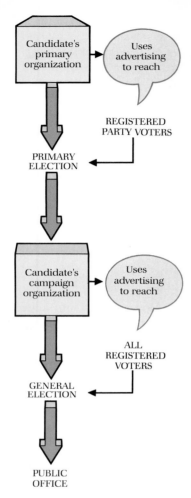

REGISTERED
PARTY VOTERS

ALL
REGISTERED
VOTERS

Figure 6-2. Media politics—the road to public office. The media politics candidate relies on his or her own organization to win the primary contest, making heavy use of campaign advertising.

MEDIA POLITICS CAMPAIGN ORGANIZATION

The inner circle

The campaign manager: in charge of overall strategy and tactics and supervision of campaign workers
Family, friends, and close advisers
Mentors and financial backers
Speech writer
Pollster
Media adviser: in charge of production and placement of political advertising
Director of press and media relations

Headquarters staff

Office manager (conversant with communications and computer technologies)
Lawyer (familiar with campaign finance and election laws)
Campaign treasurer and comptroller
Secretaries and volunteer assistants

Research

Polling organization, hired either by the candidate or by the state or national party
Issues research: on the opponent's record and votes
Position research: to develop stands on issues
Precinct targeting: to decide where to allocate field-workers
Direct-mail targeting: to decide which voters to send information

Image making

Media adviser: in charge of the overall operation and the hiring of other media professionals
Producer-director and copywriter of television and radio advertisements
Producer and copywriter for outdoor and print advertisements
Time buyer for advertisements
Graphics designer
Packaging designer for direct mail
Producer and copywriter for direct mail

Media coaching

Speech coach
Television coach
Wardrobe consultant
Makeup person

Field operations

Candidate advance: prepares site and obtains audience for the candidate
Security coordinator: works with local security and the police
Coordinator of volunteer operations
Coordinator of the voter registration drive
Coordinator for phone canvassing
Coordinator for field canvassing and election-day turnout drive
Liaison with the party and other local organizations

Image making. The purpose of creating an organization and raising funds is to get the candidate's name and message across to voters. The agency that produces the first set of advertisements tries to give the candidate *name recognition* with voters. The next set *positions* the candidate so that voters think that their beliefs and values are the same as the candidate's. The purpose is to give voters not only information but also an emotional reason to identify with the candidacy and support it.

The media consultant is central to the whole operation. Hiring a good consultant in itself establishes the credibility of a candidacy and helps raise funds. To some extent the best media consultants call the shots: they audition candidates and take on only the ones they like, and they insist on control of the entire campaign. Far from being hired hands, they have become the major political strategists in modern politics.

The consultant oversees the production of thirty- or sixty-second "spot" commercials for television and radio. "You play his song and write his movie," says Robert Goodman, a media advisor.[12] Commercials use the following techniques to maintain the audience's interest:

- *Personalize:* The candidate is a warm, concerned, committed person who cares about people, listens to them, and tries to help them. The candidate is competent and compassionate, knows how to get things done, and has new ideas. He or she has been successful in other careers and has entered politics to advance the public interest.

- *Characterize:* The candidate is pragmatic, progressive, and a dynamic liberal or a responsible conservative. But the opponent is a radical or a reactionary, too idealistic or too cynical, and out of touch with the people. The candidate is either a newcomer with energy and fresh ideas or a seasoned and experienced public official; the opponent is an inexperienced novice or else a worn-out incumbent who should be replaced.

- *Dramatize:* The commercials show the candidate doing something—listening to voters on the street or in a factory, confronting a heckler in the audience, responding to a reporter at a news conference, jogging on the beach, or even parachuting to a rally.

- *Visualize:* Since viewers are turned off by a "talking head" that fills the television screen, the commercial features dramatic visual images rather than the candidate's face, such as a city skyline, an "action shot" of crime or arson, or a missile taking off or a nuclear bomb exploding.

- *Thematize:* Each commercial concludes with a slogan that sums up the campaign. "Experience that money can't buy" works against a rich newcomer. "He (or she) is fresh and everyone else is tired" helps a challenger against an incumbent. "Leadership that works" helps an incumbent. "Send them a message" is an appeal for a protest vote.

Media consultants like David Garth argue that a series of thirty-second spot commercials can provide voters with adequate information about candidates. Garth has created an hour-long videotape presentation of his campaign advertisements for Tom Bradley, the mayor of Los Angeles, designed to convince skeptics that his work provides voters with what they need to know to make an informed decision. Studies by political scientists show that spot commercials provide more information than local television news broadcasts.[13]

Critics, especially those who are involved in more traditional party politics, agree with Edward Costikyan, a former county leader, who described spot

As party organizations decline, political consultants like David Garth have moved to fill the vacuum with media-based campaigns. (*Burt Glinn: Magnum.*)

Barney Frank's mother in a thirty-second spot appeals for votes for her son's tight congressional race. (*Photo by Barry S. Surman from "The Spot: The Rise of Political Advertising on Television," M.I.T. Press.*)

commercials as "simple words which oversimplify even simplistic thoughts."[14] Former congresswoman Millicent Fenwick observed that Alphone D'Amato, a senator from New York, had conducted a study after he was elected senator to find out why he had won and "found it owing to a commercial in which his dear mother held a bag of groceries and implored viewers to vote for her son, Al. Well, my dear," Fenwick concluded, "I cannot help thinking that is not quite what Thomas Jefferson had in mind."[15]

Mobilizing voters: Phone and field canvassing.   During the closing weeks of any campaign the candidate must try to create the kind of precinct organization which parties used to provide for their candidates.

The party organization may help a media politics candidate who agrees not to try to take over the organization or interfere in its party elections. Many candidates strike such deals with the party leaders after they have won a primary against a candidate who was backed by the organization. Unions, professional organizations, trade associations, corporations, neighborhood improvement groups, environmentalists, and civil rights groups can get their members to work in the precincts for a favored candidate.

The candidate can create his or her own *field organization*. The local phone company sells reverse-list directories, which list subscribers by street address; thus lists of voters for each precinct can be compiled. Telephone canvassers call every voter in each precinct to determine those who support the candidate, those who are opposed, and those who are undecided. A phone bank can be used to create an *instant precinct organization*. Campaign workers call people and ask whether they would like to volunteer to become precinct captains just for the last week of the campaign. Those who agree can be brought to campaign headquarters and trained to canvass their neighborhoods. They visit the people who have been listed as "undecided" by the phone canvassers.

Just like a traditional party campaign, a media politics campaign must "pull" its supporters to the polls on election day. The phone and field canvassers provide volunteers at headquarters with lists of all their supporters, precinct by precinct. On election day the campaign assigns a *poll watcher* to each precinct. As each person votes, the poll watcher, armed with the list for that precinct, checks his or her name off the list. In the late afternoon, a runner takes the list back to campaign headquarters, where phone canvassers call those who have not yet voted; then field canvassers ring their doorbells—the end of the campaign.

Media politics:
An assessment

The methods of media politics work. Even public officials who started out as party-oriented politicians admit that public opinion polls, direct mailing, and spot commercials are effective, and parties now routinely make use of them.

Media politics has improved the quality of elected officials. People can enter public life without consorting with machine politicians and becoming party hacks. Professional men and women who are skilled at raising and managing money, creating and running organizations, and communicating and motivating people are drawn into political life; one would expect that, as a result, the government would be not only less corrupt but also more effective. And it is.

But there is another side to the coin. The public can be manipulated by slick media appeals. As Edward Costikyan puts it, media politics "rewards the performer, the actor, the electronic personality, the simplifier of complex problems into thirty-second commercials."[16] Media politics appeals to people whose egos need massaging in the media and who can pay for a campaign ego trip. In the film *The Candidate*, Robert Redford, playing such a person, wins the election. He turns to his media managers and asks, "What do we do now?" Larry Sabato concludes that these managers "have sought candidates who fit their technologies more than the requirements of office and have given an extra boost to candidates who are more skilled at electioneering than governing."[17]

Media politics has become a game for the wealthy, the educated, and the urban professionals. As they dominate, if not monopolize, the paths to elective office, one may ask how the less affluent and the less well educated are to participate in politics. Are they merely to become an audience for electronic advertisements? Are their interests adequately represented by today's media politicians?

Although officials elected through the techniques of media politics are a cut above their party predecessors in terms of personal honesty, they may govern in ways which are subtly corrupting and injurious to the public welfare. To understand why this might be so, it is necessary to examine further the role of interest groups in elections; for as the power of the parties has declined, the importance of these groups has increased, and their intersection with media politics campaigns has transformed American politics.

PAC POLITICS:
THE CHALLENGE
TO PARTIES

When local and state parties had a monopoly on nominations to office, groups that were interested in certain policies would finance campaigns through the parties in return for access to the party-in-government. But the virtual evaporation of strong parties since the 1960s has left a vacuum: no longer can interest

groups maintain access to public officeholders by financing campaigns through the parties. Instead, they must contribute directly to the candidate-centered campaigns.

PACs: What are they?

Interest groups have established their own committees, which legally collect and distribute funds in campaigns; these are known as ***political action committees*** (PACs). PACs have gone far beyond the traditional (and often corrupt) relationships which have always existed between politicians and interest groups. PACs now operate within the law, but the law is skewed in their favor. Not only do they help finance campaigns, but as parties have disintegrated, they also have taken on some of their functions: they recruit candidates, finance and help manage candidates' campaigns, select candidates' media consultants, and influence public debate through their advertising.

PACs are now regulated according to the 1971 and 1974 campaign finance laws passed by Congress; although some labor and business PACs have been in existence since the 1940s, it is only in the past ten years that PACs have proliferated, as Figure 6-3 makes clear. As of 1985 there were more than 1500 corporate PACs, 650 trade association PACs, 400 labor PACs, and 940 other PACs.

Not all organized interest groups form PACs. The smaller ones find it too expensive in terms of administrative costs and compliance with federal election regulations. A group of political scientists found that only 17 percent of the interest groups it surveyed had formed PACs. Those most likely to do so are corporate interest groups, especially those with adequate funds, which think that legislative lobbying is important and are involved in conflict with other

Figure 6-3. Growth of PACs. A decade ago there were few PACs, and the majority were organized by labor unions. Since then their number has soared, with most created by corporations, trade and professional associations, and other nonlabor organizations. (Source: U.S. Federal Elections Commission.)

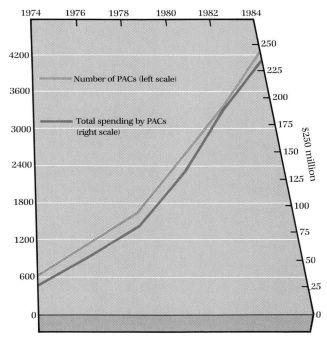

a. From January 1975 through December 1976, FEC did not identify categories of PACs other than corporate and labor PACs. Therefore, numbers are not available for trade/membership/health PACs or nonconnected PACS.

b. Includes PACs formed by corporations without capital stock and cooperatives. Numbers are not available for these categories of PACs from January 1975 through December 1976.

interest groups over significant public policies. Those which favor the status quo or believe that it is likely to be maintained in the near future have less incentive to form PACs.[18]

Corporations, unions, trade associations, and national banks may not spend their own funds in federal elections, according to laws dating back to 1907 (though in some states they can contribute to state and local elections). But they can establish PACs called *separate segregated funds* (SSFs), which may receive contributions from their own employees, stockholders, or members, and they can make contributions from these funds to candidates. Their expenses can be carried by their parent organization, and so all their receipts go directly to campaigns. Twice a year these SSFs can solicit the general public for contributions. Some of the most active groups include the National Association of Realtors, the National Association of Home Builders, the American Medical Association, the American Dental Association, the Attorneys Congressional Campaign Trust, the United Auto Workers, the Machinists and Aerospace Workers, the SeaFarer's Union, the National Education Association, the American Bankers Association, the Association of Milk Producers, the Auto and Truck Dealers Association, and the AFL-CIO.

Issue-oriented groups, such as those dealing with gun control, abortion, civil rights, the environment, and energy, may also create PACS. These differ from SSFs because they must pay their own expenses, but they can solicit funds from the public whenever they like.

There are also ideological organizations, some affiliated with parties and some independent, which contribute to conservative or liberal candidates. The most important are:

- *Democrats for the '80s*, founded by Pamela Harriman in 1980 and composed of moderate Democrats who have served in high positions, mostly in connection with matters of national security. It focuses on economic and defense issues and aids centrist Democrats.

- *National Committee for an Effective Congress* (NCEC), founded in 1948 by Eleanor Roosevelt and other liberal Democrats. It aids approximately 100 Democrats and a handful of moderate Republicans during each congressional election.

- *Independent Action*, founded by Morris Udall in 1980 and composed mostly of neoliberals who mistrust big bureaucracy and of holdovers from John Anderson's 1980 presidential campaign. It makes contributions in House elections to Democrats and will back a few Republican moderates against conservatives in their primaries.

- *Progressive Political Action Committee* (PROPAC), founded in 1982. It runs negative campaigns against right-wing candidates and is closely affiliated with the AFL-CIO.

- *Congressional Club*, organized in 1978 by Jesse Helms, the Republican senator from North Carolina. It makes contributions to right-wing Republican candidates for Congress and the Senate, mostly in the south.

- *National Conservative Political Action Committee* (NCPAC), founded in 1978. It runs negative campaigns against liberals.

- *Committee for the Survival of a Free Congress* (CSFC), founded in 1978 as a counterweight to the NCEC. It emphasizes a conservative stance on social issues and contributes to Republican candidates for the House.

President Ronald Reagan addresses a conference of conservative PAC leaders early in the 1984 presidential election campaign. (*AP: Wide World.*)

The contributors to the most liberal PACs are most likely to be professionals from urban areas who are younger and better educated than rank-and-file members of the Democratic Party. They have weak identifications with the Democratic Party and mistrust the party leadership; one survey showed that only 15 percent trusted their party on the issues. Contributors to the most conservative PACs, in contrast, are more likely to be in small business, to come from rural areas, and to be more interested in family and social issues than rank-and-file Republicans. Fewer than half (40 percent) have great confidence in their party leadership. Thus the impact of these PACs is to pull the two parties further apart on social issues and foreign policy.[19]

PAC Funding

What PACs may spend and receive according to law is indicated in Table 6-2.

PACs can evade limitations in three ways. First, they can act as a *clearing-house* for contributions to a candidate: they solicit checks made out directly to the campaign (not the PAC) and forward these checks to the candidate, thus helping to raise much more than $5000. Second, PACs can donate up to $20,000 to each party's national committee, senatorial campaign committee, and congressional campaign committee, with the understanding that these committees will spend the money on behalf of particular candidates. Third, PACs may give money to state and local parties for voter education and registration drives, supposedly not for particular candidates; in practice, however, such contributions directly benefit candidates in national elections by getting out the vote for them.

Most PACs invest in campaigns of incumbents to guarantee their access to these officials after they are reelected; this has led critics to call PAC financing

Table 6-2. Receiving and contributing PAC funds

Donor	Recipient		
	National party committee	PAC	Candidates for federal offices
Individuals[a]	$20,000 total	$5000 per PAC	$1000 to each candidate in any primary or election
PACS[b]	$15,000	$5,000 to any other PAC	$5000 to each candidate in any primary or election
Party	$20,000 from state party committee to national party committee		National parties may give $5000 to House candidates and $17,500 to Senate candidates, plus $40,000 in uncoordinated expenditures in House races and $80,000 to $1 million in Senate contests
Candidates			$5,000 each to any other candidate

a. Individuals may contribute no more than $25,000 to all types of election committees in any two-year election cycle.
b. PACs may contribute in state contests according to applicable state laws. They may also contribute soft money for state party building (that is, voter registration) which does not come under the limits for federal campaigns, although these activities may directly benefit candidates for federal office.

the "incumbent protection system." But some contribute to challengers who have a reasonable chance of defeating the people they oppose. And as some of these challengers win, other incumbents start to believe that PAC money made the difference. The result is that both challengers and incumbents begin a mad scramble for PAC funds: the challengers to mount a serious media campaign, and the incumbents to raise so much money so early that anyone thinking of mounting a challenge to them will be scared off. As Elizabeth Drew, an observer of Washington politics, noted, politicians "are signed up on a systematic basis by interests that wish to enjoy influence over their official conduct."[20]

PACs and campaigns

Choosing campaigns. How do PACs know which campaigns to fund? They get their most important clues from a few PACs that seem to know which incumbents are in trouble and which challengers could use the money effectively: BIPAC (a business group), the Chamber of Commerce listing of "Opportunity Races," and *The PAC Manager*, published by the National Association of Manufacturers, are used by business and trade PACs. Labor PACs pay attention to the AFL-CIO Committee on Political Education (COPE).

What PACs do in campaigns. PACs have taken over many of the functions of political parties: they recruit candidates and provide important campaign assistance.

RECRUITMENT. Some of the liberal, conservative, and issue-oriented PACs recruit candidates directly. All these groups rely heavily on scare tactics (if the other side wins, the republic will come to an end) and on direct-mail appeals for funds, taking their war chests to potential candidates who share their views.

CAMPAIGN ASSISTANCE. PACs help candidates by conducting polls at their own expense and then "leaking" the results to the newspapers so that candidates can make use of them. (They cannot give campaigns the results directly because that is considered a contribution in excess of their $5000 limit.) PACs can introduce potential candidates to media consultants. They may supply

campaign workers. They can help campaigns obtain good direct-mail services and can make their own lists available.

INDEPENDENT EXPENDITURES. In federal elections PACs may contribute no more than $5000 to a primary or election campaign (although they can contribute more if they take advantage of legal loopholes or violate the law); however, as a result of the Supreme Court's decision in *Buckley v. Valeo*, they may legally spend unlimited amounts to help candidates, provided that they do not coordinate their efforts with a candidate's campaign. These are called ***independent expenditures.***

NEGATIVE CAMPAIGNS. Some PACs run ***negative campaigns:*** they attack the character, the honesty, and even the patriotism of officeholders whom they oppose, sometimes years before anyone runs against them. They try to "soften up" voters and erode the incumbent's support, which will encourage someone to make the challenge in the next election. PACs can also intimidate officeholders by threatening to run such campaigns unless they change their positions.

Negative campaigns have been attacked by leaders of both parties. They go against the "Eleventh Commandment" of the Republicans—"Thou shalt not speak ill of fellow Republicans"—because some PACs threaten to run negative campaigns to unseat moderate Republicans in primaries and replace them with hard-line conservatives. They also go against the code of ethics of the American Association of Advertising Agencies, and most reputable campaign firms stay away from such tactics.

SHAPING PUBLIC OPINION. There are no legal limits on the amounts that PACs may spend to present their views on the issues. They do so even outside the campaign season, to create a climate of public opinion that influences whoever is in office. When candidates poll voters, they will find that they agree with the PACs on the issues, and the candidates will then take the same positions in their campaigns—at least so the PACs hope. And if the government's policies harm a PAC's interests, it can sponsor an initiative and allow the voters to settle the issues. The federal courts have ruled that any limits on the noncampaign spending of PACs would violate the freedom of speech of those who contribute to them.

The Federal Communications Commission balances PAC spending through the *Cullman doctrine*—its 1963 ruling—which requires radio and television stations that broadcast advertisements expressing controversial views to give free time (though not necessarily equal time) to others to present contrasting opinions. Some stations refuse to air PAC commercials because of this "free time" provision, and PACs have initiated lawsuits in federal courts arguing that this unconstitutionally restricts their access to the people.

Assessing PAC politics

PACs focus attention on issues and interests. They provide a useful corrective to campaigns which otherwise would deal mostly with personality and party loyalty. They can educate voters and get them thinking about fundamental policies. But PAC politics is *unbalanced:* there are many more business-oriented PACs than PACs favoring labor or consumers or PACs concerned about the environment. PAC politics (like party politics) offers no chance for unorganized interests or individuals to express themselves effectively.

PACs contribute to the weakening of the parties, which paradoxically means that PACs themselves cannot get what they want from the party-in-government. The problem, as Elizabeth Drew says, is that "a candidate entering politics now must systematically make the rounds of the interest groups and win

As the influence of PACs increases, so do efforts to regulate them, such as this ad campaign mounted by Common Cause in 1983. (*New York Times, Feb. 6, 1983.*)

their approval, and their money, by declaring himself, usually in very specific terms, in favor of the legislative goals they seek."[21] Some people in office end up doing little more than running errands for the interest groups that helped elect them. This makes politics more issue-oriented, but when everyone is pursuing his or her own agenda, the result is chaos. If the party structure evaporates, so does the organization which can set the government agenda, determine priorities, promote compromise, and create coalitions that can pass programs. The result is a government that seems to have no conception of the public interest and offers no coherent policies. All it offers is favors to those who invested in it; ultimately, that is not enough to retain its authority.

Party politicians oppose PAC politics. Because PACs focus on narrow issues, they make coalition building and compromise difficult. Politicians find it harder to build centrist majorities when the emotions of voters have been aroused by media techniques. They believe that PACs, in the words of Bill Brock, a former chairman of the Republican National Committee (RNC), "reduce the quality" of public officials, and that PACs engage in "all kinds of mischief," as another chairman of the RNC, Richard Richards, has said. Candidates recruited by PACs are less experienced in government and often do not have the skills or temperament necessary to make compromises. The negative campaigns that got them into office alienate potential colleagues from both parties. By 1982 Republican Party leaders were trying (unsuccessfully) to get PACs to agree not to run independent or negative campaigns in areas where local leaders opposed them—a symptom of the growing rift between pragmatic party professionals and right-wing zealots.

PACs compete with the parties for funds. "I can't believe that draining our resources is helpful," Brock argued. It is no wonder that Paul Weyrich, the executive director of the Committee for the Survival of a Free Congress (one of the more conservative PACs), says, "Both parties would have an all-night celebration if we were to go out of business."[22]

184

ISSUE AND DEBATE

PAC POLITICS. "The nation's capital is awash with cash," the vice president for federal relations of the Dana Corporation reported to his company. "It sloshes, ebbs and flows through the K Street canyon of corporations, trade associations, union headquarters and exquisitely appointed suites of special-interest law firms, around the embassies of Kalorama Road, through the pale drawing rooms of Georgetown, past the White House and, defying all laws of gravity, alternately seeps and gurgles its way uphill to the Capitol."[23]

Campaign financing by PACs has become a major issue. Some critics charge that it has led to "the best government money can buy," saying that things are now so bad that politicians can be not only bought but also rented by the special-interest groups. "Votes are given in exchange for contributions," charged William Brodhead, a former Republican representative, explaining why he had decided to retire from Congress. But Sam Melcher, a Republican senator, scoffs at these charges, claiming that contributions are small because of federal laws that prohibit PACs from contributing more than 1 percent of a candidate's campaign funds; he concludes that "no one is going to buy me for 1 percent."[24]

Do PACs corrupt the political process? Do they affect the competitiveness of elections because they give overwhelmingly to incumbents rather than to challengers? Should PACs be prohibited from contributing funds in state and national elections, or should the amounts they can give be limited? Should there be a limit on the percentage of a candidate's campaign funds which can come from PACs?

The background. Both the number of PACs and the size of their contributions have increased dramatically since the 1971 Federal Election Campaign Act and its 1974 amendments began to regulate them. In 1974 spending in congressional campaigns totaled $74 million, and PACs contributed only $12.5 million of that amount. By 1982 total spending had reached $343 million, of which PACs contributed $83.1 million. The number of PACs increased in that same period from 608 to more than 3400. Overall, PACs raised more than $189 million for state elections and federal elections in 1982, and by 1984 the total had reached well over $200 million.

The case against PACS. Critics of PACs—like Common Cause's People Against PACs, the bipartisan Citizens Against PACs, LASTPAC (a PAC whose goal is to eliminate PACs), and many concerned public officials—argue that they threaten representative government. "Poor people don't make campaign contributions," observed Robert Dole, a Republican senator, adding that "you might get a different result if there were a Poor-PAC up here."[25] PACs benefit contributors from the corporate and professional worlds and from labor at the expense of the public. Officeholders become accountable to PACs, not to the voters. Critics see a direct correlation between campaign contributions and votes, pointing to the 286 members of Congress who voted to strike down a Federal Trade Commission rule requiring used-car dealers to list each car's defects: those voting with the car dealers against the rule had previously received $742,371 in contributions from them. Critics also point to the seven companies which were affected by environmental regulations and which gave $767,000 to the members of the House Energy and Commerce Committee, as well as to the energy PACs, which contributed more than $500,000 to the members of these committees.

Critics claim that PAC contributions are investments, made to protect the interests of a PAC, not to elect the best candidate to office. Many candidates receive most of their PAC contributions from committees that represent the interests of people far away from their own constituents. In 1974, only 28 percent of House

members got one-third or more of their funds from PACs outside their districts, but by 1984 over 70 percent did so.[26] Because honest politicians do not want to mortgage their votes to PACs, they must go into debt or risk being defeated by well-financed opponents. Many decide to retire from office instead. Those who win elections today may have spent so much on their campaigns that they need PACs just to retire their debts. The system "virtually forces members to go around begging for money," charges Tom Eagleton, Democratic senator.[27] Not only can politicians who play ball with PACs get money for their campaigns, but those who were first elected before January 1980 may transfer funds from their campaigns to their own bank accounts after they leave office—even if they collected hundreds of thousands of dollars after 1980!

The case for PACs. Supporters of PACs argue that they are part of a broad increase in individual participation in politics and grass-roots organizing which started in the 1960s. They claim that in the 1950s and 1960s, when labor PACs were dominant and contributed most of their funds to liberal Democrats, the critics never complained; now, when corporate and trade association PACs are countering the contributions of labor PACs, and are making slightly more than half their contributions to Republicans, PACs have suddenly become an issue. Supporters claim that only since 1980, when corporate PACs began to make their contributions to Republican challengers rather than to Democratic incumbents, have PAC contributions dominated the liberal agenda.

Supporters of PACs argue that the funds do not buy votes—they simply help officeholders and challengers explain their positions in the campaigns, which actually promotes rather than destroys accountability. PACs help challengers overcome the advantages of incumbents. Since PACs have come into existence, turnover in Congress and state legislatures has increased. Voters are always free to reject a candidate and his or her position, and PACs give them better-financed candidates from which to choose.

The PAC system is legal, provides for full disclosure of contributors, and makes it relatively easy to see which officeholders are taking contributions from which PACs. "Today campaign finance is cleaner than it's ever been. We know who gave and who got. And we have the broadest base of political giving in our history," argues Richard Armstrong, the president of the Public Affairs Council (a nonpartisan organization of corporate public affairs executives).[28] This, defenders argue, is much better than surreptitious and illegal contributions, made by lobbyists behind closed doors, which are more likely to involve direct vote buying. Without PACs, defenders argue, candidates would have to finance their campaigns out of their own pockets or rely on "fat cat" donors. With PACs, candidates can concentrate on issues and get money from voters who care about them. Far from eroding responsibility to the people, in this view PACs make parties and candidates more responsive to voters' concerns.

Defenders of PACs argue that PAC spending does not give politics a corporate bias. All PAC contributions combined (including the contributions of labor PACs) amount to less than one-fourth of giving in federal elections. Corporate PACs provide less than 10 percent of total giving. The average contribution of a corporate PAC to a candidate for national office in 1981–1982 was $657, and 97 percent of all gifts are under $2500. This, the defenders say, cannot buy very much access, and in any event, getting access is not the same as buying votes. Richard Armstrong concludes that "by comparison with what went on in politics 15 years ago, PAC's are the Little Sisters of the Poor."[29]

PACs do favor incumbents, their defenders concede, but that is only natural: so do all other campaign contributors. Corporate PACs, in fact, are more likely to favor challengers than other types of PACs or large individual donors, and this opens up the system. And although corporate PACs are likely to favor Republicans, labor PACs are overwhelmingly Democratic; thus PAC giving reinforces tendencies toward a responsible party system rather than suppressing them.

Proponents of PACs argue that to regulate or restrict them would deny people their freedom of speech and assembly and would stifle full debate about the issues. They argue that allowing officeholders to pass laws which restrict the public's ability to fund groups that communicate to voters through the mass media would set a dangerous precedent. They believe that special interests are a condition of democratic politics and that PACs, by bringing their contributions into the open, do the best they can to promote accountable government. Considering the wide variety of PACs which contribute money, they say, the pluralism of American politics is enhanced by them rather than diminished.

Finally, defenders of PACs have public opinion on their side. A 1983 survey by Civic Services, Inc., of 1503 voters in precincts across the nation indicated that almost two-thirds of the public knew what PACs were and that a small majority (53 percent approved of their contributing to federal elections, while only 33 percent disapproved.[30] (See Figure 6-4.)

Proposed reforms.   Some of the proposed changes in campaign laws include the following:

- Reducing the maximum amount of PAC contributions, from $5000 to $1000.
- Limiting the amount of money that a campaign may accept in PAC contributions (Common Cause would limit it to $90,000 in House elections) or limiting the percentage of total campaign funds that such contributions may constitute.

Figure 6-4. Attitudes toward PACs. Public opinion toward PACs depends on the type: women's and environmental PACs are strongly favored, while business and labor PACs are seen as a negative influence. The public says it opposes candidates' accepting PAC funds—yet most incumbents who do are reelected handily. (Source: Harris Survey, no. 1, January 3, 1983.)

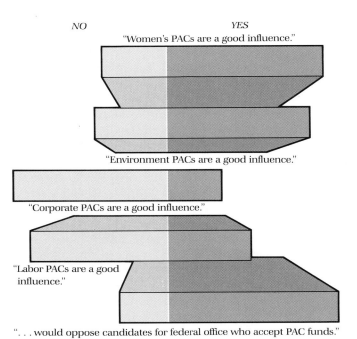

NO   YES

"Women's PACs are a good influence."

"Environment PACs are a good influence."

"Corporate PACs are a good influence."

"Labor PACs are a good influence."

". . . would oppose candidates for federal office who accept PAC funds."

- Allowing PACs to contribute only to state or national party committees, rather than to candidates, with an increase in the amounts permitted.

Critics of these reforms believe that Congress will not adopt public financing of campaigns. They think that such measures would benefit incumbents, making it more difficult for challengers to spend enough to communicate with voters. And they believe that limits on PAC expenditures would not reduce their influence in politics, since PACs could always mount their own noncoordinated campaigns.

Supporters of PACs believe that the best way to minimize any undue influence of PACs would be to allow them to contribute more, not less, to campaigns. They would like to see higher limits on individual campaign contributions and more tax deductibility to spur such donations. They would end all limits on spending by party committees on behalf of candidates and would eliminate limits on individual contributions to parties. These and similar measures, they believe, would increase the diversity of funding sources and make it even less likely that PACs could exert undue influence.[31]

PARTY RENEWAL IN THE 1980s

National and state parties remain weak, but they have tried hard in the 1980s to rebuild themselves in an effort to regain ground lost as a result of both the candidate-centered media politics and the interest-centered PAC politics of the preceding decade. They are better organized and better financed, and they provide more services to candidates.

State and local parties

Machines and rings have disappeared almost entirely. Elections are usually honest. Civil service has eliminated most machine patronage. Unions of government employees protect workers who refuse to contribute to parties. As a result of the Supreme Court decision in *Elrod v. Burns*,[32] the winning party cannot dismiss lower-level civil servants and replace them with its own supporters. The federal courts even require cities like Chicago to file plans on how they will end politically motivated hirings, dismissals, and harassment in the public work force.

Nevertheless, while remaining within the letter of the law, modern parties still compete for prizes in the game of politics: the high salaries and fringe benefits of public office and the appointments to state and city commissionerships and judgeships and to boards of public corporations that run everything from sports complexes to transit systems to airports. Elected and appointed officials in turn hire politically connected firms and consultants to provide professional services: law, architecture, engineering, accounting, management, labor relations, advertising, insurance, travel arrangements, and even market research and television commercials for state agencies (such as those dealing with tourism and industrial development).

The new patronage. Paying firms to provide these services constitutes the *new patronage* that has replaced capital construction and maintenance kickbacks, which fueled the old-time machines. The new patronage does not use extortion or bribery, and no one violates the laws.[33] Instead, professionals in these firms work for the parties as volunteers in ways that are hardly different from most civic and community improvement activity. They help elect their friends to office, and in return their friends give them the opportunity to provide professional services for large fees.

Parties and bureaucracies. Parties no longer provide goods and services directly to voters in exchange for their support. They now help constituents obtain government benefits by cutting through the red tape, explaining procedures, and providing legal advice. They become active in community development by working with local groups to obtain government grants.[34] The remaining corruption—and there is still quite a lot—is usually not organized by the party itself. Instead, most cases now involve individuals who take it upon themselves, without the sanction of the local party, to extort funds and demand kickbacks or bribes. After all, with so much legal opportunity to make money providing services to government or obtaining government contracts, only greedy or stupid people or lower-level workers will risk committing criminal acts.

Party workers. The modern party attracts different kinds of people from those who were attracted by the machines. Studies in Detroit and Los Angeles show a decline in the percentage of workers without a college education, as blue-collar workers are being replaced by white collar professionals. The majority of workers today are concerned more with issues than with personal gain, they do not need the patronage of a machine, and they are likely to enter party politics as an outgrowth of their work with community organizations.[35]

Parties and community groups. The traditional local party has evaporated over the past quarter-century. Many are now paper organizations: their precincts are not covered by captains, and they do little or nothing in the community between elections.[36] The control of such organizations has passed to mayors, county executives, and others in the party-in-government, who recruit party workers to fill seats on committees to fulfill the requirements of state election laws; thus the party organization serves as an appendage to the party-in-government.

The tasks of recruiting candidates and financing and managing campaigns are now shared with local community and civic groups: owners of newspapers and television stations, corporate and labor leaders, religious congregations, merchants' associations, neighborhood improvement groups, veterans' associations, ethnic organizations, and civil rights groups. Candidates for office are recruited by them—or they recruit themselves.[37] The support or endorsement of a party committee means less to candidates than the support of a newspaper, a union leader, or a civic association, and often the former follows the latter, as parties react to the initiatives of others. These days the *real* local and state parties are the group coalitions whose leaders recruit candidates.

The national Democratic Party

The Democrats began to transform their national party organization in the 1960s, when civil rights workers, college students, women, and activists against the Vietnamese war demanded that the party open its doors to them. Battles centered on rules for presidential nominations resulted in significant reforms between 1968 and 1976:

- *Affirmative action* programs to increase participation by women, minorities, and young people in party affairs at both the national and state levels. This put an end to overt race and sex discrimination in state and local parties.
- Women to constitute half the national committee and half the delegates to the national convention.

- The national party to be supreme over the state parties in making and enforcing these and other party rules.

The national charter. In the late 1970s the Democrats changed their party structure. They approved a charter and bylaws, in effect their first national "constitution." The Supreme Court, in *Cousins v. Wigoda*, ruled that a national party could enforce its rules on the state parties—even if state laws mandated different procedures. The Court has also decided that national party rules take precedence over state party rules.[38]

The charter and subsequent actions by the Democratic National Committee (DNC) led to the creation of the following new units within the national party:

- Judicial Council, to resolve disputes between the state parties and groups claiming discrimination or other violations of rules
- National Finance Council, to improve fund-raising
- Business Council, open to people who contribute $10,000 or more
- Labor Council, to give unions an important voice
- Equal Rights Amendment Advisory Committee, to give women's groups a greater role in the party
- Strategy Council, consisting of sixty party officials, to promote coordination of national and state campaigns
- National Education and Training Council, to improve management in local and state campaigns
- Center for Democratic Policy, to develop new policy initiatives for the national party-in-government

The midterm conventions. In 1974 the Democrats held their first *midterm convention.* That year it was used to attack the Republicans for burglarizing the DNC headquarters and committing other Watergate-related crimes. In 1978, with Jimmy Carter in the White House, the convention became a battleground for his supporters and those of Edward Kennedy, as the two sides fought over the policies of the government. In 1982 party leaders scaled down its size (from 1600 to 900 delegates), and the convention focused on issues that Democrats could run on in the upcoming congressional campaign—unemployment and the recession. It also became a forum for presidential hopefuls, who campaigned among the delegates representing local party organizations.

Aiding the state parties. In the 1980s the focus of party reform has shifted away from regulating the state parties and toward rebuilding them. The Democratic Party's National Training Academy, opened in 1981, ran three-day sessions on campaign management for candidates and campaign managers. Its talent scout program recruited candidates for local office. Funding for voter registration drives was increased. In 1982 the party started making direct financial contributions to Democrats in Congress who faced strong Republican challengers. It sponsored several issue-training conferences to brief its candidates on national economic issues. A program begun in 1981, with the unlikely name of State Party Works, trained state party officials in fund-raising, polling, and advertising.

Emulating the PACs. In the 1980s the DNC started to use the same tech-

niques as the PACs. It spent millions of dollars upgrading its direct-mail list of potential contributors. Beginning in 1982, the party mailed out millions of pieces, including:

- The Critical Issues Survey, in which Charles Manatt, the chairman of the DNC, invited contributors to express their "personal views on what is troubling our nation" and promised to "share your views with the very highest level of the Democratic Party leadership."
- Invitations to potential contributors to join the Convention Club (for $5000), the Business Council (for $10,000), the Senate Democratic Leadership Circle (for $15,000), the Democratic National Finance Council (for $5000), and the Speakers Club (for $5000) and to become card-carrying members of the Democratic Party by making contributions of $100 or more.
- "Telegrams," targeted at senior citizens, setting forth the Democrats' program to defend social security and inviting contributions to the party.
- Direct mailings, some signed by Tip O'Neill, the Speaker of the House, beginning a drive to defeat the Republicans.

By 1984 the national Democratic Party was operating as a super-PAC. By running negative campaigns against Republican candidates, it solicited funds even before the campaigns were launched. It used funds to upgrade its mailing list and to expand its direct mailings, on the sound principle that to make money one must spend money. It took out newspaper advertisements and made television commercials. It even put out slick televised responses to President Reagan's State of the Union addresses in 1983 and 1984, a far cry from its past efforts, which had put most viewers to sleep. For the 1984 elections the DNC organized "Americans for Mondale" committees as subsidiaries of each state party to raise $25 million for further party-building activities.

Although the Democrats had accomplished much, Charles Manatt, in comparing his party with the Republican party in the aftermath of the 1980 elections, admitted: "We have been out-conceptualized, out-organized, out-televised, out-coordinated, out-financed, and out-worked."[39]

The national Republican Party

The Republicans' efforts to rebuild the party began in the aftermath of the *Watergate* scandal of 1973–1974. The party made a disastrous showing in the 1974 midterm congressional elections and then lost the White House in 1976. Looking toward the 1978 contests, the party controlled only one-third of the seats in the House and the Senate and slightly less than one-third of the seats in state legislatures, and it had only twelve governors. Many commentators began to talk of a "one-and-a-half-party system" as the Republicans hit bottom. Yet by 1984, the reporter Thomas Edsell noted, "The Republican Party has become the most sophisticated and potent national political organization in this century, and probably in the history of the United States."[40]

Party finance. In the late 1970s the Republicans invested in a completely new direct-mail operation, which by 1979 provided them with a list of more than 2 million donors, up from 450,000 in 1976.[41] At the base of the pyramid were 1.6 million "sustaining members" who each contributed between $25 and $500 annually. Because they provided almost one-third of the party's funds, by 1982 the Republican National Committee (RNC) began organizing regional share-

Figure 6-5. Financing the Republican National Committee in the 1980s. The RNC receives most of its funds from small contributors, PACs, and wealthy "friends of the party." In turn it provides funds to state and local parties and candidates and encourages PACs and wealthy contributors to give to them directly. The DNC lags behind the Republicans and raises one-tenth of the funds raised by the RNC. (Source: U.S. Federal Elections Commission.)

holders' conventions; like the national conventions, they were held in big-city convention halls and attracted 10,000 contributors for briefings by top party officials.

There were the Major Donors ($500 to $999), the Associates ($1000 to $9999), and, at the summit, the Eagles ($10,000 to the legal maximum of $20,000 that an individual may donate to a party committee in a two-year election cycle). The RNC maintained a staff of four "Eagle representatives" to give the Eagles access to top officials in the Reagan White House. For $10,000 contributors could join the Senatorial Trust; for $5000, the Vice President's Club; or for $2500, the Republican Congressional Leadership Council.

The RNC encouraged PACs to contribute their legal maximum of $20,000 to the party. It told PACs, corporations, and wealthy individuals who wanted to do more that they could make unlimited contributions to Republican state and local parties for "party-building activities"—a loophole in the federal election laws. Moreover, the RNC coordinated efforts to raise these funds for state and local parties (referred to as *soft money,* to distinguish it from the more closely regulated *hard-money* contributions to the national party and candidates for national office). Funds supposedly used for registration drives or state campaigns would obviously benefit congressional and presidential candidates as well, and so soft money became an essential part of Republican national fund-raising. Its "unity dinners," attended by candidates Reagan and Bush during the 1980 campaigns, raised more than $9 million for the state parties, a reversal from the usual practice: most of the time party dinners are held to raise money at the local level and transfer it to the national party. In 1984 the national ticket helped raise more than $16.8 million for the state party-building efforts.

Hard-money contributions increased dramatically. The RNC, the Republican Senatorial Campaign Committee, and the Republican Congressional Campaign Committee raised $111 million in 1980, compared with only $18.8 million raised by the three comparable Democratic committees. By 1982 the Republican groups had raised $191 million, compared with $32 million raised by the Democrats, and in 1984 they raised $246 million, compared with $59 million raised by the Democrats. Because many Democratic candidates raised their own campaign funds, these figures do not mean that the Democrats were outspent, but merely that the national Republican Party could give more help than the national Democratic Party (Figure 6-5).

Campaign assistance. The national party also provided campaign services for the state parties, especially in the area of new campaign techniques. Since 1977 its Local Elections Division has spent more than $2 million annually on contests for state legislatures. It finances state polls which can be used by candidates for all state offices, thus avoiding unnecessary duplication. Its research and issues staff provides information on the records of vulnerable Democrats. It provides up-to-date information on the votes on Democratic state legislators and members of Congress through computer links between the national party headquarters and the state party headquarters and local campaigns. The RNC Campaign Management School trains professional campaign managers and then places them in local campaigns. The national party then contributes toward their salaries. The ultimate goal (not yet achieved) is to

place in each congressional district a salaried party agent who will recruit candidates and manage their campaigns.

Local organization. "There is no alternative to building up local party organization, county by county," according to the master blueprint for the 1980s, "A Republican Party Strategy for Controlling Government in America in This Century." Accordingly, the Republicans adopted a trickle-up theory: strengthening the party at the local level would enable it to become the majority party nationally. In 1983 Frank Fahrenkopf, the chairman of the RNC, announced plans for a buildup of local Republican organizations in the 1100 counties where they had been weak or nonexistent.

State organization. With national help in fund-raising, most state Republican parties restructured their operations.[42] They moved into permanent headquarters, hired full-time chairpersons and executive directors, and expanded their staffing. They even organized statewide advertising campaigns and beefed up their polling and direct-mail operations.

National organization. The national party completely revamped its own operations. By 1976 it had provided for a full-time paid chair and co-chair and had established eight vice chairs—one man and one woman for each of the four regions. By 1978 they were augmented by thirteen regional political directors who worked with the state parties. Regional finance directors had put the soft-money system into place by 1980. The RNC expanded its staff into several units, each designed to help local and state parties raise money, manage campaigns, and develop media images.

Candidate recruitment. For the first time in the history of the Republican Party, the regional officials directly recruited candidates to run in party primaries. They did so to counteract the influences of PACs and new politics, discouraging both issue extremists and wealthy but inexperienced newcomers from entering the races and instead encouraging seasoned and attractive politicians to run for higher office. Local mayors, city council members, and county legislators were asked to run for the state legislature; the best of the latter group were encouraged to make statewide races or to try for Congress.[43]

The Republicans' control of the White House helped them recruit good candidates. At the request of the RNC, President Reagan promised each state chair that he or she could have five "must-hire" recommendations to the White House Personnel Office, and he promised 100 jobs for Republican candidates for Congress who were defeated in the general elections. The RNC could offer candidates a package deal: a fund-raiser with personal appearances by a top-level official (possibly a Cabinet member or Vice President Bush), a televised "message from the president" to be used as a campaign ad, professional campaign management, a computerized link to Republican headquarters for research on issues, and help in preparing the media campaign. The party hired advertising agencies to develop commercials for local candidates and to run a series of ads for the entire party on network television. The White House political aides, through the "assets and priorities" group, channeled RNC and PAC contributions to candidates in "winnable" contests. Losing candidates would

receive help from the RNC in obtaining one of the federal jobs that the White House had reserved for them.

THINGS TO COME

NATIONALIZED PARTIES OR SUPER-PACs? The two parties have reversed their tendencies toward decentralization. In the future, if the national parties and their agents can recruit most local candidates and create a "career ladder" for them to climb, then the preconditions for responsible parties will exist, and PAC politics and media politics will no longer dominate the parties-in-government. The parties will be able to force members to adhere to the party line on issues by threatening them with loss of funds and campaign assistance in the next election (or even competition in the primaries) unless they do so.

But there is no reason to believe that party nationalization is the inevitable outcome of revitalization. The Democrats have maintained the same freewheeling style that once prompted Will Rogers to remark, "I'm a member of no organized political party; I'm a Democrat." Their state and local parties challenge attempts by the national party to impose rules on them. Their factionalism weakens their presidents and their presidential candidates, prevents coherent policy-making, and allows the Republicans to exploit their disunity in Congress.

The Republicans are ahead in terms of party modernization and nationalization, but that does not always translate into success at the polls. As Republican candidates are recruited and are provided with funds and services by the national party, their inclination to stray from the party line in order to appeal to their local constituencies may decrease. But only locally tailored campaigns can win the support of voters. The Democrats, with their looser ties to national party committees, are freer to follow their own political instincts. The Democratic Party remains more localized, and hence more responsive, and the Democrats win many more elections than their opponents. As of 1985 they had a 4 to 3 lead in state legislators, a 2 to 1 lead in governors, and a 4 to 3 lead in the House of Representatives.

Figure 6-6. Party and PAC politics in the 1980s. Groups in politics are either party- or candidate-oriented, and ideological or coalitional in nature.

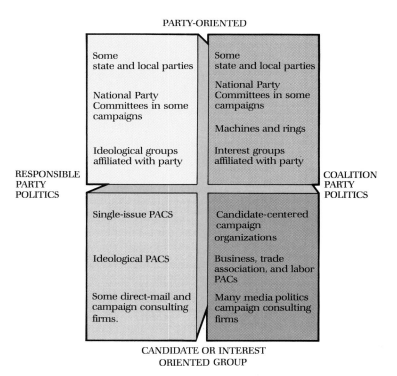

PARTY-ORIENTED

Some state and local parties

National Party Committees in some campaigns

Ideological groups affiliated with party

Some state and local parties

National Party Committees in some campaigns

Machines and rings

Interest groups affiliated with party

RESPONSIBLE PARTY POLITICS

COALITION PARTY POLITICS

Single-issue PACS

Ideological PACS

Some direct-mail and campaign consulting firms.

Candidate-centered campaign organizations

Business, trade association, and labor PACs

Many media politics campaign consulting firms

CANDIDATE OR INTEREST ORIENTED GROUP

To understand the transformation of party politics, we must return to two distinctions made earlier in this chapter: (1) the distinction between responsible and coalition parties (that is, parties which take a principled stand on issues, as opposed to those which concentrate on creating a majority coalition) and (2) the distinction between party politics and media politics. Figure 6-6 diagrams political organizations according to these distinctions: the extent to which they are coalitional, centrist, and pragmatic, as opposed to being principled, extreme, and issue-oriented, and the extent to which they are geographically based party organizations or antiparty operations, like PACs.

What kind of organization will predominate in the future depends in large measure on two factors: how existing organizations adapt to changing technologies and which style seems most likely to help candidates win elections. The new developments in television and radio would seem to give the edge to any organization that can reach an audience and motivate it to give money and listen to its message. This would seem to favor PACs (or perhaps *super-PACs*), which have experience in appealing to narrow constituencies and raising funds from them.

IN CONCLUSION

For more than a century, machines and courthouse rings dominated traditional party politics. In the past quarter-century their monopoly on the recruitment of candidates and the funding and management of campaigns has been challenged by candidate-centered campaign organizations and by political action committees. No one kind of organization, and no one style of politics, now predominates.

The erosion of party politics provides a greater opportunity for people to run for office using the methods of media politics, but by and large this has favored the wealthy. PACs have taken advantage of campaign finance laws (and loopholes), which tends to bias the system toward the interests of business.

The restructuring of the two national parties and the modernization of the state and local parties have given women and minorities more opportunities to participate in party affairs, raised the caliber of those running for office, ended much of the bribery and extortion that characterized traditional party politics, and increased party discipline and cohesion, especially in the Republican Party, although it remains to be seen whether greater centralization will help win elections.

The long-term outlook is for PACs to continue to flourish, because they help the party-in-government run effective new politics campaigns, but for the parties to adopt more sophisticated fund-raising and campaign techniques and try to counter the influence of PACs. The predominant organization of the future will be the one that politicians find most useful in winning elections.

NOTES

1. James D. Richardson, *Messages and Papers of the Presidents of the United States, 1789–1897*, vol. 1, Bureau of National Literature and Art, Washington, D.C., 1898, p. 219.
2. Samuel Eldersveld, *Political Parties in American Society*, Basic Books, New York, 1982, p. 85.
3. Austin Ranney, *The Doctrine of Responsible Party Government*, University of Illinois Press, Urbana, 1954.
4. On convergence theory see Anthony Downs, *An Economic Theory of Democracy*, Harper and Row, New York, 1957, p. 28.
5. David Truman, "Federalism and the Party System," in Arthur MacMahon (ed.), *Federalism: Mature and Emergent*, Doubleday, Garden City, N.Y., 1955.

6. Edward Costikyan, *Behind Closed Doors*, Harcourt, Brace and World, New York, 1966, p. 153.

7. Eldersveld, op. cit., p. 99.

8. James MacGregor Burns, *The Deadlock of Democracy*, Prentice-Hall, Englewood Cliffs, N.J., 1956.

9. Larry Sabato, *The Rise of Political Consultants*, Basic Books, New York, 1982, p. 286.

10. Ibid., p. 288.

11. Frank Sorauf, *Party Politics in America*, 4th ed., Little, Brown, Boston, 1982, p. 234.

12. Dom Bonafede, "Are You Planning to Run for Office?" *The National Journal*, Jan. 16, 1982, p. 104.

13. Thomas Patterson and James McClure, *The Unseeing Eye: The Myth of Television Power in National Politics*, Putnam, New York, 1976.

14. Edward Costikyan, *How to Win Votes*, Harcourt Brace Jovanovich, New York, 1980, p. 93.

15. William Geist, "Millicent Fenwick: Marching to Her Own Drum," *The New York Times Magazine*, June 27, 1982.

16. Costikyan, *How to Win Votes*, Harcourt, New York, 1980, p. 142.

17. Sabato, op. cit., p. 7.

18. Thomas Gais, "On the Scope and Bias of Interest Group Involvement in Elections," paper delivered at the annual convention of the American Political Science Association, 1983.

19. John C. Green and James Guh, "The Party Irregulars," *Psychology Today*, vol. 18, October 1984, pp. 46–50.

20. Elizabeth Drew, "Politics and Money," *The New Yorker*, Dec. 6, 1982, p. 54.

21. Drew, op. cit., p. 147.

22. Sabato, op. cit., p. 274.

23. As reported by Al Hunt, *The Wall Street Journal*, July 15, 1984.

24. Ibid.

25. Ibid.

26. Phillip M. Stern, "Pronounce PACs 'POX,'" *The New York Times*, Mar. 13, 1984.

27. *The New York Times*, Feb. 3, 1983.

28. Richard A. Armstrong, "Election Finance and Free Speech," *Newsweek*, July 18, 1983, p. 5.

29. Ibid.

30. *Attitudes toward Campaign Financing*, Civic Services, Washington, D.C., February 1983, p. 9.

31. For the anti-PAC position, see *People against PACs*, Common Cause, Washington, D.C., 1983; for a defense of PACs, see Herbert E. Alexander, *The Case for PACs*, Public Affairs Council, Washington, D.C., 1983.

32. *Elrod v. Burns*, 427 U.S. 347 (1976).

33. Costikyan, *How to Win Votes*, pp. 16–17.

34. Raymond Wolfinger, "Why Political Machines Have Not Withered Away and Other Revisionist Thoughts," *Journal of Politics*, vol. 34, no. 3, 1972, pp. 365–398.

35. Eldersveld, op. cit., p. 171.

36. Robert Agranoff, *The Management of Election Campaigns*, Holbrook Press, Boston, 1976, p. 103.

37. Frank Sorauf, "Political Parties and Political Analysis," in William Chambers and Walter Burnham (eds.), *The American Party Systems*, Oxford University Press, New York, 1967.

38. *Cousins v. Wigoda*, 419 U.S. 477 (1974).

39. *The New York Times*, Feb. 28, 1981.

40. *Washington Post National Weekly Edition*, Sept. 10, 1984, p. 23.

41. F. Christopher Arterton, "Political Money and Party Strength," in Joel L. Fleishman (ed.), *The Future of American Political Parties*, American Assembly, New York, 1982, pp. 101–139.

42. Robert Huckshorn and John Bibby, "State Parties in an Era of Political Change," in Fleishman, op. cit., pp. 70–100.
43. John F. Bibby, "Political Parties and Federalism: The Republican National Committee Involvement in Gubernatorial and Legislative Elections," *Publius*, vol. 12, winter 1979, pp. 229–236.

FURTHER READING

Agranoff, Robert: *The Management of Election Campaigns*, Holbrook Press, Boston, 1976. A nuts-and-bolts discussion of how to manage a media politics campaign.

Diamond, Edwin, and Stephen Bates: *The Spot: The Rise of Political Advertising on Television*, M.I.T., Cambridge, Mass., 1984. An illustrated history.

Fleishman, Joel (ed.): *The Future of American Political Parties*, American Assembly, New York, 1982. Essays on the relationship between the party organization and the party-in-government.

Handler, Edward: *Business in Politics*, Lexington Books, Lexington, Ky., 1982. A discussion of how business PACs work.

Pomper, Gerald (ed.): *Party Renewal in America*, Praeger, New York, 1980. Essays on party modernization.

Royko, Mike: *Boss!* New American Library, New York, 1971. An account of how Mayor Daley's Democratic machine ran Chicago.

Sabato, Larry J.: *The Rise of Political Consultants*, Basic Books, New York, 1982. A description and critique of campaign consulting firms and their work.

Sabato, Larry J.: *PAC Power*, Norton, New York, 1984. How PACs influence elections and officeholders.

THE STUDY BREAK

Burdick, Eugene: *The Ninth Wave*. Houghton-Mifflin, Boston, 1956. A novel (written by a political scientist) about a media politics entrepreneur named Mike Freeman and what happens to him in California politics. The plot mixes politics with romance and some surfing.

The Candidate. A movie starring Robert Redford as a man who knows how to win a media politics election (1972).

The Last Hurrah. A movie about a media politics candidate who runs against the incumbent mayor of Boston—a party regular who finds that he has become antiquated in the era of television (1958). Spencer Tracy plays the mayor.

Riordon, W. L.: *Plunkitt of Tammany Hall*, Dutton, New York, 1963. Reminiscences of a New York City politician at the turn of the century.

Shapley, R. E.: *Solid for Mulhooley*, Carleton, New York, 1881. A book about how ward politics was played in the old days.

USEFUL SOURCES

Campaigns and Elections. A Journal of campaign management.

Kinnell, Susan (ed.): *The Democratic and Republican Parties in America: A Historical Bibliography*, ABC-CLIO Information Services, Santa Barbara, Calif., 1983.

Roeder, Edward: *PACs Americana*, Sunshine Services, Washington, D.C., 1982. A directory of PACs.

Weinberger, Marvin: *The PAC Directory*, Ballinger, Cambridge, Mass., 1982. A guide to PAC support of candidates and parties.

ORGANIZATIONS

Democratic National Committee. 1625 Massachusetts Avenue, N.W., Washington, D.C. 20036. For more information phone 202-792-5900.

Federal Elections Commission, Office of Public Communications. 1325 K Street, N.W. Washington, D.C. 20463. For more information phone 800-424-9530.

PACs and Lobbies. 1512 Pennsylvania Avenue, SE., Washington, D.C. 20003. For more information phone 202-544-1141.

Republican National Committee. 310 First Street, S.E., Washington, D.C. 20003. For more information phone 202-863-8500.

The need to get to the people and get out the vote has never changed—only the methods have. The nineteenth century emphasized stump speaking, but today mastery of television is crucial. (*George Caleb Bingham, "Stump Speaking," Boatman's National Bank of St. Louis; AP Laserphoto.*)

CHAPTER 7

CONGRESSIONAL ELECTIONS: CLIMBING CAPITOL HILL

RUNNING FOR CONGRESS

Constitutional eligibility
Legal qualifications
Political viability
Occupational and political experience

RUNNING FOR THE HOUSE OF REPRESENTATIVES

Incumbents and challengers
Financing House elections
Campaigning for the House
Voting for the House

RUNNING FOR THE SENATE

Incumbents and challengers
Senate candidates
Financing Senate campaigns
Campaigning for the Senate
Voting for the Senate

ISSUE AND DEBATE: REFORM OF CONGRESSIONAL ELECTIONS

IN CONCLUSION

Every two years Americans elect 435 voting (and three nonvoting) members of the House of Representatives and one-third of the 100 members of the Senate. These elections shape the course of government: presidents emerge either with a cooperative Congress or with one that opposes their programs, ignores their priorities, and sets its own agenda. It is no wonder that candidates pour more than $400 million into these elections or that hundreds of thousands of people work in their campaigns. Neither is it any wonder that in the 1982 midterm elections, Tip O'Neill, the Democratic Speaker of the House, appealed for funds to hundreds of thousands of Democrats, warning: "The White House and Senate have fallen. The battle for the House is the last stand." Nor should we be surprised that Ronald Reagan wrote a letter to his backers, claiming that their "vote would decide whether or not we will continue on this new course to economic prosperity, or revert back to the discredited ideas that almost led us to national bankruptcy."[1]

Who runs for Congress, and how are candidates' campaigns organized and financed? What are the roles of parties, and of PACs, in the era of new politics? Who gets elected? Answering these questions will help us understand how Congress works, because how legislators climb Capitol Hill has a great deal to do with what happens once they get there.

RUNNING FOR CONGRESS

To be elected to Congress, one must be constitutionally eligible, legally qualified, and politically viable. Certain kinds of occupational and political experience also help candidates get elected.

Constitutional eligibility

To be elected to Congress, one must be an American citizen (for at least seven years for election to the House and for nine years for election to the Senate). A member of the House must be 25 years of age at the time the oath is taken; a senator must be 30 years of age. Both must be residents of the state. A representative need not reside in the district that he or she represents, and about 100 members of the House currently do not maintain permanent homes in their districts, although almost all have a legal residence there for political reasons. The Constitution bars any religious qualifications for office.

The separation clause states that "no Person holding any Office under the United States, shall be a member of either House during his continuance in Office." Anyone holding an executive or judicial office must give it up to take a seat in Congress. Conversely, a member of Congress must give up his or her seat to accept an executive or judicial appointment. It is easier for the president to appoint *defeated* congressional candidates to the administration than winners. Thus George Bush, after being defeated in a Senate race by Texas voters, received high-level appointments in the Nixon and Ford administrations (CIA director, ambassador to the United Nations, and emissary to the People's Republic of China).

George Bush has climbed the ladder. After serving in the House and then losing a Texas senatorial election, Bush was appointed ambassador to the United Nations, director of the CIA, and head of the liaison office in Peking before his election as vice president on the Republican tickets of 1980 and 1984. (*Office of the Vice President.*)

Legal qualifications

The states regulate congressional elections subject only to federal laws, regulations of the Federal Elections Commission (FEC), and federal court decisions. Requirements to qualify for the ballot—such as filing fees and the number of signatures on nominating petitions—differ from state to state. Candidates must comply with state party rules to enter a nominating primary, in which registered party voters (and sometimes independent voters) select the party nominee. In some states one needs only a plurality to win the nomination, but in many a majority is required, which means that a ***runoff primary*** between the top two vote-getters may be necessary. Runoffs work against extremist candidates who may obtain a plurality but lose to a more moderate member of the party in the second round. Some minority politicians claim that such runoffs discriminate against them: in a district in which close to half the voters are black or Hispanic, in the first round a minority contender may receive the plurality, but in the second round, if everyone votes on racial lines, the white candidate will win a majority.

Political viability

Nomination by a major party. Almost all serious candidates for Congress are nominated by one of the two major parties. So far, not a single member of a minor party has been elected, although in the past, several small parties— most notably the Populist Party and the Progressive Party between 1880 and 1920—achieved some representation.

Gender. Most members of Congress are male. A few wives of congressmen and senators have filled the vacancies when their husbands died. In the case of the Senate, they were appointed by the governor to fill out the term, while in the House they were chosen by local party leaders to run in special elections. These "congressional widows" were expected to keep the seat warm for other

local politicians until the next election, and often they had to fight for renomination against the local party leadership.[2]

In the past twenty years women have found ways to get to Congress other than over their husbands' dead bodies, and the number of women in the House has increased from ten in 1969 to twenty-two in 1985 (of sixty-five who ran). There are more than 1000 women in state legislatures (holding around 11 percent of statewide executive offices), two woman governors and several woman lieutenant governors, 1700 woman mayors, and a total of 17,000 elected woman officials; thus there is a large and experienced pool of woman politicians who can run for Congress. At the present rate it will take 400 years for women to constitute half of the House and Senate; clearly some breakthrough is needed if women are to have their demographic share of legislative positions.

Minorities.   Many blacks were elected to Congress in the aftermath of the Civil War; this was the result of Reconstruction policies enforced at the point of the bayonet by victorious union armies, but once these troops were withdrawn, the representation of blacks diminished, and it ended completely when southern blacks were disenfranchised in the period 1890–1910. In modern times most districts which elect blacks are urban with an average black population of 62 percent. Many districts which are 40 to 60 percent black are still represented by whites, and only two blacks were elected in the sixty-three districts in which blacks constitute between 20 and 40 percent of the voters. Black voters are willing to support white incumbents and to cross over and vote for a white against a black on issues—as some in a district with a black

Freed blacks were added to the electorate in 1867, although federal officials were needed to protect them at the polls. (*Granger Collection.*)

majority did in a 1984 Mississippi contest in which a white right-to-life candidate defeated a black pro-choice candidate. Representation of blacks in the House increased from nine in 1969 to twenty in 1985. There are approximately 6000 black elected officials in the nation, including almost 400 state legislators, and blacks make up 11 percent of the electorate; hence their underrepresentation in the House (and their lack of representation in the Senate) is due primarily to their inability to represent nonminority districts—to the unwillingness of white voters to cross racial lines and vote for blacks.

Hispanics also find it difficult to win nominations or elections except in heavily Hispanic areas. In California, Texas, New Mexico, and New York one or more "Hispanic districts" are created by the state legislature. No Hispanics were elected in the thirty-four districts in which they constitute 20 to 40 percent of the voters. There were ten voting Hispanics (and one nonvoting representative from Puerto Rico) in the House in 1985, and thus they are underrepresented in proportion to the percentage of Hispanics in the population (close to 10 percent). Overall, there are more than 3200 Hispanic officeholders.

Asian Americans do somewhat better in appealing to non-Asian voters. In 1985, two of the three in the House represented districts with an Asian-American population of less than 10 percent.

Religion. Protestants, who constitute the vast majority of the members of the House and Senate, are usually elected from districts or states with disproportionate concentrations of their denominations: the Baptists tend to come from the south, the Lutherans from the midwest, the Episcopalians from the eastern seaboard, and so on. The more evangelical sects are underrepresented, while the relatively few (but socially and economically advantaged) Episcopalians, Congregationalists, and Presbyterians are overrepresented in proportion to their numbers in the population, with more than 100 representatives and thirty-four Senators. The more numerous Baptists, Lutherans, and Methodists come next, with a total of 118 in the House and thirty in the Senate. Other Protestant groups have far fewer members in Congress. Slightly more than one-fourth of the members of the House and one-fifth of the members of the Senate are Roman Catholic, which is in rough proportion to the percentage of Catholics in the population (22.6 percent). In contrast, there are thirty Jews in the House and eight in the Senate, which is somewhat greater than the percentage of Jews in the population (2.6 percent).

Demographics. Increasingly, unmarried, divorced, and young politicians have been elected to office. (No longer need most members of Congress be happily married white males with two children.) The average age of members of the House has dropped from 50 to 47 in the past decade, and the average age of senators is just over 50. Close to 100 representatives and ten senators are under 42. The number of unmarried, widowed, or divorced members of the House has gone from twenty-nine in 1969 to close to 100 today.

Occupational and political experience

The occupational structure of our legislatures is narrow compared with those of most other western democracies. The halls of Congress are filled with lawyers and self-made business entrepreneurs; absent are the scientists, engineers, corporate executives, union leaders, novelists, poets, journalists, doctors, ministers, and blue-collar workers that one finds in other countries. In

Figure 7-1. Previous careers of members of the House, 1981–1982. How do people make the climb up Capitol Hill? People in business, advertising, banking, building, and college teaching usually serve first in state legislatures or other local and state positions before winning election to Congress. Lawyers, farmers, accountants, insurance brokers, and other teachers usually start even further down the ladder: first winning a job in city and county government, then moving to state government, and finally running for Congress. Blue-collar workers, social workers, journalists, and engineers typically require three job changes in the private and public sectors before they make it to Congress. (Source: *Congressional Directory*, 98th Congress, U.S. Government Printing Office, 1983.)

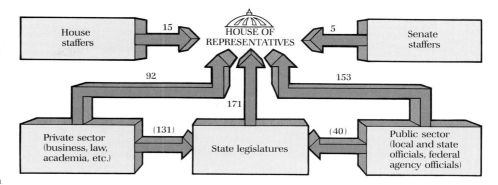

European parliamentary systems, often the party of management is pitted against the party of labor, or parties are divided along religious, linguistic, or ideological lines. Our legislators are brokers between competing interests rather than direct representatives of classes, religions, ethnic groups, or ideologies.

Occupations. In the past, the vast majority of members of both the House and the Senate were lawyers, but in the last two decades their share of seats has diminished markedly, down in 1985 to 43 percent in the House and 61 percent in the Senate. In that same year 144 representatives and thirty senators had had prior business or banking careers; thirty-seven in the House and ten in the Senate had been in education; twenty-four in the House and seven in the Senate were in farming; twenty-one in the House and seven in the Senate were in journalism; and there was a smattering of engineers, doctors, athletes, pilots, astronauts, former military personnel, and members of the clergy. Surprisingly, in our media-dominated age, there are few television producers, on-air broadcast personalities, movie stars, or people from advertising, lobbying, or public relations (Figure 7-1).

Political experience. One-fourth of the members of the House have no prior political experience. Of these, one-third are businesspeople, one-third are lawyers, and one-sixth are college professors and teachers; the rest come from the fields of banking, insurance, real estate, and the professions. These men and women are highly successful and respected in their communities—and often they are bored stiff with their roles, which is why sometime in their late thirties or early forties they decide to devote themselves to public service. Some are recruited by party leaders, but most are recruited by their bathroom mirrors.

But the other three-fourths of the members of the House, and most of the senators, are career politicians. Focusing on their occupations is misleading; they list themselves as farmers, lawyers, bankers, and the like, but rarely do they practice their professions once they are in Congress. Some get to Capitol Hill by moving up through the party organization and getting its backing, entering Congress as "ambassadors" from the party and intent on helping the organization get patronage and whatever else is to be had from the government. But local and county party jurisdictions are not coterminous with congressional district boundaries and today are not much interested in congressional nominations. Even party-oriented politicians find that the jump from a state legislature (in which help from the party organization is crucial) to Con-

gress means abandoning the party organization and creating a candidate-centered one.[3]

Interest groups are interested in and can affect nominating contests: corporate and trade associations, labor unions, and single-issue groups (such as those for or against abortion, gun control, or prayer in schools) all get involved. They may recruit, and in effect "sponsor," a potential candidate in the primaries.

The majority of those who get to Congress are experienced vote-getters. About one-third of the members of the House come directly from state legislatures, and most are well versed in local party affairs. Another third come directly from jobs with county and city governments or with state or federal agencies and also have close ties to the parties. About twenty come directly from Capitol Hill as staffers. Not only do they have local party contacts, but they also are connected to interest groups which may urge them to run.

RUNNING FOR THE HOUSE OF REPRESENTATIVES

Incumbents and challengers

It is almost impossible for an ***incumbent*** to lose a primary contest for renomination—fewer than 2 percent did so between 1956 and 1982, and only three were defeated in 1984. It is also highly unlikely that an incumbent will lose in the general election—fewer than 10 percent did so in those same years, and only seventeen lost in 1984. Elections which involve incumbents are quite different from open-seat contests, which do not.

Incumbents. In any House election approximately 4 percent of the members decide to retire, 4 percent seek higher office, and death or disability claims 7 percent. The remaining 350 to 370 incumbents will try to win renomination and reelection, and approximately 90 percent will do so, as Table 7-1 makes clear.

Not only will incumbents win, they will win big (see Table 7-2). Before 1966 about two-thirds of the incumbents won with 60 percent or more of the two-party vote, and since then 75 percent have done so. The number of *marginal seats*—those in which the incumbent won by less than 5 percent—declined from one-fifth in 1964 to around one-eighth in 1972 (and in 1984 to only 12.9

Table 7-1. Turnover in House elections, 1964 to 1984

Year	Seeking reelection	Defeated in primary	Defeated in election	Percent reelected
1964	397	8	45	86.6
1966	411	8	41	88.1
1968	409	4	9	96.8
1970	401	10	12	94.5
1972	390	12	13	93.6
1974	391	8	40	87.7
1976	384	3	13	95.8
1978	382	5	19	93.7
1980	388	6	31	90.7
1982	371	10	29	89.5
1984	392	3	17	90.1

Source: John F. Bibby, Thomas E. Mann, and Norman Ornstein, *Vital Statistics on Congress, 1980*, American Enterprise Institute, Washington, D.C., 1980, table 1-7.

Table 7-2. Landslide victories in House elections, 1972 to 1984

Year	Democrats	Republicans	House, percent
1972	185	123	70.8
1974	209	52	60.0
1976	208	89	68.2
1978	195	105	68.9
1980	173	121	67.5
1982	199	95	67.5
1984	182	140	74.0

Note: A landslide is defined as anything more than 60 percent of the total vote. This table gives the number and percentages of districts in which landslides occurred. A century ago only one-fourth of House seats were won by landslides; the number doubled to a little more than half in the period 1928–1936 and increased to two-thirds in the period 1960–1980.

percent) and has remained at that level.[4] These data are surprising because the public has little respect for Congress as an institution and yet seems to reelect most of its members.[5] Why should this be so?

INCUMBENTS' ADVANTAGES. "No Congressman who gets elected and who minds his business should ever be beaten," the former chairman of the House Democratic Campaign Committee once said. "Everything is there for him to use if he'll only keep his nose to the grindstone and use what is offered."[6] And what is offered to an incumbent amounts to approximately $1 million in staff and campaign resources, all paid for out of congressional funds. The members can make up to thirty-two free trips home each year. They are provided with funds for district offices, mobile offices, trailers, and vans so that they can help their constituents (known as *casework*) deal with government agencies (state and local as well as federal); for example, they inquire about social security eligibility, give advice on Medicare, help college students fill out loan forms, and handle problems of immigrants. Studies have shown that most voters believe that they have been helped by their representatives and view them favorably—even if they did not get what they wanted from the bureaucracy. Incumbents are often supported by such people, even voters from the opposition party.[7]

Recently elected members and those who are worried about reelection make heavy use of the House television and recording studios, which produce "news releases" about their activities for district radio and television stations. They can use the congressional frank to send out newsletters free until sixty days before an election; the cost of these newsletters (approximately 860 million pieces of mail in 1984) exceeds $250,000 per member, or more than $110 million annually. They have free WATS telephone lines that they can use to call people in their districts.[8]

Local media coverage benefits incumbents, who often help journalists from their area with features and get them access to Washington news sources. Most of the coverage by the local press is favorable, and the local media are likely to use the "canned" press releases, videotapes, and audiotapes that are sent to them, often portraying these as news coverage rather than as prepackaged material. Most incumbents are not covered by the national newsweeklies or television networks, which might be more critical of their performance.[9]

People in the districts know their representatives, and by a 3 to 1 margin in most instances they view them favorably. In contrast, most voters at the beginning of a campaign have no idea who is running against an incumbent in the primaries or the general election, do not recognize challengers' names, and do not view them positively.[10] Even by the end of a campaign, less than half the voters report having had any contact (even through newspaper articles or television coverage) with the challenger.[11]

House members claim the credit for government programs in their districts, even if they had no hand in obtaining them.[12] "Rivers Delivers" was the campaign slogan used by L. Mendell Rivers, the chair of the House Armed Services Committee, after obtaining so many military bases and hospitals that local voters in Charleston, South Carolina, joked that the city would sink below sea level. A large majority of voters think that House members care about getting the district its fair share of federal programs.[13]

How important is incumbency? We can quantify its advantages in two ways.

Geraldine Ferraro, then a representative from Queens, New York, handing out campaign literature to her constituents in 1982. (*David Burnett: Contact Stock Images.*)

First, we can compare the margin of victory in the first term with margins in subsequent terms. There is a **sophomore surge:** between 1970 and 1978 the average margin of victory between the first and second terms increased from 5.8 to 7.5 percent. In 1982 it was 2 percent for Republicans and 12.3 percent for Democrats who were reelected to second terms, and in 1984 it was 3.9 percent and 10 percent, respectively. Second, we can compare the margin of victory achieved by an incumbent in his or her last election with the margin gained by a successor of the same party in the following election—known as the **retirement slump.** The decrease in the margin of victory is usually between 6 and 11 percent.[14]

VULNERABLE INCUMBENTS. Incumbents *can* be defeated: in 1985, one-fourth of the members of Congress had beaten an incumbent to get to Capitol Hill. The odds are fairly good that an incumbent will eventually be defeated—even if the odds are low in any particular election.[15] This is so because congressional careers often follow a pattern: a close initial election victory, then vulnerability for the succeeding two elections (when the other party tries to recapture the seat), and then a constituency-building phase during which the incumbent works energetically to build support in the district. This is followed by a period in which the incumbent concentrates more on influencing decisions in Congress and forgets to cultivate the folks at home, eventually losing some support and entering another vulnerability phase, in which lower margins of victory give strong challengers an incentive to run.[16] A large number of losing incumbents slip in the previous election and win with less than 55 percent of the vote. Often a weakened incumbent faces a rematch and must run against a strong challenger from the previous election who is better known than a complete newcomer.

Corruption and scandal can be the kiss of death: twenty-six members of Congress were *convicted* of crimes between 1972 and 1982; some resigned as a result, and others were defeated. Of eighty members facing *charges* of corruption between 1968 and 1978, sixty-five ran for reelection and sixteen were defeated.[17]

207

Districting and redistricting. The Constitution apportions representation in the House among the states on the basis of their population. After each census some states gain and some lose House seats, since the size of the House has been fixed by law at 435 voting members since 1911. As a result of the Supreme Court decision in *Wesberry v. Sanders*, each district must have the same number of people.[18] Even in states that do not lose or win seats as a result of interstate reapportionment, changes in intrastate population distribution usually require new district lines after each census.

The Constitution does *not* require election to the House by districts, and before 1842 (when Congress itself prohibited it) some states elected a few members-at-large to represent the whole state. Every state legislature draws up district lines (except for six states whose population is so small that they have only one representative), and each district elects a single member by a winner-take-all plurality vote. The shape of these districts can have a substantial effect on election results, usually benefiting incumbents.

REDISTRICTING AND RACE. According to the Voting Rights Act (VRA) of 1965 and its amendments in 1982, the states cannot draw district lines to discriminate against minorities. In practice the Justice Department interprets this provision to mean that the proportion of minority voters in a district cannot be substantially reduced and that predominantly black or Hispanic districts may be created. The Supreme Court, in *Mississippi Republican Committee v. Brooks* (1984), upheld a lower court decision which held that in some circumstances, in a state with a past history of racial discrimination, the VRA could require the creation of a district with a majority of black voters.[19] In other words, in an area in which there were large concentrations of minority voters, it would be discriminatory to create two districts in which they constituted 45 percent of the voters, rather than one district in which they constituted 55 percent and another in which they constituted 35 percent—an actual issue in the *Mississippi*

Governor Elbridge Gerry's map of a Boston congressional district so resembled a salamander that the term *gerrymander* still designates artificial, politically motivated districting. (*Historical Pictures Service.*)

Figure 7-2. A gerrymandered district in California. Democrats redrew the district lines somewhat to exclude some Republican areas. They extended the district to include white working-class, black blue-collar, and Hispanic areas. The forty-fifth district, on the other hand, was created to give the Republicans a safe seat. One part, Coronado, contains many retired military people who are conservative and decidedly Republican. Another part includes the suburbs of San Diego, also solidly Republican. By making the Democratic district even more Democratic and doing the same for the Republican district, the gerrymandered lines drawn by the Democratic legislature produced the desired result: the House seat in the forty-fourth was captured by a Democrat in 1982 with an overwhelming 65 percent of the vote; the forty-fifth was taken by a Republican with 69 percent. (Source: *Congressional Districts in the 1980s*, Washington, D.C., Congressional Quarterly, 1983.)

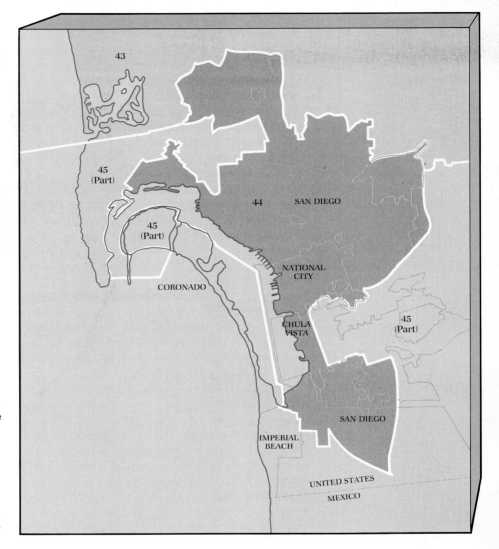

case. The creation of a few solidly minority districts benefits minority incumbents. It also benefits most white politicians, who have less to fear from minority challengers. The only politicians who suffer are minority challengers, since there are fewer districts in which minority voters form a substantial part of the electorate.

REDISTRICTING AND PARTY. Drawing district lines to benefit a party is known as *gerrymandering* (after Elbridge Gerry, an eighteenth-century governor of Massachusetts). When done on racial grounds to discriminate against minorities, it is unconstitutional, but when done by one party against another, or in collusion by both, it has not been ruled unconstitutional by the courts (Figure 7-2).

There are two ways to gerrymander. *Packing* a district means creating one in which the opposition party has total support. While that party wins the seat with just about 100 percent of the vote, every vote over 50 percent is a wasted

vote. Meanwhile, the other party keeps an edge in all the other districts, winning them with few wasted votes. The net result is that the second party wins more seats. *Cracking* a district means breaking up opposition party voters and putting them into other districts so that in each one they total less than 50 percent of the vote—and all their votes are wasted, since they win no seats.

State legislatures often gerrymander districts. The Republican National Committee (RNC) helps state parties with its Redistricting Division's $1 million computerized facilities, which are used to determine the optimum district lines for state and national elections. The Democrats, who have overwhelming majorities in state legislatures, however, rely on their political advantages to overcome the Republicans' technology.

Incumbents benefit from *collusive redistricting:* the two parties agree on a plan to preserve the maximum number of incumbents by minimizing party competition in every district. (This also has the effect of lowering turnouts.) Although redistricting helps incumbents, there is little evidence that it is a significant factor. In both gerrymandered and nongerrymandered districts in the 1970s, incumbents' margins of victory increased at about the same rate.[20]

New and open seats. Candidates have their best chances in contests for new and *open seats.* In five of the last eight elections, more party turnover occurred in open-seat races than in races against incumbents, although in 1984 fourteen new members defeated incumbents, while only seven won open seats. About half the members of Congress in 1985 had first won their seats when an incumbent retired.

CENSUS REAPPORTIONMENT. Some states gain new seats as a result of the census; after 1980 the northeastern and midwestern states lost seventeen seats, which went to the southwest and the south. In theory the new seats should benefit the Republicans—partly because an open seat always gives the minority party in the House a better chance and partly because new seats are created in the sunbelt, where the Republicans have been doing well in recent elections and where Democratic identification among voters have been weakening. Although the Republicans expected big gains in 1982, the Democrats won more new seats. They did so as a result of advantageous redistricting in states where they controlled the legislature. In California, for example, they "stole" three seats in Los Angeles by clever gerrymandering.[21] They also used gerrymanders well in New Jersey, Illinois, Missouri, and Minnesota. The Republicans turned the tables on them in Pennsylvania and Indiana; on balance, however, the Democrats came out ahead.

OPEN SEATS. Around twenty to fifty members retire each session; this is about triple the rate of the 1960s, but it is small in comparison with turnover in the nineteenth century, when one-third of the House members retired each session.[22] Older members and those in poor health are likely to retire, especially if faced with strong potential challengers in a primary or an election. More recently younger men and women, in the prime of their careers, are leaving Congress. Many are dissatisfied with the strains of holding office—burned out by the work and by commuting to and from their districts. They think that restrictions on their outside income are unfair (since they maintain two homes and many have private school or college tuition to pay). In recent years about three-fifths of the retirees have held leadership positions; seemingly some of the best are bowing out. Most won previous elections handily

Typifying a growing trend to retire early from Capitol Hill, Representative Barbara Jordan announced her decision not to run in 1978. (*David Burnett: Press Images.*)

and could have remained in office.[23] Few members resigned in 1984, however, which may mean the beginning of a low-turnover pattern.

Each session between five and twenty members of the House quit to run for higher office. They are the brave ones: most representatives never try this because the risk is too great.[24] Their odds of winning a Senate seat or a governorship are about 1 in 3. The cumulative effect of these contests is that only five or six governors, but almost one-third of senators, have served in the House.

In open-seat contests the Democrats usually hold an open primary and let the winner of this free-for-all carry the party banner.[25] The Republicans operate differently. Their state and local parties consult with the national party organization, hoping to unite around a strong politician—usually someone with experience at the state or county level. If at all possible, local parties are encouraged to avoid divisive primaries. Sometimes the national party intervenes early and supports one of the contenders, hoping to get others to drop-out.

Gender plays a role in determining who gets to run in an open-seat contest. When a party has a good chance of winning, white males usually run; when the opposition looks like a shoo-in, a woman or a member of a minority group often makes the race. In 1984, for example, forty-one women (twenty-four Republicans and seventeen Democrats) had to run against incumbents, and none won; only two Republican and two Democratic women ran in the more desirable open-seat contests. As more women become state and local party leaders (there were more than a dozen in the Republican Party in 1985, for example), fewer women should be relegated to unwinnable races.

UNCONTESTED RACES. When the south was solidly Democratic, close to 100 representatives and twenty-two senators faced no opposition in the general elections. More recently, as Republicans have built strong southern parties, most seats have been contested. Today, about 12 percent of House seats remain without two-party competition and are held by a few remaining entrenched southern Democrats and a few popular northerners who sometimes can get endorsements from the opposition.

The challengers. There is no shortage of challengers to run against incum-

211

Table 7-3. Seats lost in off-year elections, 1966 to 1982

Year	Party winning presidency	Seats gained in House in presidential election year	Seats lost in House in off-year election	Incumbents defeated from president's party
1964	Democrats	37		5
1966			48	39
1968	Republicans	5		0
1970			12	9
1972	Republicans	12		3
1974			48	36
1976	Democrats	1		7
1978			16	14
1980	Republicans	33		3
1982			26	26
1984	Republicans	14		3

bents, even though the odds are poor. In 1982 there were only fifty-eight open-seat contests and in 1984 there were only twenty-seven such contests, and so everyone else had to buck the greater odds of unseating an incumbent. Most challengers are five to seven years younger than incumbents, have less experience (only one-fifth have held elective office before), and have less funding and fewer resources.[26] How can each party recruit *strong* challengers and help them finance respectable races when the odds suggest that their best prospects are to wait for new or open seats?

PRIMARIES. One way is to defeat an incumbent in the primaries. This can be done when the incumbent is involved in a scandal, is in poor health, or has cast a particularly controversial vote. Otherwise, although one-third of the Democratic members and one-eighth of the Republican members are likely to face challengers, almost all will survive. Challengers find that it is hard to get name recognition, impossible to get news coverage in such low-key contests, and difficult to raise funds. Incumbents benefit from low turnouts in which their supporters are more likely to vote.

RECRUITING STRONG CHALLENGERS. There are good and bad nominations. In perhaps 40 contests the challenger has a real shot at the seat; in the other races the opposition party is going through the motions. When a party hack, a factional leader, or an oddball wins a nomination, it is a sign that no serious politician thought that it was worth having. But there is no difficulty in recruiting against a vulnerable incumbent; the problem is to narrow the field. The strongest challengers are those who have name recognition in the district, political experience, proven vote-getting ability, and the support of grass-roots organizations in the community.

Strong challengers give themselves better odds if they run in off-year elections against an incumbent of the president's party. In every election held in the twentieth century except that in 1934, the president's party has lost seats in the next midterm election. Off-year losses for the president's party average twelve seats in the first term (although the Republicans lost twenty-seven in 1982); in the second term losses average over twenty seats, as Table 7-3 indicates.

Financing House elections

"There are four parts to any campaign," according to Tip O'Neill, the Speaker of the House: "The candidate, the issues of the candidate, the campaign organization, and the money to run the campaign with. Without the money, you

can forget the other three."[27] Rich Bond, former deputy chairman of the Republican National Committee, quotes Lee Atwater, a White House aide, as saying, "You can't buy a district, but you can sure buy 2 percent," and 2 percent of the voters may be all that is necessary to win twenty or thirty close races.[28] In 1982, according to Tony Coelho, the chairman of the Democratic Congressional Campaign Committee, massive spending by the Republicans "saved them from an overwhelming, embarrassing defeat," an assessment shared by Republican Party officials.[29] Yet in 1984 the same spending resulted in meager gains, in spite of a Reagan landslide. Clearly money is important, but it is not decisive.

The costs of campaigning. In 1982 winners of House seats raised $124.4 million, or an average of $181,748 for each race, and losers raised $60.7 million, or an average of $101,178 per race. Money talks in House elections, although candidates need not outspend their opponents. All candidates must do is raise enough money to run a good race (that is, get themselves known and considered by most voters), whether that is more than the opposition spends or not (Figure 7-3).

The role of political action committees. PACs provide a significant amount of money for House campaigns. Winners received 26 percent of their contributions from PACs in 1976, 35 percent in 1982, and close to 40 percent in 1984. Total PAC contributions in congressional races rose from $8.5 million in 1971–1972, to $62.2 million in 1981–1982, and to close to $100 million in 1984. By 1982 PACs had displaced the small contributor as the primary source of funds for House campaigns.

Incumbents receive the lion's share of PAC funds, which means that Democrats in the House get more money than Republicans: in 1982 Democratic

Figure 7-3. The high cost of politicking. Campaign costs for primary and general elections for the Senate and House in the past decade. These costs have increased far faster than the cost of living. (Source: Citizens Research Foundation.)

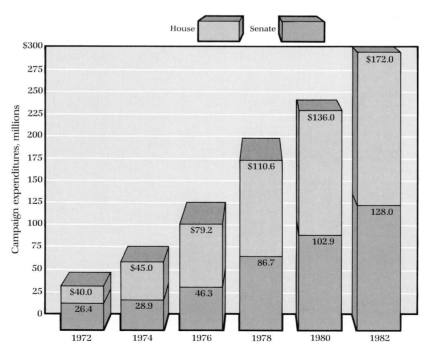

incumbents received 43 percent of their funds from PACs, while Republicans received 32 percent of their funds from this source. Incumbents in 1982 received 65.9 percent of all PAC contributions, while challengers received 13.3 percent and open-seat contestants got 14.8 percent.

Labor PACs favor Democratic candidates, while corporate and trade and professional association PACs seem to favor Republican candidates but give to Democratic incumbents as a form of "insurance" to guarantee access to them if they are reelected. In 1982 labor PACs gave 94 percent of their $20.8 million to Democrats, corporate PACs gave 66 percent of their $29.3 million to Republicans, and trade and professional association PACs gave 57 percent of their $22.8 million to Republicans. In 1984 business PACs gave 43 percent of their funds to Democrats, in response to a coordinated drive by the Democratic Congressional Campaign Committee. When funding challengers, nonlabor PACs give 9 times more to Republicans than to Democrats.

Liberal and conservative PACs play an important role in congressional races, targeting opponents for negative campaigns and providing direct contributions or services to those they favor. *Democrats for the 80s*, for example, spent $575,000 in 135 Democratic races in 1982. The *National Committee for an Effective Congress* used its Campaign Services Project that year to provide precinct targeting, polling, direct-mail, consulting, and research services, valued at $342,000, to liberal House candidates. The National Conservative PAC and other conservative PACs also spend millions, mostly on their own noncoordinated campaigns, and give little directly to House candidates.

National party finance. The national parties have become major contributors in House elections, with Republicans leading the way. Each national party committee may contribute up to $10,000 to offset the primary and general election expenses of each candidate, and each campaign may receive funds for "coordinated expenses"—party services such as polling, direct mailings, and television commercials. Figure 7-4 shows that Republican candidates have taken advantage of these provisions.

THE REPUBLICANS. The National Republican Congressional Committee has a list of more than 1.1 million donors, each of whom makes an average annual

Figure 7-4. Spending by congressional campaign committees. The Republican Party's congressional campaign committee spends far more on its candidates for election to the House than the Democratic Party's committee. This has not yet resulted in significant electoral successes in the House, since Democratic incumbents have been able to outspend their Republican challengers by raising money themselves. (Source: Federal Elections Commission, *Reports*, vol. 9, no. 6, June 1983.)

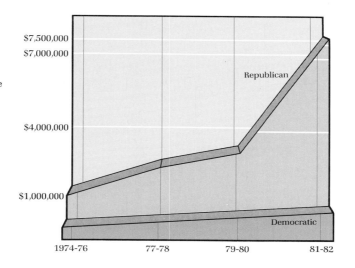

Sources of funds. It is illegal for national banks and corporations (Tillman Act, 1907), federal employees (Hatch Act, 1940), and labor unions (Taft-Hartley Act, 1947) to contribute funds to congressional candidates.

Corporations and unions may establish separate segregated funds (SSFs), which may solicit contributions from stockholders, executives, and administrative personnel (corporate SSFs) or from union members and their families (union SSFs). The sponsoring organizations may pay administrative expenses. Contributions are determined by the governing boards of the SSFs (Federal Election Campaign Act, [FECA], 1971).

Disclosing sources of funds. House and Senate campaign committees must report to the Federal Election Commission (FEC) at specified times, listing all individual and PAC contributions. The FEC issues interim, quarterly, and annual reports. Computerized files permit the data to be arranged by contributor donations or by candidates (FECA election campaign amendments, 1974).

Limitations on individual contributions. In the past, individuals could contribute no more than $5000 to congressional campaign committees (Federal Corrupt Practices Act, 1925), but candidates evaded this limitation by setting up several committees. Today, individual contributions are limited to $1000 in each primary, $1000 in each runoff primary, and $1000 in each general election contest in any two-year congressional election cycle (FECA election campaign amendments).

Individuals may contribute up to $20,000 in a two-year election cycle to national political party committees (FECA election campaign amendments). These funds may be used for congressional candidates.

Individuals may contribute no more than $5000 to any multicandidate PAC (FECA election campaign amendments).

Individuals may contribute up to $1000 in volunteer expenses for candidates (FECA election campaign amendments).

Individuals may contribute no more than $25,000 to all candidates, party committees, and PACs in a two-year election cycle (FECA election campaign amendments).

Limitations on PAC contributions. PACs may contribute no more than $5000 to each House and Senate primary, $5000 to each runoff, and $5000 to each general election contest. (FECA election campaign amendments).

Limitations on party contributions. National and state parties may contribute no more than $5000 per candidate in each primary, runoff, or general election to the House. They may contribute up to $14,720 in coordinated services in House contests. They may contribute $17,500 per candidate in Senate contests and up to 2 cents per registered voter in each state (figures as of 1980, with subsequent limits adjusted for inflation; FECA election campaign amendments).

The national party may act as the agent of a state party in collecting funds (the so-called agency agreement), which are then donated by the state party to the House or Senate candidate.

Public funding of campaigns. There are no provisions for public funding of congressional campaigns. Taxpayers may claim a $50 credit or a $100 deduction for contributions to a political campaign.

Limitations on spending. The FECA election campaign amendments of 1974 permitted candidates for the House to spend no more than $25,000 of their own funds. This provision was ruled unconstitutional in *Buckley v. Valeo*, and candidates now may spend as much of their own money as they wish in House and Senate elections.

The FECA amendments limited House campaign expenditures to $94,000 and Senate campaign expenditures to a formula based on the number of registered voters in the state. This was ruled unconstitutional in *Buckley v. Valeo*, and today there are no limitations on spending.

PACs may spend unlimited amounts, provided that their expenditures are uncoordinated and are independent of a candidate's own efforts.

contribution of $25. Republicans who are running for the House receive close to the maximum party contribution and the maximum in funds for coordinated expenses. The National Republican Congressional Committee (NRCC) handles the House campaigns for the national party. Its activities are coordinated with those of the Republican National Committee and the White House Political Affairs Office. Its priorities are (1) to protect Republicans from Democratic challengers, (2) to win open-seat contests, and (3) to assist Republican challengers in close races. It also tries to gain back seats lost to Democrats in a previous election, while new members are still vulnerable. The committee has been most successful in defeating some representatives from the liberal wing of the Democratic Party and least successful in protecting Republican incumbents and in winning open-seat contests.

Although all Republican candidates receive the maximum in party funds, the real work of the NRCC involves recruiting attractive candidates, even before the primary season; getting PACs to contribute to their campaigns; providing the close races with polling services, advertising services, and other campaign assistance; and sending in outside speakers to stump the district with the candidate (the "surrogate" program). The RNC sends "generic" direct mail to targeted House districts urging independent voters to become Republicans. In 1984 the Reagan-Bush Committee shared with House candidates the results of its phone canvasses: lists of Democrats and independents who supported the president. And it used state "party-building funds" to send canvassers to more than 4 million homes with party literature. The Republican Party also channels funds into very tight races, sometimes by taking money from races in which its candidates are strong.[30]

THE DEMOCRATS. Democratic candidates received an average of $5000 from their national committee for the 1984 elections; the national committees preferred to use their money to counter the Republican media blitz. The Democrats now have a direct-mail campaign organized through the Democratic National Campaign Committee (DNCC), which has created a national media center, but they have not yet been able to provide much assistance to most House candidates.

Other funding. Candidates typically pay for about one-tenth of their own campaign costs, but that figure varies: some wealthy self-recruited candidates can finance the entire cost of their campaigns, while some entrenched incumbents pay next to nothing and coast to victory. Individual contributions under $500 account for almost half the funds raised in House races, while contributions over $500 account for one-tenth of these funds. Republicans get a greater share of the small contributions, usually obtained by direct-mail appeals to members of single-issue groups; Democrats rely more on dinners, brunches, and cocktail parties and on wealthier givers, and so a larger proportion of their contributions is in amounts over $500.

The party that controls the White House has an advantage when it comes to fund-raising. A visit to a congressional district by the president, the vice president, or a Cabinet secretary, timed to coincide with a big fundraising event, can provide needed cash for House races. The president can encourage individuals to give money to close campaigns. In 1982 and 1984 "teleconferences," transmitted by satellite, allowed President Reagan to talk informally about the congressional elections with thousands of contributors in dozens of cities.

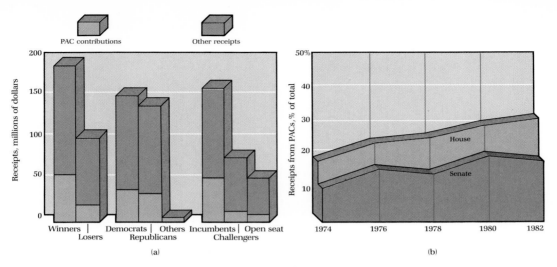

Figure 7-5. Campaign receipts in congressional elections. (*a*) In House elections, winners do significantly better than losers and receive far more PAC contributions. Incumbents, most likely to win, far outstrip their challengers. Democrats receive more funds than their Republican rivals, but only marginally. (Source: Federal Elections Commission, *Reports*, vol. 9, no. 6, June 1983.) (*b*) Percentage of contributions from PACs in general elections, for both the House and the Senate, from 1974 to 1982. (Source: Data from Michael J. Malbin, ed., *Money and Politics in the United States*, American Enterprise Institute and Chatham House, Washington, D.C., 1984, app. table A.7, pp. 288–289.)

Spending by incumbents and challengers. Incumbents have an advantage in terms of spending. As Figure 7-5 shows, incumbents raise far more money than either challengers or candidates for open seats. Since most incumbents are reelected, this advantage also shows up in two other ways: winners raise and spend far more than losers, and Democrats raise and spend more than Republicans.

Incumbents sometimes can discourage challengers by raising large war chests even before their next election. In 1985 incumbents were busy lining up support from PACs and holding fund-raisers in their districts to build up their coffers for 1986 and raise the ante on potential challengers.

Weak challengers are unable to raise, even with assistance from the national party, the $150,000 or so necessary to make a serious challenge. Thus incumbents who face such opponents need not raise or spend much while coasting to victory. (See Figure 7-6.)

But if a strong challenger can raise money, the picture changes completely. The campaign becomes a *focal point* in the national politics: the media may assign the local race some significance, saying that it is a signal about the mood of the voters, and the parties or ideological PACs may raise the ante. Out-of-state contributors may be solicited by direct mail, and the candidate may fly off to the "money centers"—such as New York City, Los Angeles, Chicago, Atlanta, Boston, Denver, and San Francisco—to meet with PAC managers and individual contributors. People who have given once in response to direct-mail appeals will give again to keep the challenger strong, and the closer the contest, the more likely they are to do so.

The incumbent then must organize a serious campaign and raise funds. But having to raise lots of money is a sign of weakness. Every dollar spent by the challenger gives him or her greater name recognition and viability. Every dollar raised by the incumbent goes toward defending his or her record and refuting charges. The more incumbents spend on House elections, the worse they do against their opponents. This is not a cause-and-effect situation; extra spending by an incumbent is a symptom of an already close race.[31]

In close races both the incumbent and the challenger are likely to spend so much money that they wind up in considerable debt. The national parties assist the winners, especially new members in Congress. After each election there is a debt-retirement party, organized by each congressional campaign

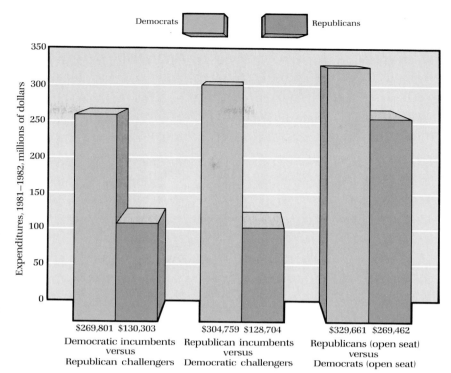

Figure 7-6. Campaign expenditures in House elections, 1981–1982. Democratic and Republican incumbents far outspend their challengers. Republicans spend more in open-seat contests than Democrats, though in 1982 more Democrats were elected to open seats. (Source: Federal Elections Commission, *Reports*, vol. 9, no. 6, June 1983.)

Democrats   Republicans

Expenditures, 1981–1982, millions of dollars

350
300
250
200
150
100
50
0

$269,801 $130,303
Democratic incumbents versus Republican challengers

$304,759 $128,704
Republican incumbents versus Democratic challengers

$329,661 $269,462
Republicans (open seat) versus Democrats (open seat)

committee even before the new House convenes, at which time members of Congress meet PAC managers who are eager to make contributions to their previous campaign.

How much is enough?   Some critics argue that we spend too much on congressional elections and that such spending forces candidates to mortgage their politics to PACs. Some comparisons may be helpful. In the United States, congressional candidates spent approximately $1.51, and presidential candidates spent about $1.75, per voter in 1980, for a total of $3.75 per voter. This compares with the figures for West Germany ($3.20 in 1983), Ireland ($3.93 in 1981), Israel ($4.34 in 1977), and Venezuela ($26 in 1983). Moreover, the figures for the United States include the costs of primary contests and PAC expenditures, while no comparable expenditures are included in the figures for the other countries.

In a system in which incumbents have so many advantages, it is necessary for challengers to spend a great deal to unseat their opponents. If we want to make elections more competitive and increase accountability in Congress, we may have to eliminate restrictions on campaign financing—not impose new limits.

Campaigning for the House

When state and local parties were strong, candidates could count on their parties to finance and manage their campaigns. House candidates were on the "party ticket," and precinct workers who brought out the vote for local candidates would also help them. Today all that has changed.

Nominating campaigns.   In recent years as many as two-thirds of the nominations have been won either by self-recruited candidates or by candidates

who have been encouraged to run by local community groups, PACs, or national party organizations. The contenders put together their own new politics organizations and field staffs. The primary vote is generally low—usually between 10 and 50 percent of the registered party voters cast ballots, which makes the electorate somewhat unrepresentative.[32] In a multicandidate contest, each candidate will rely on core supporters (for example, minorities, women, college students, union members, or ethnic or religious groups) to win the primary.[33]

Election campaigns. Congressional elections are oriented toward the techniques of media politics. By 1978 more than one-third of the campaigns no longer relied on field organizers or precinct canvassing, and fewer than one-fifth of voters are now contacted directly by party workers in House races. By 1980 most House contests used some media campaigning, and more than two-thirds of campaign expenditures now go to some form of advertising.[34] Today, the typical campaign has five full-time staffers, who are oriented toward the media rather than toward precincts.

Republican candidates rely on media politics because most run in districts in which Democrats outnumber Republicans. To win, they must appeal to independents and get voters to cross party lines. Television, radio, and direct mailings help them do this.[35] Democratic candidates have lagged in this regard, many being more comfortable with traditional grass-roots precinct canvassing.

ASSISTANCE FROM THE NATIONAL PARTY. Congressional races are not as lucrative for media consultants as statewide contests, and these consultants are abandoning the field to PACs and the parties. If the party provides services, the campaigns tend to focus on national party themes—especially economic issues—and this gives them some coherence. If ideological and single-issue PACs dominate the campaigns, the party is splintered and there is a different focus in each contest.

The Republicans are way ahead of the Democrats in unifying House campaigns and giving them a common focus. The RNC pinpoints fifty or so vulnerable Democratic seats and recruits challengers, backing them in primaries if

A Republican Party commercial attacked Democratic House Speaker Tip O'Neill in the 1982 congressional campaign. (*Photo by Barry S. Surman from "The Spot: The Rise of Political Advertising on Television," M.I.T. Press.*)

necessary. Its political education seminars and its one-week Campaign Management College, run by its Political Education Department, help campaign managers develop strategies, conduct public opinion polls, prepare commercials, and set up phone canvass banks and direct-mail operations. They can hook up local campaigns to the Republican Information Network, a computerized system which carries news of committee and floor activity in the House, presidential activities, and the position of the Republican Party on the issues, thus providing the campaign with up-to-the minute information. The NRCC will prepare advertisements and do the time buying on local media, for much less money than campaign advertising firms charge. In 1984 it used videotapes of House proceedings to make campaign commercials. (Under House rules, incumbents could not use the tapes, but Republican challengers could, and they excerpted speeches of their Democratic opponents.) To conduct these activities the NRCC has a staff of eighty-four and a budget of more than $37 million.

The DCCC has a budget of only $6 million and a staff of thirty-two. It has a national media center that makes audiotapes and videotapes, which it can broadcast via satellite to local television and radio stations. It runs a news information service that puts out press releases attacking Republican candidates. It provides computerized research on the financial reports, voting records, and positions of Republican incumbents. It runs a school for candidates, provides direct-mail services to challengers in close races, and commissions and pays for national polls in off-year elections. The DCCC spends $2 million or more on national media campaigns to counter the Republicans' commercials.

INTEREST GROUPS. Because party organizations are weak, interest groups provide volunteers, who do phone and precinct canvassing in House elections. Depending on the district, civil rights groups, women's rights organizations, labor unions, or nuclear freeze activists, for example, will take over much of the field organization of a Democratic candidate's campaign for the House, while Republican candidates benefit from the volunteer work done by corporate executives and by groups opposing gun control and abortion.[36] Environmentalists are the most bipartisan of the grass-roots groups: the Sierra Club, Friends of the Earth, and the League of Conservation Voters gave millions of dollars in assistance to candidates from both parties.

Voting for the House

After all the campaigning, it is the voters who have the last word. The outcome of an election depends not so much on which candidate has the best organization or the most funds (provided the organization and the funds are adequate) as on the size of the turnout, party identification in the district, whether one candidate was an incumbent, the candidates' personalities, and the issues.

How voters decide. House contests are less important than presidential elections and Senate races, and voters usually have less information about the candidates and fewer clues as to what would constitute a rational decision. Incumbents go to considerable lengths to take stands on issues. They introduce bills (even bills that have no chance of passage) on issues that the folks back home care about. They mail voters excerpts from their floor speeches. They vote on nonbinding resolutions and on election-year bills to put the other party on the spot.[37] They pass laws providing more benefits in election

INSURANCE RENEWAL
is now available for
MR. RICHARD M. PIOUS
in the Democratic Congressional Campaign Committee.

*Devoted to protecting the American People
against unfair and dangerous Reagan Administration policies.*

Democratic Congressional Campaign Committee

THIS

Certificate of Recognition

IS PRESENTED TO

Mr. Richard M. Pious

IN GRATEFUL APPRECIATION FOR YOUR EXTRAORDINARY
COMMITMENT TO THE DEMOCRATIC PARTY AND YOUR
GENEROUS SUPPORT TO DEMOCRATIC CANDIDATES FOR THE
HOUSE OF REPRESENTATIVES IN 1984

Thomas P. "Tip" O'Neill, Jr.   Tony Coelho
SPEAKER OF THE HOUSE   *Chairman, DCCC*

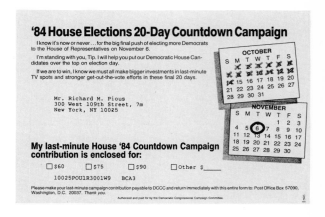

'84 House Elections 20-Day Countdown Campaign

I know it's now or never . . . for the big final push of electing more Democrats
to the House of Representatives on November 6.

I'm standing with you, Tip. I will help you put our Democratic House Candidates over the top on election day.

If we are to win, I know we must all make bigger investments in last-minute
TV spots and stronger get-out-the-vote efforts in these final 20 days.

Mr. Richard M. Pious
300 West 109th Street, 7m
New York, NY 10025

**My last-minute House '84 Countdown Campaign
contribution is enclosed for:**

☐ $60   ☐ $75   ☐ $90   ☐ Other $____

10025POU1R3001W9   BCA3

Please make your last-minute campaign contribution payable to DCCC and return immediately with this entire form to: Post Office Box 57090,
Washington, D.C. 20037. Thank you.

Authorized and paid for by the Democratic Congressional Campaign Committee

Some of the fund-raising
literature mailed to the author
during the 1984 congressional
elections.

years (such as larger social security payments) and defer new costs (such as additional social security taxes) until after the elections.

In spite of these *position-taking* activities, some studies have shown that three-fifths of the electorate cannot distinguish between the two candidates' positions on what the voters believe to be the most important issue of a campaign.[38] Fewer than one-fifth of voters can specify accurately how their representatives voted on issues.[39] With little information to go on, voters are receptive to anything which might simplify their choice.

REPUBLICAN VERSUS DEMOCRAT. One clue is party identification: voters who are Democrats can rationally support a Democrat, even if they have no other knowledge of the candidate (and Republicans can rationally support a Republican). If voters are influenced by party identification, the Democrats are favored, because there are usually more registered Democrats than Republicans in most districts. Between 1952 and 1964, when loyalty to parties was high, 9 out of 10 strongly partisan voters voted for their party's candidate, as Figure 7-7 shows.

But party ties have weakened, and the proportion of independent voters has increased; by 1980 only 6 out of 10 voters chose to vote for their party's candidate for the House simply on the basis of party identification (many did so for other reasons). This trend favors the Republicans.

LIBERAL VERSUS CONSERVATIVE. While voters do not follow most issues, they can identify themselves as liberal or conservative, and often they choose a candidate whose stance is closest to their own. The more liberal voters are, the more likely they are to vote for Democrats in House elections; the more conservative voters are, the more likely it is that they will vote for Republicans. This tendency is a rational response to the programs offered by House members of the two parties.[40] But at times liberal voters may vote for a conservative who takes a position on programs which they favor, and a significant percentage of conservative voters may help elect a liberal who supports such programs as

221

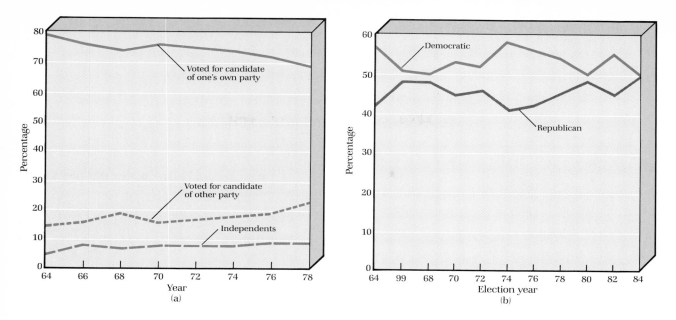

(a)

(b)

social security and Medicare. In House elections, voters are influenced more by a candidate's position on specific programs than by party ideology.

MALE VERSUS FEMALE. There are significant differences between male and female voters in some congressional elections. In 1984, for example, while a majority of both men and women voted for the Republican candidate for president, in some House and Senate races they split, with a small majority of women voting for the Democrat and a small majority of men voting for the Republican. In a number of House and Senate races this split enabled Democratic candidates to win, even against the Reagan landslide, and some analysts believe that this helped Democrats—almost all of them male—who emphasized women's issues.

INCUMBENT VERSUS CHALLENGER. Most people who defect from the party with which they are identified support incumbents of the opposition party. In 1980, 55 percent of the Democrats who defected voted for Republican incumbents in their districts, and 35 percent of the Republicans who defected voted for Democratic incumbents.[41] About three-fourths of those who defect vote for incumbents, and only one-fourth cross party lines to vote for a challenger against an incumbent.[42] This favors the Democrats.

National and local influences. "All politics are local," claims Tip O'Neill, the Speaker of the House. Most House elections are won or lost on the basis of local factors: party identification within the district and the way district lines are drawn; the skill that an incumbent demonstrates in serving his or her district and in promoting defections from the other party; the ability of challengers to raise cash and mount media campaigns; and the effect of such image making on voters.

The importance of local factors like these has increased in recent years.[43] In elections held in the 1970s, attitudes toward the candidates, incumbency, and party identification in the district could explain all but 2 percent of the vote.[44]

But national factors can still be important; even a shift of 2 percent of the vote, if based on national issues, might be enough to change the results in dozens of close races. In the 1980s, the activities of PACs and advertising by the

Figure 7-7. Opposite page: Party voting in House elections. (a) Although most voters remain likely to vote for House candidates of their own party, the percentage who vote for candidates of the other party has increased and now accounts for more than one-fifth of voters. The percentage of independent voters has also increased, weakening further the impact of party identification on congressional elections. (Source: Thomas Mann and Raymond Wolfinger, "Candidates and Parties in Congressional Elections," *American Political Science Review*, September 1980, vol. 24, no. 3, table 2, p. 620. (b) In 1984, Republican candidates for the House of Representatives won as many votes as the Democrats, a change from the normal pattern. Owing to the way Democratic-controlled state legislatures drew district lines, however, their party retained control of the House by a 252–183 margin. Some Republican analysts argued that the party could never win control of the House until it won enough state legislatures to redraw district lines favorably after the 1990 census. The Republican National Congressional Committee planned in the interim a special $5 million effort to unseat thirty of the most vulnerable Democrats in the 1986 midterm elections. (Sources: 1964–1978, *Historical Abstract of the United States: Colonial Times to 1970*, part 2, Bureau of the Census, Washington, D.C., 1975, p. 1084; 1972–1982, *Statistical Abstract of the United States*; 1984, *Congressional Quarterly Weekly Reports*, Nov. 10, 1984, pp. 2923–2930.)

national parties have tied House races more closely to presidential politics, with its media campaigns. Using national issues is a strategy that can help Republican challengers overcome their disadvantages when running against Democratic incumbents.

SUPPORT FOR THE PRESIDENT. Basing congressional elections on national issues helps the party that wins the White House in a presidential election year, but it almost always hurts that party in the succeeding off-year election. In the past, independents who have opposed the president have outnumbered those who have supported him in midterm elections. Members of the president's party who have been unhappy with his performance and have defected to the opposition have outnumbered members of the opposition party who have liked the president and have defected to support House candidates of his party.[45] To the extent that midterm congressional elections have become a referendum on the president's performance, the flow of votes has been away from his party, because protestors are more easily mobilized in midterm elections than supporters.

Most voters do not tie their decisions directly to the popularity or unpopularity of a president. The president's popularity or unpopularity had some impact in 1970 and 1974, but in other elections, such as that in 1978, polls detected none.[46] In 1982, polls indicated that most voters liked Reagan and appreciated the job he was doing; yet his party still suffered a larger-than-normal defeat in the off-year election.

THE PRESIDENT'S MANAGEMENT OF THE ECONOMY. In most congressional elections the economy is the biggest issue. The 1978 and 1982 elections were fought on that issue, both through national media campaigns and in most local contests. Democrats defeated twenty-six Republican incumbents who were identified as strong supporters of "Reaganomics." Most polls taken of people as they leave voting booths show a strong correlation between voters' attitudes toward the president's management of the economy and their party voting in House elections. A New York Times/CBS poll asked who was more to blame for economic problems—Reagan or previous Democratic policies? Of those who blamed Reagan, 87 percent voted Democratic, compared with 9 percent who voted Republican; of those who blamed the problems on the Democrats, 69 percent voted Republican and only 26 percent voted Democratic in 1982.[47]

There is a clear association between the president's popularity and per capita income figures and the percentage of the House vote that the president's party wins in midterm elections. Every decline of 10 percent in the president's popularity during the first two years costs the president's congressional party 1.3 percent of the vote. And every drop of $100 in real per capita income (due to recession or inflation) costs the president's party 3.5 percent of the vote.[48]

While acknowledging this association, political scientists have not yet found any direct connection between decisions of individual voters and economic performance. But it is not necessary for most voters to have economic concerns on their minds. Even if most people vote on the basis of party, incumbency, and local factors, a very small group of voters who decide on the basis of the economy can cause significant shifts of seats in the House.

The economy can also induce good candidates to make a race or deter them from entering it. When the economy is weak, strong challengers appear in the

Table 7-4. Split-result districts, 1964 to 1980

Year	Percent of House districts with split results[a]
1964	33.3
1968	32.0
1972	44.1
1976	28.5
1980	32.8

a. Districts carried by a presidential candidate of one party and a House candidate of another party.
Source: John F. Bibby, Thomas E. Mann, and Norman Ornstein, *Vital Statistics on Congress, 1980*, American Enterprise Institute, Washington, D.C., 1981, table 1-13, p. 19.

opposition party, while some shaky incumbents from the president's party may decide to retire before being defeated. When economic conditions are good and the president is popular, the president's party gets the good challengers and candidates for open seats, while the opposition party cannot get its best people to make the race and is likely to win fewer seats.[49]

THE PRESIDENT'S COATTAILS. At one time a strong presidential candidate at the top of the ticket could help other party candidates who were running for lower offices. This was due partly to the *party ticket:* before 1890 there were no government ballots listing all candidates, and a person cast a vote by taking a ticket (provided by a party worker) that listed all the candidates of one party and putting it in the ballot box. If a voter took the ticket showing the name of the Republican presidential candidate, this naturally helped all the other Republican candidates, and the same was true when a voter took the Democratic ticket. When voting machines were first introduced, the ***party-column ballot*** listed all candidates of the party in one column and allowed a person to make a straight-ticket vote by marking off the party box at the top. Strong party identification was more apt to lead to a straight-ticket than to a split-ticket vote.

With the weakening of party identification and the replacement of the party-column ballot in most states by the ***office-column ballot*** (in which candidates are grouped by office rather than by party and which provides no way to vote a straight ticket with a single mark), the overall rate of ticket splitting increased from 13 percent in 1952 to 25 percent by 1976.[50] The ***coattail effect*** has just about vanished.[51] As a result, the number of congressional districts which support the candidate for president from one party but also elect a representative from the other party—*split-result* districts—has increased in recent elections, as Table 7-4 shows.

Presidents rarely help most congressional candidates. In both the 1972 and the 1984 elections, popular Republican presidents won overwhelming personal victories, and yet in each case their party lost two Senate seats and won only a dozen or so seats in the House. Voters clearly differentiate between support of the president and support of the president's party: it is as if we had two distinct national electoral systems.

If presidents are unpopular (especially because of their management of the economy or as a result of a military adventure), they can do a great deal of damage to their own party. Presidents may remain out of some districts (Johnson in 1966, Nixon in 1974, Carter in 1978, and Reagan in 1982) at the request of House candidates. In 1982 many Republicans in the House focused on their incumbency and on local issues. "I know people appreciate that I'm in touch with the voters," Congressman Ed Weber observed; "I don't want people to think I've sold my soul to Ronald Reagan." "I do not support Reagan economics," said Congressman Jim Dunn; "I support Michigan economics."[52]

But in 100 districts where Reagan was popular, he appeared with Republican incumbents in commercials in which the House member was seen "briefing" him. As one party leader put it, "On a 30-second commercial, if you've got the guy briefing the President for 18 seconds, it looks like he lives over here."[53] And in 1984 the president made joint commercials with many challengers—though to little effect.

HOUSE COATTAILS. Far from being grateful for the help they supposedly get from the president's coattails, most members of the House argue that they are the ones with the coattails and that the presidential candidate of their party

benefited from their strength. In 1976 Carter won the White House with slightly more than 50 percent of the vote, while 208 Democratic congressional candidates won their districts with more than 60 percent of the vote. Carter received a total of 40,828,587 votes, but Democratic candidates for the House received more—41,749,411 in all. It was more likely that Carter benefited from the popularity of Democrats in Congress than vice versa.

In 1980 Reagan won the presidency, and 192 Republicans were elected to the House. Most owed little to Reagan, even though the White House claimed that his presence on the ballot was worth 2 points. In ninety-four districts the winning Republican received more votes than Reagan and John Anderson, the third-party candidate, combined; in 134 districts the winning Republican received more votes than Reagan; and in 149 districts he or she had a larger percentage of the two-party vote. Votes for the 192 winning Republicans totaled 24,928,623, compared with 22,607,238 cast for Reagan from these districts. The coattails belonged to the Republican candidates for the House, not to Reagan. In 1984 the president's coattails may have worked in fewer than a dozen races, since most Republicans won with a greater margin than the president, even though his victory was a landslide.

RUNNING FOR THE SENATE

Senate and House elections differ. The entire House runs for reelection every two years, while only one-third of the Senate does so. House terms are for two years, and members think constantly about reelection; senators serve for six years and therefore can take a longer view. House members run from districts (except those from states with only one member), while senators must represent an entire state. The typical House member is a virtual unknown, while the typical senator is known in the state and may even be a national celebrity. A Senate seat is considered a valuable prize by members of the House, while in modern times only a few ex-senators have subsequently run for the House.

Incumbents and challengers

While most House members have safe seats and will win landslide reelections, the prospects for senators are precarious: they have competitive primaries, they are more likely to run in close elections and to win with less than 60 percent of the two-party vote, and they are more likely to be defeated (though this was not the case in 1982 or 1984). They *feel* more vulnerable than members of the House. (See Table 7-5.)

Table 7-5. Turnover in Senate elections, 1964 to 1984

Year	Incumbents in election	Defeated in primary	Defeated in election	Percent reelected
1964	33	1	4	85
1966	32	3	1	88
1968	28	4	4	71.4
1972	27	2	5	77.1
1974	27	2	2	85
1976	25	0	9	64
1978	25	3	7	60
1980	29	4	9	55.2
1982	30	0	2	93.2
1984	29	0	3	89.7

Source: John F. Bibby, Thomas E. Mann, and Norman Ornstein, *Vital Statistics on Congress, 1980*, American Enterprise Institute, Washington, D.C., 1980, table 1-8; and author's calculations.

Senators cannot personally know a large percentage of their electorate or assist many of their constituents with casework. There are no districts to be gerrymandered to favor an incumbent. Senators, unlike House members, are covered by national news networks, weekly news magazines, and major newspapers, whose reporting is tougher than that of the local media and leaves voters more critical of them.[54]

Incumbent senators do what they can to erase negative images: in 1982 they sent 245 million pieces of mail to their constituents. Republicans (organized as the Senate Republican Conference) have set up a communications division with ten staffers whose job is to prepare press releases, packaged radio and television tapes, and columns and op-ed pieces which can be distributed to the media under the names of senators.

Most challengers are self-recruited. They tend to be statewide officeholders (sometimes governors who cannot succeed themselves according to the state constitution) or members of Congress. Occasionally, people who are not involved in politics at all—wealthy businesspeople (Frank Lautenberg of New Jersey), heirs to fortunes (John Heinz of Pennsylvania), movie stars (George Murphy of California), husband of movie stars (John Warner of Virginia, at the time married to Elizabeth Taylor), astronauts (John Glenn of Ohio and Harrison Schmidt of New Mexico), and athletes (Bill Bradley of New Jersey)—may decide to run. Presidents sometimes encourage and recruit challengers, and they may induce a weak incumbent to retire (by offering an ambassadorship or other position) in an effort to save the seat for their party.

Senate contests revolve around personalities, issues, and other statewide gubernatorial and presidential races. Party voting is relatively unimportant: one measure is the sharp rise, from fourteen in 1959 to twenty-three in 1985, in the number of states which have senators from both parties. Because many of the candidates are popular politicians or celebrities or have the money to run media campaigns, they become as well known to voters as the incumbents.[55]

One of the most effective spots ever produced propelled an Ivy-Leaguer, Malcolm Wallop, to the Senate by casting him as a hard-riding cowboy. (*Photo by Barry S. Surman from "The Spot: The Rise of Political Advertising on Television," M.I.T. Press.*)

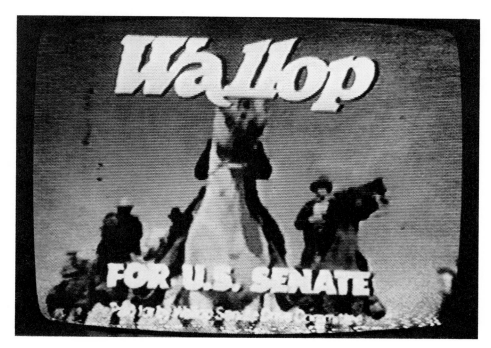

UNITED STATES SENATE

Senate staffers — 2 → UNITED STATES SENATE ← 8 — Other

16   28   10   26   10

House of Representatives   State governors   State legislatures

Private sector (business, law, academia, etc.)   State and local government

Figure 7-8. Career paths to the Senate, 1981–1982. Most senators have had previous public careers. Slightly more than one-fourth enter directly from the House. One-tenth were elected from state legislatures or governorships. Most others served in state and local government. (Source: *Congressional Directory*, 98th Congress, U.S. Government Printing Office, 1983.)

Senate candidates

Occupations. About two-thirds of the senators in 1985 listed their profession as lawyer, although only half had ever practiced. Businesspeople accounted for another fifth. About one-tenth had taught, most at the college level. A handful had been publishers, insurance brokers, journalists, farmers, bankers, or realtors.

Social characteristics. Ninety-eight senators were male in 1985. Women get nominations against strong incumbents, and a few get open-seat nominations. In 1984 a record number (twelve ran, but almost all against unbeatable men, and many got the nominations because other men and women declined, as in Oregon, Nebraska, and Rhode Island. A loosely knit group of women known as "Emily" (it stands for "*e*arly *m*oney *i*s *l*ike *y*east") encourage women in the House to run for the Senate by offering them financial backing, but as yet most of the strong potential candidates have declined to run. There were only two women in the Senate after the 1984 elections, both Republicans.

Since Reconstruction only one black has won election to the Senate (the Republican Edward Brooke of Massachusetts). No other black politician has been able to appeal successfully to a statewide electorate, and few have tried. Several Hispanic senators from New Mexico have been elected, and Arizona and California are likely to have Hispanic senators in the future. Asian Americans have been represented by S. I. Hayakawa, a former college president, who won a California seat, and by several senators from Hawaii.

Political experience. Most senators are professional politicians, and a majority start near the bottom of the ladder. In 1985, more than one-third had served in state legislatures, and one-third had served in the House of Representatives. Another third had come from state, county, or local government, and one-tenth had served as governors (Figure 7-8).

Financing Senate campaigns

In Senate elections three things are crucial: money, money, and more money. Senate elections cost more than House contests because challengers are more likely to be well financed. In 1974 only $28.4 million was raised by all the candidates, and only seven more than $1 million; in 1980 all the candidates

spent more than $76.9 million, and ten spent more than $2 million. The median spent by winners in 1982 was $1,746,230; in 1984 it was over $2 million. In North Carolina alone the two candidates spent more than $22 million in 1984 (Figure 7-9).

Heavy spending is clearly related to victory. In 1982, 27 of the 33 winners outspent their opponents. But it does not always work: in Minnesota, Mark Dayton spent $6.9 million (most of it from a fortune that he inherited) and managed to lose to the incumbent, David Durenberger, who spent half that amount. But the successful campaigns of millionaires such as Frank Lautenberg (New Jersey), Howard Metzenbaum (Ohio), John Heinz (Pennsylvania), and John Denforth (Missouri) also show that sometimes throwing money at the voters in a media campaign works.

Raising money. Some candidates provide nearly all their own campaign funds, while others contribute almost nothing: typically the contender provides one-tenth. Another tenth may come from state and national party committees, especially in the case of Republican candidates; these committees may contribute up to $17,500 to a candidate for the Senate and provide coordinated funding for services such as direct mailings or polling, paying up to 2 cents per voting-age person in the state. Another fifth come from PACs. The biggest proportion comes from individual contributions: one-fifth of all funds consist of gifts over $500, but two-fifths involve smaller amounts.[56] Republicans get more than Democrats from the national and state parties; Democrats rely more than Republicans on large individual donors.

The parties and financing. The Republicans outraise and outspend the Democrats. The National Republican Senatorial Committee (NRSC), with a staff of eighty-four, raised more than $50 million in the 1982 elections and provided more than $10 million to candidates and $2 million to a national advertising campaign. In 1984 the Republicans raised more than $80 million. The Democratic Senatorial Campaign Committee, with a staff of only six, raised only $6

Figure 7-9. Campaign expenditures in Senate elections, 1972–1982. Incumbents from both parties had a financial advantage against challengers. In open-seat contests the contenders were closely matched. Excluding Jesse Helms's expenditures, the mean for Republican incumbents in 1978 is $1,526,145. [Source: Data for 1974–1980 from Norman J. Ornstein et al., *Vital Statistics on Congress, 1984–1985 Edition,* American Enterprise Institute, Washington, D.C., 1984, table 3-4, pp. 69–70. Data for 1982 from U.S. Federal Elections Commission, *Reports on Financial Activity, 1981–1982, Final Report* (*U.S. Senate and House Campaigns*), December 1983.]

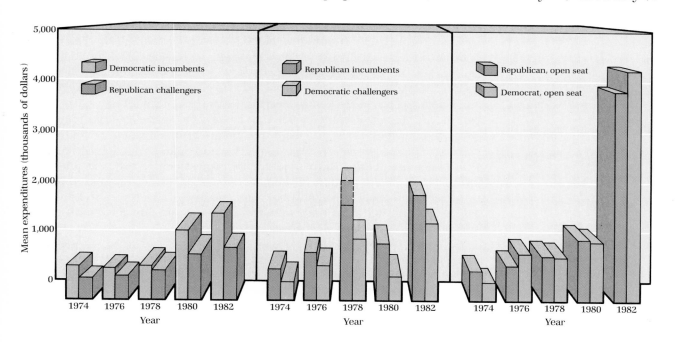

One campaign strategy is to associate an opponent with an unpopular politician. Jesse Helms of North Carolina was reelected to his Senate seat in 1984 after his opponent, Governor Jim Hunt, was tied to Mondale's losing presidential campaign. (*Sian Evans.*)

million and provided hardly any funding to its candidates in 1982, and in 1984 it did little better. Both parties could channel contributions of $20,000 made by individuals to party committees into campaigns of specified candidates. In return for large contributions, the NRSC maintained five staffers whose job it was to help contributors get access to senators or members of the administration if they had any problems. Senate rules allow members to use leftover funds for office expenses, and so the NRSC, taking advantage of this loophole, gets friendly PACs to contribute to campaigns; afterward, senators divert the money to office accounts and spend it on newsletters to solidify their support in the next election.

PACs and negative campaigns. PACs may contribute $10,000 to any Senate candidate for the primary and the general election. PACs also play an important role in fund-raising by soliciting contributions to a campaign and then sending them along as if they were made directly to the candidate. Such *bundling* of money enables a campaign to defray the costs of fund-raising by letting PACs do it.

Liberal and conservative PACs provide some money to candidates, but their most important function is to run negative campaigns against incumbents they oppose. In 1978 and 1980 conservative PACs targeted liberal Democrats for defeat. The Fund for a Conservative Majority, Citizens for the Republic, the Committee for the Survival of a Free Congress, and the National Conservative PAC (NCPAC) spent millions on so-called uncoordinated campaigns. They cast doubt on the honesty, the integrity, and even the patriotism of incumbent senators, sometimes years before an election and before a challenger had even been nominated. These campaigns eliminated six Democratic liberals from the Senate and replaced them with conservative Republicans.

In 1982 liberal PACs counterattacked. The National Committee for an Effective Congress, Democrats for the '80s, Americans for Democratic Action, and Progressive PAC sent direct mailings to liberals all over the nation, inviting them to send money to defend liberal senators and defeat conservatives. The result: PACs fought to a standoff. Senator Paul Sarbanes of Maryland, the chief target of a $1 million NCPAC negative campaign in 1982, created Marylanders for Fair and Honest Elections, a group which had on its governing board Milton Eisenhower (the brother of President Eisenhower and a former president of Johns Hopkins University in Maryland), Reverend David Leighton (an Epis-

HOW TO BUILD A CONGRESSIONAL OBSTACLE:

In North Carolina's hard-fought 1984 senatorial election, PROPAC (Progressive Political Action Committee) got in its digs at Senator Helms on behalf of Governor Hunt. (*AP Laserphoto.*)

229

copal bishop of Maryland), and Brooks Robinson (a former third baseman for the Baltimore Orioles). Sarbanes used the committee to deflect NCPAC's campaign and win reelection.

Republican Party leaders are not particularly happy about the negative campaigns of PACs. For one thing, PACs are their competitors in recruiting, financing, and staffing. PACs claim credit for electing conservatives—the same credit which is claimed by the party. Negative campaigns jeopardize potential Republican victories because Democrats raise them as an issue. In some states candidates now pledge not to take PAC money, and in 1984 Massachusetts became the first state to hold a primary (Republican) in which all the candidates took such a pledge.

Campaigning for the Senate

Campaign organization. Because Senate contests are statewide elections, the state parties have traditionally played important roles. But in the age of new politics these organizations have lost their control of nominations. Senate candidates now create their own organizations for both the nomination and the election—high on media, low on fieldwork, and only loosely coordinated with the state and local parties.

Media exposure. The media campaign becomes the centerpiece of the senatorial campaign. Unlike House contests, which media consultants find neither very profitable nor very interesting, a Senate race is both, and it attracts the best operators of new politics. The result is an increasing divergence between House campaigns, which are now largely in the hands of party-oriented campaign managers, and Senate contests. This may partly explain why Republican members of the House are likely to be "team players" who follow the national party line, while Republican senators are increasingly independent of the White House and the national party.

Voting for the Senate

How voters decide. In Senate contests neither party identification nor incumbency counts for much. The most important factor is the media campaign and how it presents personality and issues. In most states, elections are local rather than national affairs. In 1982, the national economy was the issue in House elections, as the parties tried to make them a "referendum" on Reaganomics; in Senate races the issue involved claims by incumbents that they had created jobs in their states or claims by challengers that they could bring new jobs into a state. Because there are fewer senators and because they serve for longer terms, each has more of a chance to make a record, and elections are fought partly on that record and partly on the character and accomplishments of the challenger and the incumbent.

Coattails. In the past, the president's coattails have been effective in some elections. But often the coattails work in reverse. In 1976, 20 of the 21 winning Democratic senators had greater margins of victory than Carter, and in all they won almost 1 million more votes than Carter. In 1980, eight Republican senators received more votes than Reagan, and his total vote in these senators' states just barely exceeded theirs. In 1984, 11 of the 18 winning Republican senators received more votes than Reagan in their states, and a number of Republican challengers were defeated in states in which Reagan ran well, in part a result of split-ticket voting among women.

Ticket-splitting. Surveys show a close connection between weakening party identification and ticket-splitting in Senate contests. Independents are most likely to vote for one party's candidate for president and for the other's candidate for senator; the voters who are least likely to do so are those with a strong party identification. Overall, between 1952 and 1976 the rate of ticket-splitting doubled, from 12 to 24 percent.[57] This too has weakened the effect of the president's coattails and leads most senators to believe—correctly—that they are stronger in their states than their party's presidential candidate.

ISSUE AND DEBATE

REFORM OF CONGRESSIONAL ELECTIONS. Some political scientists want to change the way we elect representatives and senators. Some reforms are designed to make it easy for presidents to lead Congress, while others would preserve congressional autonomy.

The background. Most reforms which would strengthen presidential leadership of Congress require drastic constitutional changes. One proposal is to have four-year terms for senators and representatives, with elections to be held in the presidential election year. To some extent this would focus congressional elections on national issues. All members of Congress would know that their next election would be in a presidential election year (under the present system those who are elected in a presidential election year have their next election in an off year). It would increase the impact of the president's coattails and would tie the fortunes of legislators more closely to presidential success or failure.

Another proposal is to put a limit of twelve years on service in the House and Senate. This would strengthen the presidency at the expense of Congress, since the most experienced and powerful legislators would run up against the provision for forced retirement.

Another proposal for change would automatically give the party that won the White House enough "bonus" seats in Congress to give it control. No longer could one party win the presidency and the other win the legislature, nor could the Senate be controlled by one party and the House by the other.

The case for reforms. Proponents argue that these measures would end congressional obstruction and the delay of presidential programs. They believe that Congress is too often dominated by incumbents who are out of touch with public opinion, too concerned with their own districts to recognize the national interest, and more interested in their own power than in the public interest. They believe that newly elected presidents better represent the will of the people than most legislators from safe seats.

The case against reforms. Opponents say that these changes would erode or eliminate the system of checks and balances and would go against the fundamental principles of the Constitution. Four-year terms tied to presidential elections would weaken the diversity inherent in localized campaigns. Legislators might be elected or defeated simply on the basis of a nationwide media campaign rather than on the basis of character, competence, and representation of district or state interests. The twelve-year limit, they argue, is fundamentally unconstitutional: it restricts the choice of voters, weakens the incentives of the best people to run for Congress, and converts the best legislators (that is, those who have been elected time and time again) into "lame ducks" after a decade. If the public wants "new blood," it can elect new members whenever it likes. If it wants to keep experienced incumbents, why should the Constitution be amended to prevent this?

A system of bonus seats in Congress for the party that wins the White House would just about end the system of checks and balances. Presidents, according to critics, could always get their way with the legislature, and that is not what the framers of the Constitution had in mind. Far better to require the president to persuade autonomous legislators than to provide an automatic majority.

Public opinion. Gallup public opinion polls show that by as much as a 2 to 1 margin, people favor four-year terms for representatives and senators and a twelve-year limit on service in Congress. (There have been no polls on the idea of bonus seats.)

The prospects. It is very doubtful that these reforms will be adopted. Senators do not want to lop two years off their terms. No member of Congress wants to limit service to twelve years, and so it is doubtful that such an amendment will be adopted (although an amendment did limit presidents to two terms). Finally, there is no desire among the members of Congress to add 100 or so new members to the House just so that the president can dominate congressional proceedings. Any change in Senate representation is limited by the provision of the Constitution that bars changing the arrangement by which each state is represented by two senators—the one part of the Constitution that cannot be amended.

IN CONCLUSION

How members of Congress climb up Capitol Hill has a lot to do with what happens once they get there. Representatives have an easier time getting reelected than senators but consider themselves just as vulnerable, and both representatives and senators organize their activities around reelection efforts. They finance their campaigns with their own funds and with PAC and party contributions (though in races for both the House and the Senate the major source of funds remains individual contributions from supporters), and therefore they are highly responsive to interest groups once they are in office. Increasingly, national party committees are helping in House elections, especially in terms of developing media campaigns, while Senate contests remain in the hands of independent campaign consultants.

The congressional election system maximizes the role of PACs and provides for some influence by the national parties, but it does not as yet give the parties control over legislators. The coattail effect is a factor, but the evidence seems strong that the president benefits from legislators' coattails, not the reverse, which minimizes presidential influence in Congress. Most members of Congress who are in the president's party view the president as a potential liability who may cost them the next election, rather than as an asset who can help them win.

James Madison wanted a constitutional system of checks and balances, one in which "ambition must counteract ambition." Our congressional election system has succeeded in that regard. It ensures that the fundamental constitutional understandings which create competition for power between different branches remain in place. Neither the president nor the leaders of the president's party control nominations, financing, or campaigning for Congress, and therefore they do not control legislators once they have arrived on Capitol Hill. All aspects of national government are affected by that fact.

NOTES

1. Letters sent by the Republican National Committee, Oct. 20, 1982, and by the Democratic Congressional Campaign Committee, Sept. 30, 1982.

2. Diane E. Kincaid, "Over His Dead Body: A Positive Perspective on Widows in the United States Congress," *Western Political Quarterly*, vol. 31, no. 1, March 1978, pp. 97–99.

3. Gary Jacobson, *The Politics of Congressional Elections*, Little, Brown, Boston, 1983, p. 19.

4. David Mayhew, "Congressional Elections: The Case of the Vanishing Marginals," *Polity*, vol. 6, no. 1, spring 1974, p. 305.

5. Richard F. Fenno, Jr., "If, as Ralph Nader Says, Congress Is 'the Broken Branch,' How Come We Love Our Congressmen So Much?" in Norman Ornstein (ed.), *Congress in Change: Evolution and Reform*, Praeger, New York, 1975, pp. 277–278.

6. Quoted in Gary Jacobson, *Money in Congressional Elections*, Yale University Press, New Haven, Conn., 1980, p. 113.

7. Diane E. Yiannakis, "The Grateful Electorate: Casework and Congressional Elections," *American Journal of Political Science*, vol. 25, no. 3, August 1981, p. 113.

8. Albert D. Cover, "Contacting Congressional Constituents," *American Journal of Political Science*, vol. 24, no. 1, February 1980, p. 125.

9. Michael Robinson, "Three Faces of Congressional Media," in Thomas Mann and Norman Ornstein (eds.), *The New Congress*, American Enterprise Institute, Washington, D.C., 1981, pp. 55–94.

10. Thomas Mann and Raymond Wolfinger, "Candidates and Parties in Congressional Elections," *American Political Science Review*, vol. 74, no. 3, September 1980, p. 622.

11. Roger Davidson and Walter Oleszek, *Congress and Its Members*, Congressional Quarterly Press, Washington, D.C., 1981, table 3.4, p. 86.

12. Morris Fiorina, "The Case of the Vanishing Marginals: The Bureaucracy Did It," *American Political Science Review*, vol. 71, no. 1, March 1977, pp. 177–181.

13. Warren Miller et al., *American National Election Studies Data Sourcebook*, Harvard University Press, Cambridge, Mass., 1980, table 4.20.

14. Albert D. Cover and David R. Mayhew, "Congressional Dynamics and the Decline of Competitive Congressional Elections," in Lawrence Dodd and Bruce Oppenheimer (eds.), *Congress Reconsidered*, 2d ed., Congressional Quarterly Press, Washington, D.C., 1981, p. 70.

15. Robert Erikkson, "The Advantages of Incumbency in Congressional Elections," *Polity*, vol. 3, no. 1, spring 1971, pp. 395–405; and "Is There Such a Thing as a Safe Seat?" *Polity*, vol. 8, no. 2, summer 1976, pp. 623–633.

16. Richard Fenno, *Home Style: House Members in Their Districts*, Little Brown, Boston, 1978; see also Jacobson, *The Politics of Congressional Elections*, pp. 44–45.

17. John Peters and Susan Welch, "The Effects of Charges of Corruption on Voting Behavior in Congressional Elections," *American Political Science Review*, vol. 74, no. 3, September 1980, pp. 697–708.

18. *Wesberry v. Sanders*, 376 U.S. 1 (1964).

19. Charles S. Bullock III, "The Inexact Science of Congressional Redistricting," *P.S.*, summer 1982. On the expected Republican gains and how they failed to happen, see Richard E.Cohen, "Despite the Map Maker's Best Efforts, Redistricting Won't Help Either Party," *The National Journal*, vol. 14, no. 18, May 1, 1982.

20. Davidson and Oleszek, op. cit., p. 63.

21. *The National Journal*, Apr. 6, 1982, vol. 14, no. 14, p. 1887.

22. Stephen Frantzich, "Opting Out: Retirement from the House of Representatives, 1966–1974," *American Politics Quarterly*, vol. 6, no. 3, 1978, pp. 251–273.

23. Joseph Cooper and William West, "The Congressional Career in the 1970s," in Dodd and Oppenheimer, op. cit., pp. 83–106.

24. David Rhode, "Risk-Bearing and Progressive Ambition," *American Journal of Political Science*, vol. 23, no. 1, Feburary 1979, pp. 1–26.

25. Harvey L. Schlantz, "Contested and Uncontested Primaries for the U.S. House," *Legislative Studies Quarterly*, vol. 5, no. 4, 1980, p. 550.

26. Edie N. Goldenberg and Michael W. Traugott, *Campaigning for Congress*, Congressional Quarterly Press, Washington, D.C., 1984, p. 21.
27. Jimmy Breslin, *How the Good Guys Finally Won*, Ballantine Books, New York, 1975, p. 14.
28. *The New York Times*, July 26, 1982.
29. *The New York Times*, Nov. 5, 1982.
30. Goldenberg and Traugott, op. cit., p. 71.
31. Jacobson, *Money in Congressional Elections*, Yale University Press, New Haven, Conn., 1980, p. xvii.
32. Bruce W. Robeck, "The Representativeness of Congressional Primary Voters," *Congress and the Presidency*, vol. 11, no. 1, spring 1984, pp. 59–67.
33. L. Sandy Maisel, *From Obscurity to Oblivion: Congressional Primary Elections in 1978*, University of Tennessee Press, Knoxville, 1983.
34. Larry Sabato, *The Rise of Political Consultants*, Basic Books, New York, 1980, pp. 116, 197.
35. Majorie Hershey, *The Making of Campaign Strategy*, Lexington Books, Lexington, Ky., 1974, p. 91.
36. Goldenberg and Traugott, op. cit, pp. 30–31.
37. David Mayhew, *Congress: The Electoral Connection*, Yale University Press, New Haven, Conn., 1974.
38. Barbara Hinckley, *Congressional Elections*, Congressional Quarterly Press, Washington, D.C., 1981, p. 104.
39. Patricia Hurley and K. Hill, "The Prospects for Issue-Voting in Contemporary Elections," *American Politics Quarterly*, vol. 8, no. 4, October 1980, pp. 425–448.
40. Paul Abramson et al., *Change and Continuity in the 1980 Elections*, Congressional Quarterly Press, Washington, D.C., 1981, p. 214.
41. Ibid., p. 218.
42. Cover and Mayhew, op. cit., p. 75.
43. Thomas Mann, *Unsafe at Any Margin*, American Enterprise Institute, Washington, D.C., 1978.
44. Hinckley, op. cit., p. 86.
45. Samuel Kernell, "Presidential Popularity and Negative Voting," *American Political Review*, vol. 71, no. 1, March 1977, pp. 44–66.
46. Lynn Ragsdale, "The Fiction of Congressional Elections as Presidential Events," *American Politics Quarterly*, vol. 8, no. 4, October 1980, p. 394.
47. *The New York Times*, Nov. 11, 1982.
48. Edward Tufte, *Political Control of the Economy*, Princeton University Press, Princeton, N.J., 1978.
49. Gary Jacobson and Samuel Kernell, *Strategy and Choice in Congressional Elections*, Yale University Press, New Haven, Conn., 1982.
50. Miller et al., op. cit., table 6.4.
51. George C. Edwards, "The Impact of Presidential Coattails on Outcomes of Congressional Elections," *American Politics Quarterly*, vol. 7, no. 1, January 1979, pp. 94–108.
52. *The New York Times*, Oct. 28, 1982.
53. *Newsweek*, Oct. 18, 1982, p. 36.
54. Robinson, op. cit., p. 58.
55. Davidson and Oleszek, op. cit., p. 86.
56. Michael Malbin (ed.), *Parties, Interest Groups and Campaign Finance Laws*, American Enterprise Institute, Washington, D.C., 1980, pp. 154–155.
57. Miller et al., op. cit., table 6.67.

FURTHER READING

Crotty, William: *American Parties in Decline*, 2d ed., Little, Brown, Boston, 1984. A treatise on the connections between party structure, voting behavior, and congressional elections, emphasizing the decline in party strength.

Drew, Elizabeth: *Politics and Money,* Macmillan, New York, 1983. An account of the way in which politicians circumvent campaign finance regulations in congressional elections.

Evans, Susan: *Covering Campaigns: Journalism in Congressional Elections,* Stanford University Press, Stanford, Calif., 1983. An account of news coverage of House candidates.

Fenno, Richard: *Home Style,* Little, Brown, Boston, 1978. A study of the advantages of incumbency.

Goldenberg, Edie N., and Michael W. Traugott: *Campaigning for Congress,* Congressional Quarterly Press, Washington, D.C, 1984. Surveys of campaign managers and how they run their operations.

Hinckley, Barbara: *Congressional Elections,* Congressional Quarterly Press, Washington, D.C., 1981. An account of how voters make their decisions.

Jacobson, Gary: *Money in Congressional Elections,* Yale University Press, New Haven, Conn., 1980. A book dealing with campaign finance regulations and the impact of money on campaigns.

——— : *The Politics of Congressional Elections,* Little, Brown, Boston, 1983. A comprehensive and up-to-date account of congressional elections.

——— : and Samuel Kernell: *Strategy and Choice in Congressional Elections,* Yale University Press, New Haven, Conn., 1982. A study of how the recruitment of candidates affects party competition.

Mayhew, David: *Congress: The Electoral Connection,* Yale University Press, New Haven, Conn., 1974. A discussion of how the prospect of reelection conditions almost every aspect of a House member's career.

Sabato, Larry J.: *PAC Power: Inside the World of Political Action Committees,* Norton, New York, 1984. A study of PACs and how they help in congressional campaigns.

Tufte, Edward: *Political Control of the Economy,* Princeton University Press, Princeton, N.J., 1978. A book arguing that changes in the president's popularity and the gross national product have a measurable impact on party competition in the House.

THE STUDY BREAK

Caro, Robert: *The Years of Lyndon Johnson,* vol. 1, Knopf, New York, 1983. A fascinating and detailed account of Johnson's first congressional campaign in Texas.

Clancy, Paul, and Shirley Elder: *TIP,* Macmillin, New York, 1980. A study of machine politics in O'Neill's Boston district.

USEFUL SOURCES

Barone, Michael, et al.: *The Almanac of American Politics,* National Journal, Washington, D.C., annually. Information on House and Senate elections.

Congressional Quarterly Weekly Reports, A publication that follows the campaigns and reports on election results.

Grotton, Martha V. (ed.): *Congressional Districts in the 1980s,* Congressional Quarterly Press, Washington, D.C., 1983. A source of information on district lines and relevant demographic and political data.

Martis, Kenneth C., and Ruth Anderson Rowles: *The Historical Atlas of United States Congressional Districts, 1789–1983,* Free Press, New York, 1982. A source of information on district lines.

ORGANIZATIONS

Democratic Congressional Campaign Committee. 400 North Capitol Street, N.W., Washington, D.C. 20001. For more information phone 202-789-2920.

Democratic Senatorial Campaign Committee. 400 North Capitol Street, N.W., Washington, D.C. 20001. For more information phone 202-224-2446.

National Republican Congressional Committee. 320 First Street, S.E., Washington, D.C. 20003. For more information phone 202-479-7000.

National Republican Senatorial Committee. 404 C Street, N.E., Washington, D.C. 20002. For more information phone 202-224-2351.

CHAPTER 8

PRESIDENTIAL NOMINATIONS: PRIMARIES, CAUCUSES, AND CONVENTIONS

National conventions conduct political business but today are primarily media events. Above: The Republicans nominated Benjamin Harrison at Chicago in 1888. Below: The Democrats in San Francisco in 1984. (*Brown Brothers; Eli Reed: Magnum Photos.*)

Alexander Hamilton wrote in 1788, "The time will assuredly come when every vital question of state will be merged in the question, 'Who shall be the next President?'"[1] The answer to that question depends on how the two major parties nominate their presidential candidates. The people who make up the field of contenders, how the field runs in primaries and caucuses, and what happens at the nominating conventions affect not only the general election but also the way in which our national government works.

"The system itself is becoming increasingly irrational, self-defeating and destructive," charges Walter Mondale.[2] Critics claim that nominations add little to the public's understanding of issues and shed no light on the competence and character of candidates and their associates or on the kind of administration they would form. "All told, the primary system is a disaster," says the political scientist Michael Robinson." It costs too much; it takes too long; it makes pseudo-enemies out of true political allies; and it makes pseudo-winners out of true losers. And, more importantly, the primary system has made the process of becoming President so dispiriting, so distasteful, that those would become, shouldn't."[3]

But others see things differently. "What Americans have constructed, mostly by accident," Stephen Hess argues, "is a partial stimulation of the presidency," which enables voters to see how potential presidents act under the kind of pressure they would face in the White House.[4] "Primaries are the most effective of the existing means of involving the populace in the nominating process," Thomas Cronin says, adding: "If, as the critics have remarked, primaries are democracy gone mad, the response can only be to paraphrase Shakespeare: Ah, but there is some method in this madness."[5]

This chapter will examine the method in the madness. We will consider how the field of contenders is chosen and how contenders campaign for money and votes during the primary and caucus season, and we will discuss the activities of nominating conventions. The chapter concludes with an assessment of some proposals for reform in the light of the key issues of legitimacy, authority, and the power to govern.

WHO RUNS FOR PRESIDENT?

The field of contenders for the major-party nominations is determined by constitutional, legal, social, and political factors.

Constitutional provisions

Article II, section 4, of the Constitution restricts eligibility for the presidency to natural-born citizens (those born within United States territory and presumably those born abroad of American parents) who are at least 35 years old (upon entering office) and who have spent at least fourteen years in the United States. The Constitution bars any religious tests.

Social and political factors

Social acceptability. The Constitution puts up no barriers to eligibility based on race, ethnicity, or gender. Major-party nominees must be acceptable to

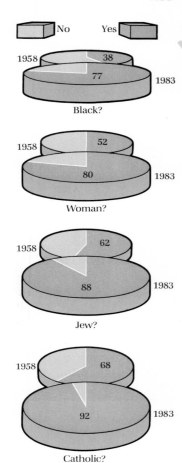

Figure 8-1. Social acceptability for presidents. In the past quarter-century the percentage of voters who say they would not vote for a woman, black, Jew, or Catholic has decreased greatly. The survey question ("Would you consider voting for a ——— for president?") may not, however, be an accurate measure of the remaining prejudice against candidates from these groups. (Source: Gallup polls.)

most of the voters. Until recently this ruled out divorced men, women, non-whites, and non-Christians, and the field was composed almost exclusively of white Protestant males of English, Scottish-Irish, or German descent. But times have changed. Two Roman Catholics—Al Smith in 1928 and John Kennedy in 1960—were nominated, and others have competed strongly (Robert Kennedy, Ted Kennedy, Edmund Muskie, and Jerry Brown). The post-Civil War bias against southerners was broken by Lyndon Johnson in 1964 and by Jimmy Carter in 1976. Ronald Reagan, though he had been divorced and had remarried, won the presidency in 1980 and 1984. Nonwhites, non-Christians, and women still have not won a major-party nomination. Residual voter prejudices would make it difficult for such persons to head the ticket, but in the near future such prejudices will, it is hoped, continue to diminish (Figure 8-1).

Political experience. Most contenders for major-party nominations have been senators, governors, vice presidents, or Cabinet members. A recent trend is for former officials to run. Richard Nixon, Jimmy Carter, Ronald Reagan, and Walter Mondale all ran as private citizens. Howard Baker retired as majority leader of the Senate and as senator in 1984 to make his bid in 1988.

When state and local bosses dominated the national conventions, governors had the best chance, and members of Congress were rarely considered.[6] After the Second World War senators were the preferred choices, and some analysts theorized that the importance of national security issues and senators' media exposure in Washington would give them permanent advantages over governors.[7] Just as these generalizations were taking hold, former governors Carter and Reagan won the White House!

Nine of the sixteen major-party vice presidential nominees between 1952 and 1984 later ran for the presidency or were considered potential presidential nominees. Of the nineteen vice presidents elected since 1901, fifteen were involved in the presidential sweepstakes in later elections. And vice presidents who succeed to the presidency, such as Truman, Johnson and Ford, are likely to win the next presidential nomination.

Party leadership. Presidents usually win renomination, even if it comes down to the wire, as it did in 1976 (when Reagan challenged Ford) and in 1980 (when Kennedy challenged Carter). Since the Twenty-Second Amendment bars a reelected president from running for a third term, usually strong potential contenders prefer to wait rather than challenge an incumbent.

The party of a president who is not running for renomination has no recognized "leader," and the same holds true for the opposition party. The defeated nominee in the prior election has no formal party position, and no function, as a European or Canadian opposition leader would. A defeated nominee who wishes to compete for the next nomination must do so as a member of the field, with no special advantage and with the disadvantage of being labeled a "loser" by opponents. For this reason, with only a few exceptions, the loser of a presidential contest usually does not get another chance. Often, however, defeated vice presidential contenders or nominees later win their party's presidential nomination: John Kennedy, Richard Nixon, and Walter Mondale, for example.

A comparative perspective: Apprentices versus entrepreneurs. In parlia-

The careers of three contemporary western European leaders illustrate different routes to top governmental positions. Helmut Kohl, chancellor of the Federal Republic of Germany since 1982, rose through the ranks in his home-state legislature, eventually becoming a state governor and federal senator. As leader of the Christian Democratic Union, he became chancellor when his party came to power. (*Regis Bossu: Sygma.*)

Francois Mitterand won the French presidency in 1981 on his third try in sixteen years. A Socialist, he ended more than two decades of Gaullist-conservative dominance. In the postwar years he had been a deputy in the National Assembly and a cabinet minister in coalition governments. (*Jean Gaumy: Magnum.*)

mentary systems leaders serve long apprenticeships before heading the government. Members of the British Parliament, like Margaret Thatcher, start in the "back benches" and demonstrate their talents on minor assignments. They become junior ministers, assisting veteran members in running a department and defending its policies in debates. Later they become ministers and eventually might be chosen as parliamentary leaders. They spend many years rising to the top of their party by gaining the respect and friendship of their colleagues. By the time such a person takes over as prime minister, he or she knows all the ins and outs of government.

In the early 1800s, presidential nominations were made by congressional parties, but since that time we have had no similar system. In the era of the boss-dominated conventions, party leaders chose novices who were easy to manipulate, like General Ulysses S. Grant, or mediocrities, like Senator Warren Harding. Today the field consists of any senator, governor, House member, or other figure who wants to run. Candidates are self-recruited entrepreneurs

who can raise the money and organize primary campaigns. The intraparty contests become bloodbaths, in which competitors find it difficult afterward to unite for the general election (Muskie and McGovern in 1972, Reagan and Ford in 1976, and Carter and Kennedy in 1980).

There is no orderly line of succession, no "shadow cabinet" in the opposition waiting to form a government if elected. Given the anti-Washington mood of voters, outsiders who know little about the ways of the capital, such as Eisenhower, Carter, and Reagan, stand a good chance of winning the nomination.

Joining the field

The exploratory committee. If you were a major-party officeholder (or former officeholder) and decided to join the field, after discussing the idea with your family and friends, you would form an ***exploratory committee,*** such as Jack Kemp's Kemp Associates or Lew Lehrman's Citizens for America. You would be able to spend up to $50,000 of your own money as well as money contributed by PACs ($5000 each) and individuals ($1000 each) to pay your expenses while you traveled around the country speaking to audiences and meeting with party leaders. The committee would be able to commission public opinion polls and pay for your speaking engagements. Later you would be able to organize your own PAC, which could make contributions (up to $5000) to candidates in congressional elections; in 1984 Jack Kemp gave 100 Republican House candidates $220,000 from his organization, the Campaign for Prosperity.

Polishing the image. You might commission a ghostwriter to provide you with a campaign autobiography or publish a book of your ideas or speeches. You would visit Ireland, Italy, and Israel (the "three I's" of ethnic politics) and arrange interviews with leaders of other nations. You would shape up and get a new wardrobe. Ray Strother (Gary Hart's media adviser in 1984) takes candidates to a video studio for rehearsals. "In that studio," he says, "we teach the candidate how to stand, how to address the camera, how to address a reporter's question."[8]

Margaret Thatcher, prime minister of Great Britain since 1979, was elected leader of the Conservative Party in 1975 after sixteen years in the House of Commons. She had served in subcabinet and minor cabinet posts in education, science, and social welfare. Her apprenticeship was unusual for a British prime minister in that it included no major cabinet portfolios. (*Stuart Franklin: Sygma.*)

If you were a Democrat, you would show up at your party's midterm convention; if you were a Republican, you would attend the annual Tidewater Conference to meet party leaders. You would go to various state conventions in the year before the nomination—nicknamed the "cattle shows"—so that county leaders could have a look at you.

The screening committee. David Broder, a columnist for the *Washington Post*, once argued that an inner club of newspaper editorialists and columnists acted as a kind of screening committee for the field. In fact, columnists such as James Reston, Tom Wicker, Jack Germond, and Broder himself were the talent scouts who sought out and identified presidential possibilities who might otherwise have been overlooked by party professionals.

Contenders will court columnists and broadcasters, hoping that what Russell Baker calls the "great mentioner" will mention them. You would know that you had hit the jackpot when you got a full-length feature story in *The New York Times Magazine;* made the cover of *Time, Newsweek,* or *U.S. News and World Report;* or were a guest on one of the Sunday morning network talk shows: *Issue and Answers, Face the Nation,* or *Meet the Press.*

MODERN NOMINATING POLITICS: PRECONVENTION CAMPAIGNS

Candidates simultaneously conduct four campaigns: for money, for supporters, for media recognition, and for votes. Doing well in one helps them in the others. These four campaigns are run in two different periods: the preelection years constitute phase 1; the three months in which primaries and caucuses are held constitute phase 2.

Phase 1: Politics in the preelection years

The first phase lasts from the preceding presidential election to January of the presidential election year.

The campaign for cash. What separates serious contenders from those who drop out early is money. The campaign must raise about $30 to $40 million for the nomination. Before 1974 candidates financed the early stages of their campaigns from the deep pockets of wealthy contributors, who made legal (or illegal corporate) contributions of hundreds of thousands of dollars. Since 1974 candidates have been able to contribute only $50,000 of their own money, and their backers are limited to $1000. "Prenomination Campaign Regulations" describes the various ceilings on contributions and expenditures.

Wealthy people are still important, but more for *whom* they know (other people who can contribute $1000) than for what they can give personally. A lawyer-lobbyist, a PAC manager, a corporate executive, a business entrepreneur, and a union leader can each hold a fund-raising party, and the small contributions add up to amounts that are donated by clearly identified constituencies interests in particular issues. Often partners in large law firms or lobbyists in trade associations will "bundle" many small checks from their friends and business associates and present them to campaign managers—who will remember later where the money came from and be responsive to those who raised it.

Candidates' PACs use initial funds to develop their direct-mail campaigns. Specialists such as Morris Dees raised $20 million from 700,000 donors in 1972 for the McGovern campaign. The Reagan-Bush '84 Committee raised $24 mil-

---

PRENOMINATION CAMPAIGN REGULATIONS

- Contenders for president and vice president may contribute up to $50,000 to their own campaigns.
- Individuals may contribute up to $1000 each year to each candidate for president or vice president (and up to $25,000 to all candidates running for federal office).
- PACs may contribute up to $5000 to each presidential contender; there is no limit on the number of such contributions.
- Contenders are eligible for matching funds from the Treasury. To qualify, a contender must obtain, in each of twenty states, $5000 in contributions (in amounts of $250 or less). The Treasury then matches, on a dollar-for-dollar basis, all contributions of $250 or less.
- The overall spending limit for a contender who accepts matching funds from the Treasury is $10 million, plus $2 million in expenses and a cost-of-living adjustment (COLA). The adjusted limit in 1984 was $24.24 million. There are ceilings on expenditures for each state based on its population.
- An amount equivalent to 20 percent of the adjusted limit may be spent on fund-raising and is not counted toward the adjusted limit.
- The national parties receive $3 million plus a COLA in public funds for the nominating conventions; in 1984 this amounted to $6.06 million.

---

lion (the maximum permitted by law) for the preconvention period in six months by using direct mailings and concentrating on small contributors, thus saving its big contributors for party-building and congressional campaign efforts. The Mondale campaign hired marketing firms with demographic data on 80 million Americans and integrated this information with its phone-bank operations so that only those people who expressed some support for Mondale would be solicited for contributions or volunteer work.

Campaign organization. Campaigns must be organized two years in advance of a primary season. Field operations in key primary and caucus states start as much as a year before an election; staffers hire organizers who have worked the state in previous campaigns and who know the local politicians. Sometimes a candidate benefits from an organization that is already in place. Jesse Jackson's victory in the Louisiana primary in 1984, for example, was due in large measure to an existing computerized network, set up in New Orleans by black politicians, which could reach 125,000 black voters by telephone or direct mail. Tape-recorded phone messages from black leaders were used in a "get out the vote" drive.

The exploratory committee begins direct-mail fund-raising. It may, like Walter Mondale's Committee for the Future of America, send out a "national issues survey" and invite contributors to join its "new agenda network." When it is announced that the contender is now a candidate, the exploratory committee is transformed into a presidential campaign committee, and contributions to it qualify for federal matching funds.

Peddling the scenario. Candidates provide media commentators with a scenario: a game plan which indicates where the candidates think they stand, what they intend to do, and how they intend to win. Walter Mondale's 1983 scenario specified that he would win a quick knockout in the first few prima-

ries and caucuses. Gary Hart saw himself as a long shot who would get to the "front tier" in Iowa; come in second in New Hampshire; go one-on-one with Mondale, whom he referred to as "mush"; and win a long, drawn-out campaign.

Phase 2: Primaries and caucuses

By the beginning of the nomination year the candidates have created their national organizations and fund-raising apparatuses. They have met with media columnists and with state and local party leaders at the cattle shows. The wire services poll county leaders, and the pollsters query voters, to see which contender has the most support. A front-runner emerges, followed by a first tier and a second tier of candidates, and the field then enters the primary and caucus season, which takes place from March to June.

Primaries: The party-in-the-electorate. In the 1970s media politics delegitimized boss-dominated politics: if the candidate-centered campaign organizations could appeal directly to voters in state and congressional races, why could they not do so in presidential nominating contests? Journalists and television broadcasters discovered that primaries make interesting news and best-selling books. They set up the primary period as a kind of pennant race— an elimination bout preceding the World Series of the general election. At the same time many party organizations asked their state legislatures to replace caucuses and conventions with primaries. They wanted to keep antiwar activists, civil rights groups, party reformers, women's liberationists, environmentalists, and others as far away from them as possible. Caucuses and conventions would only attract these people into local party politics; instituting direct primaries seemed a way of segregating local and state party matters from the national politics that concerned these groups. For the same reason most states decided not to hold their local and statewide elections in a presidential election year, and many held presidential and congressional primaries on different dates. Thus presidential nominating contests were *disaggregated* from state and local politics, and in many states the parties remained neutral and let candidate-centered organizations battle it out.

Most states adopted primaries in the 1970s, as Figure 8-2 shows. Votes for a candidate translated (directly or indirectly) into votes for delegates to the national convention.

Contenders run in most or all of these primaries. The days when a contender could compete in four primaries and win the nomination, as Jack Kennedy did in 1960, are long gone. In 1976, Jimmy Carter proved that the winning candidate must compete in all the states.

PRIMARIES AS PLEBISCITES. Primaries are plebiscites: registered voters get the chance to express their preferences in *closed primaries*; registered party voters and independents participate in *open primaries*. In the former, candidates can demonstrate their appeal to the party faithfuls; in the latter, they can appeal to a wider electorate.

The nominating convention has been transformed from a representative assembly of state parties convened to bargain with potential candidates into something quite different—a device to register the preferences of the party-in-the-electorate. The winner of each convention since 1972 (with the exception of the 1976 Republican convention) has been the candidate with the largest share of primary notes.

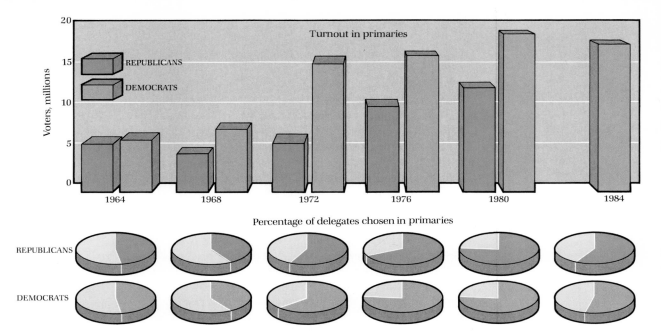

Turnout in primaries

REPUBLICANS
DEMOCRATS

Voters, millions

1964   1968   1972   1976   1980   1984

Percentage of delegates chosen in primaries

REPUBLICANS

DEMOCRATS

Figure 8-2. Growth of presidential primaries. In the past two decades, the number of primaries has increased and the numbers of voters who participate has tripled. The high point for primaries may have been 1980; since then their number has diminished. (Note: Reagan was virtually unopposed for the Republican nomination of 1984. Source: Congressional Quarterly, *Presidential Elections since 1789*, 3d ed., Washington D.C., 1983.)

PRIMARIES: THE END OF PEER REVIEW? Primaries involve an implicit contract between the electorate and the candidates. Neither voters nor the media will tolerate a return to either the congressional caucus or the boss-dominated convention. But minimizing the role of members of Congress or state party leaders ends peer review: there is no way for voters to take the measure of contenders in person and separate the ones with character and ability from the media hypesters. At most recent conventions, especially Democratic Party conventions, national politicians have been conspicuously absent, as Figure 8-3 shows.

Figure 8-3. Elected officials at Democratic national conventions. Participation of governors, senators, and representatives greatly increased in 1984 as a result of new party rules giving a greater role to the party-in-government. (Source: Democratic National Committee.)

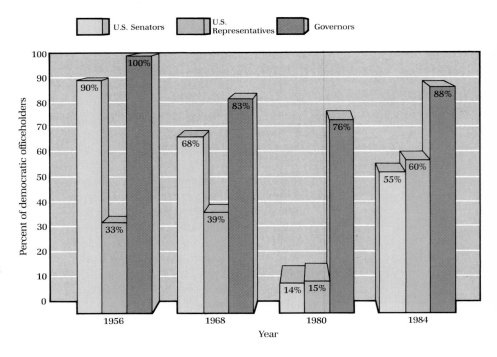

U.S. Senators   U.S. Representatives   Governors

Percent of democratic officeholders

90%   100%
33%
68%   83%
39%
76%
14%   15%
55%   60%
88%

1956   1968   1980   1984

Year

In 1984 the Democrats brought back some element of peer review. They created 566 superdelegates—14 percent of the convention—chosen from among House members (164), senators (27), state elected officials, and party leaders. It was originally thought that most superdelegates would remain uncommitted and, in a close contest, would be in a position to swing the nomination. But the candidates lobbied intensively with the superdelegates for their support. After the last primary there was a steady flow toward Mondale, who amassed the support of 85 percent of them before the convention. The superdelegates helped clinch Mondale's victory.

Critics of the primary system believe that incompetent candidates can use the media to fool voters. They point to the many impressive candidates whom professional party leaders have given the public in the twentieth century. Defenders claim that the media can expose phonies, and they point out that peer review in the nineteenth century led to mediocre nominees with whom politicians were comfortable, while only the advent of primaries has induced party bosses to back better candidates.

Critics argue that the bargaining between bosses and managers at conventions served a useful purpose: it constrained nominees by reminding them that they needed the party. But if candidates can win the nomination by going directly to the voters, they may think that they owe nothing to party leaders or workers—who may later decide that they owe nothing to them either. Nominees sever links with their own party. Primaries promote an individualistic rather than a collegial approach to politics and lead to charges of an "imperial president" who ignores the party and rides roughshod over its interests.[9]

Defenders say that the constraints which bosses placed on presidents hardly served the public interest and that we are better off without the horse-trading over cabinet posts and contracts. Presidents are constrained, but in different ways: they no longer can ignore the interests of the party rank and file, since they will have to run the primary gauntlet for renomination.

The vulnerability of an unpopular incumbent president may be the most significant problem with primaries. Do we really want a president, like Ford in 1976 or Carter in 1980, to be distracted for a whole year by nomination politics? Are the values of intraparty democracy so important that we are prepared to see presidents devote most of their time to fending off opponents within their own party? To defenders, the answers to both these questions is yes: presidents must compete in primaries to preserve accountable government. If they are unpopular, it might be a good thing to keep them vulnerable, or even to deny them renomination.

Caucuses: The resurgence of party politics. The party caucuses, which were an integral part of the boss-dominated conventions, have been modernized. Since 1972 they have been open to any registered party member who wishes to participate. From clubby meetings of party officials going routinely through the motions of sending delegates to state *nominating conventions,* caucuses have been transformed into contests between candidates' organizations. Unlike a primary (a party election, held in one of the usual polling places and involving a secret ballot), a caucus is a meeting, held in a special meeting hall (for example, a high school gym), at which people must vote openly, often by going to a designated part of the hall where their presence is counted as a vote for a candidate. This first tier of *precinct caucuses* is usually followed by

Figure 8-4. Caucus-convention system.

a second tier in which delegates attend *district conventions* (congressional, state, legislative, or county), all of which culminates in a **statewide convention** that elects delegates to the national convention. (See Figure 8-4.)

Caucuses, with their complex procedures, give local party professionals advantages over outsiders. Nevertheless, in recent years candidates have fashioned their own organizations to compete for convention delegates at every tier of the process. They do so by "flooding" the caucuses with their followers. The only way they can do this, however, is by relying on the support of unions, ethnic groups, professional associations, and others who can bring their members out to the precinct caucuses. Thus caucuses force candidates to obtain the support of interest groups and fashion effective field organizations.

Many states which adopted primaries in the 1970s abandoned them in the 1980s because of the additional expense or because their party organizations once again tried to send uncommitted delegates to the national convention. In 1984, twenty-seven states used caucuses, at which about 31 percent of the delegates (some of whom remained uncommitted until the end of the primary season) were chosen. The resurgence of state and local parties has led many to revive caucuses; some still hold preference primaries (in which no delegates are selected), but the party organizations dominate delegate selection through separate caucuses. A candidate might win the primary but lose the caucus badly—as Gary Hart did on several occasions—and therefore win few convention delegates.

CLOSE-UP

JESSE JACKSON RUNS FOR PRESIDENT. "Run, Jesse, run," the crowds roared through the winter and spring of 1984; "run, run, run." And Jesse Jackson ran with their cadenced chants.

"When you run, your enemies can't write you off and your friends can't take you for granted," he argued.

"If you run, you may lose," he told the crowds, "but if you don't run, you're guaranteed to lose. And if you run," he concluded, "you might win."

Jackson was off and running for the Democratic nomination for president, the first black candidate ever to be taken seriously, by blacks and whites alike, for the highest office. "From freedom to equality, from charity to parity," was the message he brought to the Democratic Party. "From aid to trade, from welfare to our share, from slave ship to championship—our time has come."

Reverend Jesse Jackson was the first black candidate to amass substantial delegates at a major-party convention in his 1984 run for the presidency. (*K. Hawkins: Sygma.*)

Jesse Jackson is not a career politician. Born poor, he pushed himself to academic and athletic achievements in high school and college and then went to divinity school. He became a Baptist minister, participated with the Reverend Martin Luther King, Jr., in the civil rights struggles in the 1960s, and was the leader of PUSH (People United to Save Humanity), a Chicago-based organization which organized boycotts and negotiated with large corporations to make more jobs available to minorities.

Jackson knew that he stood no chance of winning the nomination. His purpose was to send his party a message, to galvanize the minorities who constituted the most loyal of the Democratic supporters, to increase their participation, and to win them new power in party councils. It was to be a "rainbow coalition" that would bring together as many of the minorities as possible, but its effect would be to solidify a black power base in the party.

From the beginning the campaign was strong on rhetoric, issues, and ideas and weak on strategy and tactics. The idea of a rainbow coalition ignored the great differences between blacks, Hispanics, and Asians. In spite of a few publicized endorsements, most women's organizations did not join in. Jackson alienated Jews by referring to New York City as "Hymietown," and the phalanx of Black Muslim bodyguards who surrounded him and the pending indictment of his campaign manager, Arnold Pinckney, in a corruption case in Cleveland gave many other voters a negative impression. The campaign never did create a rainbow coalition—most of its support came from blacks.

Hundreds of thousands of blacks, and then more than a million, registered to vote in the primaries for him. In state after state where black voters were numerous—in the north and the south—Jackson won 10, then 20, and then 30 percent of the votes, and he won several primaries. His delegate totals mounted into the hundreds. He outlasted many of the other contenders and, along with Hart and Mondale, remained one of the three finalists. In the televised debates, he got his chance to bring his issues to the voters.

At the convention itself the Hart and Mondale delegates united to prevent Jackson from gaining enough support to bring his four platform planks to the floor of the convention: no first use of nuclear weapons, cutting the Pentagon budget, no runoff primaries (which he claimed discriminated against black candidates), and numerical quotas to end discrimination. The Mondale camp did allow a platform amendment that called for "verifiable measurements" to end discrimination, and it agreed on a "fairness commission" to study nominating rules for the next convention, so that Jackson could at least win something and would be willing to campaign for the ticket.

Jackson gave a brilliant hour-long televised address to the convention, the party, and the nation. He was once again the preacher, using his ministry for a public dialogue, rich in biblical imagery and rhyme, as when he called on the nation to join him in his mission to help "the desperate, the damned, the disinherited, the disrespected and the despised." He called for reconciliation and made his own apology: "If in my low moments, in word, deed or attitude, through some error of temper, taste or tone, I have caused anyone discomfort, created pain or revived someone's fears," he said, "that was not my truest self. . . . As I develop and serve, be patient. God is not finished with me yet." And for millions of Americans, black and white, that speech was indeed Jackson's "joy bell," ringing with the affirmation that American politics would never be the same.

Campaigning in the primaries and caucuses. PRIMARIES AND CAUCUSES AS ENDURANCE TESTS. The patchwork quilt of primaries and caucuses requires contenders to travel all over the country, in the space of fifteen weeks. Senator Bob Packwood argues that "the present system is more of a test for the Olympics than for the presidency," adding that "The test now is, can you fly from New Hampshire to California to Illinois in a day and make three intelligent speeches? This is no way to select a president."

Symptomatic of this approach is the "live shot for the locals," which is campaign jargon for a brief airport stop timed to coincide with the local evening news. Armed with minicams and microwave transmitters, a news crew can conduct a live interview with a candidate and feed it back to the local television station, and from there to the news audience. Interviews last five minutes, and so a candidate can appear on all the local stations that day.

Scurrying around the country gives candidates little time to think, to read, to reflect on the issues, or to work closely with people they might want in their administration. Staffers and media advisers with little experience in government peddle their own policies. The campaign functions in its own little universe, which negates much of the value of campaigning.

PRIMARIES AND CAUCUSES AS A STEEPLECHASE. Candidates want to avoid a poor showing and quick elimination; each wants to become the only contender from one of the wings of the party by eliminating rivals. They want to win some of the big-state primaries and accumulate enough delegates in other states to take the lead. It is not necessary to have a majority; in modern times any front-runner who has 41 percent or more of the delegates by the end of the season has won the nomination.[10]

Contenders may use a defensive strategy, trying to defeat others within the same party wing in order to remain survivors of the winnowing that occurs in the first primaries. Using an offensive strategy, candidates try to break out of the pack and distinguish themselves from the rest of the field.[11] By getting many more votes than expected in the early primaries, they hope to get good media coverage, move up in the polls, and get more PAC and direct-mail contributions, since winners get a major boost in the subsequent polls.[12]

The key primaries and caucuses are the preliminary rounds, which give extensive media coverage to the winners; the core contests, in which many delegates from the large states are chosen; and the watershed primaries, which are "do or die" for one or more contenders.

THE PRELIMINARY ROUNDS: IOWA AND NEW HAMPSHIRE. Since 1976 these two states have held a unique place in the nominating game. Iowa goes first with its caucus and convention. The contenders must organize in the state as much as a year in advance. Union members, farmers, and teachers play a major role in bringing out the vote. Jimmy Carter in 1976 and 1980 had the backing of the National Education Association and rewarded it by establishing the Department of Education after his election. Turnouts in Iowa approach 10 percent of the registered party voters, which gives the caucuses the flavor of a primary. A win, or even a strong second-place finish, propels a candidate into the front rank of contenders. (For the Democrats, this is somewhat ironic, since Iowa almost always votes Republican in the general election.) In 1984 Gary Hart took second place, and George McGovern took third (the difference between them was fewer than 1500 caucus voters), and yet Hart received an enormous amount of publicity for his showing, while McGovern was ignored.

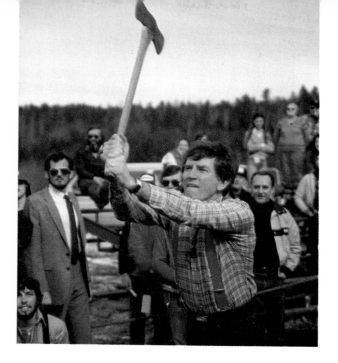

Senator Gary Hart of Colorado hit the bulls-eye with an ax at both a New Hampshire county fair and its Democratic primary in 1984. (*Ira Wynam: Sygma.*)

New Hampshire runs the first of the direct primaries. Because of the enormous media exposure it generates for the winner, it is also one of the most important primaries. Consider Jimmy Carter's experience after his first-place finish in 1976:

> Carter's face appeared on the covers of *Time* and *Newsweek*. On the inside, he got 2,630 lines. The second place finisher, Udall, got only 96 lines; in fact, all of Carter's opponents together received only 300 lines. That week, Carter got three times the television evening news coverage as his typical major candidate rival. He also got four times as much front-page newspaper coverage and over three times as much inside space.[13]

In 1984 Gary Hart's surprise victory gave him the same media boost, resulting in a huge jump in support in the polls, from about 4 to 40 percent in two weeks. Surveys of voters conducted just before and just after the network evening news for several days after the New Hampshire primary showed a surge in support for Hart following each evening's coverage. By early March he was the only Democratic contender to lead President Reagan in the "trial heats" of the pollsters.

The preliminary contests give unknowns like Carter and Hart publicity and name recognition across the country, and this boosts them in the polls and gets them funds. Rivals who do poorly begin to drop out of the race. Voters in other states reassess their tentative decisions about which candidate to support. They move from second-tier candidates who have no chance to the front-runners, and they move toward a "comer," like Carter or Hart, who seems to have momentum. In the six weeks after the new Hampshire primary in 1984, 8 percent of Democrats who supported second-tier candidates switched to Mondale and 14 percent switched to Hart, and 14 percent switched from Mondale to Hart.

CORE AND WATERSHED CONTESTS. As the primary season progresses, most contenders drop out. The core primaries and caucuses give the remaining two or three a chance to win large numbers of delegates. In some states delegates are

apportioned solely on the basis of the percentage of votes a candidate received, but in others there are "bonus" allocations or winner-take-all delegate contests (based on results in districts within the state), and these give a candidate who narrowly wins the popular vote a huge lead in delegates.

Those who do poorly in these states get unfavorable media coverage, and their expenses outrun new contributions. The watershed contests eliminate them if they fail to meet media expectations; conversely, a good finish can restore a sagging campaign, as it did for Ronald Reagan in several southern primaries in 1976.

The role of the media in primaries and caucuses. Broadcast and print journalists bring the public campaign news (where the candidates went and what they did and said—known in the trade as "here they come, there they go" stories), analysis of strategy and tactics, evaluations of candidates, and discussion of the issues. They pay too little attention to issues and too much attention to daily events and to the horse race. Dan Rather, the CBS anchor, says, "We have no apologies for covering the horserace aspect of this. They want to know who lost, who won, and why. I don't think they want a lengthy discussion of the issues."[14]

But critics fault the media for their pervasive inability even to get the horserace aspects right. The media commission polls, which they report before and after each round of primaries; these are designed to explain how people voted and why. The media also make forecasts of how campaigns will do. Most of these forecasts are incorrect. In 1968 media gurus insisted that an incumbent president could not be denied renomination, but Eugene McCarthy's near tie with Lyndon Johnson in the New Hampshire primary led to the president's decision to withdraw from the race. In 1972 the media thought that the front-runner, Edmund Muskie, had the Democratic nomination locked up and that George McGovern was a fringe candidate with no chance—several months later Muskie was gone and McGovern was the nominee. In 1976 the conventional wisdom had it that no contender could obtain a majority of delegates in a lengthy primary season, and Jimmy Carter was considered an obscure regional contender whose real goal was the vice presidency. On the Republican side, Gerald Ford was thought to have an easy run for nomination. Yet he barely held off Ronald Reagan, and eventually he lost to Carter in the general election. Going into the winter of 1980, commentators thought that Ted Kennedy could wrest the nomination from Carter; by late spring they were sure that Carter was unbeatable, and by early summer they did not know which way to bet. Few gave Reagan a chance before the 1980 primary season; by the following January he was president. A New York Times poll—conducted with technical advice from political scientists—pronounced, just before the 1984 New Hampshire primary, that Walter Mondale enjoyed the largest lead ever recorded by a Democratic presidential hopeful in the party. Yet Gary Hart proceeded to win the primary, and subsequent polls showed him advancing 30 points within two weeks.

The polls are mush, almost completely unreliable: the samples are not always valid, and voters change their opinions up to the time they step into the booths. But the savvy candidate can take advantage of the media's addiction for prediction. By peddling a scenario which downplays strength in the early caucuses and primaries and by releasing or publicizing unfavorable polls, a

candidate can keep media expectations low. Then a good performance will be taken as evidence of a surge of support, and the media will report favorably on the surprise showing. Candidates who do better than expected will win the "media primary" even though they lost the actual one. "The elimination of candidates occurs," David Broder argues, "not because of the actual votes they receive, but because they get discouraged; volunteers and contributors desert them and the press sours on them when the returns are disappointing. What happens, and what is written and broadcast, the day after the primary is more important than what happens at the polls."[15] Even winners who do worse than expected—like Lyndon Johnson in 1968 and Edmund Muskie in 1972 in New Hampshire—can "lose" the media primary even though they won the real one.

WOLFPACK JOURNALISM. A campaign can be derailed if the candidate commits a *gaffe:* makes a slip of the tongue, tells an ethnic joke, has an outburst of temper, or blows up at reporters. Consider what happened to Jesse Jackson's campaign in 1984 after he referred to New York City as "Hymietown" and to Jews as "Hymies." His remarks were reported in the *Washington Post* by Milton Coleman, a black reporter. Jackson first claimed that he did not remember making them, and then he appeared before a Jewish congregation in New Hamsphire to apologize; meanwhile, his campaign lost weeks of momentum. Later he had to disassociate himself from anti-Semitic remarks made by one of his supporters, the Black Muslim leader Louis Farrakhan (who also threatened Coleman's life). Although Jackson was successful in mobilizing black voters in the primaries, the media concentrated on these gaffes, not on the issues that Jackson wanted to discuss—which was a major reason he was running in the first place.

Other candidates have had their problems: Hart's change of name (from Hartpence) and the fact that he said that he was one year younger than he really was also dogged him for weeks, while he tried vainly to interest the media in his "new ideas" theme. And he lost the New Jersey primary in large measure because of a slip: while in California, he jokingly told a crowd of supporters that his wife was lucky to be campaigning there, while he had to go back to New Jersey and campaign at toxic-waste dumps.

CONTROLLED MEDIA: POSITIONING THE CAMPAIGN. As candidates move from one state to another, they usually concentrate on national and local themes. Gary Hart talked about new ideas to the nation, but about toxic-waste dumps to people in New Jersey and about nuclear power plants to California residents. Walter Mondale talked about experience to the nation, but about gun control to New Yorkers and about the Chrysler loan program to people in the industrial midwest. Jesse Jackson talked about the rainbow coalition to the nation, but said "our time has come" to black inner-city audiences. Candidates use direct mailings, radio and television advertisements on local stations, and local news coverage to deliver these specialized messages.

Candidates use the techniques of new politics to project their personalities. Robert Goodman, the media adviser to George Bush in 1980, used exciting theme music, actors impersonating secret service agents, and youthful crowds. Bush was featured pledging that he would move the nation "into a position of strength. We're gonna be strong, we're gonna lead, and we're gonna win." The 1976 advertisements for Gerald Ford looked like soft-drink pitches, with a bouncy "we're feelin' good about America" theme.[16]

Dan Wasserman, Los Angeles Times Syndicate; reprinted by permission.

Primary campaigns can take a negative turn. Consider one of Carter's successful advertisements in 1980:

MAN: I don't think Kennedy's qualified to be President.
WOMAN: I don't think he has any credibility. . . .
MAN: I don't trust him.
WOMAN: You're taking a chance with Kennedy.
MAN: Between Kennedy and Carter, I would definitely go with Carter myself.
    I trust him.[17]

Candidates can use commercials to position themselves on the issues. They can take an extreme or a centrist position within their party, or they can position themselves closest to the overall electorate. They can also choose direction as well as position: moving toward the center from one of the extremes or sharpening differences with the rest of the field by moving away from the center.[18]

In *closed* primaries or caucuses, candidates go either with mainstream attitudes in their party or with a faction. In *open* primaries or caucuses, they have more flexibility because they can also do well by appealing to independents. Walter Mondale, who emphasized traditional liberalism, did well in closed contests; Gary Hart, who was skeptical about interest groups and government welfare programs and who opposed gun control, did better in open primaries.

Voters in primaries often do not know or misperceive a candidate's stance on issues. Eugene McCarthy was the antiwar candidate in New Hampshire in 1968, and yet almost half of his primary supporters voted for him even though they were hawkish on the war, and some thought that he was a hawk as well. Many of the white blue-collar voters who supported Robert Kennedy in the

Trendy graphics characterized Gary Hart's primary commercials. (*Photo by Barry S. Surman from "The Spot: The Rise of Political Advertising on Television," M.I.T. Press.*)

The eight starters in the 1984 race for the Democratic nomination began the winnowing-out process with their first debate at Dartmouth College in Hanover, New Hampshire. (*John Ficara: Woodfin Camp.*)

1968 primaries later voted for George Wallace (a third-party candidate) in the general election; Wallace was opposed to most of the issues that Kennedy stood for, but nevertheless he could tap the same vein of protest against Washington that had been a theme of the Kennedy campaign.

PRIMARY DEBATES. Contenders may be invited by networks, civic groups, or universities to participate in debates. In 1984 the Democrats held six candidate forums, which had a major impact on the primary contests. Many voters, knowing that debates would be held, remained uncommitted or tentative, preferring to obtain more information about the candidates in the course of one evening's debate. The low-keyed John Glenn did poorly, while Jesse Jackson and Gary Hart picked up strength. Walter Mondale regained the offensive

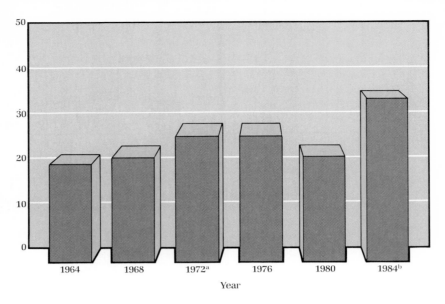

Figure 8-5. Primary turnouts, 1964–1984. Turnouts rose in the 1970s but declined in the 1980 nominating contests, even with highly competitive races in both parties. In 1984 President Reagan had almost no opposition in Republican primaries and the percentages refer only to Democratic contests. (Sources: Austin Ranney, *Participation in American Presidential Nominations*, Washington, American Enterprise Institute, 1976, and author's calculations.)

a. Nixon renominated with little serious opposition; Republican turnouts included.

b. Reagan renominated with no opposition. Republican turnouts excluded; figures are only for Democratic primaries.

against Hart, and Jackson finally reached a national audience with his ideas.

Front-runners prefer not to debate because the risks are considerable. This can backfire. In 1980 Ronald Reagan refused to debate in Iowa and lost a state he should have won. In New Hampshire the front-runner, George Bush, refused to debate in a large field, demanding to go one-on-one with Reagan; the latter made an issue of it and put Bush on the defensive. Jimmy Carter, who was ahead in the polls in the 1980 primary season, refused to debate Ted Kennedy, but this time the strategy worked.

Primaries and caucuses: How democratic are they? Are primaries and caucuses the most democratic way to choose a party nominee for president? Or are they unrepresentative charades, dominated by media manipulators and likely to produce nominees who are unrepresentative of the will of the party-in-the-electorate?

PARTICIPATION. Primaries are now mass-participation events (Figure 8-5). The average turnout in caucuses was only 2.6 percent in 1984, and that was higher than usual. Compare this with the 35 percent turnout in the Democratic primaries in 1984 and the 23 to 28 percent turnouts in preceding Republican and Democratic contests. Only 11 million people participated in primaries in 1968; by 1980 (when both parties had serious contests) that number had tripled to more than 33 million. In states which hold closed primaries, usually between 40 and 60 percent of the eligible registered voters participate. The highest rates of participation occur in states in which primaries are held before anyone sews up the nomination; in which contenders' names are on the ballot; which are closed to registered party voters; and in which primaries have been held in the past and voters have become used to them.[19]

REPRESENTATIVENESS OF THE PRIMARY VOTE. Some people argue that primaries draw a disproportionate number of voters from higher socioeconomic

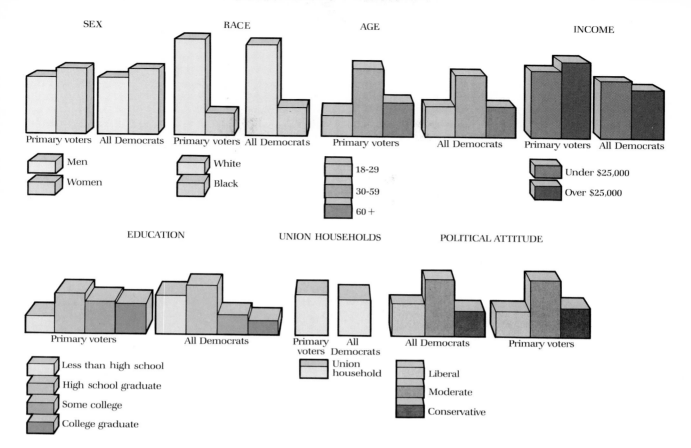

SEX RACE AGE INCOME

Primary voters   All Democrats
- Men
- Women

Primary voters   All Democrats
- White
- Black

Primary voters   All Democrats
- 18-29
- 30-59
- 60+

Primary voters   All Democrats
- Under $25,000
- Over $25,000

EDUCATION UNION HOUSEHOLDS POLITICAL ATTITUDE

Primary voters   All Democrats
- Less than high school
- High school graduate
- Some college
- College graduate

Primary voters   All Democrats
- Union household

All Democrats   Primary voters
- Liberal
- Moderate
- Conservative

Figure 8-6. Democrats in general versus Democratic primary voters, 1984. Primary voters were more likely to be white, older, liberal, well-educated, and with higher incomes than all Democrats. But most of these differences were small, and some might be accounted for by the margin of error in the poll samples. (Source: *The New York Times*, based on polls conducted in twenty-four primary states by NYT/CBS, CBS News, NBC News, and ABC News.)

groups. Although in the past this may have been true, recent surveys have shown similarities between voters in primaries and voters in general elections. The Democrats who voted in the 1984 primaries were quite similar to all rank-and-file Democrats, as Figure 8-6 makes clear, although they were better educated, older, more affluent, and slightly more liberal (in 1980 voters in primaries were ideologically similar to voters in the general election).[20] Small differences remain, but it is not true that voters in primaries are quite different from the party rank and file or that there is a marked upper-class bias in primary systems. The large turnouts of minority voters in 1984 (up 82 percent in Alabama, 43 percent in Florida, 103 percent in New York, and 38 percent in Pennsylvania from 1980) have made the system much more representative. However, those who participate in caucuses do not mirror the overall party-in-the-electorate, but overrepresent particular interest groups, extreme ideological voters, religious fundamentalists (in Republican states), and more affluent voters.

LEGITIMACY OF THE PRIMARY SYSTEM. Primaries are supposed to give the nomination to the choice of the party rank and file. Do they? In almost all cases the winner of the primary season also becomes the first choice of the party voters; this has been true in 25 of the past 26 contests (the only exception was Barry Goldwater in 1964). By virtue of the struggle itself, the winner is transformed into the party's choice.[21] In 1984, for example, by the end of the primary season Walter Mondale was the choice of 53 percent of black Democrats, and Jesse Jackson was the choice of 31 percent, event though the majority had voted for Jackson in the primaries.[22] (See Figure 8-7.)

But the legitimacy of a nomination may be called into question because of the way delegates are allotted. Consider the 1984 contest (Figure 8-8). Gary Hart won sixteen primaries to Walter Mondale's eleven, and he claimed to be the popular choice. However, because Mondale received 38.6 percent of the votes, (compared with 36.2 percent won by Hart), because he led in preference polls

Figure 8-7. Jackson's popular vote in primaries and share of delegates.

Figure 8-8. Mondale's strength was concentrated in the industrial northeast and midwest and the south, traditional areas of Democratic strength. Hart's base was the plains and western states and New England, all regions which vote Republican in most presidential elections. Many of Hart's supporters did vote for Reagan against Mondale in the general election.

of party identifiers, and because he did better than Hart in trial heats against President Reagan, Hart's claims could be dismissed. But suppose that Hart had received a larger percentage of the popular vote and had done better in the polls of party identifiers and the trial heats? Mondale still would have won the majority of delegates, but perhaps some of the uncommitted delegates and superdelegates would have gone with Hart. And the party itself would have been divided, with some claiming that Hart should have received the nomination because of the popular vote and with others claiming that Mondale should have won because he came out ahead in delegate contests.

THE NOMINATING CONVENTION

"The convention does not decide and it does not debate," concludes Senator Pat Moynihan of New York; "the rise of the primaries has made it inevitable that the nomination is settled before the convention begins."[23] Approximately 4000 Democratic and 2000 Republican convention delegates must, in a four-day period, approve the party rules and settle challenges to delegates' credentials, agree on the platform, nominate a presidential candidate, and nominate a vice presidential candidate. They must accomplish all this in such a way as to win rather than lose the support of a nationwide television audience, which they do by promoting an image of a united party rather than a divided one. The coalition that controls the convention must convert its intraparty enemies into willing allies in the general election. If it fails to do so, the other party often wins the White House, as happened to the Democrats in 1968, 1972, and 1980 and to the Republicans in 1976. An intraparty bloodbath weakens the authority even of a candidate who can win the presidency.

Managing the convention: Nominating the president

Front-runners try to hold onto their delegates, and in some cases (Carter in 1976 and Mondale in 1984) they must obtain more support for a majority. They lobby the superdelegates and convince uncommitted delegates (who are likely to come from caucus states) to join the bandwagon. Trailing candidates attempt to break up the coalition. There are only three ways to stop front-runners: challenge the credentials of rival delegates on the first day, provoke a platform fight that divides their followers on the issues on the second day, or raise a procedural issue that causes defections before the presidential nomination on the third day.

In the boss-dominated conventions these tactics worked because some bosses, nominally in one coalition, were prepared to double-cross their partners and accept a better deal from another coalition. Votes on credentials or party rules became tests to see whether a coalition could control the convention.

In most conventions front-runners have maintained control against challengers. Delegates come to the convention to nominate the candidate to whom they pledged themselves in the primaries. The front-runner's organization keeps in constant contact with delegates through an elaborate "whip" system. Instructions can be relayed from the campaign headquarters (a hotel suite in the convention city) to the communications trailer located off the convention floor, and from there by walkie-talkie to aids who can signal the front-runner's supporters. If the front-runner manages things well, delegates are not diverted by extaneous issues, nor are they interested in deal and defections.

Managing the convention for the media

Since the networks dropped gavel-to-gavel convention coverage in 1984, opting instead to broadcast only the highlights, the leading contender have had to organize the convention business into segments, each of which shows the party favorably. The Republicans in 1984 produced an eighteen-minute film introducing Ronald Reagan (at a cost of $425,000), which they showed to the delegates. The national committee and the platform and rules committees control these segments to ensure that everything will proceed according to plan.

Nevertheless, a well-managed convention, to the extent that it becomes a floor show rather than a political contest, may defeat its purpose. During the Republican convention in 1984 a Marx Brothers movie swept the television ratings in several cities. In New York City the Mets and Yankees won over the Democratic convention. All the networks got a combined share of 13 percent of all homes. Only 19 million Americans watched each convention at any one time. Usually the networks get 42 percent of the television audience in July—during the conventions their coverage got only 21 percent. As the ratings have dropped, so has the coverage: from 142 hours in 1976, to 110 in 1980, and to only 76 in 1984.

Rules and credentials

Opponents propose changes in party rules and challenge delegates' credentials to break up the front-runner's coalition. The strategy goes all the way back to Martin Van Buren, who in 1832 proposed that a two-thirds majority be required to nominate the Democratic candidate for vice president—a proposal made solely to keep the incumbent, John Calhoun, from winning renomination. Van Buren later attacked the two-thirds rule as applied to presidential nominations in his own failed attempt in 1844 (yet the rule lasted until 1936).

Front-runners use rules changes to solidify their position. George McGovern, whose party commission proposed rules changes for the Democratic convention of 1972, capitalized on the new rules to win the Democratic nomination. At the convention itself, McGovern's forces voted to seat the California delegation—chosen by a winner-take-all procedure which in principle he had opposed—because he had won the California primary. Meanwhile, party oppo-

Nancy Reagan waves to husband, Ron, watching her perform before a nationwide television audience as she delivers a short speech to delegates at the Dallas convention. (*Sygma.*)

nents, who in the past had supported the winner-take-all procedure, argued for proportional representation of the delegation because that would have reduced McGovern's proportion from 100 to 44 percent.

Consider the *pledge rule,* which binds delegates to vote at the convention for the contender to whom they pledged support in the primaries, a rule used by the Republicans in 1976 and by the Democrats in 1980 and then discarded by both. The front-runners (Ford and Carter) referred to it as the "justice" rule, arguing that it is only right that the convention enforce the primary results. Their opponents (Reagan and Kennedy) referred to it as the "robot" rule and argued instead for a "conscience" rule, which would permit delegates to vote for whomever they chose, regardless of the primary results, thus creating an "open" convention. Such a proposal is derided by front-runners, who say that it would negate the democratic principle on which the primary rests and return control to the party organization. In any event, both rules challenges failed.

Nevertheless, there is a serious argument to be made against the pledge rule. It prevents a convention from making an assessment, on the basis of new information or changed circumstances, about the merits of the contenders. And it removes the last vestiges of the representative function from conventions, converting them into registering devices, pure and simple. For these reasons, both parties have discarded the rule.

Platform politics

A party's platform specifies its principles and proposed programs. While it does not bind a candidate once in office, a majority of platform pledges are implemented.[24] Several months before the nomination the party's national committee appoints a temporary platform committee and staff members. The state parties also appoint temporary members, who, after the primaries and caucuses, are replaced by elected delegates who represent the candidates. The platform committee then holds public hearings around the country or in Washington. It then meets a few weeks before the convention for final hearings. Then it drafts the platform and any minority reports. On the second day the convention considers and adopts the platform and accepts or rejects any minority reports. In recent years party rules have prevented any amendments from the floor; this keeps things running smoothly and gives everyone an incentive to work things out in committee.

The worst thing that can happen to a nominee is to have key parts of the platform written by delegates who support other contenders. In 1976 the Republicans approved a foreign policy plank which repudiated the policies of President Ford and Secretary of State Kissinger and endorsed the approach taken by Ronald Reagan. In 1980, rather than try to win a divisive fight against Ted Kennedy's forces, President Carter compromised, and key parts of the Democratic platform incorporated Kennedy's positions. In both cases incumbent presidents demonstrated weakness that presaged trouble in the fall elections.

Republican convention delegates divide into a large conservative majority and a smaller "progressive" wing. Even conservative Republican nominees sometimes try to keep their delegates from putting strong conservative positions into their platform, since this might cost them the election, and they are likely to ignore the provisions that they do not want to run on. After the "hard right" had won most of its platform fights with the moderates, Richard

Viguerie, the direct-mail specialist for right-wing causes, cautioned his supporters, saying, "I would not advise you to bet the farm that they are going to keep the promises in this platform any better than they did in the last platform."[25]

The Democrats fragment into various "issues caucuses" that meet during the first two days of the convention. Delegates who are committed to causes—ranging from the environment to a nuclear freeze and from putting a woman on the ticket to guaranteeing full employment—meet to draft their own statements on issues, culminating several months of preconvention organizing. These caucuses often pressure the platform committee, which meets several weeks before the convention in Washington, to adopt their causes. In theory, the candidate and the candidate's deputies control all the committees which meet and can adopt their own provisions by majority vote over proposals of other nominees. But in fact, much of the content of the platform is dictated by the pragmatic compromises that the candidate has to make with these caucuses.

Nominating the vice president

On the fourth day the convention nominates a vice president. The delegates have by then ratified the choice of their presidential candidate, usually announced days or weeks before the convention meets. The purpose behind the choice for vice president, as Barry Goldwater succinctly put it, "is to get more votes."

The nominee for vice president usually balances the ticket by region and sometimes by religion: in 1960 John Kennedy, a Catholic from the north, ran with Lyndon Johnson, a Protestant from the south, and in 1964, 1968, 1972, and 1984 Catholic candidates ran for the vice presidency. In 1984 the Democrats produced the first gender-balanced ticket by nominating Geraldine Ferraro. Occasionally a liberal will choose a conservative, or vice versa, but contrary to popular belief, such balancing is rare. In most cases presidential nominees choose people whose beliefs are compatible with their own: Kennedy and Johnson, Goldwater and Miller, Carter and Mondale, Reagan and Bush, and Mondale and Ferraro, for example. Often a governor or former governor who is running for president chooses a Washington insider (usually someone who has served in Congress), though senators rarely reciprocate, usually picking someone else with experience in Washington rather than a governor. In the boss-dominated conventions the vice presidency was either a consolation prize given to a defeated coalition to unify the party or bait to build the winning coalition—tactics used to nominate Woodrow Wilson and Franklin Roosevelt for president. But coalition-building deals produced mediocre men for the vice presidency: in the nineteenth century six were not even renominated, none of the four vice presidents who succeeded to the presidency on the death of the incumbent won the nomination on their own, and only Martin Van Buren parlayed the vice presidency into a subsequent presidential nomination and election.

Since World War II the quality of nominees has improved. Men like Harry Truman, Lyndon Johnson, Walter Mondale, and George Bush all had impressive credentials when they joined the presidential ticket. In fact, between 1952 and 1984, eleven vice presidential nominees were more experienced in civilian politics than the presidential nominee. Republican presidential nominees averaged 12.25 years in public office, compared with 11.125 for their running

mates; corresponding figures for the Democrats are 12 years for the presidential nominee and 15.5 years for the vice presidential nominee (though 1984 was an exception).[26]

In the past, the major problem with the selection process has been that it has come at the end of the convention, when the candidate and his advisers were exhausted and when they may not have devoted sufficient time to their choice.

A hurried decision resulted in the selection of Tom Eagleton, a distinguished liberal Democratic senator from Missouri whose past history of shock treatments surfaced after his nomination, forcing his withdrawal from the ticket and damaging George McGovern's chances. Yet it is not at all clear that unhurried consideration, lengthy interviewing of contenders, or extensive consultation within the party produces a better nominee than the rush jobs. Last-minute nominees include Lyndon Johnson, Edmund Muskie, Robert Dole, and George Bush, all of whom were well qualified for the presidency. More leisurely consideration gave us Spiro Agnew, a mediocre and corrupt political hack who ultimately resigned from the vice presidency in disgrace after pleading no contest to charges of corruption involving his conduct as county executive and governor in Maryland and as vice president. Although Walter Mondale used a lengthy interviewing process, his staff failed to uncover any of the irregularities involving the financial dealings of Geraldine Ferraro's husband, matters which hurt her campaign.

FOCUS

A WOMAN ON THE TICKET. The memo to Walter Mondale from his campaign field director, Mike Ford, was blunt. Mondale always seemed to play it safe—always running the ball and never daring to pass. It looked at though he might do that again when choosing a vice president for his ticket. "A run is another white male," Ford wrote. "We are behind. A pass should be considered. A black, Hispanic, or woman."

Mondale called his choice for vice president "the most important decision I will make as the Democratic nominee." His list narrowed to four: Henry Cisneros, the Hispanic mayor of San Antonio; Tom Bradley, the black mayor of Los Angeles; Diane Feinstein, the mayor of San Francisco; and Geraldine Ferraro, the third-term representative of the "Archie Bunker" district in Queens, New York.

Bradley, 66, and Cisneros, 37, were dropped because of their age. A staff memo warned that choosing Cisneros might cause hard feelings among blacks. Feinstein, the mayor of a liberal city with a large gay population (to whom she had been politically responsive), might not present the right image to middle America. Ferraro could appeal to the Catholic voters of the northeast, to the descendants of southern and eastern European immigrants, and to the liberal and feminist wings of the Democratic Party.

So it was to be Ferraro.

Like anything else that happens in presidential nominating campaigns, Mondale's decision involved behind-the-scenes organization, a media campaign, political maneuvering and pressure, and a dash of luck. He picked a woman (rather than a male governor from a southern or border state or his rival, Gary Hart) because he was pushed in that direction by the women in the Democratic Party and by women's political organizations.

In the weeks before the convention the National Organization of Women (NOW)

New York Representative Geraldine Ferraro chaired the 1984 platform hearings and went on to receive the vice-presidential nomination. (*UPI; Bettmann Archive.*)

made it clear that the price for support from the women's movement would be a woman on the ticket. If Mondale chose a man, warned Judy Goldsmith, the president of NOW, "one strong possibility is a nomination from the floor," and NOW's national meeting passed a resolution to that effect. NOW's Democratic Task Force started to organize woman delegates and line up votes on the convention floor by conducting a telephone survey and generating a computerized list of delegates who would support a floor fight. The Gender Gap Action Campaign put pressure on Mondale through press conferences and advertisements in newspapers. Kathy Wilson, the president of the National Women's Political Caucus, argued that the 33 million unregistered women in the country would come out for a woman vice president. The caucus would have 400 members as delegates to the convention, and it released a poll late in June of a sample of all Democratic delegates indicating that 74 percent though that "a well-qualified woman would be a real help in defeating Ronald Reagan," while only 10 percent thought that a woman would hurt the ticket. Several state delegations and state parties—including those from New York, Louisiana, Idaho, Washington, Vermont, and Wisconsin—passed resolutions calling for a woman on the ticket. And fifteen leading Democratic women met privately with Mondale to lobby with him. Many male Democratic politicians agreed. "The real challenge is for the men of the Democratic Party to share power with the women who have done so much to make the party the progressive force it is today," argued Anthony Earl, the governor of Wisconsin, while another governor, Richard Celeste of Ohio, thought that nominating a woman would "generate fresh excitement coming out of the convention."

Geraldine Ferraro played her cards perfectly. "I don't know whether a woman would help the ticket," she confessed to one women's organization. "Quite frankly, whether I would do it would [depend] on whether it was the strongest ticket." After a meeting with Mondale, she said that she would not let her name be placed in nomination in a floor fight against Mondale's choice, and she helped organize other women in the party against an attempt to dictate to Mondale. On the other hand, she made it clear after a three-hour meeting with Mondale in North Oaks that she wanted to be on the ticket and thought that she would help the campaign. The Speaker of the House, Tip O'Neill, endorsed her candidacy;

with his backing she had become the secretary of the Democratic Caucus (the meeting of all House Democrats), a member of the House Budget Committee, and chair of the platform committee of the national convention. "Tip's comfortable with Gerry carrying on the traditional values of the party in the language of a new generation," explained Ann Lewis, the political director of the Democratic National Committee.

So were the convention delegates. Polls showed that Ferraro had the support of 23.1 percent of the woman delegates, compared with 21.7 percent who supported Hart, and was the first choice of Mondale delegates, with the backing of 21.8 percent, compared with 17.6 percent for Hart. Rank-and-file Democrats, however, were not nearly as enthusiastic. A New York Times/CBS poll showed that Hart was well ahead of Ferraro as their choice for vice president: 23 percent favored Hart, 9 percent favored Jackson, 3 percent favored Feinstein, and 2 percent favored Ferraro.

The nomination of a woman would not by itself change many votes: a New York Times/CBS poll of registered voters (taken on July 12, 1984) indicated that 6 percent of the voters were more likely, and 8 percent were less likely, to vote for the Democratic ticket, while more than 80 percent said that having a woman on the ticket would make no difference in their vote.

The delegates

Who are the **convention delegates,** and how representative can they be of the party rank and file? These are important questions: if the delegates do not reflect the preferences of party identifiers, the party may be in serious trouble when it tries to win the support of these identifiers in the fall elections.

How representative are the convention delegates? DEMOGRAPHICS. In the era of the boss-dominated conventions, all the delegates were white male local

Figure 8-9. Characteristics of convention delegates, 1968–1984. Democrats have significantly increased the percentage of blacks and women as a result of party reform rules. Jews and Catholics are overrepresented according to their proportion of the population, owing to their historic support for the Democratic coalition. Republicans have significantly increased their proportion of women but remain a forum for white, predominantly Protestant delegates. (Sources: *Public Opinion*, October–November 1980; Democratic National Committee; and *The New York Times*, reporting on 1984 CBS News and New York Times/CBS News polls.)

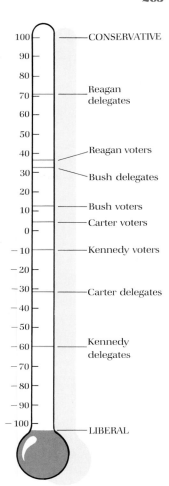

Figure 8-10. Ideological orientation of primary voters and convention delegates, 1980. Samples of voters and convention delegates were asked to place themselves on a "thermometer" with readings from 0 (coldest) to 100 (warmest). Voters were asked how they felt about liberals and conservatives: the former score would be subtracted from the latter, giving each a possible net score, or placement, between −100 (most liberal) to +100 (most conservative). The general electorate places close to 0, with equal feelings towards liberals and conservatives. There is only a loose correspondence between the placement of voters who favored a particular candidate in the primaries and the delegates pledged to that candidate. Carter voters in 1980 were on average slightly conservative, while his delegates were moderately liberal. Reagan voters were moderately conservative while his delegates were extremely conservative. (Source: Barbara Farah, "The Representativeness of Direct Primaries," fig. 1.C, "Ideological Orientation of Primary State Convention Delegates and Their Partisan Identifiers, 1980.")

party politicians. Since 1968 the Democrats have reformed their procedures to make convention delegates more demographically representative. In 1972 there were quotas for minorities and younger delegates; in 1976 these were dropped in favor of affirmative action goals. Since 1980 the rules have required that half the delegates be male and that half be female. In 1984, 50 percent of the delegates were women, 17.5 percent were black, 6.4 percent were Hispanic, 1.9 percent were Asian American, and 0.9 percent were American Indian. The Republicans have shied away from formal rules about demographic diversity; since 1976 the proportion of woman Republican delegates has increased to 44 percent, but there are few minority delegates. Figure 8-9 shows the differences between the two parties; these differences are understandable in light of the electoral support that different groups give to the parties.

SOCIOECONOMICS. Delegates from both parties are better educated and more affluent than the general population, as one would expect of any group of politicians. More than two-thirds have finished college; almost one-fifth of the Republican delegates have law degrees (slightly more than the Democratic delegates), and one-fifth of the Democratic delegates have masters and doctorates (slightly more than the Republican delegates). The Republican delegates in 1984 had higher incomes than the Democratic delegates: 57 percent of the Republicans and 42 percent of the Democrats had incomes over $50,000. More Democratic delegates are teachers and union leaders and members, while more Republican delegates are businesspeople, professionals, white-collar workers, and farmers.[27]

IDEOLOGY. Delegates are not very representative of registered party voters in terms of issues and ideology (Figure 8-10). While some come from pragmatic county and local party organizations, many are recruited as delegates by a candidate's own campaign organization, which selects people from the single-issue groups that work with the candidate in the primaries. In 1980 the National Education Association had 279 tightly organized and disciplined national convention delegates supporting Jimmy Carter at the convention; also present in large numbers were environmentalists and members of the National Women's Political Caucus, the National Organization of Women, and civil rights organizations. Although delegates will vote for the candidate, they remain free to express their own views when drafting the party platform, passing on rules changes, and acquiescing or objecting to the choice of a vice presidential nominee. The result is that Democratic convention delegates are more likely to be liberal and to be identified with particular issues or causes than Democratic party identifiers. In 1984 the ***Equal Rights Amendment*** (ERA) was supported by 9 out of 10 Democratic delegates and by 6 out of 10 Democratic

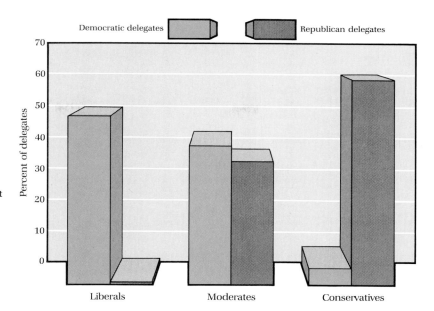

Democratic delegates   Republican delegates

Figure 8-11. Ideology of convention delegates, 1984. Most Democratic convention delegates are liberals or moderates. A majority of Republican delegates are conservative. Approximately the same results were obtained for the 1980 conventions. (Source: CBS News delegate survey.)

voters; a majority of the delegates thought that taxes should be raised, while fewer than 20 percent of the rank and file agreed; the delegates opposed the draft, while a majority of the Democratic voters favored it; and the delegates opposed military intervention against the spread of communism, while almost two-thirds of the Democratic voters favored it. Republican delegates are more conservative and more likely to be identified with conservative causes (against abortion, gun control, and the ERA) than Republican identifiers.

In 1972 the Democratic delegates, especially those who supported McGovern, were far more liberal than the Democratic voters—so much so that the Republican *delegates* were closer to the Democratic *voters!* Some have argued that this accounted for McGovern's overwhelming defeat: the convention activists who nominated him were out of touch with their own constituencies. But since then Democratic delegates have moved closer to the center; in 1984 half described themselves as liberals, 42 percent as moderates, and only 5 percent as conservatives—and they are still able to lose massively. In contrast, Republican delegates have moved further from the center, and in 1980 and 1984 they were skewed to the right: 1 percent said that they were liberals, 35 percent said that they were moderates, and 60 percent said that they were conservatives. (See Figure 8-11.) Yet in both years the Republicans won a massive victory, proving that conventions need not mirror either the electorate as a whole or even the party identifiers to win—provided that candidates do not let the ideology of their delegates determine their campaign stance in the general election.

Delegates' orientation: partisans, personalists, purists. In the days of the boss-dominated conventions, delegates were ***partisans*** attuned to the needs of state parties. Today, delegates are oriented toward candidates first and party second.

Approximately two-thirds of convention delegates have been active in some state or local party politics and have held public or party office. Some are partisans; their first loyalties remain with their home organizations. But others, the ***personalists,*** are committed to candidates rather than to their party organizations at the convention. Some delegates, the ***purists,*** are oriented toward

266

issues. They back the contender as a way to advance their causes. They will be more independent on convention business, especially on the platform. Moderates—such as Ford, Carter, and Mondale—are likely to attract party professionals and personalists; ideological candidates, like McGovern and Reagan, attract more purists.[28]

Old-style versus new-style conventions

Convention delegates differ significantly from the party rank and file, but this was so in the era of the old-style conventions as well.[29] At least the modern conventions no longer shut out women, minorities, or youthful voters. In any event, today the national conventions are accountable to voters in primary and caucus states because they accurately reflect their preferences—or at least the choice of a plurality of voters. And the very process of going through primaries seems to give the winner the support from the registered party voters that is necessary to legitimize the system.

What, then, is a modern convention good for? If it is merely a ratifying device for the party-in-the-electorate, should it not be abolished? The answer is no. A convention is useful for morale building among party activists. It sets a mood, tone, and direction for the party in the general election. "Our activists and leaders still need to meet with each other," says Newt Gingrich, a conservative representative, about Republican conventions, "to talk about what is really going on in this country, about their beliefs and about the future."[30]

And a convention sets the stage for the next nomination. It gives party leaders across the nation a chance to see potential candidates in action: holding receptions and giving interviews, making convention addresses, conducting news briefings, and participating in platform fights. The early betting line can even be established on front-runners when the media poll the convention delegates about their choices for the next contest.

THE REFORM AGENDA

NOMINATIONS. The choices boil down to three: do we want to maximize the power of the party-in-the-electorate, the party organization, or the party-in-government? Those in favor of the first alternative believe that it will increase voter participation and lessen apathy and alienation, that it will make nominees more accountable to the party, and that it will encourage contenders who have stamina and leadership qualities. Those in favor of a larger role for party politicians believe that they are more likely to bring out the vote if they have played the major role at a convention, that their relationships with the candidate are what keeps contenders responsive to the needs of the party and accountable to its members, and that professionals are most likely to recognize presidential leadership qualities. Those who want a larger role for the party-in-government point to the apprenticeship and peer review of parliamentary systems, claiming that these can produce another "Virginia line" of Washington, Jeffersons, and Madisons.

The public is not likely to accept a return to the congressional caucus, nor will it allow party bosses to dominate conventions. Party reforms that create open caucuses and mass-participation primaries are here to stay, although the mix between caucus and primary states varies from one election to the next.

New ideas, new leadership. Lengthening the primary season would give underdogs a better chance. Proportional representation of delegates, rather than winner-take-all votes at the district level, benefits underdogs, not front-runners. Outlawing "bonus" delegates for those who win the state or districts also favors them. Providing free media time for all contenders and designing debate formats that

would include the entire field would slow down front-runners. Contests could start with the smaller states (which would make less expensive personal campaigning possible) and build up to the larger, media-oriented states at the end, giving long shots more time to get the money to compete and build their organizations. The problem with this reform is that it would prolong the fragmentation of the parties and might result in brokered conventions and weak compromise candidates whose authority and legitimacy would be eroded by charges that they were tools of special interests.

Party unification. Some argue that short and intense campaigns would maximize party unity in preparation for the fall elections: either the front-runner would demonstrate strength and wrap the whole thing up early, or else another contender would make a successful challenge and win early. Reforms include statewide winner-take-all allocation of delegates; holding primaries in the large, media-oriented states first; and reducing matching public funds and raising the qualifying amounts. Another change would be to hold a national primary (or to hold all state primaries on the same day), which would require huge media expenditures and previous name recognition.

Peer review. To create an open convention in which the delegates could evaluate the field and choose the strongest candidate for the election, party officials or public officeholders could be made ex officio delegates (that is, delegates by virtue of their other offices). The Democrats allow states to fill 8 percent of their delegations committed to candidates with party officials, and they provide an additional 14 percent of elected and party officials (the superdelegates) who are officially uncommitted. To maximize peer review, half the delegates could be made into superdelegates. This reform, of course, would not mean that the convention would elect a winner. Party professionals on the Democratic side gave the nation Adlai Stevenson (twice) and Hubert Humphrey, and they overwhelmingly supported Walter Mondale; thus their judgment about winners may not be any better than that of voters in primaries. Likewise, Republican professionals were more likely to back Ford than Reagan.

A national primary. The role of the party-in-the-electorate would be maximized by a national primary, which would replace the existing state primaries and the nominating covention and would give all power to the party-in-the-electorate. The vast majority of Americans favor such a system: 72 percent in 1952 and 67 percent in 1984.[31] But the national primary would favor front-runners. It would end all peer review, leaving the way open for new politics contenders, who could successfully manipulate voters in a one-shot event. Unlike the present system, which provides a sequence of events and a chance for the nation to see how candidates react to a series of challenges, it would force a single decision on a single day. It would also provide an opportunity for voters in small states to make judgments about candidates who campaign personally among them.

The mechanisms of a national primary would also create problems. In a crowded field, no one might win a majority. Either a candidate could win with a plurality, opening the way for an extremist, or a runoff contest would be required between the top two contenders. Runoffs, as it turns out, do not necessarily produce the first choice of party voters, or even their "compromise choice," but can result in a nominee who is unrepresentative both ways.[32] Holding runoffs means yet another contest, with the attendant expense and commitment of time. It would probably reduce rather than increase turnouts. It would intensify the fragmentation of the parties, as each of their different ideological, racial, ethnic, and economic constituencies fought it out.

IN CONCLUSION

The road to the White House leads first to the primaries and open caucuses in the states and then to a national convention. The system has been transformed: power has been transferred from the party-in-government and its congressional caucus, to the party organization and its boss-dominated convention, to the party-in-the-electorate and its open caucuses and primaries. In each case technological change and the ambitions of politicians have intersected to delegitimize the existing methods and spur the adoption of new ones. Better transportation led to the national convention and increased the power of state party leaders, and advances in communication have allowed candidates to communicate to voters in primaries without using party organizations; this has resulted in the modern-day mass primaries. Telephone canvassing and direct mailings have changed the way candidates organize and fund their campaigns and have also limited the importance of state and local parties and increased the importance of obtaining the support of PACs, single-issue groups, and professional and trade organizations and unions.

The present nominating system is open and fluid: almost anything can happen if an incumbent is not running. There is no apprenticeship and no formal party leader, and so the field is wide open, though in practice it narrows down to politicians who have the money to put together a large organization to compete for delegates in the states. There is no system of peer review, and relative unknowns (such as Carter) or outsiders (such as Reagan) can obtain the nomination even though they are by no means the choice of the congressional party-in-government with whom they will later have to work. The nominating system divides presidents from their parties and leaves them with bitter intraparty enemies, thus weakening their authority.

Voters in primaries are nearly representative of all party voters, but the delegates selected are not, in terms of either personal or political characteristics. Delegates are more ideological and issue-oriented and are more committed to candidates than to party than the rank and file is. They nominate the voters' choice, but they may adopt a platform that is not fully in tune with the opinions of the majority of party followers. Candidates tend to ignore the platform during the election, though they are likely to implement a majority of its provisions once they are in office. Delegates today are no less representative of their constituents than the delegates to the boss-dominated conventions were.

The Democrats are more likely to make extensive reforms than the Republicans, but in recent years Republican nominees have won the presidency, leading some Democrats to wonder whether their efforts are not misplaced. The idea, after all, is to win the White House: even the most representative nominating procedure should be a means to an end, not an end in itself.

NOTES

1. *The Federalist,* number 68.
2. Walter Mondale, *The Accountability of Power,* McKay, New York, 1975, p. 30.
3. Michael Robinson, "An Idea Whose Time Has Come—Again," *The Congressional Record,* June 19, 1975, p. E 3336.
4. Stephen Hess, *The Presidential Campaign,* Brookings, Washington, D.C., 1974, p. 42.
5. Thomas Cronin, *The State of the Presidency,* 2d ed., Little, Brown, Boston, 1980, p. 39.
6. Moseii Ostragorski, *Democracy and the Organization of Political Parties,* vol. 2 (1902), Anchor Books ed., Garden City, New York, 1964, pp. 133–144.
7. Louis Harris, "Why the Odds Are against a Governor's Becoming President," *Public Opinion Quarterly,* fall 1959; Robert L. Peabody and Eve Lubalin, "The Making of

Presidential Candidates," in Charles Dunn (ed.), *American Democracy Debated*, General Learning Press, 1975, p. 27.

8. *The New York Times*, Mar. 26, 1984.
9. Donald R Matthews (ed.), *Perspectives on Presidential Selection*, Brookings, Washington, D.C., 1973, p. 46.
10. Steven J. Brams, *The Presidential Election Game*, Yale University Press, New Haven, Conn., 1978, p. 69.
11. John H. Aldrich, *Before the Convention*, University of Chicago Press, Chicago, 1980, p. 161.
12. James Beniger, "Winning the Presidential Nomination: National Polls and State Primary Elections," *Public Opinion Quarterly*, vol. 10, no. 1, spring 1976, pp. 22–39; see also Harvey Zeidenstein, "Presidential Primaries—Reflections of the 'The People's Choice,'" *Journal of Politics*, vol. 32, no. 4, November 1970, pp. 856–874.
13. Stephen J. Wayne, *The Road to the White House*, 1st ed., St. Martin's, New York, 1981, p. 101.
14. *The New York Times*, Apr. 14, 1984.
15. Cronin, op. cit., p. 37.
16. David Broder et al., *The Pursuit of the Presidency, 1980*, Berkeley Books, New York, 1980, p. 33.
17. Broder, op. cit., pp. 115–116.
18. Benjamin Page, *Choices Not Echoes*, University of Chicago Press, Chicago, 1980.
19. Richard Rubin, "Presidential Primaries: Continuities, Dimensions of Change, and Politicial Implications," in William Crotty (ed.), *The Party Symbol*, Freeman, San Francisco, 1981.
20. *ISR Newsletter*, winter 1981, p. 1.
21. William H. Lucy, "Polls, Primaries and Presidential Nominations," *Journal of Politics*, vol. 35, no. 4, November 1973, p. 837.
22. New York Times/CBS poll, June 23–28, 1984.
23. *The New York Times*, July 20, 1984.
24. Gerald Pomper, *Elections In America*, Harper and Row, New York, 1973, pp. 181–189.
25. *The New York Times*, Aug. 19, 1984
26. Joel K. Goldstein, *The Modern American Vice Presidency*, Princeton University Press, Princeton, N.J., 1982, p. 85.
27. Warren J. Mitofsky and Martin Plissner, "The Making of the Delegates, 1968–1980," *Public Opinion*, vol. 3, no. 5, October–November 1980, pp. 37–43.
28. *Washington Post*, Aug. 17, 1976.
29. Barbara Farah, "The Representativeness of Direct Primaries: Linkage between Partisan Voters and Convention Delegates, 1972, 1976, 1980," University of Michigan, Survey Research Center, Ann Arbor, 1982.
30. Newt Gingrich, "Transition Shaped by an Elite," *The New York Times*, Aug. 19, 1984.
31. Gallup poll, June 22–25, 1984.
32. Steven J. Brams and Peter Fishburn, *Approval Voting*, Birkhauser, Boston, 1983.

FURTHER READING

Aldrich, John H.: *Before the Convention*, University of Chicago Press, Chicago, 1980. A study of the strategies and choices open to contenders, with interesting mathematical applications.

Brams, Steven J.: *The Presidential Election Game*, Yale University Press, New Haven, Conn., 1978. A discussion of mathematical models and game theory used to explore primary strategies in multicandidate races.

———— and Peter Fishburn: *Approval Voting*, Birkhauser, Boston, 1983. An account of how multicandidate primaries distort the preferences of voters and what can be done about it.

Broder, David, et al.: *The Pursuit of the Presidency, 1980*, Berkeley Books, New York, 1980. An in-depth look at new politics contenders by *Washington Post* reporters.

Bryce, James: *The American Commonwealth*, Macmillan, London, 1888. A classic nineteenth-century critique of the boss-dominated conventions and the candidates they produced.

Ceasar, James: *Presidential Selection*, Princeton University Press, Princeton, N.J., 1979. A book by political theorist dealing with power, authority, and legitimacy in nominating systems past and present.

Chase, James S.: *Emergence of the Presidential Nominating Convention, 1789–1832*, University of Illinois Press, Urbana, 1973. A treatment of the nominating process from congressional caucuses to the convention.

Davis, James W.: *National Conventions in Age of Party Reform*, Greenwood Press, Westport, Conn., 1983. A history of nominating conventions.

Kirkpatrick, Jean: *The New Presidential Elite*, Russell Sage Foundation and Twentieth Century Fund, New York, 1976. Attitudes and behavior of delegates in the 1970s.

Rubin, Richard: *Party Dynamics*, Oxford University Press, New York, 1976. How party factions are influenced by nominating politics.

Shafer, Byron E.: *Quiet Revolution*, Russell Sage, New York, 1984. A comprehensive account of the reform of Democratic Party nominating rules from 1968 to 1972.

Wayne, Stephen J.: *The Road to the White House*, 2d ed., St. Martin's, 1984. A comprehensive account of primary campaigns and convention politics.

White, Theodore: *The Making of the President, 1960*, Atheneum, New York, 1961. The first of White's narratives of the primary seasons, including a discussion of what primaries could and could not do at the end of the era of boss-dominated coventions.

THE STUDY BREAK

Crouse, Timothy: *The Boys on the Bus*, Ballantine Books, New York, 1973. An irreverent account of journalists on the campaign trail.

Kozinski, Jerzy: *Being There* (1979). How to get nominated for vice president, the easy way; starring Peter Sellers.

The Manchurian Candidate (1962). A movie, based on Richard Condon's novel, about a plot by the Soviets to put one of their agents in the White House.

Thompson, Hunter: *Fear and Loathing on the Campaign Trail '72*. Warner Books, New York, 1983. A spacy and spicy account of campaigns.

SOURCES

Bain, Richard C., and Judith H. Parris: *Convention Decisions and Voting Records*, 2d ed., Brookings, Washington, D.C., 1973. Votes on rules, nominations, and party platforms.

Congressional Quarterly Weekly Reports. A weekly publication containing information on primaries and caucuses, including rules, political lineups, and results.

Johnson, Donald Bruce: *National Party PLatforms*, rev. ed., University of Illinois Press, Urbana, 1978, 2 vols. The texts of each party's platform, including the platforms of minor parties (supplements available for 1980 and 1984).

National Party Conventions: 1831–1980, Congressional Quarterly Press, Washington, D.C., 1983. Descriptions of each convention and its results.

1984 Presidential Campaign Summary Reports, Federal Elections Commission, Washington, D.C., 1985. A computerized index and data file on the financial activities of all presidental contenders, based on reports filed by their campaigns, including summary totals of contributions and expenditures, by category.

Presidential Elections since 1789, 3d ed., Congressional Quarterly Press, Washington, D.C., 1983. Gives complete primary and caucus results, by state.

ORGANIZATIONS

Democratic National Committee. 1625 Massachusetts Avenue, N.W., Washington, D.C. 20036. For more information phone 202-797-5900.

Federal Election Commission. 1325 K Street, N.W., Washington, D.C. 20436. For more information phone 800-424-9530.

Republican National Committee. 310 First Street, S.W., Washington, D.C. 20003. For more information phone 202-484-6764.

PRESIDENTIAL ELECTIONS: CAMPAIGNING, VOTING, AND THE PARTY SYSTEM

The first presidential inauguration, in 1789, took place at Federal Hall in New York; the most recent, in 1985 in Washington. (*New-York Historical Society; Sygma.*)

273

The humorist Russell Baker once proposed a constitutional amendment that would provide for "separation of state and race." Pointing out that "skill at running for President has little relationship to the job of being President," he suggested that winning candidates be barred from office—they would merely run on behalf of politicians who, "because of low charisma, bad teeth and distaste for looking foolish, couldn't run successfully for a bus"—let alone for the White House.[1]

Baker's proposal points up the loose relationship between running for, and serving as, president. Elections shape presidential priorities, influence the president's relationships with Congress, and affect the programs of the bureaucracies. But do campaigns tell voters about a candidate's character and competence? Do they give them real policy alternatives? Do they tell them anything about what a candidate would do in office? Can voters be relied upon to choose what is in their best interests, or are they manipulated by slick media campaigns?

This chapter will consider these issues by describing the environment in which presidential elections are waged: the three-month campaign for electoral college votes. We will look in depth at the campaigns for money, organization, image, and popular votes. The chapter concludes by analyzing some trends and assessing proposed reforms. The overall focus remains on the issues of legitimacy, authority, and power: our free democratic elections maintain the legitimacy of our government, but do they provide the president with the authority and the power necessary to govern?

THE ELECTORAL ENVIRONMENT

Presidential elections are frantic affairs: there are just three months (August, September, and October) in which to finance, organize, and campaign. On the first Tuesday after the first Monday in November, voters choose the electors whose votes determine the winner, and so it is with the electoral college that we must begin.

How the electoral college works

Everyone knows that the president and the vice president are the only two officials who are elected by all the American people—but everyone is wrong. They are the only elected officials in the American government who are *not* chosen directly by the people. The Constitution provides for their selection by an electoral college. Each state chooses its electors (equal to its Senate and House representation) by any method that its state legislature prescribes. The Constitution does not require a popular vote. In the early 1800s many state legislatures chose the electors; all the states but South Carolina had switched to the popular vote by 1832, and it changed over in 1856.

The electors chosen by the voters in each state (and the District of Columbia) meet in their state capitals on the first Monday after the second Wednesday in December (the electoral college never meets as a body) and cast secret ballots for president and vice president. These ballots are sent to the capital, where

THE ROAD TO THE WHITE HOUSE: SOME ALTERNATIVE ROUTES

On the death of a president, the vice president takes the oath of office and succeeds to the presidency, filling out the remainder of the predecessor's term, under the provisions of Article II, Section 1. The same provision applies if a president resigns.

If a president is disabled, the Twenty-Fifth Amendment provides that the vice president acts as president (but does not assume the office of president) until the incumbent can resume the office. The president can declare disability and invite the vice president to act as president. Or the vice president, together with a majority of the Cabinet, can find the president to be disabled, in which case the vice president can act as president. In either case the president determines when to resume the duties of the office. If the vice president (acting for the president) and the Cabinet disagree with the president, the final determination is made by Congress. A two-third vote by each house of Congress is required to permit the vice president to continue in office as acting president.

The Constitution, under the terms of the Twenty-Fifth Admendment, provides for a vacancy in the vice-presidency. In such a case, the president can nominate a vice president, who takes office upon confirmation by a majority vote of both houses of Congress.

If there is a double vacancy, a law passed by Congress in 1947 provides for a line of succession. The Speaker of the House is next in line for the presidency, followed in turn by the president pro tem of the Senate and the Cabinet Secretaries, in the order in which their departments were founded, starting with the secretary of state.

they are opened early in January by the incumbent (and possibly outgoing) vice president in the presence of the *newly elected* Congress. (In 1960 this meant that outgoing vice president Nixon announced that John Kennedy had defeated him for the presidency; in 1968 outgoing vice president Humphrey announced that Nixon had beaten him.)

Contingency elections. If the electoral college does not produce a majority for president—270 of the 538 votes—the newly elected House chooses from among the three candidates who received the most electoral votes. Each state's House delegation casts one vote (determined by its majority), and a majority of states elects the president (the District of Columbia has no vote). If there is no electoral college majority for vice president, that election goes to the Senate, which chooses from between the two candidates who received the most electoral votes. Each senator casts one vote, and a majority elects. If no president is elected by the House, the vice president serves as acting president until the House decides—even if it is necessary to serve the full term. Such elections are known as ***contingency elections.***

Candidates, parties, and the electoral college. Electors have always been the agents of candidates running for office. Slates of electors are put up in each state under the name of the candidate. The popular vote is cast for the presidential and vice presidential ticket, and a plurality of the popular vote in each state elects a pledged slate. The electoral college is a registering device which records the preferences of each state's voters. Only a handful of electors have violated their pledges and voted for someone else, and none has ever influenced the outcome of an election.

Sometimes the electoral college works badly. The elections of 1800 and 1824

were settled by contingency elections in the House of Representatives, amid charges of corruption and deals. The election of 1876 required a special commission to determine which set of electors in several southern states should be counted. Sometimes the college narrowly avoids a deadlock, as it did in 1960, 1968, and 1976—in 1976 a shift of fewer than 12,000 votes in Delaware and Ohio would have produced a 269 to 269 tie vote.

In several elections the candidate with the most popular votes has been defeated: in 1824, when John Quincy Adams was elected by the House, although Andrew Jackson had a plurality of popular votes; in 1876, when Rutherford B. Hayes defeated the more popular Samuel J. Tilden; and in 1888, when Benjamin Harrison defeated Grover Cleveland. In 1960, contrary to popular opinion, John Kennedy did not win more popular votes when he beat Richard Nixon—Kennedy's totals included votes in Alabama (where he was not even on the ballot) cast for uncommitted Democratic electors. If Kennedy had not had these popular votes, Nixon would have had the edge.[2] Mathematicians claim that a disrepancy between the popular majority and the electoral majority should occur in 1 out of every 3 elections in which the vote margin is less than 300,000 and in 1 out of every 4 elections in which the margin is less than 1 million; thus a problem in the future is likely.[3]

How the electoral college affects campaigns

Winner-take-all and campaign strategy. All states except Maine give all their electoral votes to the candidate with a plurality of the statewide popular vote. The other candidates get no electoral votes. In effect, the winner is rewarded with the electoral votes which the loser would have received under a system of proportional representation. Nothing in the Constitution requires this system of *winner-take-all elections.* The states can apportion electors as they wish, and some have done so by holding contests in each congressional district: South Carolina until 1856, Michigan in 1892, and Maine since 1972. But the states prefer the winner-take-all method because it makes winning a state more important to a candidate.[4]

The winner-take-all system determines campaign strategy. The general election devolves into fifty separate state contests (and one in the District of Columbia). Obviously:

- It makes sense to concentrate on states with many electoral votes.
- It is better to win more states by small margins than fewer states by large margins.
- It is more important to campaign in states which are close than in states in which the candidate will definitely win or definitely lose.

Candidates spend their time on the campaign trail according to the ³⁄₂ *rule:* take the square root of a state's electoral college vote and then cube that number. Thus in comparing New Jersey, which has sixteen votes, with Montana, which has four, the ³⁄₂ rule gives New Jersey a factor of 64 and Montana a factor of 8—which means that candidates are likely to spend 8 times as much time and effort in New Jersey as in Montana, even though it has only 4 times as many electoral college votes. (Try this out with a state that has forty-seven electoral college votes.[5]) Candidates concentrate their campaigns on the "big twelve": the eleven largest states (plus any one of three in twelfth place), which themselves provide an electoral college majority (Figure 9-1).

Geopolitical strategy. Candidates must come up with a strategy to win an

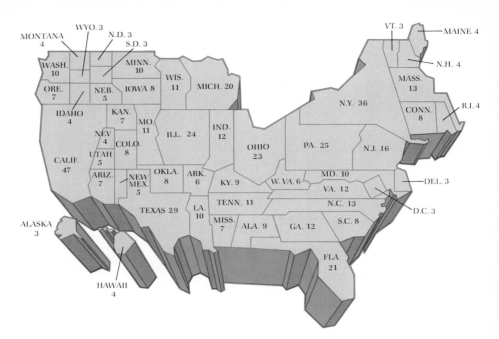

Figure 9-1. Map of the states drawn to the scale of their Electoral College votes. Note how small all the states west of the Mississippi River are, with the exceptions of Texas and California. The largest region becomes the mid-Atlantic and midwest.

electoral college majority. Between 1932 and 1944 (Figure 9-2a), Democrats won all four national elections handily by relying on their strength in the "solid south" (which after the Civil War became a one-party Democratic region) and on votes in the industrial north, which was suffering from the depression. In the post-New Deal period, 1948 to 1960 (Figure 9-2b), competition for electoral votes was more balanced. The Democrats' strength in the south and west splintered, and it eroded in the New England, upper midwest, Great Plains, and Rocky Mountain states. In the past twenty years (Figure 9-2c) the Republicans have consolidated their strength west of the Mississippi and have made the south highly competitive—in most recent elections they have trounced the Democrats everywhere but in the northeast quadrant.[6]

The Democrats win presidential elections when they hold onto a majority of southern and border states and win a majority of the large, competitive northern states, such as New York, Ohio, Pennsylvania, Michigan, and Massachusetts. They have not won a national election since 1948 without a border or southern politician on the ticket. The Republicans can win by combining the west with big states (Illinois, Michigan, Texas, Florida, and Virginia), by combining the west with the south in a sun belt strategy, or by winning a landslide in all regions (Figures 9-3 and 9-4, pages 278–279).

THE CAMPAIGN FOR FUNDS

The costs of presidential elections have skyrocketed, largely as a result of media expenditures, as Table 9-1 (page 280) shows. In spite of recent reforms, campaigners devote much of their time to raising funds and trying to outspend one another.

Past practices

The financing of general elections followed the same pattern as that for nomination campaigns until 1976. Candidates relied on their own funds, on contributions from the heirs to great family fortunes (Astors, du Ponts, Fords, Harrimans, Lehmans, Loebs, Mellons, Pews, Rockefellers, Schiffs, Scaifes, Watsons, Whitneys, and the like), and on funds from corporate executives, lawyer-lobbyists, trade association representatives, and union leaders.[7]

Figure 9-2. Electoral college competition since 1932. (a) When Republicans won the presidency in the nineteenth century they coined the phrase "As Maine goes, so goes the nation." Democrats in the New Deal period (1932–1944) responded "As Maine goes, so goes Vermont," since those two New England states were the only ones to vote solidly Republican in this period. Most states voted Democratic three or four times, including the southern and western states past the Great Plains. (b) In the post-New Deal period (1948–1960) the Democratic "solid south" broke up as Republican candidates made inroads in Texas, Florida, Virginia, and Tennessee. Republicans dominated the west and most of the midwest. States in red voted Democratic less than twice; states in blue voted Republican less than twice. (c) Between 1964 and 1984 Republicans solidified their southern and western regional bases. Not a single region of the nation could be considered solidly Democratic. The map is almost the reverse of the New Deal electoral map.

Donations were made to influence policies, gain access to the next administration, obtain lenient regulatory treatment by government agencies or favorable treatment in the tax code, or get government business. Ambassadorships to European countries were given to some contributors. Dr. Ruth Farkas, for example, contributed $250,000 to Nixon's 1972 campaign and, when offered the embassy in Costa Rica, replied, "I am interested in Europe, I think; isn't $250,000 an awful lot for Costa Rica?" For $50,000 more she got Luxembourg.[8]

Corporations and nationally chartered banks (since 1907) and unions (since

CARTER'S BASE

REAGAN'S BASE

Electoral College
78 Electoral College votes

77 Electoral College votes

KEY STATES
for Reagan to win 208

HAWAII

Figure 9-3. The Reagan strategists' first calculations in planning the general election campaign of 1980. Their strategy was based on taking several "key states," including California, Texas, Florida, Virginia, Ohio, and Illinois. (Source: Richard B. Wirthlin, "The Republican Strategy," in S. M. Lipset, ed., *Party Coalitions in the 1980s,* San Francisco, Institute for Contemporary Studies, 1981.)

"Big 12" electoral votes

Democratic   Republican

Figure 9-4. In every election the candidate who wins a majority of the "big twelve" wins the White House. (The number of electoral votes in "big twelve" states shifts each decade owing to reapportionment of seats in the House of Representatives.)

1947) cannot contribute to federal election campaigns. But corporations have made "loans" to campaigns and then written them off. They have underbilled for their services or delayed billing, in effect giving candidates interest-free loans. Unions have let their workers help out while keeping them on the payroll. By means of pay raises, bonuses, or padded expense accounts for their employees, corporations and trade associations have laundered funds to campaigns, making them look like individual contributions. George Steinbrenner, the principal owner of the New York Yankees, used this method to get funds

Table 9-1. Presidential election costs, 1952 to 1984

Year	Total costs[a]		Radio and television costs	
	Republicans	Democrats	Republicans	Democrats
1952	$ 6,608,623	$ 5,032,926	$ 2,046,000	$ 1,500,000
1956	$ 7,778,702	$ 5,106,651	$ 2,886,000	$ 1,763,000
1960	$10,128,000	$ 9,797,000	$ 1,865,000	$ 1,142,000
1964	$16,026,000	$ 8,757,000	$ 6,370,000	$ 4,674,000
1968	$25,402,000	$11,594,000	$12,598,000	$ 6,143,000
1972	$61,400,000	$30,000,000	$ 4,300,000	$ 9,081,321
1976	$21,786,641	$21,800,000	$ 7,875,000	$ 9,081,321
1980	$29,188,888	$29,352,768	$14,600,000	$19,500,000
1984	$42,563,759	$41,828,811	n.a.	n.a.

a. Since 1976 total costs have been limited by law for any campaign that chooses to use public funds.
Source: Herbert Alexander, *Financing Politics*, Congressional Quarterly Press, Washington, D.C., 1980, pp. 5, 8, 10.

from his American Shipbuilding Company to the Nixon campaign—and then had his employees cover up before a grand jury (he eventually pleaded guilty in a federal court to charges of violating campaign law). Corporations and unions have allowed law, advertising, accounting, engineering, architectural, shipping, food service, and travel firms to overbill them—with the understanding that these firms would make contributions to certain campaigns.[9]

In 1972 Nixon's fund-raisers went through the files of regulatory agencies and the Justice Department, looking for matters involving large corporations. They then met with corporate executives, brought up these cases, and set specific figures which they expected to be contributed—usually on the basis of the net worth of the top leaders of the company. A list of more than 2000 such contributors, dubbed "Rosemary's baby," was kept by Nixon's secretary, Rosemary Woods.[10] Executives of many of these corporations pleaded guilty in federal courts to charges of contributing corporate funds; most of them were fined, and their companies later rewarded them for their trouble with bonuses, salary increases, or retirement settlements.

Reforms in campaign financing

The 1974 amendments to the Federal Election Campaign Act created the Presidential Election Campaign Fund, to which individuals can allocate $1 of their taxes each year. (Almost one-third of taxpayers do so, providing about $36 million annually.[11]) Major-party candidates for president can choose to finance their campaigns entirely from this fund, in which case they receive $20 million plus a cost-of-living adjustment (COLA) ($40.4 million in 1984). The law also provides that national committees may raise funds from private sources for an election campaign, but it limits each party to spending $3.4 million plus a COLA ($6.9 million in 1984). A candidate may forgo federal funds and raise money privately (in which case there is no limitation on spending), but none has ever done so.

Minor-party candidates (defined as those whose parties received between 5 and 25 percent of the popular vote in the preceding presidential election) are eligible for a proportional share of federal funds. New parties and independent candidates must raise funds privately, but they are eligible for reimbursement by the Treasury if they receive 5 percent or more of the popular vote.

Campaign financing today

The failure of the reforms. The reforms have not ended the influence of large contributors or of corporate and union money. Congress left loopholes in the 1974 and 1979 laws.

STATE PARTY BUILDING. State parties may spend unlimited amounts on party building and voter registration in presidential election years. These efforts can be privately funded, and there are no limits on contributions. In twenty-eight states corporations may make direct contributions, and in forty-one states unions may do so. Expenditures are not charged off against the limits on spending for presidential campaigns.[12]

The national parties have set up *soft-money accounts* for their state parties; supposedly they collect funds from private donors and then give them to the state parties, but actually they determine how the money will be spent as part of the national presidential campaign. The Republicans raised approximately $15 million in 1980 and twice that amount in 1984.[13] The Democrats received $1.3 million in 1980, most of it from unions, and they raised more than $10 million in 1984. Candidates may also decide to convert their nomination PACs into a nonfederal account which can receive contributions destined for state parties.

NATIONAL PARTY SUPPORT. Private donors may give $20,000 every two years to a national party. They may also give funds to tax-exempt foundations (which gives them a tax deduction) set up by the parties; these foundations pay for the mortgages and upkeep of national headquarters or provide educational materials and training for party workers.

"NONPARTISAN" VOTER REGISTRATION. Party professionals may establish "nonpartisan" organizations to raise money from private donors for voter registration activities. Leaders of the Reagan-Bush Finance Committee set up a supposedly nonpartisan group, Leadership '84, to raise $2 million for voter registration (also tax-deductible). Most of the contributions were made by Republican Eagles and contributors to the annual Republican House-Senate dinner. This money in turn was given to Americans for Responsible Government, a conservative organization, which then funneled it to grass-roots conservative organizations that intended to register nonvoters as Republicans.[14]

NONCOORDINATED CAMPAIGNS. Individuals and PACs may spend unlimited amounts to support a candidate, provided they do not coordinate their expenditures with those of the candidate's own committee. In 1980 conservative PACs spent more than $12 million for Reagan; in contrast, campaigns for Carter totaled only $46,000. Such *noncoordinated campaigns* in the past have favored the Republicans by bringing out conservative voters. The Supreme Court has ruled that these campaigns are protected by the First Amendment—to limit them, the Court decided, would infringe on freedom of speech.[15]

Campaigning for funds: The Republicans' advantage. Because federal funding for campaigns gives each major party exactly the same amount, many people have the impression that neither party has an advantage in terms of funding for presidential elections. But loopholes in the law give the Republicans an advantage: they raise more than $4 million a month in a presidential election year—most of it from small contributors who are contacted by mail. In 1984 they kicked off their campaign by raising $10.6 million (as of August) that could go for national and state party activities; this enabled them to run

big advertising campaigns even during the Democratic primary season and the convention. Meanwhile, the Democrats were burdened with debts: their national committee owed $7 million for its new party headquarters and media center and for services that it had contracted for. Its contenders for the nomination owed $13.3 million![16] After the convention, the Democratic candidate must campaign furiously for funds to pay off nomination debts, to build up state and county parties, and to raise funds for the national party so that the Republicans' advantage can be neutralized.

CLOSE-UP

RICHARD M. NIXON AND WATERGATE. The Watergate crisis involved an attempt by President Nixon to interfere with the integrity of a presidential election—through burglary, wiretapping, intimidation, and dirty tricks—and then to cover up evidence of federal crimes when he was investigated by the FBI, congressional committees, and a federal grand jury. Ultimately, it culminated in an impeachment inquiry by the House of Representatives and in the president's resignation.

Richard Nixon entered Congress in 1946 as a Republican after defeating a Democratic incumbent with a dirty-tricks campaign. In 1950 he was elected to the United States Senate after a smear campaign against Helen Gahagan Douglas (which earned him the nickname "Tricky Dickie"). In 1952 he was elected vice president. After surviving a campaign scandal (it was revealed that he had accepted funds from some wealthy businesspeople) by means of a televised speech that won him popular support, Nixon went on to serve two terms as vice president. In 1960 he lost the presidential election to John F. Kennedy, amid charges of vote fraud by Democrats in Texas and Illinois, and in 1962 he lost the gubernatorial election in California.

Nixon seemed to have learned three lessons from his campaigns: never hesitate to use dirty tricks (his campaigns to get into the House and the Senate), never let them steal one from you (1960), and never take anything for granted (a 15-point lead dwindled to 1 in his 1968 presidential victory). Early in 1972, as the Democrats headed into their primary season, it appeared that they might nominate Edmund Muskie, a centrist candidate from Maine with a good chance of winning. The White House decided to derail Muskie and the other Democrats during the pri-

President Nixon and well-wishers on the campaign trail. (*Raymond Depardon: Magnum.*)

mary season. Dirty-tricks artists disrupted the Muskie campaign. The headquarters of the Democratic National Committee were burglarized, and phones were tapped.

On June 17, 1972, five Cubans were caught burglarizing the DNC headquarters at the Watergate complex. They named Gordon Liddy, counsel to the Committee to Reelect the President, as an accomplice. Nixon met with his two top aides, H. R. Haldeman and John D. Erlichman, and they decided to get the Central Intelligence Agency to impede the pending FBI investigation of the break-in by having the CIA claim that it was a national security matter. For a while the strategy worked, and Nixon won a landslide reelection victory.

But the break-in could not be contained. The Watergate burglars were sentenced to long prison terms by John Sirica, a federal judge, who hoped to prod them into talking. Nixon and his aides decided on a fallback strategy: if the probe pointed to higher-ups, they would blame Attorney General John Mitchell. John Dean, the White House counsel, realized that he was being set up as another fall guy for the break-in and cover-up, and he went to the Justice Department with his lawyer to confess his role in the matter and implicate other aides. On April 30, 1973, Nixon accepted the resignation of Haldeman and Erlichman, as the investigation spread to them.

The Senate Select Committee on Watergate, chaired by Sam Ervin, a senator from North Carolina, opened televised hearings. Dean's testimony implicated the president, but could not be corroborated. After Haldeman's aide, Alexander Butterfield, admitted that the White House had a taping system, the Justice Department's special prosecutor, Archibald Cox, demanded that Nixon turn over any recorded conversations about Watergate. Nixon turned over some of the evidence and then told Cox (as a Justice Department employee) not to press for the remaining tapes. Cox refused to back down, and on October 20, 1973, Nixon ordered his attorney general, Elliot Richardson, to fire Cox. Richardson resigned in protest, and Deputy Attorney General William Ruckelshaus also refused and was himself fired; finally another Justice Department official was found who would carry out Nixon's order. This "Saturday night massacre" unleashed a fire storm of protest. Shortly thereafter the House Judiciary Committee opened an impeachment investigation.

The House Committee deliberated until July 24, 1974, at which time it voted on three articles of impeachment. One involved obstruction of justice (the cover-up of White House involvement in the Watergate burglary), another involved abuse of power (misuse of the CIA, the FBI, and the Internal Revenue Service to harass opponents in the administration), and the third cited Nixon's refusal to answer committee subpoenas for evidence. Meanwhile the Supreme Court, in *U.S. v. Nixon,* ordered the president to turn his tapes and other evidence over to the federal district court judge who was trying the Watergate cases. (One of the tapes released later did, in fact, show that Nixon had conspired with his closest aides to cover up White House involvement in the Watergate crimes, in itself a crime and an impeachable offense.)

Shortly thereafter a delegation of senior Republicans in Congress, led by Barry Goldwater, a conservative, advised Nixon that the Senate would probably convict him if an impeachment trial were held. Nixon resigned from office on August 9, 1974. He was later pardoned for all Watergate-related crimes by his successor, Gerald Ford.[17]

ORGANIZING THE CAMPAIGN

Within the space of a few months, a candidate must transform the nomination organization—essentially a media operation and field unit which goes into a few states at a time—into an operation capable of waging fifty state contests simultaneously. To do so, the candidate must mesh the state and county party organizations with campaign aides, volunteer field organizations, and allied interest groups. This is easier said than done.

The inner circles

A candidate retains top advisers from the nominating campaign, but adds to them the party leaders and a few of the campaign operatives from rival camps. This results in overlapping circles, diffuse rather than clear lines of authority, a proliferation of titles ("campaign chairperson," "campaign director," "campaign manager," and so on), and general confusion. There are tensions between "the plane" (that is, wherever the candidate is and whomever the candidate is with) and "headquarters" and between both these units and the party's national committee.[18]

The party national committee

The presidential nominee takes control of the party's national committee, which conducts the state party-building and fund-raising operation and voter registration drives, encourages religious and ethnic groups to become allied with the party, and runs some of the polling efforts. By custom the nominee may name a new chairperson, although Walter Mondale's attempts to do so in 1984 met with such resistance at the convention that he backed down (he designated Bert Lance, a former official in the Carter administration who was forced to leave office after charges of improprieties in his dealings as a private banker). Usually, either candidates choose to mesh the committee with their own campaign—in which case they appoint the director and deputy director of the campaign's political operations or put their own staff aides in charge of these operations—or else they ignore the committee and run everything from their own campaign headquarters. The Republicans have gone toward complete integration of campaign efforts; the Democrats have vacillated between ignoring the committee and seeking to dominate it.

Walter Mondale chose Jimmy Carter's former budget director, Bert Lance, as Democratic National Chairman and then withdrew the nomination a few days later to avoid a party split. This was the first of many mishaps in his campaign. (*Larry Downing: Woodfin Camp.*)

The state and county parties

The state and county parties play an important role in a presidential election. If they are headed by chairpersons who are enthusiastic, they can be the focal point for the statewide contest. They can conduct effective voter registration and field canvassing operations and can deliver the state for the candidate. But often these parties favor another contender, have misgivings about the candidate, and believe that the ticket will lose. They may sit on their hands or concentrate on local elections. Candidates usually try to rally these parties by fund-raising and campaigning for local candidates, modifying their positions or taking stances that are regionally popular. But sometimes, as Goldwater, Humphrey, McGovern, Carter, and Mondale all discovered, nothing works. Failure to get state and local parties actively involved in a campaign is a good sign that the candidacy is doomed.

The Democratic Party is a bottom-up party in an election; the state and county parties concentrate on winning local elections and then give what resources and aid they can to the national ticket. They assume that a presidential nominee cannot help them, but can only snatch defeat from the jaws of their impending victories. The Republican Party is a top-down party; the Republicans rely on national funding and advertising and on the popularity of a presidential nominee to help them win state and local contests. They expect a presidential nominee to help them, although they are often quite disappointed when a state goes presidentially Republican but locally Democratic.

CAMPAIGN THEMES AND IMAGES

A candidate must develop a campaign theme and, through television, project a favorable image to more than 85 million households. Each campaign in 1984 spent more than $25 million on national advertising; the Mondale campaign estimated that it made more than 3 billion "gross impressions" on voters, with each household seeing an average of twenty commercials during the campaign. The Reagan campaign put more than forty top advertising executives in its "Tuesday group," including some who worked on the spectacular Michael Jackson advertisements for Pepsi-Cola. Marketing a presidential candidate is not dissimilar to marketing a product.

The overall theme

An incumbent president wants to run on peace, prosperity, and "you never had it so good." Consider the soft sell used in Reagan's 1984 commercials: "Life is better. . . ." "America's back. . . ." "People have a sense of pride they never thought they'd feel again." An incumbent president whose party is united can contrast this with what is happening in the opposition party. As James Lake, the director of communications for the Reagan-Bush campaign, put it, Republican advertisements during the primary season were designed to show "a positive presidency, an alternative to the trashing going on on the other side." A challenger tries to capitalize on the public's dissatisfaction with the party in power and to generate a protest vote, or a mandate for change. "If you're thinking of voting for Ronald Reagan in 1984," Mondale's campaign warned in one advertisement, "think of what will happen—in 1985." The themes and images must be unified, coherent, and fairly easy to understand. Complex arguments that are constantly shifting do more to confuse than enlighten voters. The campaigns that project the best image integrate the paid advertisements with the news coverage of the campaign: if the networks show the president dealing with foreign leaders, the advertisements also project the

One of the earliest television commercials—1952. Ike answers viewers' queries. (*These photos by Barry S. Surman from "The Spot: The Rise of Political Advertising on Television," M.I.T. Press.*)

One of the dirtiest commercials—1964. When the little girl finishes "counting down" from ten to zero as she picks petals off the daisy, an atomic bomb explodes. This anti-Goldwater ad was removed from the air by the Democrats after Republican protests.

One of the best commercials. Tanya, a Russian girl who died during the seige of Leningrad in World War II, is eulogized by President Nixon in this 1972 spot in which he promises to "work toward a more peaceful world."

One of the most boring commercials. Jimmy Carter introduces himself to the voters in 1976.

"leader" image. The operative slogan of a media campaign can be expressed in the acronym KISS ("Keep it simple, stupid.").

The political scientist James David Barber argues that the theme a campaign uses is likely to assume one of three forms: *partisan conflict* between the parties; a *crusade of conscience,* in which a hero is pitted against a villain; or a *campaign of reconciliation,* which offers the nation a chance for compromise, moderation, and the healing of wounds. The 1984 campaign was won with a campaign of reconciliation by the Republicans, who called on voters to endorse an "opportunity society" for all Americans. Barber believes that these themes run in a cycle, one following predictably after the other; even if this is not the case, his typology is useful in highlighting some of the themes candidates use.[19]

**"REACH OUT":
A THEME COMMERCIAL FROM THE 1968 NIXON CAMPAIGN**

Video	*Audio*
1. Opening network disclaimer: "A political announcement."	
2. Fade-up on zoom into the crowd. Nixon is surrounded by people.	Music up full.
3. Nixon moves through the crowd: various shots from different perspectives.	Nixon: "What has to be done, has to be done by the president and people together; or it won't be done at all. I am asking not that you give
4. MCUs of the above sequence.	something *to* your country, but that
5. WS Nixon and crowd separated by roof of a car. Zoom in to hands, as they reach toward each other.	you do something *with* your country; I am asking not for your gifts, but for your hands."
6. Montage of reaching hands and smiling faces—Nixon and people, increasing tempo.	Music up full. Music under.
7. Pull back from clasped hands of Nixon and people. Tilt from people in window to "Nixon for President" sign. Pan to CU of Nixon.	Nixon: "Together we can hardly fail, for there is no force on earth to match the will and spirit of the people of America."
8. Zoom out from CUI word "Nixon" to reveal sign "Nixon's the one" above Nixon cavalcade surrounded by cheering throngs. Hold. Fade-out.	Music up full. Music out.
9. Fade-up title: "This time vote like your whole world depended on it."	(Source: Joe McGinnis, *The Selling of the President*, 1968, Simon and
10. Dissolve to title word, "Nixon." Zoom into CU. Hold. Fade-out.	Schuster, New York, 1969, p. 250.)

Whatever else they do, candidates must offer meaningful reasons to support them—an overall theme with some excitement and drama. Examine "A Theme Commercial from the 1968 Nixon Campaign." Does this commercial really say anything? Hardly; yet with music and dramatic visual effects, it came alive on television and provided a dramatic theme.[20]

Media formats

The media formats available to candidates make it possible for them to project their themes and images in different ways.

Candidate-controlled formats. Television and radio commercials, billboards and posters, and newspaper and magazine advertising all give candidates maximum control. The message is produced solely by the campaign. The images emphasize traits which voters believe that presidents should have: strength, experience, competence, knowledge, character, and empathy.[21] Campaign commercials include "voter-in-the-street" endorsements; "feeling good" imitations of soft-drink ads; "introductions" to candidates and their families, "scare ads" claiming that opponents are warmongers or against social

security; "issues" which position candidates; "looking at the record," or attacking past performance; and "experience" ads, about candidates' careers. Incumbent presidents use "Rose Garden" commercials that show them signing legislation or dealing with national problems and meeting with foreign leaders.

Images are the key to a campaign. The producer of Nixon's campaign commercials admitted:

> Let's face it, a lot of people think Nixon is dull. Think he's a bore, a pain in the ass. They look at him as the kind of kid who always carried a bookbag. Who was forty-two years old the day he was born. They figure other kids got footballs for Christmas, Nixon got a briefcase and he loved it. He'd always have his homework done and he'd never let you copy."[22]

According to the speech writer Ray Price: "It's not the man we have to change, but rather the received impression. And this impression often depends more on the medium and its uses than it does on the candidate himself."[23] A media blitz converted Nixon from a partisan street fighter into a mature, experienced statesman.

Candidate-dominated formats. Rallies, staged news events, and news releases all offer a candidate opportunities to emphasize themes or issues. Yet they provide no opportunity for the press to question or confront the candidate. Nixon capitalized on a closed media strategy in 1968 and 1972. He re-

Before jet travel, candidates rented trains and embarked on "whistle-stop" campaigns, as Franklin D. Roosevelt and John N. Garner did. Here they are photographed at a stop in Topeka, Kansas, in their 1932 campaign. (*Bettman Archive.*)

The Illinois-born Californian Ronald Reagan and the Connecticut reared ex-Texas Congressman George Bush get a warm welcome in Texas in 1984. (*Bill Fitzpatrick: White House.*)

fused to debate his opponents and stayed away from press conferences. He would travel to a city, stage some sort of dramatic pictorial event (in time for the evening news), and deliver a speech in an auditorium. His campaign provided the media with only one event each day, and therefore he controlled the daily campaign theme. Instead of holding real press conferences (he held only seven the year he ran for reelection), Nixon made commercials in which he was "interviewed" by a celebrity—his favorite was the football coach Bud Wilkinson—and he barred reporter from the set. Jules Witcover, a reporter, after trying to question Nixon one day, recalls, "No soap. Couldn't get to him. They hustled him off. Just the idea of your going up there and confronting the candidate—the guys around him were startled, they couldn't believe their eyes that you were doing this. And they learned, very quickly, and it didn't happen much after that."[24] "Without television Richard Nixon would not have a chance," admitted Frank Shakespeare, a campaign adviser. "He would not have a prayer of being elected because the press would not let him get through to the people. But because he is so good he will get through despite the press. The press doesn't matter anymore."[25]

Ronald Reagan used a similar strategy in 1984. "Our goal is to have one set of pictures and one story a day out of the White House," according to his press secretary.[26] A July tour of the polluted Chesapeake Bay, for example, allowed the president to demonstrate his concern for the environment. When reporters tried to question him about some controversial appointments to an environmental advisory committee, worsening conditions in the bay, and condemnation of his record by environmental organizations, staffers hustled them away, turned off the lights (so that the television cameras could not function), and put their hands over the camera lenses. Reagan held no news conferences all summer or fall.

289

Reporter-dominated formats. Interviews, press conferences, public affairs panel programs, and other formats in which candidates and their key staffers respond to reporters' questions are dangerous for candidates. A reporter can edit responses, determine the emphasis on each point, and slant the story. Some candidates, including losers (like Humphrey and McGovern) and winners (like Kennedy and Carter), believed that there was more mileage to be gained by being open and accessible. Their staffs helped rather than blocked the press. The result? Stories about staff disagreements, candidates' temper tantrums, conflicts over strategy and tactics, and even attempts to stroke the media. An open campaign may even given the impression that it is trying to manipulate voters because reporters get access to the media politics practitioners. Reporters have a field day covering an open campaign critically, while doing little to uncover what goes on in a totally controlled operation.

Media-controlled formats. Documentaries, investigative and analytical reports on issues and strategy, discussion of polling data, stories on campgin financing, and voter-in-the-street interviews—these can provide a picture of a campaign that is completely at variance with the one projected by the candidate.

Most media-controlled stories fall into one of several categories. The majority of stories involve the candidate's travels and speeches, what the news producer Av Westin refers to as "here he comes, there he goes" reporting; this is the traditional "wire service" style of objective, neutral reporting. Related are the "horse-race" stories: who is in the lead and who has the momentum.[27] Some reporters make their living as tipsters, giving us the latest gossip about campaign friction, while others are "assistant district attorneys" who report on campaign financing, potential conflict of interest, and the medical histories of the candidates and their staffers. Still others, breaking away from objective reporting, act as "assistant campaign managers" and offer candidates advice or even help out with campaign tasks (for example, the columnist George Will helped prepare Reagan for the 1980 debates)—roles which other journalists believe are inappropriate.[28]

Beginning in 1980 a constructive new format was introduced. Television networks were stung by the charges of the investigative reporter Brit Hume that the media report "what one candidate said, then they go and report what the other candidate said with equal credibility. They never get around to finding out if the guy is telling the truth. They just pass the speeches along without trying to confirm the substances of what the candidates are saying. What they pass off as objectivity is just a mindless kind of neutrality."[29] Reporters now often produce analytic pieces which demonstrate candidates' inconsistencies, exaggerations, or outright falsehoods.

Note: The media as sources of campaign information. Two-thirds of voters rely primarily on television for campaign information, compared with one-third who rely primarily on newspapers. Those who read the papers are much better informed, since the typical television story is the equivalent of no more than one or two paragraphs in a newspaper. Since most stories, whether in the print or the broadcast media, involve the horse race rather than the issues, it is not surprising that the media provide less information about issues than the candidates' own campaign advertisements do. The political scientists Thomas

Patterson and Robert McClure, in their analysis of election coverage, concluded that "television news adds little to the average voter's understanding of election issues. Network news may be fascinating. It may be highly entertaining. But it is simply not informative."[30] In 1972 during the last six weeks of the campaign, ABC, CBS, and NBC devoted a total of thirty-five, forty-six, and twenty-six *minutes*, respectively, to the issues.[31]

Polls

Using and misusing the independent polls. Horse-race coverage relies on public opinion polls.[32] These polls are conducted by independent concerns such as Gallup, Harris, and Roper; by people who work for candidates, such as David Garth Associates and Peter Hart Associates; by firms that work for the media (ABC/Harris, NBC/Associated Press, CBS/New York Times, and Time/Yankelovich); and by organizations which conduct statewide polls (Eagleton in New Jersey and Field in California, for example), either by themselves or under contract to local newspapers.

Different pollsters get different results.[33] There was a 14-point spread between the support for Reagan in the first week of July 1984 recorded by NBC and ABC polls. Some pollsters present the opinions of the adult population. Others question only registered voters (Harris, Roper, and CBS/New York Times) but differ by as much as 10 percent on the proportion of Republicans in their samples. Others use a sample of "likely voters" (Gallup and Time/Yankelovich). Sometimes, as is true of the NBC/Associated Press poll, only the opinions of voters who are registered and have made up their minds are recorded. Most of the published polls match up candidates and ask voters for their preferences or voting choices. Results differ depending on the wording of the questions. Some ask for feelings about candidates (evaluation of another). Others ask whether the respondent supports or intends to vote for the candidate (self-evaluation). Results are reported as if a candidate were ahead or behind in a race. But an election is not a race; it is a single, discrete event, held on a single day. In one sense, the only poll result that really counts is the vote on election day. But the results of published polls can affect campaign contributors, workers, and even voters.[34]

Candidates who are ahead in the polls play them up. Those who are behind try to ignore them. They claim that voters have not really made up their minds and that the campaign will catch on once all its themes have been presented. They emphasize the statistical margin of error (the usual claim is that there is a 95 percent probability that the poll results are accurate to within 3 percentage points) if the results are close. They point to inconsistencies among different polls. They note the large number of undecided voters and claim that those who support their opponents are "mushy" and can be won away. They concentrate on gaining ground and momentum rather than on standings.[35] They point to the incorrect calls made by pollsters (Gallup missed in 1976, and Harris called 1968 wrong), ignoring the fact that in most elections the final Gallup and Harris polls are within 1 or 2 points of the actual results.

Candidates' polls. Presidential candidates run much more sophisticated polling operations than do news services. The Republican Party, in 1980 and 1984, used PINs (Political Information Systems), which consisted of a data bank with information on the 3041 counties: census data, economic information from the Bureau of Labor Statistics, demographic and market research data,

---

WORLD SERIES WINNER KEY TO PRESIDENCY?

Jon Margolis, a Washington correspondent for *The Chicago Tribune*, claims that if in a presidential election year the National League wins the World Series, the Democrats will win the election. Since 1903 there have been twenty-one presidential elections, and the theory has held up fifteen times.

Newton's law (not Isaac, but Wayne W.) holds that in a good vintage year for the Bordeaux wines of France, a Democrat wins the presidency.

The party that is rated ahead in the October Gallup poll on the ability to handle the nation's most important problem has won every presidential election since 1964.

The *Weekly Reader's* poll of 100,000 elementary school and high school students has picked every winner since 1956. In 1984 Reagan scored higher than Mondale in this poll, 64 to 33 percent.

---

voter registration data, voting records from past elections, spending patterns in congressional races from the Federal Elections Commission, polling data sponsored by state parties and PACs, and nightly tracking polls sponsored by the RNC. It also used a market research technique, TRACE, which allowed members of a test audience who viewed commercials or the debates to record positive or negative feelings about them on hand-held calculators; the calculators had five buttons that allowed viewers to record their reactions (ranging from most positive to most negative), and the data were fed into a computer.

This information was used to simulate the effects of any change in Republican (or Democratic) strategy, tactics, or campaign rhetoric on each county's projected vote. Should Reagan play up environmental issues, or should he play them down? Should he move to the center on social issues, or should he take a conservative position? The computerized system could forecast the effect of any move.[36]

Presidential debates

The centerpiece of recent presidential elections has been the debate between the major-party candidates. In the first three—1960 1976, and 1980—the party that controlled the White House lost the election. Mondale won a narrow victory in the 1984 debates, but changed few votes, a reversal of the previous pattern. Still, debates may be the great equalizer, offsetting advantages of incumbency, funding, and organization.

The stakes. Debates attract a huge audience: 107 million adults in 1960 and 122 million in 1976 viewed at least one in the series, while more than 100 million saw the debates in 1980 and 1984. Debates raise voters' interest and provide information. In close contests many voters wait for the debates before making their decision. Strong Democrats and Republicans are likely to watch selectively (that is, they think that the candidate of their party has won the debates), and they are least likely to reconsider their choice. Weaker identifiers, independents, and voters with doubts about their party's nominee are likely to use the debates to help them decide. Those who watch debates tend to vote on the basis of the issues, while those who do not watch are more likely to vote on the basis of personality.[37]

Debates may change votes. They can soften up viewers by dispelling negative impressions. Roper polls showed that 6 percent of the public—4 million voters—based their votes in 1960 on the debates, and of these, Kennedy won 72 percent. We cannot tell whether he would have won these votes otherwise,

Nixon and Kennedy in their fourth presidential debate in 1960. (*AP: Wide World.*)

Reagan and Mondale in 1984 continued the modern tradition of presidential debates. (*Larry Downing: Woodfin Camp.*)

but the election was close and his good performance must have helped. In 1980 polls shows that Reagan picked up ground among undecided voters and independents.[38] In 1984 after the first debate, Reagan lost a few points among undecided voters, but later he won them back.

To debate or not. The public overwhelmingly favors debates, but after 1960 none were held in 1964, 1968, or 1972, when at least one of the candidates refused to debate because he had nothing to gain. Ford challenged Carter to debate in 1976, violating the "rule" that an incumbent president does not give the challenger equal standing. But Ford was in no position to ignore his opponent. He had entered the White House via the Twenty-Fifth Amendment rather than popular election, was nominated by a badly split convention, ran as the candidate of the minority party, and was tarnished by his pardon of Nixon for Watergate-related crimes. He began campaigning 30 points behind in the polls. Why, then, did Carter agree to debate? Because his lead was slipping as a result of an interview he had given to *Playboy* in which he discussed the "lust" he sometimes felt for women and in which he used swear words.

In 1980 Carter was behind in the polls and eager to debate. He wanted to portray Reagan as an extremist. At first Reagan ducked, but then when his campaign coverage turned sour, he changed his mind. He was also worried that Carter might pull a presidential "October surprise" (like negotiating an end to the Iranian hostage crisis). Anyway, how could a former actor like Reagan resist performing on the biggest stage, and before the largest audience, of his career?

Rehearsal and performance. Candidates prepare for debates by rehearsing in studio mock-ups. Their top campaign officials prepare briefing books which provide background, as well as script segments which lay out issues, defend their record, and attack their opponents. They are coached on posture, mannerisms, and diction.

Candidates do best when they give long answers which directly address the concerns of the audience. They do worst when they try to rebut what their opponent has said or try to contradict the opponent's arguments. Scoring debating points is less important than presenting ideas and themes to a national audience. Candidates must keep on their own strongest ground, define the terms in which the issues are framed, and use vivid examples—even parables and metaphors to illustrate their point. They learn how to slide away from questions put to them by a panel of reporters or by the other candidate and to get back to a planned segment.[39] They can calculate a show of emotion. Reagan's exasperated gibe at Carter—"There you go again"—was an eloquent retort to what Reagan claimed was Carter's distortion of Reagan's positions. (Of course, Reagan was aided in the 1980 debate because his campaign had obtained access to Carter's briefing books, and therefore Reagan knew exactly what Carter would say.) In 1984, when Reagan used that line again, Mondale was prepared, and he effectively counterattacked with a direct question ("Remember when you last used that line, Mr President?") that disconcerted Reagan.

Debates give candidates a chance to neutralize an issue. Consider the second sentence of Reagan's opening remarks in the 1980 debate: "And I'm only here to tell you that I believe with all my heart that our first priority must be world peace. . . ." Later he added, "I have seen four wars in my lifetime. I'm a father of sons; I have a grandson. I don't ever want to see another generation of young Americans bleed their lives into the sandy beachheads of the Pacific . . ." and so on.[40]

Candidates aim their comments at specific groups: independents, voters who often switch back and forth, potential defects from the opposition, and

members of their party who have doubts. In 1984 Mondale, according to his pollster, Peter Hart, aimed his appeals primarily at blue-collar workers and Catholics, whom Hart described as "shaky as a bowl of Jell-O."

Media verdicts. The media not only report the debates but also announce the winner and the loser. This results in a *sleeper effect:* the cumulative impact which media coverage, subsequent analysis, and verdicts can have on viewers. Consider what happened in 1976. Ford did well in the first debate; then in the second debate he startled knowledgeable people with the misstatement that the people of eastern Europe do not live under Soviet domination. Initially most viewers were unaffected by this slip. But Ford took more than a week to admit that he had made a mistake, and the error and his refusal to concede it became a major media issue. ("Is Ford too dumb to run the country?" "Is he too stubborn to admit that he made a mistake?") Ford's campaign manager, Don Chaney, argued later that "it was not a significant item until after it received extensive comment and coverage in the press."[41]

In 1984 the first New York Times/CBS survey of voters, take just after the debate, showed that Mondale won a narrow victory over Reagan—43 to 34. After a week of media coverage, polls showed that Mondale was the winner—66 to 17. It is not always how the candidates did, but how the media say they did, that determines who won or lost a debate.

The winner of a debate can expect an infusion of cash. After Mondale's success the Democratic Victory Fund swelled with checks dated that evening. The 19,800 fund-raising parties held during the debate raised more than $4.5 million. More people had favorable views of Mondale after his victory: his favorable ratings went up in the Washington Post/ABC polls from 41 to 57 percent in the following week.[42]

But winners cannot always expect to get votes on the basis of their performance in a debate. Most voters believed that in the first debate, Reagan simply had an "off night." By defusing fears that he would cut social security and by lightly poking fun at the age issue ("I will not make an issue of my opponent's youth and inexperience"), Reagan gained more than he lost. As a result of the debates Reagan gained ground on two issues: controlling nuclear arms and keeping the nation out of war. Mondale picked up at most 3 points in the first debate and none in the second, according to Peter Hart—and thereafter began his steady slide to defeat.

ISSUE AND DEBATE

THE FUTURE OF PRESIDENTIAL DEBATES. *The background.* Debates were held in 1960 and have been held in every presidential election year since 1976 under the auspices of the League of Women Voters. A panel of reporters (acceptable to both candidates) questions the candidates, and they are given time to rebut their opponent's statements. Debates have not yet become a routine feature of presidential elections. One or both candidates may refuse to debate (as happened in 1964, 1968, and 1972). The ground rules are negotiated by their staffers and change from one election to the next. Minor candidates, such as John Anderson in 1980, may participate in a separate debate but not be invited to the main event, but there are no criteria for inclusion or exclusion.

The Proposals for reform. Some reforms would take control over the debates away from the candidates and the League of Women Voters and have them organized by a presidential debate commission. One idea is to have former presidential and vice presidential candidates from both major parties serve. A proposal to

strengthen the two-party system would allow the Republican and the Democratic national committees to sponsor party-oriented debates which would include Cabinet members, governors, and congressional leaders.

Newton Minow, the former chairman of the Federal Communications Commission, has proposed a series of such party-controlled national debates which would not be confined to the election season. He has also proposed that the national committee of the opposition party have the right of reply to any presidential radio or television address made during the ten months preceding a presidential election or the ninety days preceding a midterm congressional election. During the election season the candidates on the presidential ticket would receive six half-hour prime-time slots (minor-party candidates would receive proportional allocations).

Other proposed reforms take aim at the panels which question candidates. Some reporters ask frivolous questions or seem poorly informed. Few challenge candidates when they make errors or falsify facts. Perhaps candidates should not be able to "veto" panelists. The pool could be broadened to include presidential scholars and former officials. The television networks have proposed that distinguished public figures chair the debates and serve on the panels, but candidates have held out for newscasters. The networks have also suggested that candidates hold real debates, in which each would directly address the other and ask direct questions, with no holds barred. Candidates have refused to engage in real debates; they prefer panels of reporters and the familiar "news conference" format.

Another idea is for candidates to participate in "town meetings" so that a cross section of the public could question them; the format would be similar to that of William Buckley's *Firing Line* or public television's *MacNeil, Lehrer Newshour.*

The pros. Those who favor these proposals argue that the existing format allows a front-runner either to get away without really debating or to insist on rules that minimize the effect of a debate. Candidates can get by using their basic stump speeches. Debates do not test their knowledge or their ability to react under pressure. What is needed, the proponents of reform claim, is a lengthy series of debates on the issues, organized by the parties, that would focus not merely on presidential candidates but also on the entire spectrum of party leadership so that the public could make the most informed choice.

The cons. Those who oppose reform argue that the League of Women Voters has done an excellent job of mediating between candidates and fashioning debates that take into account the particular conditions of each campaign. They believe that a new commission at best would duplicate the league's work and at worst would lock debates into an inflexible format. They believe that reporters do ask the candidates tough questions and that their questioning is more likely to keep the candidates focused on the issues than a straight debate would. They do not believe that the public would be interested in a series of party-sponsored debates on the issues, and they claim that the audience would be small and would not include the least informed voters, who need debates the most.

The outlook. It is not likely that Congress will legislate ground rules for presidential debates, though it has been suggested that any candidate or party that accepts public funding be obligated to participate in forums devised by a national commission. The League of Women Voters, responding to criticism of the 1984 debates, is likely to reconsider some of the procedures it agreed to, especially those allowing candidates to veto panelists.

HOW VOTERS DECIDE

To understand how candidates appeal to different kinds of voters, we must discuss the way voters think about parties, candidates, and campaigns.

The American voter

Surveys conducted in the 1952, 1956, and 1960 elections showed that most voters were only mildly interested in politics, took little interest in campaigns, and did not participate in politics. Most did not think much or know much about issues. They were inconsistent, taking liberal or conservative positions on different issues, and they changed their positions from one year to the next.[43]

Party identification—the standing decision to favor one party over the other—was strong in these years and remained fixed from one election to the next. Like religious or ethnic identity, it was usually transmitted from one generation to the next within a family.[44] Straight-ticket voting was high, and even when voters defected (as many Democrats did to vote for Eisenhower), they retained their original party identification.

Although issues and candidates were more important factors in voting choice than party identification, feelings about parties conditioned how people felt about candidates and issues. Moreover, although issues and candidates might change from one election to the next, party identifications remained the same: knowing the party identifications of voters was the best way to predict voting choice.

The changing American voter. Since Goldwater's campaign in 1964, presidential politics has become more ideological and issue-oriented. Moderates and conservatives fought pitched nomination battles in the Republican Party in 1964, 1976, and 1980, and liberals and moderates have fought it out in the Democratic Party in every contest since 1968. Voters have become more ideological and issue-oriented as well. They care more and know more about issues. They have begun to array issues, candidates, and themselves along liberal-conservative dimensions. They are less likely to identify themselves as moderates. They have become more consistent in taking liberal or conservative stands on related issues, and they are less likely to change their views from one year to the next.[45]

Party identifications have become less significant in influencing voters' positions on candidates and issues, and voters rely less on party identification in deciding for whom to vote. Both parties have lost ground to independents, largely as a result of young voters' decision not to affiliate with either party; about half of young voters had become unaffiliated by 1976. Between 10 and 20 percent of voters have switched parties or have become independents between each election. They have fewer positive feelings about parties and think that the parties are not responsive on issues.[46] By 1972 almost half the voters had become ticket switchers, up from one-fourth in the 1950s. Many southern Democrats have become *presidential Republicans*—they have maintained their Democratic affiliation but vote regularly for Republican candidates in presidential elections. In the north some moderate and liberal Republicans have become more independent. (See Table 9-2.)

Since the 1964 elections, issues have become more significant for voters, and party identification has become less important, as Figure 9-5 indicates. In 1980, three-fifths of the voters surveyed could place themselves and the two major-party candidates on the issues. More than half perceived important differences

Table 9-2. Defection rates of party identifiers

	Democratic victories: 1960, 1964, 1976	Republican victories: 1968, 1972, 1980
	Percent of voters who defected from their parties	
Strong Democrats	7.7	15.3
Weak Democrats	23.7	43.7
Independent Democrats	16.7	45.3
Independent Republicans	17.3	15.3
Weak Republicans	26.0	8.7
Strong Republicans	5.0	3.7

Source: Arthur H. Miller and Warren E. Miller, "Partisanship and Performance: Rational Choice in the 1976 Presidential Elections," APSA paper, 1977; Paul Abramson et al., *Change and Continuity in the 1980 Elections*, Congressional Quarterly Press, Washington, D.C., 1982, table 8.4, p. 167.

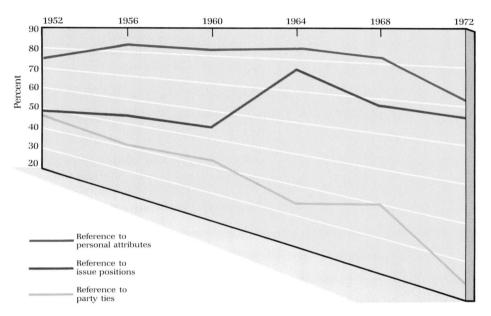

Figure 9-5. Beginning with the 1964 election, voters evaluated candidates increasingly in terms of their positions on the issues, while their party identification played less of a role. This helps account for Nixon's reelection and Reagan's two victories in a period in which the majority of voters retained their Democratic affiliations. (Source: Norman H. Nie, Sidney Verba, and John R. Petrocik, *The Changing American Voter*, A Twentieth Century Fund Study, 1976, Twentieth Century Fund, New York, fig. 10.6, p. 167.)

between Carter and Reagan; of this group, four-fifths perceived these differences correctly, and 70 percent cast their ballots for the candidate who was closer to their own position (though not necessarily because of that positioning).[47]

Voters have come to link their ideology with their party identification. In the 1980 elections, of those voters who supported a major-party candidate for president, 70 percent of the liberals voted for Carter and 30 percent voted for Reagan, while 72 percent of the conservatives voted for Reagan and 28 percent voted for Carter. These figures are associated with party identification: most Republicans backed Reagan (and most identified themselves as conservative), and many conservative Democrats also supported him; Democrats who voted for Carter were more likely to be liberal than those who defected to vote for Reagan. The ideological lineup was due in part to party identification, just as party identification was due in part to the different positions of the parties and the candidates. By the 1980s, for many voters party identification had become a *conscious* decision, based on issues and ideology, rather than simply a *standing* decision, based on habit, family ties, or social affiliation.[48]

The normal vote. The Republicans have some advantages when they begin a campaign: access to more money, better discipline within their party structure, and more effective image-making and polling apparatuses. But the Democrats also have an advantage: a majority of party identifiers, as Figure 9-6 shows.

The significance of this imbalance is best explained by using the concept of the ***normal vote:*** the calculation as to how the election would be decided if there were no candidates and no campaigning—only party identification. (The calculation also takes into account expected turnout rates.[49]) The normal vote is therefore not a prediction of the actual vote. (In this sense, *normal* is a misnomer.) It is simply a way of handicapping the contest. Since the Democrats have more identifiers, in the absence of a campaign they should win every election.

The normal-vote concept affects the strategies of the two parties. Democratic candidates emphasize party identification and party loyalty, while Republican candidates sometimes do not even mention their party affiliation.

Stable factors in voting. Party identification remains fairly stable over time. So do turnout rates (which have declined only a few percentage points from one election to the next). The tendency for different kinds of people to support one party or another often remains stable from one election to the next. Changes may occur, but they are usually minor variations. Party identification, group support of a party, and turnout rates are the ***stable factors.*** They tell us which party has the advantage going into a campaign.

Although historically the Republicans have had higher turnout rates, the Democrats have had the advantage in terms of group support: in most elections between 1932 and 1980 this included blacks, Hispanics, Jews, Catholics, eastern and southern Europeans, union members and their families, and southerners. Combined with their advantage in party identification, the Democrats have had an impressive edge in the stable factors.

But the Democrats often lose presidential elections. Between 1948 and 1980, even with their advantages, they received 291.6 million presidential votes, com-

Figure 9-6. While Democratic and Republican party identifications have declined gradually since 1936, independent identifications have increased sharply. In the wake of President Reagan's reelection many polls showed the Republicans closing the gap with the Democrats. If this holds through the 1986 midterm elections, it may signal a fundamental realignment in party identification. (Source: 1920–1944 data reconstructed by Kristi Andersen from Norman H. Nie, Sidney Verba, and John R. Petrocik, *The Changing American Voter*, A Twentieth Century Fund Study, 1976, Twentieth Century Fund, New York, fig. 5.1, p. 83. Later data from SRC, Institute for Social Research, National Election Studies.)

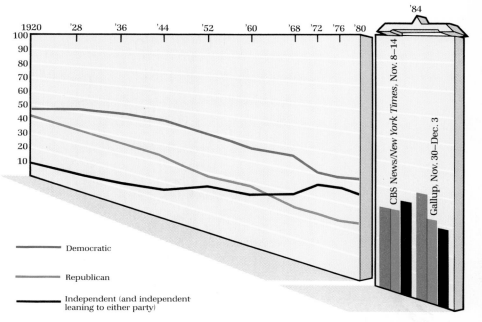

pared with 314.8 million received by the Republicans. They averaged 43 percent of the vote between 1968 and 1980, compared with 51 percent for the Republicans, and in 1984 they were crushed 60 to 40 by Reagan. Clearly, the normal vote and the stable factors cannot explain actual election results.

Dynamic factors in voting. Personality, issues and ideology, and specific events (such as the impact of Watergate in 1976, the Iranian hostage crisis in 1980, and the selection of a woman vice presidential nominee in 1984) are the *dynamic factors* in any campaign because they change from one election to the next. The stable factors *structure* a race (for example, the Democrats always have the advantage in terms of party identification), but the dynamic factors *decide it,* allowing the Republicans to overcome the initial edge of the Democrats.

In recent elections the dynamic factors have become more significant than the stable factors. There are more independents and voters whose attachments to parties are weak. Members of ethnic, religious, and economic groups are less likely to follow leadership endorsements or even to take their group affiliation into account when deciding on a candidate. Turnout rates are no longer quite so predictable. The so-called normal vote is harder to calculate and is of less value. The impact of convention coverage, campaign commercials, and presidential debates—all dynamic factors—has increased.

Retrospective voting. Voters also look at the record. They think retrospectively about how candidates and parties have acted in the past in order to make a judgment about who should govern in the future. The simplest kind of *retrospective voting* involves meting out rough justice to incumbents.[50] Voters can reward good performance and punish bad performance (in 18 of the last 22 elections through 1984, either a president or a vice president was running). There is a high correlation between a favorable evaluation of a president and a subsequent vote for reelection.[51] In a New York Times/CBS poll taken in August 1984, 72 percent of the voters who thought that the United States was better off than it had been four years earlier were planning to vote for Reagan; only 15 percent said that they would vote for Mondale. Of those who thought that the

Reprinted by permission: Tribune Media Series, Inc.

country was worse off, 58 percent planned to vote for Mondale, and only 20 percent planned to vote for Reagan.

Voters can also make *projective comparisons:* they look at the past record of the candidates and their parties in terms of missed opportunities—what would have happened if the party out of power had been in the White House for the past four years. Would things have been better or worse? Ironically, hard times might actually reinforce support for an incumbent: when unemployment goes up during a Democratic administration, most Democrats think that things would have been even worse if the Republicans had been in office; when inflation goes up during a Republican administration, most Republicans think that the Democrats would have done even worse.

Candidates ask unsophisticated voters for a protest vote, as Reagan did when, as part of his closing remarks during the debate with Carter in 1980, he asked, "Are you better off than you were four years ago?" Mondale's attempt to raise the same question in 1984 backfired: polls showed that a majority of Americans (especially younger white males, who were crucial to the Democrats' success) believed that they were better off, gave the Republicans the credit for it, and intended to vote for Reagan.

Swaying voters: Campaign strategy and tactics

The Democrats' campaign strategy and tactics are designed to reinforce existing party identifications and group allegiances; the Republicans' campaign strategy and tactics are designed to break them up and create new alignments.

Party coalitions. Parties have concentrated on different regions and on different racial, ethnic, religious, and occupational groups. This does not mean that all members of a group vote for one party or that all Republicans are members of some groups and that all Democrats are members of others. It does mean that there is a greater *probability* that some kinds of people will identify with a party and vote for its candidate than can be accounted for by chance (Figure 9-7).

ETHNIC, RACIAL, AND RELIGIOUS GROUPS. The Republicans do well among white Protestants in the north who are of English, Scottish, Welsh, Scotish-Irish, or German descent; among the wealthy and well educated; among farmers in the north and the midwest; and among male voters between the ages of 18 and 24. A majority of white Protestants have voted for Republican candidates in every presidential election since 1944 (with the single exception of

Figure 9-7. Each pie chart shows how voters from various groups split between the Democratic and Republican presidential candidates in the six presidential elections through 1980. White indicates votes for third-party candidates. (Source: *Gallup Opinion Index,* December 1980, pp. 6–7.)

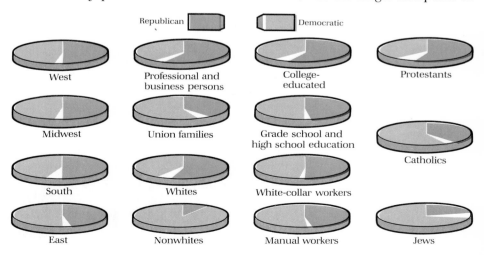

Republican ⬜   ⬜ Democratic

West

Professional and business persons

College-educated

Protestants

Midwest

Union families

Grade school and high school education

South

Whites

White-collar workers

Catholics

East

Nonwhites

Manual workers

Jews

that held in 1964). In 1980 Reagan received 61 percent of this vote, and in 1984 he received close to 70 percent.

Blacks are almost exclusively Democratic identifiers and voters. Since 1964 they have given at least 85 percent of their vote to Democratic candidates. Hispanics give a large margin to Democrats (except for Cuban Americans in Florida, who register 60 percent Republican). Together, these minorities account for one-fifth of the Democratic vote. The Democrats count on union members and their families, who provide between one-third and one-fourth of their votes. Jews since 1944 have been the most heavily Democratic of all religious groups: the Democrats won a majority from them in every election between 1944 and 1980 (when Carter won only a plurality), and in 1984 they won two-thirds of their vote. Because of their small numbers (5.7 million, a declining proportion of the total electorate), they are not as influential as other groups: in the past three elections they have provided only 1 vote in 20 received by Democrats. Nevertheless, because of the large numbers of Jewish voters in the big states (New York, California, Pennsylvania, Florida, and New Jersey), a swing in their vote can have significant consequences in the electoral college. Solid majorities of Catholics voted Democratic in 6 of the 7 elections between 1944 and 1968, but in 1972 and 1980 the Republicans won a majority of their vote, and in 1984 they won 58 percent. Upper-income and Polish and Irish Catholics are most likely to shift toward the Republicans.

GENDER. Women have become increasingly more Democratic in their party orientation. Today women constitute 60 percent of Democratic identifiers and 40 percent of Republican identifiers; for men, the figures are reversed. The gender gap (that is, differentials in voting between men and women) can favor either party. In 1980 Reagan won a far greater margin of votes from men than from women in defeating Carter. In the 1982 congressional elections, there was a wide gender gap going the other way: the Democrats won the women's vote (62 to 38), while barely winning the male vote (52 to 48). But in the 1984 presidential election, contrary to the hopes of Democratic strategists, party identification and the nomination of a woman vice presidential candidate did not keep women in the Democratic column. Only 3 percentage points separated men and women in their support for Reagan, and he won majorities from both.

While the Democrats argue that the Republicans have a "female problem," the Republicans make a more compelling case that the Democrats have a "male problem." Only 30 percent of white males now vote Democratic in presidential elections, and a sharply declining percentage of them identify with the Democratic Party. The Democrats never quite figured out how to play the gender gap in 1984. In the debates both Mondale and Ferraro tried to show how "tough" they could be on the Russians, in an unsuccessful attempt to "out-macho" the Republicans and win back the defecting white males.

INSTABILITY OF GROUP ALIGNMENTS. Unlike the situation in the New Deal period (1932–1948), today the level of *polarization* is low: in most cases the groups are split, with only a small margin between the parties; in only a few cases (for example, blacks and Jews) are groups overwhelmingly aligned with one party. Members of most groups have only weak party attachments, and so in any given election just about any group can split or provide a decisive margin to the candidate of either major party. Reagan won a majority or plurality in 1980 from several groups that traditionally support Democrats. In 1964 Johnson won large majorities from several groups that usually vote Republi-

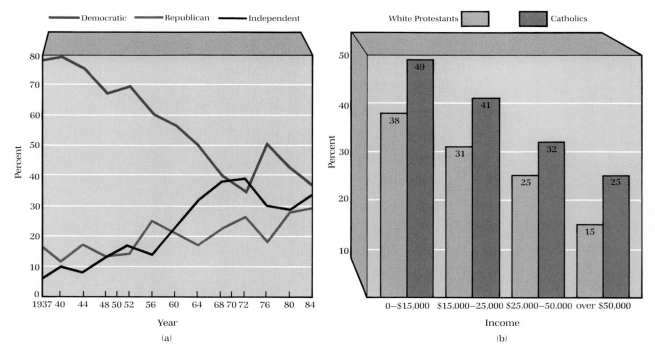

Democratic ——— Republican ——— Independent

White Protestants ☐ ■ Catholics

(a)

Year

(b)

Income

Figure 9-8. The key groups in presidential politics are upper-income Catholics in the north and upper-income white Protestants in the south. When these groups defect from the Democratic Party, its presidential candidates lose. Similarly, if Democrats can induce defections from white working-class Protestants in the north, they have a good chance of winning the industrial states. (*a*) Republicans have made small but steady gains in party identification among southern whites while Democrats have suffered large losses since 1936. Most of those defecting from the Democrats became independents and voted for Republican or third-party candidates (in 1948 and 1968). The Democrats have reversed the tide only once since 1952, when a Georgian, Jimmy Carter, headed their ticket. (Source: Gallup polls.) (*b*) The 1980 data for percent of vote received by Carter show Carter's failure to hold the votes of Catholic Democratic identifiers, even those in lower-income groups. (Source: SRC National Election Studies.)

can. The Republicans won the south in 1972, the Democrats retook it in 1976 and then lost it again in 1980, and so on.

Breaking up coalitions. The Democrats win presidential elections by minimizing defections from their existing coalition and by making inroads among lower-income white Protestant voters in the north by emphasizing unemployment and other economic issues. The Republicans win by adding to their existing base: they go after white southerners, conservative Democrats in all regions, and upper-income Catholic and Jewish voters. The Republicans win by keeping white Protestants together, regardless of class differences, while splitting Catholic voters on class lines. The Democrats win by keeping Catholic voters with them, while splitting Protestant voters along class lines. (See Figure 9-8.)

THE SOUTH. The Republican Party promotes itself as the party of states' rights, decentralization, local control, neighborhood schools, and new federalism. The new breed of Republican "populists" attack the Democrats for high interest rates and inflation, which hurt working-class people as well as the wealthy. They paint the Democratic Party as the party of big government trampling on states' rights, beholden to minorities, and willing to weaken the country's defenses. Their appeal to white voters in the south has increased. The south no longer votes Democratic in presidential elections, as it did (with few exceptions) for a century after the Civil War.

THE NORTH. The Republicans have broken up the New Deal coalition of union members, Catholics, and Jews. They portray the Democratic Party as a "permissive" party when it comes to abortion, gay rights, prayer in schools, drugs, crime, busing, and other social and family issues. The Republicans favor aid to parochial and private schools, an issue which unites Protestant fundamentalists and Catholics. They no longer emphasize issues such as prohibition of gambling or the sale of alcoholic beverages—issues which once divided

303

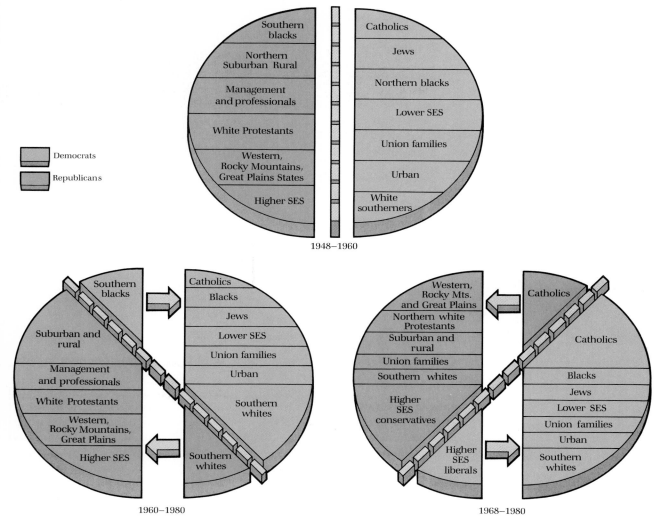

Democrats

Republicans

Southern blacks

Northern Suburban Rural

Management and professionals

White Protestants

Western, Rocky Mountains, Great Plains States

Higher SES

Catholics

Jews

Northern blacks

Lower SES

Union families

Urban

White southerners

1948–1960

Southern blacks

Suburban and rural

Management and professionals

White Protestants

Western, Rocky Mountains, Great Plains

Higher SES

Catholics

Blacks

Jews

Lower SES

Union families

Urban

Southern whites

Southern whites

1960–1980

Western, Rocky Mts. and Great Plains

Northern white Protestants

Suburban and rural

Union families

Southern whites

Higher SES conservatives

Higher SES liberals

Catholics

Catholics

Blacks

Jews

Lower SES

Union families

Urban

Southern whites

1968–1980

Figure 9-9. The majority New Deal coalition put together by the Democratic party pitted unions against management, and religious and racial minorities and working-class voters against wealthier white Protestants in the North; and it took advantage of the "solid south" heritage of the Civil War. After 1964 Republicans broke up this coalition. First they emphasized their opposition to busing and used a "southern strategy" to become competitive in the south. As southern whites joined the Republican party, southern blacks left and became Democrats: on balance the Republicans gained. Later, Republicans emphasized the "social issues" to bring northern Catholics and southern fundamentalists to their party. In response to their conservative stance, some moderate Republicans in the north defected; but once again on balance the Republicans gained many more voters than they lost, especially in presidential elections.

Protestants and Catholics. Instead, they unite these groups with calls for a war on drugs and pornography. Issues of race (for example, busing, quotas, and affirmative action) and morality displace issues of class, on which the Democrats often have greater appeal. "We are for life and against abortion," Reagan told parishioners at St. Ann's church in Newark during the 1984 campaign. "We are for prayer in the schools, we are for tuition tax credits and, in Central America, we are rather more inclined to listen to the testimony of his holiness the Pope than the claims of the Communist Sandinistas."[52]

CROSSCUTTING ISSUES. The Republicans have found issues which cut across existing divisions, break up the New Deal coalition, unite their followers, and divide the Democrats. Their stand on racial issues may alienate the small number of liberal Republicans, but meanwhile the Democrats are bitterly divided: blacks debate Jews on quotas and affirmative action; southern conservatives who are opposed to busing fight black activists in the courts; and many Democrats switch to the Republican Party. On family and social issues the Republicans have lost the liberal wing, but they have gained support from southern Protestant fundamentalists and northern Catholics (Figure 9-9).

REFERENCE GROUPS. Campaigns also try to get voters to think of themselves as members of groups which the party has helped. People have many group affiliations; they may be veterans, union members, suburbanites, or churchgoers, for example. Usually they identify with a party and support a candidate on the basis of a few of these identifications. The campaign gets voters to make other self-identifications: union members who expect to vote Democratic may start thinking of themselves as suburbanites concerned about inflation and interest rates—which may induce them to vote Republican.

The Democrats campaign by reaffirming traditional party identifications and reassuring voters that their party is still better for the unions, Jews, blacks, the south, and so forth. Rather than try to convince voters otherwise, the Republicans have created a set of reference groups with which voters can identify—for example, middle Americans, forgotten Americans, and the new American majority. Their campaign advertising is geared toward convincing people (such as family-oriented middle- and working-class taxpayers) that they are members of these groups and that their interests are best served by the Republicans. In addition, their rhetoric creates reference groups with which a majority of people do not identify—welfare cheats, career criminals, liberal elitists, secular humanists, drug abusers, and women's liberationists—suggesting that the Democratic Party is the party of these and similar groups.

TRENDS: ELECTION RESULTS AND THEIR MEANING

Election results tell us much more than which candidate will occupy the White House for the next four years. The voting returns are connected to governance: how a candidate campaigns and how voters make up their minds have much to do with how the country will be governed.

Types of presidential elections

We can classify elections according to their impact on the stable factors: party identification, party coalitions, and turnout rates. In some elections the campaigns make no impact on these factors, while in others there are dramatic changes.[53] Each type of election has a different impact on presidential power, the prospects for presidential leadership of Congress, and the policies that the White House might pursue.

The maintaining election. An election in which there is little or no measurable change in the stable factors and in which the party with the normal-vote advantage wins is a *maintaining election.*

The reinforcing election. An election that is won by the party with the normal-vote advantage, which gives it even greater strength in terms of the stable factors, is a *reinforcing election.* It gives the president great influence

with the party; not only has the president won, but the victory also helps other candidates on the ticket and attracts new party supporters.

The critical election. Conversely, consider an election which is won by the party with the normal-vote advantage but in which the advantage in terms of the stable factors decreases. Voters defect from the party, one or more groups leave the party coalition, and turnout among supporters is down. Even though the party won, the new president may be in trouble: the president may have lost some partisans in Congress, will have trailed the ticket in many areas, and will be subject to criticism for having conducted a poor campaign. This is a *critical election.*

Alternatively, there is the election in which even though a party wins a great victory, a particular group has shifted its party identification. Although Herbert Hoover a Republican, won a landslide victory in 1928, his election can be considered critical rather than reinforcing because northern urban Catholics supported a Catholic Democratic candidate and began a massive shift to the Democratic party.[54]

The deviating election. An election that is won by a popular candidate of the minority party who appeals to voters on issues or whose candidacy is a protest is a *deviating election.* The candidate takes advantage of the dynamic factors and wins a personal victory, but there is no change in party identification or underlying group allegiance to the majority party. Voters defected to the candidate, but still do not identify with the minority party. This is a deviation from the normal vote. The newly elected president may be confronted with a hostile Congress controlled by the opposition. Members of the president's own party remain somewhat dissatisfied because the personal victory did not help them. The Republicans won deviating elections in 1952, 1956, 1968, 1972, and 1980.

The reinstating election. After one or two deviating elections the party with the normal-vote advantage eventually regains the White House in a *reinstating election.* A newly elected president comes into conflict with leading members of the winning party in Congress, who see the reinstating election as their opportunity to implement their own priorities. Kennedy and Carter both had problems with their own party after such elections.

The realigning election. In a *realigning election,* the minority party uses crosscutting issues and reference groups to break up the majority coalition. It gets large numbers of people in critical groups not only to defect in their vote but also to switch their party identification—either in that presidential election or the subsequent one. The minority party, by virtue of these defections, becomes the majority party. Such elections involve drastic changes in the stable factors: the advantage in terms of party identification shifts, groups swing decisively from one party to the other, regional political competition changes, and turnout rates may suddenly move up or down by as much as 20 percentage points. After such a political earthquake there is usually a thirty- to sixty-year period in which most factors remain fairly stable—until there is another realigning election. The Republicans won a realigning election in 1896, when they won over many white working-class factory employees and immi-

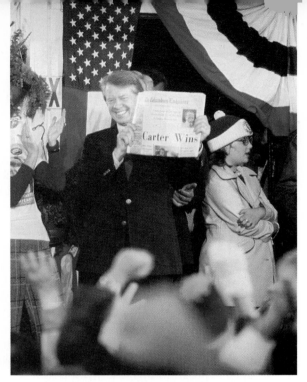

President-elect Jimmy Carter
savors the newspaper headlines
in 1976. (*Sygma.*)

grants. The Republican Party remained the dominant party in Congress and at the state level for almost forty years. The Democrats realigned the party system in the elections of 1932 and 1936, creating the New Deal coalition. Since then, they have lost deviating elections (1952, 1956, 1968, 1972, and 1980), won reinstating elections (1960 and 1976), and once, in 1964, managed to win a reinforcing election. In 1984 Republicans almost pulled even with Democrats in party identification within the electorate, leading some Republicans to argue that the 1980 and 1984 elections had produced a realignment of two-party competition.

Obviously, the minority party would much rather win a realigning election than a deviating election. For one thing, it is then less likely to lose the subsequent election and more likely to run off a string of victories. Winning a realigning election also gives other party candidates the normal-vote advantage, making their races easier. It gives the president partisans in Congress and the state legislatures, which helps the president implement programs (though there is usually a lag of four to eight years before a realignment at the national level is fully reflected in state politics).

Election results and governance

While elections have some impact on policy, it would be grossly misleading to state that they are the major determinant. Nevertheless, history allows us to make some tentative generalizations. Reinforcing and realigning elections are associated with policy breakthroughs. A party wins big because voters are attracted to a presidential candidate's vision of the future. Once in office, the president can capitalize on public opinion, at least in the first year, to get proposals through. Franklin Roosevelt's New Deal and Lyndon Johnson's "great society" involved regulation of the economy or redistribution of resources and were implemented after the incumbent went to the country and made appeals on the basis of his election mandate.

Maintaining, critical, and reinstating elections are associated with more erratic presidential performance. Truman, Kennedy, and Carter all found it hard

to get along with Congress—including members of their own parties. There were few great policy breakthroughs; more often, there were incremental changes in existing programs. Presidents who have won in such elections have found it hard to lead the public and hard to claim a mandate or implement one.

Deviating elections usually lead to centrist accommodations with an opposition congressional majority (the Eisenhower pattern), to intense confrontations between the two branches (the Nixon pattern), or to an attempt to replicate the election success by going to the country and putting the pressure of public opinion on Congress (the Reagan pattern).

But these generalizations do not always hold true, especially as the memory of the election results fades and as the parties look toward the next set of congressional and presidential contests. The winner of a deviating election is not always weaker than the winner of a realigning or a reinforcing election. Woodrow Wilson and Ronald Reagan both implemented most of their far-reaching domestic programs in their first terms.

Although it seems logical that a president who wins a reinforcing election will be a strong leader, it does not always work out that way. Franklin Roosevelt's 1936 election was followed by open revolt within his party and paralysis of much of his program by 1938. Lyndon Johnson's reinforcing election of 1964 was followed in 1966 by defections in Congress over issues of foreign policy, a result of the unpopularity of the Vietnamese war.

Dealignment theory

The preceding discussion assumes that the stable factors really are stable. This is debatable. The coalition that elected Franklin Roosevelt in 1932 was somewhat different from the one that elected John Kennedy in 1960, and that coalition was quite different from the one that elected Jimmy Carter in 1976. The demographic characteristics of voters, their turnout rates, and their group affiliations changed somewhat. The above discussion also assumes that the stable factors are critically important and can still structure party competition. This too is debatable in the era of weakening party identification and media manipulation through the techniques of media politics.

The long-awaited realignment predicted by the election typology still has not occurred. Analysts thought that Nixon's reelection in 1972 would be the breakthrough, but Nixon was unable to win congressional majorities, and by 1976 his party not only had lost the White House but also had been thumped in congressional and state elections, leaving what some analysts referred to as a "one-and-a-half" party system. In 1980 Reagan won the White House, and the Republicans won the Senate, but during Reagan's first term the Republicans barely made a dent in the Democrats' advantage in terms of party identification. They did poorly in the 1982 midterm congressional elections, and their modest gains in governorships and state legislative seats were rolled back. In 1984, even Reagan's landslide could not make up for those losses. However, the Republicans did make some gains in southern state legislative seats, which indicated that realignment might be taking place.

The joke on economic forecasters is that they have predicted five of the last two recessions. So, too, realignment theorists have predicted four Republican realignments (1952, 1972, 1980, and 1984), but none has yet occurred. When a theory, no matter how elegant, has little predictive value, it may be time to consider a new one.[55]

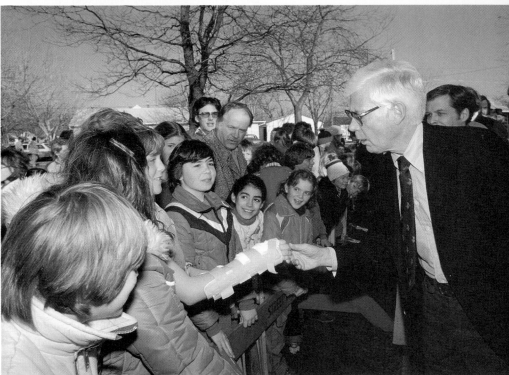

Third-party and independent candidacies can play a significant role. Governor George Wallace of Alabama created the American Independent Party for his 1968 run for the presidency; John Anderson ran as an independent in 1980. (*Constantine Manos: Magnum; Susan McElhinney: Woodfin Camp.*)

Voters are becoming unmoored from party and group orientations. Most are weak or independent party identifiers or pure independents. Voters have become ticket splitters and habitual defectors in presidential elections. In 1968 and 1980 many people voted for third-party candidates as a stopover on their

way to switching parties. Voters decide on the basis of issues, ideologies, and retrospective evaluations, not party identification or group affiliations. Politics has become nationalized as a result of the impact of the news media and campaign advertisements: no longer is it class against class, region against region, or religion against religion, in predictable patterns. Like unsecured cargo on a ship, most groups can swing from one side to another, depending on the political weather.

The stable factors are not very stable. Normal-vote patterns no longer exist. The dynamic factors are the key to the vote, and therefore to any meaning which an analyst can find in it.

The party system may be involved in voter dealignment rather than realignment; if the trends discussed above continue to dominate electoral choice.

THE REFORM AGENDA

ELECTING THE PRESIDENT. During the past two centuries our electoral process has been transformed; we have gone from limited suffrage to mass suffrage, from congressional caucuses to open nominations decided by the voters, from a one-party system to a two-party system (including five different party alignments), and from canvassing by local party workers to new politics advertising. There is no reason to assume that our political institutions and practices will not change in the future.

The electoral college. Why keep the electoral college—an archaic system with a great potential for disaster? There are several reasons. First, it discourages minor parties and independent candidates unless they can win states outright— they get nothing for winning less than a purality. Second, the smaller states get more representation than they would be entitled to on a pure arithmetic basis: Alaska, for example, has three electors who represent 140,000 persons each, while California has forty-seven electors, each of whom represents more than 500,000 people. Third, the influence of voters in the large states is maximized because of the winner-take-all system. (Suppose that in an election voters in Alaska and California were tied and that you could cast a vote in either state to break the tie. Which state would you choose to vote in? You would pick California, because your vote would determine forty-seven electoral college votes.)

Those who are opposed to the electoral college system argue that it breaks down and that it can give an election to the less popular candidate. Opponents have proposed several changes. The simplest would be to abolish the position of elector and count votes automatically. The most drastic change would be to eliminate the electoral college and hold direct popular elections.[56] The winner would have to receive 40 percent of the vote, or else there would be a runoff between the top two contenders. (Another variation would provide for a runoff between the top three contenders, with Congress deciding if no one received 40 percent of the vote on the second round.)

Critics of direct popular elections argue that they might result in a proliferation of minor-party candidates. The 40 percent rule might lead to presidents elected by plurality rather than majority vote. Major-party candidates would probably make deals with small parties that represented ideologies, single-issue groups, or racial and ethnic constituencies, thus fragmenting the parties and increasing public disillusionment. Runoff elections would probably result in lower turnouts and less interest on the part of voters, since they would become saturated with campaigning.

Two proposals would retain the electoral college while solving some of its prob-

lems. First, the electoral college vote could be apportioned within each state according to the popular vote. This would ensure that the popular and electoral winners were the same and would deemphasize the importance of the large states and swing voters within them. But it would encourage minor-party candidacies, with all their attendant problems. Second, we could use congressional district lines to select 435 electors and use state contests to select 103 electors from the states and from the District of Columbia. The Republicans favor this plan; if it had been in operation in 1960, Nixon would have won the election because Republicans often "win" more congressional districts in presidential voting than Democrats. This proposal would inhibit many minor-party candidates but would encourage those with regional support or support from minority racial and ethnic groups. Third-party or minority-group electors might hold the balance of power in the electoral college, which would lead to bargaining or even to a House contingency election.

Another proposal, this one put forth by the Twentieth Century Fund's Commission on Presidential Selection, would give a bonus of 102 electoral votes to the person who won a plurality of the popular vote. This would keep all the advantages of the present system, while ensuring that the winner of the popular vote also won a majority in the electoral college.

Campaign financing. The public is unhappy with the existing system of campaign financing. An Associated Press poll conducted in July 1984 indicated that 86 percent of the public think that candidates spend too much and that 82 percent favor more restrictions on campaign financing. The national party committees, rather than the candidates, could be given public funds, which would tie a candidate more closely to the party organization. Limits could be placed on contributions for state party building, and unions, corporations, and banks could be prohibited from contributing to state party accounts that spend money directly or indirectly on presidential campaigns. A candidate who was attacked by an independent committee could be given extra federal funds as an equalizer or free media time to respond. But the prospects for reform are poor: the Republicans do not want their soft-money state accounts touched, and the Democrats do not want reforms to inhibit union support for their candidates. Limits on contributions to parties are likely to be raised, but serious limits on spending are not likely to be enforced.

Election-night coverage. Proposed federal legislation would bar network projections of the winner (based on exit polls or actual precinct tallies) until the last state voted; this would prevent any possibility that voters in western states might choose not to go to the polls if a projected winner had already been announced. Other proposals include voluntary agreement by the networks to forestall such a law and a synchronized set of voting hours so that the forty-eight continental states could complete their voting at exactly the same time. The networks claim (and some empirical studies back them up) that very few people decide not to vote on the basis of network projections and that in almost no congressional or presidential contests have such decisions made any difference in the outcomes.

Responsible parties. In addition to these piecemeal proposals for reform, some political scientists have suggested comprehensive reforms that simultaneously strengthen the party structures (by providing that all financing go through them), link ***presidential parties*** and ***congressional parties*** (by providing for simultaneous four-year terms for House members, senators, and the president), and give the president a working majority in Congress, which would end the possibility of a deviating election (by giving the party that wins the White House a

"bonus" of 100 or so seats in the House). These reforms would create a system of presidential government quite at odds with our original constitutional understandings. If we amend the Constitution we can have such a system, but we should be clear about what we are doing: trading the safeguards of separate institutions that compete for power for the possibility that presidential government will be effective enough to solve national problems. Instituting such reforms would be quite a constitutional gamble, and as yet there is no indication that the nation is prepared to take so drastic a step.

IN CONCLUSION

Presidential campaigns, unlike primary contests, are short, intense affairs which involve campaigns for money, organization, image, and finally votes. The Republicans do better at funding and organization, and they have pioneered in media politics, which offset the Democrats' advantages in terms of party identification and group affiliation. Even though the Democrats have the normal-vote advantage, the Republicans have won more than half the elections since 1952. The Republicans Party has not, however, been able to convert itself into the majority party. We seem stuck in a pattern of deviating and reinstating elections, which leaves presidents of both parties weakened in dealing with Congress and their state parties. The system may now be so unmoored from its traditional bearings that no fundamental realignment is possible, and most trends seem to point to a party system that is more ideological, functioning in a nominating system that is more fluid and open to change. The consequences are that candidates, their coalitions, and their ideas can change drastically from one election to the next. There is a lengthy agenda of reforms, but most of them are unlikely to be adopted, especially proposals for a responsible party system.

NOTES

1. Russell Baker, "Observer," *The New York Times*, Apr. 12, 1980.
2. Lawrence Longley and Alan Braun, *The Politics of Electoral College Reform*, Yale University Press, New Haven, Conn., 1972, p. 3.
3. Ibid.
4. Lucius Wilmerding, *The Electoral College*, Rutgers University Press, New Brunswick, N.J., 1953, pp. 47–61.
5. Raymond Tatelovich, "Electoral Votes and Presidential Campaign Trails: 1932–1976," *American Politics Quarterly*, vol. 7, no. 4, October 1971, pp. 489–497; Steven J. Brams and Morton D. Davis, "The ½'s Rule in Presidential Campaigning," *American Political Science Review*, vol. 68, no. 1, March 1974, pp. 113–134.
6. Michael Goldstein, *A Handbook for Presidential Campaigns*, Public Affairs and Communications, Washington, D.C., 1984.
7. Herbert Alexander, *Financing Politics*, Congressional Quarterly Press, Washington, D.C., 1980, p. 10.
8. *Final Report of the Senate Select Committee on Presidential Campaign Activities*, 93d Cong., 2d Sess., 1974, p. 904.
9. Herbert Alexander, *Financing the 1968 Elections*, Heath, Boston, 1971, chap. 10.
10. The list was printed in *The New York Times*, Mar. 20, 1974.
11. Alexander, *Financing Politics*, op. cit., p. 159.
12. Elizabeth Drew, "Politics and Money," *The New Yorker*, Dec. 11, 1982, p. 64.
13. *The Wall Street Journal*, July 5, 1984, p. 1.
14. Ibid.

15. *Federal Elections Commission v. National Conservative Political Action Committee et al.*, 53 Law Week, 4293, March 19, 1985.
16. Brooks Jackson, "Democrats Must Stump for Dollars," *The Wall Street Journal*, July 3, 1984.
17. Researched by Arthur Larkin, Columbia College.
18. John Kessel, *Presidential Campaign Politics*, 2d ed., Dorsey, Homewood, Ill., 1984.
19. James David Barber, *The Pulse of Politics*, Norton, New York, 1980, pp. 3–4.
20. Richard Jensen, "Armies, Admen and Crusaders: Strategies to Win Elections," *Public Opinion*, vol. 3, no. 5, October–November 1980, pp. 44–53.
21. Benjamin Page, *Choices and Echoes in Presidential Elections*, University of Chicago Press, Chicago, 1978, pp. 232–265.
22. Joe McGinnis, *The Selling of the President, 1968*, Pocket Books, New York, 1969, p. 54.
23. Ibid., p. 31.
24. Timothy Crouse, *The Boys on the Bus*, Ballantine Books, New York, 1973, p. 303.
25. McGinnis, op.cit., p. 54.
26. *The New York Times*, July 16, 1984.
27. Av Westin, *Newswatch*, Simon and Schuster, New York, 1982, p. 93.
28. David S. Broder, "Political Reporters in Presidential Politics," in James I. Lengle and Byron E. Shafer (eds.), *Presidential Politics*, St. Martin's, New York, 1980, p. 497.
29. Crouse, op. cit, p. 323.
30. Thomas Patterson and Robert McClure, *The Unseeing Eye*, Putnam, New York, 1976, p. 58.
31. Ibid.
32. Irving Crespi, "Polls as Journalism," *Public Opinion Quarterly*, vol. 44, no. 4, winter 1980, pp. 516–517; C. Anthony Broh, "Horse-Race Journalism," *Public Opinion Quarterly*, vol. 44, no. 4, winter 1980, pp. 516–517.
33. Seymour Martin Lipset, "Different Polls, Different Results in 1980 Politics," *Public Opinion*, vol. 3, no. 4, August–September 1980, pp. 19–20; Barry Sussman, "Reagan vs. Mondale: Who's on First and Who's on Second," *Washington Post National Weekly Edition*, Aug. 6, 1984, p. 37.
34. Michael Wheeler, "Reining in Horserace Journalism," *Public Opinion*, vol. 3, no. 1a, February–March 1980, pp. 41–45; Burns W. Roper, "The Media and the Polls," *Public Opinion*, vol. 3, no. 1a, February–March 1980, pp. 46–49.
35. Roper reports, August–September 4, 1976.
36. Elizabeth Drew, "A Political Journal," *The New Yorker*, Sept. 10, 1984, pp. 102–106; Oct. 8, 1984, pp. 118–120.
37. Evron Kirkpatrick, "What Can We Learn from 1960?" in Austin Ranney (ed.), *The Past, Present and Future of Presidential Debates*, American Enterprise Institute, Washington, D.C., 1979, pp. 26–29; Steven H. Chaffee and Jack Dennis, "Wisconsin Panel Survey," as reported in Chaffee and Dennis, "Presidential Debates: An Empirical Assessment," in Ranney, op. cit., pp. 90–94.
38. *The New York Times*, Oct. 30, 1980, p. A-1; Paul Abramson et al., *Change and Continuity in the 1980 Elections*, Congressional Quarterly Press, Washington, D.C., 1982, pp. 129–134.
39. Marilyn Jackson-Beeck and Robert G. Meadow, "The Triple Agenda of Presidential Debates," *Public Opinion Quarterly*, vol. 43, no. 2, summer 1979, pp. 173–180.
40. Washington Post, *The Pursuit of the Presidency, 1980*, Berkely Books, New York, 1980, p. 361.
41. Richard Chaney, "The 1976 Debates: A Republican Perspective," in Ranney, op. cit., p. 128.
42. Barry Sussman, "How T.V.'s Power Has Again Transformed Public Opinion," *Washington Post National Weekly Edition*, Oct. 15, 1984, p. 37.
43. Norman Nie, Sidney Verba, and John Petrocik, *The Changing American Voter*, Harvard University Press, Cambridge, Mass., 1979, pp. 21, 26–27, 33.

44. Ibid., p. 29.

45. Ibid., pp. 97–99, 105–109, 113, 133, 143–150, 199–205.

46. Ibid., pp. 57, 105.

47. Abramson et al., loc. cit.

48. Morris Fiorina, *Retrospective Voting in American National Elections*, Yale University Press, New Haven, Conn., 1981, chap. 5.

49. Angus Campbell et al., *Elections and the Political Order*, Wiley, New York, 1966, chap. 1.

50. V. O. Key, *Politics, Parties and Pressure Groups*, 5th ed., Thomas Y. Crowell, New York, 1964, p. 588.

51. Fiorina, op. cit., p. 85–89, 102, 185.

52. *The New York Times*, July 27, 1984.

53. Walter Dean Burnham, *Critical Elections and the Mainsprings of American Politics*, Norton, New York, 1970, pp. 135–195.

54. V. O. Key, Jr., "A Theory of Critical Elections," *Journal of Politics*, vol. 17, no. 1, 1955, pp. 3–18.

55. On elections and party systems, see Seymour Martin Lipset (ed.), *Party Coalitions in the 1980s*, Institute for Contemporary Studies, Berkeley, Calif., 1980.

56. Stephen J. Wayne, *The Road to the White House*, St. Martin's, New York, 1980, pp. 15–22.

FURTHER READING

Alexander, Herbert: *Financing Politics*, 2d ed., Congressional Quarterly Press, Washington, D.C., 1981. A comprehensive and critical discussion of present-day campaign financing.

Altshuler, Bruce E.: *Keeping a Finger on the Public Pulse*, Greenwood Press, Westport, Conn., 1982. An account of the role of private pollsters in presidential elections.

Barber James David: *The Pulse of Politics*, Norton, New York, 1980. A treatment of campaign rhetoric.

Drew, Elizbeth: *Portrait of an Election*, Simon and Schuster, New York, 1981. A journalistic account, including a shrewd discussion of strategy, tactics, and personalities.

Fiorina, Morris: *Retrospective Voting in American National Elections*, Yale University Press, New Haven, Conn., 1981. A study of the way people's thoughts about the past and the future influence their vote.

Heard, Alexander: *The Costs of Democracy*, University of North Carolina Press, Chapel Hill, 1960. A classic study of traditional campaign financing.

Jamieson, Kathleen H.: *Packaging the Presidency: A History and Criticism of Presidential Campaign Advertising*, Oxford University Press, New York, 1984. A study of the development of new politics in presidential campaigns.

Kessel, John: *Presidential Campaign Politics*, 2d ed., Dorsey, Homewood, Ill., 1984. A study of the way campaigns are organized.

Lengle, James I., and Byron E. Shafer (eds.): *Presidential Politics*, 2d ed., St. Martin's, New York, 1983. Articles on election politics, focusing on the rules of the game.

Linsky, Martin (ed.): *Television and the Presidential Elections*, Lexington Books, Lexing-

ton, Mass., 1983. Proceedings of a conference held at the Institute of Politics, Kennedy School of Government, Harvard University.

Nie, Norman H., Sidney Verba, and John R. Petrocik: *The Changing American Voter*, Harvard University Press, Cambridge, Mass., 1976. A treatise on voting behavior and how it has evolved in the past thirty years.

Page, Benjamin: *Choices and Echoes in Presidential Elections*, University of Chicago Press, Chicago, 1978. A study of how candidates position themselves on the issues.

Patterson, Thomas: *The Mass Media Election*, Praeger, New York, 1980. An analysis of the 1976 elections.

Ranney, Austin (ed.): *The Past, Present and Future of Presidential Debates*, American Enterprise Institute, Washington, D.C., 1979. A collection of essays on presidential debates.

Robinson, Michael, and Margaret Sheehan: *Over the Wire and on T.V.: CBS and UPI in Campaign '80*, Russell Sage, New York, 1980. A discussion of how networks and wire services cover campaigns.

Rosenstone, Steven: *Forecasting Presidential Elections*, Yale University Press, New Haven, Conn., 1983. A discussion of the techniques used by political scientists.

Rubin, Richard: *Press, Party and Presidency*, Norton, New York, 1981. A book that traces the changing relationships between the media and presidential campaign politics and develops implications for government.

Schramm, Martin: *Running for President, 1976*, Stein and Day, New York, 1977. A journalist's account of the Carter campaign, containing strategy memorandums from both camps.

Twentieth Century Fund Task Force: *With the Nation Watching*, Lexington Books, Lexington, Mass., 1979. A report on presidential debates.

Wayne, Stephen J.: *The Road to the White House*, 2d ed., St. Martin's, New York, 1984. An overview of presidential election politics.

THE STUDY BREAK

Crouse, Timothy: *The Boys on the Bus*, Ballantine Books, New York, 1973. A book about how the media covered the 1972 campaign.

McGinnis, Joe: *The Selling of the President, 1968*, Pocket Books, New York, 1969. An account of Nixon's media campaign, including some hilarious stories about the candidate.

USEFUL SOURCES

Roseboom, Eugene: *A History of Presidential Elections, from George Washington to Jimmy Carter*, 4th ed., Macmillan, New York, 1979. Short histories of presidential campaigns from Washington's time to 1976.

Scammon, Richard (ed.): *America Votes, 1984*, vol. 16, Congressional Quarterly Press, Washington, D.C., 1985. Voting statistics on the 1984 presidential election. A new volume is published the year after each presidential election.

Schlesinger, Arthur M., Jr. (ed.): *The Coming to Power: Critical Presidential Elections in American History*, Chelsea House, New York, 1981. Important campaigns, as described by distinguished historians.

Abraham Lincoln near the front at Antietam and Ronald Reagan at the DMZ between North and South Korea illustrate the president's responsibilities as commander in chief. (*Culver Pictures; Bill Fitzpatrick: White House.*)

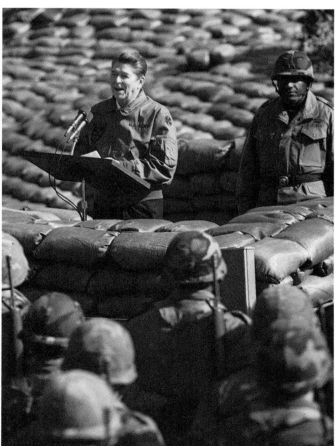

CHAPTER 10

PRESIDENTIAL POWER: CONSTITUTIONAL PREROGATIVES AND POLITICAL LEADERSHIP

PREROGATIVE POWERS

Using prerogative powers
Legitimizing prerogative powers
Risks of using prerogative powers
Criteria for use of prerogative powers

POWER AND LEADERSHIP

The power problem
Limits to power politics
Principles and power

IN CONCLUSION

President Nixon conferring with former president Lyndon Johnson in 1970. Both men's use of their powers as commander in chief contributed to what some political scientists call the *imperial presidency*. (*Elliott Erwitt: Magnum.*)

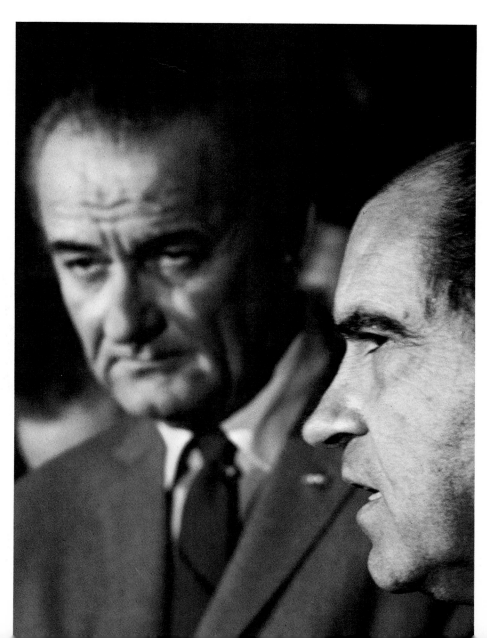

The presidency, Theodore Roosevelt once said, is a "bully good pulpit." It is the keystone of our government. The president is chief of state, representing our sovereignty; chief diplomat, communicating with other nations; commander in chief, presiding over the armed forces in peace and war; chief executive, overseeing the departments; chief legislator, presenting new programs and the federal budget to Congress; chief economist, proposing new taxing and spending policies; and, finally, chief of a political party. The president can be a catalyst for social change or a consolidator; a defender of existing economic interests or a proponent of new ones. At times the presidency functions, in the words of James MacGregor Burns, as "a weapon that has served Americans well in the long struggle for freedom and equality at home and in the search for stable and democratic politics abroad."[1] At other times it has been an *imperial presidency*, riding roughshod over civil liberties, the constitutional powers of the other two branches, and even international law.

If we have a president who is strong enough to govern, is that, as Alexander Hamilton asked, "inconsistent with the genius of republican government?"[2] Do we have, as former president Gerald Ford suggests, an *imperiled* rather than an *imperial* presidency? Or has Ronald Reagan, as Arthur Schlesinger argues, "dispelled doubts about the ability of a President to govern and revived national confidence in the workability of the system?"[3]

CHIEF SCAPEGOAT: EVALUATING PRESIDENTS

"Before you get to be President you think you can do anything," Lyndon Johnson told Richard Nixon, as he left the White House, "but when you get in that tall chair, as you're gonna find out, Mr. President, you can't count on people. You'll find your hands tied and people cussin' you. The office is kind a like the little country boy found the hoochie-koochie show at the carnival, once he'd paid his dime and got inside the tent: 'It ain't exactly as it was advertised.' "[4] Johnson's disappointment in the office matches the disappointment that the American people often have in those who occupy it; presidents are the chief scapegoats in American politics. Their performance almost always falls short of our expectations.

We are ambivalent about presidents and their powers. We want the occupant of the Oval Office to take charge, and yet we are fearful and suspicious of presidential powers. We want a strong president, but one who works with Congress within the system of checks and balances. We believe in checks and balances and in separation of powers, but we give high marks to presidents who lead and to Congresses which follow.[5] We want the president to have the aristocratic bearing of Franklin Roosevelt and the common touch of Harry Truman, to project the father image of Dwight Eisenhower and the youthful energy of John Kennedy, to possess the political instincts of Lyndon Johnson and the moral bearing of Jimmy Carter, and to display the combativeness of Teddy Roosevelt and the geniality of Ronald Reagan.[6]

We compare presidents' accomplishments with those of their predecessors:

George Washington and the founding of the union, Abraham Lincoln and its preservation, and Theodore Roosevelt and Franklin Roosevelt and the emergence of the United States as a world power. We consider the great ones, as the former White House counselor Ed Meese observed, to be "leaders who put the stamp of their own personality on the office and the nation—men who swashbuckled their way through great events, who delighted in battle, despised the status quo, and never shied away from the use of the personal pronoun. Men, in short, who centralized authority and personified change."[7] The greatest of them created new political movements or parties or led the nation to military victories; yet while in office, even they were not perceived as great.

When asked to choose, the public prefers moral qualities such as courage, honesty, and convictions to political skills in its presidents. We want someone who acts for the good of the nation rather than for personal power or for narrow party interests—a leader rather than a politician.[8] We prefer people with convictions even if they do not always follow public opinion.

The impression that most people have about the presidency is that if only good people who knew how to govern were chosen for the office, the problems facing the nation could be solved. This belief is based on an underlying set of assumptions:

- Presidents head the government.
- Congress and the bureaucracy work under them.
- By virtue of their election they receive a mandate.
- Their own party should support them.
- Congress should pass their programs.

These assumptions are wrong. The best of presidents—with all the requisite political skills and moral qualities and the expertise of advisers—cannot lead Congress or their party on most issues most of the time.

PRESIDENTIAL POWERS

The constitutional principles that make the president the chief executive in theory hinder exercise of power in fact, because the Constitution itself assumes that power should not be concentrated in a single institution, but is to be divided, checked, and balanced in separate institutions. The politicians who run for office in these institutions are to share in, and compete for, the power to govern. Presidents must come to grips with this constitutional legacy.

The Constitution is not a blueprint which defines powers with precision: it is undefined, underdefined, ambiguous, incomplete, or silent on some important points. Nothing in the Constitution gives the president full responsibility to conduct foreign affairs, manage the economy, solve social problems, or even supervise government agencies. But nothing in the Constitution prevents the president from trying to do these things. "We elect a king for four years," Secretary of State William Seward observed during the Civil War, "and give him vast powers, which after all he can interpret for himself."

Constitutional powers

The executive power. Article II of the Constitution invests the president with the *executive power* of the United States. This power permits the president to make policy and to command subordinates, and it is constitutionally exercised solely by the president. Although for a period of about twenty years

in the early 1800s presidents governed through Cabinet consensus, most later incumbents have followed Lincoln's approach: once, when his entire Cabinet disagreed with a decision he was about to make, he announced the results of the deliberations by saying, "Six nays and one aye, and the ayes have it."

Running the government. Presidents have few explicit powers over government agencies. Their nominations to office must be consented to by the Senate. Their right to fire subordinates is not explicitly mentioned in the Constitution, although the courts have accepted it since the 1920s. They may require department secretaries to give their opinion in writing on any matter. Congress can also issue instructions to officials through laws, and the courts do the same in their decisions, and if presidential orders conflict with these, the courts may nullify them.

Commander in chief. The president is commander in chief of the armed forces and of the state militias (that is, the National Guard) when called into federal service. But the Constitution does not list any express powers which presidents might exercise. Can they command troops, direct military officers, or make war policy? Can they commence or end hostilities? Can they do these things without obtaining the approval of Congress? May Congress restrict presidents when they exercise their powers, by using the necessary and proper clause? Congress itself has many war powers which potentially conflict with the president's: it declares war, punishes offenses against international law, raises and supports the armed forces and issues regulations concerning them, and raises and organizes the state militias, and the Senate consents to or rejects presidential commissions for the officer corps.

Diplomatic powers. The president receives foreign ambassadors and, by and with the advice and consent of the Senate, nominates our ambassadors. Does this entail the power to grant or refuse recognition to other nations? The Constitution does not say. The president, by and with the advice and consent of the Senate, makes treaties with other nations. Does this mean that the president decides to ratify them (that is, put them in force) after Senate approval? Or must the president also obtain the consent of the Senate to put a treaty in force? What if conditions change or if the other side refuses to abide by the terms of a treaty? Can the president abrogate the agreement unilaterally or only with the consent of the Senate? The Constitution is silent on these points, though in all such cases presidents have successfully expanded their powers.

Economic management. The president has no explicit constitutional power to manage the economy, in contrast to Congress, which has the power to tax and spend, to regulate the currency and coinage, to regulate commerce between the states and foreign commerce, to manage the national debt, and to exercise all "necessary and proper" powers. Yet presidents take the responsibility for proposing economic policies, including tax programs, the budget, and regulatory policies.

Interpreting constitutional powers: Four strategies. Presidents cannot confine themselves to the literal Constitution of 1787. Instead, they must interpret their powers expansively by invoking the *living Constitution*, which has

the adaptability to give them enough powers to meet national needs.[9] "The President is at liberty, both in law and in conscience," Woodrow Wilson argued, "to be as big a man as he can. Only his capacity will set the limit."[10] Presidents expand the Constitution, not as a matter of abstract legal reasoning, but to give themselves *legitimacy* when they make important decisions. They look at the Constitution as a power base, useful to them insofar as it permits them to act decisively. No matter if a provision has been interpreted in the past by the courts or Congress as a limitation or boundary that restricts their power: presidents often are willing and even eager to break new ground and cut through parchment barriers.

CLAIMING THE SILENCES. Presidents argue that any function not mentioned in the Constitution should be assigned to them by virtue of the oath of office, the executive power, and clauses naming the president commander in chief. This was the argument that George Washington used in 1792 when he declared neutrality in a war between Britain and France—even though the Constitution does not mention such a power.

EXPLOITING AMBIGUITIES. Incumbents argue that *the executive power* is a general term, which gives them all the powers that any executive would have unless specifically excluded by the Constitution. Thus they claim that they have the power to set policies and to fire officials, give them orders, and supervise their work.

PYRAMIDING RESPONSIBILITIES. Presidents can point to specific duties and then claim all related responsibilities. They argue that their duty to receive foreign ambassadors and to nominate ours makes them the "sole voice" in communicating with other nations. They then argue that the president is responsible for the entire field of foreign affairs, with only such exceptions as the Constitution provides for Congress—and that these are to be construed narrowly.

COMBINING POWERS. Presidents combine several constitutional provisions to create powers. They fuse the executive power, the oath of office, and the commander-in-chief clauses, claiming the general responsibility to do all that is not specifically forbidden by the Constitution, even if that involves exercising powers not mentioned in the Constitution or exercising powers given to Congress. The idea is that presidents are allowed to do anything that the Constitution does not forbid them to do.

Delegated powers

Most of the powers that presidents exercise, including some war and emergency powers, are delegated by Congress, using the necessary and proper clause. In a national emergency, the president uses delegated power to confine persons who are considered threats to national security, restrict travel in and out of the country, require persons to register with the government, control employment in the public and private sectors, deny jobs to persons who are considered security risks, stockpile strategic raw materials, impose rationing, institute import and export restrictions, allocate materials and personnel for defense, require companies to give priority to government contracts, seize plants, fix wages and prices, set standards for working conditions, and regulate communications. Congress makes a *conditional delegation*: the president must declare that a national emergency exists and report to Congress periodically. Congress may at any time end the state of emergency by passing a joint resolution (subject to presidential veto).

Congress is of two minds about presidential power: it wants to defend its own prerogatives, but public opinion usually favors legislators who cooperate with the administration. Often Congress passes the buck to the White House, delegating responsibilities that it wants to avoid because of the potential political fallout such as setting tariffs for imports and pay scales for federal employees.

Congress often grants presidents responsibility but circumscribes them with detailed rules and regulations in subsequent laws. Often the president acts as a *clerk* for the bureaucracy, members of Congress, or state and local officials and takes action, but according to *their* priorities and for *their* interests.[11] While Congress often delegates conditionally or restrictively, presidents assume that when Congress gives them powers, these should be interpreted permissively. They exploit any ambiguities and omissions in the laws as well as in the Constitution. President Carter did this, for example, when he interpreted a law dealing with foreign trade in a way that enabled him to conclude an agreement with Iran that traded Iranian assets frozen in the United States in return for American diplomats held hostage. To do so, Carter had to infringe on the rights of American individuals and companies to sue Iran in American courts for damages claimed to their interests—yet the Supreme Court, in reading the provisions of the law, interpreted them almost out of recognition in order to uphold presidential diplomatic authority in this crisis.

PRESIDENTS AS POPULAR LEADERS

Presidents engage in a kind of high-wire balancing act as they interpret the Constitution and the laws which delegate them power: their safety net becomes public support. "Public sentiment is everything," Lincoln said as he expanded the powers of the presidency during the Civil War; "with public sentiment nothing can fail; without it nothing can succeed." Woodrow Wilson, writing about Theodore Roosevelt's presidency, concluded that the presi-

President John F. Kennedy calling on the public to support his "new frontier" program. (*Cornell Capa: Magnum.*)

dent's power is based on public opinion: "Let him once win the admiration and confidence of the country, and no other single force can withstand him; no combination of forces can easily overpower him." Walter Mondale thought that Jimmy Carter had spent too much time sweating the small stuff and not enough time leading the public. "I'd rather give up the veto than the bully pulpit," he concluded.[12] Presidents need not obtain public approval for all, or even most, of their policies. But no president can sustain important policies for very long in the face of severe public disapproval.

But just as the Constitution does not give presidents all the powers they need to govern, neither does the public or the party give them sufficient political support. Just as they interpret the Constitution in such a way as to obtain the powers they need, so too they must work to maintain their legitimacy and authority. Presidents like Franklin Roosevelt, Dwight Eisenhower, and Ronald Reagan use their successes as popular leaders to expand their powers, pass much of their legislative programs, and win reelection landslides. Presidents who fail to retain their authority or to defend the legitimacy of their actions may be characterized as "imperial presidents" (Lyndon Johnson and Richard Nixon), find their legislative programs stalled (Harry Truman and Gerald Ford), decide not to seek renomination (Harry Truman and Lyndon Johnson), or be defeated in the next election (Gerald Ford and Jimmy Carter).

Presidential approval scores

Slightly more than half of those who are eligible to vote in presidential elections do so, and of these, slightly more than half vote for the winner: most presidents enter office with the expressed support of little more than one-fourth of the adult population. Initially they start with a much larger base, as a result of the ***honeymoon effect***: the tendency of most Americans to wish a new president well and to rally together after a divisive political campaign. Figure 10-1 compares the percentage of the voting-age population which supported several presidents with their approval ratings in early public opinion polls.

The honeymoon does not last long. Presidential approval ratings (Figure 10-2), traditionally start fairly high, then fall during the term, and finally rise

Figure 10-1. The initial approval score for each president has been much higher than his percentage of the popular vote. (Source: Gallup polls.)

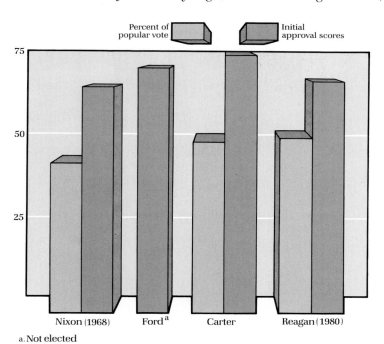

a. Not elected

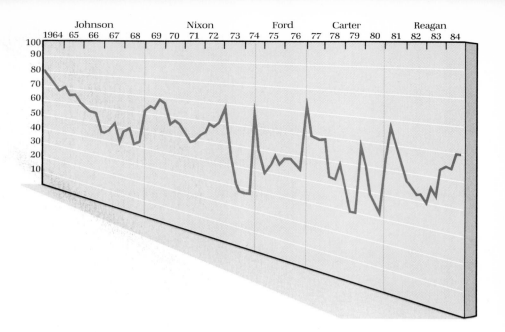

Figure 10-2. Presidential approval ratings, 1964–1984. (Source: *Gallup Opinion Index.*)

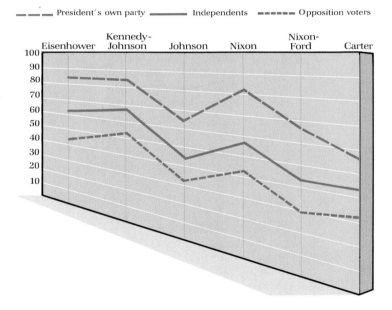

Figure 10-3. Approval scores for presidents, by party. Presidents receive their greatest support from members of their own party, followed by independents and opposition party identifiers. (Source: Gallup polls.)

near the end, though not to the initial levels. Party identifiers continue to support the president long after opposition identifiers and some independents have begun to fall away (Figure 10-3). The declines in public support tend to be quite sharp, to occur fairly early in the term, and to leave the president for much of the term in office with fairly low approval ratings (Ronald Reagan's rise in popularity during his third and fourth years in office is an exceptional case). The ratings are volatile: within a few months a president can rise or sink dramatically. One reason is the *rally-round-the-flag effect*: the rise in support when the president faces a major international crisis, even if it is not handled particularly well.

327

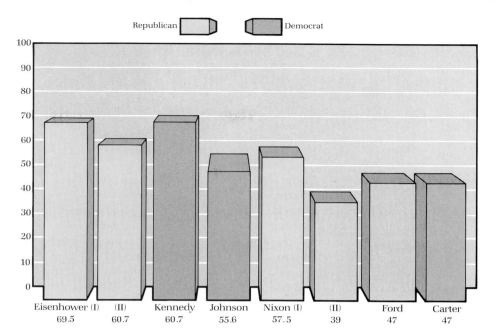

	Eisenhower (I)	(II)	Kennedy	Johnson	Nixon (I)	(II)	Ford	Carter
	69.5	60.7	60.7	55.6	57.5	39	47	47

Figure 10-4. Mean presidential approval scores, 1953–1980. In recent years presidents have had lower approval scores than their predecessors. President Reagan, however, may reverse the trend in his second term. (Source: *Gallup Opinion Index.*)

The overall level of public support for presidents is lower today than it was in the 1950s and 1960s. Moreover, each president since Eisenhower has begun office with lower ratings than the last president of his own party (Figure 10-4). According to some political scientists, this is in some measure the result of greater cynicism, skepticism, or apathy on the part of the public due to government policies and to the legitimacy crises brought about by Watergate and the Vietnamese war. Others correlate the high rates of inflation and the lower growth rates of the late 1960s and early 1970s with lessened popularity.[13] Approval of presidents has declined along with support for most other governmental and social institutions. A related explanation focuses on changes in campaigns: the public's inflated expectations, which are due to the hype of new politics campaign commercials, are followed by disillusionment when presidents' performance fails to match their promises and when the media harp on the administration's in-fighting and friction with Congress. The lower percentage of partisan voters and the increase in the proportion of independents are one explanation for the volatility in the approval scores. Finally, the decline in support scores may occur because presidents cannot keep their promises to all the groups that initially support them. It is only natural that during the course of a term the president will retain the support of those who are satisfied and will lose the support of those who are disappointed.[14]

Reagan: The Teflon presidency

Ronald Reagan has confounded most of these political orthodoxies. True, he began with high approval ratings and then suffered a sharp decline, but during his third and fourth years in office his ratings rose sharply, into the high 50s and 60s. "Such a strong upward trend on the part of an incumbent president seeking reelection is without precedent in Gallup's 50 years of polling experience," George Gallup noted.[15] Reagan's popularity increased even though voters disapproved of some of his specific policies—in Lebanon, in Central America, and regarding the environment. "He walks away from more political car crashes than anyone," says his longtime adviser, John Sears.[16] Representative Patricia Schroeder, a Democrat from Colorado, charged in a speech to the

House that Reagan was "perfecting the Teflon-coated presidency." Nothing stuck to him, and voters refused to hold him personally responsible for his policies. One possible explanation: "When Reagan talks, the government is never 'we'; it's always 'them,'" according to the pollster Peter Hart. "Things never become his problem; they're always the government's problem."[17]

But another explanation is more satisfying to Republicans. A Washington Post/ABC survey taken early in 1984 indicated that most voters could distinguish between Reagan and his policies. Those who liked Reagan *and* his policies voted for him, but most of those who liked him and *not* his policies were prepared to vote against him.[18] By the time of the election Reagan's landslide could be explained, in terms not of Teflon but of policy: the public agreed with many of his policies and supported them. Polls taken throughout the election year showed that his economic program (tax cuts and lowered inflation) and foreign policy (the promise of new negotiations with the Soviets, the withdrawal of American troops from Lebanon, and the invasion of Grenada) commanded wide support, a reversal of the normal pattern, in which support for presidential policies erodes.

CLOSE-UP

PRESIDENT DWIGHT DAVID EISENHOWER. President Eisenhower was overwhelmingly elected to two terms (1953 to 1961), and had it not been for the Twenty-Second Amendment, he could easily have been elected to a third. During his administration the Korean war ended, involvement in Vietnam was averted, and the nation remained at peace. Inflation was low and the standard of living surged, in spite of two severe recessions. Yet two decades ago most historians and political scientists viewed Eisenhower as a political amateur who reigned too much and ruled too little, as an intellectual lightweight, and as a passive nonleader. "This man neither liked the game he was engaged in nor had gained much understanding of its rules," argued Richard Neustadt in 1960.[19] Was this true? Hardly.

Dwight D. Eisenhower. (*Bettmann Archive.*)

For one thing, Eisenhower was highly political while serving in the Army. He was a deputy to the assistant secretary; he was chief aide to General Douglas MacArthur (a highly political officer) in the Philippines, where he worked closely with its civilian government as chief of staff of the Third Army; he served in the Planning Division of the War Department after Pearl Harbor; and in 1942 President Roosevelt appointed him commanding general of the European theater of operations. In his last post he had to smooth over disputes between Allied officers and negotiate with French officials in the Vichy government over the landings in north Africa, and eventually he worked closely with Roosevelt, Churchill, de Gaulle, Stalin, and other world leaders as the Allied armies moved toward victory.

Fred Greenstein, a political scientist at Princeton, analyzed Eisenhower's military career and found that while in the military, he developed a leadership style with five important characteristics that later served him well in the White House:

- *Hidden-hand leadership.* Eisenhower was a skilled political operator who chose not to let others realize that fact. He camouflaged his participation in politics by relying on others to conduct his political business and concealing his own role.
- *Use of language.* Eisenhower often used language that was deliberately ambiguous or spoke in an evasive, noncommittal, or seemingly confused way in order to make his adversaries (or the press) underestimate him or to get himself off the hook in a controversy. His use of jumbled syntax at press conferences was a deliberate ploy that allowed him to avoid making a comment when he did not wish to.
- *Avoiding personal comments.* Eisenhower tried never to attack anyone else's motives or to make personal comments about his political rivals or convert them into enemies. He could mask his own negative feelings about those with whom he had to work (such as his own congressional leaders).
- *Personality analysis.* Eisenhower could step into other people's shoes, understand how they viewed a situation and how they were likely to respond, and then shape his own strategy and tactics accordingly. He could figure out how to use the strengths of his subordinates and get around their weaknesses.
- *Selective delegation.* Eisenhower delegated responsibility, but never to the extent that he lost control of policy. He supervised Secretary of State Dulles closely (because he personally knew most of the world leaders) and in effect ran his own Defense Department. He would share credit for the successes of subordinates, but even more important, he would diffuse blame for failures, preserving his image as head of state while allowing others to take the heat for partisan politics or failing policies.[20]

Eisenhower's admirers believe that his hidden-hand style of leadership was effective. He managed to defuse the destructive attempts of Joe McCarthy, a Republican senator from Wisconsin, to meddle in military and diplomatic matters while on a supposed hunt for communist spies in government. He forged a bipartisan consensus in foreign policy that kept us at peace, while allowing intelligence agencies to influence foreign governments and even help replace several unfriendly regimes (in Iran and Guatemala, for example). On the domestic front he presided over the consolidation of the New Deal social programs and even expanded them, in the process creating the Department of Health, Education and Welfare—again by working with leaders of both parties in Congress.

While conceding these points, Eisenhower's critics remind us that the hidden hand often was so well hidden that no one could detect Eisenhower's leadership.

True, he preserved his own reputation and popularity, but he never transferred these to his party, which suffered disastrous defeats in state and congressional elections in 1958 and then lost the presidency in 1960. He exerted no moral leadership on one of the key domestic issues of the time: racial desegregation of public schools. And his economic policies resulted in slow rates of growth and two severe recessions. He never groomed anyone to succeed him, and he left his party in considerable disarray, with no prospect of a realignment.

Why do we care whether Eisenhower was an effective politician or an amateur? It is an important consideration because it raises the question of the leadership styles of other presidents. Many political scientists and journalists now say the same things about Reagan that used to be said about Eisenhower; perhaps in twenty years, Reagan's presidency will be similarly reassessed.

PARTY LEADERSHIP

While presidents retain the support of their party rank and file, they cannot translate that support into long-term leadership of their party-in-government. More damage is done to presidents by their own congressional leaders than by the opposition. "Party loyalty or responsibility means damn little," President Kennedy observed; "they've got to take care of themselves first."[21] "It doesn't matter what kind of majority you came in with, you've got just one year when they treat you right, before they start worrying about themselves," Lyndon Johnson said. "They'll come along and they'll give you almost everything you want for awhile, and then they'll turn on you. They always do. They'll lay in waiting, waiting for you to make a slip and you will. They'll give you almost everything and then they'll make you pay for it."[22]

Party competition

Thomas Jefferson early in his first term, Andrew Jackson with his bank veto, Franklin Roosevelt with his 100 days, and Ronald Reagan with his supply-side economics—all capitalized on the momentum of election landslides, and their major legislative accomplishments all came early rather than late in their terms. Under what circumstances are presidents effective party leaders? Most often when they represent political and economic interests that seize the public's imagination, capitalize on crises, and replace worn-out ideas and practices with something new.

Such periods of energetic presidential leadership often coincide with, and are intimately related to, party competition. When the dominant party, because of its approach to public policy, loses its authority, the result is a party realignment. Coincidental with realignment is effective presidential party leadership. Later, when the party has run out of new ideas and is merely marking time, deviating, critical, and reinstating elections are likely; in such circumstances presidents of neither party do very well. The dominant party may reinvigorate itself, as the Democrats did under Lyndon Johnson and his "great society" program, but eventually a new realignment occurs, the opposition assumes power, and the cycle begins again.[23] But unless we have a president who founds a party (such as Jefferson) or leads one to realignment or a reinforcing election, the prospects for sustained party leadership in the White House are poor.

The legislative party

Thomas Jefferson got on so badly with his House majority leader that he attempted to engineer his defeat in the next congressional election. Abraham

Lincoln fought with congressional leaders over the conduct of the Civil War. Woodrow Wilson could not obtain the support of several congressional leaders for his policy that led the United States to enter World War I. Members of Franklin Roosevelt's own party stopped his efforts to "pack" the Supreme Court, and their alliance with Republicans stalled the New Deal economic program after 1937. Dwight Eisenhower was openly contemptuous of his congressional leaders, and at one point he threatened to create a new political party if they did not give his programs more support. The major opposition to John Kennedy's civil rights initiatives and Lyndon Johnson's Vietnamese war policies came from Democratic committee leaders. The pressure of Republican Senate leaders finally convinced Richard Nixon to resign from office rather than fight impeachment charges.

Jimmy Carter's programs were modified beyond recognition by committees controlled by his own party. He had no strong supporters among the leadership. When a reporter asked Jim Wright, the majority leader, whether the president was "big enough" for the job, Wright replied, "No one is big enough for the job, so we have to settle for what we've got."[24] Ronald Reagan, after initial successes with his economic program, found that his party leaders were insistent on modifying his tax program, reforming the Environmental Protection Agency, changing his posture at arms talks with the Soviets, ending the mining of the harbors of Nicaragua, and stalling his proposals for constitutional amendments concerning prayer in schools, abortion, busing, and a balanced budget. At the start of his second term, Reagan's new majority leader, Robert Dole, announced that Senate Republicans would substitute their own deficit-reduction plan for the budget that even then was being prepared by the president.

The original constitutional arrangements are at the root of all presidents' friction with their own party. As James Madison explained in *Federalist* 51, it is necessary for each branch to "have a will of its own." This could be achieved by "giving to those who administer each department the necessary constitutional means and personal motives to resist the encroachments of the others. . . ." Under this arrangement, "Ambition must be made to counteract ambition. The interests of the man must be connected with the constitutional rights of the place." Today this means that the ambition of the president to lead Congress collides with the ambitions of party leaders to develop their own programs, extend their own powers, and advance their own careers. Every president comes to agree with Kennedy's assessment that "the Congress looks more powerful sitting here that it did when I was there. . . . But that's because when you're in Congress you're one of a hundred in the Senate, or one of 435 in the House, so that your—the power is divided. But from here I look at a Congress and I look at the collective power of the Congress, particularly to block action, and it's substantial power."[25] As one of Reagan's advisers explained, "You can push Congress only so long. Eventually they get tired of the pressure, tired of the complaints back home about some program that's being cut, and they get mad."[26]

Constitutional arrangements for elections mean that after a presidential election every member of Congress next runs in a midterm election, in which no presidential coattails can help. Members of the president's party will *distance* themselves from unpopular presidential policies. Survey research indicates that in midterm congressional elections people who oppose the president are somewhat more likely to vote than supporters. Party identifiers who

dislike the president's performance are 3 times more likely to vote for a congressional candidate of the other party than members of the other party who like it are to vote for a congressional candidate of the president's party.[27] Members of the president's party have always realized that he could not help them with a good effort but could hurt them badly with a poor one, and have therefore been his strongest critics. The president controls none of the important elements in a successful congressional career: nominations, campaign financing, advertising, polling, and local party organizations. What the Constitution separates, the president's policies cannot reunite.

The president as titular party leader

The president is chief of the party, but that does not entail much power over the party organization. Some presidents become fierce partisans, like Franklin Roosevelt, Jack Kennedy, and Ronald Reagan, helping build up state organizations and win their support; others disdain party leaders, ignore party committees, and govern in a more personal way—Lyndon Johnson, Richard Nixon, and Jimmy Carter, for example. But whether they are attracted to, or repelled by, party affairs, most presidents find themselves performing chores for their parties—fund-raising, campaigning, and appointing party members to office and getting very little in return.[28]

The president can get supporters elected as chairs and deputy chairs of the national party committee. A Republican president can also dominate the House and Senate congressional campaign committees, which are tied in closely with the Republican National Committee (RNC); a Democratic president has no such influence over the party's congressional campaign committees, which have traditions of complete independence from the White House. But even on the Republican side, the party committees have little influence on legislators. Rich Bond, the deputy chair of the RNC, told Republicans to vote for Reagan's tax program in 1981, warning them that he would "nail them to the wall" on campaign funding if they voted against the administration. But after a congressional uproar Richard Richards, the chairman of the RNC, apologized, saying, "It has never been, and never will become, the policy of the RNC to put pressure on members of Congress."[29]

ISSUE AND DEBATE

CABINET GOVERNMENT? *The background.* Should we abandon separation of powers and the system of checks and balances and adopt cabinet government? This question has been asked for more than a century.

Henry C. Lockwood, in his book *The Abolition of the Presidency* (1884), proposed to abolish the presidency by constitutional amendment: Congress would appoint department officers to an executive council, chaired by the secretary of state; the members would sit in Congress, initiate legislation, and participate in debates. They could be removed by Congress. Even earlier, Woodrow Wilson's article in *The International Review*, written when he was a senior at Princeton, proposed that the president select members of the Cabinet from Congress. They would retain seats in Congress and have the power to initiate legislation. They would resign if Congress rejected their programs; thus the majority party would determine the president's Cabinet.

Others have called for joint councils of legislators and Cabinet secretaries to coordinate government policies. For example, in 1946 Thomas Finletter proposed a "joint cabinet of Congress" consisting of eighteen congressional committee chairs; nine of these chairs and nine Cabinet secretaries would constitute a "joint

executive-legislative cabinet." In 1979 Representative Henry Reuss proposed a constitutional amendment that would permit up to fifty legislators to serve in high executive offices while remaining in Congress.

Other proposals would allow Congress to vote "no confidence" in presidents and call for new presidential elections, and allow presidents to dissolve Congress and require new congressional elections if it refused to pass their programs. Each would require a constitutional amendment.

The pros. Proponents of cabinet government argue that it would reduce friction and increase coordination between the executive and legislative branches. It would lessen congressional resistance to a president's program and would allow electoral mandates to be translated into policy sooner. It would centralize the powers of government in the executive branch, but would make the executive branch accountable to congressional majorities and would reduce the possibility of an imperial presidency. Party discipline would increase, since the majority party would have to support the administration to keep it in power. Since the cabinet would enjoy the confidence of a majority of Congress (or else it would resign), there would be no need to rely on presidential prerogatives to push through policies; like the prerogatives of the crown in England, these powers would become mere formalities, and all that needed doing could be accomplished by legislation and by delegation of power from Congress to the president.

The cons. Opponents argue that the friction between the executive and legislative branches is useful; for example, it clipped the wings of an imperial presidency in the 1970s. Coordination, they believe is only a euphemism for presidential control of the government, even when it appears that Congress will control the Cabinet: in the British system, Parliament has become a rubber stamp for the prime minister as leader of the majority party. Opponents believe that the two legislative parties have just as much of an electoral mandate as the president, and they favor retaining midterm elections because they permit voters to renew or modify their mandate every two years.

Opponents argue that centralizing power eliminates the beneficial effects of redundancy and load sharing. Voters can use the two branches to exercise a double control on the bureaucracy: the president holds appointees responsible for implementing policies and may dismiss them if the public demands it; and an independent Congress can also influence the bureaucracy by means of laws, appropriations, and investigations to win public support, thus allowing voters to choose which branch to support when the branches come into conflict over their attempts to control the departments.

The outlook. At present none of the proposals for cabinet government are likely to pass Congress as constitutional amendments. Even at the height of the furor over the imperial presidency, proposals for the "vote of no confidence" went nowhere. Legislators want to make their own proposals and criticize the president without being part of a supercabinet that might inhibit their freedom of action or force them to share accountability for presidential decisions.

THE INSTITUTIONALIZED PRESIDENCY

No one person can meet all the demands of the presidency. The president needs help, and gets it from a number of agencies which constitute the *presidency*. These give the office some permanence, a routine, and a "memory" of how things are done; thus we say that we have an ***institutionalized presidency.*** The presidency consists of more than a dozen agencies and thousands of officials. They help the president communicate with the public and the

media, develop new programs, and formulate a budget. But these agencies, while sometimes a great help to the president, also can create as many problems as they solve.

Presidential institutions

The White House Office. The president's personal and political aides are located in the White House Office (Figure 10-5). These staffers give the president advice on political matters; maintain liaison with congressional leaders,

Figure 10-5. Organization of the White House Office, 1981: the formal table of organization for the White House Office in President Reagan's first term. In 1985 the new chief of staff, Donald Regan, scrapped this structure and replaced it with an entirely new system in which all officials reported through him to the president. (Source: Presidency Research Group Newsletter, vol. 3, no. 2, April 1981.)

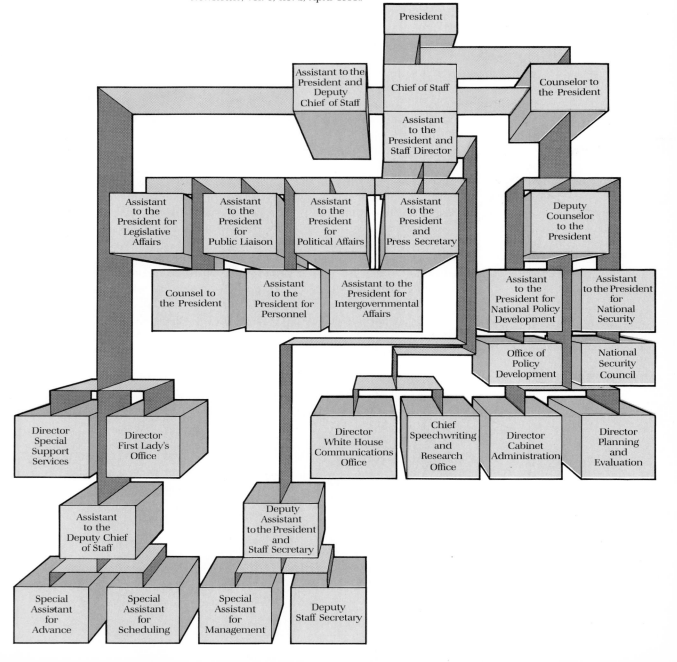

governors, mayors, and interest groups; supervise the department secretaries on matters of presidential concern; prepare messages and documents; draft presidential speeches; and give advice and counsel on the constitutionality and legality of proposed presidential actions. Support staff members run the White House and its grounds, assist the First Lady (they will someday assist the First Husband) and the First Family, and do the advance work for presidential trips. The way the Reagan White House was organized is shown in Figure 10-5.

The staff has grown enormously since it was created in 1939. Today it works out of two White House wings and the basement, and it overflows into the Executive Office Building next door. The staff consists of four groups: an inner circle of five to seven senior aides who consult regularly with the president; a second tier of top-level aides, each of whom is responsible for a particular function and runs his or her own "shop" with several assistants (but reports to someone in the inner circle rather than directly to the president); the remaining professional employees who report to a top-level aide; and, finally, the several hundred clerical and administrative workers who provide support. In addition to White House staffers, department personnel may be *detailed* to work in the White House; this expands the staff without enlarging the White House payroll. Figure 10-6 shows the great increase in staffing.

The Executive Office of the President. The president is also assisted by several agencies, known collectively as the ***Executive Office of the President*** (Figure 10-7). Unlike the White House staff, these agencies are concerned more with policies and processes than with communication and image—both are concerned with politics, but approach it from different angles. The Office of Management and Budget prepares the president's budget proposals to Congress, promotes more effective management of the bureaucracy, reviews proposed legislation from the departments and can recommend them to Congress as part of the president's program, and advises the president on whether to sign or veto bills passed by Congress. The Council of Economic Advisors

Figure 10-6. Growth of the White House Office, from Roosevelt to Ford. The White House staff and employees detailed from the departments have increased enormously since creation of the White House Office in 1939. About half the employees are clerical or support and half are professional and political. (Source: Hugh Heclo, *Studying the Presidency: A Report to the Ford Foundation*, New York, 1977, pp. 36–37.)

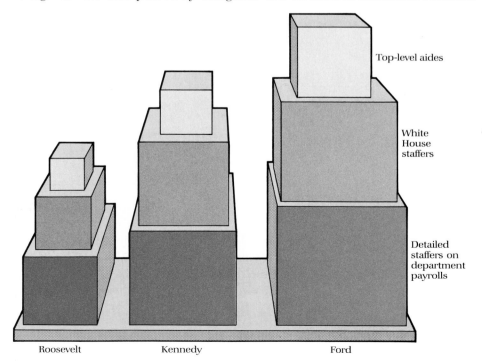

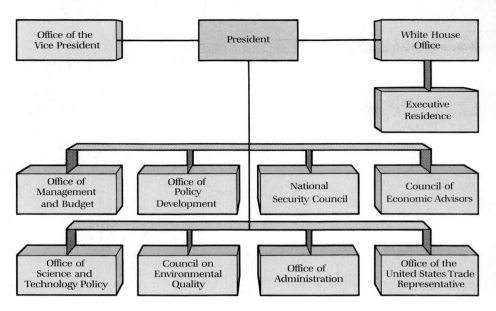

Figure 10-7. The Executive Office of the President comprises several agencies. (Their addresses and telephone numbers are given at the end of the chapter.)

prepares the president's economic report and advises on economic policy. The National Security Council deals with important military and diplomatic issues. These and other presidential agencies formulate programs to be submitted to Congress, coordinate activities that cross departmental boundaries, resolve conflicts between departments, impose presidential priorities on lower-level officials, implement important presidential orders, and help defend the White House program before Congress and in the media.

The presidential advisory system. To make decisions, presidents need advice and information. They can draw on a wide variety of sources:

- *The Cabinet*, which in some administrations meets frequently, but in others meets hardly at all. Usually the Cabinet is convened to give the president political advice, to serve as a sounding board for the president's ideas, or to make sure that top officials understand and speak for the president's policies.
- *Cabinet councils*, consisting of several Cabinet secretaries who work together on problems cutting across departmental boundaries.
- *Interagency task forces*, consisting of lower-level officials who work together on problems. In recent years these have included task forces on famine relief for African nations, child abuse, and immigration.
- *National commissions*, consisting of leaders from business, labor, and government, which advise the president on major national problems, such as juvenile delinquency, the environment, and the social security system. Experts are hired by the commission, and expert witnesses testify and propose new policies. Eventually the commission issues a report to the president.
- *"The wise men,"* usually former government officials who have served at the highest levels or former presidents, whom the president consults. They may also be asked to take on assignments, such as delivering messages to foreign leaders. They are often asked to serve as members of special study groups or national commissions.
- *"On-line" computer conferences*, such as the one held by the White House for 200 top business executives who made recommendations to a White House conference on productivity in 1983.

337

President Reagan confers with Vice President Bush in the White House oval office. (*Michael Evans: White House.*)

• *The vice president*, whose only function used to be to inquire after the health of the president. Today all that has changed. A "new vice presidency" has emerged as a result of the efforts of Nelson Rockefeller, Walter Mondale, and George Bush. While vice presidents still stand in for the president at apple-blossom festivals and homecomings, they also stand in at Cabinet meetings and represent the president on diplomatic visits abroad. They play a key role in midterm campaigns, are lobbyists for the president with Congress and governors, and serve as top presidential advisers. They have offices in the west wing, close to the president; large staffs which parallel the presidential agencies (Bush has about seventy aides); and even a mansion for entertaining. Provided they are team players, give the president all the credit for success and shoulder some of the blame, and do not leak stories to the press about their frustrations, vice presidents can play an important role in formulating policy.[30]

The advisory system allows presidents to make two claims: (1) that they have obtained the best advice available and (2) that by virtue of being the only nationally elected officials (other than vice presidents), their perspective and therefore their programs best represent the national interest.[31]

But these are only claims, designed to legitimize a program that may be quite political and partisan. The presidential counsels and councils, experts and advisers, have usually not been able to give the president proposals which were so persuasive on their merits that he could, simply by making them public, convince Congress and the nation to embrace them. The theories may be unproven, the proposed methods controversial. Critics cry doom even before the results are in, especially those who work for Congress, interest groups, and the media.

Problems with the institutionalized presidency

Sometimes the institutionalized presidency hurts presidents more than it helps them. For one thing, there are too many aides. They trip over one another trying to maintain their access to the president. They undercut one

another, and their feuds are picked up by the media, which present the image of an administration in disarray. Even without the office politics, the White House Office would still be a hotbed of conflict: aides, by the nature of their job, have problems with Cabinet secretaries who resent their attempts to transmit orders in the name of the president, especially relatively junior aides who give orders to their seniors. The White House staff tries to insulate the president from the demands of Cabinet secretaries and may keep a secretary away from the Oval Office for months. The secretaries of state, defense, and the Treasury always square off against staffers whom they accuse of meddling. Meanwhile, presidential agencies become embroiled in a three-way tug-of-war with White House aides and Cabinet secretaries over who will make policy.

In actuality, all administrations are organized not according to formal tables of organization, but rather according to the way in which confidence flows down from the president to subordinates. Those whose power is increasing are those to whom the president listens and gives assignments; the others, no matter what their title or job description, are of less weight. Since there is no way to measure one's "confidence level" with the president accurately, aides are insecure, somewhat paranoid, and rather compulsive about serving their boss. "You don't understand," Henry Kissinger once chided a reporter, who was complaining about the way he hovered around Nixon; "when I'm not talking to the president, someone else is."

All this maneuvering around the president involves *court politics*. George Reedy, who served as press secretary in Lyndon Johnson's White House, described it as "a mass of intrigue, posturing, strutting, and cringing"; he considered this kind of politics to be nothing more than a conspiracy of "the untalented, the unpassionate, and the insincere. . . ."[32] Presidents may be surrounded by sycophants who are adept at telling them what they want to hear rather than what they ought to hear; and this may happen because, with dozens of aides to pick and choose from, presidents want it that way.

Presidents are faced with a no-win situation in staffing the White House. If they delegate great responsibility to staffers or presidential agencies, the media charge them with overdelegating and characterize them as lazy, inattentive, ignorant, and stupid. Eisenhower, Ford, and Reagan faced such charges. But if presidents immerse themselves in the details of most issues, keep their aides on a tight string, and closely guard all the important decisions, they are likely to become exhausted by the sheer mass of government business they must face. Then the media portray them as "grinds" who are too immersed in the details to understand the big picture or inspire the public—the charge made against Carter.

Organizational strategies

Presidents organize their staffs and presidential agencies differently, but the best of them recognize that the most important problem is not administrative efficiency but political efficacy. Some, like Dwight Eisenhower and Ronald Reagan, create highly formalized systems in which all issues move up a "ladder" for full consultation and briefings (Reagan even has a computerized system for tracking the progress of issues through the advisory system). Others, like Franklin Roosevelt, John Kennedy, and Lyndon Johnson, organize their operations more informally, making specific assignments to staffers who report back to them.

Those who prefer the staff-and-briefing system argue that it ensures that problems arrive at the president's desk after all options have been examined,

all affected interests have been consulted, and all agencies have had their say. Critics claim that such a system is cumbersome, cautious, and slow and that it makes the president a captive of the staff. Presidents' options may be narrowed down by staffers; and presidents may be faced with a staff consensus that they have had no part in shaping. The informal system, however, sometimes loses track of important issues, especially if aides don't tell presidents about all the options or issues.

Presidents can sometimes take action to keep their staffers and agencies in line. Franklin Roosevelt fostered *competition*: he gave aides and even Cabinet officials overlapping assignments or jurisdictions and then waited for the fireworks. All officials found that others were interfering with or duplicating their functions, and each went to the president with negative information about a rival. Roosevelt obtained all the information and proposals he needed from the rivals, and therefore he knew more about every situation than any single aide.[33] The drawback with the competition approach, of course, is the sheer amount of time and energy that a president must invest to make it work.

A second approach is to allow one agency to carry out an assignment, but if it fails to produce, is criticized by the media, or acts contrary to presidential wishes, allow another agency to take over. *Redundancy* has been used by presidents as diverse as Nixon, Ford, Carter, and Reagan, who alternated between officials in the State Department, the National Security Council, the Defense Department, and the CIA in carrying out sensitive national security policies.

Multiple advocacy involves organizing the advisory system in such a way that the ideas of all those with different viewpoints and options are debated in the hearing of the president. This approach complements the staffing system but gives presidents a personal role; they can ask questions, uncover biases, and prevent officials from compromising over differences and presenting a consensus that forecloses the president's own options.[34]

PRESIDENTIAL LEADERSHIP: THE POWER TO PERSUADE

Presidents rarely have the constitutional powers or political support to do what they want to do, what the public expects them to do, and what they think they must do. The idealized version of presidential government, in which staffers and department secretaries work together smoothly, under the direction of the White House, does not exist. As Richard Chaney, the former chief of staff in the Ford administration, put it, "While you're here trying to do things, you are far more aware of the constraints than you are of the power. You spend most of your time trying to overcome obstacles getting what the President wants done."[35]

But some presidents succeed. Like Theodore Roosevelt and Richard Nixon, they conduct new diplomatic initiatives. Like Woodrow Wilson, Franklin Roosevelt, and Lyndon Johnson, they get major legislation through Congress. Like Ronald Reagan, they completely reverse the course of a generation of politicians before them. How do they do it?

Negotiating, compromising, and bargaining

To get what they want, presidents must bargain, even with members of their own party. American politicians are used to negotiation. It is the essence of the American political style. Listen to Ronald Reagan on the subject:

> My belief is that in this democratic process which entails compromise, you seek what you think should be done and if you only get half of it, three-quarters of it,

and politically it's impossible to get beyond that, I don't think it makes any sense to dig in your heels and say, then "I won't play." No, you take what you can get and tuck it away in your mind that you'll wait and come back another time and try to get the next bite. . . . And suppose even at the very end you've only gotten 70 or 75 percent of the goal. Well, that's a lot better than being back where you started.[36]

The president can provide things that other politicians want: patronage appointments for their supporters, contracts and programs for their constituents, and help for their projects. The president's powers can be used for their purposes. Sometimes the president trades powers for their help on other matters as a quid pro quo—a specific exchange of favor for favor. White House aides may organize a large package deal that offers tangible benefits to many legislators: they can point out the exact number of job-training slots allotted to a congressional district, the amount of money that each urban area will get as a result of a new housing bill, or the number of jobs that a construction measure will bring to each state.

The president has *vantage points*: formal powers which can block things that other politicians want. Presidents can threaten to veto pork-barrel bills and then lift their veto in return for promises to support bills they want. Franklin Roosevelt reportedly asked his aides occasionally to "give me something I can veto," just so that he could remind Congress that he had the power. Presidential vetoes are rarely overturned. (Vetoes of recent presidents are noted in Table 10-1.) The threat of a veto often results in compromises between the president and Congress, and so its influence is important, even though it may not actually be used.

Presidents do not always trade in specific favors. For one thing, if they trade with people who initially oppose their programs, the word gets out that the best way to get something from the White House is to announce opposition to the president's program. For another, people who support the president and get nothing in return will feel that they were taken for granted.

Table 10-1. Presidential vetoes, 1961 to 1985

John Kennedy	21
Lyndon Johnson	30
Richard Nixon	43
Gerald Ford	66
Jimmy Carter	31
Ronald Reagan (first term)	39

President Harry Truman's veto of the 1947 Taft-Hartley Act limiting the power of labor unions was overridden by a Republican-controlled Congress. (*Culver Pictures, Inc.*)

So presidents trade in *favor* rather than in *favors*: a relationship in which the people involved expect to help one another and therefore benefit from mutual support.[37] Presidents bestow their favor on legislators who support them most of the time, and they withdraw favor from those who desert them on crucial issues. They minimize the number of specific deals they enter into with the rule that they will reward an overall pattern of support rather than specific votes. (Sometime, of course, they have to abandon this rule when they are dealing with a particularly important party or committee leader or with someone who can cast a key vote at a crucial stage.) Sometimes presidents will not deal because they have neither the time nor the energy, because they cannot deliver, or because they are unwilling to offer what a legislator wants. They must then use other methods.

Persuasion

Presidential power largely consists in the ability to persuade people to do what the president wants them to do and to convince them that it is in their best interests to do it. "A leader is a man who has the ability to get other people to do what they don't want to do, and like it," Harry Truman said.[38] A president who can get people to take action of their own volition has converted them from trading partners into willing allies.

Lyndon Johnson used "the treatment." He brought his prey into the Oval Office, where he would argue, cajole, buttonhole, plea, browbeat, and wear down his opponent with every psychological ploy he could think of. The opposite approach is to "stroke" legislators, by offering them seats in the presidential boxes at Kennedy Center and inviting them to lunches, dinners, and diplomatic receptions, all in an effort to "break the ice" and trade friendship for support. Eisenhower's late-night poker games with congressional leaders of the opposition party did him more good than any lobbying ever could have.

Presidents persuade by pointing out to others that what they want them to do is what their own appraisal of their political position should impel them to do in their own interest. A president can point out not only the objective merit of a proposal, but also its political merits, and why in the long run it may help others, even though in the short run it may cost them some support. Or a president may offer people *compensation* if they take political heat: funding and campaign speeches in the next election and even a job with the administration if they lose.

There is the *grass-roots* strategy: the White House can pressure a legislator by appealing to influential constituents. Members of Congress may hear from defense contractors who want them to support the president's military budget, from business executives who want them to vote for a tax program, or from bankers who want them to vote for a new mortgage program for housing.

Finally, there is always *persuasion on the merits*. If a difficult policy issue offers no rewards and may present a danger to the public if it is not dealt with—such as toxic-waste disposal, acid rain, air and water pollution, or the soundness of the social security system—presidents may offer Congress a way out. They can appoint national commissions on a bipartisan basis which deal with the problem primarily in terms of expertise and the public interest and allow each party to share the credit and the blame for the proposal equally.

Presidential reputation and the power to persuade

No president can find the time to persuade or bargain with hundreds of legislators and top administration officials, let alone fifty governors, thousands of majors, and all the lobbyists in Washington.[39] Presidents must therefore find a

way to cut down on face-to-face and telephone communications. The other people, in turn, must find a way to take the measure of a president, even without direct communication. Both sides solve their problem by considering the president's *reputation*.[40]

Reputation and anticipated reactions. Politicians make calculations about what the president might do under certain circumstances and then modify their own behavior accordingly. They do so because of the law of *anticipated reactions*: what you do in any situation is based in part on your assumptions about how other people will respond to your action. Politicians take reputation into account as they calculate the president's probable response to anything they might do—even though the president may not be talking directly with them or even know who they are.

All presidents come to Washington with a reputation, based on their conduct during the campaign and the transition period and on their previous record in public life. Those who have to work with the president have questions: Is the president a lightweight, a deep thinker, or a person of action? A compromiser and bargainer, or a tenacious fighter for all goals? Can the president see others' points of view and be sympathetic to their concerns—or, on the other hand, is the president self-centered? Does the president reward friends and punish enemies, or forget friends and buy off enemies? Is the president's word to be trusted?

Guarding reputation. By what they do, the presidents can influence answers to these and other questions. Suppose that a presidential aide is accused in the newspapers of corruption. You might think that the president should suspend that official, pending the outcome of an investigation. But consider the issue in terms of reputation. If the staffer is suspended, all the other officials will feel vulnerable and will assume that the president will abandon them at the first sign of trouble. Opponents will calculate that they can neutralize other assistants by threatening to make similar accusations. Presidents are better off sticking by their aides and striking back hard at those who make charges. By doing so, they send a message: an attack on an aide will be treated as an attack on the president. Morale in the administration is protected, and opponents come to understand that they had better be justified in making charges and that making them should be worth incurring presidential wrath.

Suppose that a president submits a highly controversial bill to Congress and stitches together a coalition of supporters by bargaining and persuasion. Now along come the president's economic advisers, who want to abandon the bill because of its expense. The president must, once again, consider reputation. A coalition of supporters who are risking their political careers has been created. What kind of reputation will the president have with them if they find themselves suddenly deserted? Are they likely to join another such coalition in the future? If the president decides to retreat, it must be done in a way that protects supporters.

Presidents who fail to guard their reputations will be viewed by others as ignorant, irresolute, and indecisive. Officials will assume that such presidents cannot help them and must fail in what they attempt. It is better to distance oneself from presidents like this than to work with them. And the president's problems will multiply.

NATIONAL AGENDA POLITICS

How national agenda politics works

Presidents who find themselves losing a political struggle in one arena may move it to another in which they have an advantage. If presidents cannot get what they want by using bargaining and persuasion with Washington insiders, they might try to appeal to the public using a strategy of **national agenda politics**. The president might follow the advice of Carter's pollster, Pat Cadell, who argued that "governing with public approval requires a continuing political campaign."[41] Increasingly, presidents have "gone public." They have increased their prime-time televised addresses, and there has been a fivefold increase in minor presidential speeches and public appearances in the past two decades.[42]

National agenda issues. Consider two examples of national agenda issues. First, when Richard Nixon was president, some Democrats called for comprehensive health insurance that would cost upward of $20 billion. In a bold move, Nixon gained control of the health care issue by redefining it. He argued that the way to improve health care was not to provide more aid to those who were already ill, but rather to do more basic research and conquer dreaded diseases. Focusing on cancer, Nixon announced the creation of a National Cancer Institute and a "war on cancer." By redefining the issue, Nixon avoided a major budget commitment; he spent only a few hundred million dollars on the cancer center, and even that money was transferred from other programs.

Second, the Democrats made "excellence in education" a major theme of

President Woodrow Wilson on a nationwide speaking tour to win public support for the League of Nations, at the San Francisco City Hall. (*Culver Pictures.*)

The constitutionally mandated state of the union message was usually sent to Congress in the nineteenth century. Today presidents deliver it in person to a national television audience. (*Wally McNamee: Woodfin Camp.*)

the 1984 presidential campaign. Reagan was able to redefine and take control of the issue. Instead of agreeing that major new funding was needed, the president proposed "merit pay" for excellent teachers, more local control of schools, and a "back to basics" approach—none of which would cost any federal money.

Presidents use national agenda politics to push their programs through Congress. Franklin Roosevelt's 100 days of recovery legislation in the midst of the depression included radio addresses that explained what Congress was doing; this maintained his authority, enhanced his reputation, and gave Congress the confidence to continue. Lyndon Johnson's "great society" programs were passed amid a blitz of television, radio, newspaper, and magazine publicity for his proposals, especially those dealing with antipoverty efforts. Ronald Reagan used a national agenda strategy to get Congress to pass his supply-side tax and spending cuts.

The January messages. Each year the president has the first shot at the national agenda, delivering several *January messages* to Congress. These include the state of the union address, usually delivered in person to a joint session of Congress; the economic message, which accompanies the *Report of the Council of Economic Advisors*; and the budget message, which accompanies the *Budget of the United States*. At times the president may make an address to the nation about an economic program or budget shortly after submitting it to Congress. These messages and speeches form the core of the president's program. The White House press officials highlight the most important parts for the media in briefings just before their release. Interviews are arranged with the president, Cabinet secretaries, and other top officials to further the administration's viewpoint. These messages and reports always give the president the political initiative: politicians from both parties must react to the president's agenda.

It takes several months (in the case of the budget, almost a year) to prepare the January messages. The White House asks the Cabinet secretaries and ca-

reer bureaucrats for their ideas. Outside experts are consulted. The presidential agencies consider these proposals and make their own recommendations. Differences are thrashed out in Cabinet councils. Eventually the president and a small group of senior aides determine the priorities. The president then calls in speech writers and outlines proposals. Competing drafts for speeches become a battlefield on which aides and Cabinet secretaries can make their arguments.

The January messages, speeches, and reports are prepared through ***action-forcing cycles***: they require the administration to (1) canvass departments and the advisory system to develop new programs; (2) debate the priorities and policies of the government; (3) make decisions and resolve disputes; and (4) present a program to Congress by a specific date. Then the process starts all over again in a new annual cycle. It therefore becomes convenient for all those involved to organize their work around the four cycles in a presidential term. Because of the length of time involved, the president can allow aides to float trial balloons: leaks to reporters about possible programs. Thus public reaction can be gauged before it is decided whether to put them in the messages.

Presidential television.   Presidents make other televised addresses to the nation. They may address a joint session of Congress, either during a crisis or when they introduce a major piece of legislation. They may speak to the public directly from the White House by obtaining free time from the major networks. Some observers believe that presidents can overwhelm the opposition using television, and proposals have been made to give the other party a formal right of reply and to provide for regular "national debates" between the two parties.[43] The opposition does receive free time from the networks to reply to the State of the Union address and some other speeches, but the time slots are less favorable, and not all networks carry them. The White House cues in the media before, during, and after the presidential address, highlighting the argument

Public persuasion is an important presidential resource. President Kennedy consults with his speechwriter, Theodore Sorensen (far right). (*Jacques Lowe: Woodfin Camp.*)

President Reagan dramatizes his "back to basics" theme by sitting in on a high school English class. (*Michael Evans: White House.*)

and giving reporters summaries of the speech and the key points. Important columnists may get interviews with the president. But media coverage of presidential speeches is often skeptical and sometimes hostile. Attempts by the White House to spoon-feed reporters and influence coverage become an issue that is critically reported.

Televised presidential addresses have not unbalanced American politics. Occasionally, a White House request for network time will be denied if it seems partisan. More often, the networks negotiate on timing so as not to disrupt their schedules. Presidents themselves are reluctant to bump popular programs off the air (they even postpone the inaugural ceremony if it conflicts with the NFL Superbowl game) and they find that taking to the airwaves too often results in lower ratings and lessened impact. Presidents' use of television is self-regulating: too much exposure to the Oval Office jades the audience, and so the White House limits it.

Pseudo events. Presidents rely on ***pseudo events*** in their use of television. Carter's "town meetings" and Reagan's visits to schoolhouses, where he read Shakespeare to students, are examples. Presidents leave Washington and campaign for their programs because it is fun to be on the road and because it permits them to bypass the critical Washington press corps and gain coverage from a local press, which is more likely to be favorable.[44] Even some of the summit conferences, such as the annual economic summit for the heads of major noncommunist industrial powers, are primarily public relations showcases. (The Reagan White House put on an election-year road show in 1984, including trips in the spring to Korea, Japan, China, and Ireland, capped by a London economic summit.) One event a day is planned, held early so that it will make the evening news. It is packaged to provide good "visuals," and ample "photo opportunities" are arranged each day by the White House Photo Office—but no opportunity for reporters to question the president.

The president's relations with the media are sometimes cooperative, sometimes antagonistic, but usually difficult and uncertain. Presidents seldom get an opportunity to show their frustration with the media. Addressing the 1983 White House press photographers' dinner, President Reagan felt free to poke fun at his hosts, believing that the event was off the record. It wasn't. (*Gerald Martineau: Washington Post.*)

News conferences. News conferences, which were started by Woodrow Wilson, were first used extensively by Franklin Roosevelt, who had twenty or so White House reporters crowd into the Oval Office periodically for interviews. This informal approach was transformed by Dwight Eisenhower into a staged conference, held in a larger room and filmed and shown on television. John Kennedy moved his news conferences into an auditorium and permitted live television coverage. Presidents use news conferences to address the nation directly. "I would rather have 60 million people watch President Reagan than have 30 million people seeing him interpreted by Sam Donaldson on the evening news," says Michael Deaver, a former Reagan aide.[45] The president makes a brief opening statement, which is followed by reporters' questions: first from AP and UPI wire service reporters, and then from correspondents for the three national networks, and then from other reporters.

The president prepares for news conferences during briefings conducted by the staff and important Cabinet officials. The purpose of these sessions is to rehearse positions on existing policy, and they may also be used as action-forcing processes to spur the development of new policies in anticipation of a question. The president can use a news conference to signal policy changes to members of Congress and to foreign governments.

Presidents need not hold news conferences when they are on the defensive, since the conferences are scheduled solely at the president's discretion.[46] Some presidents are more accessible than others. Roosevelt and Kennedy held frequent conferences; Johnson held many early in his term, when things were going well, and then he tapered off; and Nixon held few, especially during his second term. Carter held fifty-nine, but Reagan held only twenty-seven during his first term. The average for all presidents is around one conference a month.

Recently the White House has decided to bypass the national media and work more closely with local reporters. A White House wire and computer service feeds documents, speeches, and press releases directly to local news desks. In 1985 the White House television studio began to set up teleconfer-

ences so that local reporters could interview Washington officials; the video-tapes were sent by satellite to local stations for rebroadcast.

Public liaison. Presidents communicate with leaders of labor, business, scientific, cultural, religious, and ethnic groups. Presidential aides give these people briefings and information and invite them to lunches and meetings with the president and Cabinet leaders. The president bestows favor for their support, and they have access to the president when they want the government to do something for them. The president hopes that in return, they will influence Congress.

Sometimes the White House simulates support. It may orchestrate a series of phone calls, letters, and telegrams, supposedly from people supporting the president after a speech, but actually coming from political operatives and local party workers in each state. The White House may channel leftover campaign funds to its supporters so that they can take out newspaper advertisements praising the administration's decisions.[47]

Pollsters. The same pollsters who help presidents during the campaign are hired by the party to conduct polls during their administrations. Polls help the president shape not only national agenda politics but also a whole program.

President Reagan relies on Richard Wirthlin, who does nightly "tracking" polls to detect shifts in attitudes. He also does monthly "eagles," which are in-depth polls for the White House and the RNC. His firm, Decision Making Information, receives close to $1 million annually from the RNC.[48] Wirthlin meets with White House aides regularly and with Reagan once a month to discuss political strategy.

Limits to national agenda politics

Presidential shortcomings. National agenda politics is not a cure for a president's weakness. For one thing, most presidents (Reagan aside) have been poor media performers. Theodore Sorensen, a speech writer for President Kennedy, noted a "longterm decline over several administrations in the quality of English spoken at the White House."[49] Presidents Johnson, Nixon, Ford, and Carter were ineffective in front of cameras and microphones.

Most presidential speeches that try to sway public opinion are unsuccessful. President Ford's speech unveiling his economic program, complete with its WIN button (standing for "whip inflation now"), became a national joke. The more President Carter appealed for support for his energy program, the lower his approval ratings fell. After delivering five speeches, he canceled a sixth one at the last minute because he knew that it would just make things worse. Only one-third of the public believed that the energy crisis was real and approved of his handling of it.[50] One study by political scientists of fifty-six public issues between the early 1930s and the early 1970s showed that on only a few did a president sway public opinion, and then only when he was popular; otherwise, his efforts often made things worse.[51]

Presidents may lose control of the timing of national agenda politics, as Kennedy did when he had to advance his own schedule for the introduction of civil rights legislation after massive demonstrations by civil rights marchers in the south. Presidents may also lose control of the definition of an issue, as Nixon did when a combination of Harvard medical researchers and members of Congress discovered that people were hungry in the United States; the result

was a massive expansion of the food stamp program. Moreover, presidents may not communicate their own sense of urgency; this happened to Reagan in dealing with El Salvador and Nicaragua. Finally, a president may even lose the debate on an issue, as Truman found out when the American Medical Association convinced the public that his plan for health insurance was a form of "socialized medicine."

The media and the national agenda. The national news media may have more influence on the national agenda than the president. Commentators can raise issues, and news departments can cover events, provide their own context and explanations, and challenge the administration's version. Some network news programs cover the president using the *diary* format: what the president did that day. Others use the *tipster* approach, offering the "inside story" as to why the president did something. The White House becomes most upset, however, if a network takes the *populist* approach, focusing on the impact of a presidential decision by suggesting that ordinary people are going to suffer because the president is favoring the "interests" of the wealthy. According to a study conducted for *TV Guide*, over a two-week period in 1983 the networks differed significantly in their reporting of news about the president. While NBC and ABC concentrated on the diary and analysis approaches, CBS took the populist approach. It presented more stories about the White House, and most of them, by a 7-to-1 margin, were negative.[52] The CBS anchor, Dan Rather, has complained strongly about White House pressure on his network superiors to change the tone of his coverage.

The White House complains most bitterly about lengthy documentaries which seek to influence the national agenda. In 1982 CBS produced a documentary entitled *People Like Us*, which depicted three families and a church program, all of which were affected by Reagan's cutbacks of social programs. The network denied the administration's request to reply. As one White House official put it, "This was a powerful emotional documentary, to which we had no way of responding. It was like being hit with a two-by-four."[53]

The media can publicize other national agenda challenges to the president. It is always a story when someone who is invited to the White House attacks a presidential policy. Consider a 17-year-old high school student, Ariela Gross, who was to receive an award as a "presidential scholar." She decided to present Reagan with a petition urging his support for a congressional nuclear freeze resolution. After the story hit the papers, the White House invited her to a twenty-minute meeting in the Oval Office. Ms. Gross had her meeting with Reagan, and then she gave interviews on the White House lawn, concluding: "He said here today that we should be proud of a country that wants to remain strong. And I say that I am ashamed of the leaders of this country who can vote for nuclear freeze and then turn around and vote for the most dangerous and expensive missile system that this country has ever suggested."[54] All in all, it was quite a good day for Ms. Gross, and a bad one for the president.

Runaway national commissions and task forces can also embarrass the president. The White House Conference on Civil Rights in 1966 had an agenda that went considerably further than President Johnson's, and his attempts to manipulate the delegates were uncovered by the media, to his embarrassment. The Kerner Commission, which blamed urban unrest on "white racism," was disavowed by Johnson, who feared white backlash against these charges. Rich-

Presidents can use Air Force 1 to crisscross the nation, making brief airport speeches in support of their programs. (*Max Winter: Picture Group.*)

ard Nixon repudiated the findings of the Eisenhower Commission on Campus Unrest because it did not pin the blame on student demonstrators, whom Nixon called "bums." When Ronald Reagan's Private Sector Survey on Cost Control issued a report detailing a plan that it believed could save the government $54 billion, Reagan found the proposals to be so politically controversial that he distanced the White House from them. Instead of allowing Peter Grace, the chairman, to present his report in person at the White House, Reagan arranged for a briefing to be held in a Commerce Department auditorium, and he did not attend. One White House official, asked about the site, responded that the briefing should have been held in Siberia.[55]

Presidents often resort to overblown rhetoric and hyperbole. They declare "war" on poverty, cancer, and crime. They proclaim that a summit meeting with the Chinese is the most important event of the twentieth century or that a treaty between Egypt and Israel is the diplomatic triumph of the decade. They appoint a "czar" to coordinate government efforts to solve one crisis after another. This rhetorical excess leaves the public with inflated expectations, and when the euphoria wears off, the burden of proof is on the president. The White House tries to lead, but many people do not have the energy or the interest to follow.[56] Instead of sounding good, the president appears to be sounding off.

The public these days is therefore more likely to trust media sources than the White House. Summing up the problem, the political scientist George Edwards concluded that "presidents cannot depend upon leading the public any more than they can rely on understanding public opinion."[57] Or, as put more elegantly by John Travolta, "I can do all that Reagan does. I do it all the time and have a bigger audience."[58]

PREROGATIVE POWERS

Presidential ***prerogative powers*** are those powers granted to the president by the Constitution. They include ***express powers,*** which are explicitly men-

tioned, such as the veto and appointment powers; **implied powers,** which presidents say they need in order to accomplish what is expressly permitted; and **inherent powers** (that is, all executive functions) which the president claims because of separation of powers.

The **Lockean prerogative,** named after the English philosopher John Locke, is the power to act without reference to the law, and sometimes even against it, in a crisis when the existence of the nation is at stake.[59] Presidents never forget that to protect the people, they may have to go beyond the confines of the Constitution or temporarily suspend the execution of the laws, even though they will be acting illegally or unconstitutionally (though no president admits to that). In some nations emergency power is provided in the constitution itself, which provides for martial law or for a state of emergency or a state of siege. Our Constitution makes no mention of such powers or of the Lockean prerogative. Presidents fashion their own such powers, although they claim that they are not violating the Constitution when they do so. Richard Nixon even argued, after he resigned from office, that a president cannot violate the Constitution or laws because "if the President does it, it is legal."[60] The Supreme Court has ruled that presidents may not be sued for their acts committed while in office, no matter how damaging (which goes a long way toward ratifying Nixon's idea), although aides may be sued and the president remains liable for criminal prosecution and impeachment.[61]

Using prerogative powers

Presidents have used prerogative powers when they could not get what they wanted by persuading Congress. George Washington declared neutrality in the wars between Britain and France on his own authority because he knew that Congress would not do so. Thomas Jefferson purchased the Louisiana Territory from Napoleon without law or appropriation. James Polk, on his own authority, maneuvered American forces in disputed territories to begin the Mexican-American war. Abraham Lincoln used emergency powers to raise military forces, provide weapons to union loyalists in West Virginia, suspend the writ of habeas corpus, and arrest suspected Confederate sympathizers; then he called Congress into session to retroactively ratify these and other actions taken at the outset of the Civil War. Theodore Roosevelt mediated a war between Russia and Japan and won a Nobel peace prize for his efforts, even though no such responsibility is mentioned in the Constitution. Woodrow Wilson invaded Mexico and the Soviet Union without congressional sanction. Franklin Roosevelt ordered the Navy into a shooting war with Axis ships in the north Atlantic before the United States entered World War II. On their own authority, Harry Truman, Lyndon Johnson, and Richard Nixon sent American forces to fight undeclared wars in Korea, Vietnam, and Cambodia. Jimmy Carter abrogated a mutual security treaty with Taiwan to cement a diplomatic relationship with China.

The exercise of prerogative powers follows a characteristic pattern. Presidents make decisions with the help of a circle of close and trusted advisers, often keeping their intentions secret not only from Congress but also from career officials. They issue orders to their subordinates, who are expected to carry them out without regard to their legality. In a crisis, the president may bypass many layers of bureaucracy and establish a direct chain of command with officials at the scene. The policies are implemented suddenly, as *faits accomplis* (accomplished facts), and then presented to Congress and the nation, often in a televised presidential address.

Departments and agencies rarely participate in deliberations, as in national agenda politics. There is no bargaining with, or persuasion of, subordinates and members of Congress before action is taken, as there is in routine negotiating politics. In fact, legislative leaders are just as much in the dark about what the White House is up to as is the American public.

Legitimizing prerogative powers

The use of prerogative powers leaves presidents open to charges that they are abusing their own powers, usurping those of Congress, and instituting an imperial presidency. They must therefore legitimize their actions with the public. Voters want strong, decisive leadership, but they trust congressional decision making more than presidential decision making in foreign affairs as well as domestic issues, and they are reluctant to grant prerogative powers to presidents.[62] Close to three-fifths of the people want Congress and the president to share responsibility, while fewer than one-tenth want the president to make decisions unilaterally.[63] Presidential approval ratings rise when both branches work together, and they fall when the branches confront each other.

Party conflict. The White House tries to unify the president's party and split the opposition. It briefs legislators and prepares speeches which they can deliver on the floor of Congress. It gives classified information to them so that they can discredit charges by critics. But usually the president's own party splits badly, while the opposition unites. This was the case in 1808, when Jefferson's foreign policy was repudiated by Congress; in 1832, when Jackson's vetoes and his firing of a Treasury secretary led many Democrats to leave his party and unite with the new Whig Party; and in 1968, when the fiercest opposition to the Vietnamese war came not from Republicans but from a Democrat, William Fulbright, the chair of the Senate Foreign Relations Committee.

Public support. Presidents often lose the battle for public support. After Truman seized the steel mills in 1950 to keep production going during a labor dispute in the midst of the Korean war, the mill owners fought back with charges that he was paying off a political debt to the unions. Public opinion swung against the president. Eventually the Supreme Court found the seizure unconstitutional, which was a major blow to presidential war powers. Truman, Johnson, and Nixon all lost home-front battles for public support of the wars in Korea and Indochina as casualties mounted; ultimately this resulted in settlements that were less advantageous than might otherwise have been obtained. In the post-Vietnam era, Reagan felt so constrained by public opinion that he could not keep marines in Lebanon after 250 had been killed in a suicide bombing, and he could not continue mining the harbors of Nicaragua after the role of the CIA was disclosed by the media.

The case for the president. In their attempts to legitimize the use of prerogative powers, presidents are assisted by the legal counsel in the White House, who runs a seven-person "law firm for the president," and by the attorney general and the assistant attorney general in charge of the Office of Legal Counsel, who prepare briefs defending the presidential exercise of power. These officials see their main function as defending and expanding the powers of the presidency in the face of attacks by critics. (The attorney general may submit a formal *opinion* in advance of an important presidential order, as Robert Jackson did when Franklin Roosevelt transferred destroyers to Great

Britain during World War II, in spite of congressional laws which seemed to forbid that action.) Counsel for the Defense Department and the State Department prepare legal briefs which set forth the gravity of a situation and justify presidential powers. They emphasize administration intelligence which cannot be revealed. Spokespersons for presidents claim that they are acting in the national interest and that opponents lack the information and expertise necessary for correct decisions. They cite the presidential oath of office and responsibility to protect the nation.

Assessing presidential claims. We need not accept all these presidential claims at face value. Presidents do not restrict their use of prerogative powers to crises. They use secrecy, commands, vetoes, appointments and removals, withholding of funds, and suspension of the execution of laws as vantage points, creating bargaining opportunities in routine politics. And presidents use emergency powers in situations that are not really emergencies, as the Supreme Court found when it chastised Truman for seizing the steel mills when other ways to settle the dispute were available.

Presidents claim that they have more information and expertise than their critics, but this is not always true. Nixon, for example, invoked ***executive privilege*** and claimed that Watergate involved "national security matters," which justified his refusal to testify before Congress and to provide evidence to the courts. But this claim was merely a ploy to get the FBI to stop investigating the burglary of the Democratic National Committee headquarters. Even when wars or covert intelligence operations are involved, the main issue between the president and the critics is the wisdom of the policy, and it is rare that any particular bit of secret information that the president has would be decisive in discrediting the arguments of critics.

Checking prerogative powers. Congress can exercise the impeachment power, but it will not do so when the president invokes prerogative powers for diplomatic or military purposes, however controversial. And the process itself may be stalled or nullified by presidents who keep their actions secret, classify vital information, or invoke executive privilege against Congress and the courts. A president may even be able to stave off inquiries into impeachable offenses. Presidents can also use their pardon prerogative for the benefit of people caught breaking the law on their behalf (although they may not pardon anyone in an impeachment proceeding); this might induce people to withhold testimony or to lie for the president during an inquiry.

It is true that the ultimate check remains: retribution by the voters at the polls. But even this can be threatened by prerogative powers if they are used for surveillance of opponents to obtain political intelligence; for blackmail, intimidation, or dirty tricks to harass and disrupt the opposition; or for secrecy to keep such sordid operations from the public.

Risks of using prerogative powers

Using prerogative powers is risky. It can result in the *frontlash* effect: the president resolves a crisis successfully and, by doing so, establishes a consensus in the parties and in Congress that the exercise of the powers involved is legitimate. Examples include George Washington's diplomacy and proclamation of neutrality in the 1790s, Franklin Roosevelt's diplomatic and war powers during the Second World War, and Jimmy Carter's observance of SALT II limitations in

The first and only president to resign the office, Richard Nixon departs for California on August 10, 1974. (*Holland Freeman: Magnum Photos.*)

the absence of a treaty with the Soviet Union. But there is also a possibility of a *backlash*: the president controls the situation, but the president's own party splits on the issue, and there is considerable opposition in Congress, which may pass laws that curb powers or regulate presidential powers; and the Supreme Court or lower federal courts may declare the exercise of power unconstitutional. The president may retire or be defeated at the polls. Examples include controversies surrounding Andrew Jackson's use of the veto and removal power, Harry Truman's seizure of the steel mills and entry into the Korean war, Lyndon Johnson's involvement in the Vietnamese war, and Richard Nixon's refusal to spend funds appropriated by Congress.

There is the *overshoot and collapse* effect: to members of Congress and to much of the public, the exercise of prerogative powers seems to involve a serious abuse of power. The actions seem illegitimate, and congressional leaders hold hearings in order to force the removal of lower-level officials and repudiate a policy or even begin proceedings to censure (Andrew Jackson and John Tyler) or impeach (Andrew Johnson and Richard Nixon) the president.

No president has ever been convicted and removed from office as a result of impeachment proceedings. Only Andrew Johnson was actually impeached and tried, and Richard Nixon resigned before the House took any action; in both cases, however, efforts to impeach were accompanied by a resurgence of congressional power and a major reshaping of the presidency. Johnson sur-

355

vived impeachment, but only by giving up several claims to power and agreeing to follow Congress on most issues. During the months leading up to Nixon's resignation, Congress passed laws regulating presidential war powers and preventing the president from withholding funds appropriated by Congress; and the Supreme Court indicated that the judiciary, not the White House, would determine the president's proper use of the executive privilege and would examine any evidence in the president's possession.

Criteria for use of prerogative powers

We can make a distinction between an *imperial presidency* and a *crisis presidency*: the former undermines the system of checks and balances to institute unrestrained presidential government. While Congress and the courts remain, they have no independent power; in ancient Rome, this happened to the senate after the assumption of almost total power by the Caesars. The crisis presidency, however, is instituted to *preserve* the fundamental values of a democratic and constitutional government when the very life of the nation may be at stake.[64] To distinguish between the abuse of power and its vigorous use in crises, the following standards may be helpful:

- Emergency powers should not be used for personal or party advantage.
- There should be no interference with the next elections.
- Controversial prerogative powers should be exercised only when a crisis is extreme, when a delay might prove fatal, and when the regular constitutional procedures would involve such a delay.
- These powers should be exercised only when no laws provide viable alternatives and when nothing in the Constitution expressly prohibits the action.
- The use of these powers should be preceded by the widest possible advance consultation among top officials and, if possible, congressional leaders.
- The president should make available to Congress and the judiciary (when court cases are involved) the full record of actions in the crisis. The courts should make the final determination if the president wants to withhold information and claims executive privilege.
- After the emergency, Congress should legislate and put presidential powers and actions under law, retroactively if necessary.
- Congress by law should be able to override presidential actions.
- The impeachment powers should function throughout the emergency.[65]

President Lincoln, whose statesmanship in preserving the union created the standard by which we still evaluate the performance of presidents in crises today. (*Culver Pictures.*)

If presidents act as Lincoln did during the Civil War—if they hold elections, respect the system of checks and balances, and confine the use of prerogative powers to an emergency—then these powers, even those which seem to disregard the Constitution, can be accommodated by our political system. Even so, it is always useful to remember the warning given by the Supreme Court, at the end of the Civil War, when it observed that "wicked men, ambitious of power, with a hatred of liberty and contempt of law, may fill the place once occupied by Washington and Lincoln."[66]

POWER AND LEADERSHIP

Leadership is at the core of presidential power. Presidents must have a sense of timing and pace, and they must know how to bluff, how to compromise, how to persuade, and how to bargain. They have to know the pros and cons of negotiating, setting the national agenda, and using prerogative powers—and

they must know how to combine these tactics into an overall strategy suitable for each issue. They have to have the personal skills necessary to inspire their supporters, and they must be able to build different coalitions on different issues, converting adversaries on one issue into backers on another. They have to know when to press their advantage and when to stop, so that adversaries will not become enemies. They must know how to advance, but just as important, they have to know how to retreat and cut their losses. And above all, presidents must understand power.

The power problem

"What Presidents do every day," according to Richard Neustadt, a political scientist and former White House aide, "is to make decisions that are mostly thrust upon them, the deadlines all too often outside their control, on options mostly framed by others, about issues crammed with technical complexities and uncertain outcomes."[67] Or, as Ronald Reagan put it, "Sometimes I have to read the papers to find out what I did yesterday." Under these circumstances presidents may become "clerks" whose powers are exercised as often for the benefit of others as for themselves, unless they extricate themselves from the pressures converging on them and find some room to maneuver.

At the heart of an effective presidency is the incumbent's search for *personal influence*. Presidents get advice from aides and experts, but only they can understand their own stakes and guard their own reputation. Presidents must want power and feel comfortable exercising it. Presidents must influence the calculations and behavior of people who make and carry out policy. Presidents must use their resources for their own purposes. No one with whom they deal, whether legislators, department secretaries, or interest-group lobbyists, has their responsibilities or their viewpoint. Presidents must come to their own decisions in terms of stakes and political risks—but they must also recognize the stakes and risks of others and extend their authority by communicating their reasoning effectively to others.

Much of the public believes that effective presidents first figure out their goals, in terms of the national interest, and then develop political strategy and tactics. This view is dead wrong. Principles do not precede political strategy, and the *ends* do not determine the *means.* Instead, the *means* often determine the *ends.* The power stakes of presidents often determine what they decide they want to do. As presidents examine issues, they think about their own reputations, their own authority, and even their own legitimacy. They consider how any decision made about an issue today will boost or diminish their chances for winning another contest tomorrow. They consider how a particular issue will help them unify a coalition of supporters and split the opposition party; how they can develop a reputation as a winner; how they can time decisions so that unpopular sacrifices come early in the term and benefits to voters come in the third and fourth years, in time for renomination and reelection.

Those who believe that presidents should consider power stakes and use them to determine goals argue that there is no such thing as the "national interest" which can be considered apart from presidential power. Richard Neustadt argues that "the things a President must think about if he would build his influence are not unlike those bearing on the viability of public policy. The correspondence may be inexact, but it is close. And because the President's own frame of reference is at once so all-encompassing and so political, what he sees as a balance for himself is likely to be close to what is viable in

terms of public policy."[68] As Neustadt concludes, "In a relative but real sense one can say of a President what Eisenhower's first Secretary of Defense once said of General Motors: What is good for the country is good for the President and vice versa."[69]

Limits to power politics

The power politics approach to the presidency has left many people dissatisfied.[70] For one thing, in the post-Watergate era, it is difficult to sustain the proposition that what is good for the president is always good for the country. A president like Nixon who condones and covers up a violation of the Constitution and the laws is a danger to the country, and when such a president guards power stakes, it is not in the public interest. For another, it is not always clear how a president goes about guarding power stakes. As Neustadt admits, "The insights power offers into policy diverge, pointing many ways at once, thus limiting their usefulness as guides to viability."[71] To tell presidents that "insights diverge" may leave them muttering about consulting the stars or tea leaves, if that is the best their advisers can do. Presidents must remember that power is not the only value to be considered: the legitimacy of presidential action is also at issue (as Neustadt recognizes), and it is as important to keep within the bounds of law and propriety as it is to exercise maximum influence.

Perhaps most important of all, a presidency that is based on bargaining, persuasion, manipulation of public opinion, and prerogative actions may ultimately leave the American people without ideals, without principles, and without faith in the government or its leaders. Moving the nation may involve more than instrumental use of political techniques, for as James MacGregor Burns asks, "In protecting themselves—their reputations, choices, resources— what are chief executives guarding? If they constantly protect themselves, to what extent are they also guarding the *purpose* they are supposedly ultimately to be serving? How do they draw the line between preserving power for themselves and expending it for broader goals?"[72]

Principles and power

Ultimately presidents can lead the nation only if they inspire it through an appeal to principle. They must have a vision, not merely of their own power stakes but also of a better future, and they must communicate that vision to the people in a way that enhances their authority.

Most of our great presidents exercised what James MacGregor Burns has called ***transformational leadership***: they went beyond the existing divisions and deals of the politics of their time and summoned politicians and the people to enter new and uncharted territory. They possessed a deep-felt sense of where they wanted to take the country. They transformed the nature of the debates, the terms of reference, and even the style of politics. They created new constitutional arrangements, as George Washington did with the formation of the union, as Abraham Lincoln did with its preservation, and as Franklin Roosevelt did with the country's assumption of vast new powers in economic matters. They transformed the party system by shaping new electoral coalitions. They were able to simplify issues down to the bare essentials so that everyone would be emotionally as well as intellectually affected by their arguments. They provided a sense of common and overriding national purpose rather than a set of bargains. Presidents who exercise transformational leadership may be rare, but they accomplish more in one or two terms than a generation of other presidents do through politics as usual.

An appeal to principle may well turn out to be the way to reverse the declin-

ing fortunes of the modern presidency. A reputation for statesmanship and principled leadership may yet turn out to be the best presidential politics.

IN CONCLUSION

The powers of the president are not clearly defined by the Constitution, which remains silent, ambiguous, and underdefined on some important points. Except in periods of realignment or reinforcement of the party system, presidents control neither the party as organization nor the legislative party, which means that they do not lead disciplined party majorities as in a parliamentary system. To exert effective leadership, presidents must create coalitions: they do so by bargaining, and if that fails they go to the people by dominating the national agenda. In recent years presidents have relied increasingly on use of the media, at a time when presidential popularity has declined. Presidents may also use prerogative powers unilaterally to resolve issues when they believe that they cannot get support from Congress. The exercise of such powers may lead to a frontlash effect, which expands our conception of the presidency; to a backlash effect, which diminishes the powers of the office; or, in rare cases, to a collapse in the authority and legitimacy of an administration. The most effective presidents know how to guard their reputations, recognize their power stakes, and understand that means and ends are inextricably linked. But the truly great ones are also transformational leaders, who move the nation more by force of argument and vision than by the maneuvers they make and the prerogative powers they must exercise.

NOTES

1. James MacGregor Burns, *Presidential Government*, Avon, New York, 1965, p. 351.
2. *The Federalist*, number 70.
3. *Time*, Nov. 10, 1980, p. 30; "Making Reagan Accountable," *The Wall Street Journal*, Apr. 20, 1984.
4. Bobby Baker, *Wheeling and Dealing*, Norton, New York, 1971, p. 265.
5. Michael Nelson, "Evaluating the Presidency," in Michael Nelson (ed.), *The Presidency and the Political System*, Congressional Quarterly Press, Washington, D.C., 1984, pp. 5–28.
6. Thomas Cronin, *The State of the Presidency*, 2d ed., Little, Brown, Boston, 1980, p. 5.
7. Edwin Meese, "The Institutional Presidency: A View from the White House," *Presidential Studies Quarterly*, vol. 13, no. 2, spring 1983, p. 191.
8. George Edwards III, *The Public Presidency: The Pursuit of Popular Support*, St. Martin's, New York, 1983, pp. 187–210; Eric B. Herzik and Mary L. Dodson, "The President and Public Expectations: A Research Note," *Presidential Studies Quarterly*, vol. 12, no. 2, spring 1982, pp. 168–173.
9. Jeffrey Tulis, "The Two Constitutional Presidencies," in Nelson, op. cit., pp. 59–86.
10. Woodrow Wilson, *The Principles of Constitutional Government*, Columbia University Press, New York, 1908, p. 30.
11. On the concept of clerkship, see Richard Neustadt, *Presidential Power: The Politics of Leadership from FDR to Carter*, Wiley, New York, 1980, p. 6.
12. Quoted in Jack Valenti, *A Very Human President*, Norton, New York, 1975, p. 261; Wilson, op. cit., p. 30; *The National Journal*, Oct. 16, 1984, p. 1870.
13. James Stimson, "Public Support for American Presidents: A Cyclical Model," *Public Opinion Quarterly*, vol. 40, no. 1, spring 1976, pp. 1–21; Henry Kenski, "The Impact of Economic Conditions on Presidential Popularity," *Journal of Politics*, vol. 39, no. 3, August 1977, pp. 764–773; Samuel Kernell, "Expanding Presidential Popularity," *American Political Science Review*, vol. 72, no. 3, June 1978, pp. 506–522.
14. Stephen J. Wayne, "Great Expectations: Contemporary Views of the President," in Thomas Cronin (ed.), *Rethinking the Presidency*, Little, Brown, Boston, 1982.

15. Lou Cannon, "They Don't Call Reagan the Teflon President for Nothing," *Washington Post National Weekly Edition*, Apr. 30, 1984.
16. *The Wall Street Journal*, Apr. 20, 1984.
17. Cannon, op. cit.
18. Barry Sussman, "Reagan's Policies Are the Key—Not His Personality," *Washington Post National Weekly Edition*, Feb. 13, 1984, p. 37.
19. Richard Neustadt, *Presidential Power*, Wiley, New York, 1960, p. 121.
20. Fred Greenstein, *The Hidden-Hand Presidency*, Basic Books, New York, 1982.
21. Theodore Sorensen, *Kennedy*, Bantam, New York, 1966, p 387.
22. Godfrey Hodgson, *All Things to All Men*, Simon and Schuster, New York, 1980, p. 31; David Halberstam, *The Best and the Brightest*, Random House, New York, 1969, p. 516.
23. Steven Skowrenek, "The Presidency and Political Time," in Nelson, op. cit., pp. 87–133.
24. *The New York Times*, Mar. 7, 1979.
25. PBS transcript, Apr. 26, 1973, p. 3.
26. Elizabeth Drew, "Reporter at Large," *The New Yorker*, June 8, 1981, p. 138.
27. Samuel Kernell, "Presidential Popularity and Negative Voting," *American Political Science Review*, vol. 71, no. 1, March 1977, pp. 44–66.
28. Roger G. Brown and David M. Welborn, "Presidents and Their Parties," *Presidential Studies Quarterly*, vol. 12, no. 3, summer 1982, pp. 302–315.
29. *The Wall Street Journal*, Aug. 19, 1982.
30. Paul Light, *Vice-Presidential Power*, Johns Hopkins Press, Baltimore, 1984.
31. Thomas Cronin, "The Textbook Presidency and Political Science," paper delivered at the American Political Science Association Convention, 1969.
32. George Reedy, *The Twilight of the Presidency*, New American Library, New York, 1970, p. xiv.
33. Arthur Schlesinger, *The Coming of the New Deal*, Houghton Mifflin, Boston, 1958, sec. 8, pp. 511–588.
34. Alexander George, *Presidential Decisionmaking and Foreign Policy*, Praeger, New York, 1982, pp. 191–208.
35. Cited in Stephen J. Wayne, "Working in the White House: Psychological Dimensions of the Job," paper presented at the annual meeting of the Southern Political Science Association, New Orleans, 1977, p. 10.
36. *Newsweek*, Feb. 16, 1984, p. 12.
37. John Manley, "Presidential Power and White House Lobbying," *Political Science Quarterly*, vol. 93, no. 2, summer 1978, pp. 255–275.
38. Meese, op. cit., p. 192.
39. Peter W. Sperlich, "Bargaining and Overload: An Essay on Presidential Power," in Aaron Wildvasky (ed.), pp. 168–192.
40. On reputation, see Neustadt, *Presidential Power: The Politics of Leadership from FDR to Carter*, pp. 46–49.
41. Cited in Richard A. Watson and Norman Thomas, *The Politics of the Presidency*, Wiley, New York, 1983, p. 165.
42. Samuel Kernell, "The Presidency and the People," in Nelson, op. cit., pp. 233–263.
43. See the proposals made in Newton Minow et al., *Presidential Television*, Basic Books, New York, 1973, pp. 159–166.
44. On the use of the local strategy, see Robert Locander, "Modern Presidential In-Office communication," *Presidential Studies Quarterly*, vol. 13, no. 2, spring 1983, pp. 242-254.
45. *The New York Times*, Feb. 16, 1982.
46. William Lammers, "Presidential Press Conference Schedules: Who Hides and When?" *Political Science Quarterly*, vol. 96, no. 2, summer 1981, pp. 261–267.
47. Edwards, op. cit., p. 77.
48. *The New York Times*, Nov. 16, 1981; Barry Sussman, "Why the GOP Pays Richard Wirthlin $1 Million a Year," *Washington Post National Weekly Edition*, Dec. 26, 1983, p. 35.

49. Theodore Sorensen, "Presidents and the King's English," *The New York Times*, Aug. 19, 1979.
50. New York Times/CBS poll, July 18, 1979.
51. Benjamin Page and Robert Shapiro, *Presidents as Opinion Leaders: Some New Evidence*, National Opinion Research Center, Chicago, June 1983.
52. John Weisman, "Who's Toughest on the White House—and Why," *TV Guide*, Aug. 27–Sept. 2, 1983.
53. *The New York Times*, Apr. 23, 1982.
54. *The New York Times*, June 17, 1982.
55. *The New York Times*, Apr. 6, 1983.
56. James Ceasar et al., "The Rise of the Rhetorical Presidency," *Presidential Studies Quarterly*, vol. 11, no. 2, spring 1981, pp. 159–160.
57. Edwards, op. cit., p. 4.
58. *California Magazine*, May 1982.
59. John Locke, *Two Treatises of Government*, Cambridge University Press, Cambridge, 1960, p. 422.
60. Nixon is quoted in Christopher Pyle and Richard Pious, *Presidents, Congress and the Constitution*, Free Press, New York, 1984, p. 74.
61. *Nixon v. Fitzgerald*, 457 U.S. 731 (1982).
62. Hazel Erskine, "The Polls: Presidential Power," *Public Opinion Quarterly*, vol. 37, no. 3, fall 1973, pp. 488–503.
63. Robert E. DiClerico, *The American President*, Prentice-Hall, Englewood Cliffs, N.J., 1983, table 5–3, p. 156.
64. Clinton Rossiter, *Constitutional Dictatorship*, Princeton University Press, Princeton, N.J., 1948.
65. Similar lists compiled by Rossiter and Schlesinger appear in Pyle and Pious, op. cit., pp. 140–143.
66. *Ex Parte Milligan*, 71 U.S. 125 (1866).
67. Neustadt, *Presidential Power: The Politics of Leadership from FDR to Carter*, p. 185.
68. Ibid, p. 135.
69. Ibid., p. 136.
70. Useful critiques of this approach include Thomas E. Cronin and Rexford G. Tugwell (eds.), *The Presidency Reappraised*, Praeger, New York, 1974; and Sperlich, op. cit, pp. 168–192.
71. Neustadt, *Presidential Power; The Politics of Leadership from FDR to Carter*, p. 189.
72. James MacGregor Burns, *Leadership*, Harper and Row, New York, 1978, p. 396.

FURTHER READING

Barber, James David: *The Presidential Character*, Prentice-Hall, Englewood Cliffs, N.J., 1972. An analysis of the character of several presidents, including predictive theory of how presidents behave in office.

Bessette, Joseph M. and Jeffrey Tulis (eds.): *The Presidency in the Constitutional Order*, Louisiana State University Press, Baton Rouge, 1981. Articles on presidential powers.

Burns, James MacGregor: *Roosevelt: The Lion and the Fox*, Harcourt, Brace and World, New York, 1956. A biography of Franklin Roosevelt, emphasizing his political skills.

Cronin, Thomas: *The State of the Presidency*, rev. ed., Little, Brown, Boston, 1980. A textbook based on original research on the workings of the presidential agencies and advisory system.

Edwards, George C. III: *The Public Presidency: The Pursuit of Popular Support*, St. Martin's, New York, 1983. A study of national agenda politics and presidential successes and failures.

————and Stephen J. Wayne: *Presidential Leadership*, St. Martin's, New York, 1985. A textbook that emphasizes empirical data about the performance of presidents as leaders of their party, Congress, and public opinion.

Fisher, Louis: *Constitutional Conflicts between Congress and the President*, Princeton University Press, Princeton, N.J., 1985. An up-to-date analysis of conflicts between the two branches over important administrative and foreign affairs powers.

Glad, Betty: *Jimmy Carter: In Search of the Great White House*, Norton, New York, 1980. A book about Carter's quest for the presidency and his performance in office.

Greenstein, Fred I.: *The Hidden-Hand Presidency*, Basic Books, New York, 1982. An account of political strategy and tactics used by Eisenhower, revealing him to have been a thoughtful and savvy politician.

Grossman, Michael, and Martha Kumar: *Portraying the President: The White House and the News Media*, Johns Hopkins, Baltimore, 1981. An account of the way the White House and the news media interact.

Kearns, Doris: *Lyndon Johnson and the American Dream*, Harper and Row, New York, 1976. A biography of Johnson by a political scientist who served in the White House.

Koenig, Louis: *The Chief Executive*, 4th ed., Harcourt Brace Jovanovich, New York, 1981. A leading textbook emphasizing the benefits of vigorous presidential leadership.

Leuchtenberg, William: *In the Shadow of FDR*, rev. ed., Cornell University Press, Ithaca, 1985. An account of the impact of Franklin Roosevelt's activist administration on later presidents.

Light, Paul C.: *The President's Agenda*, Johns Hopkins, Baltimore, 1984. A discussion of how issues reach presidents and how presidents set their priorities.

Lowi, Theodore J.: *The Personal President*, Cornell University Press, Ithaca, 1985. A study of the plebiscitary presidency.

Nelson, Michael (ed.): *The Presidency and the Political System*, Congressional Quarterly Press, Washington, D.C., 1984. Articles by scholars assessing the modern presidency.

Neustadt, Richard: *Presidential Power: The Politics of Leadership from FDR to Carter*, Wiley, New York, 1980. A classic study of presidential power as influence.

Pious, Richard M.: *The American Presidency*, Basic Books, New York, 1979. A treatment of presidential power as prerogatives.

Pyle, Christopher, and Richard Pious: *Presidents, Congress and the Constitution*, Free Press, New York, 1984. Cases and materials on presidential powers and congressional and judicial responses.

Rockman, Bert A.: *The Leadership Question: The Presidency and the American System*, Praeger, New York, 1984. A book that puts the presidency in the context of the American political culture, discusses its relationship to three time cycles of politics, and provides a comparative perspective with leadership positions in other nations.

Rubin, Richard: *Press, Party and Presidency*, Norton, New York, 1981. A theoretical and empirical analysis of the influence of the mass media on presidential powers.

Schlesinger, Arthur M., Jr.: *The Imperial Presidency*, Houghton Mifflin, Boston, 1973. A study of the growth of presidential powers and the dangers inherent in an unbalanced presidency.

———: *A Thousand Days*, Houghton Mifflin, Boston, 1965. An account of John Kennedy's presidency written by a historian who served in his administration.

Watson, Richard, and Norman Thomas: *The Politics of the Presidency*, Wiley, New York, 1983. A comprehensive and up-to-date text.

Wayne, Stephen J.: *The Legislative Presidency*, Harper and Row, New York, 1978. A book about the way administrations develop legislation and win support for it in Congress.

THE STUDY BREAK

Eleanor and Franklin: The White House Years. An award-winning television movie, produced in 1977 and starring Jane Alexander, adapted from Joesph Lash's Pulitzer prizewinning biography, *Eleanor and Franklin*.

John F. Kennedy: Years of Lightning, Day of Drums. A movie commissioned in 1966 by the United States Information Agency for foreign distribution. A classic, it is now shown on television in this country.

The Man. A 1971 movie about a black vice president who is suddenly elevated to the Oval Office, starring James Earl Jones and Burgess Meredith and adapted by Rod Serling from a book by Irving Wallace.

The President's Analyst. A satiric movie, released in 1967, about what happens to the president's analyst (played by James Coburn) when he quits his job. A brilliant parody of Washington politics.

USEFUL SOURCES

Dennis A. Burton, et. al. (eds.), *A Guide to Manuscripts In the Presidential Libraries*, Research Materials Corp., College Park, Maryland, 1985. Indexed descriptions of manuscripts, microfilms, and oral histories in seven presidential libraries.

Byrne, Pamela R. (ed.): *The American Presidency: A Historical Bibliography*, ABC-CLIO, Santa Barbara, Calif., 1984.

Congressional Quarterly Weekly Reports. Reports on the presidential program and Congressional responses.

Edwards, George III, and Stephen J. Wayne: *Studying the Presidency*, University of Tennessee Press, Nashville, 1983. A book containing several articles on how to use sources and how to work in presidential libraries.

William M. Goldsmith, *The Growth of Presidential Power: A Documentary History*, Vols I–III, Chelsea House, New York, 1974. Key speeches, executive orders, legal opinions and court cases involving presidential powers.

The Journal of Law and Politics. A journal devoted to presidential and congressional powers.

The National Journal. A weekly journal on politics in the executive branch.

Presidential Studies Quarterly. A journal containing articles on the institutionalized presidency.

Presidents and Congress. A journal covering relations between the president and Congress.

Public Papers of the Presidents of the United States, GPO, Washington, D.C., issued in several volumes for each president, annually as their terms progress. Bound volumes containing some significant presidential documents, though not the classified or limited-distribution documents.

Weekly Compilation of Presidential Documents, GPO, Washington, D.C. Speeches, transcripts of news conferences, and executive orders and proclamations issued each week by the White House. (Much of this material can be accessed by commercial computer services, which since 1985 have been supplied with these documents by the White House.)

ORGANIZATIONS

Center for the Study of the Presidency. 208 East 75th Street, New York, N.Y. 10021. For more information phone 212-249-1200.

The Executive Office of the President (see also Figure 10-7) comprises the following:

Council of Economic Advisors. Old Executive Office Building, Washington, D.C. 20500. For more information phone 202-395-5042.

Council on Environmental Quality. 722 Jackson Place, N.W., Washington, D.C. 20006. For more information phone 202-395-5080.

National Security Council. Old Executive Office Building, Washington, D.C. 20506. For more information phone 202-456-2255.

Office of Administration. Old Executive Office Building, Washington, D.C. 20500. For more information phone 202-456-7052.

Office of Management and Budget. Old Executive Office Building, Washington, D.C. 20503. For more information phone 202-395-3000.

Office of Policy Development. Old Executive Office Building, Washington, D.C. 20500. For more information phone 202-456-6515.

Office of Science and Technology Policy. Old Executive Office Building, Washington, D.C. 20506. For more information phone 202-456-7116.

Office of the United States Trade Representative. Winder Building, 600 Seventeenth Street, N.W., Washington, D.C. 20506. For more information phone 202-395-3204.

Office of the Vice President. Old Executive Office Building, Washington, D.C. 20501. For more information phone 202-456-2326.

The White House Office. 1600 Pennsylvania Avenue, N.W., Washington, D.C. 20500. For more information phone 202-456-1414 (executive residence, 202-456-2957).

CONGRESSIONAL POWER: REPRESENTATION AND LEGISLATION

The creation of a new national capital with impressive national monuments was part of the agenda of the young republic. The view toward Capitol Hill was already such a sight in 1837. Today the Hill is crowded with office buildings housing congressional staffers and agencies. (*Granger Collection; Owen Franken: Sygma.*)

How does Congress work? How do bills become law? A good way to start to understand the legislative process is to see it through the eyes of Eric Redman, who in 1971 was 22 years old and just out of college (but still writing his senior essay so that he could get his degree from Princeton). Redman had just gotten a job with Senator Warren Magnuson, a Democrat from Washington, who had been put in charge of a bill to create a national health service corps—the pet project of a pediatrician who was a friend of the senator.[1]

Redman tried to get officials in the Nixon administration to support the bill, but when he could not get their help with a big program, he decided to press for a small "demonstration" project that would put a few dozen doctors from the Public Health Service (PHS) into several communities. Following the advice of some seasoned staffers, Redman explored the possibility of putting such a pilot program into operation without any new legislation by getting the PHS to agree to reallocate some of its funds for the project. However, the Senate's legislative counsel told him that a new law would be needed.

Redman realized that he would have to run the entire legislative gantlet with his little project; this lowered the odds, since only 1 in 20 bills introduced ever passes Congress. Fortunately, Senator Ralph Yarborough, chair of the Education and Labor Committee, agreed to hold hearings because he was incensed that Nixon had threatened to kill the entire PHS as part of a proposed health care reorganization plan: this bill would be a way of signaling Nixon to back down. Unfortunately, however, the Republicans were boycotting the committee because they did not want it to report some other, completely unrelated measure; their boycott meant that no bills would be reported from the committee.

Eventually the boycott ended when Yarborough made a deal with the Republicans on another bill. Redman's measure got through the committee and went to the Senate floor. But when it came up for a vote, both Magnuson and Yarborough were out of town, and there was no senator to act as floor manager for it—to explain its provisions to members in the Senate debate. Magnuson's staff rounded up Senator Peter Dominick, a conservative Republican, who agreed to shepherd it through as a favor to Magnuson. The bill passed, even though most senators had never heard of it before: no one wanted to vote against it and incur Magnuson's wrath, since he chaired the appropriations subcommittee that funded health care and hospitals.

Meanwhile, time was running out; the congressional session was nearly over, and the House committee had yet to hold hearings or report the bill to the full House. Luckily, Paul Rogers, who ran the subcommittee in the House that would consider the measure, needed Magnuson's help on a different bill and was willing to cooperate. The chair of the parent committee, Harley Staggers, was being pressured by medical school students and faculty members in West Virginia to support the bill, and so he too agreed to help. The subcommittee and the committee approved the bill.

Next it went to the House Rules Committee, which had to provide a rule that

set the procedures for debate. Not all bills get rules near the end of the session, but for some reason Nixon pressured the committee to report all its pending measures (so that he could get some of his bills out of committee), and the PHS measure was swept through as well. The next hurdle was the end-of-session traffic jam on the floor. After another long delay the House approved the bill, but in a form slightly different from the Senate's version.

This presented a problem, since all laws must be passed by both chambers with exactly the same wording. With time running out, there was no way to reconcile the two bills, and so Yarborough's Senate committee agreed to accept the House bill, and it was taken directly from the House to the Senate floor and was repassed by the Senate. Congress finally had passed the bill into law.

The bill went to President Nixon within ten days of the scheduled adjournment of Congress; and in that time period, the Constitution permits the president to "pocket veto" a measure. But Nixon had recently used the pocket veto on the Family Practice Act, another health measure, and had touched off a storm of protest. (It seems that he used it while Congress was on vacation, which might have been unconstitutional, since Congress had recessed rather than adjourned.) With members of Congress threatening a lawsuit over presidential power (a case which Senator Edward Kennedy eventually took to the Supreme Court and won), Nixon's political advisers recommended that he not veto another health bill, and so he signed it.

Redman later wrote a book, called *The Dance of Legislation*, about his experiences working on this bill. The "dance" he refers to is the informal whirl of personal motives and friendships, favors given and received, accidents, and luck—all going on in the hectic atmosphere of a congressional office. How Congress actually works is far different from the way the smooth flowcharts in most textbooks describe the "legislative process." In the case of Redman's bill, much depended on personalities, favors, and luck. Had Redman not been on the Senate floor when the bill was suddenly called up (which made it possible for him to get Dominick to act as floor manager), it would have died then and there. Favors and influence (in this case, Dominick's friendship with Magnuson and Roger's need to deal with Magnuson's committee) are at least as important as party and ideology. Bills going through Congress are like canoes shooting the rapids.

**CONGRESS:
THE FIRST BRANCH?**

The Constitution makes Congress the "first branch" of government, and so did the architects of the District of Columbia: Congress meets atop Capitol Hill, which looms over the White House and the executive departments on the mall. From the vantage point of the president and foreign leaders, Congress shares the power to govern: it can check and balance, and every president knows that confrontations with the legislature can weaken or even destroy an administration.

But some observers consider Congress the worst branch. It is "the greatest menace in our country to the successful operation of the democratic process," according to Joseph Clark, a former senator. "It is gutless beyond my power to describe it to you," said one representative.[2] Howard Baker, a former Republican Senate majority leader, proposed that members of Congress get out of town for six months every year to find out what was going on in the country.

A congressman, Les Aspin, at work in Washington. (*Sepp Seitz: Woodfin Camp.*)

And one Cub Scout in Oklahoma, asked by Representative Mike Synar to explain the difference between Congress and the Cub Scouts, replied, "We have adult supervision."[3]

The case against Congress is that it is not responsive enough to the national interest, too responsive to special interests, lazy (it operates on a Tuesday-to-Thursday schedule), slow, and inefficient. It does not operate according to laws it passes: it exempts itself from the Civil Rights Acts, the Equal Pay Act, the National Labor Relations Act, the Fair Labor Standards Act, the Occupational Safety and Health Act, the Social Security Act, the Privacy Act, and the Age Discrimination Act.[4] A majority of the public believes that legislators would take bribes and rates Congress low on lists of important institutions.[5]

Yet most members of Congress are honest, hardworking men and women whose twelve-hour working days leave them little time for a private life. They are on a Capitol Hill treadmill, running from one committee meeting to another, meeting and serving constituents (and traveling back and forth from their home states or districts just about every weekend), supervising their staffs, and responding like Pavlov's dogs to the sound of the bell calling for their presence on the House or Senate floor for a vote. While public approval of Congress declined from 60 percent in 1964 to 20 percent in 1980, most voters rate their own members highly and elect them again and again.[6]

"The Senate and the Congress as a whole is choking on its own processes," says Sam Nunn,[7] a senator from Georgia. Why is Congress—so frustrating and seemingly unworkable to those on the inside—so formidable to presidents and heads of foreign governments? Why is it so slow and cumbersome, and yet also so innovative when it tackles big issues? Why does the public rate it so low as a collective body, and yet think so highly of its individual members? We will consider these questions by focusing on the members and leaders of Congress and on their formal and informal powers. Our concern will be the problem of congressional power: how can legislators—who represent separate geographic jurisdictions and competing interests, are organized into two separate chambers, and are divided into two parties—make Congress work?

ON CAPITOL HILL

There are 535 voting members of Congress. They come to their jobs with different talents, temperaments, and goals. Reconciling their individual goals to fashion lawmaking majorities is what legislative politics is all about.

What legislators want

As soon as legislators are elected, they start to worry about being reelected. House members know that sooner or later one-third of them will be defeated, and so they are understandably nervous. Senators serve for six years, but they are more likely to lose in their next election, and so they also run scared. "The President does not have to run for reelection anymore," Bob Dole, the Senate majority leader, explained to reporters who wanted to know why he announced his intention to oppose much of Reagan's budget plan in 1985, "but a lot of the rest of us do."[8] Legislators look for soft landings if they lose: jobs in the executive branch or as lobbyists or registered agents for foreign governments, positions held by 250 former representatives. For example, Paul Rogers, a former congressman from Florida, monitors bills involving savings and loan institutions; former congressman James Corman represents the Tobacco Institute; and former congressman Jack McDonald lobbies for the American Express Company.[9]

Legislators are hospitable to constituents and important fund-raisers and to PACs who can help them stay in Congress or help them when they leave. They build up hundreds of thousands of dollars in campaign warchests out of contributions from interest groups; members who were elected before 1980 may transfer these funds to their own bank accounts after they retire or fail to win reelection. They are sensitive to ideological groups and single-issue organizations which "scorecard" them and publicize their votes on controversial issues.

Legislative roles

Members must decide on the roles they will play in Congress. Some become *legislative party leaders,* like Jim Wright, the House Democratic *majority leader* from Texas, and Bob Michels, the House Republican *minority leader* from Illinois. They communicate with different factions and leaders, make deals to unite the disparate interests, unify their parties, and tamp down intraparty friction. Others—like Russell Long, a Democratic senator from Louisiana,

Senator Henry "Scoop" Jackson, who was one of the most powerful men in Congress in foreign affairs, advises president-elect Reagan during the transition in 1980. (*AP Laserphoto.*)

and Orrin Hatch, a Republican senator from Utah—become **committee leaders,** whose influence comes from their policy expertise and committee jurisdictions. Other members become *policy experts;* Daniel Moynihan of New York, Sam Nunn of Georgia, and Bill Cohen of Maine, for example, are looked to by others for guidance on policy.

Democratic legislators like Edward Kennedy of Massachusetts and Gary Hart of Colorado and Republicans like Jack Kemp of New York and Robert Dole of Kansas are *presidential hopefuls;* they use Congress as a stage to reach a national audience. *Factional leaders,* like Jesse Helms of North Carolina and Paul Sarbanes of Maryland, seek to move their party to the right or the left. *Gadflies,* such as Lowell Weicker of Connecticut and William Proxmire of Wisconsin, are mavericks who treasure their independence and can raise new issues for the public.

Representative roles

Area representation. Congress represents the "scuffle of local interests," as the journalist Henry Jones Ford put it at the turn of the century, and surveys have shown that almost half the House members would put their local interests ahead of the national interest.[10] "I'm here to represent my district," said one, "What is good for the majority of my district is good for the country. What snarls up the system is those so-called statesmen-congressmen who vote for what they think is the country's best interest." "I've got many, many families in my district who make a living on tobacco," said another, who was about to cast a vote for tobacco subsidies, because "If you don't you aren't going to be around here very long."[11] Yet over half the members weigh national factors when voting, and on the most important issues almost all can rise above their districts.

Functional representation. On issues which are public and on which voters have strong views, some legislators are **delegates;** they simply determine the wishes of some group in their district or in the nation and then vote accordingly. But on many issues they find that their constituents have no views, care little, or are uninformed. Then they may become **trustees** for their constituents: they protect their interests. "Your representative owes you, not his industry only, but his judgment," wrote the British parliamentarian Edmund Burke to his constituents 200 years ago, "and he betrays, instead of serving you, if he sacrifices it to your opinion."[12] Senator Robert Byrd of West Virginia used almost the identical words when he explained to voters in his state why he had defied their wishes and voted for the Panama Canal treaty.

Some legislators are wheeler-dealers, willing to bargain and trade their votes on one issue if this will help their careers and their constituents on another. These **politicos** will "vote the district" on issues that affect their chances for reelection, "vote the conscience" on issues of national security, and trade votes on everything else. Representatives from Texas helped New York City get loan guarantees in the 1970s. "We were very interested in the problems of Brooklyn and the Bronx," recalls Congressman Charles Wilson of Texas, "but we also expected they'd remember." The New York delegation reciprocated on defense and agriculture bills which helped Texas.

Personal representation. Legislators bring their experiences and interests to their work. Cecil Heftel, a representative from Hawaii who was severely

injured in a car crash, later became the sponsor of automobile safety legislation. Paula Hawkins, a senator from Florida, suffered sexual abuse as a child and has fought for laws against child abuse. Senator Edward Kennedy, whose two brothers were assassinated, has sponsored legislation banning handguns. Senator Robert Dole, who was badly wounded and permanently disabled in World War II, fights for aid for the handicapped and veterans.

Interest-group representation. Most legislators have received direct PAC funds, "bundled" funds, or individual contributions stimulated by PAC direct-mail campaigns. Once winners arrive in Washington, however, they are greeted by PACs and by lobbyists who represent labor, corporations, trade associations, and professional groups—close to 20,000 of them. They want access to members of Congress so that they can press for new legislation or block measures that would be harmful to the groups they represent. They can be extremely helpful to members: they do research, draft proposed bills and supporting speeches, make introductions and help new members get the committee assignments they want, and even help new members and their families get oriented to Washington. They invite members on all-expenses-paid trips and give them honorariums (that is, fees) for speaking engagements.

PACs expect members of Congress to represent their interests in committees and to vote for their bills on the floor. The American Medical Association and the American Dental Association gave more than $3 million in campaign contributions to House members just before a vote that would exempt doctors and dentists from certain federal regulations. Used-car dealers gave more than $1 million to overturn a Federal Trade Commission ruling requiring that certain information about used cars be disclosed to potential buyers. Three dairy PACs gave more than $1 million to prevent Congress from removing dairy price supports.[13]

PAC lobbyists argue that they do not trade money for votes, but simply give to members who would be likely to support them anyway. Political scientists have examined these claims, and some have determined that PAC contributions measurably increase the probability that members will vote the way the PAC wishes and that such votes substantially increase the amount of later contributions that PACs make to these members.[14]

Getting along on the Hill

In the past, new members went along with the traditional ways in which their chamber conducted its business; otherwise, they earned reputations as mavericks and outsiders and were frozen out by the leadership. Senior members judged junior members: some were considered thoughtful, hardworking "comers" who would gain powerful mentors; and others were dismissed as lightweights, publicity hounds, or just plain bad news—they would be expected to lose out on good committee assignments, have their pet projects stalled, and be denied advancement. "There are two kinds of congressmen," Carl Hayden was told when he arrived in Washington, "show horses and workhorses. If you want to get your name in the paper, be a showhorse. If you want to gain the respect of your colleagues, keep quiet and be a workhorse."

Today these traditions and norms are less important. New members speak up more and expect to do more early in their first term: they have to, in order to get the media publicity and the PAC contributions they need to be reelected.

There is no longer any real apprenticeship or mentorship on the Hill, and that makes it more difficult than ever for Congress to work effectively.

Specialization. Members of the House are expected to specialize in a few areas, while senators are more likely to be generalists. New representatives are expected to work hard on their committees, provide "language" for bills initially only on minor matters, and master the complicated parliamentary rules according to which the House does its business. They are asked by party leaders to remember Speaker Sam Rayburn's advice: "To get along, go along." Members are supposed to make some sacrifices to help their party pass its programs. "To serve his constituents at home," Rayburn said, a member of Congress "must also serve his colleagues here in the House."[15]

Deference. In the past, senators were expected to wait a year or more before making a "maiden" speech. "You just *had* to talk, didn't you," hissed a colleague to Senator Carl Hayden after his first Senate speech. "Keep your mouth shut for a while," was Senator Hubert Humphrey's advice to Joseph Clark, a newcomer.[16] Today senators arrive on the Hill with their mouths still open from nonstop media campaigning. They get subcommittee chairs within two years (all Republican senators have such assignments) and are assigned important committee responsibilities in their first term. They can become floor managers for important bills. "The point is to get things done," concluded Senator Bill Bradley—no senator wants to remain on the bench while others carry the ball.[17]

At one time, House members were also expected to know their place. "When you pass a committee chairman in the hall, bow low from the waist," John McCormack, the Speaker of the House, told incoming freshmen in the 1960s. But today newcomers bow to no one. Most come from marginal districts and need to make a name for themselves and accomplish something for their districts to solidify their base. They can hire experienced staffers (whose former bosses resigned or were defeated) to get them off to a fast start. They band together with other freshmen to force party leaders to give them decent committee assignments.[18]

Reciprocity. Every member can help a colleague, knowing that sooner or later the favor will be returned. The Republican House leader, Bob Michel, trades favors on scheduling and debate with the Democratic House leader, Jim Wright. Southern tobacco and cotton growers deal on issues of farm benefits with the wheat growers of the midwest and then get urban legislators from northern cities to join with them in return for support on a mass-transit bill. "Milt, I would just like you to tell me how to vote about wheat and sugar beets and things like that," said Senator Sam Ervin of North Carolina to Senator Milton Young of North Dakota one day, "if you just help me out on tobacco and things like that."[19] Senator Gaylord Nelson of Wisconsin, on arriving late to a meeting of the Senate Finance Committee, requested Russell Long, the chairman, to accept an amendment to a bill to give some tax breaks to ferry operators in his state. "I'll be happy to give you that one," Long replied, "but I expect you in exchange to vote for this next tax credit we're about to discuss."[20]

These alliances cross party and ideological lines. Henry Waxman, a liberal House Democrat, and Orrin Hatch, a conservative Republican senator, are

Congress relies on its own staff for technical expertise. Alice Rivlin, then the Congressional budget director, testifies before the Senate Finance Committee. (*UPI; Bettmann Archive.*)

THE UNELECTED CONGRESS: STAFFERS ON THE HILL

There are close to 20,000 legislative and committee staffers: they are the unelected "representatives," and they have a great impact on Congress.[a]

Each representative receives a clerk-hiring allowance of more than $400,000 annually and has fifteen or so workers. Senate allowances are based on state population and range from $600,000 to more than $2 million; the number of employees averages thirty-one. Each committee has approximately thirty staffers, most of whom work for subcommittees. The majority party hires two-thirds of them, and the minority party hires one-third.

Most staffers are under 45, two-thirds are men, and a few are minorities. Half have undergraduate college degrees, one-fifth have M.A.s, and one-tenth have Ph.D.s; half of the staffers in the Senate, and one-fourth of those in the House, are lawyers.

Staffers answer the 40 million letters sent to House members and the 29 million letters sent to senators each year. They do casework for constituents. They prepare newsletters, press releases, and videotapes and audiotapes of their bosses at work. They research and draft bills, negotiate with lobbyists, prepare for hearings, suggest changes in language when bills are revised in committee, and write speeches and drafts of committee reports.

Most legislators rely heavily on their staffers. A 1977 study showed that three-fifths of the House members had staffers give them briefings on their committee work or cue them about how to vote on bills from other committees. Half relied on staffers to brief them on important national issues.[b]

The *neutral professionals* are expert technicians who facilitate the goals of their bosses. The *policy entrepreneurs* have their own agendas. "We see it as part of our job to present alternatives to the senator," said one, "to lay out things before him that he might want to do."[c] "This committee spends most of its time arguing with its own staff," said Senator Robert Griffin, "summing up the negative side of working with ambitious staffers."[d] But staffers have strengthened laws dealing with automobile safety, health, education, consumer protection, and nuclear energy. The neutral professionals, on the other hand, have been closely connected with taxing, appropriations, revenue sharing, and agriculture—matters on which members have clear priorities but need technical expertise. Staffers may be delegated responsibility by a lazy or indifferent legislator, sit in on committees, negotiate and trade for votes, and go off on tangents with their own pet projects. Legislators may become clerks for their own staffers. An informal network of staffers, lobbyists, and officials at the sub-Cabinet level may negotiate their own deals, and sometimes the results are different from what would have been obtained had their bosses been involved. Alternatively, personality conflicts lead to situations in which deals fail because staffers cannot agree, even though their bosses might have come to an understanding. The influence of the unelected representatives is strong, and the problems they pose are serious. But Congress would get far less done without them.[e]

a. Harrison W. Fox and Susan W. Hammond, *Congressional Staffs*, Free Press, New York, 1977, p. 171; Roger Davidson and Walter Oleszek, *Congress and Its Members*, Congressional Quarterly Press, Washington, D.C., 1981, p. 238.
b. David Vogler, *The Politics of Congress*, 4th ed., Allyn and Bacon, Boston, 1983, p. 131.
c. David E. Price, "Professionals and Entrepreneurs: Staff Orientations and Policy Making on Three Senate Committees," *Journal of Politics*, vol. 33, no. 2, May 1971, p. 324.
d. Norris Cotton, *In the Senate*, Dodd, Mead, New York, 1978, p. 67.
e. Michael Malbin, *Unelected Representatives*, Basic Books, New York, 1980.

called "the odd couple" because of their alliance in pushing for health care legislation. Waxman helped Hatch get aid for Utah residents who claimed that their leukemia had been caused by atom bomb tests in the 1950s; Hatch

---

THE CONGRESSIONAL AGENCIES

Congressional Budget Office (CBO). This agency was established in 1974 to give Congress information about tax receipts, department expenditures, and the impact of pending legislation on the federal budget. The CBO also studies and evaluates presidential budget requests and provides alternatives for Congress.

Congressional Research Service (CRS). This agency is part of the Library of Congress. Formerly the Legislative Reference Service, it has been in existence since 1946. Its 400 researchers draft bills for members and work on more than 450,000 questions that they assign annually, preparing over 50,000 studies or briefs.

General Accounting Office (GAO). This agency was created in 1921 as an independent agency accountable to Congress. Its comptroller general is appointed by the president and confirmed by the Senate for a fifteen-year term. The GAO is a watchdog over government expenditures. It conducts field audits of agencies' accounts, suggests improvements in agencies' accounting and auditing procedures, and rules on the legality of government expenditures.

Office of Technology Assessment (OTA). This agency was created in 1972 and assists members of Congress in understanding scientific and technical matters. It drafts bills and conducts policy evaluations at the request of committees. It helps legislators obtain the best scientific advice from outside experts, and it contracts with universities and think tanks for some of its research studies.

---

helped Waxman with a bill that would encourage manufacturers to develop certain new drugs that were not likely to be profitable.

Respect. Most members, especially those who become party leaders, learn to respect their political opponents and stop attacking their motives or their sincerity. "The reality is that there are responsible and often persuasive arguments on both sides of an issue," says Steven Solarz, a representative from Brooklyn, "and that no one has a monopoly on truth and wisdom."[21] Opposing committee and party leaders must work with one another to schedule their business. Sometimes this leads to friendships: Tip O'Neill, the Democratic Speaker of the House, is a golfing companion of Bob Michel, the Republican minority leader; Senator Gary Hart, a Democrat, wrote a detective novel in collaboration with Senator Bill Cohen, a Republican. The web of friendships makes it possible for bipartisan majorities to form.

THE CONGRESSIONAL POWER STRUCTURE

Constitutional leaders

Article I, Section 2, of the Constitution provides that the vice president of the United States is also the president of the Senate—the presiding officer with the power to vote in case of a tie. The president of the Senate may also issue rulings on Senate procedure which can be important in controlling debate. In the absence of the president of the Senate, the chief constitutional officer is the *president pro tem,* who presides over the Senate. Since 1910 the president pro tem has been the most senior member of the majority party (usually turning over the job of presiding to the most junior senators). The president pro tem signs bills sent to the president and appoints senators to serve on conference committees that negotiate the final drafts of bills with the House. The *Speaker of the House* is the constitutional leader of the Senate. The Speaker almost always presides (and rarely votes)—the reverse of the role of the president pro tem of the Senate. The Speaker also signs bills sent to the president and appoints the House members of conference committees.

Congressional leaders enjoy high status at the White House. Bob Michel, the House minority leader, speaks to the press on a compromise worked out with the White House staff on the MX missile. (*UPI; Bettmann Archive.*)

Party leaders

Party leaders include the Speaker of the House, the House majority and minority leaders, and the majority and minority leaders of the Senate. They are chosen by, and remain responsible to, the legislative parties of Congress: House and Senate Republicans and House and Senate Democrats. "When I'm talking about my party," says Speaker Tip O'Neill, "I'm talking about the House [party]."[22] They remain independent of the White House and national party leaders; at the beginning of President Reagan's second term, for example, a moderate group of Republicans took over the party leadership posts in the Senate, and none were beholden to the White House.

Party leaders schedule the business of their chamber and control floor proceedings. They assign bills to committees and try to coordinate the committees' work. They attempt to instill party spirit and loyalty and to round up votes for the party position. They are spokespersons on the nightly news and the talk shows. They serve as intermediaries between the White House and their legislative parties. Some are potential presidential candidates who will try to position themselves for the next nominating season. But they do not control their legislative parties. "You have a hunting license to persuade," according to Jim Wright, the House majority leader; "that's about all you have."[23]

House caucuses and party leaders. The Democrats organize as the House Democratic Caucus, and the Republicans organize as the House Republican Conference—but each party's meeting is known as its *caucus* (Figure 11-1). Membership is open to those elected on the party line and to independents (if any). Members must vote with the party at the beginning of each session, when the House elects the Speaker and the committee chairs and assigns committee members. Otherwise, they are free to vote as they wish.

The leader of the majority caucus becomes the Speaker of the House. In modern times he has always been a senior member, averaging more than twenty years in Congress before his election and serving for an average of six years thereafter. The majority caucus also elects a majority leader (a post created in 1899), who leads the party in floor debates, while the Speaker presides. The minority caucus elects its own minority leader (referred to by the Republicans as the *Republican leader* rather than the *minority leader*).

Each caucus elects a chief whip and various deputy and assistant whips (posts created by the Republicans in 1897 and by the Democrats in 1900); their function is to find out how members intend to vote.

Figure 11-1. Party leaders in the House: (a) Democrats; (b) Republicans. All party committees and leaders are formally chosen by the caucus or conference.

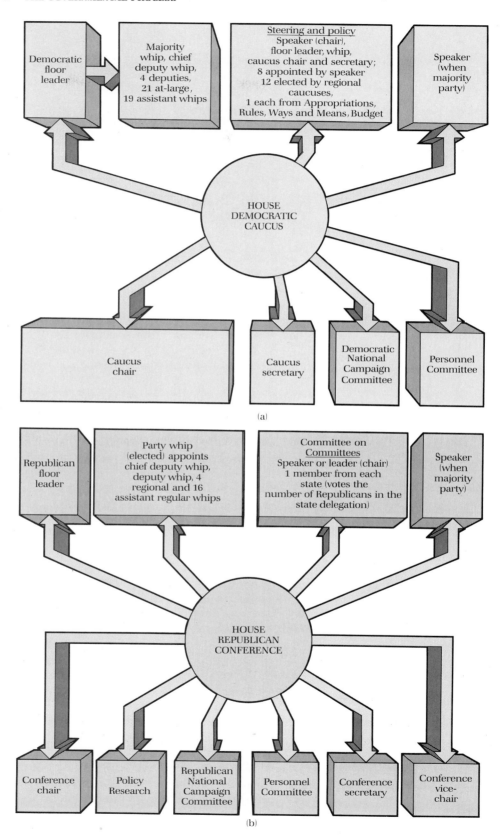

Democratic floor leader

Majority whip, chief deputy whip, 4 deputies, 21 at-large, 19 assistant whips

Steering and policy
Speaker (chair), floor leader, whip, caucus chair and secretary; 8 appointed by speaker 12 elected by regional caucuses, 1 each from Appropriations, Rules, Ways and Means, Budget

Speaker (when majority party)

HOUSE DEMOCRATIC CAUCUS

Caucus chair

Caucus secretary

Democratic National Campaign Committee

Personnel Committee

(a)

Republican floor leader

Party whip (elected) appoints chief deputy whip, deputy whip, 4 regional and 16 assistant regular whips

Committee on Committees
Speaker or leader (chair) 1 member from each state (votes the number of Republicans in the state delegation)

Speaker (when majority party)

HOUSE REPUBLICAN CONFERENCE

Conference chair

Policy Research

Republican National Campaign Committee

Personnel Committee

Conference secretary

Conference vice-chair

(b)

The Democratic caucus has a Steering and Policy Committee; the members are elected by regional caucuses, selected by the Speaker, or sit by virtue of other party office. This committee makes Democratic assignments to legislative committees. House Republicans use a Committee on Committees to make their legislative committee assignments, and they have separate policy and research committees to set their agenda.

FOCUS

SPEAKERS REED AND CANNON Almost a century ago the House engaged in a twenty-year-long experiment in strong party government. Its failure sheds some light on the difficulties that presidents and party leaders have today in getting the House to act according to a party program.

The Speaker—Thomas "Boss" Reed, elected in 1889—changed House rules so that he could control floor debates and end minority-party obstruction of the Republican program. He packed two important committees (Ways and Means and Appropriations) with his allies and controlled the flow of tax and spending favors to the members. He chaired the Rules Committee, which determined procedures for each bill on the floor, and when he came up with an unfair rule, he cheerily informed the Democratic minority: "Gentlemen, we have decided to perpetrate the following outrage." He made all appointments to committees and could remove members if they defied him. His successor, Joe ("Uncle Joe") Cannon, instituted a binding rule in the Republican caucus so that members would vote in committee and on the floor in accordance with caucus instructions. Speaker Cannon also saw that some important bills in a session were passed before making committee assignments, thus forcing members to demonstrate their loyalty.

Both Reed and Cannon acted according to the doctrine of party responsibility. The only function of the minority party was to oppose, and the majority party would not permit it to obstruct the working of the House. The function of the majority party was to govern—to pass laws and make policy and to take the responsibility for the consequences in the next elections. As early as 1891, Albert Hart, a professor at Harvard, commented on this situation, saying that "the Speaker is likely to become, and perhaps is already, more powerful, both for good

Thomas Reed. (*Bettmann Archive.*)   Joe Cannon. (*Bettmann Archive.*)

and for evil, than the President of the United States.[24] In 1896, Mary P. Follett, a political scientist, referred to Reed in her definitive study of the role of the Speaker as the "Speaker-Premier" of government—a clear reference to the power of the British prime minister.[25] Woodrow Wilson, then president of Princeton University, wrote in 1908 that "when matters of legislation are under discussion the country is apt to think of the Speaker as the chief figure in Washington rather than the President."[26]

Eventually public opinion, newspaper editorialists, and many members of Congress turned against "Czar" Cannon. In 1910 a combination of Democrats and disgruntled Republicans staged a revolt and changed some of the House rules to minimize his powers. They also removed him from the Rules Committee. In the subsequent elections, the Democrats became the majority; committed to a weak Speaker system, they gave the power to make committee assignments to their members on the Ways and Means (that is, taxation) Committee. They also made its chairman their floor leader, weakening the Speaker even more, and in 1919 they created a separate majority leader, further diffusing power.[27] Since the 1910 revolt, neither Democrats nor Republicans have tried to institute centralized control or party government in the House.

Senate caucuses and party leaders. Senate Democrats meet as the Democratic Conference (Figure 11-2a). They elect a leader, who chairs the conference, as well as the Policy Committee (made up of nine senators who plot legislative strategy) and the Steering Committee (which consists of twenty-two members who make committee assignments). The conference elects a party whip, but the chief deputy whip and the deputy whips are chosen by the leader.

The Republicans use collective leadership (Figure 11-2b): their conference elects a leader, but he or she does not chair any other committees. Instead, the conference elects a chair, who chooses a seventeen-member Committee on Committees (with its own chair), which makes legislative committee assignments. A Policy Committee (with its own chair), develops legislative strategy.

Power and influence of party leaders. Leaders do not have formal powers which enable them to dominate the legislative parties. They do not control committee assignments or choose committee or subcommittee chairs. The party caucuses cannot bind members to vote the "party line" on pending bills. Both parties used such rules only briefly—the Republicans between 1890 and 1910, and the Democrats between 1911 and 1915. Leaders can influence their party Committee on Committees when they make assignments. They can make newcomers their protégés, as Senator Robert Kerr did with Lyndon Johnson and as Speaker Tip O'Neill did with Geraldine Ferraro. They can make a member's priority their own and bring it to the caucus. They can intercede with the White House and get someone a favor. They can introduce members to important lobbyists and PAC managers who might fund their future campaigns. And, like the president, they can offer *favor*—they can reward those who work with them.

Party leaders rely mostly on influence rather than pressure. "You can't do those things by arm-twisting. I don't believe in that. You have to reason with them," says Tip O'Neill.[28] And so he reasons group by group, though he admits

Figure 11-2. Party leaders in the Senate: (a) Democrats; (b) Republicans. The Republican conference chooses all the party leaders. The Democratic conference chooses the majority or minority leader, who then select most other party leaders.

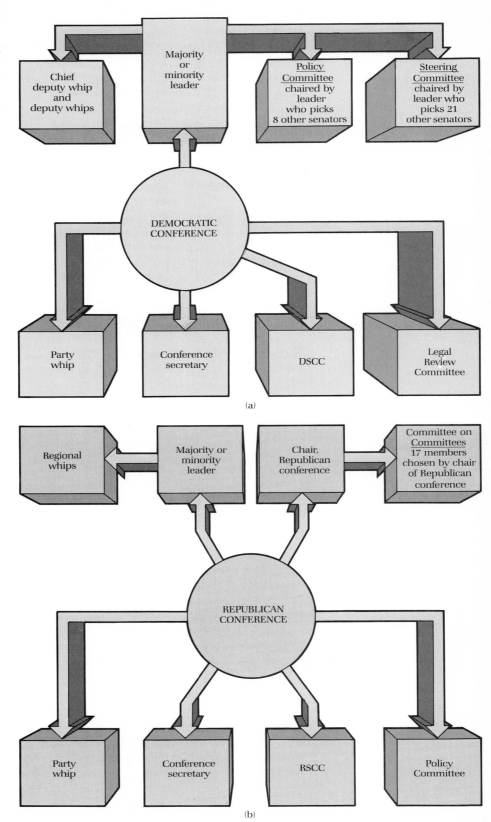

that "in any other country in the world, the Democrats would be five different parties." "I've never even once threatened to punish a member," says Ted Stevens, a former Senate Republican whip. "We probably don't even have the power to do so if we wanted to."[29] Influence comes more through force of personality than through formal powers. Lyndon Johnson was a master of persuasion. He knew everybody's weaknesses and strengths. "The treatment," which was administered in the Senate cloakroom, on the Senate floor, or in his office, was "an almost hypnotic experience and rendered the target stunned and helpless," according to reporters who observed its effects.[30] Johnson was a tireless negotiator and a shrewd compromiser. Yet even he could not control his colleagues: he was a protégé of a small clique of senior senators who had chosen him to handle their exhausting chores. Often it was their public backing for a bill that convinced hesitant colleagues to go along.

Although Johnson was successful, he was no better—as measured by the percentage of senators who supported the party and by the percentage of bills passed—than his low-key successor, Mike Mansfield, who relied on mild persuasion.[31] The success of Howard Baker (another mild-mannered leader on the Republican side) in the 1980s shows that more than one style of party leadership can work.

Committees and their leaders

"It is not far from the truth," Woodrow Wilson wrote a century ago, "to say that Congress in session in its Committee rooms is Congress at work."[32] All the 10,000 to 20,000 bills introduced in Congress are immediately referred to one of the House and one of the Senate standing committees, which can take the following actions:

- Conduct *hearings* so that officials in the executive branch, interest-group lobbyists, and academic experts can offer opinions or suggest amendments.
- Hold *markup* sessions, at which time (by majority vote) committee members can rewrite a bill or even substitute a completely new version.
- Write and submit to Congress a *report* discussing a proposal, complete with minority and dissenting views.

Committee members lead the floor debate, for or against a measure, when it is considered by the entire chamber. They work with party leaders to round up votes for their position, briefing members who are unfamiliar with the issues. Some serve on the Conference Committee, which reconciles the versions passed by each chamber and reports back a single version to be repassed in identical language before being sent to the president.

There are twenty-two standing committees in the House and sixteen in the Senate. In addition, there are three Senate and four House select committees, which may study issues and report to Congress but which do not handle legislation. (There are also four joint committees, two of which study economic and tax issues, and two of which handle the Government Printing Office and the Library of Congress.)

The committees are composed of subcommittees: 103 in the Senate and 144 in the House, as of 1985. They do the preliminary work on measures referred to full committees; increasingly, they hold the hearings and draft the report, and the full committee modifies their initiatives. Representatives serve on an average of 1.7 committees and 4 subcommittees, while senators serve on an av-

HOUSE AND SENATE COMMITTEES

House committees

Rules: Gives each bill reported to the floor a "rule" specifying the procedures for debate. It is an arm of the majority caucus and leadership.

Five major committees

Ways and Means: Handles all revenue measures and funding for many important programs which do not require appropriations.
Appropriations: Handles all appropriations bills, which fund about half of all government agencies.
Budget: Reports resolutions which set taxing and spending targets for the federal budget.
Armed Services: Handles all bills involving the military, including base construction and weapons procurement.
Foreign Affairs: Handles the foreign aid program, the State Department, and international agreements.

Other important committees

Education and Labor
Science and Technology
Judiciary
Agriculture
Banking, Finance, and Urban Affairs
Energy and Commerce
Merchant Marine and Fisheries
Public Works and Transportation
Interior and Insular Affairs

Minor committees

Veterans Affairs
Small Business
Government Operations
Post Office and Civil Service
District of Columbia
Standards of Official Conduct
House Administration

Select committees

On Aging
On Children, Youth and Families
On Intelligence
On Narcotics Abuse and Control

Senate committees

Five major committees

Finance: Handles revenue measures and funding for programs that do not require appropriations.
Appropriations: Funds about half of all government agencies through appropriations bills.
Budget: Reports resolutions which set taxing and spending targets for the federal budget.
Armed Services: Legislates on the military services.
Foreign Relations: Has jurisdiction over treaties, nomination of ambassadors and important national security officials, foreign aid programs, and the State Department.

Other important committees

Labor and Human Resources
Commerce, Science and Transportation
Judiciary
Agriculture
Banking, Housing and Urban Affairs
Energy and Natural Resources
Environment and Public Works

Minor committees

Small Business
Governmental Affairs
Rules and Administration
Veterans Affairs

Select committees

On Ethics
On Indian Affairs
On Intelligence

Special committee

On Aging

erage of 2.3 committees and 8.1 subcommittees. Because they have fewer assignments, House members are better able to specialize.

Party control of committees. Since the 1830s all committees have been controlled by the majority party in the chamber—even if the other party has controlled the White House—and the majority party determines how many seats are allocated to each party. The ratio of Republican to Democratic committee members follows the party ratio in the chamber: if there are sixty Republicans and forty Democrats in the Senate, Republicans will constitute 60 percent of most committees. On important committees the majority party sometimes increases the ratio to ensure its control even if one or two of its members defect. The majority party also gives itself a disproportionate number of subcommittee seats, and it chairs every subcommittee.

Committee assignments. Once the ratios have been determined, each legislative party makes its own committee assignments, which are rubber-stamped by Congress. The White House and the national party committees have no influence. Moreover, committee members are almost never dropped or reassigned from one committee to another without their consent (this has not happened since 1853 in the Senate and since 1870 in the House), which means that neither the president nor any party leader can discipline members by threatening to take away their committee seats.[33]

To get on a committee (or to be reassigned to a better one), a member puts in a request to the legislative party's Committee on Committees, just before the new Congress convenes. In making assignments, the Committee on Committees heavily weighs ***chamber seniority***—years of uninterrupted service in the House or Senate. The committee also tries to accommodate party leaders, who want members (preferably from safe seats) who will vote with the party. Committee chairs also have their favorites. Lobbyists push for members who are sympathetic to their causes. They remind the committee how useful their PACs have been in previous elections. Seats are denominated by geographic *zones* so that no more than two members from the same zone may serve on a committee in the House. About two-fifths of the seats on committees are informally reserved for particular states by past custom: for example, New York always gets a seat on the taxing and spending committees, while members from western states always get assignments to committees dealing with water and public lands.

The "freshman class" always pressures the committee for good assignments. When control of the Senate shifts from one part to the other, freshmen from the new majority party get better assignments than at other times.[34] Otherwise they take whatever they can get. In 1979 James Shannon of Massachusetts, a freshman, got on the Ways and Means Committee, a plum assignment, in part because he had written his master's thesis in political science on Tip O'Neill, the Speaker of the House. Another freshman—Robert Mrazek, a Democrat from New York—went in to see the Speaker in 1983 to ask about getting on the Appropriations Committee. O'Neill told him that the committee would never assign a freshman, but then asked whom he had defeated to get to the House. Mrazek replied, "LeBoutillier," a Republican who had once compared Tip O'Neill to the federal budget, saying that they were both "fat, bloated, and out of control." Later, according to a member of the Committee on Committees,

O'Neill kept saying, "He beat LeBoutillier, he beat LeBoutillier"—and the freshman got his committee assignment!

Committee lineups. Party lineups mean less than the ideologies of the members or the interests they represent. Some committees, such as the House Education and Labor Committee and the House Foreign Affairs Committee, are dominated by liberals. Others, such as the House Appropriations Committee and the House Ways and Means Committee, are dominated by conservatives and moderates. Republicans control both the Senate Foreign Relations Committee and the Senate Armed Services Committee, but the former is run by moderates and liberals, and the latter is run by conservatives, which means that the two committees often square off against each other.

Members of committees dealing with agriculture, public works, water projects, and natural resources usually work closely with interest groups and career bureaucrats to get projects and services for their constituents and contracts or changes in the laws for their local companies—and their interests usually cross party and ideological lines. Some committees work in a very

---

COMMITTEE ASSIGNMENTS IN CONGRESS

House Democrats. Requests for assignments and reassignments go to the Steering and Policy Committee, which is chaired by the Speaker. Every member must receive at least one good committee assignment. The list of proposed assignments is accepted or rejected by the entire Democratic caucus at the beginning of the congressional session.

Committee chairs and the subcommittee chairs of the Appropriations Committee are nominated by the Steering and Policy Committee, almost always on the basis of seniority. Nominations are voted on by the Democratic caucus.

Other subcommittee chairs are elected by the Democrats on the parent committee. No member may chair more than one subcommittee on each committee.

The Speaker selects the Democratic members and the chair of the Rules Committee.

House Republicans. Requests for assignments and reassignments go to the Committee on Committees, which is chaired by the Republican leader. Its Executive Committee makes nominations, which are approved by the committee and then by the Republican House Policy Committee.

Ranking minority members of committees and subcommittees (or chairs) are chosen on the basis of seniority. The House Republican Conference approves the nominations by secret ballot.

Senate Democrats. Requests for assignments and reassignments go to the Steering Committee. Each Democrat must receive one good committee assignment before any senator receives a second good committee assignment. The Democratic Conference approves all nominations.

The ranking Democrat (or chair) is selected according to the rule of seniority, subject to approval by the conference if one-fifth of the members request a vote.

Senate Republicans. Requests for assignments and reassignments go to the Committee on Committees, whose members are appointed by the chair of the Republican Conference. Members receive preference according to seniority. No member may serve on more than one of the "big four" (Appropriations, Armed Services, Finance, and Foreign Relations) until all others who have applied are accommodated.

The chairs (or ranking minority members) are chosen on the basis of seniority. Nominations are subject to vote by committee Republicans.

Table 11-1. Seniority in the House, 1881 to 1963

Congressional sessions	Percentage of positions as chair in which seniority rule was not followed
1881–1889	60.4
1891–1899	49.4
1901–1909	19
1911–1919	30
1921–1929	26
1931–1939	23
1941–1949	14
1951–1963	0.7

Source: Data reworked from Nelson Polsby et al., "The Growth of the Seniority System in the U.S. House of Representatives", *American Political Science Review*, vol. 53, no. 3, September 1969, table 1, p. 792.

partisan fashion (usually liberal Democrats confront conservative Republicans), while others have always worked in a bipartisan spirit (usually moderate Republicans and Democrats hold the balance of power). And when it comes to getting "goodies" from the government, conservative legislators like Barry Goldwater and Jesse Helms are just as likely as liberals to feed at the federal trough. In fact, in 1985 Helms refused to accept the position of chair of the Senate Foreign Relations Committee (where he could have advanced his principles) so that he could remain chairman of the Senate Agriculture Committee (where he could advance the interests of the tobacco industry in his home state).

Committee leadership. Committees are always chaired by a member of the majority party. Other leaders include the ranking majority member (next in line to be chair) and the ranking minority member (who would become chair if his or her party controlled the chamber). If you examine a committee roster, you will notice that all Democrats are ranked on one side and that all Republicans are ranked on the other, according to *committee seniority:* years of uninterrupted service on the committee. *Chamber* seniority gets people on a committee, but only *committee* seniority gets them ahead within the committee. Someone with twenty years of chamber seniority starts at the bottom when going on a new committee.

Usually the position of chair is assigned according to strict committee seniority, a practice known as ***seniority rule*** (Table 11-1). In most cases, subcommittee chairs are also assigned on the basis of seniority, with high-ranking members most likely to be chosen by other committee members or by the party caucus.[35] Since 1921 the Senate has used the seniority rule for assigning most chairs (before that time, chairs were appointed by the president of the Senate, by the president pro tem, by the entire Senate, or on the basis of chamber seniority). In the House, the rule gradually took hold between 1880 and 1950.

ISSUE AND DEBATE

THE SENIORITY SYSTEM. *The background.* The seniority system favors legislators from states or districts that do not have a competitive two-party system, because they can be elected time and time again and accumulate more and more chamber and committee seniority. "We pick 'em young, we pick 'em honest, and we send 'em back," is how Speaker Sam Rayburn described the way so many Texans became chairs from the 1930s through the 1960s, when Texas was a one-party state. Up until the 1970s, southern Democrats had far more than their proportional share of positions as chairs, which gave Congress a conservative cast. But these things change: by the 1980s western Republicans were having their turn in the Senate, and northern liberals and minorities in the House were benefiting from their seniority (William Gray, a black representative, became chairman of the powerful House Budget Committee, for example), while the proportion of chairs controlled by the south plummeted as a result of the emergence of a two-party system and the retirement and death of many elderly southern members.

The cons. The seniority system may be ideologically unrepresentative. Conservatives from the south had a disproportionate amount of influence in the 1950s; in the 1980s, a minority of moderate Republican senators have had much more influence than a majority of their more conservative (but junior in terms of seniority) colleagues. When the country shifts direction, Congress is likely to lag.

The seniority system retards political change. The most powerful leaders in Congress now come from the least competitive districts. They won their first elections one or two decades ago, and they represent the political currents of the past. The freshmen, who are more attuned to changes in the electorate and are more likely to have won in competitive districts by being responsive to new ideas, are relegated to the bottom of the congressional power structure. When women and people from religious, racial, and ethnic minorities gain more representation in Congress, their legislators also start at the bottom. Nader's Raiders (a group affiliated with Ralph Nader, a consumer activist) referred to the seniority system as the "senility system" because it keeps elderly members in important positions long after they are past their prime. "It is tired, it is old, it is insane," was how John Rhodes, the House Republican leader, characterized it.[36]

The pros. The seniority rule helps preserve the cohesion and autonomy of the legislative party. It dispenses formal leadership positions on committees in a clockwork, automatic fashion. There are no contests or jockeying for position by committee rivals when the rule is fully in effect. Moreover, the selection of leaders is no longer bound up with the election of the Speaker or of Senate party leaders, as was the case in the nineteenth century. Congress is no longer torn apart at the beginning of each session by ambitious members struggling to become chairs. Most important, presidents have no influence in the selection of committee leaders. They must work with whomever the rule generates as leaders in the next congressional session. The combination of chamber and committee seniority rules gives the president almost no influence in distributing the coveted prizes to legislators, and this preserves their autonomy in the face of pressure from the White House.

The 1970s reforms in the seniority rule. Rules changes in the 1970s made seniority leaders more responsive to the party caucuses. Since 1975, committee and subcommittee chairs have been voted on by the party caucuses (or by party members of the committee involved). "Chairmen are not serving by divine right," the reformer Jack Bingham observed after the rules change, "but as representatives of the caucus."[37] They now follow the caucus priorities and policies and are not likely to obstruct the party leaders. While most assignments are still made on the basis of the seniority rule, in 1975 House Democrats removed three chairs from their posts because they had abused their power, violated committee procedures, or were out of touch with their members.[38] Later, two others who were involved in sex scandals resigned because of pressure from party leaders. Several subcommittee chairs were removed from their posts in 1977 and 1983 for conduct unbecoming a member, and in 1985 Melvin Price, the elderly chair of the House Armed Services Committee, was replaced by the caucus with seventh-ranked Les Aspin, a strong critic of waste in the Pentagon.

Power of committee chairs. Until recently, chairs reigned supreme. "You can go to hell," the chairman of the Rules Committee once told his colleagues; "it makes no difference what a majority of you decide; if it meets with my disapproval, it shall not be done. I am the committee."[39] Chairs set meeting times, convened or adjourned committees at will, controlled the workload and the agenda, set priorities, and determined which bills would be taken up. They appointed the entire staff, created subcommittees, defined their jurisdiction, and appointed their members.[40]

Chairs used their power to exchange favors and keep junior members in

line. They could bargain with the president for favors, since they controlled a "choke point" through which the president's program had to pass. They dominated Cabinet departments in the same way, with jurisdiction over their authority and their funds. "Uncle Carl" Vinson, who served for half a century in the House as chairman of the Armed Services Committee, used to ask generals, "Boy, what did you say your name was?" when they testified before him. "I'd rather run the Pentagon from up here," was the way he put it when declining offers to serve as secretary of defense.[41] NASA even had to allow Jake Garn, a Republican senator from Utah, to fly in the space shuttle simply because he headed the subcommittee which had jurisdiction over NASA's budget.

Committee leaders controlled (and could deliver) their committees, and the committees in turn could usually deliver the votes in the chamber to pass a bill. The president had to deal with only a few party and committee leaders. All this has changed. Committee chairs are now responsive to their committee members and to party caucuses, who can replace them if they are abusive or obstructive. Committee majorities now make the rules, set the agenda, and determine priorities. Chairs cannot keep junior members in line; they must bargain with them and trade for favors. Chairs no longer can automatically deliver their committees. It does presidents no good to bargain just with a chair; they must obtain the backing of a majority of the committee.

Subcommittee government.   The number of subcommittees has increased. They have their own budgets, jurisdiction, and staff. In 1973 the House Democrats wrote a Subcommittee Bill of Rights, which guarantees their right to receive bills from committees and requires committees to take up their reports. Since 1971 subcommittee chairs have had the right to manage bills on the floor of the House, and they are now the floor leaders on two-thirds of the bills reported out of the full committee.[42] The subcommittee chairs and ranking minority members are no longer selected by the committee leaders, but instead are chosen either by the legislative caucus (through its Committee on Committees) or by party members on the parent committee. They cannot be removed by the committee chair (although they can be replaced by committee members or the party caucus). Committee chairs no longer control the subcommittees. Often a subcommittee obtains a majority for its own proposal and gets it to the floor against the wishes of the committee chair.

Subcommittees make it difficult for the White House to influence the legislative agenda. Work is conducted by 250 subcommittees, each of which jealously guards its independence. "We're becoming a mobocracy," is how John LoFalce, a Democrat from New York, put it; "the leadership has . . . said to its members, do your own thing."[43] The committee government of the past has become today's subcommittee government, which is free-lance government, as individual legislators go whichever way their spirit and their staff aides move them.[44] A subcommittee chair becomes a soapbox for junior members—a way for them to conduct hearings and get a twenty-second spot on the network news or a local station.

POWERS OF CONGRESS

This section considers what Congress does—that is, its formal and informal powers.

Legislative powers

Article I of the Constitution grants Congress substantial powers—"all legisla-

tive powers herein granted"—and Section 8 of that article enumerates seventeen specific powers. The eighteenth clause gives Congress the power "to make all laws which shall be necessary and proper for carrying into execution the foregoing Powers, and all other Powers vested by this Constitution in the Government of the United States, or any Department or Officer thereof."

This so-called elastic clause allows Congress to make laws that are necessary and proper to execute *its own powers*. But it also lets Congress pass laws that are necessary and proper for *the other two branches*—the presidency and the judiciary—to operate. It establishes the lower court system. It establishes and funds the Executive Office of the President. It delegates authority to the executive branch. It creates and funds the departments of government.

Policy innovation

Congress can pass the president's program intact, make major changes, or reject parts of it. Although the administration does not have formal control over the congressional calendar, its important measures are always considered by committees, and party leaders usually see that they are taken up within a reasonable time. Yet only during the initial "honeymoon" phase of the presidency or in a national emergency do bills go through Congress without substantial change. Usually bills are thoroughly "marked up" by committees and are further amended on the floor.

Congress must reauthorize existing programs, and that in turn usually means substantial amendment. Even in the case of programs that are initially proposed by the president, such as the "war on poverty" of 1964 and the Voting Rights Act of 1965, two decades of congressional action are likely to convert them into laws which mirror congressional priorities. Presidents and Cabinet secretaries often use national agenda politics to obtain a national consensus for a new program, but long after the media and the public have lost interest, legislators reshape the laws for their own purposes.

Congress may also pass its own measures. Many important bills—such as the National Labor Relations Act, the Taft-Hartley labor law, national pensions legislation, and environmental protection and consumer safety measures—originated in Congress. Sometimes Congress has "incubated" an idea for a substantial time, holding hearings without taking action, until a new president picked it up and made it part of his program. Much of John Kennedy's "new frontier," including the Peace Corps, had been developed by congressional Democrats in the four years preceding his term. Similarly, Reagan's 1981 supply-side tax cuts and his proposals for a flat tax in 1985 were originated by House Republicans.

Informal checks

Congress can use the threat of legislation to get executive officials to respond to its wishes. It can threaten to hold controversial hearings to get them to delay or modify decisions. It can hold hearings which become media events and influence the national agenda. Committees can conduct full-scale investigations (on the basis of the necessary and proper clause) which can put the president on the defensive; they can force resignations (the Senate Select Committee on Campaign Activities that investigated Watergate-related crimes forced the resignation of four top Nixon staffers, for example) or policy shifts (such as the 1983 housecleaning in the Environmental Protection Agency); and they can provide a legislator with a springboard for a future presidential race (for example, Jack Kennedy's investigation of labor unions and Lyndon John-

Senators Sam Ervin (D.-N. C.) and Howard Baker (R.-Tenn) examine a letter from the Nixon White House as other senators and staffers look on, during the Judiciary Committee's investigation of Watergate crimes. (*J. P. Laffont: Sygma.*)

son's hearings on defense preparedness were useful in their 1960 presidential nomination bids).

Congressional headline hunters can abuse their power. In the 1950s Senator Joe McCarthy, a Republican from Wisconsin, charged that communists had infiltrated the State Department and the Army. His Permanent Investigations Subcommittee smeared the reputation of many loyal Foreign Service and Army officers without uncovering any evidence of communist subversion. Senators who spoke out against his lie and smear tactics (which made the word *McCarthyism* part of the American political vocabulary) were defeated for reelection after he campaigned against them in 1952. An intimidated President Eisenhower allowed McCarthy to control the personnel policies of the State Department, leading to the resignations of some of the most able career diplomats. Eventually McCarthy attacked the secretary of the Army in televised hearings, and public opinion turned against him when he failed to produce any evidence. The Senate ultimately censured McCarthy for "conduct unbecoming to the Senate," and he died a few years later, a broken and powerless outcast.

Censure and impeachment: Checks and checkmate

Either chamber may vote a resolution of **censure** against the president or any other official, although there is no mention of this power in the Constitution. President Jackson was censured by the Senate after removing Treasury Secretary Duane from office. After Jackson left office, his supporters got the Senate to expunge the resolution. His censure played a major part in the formation of the pro-Jackson Democratic Party and the anti-Jackson Whig Party. A House committee censured President Tyler for vetoing several bills. President Buchanan was censured by the House for alleged bribery involving a federal appointment. In each case the opposition used the censure to score political

points, and the president argued that censure was unconstitutional and challenged Congress to impeach him.

The process. Although no president has ever been removed from office, impeachment has been used successfully against several federal judges. First, a resolution of impeachment is introduced by a member of the House and is referred to the House Judiciary Committee. The House must approve committee hearings. The committee then drafts and votes articles of impeachment, laying out its charge. It sends them, together with a report, to the House, which debates the charges and by majority vote can adopt one or more of them. Andrew Johnson was the only president ever to be impeached; Richard Nixon would have been the second, had he not resigned.

Once the House has voted to impeach, it appoints five managers (that is, prosecutors) who read the articles to the Senate, which then conducts a trial; the members of the Senate serve as the "jury," and if the case is against the president the chief justice of the Supreme Court presides as the "judge." The House managers and the counsel for the official who is being impeached can submit legal briefs, call witnesses and cross-examine them, and enter evidence. After the trial, each article is voted on separately. If two-thirds of the senators present vote for any of them, the official is convicted and removed from office. (In the trial of a president, the vice president of the United States would then be brought immediately into the chamber after the voting to take the presidential oath.)

Grounds for impeachment. Both Andrew Johnson and Richard Nixon argued that grounds for impeachment must be limited to serious federal crimes. The Republicans and the Democrats reversed their positions in the two proceedings: in the Johnson case, the Republicans argued that *abuse of power* (which might not involve a criminal violation) could be grounds for impeach-

The Senate has been called the "most exclusive club in the world." Like a club, it is mostly self-policing. Senator Joseph McCarthy (left) was eventually censured for intemperate conduct during his anti-Communist hearings in the 1950s. (*UPI; Bettmann Archive.*)

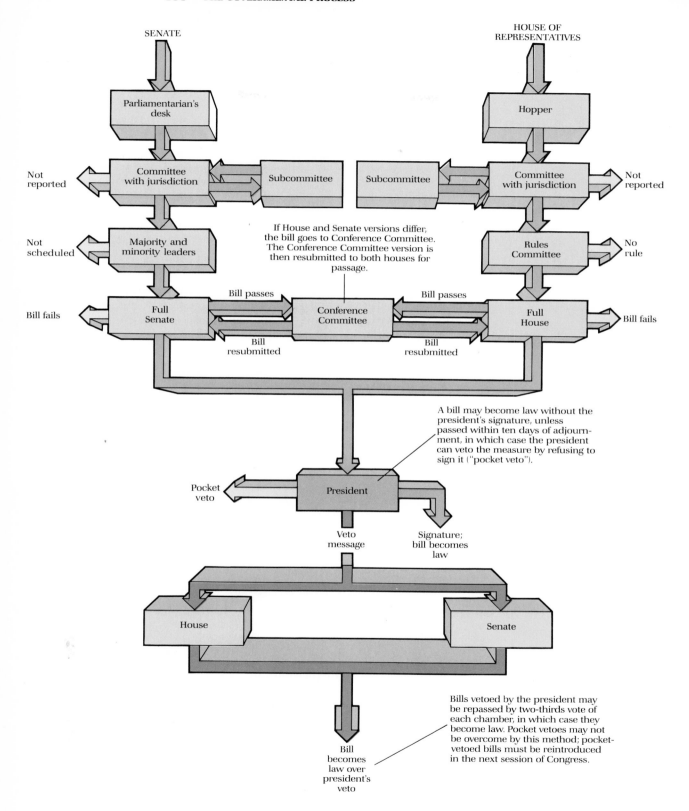

SENATE

HOUSE OF
REPRESENTATIVES

Parliamentarian's
desk

Hopper

Not
reported

Committee
with jurisdiction

Subcommittee

Subcommittee

Committee
with jurisdiction

Not
reported

Not
scheduled

Majority and
minority leaders

If House and Senate versions differ,
the bill goes to Conference Committee.
The Conference Committee version is
then resubmitted to both houses for
passage.

Rules
Committee

No
rule

Bill fails

Full
Senate

Bill passes

Conference
Committee

Bill passes

Full
House

Bill fails

Bill
resubmitted

Bill
resubmitted

A bill may become law without the
president's signature, unless
passed within ten days of adjournment, in which case the president
can veto the measure by refusing to
sign it ("pocket veto").

Pocket
veto

President

Veto
message

Signature;
bill becomes
law

House

Senate

Bills vetoed by the president may
be repassed by two-thirds vote of
each chamber, in which case they
become law. Pocket vetoes may not
be overcome by this method; pocket-
vetoed bills must be reintroduced
in the next session of Congress.

Bill
becomes
law over
president's
veto

After the House had exercised its power to impeach a president for the first and only time, in 1868, President Andrew Johnson was summoned to trial by the Senate, where conviction failed by one vote. (*Granger Collection.*)

ment; later, when Nixon was involved, they reversed themselves. The Democrats, who defended Johnson by demanding evidence of a crime, later argued that Nixon could be impeached without having violated federal law. *Abuse of power* is a vague term. A congressional majority could remove a president whose policies it disagreed with. But thus far, Congress has acted responsibly.

THE LEGISLATIVE STRUGGLE

Now that we know something about life on the Hill, the power structure, and the formal powers of Congress, we can consider the legislative process: the sequence of events from the introduction of a bill to its final passage (Figure 11-3).

The process

Figure 11-3. Opposite: How a bill becomes a law. How bills are introduced, dealt with by committees and party leaders, considered by each chamber and sent to conference, and finally sent to the president for signature or veto. The actual progress of any particular bill is likely to diverge significantly from this chart, and most bills never make it all the way to final passage.

Referral to committee. Bills are drafted by members (or by their aides, with the assistance of congressional agencies or the House or Senate legislative counsel). They are dropped into the House hopper, a mahogany box at one end of the Speaker's desk, or are put on the desk of the Senate parliamentarian (the Senate employee who advises the presiding officer during debate). Party leaders then refer bills to the committee with jurisdiction. In some cases the choice may be crucial; in 1964, for example, civil rights measures were sent to the Judiciary Committee in the House but to the Commerce Committee in the Senate because the Senate Judiciary Committee would have killed them. In 1978 energy legislation went to several House committees for preliminary work and were then referred to a select committee dominated by House Democratic leaders, who put together a comprehensive package.

Subcommittees conduct hearings and report back to the full committee,

391

usually taking a leading role in revising the language of the bill in the committee, when it marks up the bill line by line and makes revisions, by majority vote. The bill is then reported to the chamber, accompanied by a printed report expressing majority and minority views.

Scheduling in the House and Senate. In the House, bills reported by committees must go to the Rules Committee, which since 1961 has been an arm of the majority party leadership and whose members are appointed by the Speaker, where they are given a special rule governing debate. An *open rule* allows members to amend the measure on the House floor; a *closed rule* restricts amendments to members of the committee with jurisdiction. Most rules provide for no more than two hours of debate. The Speaker of the House then schedules debate (in consultation with the minority leader) and the vote for final passage. In the Senate the majority leader schedules legislation by working out *unanimous-consent* agreements with the minority leader; these suspend the formal Senate rules (which usually provide for unlimited debate) and replace them with ad hoc rules that move the bill along much faster.

Senate filibusters. In theory, senators have the right of unlimited speech, though in practice they usually abide by unanimous-consent agreements and limit their remarks. Occasionally one or more senators who strongly oppose a measure will *filibuster:* they require the Senate to abide by its rule that a senator who has the floor need not relinquish it, and they make extended speeches, hoping to force the leadership to drop consideration of a measure. A filibuster can be ended only if three-fifths of the senators vote for *cloture* (an end to debate). Cloture was first used in 1919 in a filibuster against the Treaty of Versailles and was later employed in the 1950s and 1960s when southerners filibustered against civil rights bills. In the past two decades liberals such as Howard Metzenbaum have filibustered to protest energy and environmental legislation favoring business. Gary Hart filibustered against the MX missile to boost his presidential chances. There were thirty votes to impose cloture between 1981 and 1985, cast so that the Senate could continue to function.

Each senator's privilege of almost unlimited speaking time—the filibuster—can make for long nights in the Senate when an issue is hotly contested. (*George Tames: New York Times.*)

Debate and amendment. Congressional debate sometimes strongly influences the final version of a bill. Often provisions are poorly drafted or are ambiguous. The sponsors and the floor managers can discuss the language and explain what is means or how the bill might apply in specific circumstances. These discussions become part of the *legislative history* of a bill: along with hearings and the reports, they are used by judges and administrators to determine how the law should be applied.

Usually the committee supports *friendly amendments* which clarify the language of a bill, strengthen its provisions, or add to its roster of supporters. *Christmas tree amendments* are put on measures to give legislators and their constituents presents (such as tax loopholes), and this ensures the necessary votes for passage. *Unfriendly amendments* are put on if opponents try to gut a measure, limit its scope or duration, or make it unworkable. Some amendments are designed to split the majority by introducing extraneous issues. Opponents of a bill vote with one group of its supporters to tack on an amendment that another group opposes strongly; then they join with the second group to kill the whole measure. In 1919, for example, the Senate killed the Treaty of Versailles and kept the United States out of the League of Nations. Opponents of the treaty combined with a group that favored it and put some reservations into the treaty draft; an infuriated President Wilson then asked his supporters to vote against the whole treaty with its unacceptable amendments, and this group, combined with the antitreaty group, killed the entire bill.

Final motions. The final maneuvering comes after a bill has been amended. First, opponents make a motion to recommit the bill to its original committee. This is actually a vote to kill the bill, even though it looks like a mere procedural vote. If the motion fails, the next vote is for final passage. This twofold system allows people who tried to kill a popular measure to get on the bandwagon and vote for final passage. Thus members can have it both ways: first they get a chance to defeat a bill on a procedural vote, which most voters will never know about; but if that fails, they can support a popular bill.

Conference. Since the House and Senate usually pass different versions of the same bill, they must reconcile the differences. Sometimes a bill passed by one chamber is voted on by the other chamber (even without full committee consideration) if the session is ending. Otherwise, each chamber appoints members to a ***conference committee:*** an ad hoc group which meets to iron out the differences and come up with a single version. The committee need not limit itself to reconciling the language of the two versions. It can write new provisions which had not previously been considered by either chamber—a practice used extensively in 1981 and 1982 in connection with tax and spending measures. The committee can modify, compromise on, or even remove language which both chambers had previously agreed to. At this stage the president has a last chance to threaten to use the veto, which is sometimes effective in getting the conference committee to modify a bill to meet the president's objections.

The conference report. The conference committee produces a single bill—known as the ***conference report***—which is sent back to each chamber to be

voted up or down (but which cannot be amended). If both chambers approve the conference report, the bill is signed by the Speaker of the House and the president pro tem of the Senate and is sent to the White House.

Politics of the legislative process

The above description of the sequence of events is not an accurate picture of what really goes on in Congress. During every session, between 10,000 and 20,000 bills are introduced, and fewer than 1000 are enacted into law. Many bills are introduced without any expectation that they will be passed. The most important function of Congress is to bury proposed legislation, and the committees are the graveyards. Important administration measures are considered, but the pet projects of individual legislators are dealt with on a reciprocal basis. A subcommittee may take up a measure in return for a member's vote on a completely unrelated matter. It takes time and effort to schedule hearings, and the legislative agenda is crowded; one "buys" time from colleagues only in exchange for something of equal value—favor for favor.

Even so, more bills get out of committee than Congress can deal with. Party and committee leaders bargain with one another for floor time. Some bills must be moved back to the end of the session or are bumped from the calendar entirely. Bills are bottled up, delayed, amended, gutted, and killed. They can be defeated by any obstructive majority in a subcommittee, in a committee, or on the floor in either house. The process favors those who want to derail a measure, and sometimes it seems a miracle, given all the confusion and obstacles, that any bills are passed at all. Near the end of a session, however, discipline breaks down. Appropriations bills, debt extension measures, and continuing resolutions to allow the government to spend (until appropriations have passed)—all become vehicles onto which riders, amendments, and even whole bills can be attached, making them resemble a freight train lumbering down the tracks.

Coalition building. How does Congress get anything done? It accomplishes its work by building coalitions through compromise and negotiation, which it

Members of Congress introduce many bills just for home consumption, such as H. R. 7349, which needless to say was never enacted into law.

96TH CONGRESS
2D SESSION

H. R. 7349

The Former Presidential Enough Is Enough and Taxpayers Relief Act of 1980.

IN THE HOUSE OF REPRESENTATIVES

MAY 14, 1980

Mr. JACOBS introduced the following bill; which was referred to the Committee on Government Operations

---

A BILL

The Former Presidential Enough Is Enough and Taxpayers Relief Act of 1980.

1   *Be it enacted by the Senate and House of Representa-*

2   *tives of the United States of America in Congress assembled,*

3   That the total annual Government expenditures for the care

4   and feeding of a former President shall not exceed ten times

5   the poverty level income for one urban family of four.

does by drafting and revising bills so that they will appeal to a majority coalition and by means of presidential and leadership lobbying of the rank and file. This is known as **coalition building.** Even before bills are introduced, legislators modify their bills to attract potential supporters on the important subcommittees and committees. One good strategy is to give things to committee members; in the case of a 1983 jobs bill, for example, Bob Mrazek explained that "all members of the subcommittee worked together to select worthwhile projects," adding: "Needless to say, for most of us these projects were in our districts."[45] Members engage in the classic *logroll:* they include pet projects for many different committee members so that each one finds something to vote for in a large bill. On measures involving public works, rivers and harbors, job training, housing, and transportation, it is common to provide members with computer printouts showing exactly how much money will go to each state and each congressional district so that all those involved can see what they will get if they vote for the measures. In the case of a *time logroll*, one group will gain from a bill and therefore solicits the support of other committee members, promising them that in a later bill their help will be reciprocated. If northern Democrats vote today for a farm bill and rural public works and water projects, for example, later in the session southern and western Democrats will vote for housing and mass-transit bills.

The reverse of the logroll is the **package deal:** the logroll is organized from the "bottom up" by members who want their pet projects included, while the package deal is organized from the "top down" by the White House. It offers a comprehensive solution to a set of hard problems, incorporated into one single measure. The president tells Congress to take it or leave it, threatening to use the veto if anything in the package is changed and appealing to the public "over the heads of Congress," as Reagan did successfully with his economic program. The inducement for supporting the deal is that it takes care of the problem with a single vote, and if enough people agree to support it, the risk of voting for an unpopular measure is shared by both parties. In fact, the legislators can even gain a measure of credit for their political courage.

To get support, it is sometimes necessary for party leaders or the White House to offer favors which have nothing to do with a bill under consideration; these are known as **side payments.** Party and committee leaders may offer to schedule hearings on someone's pet project or to consider a coveted assignment to a committee. Lobbyists may offer campaign contributions from their PACs. The president may offer help in getting a federal appointment or contract for a legislator's friend.

Conflict resolution. Sometimes the sponsor of a bill can make modifications to split the opposition coalition. Some measures lend themselves to *compromise:* each side moves to the center from an extreme position. Bills with "more or less" provisions—like the amount of funding—are ideally suited for compromises. But not all issues have such provisions: social issues like prayer in schools, busing for racial integration, handgun control, and abortion are "either-or" issues by their nature, and it is hard to find room to compromise on such issues of morality. Consequently, the legislators of the new right who are concerned with them have a reputation for being uncompromising and rigid.

On some issues it is possible to *horse-trade:* each side gives up something it wants if the other side does likewise. Trades can be negotiated when a bill

contains many small but discrete items (or when a policy can be broken up into discrete components), such as coverage and contingencies. An example is minimum wage legislation: it is a *compromise* if those who want the minimum wage to be $6 and those who want it to be $3 agree on $5—it is a *horse trade* if they agree that agricultural and laundry workers will receive the minimum wage, but not people under the age of 16 or immigrant workers.

Sometimes sponsors make important provisions *ambiguous* so that all those in their coalition can read into a bill what they wish. Later the judges and administrators can sort things out, after the bill has passed. Support can be obtained by adding *loopholes* (so that people can avoid the impact of the law), *exemptions* (or certain categories of people or businesses), or *contingency provisions* (so that the law takes effect only under certain circumstances). *Timetables* for implementation can be extended to ease the impact of a measure and provide for a transition.

All these techniques are used in regulatory bills, such as those dealing with air and water quality, as environmental groups push for stricter standards and speedy timetables and as industry groups fight for weaker provisions.

Party politics

To win anything from Congress, the president or party leaders must put together transitory coalitions, which form for each bill and then dissolve. One month, a Dole-Bradley energy bill amendment brings together a Republican senator and a Democratic senator who are trying to forge a bipartisan coalition; a short time later, Dole leads the charge against Bradley's amendment to tax windfall profits of oil companies. There are no permanent friends or enemies in Congress.

The majority of roll-call votes in the House and Senate are **bipartisan:** majorities of both parties support, and minorities of both parties oppose, close to 7 out of every 10 bills. But *partisan voting*—in which a majority of one party opposes a majority of the other—is high on the important bills of the president's program, especially those involving the budget and controversial defense and foreign policy measures.

With all the problems that party leaders have in dealing with committees and rank-and-file members, legislators can be counted on to vote with a majority of the members of their party about 70 percent of the time. Moreover, the influence of party membership is stronger than the influence of constituency.[46] Rural Democrats, for example, are more likely to support big-city legislation than urban Republicans.[47] Logrolls and side payments organized by party leaders, reciprocity, and the desire to join the party majority—all these can counterbalance conflicting pressures from constituencies.

Coalition splitting and ideological wings. Often members break away from their party, usually on ideological grounds. A **conservative coalition** forms when southern Democrats (organized since 1980 in the House as the Conservative Democratic Forum and before that time known informally as the "Dixiecrats") join with Republicans (the most conservative of whom have organized the Conservative Opportunity Society). Republican presidents and party leaders usually do well when they can engineer such a coalition. It forms on approximately one-fifth to one-sixth of the votes (more when a Democrat is in the White House), it wins three-fifths to nine-tenths of the time, and its chances improve about 20 percent when a Republican president can give some help by

lobbying and offering side payments.[48] The conservative coalition usually allies with a Republican president, supporting the administration's bills 75 percent of the time and opposing them only 25 percent of the time; it supports fewer than 10 percent of a Democratic administration's bills. (Of course if a moderate Democrat like Lyndon Johnson wins a huge victory and the Democrats enlarge their majority in the House, the conservative coalition, when it appears, is likely to be on the losing side more than half the time, as it was in 1965 and 1966.)

A majority of Democrats belong to the Democratic Study Group (DSG), which consists of approximately 180 liberal to moderate members, almost none from the south. They try to avoid an open split with the Conservative Democratic Forum by giving them leadership positions and promoting enough reciprocal deals to keep them from defecting to the Republicans. They promote geographic splits, trying to pick up support from New Englanders from Republicans in the mid-Atlantic states and the midwest. They try to get votes from the thirty or so moderate, urban-oriented northern Republicans (known as the "Gypsy Moths" in the House) and from the "Gang of Six" Republican liberals in the Senate.

Nonparty coalition building. Thirty groups with staffing and funding provided by Congress—such as the Congressional Black Caucus, the Hispanic Caucus, and the Women's Caucus—as well as hundreds of informal groups serve as the focal point for PACs and lobbyists trying to gain access to Congress and trade campaign contributions for support of their bills. They provide a network that can lobby with other members on various committees to push bills. If members exert pressure, they can trade their votes with the leadership in return for favorable floor scheduling. The legislative party then becomes the sponsor of interest-group rather than party legislation. Often both parties join in a bipartisan coalition organized by a caucus and share the credit and future campaign contributions.

Far from being monolithic, Congress consists of many political groups. Mondale seeks the support of the Congressional Black Caucus during the presidential campaign in 1984. (*Larry Downing: Woodfin Group.*)

Table 11-2. Support for the president's program, by party, 1954 to 1984

President	House		Senate	
	Presidential party	Opposition party	Presidential party	Opposition party
Eisenhower	68	54	80	52
Kennedy	83	41	75	47
Johnson	81	49	71	56
Nixon	73	53	73	50
Ford	65	41	72	48
Carter	69	42	74	52
Reagan (1981)	68	42	80	49
Reagan (1982)	64	39	74	43
Reagan (1983)	70	28	73	42
Reagan (1984)	60	34	76	41

Sources: Randall Ripley, *Congress: Process and Policy*, 3d ed., Norton, New York, 1983, table 9.2, p. 360. The data on Reagan are from *Congressional Quarterly Weekly Reports*, Jan. 15, 1983, p. 96; Dec. 15, 1984.

The White House and floating coalitions. Presidents run a substantial lobbying operation from the White House; an Office of Congressional Liaison and about twenty staffers cover the House and Senate. Presidents also use their Cabinet secretaries and sub-Cabinet officials and their contacts in business and labor to lobby on the Hill.

One might think that an incumbent who is a master at lobbying and has previous experience in Congress, like Lyndon Johnson, would do better than a newcomer without such experience, like Jimmy Carter. As it turns out, the impact of these lobbying activities is less important in getting votes than presidential popularity ratings: Carter did as well as Johnson in getting congressional support, probably because neither of them remained popular very long.[49] Presidents do best, of course, when their popularity is high and climbing. They always get more support from their own party than from the opposition (Table 11-2), but they must contend with the possibility of defectors, which means that they must usually get votes from the other party. To do this, they use one or more *floating coalition* strategies:

- Keeping most of their own party and obtaining a majority with the help of a splinter opposition group, by offering either compromises or side payments
- Obtaining a bipartisan majority by forgoing political advantage and sharing credit or blame, often by creating a bipartisan study commission
- Holding a minority of their own party but gaining a majority of the opposition (a rare gambit)

Presidents get more support from their own party when the economy is doing well, when they are riding high in the popularity polls, and when it is likely that their party is headed for victory in the next elections. They do worst either when Congress is controlled by the opposition or when their own party splits over a presidential action involving war or another foreign policy crisis.

IN CONCLUSION

ASSESSING CONGRESSIONAL POWER. There are two sources of influence on Congress. Pressures from the top down come from the White House, national

party leaders, and ideological PACs, all trying to organize broad-based coalitions to deal comprehensively with important national problems. Pressures from the bottom up come from a "scuffle of local interests," including constituency groups, state delegations, and narrowly focused legislative caucuses and affiliated interest groups. In the absence of a strong national party organization or presidential control over the legislative party, the balance tilts toward the interest groups and toward the concerns of constituencies—unless the president can dominate the national agenda and build a temporary coalition to address national problems.

If left to its own devices, Congress usually delays, obstructs, or waters down measures. It delegates its powers and policy-making responsibilities to the bureaucracy, or else it ties the bureaucracy in knots with petty restrictions. It distributes goods and services in "shotgun" fashion, by logrolling so that everyone gets a piece of the action. It creates many small programs with overlapping and competing jurisdictions in fields such as job training and vocational education, programs which are explainable only in terms of subcommittee and committee turf. Congress is oriented toward pressures from organized interest groups and is less responsive to the unorganized and politically unsophisticated. It decentralizes power by giving states, counties, and cities a large role in administering federal programs. Because of logrolling and reciprocity, it honors so many claims and gives in to so many special interests that the overall scope of government activity increases—even when action by the federal government cannot solve local problems.

Congress is prone to making false starts. Subcommittee chairs posture and introduce measures or hold hearings when their proposals have no chance of passage. There is a great deal of media smoke and not much legislative fire. The system is clogged with pet projects in a topsy-turvey Hill: energy and attention are focused on the small stuff rather than on national issues. "We have diffused power to such an extent that there is no power anywhere," argues Senator Don Quayle, Republican from Indiana.[50]

But sometimes the top-down system transforms Congress. It debates key issues. Committees conduct important hearings on the president's program or on misconduct in office. Parties line up against each other (most notably on budgets, taxes, and deficits). The American people witness a real debate on alternatives, and public opinion, as transmitted to the White House and Congress via the polls, has a significant effect on policy.

So there are really two Congresses. One is a parochial, pluralistic, inward-looking, and inefficient legislature, deadlocking American democracy with its inaction and its irresponsibility. The other is a powerful branch of government, collaborating with the administration or checking its excesses and legislating seriously and comprehensively on important issues.

The current fragmentation of Congress reinforces its twofold character. The more it is democratized, the more it lets relatively junior members in on the action, and the less likely it is to work effectively except in a crisis. The decentralization of congressional power has resulted in legislative impotence and the resurgence of the post-Watergate presidency.[51] Paradoxically, in order for there to be a resurgence of congressional power, legislators may have to sacrifice some of their autonomy, modify the seniority system and the committee structure, and be willing to get into the party harness. The balance between representational and legislative functions may require a new shift.

NOTES

1. This account is taken from Eric Redman, *The Dance of Legislation*, Simon and Schuster, New York, 1973.
2. Joseph Clark, *Congress: The Sapless Branch*, Harper and Row, New York, 1964, p. 23; *Washington Post*, Oct. 16, 1978, p. A-6; Richard Fenno, *Homestyle: House Members in Their Districts*, Little Brown, Boston, 1978, p. 97.
3. Gregg Easterbrook, "What's Wrong with Congress?" *The Atlantic*, December 1984, p. 57.
4. Martin Tolchin, "Some Rules to Live by, for Everyone Else Only," *The New York Times*, Mar. l, 1983.
5. CBS/New York Times survey, February 1980.
6. David J. Vogler, *The Politics of Congress*, 4th ed., Allyn and Bacon, Boston; 1983, p. 7.
7. *The New York Times*, Nov. 30, 1984.
8. *The New York Times*, Jan. 9, 1985.
9. Dom Bonafede, "Life after Congress—Former Members Stay in Town as Political Insiders," *The National Journal*, vol. 14, no. 36, Sept. 4, 1982, pp. 1507–1511.
10. Roger H. Davidson, *The Role of the Congressman*, Bobbs-Merrill, Indianapolis, 1969, pp. 117–122.
11. Lewis A. Dexter, "The Representative in His District," in Robert Peabody and Nelson Polsby (eds.), *New Perspectives on the House of Representatives*, Rand McNally, Chicago, 1969, p. 6.; John Kingdon, *Congressmen's Voting Decisions*, 2d ed., Harper and Row, New York, 1980, p. 37.
12. *The Works of the Right Honorable Edmund Burke*, John Nimmo, London, 1899, vol. 2, "Speech to the Electors of Bristol."
13. John B. Oakes, "The PAC-MAN Game: Eating Legislators," *The New York Times*, Sept. 6, 1984.
14. See W. P. Welch, "Campaign Contributions and Legislative Voting: Milk Money and Dairy Price Supports," *Western Political Quarterly*, vol. 35, no. 4, December 1982, pp. 478–495; Henry W. Chappell, "Campaign Contributions and Congressional Voting," *The Review of Economics and Statistics*, vol. 64, no. 1, February 1982, pp. 77–83; Kirk F. Brown, "Campaign Contributions and Congressional Voting," paper presented at the annual meeting of the American Political Science Association, Chicago, Sept. 1–3, 1983.
15. Roger Davidson and Walter J. Oleszek, *Congress and Its Members*, Congressional Quarterly Press, Washington, D.C., 1981, p. 10.
16. Clark, op. cit., p. 2; Ross K. Baker, "Upstart Senate Frosh," *The New York Times*, Nov. 13, 1979.
17. Martin Tolchin, "Senate Freshman Class Doesn't Defer to Anyone," *The New York Times*, Dec. 11, 1979, p. B-20.
18. Herbert Asher, "The Changing Status of the Freshman Representative," in Norman Ornstein (ed.), *Congress in Change*, Praeger, New York, 1975, pp. 216–239.
19. Randall P. Ripley, *Congress: Process and Policy*, 3d ed., Norton, New York, 1983, p. 129.
20. Ibid., p. 183.
21. *The New York Times*, Aug. 7, 1984.
22. *The New York Times*, Mar. 27, 1977.
23. Vogler, op. cit., p. 125.
24. Albert B. Hart, *Practical Essays on American Government*, Longmans, London, 1894, p. 19.
25. Mary P. Follett, *The Speaker and the House of Representatives*, Longmans, London, 1896, p. 274.
26. Woodrow Wilson, *Constitutional Government in the United States*, Columbia University Press, New York, 1908, p. 107.
27. Charles Beard and C. R. Atkinson, "The Syndication of the Speakership," *Political*

Science Quarterly, vol. 26, no. 3, September 1911, pp. 381–414; George R. Brown, *The Leadership of Congress*, Bobbs-Merrill, Indianapolis, 1963.

28. *Congressional Quarterly Weekly Reports*, Sept. 13, 1980, p. 2696.
27. Ibid., p. 2698.
30. Rowland Evans and Robert Novak, *Lyndon B. Johnson: The Exercise of Power*, New American Library, New York, 1966, p. 104; Ralph K. Huitt, "Democratic Party Leadership in the Senate," *American Political Science Review*, vol. 55, no. 2, June 1961, pp. 333–344.
31. John G. Stewart, "Central Party Organs in Congress," in Harvey C. Mansfield, Sr. (ed.), *Congress against the President*, Academy of Political Science, New York, 1975, pp. 20–33.
32. Woodrow Wilson, *Congressional Government*, Houghton Mifflin, Boston, 1886, p. 69.
33. There have been occasional purges. Thirteen Republicans were stripped of their committee posts for supporting the Progressive presidential candidate in 1924. Democrats purged two members from Mississippi who did not support the national ticket in 1964. But in 1948, 1956, and 1980 Democrats who backed other candidates went unpunished.
34. Richard A. Champagne, "Realignment in the Senate," *Legislative Studies Quarterly*, vol. 8, no. 2, May 1983, p. 233.
35. Barbara Hinckley, *Stability and Change in Congress*, Harper and Row, New York, 1983, p. 163.
36. John Rhodes, *The Futile System*, EMS Publications, Garden City, N.Y., 1976, p. 72; Mark Green, *Who Runs Congress?* 3d ed., Viking, New York, 1979, pp. 64–66.
37. *The New York Times*, Jan. 24, 1975.
38. Glenn R. Parker, "The Selection of Committee Leaders in the House of Representatives," *American Politics Quarterly*, vol. 7, no. 1, January 1979, pp. 71–93.
39. Richard Bolling, *House out of Order*, Dutton, New York, 1966, pp. 17–42.
40. Donald R. Matthews, *U.S. Senators and Their World*, Random House, New York, 1960, pp. 147–165.
41. Bolling, op. cit., p. 88.
42. Christopher J. Deering, "Subcommittee Government in the U.S. House: An Analysis of Bill Management," *Legislative Studies Quarterly*, vol. 7, no. 4, November 1982, p. 537.
43. *The New York Times*, Oct. 25, 1979.
44. Lawrence C. Dodd and Bruce I. Oppenhemier, "The House in Transition: Change and Consolidation," in Lawrence C. Dodd and Bruce I. Oppenheimer (eds.), *Congress Reconsidered*, 2d ed., Congressional Quarterly Press, Washington, D.C., 1981, pp. 31–61.
45. *The New York Times*, Mar. 2, 1983.
46. Ripley, op. cit., p. 319.
47. Demetrios Caraley, "Congressional Politics and Urban Aid," *Political Science Quarterly*, vol. 91, no. 1, spring 1976, p. 26.
48. Mark C. Shelley II, "Presidents and the Conservative Coalition in the U.S. Congress," *Legislative Studies Quarterly*, vol. 85, no. 1, February 1983, p. 81.
49. "Presidential Support Scores," *Congressional Quarterly Weekly Reports*, vol. 42, Oct. 27, 1984, p. 2802.
50. *The New York Times*, Nov. 25, 1984.
51. Lawrence Dodd, "Congress, the Constitution and the Crisis of Legitimation," in Dodd and Oppenheimer, op. cit., p. 415.

FURTHER READING

Baker, Bobby: *Wheeling and Dealing*, Norton, New York, 1978. A book about the wheeling and dealing done by senators Robert Kerr and Lyndon Johnson, written by their former staffers.

Baker, John (ed.): *Member of the House*, Scribner, New York, 1962. Letters to constituents by Clem Miller, describing the House in its prereform era.

Davidson, Roger H., and Walter J. Oleszek: *Congress and Its Members*, Congressional Quarterly Press, Washington, D.C., 1981. An excellent description of how Congress works.

Dodd, Lawrence C., and Bruce I. Oppenheimer (eds.): *Congress Reconsidered*, 2d ed., Congressional Quarterly Press, Washington, D.C., 1981. Essays describing Congress in transition.

Harris, Fred R.: *Potomac Fever*, Norton, New York, 1972. An account of the experiences of a Democratic senator from a plains state.

Hinckley, Barbara: *Stability and Change in Congress*, 3d ed., Harper and Row, New York, 1983. A study of Congress, emphasizing what has changed and what has not changed in the recent reform period.

Jones, Charles O.: *The United States Congress: People, Place and Policy*, Dorsey, Homewood, Ill., 1982. A study of Congress in the postreform era.

Redman, Eric: *The Dance of Legislation*, Simon and Schuster, New York, 1973. An account of young Senate aide's efforts to get his pet project passed into law.

Ripley, Randall: *Congress: Process and Policy*, 3d. ed., Norton, New York, 1983. A book linking the structure of power in Congress to the policies it adopts.

Rovere, Richard: *Senator Joe McCarthy*, Vintage Books, New York, 1960. A study of the damage that McCarthy inflicted on American institutions chronicled by a reporter.

Vogler, David: *The Politics of Congress*, 4th ed., Allyn and Bacon, Boston, 1983. A short but comprehensive treatment of how Congress works.

THE STUDY BREAK

Mr. Smith Goes to Washington. A late-night movie, made in 1939, about how the Washington establishment tries to corrupt innocents from Main Street, U.S.A.

The Seduction of Joe Tynan. A 1979 movie, starring Alan Alda and Meryl Streep, about a senator's moral dilemmas.

Tail Gunner Joe. A movie made in 1977 starring Peter Boyle as Senator Joe McCarthy, chronicling his rise and fall.

Washington-Merry-Go-Round. A 1932 movie about an idealistic young member of Congress who gets into trouble when he opposes a key appropriations bill.

USEFUL SOURCES

Barone, Michael, and Grant Ujifusa: *The Almanac of American Politics*, The National Journal, Washington, D.C.; annually. A compendium of the political careers of every member of the House and Senate, complete with their past electoral records and their present-day interests.

CIS Microfiche Library, Congressional Information Service, Washington, D.C. The complete texts of congressional hearings, reports, and documents, filmed and distributed monthly to subscribing libraries.

C-Span. Cable television coverage of Congress.

Congress and the Nation, Congressional Quarterly Press, Washington, D.C., vols 1–6. Massive volumes which record congressional actions over a four-year period, arranged topically for easy reference.

Congressional Committee Prints Index and *Congressional Committee Hearings Index*, Congressional Information Service, Washington, D.C. A monthly, quarterly, and annual index of all hearings, reports, and committee prints published during each session of Congress, listed by subject matter and committee.

Congressional Directory, 99th Congress, Publications Office of the Joint Committee on Printing, Washington, D.C., 1985. A source listing members of Congress, committee assignments, office addresses, and telephone numbers.

Congressional Monitor. A daily report on committee and floor actions, complete with advance hearing schedules and a weekly update on the status of all pending legislation.

Congressional Quarterly Weekly Reports. A weekly guide to congressional activities, including the status of legislation, committee actions, and voting records.

The Congressional Record, GPO, Washington, D.C. A transcript of the proceedings on the floor of the House and Senate, published and distributed daily.

Congressional Staff Directory Advance Locator for Capitol Hill, 1984, Congressional Staff Directory, Mount Vernon, N.Y., 1984. A who's who of congressional staffers, with offices and phone numbers.

Digest of Public General Bills and Resolutions, GPO, Washington, D.C. Descriptions of all bills and resolutions introduced into Congress, in five annual issues.

Elliot, Jeffrey M., and Sheikh R. Ali: *The Presidential-Congressional Political Dictionary*, ABC-CLIO, Santa Barbara, Calif., 1984.

Goehlert, Robert: *Congress and Law-Making: Researching the Legislative Process*, ABC-CLIO, Santa Barbara, Calif., 1979. A guide for beginners, telling how to trace the progress of legislation from the introduction of a bill through final passage.

———— and John Sayre: *The United States Congress: A Bibliography*, Free Press, New York, 1982. A guide to books and articles on Congress.

Guide to Congress, 3d ed., Congressional Quarterly Press, Washington, D.C., 1982. A massive compendium of information on congressional structure and process.

United States Code, GPO, Washington, D.C. A codification of the laws passed by Congress, published every six years (with interim updates).

U.S. Code Congressional and Administrative News, West, Saint Paul, Minn., monthly. Committee reports on selected bills and the text of all laws passed by Congress.

ORGANIZATIONS

LEGI-SLATE. 111 Massachusetts Avenue, N.W., Washington, D.C. 20001. A computer-based service containing all votes from the start of the Ninety-sixth Congress (1979), together with programs to create customized voting analyses. For more information phone 202-898-2300.

JUDICIAL POWER: THE LEAST DANGEROUS BRANCH

Opposite page, above: The Supreme Court meets in this white marble building, located just behind the Capitol. (*Alex Webb: Magnum.*) Below: Ira Brown, a federal district judge, presiding over lawsuits involving asbestos-related diseases. So many suits were filed that the case was heard in Nourse Auditorium in San Francisco. (*Eli Reed: Magnum.*)

lexis de Tocqueville, the greatest foreign commentator on American society, once said, "Scarcely any political question arises in the United States that is not resolved, sooner or later, into a judicial question."[1] Our judicial issues are political because our Constitution is the highest law of the land and because judges hold the actions of government to constitutional and statutory standards. And court decisions are political because they impose costs and confer benefits; they help determine who gets what, when, and how.

In *The Federalist*, Alexander Hamilton called the Supreme Court the "least dangerous branch," lacking both sword and purse and therefore needing the cooperation of the other two branches and public support.[2] Robert Dahl, a political scientist at Yale, has argued that "the policy views dominant on the Court are never for long out of line with the policy views dominant among the lawmaking majorities of the United States."[3] But throughout American history the judiciary has been involved in controversy. President Thomas Jefferson had Congress impeach Justice Samuel Chase (he was acquitted), impeach and convict a lower court judge, pass a law preventing the Supreme Court from sitting for a year, and revoke a law establishing new federal judgeships—all in a vain attempt to bring the Court into line with the policies of his party. Populists in the 1890s made the Supreme Court into an election issue, attacking it for decisions favoring Wall Street over Main Street and calling for popular election of judges. President Franklin Roosevelt in the 1930s unsuccessfully tried to "pack" the Court by proposing a law that would have let him add new members in order to overturn decisions invalidating part of his New Deal. In the 1980s the new right has tried to strip the federal courts of jurisdiction in cases concerning abortion, prayer in schools, and busing.

The danger that such controversies create for the courts was understood by Hamilton, who argued that the judiciary "is in continual jeopardy of being overpowered, awed, or influenced by its co-ordinate branches."[4] That is the power problem for the judiciary, and this chapter will consider how the courts try to solve it.

JUDICIAL POWERS

What the federal courts do

Article III of the Constitution provides that "the Judicial Power of the United States" is vested in the Supreme Court and such other courts as Congress may establish by law. The federal courts decide cases involving national or state laws, administrative regulations, and actions of the executive branch, provided they contain a constitutional issue or legal issue involving a "substantial federal question."

Statutory interpretation. In most cases the courts determine the meaning of existing laws or administrative rulings and apply them to the facts at hand; this is ***statutory interpretation.*** "A federal statute finally means what the Court says it means," said Chief Justice Charles Evans Hughes.[5] The federal courts have to "fill in the blanks" after Congress passes laws. When college faculty

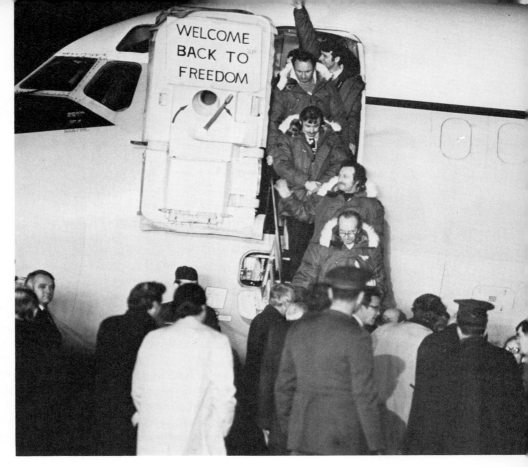

Former president Jimmy Carter welcoming back the first of the American diplomats and servicemen freed from Iran, at a military base in Wiesbaden, Germany. His executive agreement with Iran which led to the release of the hostages, signed on his last day in office, was later tested in the federal courts by American companies which objected to the provision for an international claims tribunal. The Supreme Court interpreted federal laws expansively in order to uphold the agreement. (*Sigma*.)

members organize a union and the board of trustees refuses to recognize it, claiming that the faculty members are not "workers" covered by federal labor laws, for example, it is up to the courts to interpret the laws and decide whether the faculty members are covered. The courts have interpreted federal copyright laws to permit home videotaping of movies, something that Congress could not have foreseen when it passed the original copyright laws.

Sometimes Congress passes laws which are unclear in order to keep a coalition intact. It assumes that the courts can deal with the problems created by the ambiguous language.[6] If Congress does not like the way the courts interpret a law, it can always amend its original law to overturn the courts' decision. Any judicial decision which interprets a federal law or an administrative ruling is *provisional:* it can always be changed by Congress. In 1978 the Supreme Court, in *Zurcher v. Stanford Daily,* ruled that police officers armed with a warrant could make an unannounced search of a campus newspaper office to obtain evidence involving a criminal case, even though the paper was merely reporting the crime and had no involvement in it.[7] The paper argued that the police should have obtained a court subpoena, rather than make an intrusive search and disrupt the newsroom. Congress then passed a law which prohibits federal, state, and local police officers from searching or seizing the "work products" of news organizations, including notes, photographs, and other documents, unless a reporter is suspected of having committed a crime or the materials are needed immediately to prevent a death or injury. The large majority of laws overruling court decisions involve commerce, labor-management disputes, and environmental issues.

Table 12-1. Judicial review and the Supreme Court, 1800 to 1983

Period	Number of laws of Congress overturned	Number of state laws overturned
1800–1859	2	35
1860–1919	35	297
1920–1983	88	700 +

Source: Congressional Research Service.

Judicial review. The state and federal courts have the power to declare actions of the national government and the state governments unconstitutional (Table 12-1). The power of **judicial review** encompasses every action of government: laws, treaties, interstate compacts, executive agreements, administrative regulations, rulings by independent commissions, provisions of state constitutions, initiatives and referendums, and actions or decisions of state courts. Only the Constitution or its amendments cannot be overturned. The Supreme Court has increasingly made use of this power, making it a "continuous Constitutional Convention," in the words of Justice Robert Jackson.[8]

Judicial actions. The parties involved in a federal court case hope to obtain specific court orders. Even before the trial they may seek a *restraining order*, which prevents someone from taking action until a hearing can be held, and a *temporary injunction*, granted after the hearing, which prevents action from being taken until a trial is held. After trial, the court issues a *decision* in favor of one of the parties and issues one or more *orders*, which include:

- *Permanent injunction*, which requires a party to refrain from taking action
- *Mandatory injunction*, which requires a party to do something and specifies how it must be done
- *Writ of mandamus*, which directs a government official to perform certain duties
- *Declaratory judgment*, which gives the opinion of the court on a legal question but does not require that anything be done (used to guide lower courts)

The higher federal courts supervise both the lower federal courts and the state courts: they may *affirm* a lower court decision, *modify* it in crucial ways, or *overturn* it, in which case they will *vacate* the orders of the lower court and substitute their own. They may also *stay* the execution of a lower court order (similar to the temporary restraining order). They may *remand* a case to a lower court for retrial on a new issue so that the lower court can issue final decrees which follow the instructions of the higher court.

Class action suits. Some cases are *class actions:* the decision of the court affects not only the party which brought the case but also "all members of the class similarly situated." When the National Coalition of Independent College and University Students asked a federal court to prohibit collection of fees by the College Entrance Examination Board and the American College Testing Program, claiming that this violated a 1980 law prohibiting charging low-income students such fees, more than 500,000 students were in a class affected by the ruling. Class action suits are often brought in cases involving civil rights, price-fixing, product liability, consumer rights, and environmental issues.

Judicial powers in the context of government

Shared powers. Statutory interpretation gives the courts a share in legislative power: their decisions flesh out the bare bones of statutes and provide explicit guidance to cover contingencies, as the tax courts do with the internal revenue laws, for example. Because of their powers to issue injunctions, writs of mandamus, and other judicial orders, the courts also share in the executive power. For example, a federal judge, by issuing a stream of orders in a single case, can to all intents and purposes take over the responsibility for health care in a hospital, the busing of children to desegregate a school system, or the recruitment and promotion policies of a police or fire department. While such *judicial administration* is rare, it can be quite sweeping: in the 1970s a federal judge in Alabama controlled the state police, prisons, and mental hospitals.

Judicial enforcement. Judicial orders are delivered to the parties by federal marshals assigned to each district court. Anyone who refuses to obey these orders is in *contempt of court:* civil contempt involves refusal to obey an order granted to one of the parties in a case; and criminal contempt involves acts which disrupt the courts or the administration of justice or which show disrespect for the courts' enforcement powers. Civil contempt is usually followed by a fine and imprisonment until the individual agrees to obey the court. Criminal contempt involves fines and a jury trial if the jail term imposed exceeds six months.

The courts' enforcement powers rest not with a few marshals in each district, but with the full power of the national government. Presidents have the constitutional duty to maintain the supremacy of the Constitution. They may place state National Guard troops in national service to enforce an order, as President Eisenhower did in 1957 when mobs tried to prevent the desegregation of Little Rock Central High School. They may send in armed marshals and even federal troops, as President Kennedy did in 1961 in upholding court orders desegregating the universities of Mississippi and Alabama. Such instances are rare; usually the mere presence of a federal marshal ensures compliance with a court order.

FOCUS

THE SUPREME COURT EXPANDS ITS POWERS. The judicial branch checks and balances the other two branches with judicial review: the power to declare laws and official acts unconstitutional. This power itself is nowhere explicitly assigned to the federal courts by the Constitution. The Supreme Court gained it in *Marbury v. Madison*, a case which it decided.

When the Supreme Court started hearing cases in 1790, it had no power of judicial review. The power was not unknown, however; in England it had been asserted more than 100 years earlier to strike down laws of Parliament, although it had not been used much thereafter. State courts had used it at least eight times against state legislatures before the Constitutional Convention, and thereafter ten state courts gained the power.

The supremacy clause of the Constitution gives the federal courts the power to review and, if necessary, overturn decisions of the state courts involving interpretations of federal law, a power which Congress recognized in passing the Judiciary Act of 1789. But did the Constitution also allow the Supreme Court and the lower federal courts to use judicial review against Congress and the president and against executive officials?

Debates during the Constitutional Convention shed little light on the issue.

Gouverneur Morris argued that the courts could not "be bound to say that a direct violation of the Constitution was law."[9] But John Mercer of Delaware argued against "the doctrine that the judges as expositors of the Constitution should have the authority to declare a law void."[10] Charles G. Haines, the leading historian on judicial review, has concluded that the convention delegates in favor of granting judges such authority—including Washington, Madison, Morris, and Hamilton—decided "to allow the definite assertion of the right of judicial review to come through interpretation . . . rather than arouse controversy and suspicion by incorporating a direct grant to the judiciary."[11]

The issue became bound up in the politics of the first party system. The Federalist Party favored judicial review. As Alexander Hamilton put it, "Whenever a particular statute contravenes the Constitution, it will be the duty of the judicial tribunals to adhere to the latter and disregard the former."[12] But the Republicans, faced with Federalist judges when they took control of the White House and Congress in 1801, opposed giving judges this power, since they might declare laws of the new Congress unconstitutional.

Before surrendering power, the outgoing Federalist Congress passed a judiciary act that increased the number of federal judges. President John Adams nominated, and the outgoing Senate confirmed, loyal Federalists for these positions. When the Republicans took office, seventeen of the commissions had not yet been delivered. The incoming Republican secretary of state, James Madison, literally tossed his predecessor, John Marshall, out of the office and then kept the commissions under lock and key, refusing to deliver them to the Federalist appointees and arguing that the final decision to give out the commissions was a political act to be taken at the discretion of the new administration. Then Congress passed a law which revoked the judgeships and provided that the Supreme Court was not to meet for more than a year; it also impeached and convicted a federal district judge, as a clear warning to the judiciary not to oppose the Republican program.

William Marbury went to the Supreme Court when it reconvened and asked it to rule that Madison had acted illegally and unconstitutionally by withholding his commission. The Supreme Court, dominated by Federalists and headed by none other than John Marshall (who had been named chief justice by the outgoing Federalists in 1800), now had a golden opportunity. It could declare Madison's actions unconstitutional and exercise the power of judicial review against the executive. It could order President Jefferson and Secretary of State Madison to deliver the commissions, establishing the principle that executive officials must obey the Constitution as interpreted by the Court.

Or could it? Suppose that Marshall had ordered Madison to release the commissions. Madison would not have obeyed. "Judicial supremacy may be made to bow before the strong arm of Legislative authority," warned Caesar Rodney, one of Jefferson's followers, a week before the decision.[13] The Republicans were looking for an opportunity to weaken the Supreme Court and, in Rodney's words, to show the nation who was "master of the ship." John Marshall recognized the power problem: he had to prevent the Republicans from disobeying a Supreme Court order. But how could the Court extricate itself without admitting defeat? If Marshall had ruled in favor of the Republicans, he would have sanctioned Madison's illegal withholding of the commissions and rendered a personally humiliating judgment, since he was the person who had surrendered the commissions to Madison in the first place! The White House would have intimidated the Court—hardly a way to protect its power.

John Marshall, chief justice of the United States. (*New York Public Library.*)

But Marshall's choices were not limited to a humiliating run or a suicidal fight. He conceived a plan which let the Republicans gain the political victory but which allowed the Federalists to establish the principle of judicial review—and which could not be disobeyed. Before considering the merits of cases, courts first take up procedural issues. Among them is the question of *jurisdiction:* Marbury took his case directly to the Supreme Court, bypassing the lower federal courts. He acted according to Section 13 of the Judiciary Act of 1789, which allowed the Supreme Court to issue writs of mandamus to compel national officials to perform their duties—in this case, to give Marbury his commission. Marshall seized upon a jurisdictional question: Was Marbury entitled to bring his case directly to the Supreme Court?

To answer that question, the Supreme Court had to look at what the Constitution says about its jurisdiction. In Article III the Constitution sets forth the cases in which the Supreme Court has original jurisdiction. But nowhere in the Constitution are writs of mandamus mentioned; such original jurisdiction came solely from the Judiciary Act of 1789. Now Marshall asked the key question: Could an act of Congress add to the original jurisdiction of the Court? Marshall compared the grant of original jurisdiction in Article III with the provisions of Section 13 of the law passed by Congress and found the two provisions to be inconsistent—the law added jurisdiction that was not contemplated by the Constitution. Marshall concluded that "a law repugnant to the Constitution is void."[14] And because Section 13 was unconstitutional, the Supreme Court did not have original jurisdiction over the case and could not issue the write of mandamus against Madison. Marbury would have to go to the lower courts first. The Court exercised the power of judicial review by striking down a provision of a law passed by Congress. The decision was implemented by the Court itself, which refused to give Marbury the writ. Thus the Court established its power of judicial review without confronting Congress or the president. It could make the decision stick without the cooperation of the Republican president or of Congress. In fact, the Republicans had no way of disobeying the decision. They could still argue that the courts could not overturn a law passed by Congress, but Marshall had already done so.

Marbury v. Madison illustrates some of the principles of judicial power. Marshall considered the power problem of the Court: the need to protect the judiciary from elected politicians ready to disobey it or strike out against it. He had to protect the Court's authority and legitimacy against the stronger branches. Thus he would not make a decision that could not be enforced. Marshall gained additional authority for the Court, even though he had to give up some power to do it. The Supreme Court not only let Madison keep the commissions but also gave up the power to issue writs of mandamus against federal officials as part of its original jurisdiction. This was realistic: Marshall gave up commissions that he could never hope to obtain physically and a power to issue writs which he knew would never be obeyed—in reality he gave up nothing that the Court might reasonably have ever possessed. An awareness of power stakes, an understanding of the limits of judicial power, an emphasis on procedure, and a desire to minimize political confrontations with the other two branches—these are the things that distinguish the successful exercise of judicial powers.

THE JUDICIARY AND GROUP CONFLICT

The federal courts often decide controversies between interest groups and between these groups and the government. Parties bring cases to the federal

courts to win victories that have eluded them in Congress, government agencies, and state government.

Which groups litigate?

Interest groups view litigation as one political strategy which complements others. Trade associations, unions, and professional associations may litigate against one another or against state and federal officials. Just as interest groups create PACs for electoral politics, so too they create or support litigating organizations, such as the probusiness Capital Legal Foundation, the Washington Legal Foundation, the Pacific Legal Foundation, and the Mountain States Legal Foundation, which oppose environmental and consumer groups, such as Consumer's Union (product safety), the Sierra Club (the environment), and Common Cause (campaign financing laws).

What interest groups do

An interest group may exercise complete control over a case by having someone test a law or challenge an administrative ruling. This enables it to set up the facts of the case in a favorable way; groups that challenged government funding of religious activities, for example, preferred to choose plaintiffs who were themselves religious, were pillars of their communities, but favored separation of church and state. Interest groups conduct research and prepare legal briefs, as the National Consumer's League did in defending state wage and hour laws against a hostile federal judiciary in the early 1900s and as the National Association for the Advancement of Colored People did in arguing the landmark 1954 case that ended racial segregation in public schools. A group picks the lawyers, develops the legal strategy, and pays the hundreds of thousands of dollars necessary to carry a case all the way to the Supreme Court. A more limited way to participate is by filing an amicus curiae (literally, "friend of the court") brief in a case started by other parties.

Groups may bring cases even when they do not expect to win. Their use of the courts may be a delaying strategy: an environmentalists group, for example, can bring a case which ties up the construction of a power plant or a transportation system for years; then, as costs mount and as plans become outdated, the delay itself may result in the project's being dropped or modified to meet the group's objections.

The increase in group-sponsored litigation

Group-sponsored litigation has increased in the federal courts in the past sixty years. Supreme Court cases in which such groups filed amicus curiae briefs increased from fewer than 2 percent between 1928 and 1940 to more than 53 percent between 1970 and 1980. Interest groups litigate most cases of race or sex discrimination and most civil liberties cases; they are involved in slightly more than one-third of criminal cases and cases involving commercial matters. Between 1951 and 1971, sixty-seven church-state cases were decided by the Supreme Court; three groups that were opposed to government funding of religious institutions—the American Civil Liberties Union, the American Jewish Congress, and Americans United for Separation of Church and State (a Protestant group)—were involved in fifty-one of them.[15] Group-sponsored litigation activity has increased because more public interest groups have organized and see the judiciary as a favorable forum; because these groups have a stake in interpreting hundreds of new federal laws providing rights, benefits, or entitlements to goods and services to their members; and because the Supreme Court is more likely to accept their appeals than those from individuals.

THE FEDERAL COURTS

Constitutional courts and legislative courts

Figure 12-1. The American judicial system consists of fifty state court systems (and federal courts for the District of Columbia and American territories), as well as federal constitutional and statutory courts created by Congress with jurisdiction over federal law and federal questions throughout the union. (In recent years Chief Justice Warren Burger has proposed still another federal court, one that would handle the thirty or so cases each year that involve conflicting rulings by different federal courts of appeals.)

Congress has established **constitutional courts,** which deal with all matters of constitutional law and most matters of statutory law, and **legislative courts,** which deal with specific statutes (Figure 12-1).

Constitutional courts. The states and territories of the United States are divided into ninety-five judicial districts, each with jurisdiction over federal cases within its area. None of the districts crosses state lines, and the 515 or so federal judges must by law reside in their districts. The judges, who are appointed for life, preside over cases involving federal civil and criminal law, diversity cases between citizens of different states (involving amounts over $10,000), cases involving a "substantial federal question" (where federal law or the Constitution is involved), rulings of administrative agencies, and admiralty and maritime cases.

The losing party in any federal case may challenge the decision in one of thirteen circuit courts of appeals. Eleven circuits cover the states, one covers the District of Columbia (it handles a majority of cases involving federal agencies), and one handles customs and patent cases; these courts are staffed by 144 or so judges, who are also appointed for life.

Legislative courts. The military courts and the Court of Military Appeals handle cases involving the armed forces (including courts-martial). Customs and tariffs issues go to the Court of Trade. The tax laws are considered by the United States Tax Court. Suits against the federal government are handled by the United States Court of Claims. Requests from the FBI or the CIA for judicial warrants to conduct surveillance for foreign intelligence are considered by the

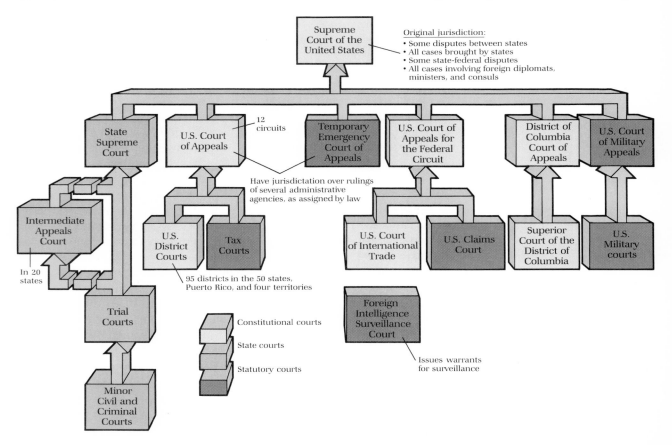

FISA Court, which is a closed-door panel of seven federal district judges appointed by the chief justice of the United States to administer the Foreign Intelligence and Surveillance Act of 1978. Judges on these courts are appointed for fixed terms.

Relationship between state and federal courts

Each state has its own court system, including lower trial courts, intermediate appeals courts, and a court of last appeal. All told, there are 17,000 state courts which hand down millions of decisions each year—about 95 percent of all cases decided.[16] They have exclusive jurisdiction when cases involve purely state matters and concurrent jurisdiction with the federal courts over other matters, such as corporate cases and bank robberies. The state courts have powers of judicial review and statutory interpretation, and they construe the United States Constitution and federal laws and regulations as well as their state constitutions and laws.

The Supreme Court reviews state court rulings which hold federal laws unconstitutional or which uphold state laws or constitutions against claims that they violate the United States Constitution, treaties, or interstate compacts.

Cases in which one of the parties claims that federal law is in conflict with state law may involve a "substantial federal question," and when they have worked their way through the state court of last appeal, they may be appealed in the Supreme Court, which is limited to reviewing the federal questions presented by these cases. It decides such questions and then sends the cases back to the state courts, which render final decisions "not inconsistent" with the decisions of the Supreme Court.

Cases in federal courts

The courts' caseloads. THE LOWER COURTS. Each year the federal district courts decide approximately a quarter of a million civil cases and 35,000 or so criminal cases. The courts of appeals handle approximately 30,000 cases annually. The civil caseload of the federal courts has increased greatly in the past twenty-five years; in 1960 federal judges decided an average of 242 cases per year; in 1981 the figure had increased to 350 per judge. The number of cases in the courts of appeals more than doubled between 1975 and 1985, with each judge handling more than 200 cases each year.[17]

Why the huge increase? Congress has passed more laws of greater complexity, requiring more statutory interpretation. More lawyers (350,000 in 1970 and 700,000 in 1986) mean more cases, and more cases mean more appeals.

THE SUPREME COURT. On the average, the Supreme Court handles more than 5000 cases each year. It decides most of them summarily (without legal briefs or oral argument, but simply on the basis of the petitions for review). It decides about 125 cases with written briefs, but without hearing oral argument from the lawyers. It hears about 175 cases with full argument. Of these, 150 or so are decided with signed, written opinions of the justices, and another 25 are decided per curiam (by the entire Court, without written opinions).[18]

In recent years, justices have complained about the number of cases on their dockets, which increased from 1000 a year in the 1930s to 2000 in the 1950s and is now heading toward 6000. "Supreme Court justices must now work beyond any sound maximum limits," warns Chief Justice Warren Burger, adding that "the precious time for reflection so necessary to a court that decides cases with far-reaching consequences has been reduced to, and possibly below, an absolute minimum."[19] As a consequence, more cases are decided

A camera operator for WPBT-TV records *Florida v. Zamora,* a case in which Florida allowed local stations to televise trials without the consent of the participants. The Supreme Court later ruled that televising the trial did not violate the defendant's constitutional rights. (*Public Broadcasting System.*)

**HOW THE SUPREME COURT REVIEWS CASES:
APPEALS AND CERTIORARI**

Cases reaching the Court by appeal (10 percent)
From the state court of last appeal:

1. When it has declared a federal law or treaty (or a provision) unconstitutional
2. When a state court has upheld a state law or a provision of the state constitution against the challenge that it conflicts with the Constitution, treaties, or laws of the United States

From the federal constitutional courts:

1. When a state law or a provision of a state constitution has been struck down because of a conflict with the Constitution, treaties, or laws of the United States
2. When a federal law has been held unconstitutional and the United States is a party to the suit
3. When the United states is a party to a suit involving interstate commerce, communication, or antitrust laws
4. When a district court has granted or denied an injunction in a suit brought to restrain enforcement of federal or state statutes or orders of state administrative agencies

From other courts of the United States (such as a court of claims or a court of customs and patent appeals):

1. When a federal law has been declared unconstitutional, provided that the United States is a party to the case

Cases reaching the Court by writ of certiorari (90 percent)
From the state court of last appeal
From the United States Court of Appeals and other courts of the United States:

1. When a case involves the application or interpretation of the Constitution, treaties, or laws of the United States
2. When the court has upheld a state law or a provision of a state constitution against the challenge that it conflicts with the Constitution, treaties, or laws of the United States

The conference room of the justices, being prepared for consideration of petitions for certeriori and appeals. (*Supreme Court Historical Society.*)

summarily (which usually means that the claim of the government is upheld against that of someone who is complaining about official actions) or are decided without adequate attention to the issues.

How the Supreme Court controls its agenda. The huge caseload of the federal and state courts gives the Supreme Court an opportunity to pick and choose the cases involving the most important issues. "How the Supreme Court Reviews Cases" describes the way cases are filed.

CERTIORARI. The most common method involves the petition of *certiorari* (from the Latin, meaning "to be informed"). These petitions may be no more than thirty pages long; accompanied by a $200 fee, they set forth the reasons why the losing party believes that there is a constitutional question of interest to the Supreme Court which has been decided improperly by the lower courts. (Convicted criminals may file in forma pauperis, which requires no fee.)

APPEAL. In theory, certain cases must be heard by the Supreme Court on appeal, especially those involving state laws or constitutional provisions. Even so, the Supreme Court does not always give such cases full consideration. Most are decided summarily, simply by affirming the decision of the lower federal court without a full hearing or even a written opinion. Even if the decision of the appeals court is reversed, the Supreme Court may simply issue a *per curiam* opinion: one which expresses the opinion of the Court without identifying the author and without even hearing argument by the parties. Only in a few appeals will the Court permit full consideration: argument by opposing counsel, full discussion in conference, and lengthy signed opinions.

How the Supreme Court decides what cases to hear. Each of the nine Supreme Court justices has four law clerks (recent law school graduates) who

416

THE COURT CALENDAR

The term. The term lasts from the first Monday in October to the end of June or the first week of July. The term is designated by the year in which it begins.

The month. Each term is split into *sittings*, which last two weeks, and *recesses*, which also last two weeks. The Court hears cases and holds conferences during its sittings (some conferences are held during recesses). Opinions are written during recesses. The Court sits through the entire months of May and June.

The week. During sittings the Court holds *open sessions* on Mondays, Tuesdays, and Wednesdays for two weeks. It holds two conferences during each week that it is sitting: Wednesdays and Fridays.

The day. Open sessions are held from 10 A.M. until noon and from 1 P.M. to 3 P.M. The Court hears two cases in the morning and two in the afternoon. One hour for argument is allotted to each case, with each side receiving thirty minutes.

---

review the petitions and appeals. They recommend the most significant cases (fewer than one-fourth of those filed). The chief justice then puts these cases on a "discussion list" for consideration in conference. To "grant cert," four justices must agree to hear a case; if three feel strongly enough about it, another justice may "lend" a vote. Only 5 percent of the petitions for cert, fewer than 1 percent of the in forma pauperis filings, and fewer than one-third of the appeals will go to argument and decision.

The Supreme Court chooses cases that interest it, including those which develop new doctrines of constitutional law, especially cases involving separation of powers, civil rights and liberties, and federalism. It also resolves conflicts between different circuit courts in order to ensure uniformity in federal case law. Yet about 90 percent of conflicting lower court decisions do not even reach the Supreme Court because it does not consider the issues important enough to resolve.

The Court accepts approximately two-thirds of the cases brought by the government itself, represented by the solicitor general, who is the third-ranking official in the Justice Department. It also gives preference to cases brought by private parties if they are accompanied by a brief from the Justice Department asking the Court to take them. (In contrast, the Court accepts fewer than 3 percent of petitions submitted by private parties without such a brief.) The Court is more likely to consider government cases because the solicitor general has already screened them and weeded out those of lesser importance.[20]

Federal judges and Supreme Court justices

Most men and women who become judges have the backing of their party organizations, senators, and professional bar associations. They are hardly a cross section of the American public, or even of the legal profession.

Lower court nominations. There are no constitutional requirements to be a federal judge, since the Constitution makes no mention of federal judges. Congress by law has provided that the president nominates federal judges and appoints them with the advice and consent of the Senate. Each year the president nominates from forty to fifty judges for district and circuit courts and specialized legislative courts. These nominations are made after the White House consults with the attorney general and with members of the president's party in Congress.

Since 1840, senators of the president's party from states in which there are vacancies have been able to block a Senate vote on a nomination. Each senator extends to every other senator this *senatorial courtesy,* which is in effect a "veto" over the nomination of federal judges in his or her state. Thus the president must discuss proposed nominations with the affected senators in advance. In consultation with local party leaders, senators make suggestions for filling vacancies, and the president and the attorney general may exercise a veto over *their* choice. (When one senator is from the opposition party, he or she is usually given 25 percent of the nominations.) Since 1978 about half the senators have established their own "screening panels" to ensure that their choices are professionally qualified.

Nominations for the courts of appeals are usually made by the president, after consulting with members of the Senate for a "clearance" but without conceding them a veto power. Since the circuits comprise several states, no senator can dictate nominations. The White House itself has its own screening committee.

PROFESSIONAL STANDARDS. Nominees are subjected to intensive scrutiny. The FBI runs a background check. The Standing Committee on the Federal Judiciary of the American Bar Association (ABA) rates all nominees— exceptionally qualified, highly qualified, qualified, or not qualified (Table 12-2). Between 1953 and 1977 it was consulted by all attorneys general, who referred lists of prospective nominees to it.[21] Some presidents have even given the committee a virtual veto on nominations or have withdrawn the names of those whom the committee found unqualified. Presidents rarely nominate someone who is unqualified, although John Kennedy got eight such persons through the Senate, Gerald Ford got one, and Jimmy Carter got three.[22]

PARTY AFFILIATION. Presidents nominate members of their own party at better than a 90 percent rate. Party affiliation has a direct bearing on how federal judges decide cases. Democratic judges are more likely to favor defendants in criminal prosecutions, regulatory agencies in conflict with corporations, consumer and environmentalist groups suing corporations, minorities and women in affirmative action cases, and individuals in civil liberties cases against the government. Republican judges are more likely to favor the government in criminal and civil liberties cases and corporations in suits brought against them by environmentalists, labor, consumer, and minority groups.

Table 12-2. ABA ratings of lower court nominees

	Exceptionally well qualified	Well qualified	Qualified	Unqualified
Eisenhower	17.1	44.6	32.6	5.7
Kennedy	16.6	45.6	31.5	6.3
Johnson	12.2	43.3	41.7	2.8
Nixon	6.3	42.8	50.9	0
Ford	3.0	47.0	48.5	1.5
Carter	6.1	49.6	43.1	1.1
Reagan (first term)	9.6	40.7	49.7	0

Sources: The statistics on Eisenhower, Kennedy, and Johnson are adapted from Harold W. Chase, *Federal Judges: The Appointing Process,* 1972. The statistics on Ford are from a study by Sheldon Goldman of the University of Massachusetts at Amherst. The statistics on Carter, Nixon, and Reagan were compiled by Congressional Quarterly from data of the American Bar Association. This table is reprinted from *Congressional Quarterly Weekly Reports,* Dec. 8, 1984, p. 3074.

Table 12-3. Women and minorities in federal judgeships

	United States courts of appeals				United States district courts		
	Women	**Blacks**	**Hispanics**		**Women**	**Blacks**	**Hispanics**
Democrats:				Democrats:			
Johnson	2.5	5.0	n.a.	Johnson	1.6	3.3	2.5
Carter	19.6	16.1	3.6	Carter	14.1	14.1	6.8
Republicans:				Republicans:			
Nixon	0	0	n.a.	Nixon	0.6	2.8	1.1
Ford	0	0	n.a.	Ford	1.9	5.8	1.9
Reagan	9.1	3.0	3.0	Reagan (first term)	9.2	0.8	5.4

Sources: The statistics on Johnson, Nixon, and Ford are from a study by Sheldon Goldman of the University of Massachusetts at Amherst. The statistics on Carter and Reagan were compiled by Congressional Quarterly on the basis of figures from the Justice Department and the Senate Judiciary Committee. This table is reprinted from *Congressional Quarterly Weekly Reports,* Dec. 8, 1984, p. 3075.

OCCUPATION. About two-fifths of judges are lawyers with close ties to sponsoring senators and party organizations. Another one-fourth come directly from state courts, and two-thirds have had some previous judicial experience or have been prosecuting attorneys. About 5 percent are state legislators, and 5 percent are state or federal officials. Only a sprinkling have been law school professors or businesspersons. In the past thirty years hardly any have come from Congress.

Nominees to the circuit courts are likely to be lawyers in private practice (one-third) who are well connected to the White House or important senators. About one-fifth come from state or federal courts, and one-eighth are former national officials. One-tenth are from state legislatures or executive agencies. There are considerably more former law professors than at the district court level. Again, almost none come from Congress.

SOCIAL CHARACTERISTICS. The majority of federal judges are white male Protestants from affluent families. Democratic presidents are much more likely to nominate women, blacks, Hispanics, Catholics, and Jews, reflecting their electoral coalitions, as Table 12-3 indicates.

As of 1982, 47 women were federal judges (7.6 percent), compared with 619 men. (In contrast, 17 percent of state judges were women.) Considering that women constitute more than 15 percent of all lawyers and 35 percent of all law students, it is clear that they have not achieved representation proportional to their numbers in the legal profession.

POLICY ORIENTATIONS. Presidents try to appoint judges who agree with them on the issues. The Reagan administration appointed judges to the circuit and legislative courts whose judicial philosophy was consistent with the 1980 Republican Party platform, which called for judges who believed in "the decentralization of the federal government and efforts to return decision-making power to state and local elected officials." Reagan appointed conservatives to the traditionally liberal Court of Appeals of the District of Columbia, and by 1985 it had a 6–6 balance of liberal and conservative judges. During Reagan's second term most of the other circuit courts have had conservative majorities as a result of his appointments.

To find nominees, Reagan relied on the Justice Department's Office of Legal Policy, which solicited names from interest groups allied to conservative and

right-wing Republican PACs and legislators. Names were sent to White House aides, who sent prospective nominees to the president after an FBI field check and consultation with ABA's Standing Committee on the Federal Judiciary and with sponsoring senators. Democratic presidents consult with liberal law professors and think tanks and with litigating organizations for the poor, minorities, women, and environmentalist groups, as well as with party organizations.

Supreme Court nominations. Presidents appoint an average of two Supreme Court justices a term, which in theory means that even during two terms they cannot appoint a majority. But averages are deceiving: in four years Carter appointed none, Nixon appointed four, and Reagan appointed one. No other appointments that a president makes have a longer-term impact on government. A president like William Taft or Franklin Roosevelt can appoint six justices, thus creating a majority that controls the Court for several decades. In a period of eight years, Richard Nixon and Gerald Ford made 5 out of 9 Supreme Court appointments. The quality of appointees to the Supreme Court is a measure of presidential performance, and for that reason alone no incumbent cedes this prerogative to senators or to the Justice Department.

Although no senatorial courtesy is involved in Supreme Court nominations, pressure is exerted on presidents by leading members of their party. Justices themselves may influence presidential nominations. On at least sixty-six occasions they have made suggestions for filling vacancies.[23] Warren Burger recommended Harry Blackmun, his colleague from Minnesota, to Nixon, and William Rehnquist lobbied Reagan on behalf of Sandra Day O'Connor, one of his classmates at Stanford Law School.

PROFESSIONAL QUALIFICATIONS. The Constitution includes no requirements for Supreme Court justices—not even a law degree, though all have been lawyers. Some have served as distinguished private counsels in corporations or have been partners in firms which represent corporations. Occasionally a president chooses a lawyer who has represented labor, the poor, or minorities (Woodrow Wilson's choice of Louis Brandeis or Lyndon Johnson's choice of Thurgood Marshall, for example). The majority have been judges (three-fifths), but only a little more than two-fifths have served five years or more on another court. Some come from high state courts (William Brennan and Sandra Day O'Connor, for example), while others (such as Warren Burger, Harry Blackmun, and John Stevens) have come from the federal circuit courts. Eight chief justices, including Earl Warren, had no prior judicial experience.

Of the 102 justices who have served thus far, one had been president. Thirty-one had served in the executive branch (twenty-one of them in the Cabinet), and of these, twenty-two went directly from the executive branch to the Court. Eight attorneys general (none recently) and nine other Justice Department officials have been appointed. Twenty-eight had served in Congress: only five senators and seven representatives in the twentieth century.

Republican presidents are likely to choose former state or federal judges or leading corporate lawyers (they have done so in 26 out of their 29 nominations). Democratic presidents lean toward politicians, who have served in high executive positions. Since the 1860s they have made 17 out of their 29 appointments from outside the judiciary.[24]

Democratic presidents sometimes pick their political buddies: Harry Truman nominated a Republican, Harold Burton, who had served with him on the

The justices of the Supreme Court. Left to right: Blackmun, Marshall, Brennan, Burger (chief justice), O'Connor, White, Powell, Rehnquist, Stevens. (*Bill Fitz-Patrick: White House.*)

"Truman committee" during World War II, investigating abuses in defense industries. He also elevated Sherman Minton, a senator who had a desk adjoining Truman's. John Kennedy picked his touch-football buddy, Byron White, and Lyndon Johnson chose Abe Fortas, a close adviser who handled some of his legal matters.

ABA's Standing Committee on the Federal Judiciary rates nominees as exceptionally qualified, highly qualified, qualified or not qualified. It has *never* rated a nominee, no matter how poorly qualified, as not qualified. Some presidents have sought the ABA's approval before publicly announcing their nominations. Nixon followed Eisenhower's practice of consulting with bar leaders in advance, but after several leaks to the press he ended such consultations. Ford allowed the ABA to screen a list of potential nominees before he made his final choice, but neither Carter nor Reagan did so.

PARTISANSHIP. Republican presidents have nominated only 9 Democrats out of their 29 appointments, and Democratic presidents have nominated only 3 Republicans out of their 29 appointments (since 1860). Dwight Eisenhower chose William Brennan to win support among northern Catholics, while Richard Nixon nominated a Virginia Democrat, Lewis Powell (and nominated two other southerners who were not confirmed by the senate), as part of his southern strategy.

SOCIAL CHARACTERISTICS. Like their counterparts in the lower courts, the justices have been almost exclusively white males (only one woman and one black have ever served). Most have been over 50 and have come from middle-class or upper-middle-class professional backgrounds. Most have served in the military (six on the president Court served in World War II). Ninety-one have been Protestants, six have been Catholics, and five have been Jewish. There has been a "Catholic seat" since 1898 (there were Catholic justices even earlier),

421

and between 1916 and 1969 there was a "Jewish seat" as well. Nixon dropped the Jewish seat on the Court in 1969 when he revived the notion of a "southern seat" with two unsuccessful nominations and the subsequent appointment of Justice Powell.

Justices do not represent their race, class, gender, or religion on the bench. A Court consisting almost entirely of wealthy white males has rendered many decisions favorable to women, minorities, and the poor. Nevertheless, such a Court is likely to move slowly on most issues involving social change: it took almost a century for the Court to move decisively on issues of racial segregation, and its approach to issues of gender has been cautious.

POLICY ORIENTATIONS. Presidents consider carefully the policy orientations of potential justices. "I should hold myself as guilty of an irreparable wrong to the nation if I should put any man on who was not absolutely sane and sound on the great national policies for which we stand in public life," said Theodore Roosevelt. In justifying his nomination of a Democrat, Horace Lurton, he pointed out that although Lurton was from the other party, "he is right on the Negro question; he is right on the power of the federal government; he is right on the insular business; he is right about corporations; and he is right about labor."[25]

Presidents who choose lower court judges for the Supreme Court are least likely to be disappointed, since these justices usually continue along the same path they followed in the lower courts.[26] Sandra Day O'Connor, for example, wrote an article for a law review the summer before her nomination in which she argued that state judges should be given more leeway and be subjected to less oversight by the federal courts. On the Supreme Court she figured in several major decisions in which the Court agreed to do just that.

Yet justices often disappoint presidents. Chief Justice Salmon Chase (who had been Treasury secretary during the Civil War) was put on the Supreme Court to uphold the government's wartime currency; yet he wrote the Court opinion holding the system unconstitutional. Harry Truman, when asked about the biggest mistake he ever made as president, said that it was his appointment of Justice Tom Clark. When asked why, he responded, "He was no damn good as Attorney General, and on the Supreme Court . . . it doesn't seem possible, but he's even worse. He hasn't made one right decision that I can think of."[27] Truman later observed that "whenever you put a man on the Supreme Court he ceases to be your friend."[28] After Chief Justice Earl Warren marshaled the Court for the decision overturning racial segregation in public schools, President Eisenhower is said to have remarked that appointing Warren was "the biggest damnfool mistake I ever made."[29]

"When one puts on the robe," says Justice Rehnquist, "one enters a world of public scrutiny and professional criticism which sets great store by individual performance and much less store upon the virtue of being a 'team player.'"[30] The justices wish to demonstrate their independence from the White House; no justice wants a reputation as a presidential flunky.

SENATE CONSENT. The Constitution requires Senate consent for Supreme Court nominations. There have been 140 nominations (some of the 102 justices received a second nomination for chief justice), and of these, 113 have been approved, 11 have been rejected, and 16 have been withdrawn or permitted to lapse. Since 1894, only 5 out of 53 nominations have been rejected or withdrawn: Robert Parker (1932), Abe Fortas for chief justice and Homer Thornberry

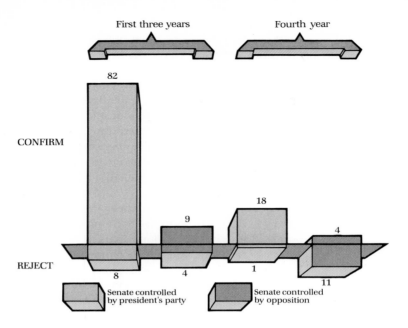

First three years   Fourth year

CONFIRM

82

18

9

4

REJECT

8

4

1

11

Senate controlled
by president's party

Senate controlled
by opposition

Figure 12-2. Senate action on Supreme Court nominations, 1789–1984. Most presidential nominations are consented to by the Senate, although the success rate is lower when the Senate is controlled by the opposition party, especially in the president's fourth year in office. (Source: Adapted from Robert Scigliano, *The Supreme Court and the Presidency*, Free Press, New York, 1971, p. 99. Copyright © 1971 by Robert Scigliano. By permission of The Free Press, a Division of Macmillan, Inc.)

for his post as associate justice (1968), Clement Haynesworth (1969), and Robert Carswell (1970).

Although Senate consent is no certainty, the odds favor the president. When the president's party controls the Senate, better than 90 percent of the nominations are approved; when the opposition controls the Senate, the approval rate drops to 48 percent. Presidential nominees are also more vulnerable in an election year (in such years the opposition party has refused 11 out of 15 nominations, hoping that it would win the White House) and in the lame-duck period before a change of party in the White House.[31] (See Figure 12-2.)

The Senate considers the integrity, judicial competence, and issue orientation of nominees. Parker was turned down because of antilabor decisions in a lower court; Haynesworth, because of his segregationist views; and Carswell, because of mediocrity—many of his decisions had been reversed by higher federal courts. Abe Fortas, who was already an associate justice, was defeated by the Senate because of conflicts of interest (he received payments from a foundation while on the bench), and later he resigned from the Supreme Court to avoid being impeached.

CLOSE-UP

ASSOCIATE JUSTICE SANDRA DAY O'CONNOR. Sandra Day O'Connor is the first woman to serve on the Supreme Court. In 1952 she graduated from Stanford Law School, where she was an editor of its law review and ranked among the top ten students in her class. Despite her brilliant record, she could not get a job in a law firm. When she applied to the firm in which William French Smith (an attorney general in the Reagan administration) was a partner, she was offered a job as a legal secretary.

O'Connor served as a deputy county attorney in San Mateo, California, and then as an assistant attorney general in Arizona, where she became active in Republican Party politics. She became a state senator in Arizona and eventually Senate majority leader (the first woman in the nation ever to hold such a state legislative position). She was then elected county judge, a position that she held for five

Associate Justice Sandra Day O'Connor. (*Supreme Court Historical Soiety.*)

years. Governor Bruce Babbit then appointed her to Arizona's highest court of appeals, where she served between 1979 and 1981.

When Justice Potter Stewart announced his resignation from the Supreme Court, President Ronald Reagan chose O'Connor to replace him, fulfilling a 1980 campaign pledge that "one of the first Supreme Court vacancies in my administration will be filled by the most qualified woman I can find." O'Connor was a woman, a westerner, a conservative, and a state court judge—all this was in her favor, as was the enthusiastic backing of Senator Barry Goldwater of Arizona, dean of the Republican conservatives. Also working for her was Associate Justice William Rehnquist, a classmate at Stanford (and also among the top ten students in the class).

Liberals such as Representative Morris Udall and Senator Edward Kennedy and women's groups such as the National Organization of Woman praised the nomination. But right-wing groups charged that O'Connor favored abortion and ratification of the Equal Rights Amendment, then pending in state legislatures. Jerry Falwell, the head of the Moral Majority, said that her nomination was a disaster. But the American Bar Association's Standing Committee on the Federal Judiciary found her "qualified" for the Supreme Court.

O'Connor breezed through the nomination hearings conducted by the Senate. Most members congratulated her in advance of her testimony. In her testimony O'Connor argued that "the personal views and philosophies . . . of a Supreme Court Justice and indeed any judge should be set aside insofar as it is possible to do that in resolving matters that come before the Court." She said that she personally was opposed to abortion and mentioned her "own abhorrence of abortion as a remedy." But she also said, as most nominees do in such hearings, that she could not promise anyone what she would do in future cases, could not comment on pending cases, and would not comment on previous cases. She also said that she felt it would be inappropriate for a Supreme Court justice to speak out on behalf of the Equal Rights Amendment. She was confirmed by the Senate Judiciary Committee by a 17–0 vote and by the entire Senate by a 99–0 vote.

In her few years on the Court, O'Connor has made a large impact. She has voted consistently with conservative justices on most issues, creating a cohesive 6–3 bloc that upholds most exercise of executive and legislative power at the national level, and she has broadened the powers of the state and local police. Her opinions are noted for their sharp and acerbic flavor, and she is part of the combative judicial tradition, more likely to polarize than to conciliate her colleagues. A Republican president might well consider her for the next "first"—chief justice of the United States.

Deciding cases

Each branch of government has its own power problem: for the president, it is the problem of reconciling prerogative and persuasion; for Congress, it is the difficulty of reconciling representational and legislative functions; and for the judiciary, especially the Supreme Court, it is the problem of reconciling its legal function with its political environment. The judiciary must uphold the rule of law, while at the same time remaining responsive to public opinion and deferential to the power of the other two branches.

The judicial vantage point: Access to the courts. By opening or closing access to the courts on procedural grounds, as in *Marbury v. Madison*, the

courts can determine—without seeming to do so—important political and constitutional issues.

STANDING. A court may decide that a party bringing a case has no right to sue. The federal courts do not usually grant *standing* to taxpayers alleging that the government would be spending their money unconstitutionally or illegally. Consumers are limited in suing corporations under federal antitrust laws. In most instances states may not sue the national government on behalf of their citizens. But if the courts wish, they may reverse these rules: in some instances taxpayers, consumers, and states have obtained standing to sue.

CASE OR CONTROVERSY. A court does not issue advisory opinions, but requires a real case. It can sidestep requests by government officials for "advance approval" and maintain its freedom to use judicial review to strike down their actions.

RIPENESS. A court may decide that an issue presented by a case is not ready for decision; sometimes this is done to avoid taking sides in a controversy between the president and Congress.[32] In 1979, for example, President Carter abrogated the defense treaty with Taiwan, a condition insisted on by the People's Republic of China before it would exchange ambassadors with the United States. Several senators challenged Carter's action, arguing that the Constitution did not give him such power. They claimed that since the Senate had consented to the treaty in the first place, it had to approve any subsequent abrogation. The district court ruled that Congress had to share in the power to abrogate; the appeals court reversed this decision and ruled that the president did have the constitutional power to act alone. The Supreme Court dismissed the case; many of the justices felt that it was not ripe, arguing that Congress as a whole had not challenged the president by law or resolution (only a few members of Congress had gone to court on their own initiative). The Court let Carter's decision stand, but it did so without legitimizing his action.[33]

MOOTNESS. A court will not decide a case in which, because of changing circumstances, its opinion no longer can have any effect. This rule favors the executive branch, which can take unilateral actions to resolve an issue or negotiate and reach a settlement before the court has had a chance to rule on the constitutional issues.

EXHAUSTION OF REMEDIES. Usually a higher court will not hear a case until the issues have been fully considered by officials in the executive branch and the lower courts. Only when all administrative appeals for redress have been exhausted and when the trial courts have issued a decision can the case be appealed. This principle favors the government at the expense of private parties, since it is time-consuming, expensive, and emotionally draining to pursue remedies.

The courts may disregard this principle when they want to decide certain kinds of cases. The Supreme Court has ruled that certain civil rights matters based on the Civil Rights Act of 1871 may be taken to a federal district court before state administrative remedies are exhausted.

POLITICAL QUESTIONS. A court may identify certain controversies as *nonjusticiable:* not subject to a judicial remedy. It turns these cases back to the president and Congress or to the state government. Such cases include those in which there is a need for the government to speak with a single voice (some diplomatic or national security issues); in which the Constitution clearly confides resolution of the issue to the political branches; and in which the courts

are not competent to create a manageable standard of judgment. These are vague criteria. How can one tell whether a case is or is not justiciable? Critics of the doctrine of **political questions** claim that the courts use it as a cop-out for any set of cases which are too controversial for them to decide, such as those involving presidential war powers.[24]

Judicial restraint versus judicial activism. Judges must decide whether to give the other two branches maximum scope in policy-making and pay deference to their interpretations of the Constitution and the laws or whether to play a policy-making role—whether to practice **judicial restraint** or **judicial activism.** "In a constitutional democracy the moral content of the law must be given by the morality of the framer or the legislator, never by the morality of the judge," argues Robert Bork, a judge on the Court of Appeals.[35] In contrast is the approach taken by Chief Justice Earl Warren, who at times would cut through the complicated legal arguments of his colleagues to pose the question, "But is it just?" and if Warren thought that something was unjust, he and other judicial activists were prepared to strike it down, using broad constitutional principles rather than narrow, technical interpretations of the laws if necessary.

THE BURDEN OF PROOF. Judicial restraint emphasizes presumptive governmental rationality: the courts must assume that the elected officials know what they are doing. Justice Frankfurter cautioned his colleagues that "the Constitution has not authorized the justices to sit in judgment on the wisdom of what Congress and the executive branch do. . . ."[36] The burden of proof is on the complainants to demonstrate beyond a reasonable doubt that the government has acted irrationally, unconstitutionally, or illegally—the benefit of the doubt goes to the government.

Judicial activism relies on the principle of suspect governmental action: the courts must protect the people against intrusions on their rights and liberties. In certain kinds of cases (civil liberties cases, for example), the courts must be especially vigilant: the government must show that any action it took was constitutional and legal and that it had no alternative except to act as it did. In the areas of economic and social policy, judicial activism can sometimes give way to policy activism, in which judges may deliberately or inadvertently substitute their own notions of what would be best public policy for those of the legislature.

STARE DECISIS: PRECEDENTS. A court decides cases in part by examining the precedents—previously decided cases (even those decided 200 years ago). These are brought to the attention of the court in the legal briefs filed by the parties. The judges can *rely* on these precedents (that is, rule the same way) or *distinguish* the present case from them and determine that they do not apply. A court may also *overrule* a precedent by issuing a decision that establishes new rules to decide the present case and those to follow.

Consider the strength of precedent in the cases involving major-league baseball. In 1922, in the Federal League case, Justice Oliver Wendell Holmes decided that organized baseball was not subject to the Sherman Anti-Trust Act, a decision which benefited owners at the expense of players. This precedent was reaffirmed in *Toolson v. New York Yankees* in 1953. In 1957, however, the Supreme Court, in *Radovich v. NFL*, decided that organized football was subject to the Sherman act. In 1971, the baseball star Curt Flood sued organized baseball, hoping that the Supreme Court would follow the Radovich case. In-

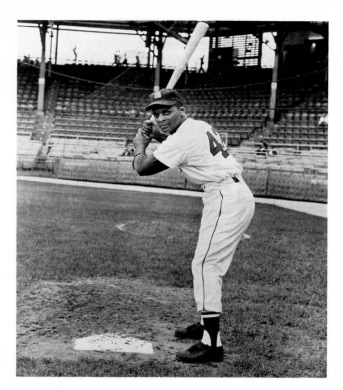

Curt Flood, a star ballplayer for the St. Louis Cardinals, sued major league baseball for restraint of trade. (*St. Louis Cardinals.*)

stead, Justice Blackmun based his decision on the precedents set in the two earlier cases involving baseball, ruling that the exemption for baseball remained "a confirmed aberration" in antitrust law which the Court would not overturn. Sometimes, as justices are apt to say, "it is more important that the law be settled than that it be settled right."

The courts often decide on the basis of ***stare decisis:*** to stand by that which has been previously decided. A court which gives great weight to this principle will not interfere with legal doctrines decided in the past and will uphold them even though, in their absence, it might have decided a present case differently. Judges who believe in judicial restraint rely heavily on this doctrine; they uphold precedent where they can, and instead of overruling, they prefer to distinguish a present case. Judicial activists, on the other hand, seek opportunities to transform existing legal doctrines and overrule outmoded precedents. In their view, predictability and certainty are far less important than making the law rational and equitable. Justice William Douglas argued that the good judge "remembers above all else that it is the Constitution which he swore to support and defend, not the gloss which his predecessors may have put on it."[37]

Between 1810 and 1956 the Supreme Court overruled its previous decisions only ninety times, but recently it has overturned an average of four of its own decisions each year.[38] But this understates matters: large numbers of other decisions are simply disregarded by the courts and lose their precedential value.

REACHING CONSTITUTIONAL ISSUES. An activist judge always wants to reach the heart of the matter in any case: the crucial statutory or constitutional issues. But the order in which the courts must consider issues is weighted toward judicial restraint. The courts fully consider procedural issues, and often there are grounds for disposing of a case without consideration. Even when substantive issues are reached, the courts are required, by their own

rules, to consider statutory grounds on which a decision might be based before reaching constitutional issues.[39] Judicial review may be used only when no other approach to a case can settle the issues.

LANDMARK VERSUS INCREMENTAL DECISIONS. The greatest difference between judicial activists and those who favor restraint involves the kind of decision they prefer. Activists prefer **landmark decisions,** in which broad principles of law are announced, new private rights and liberties are recognized, new definitions of governmental powers are established, or controversies between the president and Congress over the scope of their powers are settled. Supreme Court decisions such as those in *Gideon v. Wainright* (which established the right of defendants to have lawyers in state criminal trials) and *Roe v. Wade* (which guaranteed the right of women to have an abortion in the first trimester of pregnancy) are landmark decisions. In each, the Court overturned scores of state laws, administrative regulations, and previous cases.

Those who favor judicial restraint craft decisions to minimize their impact. Their opinions may limit a decision to the particular issues at hand rather than fashion general principles. And they prefer a series of small steps—each one seemingly inconsequential, but adding up to a significant transformation. Thus the Supreme Court has extended the rights of women in the workplace over the past two decades, but it would be difficult to think of any one landmark ruling.

Litigating strategies. At the appeals stage, a lawyer must make some decisions about his or her brief: a document which sets forth arguments about the facts and the law. It is an old legal maxim that you argue the facts when you do not have good law on your side and that you argue the law when you do not have good facts. Arguing the facts, in the context of a federal case, means using economic, sociological, psychological, and other evidence provided by experts to present the facts of a situation (air pollution, for example). The purpose often is to show that the policy of the government is not rational. Such a factual argument can shake judges' confidence that they can rely on judicial restraint and presumptive governmental rationality. It invites them to distinguish precedents or take a policy-making role or to look for new constitutional doctrines that might apply. Briefs based on factual arguments are sometimes called **Brandeis briefs,** after Louis D. Brandeis, an attorney (and later a Supreme Court justice) who won several cases before the Court by marshaling a tremendous amount of evidence about industrial conditions in the early 1900s.

THE AMICUS CURIAE BRIEF. The courts permit briefs to be filed by groups which are not parties to, but are interested in the outcome of, a case; these are **amicus curiae briefs.** Supposedly, the function of these briefs is to bring to the attention of a court information which it might otherwise not obtain. The real purpose of filing such briefs is to lobby the court, much as Congress is lobbied when organizations submit written statements for committee hearings. There may be amicus curiae briefs on both sides of an important case, which gives the court some indication of group concerns. In addition, the solicitor general may direct the Justice Department to submit its own brief outlining the position of the government.

INFLUENCING JUDICIAL OPINION. Judges are not cloistered monks and nuns, oblivious to what goes on around them. They are affected by the intellectual and political currents of their day. The "hot" issues are usually treated in

Louis D. Brandeis as a young litigator. His "Brandeis briefs" changed the way cases involving economic issues were argued in federal courts. He later became the first Jewish justice appointed to the Supreme Court. (*Supreme Court Historical Society.*)

articles in law reviews (published by law schools and containing notes by student editors and articles by professors, judges, and practitioners), even as the courts are dealing with them. Often the purpose of such an article is not to describe doctrines that are already shaped but rather to influence the federal courts in considering current cases. Litigating organizations may assist in the preparation of these articles; reciprocally, the authors may help prepare briefs or even argue cases. Articles in law reviews are cited in briefs and sometimes in judicial decisions.

The justices decide.   After argument by the attorneys, the justices meet in the conference room to argue and decide the cases they have heard. This small-group environment has an effect on how the justices decide.

THE RULES OF THE GAME.   The justices consider cases at their all-day Friday conference and on other afternoons in their conference room, behind locked doors. No one but the justices may enter the room, and the deliberations remain secret. The chief justice presides at a large rectangular table. The chief justice's own views are presented first, followed by those of the other justices in order of seniority. Voting follows reverse seniority, with the most junior members going first. The Supreme Court decides cases by majority vote (a tie vote upholds the decision of the lower court). If chief justices join the majority, they assign the decisions; if they do not, the most senior justice on the majority has that prerogative. Drafts are written and circulated for review and discussion by all the justices, sometimes several times before a final vote is taken.

THE INFLUENCE OF CHIEF JUSTICES.   Chief justices are only first among equals, but they often can move the Court in their own direction. They may get the vote of a wavering justice by assigning an opinion to that justice. They may take an opinion themselves in order to make the concessions necessary to build a larger majority. Charles Evans Hughs admitted that if he needed the vote of a justice, he would put that justice's argument into the opinion, even if it conflicted with his own, and "let the legal commentators sort it all out." Chief justices may hold additional conferences and schedule more discussion in order to keep or enlarge their majority. In the most significant cases, the pressure to "marshal the Court" and obtain a unanimous opinion may lead chief justices to withhold final voting and announcement of a decision until they have gained as many votes as they can, as Chief Justice Earl Warren did in the 1954 decision to desegregate public schools.

JUDICIAL STRATEGIES.   No matter how brilliant or eloquent a jurist is, the key to gaining judicial power is to get the support of at least four colleagues. This puts a premium on knowing how to win friends and influence justices.[40] A talent for negotiation is helpful, since conceding on certain points or incorporating arguments of other justices helps create a coalition. Justice Stone once wrote to his colleague Frankfurter proposing such an arrangement: "If you wish to write [the opinion] placing the case on the ground which I think tenable or desirable, I shall cheerfully join you. If not, I will add a few observations for myself."[41] Between the first and final votes there are shifts in three-fifths of Supreme Court cases, indicating that persuasion and bargaining are pervasive.[42] In these instances justices in the minority gave in and supported the majority. In fact, in 14 percent of the cases a skillful justice converted a minority opinion into the majority decision.[43]

LOSING INFLUENCE.   Justices who antagonize their colleagues may have repu-

tations as brilliant jurists outside the Court but little influence within it. A supercilious justice who picks fights and tries to embarrass colleagues by showing them up in written decisions is likely to lose support. A justice who refuses to compromise may author brilliant dissents (which are studied in the law schools as models of legal reasoning), but they are dissents nonetheless.

THE LEAST DANGEROUS BRANCH

To many Americans the judiciary seems to be stronger than the other two branches of government because of judicial review. Nothing could be further from the truth. The size, jurisdiction, structure, and powers of the judicial branch are subject to presidential and congressional control, and the federal courts remain subject to political forces which greatly influence how and what they decide.

The scope of judicial power

Judicial supremacy. The doctrine of *judicial supremacy* rests on three principles: (1) the Supreme Court's power of judicial review provides a definitive interpretation of the Constitution; (2) this interpretation must be accepted by the other two branches; and (3) these branches must obey and enforce the Court's decisions and not evade or overturn them. This doctrine was used by Chief Justice John Marshall, who not only declared an act of Congress null and void in *Marbury v. Madison* but also voided an executive order issued by President John Adams on the grounds that it conflicted with an act of Congress, thus establishing judicial review over the presidency as well.[44]

Legislative supremacy. The doctrine of *legislative supremacy* assigns a very different role to the federal courts. Laws passed by Congress may be interpreted by the courts, but the courts must begin with the premise that all acts passed by Congress are constitutional. This doctrine was advanced by Jefferson's followers in Congress, by the Whig Party, by Populists at the turn of the century, and by New Dealers in the 1930s. Although the Supreme Court opposes this doctrine, it is by no means a crackpot approach to judicial powers. There is no power of judicial review of the acts of Parliament in Britain or in most other democracies.

Coordinate powers. Most presidents argue that each branch must interpret the Constitution for itself. Judicial review may be used only for a particular case, and decisions are not to be taken as general principles in guiding or limiting Congress or the president in future matters.[45] Although the Supreme Court ruled that Congress could create a national bank, for example, President Jackson later vetoed a bill rechartering it on the grounds that he believed a national bank to be unconstitutional. In his message to Congress he argued that "the opinions of the judges have no more authority over Congress than the opinion of Congress has over the judges, and on that point the President is independent of both."[46]

The reality: Concurrent review. The reality is more complex than any doctrine: the Constitution and laws are interpreted every day by all units of government. When the courts exercise judicial review, they are exercising not an exclusive function, but one that is shared throughout the government. Judicial review is followed by political review in which the public, the parties, and the

politicians either accept the judicial decision or create the conditions under which it can be modified, evaded, or overturned.

The judiciary as referee among the branches

Richard Neustadt argues that "the Constitutional Convention is supposed to have created a government of 'separated powers.' It did nothing of the sort. Rather, it created a government of separated institutions sharing powers."[47] And, one might add, it created a government of separated institutions that compete fiercely for these powers. The federal courts are often called upon to settle the legitimacy of claims to power.

The courts and presidential power. DEFENDING PRESIDENTIAL PREROGATIVE POWERS. After presidents use a controversial prerogative power, they legitimize their action by claiming:

- That their power to act came from the express or implied provisions of the Constitution
- That they acted according to laws passed by Congress
- That Congress has not protested and therefore has acquiesced or has taken other actions that advance and "ratify" the policy
- That in an emergency or when national security is involved, the courts should construe the president's legal and constitutional authority broadly
- That the courts should show maximum deference to the president and recognize the limits of their own competence to judge complex national security matters
- That boundary disputes between the president and Congress are "political questions" and are beyond the competence of the courts to decide

Let us consider how these claims intersect with judicial powers by looking at the cases decided by the federal courts during the Vietnamese war. Some draftees argued that the war was unconstitutional because it had not been declared by Congress. They claimed that it was unconstitutional and illegal for the president and the secretary of defense to send them to Vietnam to fight. Officials in the Johnson and Nixon administrations argued that the power to wage war was a sovereign power of the nation which could be exercised *either* by Congress through a declaration of war *or* by the president as commander in chief. They argued that the president could send draftees anywhere, since this was a power of the commander in chief and was not shared with Congress or subject to review by the courts. Then they argued that Congress had acquiesced and collaborated in the war effort: that it had renewed the draft and provided budgeting authority. Administration officials said that the war was a collaborative effort, not a presidential usurpation of power. Finally, they claimed that arguments over war powers are political questions—that it is up to Congress, if it believes that its powers have been usurped, to act against the president. By and large, the federal courts in the forty or so cases brought before them agreed with these arguments.

CHECKING PRESIDENTIAL POWER. The Federal courts rarely use judicial review to nullify actions of the president or the executive branch. Between 1789 and 1956 the Supreme Court declared sixteen presidential orders unconstitutional, and only eight more between then and 1975.[48] Most involved cases in which the president made a national security claim in matters involving partisan,

domestic politics and in which Congress and at least one of the political parties strongly opposed the president; in which the president had made a sweeping claim of power and had denied the power of the courts to interfere; and in which the courts believed that the integrity of the constitutional system had been undermined by a presidential action.

The courts sometimes check the president indirectly. A case may involve a presidential policy and a claim of presidential power, but it is decided as if a subordinate were acting without reference to presidential orders.[49] President Nixon argued that he had the constitutional power to refuse to spend funds appropriated by Congress and that he had been given legislative authority to do so under certain economic stabilization laws. The federal courts narrowed down the issue to the simple question of whether Congress had directed that the money be spent. Finding that it had, they ordered officials to comply with the law; the courts never directly confronted the president.[50]

Occasionally the Supreme Court overturns a presidential policy. In *Ex Parte Milligan* the Supreme Court lectured President Lincoln about the impropriety of using courts-martial to try civilians in states in which the regular courts remained open during the Civil War. But this case was not quite a great confrontation between judicial civil power and presidential military power: the war had already ended and Lincoln himself was dead.[51]

In modern times, the most celebrated case involving judicial review of a president's actions had to do with the steel strike of 1952. Steelworkers went on strike, and compromises proposed by the government were rejected by the steel companies. Truman decided to bring pressure on them to settle by seizing the mills and ordering a resumption of production with a pay raise for the workers. He justified his action with the claim that the Defense Department needed steel to fight the Korean war.

The steel companies went to federal court, arguing that nowhere in the Constitution or laws was Truman given the authority to seize the mills. A majority of the Supreme Court agreed. Brushing aside the claims of national emergency, the majority decided that Truman had disregarded a procedure established by Congress to settle strikes and had seized the mills without any power to do so. In a concurring opinion, Associate Justice Robert Jackson (a noted supporter of expanded presidential powers) set out a threefold test for the federal courts to apply in evaluating presidential actions: (1) When the president acts pursuant to law, presidential authority is at a maximum; (2) when the president acts without congressional authorization, the courts should scrutinize the action carefully, but "there is a zone of twilight in which he and Congress may have concurrent authority, or in which its distribution is uncertain," and therefore the courts might well uphold the action; and (3) when the president acts in ways that are incompatible with the expressed or implied will of Congress, "his power is at its lowest ebb, for then he can rely only upon his own constitutional power minus any constitutional powers of Congress over the matter."[52]

The strategy for presidents is clear enough: any claim of power should be placed in the first category, by arguing that Congress has explicitly or implicitly collaborated in its exercise, or in the second category, by arguing that Congress has acquiesced in the matter or even invited the president to act. If possible, presidents should avoid the third situation, in which they act against the express or implied will of Congress.

The courts and congressional power. The courts rarely overturn acts passed by Congress. After *Marbury v. Madison*, it was more than fifty years before another provision of Congress was declared unconstitutional. But occasionally the courts have decisively confronted Congress. Consider what happened in the 1930s when six conservative justices squared off against Franklin Roosevelt, the Democratic Congress, and the New Deal program for economic recovery.

STRIKING DOWN NEW DEAL LAWS. Roosevelt recommended, and Congress enacted, measures to stabilize prices against decline by regulating the supply of goods provided on the market. Instead of having a free market and fluctuating prices, prices were set by government-industry committees. Although these programs were supported by many business groups (and many were initiated by such groups) and were favored by a majority of the public, the federal courts struck them down, arguing that Congress could not delegate such vast powers to administrative agencies. In 1935, in *Schechter v. United States*, the Supreme Court invalidated the entire industrial recovery program; in the same year, in *Carter v. Carter Coal Co.*, it struck down a federal tax on coal producers who had not accepted the coal association's production code; and in 1936, in *United States v. Butler*, it struck down the Agricultural Adjustment Act, which involved a processing tax used to pay subsidies to farmers who accepted acreage controls or production quotas set jointly by farmers' associations and the Department of Agriculture.[53] All told, between 1935 and 1937 the Supreme Court struck down seventy-six laws passed by Congress, almost all of them regulating the economy.

THE SWITCH IN TIME SAVES NINE. But in 1937, after Roosevelt's reelection, the Court reversed itself and accepted the constitutionality of revised New Deal laws. Why did it back down? It was threatened by a presidential court-packing scheme which would have added an additional justice for each one who had reached the age of 70. Had Congress passed the measure, Roosevelt could have nominated six new justices and gained a majority on the Court. Faced with this threat, Chief Justice Hughes and Justice Roberts began to vote with three pro-New Deal justices to create a 5–4 majority that would uphold congressional measures. The upshot was a series of cases signaling the withdrawal of the federal courts from judicial review of economic legislation. In 1937, the Court upheld the National Labor Relations Act in *NLRB v. Jones and Laughlin* and the unemployment insurance and social security programs in *Seward Machine Co. v. Davis* and *Helvering v. Davis*. In 1941, in *United States v. Darby*, the Fair Labor Standards Act, which regulated wages and hours and prohibited child labor, was upheld.[54] As the Court backtracked, Congress refused to support the president's plan.

Since 1937 the federal courts have not struck down any important laws regulating the economy, and instead have turned to issues of state economic legislation and civil rights and liberties, rather than continue constitutional confrontations with the president and congress over economic powers.

Protecting judicial power. The Supreme Court uses judicial review to protect its powers against challenges by the executive and legislative branches, as in *United States v. Nixon*. The constitutional issue boiled down to whether President Nixon could use executive privilege to withhold information about

Watergate-related crimes committed by him and his associates from the grand jury of a federal district court. It is a maxim in American law that a jury is entitled to hear evidence from everyone involved. There is no Fifth Amendment right to remain silent in a grand jury proceeding, although testimony that incriminates a witness may not be used in a subsequent trial unless the witness "waived immunity" when testifying before the grand jury. But Nixon claimed that he alone would determine what evidence to turn over to the grand jury. The Watergate special prosecutor, taking Nixon to court over the issue, argued that in matters involving criminal offenses, executive privilege must yield to the right of the grand jury to have evidence.

The Supreme Court acted to uphold judicial prerogative powers. It made it clear in its decision that in ordinary criminal cases, the grand jury was to have evidence from the president. And in any kind of case, the Court went on, it,

The scope of executive privilege in judicial proceedings was argued before the Supreme Court by James St. Clair, White House counsel, and Leon Jaworski, the Justice Department's special prosecutor. In *United States v. Nixon*, the Court decided that the president could not withhold from the federal courts evidence involving a crime. (*James St. Clair—A. Grace: Sygma. Leon Jaworski—J. P. Laffont: Sygma.*)

not the president, would be the federal trial judge, and it would determine what evidence would be made public, what would be revealed to a grand jury in secret, and what would be withheld from a grand jury. The president and the president's lawyers could never withhold evidence from judicial scrutiny.[55]

Checks and balances and judicial power

The courts treat presidents and Congress with deference. They legitimize most presidential actions or stay out of presidents' way in cases involving national security, diplomacy, and war powers. They immunize presidents from civil lawsuits and make it difficult for their subordinates to be sued.[56] They accept claims of executive privilege in national security matters. Only when presidents flagrantly violate the Constitution on domestic issues or defy the courts will they try to check the White House. Even then they wait until they have public and congressional support. At the same time, presidents have shown increasing deference to the courts. Nineteenth-century attacks on the legitimacy of judicial review, threats to impeach federal judges, evasion or defiance of court orders, and other forms of coercion have given way to presidents' acceptance of decisions directed against them: Truman turned the steel mills back to the companies, and Nixon turned the evidence over to the Watergate special prosecutor. Presidents enforce court decisions with which they strongly disagree, as Eisenhower did when he used the military to desegregate public schools.

The question remains: Why should the courts defer to presidents and Congress? To understand why they do, we must examine the potential and actual application of checks and balances against the judiciary.

Jurisdiction. The federal courts can lose power if Congress exercises its constitutional power to regulate the appellate jurisdiction of the Supreme Court and the original jurisdiction of the lower federal courts. In 1868 Congress passed a law providing that the Supreme Court could not review circuit court decisions involving petitions for habeas corpus, and in 1914 it passed the Clayton Act, which established the Federal Trade Commission and removed certain cases from the federal courts. In order to prevent federal judges from issuing injunctions in peaceful labor disputes, Congress has also restricted their power to hold people in contempt of court.

Attempts to strip the Supreme Court of jurisdiction may influence its subsequent decisions. In 1957, after the Court began protecting the civil liberties of communists, Senator Jenner introduced a bill to strip the Court of jurisdiction in matters involving contempt of Congress, the hiring and firing of federal employees on national security grounds, and the admission of communists to state bars. Although Congress did not pass this bill, the Court backtracked in several other civil liberties cases, and its rejection of such claims soared from one-fourth in 1957 to one-half in 1958.

New right politicians—upset with Supreme Court decisions outlawing voluntary prayer and Bible reading in public schools, requiring busing to overcome racial imbalance, and allowing abortions—have sponsored legislation to curb the jurisdiction of the courts. These forty or so bills do one or more of the following: (1) remove certain cases from court consideration, (2) require the courts to make certain findings or apply certain legal rules, and (3) limit the

kind of orders which the courts may issue. The Senate passed one measure, the Neighborhood Schools Act, which bars the federal courts from ordering children who live more than 5 miles or 15 minutes away from their schools to be bused to overcome racial imbalance. Another bill would establish that at conception a fetus is a person within the meaning of the Fourteenth Amendment and would prevent the federal courts from striking down any national or state laws regulating or prohibiting abortions.

Liberal and conservative opponents, including the dean of congressional conservatives, Barry Goldwater, have argued that such measures are inconsistent with the Constitution and are at odds with the intentions of the framers. Robert Bork, a former solicitor general and acting attorney general in the Nixon administration, argued that it "would not be in keeping with the spirit of the Constitution, nor would it be in keeping with its structure."[57] Six former Justice Department officials, spanning four administrations, agreed. The American Bar Association's House of Delegates passed a resolution opposing court stripping in 1981.

The Reagan administration has not supported these measures. In part this may reflect the desire of Justice Department lawyers not to antagonize federal judges before whom they try their cases. And President Reagan and William French Smith, the former attorney general, have indicated that they would rather use constitutional amendments than court-stripping.

It is not even clear that Congress has the constitutional power to strip the courts of whole categories of its jurisdiction. Some lawyers argue that the Constitution provides federal courts with their jurisdiction and that Congress may legislate only to create the court system and assign different kinds of cases to different federal courts—it cannot simply remove whole categories of cases from the federal courts. The Supreme Court itself ultimately can determine whether such legislation is constitutional. In several cases already decided, the Court has hinted that it would not acquiesce in the wholesale elimination of categories of cases. Whenever it has upheld congressional legislation involving its jurisdiction, it has been careful to observe that there were still ways for the cases to reach the federal courts. The Supreme Court has indicated that Congress can regulate the jurisdiction of the courts only in a manner that is consistent with judicial independence. It may not change the Supreme Court's jurisdiction as a way of affecting policy indirectly—as a means to a legislative end.

Amending the Constitution. Decisions based on judicial review may be overturned by a constitutional amendment. The Eleventh Amendment was adopted in 1795 in response to a Supreme Court decision permitting a state to be sued by a citizen of another state. This amendment was itself held constitutional in 1798 by the Supreme Court, which recognized that any amendment to the Constitution, by definition, was not subject to judicial review.[58] In 1895 the Court ruled that an income tax law passed by Congress was unconstitutional.[59] The Sixteenth Amendment, ratified in 1913, overturned that ruling. In 1970 the Supreme Court ruled that Congress could not reduce the voting age in state elections to 18; the following year the Twenty-Sixth Amendment was ratified, giving Congress that power.[60]

The main impetus to amend the Constitution to overturn court decisions

Jerry Falwell, the leader of Moral Majority, and Senator Jesse Helms (R.-N.C.) confer at the White House after hearing President Reagan endorse a school-prayer amendment to the Constitution in May 1982. (*Shepard Sherbell: Picture Group.*)

today comes from conservative, right-wing, and "profamily" groups concerned with **social issues.** "The purpose of the constitutional amendment is to circumvent the Supreme Court and put it out of their reach," says Jerry Falwell, the head of the Moral Majority.[61] He was referring to an amendment proposed by President Reagan that would permit voluntary prayer and Bible reading in schools. Another proposed amendment, the Human Life Federalism Amendment, would give both the states and Congress the power to outlaw abortions.

Supporters argue that adopting these amendments would be a legitimate way to settle political issues. They view the amending process as a way for the people to overturn federal court decisions which depart from the will of the majority (as they count noses).

Opponents argue that it is unwise to resolve policy disputes by amending the Constitution. The adoption and later repeal of the Prohibition amendment is cited as evidence that policies should be settled in the political branches, where transitory majorities can pass, amend, and even repeal laws to their hearts' content. They say that the Constitution should remain the fundamental law, a higher law that concentrates on procedures rather than substance and on means rather than ends; to use the Constitution to embody opinions on divisive social issues will, in the long run, diminish respect for it and weaken its authority.

IN CONCLUSION

The federal court system consists of constitutional and legislative courts, each of whose appellate jurisdiction and structure are determined by Congress. Judges and justices are nominated by the president and appointed with the advice and consent of the Senate; in practice, senatorial courtesy and senatorial clearance

give Congress a strong voice in the selection of lower court judges. Most judges have had extensive government or judicial experience and have been rated as qualified or as highly qualified by professional associations. The vast majority are white male Protestants, although Democratic presidents have increased the representation of racial and religious minorities and of women.

The federal courts use access to the judicial system as a means of gaining influence over the other two branches, as demonstrated in *Marbury v. Madison*, which established the power of judicial review. Individual members of the Supreme Court choose whether to be activists or to embrace the principles of judicial restraint. They also gain more or less influence with their colleagues depending on their willingness or unwillingness to bargain and compromise when they write decisions.

The courts remain subject to the checks and balances of the other two branches, vindicating Hamilton's observation that they suffer from strategic weakness. Because of threats to their jurisdiction and powers, the overturning of their decisions by new statutes and constitutional amendments, and changes in their personnel, the courts do not remain long apart from the national consensus on issues. The judiciary usually does not engage in direct confrontations with the president, and it overturns far more state statutes than congressional statutes. It remains the weakest of the three branches.

NOTES

1. Alexis de Tocqueville, *Democracy in America*, Knopf, New York, 1945, vol. 1, p. 280.
2. *The Federalist*, number 78.
3. Robert Dahl, "Decision-Making in a Democracy: The Supreme Court as National Policy-Maker," *Journal of Politics*, vol. 6, no. 2, 1958, pp. 279–295.
4. *The Federalist*, number 78.
5. Charles Evan Hughes, *The Supreme Court of the United States*, Columbia University Press, New York, 1927, p. 230.
6. Arthur S. Miller, "Statutory Language and the Purposive Use of Ambiguity," *Virginia Law Review*, vol. 42, no. 1, January 1956, pp. 23–39.
7. *Zurcher v. The Stanford Daily*, 436 U.S. 547 (1978).
8. Robert Jackson, *The Struggle for Judicial Supremacy*, Knopf, New York, 1941, pp. x–xi.
9. James Madison, *Notes of the Debates in the Federal Convention*, Ohio State University Press, Columbus, 1966, p. 463.
10. Ibid., p. 462.
11. Charles G. Haines, *The American Doctrine of Judicial Supremacy*, 2d ed., Russell and Russell, New York, 1959, p. 134.
12. *The Federalist*, number 78.
13. Charles Warren, *The Supreme Court in United States History*, Little, Brown, Boston, 1923, vol. 1, p. 229.
14. *Marbury v. Madison*, 1 Cranch 137 (1803).
15. Frank Sorauf, "Winning in the Courts: Interest Groups and Constitutional Change," *The Constitution*, vol. 1, fall 1984, pp. 12–14.
16. Henry Glick, *Courts, Politics, and Justice*, McGraw-Hill, New York, 1983, p. 33.
17. Administrative Office of the United States Courts, 1985.
18. *Annual Report of the Administrative Office of the United States Courts*, GPO, Washington, D.C., 1985, table A-1.
19. *The New York Times*, Dec. 30, 1984.
20. Robert Scigliano, "The President and the Judiciary," in Michael Nelson (ed.), *The*

Presidency and the Political System, Congressional Quarterly Press, Washington, D.C., 1984, p. 400.

21. Joel Grossman, *Lawyer and Judges: The ABA and the Politics of Judicial Selection*, Wiley, New York, 1965.

22. Robert G. Scigliano, *The Supreme Court and the Presidency*, Free Press, New York, 1971, pp. 109–123.

23. Henry J. Abraham and Bruce A. Murphy, "The Influence of Sitting and Retired Justices on Presidential Supreme Court Nominations," *Hastings Law Quarterly*, vol. 3, no. 1, winter 1976, pp. 37–63.

24. Scigliano, op. cit., p. 115.

25. Ibid., p. 196.

26. David W. Rohde and Harold J. Spaeth, *Supreme Court Decision-Making*, Freeman, San Francisco, 1976, pp. 107–109.

27. Merle Miller, *Plain Speaking*, Berkley Publishing, New York, 1974, p. 226.

28. Henry J. Abraham, *Justices and Presidents: A Political History of Appointments to the Supreme Court*, Oxford University Press, New York, 1974, p. 62.

29. Steve Neal, *The Eisenhowers: Reluctant Dynasty*, rev. ed., University Press of Kansas, Wichita, 1984, p. 382.

30. *The New York Times*, Oct. 20, 1984.

31. Baum, p. 45.

32. See Felix Frankfurter's opinion in *Maryland V. Baltimore Radio Show, Inc.* 338 U.S. 912 (1950).

33. *Goldwater v. Carter*, 444 U.S. 996 (1979).

34. Philippa Strum, *The Supreme Court and "Political Questions": A Study in Judicial Evasion*, University of Alabama Press, 1974.

35. *The New York Times*, Jan. 4, 1985.

36. *Trop v. Dulles*, 356 U.S. 86 (1958).

37. Alan Westin (ed.), *The Supreme Court: Views from the Inside*, Norton, New York, 1961, p. 123.

38. Albert P. Blaustein and Andrew H. Field, "Overruling Opinions in the Supreme Court," *Michigan Law Review*, vol. 57, no. 4, December 1958, pp. 151–194.

39. See Justice Brandeis's opinion in *Ashwander v. T.V.A.*, 297 U.S. 288 (1936).

40. Walter Murphy, *Elements of Judicial Strategy*, University of Chicago Press, Chicago, 1964, pp. 37–91.

41. Alpheus T. Mason, *Harlan Fiske Stone: Pillar of the Law*, Viking, New York, 1956, p. 501.

42. Glick, op. cit., p. 265.

43. Ibid.

44. *Little v. Bareme*, 2 Cranch 170 (1804).

45. Quoted in Walter Murphy, *Congress and the Court*, University of Chicago Press, Chicago, 1962, p. 25.

46. Andrew Jackson, "Bank Veto Message," in Richardson (ed.), *Messages and Papers of the Presidents*, Bureau of National Literature and Art, Washington, D.C., 1900, vol. 2, pp. 576–591.

47. Richard Neustadt, *Presidential Power: The Politics of Leadership from FDR to Carter*, Wiley, New York, 1980, p. 26.

48. Scigliano, op. cit., p. 408.

49. Ibid., pp. 406–410.

50. *Train v. City of New York*, 420 U.S. 35 (1974).

51. *Ex Parte Milligan*, 71 U.S. 2 (1866).

52. *Youngstown Sheet and Tube Co. v. Sawyer*, 343 U.S. 579 (1952).

53. *Schechter v. United States*, 295 U.S. 495 (1935); *Carter v. Carter Coal Co.*, 298 U.S. 238 (1936); *United States v. Butler*, 297 U.S. 1 (1936).

54. *NLRB v. Jones and Laughlin*, 301 U.S. 1 (1937); *Seward Machine Co. v. Davis*, 301 U.S.

548 (1937); *Helvering v. Davis*, 301 U.S. 619 (1937); *United States v. Darby*, 312 U.S. 100 (1941).

55. *United States v. Nixon*, 418 U.S. 683 (1974).
56. *Nixon v. Fitzgerald*, 457 U.S. 731 (1982).
57. *Congressional Quarterly*, May 30, 1981, p. 948.
58. *Hollingsworth v. Va.*, 3 Dallas 378 (1798).
59. *Pollock v. Farmers Loan and Trust Co.*, 157 U.S. 429 (1895).
60. *Oregon v. Mitchell*, 400 U.S. 112 (1970).
61. *The New York Times*, May 7, 1982.

FURTHER READING

Abraham, Henry J.: *Justices and Presidents: A Political History of Appointments to the Supreme Court*, Oxford University Press, New York, 1974. A discussion of the politics of presidential nominations.

Bickel, Alexander: *The Least Dangerous Branch*, Bobbs-Merrill, Indianapolis, 1962. A study of the political context in which the Supreme Court operates.

Cardozo, Benjamin: *The Nature of the Judicial Process*, Yale University Press, New Haven, Conn., 1921. An introduction to what judges do and how law is made.

Hughes, Charles Evans: *The Supreme Court of the United States*, Columbia University Press, New York, 1928. Lectures by the chief justice on the functions of the Supreme Court.

Glick, Henry: *Courts, Politics, and Justice*, McGraw-Hill, New York, 1983. An introduction to the state and federal courts.

Jackson, Robert H.: *The Supreme Court in the American System of Government*, Harvard University Press, Cambridge, Mass., 1955. A discussion, by an associate justice, of the role of the Supreme Court.

Murphy, Walter F.: *Congress and the Court*, University of Chicago Press, Chicago, 1962. An account of controversies between the Warren Court and congressional conservatives.

Scigliano, Robert G.: *The Supreme Court and the Presidency*, Free Press, New York, 1971. A book about confrontations between presidents and the judiciary.

THE STUDY BREAK

The First Monday in October. A movie, made in 1981, about the collision between the first woman Supreme Court justice (played by Jill Clayburgh) and her brethren, especially a crusty conservative, played by Walter Matthau.

The Magnificent Yankee. A 1950 movie about the life of Justice Oliver Wendell Holmes.

Twelve Angry Men. A movie made in 1957, with a brilliant cast, about the attempts of one man (played by Henry Fonda) to convince his fellow jurors of the innocence of a boy on trial for murder.

Woodward, Robert, and Scott Armstrong: *The Brethren*, Simon and Schuster, New York, 1979. An inside account by some law clerks of how the Supreme Court operates.

USEFUL SOURCES

Biographical Directory of the Federal Judiciary, Gale Research Company, Detroit, 1976. Data on the lower federal courts.

Congressional Quarterly's Guide to the U.S. Supreme Court, Congressional Quarterly Press, Washington, D.C., 1979. A thorough description of the Court and its justices.

Fein, Bruce E.: *Significant Decisions of the Supreme Court*, American Enterprise Institute, Washington, D.C. An annual review of the work of the Supreme Court.

Freund, Paul A. (ed.): *History of the Supreme Court of the United States*, Macmillan, New York, 1969–1974. A multivolume definitive history of the courts.

Friedman, Leon, and Fred L. Israel (eds.): *The Justices of the United States Supreme Court, 1789–1971*, Bowker, New York, 1978, 5 vols. Biographical information on the justices and their most important opinions.

Kurland, Philip, and Gerhard Casper (eds.): *Landmark Briefs and Arguments of the Supreme Court of the United States: Constitutional Law*, University Publications of America, Washington, D.C., 1975. Briefs, oral arguments, and decisions between 1793 and 1973.

United States Law Week, Bureau of National Affairs, Washington, D.C. A weekly compendium of the work of the Supreme Court.

United States Reports, GPO, Washington, D.C. Daily "slip opinions" and annual bound volumes of the decisions and proceedings of the Supreme Court.

ORGANIZATIONS

Supreme Court of the United States. U.S. Supreme Court Building, 1 First Street, N.E., Washington, D.C. 20543. For more information telephone 202-252-3000.

Administrative Office of the United States Courts. Washington, D.C. 20544. Handles personnel, budget and administrative matters for all federal courts (except the Supreme Court) and publishes an annual report on judicial performance. For more information telephone 202-633-6097.

Federal Judicial Center. Dolley Madison House, 1520 H Street, N.W. Washington, D.C. 20005. Conducts research on the operations of the federal judiciary. For more information telephone 202-633-6011.

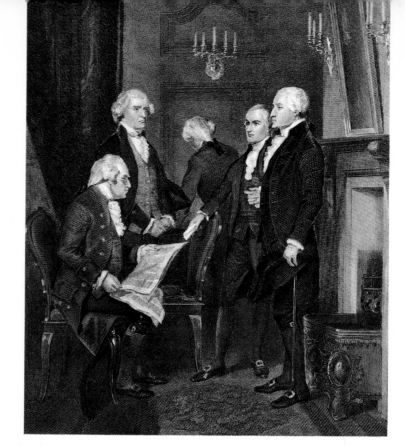

The original cabinet consisted of Henry Knox, secretary of war; Thomas Jefferson, secretary of state; Edmund Randolph, attorney general; and Alexander Hamilton, secretary of the treasury. The modern cabinet is three times as large, but less influential. (*Granger Collection; Sebastiao Selgado, Jr.: Magnum.*)

CHAPTER 13

BUREAUCRATIC POLITICS: IRON TRIANGLES AND ISSUE NETWORKS

$\mathbf{T}$he bureaucracy is the "fourth branch" of government; it is deeply involved in politics and highly responsive to the other three branches. Officials must respond to pressures from clienteles and interest groups that have a stake in their operations, and their activities can become a national agenda issue. Governmental effectiveness is primarily a political rather than a managerial problem.

Critics charge that bureaucrats are too rigid—that they drown the nation in paperwork and red tape and do things "by the book," disregarding the human consequences. But they also charge that bureaucrats are too political: prone to favoritism and special exceptions. Surveys have shown that the public rates the federal bureaucracy last among the major institutions in terms of ability to get things done.[1] Yet the public strongly supports most domestic programs and wants greater federal involvement in the areas of pollution control, consumer protection, toxic-waste disposal, and disaster relief. Presidents come into office pledging to cut the size of "big government," freeze hiring, and reduce the size of the federal work force. Yet each president adds to the government's activities.

This chapter will examine the political setting of the bureaucracy. It will consider how presidents, Congress, and the judiciary try to cope with this fourth branch; how officials forge alliances with congressional committees and interest groups; and whether big government is really the crucial problem or whether there are more important issues involved in making government more efficient and accountable.

WHAT IS BUREAUCRACY?

Bureaucratic organization

A bureaucracy is an organization which functions according to set procedures, usually embodied in formal rules and regulations and in informal "norms" of acceptable employee conduct. The activities of an organization are assigned to units, and the power to command is given only to officials who run them.[2] Employees are trained to perform complex tasks. They are appointed on the basis of assessments of their merit, rather than because of their family ties or social connections, as would happen in a tribal or feudal system.[3] Their career advancement depends largely on their performance.

What bureaucracies do

Making goals operational. Officials take general goals (for example, ending hunger in the United States or improving the quality of our air) and turn them into specific targets with measurable indicators.[4] To end hunger, they can identify everyone whose caloric intake is 20 percent lower than the minimum recommended level and then devise a program to raise these people's intake to that level. To clean the air, they can measure particulates (dust and smoke) and then attempt to reduce the particulate levels. Operationalizing a goal helps define it more clearly, allows for gradual improvement, and enables officials to measure progress and quantify performance.

HUD officials at the New England regional office review disaster-relief claims processed by field workers. (*Department of Housing and Urban Development.*)

Developing programs. Bureaucracies devise programs: sequences of activities, such as forecasting the weather or mailing social security checks. Each program can be subdivided into routines which require a repertoire of skills or techniques that employees acquire through training or on the job. A weather forecast, for example, involves field measurement and reporting, computer-assisted data analysis at headquarters, preparation of maps and tables, and transmission of information to the media and to subscribers to special services. Division of labor enables an organization to perform complex tasks.

Evaluating programs. Programs must be monitored to see whether they are meeting performance standards or implementation timetables and are remaining within their budgets. Sometimes agencies do their own evaluations, but often they contract out to management consultants, academic think tanks, or even interest groups. Officials are evaluated by presidential and congressional staff agencies and by public interest groups. Poor performance may become a national agenda issue and lead to shake-ups and firings.

The federal bureaucracy

The federal bureaucracy consists of thirteen departments and other nondepartmental agencies within the executive branch, agencies outside the executive branch, a few dozen independent regulatory agencies, and government corporations.[5] Each of these organizations divides itself into smaller units (known as *offices*, *services*, *bureaus*, or *divisions*) which run programs; examples are the Passport Office and the Bureau of Labor Statistics (Figure 13-1).

Government agencies are established and funded by Congress, which also sets general rules of procedure and defines and limits the duties of all officials. They operate according to internal agency rules based on these statutes.

Figure 13-1. An executive department and an agency located within it. The table of organization for the Department of State (above) and for one of its affiliated agencies, the Arms Control and Disarmament Agency (opposite). Each of the other agencies located within the Department of State has its own table of organization. (Source: *U.S. Government Organization Manual,* 1984.)

Politics versus administration. Both national and state agencies were organized in the nineteenth century as repositories for party patronage and people with good social connections.[6] They were not expected to act impartially: the operative rule was, "To the victor belong the spoils." Their regulations and procedures for awarding contracts or making payments benefited friends of the party in power. Almost a century ago reformers and some political scientists argued that administration could be separated from politics. Congress and the president could be confined to giving policy direction to officials, who would then impartially apply the law and rules to specific cases with all the demeanor and honesty that one associates with federal judges.[7] In practice, bureaucrats have always cultivated good relations with those close to the president, with congressional committee leaders, and with interest-group lobbyists—and the way to get on with these people is to bend, and sometimes even to break, the rules in their favor. Bureaucrats are as much politicians as they are managers.

Agency missions. Officials of an agency use their positions to form policy, even as they execute it, by defining the mission of the agency and by operationalizing its goals. All its programs, and indeed its mission itself, are subject to challenge by those wanting it to adopt a different mission, operationalize its goals differently, or create new programs. This is the reason for the conflicts within the Interior Department between probusiness officials, who see its mission as involving "multiple use" of land for recreation and business, and conservationists, who believe that certain areas should remain completely protected wilderness.

Empire building. "No one with a day's experience in government fails to realize that in all bureaucracies there are three implacable spirits," warned Herbert Hoover, a former president and the head of two national commissions on bureaucratic reform: "self-perpetuation, expansion, and an incessant demand for more power".[8] Officials want higher salaries; more assistants; better benefits, offices, and facilities; and funds for training and retraining, for conferences and travel, and for research and evaluation. "Gradually a hierarchy of administrative officers, executive officers, budget officers, congressional liaison officers, and public relations officers grows up, almost the sole purpose of which is fund-wheedling," says one.[9]

Bureaucrats are ambitious: programs want to become bureaus, bureaus want to absorb other bureaus with related functions and become a large agency within a department; and the very largest agencies may eventually want to become full-fledged departments with Cabinet status. Alternatively, they try to become independent executive agencies or public corporations, legally insulated from White House control.

Direct and indirect services. Some federal agencies, such as the FBI, the Selective Service, the Internal Revenue Service, and the Immigration and Naturalization Service, deal directly with the public. But most have an indirect relationship: government and private organizations at the state and local levels receive contracts to perform services or provide goods. The Job Training Partnership Act provides an example. The Labor Department distributed $3.5 billion to state personnel offices, which in turn contracted with private companies and vocational schools for actual job training. Planning for the program

was conducted in 500 "service delivery areas," where industry councils composed of the heads of leading local corporations determined the kind of training most suitable for the local economy. Many bureaucracies use partnerships to deliver services; once the private groups are involved, they become constituencies which put pressure on Congress and the president to expand these programs.

Administrative pluralism. Congress often requires bureaus to work closely with state and local agencies or private groups. It may give the governor or local agencies the option of participating in, or staying out of, programs, such as those involving social services. It may give them a veto over the activities of federal agencies (such as legal services for the poor.) It may route funding through state offices and require them to coordinate their plans with a state planning agency concerned with transportation or the environment, for example. Local community planning boards may have a veto over federally assisted construction (housing and urban renewal programs). Congress allows private interest groups to help administer and evaluate federal programs, conduct research and development for them, and even provide direct services (such as job training). Often the federal officials who work in regional or district offices are there because their state congressional delegations recommended them (or had an informal veto over their appointment). If such federal officials antagonize the governor or the mayor, they may find themselves transferred.

Sometimes a federal agency is really a hollow shell that provides funds, statistical information, or technical assistance to private groups. Scientists receive most of their funding for basic research from the federal government: federal agencies delegate the funding decisions to outside review panels—consisting of scientists.[10]

FOCUS

TECHNOLOGY AND TURF WARS. In January 1984 West German officials seized a Digital Equipment Company VAX 11-782 minicomputer just minutes before it was to be sent to the Soviet Union. The VAX could have helped the Russians with their air defense system in Europe. The United States Customs Service and the Treasury Department held a new conference, with the computer on display, and Treasury Secretary Donald Regan called the incident an "espionage coup" for the United States. But was it? "Dozens of VAXs are missing," said Richard Perle, an assistant secretary of defense, "and we presume the Soviets have them."[11]

The Soviet Union seeks American technology involving supercomputers and minicomputers, metallurgy, semiconductor design and manufacture, telemetry, radar, lasers, telecommunications, and biotechnology. The Soviets try to bring manufactured products incorporating advanced technology into their country, in spite of American export regulations which prohibit the export of items on the Pentagon's "militarily critical technologies list." In 1979 Congress passed the Export Administration Control Act, which authorizes the Commerce Department's Office of Export Administration to make regulations involving these manufactured goods. Customs agents do not allow these goods to leave the United States without licenses issued by the Commerce Department. There are more than 300,000 items which require special permission to export. But the Soviets get around the law by setting up, or working with, trading corporations in other nations, which order goods from an American company or its foreign distributor or subsidiary.

More than 750 high-tech corporations export over $20 billion annually in manu-

Customs agents control the movement of goods and people at the entry points to the United States. (*Department of the Treasury.*)

factured goods. They have a vital stake in the regulations, as do the states in which they operate. Governors, company lobbyists, and trade association representatives come to Washington and meet with bureaucrats and presidential aides whenever new regulations are proposed, claiming that tough laws would add to their costs, cause delays in shipping that would lose them sales to legitimate distributors, and do nothing to prevent the Soviets from obtaining the technologies. They also call for the Commerce Department to appoint industry representatives to a technical advisory committee, as authorized by law, to give officials advice and play a role in the administration of the law. In 1985 they got the Commerce Department to agree to new regulations emphasizing industry self-regulation: companies must institute their own control programs and screen the companies to which they export.[12]

The export control issue has sparked a turf war in the Washington bureaucracy. We need the cooperation of our allies, especially the fifteen advanced industrial nations who are members of a coordinating committee dealing with such trade (COCOM). But who in the American government should represent the United States at COCOM? The State Department and its Bureau of East-West Trade? The deputy assistant secretary of defense, who prepares the critical technologies list? The White House Office of Special Trade Representative? And who should chair the working group of senior officials from different departments who must make policy? The secretary of commerce? The Secretary of the Treasury, who chairs the Senior Interagency Group on International Economic Policy? And, finally, which government agency should administer the export control program? The Strategic Investigations Division of the United States Customs Service (which lets goods in and out of the country) or the Commerce Department's Office of Export Administration (which grants the licenses)?

Answers to these questions affect policy. The Commerce Department works closely with high-tech corporations and wants to export as much as possible. The Custom Department scornfully refers to the Commerce Department's proposals as the "KGB relief bill," arguing that they will make the efforts of the Soviet intelligence agencies that much easier. At the Pentagon, Richard Perle, who favors the toughest possible restrictions, calls the Commerce Department's export control office "hopelessly parochial and turf conscious." At the Commerce Department, Assistant Secretary William Archey says that the Pentagon should keep out of the matter, since "all they seem to do is sit around contemplating their navels, while companies lose sales."[13]

Eventually Congress must decide. The Export Control Act lapsed in 1984, and since then the authority to restrict exports rests on a presidential executive order. In 1985 the House and Senate were deadlocked on the bureaucratic issues: the House favored the Commerce Department, and the Senate favored the Customs Service. While the two branches fought it out, the Senate Investigations Subcommittee warned in its own report that the continuation of the turf war "can only mean less effective enforcement and the continued loss of important technology to potential adversaries."

RUNNING THE BUREAUCRACY

The officials who run the federal bureaucracy include the 1000 or so political executives appointed by the presidents, 3500 top-level officials who are in positions which by law may be offered to career officials or political appointees, 3500 other top career officials in the Senior Executive Service, middle managers

in the civil service, and lower-level employees and temporary workers who implement the programs—the "line" workers.

Political executives

Most political executives are appointed by the president with the advice and consent of the Senate. The most important are the thirteen department secretaries and the dozen or so agency directors (such as the director of the Central Intelligence Agency). They propose new programs and defend agency budgets in testimony before congressional committees, supervise the bureaus and coordinate their work with the work of other agencies and of state and local governments, and maintain good relations with interest groups. They are spokespersons for the administration, especially during a campaign season.[14]

The inner and outer circles. The top officials can be divided into two groups: the inner circle, which consults regularly with the president, and the outer circle, which rarely gets access. The inner circle includes the secretaries of defense, state, and the Treasury; the director of the CIA; and the national security adviser. Sometimes other officials, such as the attorney general, may be included. The president sees them individually on a weekly or even a daily basis or in small, informal group settings.

The outer circle consists of the "clientele departments" (Education, Commerce, Labor, and Agriculture), whose secretaries have close ties with interest groups affected by agency operations. They may have been appointed to satisfy these groups during an election campaign. Some owe as much allegiance to their constituencies as to the president. Their advice on issues other than those directly affecting their programs is not valued or sought by the president or the president's advisers. The White House staff usually protects the president from their requests for meetings, and they are confined to ceremonial occasions and rare formal Cabinet meetings. They see the president when the president finds fault with them or has to deny their budget requests. The president wants them to hew to the White House line, run their agencies without public controversy, and prevent lower-level officials from getting to Congress with requests for more money.

These secretaries usually mediate between the White House and their departments. Margaret Heckler, former secretary of health and human services in the Reagan administration, for example, was a moderate Republican congresswoman who once declared that she was "not a Reagan clone." Heckler's aides passed the word that her first allegiance was to her department. She tripled funding for research into the cause of AIDS, in spite of White House objections. She ended a crackdown on recipients of social security disability assistance which had been ordered by the White House. At the same time, she strongly stumped for Reagan in his reelection campaign and defended his program against the Democrats' charges of unfairness, thus temporarily retaining her political value to the administration.[15]

Sub-Cabinet officials. Below the secretaries are the 1000 or so deputy secretaries, under secretaries, assistant secretaries, and deputy assistant secretaries who staff the departments. They are appointed by the president with the consent of the Senate. Many of them are appointed on the recommendation of members of Congress or interest groups. In the past, these "nominations" have enabled the president to win political support but have made it more difficult

Figure 13-2. Appointments clearance process in the Reagan administration, July 1981. This flowchart shows the steps, from top to bottom, which were taken to make appointments in the first year of the Reagan administration. (Source: G. Calvin Mackenzie, "Cabinet and Subcabinet Personnel Selection in Reagan's First Year: New Variations on Some Not-So-Old Themes," APSA Annual Meeting, New York, City, September 1981.)

The flowchart contains the following labels:

- Candidates recommended by Cabinet secretaries
- Candidates recommended by presidential Personnel Office
- Preferred candidates
- Domestic policy advisor
- National security advisor
- Political affairs advisor
- White House counsel
- FBI "name check"
- White House congressional liaison office — Obtains congressional clearance
- Top presidential aides
- White House counsel
- FBI "full field investigation"
- President
- Senate

for him to run the executive branch, since these officials have been "his" in name only. Figure 13-2 shows the appointment process during Reagan's first term.

The number two person is the deputy secretary. Most deputy secretaries come from large corporations, law firms, or financial institutions, rather than from public service. Below them are one or two under secretaries, who take charge of policy formulation, department administration, or some important matter given to them by the secretary or the president.

Below these officials are the assistant and deputy assistant secretaries in charge of the bureaus. They are responsible for implementing the presidential and departmental programs. In a sense they are caught in the middle: they must represent the president's program to the career officials and the interests of the bureaus to the White House. If they are too "presidential," the lower bureaucrats may circumvent or ignore them, leak their mistakes to the media, or isolate them. But if they champion the interests of the bureaucracy, the White House assumes that they have been "captured" by the bureaucracy or have "gone native," and it ignores or replaces them.

Most of these appointees come from business, finance, and the law; a few are from academia, labor, and nonprofit organizations. Often the president appoints people from agribusiness to the Agriculture Department, people from Wall Street to the Treasury Department, people from large corporations to the Commerce Department, people from unions to the Labor Department, and people involved in ranching, mining, or logging to the Interior Department. As is true of the judiciary, Democratic presidents are much more likely than Republican presidents to appoint minorities and women (though Reagan has appointed more women to Cabinet-level positions than any Democrat): 21 percent of Carter's appointees were from minority groups, and 22 percent were women; 7.6 percent of Reagan's appointees were from minority groups, and 14.3 percent were women.[16] These figures reflect each party's electoral coalition.

452

The typical department secretary keeps the job for two or three years, while assistant secretaries remain on average eighteen months. Many of these positions remain vacant for months at a time; in 1983 five departments lacked deputy secretaries and in 1985 many important slots for assistant secretary were not filled. The reason? Appointees have to move to Washington, where the costs of housing and education are high, and usually they take a substantial salary cut if they have come from business. Many would be precluded from returning to their old jobs if their government position involved distributing contracts. They must sell investments which might involve a conflict of interest and then take up the confirmation gauntlet in the United States Senate. It is not easy to get potential appointees—especially those at the peak of their careers—to come to Washington or stay under these circumstances.[17] Many political executives hardly have time to learn their jobs before they move on, which makes it more difficult for them to translate administration policy into bureaucratic performance. Lower-level officials simply outlast them.

Layering. Half a century ago presidents got along with few officials. There were ten Cabinet secretaries and forty to fifty assistant secretaries. They handled congressional relations and political matters (such as getting spoils for some local party leaders). Since then, departments have added layer upon layer of officials with new staff functions (budgeting, accounting, and auditing personnel; inspectors general to stop corruption; legal advisers; personnel managers; training and program evaluators; policy planners; public affairs personnel; and congressional liaisons, for example) and have expanded their programs. Figure 13-3 shows what has happened in the Labor Department.

A GOVERNMENT OF STRANGERS. Presidents cannot possibly know more than a few of these officials. They preside, according to Hugh Heclo, over a "government of strangers."[18] In fact, they may not even know their own secretaries; President Reagan, at a meeting of the U.S. Conference of Governors, said, "Hello, Mr. Mayor" to his own secretary of housing and urban development, Samuel Pierce, seeming not to recognize him until he had been briefed by his aides. The secretaries do not know the president, other members of the Cabinet, or their own subordinates very well. "A secretary rarely gets to pick his own deputy, and so the two men are often at the disadvantage of being absolute strangers before they begin working together," according to Robert Wood, a former deputy secretary.[19]

Most political executives have never held elective office or worked in party politics. They are corporate executives, lawyers, investment bankers, academics, trade association lobbyists, or state or local officials. They usually have little knowledge of, or patience with, the ins and outs of legislative politics.

CENTRALIZING WHITE HOUSE CONTROLS. Because they have no public following, political executives are not able to challenge increasing centralization by the White House. "The typical cabinet officer's immediate superior is one or more members of the White House staff," says Joseph Barlett, a former undersecretary of commerce.[20] They must carry out presidential policies and the orders of White House aides and directors of presidential agencies. In recent years the influence of the White House has increased, in part because of a computerized executive data link system, which connects several hundred top officials with one another and with the White House. Speeches, congressional testimony, and policy proposals can all be monitored by presidential aides.

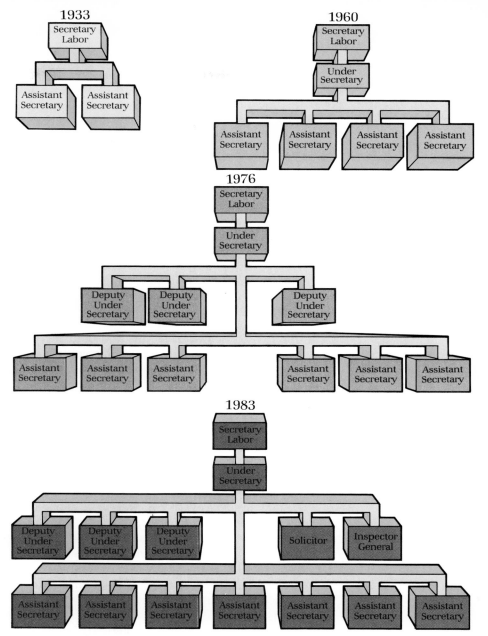

Figure 13-3. Political executives in the Labor Department. Between 1933 and 1983, the number of assistant secretaries increased from two to seven, and two supervisory layers were added between the secretary and the assistant secretaries. (Source: *U.S. Government Organization Manual*, 1984.)

The Office of Management and Budget, for example, can negotiate with departments on budgets, spending totals, and proposed congressional testimony, taking half an hour to communicate by electronic mail; this used to take days and require formal meetings. The assistant secretaries for management, congressional liaison, and budgeting are all plugged into the new network.[21] If differences with presidential aides are irreconcilable, officials resign. They do so quietly and with little fanfare, citing personal reasons, to keep their reputations for being discreet, to avoid being labeled troublemakers, and to stay in line for other assignments in the future.[22]

The Senior Executive Service

Below the political executives are the 7000 officials in the ***Senior Executive Service*** (SES) and the 1500 top-ranking officials in the State Department and its

related agencies. Most are career civil servants, though by law 10 percent of the SES positions (and all the top foreign affairs slots) may be filled with political appointees.[23] The SES was created in 1978 to make top-level civil servants more responsive to the administration; members are given greater responsibility and can get pay increases and bonuses on the basis of superior performance. But they give up some of the protection of the civil service system: it is easier for their superiors to transfer them or put them in less important positions, to demote them back to the civil service, or even to fire them. Reagan has filled 850 SES posts with his own political executives: political appointees now operate at lower levels in the bureaucracy than ever before. Meanwhile, the Office of Personnel Management began awarding pay raises on the basis of performance appraisals in the other services in order to make lower-level officials more responsive to the White House.

Critics of the SES contend that it fosters favoritism, politics, and slavish adherence to the administration by civil servants angling for more pay. Supporters say that it gives the president more flexibility, creates a more responsive bureaucracy, and makes for better relations between political executives and senior civil servants.

The civil service and other services

More than 99.8 percent of all government employees are in the government services: the Postal Service employs almost half a million people; the technical and professional services (such as the Foreign Service, the Public Health Service, and the Forest Service) have about 100,000 workers; and there are 1.2 million employees of the General Service (GS), which staffs most federal departments and agencies. The total civilian federal work force numbered about 2.6 million in 1985, down 75,000 since 1981.

Grade levels. Civil servants are nonpartisan employees who get their jobs on the basis of competitive entrance examinations and personal interviews. Skilled positions are competitive: there are more than twenty applications for each high-level administrative and professional job and more than thirty applications for middle-management positions for every available opening. Employees are given grades on the basis of education, experience, and responsibilities.

Emergency relief is directed to victims of flooding in Kentucky. (*Department of Housing and Urban Development.*)

There are eighteen grades: GS 1 to GS 5 (clerical and office workers), GS 6 to GS 11 (more skilled office workers and newly hired managers), GS 12 to GS 15 (experienced managers and technical and scientific employees), and GS 16 to GS 18 (the very top officials covered by civil service protections, most of whom have left to join the SES, with its higher pay and larger bonuses).

Merit systems. The premise of the *civil service* and other services is that recruitment, promotion, assignment, and pay are to be based on merit, not partisan politics. The Hatch Acts, passed by Congress, provide that officials may not contribute to political campaigns or work in them (these laws, originally designed to protect workers from pressure by political executives, have been weakened by the courts as workers have insisted on their right to participate in political campaigns). Officials cannot run for office and remain federal employees.

Their tenure in office is protected by an elaborate system of disciplinary hearings, agency appeals procedures, and finally systemwide hearings and appeals. Although civil service tenure was originally designed to protect officials against wholesale firing after a change of party in the White House, today its critics charge that it protects incompetent officials from being disciplined, demoted, or fired and that it lowers morale among good employees.

Size of the work force. In absolute numbers, the federal work force has expanded from 2.3 million employees in 1955 to 2.6 million in 1985 (Figure 13-4). But federal workers accounted for 37 percent of all government workers in 1955 and for just 16 percent in 1985 (state and local workers accounted for the rest), and as a proportion of the total civilian work force, they declined from a high of 3.8 percent in 1968 to 2.5 percent in 1985.

What accounts for the notion that big government is getting bigger? The pay scales and perquisites of federal employees have improved dramatically in the past two decades. Congress requires "pay comparability" with the private sector in order to attract a qualified work force. This provision has been interpreted generously, by comparing government pay scales with those of corporations paying the highest salaries. Although the federal work force has not expanded greatly because many programs are implemented by state and local governments or by organizations in the private sector, the number of state and

Figure 13-4. Growth of federal civilian employees, 1789–1986. The large upsurge in employment is accounted for by the Second World War. Since the end of the Korean War, federal employment has leveled off at around 2.6 million workers. (Source: Office of Personnel Management.)

Not all federal office workers are paper-shufflers. Many, like this park ranger, work directly with the public. (*Richard Frear: National Park Service.*)

local government workers has increased greatly in recent years, and there are close to 6 million people in the private sector whose activities are funded by the national government. As the government takes on more functions and issues more regulations, the visibility of officials increases, and so we think that there must be more of them.

Unions and the civil service. Labor unions have been recognized for collective bargaining since President Kennedy signed an executive order in 1962. In 1978 Congress gave civil service workers (other than FBI, CIA, and military personnel) a statutory right to organize. Today more than ninety unions represent almost 60 percent of all federal workers. The biggest include the Postal Workers, the American Federation of Government Employees, the National Association of Government Employees, the Metal Trades and Machinists, and the National Treasury Employees Union. The Federal Labor Relations Authority conducts union elections and decides which bargaining units to recognize. A union may not organize a union shop (in which everyone must belong to the union in order to work), and so many people work under union contracts but

Federal employees have the right to organize and bargain collectively, but no right to strike. (*John Ficara: Woodfin Camp.*)

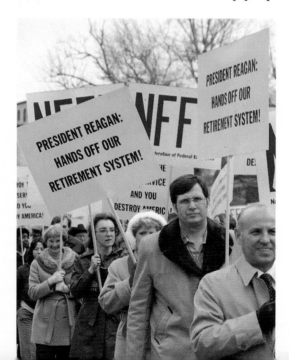

are not union members—only about 35 percent of workers covered under union contacts actually *belong* to the unions that represent them. Unions sometimes get involved in policy-making. They have brought court cases against officials in the Nixon and Reagan administrations who tried to cut funding for agencies below levels set by Congress or even to dismantle them when Congress had authorized them to keep operating.[24]

Managers and policy-making. Civil servants usually begin and end their careers in government, working for only one or two agencies. Top managers average twenty years of service by the time they are put in charge of programs of bureaus. They identify strongly with the goals and missions of their units. They fight to maintain programs that their superiors want to modify or eliminate. They put their bureaucratic and career interests ahead of the interests of the current administration. They tend to discount the priorities of the "two-year wonders" who show up as assistant secretaries through what seems to be a revolving door. They do not take kindly to directives instructing them that, for the good of a president who may serve for only four years, they should sacrifice programs for which they have worked all their lives.

So in dealing with political executives, civil servants engage in "education from below." Instead of stating flatly that they will not carry out orders, they present their superiors with unpleasant alternatives; for example, if budget cuts are instituted, essential services must be cut, or if procedures are changed, constituencies will be inconvenienced. Most activities have been created by statute, and career civil servants may inform their superior that, much as they would like to institute the administration's policies, it would be illegal to do so. They force their superiors to confront reality: bureaucracies usually provide services which Congress has mandated and which the public wants, and one cannot simply modify or cut services without incurring political costs.

These tactics do not always work. When William B. Reynolds took over as head of the Justice Department's Civil Rights Division, he instructed it to oppose busing for desegregation of public schools and also to oppose affirmative action to end job discrimination, and he started to negotiate with, rather than litigate against, mental hospitals and prisons that were accused of violating civil rights. The staff lawyers opposed his new policies but were unable to slow him down or change his approach; instead, sixteen of the eighteen staff lawyers resigned.

The line employees

The line workers who implement programs and deal with the public also can affect policy. Their operations are at a level where supervision is minimal and their discretion is high. Their own values, priorities, and ways of working may determine what actually gets done (or what does not get done, as the case may be). At some airports flight controllers follow all safety rules, while at others they bend the rules so that more flights can be scheduled. Agricultural extension agents choose which farmers to assist in their communities; often they work with the more prosperous ones and let the others continue to use obsolete methods until eventually they leave their land. Lawyers for the poor can concentrate on individual cases (which are the least controversial) and build up local connections before leaving government service for private practice, or they can adopt more militant tactics in representing the poor. During the Vietnamese war some local draft boards made it hard for conscientious objectors, while others gave them deferments or exemptions.

Employees who disagree with the policies of their superiors can become *whistle-blowers:* they can photostat documents and leak them to the press or to congressional committee staffers. When corruption, cutbacks, or poor performance is at issue, the result may be a congressional investigation. Whistle-blowers have forced the resignation of many top officials, and Congress does what it can to shield them against reprisals by agency officials in order to protect its sources of information in the future. Lower-level officials in the Environmental Protection Agency, for example, circulated memos in 1983 detailing attempts by Reagan appointees to undercut full enforcement of laws concerning toxic-waste disposal; in the resulting furor, top officials had to resign, the agency was completely revamped, and the White House appointed a "Mr. Clean" to undo the damage.

CONTROLLING THE BUREAUCRACY

Most people believe that all national departments and agencies are part of the executive branch and that the president supervises them through a chain of command, as shown in Figure 13-5 (page 460).

The reality is quite different. To begin with, the Constitution makes no mention of an executive branch. When it mentions the "executive power" of the United States, it refers only to the president as a political officer with certain express and implied constitutional powers—some of which involve the departments. The Constitution does not prevent Congress or the judiciary from supervising national officials.

It is more accurate to think of a "fourth branch"—a separate bureaucratic establishment which is supervised by the other three branches. Thus presidents who enter office expecting to overhaul the work of the departments or to cut back on their functions find themselves checked and balanced by the courts and stalemated by Congress. The only way for the president and Congress to gain control of the bureaucracy over the long term is to cooperate. And that is easier said than done because of the decentralized nature of the parties, the diffusion of power, and the systems of checks and balances.

Congressional control

Historically, Congress has had the most influence on the departments. In fact, during most of the nineteenth century, the secretaries worked closely with the committee chairs. Most secretaries were politicians (and many had served in Congress), and so they knew how important it was to cultivate good congressional relations. Many had presidential ambitions and believed that the best way to advance was to get support from Congress. Woodrow Wilson made his academic reputation as a political scientist with *Congressional Government,* published in 1885, in which he showed how Cabinet secretaries were influenced by congressional leaders.[25] The president then was little more than a clerk, lacking control of the departments' budgets and legislative requests to Congress and with little power to make policies involving the departments. Figure 13-6 outlines this post-Civil War system of congressional government.

Today, Congress no longer dominates the departments, but it still has considerable powers.

Creation and reorganization. By laws, Congress creates and abolishes all departments, agencies, bureaus, and programs and specifies their exact organization. By joint resolution, it approves or vetoes plans for reorganization submitted by the president. It creates, defines, and limits all offices, and it

Figure 13-5. Left, above: The illusion of presidential government. Presidents and their advisors issue orders to cabinet secretaries, who transmit them to political executives, down through the chain of command to bureaucrats who implement them. In reality presidents transmit few direct orders this way, and there is no "chain of command" that can ensure that a president's orders or suggestions will always be carried out in a timely and responsive manner.

Figure 13-6. Left, below: Congressional government. In the nineteenth century Congress directed department business through laws and appropriations. Department secretaries reported to the president, who sent their budget and legislative requests directly to Congress. The main executive function of the president was to see that the laws were faithfully executed and to provide the patronage demanded by the party leaders.

specifies job qualifications. It determines grades and salaries and may set ceilings on how many officials can be hired and at what levels. It determines which positions are filled by political executives, SES officials, or lower-level civil service workers. It can determine travel allowances, expense accounts, office facilities and furnishings, and other "perks."

Appointment to office. The Senate must advise on and consent to presidential appointments of political executives. It may not directly attach conditions to its assent, nor can it require a nominee to promise to take certain actions. But informally it may gain reassurances from a nominee who is worried about rounding up a majority on the committee considering the nomination.

Senators "nominate" officials for positions affecting their states; these include regional and district personnel and federal judges, attorneys, and marshals. At times senators are given a veto by the administration. Senatorial courtesy enables the senator of a state affected by any nomination subject to Senate confirmation to declare that a prospective nominee is "personally obnoxious," in which case the Senate will hold up the nomination indefinitely.

Senate committees can put nominations on hold until the president or the president's nominee provides assurances on policy. They can cast a negative vote and refuse to send the nomination to the full Senate. The Senate can pass a resolution requesting the president to withdraw a nomination, or if necessary it can defeat the nomination on the floor.

The Senate usually does not block presidential appointments. Most investigations involve conflict of interest, divestiture of stocks and other investments before entering government service, or allegations against the character of a nominee. Many investigations are superficial, even when there is some evidence that a nominee has had unsavory business connections or links to organized crime. The Senate usually takes the position that presidents are entitled to have whomever they want in their administrations.

But there are some exceptions. A nominee whose background involves racial discrimination is in for rough sledding. Nominees who lack the background and skills necessary for the position may withdraw rather than face criticism, although some, especially those who are nominated for foreign affairs posts, promise the Senate that they will be "quick learners" if confirmed (one potential ambassador to Ceylon could not tell the Senate Foreign Affairs Committee the name of its capital, for example). A nominee who in a previous government position was abusive to senators may face defeat; for just such a reason Senator Clinton Anderson of New Mexico managed to clobber the Eisenhower administration when it nominated Lewis Strauss to be secretary of commerce. The word gets around that officials should be responsive and honest in dealing with legislators if they plan on serving in higher positions.

460

Most high federal positions require confirmation by the Senate. Theodore Sorensen (center), nominated by President Carter in 1977 to be director of the CIA, withdrew in the face of strong opposition, one of the few nominees for high office who failed to win quick backing from the Senate. (*AP/Wide World.*)

The Senate occasionally blocks a series of nominations to prevent the president from gaining control of an independent agency—especially if it believes that the president would use such control to dismember it. President Reagan made twenty-five nominations at various times for the Legal Services Corporation's eleven-member board of directors and was unable to get a single appointment past the Senate in his first term.

Nevertheless the president can sometimes evade senatorial checks by filling posts with temporary appointees when the Senate is in recess. Reagan used this strategy to make changes in the operation of the Legal Services Corporation. He made eleven appointments to its board while the Senate was in recess, filling the vacancies with people whom the Senate had previously refused to confirm!

Authorizations. Congress gives agency officials all their powers through various *statutory authorizations.* These are granted for one year, or several years, or they may be permanent. Usually they are accompanied by informal understandings between members of committees and agency officials as to how the agency will operate after it has been given its grant of power. Congress often places restrictions on these powers, specifying in detail what an agency may not do (for example, use federal funds for abortions or for school busing). It gives *conditional* authority: the president may reorganize agencies during wartime, for example, but these emergency powers end once the war is over. Congress also gives *contingent authority;* thus it may provide for extension of unemployment payments to jobless workers, but only if the unemployment rate in a state exceeds a specified percentage. It can give *standby authority,* which may later be triggered by a presidential certification or by a congressional resolution (standby wage and price controls in case of runaway inflation are an example). It provides for *concurrences:* agencies cannot act until they receive approval from a state or local government or from interest groups.

These authorizations may be delegated to the president, who in turn

Officials in regulatory agencies are particularly vulnerable to charges of conflicts of interest. Anne Burford stepped down as head of the Environmental Protection Administration because of such a controversy. (*Sebastian: Sygma.*)

subdelegates them to departments and agencies; this gives the president the most power to direct the bureaucracy. Alternatively, Congress may delegate power directly to lower-level officials, specifying what they are to do and how they are to do it—a sign that the president is not expected to interfere. A president who does interfere may be checked by the courts.

Oversight. Congress can examine how agencies are implementing the laws through *legislative oversight.* It may hold investigations and public hearings, which can turn the spotlight on corruption, conflicts of interest, and lack of enforcement. It can force the resignation of high-ranking officials and changes in agency procedures, and it can recommend new laws to restrict an agency. The General Accounting Office audits agencies and can disallow unlawful expenditures.

Members' inquiries. Representatives or senators can ask agencies to help their constituents. In addition, they pressure agencies to institute special programs, often going through the White House and presidential agencies. Senator Al D'Amato, a Republican from New York, earned a reputation for being "tough on crime" by getting the Reagan administration to assign thirty-eight agents from the Drug Enforcement Administration to New York and its "operation pressure point" program, aimed at ridding the Lower East Side of drug pushers.

The legislative veto. Until 1983 Congress could also impose a legislative veto: one or both chambers of Congress, or even one of its committees, could by law "veto" a proposed decision of an agency. For example, Congress could pass a law allowing the secretary of defense to close down military bases—unless his decision was "vetoed" by the Armed Services Committee. Such vetoes could be used in connection with sales of arms and nuclear reactors to foreign nations, the construction of atomic reactors, presidential states of emergency, impoundments of funds, presidential requests for reorganization, and about 200 other matters. The Supreme Court in 1983 ruled these legislative vetoes to be unconstitutional violations of the separation of powers because they allowed Congress to interfere in administrative actions. Moreover, the Court argued

that these vetoes constituted "acts of Congress," which under the Constitution should have been taken by both chambers and sent to the *president* for approval or veto.[26] Congress now uses a *joint* resolution when it vetoes an agency action, which is then sent to the president for approval or veto, thus attempting to meet the objections of the Court.

Sunshine and secrecy. Congress regulates disclosure of information. It can provide criminal penalties for disclosure and transmission, as it does with military and atomic secrets. Its "sunshine laws" may require agencies to conduct open meetings, give greater access to government files (the Freedom of Information Act), and regulate the government's computer files. Loopholes allow agencies to protect information about "ongoing operations" or "pending decisions." Critics charge that these acts have been ineffective because government agencies are reluctant to comply with them. Defenders argue that many of the requests would damage government operations or result in the disclosure of valuable private trade secrets.

Presidential control

Early in our history, presidents presided as figureheads over the departments, compiling their reports and budget requests and transmitting them to Congress for action. But in the twentieth century presidents have become chief executives whose aides and agencies attempt, often with success, to supervise the bureaucracy.

Nominations. Presidents nominate all political executives in departments, in executive agencies, and even in the independent agencies and corporations. Each year one-fourth of these positions open up (closer to half of sub-Cabinet positions in executive agencies), and so presidents have regular opportunities to make policy through appointments.

Removals. Presidents have the power to remove executive agency appointees. Most of the time they need not resort to this power: they can usually arrange a "negotiated departure" instead of firing someone. They may even request undated letters of resignation as a condition of an initial appointment, or they may request such letters later (as Lincoln did during the Civil War with his entire Cabinet). Presidents' aides can leak stories to the press that the White House would like an official to resign. By law, presidents, their Office of Personnel Management, and their appointees may promote, transfer, demote,

Policies on civil rights changed dramatically after President Reagan appointed Clarence M. Pendleton, Jr., to chair the Civil Rights Commission in 1981. (*U.S. Commission on Civil Rights.*)

THE PRESIDENTIAL REMOVAL POWER

The presidential removal power is not directly specified by the Constitution. Presidents have claimed it on the basis of the executive power, their oath of office, and their duty to see that the laws are faithfully executed. James Madison, while serving in the first Congress, argued that separation of powers required the president to be able to remove officials; otherwise, the president's responsibility for executing the laws according to the Constitution could not be fixed. Madison believed that a president who had this power would be more, not less, accountable to Congress.

During the nineteenth century Congress claimed the power as its own. After Andrew Jackson fired William Duane, the secretary of the Treasury, the reaction against "King Andrew" was so strong that it led to the formation of the opposition Whig Party and a motion of censure against the president. After the Civil War, Congress passed tenure-of-office acts that prevented the president from removing top officials until the Senate had consented to their successors—in effect giving the Senate the final way on removals. The House voted to impeach Andrew Johnson after he removed Edwin Stanton, the secretary of war, in violation of this law.

The issue between presidents and Congress simmered for another sixty years. Congress eventually modified and later repealed the tenure-of-office laws for high-level officials, but kept some protections for lower-level civil servants, who went to court to get damages when removed by presidents. The issue was finally settled by the Supreme Court in two key decisions. In 1926, in *Myers v. United States*, Chief Justice (and former president) William Taft ruled for the majority that Congress could not by law restrict the president's power to remove officials whom the president had appointed. This sweeping decision was modified in 1935, in *Humphrey's Executor v. United States*, in which the Court ruled that the president's power to remove officials could be limited by Congress in the case of "administrative agencies" which issued "quasi-legislative" rules or made "quasi-judicial" decisions in cases involving administrative law. These agencies include all the independent regulatory commissions; other agencies, such as the Federal Reserve Board; and most independent government corporations.

or even fire officials in the Senior Executive Service. By the end of their first year in office, presidents can have senior officials working for them who are responsive to their wishes.

Policy direction. Presidents construe the executive power of the United States and their duty to see that the laws are faithfully executed to mean that department offificials are their subordinates who must obey their orders. As President Franklin Roosevelt put it in a 1939 report on administrative reform, "The Presidency was established as a single strong Chief Executive Office in which was vested the entire executive power of the National Government."[27] Congress argues that officials must obey the laws of the United States and therefore are also subordinate to Congress. The federal courts, refereeing this conflict, distinguish between routine *ministerial duties*, which involve no discretion, and *executive duties*, which involve discretion and political judgments. The courts agree that Congress may by law direct officials to perform ministerial duties, and they will enforce these laws even if the president has issued orders to the contrary. But the president may issue orders involving executive duties. The upshot is that both Congress and the president may direct officials, but in different ways, and the boundary lines remain unclear and subject to judicial resolution on a case-by-case basis.

Presidential agencies. Presidents cannot take the time to supervise officials personally; they must rely on White House aides, presidential agencies, department executives, and SES officials, layers which stand between them and the bureaucrats and which make it difficult for them to understand what the bureaucrats want, and vice versa.

What presidents cannot do personally their agencies may do for them. Aides in the White House Office may take on functions which involve them in the work of departments, as when they negotiate directly with a foreign government or a governor. Or they may act as "fire fighters," resolving an issue that has generated bad publicity. They may also be coordinators, heading off impasses between departments, smoothing personal relations, and suggesting compromises.

The Office of Management and Budget (OMB), whose director is also a presidential assistant, helps supervise the bureaucracy. All department legislative proposals since the 1940s and all agency regulations since 1981 have had to be submitted to the OMB for clearance: the president then decides whether they are to be part of the program, can stand on their own, or are to be shelved. All budget requests similarly go to the OMB. Bills passed by Congress go to the OMB (which recommends signature or veto) for review before being sent to the president.

The OMB's Management Division tries to get agencies to introduce new management and budgeting methods. These attempts are not usually effective, since departments often resist innovations. A special unit, the Management Reform Task Force, is in charge of instituting "Reform 88," a special effort to upgrade the way departments manage themselves. The OMB is more successful with spending controls: its Budget Division can order reprogramming of funds within an agency or even a transfer of money from one activity to another, crossing agency lines. Usually these transfers receive informal approval or veto from congressional committees with jurisdiction. Proposed executive agency regulations are sent to the OMB's Division of Information and Regulatory Affairs for cost-benefit analysis and for confirmation that they conform to the presidential program of regulatory reform. During Reagan's first three years in office, the administration's special Task Force on Regulatory Relief, chaired by Vice President Bush, reviewed 6700 existing regulations and got agencies to withdraw 3 percent of them, claiming savings for consumers and companies of more than $150 billion in the next ten years. The OMB's Division of Federal Procurement Policy recommends ways of cutting procurement costs, which are far higher than procurement costs in the private sector.

The Office of Personnel Management (OPM) recommends changes in pay and benefits (increases or decreases) and supervises agency recruitment, training, promotion, and other personnel practices. It prods agencies into meeting presidential targets for reductions in the federal work force.

Presidential policy agencies and councils—such as the National Security Council, the Council of Economic Advisors, the Council on Environmental Quality, and the various Cabinet councils—are also involved with departmental operations. They are supposed to set overall policy and to coordinate agency activities and media relations. They try to control sub-Cabinet appointments to agencies, putting their loyalists in control, and they also try to influence transfers and promotions in the SES and to establish "clearance" procedures to dominate departmental legislative and budget requests. Needless to say, they come into conflict with department secretaries.

For the White House, the resulting friction (and even the chaos) is useful: it allows presidents to make choices. They can side either with a department secretary or with the head of a presidential agency or council. Thus presidents do nothing to prevent, and often they encourage, these conflicts, and some have become Washington institutions: the secretary of the Treasury versus the chair of the Council of Economic Advisors; the secretary of state versus the presidential assistant for national security affairs; the president's science adviser versus NASA; and the White House Domestic Council versus the secretary of health and human resources and the secretary of education.

Rewarding and punishing agencies. Formal powers are used by presidents and White House officials to reward or punish agencies. An agency which the president wants to boost is reorganized into a larger unit and is given more responsibilities (the new Department of Education in the Carter administration, for example). The president encourages new proposals and larger budget requests for the agency; it becomes the lead agency in interdepartmental councils and task forces, and with White House backing it coordinates other agencies. The White House may tie its own political fortunes to the agency's programs, in which case the presidential aides will handle public relations for the agency.

An agency that is marked for retrenchment, extinction, or scapegoating for the failure of a preceding administration is given different treatment—the Occupational Safety and Health Administration in the Reagan administration is an example. The president appointed officials who were hostile to the agency's mission, and they assigned SES managers who cut back on its activities and powers of enforcement; the number of inspectors was reduced, and voluntary compliance programs were instituted instead of legal actions. The results: In 1982 there were only eighteen fines of more than $10,000 whereas in 1980 there had been ninety-eight, and the number of fines over $5000 dropped from 600 to fewer than 25. Vulnerable agencies also find that their budget requests are slashed, that their quarterly allotments are reduced by the OMB, and that their personnel ceilings are lowered by the OPM. An agency may even be ordered to shut down its operations in anticipation of a presidential request to Congress—although until Congress acts, the courts will require that the agency remain open.

Bureau autonomy and professional standards

Bureaus may win autonomy by claiming that professional standards must control their activities. These may involve formal arrangements which include:

- The requirement that top officials have certain professional qualifications or experience
- A fixed term for an agency or program director
- A professional service, like the Foreign Service, the Forest Service, or the Public Health Service, with its own code of ethics and professional standards

Some of these arrangements make a professional association or interest group, such as the American Bar Association (ABA) or the American Medical Assocation (AMA), the arbiter of what constitutes professional conduct in the bureaucracy. This enables career officials to balance presidential or congressional directives with the claim that to obey would compromise them profes-

sionally. Thus antipoverty lawyers argue that to prevent them from representing the poor in cases involving divorce or abortion would violate the ABA Canons of Professional Ethics, since the poor are entitled to be represented in all legal matters. The AMA argues that its codes of professional conduct should take precedence over federal regulations aimed at limiting the kind of medical care that Medicare or Medicaid patients may receive.

CLOSE-UP

J. EDGAR HOOVER AND THE FBI. "In politics you do not attack Santa Claus and you do not attack God," one senator said, by way of explaining how J. Edgar Hoover escaped congressional criticism for his administration of the Federal Bureau of Investigation. For forty-eight years Hoover was its director, and he kept it virtually immune from effective control by the White House or Congress. Dean Rusk, secretary of state during the Kennedy and Johnson administrations, observed that "he had created a kind of kingdom . . . almost unparalleled in the administration branch of our Government, a combination of professional performance on the job, some element of fear, very astute relations with Congress, and very effective public relations."[28]

Hoover was the consummate bureau chief, concerned with professional performance rather than partisan politics, and he took the directorship in 1924 only after informing Attorney General Harlan Stone that all appointments within his agency would be based on merit. During the 1930s the FBI concentrated on arresting gangsters, such as John Dillinger and "Machine Gun" Kelly. During World War II it was responsible for counterespionage. It has always done effective work in investigating bank robberies, automobile theft, and kidnappings. Critics point out, however, that the FBI was slow to develop effective techniques against organized crime, had a poor record in civil rights enforcement, and violated the civil liberties of many individuals and organizations through programs of domestic surveillance and mail interception.

Hoover's power rested partly on fear. Few people dared to speak out against FBI abuses; because of Hoover's information networks, his informers, and his powers of surveillance, he had information about the private lives of too many people in Washington. But he also cultivated members of Congress, especially those in the conservative wing. Criticism of the FBI would lead them to counterattack. Finally, Hoover was a master of public relations. Public opinion polls gave him and the FBI overwhelming support: in 1971 a Gallup poll showed that 80 percent of the public rated his work as good or excellent. Hoover's personal popularity helped the bu-

J. Edgar Hoover (seated). (*Bettmann Archive.*)

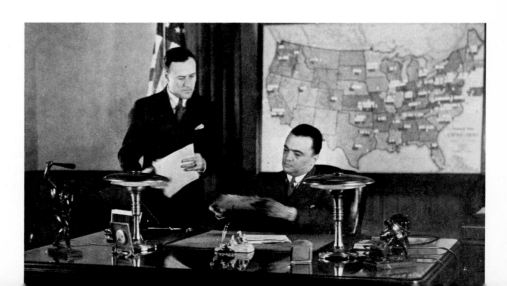

reau. The House Appropriations Committee always gave him all the money he asked for and sometimes more, while the Senate Appropriations Committee approved these requests without even asking him to testify.

When Robert Kennedy, Hoover's nominal superior as attorney general, showed up one day at the Justice Department building without a pass, the guard refused to let him in, remarking, "I don't care if you're J. Edgar Hoover himself, you don't get in." That gives some indication of how Hoover was regarded in Washington. When he reached the mandatory retirement age of 70, President Johnson waived it, telling him, "The nation cannot afford to lose you." Nixon also asked Hoover to remain in office. Only the Kennedy administration tried to bring the director under control. Robert Kennedy insisted on approving Hoover's public speeches, communicated directly with FBI field offices without going through the director, and forced the agency to protect civil rights demonstrators. But the problems Hoover had with the Kennedys were unusual. For the most part, Hoover was untouchable—the most powerful bureau chief that Washington has ever known.[29]

Judicial control

The federal courts can also control officials. They provide access to government employees unions, interest groups, state and local governments, and other interested parties who seek to have agencies comply with the Constitution and the laws. The courts can declare an agency's actions to be unconstitutional or illegal, and they can also interpret the laws to define their powers. They also ensure that agencies operate according to due process of law.

Adhering to procedures. The courts make agency officials act in conformity to procedures already established by the agency itself; thus bureaucrats cannot change their own rules in midstream simply because the rules are inconvenient. In 1984, for example, the Interior Department settled a lawsuit brought by environmentalists charging that it was disregarding its own rules by failing to enforce regulations requiring strip-mining companies to restore land to its original contours. The courts also require officials to follow procedures mandated by Congress. After Congress passed a law requiring the Department of Transportation to consider safety data in making a decision about whether to require air bags in cars, the department used a different approach: it weighed the costs of the bags against the total number of lives which might be saved and concluded that requiring air bags would cost too much. An insurance company sued the department, arguing that Congress wanted not a cost-benefit analysis, but only a safety-risk analysis; the Supreme Court required the department to reverse its decision.[30]

Upholding the laws. The judiciary requires agencies to conform to laws. When Congress directs or prohibits something, it must be obeyed. What Congress appropriates must be spent. Thus federal district judges in 1984 required the Legal Services Corporation to spend money which its board of directors had attempted to withhold. Sometimes Congress gives people ***entitlements:*** the rights to receive something from the government, such as welfare or unemployment checks, medical care, access to transportation for the disabled, and bilingual education for linguistic minorities. Such people can go into the federal courts if their entitlements are reduced or taken away. The Labor Depart-

ment spent only $25 million of $123 million in job-training funds which Congress appropriated for workers who had been laid off because of foreign competition; the United Auto Workers sued the department, and a federal judge ordered that the full amount be spent. In another case, a federal judge described the Department of Health and Human Services as "a heartless and indifferent bureaucratic monster destroying the lives of disabled citizens" in a decision ordering the department to end procedures denying certain disabled people social security benefits mandated by Congress. In the 30,000 or so disability cases heard in the federal courts in Reagan's first term, the reversal rate against the department was 49 percent.[31]

BUREAUCRACIES AND THEIR ALLIES

Bureaucrats deal with the political branches by playing them off against one another and by looking for allies among the groups and clienteles they serve; these activities have consequences for policy-making and policy implementation.

The iron triangle

The classic description of bureaucratic alliance building is the *iron triangle,* also known as the *subgovernment* or the *triple alliance* in political science literature (Figure 13-7): it refers to the relationships between top-level agency officials, lobbyists for a group that the agency serves, and congressional committee leaders with jurisdiction. The triangle may exist at the departmental, bureau, or program level.[32]

Agency officials consult with lobbyists on new legislation, budget submissions, reorganization plans, personnel matters, and proposed regulations. Such consultation is often formalized in group membership on an agency advisory committee. Often industry representatives are named by the president to administer an agency or are put in sub-Cabinet positions in the departments. In return, the bureau expects the interest group to endorse its work in congressional testimony and in the media.[33]

Bureaucrats and lobbyists work closely with congressional committees and subcommittees. They provide services for constituents, assist staffers in preparing for hearings (even going so far as to tell them the questions that legislators will ask), and offer amendments to bills which a committee may adopt. In return for being so solicitous of the committee's interests, they hope that the committee will champion their budgets and authorizations before the entire Congress and protect them from White House cuts.

The iron triangles maintain themselves because of the close professional relationships of the participants: lobbyists and top bureaucrats may work together for twenty years or more. By helping reelect allies in Congress and by getting sympathetic newcomers on committees, the PACs behind the lobbyists also reinforce the system. PACs also try to influence committee and party leaders to appoint sympathetic newcomers so that the triangle will perpetuate itself.

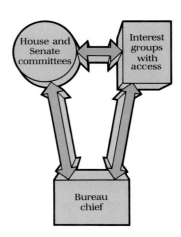

Figure 13-7. The iron triangle. The iron triangle or "subgovernment" consists of a bureau chief or program director who works closely with House and Senate committee leaders and their key staffers, as well as with the Washington lobbyists for interest groups affected by their operations. There are hundreds of such subgovernments in Washington.

Examples of iron triangles. The Department of Agriculture was established because of farm organizations, which permeate its bureaus and work closely with subcommittees of the two agriculture committees. The Interior Department works with ranchers, farmers who need irrigation on dry western lands, and forestry and mining companies. The Nuclear Regulatory Commission maintains close ties with nuclear plant operators, especially on matters of

plant shutdowns. The Public Health Service, the maritime unions, and the House Merchant Marine and Fisheries Committee protect hospitals that benefit members of the merchant marine. The United Mine Workers, the Labor Department, and the House Education and Labor Committee protect the black-lung program from proposed cuts by the OMB.

Iron triangles and policy formulation.   Iron triangles provide continuity in policy-making. They have expertise and technical skills that political appointees can rarely match. They give groups access to government decision making and implementation, a load-sharing device which takes some of the burden off presidents in times of crises, especially when they are preoccupied with foreign affairs or the economy. During the Civil War, for example, while Lincoln dealt with the secession, the iron triangles revamped banking and the currency, land use, and the agricultural policies of the nation; one result was the creation of the land-grant colleges, which are now the great southern and midwestern state universities.

But iron triangles have their disadvantages. Continuity is not always good. Sometimes the people vote for innovation and new policies. Then the president will be frustrated by these alliances, and presidential rhetoric will not be matched by accomplishment, which further erodes public support of the government. Iron triangles lead to corruption and conflicts of interest. Many political appointees, members of the SES, and top civil servants intend to leave government service and go into the private sector. They may decide to arrange a "soft landing" by taking actions favorable to the industries they are supposed to regulate. They may give contracts for research to the "beltway bandits" (the research firms that line the beltway surrounding the capital) and then join these same outfits later.

Iron triangles are created either to get things from the government or to get the government out of their business. Lax regulation enables interest groups to cut their costs in such areas as environmental protection and health and safety regulations. Iron triangles reinforce private-sector dependence on government largesse, which in turn prevents the free market from disciplining inefficient businesses or superfluous nonprofit organizations. They substitute political influence for market competition in allocating resources. They wheedle contracts for goods and services, research and development, and capital construction, which the government may not need. They obtain subsidies, guaranteed and below-market-rate loans, and tax expenditures. They get regulations which freeze out competitors and just about guarantee them a profit. They substitute connections and influence for the impartial administration of the law.[34] And as one group or industry establishes such an arrangement and distorts the operation of market forces, others must also do so in order to survive.

Finally, iron triangles guarantee some groups access and preferences at the expense of others. Wealthier family farmers and agribusiness dominate the Department of Agriculture, while poorer farmers—tenants and sharecroppers—have less access to services and are forced off the land. Environmentalists get frozen out of policy-making in the Interior Department, which favor companies doing business on public lands under the theory of multiple use. The iron-triangle system penalizes groups that are unorganized (the poor), have organized late (consumers and environmentalists), have innovative ways

of doing business, or are more concerned with broader public policy than with their own immediate economic interests. It benefits members of groups, especially corporate and trade associations, which establish PACs and make campaign contributions; which hire the best public relations, lobbying, and law firms; and which know the ins and outs of Washington politics.

Issue networks

Sometimes iron triangles are superseded by *issue networks:* more complex but somewhat looser networks of relationships between bureaucrats, journalists, academics, foundation officers, White House and congressional staffers, lobbyists, and others who represent interest groups.[35] They think about issues in a broader context and are interested in rational problem solving, efficient allocation of resources, and the use of new decision-making techniques. They are professionals who get satisfaction from influencing policy, exercising power, and enjoying the respect of their peers, and they are less interested in bureaucratic empire building, lobbying for the benefit of a particular industry, or their own personal economic gain. They concentrate on innovative policies or major redistributions of wealth rather than on narrow regulatory or distributive outcomes. A distinction made in Chapter 6 about party professionals applies here: participants in iron triangles live *off* politics (in the sense that they are involved for the purpose of making an economic gain, establishing bureaucratic careers, or winning reelection), while participants in issue networks live *for* politics (because they measure their success in terms of policy influence).

Examples of issue networks. The difference between iron triangles and issue networks is best explained by an example. Agricultural policy has traditionally been dominated by iron triangles consisting of bureaus in the Agriculture Department, subcommittees organized around particular crops in the Agriculture Committee, and the national farmers' organizations. Their goals have been to dominate decision making in the department, obtain funds for their organizations, and get higher income for farmers. Contrast this alliance with the issue network devoted to feeding malnourished Americans: foundations have awarded several "think tank" grants to groups such as the Food Research and Action Center to find out how many people in this country are going hungry and why; the Senate Select Committee on Nutrition was created after a national agenda campaign to make hunger a major issue; and Congress is pressured by Bread for the World and the Child Nutrition Forum (two citizens' lobbies) to stop cuts in food programs for the poor. Various antipoverty agencies, legal services lawyers, local community groups, and others involved in the National Anti-Hunger Coalition have gone into the federal courts to obtain orders making it easier for people to obtain food stamps and other government assistance.

Usually issue networks must contend with entrenched iron triangles. This is the case when defense analysts attack procurement decisions that benefit specific companies, when environmentalists concerned about acid rain are opposed by congressional spokespersons for "smokestack industries," and when transportation safety experts and insurance companies square off against automobile manufacturers over the issue of air bags and seat belts.

The work of the issue network involves policy analysis, national agenda politics, and the formation of broad citizen coalitions to pressure Congress; in

Figure 13-8. The issue network and executive agencies. Members of an issue network may join together in a coalition to influence government policy at the program, bureau, or department level; or they may bypass the bureaucracy and try to influence congressional committees or the White House.

contrast, the iron triangles have fewer participants, eschew publicity, and focus on economic benefits for the producers and campaign contributions to sympathetic members of Congress (Figure 13-8).

Network activism. Networks form when some of the people concerned about an issue realize that they have similar points of view and use similar methods of analysis. They may have communicated at academic conferences or in national commissions or task forces, or they may have read one another's books and articles. They may even be linked together by computer networks formed to study and exchange views on issues. Eventually they may try to influence policy. Their strategy is threefold: to convince the White House and Congress that their analysis is correct; to get the president to name a key member of the network to a high position, who in turn can bring others into sensitive posts; and to win over the presidential advisory system and obtain a mandate from the president to control the resolution of the issue.

USING THE MEDIA. Issue networks gain much of their strength through their effective use of the media. They try to isolate, discredit, and eventually remove their opponents from the administration. They may leak government documents and information about agency plans to favored reporters, who in effect become publicists for them. Well-timed and well-publicized op-ed articles in newspapers, research reports, articles, books, interviews on the Sunday television talk shows, and congressional testimony can discredit their opponents.

GOVERNMENTS IN EXILE. Think tanks and private research institutes—such as the conservative American Enterprise Institute, Heritage Foundation, and Hoover Institution; the centrist Brookings Institution; and the radical Institute for Policy Studies—have resident scholars who follow and analyze public policy. Many are former officials who left office after a change of control in the White House. Loose networks of these former officials and others in law firms or universities constitute a kind of "government in exile" whose members are available for high government positions after a change of party control of the White House. Often presidents make policy by deciding on the "crowd" they intend to tap for their administrations.

RATIONAL DECISION MAKING. Issue networks emphasize rational decision making based on all the relevant data. Consider the 1984 decision by the Department of Transportation to speed up the passage of rules banning lead from gasoline. Traditional iron-triangle politics would have involved delays, exemptions, and loopholes favoring the refiners of leaded gasoline. Yet even within the Reagan administration, dedicated to deregulation, the evidence that leaded gasoline was causing irreparable damage to children (especially inner-city youngsters) proved compelling, and that evidence was gathered and evaluated through an issue network devoted to the relationship between the environment and transportation policy.

PRESIDENTIAL OPTIONS. While iron triangles tend to frustrate presidents, limit their options, and slow down change, the issue networks have the reverse effect. All presidents find themselves caught in the middle of conflicts between different networks: supply-siders versus fiscal conservatives in economic policy; hawks versus doves on arms control; and advocates of nuclear energy versus advocates of coal and oil in energy policy. Often the media coverage, fueled by the leaks of sensitive documents from competing issue networks, gives the impression of an administration in disarray. But in fact the competition between different issue networks is good for the president. It brings more

participants and a wider range of views before the public and the administration. It provides a constant launching of trial balloons, enabling the president to gauge public opinion. It allows participants to "get out in front" of the White House, bring the public and Congress around, and then get the president to "sign on" and support their plans. It enables groups which are weak politically to win arguments through the force of their ideas. It serves as an antidote for entrenched bureaucratic interests, secrecy, and political privilege.

Presidents encourage conflict between issue networks because it gives them information and options. It makes each network dependent on the White House for a final resolution. Presidents often organize their staffs and agencies in such a way as to encourage the networks to have it out with one another. One may control the Council of Economic Advisors, but it will be balanced by another which dominates the Treasury. One may control the disarmament agency, but another will be in charge at the State Department. Presidents act as magistrates: they listen to the arguments, gauge public opinion, canvass Congress and their advisers, and then make a final decision on policy.

PROBLEMS WITH THE BUREAUCRACY

There are two important problems with the federal bureaucracy: erosion of authority and lack of accountability.

Authority

Officials in government agencies do not always know what they are doing. They usually work with incomplete, inaccurate, and out-of-date information. Their planning and budgeting systems are poorly designed and often yield ludicrous results which even the bureaucrats ignore as useless. Sometimes they operate on the basis of controversial and unproven theories: in the 1960s this was the case with the liberal antipoverty programs, and in the 1980s it has been true of the conservative programs aimed at stopping crime, drug use, and pregnancy among teenagers. The program evaluations of officials in government agencies are often self-serving.

Most government agencies do not handle routine management functions well. Their financial control systems (accounting, bookkeeping, and auditing) are antiquated. Their computer systems have not been state-of-the-art since the late 1960s. Their recruitment, training, classification, and merit systems do not match up to those in the private sector. They are overstaffed. Their procurement costs are enormous, compared with those of private organizations.

The federal government structure is inefficient. Agencies often duplicate one another's work, have overlapping jurisdictions, or leave crucial matters unattended to; in the 1980s, for example, there has been no government agency with jurisdiction over the release of new genetic material into the environment, even though such release could have catastrophic consequences. Agencies cover up mistakes and mishaps (such as the Three Mile Island nuclear reactor shutdown), hide behind loopholes in the Freedom of Information Act, and stonewall when confronted with evidence of incompetence. They punish whistle-blowers rather than reward them.

The bureaucracies are inflexible where they should be flexible (in providing people with services), and they are freewheeling and highly politicized where they should not be (in dealing with interest groups and organized constituents). They bend or break the rules for the powerful, while adhering to them with a vengeance against everyone else.

The end result is a crisis of authority. Everyone running for office attacks big

government, and yet no one does anything about it because it is not the problem. The size of government cannot be reduced substantially because the public wants fairer and more efficient administration of programs, not their elimination. Thus the politics of baiting the bureaucracy misses the point, however better it makes voters feel.

Accountability

In theory, the fourth branch is supervised by the other three branches. In practice, the decentralization of congressional power, the autonomy of the legislative parties, and the competition for power within the institutionalized presidency all limit that supervision. It remains extremely difficult for the White House to impose a chain of command on most bureaus and to control the workings of most programs. Congressional oversight remains intermittent and works best in controlling distributions or tempering regulations for the benefit of the iron triangles. Supervision by the judiciary is intermittent, and its legitimacy is denied by an increasing number of conservative judges who have been appointed in the past few years.

The question of to whom the bureaucracy should be accountable has never been resolved.[36] The president and Congress contend for control, and the courts referee their dispute. Meanwhile, the alliance of professional associations, interest groups, and bureaucrats works for agency autonomy, insisting that professionalism rather than partisan politics should be the standard for agency operations. In turn, a looser issue network tries to use national agenda politics to assert a public interest, often at the expense of the political branches and the career bureaucrats.

The public usually remains confused by this conflict, especially since there are good arguments to be made on all sides. Agencies should be responsive to their clienteles, but they also should maintain professional standards. They should be responsive to the president, but they should also follow the laws laid down by Congress. If issue networks have better ideas, perhaps the existing iron triangles should be overturned.

How do we ensure that bureaucracies are accountable to the public interest? There are no easy answers. Iron triangles form in response to pressures on bureaucrats which are unlikely to fade away. But the White House, through the kind of appointments it makes, can bring in more policy experts from the issue networks. The presidential agencies can foster *multiple advocacy* so that the issue networks will compete with one another and the president can choose from among many options. The resulting interactions between presidential agencies, departments, and issue networks would involve a good deal of competition and redundancy, and different combinations of presidential agencies and bureaus would be ready to implement proposals, once the president approved them. It would be a messy system; but the more councils, boards, and presidential agencies there are, the more flexible the top levels of the administration are and the more options the president and Congress have. That might increase the accountability of the fourth branch to the other three.

IN CONCLUSION

Bureaucratic organization, which involves a chain of command, formal procedures, division of labor, and specialization, is the predominant way of organizing public and private activities. The national government is organized bureaucratically: there are thirteen major departments, as well as other executive and nonexecutive agencies and independent commissions. These are run by political

executives appointed by the president to make policy; a Senior Executive Service, responsive to the president to oversee implementation; a career civil service to administer departments; and line personnel to carry out orders and see to implementation. There is no separation of politics from administration: each level of officialdom has its own ideas, priorities, and political interests.

The fourth branch is supervised by the other three branches. Presidential agencies use the appointment and removal power, budget and legislative clearances, and centralized management to impose a chain of command on executive agencies. Congress uses its power to consent to presidential appointments, its power of authorization and appropriation, and legislative oversight to influence what departments do. The judiciary referees the struggle between the executive and the legislative branches, sometimes making officials follow presidential or departmental orders, but enforcing laws where they conflict with these orders.

The bureaucracies try to gain autonomy by emphasizing professional standards rather than political supervision and by joining in the iron triangles with interest groups and congressional committees. In turn, these triangles may be challenged by issue networks, which use national agenda politics or persuasion based on research and policy analysis to propose policies that are in the public interest.

While most reforms would strengthen presidential control or congressional oversight of the bureaucracy, few are likely to be adopted, and most miss the point—which is to make officials more accountable to the public and less likely to betray the public's trust and promote narrow interests. The increasing strength of issue networks will have a greater effect on the way government works than any proposed reforms.

NOTES

1. Seymour Martin Lipset and William Schneider, *The Confidence Gap*, Free Press, New York, 1983, pp. 48–49.
2. H. H. Gerth and C. Wright Mills, *From Max Weber: Essays in Sociology*, Oxford University Press, New York, 1958, pp. 196–198.
3. Max Weber, *The Theory of Social and Economic Organization*, A. M. Henderson, (trans.) and Talcott Parsons (trans.), Free Press, New York, 1947, "The Essentials of Bureaucratic Organization: An Ideal Type Construction," pp. 329–347.
4. Alice Rivlin, *Systematic Thinking for Social Action*, Brookings, Washington, D.C., 1971.
5. *U.S. Government Organization Manual, 1985*, Government Printing Office, Washington, D.C., 1985.
6. Leonard White, *The Jacksonians and the Republicans*, Macmillan, New York, 1955.
7. Woodrow Wilson, "The Study of Administration," *Political Science Quarterly*, vol. 2, no. 2, June 1887, pp. 197–222.
8. Herbert Hoover, *The Challenge to Liberty*, Herbert Hoover Presidential Library Association, Rockford, Ill., 1971, p. 114.
9. Charles Peters, *How Washington Really Works*, 2d ed., Addition-Wesley, Reading, Mass., 1983, p. 38.
10. Donald K. Price, *Government and Science*, Galaxy Books, New York, 1962, pp. 66–78.
11. *The New York Times*, Jan. 1, 1985, p. 38.
12. "High Tech Firms Push for New Export Controls," *High Technology*, vol. 4, no. 12, December 1984, p. 83.
13. *The New York Times*, Jan. 1, 1985, p. 38.
14. Richard Fenno, *The President's Cabinet*, Vintage Books, New York, 1959, chap. 6.
15. Linda Demkovich, "Margaret Heckler Shows Fighting Style," *The National Journal*, vol. 16, no. 19, May 19, 1984, pp. 977–981.

16. U.S. Commission on Civil Rights, *Equal Opportunity in Presidential Appointments*, GPO, Washington, D.C., 1984.

17. Calvin McKenzie, John W. Macy, et al., *America's Un-elected Government*, Ballinger, Cambridge, Mass., 1984.

18. Hugh Heclo, *A Government of Stangers: Executive Politics in Washington*, Brookings, Washington, D.C., 1977.

19. *The New York Times*, July 21, 1983.

20. Joseph Barlett and Douglas Jones, "Managing a Cabinet Agency," *Public Administration Review*, vol. 34, no. 1, January 1974, pp. 62–70.

21. David Burnham, "White House Link: Computer in Ohio," *The New York Times*, July 15, 1983.

22. Thomas M. Franck and Edward Weisband, *Resignation in Protest*, Viking, New York, 1976, p. 59.

23. U.S. Senate Government Operations Committee, *U.S. Government Policy and Support Positions*, GPO, Washington, D.C., 1985.

24. *Local 2677, The American Federation of Government Employees v. Phillips*, 356 F. Supp. 60 D.D.C (1973).

25. Woodrow Wilson, *Congressional Government*, Houghton Mifflin, Boston, 1885.

26. *Chadha v. INS*, 77 L. Ed. 2d 317 (1983).

27. President's Committee on Administrative Management, *Report with Special Studies*, GPO, Washington, D.C., 1937, p. v.

28. Arthur Schlesinger, Jr., *Robert Kennedy and His Times*, Houghton Mifflin, Boston, 1978, p. 250.

29. This biography was prepared with the assistance of Jeff Adler of Columbia College.

30. *Motor Vehicle Manufacturers Association v. State Farm Insurance Co.*, 103 S. Ct. 2856 (1983).

31. *The New York Times*, June 8, 1984

32. J. Lieper Freeman, *The Political Process*, Random House, New York, 1965.

33. Grant McConnell, *Private Power and American Democracy*, Knopf, New York, 1966.

34. Theodore Lowi, *The End of Liberalism*, Norton, New York, 1969.

35. Hugh Heclo, "Issue Networks and the Executive Establishment," in Anthony King (ed.), *The New American Political System*, American Enterprise Institute, Washington, D.C., 1978, pp. 87–124.

36. Frederick Mosher, *Democracy and the Public Service*, Oxford University Press, New York, 1968.

FURTHER READING

Cater, Douglas: *Power in Washington*, Vintage, Books, New York, 1964. A journalistic account of how iron triangles work.

Downs, Anthony: *Inside Bureaucracy*, Little Brown, Boston, 1967. A classic account of the principles of bureaucratic organization.

Heclo, Hugh: *A Government of Strangers: Executive Politics in Washington*, Brookings, Washington, D.C., 1977. An account of the way top executives are recruited into the administration and why they cannot work as a team.

Lowi, Theodore J.: *The End of Liberalism*, Norton, New York, 1969. An argument for a return to statutory standards and less delegation of power from Congress to officials, including a description of the performance of programs in the 1960s.

Lynn, Laurence E., Jr.: *Managing the Public's Business*, Basic Books, New York, 1981. Suggestions by a former staffer in three departments and the National Security Council about how officials could improve their performance.

McConnell, Grant: *Private Power and American Democracy*, Knopf, New York, 1966. A study of the way government policies are shaped by private groups which share in the administration of programs.

Nathan, Richard: *The Administrative Presidency*, Wiley, New York, 1983. An account of the strategies used by Nixon and Reagan in dealing with the bureaucracy.

Peters, Charles: *How Washington Really Works*, 2d ed., Addison-Wesley, Reading, Mass., 1983. A journalist's look at the foibles of bureaucrats.

Pressman, Jeffrey, and Aaron Wildavsky: *Implementation*, University of California Press, Berkeley, 1973. An account of how federal programs are actually run at the local level, including a theory as to why they diverge from the intent of national policymakers.

Seidman, Harold: *Politics, Position and Power*, 2d ed., Oxford University Press, New York, 1975. Shrewd observations by a former Budget Bureau official about the games that federal bureaucrats play.

THE STUDY BREAK

Parkinson, C. Northcote: *Parkinson's Law*, Houghton Mifflin, Boston, 1962. Just as the British Empire was breaking up after World War II, the British Colonial Office was expanding its personnel and budget. The author tried to discover why, and in the process developed some very funny laws about bureaucratic empire building.

The Right Stuff. A 1984 movie, based on a novel by Tom Wolfe, about the space program and the clash between the worlds of bureaucrats and test pilots.

USEFUL SOURCES

Adzigian, Denise A. (ed.): *Encyclopedia of Governmental Advisory Organizations*, 4th ed., Gale Research Company, Detroit, 1983. A directory of advisory groups attached to bureaucracies.

Budget of the United States Government, GPO, Washington, D.C. Annual budgetary data for the bureaucracy.

Encyclopedia of Associations, Gale Research Company, Detriot, 1983. A directory of interest groups.

Federal Yellow Book, The Washington Monitor, Washington D.C., 1985. Names and phone numbers of 29,000 top officials in the White House, presidential agencies, and federal departments and agencies.

The Federal Register, GPO, Washington D.C. A daily compendium of proposed and adopted agency rules.

The National Journal. A weekly journalistic account of the activities of important government agencies.

Public Administration Review. A quarterly journal devoted to improvement in public administration.

U.S. Government Organization Manual, GPO, Washington, D.C. An annual compendium of all government agencies and the top officials in each, including addresses and phone numbers and the table organization of each department and agency.

The Washington Monthly. A magazine with many articles detailing the empire-building tendencies of bureaucrats.

ORGANIZATIONS

General Accounting Office. General Accounting Office Building, 441 G Street, Washington, D.C., 20548. Conducts audits and policy analyses of the bureaucracy for Congress. For more information telephone 202-275-2812.

Committee on Post Office and Civil Service. U.S. House of Representatives, suite 309, Cannon House Office Building, Washington, D.C. 20515. Issues reports on the personnel practices of the bureaucracy. For more information telephone 202-225-4054.

Office of Management and Budget. Executive Office Building, Washington, D.C. 20503. Management units monitor agency compliance with presidential priorities and attempt to strengthen presidential controls. For more information telephone 202-395-3080.

Office of Personnel Management. 1900 E Street, N.W., Washington, D.C. 20415. Administers the appointment, promotion, and other personnel policies for the President. For more information telephone 202-632-5491.

Committee on Government Operations. U.S. House of Representatives, suite B-377, Rayburn House Office Building, Washington, D.C., 20515.

Committee on Governmental Affairs. U.S. Senate, suite 342, SDOB, Washington, D.C., 20510. Both the Committee on Government Affairs and the Committee on Government Operations study the overall effectiveness of the departments and issue reports and studies. For more information telephone 202-225-4407 (House) and 202-242-4751.

Budget planning involves close cooperation between executive and legislative leaders. The federal budget affects, and is affected by, the entire economy, including the New York Stock Exchange. (*Michael Evans: White House; Sepp Seitz.*)

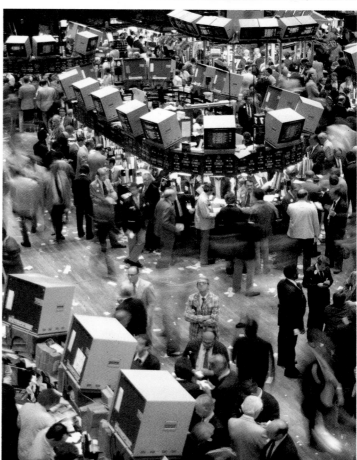

CHAPTER 14

BUDGET POLITICS: CONTROLLING UNCONTROLLABLES

To budget is to govern. To control what goes into a budget answers the key political question, "Who gets what, when, and how?" "There are no money questions of any moment which are not also policy questions," says a high-ranking budget official. Robert Michel, the House Republican leader, observed that in budgeting, "The issue is not one of figures, but philosophy; it spells out who we are and where we are going."[1]

"To find out how anything really works," according to a House member, "you have to look at the budget."[2] This chapter begins with a discussion of the functions of a budget; then we will see how presidents put their budgets together, and we will look at the congressional budget process. The chapter concludes by examining presidential budget strategies; thus it is also a case study of presidential-congressional relations.

WHAT A BUDGET DOES

First let us consider what a budget does and how the *Budget of the United States Government* is organized.

A budget—whether for a household, a corporation, a university, or a government—does several things:

- It plans activities for the coming year.
- It specifies priorities and timing for these activities. It decides among alternatives and among claimants for scarce resources.
- It determines what agencies can do during the year.
- It is a source of prizes and payments, which those who control it can use to reward others who cooperate with them.

The government budgets according to a fiscal rather than a calendar year. The *fiscal year,* FY, begins October 1 and ends September 30, taking its number from the year in which it ends. FY 1986 begins October 1, 1985, and ends September 30, 1986.

The national budget not only determines what goes on inside the government but also influences the allocation of national wealth. It can redistribute income, by taxing those who earn and providing payments and services to nonworkers or low-paid workers, or it can be neutral, providing services to people that cost about the same as they paid in taxes.

The budget can affect the size, composition, and performance of organizations in the private sector. Agencies can be funded to compete with private companies, as in the field of telecommunications satellites. The government can subsidize corporate research and development, as it did with the space shuttle. The budget determines which sectors of the economy get subsidies, loans, loan guarantees, contracts, and insurance.

The budget is a claim on national wealth. It shows not only the activities of the government but also the proportion of the gross national product (GNP) that its activities consume. Both the government's expenditures and its share of the GNP have increased in recent years. Spending has gone from $728.4

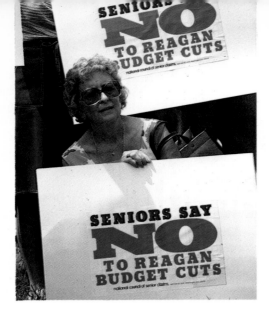

Senior citizens protest Reagan's budget cuts. Congress is traditionally protective of popular programs and usually rejects attempts to cut them. (*John Ficara: Woodfin Camp.*)

billion in FY 1982 to more than $1 trillion in FY 1986, while its proportion of the GNP has gone from 20.4 percent in FY 1972 to 24.4 percent in FY 1985. Liberals who believe that the government should make decisions about the investment and consumption of national wealth look favorably on these developments; their goal is to emulate the mixed economies of western Europe, in which governments typically allocate from 30 to 50 percent of the GNP. Conservatives argue that there should be a gradual movement downward, perhaps to 15 percent of the GNP, with the government concentrating only on national security and essential domestic activities. Both are likely to be disappointed: the most liberal and the most conservative American administrations will probably not move out of the 20 to 25 percent range. (See Figure 14-1.)

Budgets also allow politicians to make promises about the future, to take

Figure 14-1. In recent years the largest increases in government expenditures have involved military spending and direct payments to individuals. Note the increase in interest payments on the national debt and the sharp decrease in other programs. The figures are in 1972 dollars adjusted for inflation. In current (1985) dollars the expenditures are close to $1 trillion. (Source: Office of Management and Budget.)

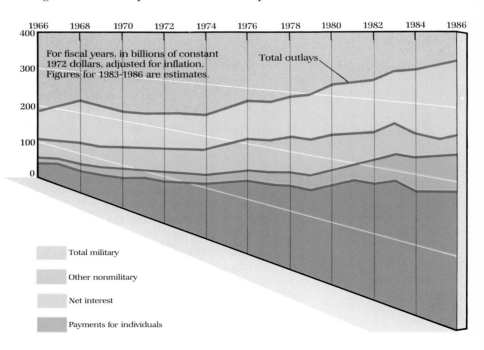

\pos

positions on issues, to reassure constituents, and to campaign for votes. Both the Democrats and the Republicans gear much of their national television advertising toward taxing and spending issues. But there is more to budgeting than just campaign rhetoric. Budgets are highly sensitive to changes in party control of government: it makes a difference who wins an election. Overall spending and levels for particular programs shift greatly when a different party takes power, just as they do in other democratic nations.[3] The White House and legislative parties circle warily around the budget, trying to develop strategies for the next elections. Should the president promise more programs or become "curtailer in chief" and promise to curb big government? Should the president's party in Congress support the president, or should members distance themselves from unpopular proposals? Should the opposition cooperate with or confront the president?

Each party plays it differently. The Democrats are good at winning votes by promising more programs. But their "spend, spend, elect, elect" approach to coalition building makes it difficult for them to restrain spending without alienating core supporters, and they have little credibility when they shift gears and pose as budget cutters. The Republicans have credibility as budget cutters (at least for domestic programs), but that is as much a liability as a benefit. Senator Mark Hatfield, a Republican, observed that his party was viewed by many Americans as an instrument to transfer wealth "from the needy to the greedy," because of cuts in programs for the poor.[4] The Republicans have their own electoral constituencies, which simultaneously want smaller budgets and greater spending on domestic programs that benefit them.

THE FEDERAL BUDGET: A CLOSER LOOK

Income and expenditures

By FY 1986 the income and outlays of the federal government each added up to around $1 trillion, organized in the following overall aggregates:

- *Total receipts.* These include the total income that the government expects to receive. The money comes from borrowing by the Treasury (20 percent), personal income taxes (36 percent), social security and unemployment insurance taxes (29 percent), corporate taxes (8 percent), excise taxes (on gasoline and tobacco, for example, 4 percent), and estate taxes, gift taxes, customs fees, and taxes on the sale of property and other income (3 percent). In good times receipts soar, while during recessions they drop. Usually there is much greater fluctuation in receipts than in spending, which accounts for most of the changes in the deficit. Revenues (other than borrowings) totaled over $800 billion in FY 1986.
- *Total outlays.* These are the total expenditures for the fiscal year. They include direct payments to individuals (42 percent); defense spending (29 percent); interest on the national debt (13 percent); grants to states, counties, and cities (1 percent); and all other federal operations (5 percent). They totaled over $990 billion in FY 1986.
- *Deficit or surplus.* The difference between receipts and outlays yields the deficit or surplus for the fiscal year. In almost every year a deficit is recorded. In FY 1983 it was $195 billion, and in FY 1984 it was $175 billion—figures far greater than in any other peacetime year.
- *National debt.* Not to be confused with the *deficit* for a single fiscal year, the national debt includes money owed from previous years (from the sale of Treasury savings bonds, bills, and notes). It also includes new borrow-

ing for the deficit in the fiscal year, as well as the interest on the debt. In recent years, because of high interest rates and the soaring size of the debt, interest payments have accounted for as much as 15 percent of the budget. The total national debt now approaches $2 trillion, which represents 22 percent of all public (national, state, and local) and private debt.

Government expenditures

Types of spending. TAX EXPENDITURES. The government spends money in different ways. There are *tax expenditures:* income which the Treasury forgoes through loopholes in the tax laws designed to encourage people to do certain things. For example, if an industry cannot get the government to spend money to clean up toxic wastes, it might get tax breaks if it installs nonpolluting equipment. Disadvantaged youths age 16 and 17 who are employed during the summer provide tax breaks of 85 percent of their salaries, up to $2555 per worker, to employers. By 1985 there were 104 such tax expenditure programs, equaling 25 percent of actual government outlays (more than $250 billion), and therefore they constitute a major part of government "spending."

The biggest break, $40 billion, goes to homeowners, who can deduct interest on their mortgages and (unless Reagan's 1985 tax proposal is passed by Congress) another $15 billion in local property taxes. Contributors to charities (and the organizations that receive them) benefit from $15 billion in deductions. Future retirees benefit from more than $40 billion that is exempt from taxes until their retirement benefits are paid. Corporations receive more than $25 billion in investment credits, $2.2 billion in oil and gas depletion allowances, and $2.4 billion in state and local industrial development bonds. Deductions for state and local income taxes (at risk under Reagan's 1985 tax proposal) amounted to $40 billion for individuals who itemize. Even college students and faculty members get breaks: a $600 million exemption of scholarship and fellowship income.

OUTLAYS. Next come actual government payments to individuals, corporations, nonprofit organizations, and state and local governments. When Congress approves presidential budget requests, it means that agencies can incur *obligations:* they can hire employers, rent office space, buy goods and services, and so forth. *Total obligational authority* (TOA) is the amount that the government can commit in the current fiscal year and future fiscal years. TOA in turn can be divided into *previous year authority* (money allocated in previous years but not yet spent) and *new obligational authority* (NOA), which is money requested for the current fiscal year. These figures in the budget indicate how much the government is permitted to spend, but *not* the actual amounts it pays out. These are *outlays;* payments made in the fiscal year in the form of checks, cash, bonds or debentures, and accrual of interest on agency debts in order to liquidate obligations. As Figure 14-2 shows, annual spending outlays are a mixture of previous and new obligational authority. Figure 14-3 shows the relationship between obligational authority, obligations incurred, and outlays.

Often yearly outlays exceed new obligational authority (because of spending based on previous authority)—there is no close relationship between either TOA or NOA and annual spending. This means that when the administration and Congress try to control spending by limiting budget TOA or NOA, actual outlays may remain quite high; this often happens with military spending. Alternatively, some programs may be given large budget authority, but actual

Figure 14-2. The mix of government spending. Government agencies are permitted to spend money based on prior years and new obligational authority (laws passed by Congress). This budget authority provides for spending in the current fiscal year as well as in future fiscal years. Thus Congress cannot simply pass new laws which immediately reduce spending in the current fiscal year by large amounts; the impact of its decisions is usually spread over several years.

Figure 14-3. Obligations, outlays, and budget authority. After Congress provides agencies with their budget authority (TOA), they may incur obligations and pay for them with checks drawn on the United States Treasury. The TOA which is not obligated by agencies at the end of the fiscal year is returned to the Treasury or carried forward into future fiscal years if Congress has provided for multiyear authority.

outlays may be much lower if the program runs for several years, if there are delays, or if the administration decides not to spend all the money.

Spending authority: Budget authority versus legislative authority. Congress grants two kinds of spending authority: legislative authority and budget authority. *Legislative authority* gives an agency permission to do something and may set a ceiling on the amount that can be spent. Permission is not the same as funding, however; the actual money comes from **budget authority,** which requires one or more of the following from Congress:

- *Appropriation:* a bill reported by the appropriations committees for annual, multiyear, or permanent funding of a government agency, specifying the amounts (and staying within the limit of the legislative authorization). An example is military procurement. Two-fifths of all government expenditures come from appropriations.

- *Contract authority:* a bill reported by any standing committee which allows an agency to contract for goods or services with public or private agencies. Congress pledges its full faith and credit: it will provide appropriations when needed to meet the contractual obligations. Certain farm programs involve contracts between the government and growers, for example.
- *Loan or credit authority:* a bill which allows an agency to make a loan or extend credit to individuals, corporations, cooperatives, and state, local, and foreign governments. The government may also buy loans made by financial institutions to individuals, making more credit available for new loans; the student loan program is an example.
- *Loan guarantee authority:* a bill which allows an agency to guarantee bonds issued by, or a loan made to, a local government or corporation. The guarantee provides funds to near-bankrupt operations (such as Chrysler, Lockheed, and New York City in the 1970s) or allows them to obtain funds at below-market rates.
- *Borrowing authority:* a bill which allows an agency to borrow money from the Treasury or the private bond markets to finance its operations, with interest and principal to be repaid by fees collected. Certain government corporations, such as the Tennessee Valley Authority and COMSAT (space communications), finance their capital construction this way.

Agencies must obtain both *legislative* authority, which gives them permission to do certain things; and *budget* authority, which directs the Treasury to fund these activities or allows the agencies access to private money markets. Congress usually forbids agencies to ask for budget authority until their legislative authority has been granted. In most instances, legislative authority establishes a ceiling beyond which budget authority does not go. "Never lose sight of the fact that the Appropriations Committees are the saucers that cool the legislative tea. Just because you have an authorization doesn't mean a thing to us . . . ," Representative John Rooney once told a State Department official who reminded him that the department had received large legislative authorizations.[5]

Congress maintains the twofold system of legislative and budget authority as its own internal check: the system fragments congressional power and sets the legislative committees (which like to increase funding for their pet projects) off against the appropriations committees. When the latter get too niggardly with their funding, other committees can often get changes in congressional rules which allow them to provide loan, contract, or borrowing authority to agencies; this is known as *backdoor funding.* In recent years federal credit and guaranteed loans from government agencies and government-sponsored corporations have increased from less than $275 billion in FY 1971 to more than $1 trillion in FY 1985, as Figure 14-4 (page 486) shows.

Controllable and uncontrollable expenditures. Expenditures can also be categorized as relatively controllable or as uncontrollable. Uncontrollable expenditures involve government provision of goods and services to people who can legally make a claim to them. They include social security, Medicare, Medicaid, and welfare payments to individuals; pensions for military personnel and civilian workers; interest on the national debt; and payments for long-term

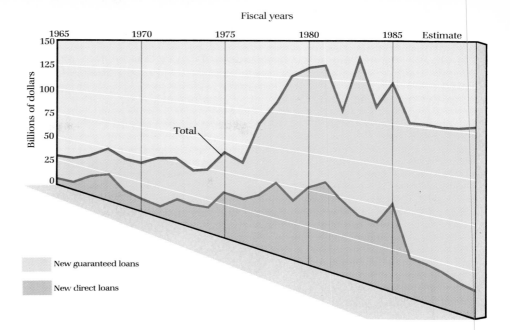

Figure 14-4. The large increases in federal loans and guaranteed loans (made by financial institutions) triggered an effort by the Reagan administration to cut back on these politically popular programs in 1986. (Source: *Budget of the United States Government, FY 1984*, Special Analysis F, p. f-7.)

capital construction contracts. Such expenditures are uncontrollable in the sense that it is politically difficult to change the laws that guarantee the payments; but occasionally when the deficits loom too large, it is possible to make cuts in these programs (though not in interest payments).

Personnel costs, such as salaries and benefits, are also relatively uncontrollable. By law, these payments must be competitive with the payments in the private sector. By 1984 the government's own pay commission estimated that increases averaging 20 percent would be needed to compete with pay in the private sector.

What is left is *discretionary* or *controllable* spending: spending for military and civil programs that are not locked into long-term contracts and are not part of the entitlement system. *Only 20 percent of the entire budget fits into this category.* For example, only 4 percent of the expenditures of the Department of Health and Human Services do not involve personnel costs or entitlement programs. Thus it is impossible to make meaningful spending cuts without going after these entitlement programs. It is easier to cut new obligational authority in discretionary programs, but not much money is saved by doing so. If really big amounts are involved, either all the controllable programs must be eliminated, or the government must make cuts in the uncontrollable programs. Either way, those who would limit government expenditures face excruciatingly difficult choices.

Expenditure equivalents. Sometimes legislative authority has an impact equivalent to that of budget authority, and the government can propose expenditure equivalents as a substitute for new spending. When Congress passes regulations, it imposes costs. Regulatory relief, as implemented by the Reagan administration, either for a company or for industry, may be just as useful as federal funding. Regulatory changes and lax enforcement of existing laws can lower the cost of toxic-waste disposal and mine-tailing cleanups, for example, which for the affected companies is the equivalent of federal funding. If state and local governments cannot obtain enough money to build ramps and other

means of access for the handicapped, they will propose weakening existing regulations that require them to provide such access. If Congress cuts Medicaid funding, it will soften the blow to state governments by changing eligibility requirements and reducing services. Imposing tariffs or quotas on foreign goods may be just as useful to companies that are threatened by foreign competition as giving them tax expenditures (in the form of investment tax credits) or subsidizing their research costs. Expenditure equivalents may reduce interest-group pressure for government funds.

FOCUS

BACKDOOR BUDGETING. Many government agencies are not funded by appropriations, but instead have backdoor access to the Treasury. Some are not even listed in the *Budget of the United States Government.* Most of these make loans, borrow money, or charge fees; they include the Federal Reserve Board, the Strategic Petroleum Reserve, the Postal Service, the United States Railway Association, the United States Synfuel Corporation, and the Federal Financing Bank (FFB).

The largest off-budget entity is the FFB, which made more than $14 billion in loans to other government agencies in FY 1984 and has a total of more than $110 billion in loans outstanding. It is the second largest "bank" in the United States. It makes loans to other government agencies—known as *sponsored borrowing*— such as the Student Loan Marketing Association (Sallie Mae). Here is how the system works: Banks make loans to students so that they can attend college. These loans are then sold to Sallie Mae, which provides the banks with more money for more student loans. In turn, Sallie Mae markets the loans to the FFB, which gives it money so that it can buy more loans from the banks. Where does the FFB get the money to buy the loans from Sallie Mae? It raises money from the Treasury, which lends it funds (using the original student loans as collatoral).

Why go through this tortuous process of raising money? For one thing, the FFB makes loans to Sallie Mae at below-market rates, which ultimately means that the banks can lend students money at low rates. For another, if many government agencies raised money by borrowing, the money markets would be flooded with strange bonds; the existing process eliminates most agency financings, leaving it up to the Treasury to market its well-known bonds and bills in private money markets. Finally, the process operates as a revolving door with no limits, something that sponsors of student loans, farmers' housing, and other programs like. Loans to farmers soared from $4 billion in 1974 to more than $16 billion in 1980, with more than $40 billion outstanding; this would have been impossible if the program had been subject to annual appropriations.

THE BUDGET PROCESS

Budgeting as an action-forcing process

Budgeting is like preparing the state of the union message: it is an action-forcing process, requiring advance preparation to meet deadlines. Fourteen days after the Monday on which Congress convenes each January, the president sends the budget to Congress. To meet the deadline, the budget must be at the printer's in early January. That requires the president, along with the *Office of Management and Budget* (OMB), to finish work on the budget in late December. In turn, the OMB and the executive departments must complete their work early in the fall, which means that agency officials must start sometime in the preceding spring. Most planning for new programs, drafting bills

for Congress to consider, and evaluating existing activities, is tied to budget deadlines and is part of the budget process.

Budgeting takes a long time. Consider the budget enacted for FY 1986. It was developed by agencies and departments in the winter and spring of 1984 and was then submitted in the summer to the OMB, which prepared its draft budget for the White House in the fall. In January 1985, the president sent the budget to Congress, which considered and modified it for nine months. It went into effect on October 1, 1985, and remained in effect until September 30, 1986. Departments had to plan a budget in 1984 that would determine their spending through most of 1986 (and in 1984 they were spending money they had planned for in 1982).

The length and the complexity of the process tend to slow down innovation. Abolishing or reducing the size of programs also takes a long time—often until the legislative and budgetary authority expires, which may be several years. It helps to take a long perspective when you budget.

Budgeting is a bit like driving a huge truck, loaded with lumber, down an icy mountain road. Decisions that you made 100 yards back about whether to use the brakes or downshift affect what you can do now to control the truck. The way you handle it now will limit your options 100 yards down the road. It is snowing, visibility is low, and a competitor is ready to take over your job as soon as your truck overturns.

Steps in the budget process

The budget process can be divided into the time before the fiscal year when the budget is prepared; the fiscal year itself, when outlays are expended from previous and current budget authority; and subsequent fiscal years, when some of the funds authorized will be spent.

The budget call. The OMB requires departments to submit their budgets two years before the president's version is sent to Congress. Its budget call instructs them to plan on the expansion or contraction of their programs, on the basis of economic forecasts.

Agency budgeting. Agencies within each department estimate what it would cost to maintain programs at their existing levels in the next fiscal year (taking inflation into account); this becomes their *current services budget*, also known as their *base*. Next, they ask for what they consider to be their *fair share* of any increases in federal spending. Most agencies expect to make only minor changes in activities in any single year. Thus they budget incrementally, rarely asking for more than 10 or 15 percent in additional funds.[6]

Department budgeting. Department officials review agencies' requests. Most departments make nonincremental changes; they add to some programs and cut others, even though overall department budgets do not change very much from year to year.[7] In the past, agencies that "thought big" and asked for major increases were likely to get them; the size of the request, especially if it was backed up with good arguments, not the existing base, seemed to be the key to additional funding.[8] More recently, departments have been asked by the White House to "freeze" many of their operations, and agency officials who ask for large increases and who aggressively lobby for them may be reprimanded by higher-ups.

Some department budget officials use program budgets: they compare the fit between an agency's goals and line-item requests, and they may reject parts of the budget if it does not have immediate relevance to the agency's goal. Others use cost-benefit analysis to rank projects in terms of costs versus projected benefits, rejecting those with the lowest ratios. Sometimes programs from different agencies are put into the "pit" against each other, and the ones with the lowest cost-to-benefit ratio are cut back or ended. Some departments even experiment with *zero-base budgeting:* no agency has a guaranteed base, and all must justify the next year's expenditures starting from zero.

OMB budget guidance.   The OMB guides departmental review of agency budget submissions. In relatively flush years the word goes out to prepare new programs and accept agencies' incremental requests. In leaner years the OMB requires departments to use restrictive definitions of the base—small inflation adjustments (or none at all) or exclusion of low-priority programs. It may instruct agencies to make across-the-board percentage cutbacks, to make cuts in functions (like regulatory enforcement), to freeze all new programs and hiring, or to ban or limit activities such as nonessential travel or publications.

OMB budget review.   Departments submit their proposed budgets to the OMB for review. These include *language sheets*, which estimate spending authority, and *green sheets*, which estimate outlays. They are reviewed by the OMB's Budget Review Division; its examiners make recommendations for every agency and program in the department. These in turn go to the OMB program associate directors, political appointees who make sure that the recommendations follow the administration's policies. Finally, the budget director holds "review sessions" with top White House staffers, during which department secretaries can plead their cases before the director briefs the president.

Presidential budget review.   Presidents consider spending proposals in the context of their overall economic program. They meet with political advisers and with officials from residential advisory agencies before changing the OMB's recommendations. Sometimes department secretaries get one last chance to appeal directly to the president. Truman, Ford, and Carter listened to such appeals carefully, acting like judges deciding cases. Other presidents, such as Nixon and Reagan, have had an intermediate "appellate level" consisting of the OMB director and several White House aides to screen appeals. Few presidents ever reverse the decisions of their budget directors; to do so would simply invite more appeals and weaken their authority. In some administrations (Kennedy's and Reagan's, for example) the OMB must appeal against Pentagon budget requests, rather than the other way around.

Figure 14-5 (page 490) shows in more detail all the formal steps involved in the formulation of the budget; but the actual sequence can be far messier and more out of step than these neat flowcharts indicate.

The budget game

Imagine a game in which the players come on or off the field at will; in which the rules change from one season to the next; in which the object of the game may be to put more points on the board—or fewer; in which a new team forms on every play, only to dissolve before the next play; in which no one, even

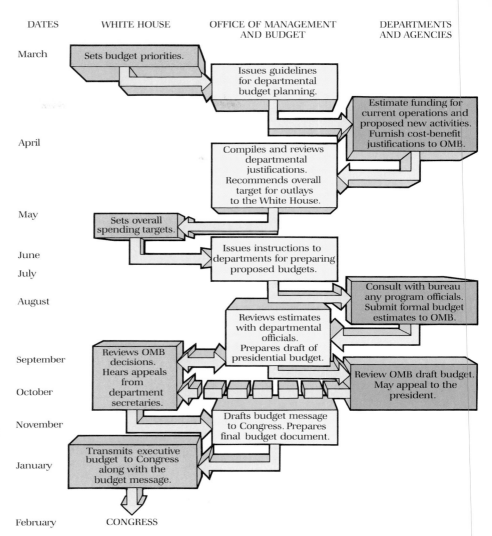

DATES	WHITE HOUSE	OFFICE OF MANAGEMENT AND BUDGET	DEPARTMENTS AND AGENCIES
March	Sets budget priorities.	Issues guidelines for departmental budget planning.	
April		Compiles and reviews departmental justifications. Recommends overall target for outlays to the White House.	Estimate funding for current operations and proposed new activities. Furnish cost-benefit justifications to OMB.
May	Sets overall spending targets.		
June		Issues instructions to departments for preparing proposed budgets.	
July			
August		Reviews estimates with departmental officials. Prepares draft of presidential budget.	Consult with bureau any program officials. Submit formal budget estimates to OMB.
September	Reviews OMB decisions. Hears appeals from department secretaries.		Review OMB draft budget. May appeal to the president.
October			
November		Drafts budget message to Congress. Prepares final budget document.	
January	Transmits executive budget to Congress along with the budget message.		
February	CONGRESS		

Figure 14-5. Preparation of the executive budget. The Office of Management and Budget (OMB) takes primary responsibility for translating general presidential priorities into specific instructions which guide departments and agencies when they submit their budget requests. The OMB eventually prepares the budget of the United States for submission by the president to Congress, a process which takes almost a year to complete.

those on the same team, gives anyone correct information; and in which the scoreboard always exaggerates. If you can imagine such a game, you are ready to play executive budget politics.

The agencies. The submissions that agencies make to their departments are not exactly what they need, or even what they want. Instead, they are padded, in anticipation of departmental and OMB cuts. If agencies think that the president will increase their funds, the president gets their support. Otherwise, they plan end runs around the OMB to the more sympathetic Congress. They find interest groups to serve, as the Department of Agriculture has done with farmers, as the Pentagon has done with contractors and subcontractors of weapons systems, and as the Department of Health and Human Services has done with doctors and hospital administrators. Officials include programs and services for important committee leaders so that they can build a coalition that will make their higher-ups think twice before suggesting cuts. They may even use federal funds to organize their constituents into interest groups; this technique was pioneered by the Agriculture Department with farmers and then

was used by antipoverty agencies in the 1960s. Federal money can even be used to lobby Congress for more funding, something that Pentagon contractors specialize in.

To protect themselves against cuts, agencies can mount their own national agenda campaigns. Some advertise their mission, like the National Guard with its television commercials and the Forest Service with Smokey the Bear. The military cites Soviet arms buildups just before its budget requests are reviewed by the White House. The United States Geological Survey makes widely publicized predictions about earthquakes when its budget is in danger, and the Weather Service mounts new hurricane, tornado, and flood watches.

Agencies that are pressured to make cuts may announce that the cuts will be made in popular programs. The Coast Guard claims that it will not be able to stop illegal immigrants from entering the country. The Postal Service says that it will have to stop Saturday mail delivery. The Park Service says that it will have to restrict visiting hours at the Washington Monument and reduce the number of rangers in the national parks. The Securities and Exchange Commission says that it will have to close the office that handles investors' complaints. The idea is to get interest groups and voting constituencies to pressure the administration not to make the cuts.

The departments. Sometimes the departments play games with the agencies. They may impose restrictive new budgeting methods in order to change an agency's priorities. Top Defense Department officials use the budget to discipline the military services and force them to coordinate their missions and programs. When heavy cuts are required, sometimes a department secretary engages in an elaborate hoax with the OMB: instead of letting the secretary be the villain, the OMB does the heavy cutting—even making cuts which the department itself secretly proposed. When departments want more money, of course, they try to build a coalition that includes the leading members of the legislative and appropriations committees so that they will be able to stand up to the OMB and the White House.

Secretary of Agriculture John Block prepares the USDA budget. (*United States Department of Agriculture.*)

The OMB. The OMB has its own games to play. Often it tries to cut department submissions. Its examiners look for padding and duplication in agency and department submissions. It requires departments to use restrictive budget techniques and penalizes them if their submissions do not comply. It may force departments to plan for lower outlays than its obligational authority would indicate. It has the power to make quarterly allotments of funds, and it can provide less money than Congress gave. But sometimes the OMB tries to moderate demands for severe budget cuts. Then it takes an optimistic view of the economy, forecasting major increases in tax revenues and shortfalls in projected outlays—all in an effort to reduce projected deficits and therefore lessen the pressure on the president to make more spending cuts. Its forecasts in turn may be challenged by the Treasury (which is likely to be more pessimistic) or the Council of Economic Advisors.

The OMB may even disavow the president's budget if it cannot get its own way, as it did in 1984, when in congressional testimony David Stockman, the budget director, called on Congress to enact spending cuts (especially in defense) and tax increases that were not even mentioned in the presidential budget.

The White House. Presidents must decide how deeply involved in budget politics they want to become. Some lobby heavily with Congress to get their budgets enacted, as Reagan did in 1981 and 1985; others walk away from their own budget submissions, refuse to defend the figures, and distance themselves, as Eisenhower did in 1958 and as Reagan did in 1983.

Some presidents, such as Kennedy and Johnson, are fortunate enough to budget in periods of economic expansion. During their administrations, tax receipts soared along with the GNP, and there was money for new domestic programs. Between 1961 and 1964 domestic spending increased 35 percent, and it increased another 24 percent between 1964 and 1968. Budget choices for the White House in such times are simply choices between what to do first and what to delay. The OMB becomes a programming agency; its examiners organize task forces to plan new government activities, and then they take the lead in getting these programs through Congress and seeing that they are implemented.

Other presidents—including Nixon, Ford, and Carter—have had to budget

President Reagan discusses the growing federal deficit in a speech at the White House, April 29, 1982. (*J. T. Atlan: Sygma.*)

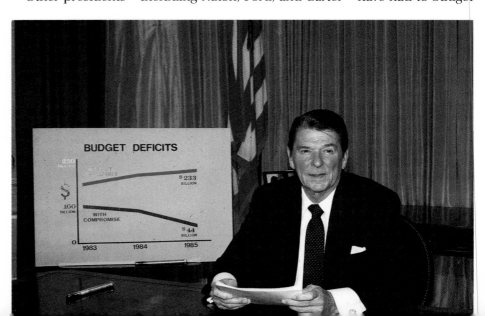

in periods of recession or ***stagflation*** (high inflation and low economic
growth). They had to become "curtailers in chief." But spending during these
presidents' administrations continued to rise (25 percent between 1969 and
1972 and 31 percent between 1973 and 1976), even though receipts did not
keep pace. The result was growing pressure to "do something" about the deficit. The budget game changed significantly in 1978, when Carter proclaimed
that retrenchment was the order of the day. As one OMB official, W. Bowman
Cutter (!), observed about Carter, "He was puzzled and irritated by the fact that
the choices were so brutal. He grew to hate the budget process."[9] Reagan
managed a 5 percent cutback in domestic spending between 1981 and 1984,
halted cutbacks for the 1984 elections, and then proposed sweeping and drastic new cuts in 1985. Yet overall outlays still rose.

When the media cover the presidential budget, they focus on the overall size
and on the projected deficits. Presidents do what they can to minimize the
damage. After a change of party in the White House, entering presidents submit a budget designed to embarrass their predecessors (claiming that they
underestimated the problems), and they exaggerate the gravity of the situation.
On leaving office, most presidents submit a final budget document that overes-
timates income and underestimates expenditures, showing a plan for a balanced budget in one or two years. These are fairy-tale figures, cooked up to
make the outgoing president look good and the incoming president look bad;
they are revised in mid-March, when the new president claims to have inher-
ited an unbelievable mess.

Most presidents forecast balanced budgets several years in the near future,
no matter what the present deficit is, reminding one of the queen in *Through
the Looking Glass* who promised jam yesterday and jam tomorrow, but never
jam today. Reagan used this trick in his 1981 budget submissions and in the
1984 elections, when he argued that the huge deficits would be reduced by the
end of his second term. Other presidents use accounting tricks to avoid passing crucial milestones; Johnson even postponed some expenditures for a year
to avoid spending $100 billion in 1964, and Reagan did the same thing two

493

decades later, when the deficit approached the $1 trillion mark. Candidates who are running for office decry huge deficits; once in office, they tend to minimize the problem and focus on other economic data. If the economy is doing poorly, they argue that deficit spending will stimulate it to recovery; if the economy is booming, they argue that the deficit will soon come down and that the nation can afford it anyway.

CLOSE-UP

DAVID STOCKMAN. David Stockman spearheaded the 1981 and 1985 drives of the Reagan administration to slash domestic spending. He was a liberal antiwar activist in the 1960s at the University of Michigan, and then at Harvard he became a neoconservative under the influence of two political scientists, Daniel Moynihan (now a senator from New York) and James Q. Wilson. Stockman worked as a congressional aide for John Anderson, and in 1976 he was elected as a representative from Michigan. In Congress he was a hardworking and principled conservative: he was the only legislator from his state, the automobile capital of the nation, to vote against the Chrysler bailout.

After the 1980 elections, Reagan made Stockman director of the OMB. Shortly before the inauguration, he and Representative Jack Kemp teamed up on a memo to Reagan which proposed tax reform and reductions, spending cuts, deregulation of business, and decontrol of oil prices. In January he began to implement his own spending recommendations, making a proposal for a first round of cuts totaling $40 billion. Many of the programs involved were political sacred cows that had previously been immune to cuts. Stockman argued that cuts should be made regardless of who would be hurt: "We are interested in cutting weak claims rather than weak clients; . . . we have to show that we are willing to attack powerful clients with weak claims."[10] But the largest cuts were made in social service agencies with politically weak clienteles; defense contractors, large corporations, farmers, the elderly, and other organized interests were affected far less.

Stockman played an important role in getting Congress to go along. He consulted closely with legislators from both parties, making compromises when necessary. When Howard Baker, the Senate majority leader, insisted on funding the Clinch River nuclear reactor in Tennessee, Stockman backed off. "It just wasn't worth fighting," he said. "The package will go nowhere without Baker and Clinch River is just life or death to Baker."[11] Stockman was unable to dominate the administration's revenue program. He favored a flat tax with only minor reductions in revenue, and he did not believe the supply-siders' argument that large cuts would stimulate the economy and result in increased revenues. "I was a budget cutter before I was a tax cutter," he said.[12] To make the system fairer and produce more revenue, he tried to increase user fees for government services and elimi-

As director of the OMB, David Stockman had final responsibility for presenting the administration's budget proposals to Congress. (*Shephard Sherbell: Picture Group.*)

nate some tax loopholes, deductions, and exemptions. President Reagan turned down some of these proposals and Congress rejected others. The bill as passed reduced revenues by $750 billion over the period 1981–1986.

At the end of his first year in office, Stockman faced another setback. In November 1981 William Greider, a Washington reporter, published an article in *The Atlantic* based on extensive personal interviews with him. In the article Stockman conceded that the main purpose of the tax cuts was to reduce the rate for the rich. He admitted that neither he nor anyone else had confidence in many of the budget numbers which had been used and that the computer models had been changed on the basis of some optimistic assumptions and unproven theories. The Democrats pounced on these admissions and took some of them out of context, charging that Stockman was dishonest, incompetent, and duplicitous. Tip O'Neill, the Speaker of the House, said that Stockman "knew firsthand the fundamental weaknesses in the Reagan program and chose to cover them up."[13] Many Republicans urged him to resign. After a well-publicized lunch with President Reagan, Stockman came out and informed reporters that the meeting was "in the nature of a visit to the woodshed after supper."[14] His offer of resignation had not been accepted.

Stockman recovered from this political blow but never regained his former authority with his colleagues or with Congress. In part this may account for the fact that Reagan's 1982, 1983, and 1984 budgets were virtually ignored by members of Congress, including Republicans in the Senate, and for the fact that his 1985 proposals were under attack by his own party in Congress even before he submitted them.[15] Stockman resigned his post in 1985.

CONGRESSIONAL ACTION ON THE PRESIDENTIAL BUDGET

The president submits the *Budget of the United States Government* to Congress in January (Figure 14-6). It is an accurate description of current budget authority and past outlays—but it is only a set of recommendations for the next fiscal year. Most of the figures are agreed to by the OMB and the White House, although Congress, by law, has required that the budget contain the recommendations of several agencies (the Consumer Product Safety Commission, the Federal Elections Commission, the Interstate Commerce Commission, and the Federal Energy Regulatory Commission), along with the final OMB figures.[16]

Congress, by law, requires the president to propose a budget, but the Constitution, in Article I, Section 9, provides that it is Congress that disposes of the budget, through the provision that "no Money shall be drawn from the Treasury but in Consequence of Appropriations made by law." As James Madison once said, "The legislative department alone has access to the pockets of the people."[17] The president's requests are converted by Congress into budget authority. Officials in the executive branch know that the figures in the presidential budget are not written in cement—these officials have one more chance to get what they want from Congress.

The budget committees

The House and Senate budget committees report resolutions in March and September before the beginning of the fiscal year; this enables Congress to set total tax and spending levels as well as targets for thirteen or so large categories of spending—defense and agriculture, for example. (See Figure 14-7.) "Per-

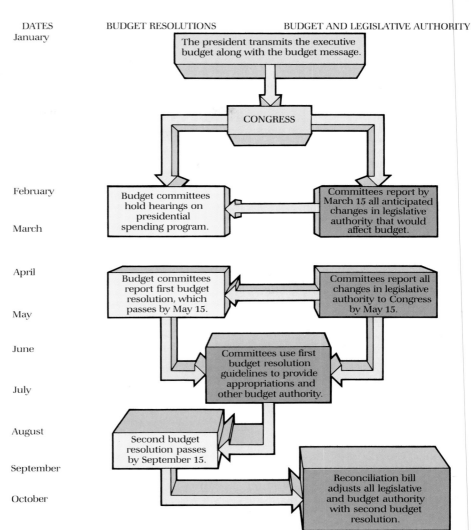

DATES
January

BUDGET RESOLUTIONS

BUDGET AND LEGISLATIVE AUTHORITY

The president transmits the executive budget along with the budget message.

CONGRESS

February

March

Budget committees hold hearings on presidential spending program.

Committees report by March 15 all anticipated changes in legislative authority that would affect budget.

April

May

June

Budget committees report first budget resolution, which passes by May 15.

Committees report all changes in legislative authority to Congress by May 15.

Committees use first budget resolution guidelines to provide appropriations and other budget authority.

July

August

September

October

Second budget resolution passes by September 15.

Reconciliation bill adjusts all legislative and budget authority with second budget resolution.

Figure 14-6. The Congressional budget process. Committees which provide legislative and budget authority are linked with the budget committees and their first and second budget resolutions in this complicated and lengthy process. Although the flowchart indicates dates by which Congress must complete action, often the deadlines are not met, and the resolutions are delayed or not enacted. The White House maximizes its influence if the reconciliation bill which normally is passed at the very end is moved up toward the beginning of the process.

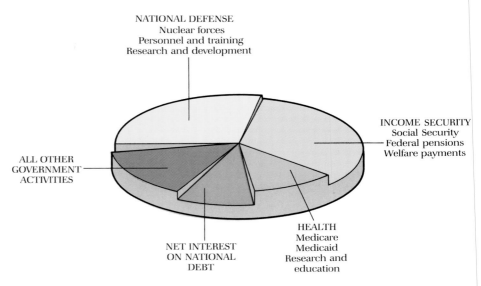

NATIONAL DEFENSE
Nuclear forces
Personnel and training
Research and development

INCOME SECURITY
Social Security
Federal pensions
Welfare payments

ALL OTHER
GOVERNMENT
ACTIVITIES

HEALTH
Medicare
Medicaid
Research and
education

NET INTEREST
ON NATIONAL
DEBT

Figure 14-7. Outlays of the national government for fiscal year 1985. (Source: *Budget of the United States Government, FY 1985*, table A-4, Special Analysis A.)

haps the most important aspect of the resolution," according to Brock Adams, a former House chairman, "is the fact that it contains the budget of Congress and not that of the President."[18]

The House Budget Committee has thirty-one members, five of whom come from the Appropriations Committee and five from the Ways and Means Committee. The House party leaders also choose several, and the House legislative caucuses choose the remainder. The Democrats, who control the House, give themselves a large majority ratio. The House Budget Committee is highly partisan, with liberal Democrats confronting conservative Republicans. The Democrats write their own budget resolution and ignore the Republicans. Yet the members are more pragmatic than their ideological stances would suggest. "One thing that happens, regardless of philosophical stripe," says Jim Jones, a former chairman, "is that once they sit on the Budget Committee they become pragmatic. They become driven by the numbers."[19] House members can serve on the committee for only four years in any decade, and so they do not gain much expertise, nor do they have much incentive to build up the committee's power at the expense of other House committees. They are usually inclined to compromise with the Appropriations Committee and the Ways and Means Committee.

The Senate Budget Committee consists of twenty members. They too are pragmatic. Unlike their counterparts in the House, they usually form a centrist bipartisan coalition, freezing out extremists.[20] The members can serve for as long as they wish, which gives them an incentive to expand their power at the expense of other committees. They have had many battles with the Appropriations Committee, the Finance Committee, and the Armed Services Committee because their budget recommendations often attempt to predetermine policies to be considered later by these committees.

The appropriations committees

The two appropriations committees report out thirteen bills (and several supplemental bills) which provide about two-fifths of the total budget authority. At one time members prided themselves on their role as "guardians of the Treasury." Members were strongly conservative, and Republicans combined with southern and border-state Democrats to fashion a bipartisan majority. According to one representative, "No subcommittee of which I have ever been a member has ever reported out a bill without a cut in the budget."[21] Between 1947 and 1959 the House Appropriations Committee cut estimates more than three-fourths of the time in thirty-seven agencies.[22] (This did not mean that agencies took cuts below their base; most of the time the committee simply cut a part of the *increase* proposed in the president's budget.) In the 1970s the committee changed. Republican presidents began suggesting absolute cuts or small increases, and the committee Democrats championed these programs.

There are thirteen subcommittees—one for each appropriations bill. They see the budget as a storehouse of goodies. The unit with jurisdiction over the Interior Department, for example, received requests from 260 members to include their pet projects in the appropriations bill in 1984. As the former director of the OMB David Stockman observed, "There is no such thing as a fiscal conservative when it comes to his district or his subcommittee."[23] Funding defense contracts, military bases, highways, hospitals, airports, and harbors helps committee members get reelected, and they also can use job-training, education, and health programs as a form of "human resources" pork barrel,

Urban representatives are especially sensitive to cuts in expenditures for bridges, tunnels, and mass transit. (*Gerard Rancinan: Sygma.*)

creating their own political machines with the aid of officials who receive federal grants. Members of Congress get on subcommittees that have jurisdiction over programs which benefit their districts or states. New committee assignments and transfers bring on people who want to increase funding and expand programs.[24]

The Senate Appropriations Committee has always counterbalanced the House Appropriations Committee. In the 1950s and 1960s, when the House cut presidential requests, the senators acted as a "court of appeal" for executive agencies: they could testify before the Senate committee and try to get it to recommend more money than its counterpart in the House. Senate rules reinforced the tendency of the committee to up the ante; subcommittee meetings are open to senators who are not on the full committee but who express an interest in programs being considered by the committee—and mostly they come to boost these programs. Since the Republicans took control of the Senate in 1981, the committee has served as a buffer between right-wing Republican senators intent on making very large cuts (even larger than those proposed by the president) and moderate to liberal House Democrats intent on preventing all cuts proposed by the OMB.

The congressional budget process

The president's budget is referred simultaneously to the budget committees, which consider overall tax and spending policies, and to the appropriations committees and other committees which have jurisdiction over spending. The committees that deal with legislative authority report out new authorizations no later than May 15. On the same date Congress passes the ***first budget resolution,*** setting overall spending limits and providing targets for specific categories. As the appropriations committees begin their work, they are caught between authorizing committees that want Congress to approve new activities and budget committees that call for cutbacks.

Granting budget authority. The committees that report bills granting budget authority (the most important of which are the appropriations committees) have several options. They have the ***current services estimate*** in the presidential budget, which tells them what it would cost simply to continue funding an agency at existing levels. They have the president's request. At hearings they

498

can find out what an agency or department originally asked for. They have alternatives prepared by the Congressional Budget Office. And they have target figures from the budget resolutions.

Officials in agencies in the executive branch testify before the subcommittees, sometimes daring to ask for more money than the president requested. "Mr. Chairman, you would not think that it would be proper for me to be in charge of this work and not be enthusiastic about it and not think that I ought to have a lot more money, would you?" asked an assistant chief of the Forest Service.[25] Such witnesses are followed by lobbyists for interest groups, who ask for even more money.

Members of the subcommittees have so many programs to consider and so many numbers to deal with that they must adopt a strategy to simplify their calculations. They cannot go through every line in the budget or consider every program in detail. Instead, they assume that most programs should be funded at past levels (adjusting for inflation), matching the incremental approach of the agencies whose budgets they are considering. In the case of certain sacred cows, such as the Federal Bureau of Investigation, they always follow or even exceed the president's requests. A program is reviewed carefully if the president proposes major changes, if committee members strongly like or dislike it, or if the program can help members get reelected. Subcommittee members specialize and defer on minor matters to others with expertise. Specialization and reciprocal deference help members cope but mean that they take a fragmented view: they see small parts of the budget, not the whole picture.

The committees *mark up* the president's budget and substitute their own figures. They may keep the current level of funding, make across-the-board increases or cuts, or develop their own budgets. They may also attach restrictions, prohibitions, exemptions, waivers, and other provisions which specify how money may and may not be spent; these *limitation riders* generally begin with the words "no funds appropriated" and go on to specify the restriction. Recent examples include prohibitions on using federal funds for abortions or

Members of Congress from rural areas usually seek assignments to committees and subcommittees affecting farmers. By 1985 farm programs cost more than $30 billion annually. (*United States Department of Agriculture.*)

school busing. About forty or fifty such riders are adopted during each session. (Unlike regular statutes, a prohibition expires with the funding.)

Committees write bills so that they can build a majority coalition on the floor. They report measures that will result in particular and tangible benefits to the majority. These involve packages with many different projects or logrolls. Projects are funded on the basis of horse trades for votes rather than high cost-benefit ratios. Agencies must disperse their facilities into areas where costs are high and coordination becomes difficult. Funds for slum removal, public housing, and mass transit go to smaller towns that have little need for them, while large cities decay, so that the gravy can be spread.

Yet such budgeting makes political if not economic sense. Bills get the acquiescence, if not the strong support, of a majority. Rural areas vote for programs that benefit cities in return for programs that aid their interests. Research programs gain greater support when laboratories and clinics are located throughout the country, not in just a few centers. There are good reasons for having federal facilities located at the grass roots and not centered in Washington, especially at a time when mistrust of government is high. Programs which are paid for by all taxpayers but which benefit only a few are not as likely to be popular, and those voting for them are vulnerable; bigger packages with something for everyone help legislators with their constituents.

Committee conflict. Just as different units in the executive branch play games with one another, congressional committees try to influence the budget at the expense of their rivals. Conflict occurs when the budget committees face off against committees that report bills with excessive budget authority, as well as when attempts are made to put together deficit-reduction packages. Usually the result parallels the legislative process: it is not a case of the president versus Congress, but rather a matter of shifting alliances in order to pit some presidential agencies, departments, and committee majorities against others.

BUDGET RESOLUTIONS VERSUS BUDGET AUTHORITY. Bills providing budget authority are due to be passed into law on the seventh day after Labor Day. By September 15, Congress is also supposed to pass its **second budget resolution.** This timetable pits the budget committees, with their comprehensive "top-down" approach, against the legislative and spending committees, with their "bottom-up" approach. Conflict is virtually guaranteed. The Senate Budget Committee and the Armed Services Committee have squared off over the size of the defense budget, and the Finance Committee has fought the Budget Committee over backdoor spending measures.

Sometimes the second budget resolution is not reported or passed, either because of the crush of business near the end of the session (or in an election year when Congress recesses) or because the Budget Committee does not have the votes. (The House has a rule which provides that the first resolution substitutes for the second resolution.) Congress then simply passes the money bills reported by other committees. Other times the appropriations bills are not reported because they could conflict with budget ceilings, and Congress funds the government by **continuing resolution** (keeping spending at the existing rate). Sometimes a second budget resolution passes but simply ratifies what the spending committees have decided to do. The process is preserved, but hard choices are postponed to avoid conflict—what Louis Fisher refers to as "escapist budgeting."[26]

Occasionally the budget committees stand up to the spending committees

and get a strong second resolution through Congress. This may be followed by a ***reconciliation bill:*** a proposed law which implements changes in other spending measures that have already been enacted. Such reconciliation is rare, although it remains the goal of the budget committees.

DEFICIT-REDUCTION BILLS. Yet another crunch occurs when the budget and taxing committees put together a package of proposed spending cuts and tax increases to cut the deficit, as they did in 1984 and 1985. With the participation of the White House, congressional leaders may put together a large package in one bill—as they did in 1981 and 1985—which short-circuits not only the regular budget process (and may even precede the adoption of budget resolutions) but also most appropriations measures. The deficit-reduction measure may contain multiyear "caps," or ceilings, on expenditures, which if enacted are taken as definitive directions to the spending committees.

PRESIDENTIAL BUDGET STRATEGIES

Thus far, this chapter has presented a pretty bleak picture of budget politics. Presidents present comprehensive budgets, but their own agencies and departments have an incentive to sabotage them and demand more. Congress has the power, through its budget resolutions and reconciliation bills, to implement a comprehensive program, but friction between committees, pressure from lobbyists, and escapist budgeting are the norm. Congress often undercuts its budget committees, and the result is "bottom-up" incremental increases rather than hard decisions.

Faced with the complexity of the budget process, presidents have adopted several different strategies. Looking at some of them provides a better understanding of relations between the legislative and the executive branches: how hard it is for presidents to get what they want and how wrong moves and missteps can backfire disastrously—but how well-thought-out strategies and bold maneuvers can yield great dividends.

The veto strategy

Presidents can threaten to veto any of the spending measures (such as the thirteen appropriations bills and the supplemental bills) which Congress passes, claiming that they will "bust the budget." For several reasons, such threats may not be very effective. For one thing, presidents lack the *item veto*, suggested by Eisenhower and Reagan, which would allow them to veto particular items in a spending bill rather than the whole measure. (Forty-three governors have such a power.) Usually Congress can design a bill which contains many things that the president wants and only a few that the president does not want, making it hard to veto.

Congress usually upholds the rare presidential veto. Sometimes more than one-third of the members of one chamber will pledge in advance to support a veto, giving the president some bargaining chips in negotiations with a spending committee. More than 144 Republicans, for example, sent a letter to Reagan making such a pledge in 1983.

Sometimes Congress can maneuver the president into casting an unpopular veto or accepting an unpalatable bill. In 1983 the Democrats wanted to put Reagan on the defensive; they hoped that he would veto public service jobs, extensions of unemployment insurance, medical insurance for the unemployed, and government assistance to prevent mortgage foreclosures so that they could charge "unfairness" in the next election. If Reagan had signed the

measures, they could have taken the credit for them. Often legislators from the president's own party urge the president to sign election-year appropriations bills, especially the end-of-session supplemental bill, which usually contains expenditures designed to help members who are running in tight races.

The veto is a defensive weapon. It can keep Congress from funding at higher levels than the president would like, but not from giving less than the president wants—as in defense programs. The veto threat works best when the president wants to cut and Congress wants to increase; that has been the case for most nondefense programs since 1978.

The impoundment strategy

After Congress grants budget authority and the fiscal year has begun, on October 1, the president may use the **impoundment** strategy: have the Treasury and the OMB withhold funds from agencies. Congress never actually gives *money* to agencies when it grants budget authority; it simply authorizes the Treasury to honor checks written by them to cover their expenses. Therefore, it is impossible for Congress to prevent the OMB from telling an agency not to spend money or to prevent the Treasury from refusing to honor checks that go over its allotments.

In the past, presidents have relied on their constitutional powers as commander in chief and chief executive to impound money for weapons or funding for domestic programs in wartime as Roosevelt did with public works projects during the Second World War. Truman, Eisenhower, and Kennedy all stopped development of weapons systems which they opposed, and Truman refused to make a loan to the Spanish government which Congress had ordered.

Presidents have also used impoundment powers given to them by Congress. One law specifies that if an authorized activity can be carried out for less money than the amounts appropriated, the president need not spend the extra money. Other laws direct the president to impound money intended for state or local governments if they do not comply with federal laws, such as those prohibiting racial discrimination. Sometimes presidents ask Congress for special resolutions or laws which allow them to make across-the-board spending cuts or impose a spending freeze. Johnson and Nixon did so during the Vietnamese war to restrain inflation and redirect spending into defense. But Congress usually gives presidents less authority than they ask for, and it exempts so many programs that the "cuts" are symbolic; Nixon called one a "rubber ceiling" because it could stretch to accommodate any further spending mandated by Congress.[27]

President Nixon made the most use of impoundment powers. As of 1973 he had impounded more than $20 billion, and his budget for FY 1974 contained a list of 109 reductions that he intended to make, 101 of which he claimed would require no congressional action.[28] Nixon justified these cuts by arguing that Congress had implicitly given him the power to make them when it passed the Economic Stabilization Act of 1971 (which allowed him to control wages and prices and take related actions to cure runaway inflation and an international currency crisis, but which did not specifically mention impounding funds).

But Nixon was not impounding funds to stabilize the economy. Instead, he was making *policy impoundments*; he was cutting funds and even completely eliminating programs that he opposed, even though they had been given legislative and budget authorizations by Congress. Nixon targeted pork barrel pro-

grams—such as electrification of rural areas; antipoverty programs, including programs for community action, public housing, and urban renewal; and environmental programs—using impoundments as a substitute for getting Congress to pass laws reducing or eliminating these programs.

These impoundments struck at the heart of congressional politics. If the president could make them stick, he would control favors, side payments, pet projects, and logrolls. No committee could maintain its pattern of trades and its ability to forge coalitions if members thought that the deals could be undone and the funding terminated. And on the loftier plane of constitutional principle, as Senator Sam Ervin explained, "He has no authority under the Constitution to decide which laws will be executed, or to what extent they will be enforced. Yet, by using the impounding technique, the President is able to do just that."[29]

Interest groups, federal employees' unions, and state and local governments took the Nixon administration to court, where it lost about fifty federal cases. Judges ruled that Nixon had no legal authority to impound funds. Congress then passed the Budget and Impoundment Act of 1974, which provided that deferrals of spending to future fiscal years would go into effect after forty-five legislative days unless either chamber of Congress disapproved. Rescissions (in this case, funding cuts) would require Congress to pass a ***rescission bill*** in the regular legislative process.

The one-chamber veto was invalidated by the Supreme Court in 1983, and so Congress uses regular or supplemental appropriations bills to approve or disapprove of presidential requests for deferrals.[30] But Congress usually grants deferrals; in most years 90 percent are allowed. As for rescissions, that is a different story: approvals have ranged from 80 percent in 1979 to none in 1980, and usually a president winds up with fewer than half.[31]

The reconciliation strategy

In 1981 the Reagan administration dominated budget politics by temporarily changing the process. Reagan's program called for spending cuts of $41.3 billion from the proposals of the outgoing Carter administration and for a total of $130 billion in the first three fiscal years of his term. Ordinarily, new presidents present their program to legislative authorizing committees in piecemeal fashion. To cut budget authority, they must fight thirteen separate appropriations battles (one for each bill) and deal with backdoor spending and various committees that have jurisdiction.

If Reagan had fought his battles one by one, he would have dissipated his election mandate to cut spending. His proposals would have been stalled, gutted, or modified. Interest groups could have logrolled with one another, and congressional committees could have created majority coalitions against his cuts ("I'll vote against your cuts, and you vote against mine").

The fast track. Ordinarily, the first budget resolution sets goals for congressional committees, and the second resolution sets the actual ceiling on expenditures, with a reconciliation bill modifying committee authorizations that go above those levels. This timetable leaves hard choices for last. Reagan's supporters decided to reverse the process. Reagan decided to put his entire budget program—including all proposed cuts—into the first budget resolution and to follow it up immediately with a reconciliation bill.

The first budget resolution contained *binding* instructions to authorizing

President Reagan and his advisers planned a successful budget campaign in 1981. (*Larry Downing: Woodfin Group.*)

committees. They were required to report changes in laws necessary to conform to the budget totals within thirty days. These changes were then compiled by the budget committees into a single, omnibus reconciliation bill. Thus all Reagan's proposed budget shifts came early in the congressional session, all at one time, and on a single all-or-nothing bill.

The national agenda. The president used a national agenda strategy to win over public opinion before the important votes were cast. Public opinion about spending is usually uninformed and contradictory. Large majorities believe that the government consumes too much of the GNP and operates wastefully, and three-fourths of the public think that the size of government should be reduced. Around four-fifths support a constitutional amendment which would require a balanced budget (which they think would lower spending, not raise taxes). But large majorities favor increases for most specific government programs, including many social insurance programs that benefit the middle and working classes. With the exception of a few programs narrowly targeted at the poor, such as food stamps, welfare, and Medicaid, there was no support for cutting most domestic activities. Even in the case of programs for the poor, the public supports cuts to eliminate fraud and waste, not to deprive the truly needy. Conservatives try to win over the public by focusing on the general principle that spending should be cut. Liberals counter by talking about the effects that specific cuts will have on programs which the public supports.

Reagan hammered away on general principles. Just before the first budget resolution passed, a Gallup poll reported that 68 percent of the public approved of Reagan, 58 percent liked the way he was handling the economy, and 48 percent thought that they would personally benefit from his proposals. A Harris poll showed that 64 percent of the public thought that too much federal spending was the major cause of their own financial troubles. The White House organized closed-circuit television broadcasts to 15,000 Reagan supporters around the country to get them to sell the program at the grass roots, sponsored briefings for newspaper editors and publishers, arranged for press conferences and speeches around the country, and used other national agenda techniques. "We're facing a popularity issue," Tip O'Neill recognized, just before the vote on the resolution; "he's done the greatest selling job I've ever seen."[32]

The resolution passed the Republican-controlled Senate with ease. But the Democrats controlled the House. The White House Congressional Liaison Office created a bipartisan coalition of Republicans and conservative southern Democrats. The president held 69 meetings in the Oval Office, and more than 60 Democrats met with him during the three weeks preceding the vote. Reagan even telephoned members while the House was voting to round up support. Along with the carrot went the stick: the White House orchestrated a mail campaign to influence wavering southern Democrats, while Republican Party operatives told Republican moderates that unless they voted for it, they would face opposition in the primaries and would receive no funds from the party. The result: all 190 Republicans and 63 Democrats voted with the administration.

Next, the Senate Budget Committee reported a reconciliation measure to implement the resolution's cuts. The Senate quickly passed the measure. But House committees, controlled by liberal and moderate Democrats, ignored many of the first resolution's cutting instructions, and many of their changes were ploys which would salvage programs and prevent real cuts. So Reagan's supporters offered their own bill, and again the coalition passed it. Finally, 72 senators and 183 representatives attended a mammoth conference, which divided itself into 58 subconferences, and eventually reported out an omnibus reconciliation bill. As passed, it repealed or amended 436 laws and affected 266 of the 1310 spending accounts in the budget. Projected cuts in outlays in Reagan's first term totaled $140 billion, and his approval ratings soared to new highs, with 68 percent of the public supporting these cuts.[33]

Why early reconciliation worked. Reagan was able to dominate budget politics because he compressed the budget process, capitalized on his election mandate, exploited divisions among the Democrats, and retained public support during his "honeymoon" period. By putting together a single package, Reagan made the budget cuts highly visible and dramatic—susceptible to national agenda politics. This raised the stakes for his party, discouraged defections, and limited the negotiating room of his own leaders. Reagan created the equivalent of a parliamentary "vote of confidence": no member of his party could afford to undercut him on such an important bill so early in his first term.

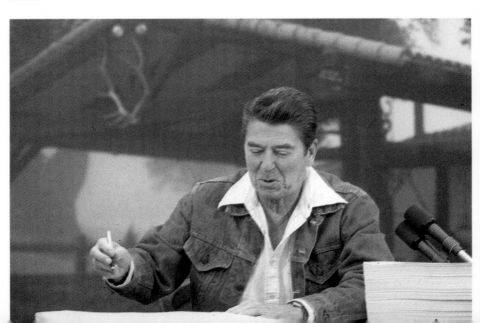

The end of the process for one year: President Reagan signs the 1981 tax cut and budget bill at his California ranch. (*AP Photocolor.*)

The Democrats hoped to stretch out the process. They wanted to split the reconciliation bill into six separate measures, each of which would require a separate vote, so that different floating coalitions could be formed against the administration. Instead of casting a single vote for or against Reagan, they wanted Congress to cast many votes—on numerous amendments and on the final bills—which would put legislators on record about particular programs and keep them susceptible to pressures from interest groups and constituencies. Moreover, the Republicans would then be able to vote for Reagan on some issues but defect on others without being branded party traitors. The issue would turn from big government to a set of mini-issues: welfare, housing, transit systems, social security, and so forth. The House, controlled by Reagan's coalition, beat back all attempts to split up the omnibus bill, and its rules called for a single up or down vote with no amendments. "Do we have the right to meet our target, or can he in one package deregulate, delegislate, the things that have taken years to do?" Tip O'Neill asked before the crucial procedural votes were cast.[34] The answer came back: Reagan could and would.

Limits on early reconciliation.   Presidents can rarely use the reconciliation strategy. When Reagan proposed $13 billion in cuts the following September, many southern Democrats and moderate Republicans defected from his coalition; he prevailed only after promising the "Gypsy Moth" Republican moderates that he would restore funds for some of their favored programs. Later they charged that he had not kept his promises, prompting Tip O'Neill to remark, "Republicans are fighting Republicans. My strategy is don't block the view."[35] The defeat marked the end of the Reagan budget coalition.

Congressional leaders of both parties refused to go along with early reconciliation the following year. And after the 1982 congressional elections, the conservative coalition no longer dominated the House, as a result of the Republicans' losses. In the Senate, Republican Party and committee leaders followed their own priorities on taxes and spending and began to distance themselves from the administration. By 1983 the budget process was completely out of presidential control.

Reagan decided to walk away from the entire budget process. He warned Congress that he would veto "budget-busting bills," but then did nothing as spending targets exceeded OMB totals. For the four years of Reagan's first term, spending increased by 41 percent, which hardly indicated much success for the "curtailer in chief." The president had learned that the organized constituencies favoring increased spending for programs could outlast his initial honeymoon period and his temporary successes with national agenda politics. The lesson was obvious: a new president should go for broke in the first two years with a large package of cuts and a national agenda campaign, because after that the presidential program faces legislative gridlock or reversal.

By 1985, having had three consecutive failures after one stunning initial success, the president was ready to exploit his second-term postinaugural honeymoon period. Again he introduced a package of large expenditures and tax cuts. Again he used national agenda politics to win public support for his program. But this time he was a lame-duck president, facing opposition from his own Senate Republicans, and the failure of his program to emerge intact once again demonstrates how hard it is for presidents to dominate the budget process.

FOCUS

THE REFORM AGENDA. Some reforms would increase presidential control, others would enable Congress to make more rational and comprehensive decisions, and still others would require both branches to observe certain limits.

Presidentialist reforms. Presidentialist reforms would allow the president to introduce the budget as a single bill, which would have priority on the congressional calendar. It would be voted on early in the session. A reconciliation measure, which would also have priority, could be introduced by the administration after the resolution passed. It would not be subject to amendment. These changes would give presidents an annual "vote of confidence" and would require them to conduct a national agenda campaign each year to obtain support for their budget. If they failed to do so, and if Congress passed a substitute budget based on its committee work, the lines would be clearly drawn between presidents and their opponents, which would make budget politics central to the following election and would promote a more responsible party system.

Congress could give the president greater discretion in deferring or rescinding spending during the fiscal year, or a constitutional amendment could give the president an item veto over appropriations. But Congress is not likely to pass any measures that give up its budget powers to the president.

Congressionalist reforms. Some reforms would strengthen the budget committees. The first budget resolution could establish binding ceilings rather than just suggest targets. The budget committees could give binding directions to taxing and spending committees. Conceivably, the work of the appropriations committees and their subcommittees could be transferred to enlarged budget committees. But because of the power of the taxing and spending committees, it is more likely that the top-down budget process will be weakened than that the committees, with their bottom-up approach, will lose their powers or have their functions consolidated. The budget committees and the budget resolutions are in danger of being reformed out of existence—not the appropriations committees.

IN CONCLUSION

Budget politics has always involved a free-for-all within the executive branch, as agencies have fought with departments to increase spending and as the OMB has fought with departments to lower it. The presidential budget then entered the legislative arena, where legislative and budget authority committees make their modifications. The result was a set of outcomes, based on the results of the legislative struggle, rather than budget policy. The system was suited for the legislative logroll and compromise.

The budget process was modified substantially in 1974 in the aftermath of the crisis over Nixon's impoundments. It was supposed to create top-down budgeting: Congress would have to make hard choices and formulate comprehensive policies. The Congressional Budget Office would give Congress the technical expertise to challenge the OMB and develop its own options. This might encourage a more responsible party system, since the majority party in Congress could formulate its own budget and take responsibility for it in the next election.

Sometimes the new process works as intended, with the two congressional parties confronting each other. On occasion the White House dominates budget politics by using early reconciliation during the honeymoon period. But often the process does not work. Bottom-up budgeting is still favored by legislators. Spending remains oriented toward district and state interests. Agencies spend on the

wrong things—pet projects or services for the most highly organized and politically influential groups. Meanwhile, the government underfunds scientific research and social services, underpays its employees, and allows its facilities to deteriorate. Too little money is spent on management and program oversight.

Often budget resolutions are reported and voted on late. The second resolution may not even be enacted. Reconciliation has been used sparingly: in 1980 to trim $5 billion and in 1981 after the first budget resolution—and since then not at all. Sometimes Congress votes to suspend rules requiring the second budget resolution to be adopted before the final vote on appropriations bills, and instead considers the appropriations first (as it did in 1983 and 1984). At other times appropriations bills and other budget authority bills are not passed on time (except for the one funding Congress!), and as a result the fiscal year begins with the passage of a continuing resolution (providing funding at existing levels) until Congress acts. Sometimes that resolution serves for the entire year and no other authority is passed; continuing resolutions controlled the foreign aid program for several years, for example. The national government and the state governments cannot plan for the coming fiscal year when they do not know whether or when new funding levels will go into effect.

There are too many committees, and they get in one another's way. Budget committees issue targets and instructions which legislative committees ignore. Authorizing committees write backdoor provisions that circumvent appropriations committees, which in turn undercut the instructions of budget committees and infringe on other committees when they attach "riders." In most years, neither the president nor party leaders can control these committees; negotiation and compromise among them shape the final outcomes.

There are many reforms which could create comprehensive and rational budgeting, dominated by the president or by the majority party in Congress. Few are likely to be adopted, because they do not offer legislators any political advantages. "We want more government than we can pay for," observes Alice Rivlin, a former CBO director, "and no process can help solve that problem."[36] Proposing changes in the process without protecting the power stakes of the participants is putting the cart before the horse. Only when a coalition can be organized that insists on comprehensive, top-down budgeting and can win the battles with other congressional committees and then maintain itself through the subsequent midterm elections will fundamental change in budget politics occur.

NOTES

1. Kermit Gordon, "Reflections on Spending," *Public Policy*, vol. 15, p. 11; *The New York Times*, May 8, 1981.
2. *The New York Times*, Apr. 11, 1980.
3. Valerie Bunce, "Changing Leaders and Changing Policies: The Impact of Elite Succession on Budgeting Priorities in Democratic Countries," *American Journal of Political Science*, vol. 24, no. 3, August 1980, pp. 373–396.
4. *The New York Times*, Mar. 14, 1983.
5. Aaron Wildavsky, *The Politics of the Budgetary Process*, 1st ed., Little, Brown, Boston, 1964, p. 100.
6. Mark Kamlet and David Mowery, "The Budgetary Base in Federal Resource Allocation," *American Journal of Political Science*, vol. 24, no. 4, November 1980, pp. 804–808; Otto Davis, M. A. H. Dempster, and Aaron Wildavsky, "A Theory of the Budgetary Process," *American Political Science Review*, vol. 60, no. 3, September 1966, pp. 529–547.

7. Peter Natchez and Irving Bupp, "Policy and Priority in the Budget Process," *American Political Science Review*, vol. 67, no. 3, September 1973, pp. 951–963.

8. Lance T. LeLoup, "Agency Policy Actions: Determinants of Nonincremental Change," in Randall Ripley and Grace Franklin (eds.), *Policy-Making in the Executive Branch*, Free Press, New York, 1975, pp. 65–90.

9. W. Bowman Cutter, "The Battle of the Budget," *The Atlantic*, March 1981, p. 64.

10. William Greider, "The Education of David Stockman," *The Atlantic*, no. 247, December 1981, p. 30. This "close-up" was prepared with the assistance of Len Kreynin, Columbia College.

11. Ibid., p. 36.

12. *The Wall Street Journal*, Feb. 9, l981.

13. *Newsweek*, Nov. 23, 1981, p. 41.

14. *The New York Times*, Nov. 22, 1981.

15. Louis Fisher, *Constitutional Conflicts between Congress and the President*, Princeton University Press, Princeton, 1985, p. 231.

16. Ibid., p. 229.

17. *The Federalist*, number 48.

18. LeLoup, op. cit., p. 126.

19. *Congressional Quarterly Weekly Reports*, vol. 41, no. 9, Mar. 5, 1983, p. 459.

20. John Ellwood and James Thurber, "The Congressional Budget Process Re-examined," in Lawrence C. Dodd and Bruce I. Oppenheimer (eds.), *Congress Reconsidered*, 2d ed., Congressional Quarterly Press, Washington, D.C., 1981, pp. 246–274.

21. Richard E. Fenno, *The Power of the Purse*, Little, Brown, Boston, 1966, pp. 311–312.

22. Ibid., p. 312.

23. Kenneth Shepsle, "The Failure of Congressional Budgeting," *Society*, vol. 20, May–June 1983, p. 5.

24. Bruce A. Ray, "Federal Spending and the Selection of Committee Assignments in the U.S. House of Representatives," *American Journal of Political Science*, vol. 24, no. 3, August 1980, p. 494.

25. Wildavsky, op. cit., p. 19.

26. Fisher, op. cit., p. 241.

27. James L. Sundquist, *The Decline and Resurgence of Congress*, Brookings, Washington, D.C., 1982, pp. 220–221.

28. Ibid., p. 205.

29. Sundquist, op. cit., p. 206.

30. Louis Fisher, "The Impact of *Chadha* on the Budget Process," *CRS Review*, 1983, pp. 12–14.

31. Ellwood and Thurber, op. cit., table 11–15, p. 266.

32. *The New York Times*, May 11, 1981; *The Gallup Report*, May 1981, p. 11.

33. *Congressional Quarterly Weekly Reports*, June 27, 1981.

34. Lance LeLoup, "After the Blitz—Reagan and the U.S. Congressional Budget Process," *Legislative Studies Quarterly*, vol. 7, no. 3, August 1982, p. 321.

35. Shepsle, op. cit., p. 8.

36. *The New York Times*, July 13, 1984.

FURTHER READING

Boskin, Michael, and Aaron Wildavsky (eds.): *The Federal Budget: Economics and Politics*, Institute for Contemporary Studies, Berkeley, Calif., 1982. Articles on trends in spending in the 1980s and on Reagan's budget strategies.

Fisher, Louis: *The Presidential Spending Power*, Princeton University Press, Princeton, N.J., 1975. A study of how the executive branch controls spending and avoids congressional mandates.

Ippolito, Dennis S.: *The Budget and National Politics*, Freeman, San Francisco, 1978. An overview of the modern budget process.

LeLoup, Lance T.: *Budgetary Politics*, Kings Court Communications, Brunswick, Ohio, 1977. A book about who wins and who loses in budget politics.

Schick, Allen: *Congress and Money*, Urban Institute, Washington, D.C., 1980. A comprehensive account of budgeting, emphasizing relations between different congressional committees.

Sundquist, James L.: *The Decline and Resurgence of Congress*, Brookings, Washington, D.C., 1982. An account of how Congress regained the power of the purse in the 1970s.

Wildavsky, Aaron: *The Politics of the Budgetary Process*, 3d ed., Little, Brown, Boston, 1979. A classic exposition of agency strategies in dealing with the OMB and the appropriations committees.

THE STUDY BREAK

Americathon. In this movie, made in 1979, the United States is so broke that only a telethon will save it from bankruptcy. A late-night bomb.

Greider, William: "The Education of David Stockman," *The Atlantic*, vol. 247, no. 12, December 1981. This article, containing the OMB director's admissions about what really went on in the first year of the Reagan administration, was a bombshell. Stockman was almost fired because of it.

USEFUL SOURCES

An Analysis of the President's Budgetary Proposals for the Fiscal Year, Congressional Budget Office, Washington, D.C., annually. The CBO's own projections for revenues and expenditures, as well as its analysis of presidential proposals. The CBO also issues a report in three volumes to the budget committees each February: *Part I, The Economic Outlook; Part II, Baseline Budget Projections for Fiscal Years____* (the years for which the budget is projected); and *Part III, Reducing the Deficit: Spending and Revenue Options.* These constitute alternatives to the administration's program.

The Budget in Brief, GPO, Washington, D.C., annually. Eighty pages summarizing important decisions, trends, and budget totals, including useful charts and tables.

Budget of the United States Government, GPO, Washington, D.C., annually. A volume consisting of more than 650 pages, half of which contain proposed expenditures for coming fiscal years.

Budget of the United States Government, Appendix, GPO, Washington, D.C., annually. This volume specifies, item by item, how much will be spent for each program, by each agency, and for what (salary, transportation, and so forth).

Budget of the United States Government, Major Themes and Additional Budget Details, GPO, Washington, D.C., annually. A publication covering many of the large program categories.

Special Analyses: The Budget of the United States Government, GPO, Washington, D.C., annually, 11 vols. Each volume deals in great detail with a particular function of government. One especially important volume covers the current services estimates, borrowing and debt management, federal credit, tax expenditures, and intergovernmental transfers of funds.

The Grace Commission, *President's Private Sector Survey on Cost Control, Final Report,* GPO, Washington, D.C., 1983, parts 1 and 2. A study of government waste and incompetence, containing materials on budgeting and financial controls.

Pechman, Joseph (ed.): *Setting National Priorities: The 1984 Budget,* Brookings, Washington, D.C., 1983. A Washington think tank assesses the presidential proposals and offers alternatives.

ORGANIZATIONS

Congressional Budget Office. House Annex 2, Second and D Streets, S.W., Washington, D.C. 20515. For more information telephone 202-226-2621.

House Budget Committee. Suite 214, Annex No. 1, Washington, D.C. 20515. For more information telephone 202-226-7200.

Office of Management and Budget. Executive Office Building, Washington, D.C. 20503. For more information telephone 202-395-3080.

Senate Budget Committee. Room 203, Carroll Arms Annex, 301 First Street, N.E., Washington, D.C. 20510. For more information telephone 202-395-3080.

PART FOUR
THE POLITICS OF GOVERNMENT

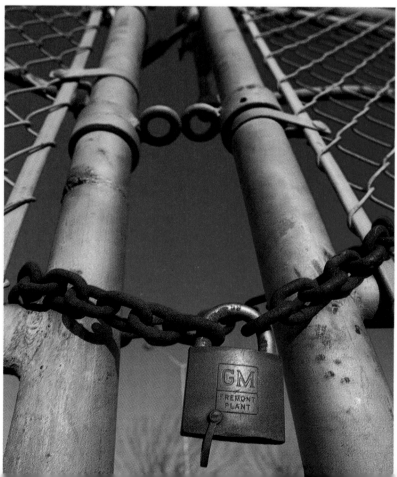

CHAPTER 15

MANAGING THE ECONOMY: FISCAL, MONETARY, AND REGULATORY POLICIES

Lee Iacocca, with the help of union concessions and federal loans, restored Chrysler Corporation to profitability, but in the early 1980s the automobile industry faced layoffs and plant closings, as at the General Motors plant in Fremont, California. (*Stephen R. Brown: Picture Group; Eugene Richards: Magnum.*)

President Coolidge observed, "The business of America is business," and it is the business of politicians as well. They know that a strong economy helps them get reelected. Since 1948, whenever economic growth has exceeded 3.5 percent in an election year, the party in power has retained the White House; otherwise, the opposition has won. Presidents Ford and Carter were defeated for reelection largely because of economic failures (when Carter left office, the inflation rate was in the high double digits, and the interest rate was around 20 percent). President Reagan was reelected in large measure because of the pocketbook vote: lowered inflation and lowered interest rates combined with large tax cuts.[1]

In the past three decades our economy has performed erratically, with periods of high **inflation** and low growth (**stagflation**), **recession** (low or no growth and high unemployment), or high growth coupled with huge deficits and an unfavorable balance of trade. In the 1950s our economy was blessed with low unemployment (4.5 percent), low inflation (2.1 percent), and high productivity (2.6 percent). By the 1980s we had exactly the reverse: higher unemployment (7.4 percent), higher inflation (4 to 5 percent), and lower productivity (1.4 percent). Clearly, something was wrong.[2] In the 1980s, with projections of $200 billion budget deficits and $100 billion trade deficits, both the Democrats and the Republicans agree that radical changes in government policy will be needed to manage the economy successfully.

This chapter focuses on fiscal, monetary, and regulatory policies and concludes with an examination of the pros and cons of the proposals for a "new industrial policy."

POLITICS AND MARKETS

The American economy is based on the **market:** the mechanisms which allows buyers and sellers to exchange goods and services for money or barter. In a **free market** there are many sellers and buyers, none of whom can set prices. Instead, prices are influenced by the supply of, and the demand for, goods and services and are set for each transaction when a buyer and a seller agree. Other things being equal, increased supply lowers prices, and increased demand raises them.[3]

Government and the market

The national government fosters the free market by guaranteeing the right of citizens to hold private property, by enforcing contracts, and by providing that property may not be taken away without due process of law—all provisions of the Constitution. It creates and regulates currency. It prevents anyone from coercing buyers and sellers and ensures that exchanges are voluntary. It sees that potential buyers and sellers can obtain the information they need to make informed decisions, and it can prohibit transactions based on "inside information" which gives one party an advantage in a sale. Through antitrust laws, it can prohibit combinations in restraint of trade which rig markets.

Markets may be regulated with help from the government. An industry may

obtain protection from foreign competition through **tariffs** or, in the case of automobile and steel, through negotiations with foreign governments to "voluntarily" restrict their imports. An industry can be shielded from domestic competition if the government permits a monopoly (such as a regional telephone or power company) or restricts the number of enterprises (for example, the number of television and radio stations). Farmers may by law enter into marketing agreements to restrict the supply of goods and support prices, let fields lie fallow, plow under crops, or store crops in government warehouses and sell them to the government for a "floor" price.[4]

The American economy is a **mixed system:** resources may be allocated by free or regulated markets. There is a built-in tension between politics and markets. Economic policy-making involves decisions about when and under what circumstances nonmarket or regulated market allocations of goods should substitute for the free market.[5]

The public and private sectors

"I do not mind paying taxes," Justice Oliver Wendell Holmes told his law clerk, "because with taxes I buy civilization." But how much civilization should the public buy? Those who favor the "nightwatchman state" say that the government should restrict itself to protecting private property, regulating the free market, and handling national security matters. Those who favor the positive state believe that the government should also spend money on educational, cultural, and social welfare programs, as well as on programs that foster economic growth, such as job training, capital construction, and industrial research and development.

Advocates of the positive state have won the day. The national government now spends one-fourth of the gross national product—the highest percentage ever spent in peacetime, and far more than the 5 percent spent just before the depression or the average of 1 percent spent in the nineteenth century.[6]

Because the government spends so much, there is no neat separation between public bureaucracies and programs that operate outside the markets and private enterprises that operate within the markets. Public enterprises are subject to some market forces. They compete for labor, pay rent and bills for supplies, and even compete with private enterprises for customers; the Postal Service and federal power utilities are examples. In fact, some government agencies, such as COMSAT and the Inland Waterways Corporation, are set up as quasi-public corporations, with boards of directors, stockholders, and the right to raise money in private capital markets. They compete in the market with private companies which supply similar services.

Many nominally private enterprises, such as large defense contractors, are more public than private. Their plants were built with money from the Pentagon, which also funds their research and development for new weapons. The market forces do not operate: the government may allow cost-plus contracts and noncompetitive bidding, and it may prohibit foreign firms from bidding.

Government and entrepreneurs

Entrepreneurs are important links between the public and the private sectors. They are the men and women who start up new enterprises with their own or borrowed capital. They are especially important in high-tech fields, such as home computers and software, bioengineering, medical devices, and telecommunications. Their enterprises create 4 out of every 5 new jobs in the econ-

The lush farmland in California's Salinas Valley is no gift of nature. The federal government dammed the Colorado River to provide irrigation water and built the roads and power lines that make the Salinas and Imperial valleys so productive. (*Baron Wolman: Woodfin Camp.*)

omy. But they also take the greatest risks; 4 out of 5 new businesses go bankrupt each year.

Entrepreneurs want the government to foster their activities. They want low taxes on their profits. They want investment tax credits, accelerated depreciation and other special deductions, and tax shelters so that they can attract other investors.[7] They ask for patent, copyright, and licensing laws that give them a transitory monopoly on their inventions; otherwise, their ideas or products could be copied, and they would have no incentive to take any risks.

Some economists believe that entrepreneurs want only to be allowed to compete without restrictions in the free market.[8] Sometimes this is the case, but often entrepreneurs work closely with government. Consider the farmers of the Imperial Valley in California, who got the state government and the national government to construct roads, dam the Colorado River, and provide new agricultural technologies, extension services, power stations, and transmission lines. Their investment in land and farm machinery would have been worth little without the government's help. Similarly, those who invested in railroads in the 1880s needed government mail and freight contracts, as did those who invested in airlines in the 1920s. Indeed, sometimes it is only when such help is assured that entrepreneurs make the investment.

Entrepreneurs almost always create new products, form new companies, and invest in new industries on the basis of their calculations about what the local, state, and national government policies will be with regard to their enterprises. The worth of a venture is to a large extent determined by its relationship to all levels of government. An entrepreneur's ability to engineer a change in that relationship (by getting a tax subsidy or a contract, for example) can turn a poor investment into a good one.

The privileged position of business

Business leaders are "public officials" in both markets and politics. They have a privileged position in dealing with their counterparts in government, a position that no other group—not organized labor, scientists, or educators—has achieved.[9] Since the depression the government has sponsored industry associations and councils which, by law, are guaranteed access to government agencies, usually in the form of advisory committees. These associations and councils work closely with bureaucrats to promote their interests. The 6000 committees are consulted in matters of developing agency regulations and

516

guidelines, proposing new legislation, distributing contracts, and funding projects. The makers of medical devices, such as artificial limbs and pacemakers, are represented on a committee in the Food and Drug Administration, and they decide which regulations apply to which devices.

Sometimes program administration is left to industry or agricultural associations: they can determine how laws are enforced, evaluate agency activities, and even do research and development under an agency contract. Sometimes, as in the case of agricultural committees during the depression, such groups help determine output and administer prices, substituting political allocations for free market allocations.[10]

Many of the top political executives in the agencies are recruited from corporations affected by their programs. Trade and industry associations have a "veto" over nominations because the Senate is unlikely to confirm nominees against their strong opposition. They may also try to conduct "purges" of agency personnel at lower levels and send "hit lists" to the White House for action, as antienvironmentalist groups did with the Interior Department in 1981. Corporate leaders can also talk directly to top economic policymakers in the government at sessions of the Business Roundtable and the Business Council, two corporate groups which hold meetings quarterly between top executives and the secretaries and deputy secretaries of the departments.

The pluralist economy

The American economy is pluralist. Different sectors of the economy and different companies, along with their political allies, compete with one another both in the marketplace and in politics. Some of the fiercest competition for influence in the government occurs between the large money-center banks (such as Chase, Citibank, and Bank of America) and the financial services companies (such as Sears, Merrill-Lynch, and Prudential-Bache). General Motors and Ford opposed the government bailout of Chrysler in the 1970s; in the 1980s a revived Chrysler attacked the government for allowing GM to go ahead with Toyota on a coproduction venture in California. The emerging "sunrise" industries of the high-tech revolution clamor for government funding against the claims of the "sunset" industries, like steel and machine tools. The sun belt companies of the south and southwest compete with the frost belt industries of the midwest and east. The copper and steel producers demand protection against imports, but they are opposed by manufacturers who want lower-cost metals and by farmers who fear a trade war that will wipe out their export markets.

There is no single group of capitalists running the American economy or government—no dominating **_power elite._** Politicians, bureaucrats, and corporate executives form competing alliances to push policies that will benefit particular industries, companies, and geographic regions. Congressional delegations representing different states and regions travel all over the world, drumming up foreign investment for their districts or touting the products they sell, such as advanced aircraft; and when they do, they find themselves up against delegations from other regions.

FISCAL POLICY-MAKING

The national government tries to influence the economy through its fiscal policies involving taxing and spending. In particular, it tries to moderate the boom and bust phases of the business cycle, maintain price stability, and keep unemployment low.

**Politics and the
business cycle**

Today, even relatively minor changes in economic conditions can result in gains or losses of congressional seats for both parties. Presidents ride an economic roller coaster, with large drops and rises in their popularity dependent on relatively small changes in unemployment and inflation rates.[11] (See Figures 15-1 and 15-2.) The performance of the economy in an election year itself is critical. During the Carter administration the growth rate was 2.96 percent annually, and during Reagan's first term it was 3.02 percent. Personal income rose 7.3 percent under Carter and 9 percent under Reagan in their first terms. And during the Carter years employment shot up 12.5 percent—far more than during the Reagan years (8 percent). But consider the last year for each presi-

Figure 15-1. Inflation rates, 1960–1984. Inflation rates were considerably higher in the 1970s than in the 1950s and 1960s. Although inflation appears to move in a cycle, in recent years each peak has hit a new high. Percentages show year-to-year changes in the Consumer Price Index. (Source: Bureau of Labor Statistics.)

Figure 15-2. Unemployment and presidential popularity. The sharp decline and equally sharp rise in President Reagan's popularity during his first term coincide almost perfectly with the rise and then the decline in the unemployment rate. (Sources: Bureau of Labor Statistics; Gallup polls.)

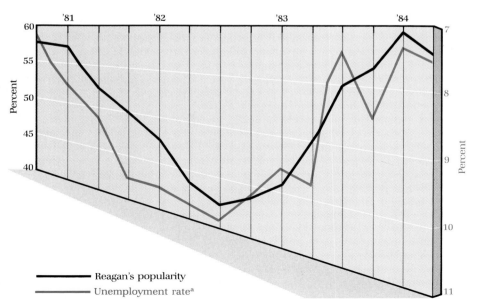

Reagan's popularity
Unemployment rate[a]

a. Not including military.

THE DISCOMFORT AND MISERY INDEXES

The discomfort index combines the unemployment rate with the inflation rate (as measured by the consumer price index). The two rates totaled about 20 percent in 1980, a good indication that President Carter would be in trouble in the election. The misery index adds on the interest rate (as measured by the prime rate, or the rate charged by banks to their best customers). In 1980 that placed the misery index at about 40 percent, almost an insurmountable obstacle.

The discomfort index for Reagan in the summer and fall of 1984 was approximately 12 percent, while the misery index stood at approximately 24 percent. These rates were low compared with those during the Carter administration, although they were high compared with most rates in postwar elections.

---

dent: growth declined 0.8 percent during Carter's last quarter, compared with a 6 percent increase during Reagan's; employment was flat in Carter's last year, compared with a gain in Reagan's fourth year of more than 5 percent. Things were getting worse for Carter and better for Reagan in their fourth years, which accounts in large measure for the former's defeat and the latter's massive reelection victory.

Presidents try to manipulate the business cycle so that downturns will occur in the first years and prosperity will reappear in the election year. Between 1946 and 1984 the gross national product rose 1.9 percent in nonelection years, 2.8 percent in congressional election years, 2 percent in presidential election years in which the president did not run for reelection, and 3.7 percent in years when the president was running for reelection. Presidents

By Toles for The Buffalo News. Reprinted by permission of Universal Press Syndicate.

Table 15-1. Presidents and unemployment

Democratic presidents	Unemployment rate, change	Republican presidents	Unemployment rate, change
John Kennedy	−0.9%[a]	Dwight Eisenhower	+3.7%
Lyndon Johnson	−2.3%	Richard Nixon	+1.0%
Jimmy Carter	−0.1%	Gerald Ford	+3.1%

a. The percentages given are the changes in the unemployment rates during the administrations of these presidents, not the rates themselves.

choose the four-year "quick fix" rather than longer-range policies. They boost employment and raise incomes in an election year with massive spending, knowing that new rounds of inflation or unacceptable deficits will result afterward. Most presidents accept large deficits and propose tax cuts in the fourth year of their first term (Johnson, Nixon, and Ford did so). Presidents and Congress pass "dipsy doodle" policies which provide the benefits before the election and levy the costs afterwards. In the aftermath of Reagan's second-term victory, for example, the president's proposed budget slashed benefits for the middle-class voters who had propelled him to victory.

The performance of the economy during a president's fourth year is crucial because many voters decide on a prospective basis: if the economy is picking up, they assume that things will be even better in the next four years. The question, "Under which candidate will I be better off financially in the years to come?" becomes a key determinant of who gets the vote. Thus in 1984 voters who answered that question with "Reagan" but opposed the president on his foreign or social policies nevertheless voted to reelect him by better than a 2–1 margin.[12] Each party's fiscal policy maximized benefits to its own voter coalition. Most Democratic presidents try to lower the unemployment rate because unionized workers, blue-collar workers, service workers, minorities, and women are most affected, and they are disproportionately Democratic. Most Republican presidents concentrate on the inflation rate because their party identifiers are disproportionately from higher-income groups. Thus President Reagan lowered inflation from 12 to 4 percent, while unemployment went from 7.4 percent when he took office up to a high of 10.7 percent by 1982 and then went down to 7.3 percent when he won reelection. Table 15-1 indicates how recent Republican and Democratic presidents have fared in dealing with unemployment.

Neither Democratic nor Republican presidents relish giving the public a dose of hard economic medicine. In 1976 *candidate* Ford promised full employment if he were given another four years in office, but *President* Ford submitted a budget calling for high unemployment in order to lower the inflation rate. *Candidate* Carter promised a balanced budget in four years to lower inflation, but after the election *President* Carter submitted unbalanced budgets. In 1980 *candidate* Reagan claimed that he could increase defense spending, cut taxes, and balance the budget, which led his primary opponent, George Bush, to say that his program was "voodoo economics" and could be accomplished only with "blue smoke and mirrors." When that turned out to be the case (the national debt increased by 50 percent during Reagan's first term), *President* Reagan downplayed the importance of these issues until he was safely reelected.

The president and fiscal policy

The presidential advisory system. The president receives advice on fiscal policy from the secretary of the Treasury, who is the president's principal

spokesperson before Congress, the Council of Economic Advisors (CEA), and the director of the Office of Management and Budget (OMB). Presidents may also create an economic policy board or a cabinet council to give other departments a say. The result is a great deal of infighting among officials and issue networks.

Tax proposals illustrate the typical conflicts within the advisory system. Sometimes the CEA proposes tax cuts to stimulate the economy, as it did in 1962 and 1981, claiming that the immediate loss in revenues would be more than offset by additional receipts when business conditions improved. Its cuts are likely to be opposed by the Treasury, which must consider how additional debt will be financed, and by the departments, which think that tax cuts will mean lower revenue, which in turn might force cuts in their programs. Alternatively, when the CEA proposes higher taxes (as it did in 1966 and 1983), it gets in trouble with the White House staff, which is mindful of the political effects.

Presidents must make the final decisions. In 1954 Eisenhower sided with the CEA and against the Treasury Department in proposing a tax cut, and Kennedy did the same in 1962 over the opposition of the Treasury Department and the Defense Department. In 1975, when a Democratic Congress passed its own tax-reduction measure, the CEA and the OMB urged Ford to sign it, while the Treasury Department unsuccessfully sought a veto. In 1977, however, Carter sided with the Treasury Department and the OMB against the CEA in deciding to withdraw a proposal for a $50 tax rebate.

Presidents usually overrule advisers who suggest raising taxes. In 1966 the CEA proposed an increase, but Johnson refused, thus fueling the inflation caused by the Vietnamese war. Reagan, acting against the unanimous advice of the CEA, the OMB, the Treasury Department, and even political advisers, refused to consider increases in personal income taxes in 1982, 1983, and 1985,

---

THE COUNCIL OF ECONOMIC ADVISORS

Recognizing that the government would have to play an active role in economic management, Congress passed the Employment Act of 1946 (sometimes erroneously called the Full Employment Act). This law, passed by a liberal-labor coalition, established the *Council of Economic Advisors,* which consists of three members, assisted by a staff of professional economists. The law requires the president to submit an economic message and an annual report of the council to Congress each year. The report and the message are submitted late in January, at about the same time the budget is sent to the Hill. The law requires the government to do the following:

. . . Coordinate and utilize all its plans, functions and resources for the purpose of creating and maintaining in a manner calculated to foster free competitive enterprise and the general welfare, conditions under which there will be afforded useful employment opportunities, including self employment, for those willing, and seeking to work, and to promote maximum employment, production, and purchasing power.

The law does not require the government to promote full employment at the expense of price stability or growth. It sets no priorities among these goals, nor does it specify trade-offs between goals. As a consequence, the Humphrey-Hawkins Act, passed by Congress in 1978, made full employment a national economic priority and required the president to report on progress toward this goal. But neither law requires the government to take any specific actions toward the goal.

Early in his first term President Reagan relied on a "troika" of economic advisers. Left to right: David Stockman at OMB, Donald Regan at Treasury, and Murray Weidenbaum of the Council of Economic Advisers. (*G. Franken: Sygma.*)

giving a new twist to Truman's comment about the Oval Office that "the buck stops here."

The OMB and the Treasury Department usually have different estimates of revenues (the OMB's is higher) and of outlays (the Treasury Department's is higher). The CEA squares off against the Treasury Department over the impact on the economy of large deficits. Each of these agencies tends to support its own predictions and projections and attempts to discredit the other's. Consider the following testimony in a congressional hearing when Donald Regan, then secretary of the Treasury, was asked whether the director of the OMB spoke for the president in suggesting new spending cuts. "I'll let Mr. Stockman describe his point of view," Regan responded, adding: "I think the President expressed the administration's view." Similarly, when asked by Senator Donald Riegle, a Democrat, about the usefulness of the economic report of the president, prepared by the CEA for Congress, Regan responded, "As far as I'm concerned, you can throw [it] away."[13]

Economic advisers differ on how to give their advice. Some, like Edwin Nourse, the first chair of the CEA, believe that they should be neutral advocates, speaking for the economics profession to presidents. Others, like the CEA chair, Arthur Okun, think that they should offer advice framed to reflect the presidents' political problems in order to maintain rapport with them and have influence with them. Presidents want advisers who are committed "point men," advancing the presidential program. What presidents do not want is condescending experts who talk down to them or become embroiled in public disputes with Cabinet members and legislators.

Advisers can help presidents understand the complexities of economic policy, but some are frustrated by the economic ignorance of the person in the Oval Office. This was the case throughout Reagan's first term, as his advisers continually indicated to him that the burgeoning deficits could not be reduced by economic growth. When Martin Feldstein, the chair of the CEA, went public with his complaints, he was reprimanded by others in the administration, was frozen out of decision making, and resigned.

Presidential fiscal policies. Every president relies on *fiscal policy,* based on the idea that when the nation is sliding into recession because investment and

consumption are too low, the government may increase expenditures or lower tax rates to increase demand; when the economy overheats because demand is greater than supply, the government can raise taxes or decrease outlays, thus lessening demand. Each president has had his own variation on this theme. Eisenhower used a *compensatory* policy: in boom years the government would try to run a surplus, and in recessions it would run a deficit. The budget would balance over the course of the entire business cycle, not in each and every year. Kennedy proposed a *propulsive* policy, by which he tried to increase the growth rate, in part so that we would be a better example than the Russians to the developing nations.[14] Nixon and Ford used *corrective* policies: they would tolerate negative growth rates and an increase in unemployment in order to bring down inflation. On the campaign stump Carter said that a balanced budget was necessary, but he began his term by asking Congress to give everyone a $50 tax rebate in order to stimulate the economy. He dropped that plan within a few months in order to combat inflation with a *restrictive* policy.

Reagan's approach was based on supply-side economics. It abandoned the postwar consensus that the best way to rev up the economy was to stimulate demand. Instead, he argued that growth could be achieved, and inflation and unemployment reduced, by lowering tax rates and deregulating the economy.[15] The idea was that people would work harder if they could keep more of what they earned, entrepreneurs would be encouraged to develop new products, and corporations would invest more in new plants and equipment, all of which would stimulate the economy. Lower taxes would encourage savings, which would mean lower interest rates and even more investment, further expanding the economy. As the supply of available goods increased, prices would stabilize, bringing down inflation.

Supply-side economics had mixed results. Reagan got Congress to adopt most of the elements of his taxing, spending, and deregulation program in his first year. The tax reductions increased the demand for goods and services, but there was no evidence that savings increased. Nor did investment increase: between the last quarter of 1981 and the third quarter of 1983 it actually declined, even after the tax cuts had been implemented. The growth in investment under Carter averaged 5.4 percent, while under Reagan it declined for two years and then rose in 1984 only to where it had been when he took office. The inflation rate was cut substantially, from 12.8 percent to between 3 and 5 percent, initially because of a steep recession induced by cuts in government expenditures and a tight monetary policy. Later Reagan was helped by bumper crops, which lowered food prices; a glut of oil, which eroded the power of OPEC; and deregulation and foreign competition, which put downward pressure on consumer goods and services. But only 5.1 million jobs were created during Reagan's first term, compared with 10 million under Carter.

Reagan's program eventually succeeded because it stimulated consumer demand in 1982 and 1983, as the tax cuts took effect. The change in tax rates did not induce most people to work or save more. For the top 2 percent of the population, tax receipts increased, indicating that these people may have worked more or invested their money well. For all other groups, tax receipts declined, indicating that the tax cuts were not self-financing—revenues lost as a result of the cut in rates could not be regained by higher levels of economic activity. In fact, for every dollar that Reagan cut in taxes, he got back only 30

THE POLITICS OF GOVERNMENT

cents because of increased economic growth.[16] This led to an imbalance between revenues and expenditures. As government outlays as a share of the GNP rose, from 21 percent at the end of the Carter administration to 26 percent by the end of Reagan's first term, the national debt increased by 50 percent, from $1 to $1.5 trillion, in just four years. Meanwhile, the country's borrowing to finance its deficit and its trade imbalances led it to become a net debtor for the first time since 1917.

Congress and fiscal policy

The Constitution grants Congress plenary powers over domestic interstate and foreign commerce, taxation, currency, and appropriations. Congress may exercise its powers or delegate them by law to the president. Yet however much Congress is influenced by the White House, while the initiative in economic policy rests with the president, its disposition remains with Congress.[17]

The Budget and Impoundment Control Act. On the basis of the provisions of the 1974 Budget and Impoundment Control Act, Congress passes a first and a second budget resolution, and if necessary a reconciliation bill, all of which attempt to set fiscal policy. The House and Senate budget committees hold hearings on the presidential program, using the analyses prepared by the Congressional Budget Office and the Joint Economic Committee of Congress (which may not report bills but which functions as a high-level seminar to educate members on fiscal policy). The committees recommend their own expenditure and revenue figures, which usually differ from the OMB's forecasts. After the committees report, each chamber passes its version of the first budget resolution, and by May 15, after conference, Congress passes the compromise version. By September 15 the second concurrent resolution passes. This one, unlike the first, is binding. Under its provisions, no law or appropriation that would modify its fiscal impact may be passed during the fiscal year without forcing a reconsideration of the second budget resolution.

In theory, fiscal policy is paramount, and specific taxing and spending measures are subordinated to policies agreed upon in the resolutions. In practice, things are not quite so neat. The leaders of the budget, taxing, and appropriations committees are all rivals for influence within party caucuses. Often splits within the parties (Republican supply-siders versus balanced-budget proponents and Democratic liberals versus conservatives, for example) are reflected in the committees' rivalries.

The president's congressional party. Presidents face strong opposition from members of their own party. Eisenhower was badgered by conservative Republicans who pressed for large budget cuts and reductions in business taxes. Kennedy had to delay proposals for a tax cut because of the opposition of Democratic leaders. Johnson routinely negotiated with Wilbur Mills, the Democratic chair of the House Ways and Means Committee, not only on tax measures but also on the size of the deficit, and he could not get a tax surcharge bill out of Mills's committee until he agreed to cuts in expenditures. Ford's tax-cut proposals met with strong opposition from Republicans on the Senate Budget Committee, and Carter's $31 billion counterrecessionary expenditure program was criticized by Democrats on the Joint Economic Committee as being too little and too late. Democrats on the tax committees rewrote Carter's tax reform bill into a set of special-interest raids on the Treasury,

based on Senator Russell Long's ditty: "Don't tax you, don't tax me, tax the fellow behind the tree."

Reagan had to compromise on his tax-cut program in 1981, dropping reductions from 30 to 25 percent, and eventually he had to raise other taxes. During his second term he had to fend off pressure from the Republican majority leader, Robert Dole, to increase personal income tax rates to cut the deficit.

White House lobbying. Presidents try to put together congressional coalitions which will adopt their fiscal program. Republican presidents go for bipartisan majorities in the House, usually by targeting fifty southern and border-state Democrats from the Conservative Democratic Forum. The president may offer them specific programs (such as increased funding for water and river bills and more defense spending in their districts) or use their fiscal policy as a point of departure (as Reagan did in 1981 with certain tax provisions). The president can promise that if they vote for the economic program, they will not be faced with opposition from the White House when they run for reelection. But if presidents get a bill they like from the House, they may find that the Senate party opposes it, and vice versa, a situation that Reagan faced in 1982 and 1983.

Democratic presidents usually find that their party is fragmented between liberals and conservatives and that their committee leaders are at odds with one another and with the Speaker of the House and Senate party leaders. Their best approach is to try to unify the party in the caucuses, but no president has been very successful at this.

If worse comes to worst, presidents can walk away from fiscal policy-making and acquiesce in the budget resolutions negotiated by congressional leaders themselves. Ford, Carter, and Reagan all abandoned the budget process at least once in their terms. The budget process may fall apart entirely if no compromises can be reached and no majority coalition forms. This may well happen when the president fails to assert leadership, especially in an election year. Thus Reagan's budget proposals were "dead on the Hill" in 1982, 1983, and 1984, and the budget process sometimes stalemated and sometimes collapsed completely.

One of David Stockman's primary functions as director of the OMB was liaison with Congressional leaders. (*AP Laserphoto.*)

When it works, congressional fiscal policy-making becomes a form of ***party government:*** the president and the president's party square off against the opposition on fundamental issues of taxing, spending, and overall economic strategy. Increasingly, most Democrats have opposed most Republicans on the important issues (as recorded in roll-call votes on the budget resolutions), and responding to the congressional party attitudes, the 1980 and 1984 presidential candidates presented voters with clear choices and a chance to influence fiscal policy. The congressional budget process has increased the differences between the parties, contributed to the political debate, and made it easier for legislators to put new ideas about the economy before the public.[18]

FOCUS

DEFICIT POLITICS. The crucial issue for the American economy in the 1980s has been the ballooning federal ***debt*** (the total obligations of the government) and the annual ***deficit*** (the difference between what the government receives in revenues and what it spends in outlays in a fiscal year). The debt was up past $1.8 trillion at the beginning of FY 1986: annual debt payments of $111 billion represent 12.7 percent of all federal outlays and 3.4 percent of the GNP. The projected deficit for FY 1986 was $180 billion if Reagan's economic program was implemented and more than $218 billion if it was not. (See Figure 15-3 for the recent history of the deficit as a percent of the GNP.) Each year the debt payments increase by another $20 billion, and by 1990 the annual interest alone might reach $200 billion.

*A **structural deficit?*** Although President Reagan has argued that economic growth will provide the revenues needed to reduce the deficit, many economists, including those in his own administration, believe that the nation is now running a ***structural deficit:*** even if there were full employment and maximum production, the government would still be spending more than it could take in. This was the position taken by three former Democratic and three former Republican secretaries of the Treasury, who in an open letter appealed to Congress to raise taxes in 1983. They argued that "the federal budget is now out of control. It is primed to generate immense deficits, year after year, for decades ahead, deficits far larger than any in our history. This fiscal course is senseless."

Figure 15-3. Yearly deficit as percentage of GNP, 1960–1984. In Reagan's first term, huge deficits resulted in a historic increase in the ratio of deficit to yearly gross national product, breaking the 6 percent line in FY 1983. The goal of the administration was to bring that percentage down to less than 4 percent by 1989. (Sources: Office of Management and Budget, "Federal Government Finances: 1984 Budget Data"; Congressional Budget Office, "The Economic and Budget Outlook: An Update," August 1984.)

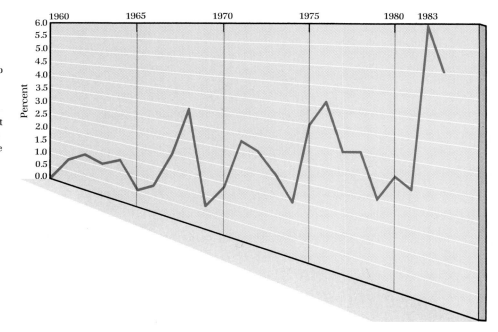

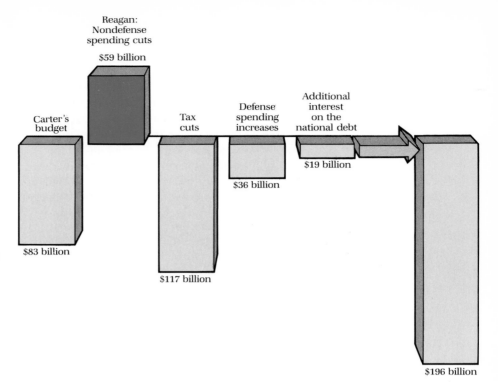

Reagan:
Nondefense
spending cuts

$59 billion

Carter's
budget

Tax
cuts

Defense
spending
increases

Additional
interest
on the
national debt

$19 billion

$36 billion

$83 billion

$117 billion

$196 billion

Figure 15-4. The tax and budget changes which Congress enacted in 1981 as part of the Reagan administration's program have added substantially to the deficit that would have existed had the Carter administration's programs continued in effect. (Source: Congressional Budget Office.)

Reagan came into office with a supply-side program that promised to balance the budget by the fourth year of his first term and provide a $7 billion surplus by 1985. However, once his tax cuts were passed, Reagan abandoned his goal and announced in November 1981 that he would rather accept deficits than support any new taxes. During his first term the deficits increased from $110 billion, far above the previous high of $60 billion during the Ford administration, to $185.3 billion in the fourth year (Figure 15-4).

Supply-side economists were quick to defend the president's program against charges that large deficits would destroy the recovery. They argued that those economists and administration officials who in the past had warned of the dangers of large deficits had always provided erroneous forecasts. Jude Wanniski of Polyconomics claimed in 1984 that deficits could be eliminated by 1988 as the recovering economy provided additional tax revenues. The administration's 1984 budget forecast that the deficits would be reduced gradually to $122 billion by 1989. Measured in terms of the ratio of the debt to the GNP, the administration projected a decline from 5.8 percent in 1984 down to 3 percent by 1988.

The Congressional Budget Office responded by arguing that the deficit would climb to about $263 billion annually by 1989 and that the size, the interest payments, and the ratio of the debt to the GNP could soar above 8 percent.

Some economists argued that large deficits were a good thing and that acting prematurely to reduce them would plunge the economy into a deep recession. In periods of high unemployment and low industrial output, a government deficit (or a massive increase in its size) could stimulate the economy. Since labor, capital, and industrial capacity would be available, this *stimulative deficit* would lead to increased output without necessarily triggering a rise in interest rates or prices. Politicians who believed that a reduction in the deficit could be achieved only by means of painful cuts in domestic spending, which their constituents would not accept, were quick to accept these views.

Before the 1984 election Reagan cast his lot with supply-side economists and argued that there was no evidence that budget deficits could be linked to inflation or interest rates. The president and the secretary of the Treasury refused to consider raising taxes. Reagan's economists pointed to France, with its low deficit, recessions, and high interest rates, and compared it with Japan, with its huge deficits, booming economy, and low interest rates. The Treasury economist Manley Johnson, in a 1983 study, concluded that "existing empirical evidence points toward no systematic relationship between government budget deficits and interest rates." Reagan echoed this position, referring to critics as "doom criers" in radio broadcasts to the nation just before introducing his economic program for 1984. David Stockman, then the director of the OMB, observed that the prospects of cuts in domestic programs were nil because the American people would not support them. Republicans in Congress did not call for tax increases or major spending cuts in the election year. As Jack Kemp put it, "Republicans no longer worship at the shrine of a balanced budget."

But the president and Republican members of Congress also played the other side of deficit politics *after* the election. They called for a dramatic new "flat tax" initiative which would lower tax rates while closing off loopholes. The president also called for a bipartisan congressional group to negotiate with the administration on cuts that would, between 1984 and 1987, pare $100 billion from federal expenditures as a "down payment" on closing the budget gaps. Reagan's economic program submitted in February 1985 called for $47 billion in new cuts, four-fifths of which would be made in domestic programs (even as military spending would rise by $31.2 billion).

The balanced-budget amendment.   President Reagan also called on Congress to pass a balanced-budget amendment in his 1985 state of the union address. Congress would have had to adopt a fiscal plan whereby revenues could not increase faster than projected increases in national income and whereby expenditures could not exceed planned outlays. An increase in the national debt would be allowed only if three-fifths of the members of Congress approved or if the nation was at war.

By 1984 advocates of such an amendment won resolutions from thirty-two state legislatures directing Congress to call a constitutional convention; only thirty-four states are required to petition Congress. Meanwhile, the Senate Judiciary Committee is drafting a constitutional convention implementation act which would provide for the popular election of delegates to any such convention—one from each congressional district and two from each state.

A convention would be limited by the act to considering only a balanced-budget amendment; it would not, as some critics have claimed, be able to run amok and revise the entire Constitution. And in any event, such a convention would itself be checked by the thirty-eight state legislatures whose approval is necessary to ratify any constitutional amendment.

Critics charge that the amendment would be a con job. Either it would put the government in a fiscal straitjacket—preventing emergency action, contingency planning, and necessary capital investment—or else it would have loopholes, become a dead letter, and soon be ignored. Gardner Ackley, a former president of the American Economics Association and, the chair of the CEA, spoke for much of the economics profession when he suggested that the loopholes in the provision itself are "strong reason not to clutter up our Constitution with unwarranted and indefensible economic nonsense." Burke Marshall, a professor at Yale Law

School, argued that "it trivializes the Constitution to try, for the first time, to write into it what are essentially economic and social legislative policies."[19]

Alternative ways to cut the deficits. Those who oppose the balanced-budget amendment believe that a more flexible approach, based on statutes rather than the Constitution, would be better. Some, like Alan Greenspan, a former chair of the CEA, have called for a bipartisan committee to come up with a plan—much as the Social Security Commission, which he chaired, was able to do. Others, such as Walter Mondale, called for increases in income taxes and a slowdown in defense spending. Still others preferred to rely on increases in taxes such as the excise taxes on cigarettes, gasoline, and liquor and on the enactment of a tax on crude oil imports. Some of the $225 billion in outstanding government loans could be sold to private banks and other institutions. The cash obtained could be used to reduce the total debt, which would result in a saving of interest payments of about $10 billion annually.

Rethinking the deficit problem. Some corporate accountants and economists argue that the size of the deficit is misleading. It includes capital expenditures (which are repaid by fees or which improve productivity), not just yearly consumption. It includes money that the government borrows which is then loaned to individuals and businesses and which will eventually be repaid. The total debt should be balanced off against the hundreds of billions of dollars of assets (in land, buildings, technology, and claims) held by the government.

As the economist Robert Heilbroner has pointed out, when private business borrows, it is known as *investing*, but when the government borrows, it is called *spending*. This suggests that the real question is not the size of the annual deficit, but rather how productively the government is investing its money.

MONETARY POLICY-MAKING: THE FEDERAL RESERVE BOARD

The government also influences the economy by influencing the quantity and cost of money. ***Monetarists*** believe that controlling money is the key to managing investment and consumption decisions and that ***monetary policy*** rather than fiscal policy is therefore the key to controlling inflation and stimulating growth. A restrictive policy which tries to contract the money supply or reduce its rate of growth may damp down a boom and control inflation, but it also can plunge the nation into a recession or choke off a recovery—as happened in the 1930s. A permissive policy which expands the money supply rapidly may fuel a boom but lead to runaway inflation and ultimately end growth, as interest rates are forced up; this happened in the 1970s.

The ***Federal Reserve Board*** (the Fed) has managed the money supply since its creation in 1912. Its powers are delegated by Congress, which according to Article I of the Constitution has the power "to coin money and regulate its value." The Fed is an independent agency, not directly subject to presidential control, although the president nominates the chair for a four-year term (which does not coincide with the president's own) and the seven other members of the board, each of whom serves for seven years. The president cannot remove board members.

As Arthur Burns, a former Fed chair, points out, the Fed is less independent in fact than it is in theory. It is influenced by both the president and Congress and is subject to provisions of the Employment Act of 1946 and other laws setting forth economic policy.

THE INSTRUMENTS USED BY THE FED

The Fed influences interest rates by setting the *discount rate* on its loans to member banks. If it raises the rate, it forces banks to raise their interest rates, which should work to dampen business activity. But raising interest rates does not always accomplish this. First, it may lead foreign investors to transfer funds into the United States in order to take advantage of higher rates, thus providing more money for investment. In the 1970s, when interest rates rose, the inflow of foreign funds increased the total money supply sharply. Second, if business thinks that rates will go even higher, corporations may take rising rates as a signal to borrow now rather than pay higher rates later.

The Fed sets a *reserve requirement* for member banks: the requirement that a bank maintain a specified ratio between its deposits and the loans it makes. Raising the reserve requirement means that banks must keep more funds on hand and may lend less. Lowering the reserve requirement makes more credit available. But such a requirement no longer affects enough commercial banks and other financial institutions to control the money supply. Corporations can finance their investments by issuing stock or commercial paper; by obtaining loans from foreign investors, companies, and banks; or by turning to financial services, insurance companies, and pension funds, none of which are subject to a reserve requirement.

The Fed controls the money supply through its *open market* operations. It buys and sells government securities from commercial banks. When it sells securities, the banks or their customers pay by check, which drains money from the banking system and thus reduces the amount of available credit; when it buys securities, it pays the banks by check, which injects money into the banking system and increases the amount of available credit.

These open market operations bring the Fed into close proximity with the fiscal policy of the Treasury and the administration. If the Fed decides to buy debt issued by the Treasury (known as *monetizing* the debt), the result will be an expansion of the money supply, which will stimulate the economy. But if the Fed refuses to buy Treasury debt (either directly or from commercial banks), then the individuals who do buy the debt must pay for it by check, which reduces the amount of available credit in the banking system for other purposes. This is a restrictive policy which will cool down the economy. Thus the Fed, by buying or selling government debt, can either reinforce or counterbalance the administration's fiscal policy.

The Fed sends signals to entrepreneurs and corporate managers, and these affect their decisions about investments. The confidence that the investment and business communities have in the Fed is as important as any specific actions it takes. These communities want a board that can resist presidential pressure to expand the money supply unduly in an election year to fuel a preelection boom that benefits the presidential party (but later brings inflation, which reduces the value of their investments). But they also want a board that does not restrict the money supply so unduly that business cannot obtain the money it needs at reasonable rates.

The Fed and monetary theory

One of the problems in making monetary policy is the lack of consensus among economists as to what effect interest rates or the money supply has on the economy. Some argue that every 1 percent increase in the money supply yields close to a 1 percent increase in the GNP. Others claim that the increase is only temporary or that increased inflation washes out the benefits. Some say that decreases in the money supply will raise interest rates and slow inflation

and growth. Others say that raising interest rates is itself inflationary and will make matters worse in an overheated economy, especially if people and corporations start to borrow in the expectation that rates will go even higher. Falling rates are supposed to increase the demand for money, but they may not do so if people think that if they wait awhile, rates will go even lower.

The Fed has only an imprecise idea of the size of the money supply (there are seven definitions from which to choose) or of how fast and by how much the supply is changing. Fed officials often revise their estimates, correcting themselves by as much as $3 to $4 billion. This means that the Fed's ability to signal its intentions to business is limited, since often a rise in the money supply is later revised to indicate a decline, or vice versa.

Monetarists are divided into two camps over the role the Fed should play. Some think that the money supply or interest rates can be controlled through continual intervention. Others, among them the Nobel prizewinning economist Milton Friedman, have argued that there should be an automatic expansion of the money supply by a specified amount each year so that business can make its plans accordingly.[20] Still others think that the best thing the Fed can do is "lean against the wind" and counterbalance the administration's fiscal policy.

The Fed versus the administration

Relations between the Fed and the administration range from forced cordiality to open hostility. A conflict between the Fed and the Treasury in 1951 over interest rates forced the intervention of President Truman, who presided over negotiations which produced an "accord" that had all the trappings of a peace treaty between two sovereign nations.

Presidents who are in economic trouble are likely to become monetarists who blame the Fed for the problems rather than their fiscal policy—giving new meaning to the term *buck-passing*. Johnson called the Fed chairman down to his Texas ranch in 1965 after the Fed raised the discount rate and dressed him down for making Johnson politically vulnerable; then he blamed the Fed for the 1967–1968 inflation. Carter attacked it in 1980 for its ill-advised policies, which he claimed had driven interest rates sky-high, and he had his Treasury secretary and CEA chair launch attacks on the Fed for several weeks.

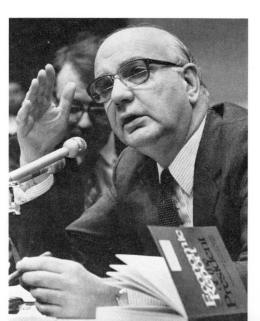

Heads of independent regulatory agencies do not always bear good news for the administration. Paul Volcker, chairman of the Federal Reserve Board, warns the House Banking Committee that the United States may soon become the world's largest debtor nation. (*UPI; Bettmann Newsphotos.*)

The Fed and the administration often disagree on fiscal policy. The Fed can use its open market operations to counterbalance the administration's fiscal policy, which it did in 1957, from 1966 to 1969, and in 1974 and 1975. The president may try to forestall this by including the chair of the Fed in the informal "quadriad" of economic advisers, and the president has the power to reappoint the chair and appoint members who support the chair's positions, which gives some powerful leverage. The negotiations between the Fed and the president may involve an agreement to keep the deficit below a certain figure. Examples include the 1961–1965 expansion; the 1970 accord between Nixon and Burns, which ended a tight money policy and culminated in a major expansion of the money supply by the 1972 elections; and the cooperation from 1983 to 1985 between the Fed and the Treasury in financing the huge deficits.[21] The Fed and the Treasury "frontloaded" the deficit financing by doing most of it early in 1984 so that there would be no crowding out of private borrowers in credit markets just before the presidential election.

Some observers have argued that most of the time the Fed delivers the policies which the administration requests. Usually significant changes in monetary policy occur shortly after a new administration takes office, and these accommodate the fiscal policies it has introduced.[22] The Fed usually adopts the policies of the administration with regard to employment, growth, and price stability.[23] The Fed always denies charges of political accommodation. It points out, and rightly so, that it cannot favor one party at the expense of the other for fear of congressional reaction. Hardly anyone at the Fed expects to get a higher political position or intends to run for office. People at the Fed claim that it has "built-in protections against political influence" and that "non-involvement in partisan politics is . . . central to its ethos."[24] But this defense fails to address the main point: the Fed may accommodate presidents not for personal or partisan reasons, but to maintain its autonomy. A hostile president might propose that the Fed be put into the Treasury Department, which would then function as a central bank in the European manner, or that the secretary of the Treasury serve also as its chair. Congress might allow presidents to appoint members for a term concurrent with theirs and to fire them at will.

During Reagan's first term the Fed pursued tight monetary policies, while the administration wanted it to loosen up. The undersecretary of the Treasury, Beryl Sprinkel, was given the go-ahead by Reagan to launch a "study" of the structure of the Fed, and the Treasury created an Office of Domestic Monetary Policy to keep tabs on the Fed's operations. A visit to the Fed by the White House staffers Baker and Meese led it to become more responsive to Reagan's policy. Similarly, early in Reagan's second term the secretary of the Treasury, Donald Regan, announced that the structure of the Fed was under review.

Congress may protect the Fed from these pressures. It does not by law require the Fed to coordinate policy with the administration. But Congress may threaten it with laws that would require it to keep the money supply or interest rates within certain "targets," and to report periodically on its efforts. At present the Fed must report to Congress on it policies at least twice a year.

REGULATORY POLITICS

The national government regulates the economy in order to reconcile private economic power with public purposes. At present there are more than 100 government agencies and 100,000 officials who create and enforce federal regulations.

Types of regulation

Wage and price controls. The government may attempt to regulate the entire economy through wage and price controls passed by Congress. Controls are implemented in wartime, and only in 1971 were they imposed in peacetime. President Nixon imposed a ninety-day freeze on wages, prices, rents, and interest rates in an effort to halt runaway inflation. Later, wage and price boards considered applications for increases. The experience of the years 1971 to 1973 is instructive for anyone who thinks that government controls can stop inflation. Economists have concluded that the program worked politically (prices were controlled through the 1972 elections) but not economically: inflation zoomed, as if to make up for lost time, after the program was dismantled. Wealthier people received income from stock dividends and capital gains, and executives were compensated through stock options, which were not subject to controls. The brunt of controlling inflation fell on middle- and lower-income people.[25]

Industry regulation. Usually government regulations cover a specific industry (for example, milk producers) or deal with a specific problem (such as prohibiting child labor). Most do one or more of the following:

- Establish performance standards for companies, such as a reduction in automobile or smokestack emissions
- Designate the process or technology which a company must use, such as a particular form of emission control
- Require that end products meet certain standards or that they incorporate safety devices, as in the case of pharmaceuticals and automobile seat belts
- Establish targets or goals which must be met on a timetable, such as a reduction in discharge of waste into rivers
- Require the disclosure of information to potential consumers and to stockholders and people considering investments
- Regulate conduct by making certain actions subject to criminal penalties or civil penalties, such as violating the provisions of antidiscrimination laws
- Control conflict between groups, as through labor-management laws and regulations
- Limit the political influence of economic groups, as with campaign contribution laws

Regulating means testing and, sometimes, failing. A Boeing 720 built of new, supposedly flame-retardant materials ignited on ground contact during a test crash. (*AP/Wide World.*)

All this activity is fertile ground for politicians and lobbyists. Who sets the goals? Who enforces them? How can they be changed? These are the important issues in regulatory politics.

The regulatory agencies

Congress establishes regulatory agencies for different sectors of the economy. They are delegated the legislative power to make general rules for an industry and to apply them in specific cases (a quasi-judicial power). Because of the nature of their powers, the regulatory agencies have commissioners who are appointed by the president on a bipartisan basis (half are Democrats, and half are Republicans), and the president may not remove them except for reasons having nothing to do with their decisions. They are expected to exercise their own judgment rather than simply follow the White House. The most important of these include the *regulatory commissions:* the Interstate Commerce Commission (trucking and railroads), the Federal Trade Commission (advertising and trade practices), the Securities and Exchange Commission (stock exchanges and offerings), the Federal Communications Commission (radio and television broadcasting), the Consumer Product Safety Commission, and the Nuclear Regulatory Commission (the licensing and inspection of nuclear plants). In addition, there are some *independent agencies* whose officials are appointed by the president but do not report to the president and are not subject to the presidential removal power (these include the Federal Reserve Board and the National Labor Relations Board), and there are many *regulatory offices* within the departments.

Agency operations. Congress governs the way all these agencies work when they make regulations through the Administrative Procedures Act of 1946. Formal rule making requires a hearing so that the commissioners can hear from industry spokespersons. Conducted much like a trial, a formal hearing includes expert testimony and cross-examination. Because this is time-consuming, an informal rule-making system is often substituted. In about four-fifths of the cases an agency simply publishes a description of its proposed rule in the *Federal Register* and lets interested groups comment on it. The agency may then modify the rule before it goes into effect.

The regulatory cycle. Sometimes new agencies are created as a result of national agenda politics, through exposure of some abuse of the public interest; for example, unsanitary conditions in meat-packing plants led to the passage of pure food laws and the creation of the Food and Drug Administration, and the unfair practices of railroads in dealing with farmers resulted in the creation of the Interstate Commerce Commission. Initially, public outrage leads the president and Congress to establish a watchdog agency to curb an abuse by issuing stiff regulations; later the agency is captured by interest groups, and the result is, in Woodrow Wilson's words, a "government of cartels and clients," with the regulatory agencies protecting and promoting the interests of groups that they were originally supposed to regulate.[26]

But often new agencies are created with the active cooperation of interest groups which themselves want regulations in markets, especially regulations which set up barriers to entry that restrict competition to existing businesses or which set rates that virtually guarantee high profits. Trucking companies, railroads, and airlines, for example, all did well under regulations which lim-

ited the ability of new companies to compete for routes—unless they had political connections. Similarly, doctors, lawyers, saloonkeepers, liquor-store owners, barbers and people in other professions and trades promote government licensing, examination, and regulation to restrict entry into their fields.

Sometimes producers accept government regulation that *socializes risks:* that forces the public to accept some of their risks of doing business. The methods include guaranteeing profits through cost-plus contracts (defense), creating legal monopolies and setting rates (telephone, gas, and electric companies), insuring against loss (export insurance), guaranteeing or subsidizing loans (housing), putting a floor on prices (agriculture), and ending competition. Thus in allocating limited radio-band channels for cellular radio telephones (so-called Dick Tracy communication), the Federal Communications Commission encouraged the competing companies to join together into new enterprises that would split the channels and markets amicably rather than compete with one another.

Other regulation involves ***protective legislation:*** an industry that is in trouble because of foreign competition—such as the steel, machine tool, shoe, or textile industry—may call for tariffs and quotas or for various product safety and environmental standards which foreign companies may find hard to meet. Or it asks for domestic content laws, which require foreign companies to include a certain percentage of American parts in their products.

Self-regulation and reregulation. Much economic regulation involves ***self-regulation.*** The government encourages industries to come up with voluntary codes and fair practices, which it then incorporates into its own regulations or statutes. These industry groups and the advisory committees have the legal right to review and comment on proposed agency regulations, and they are usually consulted before the regulations are issued. They can press officials for lenient enforcement, exemptions, postponements, and changes in interpretation—they can even ask for nonenforcement of what they claim are "unworkable" provisions. For example, in 1985 the Transportation Department lowered the fuel-economy standards for 1985- and 1986-model light-duty trucks, a deci-

To regulate or not? In 1978 James Schlesinger, then the secretary of energy, warned that oil demand would outstrip supply by 1985 without government regulation. The Reagan administration dismantled the regulatory structure of the 1970s. In 1985 there was an oil glut, not the shortage Schlesinger predicted. (*AP Laserphoto.*)

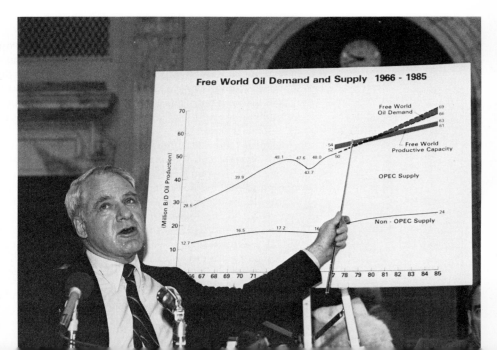

sion that saved Ford and General Motors hundreds of millions of dollars in plant investment and fines.

Sometimes companies believe that they would be better off "getting the government off their backs" and propose to deregulate their industries. A few years later, sadder but wiser, they call for **reregulation.** The trucking industry, for example, wants Congress to issue new regulations to control entry by new trucking companies. The insurance industry wants laws that will prohibit banks from issuing insurance policies.

Social versus economic values. The government may regulate the market to promote social, cultural, or environmental values, even though this may result in higher costs for producers and higher prices for consumers. Since the costs of polluted air or water are borne by the public rather than by the company which made a product or by the consumer who bought it (economists refer to these costs as *externalities,* since third parties bear them), the government may regulate the market to impose the costs directly on those who produce and consume a product. In 1984, for example, the Environmental Protection Agency issued stiff new standards concerning the amount of lead in gasoline; these were based on overwhelming medical evidence that leaded gasoline is hazardous to young children in urban areas. The new standards would reduce airborne lead by 31 percent in the next eight years. "If left to its own," says Joseph A. Cannon of the Environmental Protection Agency, "the market would not achieve this goal. Ergo, government regulations."[27]

The government may regulate according to public morality, as when it outlawed child labor in 1940 and when it restricted the number of hours which could be worked and provided for minimum health, sanitary, and safety conditions in the workplace. Similarly, in the 1960s and 1970s laws were passed prohibiting discrimination in employment on the basis of race, age, or gender. While antidiscrimination laws lower the cost of doing business (by increasing

---

LABOR-MANAGEMENT LAWS

Norris-LaGuardia Act of 1932. This act grants labor the right to organize into unions and outlaws the yellow-dog contract, by which a corrupt union negotiates with management at the expense of workers.

National Labor Relations Act of 1935. This act makes illegal any interference with workers who are organizing a union or engaging in collective bargaining, outlaws company unions, prevents firings for union activities, and requires management and unions to bargain collectively and in good faith.

Fair Labor Standards Act of 1938. This act establishes a forty-hour workweek, requires time and a half for overtime, and establishes a minimum wage for workers in interstate commerce.

Federal Labor Standards Act of 1940. This act prohibits child labor.

Taft-Hartley Labor-Management Relations Act of 1947. This act outlaws the "closed shop" requirement that a worker join a union in order to get a job in a company, outlaws jurisdictional strikes and secondary boycotts, and provides for an eighty-day labor injunction and cooling-off period, declared by federal judges during strikes at the request of the administration's labor mediators.

Occupational Safety and Health Act of 1970. This act established the Occupational Safety and Health Administration, provides that OSHA may establish health and safety standards and inspect for violations, and provides for fines and other court actions against employers who do not comply with regulations.

the number of eligible workers in the labor market and by expanding the pool of talented workers available for any job), all these regulations and laws involve paperwork and compliance costs, and many raise the cost of doing business (such as the minimum wage and antipollution laws). Sometimes this means that the laws have a perverse result: jobs are transferred by companies to places in the United States where the laws can be violated. For example, illegal sweatshops are established which employ children, illegal immigrants, and others who are grateful to get any work at all. Or jobs can be exported to foreign countries that do not have these regulations. As the costs of American products rise, the way is opened for foreign producers to undercut the prices or to manufacture counterfeit brand-name products (such as Levis jeans, Capitol records, and Mark Cross pens) and sell shoddy, defective, or even dangerous products at low prices. Such activities cost American workers at least 131,000 jobs and American companies at least $6 billion in lost sales in 1983, according to the United States International Trade Commission. How to provide decent working conditions and a good wage for American workers remains a major problem in a world that has an excess supply of labor and people who are willing to work under any conditions.

How independent are the independent regulatory agencies? In theory, the regulatory agencies are independent, but it would be naive to think that they are so in fact. The White House and Congress dominate them.

PRESIDENTIAL INFLUENCE. The president, with the advice and consent of the Senate, appoints the commissioners and the chairs. Even though the terms are staggered, and the president makes only a few appointments at a time, commissioners serve an average of fewer than three years (of their four-year terms), and so a two-term president can pack the agencies. Presidents influence regulatory politics through their appointments to commissions and agencies. They can appoint people from issue networks who are interested in effective public policy or representatives of an industry that is being regulated; these representatives prefer self-regulation and lenient enforcement of the law. For example, President Reagan named James C. Miller, who headed his task force on regulatory relief, to chair the Federal Trade Commission. As a result, fewer rules were drafted, enforcement was weakened, and the agency's budget was slashed and its staff was cut—all Reagan's policies.

Presidential agencies such as the OMB or special task forces may establish regulatory review mechanisms which pass or veto regulations proposed by agencies in the executive branch. Their budget and reorganization requests may affect the ability of an agency to implement and enforce its regulations. Finally, the White House may intervene in specific cases in favor of corporations that are accused of violating a regulation or law (known as *ex parte* contacts with regulatory officials), although this is against the law.

The White House can also take the lead in attempting to deregulate industries, especially those in which the regulatory commissions have been captured. The Carter administration deregulated the trucking and airline industries, resulting in lower prices. The Reagan administration deregulated financial services, the television and radio industry, and the telecommunications industry. Proponents argue that the competition which results will lead to lower prices and better service. Opponents claim that deregulation results in higher prices (often through a rigged market), worse service, and serious violations of health and consumer safety laws. Often deregulation allows com-

panies to retain regulations which they favor and eliminate those which impose costs on them; thus, in spite of deregulation of the television industry, the number of stations is still limited, and profits are virtually guaranteed; at the same time, the limitations on the number of commercials that can be broadcast each hour have been lifted.

CONGRESSIONAL OVERSIGHT. Congress establishes these agencies and provides them with their jurisdiction and powers. Its committees oversee the agencies' operations. Congress often passes laws which overturn the agencies' rules. It changes their jurisdiction, as it did in 1980, when it prevented the Federal Trade Commission from regulating television advertising aimed at children. Congress not only controls the agencies' budgets and personnel but also can reorganize them either to expand or to contract their jurisdiction and put them back in the department structure or abolish them altogether, as it did with the Civil Aeronautics Board.

Congressional committees, working closely with PACs and lobbyists, are likely to pressure the president into appointing sympathetic officials and giving interest groups access to the agencies. But congressional committees, especially in election years, may also revive reform efforts by investigating a captured agency and calling for its shake-up. Investigating cover-ups, conflicts of interest, lenient enforcement, and other scandals can give legislators, especially those running for reelection, a national forum. The result may be the resignation of officials, a reorganization of an agency, or even the passage of tougher regulations.

Individual legislators attempt to win waivers, exemptions, or delays for their constituents as a result of the impact of regulations. The Alaskan congressional delegation, for example, won amendments to a clean water act in 1984 that gave two paper and pulp plants a waiver allowing them to use inferior pollution control equipment. Legislators who are close to the automobile industry fight to extend deadlines for emission controls and to prevent regulations requiring seat belts or air bags.

A good way to understand the role of Congress in regulatory politics is to look at costs and benefits. The costs and benefits of a regulation may involve many or few people. When they involve many people (as in the case of taxa-

Elizabeth Dole, secretary of transportation, talks to Robert Dole, chairman of the Senate Finance Committee, before testifying. (Yes, they are married to each other.) (*AP Laserphoto.*)

tion), it is likely that Congress will be responding to an executive policy in national agenda politics. When many people pay the costs (in the form of higher prices) but only a few people benefit, the result is a form of client politics, and Congress takes low-visibility actions, such as amending an existing law. Instead of an overall policy, the result is a system of brokerage and favoritism: only when a public-interest "watchdog" can rouse the public against the favor is the president likely to get involved. When the costs are borne by only a few companies but the benefits are reaped by most people (as in the case of automobile and consumer safety laws), public-interest groups, acting on behalf of "the public," try to influence the national agenda. Opposing them are the PACs that represent the affected companies; they try to lessen the public's apprehension, discredit the public-interest groups, and keep policy-making low-key and less visible. Finally, when the costs and benefits involve only a few groups, the standard iron triangle emerges, with a trade association, a congressional committee, and a government agency dominating policy without effective interference by public-interest groups.[28]

JUDICIAL INFLUENCE. The courts play a secondary role in regulating the economy. They do not set policy directly, as Congress or the executive agencies do, but nevertheless they can check and balance the other branches. For one thing, they require the agencies to follow due process of law: the agencies must give affected individuals and corporations various statutory legal protection before promulgating or enforcing regulations affecting them. For another, the rulings of the courts often amplify and extend the meaning of statutes and regulations; much of antitrust law, for example, has been developed by the courts rather than by Congress. Finally, the courts monitor the extent to which Congress may delegate its powers to government agencies: they usually permit vast delegations, but they will not allow Congress to delegate to agencies its constitutional power of taxation, for example.

ISSUE AND DEBATE

AN INDUSTRIAL POLICY? The ability of American business to compete in the international marketplace has been slipping for more than two decades. In 7 out of 10 high-tech industries (pharmaceuticals, electrical equipment, plastics, industrial chemicals, and scientific instruments, for example) and in many other fields, foreign companies have overtaken us in terms of technology and manufacturing. While our exports have increased, a flood of imports has caused a severe erosion in the balance of trade (Figure 15-5), and American companies have lost their commanding share of many markets.[29]

The American economy does not rely on centralized government planning to solve problems like these.[30] Instead, the government fosters free or regulated markets, offers incentives to invest in certain activities, and then leaves actual decisions to companies in the private sector. Nevertheless, a considerable amount of planning is done by individuals, entrepreneurs, and corporate managers who make decisions about how to maximize the return on their capital and how to manage the risks of their enterprises. The government's management of the economy is indirect and reactive: it involves signaling these entrepreneurs and managers about shifts in fiscal, monetary, and regulatory policy. The goal is to get them to take into account what the government is doing so that they will see that it is in their own best interest to adjust their behavior. In this sense, economic management is somewhat akin to presidential power: it is the power to persuade people to do things of their own volition.

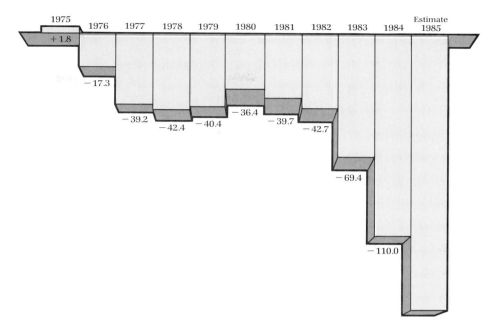

Figure 15-5. Right: The United States trade imbalance, 1975–1985. Because of high interest rates and the unprecedented influx of foreign funds, the value of the dollar relative to other currencies increased as much as 40 percent between 1982 and 1984. The result? Foreign goods cost less, and American exports cost more—resulting in a flood of imports and a weakening of our export market. The imbalance of trade reached historic highs by 1985. (Source: Department of Commerce.)

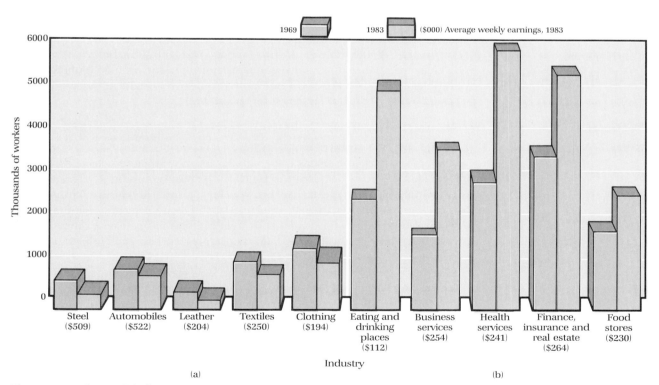

Figure 15-6. Above: While "smokestack" industries have declined since 1969, service industries have enjoyed spectacular growth. (a) Total employment in American manufacturing industries in thousands of workers, 1969 and 1983. The average weekly earnings in 1983 are shown in parentheses below the bar graphs. (b) Total employment in American service industries, 1969 and 1983. Again, the average weekly earnings in 1983 are shown. (Source: U.S. Bureau of Labor Statistics.)

The background. In the 1980s the business community was receiving more than $70 billion annually in government grants, loans, loan guarantees, and other subsidies—twice the amount when Carter left office. The Reagan administration has routinely given assistance to favored firms and industries when it came to protection against foreign competition. According to the Center for the Study of American Business, export loans and loan guarantees amounted to $13 billion in 1984, agricultural price supports cost $21 billion, and other agricultural and rural programs cost $18 billion. Over $2 billion went to small businesses (those with fewer than 500 employees), and some went to the newly created Office of Research, Innovation and Technology, which intends to fund close to $500 million in research and development by 1988. The federal government funds much of the research for the aircraft, transportation (except for automobiles), metals, communications, and scientific instruments industries. A consortium of computer manufacturers (given exemption from antitrust laws) has created a company to develop its research in the next generation of supercomputers using new silicon chips—its research is paid for by the government. Various "tax expenditures" have exempted businesses such as paper and wood producers, railroads, commercial banks, oil and petrochemical companies, and aerospace industries from paying much in the way of corporate taxes. All these outlays and tax expenditures were made without any central planning or coordination, without any rhyme or reason; they were based simply on the political pressure exerted by influential interest groups. In this respect, our government support for business can be distinguished from the strategic approach taken by Japan and France.

Proposals for an industrial policy. In the 1984 elections the Democratic Party—through its congressional study groups, its Center for National Policy, and its contenders for the presidential nomination—proposed to replace the present chaotic distribution of government benefits with a national industrial policy. The government would, in cooperation with business and labor, develop a strategy for industrial competition.

Although the Democrats have embraced the idea of an industrial policy, different constituencies in the party mean different things by the term.[31] In one version, the effort would be concentrated on restoring our declining "smokestack" industries (Figure 15-6) in order to bring back some of the 1.5 million jobs that

Will these unemployed Detroit automobile workers ever go back to their plants? Some experts advocate restoring the "smokestack industries"; others see no future there. (*Alon Reininger: Contact.*)

Many experts on industrial policy urge concentration on high tech, such as electronic chip fabrications. (*Rick Browne: Picture Group.*)

have been lost in the past decade and protect the remaining workers from unfair and predatory foreign competition. The emphasis would be on protecting American companies to the extent that foreign governments subsidize their steel, automobile, and other basic industries. We would institute quotas or obtain voluntary restraints on exports. We could require local coproduction ventures and domestic content in foreign products, and we could vigorously enforce antidumping laws (which impose fines on companies that dump surplus products in the United States at below their production cost). House Democrats have proposed an $8.5 billion bank for industrial competitiveness, which would make government loans to modernize old industrial facilities at low interest rates; a council on industrial competitiveness, which would consist of representatives from business, labor, government, and universities, who would propose new policies; and a federal industrial mortgage association, which would buy up long-term loans made by commercial banks to businesses and thus provide additional credit, much as is done in the private housing markets.

Those who propose this kind of industrial policy point to the fact that in the twenty fastest-growing industries the average weekly earnings are $210, while in the twenty declining industries the average weekly earnings are $310. They argue that the only way to ensure well-paying jobs for most new American workers (rather than the low-paying jobs in the service industry) is to embed new technologies into the products of existing industries—cars, rolled steel, machine tools, and so forth.

The other version of the policy would have the government ensure that capital is channeled into the emerging high-tech "sunrise" industries; it would let most of the "sunset" industries die. Policy would be made by a high-level tripartite economic coordinating council (consisting of representatives from business, labor, and government), which would coordinate government research and development and procurement contracts. Tax incentives and below-market-rate loans could be given to companies in these industries. Protection and market rigging for inefficient industries would be eliminated; as they failed, more capital would become available for the industries in which the United States is most competitive. Tax credits could be given to corporations that retrained displaced workers for newer and more technologically advanced jobs, and the government would also fund more university-based scientific and technical education and training.[32] The benefits and distributions given by the iron triangles to particular industries could

be examined by the tripartite board, and many could then be eliminated.[33] A weakened version of the same plan would establish a high-level council to collect information about American industry and monitor government assistance and contracting across important industries. It would recommend to Congress and the president ways to redirect such aid.[34]

Those who embrace the high-tech approach argue that we are losing international markets in many technologies. While our exports in these areas have grown, other countries have taken larger market shares, and even our imports of high-tech products from other nations have grown. The high-tech advocates say that we are losing ground to the Japanese in semiconductor memory chips, to the Germans and the Japanese in machine tools, and to the Japanese in fiber optics. They claim that such planning as we do in the high-tech industries is increasingly directed by the Pentagon, for military applications, and does not allow us to capitalize on our scientific and technological leads.

The Republicans have been in no hurry to embrace these proposals. Unless and until the Democrats win control of the White House, the prospects are dim that any national industrial policy will take the place of the existing system of distributive politics. Nevertheless, some business organizations, such as the Labor-Industry Coalition for International Trade, the American Business Conference, and the National Association of Manufacturers, have joined with Republicans in Congress to propose a high-tech initiatives program. Their proposals, together with those of the President's Commission on Industrial Competitiveness (which reported its findings in 1985), push for new trade reciprocity laws which would penalize unfair competition, relaxation of antitrust restraints in high-tech areas so that American companies could collaborate (especially in research and development), new tax incentives and tax credits for research and development, and more federal funding for research and development—in other words, for more of the same kind of distributive aid. Better coordination of policy could be achieved by combining the Office of United States Special Trade Representatives and the Department of Commerce into a new department of international trade and industry—a proposal which Reagan made in 1982 but which was stalemated in Congress.

By Toles for The Buffalo News. Reprinted by permission of Universal Press Syndicate.

Pros and cons of an industrial policy. Proponents of a national industrial policy point to the successful experience of Japan and Taiwan in developing strategies to compete in international markets. They argue that because of our present distributive politics approach, we spend too much government money and get too little for it. We subsidize inefficient industries that cannot hold up against foreign competition, which in turn raises the costs of investment and labor for our more efficient and competitive enterprises. They believe that a national industrial policy would allocate capital more efficiently than the private sector and would be less expensive than the present political distributions. They argue that if we stay on our present course, the manufacturing sector will continue to shrink, the gross national product will remain stagnant, and we will be unable to make a smooth transition to new high-tech industries.

Opponents of a national industrial policy believe that the critics do not understand how the economy has performed in the past decade or the best way to manage prosperity in the future. They point out that in the 1980s the United States has had the fastest growth rate of any industrial economy (including Japan). It had more investment and more advances in high tech than any other nation. Even in the 1970s, employment was up 24 percent, compared with 9 percent in Japan. And in the 1970s only the United States, Canada, and Italy, among all the industrial nations, had an increase in manufacturing jobs. In the 1980s even some of the smokestack industries, such as the automobile industry, have rebounded dramatically from their previous problems without a coordinated industrial policy.

Our decentralized, entrepreneurial approach has won the approval of many foreign observers, including the Japanese. Our "Silicon Valley" style, which involves the creation of small high-tech companies, seems more flexible than the bureaucratic approach taken by large Japanese companies and their government bureaucracies that control new investment.[35] Many economists, including some who were closely affiliated with past Democratic administrations—such as Charles Schultz, a former chair of the CEA—argue that the government will not be more efficient in allocating capital than the private sector. There is no reason, they think, to believe that the bureaucrats will know enough to pick the future winners in the struggle for world markets. A tripartite board would be more likely to increase the distortions and inefficiencies in allocations of capital because it would use political rather than economic criteria. They believe that it is high interest rates, the overvalued dollar, and unfair trade practices that cost us exports and jobs—and that with the proper mix of fiscal, monetary, and regulatory policies (as well as diplomatic efforts to open up foreign markets), these problems can be solved.

IN CONCLUSION

Today the government plays a larger role in economic management than ever before; this is due to the impact of its taxing and spending on the gross national product, its management of the currency, and its role in regulating markets. Under what circumstances the government should step in and substitute political for economic allocations is the central issue in the government's relationship with the private sector.

The government has three instruments for influencing the economy. It uses fiscal policy (taxing and spending) to stimulate demand or restrain the economy. Policies are proposed by the president and modified by Congress through its first and second budget resolutions. It uses monetary policy, developed by the Federal Reserve Board, an independent regulatory agency which usually coordinates its

policies with those of the Treasury Department but which may act against the administration's policy. It also uses regulatory policies, based on laws passed by Congress, and regulations made by executive agencies and independent commissions and interpreted by the courts. Some regulatory policies are proposed to curb the excesses of companies operating in free markets, while others are proposed by these companies in order to regulate the market with government assistance. A fourth approach, centralized planning and a strategic approach to international competition, has been proposed by leading Democrats in Congress but is not favored by the Republicans and is not likely to be adopted until the Democrats control the White House.

The government's performance in managing the economy has been poor: it has proved to be unable to control the economy through its mixture of fiscal and monetary policy. Irresponsible but politically attractive policies are pursued, while hard choices are postponed and the public is deceived. The most important political reforms therefore turn out to be intellectual: economists and others are recognizing that there is a limit to how much good they can do and how much influence they can have on the economy. They have often promised to obtain the unobtainable, and there has been a poor match between their competence and the public's expectations. As a consequence, their authority, and the authority of the government, has diminished. Under a system of decentralized planning, pluralist representation, and divided constitutional government, it is unlikely that the government can organize itself to fine-tune the economy or effectively administer an industrial policy.

NOTES

1. Barry Sussman, "The Pocketbook Counts More than the Risks of Nuclear War," *The Washington Post National Weekly Edition*, Oct. 1, 1984, p. 37.
2. Robert J. Samuelson, "The Failure of Economic Management," *The Atlantic*, vol. 255, no. 2, August 1984.
3. On the concept of the free market, see Adam Smith, *The Wealth of Nations*, Modern Library, New York, 1937 (originally published in 1776); see also Milton Friedman, *Capitalism and Freedom*, University of Chicago Press, Chicago, 1962.
4. Thurman Arnold, *The Folklore of Capitalism*, Yale University Press, New Haven, Conn., 1937, pp. 209–230.
5. On allocations, see Charles Lindblom, *Politics and Markets*, Basic Books, New York, 1977, pp. 93–119.
6. *Budget of the United States Government, FY 1985*, GPO, Washington, D.C., 1984.
7. Joseph Pechman, *Federal Tax Policy*, Brookings, Washington, D.C., 1981.
8. George Gilder, *Wealth and Poverty*, Basic Books, New York, 1979, pp. 75–86.
9. Lindblom, *op. cit.*, pp. 170–189.
10. Grant McConnell, *Private Power and American Democracy*, Knopf, New York 1967, pp. 230–243.
11. Richard Rubin, *Press, Party and Presidency*, Norton, New York, 1981, pp. 230–243.
12. Sussman, loc. cit.
13. *The New York Times*, July 28, 1984, sec. 3, p. 2.
14. Walter Heller, *New Dimensions of Political Economy*, Norton, New York, 1967, p. 62.
15. On early supply-side theory, see Jude Wanniski, *The Way the World Works*, Simon and Schuster, New York, 1978.
16. "Tax Data Seen Deflating Claims of Supply-Side Economists," *The New York Times*, Sept. 18, 1984; Barry Bosworth, *Tax Incentives and Economic Growth*, Brookings, Washington, D.C., 1984.
17. David Truman (ed.), *The Congress and America's Future*, Prentice-Hall, Englewood Cliffs, N.J., 1965; Harvey Mansfield, Sr., "The Congress and Economic Policy," pp. 121–149.

18. Allen Schick, *Congress and Money*, Urban Institute, Washington, D.C., 1980, pp. 227–301; John Ellwood and James Thurber, "The Politics of the Congressional Budget Process Re-examined," in Dodd and Oppenheimer (eds.), *Congress Reconsidered*, Congressional Quarterly Press, Washington, D.C.; 1981, pp. 246–274.
19. *The New York Times*, July 30, 1982; *The New York Times*, July 16, 1982.
20. Milton Friedman, "A Monetary and Fiscal Framework for Economic Stability," *American Economic Review*, vol. 38, no. 3, June 1948.
21. Richard Pious, *The American Presidency*, Basic Books, New York, 1979, p. 314.
22. Robert Weintraub, *The Political Economy of Inflation*, Joint Economic Committee, Washington, D.C., 1981.
23. Dudley Luckett and Glenn Potts, "Monetary Policy and Partisan Politics" *Journal of Money, Credit and Banking*, vol. 12, August 1980, pp. 540–546.
24. David R. Eastburn, letter to *The Wall Street Journal*, Jan. 30, 1984.
25. Marvin Kosters, *Controls and Inflation*, American Enterprise Institute, Washington, D.C., 1975, pp. 47–53.
26. Marver Bernstein, *Regulating Business by Independent Commission*, Princeton University Press, Princeton, N.J., 1955, pp. 74–106.
27. Cass Peterson, "The Crackdown on Leaded Fuel," *The Washington Post National Weekly Edition*, Sept. 10, 1984.
28. James Q. Wilson (ed.), *The Politics of Regulation*, Basic Books, New York, 1980.
29. President's Commission on Industrial Competitiveness, *Global Competition: The New Reality*, GPO, Washington, D.C., 1985.
30. Lindblom, op. cit., pp. 313–324.
31. Simon Lazarus and Robert Litan, "The Democrats' Coming Civil War over Industrial Policy," *The Atlantic*, vol. 255, no. 3, September 1984.
32. Business–Higher Education Forum, *America's Competitive Challenge: The Need for a National Response*, final report, 1984.
33. James Cook, "A Case for Reindustrialization," *Forbes*, vol. 133, no. 3, Jan. 30, 1984.
34. Robert B. Reich, "What Kind of Industrial Policy?" *The Journal of Business Strategy*, vol. 5, no. 1, summer 1984, pp. 10–17.
35. Joel Kotkin, "Industrial Policy? Japan and Europe Are Trying to Copy Us," *The Washington Post National Weekly Edition*, May 14, 1984, p. 12.

FURTHER READING

Bach, George L.: *Making Monetary and Fiscal Policy*, Brookings, Washington, D.C., 1971. A comprehensive account of the major tools of fiscal policy and monetary policy as they relate to each other.

Burns, Arthur F.: *The Management of Prosperity*, Columbia University Press, New York, 1966. An attack, by an official in the Eisenhower administration (and later the chair of the Federal Reserve), on the proposition that the economy can be fine-tuned with fiscal policy.

Friedman, Milton: *Capitalism and Freedom*, University of Chicago Press, Chicago, 1981. A presentation of a theory concerning the virtues of the free market system and how it promotes individual liberty.

Gilder, George: *Wealth and Poverty*, Basic Books, New York, 1980. An analysis of the critical role of the entrepreneur in creating new wealth and opportunity.

Heller, Walter: *New Dimensions of Political Economy*, Norton, New York, 1967. A discussion of fine-tuning the economy written by a chair of the CEA.

Jacoby, Neil H.: *The Business-Government Relationship*, Goodyear, Pacific Palisades, Calif., 1974. A reassessment by social scientists of the relations between government and business, including new theories about their interaction.

Kuttner, Robert: *The Economic Illusion: False Choices between Prosperity and Social Justice*, Houghton Mifflin, Boston, 1984. A comparative study of industrialized economies, arguing that social welfare states have higher growth rates, and an attack on supply-side economics.

McGraw, Thomas K.: *Prophets of Regulation*, Harvard University Press, Cambridge, Mass., 1984. A biographical history of the regulatory movement.

Noll, Roger, and Bruce Owen (eds.): *The Political Economy of Deregulation: Interest Groups in the Regulatory Process*, American Enterprise Institute, Washington, D.C., 1983. A study of the politics of deregulation.

Stein, Herbert: *The Fiscal Revolution in America*, University of Chicago Press, Chicago, 1969. A study of the development of fiscal policy tools, written from the point of view of a conservative Republican.

————: *Presidential Economics*, Simon and Schuster, New York, 1984. A debunking of attempts to fine-tune the economy written by a Nixon appointee as chair of the CEA.

Thurow, Lester: *The Zero-Sum Society*, Basic Books, New York, 1981. An economist's argument that in the future there will be no growth and an examination of the consequences for economic, social, and political policies.

Tobin, James: *The New Economics: One Decade Older*, Princeton University Press, Princeton, N.J., 1974. A "new frontier" economist's reflections on the Council of Economic Advisors and on fiscal policy in the 1960s.

Tolchin, Martin, and Susan Tolchin: *Dismantling America: The Rush to Deregulate*, Houghton Mifflin, Boston, 1983. The case against deregulation of industry.

Tufte, Edward: *The Political Control of the Economy*, Yale University Press, New Haven, Conn., 1978. An account of presidential manipulation of the business cycle and its political consequences.

Weidenbaum, Murray L., and Robert DeFina: *The Cost of Federal Regulation of Economic Activity*, American Enterprise Institute, Washington, D.C., 1978. Two economists' arguments for some deregulation.

Wilson, James Q. (ed.): *The Politics of Regulation*, Basic Books, New York, 1980. Patterns of government-industry relations in state and federal regulatory agencies.

THE STUDY BREAK

The China Syndrome. A 1979 thriller, starring Jane Fonda and Jack Lemmon, about a nuclear plant that almost has a meltdown. The movie probes media-industry and media-government relations.

Sinclair, Upton: *The Jungle*, Vanguard Press, New York, 1928 (originally published in 1906). A muckraking book that led to some regulatory reforms of meat packing.

USEFUL SOURCES

Banks, Arthur S. et al. (eds.): *Economic Handbook of the World*, McGraw-Hill, New York, annually. World economic statistics.

Budget of the United States Government, Office of Management and Budget, Washington, D.C., annually. Revenue and expenditure projections, as well as recommended fiscal policies.

Council of Economic Advisors: *Annual Report*, GPO, Washington, D.C., annually. A report on the fiscal policies recommended by the council to the president.

Pearce, David W. (ed.): *The Dictionary of Modern Economics*, M.I.T., Cambridge, Mass., 1981. Defines key economic vocabulary.

World Economic Outlook, International Monetary Fund, Washington, D.C., annually. Forecasts of national and regional economic performance.

ORGANIZATIONS

Congressional Budget Office. House Annex 2, Second and D Streets, S.W., Washington, D.C. 20515. For more information telephone 202-226-2600.

Council of Economic Advisors. Executive Office Building, Washington, D.C. 20506. For more information telephone 202-395-5084.

Department of the Treasury. 15th Street and Pennsylvania Avenue, N.W., Washington, D.C. 20220. For more information telephone 202-566-2000.

Office of Management and Budget. Executive Office Building, Washington, D.C., 20503. For more information telephone 202-395-3000.

U.S. Congress, Joint Economic Committee. Room 5D-601, Cannon House Office Building, Washington, D.C. 20515. For more information telephone 202-224-5171.

CHAPTER 16

SOCIAL POLICY: INSURANCE, ENTITLEMENTS, AND SAFETY NETS

The great depression traumatized the nation, leading to enactment of a safety-net policy in the 1930s. In the 1980s, though, what to do about the growing numbers of the poor is the central issue in social policy. (*Dorothea Lange: Magnum; Alon Reininger: Contact.*)

In the midst of the depression, President Franklin Roosevelt called on Americans to aid the "one-third of the nation" that were "ill fed, ill housed, and ill clothed." Today, one-seventh of the population remain below the poverty line. Most people recognize that those who cannot support themselves—the elderly, the disabled, the ill, and the handicapped—need some government assistance, or a *safety net*. One American in four would be living in poverty if it were not for government payments and services, including half the elderly. But there is no consensus on what to do about younger, able-bodied people who cannot find work or support themselves or their families. Should the government let them fend for themselves, or should it offer them welfare, job training, and public service jobs? Should the poor get health, education, and housing benefits, or would that take away their incentive to work? Is it government's job to help people become self-sufficient, or is it unfair to take the taxpayers' money and give the poor more than the bare necessities? This chapter considers these and other issues of social policy.

BACKGROUND: THE POLICY PARADOX

Poverty in the United States

Each year the Census Bureau surveys 62,000 households to determine the social and economic characteristics of the entire population. Those individuals or families who fall below a predetermined income level are classified as poor. In 1964 the **poverty line** was set at $4000 for a family of four, and approximately 20 percent of the population fell below it.[1] The number of poor people fell from 34 million to about 24.5 million by 1978, for an overall rate of 11.4 percent. But the inflation of the late 1970s and the recession of the early 1980s, the deepest in the postwar period, reversed that trend; the number of poor people increased by 1.6 million in 1982 alone. By 1983, when the poverty line was set at $10,178 for a family of four, the number of poor people had jumped to 34.4 million, a poverty rate of 15 percent. One-fourth of the children under the age of 6 lived in families that were below the poverty line. And among the poorest one-fifth of the nation's families, average disposable income fell by 9.4 percent between 1978 and 1983 (compared with a decline of less than one-half of 1 percent for the richest one-fifth of all families).[2] The number of homeless people reached levels not seen since the depression.

The poverty line is only a crude measure of who is and who is not poor. Most students and many writers, poets, and artists fall below the poverty line but would not consider themselves "poor." Others whose income puts them slightly above the poverty line may have financial burdens such as child support, alimony, or large medical bills that make their standard of living lower than the statistics would suggest. On the other hand, poverty measurements do not include the value of food stamps, Medicare and Medicaid, or housing subsidies. If these are counted as income, the poverty rate would be lower—between 10 and 13 percent.

The saying is that the rich get richer and the poor get poorer. Today the bottom one-fifth of American families earn only 4.2 percent of the national income, while the top one-fifth receive 47.7 percent. The workings of the marketplace tend to reinforce these disparities; the tax system results in a slight leveling effect; and social welfare policies, especially those involving the transfer of income to the elderly and the poor, tend to redistribute income downward.[3] Nevertheless, in the past two decades the middle class has shrunk as more Americans have sunk back into poverty or near poverty or have joined the ranks of the affluent. In the past two decades the percentage of Americans who earned between 125 and 75 percent of the median income declined from 28.2 to only 23.7 percent; those earning less accounted for 37.7 percent of all households, and those earning more accounted for 38.6 percent. During President Reagan's first term the income of the poorest one-fifth declined by 8 percent, while the income of the top one-fifth rose by 9 percent.[4]

Meanwhile, the value of welfare, food stamps, and other cash benefit programs which help the poor has declined by 40 percent in the past fifteen years as a result of inflation. The average taxes paid by the wealthiest one-fifth of American families declined from 31.6 percent of their income to 31.1 percent between 1978 and 1983, while the average taxes paid by the poorest one-fifth have increased from 9.7 to 11.9 percent of their income. Even those below the poverty line paid 10.4 percent of their income in federal taxes in 1984, compared with 4 percent in 1978.

Dealing with poverty

Laissez-faire and social Darwinism. Up until the early part of the nineteenth century, colonial and state governments based their policies on the application of the "poor laws" of Elizabethan England to the situation in this country. English local authorities built workhouses, where those in poverty were forced to live, submit to discipline, learn trades, and earn wages in useful employment. American counties had their almshouses and poorhouses, an early form of state intervention to "improve" the poor. But we were a nation of "rugged individualists," and most Americans assumed that all families were responsible for taking care of themselves. Beyond the family were the church and the community, which extended help to those who were temporarily in distress. Usually, people in each locality could limit their benevolence in two ways: (1) by distinguishing between "outsiders" and "insiders" so that the community's limited resources could be reserved for its own members; (2) by distinguishing between those who were worthy of temporary assistance, because they led virtuous lives, and those who were unworthy, because they were dissolute and likely to misuse any aid given to them. By midcentury, most of the postcolonial poorhouses had been abandoned, and people had begun to believe that poverty was the result of a lack of ability and virtue and that the government should not help alleviate the miseries of the poor.

Some economists of the late eighteenth and early nineteenth centuries—including Adam Smith, Thomas Malthus, and David Ricardo—argued that the poor were responsible for their own poverty, that wages could not rise above the subsistence level for most workers, and that certain "natural laws" (for example, supply and demand) governed the economy and could not be altered for the benefit of the poor. Herbert Spencer's *Social Statistics* contains a gloomy passage stating that poverty, distress, and starvation are "the decrees of a large, far-seeing benevolence." Giving the poor assistance would only

In the nineteenth century, it was thought that altering the inexorable workings of supply and demand to alleviate poverty would distort society. Thus this little boy was "free" to contract with his employer at mutually agreeable wages and hours. In practice such children were brutally exploited in sweatshops. (*Lewis Hine: Culver Pictures, Inc.*)

lower their morals and lead them into drinking and other vices. The ***laissez-faire*** theories reached their high point near the end of the nineteenth century, when they were combined with Charles Darwin's findings on biological evolution and were fused into the theory of ***social Darwinism.*** The social Darwinists believed that humankind, no less than the animal kingdom, followed the laws of nature, among them the law of "survival of the fittest." "American society saw its own image in the tooth-and-claw version of natural selection," according to the historian Richard Hofstadter; "its dominant groups were therefore able to dramatize this vision of competition as a thing good in itself."[5] The competition in a capitalist society was ideally suited, they believed, to weed out those who were weakest—those whose skill, intellect, or physical capacity was below the minimal level necessary to survive.

Philanthropy. Some wealthy Americans believed that private philanthropists rather than the government should help the poor. This approach had a religious underpinning—the social gospel, which condemned the laissez-faire philosophy, arguing that human beings should not be measured in terms of dollars and cents or their worth to employers. By the end of the nineteenth century a large network of philanthropic institutions had been created to care for the poor, the needy, and the elderly. These included settlement houses (in which social workers helped young people get an education and assimilate into American society), voluntary hospitals, soup kitchens, and other forms of relief. "In works of active beneficence, no country has surpassed, perhaps none has equalled, the United States," Lord Bryce wrote in the 1890s. "Not only are the sums collected for all sorts of philanthropic purposes larger relative to the wealth of America than in any European country, but the amount of personal interest and effort devoted to them seems to a European visitor to excel what he knows at home."[6] This remains the case today, as more than $74 billion is collected annually for private philanthropies each year, of which about half goes to religious organizations, one-seventh goes to hospitals, and one-tenth goes to other groups providing social services.

Table 16-1. Percentage of the population receiving government benefits

Program	Percentage of the population receiving benefits
Social security	14.1
Medicare	11.9
Veterans' compensation and pensions	2.1
Education assistance	1.6
Unemployment compensation	1.4
Food stamps	8.3
Medicaid	7.8
AFDC (welfare)	4.2
Public or subsidized rental housing	3.8
SSI (welfare for the elderly, the blind, and the disabled)	1.4
Child nutrition programs	1.1
Total receiving benefits	29.6

Source: Bureau of the Census, data for the third quarter of 1983.

The positive state. The failure of private philanthropies to meet the needs of the "one-third of the nation" in distress during the depression led to an expanded role for all levels of government. Today, as George Bush pointed out in the 1984 vice presidential election debate (and as the figures in Table 16-1 suggest), the national government spends more money on social programs than ever before. Between 1967 and 1982 outlays for social programs for the poor and the middle class (including welfare, food stamps, unemployment compensation, medical payments, social security, and retirement benefits) rose from $37.6 to $312.1 billion—or 300 percent, when adjusted for inflation. Government payments to individuals during this period rose from 4.5 percent of the GNP to more than 13 percent. Between 1970 and 1984 the entitlement programs (those to which people legally make claims, such as social security, federal pensions, medical payments, unemployment insurance, welfare, and food stamps) rose from 29.2 percent of the federal budget to 50 percent, far outstripping any other expenditure category—even defense. Payments to the

By the late nineteenth century harsh social Darwinism was modified by a social gospel stressing philanthropy. Jane Addams founded one of the first settlement houses—Hull House in Chicago—for helping slum families cope. (*Culver Pictures, Inc.*)

poor in the conservative Reagan administration increased from $47 billion in 1980 to $64 billion in 1984.

More money is spent on the poor than ever before, and yet increasing numbers of people are poor: it is this paradox that lies at the core of social welfare politics. The policy debate turns not on whether government should help the poor, but rather on how it should do so. The following section describes our present social welfare programs and some of the important issues they raise for policy-making in the future.

SOCIAL WELFARE PROGRAMS TODAY

Our present social welfare policy and social programs are in part a legacy of our historical attitudes toward the poor. We have no general welfare program that covers all poor people. Instead, we have specific programs that give certain people money or services, combined with restrictive eligibility and regulations designed to distinguish between those who have "earned" benefits or services and those who are receiving government charity. We spend more than $200 billion annually on social programs for the middle class and a small fraction of that amount on programs for the poor—a reflection of who votes and to which groups politicians remain accountable.

Social insurance

Between the 1880s and the 1940s, the Populist, Progressive, and New Deal political movements instituted a number of social programs, most of which had been adopted previously in Europe. They were designed to preserve capitalism by "insuring" workers against economic hardship during changes in the business cycle.

The social security program was a national pension plan created in 1935; most of the poor were excluded, especially low-wage agricultural workers. Today, most workers are covered. There are more than 25 million retirees and 11 million other dependents or disabled individuals in 1985 receiving more than $195 billion annually in pensions. Their benefits averaged over $8865 but could go up to as much as $12,000 per year. Only a small fraction of the population was below the poverty line.

The Medicare program, created in 1965 to assist the elderly with medical bills, has spent more than $53 billion annually on 27 million elderly and 3 million disabled individuals: of this amount, $15 billion each year has been spent on elderly people with annual incomes over $30,000. Overall, 86 percent of those served by Medicare were above the poverty line.

The unemployment insurance program, which involves payments to people who are temporarily out of work and disability insurance (payments to those who have suffered injuries at work) initially covered the better-paid industrial workers and only gradually was extended to cover service workers. These programs do not benefit the poor.[7]

Most of the *social insurance* programs were designed to benefit those workers who had suffered greatly from the effects of the depression. They were instituted to solidify support for the Democratic Party, and therefore they provided benefits to the broad mass of middle-income and working-class people—in no small measure because that was where the votes were. As the Swedish sociologist Gunnar Myrdal observed, "In almost all respects—minimum wages, social security, agriculture, housing, etc.—American economic and social policies show a perverse tendency to favor groups that are above the level of the most needy."[8]

People who received payments or benefits from these programs were not stigmatized as "poor" or as recipients of "charity." Rather, the programs were structured as **entitlements.** Those who received social security payments, unemployment benefits, or disability payments had established their eligibility—and their legal right to payment was enforceable by the courts—by making contributions to the program. There were no means tests to establish financial need. These programs were considered "insurance": by paying in premiums to the government, one was insured against disability, unemployment, or loss of income in old age. One did not apply for assistance to the government; rather, one made a "claim," as with an insurance company.

The notion that the recipients of the benefits of these social insurance programs had paid for them was, however, a myth. Although people were given social security cards and individual accounts for their contributions to the "trust funds," in fact the programs were never run on an actuarially sound basis. At first, far more people were making contributions than were drawing pensions or making claims, and so the funds always had more money coming in than going out. In 1950 there were 16 workers making contributions for every person receiving a pension. But this changed in the 1980s; by that time only 3.2 persons were contributing for every pensioner, and it was projected that by the year 2020 the ratio would be 2.1 to 1. It was predicted that the social security trust funds would go bankrupt in the 1980s, and so a bipartisan commission recommended changes which Congress adopted to keep the system afloat. These included payroll tax increases and minor cuts in benefits.

The social security program was considered "untouchable" by budget cutters, though its $189 billion cost (including Medicare) in FY 1985 presented a tempting target. Although politicians of both parties pledged never to cut the program, options to reduce costs included delays in cost-of-living increases (a one-year delay would save $40 billion in five years), further increases in payroll taxes, and an increase in the level of income subject to such a tax ($39,000 in 1985).

Meanwhile, skyrocketing medical costs, advances in medical science, increased use of surgical and other procedures, and the large number of elderly people all put an added strain on the Medicare system. It too faced major cuts to stave off bankruptcy.

Because of the higher taxes being paid into the system today by young workers—the payroll tax increased 2000 percent between 1950 and 1980—and the cutbacks in benefits, young workers in the 1980s will receive lower benefits than previous generations. The value of their benefits may not exceed the value of their contributions. But a combination of tax policy and private-sector initiatives will probably reduce the pressure on the social security system. About 56 percent of American workers have corporate pension plans, and 71 percent are covered by private health insurance. The tax laws encourage workers to put $2000 each year into supplemental retirement plans (IRA accounts). Public opinion surveys show that only 18 percent or so of the public believe that the government should provide most retirement income.[9] It is likely that future "reforms" of social security will raise the retirement age, lower benefits, and eliminate inflation indexing. For most Americans, social security will be a component of retirement planning rather than its centerpiece.

Public assistance

Before the 1930s cities and counties made only limited "outdoor relief" ex-

penditures for the poor—including the elderly poor not eligible for social security; young, unskilled, and uneducated dropouts; pregnant women; families with a female head of household; and the ill. In the 1930s some states created their own welfare programs, but payments were quite low. In the midst of the depression the federal government had to act to prevent mass starvation after private charities and the states had been overwhelmed. In 1933 a new agency, the Federal Emergency Relief Administration, provided $500 million to existing state agencies. In 1935 the Emergency Relief Appropriation Act granted $4.8 billion for job programs. But even that was not enough.

By 1935, pressure from social workers, settlement houses, governors, and mayors led Congress to create a national welfare system. The federal government would make grants to states for the disabled, the blind, the elderly (those not eligible for social security), and mothers with dependent children (but not those living with a husband or another man in the house). These payments would be supplemented by the states, which would set the levels and actually administer the programs. In the 1960s welfare was supplemented with Medicaid—a program of medical assistance to the poor, paid for by the federal government and the states—and a federal food stamp program. In 1972 the Nixon administration nationalized the welfare programs for the elderly, the disabled, and the blind; for the elderly poor, there is now supplemental security income, an $8 billion program serving 4.2 million old people and providing a minimal payment each month.

The **welfare** system was originally designed to give temporary assistance, not make payments on a permanent basis, and it did not contemplate an ever-increasing number of individuals "on the dole." Nevertheless, the rolls expanded: in 1950 there were 2.2 million persons receiving AFDC (aid to families with dependent children); and by 1985 it cost the federal government $9 billion for approximately 9 million recipients. About one-fourth of all American

Most of the working poor, like this family in Detroit, need welfare temporarily. (*Alon Reininger: Contact.*)

Figure 16-1. Patterns of welfare use among the United States population, 1969–1978. More than one in every four Americans received some income from welfare during the ten-year period under study. Nearly half the recipients were aided no more than two years of the ten. Fewer than one in twelve of the recipients were heavily dependent on welfare for more than seven years out of ten. (Source: Greg J. Duncan et al., *Years of Poverty, Years of Plenty,* University of Michigan, Institute for Social Research, Ann Arbor, 1984; reprinted in *IRS Newsletter,* winter 1983–1984, p. 4.)

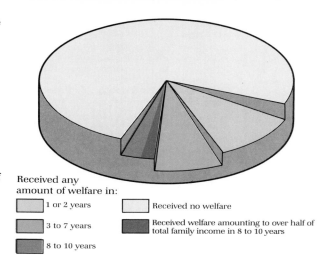

Received any
amount of welfare in:

☐ 1 or 2 years   ☐ Received no welfare

☐ 3 to 7 years   ■ Received welfare amounting to over half of
                              total family income in 8 to 10 years

☐ 8 to 10 years

families need welfare from time to time, but most return to self-sufficiency when a family emergency ends or when a breadwinner returns to work. Only 2 percent of all American families, or 8 percent of all those obtaining welfare, can be considered welfare dependents (those who are on welfare for 7 out of 10 years). (See Figure 16-1.) Moreover, most children raised on welfare do not themselves go on welfare once they leave home (though their chances of doing so are greater than those of children from more affluent families). There is little evidence that the welfare system has created a permanent underclass, doomed to live most of their lives in poverty as a burden to taxpayers.[10]

The welfare system may be sharply distinguished from the social insurance system. Welfare is considered by both the giver and the recipient to be charity supplied by taxpayers. The recipient has not earned the assistance and has no "right" to it. Aid provides subsistence, not a decent standard of living. There are means tests, and the presumption is that those who receive aid would "chisel" if they had the chance. Welfare officials say that there is a constant need for supervision, for investigation of the circumstances of recipients, and for regulation of the private lives of individuals to prevent immoral or illegal behavior.[11] They assume that one of the major causes of the poverty of their clients is their inability to obtain or hold a job as a result of a lack of education and skills or because of various personal problems.

Antipoverty programs

Ways to aid the poor other than welfare include programs which provide social services, protect against discrimination, provide training and employment opportunities, or organize poor communities to help themselves.

Social services. Some social welfare theorists believe that some personal failing or shortcoming of the individual accounts for his or her condition.[12] In their view, the only way to solve the problem would be to spend the money to hire more social workers, each of whom would supervise a group of welfare clients. The social workers would coordinate better medical care for their cases, encourage them to get an education, enter them in job-training programs, and try to place them in new jobs. They would also deal with their cases "clinically," attempting to adjust each one to his or her situation and

Social workers counsel clients on a wide range of social and economic problems. (*Department of Housing and Urban Development.*)

eliminate such problems as excessive drinking, drug abuse, child abuse, and delinquency.[13] Approximately two-thirds of all federal money (block grants) spent on domestic social services eventually goes to private organizations, usually community-based nonprofit groups.

Recent studies have cast doubt on the notion that there is a culture of poverty that dooms the poor and their children. One study of 500 white youths in Boston who had been raised in poverty by families with histories of child abuse, alcoholism, welfare dependency, and other problems showed that four-fifths of them escaped poverty and that most held steady, well-paying jobs. Another study, of 123 black children, half of whom received preschool education two decades ago, demonstrated the value of providing social services: those who had been enrolled in the preschool program accomplished far more in school and work and had a much lower crime rate than those who had not been enrolled.[14]

Family support. The poor and those with severe social problems often live in families with a female head of household. Between 1960 and 1980 the divorce rate among blacks jumped 400 percent to 178 per 1000 marriages, double the rate among whites. And black couples separate at 5 times the rate of whites. In the 1980s about 15 percent of all families (and 51 percent of black families) had a female head of household. These were the families with the lowest incomes: 48 percent of all families below the poverty line had a female head of household. While a two-parent black family in 1984 had an average income of $19,500, a one-parent black household had an average income of $7802, and 60 percent of such families lived in poverty. Welfare payments could not be made to married couples, a policy that encouraged the breakup of the family. Reformers proposed eliminating disincentives against the family and providing "family allowances" for children so that stable households with children would be encouraged. No such system has yet been adopted.

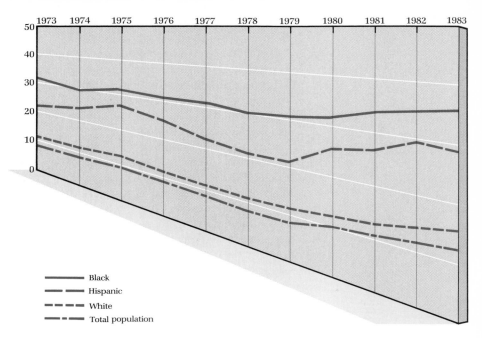

Figure 16-2. Poverty rates in the United States, 1973–1983. Lines show the percentage of blacks, whites, and Hispanics in poverty for each year, as well as poverty rates for the entire population. Rates for all groups, but especially for minorities, increased dramatically during the recession of 1980 and the subsequent first two years of Reagan's presidency. (Source: U.S. Bureau of the Census.)

Fighting discrimination. Two-thirds of the poor people in the nation are white, but a disproportionate percentage of blacks, Hispanics, and American Indians are poor: only 12.1 percent of all whites live in poverty, compared with 35.7 percent of all blacks and 28.4 percent of all Hispanics (Figure 16-2). Poverty is inextricably tied to the problems of racial and ethnic discrimination. The postwar recovery from the depression had removed the majority of white workers from the ranks of the poor, and unionization had given white and minority workers wages far above the minimum necessary for mere subsistence. But the people left behind included the rural poor, especially in the south and Appalachia, who were disproportionately black, as well as the urban poor—among them the ever-increasing numbers of families with a female head of household (usually an unmarried mother and her children)—who

Young children receive preschool educational and social services at day care centers like this one. (*Sepp Seitz: Woodfin Camp.*)

were disproportionately black or Hispanic. By 1980 fully one-half of black children and one-third of Hispanic children were born into families below the poverty line. Between 1967 and 1982 employment among black males decreased at an annual rate of 1.6 percent, the family income of blacks declined (5.3 percent between 1980 and 1983), and more black families slipped below the poverty line, at twice the rates of whites.[15] The average black family lost 3 times what the average white family lost as a result of government cuts in social programs in the early 1980s.

Some see the problem of poverty as a women's issue: two-thirds of the poor are women and their children. Only 7 percent of families with a male head of household live in poverty, compared with 32 percent of families with a female head of household. Among the elderly, 17 percent of the women live in poverty, compared with 10 percent of the men.[16] Day care programs, equal or comparable pay, an end to gender discrimination, efforts to track down fathers and make them pay child support, and other programs on the feminist agenda could make a substantial difference in the number of people who live in poverty.

Employment. If more industrial jobs could be made available, most of the poor, especially the young, would be able to support themselves. To the extent that skills were needed, they could be gained on the job, or companies could train their work forces. Or perhaps existing vocational schools could reorient their curriculums. Therefore, in the view of some people, money for new programs should go to encouraging companies, perhaps by means of tax breaks or subsidies, to locate in pockets of hard-core unemployment. The government could offer a job to everyone who wanted to work. There are also calls to raise the minimum wage so that all those who were employed would be above the poverty level.[17] Some programs improve job skills and coordinate placement to match young unemployed people with jobs.[18] In still another approach, pioneered in North Carolina, a local work force is trained, and then companies are persuaded to relocate. Federal grants are used to establish a network of state-run vocational and technical schools. Federal and state tax breaks for businesses which relocate in certain depressed areas, loans and subsidies for area redevelopment, and student loans for vocational education may all be part of a local industrial strategy designed to bring in or keep industrial and service jobs.

Community organization. Many programs provide money, services, or supervision to the poor. Some observers say that each program runs itself, according to its own professional standards, resulting in chaotic and ineffective services for the poor.[19] Getting one benefit might cancel out eligibility for another, thus leaving the recipient worse off (for example, no longer eligible for food stamps or public housing). Some have suggested that "top-down" control by city hall might be the best approach. Others have thought that "community action" programs, with boards elected by residents of the neighborhoods to be served, should direct all social programs—a form of "bottom-up" accountability.[20] Still others have preferred confrontation; they would organize the poor or other groups with social problems so that they could articulate and voice their demands to the politicians. They could then try to build voting coalitions with other groups (notably labor, civil rights, and liberal organizations) so that, as

part of a winning coalition at the local, state, or national level, their demands would be translated into greater services or payments to the community.[21]

In the 1960s a pattern emerged which Daniel Moynihan labeled "professionalization of reform." Increasingly, it was the middle-class professionals—social workers, teachers, college professors, foundation consultants, psychiatrists, doctors, lawyers, and journalists—who both defined the problem of poverty and came up with the solutions to it. The representatives of the poor themselves—labor leaders, ministers, and wealthy benefactors, who had traditionally been the definers—were now taking second place. Professional practitioners, foundation executives, and government officials created issue networks to propose new programs to deal with poverty.[22] The "war on poverty" and its programs of community action, the program of legal services for the poor, community health programs, job-training efforts, and the Head Start program for prekindergarten-age children all involved teachers, lawyers, doctors, vocational educators, and community organizers forming political coalitions to get federal funding for their programs; often they were aided by foundations which provided the "seed money" for initial demonstration programs.

Some of the people who were involved in the issue networks in the 1960s are now involved in new networks that are attempting to make rational cuts in the decade of retrenchment. The Ford Foundation, for example, which was instrumental in proposing many antipoverty programs, recently funded a multimillion-dollar research effort which will link academics and social welfare practitioners together with politicians to make proposals for cuts in entitlement and welfare programs in the next decade.

CLOSE-UP

DANIEL P. MOYNIHAN. Daniel P. Moynihan is a United States senator from New York whose career illustrates the "professionalization of reform."[23] He has made a major contribution to social policies through his research and his innovative proposals. While few have been adopted as he proposed them, eventually the issues he raised became part of the national agenda, and many have been incorporated into social welfare policy.

Born in the "Hell's Kitchen" Irish-American neighborhood on the west side of Manhattan (home of many of the most famous nineteenth-century political bosses), Moynihan went to Harvard University and became a sociologist. Well connected with local Democratic politicians, both regulars and reformers, he became an aide to the governor of New York, Averill Harriman. He entered the federal government in 1961 as special assistant to Secretary of Labor Arthur Goldberg. In

Senator Daniel Moynihan of New York (left) once recommended a policy of "benign neglect" of the minority poor while he served in the Nixon administration. (*Michael Evans: Contact.*)

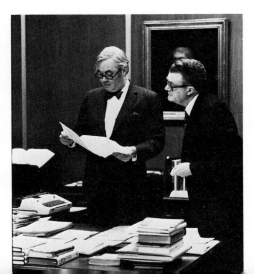

1963 President Kennedy appointed him assistant secretary of labor for policy planning and research. He joined the task force which planned President Johnson's antipoverty program, and along with other Labor Department officials he strongly opposed the "community action" approach to the war on poverty, believing that it would be a bureaucratic fiasco: instead, he advocated job training and public service work. Although his ideas were rejected, his critique of the community action programs, embodied in his book *Maximum Feasible Misunderstanding,* later helped its critics undo the program.

Moynihan prepared a Labor Department report in 1965 called *The Negro Family: The Case for National Action.* It concluded that millions of blacks were trapped in a cycle of poverty caused by instability in the family and discrimination. "The children of our slums are being cheated by society," he said, "which thinks it is too sophisticated to care about whether children have fathers and mothers have husbands."[24] That study became the basis for President Johnson's historic speech at Howard University, in which he called for a conference on the problem of black ghettos. But when the text of Moynihan's report was made public, black leaders unexpectedly attacked it, calling it paternalistic and racist.[25] When the White House conference met in November, it produced a report which denied that the black family was disintegrating. A subsequent White House conference on civil rights in 1966 did not even address the issue of the black family. Ultimately the facts proved impossible to ignore: by the 1980s the condition of the black family was at the top of the civil rights agenda.

Moynihan left government and ran unsuccessfully for president of the New York City Council. He then became director of the Harvard–M.I.T. Joint Center for Urban Studies. In 1969 President Nixon asked Moynihan (a lifelong Democrat) to join his administration as assistant to the president for urban affairs and secretary of the Urban Affairs Council, placing him in charge of developing new social welfare proposals. Moynihan proposed a family assistance program (FAP), which would have provided a minimum of $1600 for every family of four (and more for families with additional children). The proposal, even after several extensive revisions, was not passed by Congress.

In 1970 black leaders again attacked Moynihan, this time for a memorandum he submitted to Nixon arguing that "the time may have come when the issue of race could benefit from a period of 'benign neglect'" and adding that "we may need a period in which Negro progress continues and racial rhetoric fades."[26] Civil rights groups which wanted to reshape public opinion about racial issues differed with this strategy and called for his resignation. Moynihan eventually left the Nixon administration, returned to academia, and then in 1976 won his seat in the Senate, where he has become an outspoken critic of the Reagan administration's social welfare policies.

| POLITICS OF SOCIAL WELFARE | This section discusses the way new programs are formulated, passed by Congress, and implemented, and the ways in which existing programs are cut back or eliminated. |

Program development   **Recognizing and defining problems.** The first step in creating social welfare programs is to discover and define a social problem. This is political, because people disagree about definitions. Is a 15-year-old who commits a robbery a

"juvenile delinquent" whose conduct is attributable to child abuse, a broken home, poverty, and no prospect of employment? An affirmative answer suggests the need for programs ranging from community mental health programs to counseling and job-training programs. Or is this 15-year-old simply a young "career criminal"? An affirmative answer suggests the need for more police protection and more effective criminal justice.

Social scientists, many of them in universities or research institutes, take the lead in discovering and defining social problems. The war on poverty grew out of social theories that stressed a link between lack of economic opportunity and an increase in crime among juveniles, which Congress responded to when it passed the Economic Opportunity Act of 1964 and created the Office of Economic Opportunity. Similarly, the problem of hunger in the United States was addressed in the 1960s by researchers at several medical schools, who discovered that malnutrition was rampant in many rural counties and existed in some inner-city locations, even though there was hardly any actual starvation.

Demonstration programs. The ideas for social programs may come from several different sources. Most European nations already have such programs, and so we have their experiences to draw upon.[27] Some states may have already established programs, as in the case of welfare, child abuse and juvenile delinquency services, family planning services, mental health services, workers' compensation, and aid for the homeless. Often demonstration programs are funded first by foundations, together with local governments, to test their feasibility. Later the national government may also fund a small number of demonstration programs; this was done with legal services, community action corporations, rent vouchers (to help the poor afford decent housing), and even a guaranteed annual income. If the demonstration program is successful, the administration may decide to go to Congress with a full-scale program, as it did with legal services and community action.[28]

Demonstration programs attract the most skilled administrators and professionals, and so the level of talent is higher than it is when many programs are in operation. Demonstration programs pick clients who are likely to succeed, a system known as *creaming*. In a job-training program, for example, this may mean taking youths who do not have police records, whose work attitudes are good, and who have few personal problems. Thus a demonstration program has good results, but these will not be replicated when the program serves a larger group.[29]

Programs and issue networks. The next step in program development usually involves an issue network, often centered on university professors or other researchers. For example, Milton Friedman and James Tobin, two leading economists, have proposed a negative income tax and various vouchers so that poor people could purchase services (such as education or housing) on the open market instead of receiving them from the government. Dr. Jean Meyer, a nutritionist (and later the president of Tufts University), proposed action by the national government to end hunger and malnutrition in the United States. Eli Ginsberg, a business professor, developed job-training programs. Daniel P. Moynihan, as a "counselor" to President Nixon, proposed a family assistance program to replace the existing welfare system. The political scientists Hugh

Heclo and Charles Hamilton, at the Ford Foundation, were involved in a study of the reorganization of entitlement programs.

The issue networks try to build bureaucratic support at the state and national levels. Officials may become part of the network and attempt to win departmental support for a new program. The department then lobbies Congress and the president. The new initiative, such as the war on poverty, may offer something for everyone, and so each major department gets a share of the program to be developed. A logroll can be put together so that several issue networks will support a large package to get funds for several programs, as with community action, urban development, and job-training programs.

National agenda politics

One way to get a program past the White House and the Office of Management and Budget (OMB) is to build public support through a national agenda campaign, as was done by an issue network involved in programs to end hunger in the late 1960s and early 1970s. The goal was to convert a voluntary program of surplus food distribution into a major commitment by the government to feed the hungry through a massive expansion of the food stamp program rather than through an optional program with a small budget. Under this program, people who have little money (welfare recipients and some others) are eligible for food stamps, which grocery stores must accept in lieu of money.

The public campaign for support began in 1967 when a team of university researchers reported on malnutrition in rural Mississippi. The following year a Senate Select Committee on Nutrition and Human Needs was created, chaired by Senator George McGovern. It held widely publicized hearings in poverty areas, and malnourished people came before it to testify. Responding to the political winds, in 1969 the White House held a conference on food, nutrition, and health, with President Nixon declaring that "the moment is at hand to put an end to hunger in America itself." A network television documentary, prepared with the assistance of the original team of nutritionists, was broadcast. Newspapers were encouraged to publish editorials decrying the existence of hunger. Books and magazine articles on the subject appeared. (The campaign resembled the ones conducted in the early 1900s against sweatshops and child labor and the one run between 1962 and 1964 before the declaration of the war on poverty.) With public opinion mobilized, it became good politics for the Republicans and the Democrats alike to support a program of food stamps, and each party tried to get the credit for it. Expenditures for food stamps jumped from $1.1 billion in 1969 to $18 billion in 1983.

Congressional politics

To get programs passed, it is necessary to build a coalition of congressional supporters. The food stamp program was proposed by members of Congress, including Senator Bob Dole, a Republican, who put together a logroll involving representatives of the wheat producers of the midwest, the agribusiness growers of the sun belt, and the urban welfare recipients, all of whom would benefit if the food needed by the poor could be funded by the national government. This coalition dominated food policy, even though Nixon initially opposed the legislation. During the Reagan administration a logroll was put together that involved members who supported both a program of rent vouchers proposed by the Department of Housing and Urban Development (HUD) and some loans for the World Bank favored by the White House. A small demonstration program costing less than $200 million was to be converted into a billion-dollar

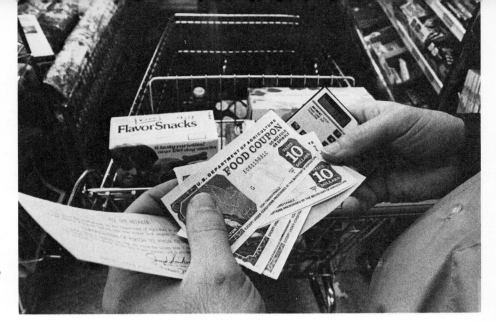

Food stamps are a kind of grocery store currency issued to welfare recipients and the working poor. (*Douglas Kirkland.*)

program in which local housing authorities would pay part or all of the rent to landlords, who would then rent to the poor in the private housing market.

Legislators treat social welfare programs as distributions—much as they treat military construction, rivers, and harbors for example—and so representatives try to obtain grants for new services in order to bring federal dollars into their communities. This means that to be passed in Congress, most social programs must provide benefits to a majority of districts.

Sometimes a program is the pet project of a committee leader, and as a minor provision attached to a bill, it is simply passed into law without much consideration or change. Or a program may be saved from the ax, as the Job Corps was in 1981, because a highly placed committee chair (in this case, a Republican senator, Orrin Hatch of Utah) happens to believe in it and will fight for it at the White House. The issue networks and the iron triangles look to congressional committees to secure their interests, since the president has no time for them. They want members of Congress to lobby the White House for the appointment of sympathetic officials (either from within the bureaucracy or from outside it) to run the new programs. They want committees to ensure their access to program officials so that the guidelines and government regulations adopted for the programs will suit them. They even want to evaluate the programs, using government research and evaluation funds, so that their initial reports can criticize agency operations when they run counter to their demands.

Most social programs are run on a limited authorization, and so within two years they are up for renewal once again. This time around, plenty of amendments to a program can be expected. Many are part of regulatory politics, bound up with the important issues of social behavior. In the 1950s, for example, amendments to health programs often involved attempts to bar racial segregation in hospitals. In the 1980s the standard amendments to social services programs include a prohibition on funding abortions or assisting clients with abortions, a prohibition on organizing for political activities, and a prohibition on lobbying any level of government for any purpose, including changing state laws or local ordinances that adversely affect the clients. Other amendments are friendly, designed to clarify the authority of the agency and

take care of routine operating problems. They may also propose a large expansion in a program to take care of more clients.

Those who opposed a program initially but were outvoted may also get their chance later when the program comes up for reauthorization or new appropriations. At the hearings they get their chance to score points with voters before the congressional elections. Here the typical approach is to charge local contractors or the officials who actually implement the program with fraud, corruption, or other misuse of funds. The so-called poverty pimps who rip off taxpayers by swindling the government may be exposed; they include the people who contract to provide various job-training or other educational services to the poor and then fail to do so, pocketing much of the money and submitting inflated expense vouchers, and the people who provide substandard housing, day care, or drug treatment. A mismanaged program, such as federally assisted rehabilitation of inner-city housing, may be in for large cuts once Congress gets around to an investigation.

Public opinion

Public attitudes toward social problems and social welfare policy are contradictory. The heritage of laissez-faire and social Darwinism remains embedded in American thought; a majority of the people believe that individuals, not the government, should take the responsibility for their lives, and on the level of abstract principle a majority consider themselves conservative. Yet when pollsters ask about specific programs, such as food stamps for the needy and Medicaid for the sick, the majority support them, criticizing "waste" or "fraud" rather than the programs themselves. The majority of the people approve of aid to the elderly, the handicapped, and children; this is why the welfare program for unmarried mothers is labeled *aid to families with dependent children.* In 1985, for example, a Washington Post/ABC survey indicated that by a 62–35 margin, the public believes that the government should not cut spending on domestic social programs.[30]

Public opinion distinguishes sharply between welfare and social insurance programs. The latter enjoy overwhelming public support—from liberals and conservatives and from Democrats and Republicans alike. Politicians try to avoid making substantial cuts in social security, unemployment insurance, or Medicare programs (although occasionally modest changes or cuts are made when there is a budget crisis), since these programs benefit middle-class and working-class voters. In fact, the first major defeat that Reagan suffered in Congress during his first term came when the Senate voted 96–0 to prevent two changes he proposed in social security that would have cut benefits. Lawrence Kudlow, an official in the OMB, recounts that when Reagan's pollster, Richard Wirthlin, took surveys, "the polling showed the majority of Social Security recipients were significantly above the poverty line and mostly Republican."[31] That put a damper on efforts to cut back on payments in order to lower the budget deficit.

Substantial cuts are routinely made in welfare and Medicaid programs, most of whose recipients are poor and are nonvoters. Between 1981 and 1983 the administration cut $16 billion from expenditures which otherwise would have been made to the needy. Such cuts are usually justified as reforms which will eliminate abuse or as efforts to "retarget" assistance to the "truly needy." The Advisory Commission on Intergovernmental Relations found that welfare headed the list of programs which the public believes should be cut if there

were a budget crisis. Many people believe that there are plenty of able-bodied people on the welfare rolls and that they should be forced to work for their benefits or should be removed from the rolls.[32] But the public remains split on conservative efforts to cut back on programs for the poor: almost half think that the Reagan administration has gone too far, one-fifth think that it has not gone far enough, and one-fifth think that the cuts are about right.[33]

Party politics

During the New Deal, the Democrats joked that their electoral strategy was "tax, tax, spend, spend, elect, elect." Until the 1950s, the Republicans played into their hands by opposing most social programs. Eisenhower, with his brand of middle-of-the-road Republicanism, recognized that most Americans wanted to keep the social insurance programs as well as provide for the poor. It was under his administration that the Department of Health, Education and Welfare was created and expenditures were increased. Similarly, the Nixon and Ford administrations presided over huge increases in expenditures for social welfare.

But in the 1980s the Democrats are not emphasizing new social programs; instead, they are calling for tax increases to fight budget deficits and for responsible cutbacks in social programs. They speak about fairness and compassion, but not about major new commitments such as national health insurance. The Republicans, on the other hand, have returned to their hard-line opposition to many social programs. The Reagan administration, in its first-term budgets, proposed cuts in social security, Medicare, and Medicaid; programs for weatherizing and heating homes for the poor; summer food and job programs; community service block grants; legal services programs; the food stamps program; and some welfare benefits. Most of these proposals were aimed at minorities and poor whites, who are overwhelmingly Democratic. Blacks, for example, constitute 44 percent of welfare recipients, 34 percent of food stamp recipients, and 36 percent of public housing tenants, and they receive 90 percent of public service jobs—all programs that suffered the most cuts. The most severe cutbacks were blocked by the Democrats in Congress.

Election-year politics

Candidates and election-year politics. Some of the most important initiatives are developed by presidents or presidential candidates in election years. The idea is to put the other party on the defensive. Until 1980 the Democrats usually proposed major new programs, involving massive expenditures, and accused the Republicans of being heartless and lacking compassion for the underprivileged in society. Thus Kennedy proposed regional development programs for depressed areas, job-training programs, and an expansion of public housing, and his successor instituted the war on poverty just before the 1964 elections. Republican candidates argued that programs often do not work well, are wasteful of resources that could be better utilized, and should be restructured so that aid will be targeted only at the "truly needy." They may campaign, as Nixon and Reagan did, against bloated government and may even target specific programs for reform, concentrating on the "welfare mess."

In the 1984 elections, for example, the Democrats pointed out that many people in need were not given aid, because programs were underfunded. They referred to Reagan's "deny-side" policies and charged that he would once again propose cuts in social security if he was reelected. The Republicans claimed that many people who were given aid did not qualify and abused the

system, and they accused the Democrats of trying to frighten old people with talk of pension cuts. President Reagan even went so far as to pledge that he would never cut social security benefits. Each party, mindful of the need to capture the center, tried to have it both ways: the Republicans came up with a proposed rent voucher program and an increase in social security payments to blunt charges about "fairness," and they appointed a presidential commission to study hunger in order, as White House aides put it, to "reposition" the president in an election year. The Democrats agreed that there was too much red tape and "fat" in the welfare system, and they talked about aiding the "truly needy."

While the Democrats concentrated on the Republicans' budget cuts for specific programs, the Republicans countered by showing that the overall amounts spent on social welfare programs had increased. They claimed that the high inflation during Democratic administrations hurt the poor, while the lower inflation and lower interest rates during their administration helped the poor. They argued that their "opportunity society," with its economic recovery, would lift the remaining poor above the poverty line.

Issue networks. Issue networks can often take advantage of election-year politics. Presidential campaigns get their ideas about new programs from these issue networks, and well-placed policy entrepreneurs can convince a candidate that it is good politics to take up a specific program. Consider the issue of hunger in the United States during the 1984 campaigns. An issue network, centered on the Food Research and Action Center in Washington, D.C., together with various schools of public health, church coalitions, local

"YEAH, MAN, THIS SURE BEATS GOING TO A NICE WARM RESTAURANT AND BUYING A REGULAR MEAL"

From "Herblock through the Looking Glass," W. W. Norton, 1984.

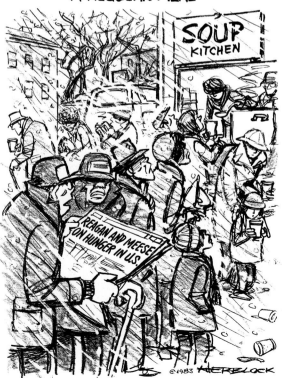

and county officials, and local nutrition centers, fought successfully to maintain and expand the food stamp program in the face of efforts by the Reagan administration to cut it. Edwin Meese, then a presidential staffer, said on a radio program that the government did not have any solid evidence that people were going hungry and that a presidential task force on food assistance was busy evaluating the data and would soon make a report. But then he followed these remarks with the comment that "people go to soup kitchens because the food is free and that's easier than paying for it." The media used this off-the-cuff remark as an example of the insensitivity of the Reagan White House. Although the president disavowed the comments and Meese himself was brought to a news conference to "clarify" his remarks, the damage was done. The Democratic candidates and congressional leaders pounced on the "fairness issue." Walter Mondale toured a soup kitchen and asked people whether they could afford to eat elsewhere.

Local and network television news covered soup kitchens to determine whether people were really going hungry. Local efforts to distribute food to the poor received wide publicity. Senator Edward Kennedy, describing the Reagan administration's policies on food assistance as "inhumane" and "indecent," called for a $2.5 billion increase in federal spending to aid the hungry in the next year and issued a 177-page report to the Senate Committee on Labor and Human Resources calling for a reestablishment of the Select Committee on Nutrition. The Citizens Commission on Hunger in New England, consisting of medical school professors from Boston University, Brown, Harvard, and Yale, invited reporters to make their rounds with them as they examined children for malnutrition. The Massachusetts Department of Health issued a report saying that over 10,000 children in that state alone suffered from nutritional deficiencies; this prompted Governor Michael Dukakis, a Democrat, to claim that the study "provides sound, reliable evidence that serious nutritional deficiencies constitute a major health problem among poor young people in the Commonwealth."[34]

An administration that was spending $12 billion on food stamps was placed on the defensive by the media blitz. Yet it should be remembered that in 1981 the Reagan administration itself had proposed to slash food stamp expenditures by $7.1 billion between 1983 and 1985 and that Congress had scuttled the plan, approving cuts of less than $1.9 billion. By early 1984, the administration let it be known that it would propose increases rather than cuts in the food stamp program in its next budget, an election-year response which was in sharp contrast to its original policy goals.

Implementation politics   **Delivery of social programs.** The heritage of laissez-faire philosophy, philanthropic impulse, and social work practice still influences our social welfare programs. Those run by the national government are administered with the participation of traditional social welfare organizations. Church groups teach illiterates, distribute surplus food, provide shelter for the homeless, and build housing in slums. Private hospitals and doctors receive federal and state funds to take care of the medically indigent (those too poor to pay for doctors) and the elderly. The private legal aid societies, organized at the turn of the century to see that legally indigent individuals had lawyers in court cases, now run federally funded legal services for the poor. The United Way and the Community Chest give their money to local groups that receive about half of their

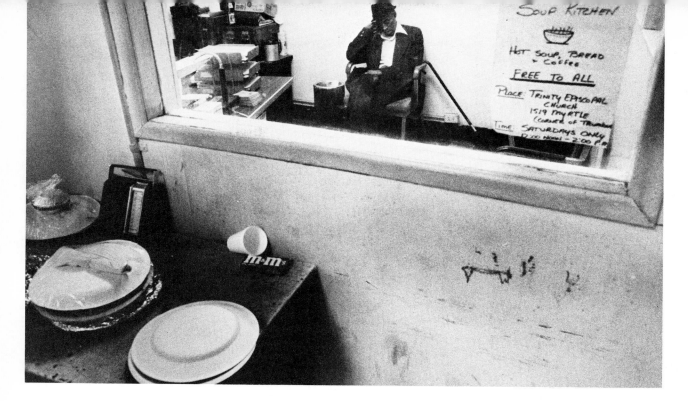

Private charity plays a large social role, as at this Kansas City soup kitchen. (*Mike Maple: Woodfin Camp.*)

funds from the federal government. Foundations now make million-dollar grants to provide food, medical care, and shelter for the homeless.

Federal social policy continues to emphasize the responsibility of localities to develop policies and set standards. Most social programs are administered by state, county, and local governments, which have the ultimate responsibility for delivering services.[35] They usually have considerable leeway in setting levels of assistance; thus some states and cities can provide much more in the way of benefits and services than others. Many national programs are optional: local authorities need not have a legal services program, put up public housing for the poor, or participate in job-training programs. Each locality develops its own program mixture on the basis of its own needs.

Some programs are put in place too quickly, without adequate screening of the local government or the private groups which will provide the services. Or these groups may be chosen on political grounds, which is practically an open invitation to rip off the system. There may be inadequate supervision or oversight from Washington, and so abuses are not uncovered for a year or more. Child pornography rings, for example, have taken advantage of lax supervision of federally funded day care centers. Organized crime figures, corrupt contractors, and poverty pimps all put social welfare programs at risk and play into the hands of those who are opposed to them.

The heritage of laissez-faire and rugged individualism shows up in several different ways in government social programs. Many continue to distinguish between "deserving" and "undeserving" recipients. There is no obligation, on the part of any level of government, to provide a safety net beneath which no American may fall. In fact, no such safety net exists, because some people remain ineligible for any form of government assistance, no matter how destitute they are. County welfare agencies operate under state rules, and in many states an "able-bodied" single man or woman who is judged capable of work-

570

ing is not eligible for any assistance, no matter how desperate that person may be. "Because of the way we feel about poor people in the United States," says the sociologist Alvin Schorr, "we build stigmas and limitations into the programs designed for them. In the end, these programs deteriorate and they are administered in a demeaning and uncaring way."[36] People are expected to accept aid only as a desperate last resort, and those who continue to receive benefits earn the stigma of "welfare drones." Recipients are required to submit to a "means test" which establishes that they are truly needy and are not trying to rip off the system. Their finances and their personal lives are subject to investigation by local officials. Both the federal government and the state governments have experimented, usually with little success, with programs requiring able-bodied recipients to work for their benefits.

Many people refuse to take government assistance because of the stigma attached. In 1980 the Census Bureau found that only 58 percent of poor households received noncash assistance, while in 1983 only about half of those who were eligible for unemployment insurance took it. Far fewer people than are eligible use Medicare and Medicaid.

Services for the poor are badly targeted. Communities which do not need them are eligible and apply because of the way laws are written. People who do not need them or could succeed without them are often given benefits, while those who are more in need are not taken into the programs. The Job Training Partnership Administration, for example, trains high school graduates, but hardly anyone in its program comes from a family living in poverty.

The plight of the homeless in Washington, D.C. (*Alex Webb: Magnum.*)

Judicial intervention. The federal courts have an important role to play in the way programs are implemented. Issue networks often bring cases to court against the administration. The Office of Economic Opportunity (OEO) was saved temporarily in the 1970s, when appointees in the Nixon administration tried to abolish it, because the courts found that they had exceeded their authority. Similarly, in the 1980s the Legal Services Corporation was embroiled in several cases brought by its staff against its board of directors; the staff charged that the board was violating the law in an effort to make the program more responsive to the administration's wishes. In 1982 the child care food program, which provided meals for 843,500 children in day care and family care centers, was to be cut 10 percent by law; when Reagan's appointees tried to institute a 20 percent cut in funding through a new Agriculture Department regulation, a federal court prevented it, in a case won by the Food Research and Action Center. Another lawsuit that same year kept the national summer lunch program going.

In 1981 the Reagan administration tried to purge the rolls of hundreds of thousands of disabled persons who were receiving social security payments, arguing that they were no longer eligible. By 1983, 491,300 people had been deprived of their benefits. Local authorities, such as in New York City, brought class actions in federal courts, charging that recipients had been removed from the rolls without any hearing, which was a violation of the law and of their due process rights. More than 200,000 recipients were ordered back on the rolls, although Margaret Heckler, the secretary of health and human services, ordered her department to pursue a policy of "nonacquiescence" to judicial orders. Eventually Congress intervened, passing a law which prevented further mass removals of recipients from the rolls and which required pretermination hearings.

White House retrenchment and targeting: The Reagan administration. Conservative politicians who do not need the votes of the poor have proposed that a safety net (see Table 16-2) be maintained for the poor and the elderly, but that other programs be cut substantially.[37] "We will continue to fulfill our obligations that spring from our national conscience," President Reagan told Congress in his first budget proposals in 1981; "those who through no fault of their own must depend on the rest of us, the poverty-stricken, the disabled, the elderly, all those with true need, can rest assured that the social safety net of programs they depend on are exempt from any cuts."[38] These safety-net programs include AFDC, Medicaid, food stamps, job training and summer job programs, Head Start, and school nutrition programs (as well as social security, Medicare, and veterans' pensions).

During his first term, President Reagan and the OMB used the language of "reform" in making severe cuts, even in the safety-net programs. They claimed that they could review, tighten up, redirect, and better target programs. In doing so, they distinguished sharply between the "truly needy," below the poverty line, and others who might be receiving government payments or services. The OMB took aim at people in families whose income exceeded 150 percent of the poverty level—a group that, according to government figures, was receiving 44 percent of the Medicaid funds and 14.2 percent of the AFDC payments. These households, comprising 12.7 million people, were made inel-

Table 16-2. The safety-net programs

Program	Percentage of families receiving assistance	Percentage of families receiving assistance below the poverty line	Race of recipients		Average payment per family or household	Percentage of the cost borne by the federal government	Amount paid by the federal government in FY 1982 (billions)	Spending increase, 1970–1979, percent, adjusted for inflation
			White	Black				
Aid to families with dependent children (AFDC)	4.6[a]	100.0	52[b]	43	$3800[c]	53	$7.8	46.8
Food stamps	7.2	73	62.6	35.1	$ 812	100[d]	$12.2	546
School lunches	5.6[e]	54	62	34	—	85	$3.9	181
Subsidized housing	3.2	52	67[f]	33[f]		93	$8	421
Medicaid	8.1	59	67	30	$ 900	55	$24	186

a. 12.2 percent of all children under 18 years of age receive AFDC.
b. Includes 13 percent Hispanic.
c. The average family had 2.2 children.
d. The federal government pays 100 percent of the benefits and splits the administrative costs with the states.
e. School lunches are received by 16.1 percent of children under 18 years of age.
f. The breakdown by race is for 10.5 percent of families who rent.

igible for aid. The OMB also eliminated 21 percent of food stamp payments. More than 3.5 million children were eliminated from the school food programs because their families' incomes were just over the poverty line. More than 700,000 children lost free health care for the same reason.[39] The largest day care program was cut by one-third, and many working mothers and their children were eliminated. More than 725,000 persons lost the services of community mental health centers.[40] The rent charged for the 2.4 million families living in public housing was increased from 25 to 30 percent of their income.

Perhaps the most ironic cuts, coming from a conservative administration which extolled the work ethic, were made in the welfare program. In 1969 Congress had passed a law which allowed welfare recipients to keep the first $30 earned each month and one-third of any additional monthly wages; the remainder would be deducted from their welfare checks. The administration had Congress repeal this law in 1981, and almost 500,000 children lost some or all of their welfare benefits because their mothers were working.

FIRST-TERM BUDGET CUTS. Reagan halted the growth of some federal programs during his first term. Between 1981 and 1983 there was a small reduction in the number of households (slightly more than 14 million) receiving benefits from the food stamp program, Medicaid, the school lunch program, or the housing assistance program, even though the poverty rate increased. The main reason for this seemed to be stricter eligibility rules aimed at targeting benefits to the lowest-income groups and cutting overall expenditures. Federal "quality control reviewers" calculated overpayments by the states and deducted a percentage of federal reimbursement payments to the states for welfare and Medicaid, thus giving the states an incentive to tighten up on eligibility. Medicaid expenditures, for example, were cut when new federal guidelines forced the states to adopt cutbacks in their programs: thirteen states began making small charges for drugs, glasses, shoes, and hearing aids and other devices; ten set limits on the number of days that patients could use hospital services; twenty-two limited certain optional services or eligibility for care;

nine curtailed use of emergency rooms for nonemergencies; eleven tightened eligibility criteria by eliminating coverage of welfare recipients under 21; and eleven adopted measures to limit or decrease reimbursements to hospitals, nursing homes, and physicians. Over 500,000 people were cut from the Medicaid rolls.[41]

Other cuts were made by means of legislation or lower appropriations. In the FY 1984 budget, the culmination of retrenchment politics, overall spending for domestic programs was down 7.4 percent, in inflation-adjusted terms. Between 1981 and 1985 the ax fell most heavily on the following programs:[42]

- Social security: 4.6 percent
- Medicare: 6.8 percent
- Welfare (families): 14.3 percent
- Food stamps: 13.8 percent
- Child nutrition: 28.0 percent
- Medicaid: 2.8 percent
- Social services: 23.5 percent
- Community services: 37.1 percent
- Job training: 38.6 percent
- Public service jobs: 100.0 percent

The local organizations that provide social services took the brunt of these programs cutbacks. Their budgets shrank by 27 percent or $4.5 billion during the first three years of the Reagan administration.

These cuts by a conservative administration stand in contrast to the Democrats' record, which almost always involves loosening eligibility for programs and expanding the rolls of recipients. Each party expands those programs which benefit the voters who support it and contracts those programs which benefit the opposition. The Congressional Budget Office estimates, for example, that families with incomes below $10,000 (overwhelmingly Democratic) lost $23 billion in after-tax income and benefits between 1981 and 1983, while families with incomes above $80,000 (overwhelmingly Republican) gained about $35 billion. One study, conducted by the Urban Institute, found that the cuts in benefit payments and other programs "disproportionately [affected] those below the average income level"; the study also found that federal payments benefiting the poor and the working poor were cut the most and that payments benefiting the middle class were least affected.[43]

In 1984, demonstrations against proposed cuts in social security by the Reagan administration proved effective. (*R. J. North: Picture Group.*)

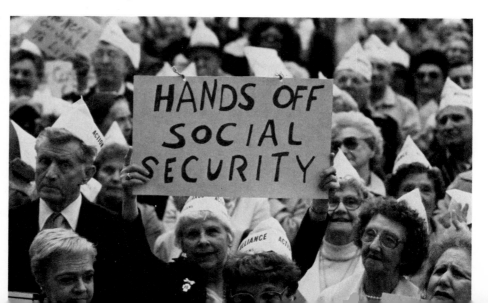

A city shelter being prepared for the night's homeless in 1983. (*Jim Anderson: Woodfin Camp.*)

These cuts prompted protests from many of the private organizations that were helping the poor. Typical was the statement signed by the Synagogue Council of America, the United States Catholic Conference, the National Council of Churches, and Evangelicals for Social Action, which declared that "the stark reality is that the available resources of the churches and synagogues, or of the entire private sector, simply will not be sufficient to replace Federal human needs programs."[44] These program cuts were attacked by some women's groups, who argued that they had a disproportionate effect on poor women. Cuts in legal services affected the 70 percent of the clients who were women. Cuts in food stamp eligibility affected the 61 percent of eligible households that were headed by women. Raising the rent for public housing affected the 70 percent of the tenants who were women.[45] Hispanic and black organizations also called for increases, not decreases, in social welfare expenditures.

PROPOSED SECOND-TERM CUTS. For FY 1986 the Reagan administration proposed to make $34 billion in nondefense cuts. Many of these would fall heavily on the poor. The job corps program (which provides job training for inner-city youth) would be eliminated, as well as legal services, urban development grants, and revenue sharing. There would be a freeze on Medicaid reimbursement levels to hospitals serving the poor. There would be cuts in housing aid for the poor, the elderly, and the handicapped; in child nutrition programs in schools; and in the food stamp program for women, infants, and children. There would be a freeze on food stamp payments, and the poor would suffer from the effects of any inflation.[46]

FOCUS

THE REFORM AGENDA. Three major reforms have been proposed to alleviate poverty: nationalization of welfare, family assistance, and a negative income tax.

Nationalization of welfare. One proposal is to *nationalize* the welfare system: the federal government would pay for the entire program. This would also increase workers' mobility, since recipients could go anywhere in search of employment and still receive their benefits. These would be set at an equivalent level in all states (varying only to reflect differences in the cost of living); thus all recipi-

576   THE POLITICS OF GOVERNMENT

ents would be treated equally, and there would be no incentive for the poor to move from low- to high-benefit states. This proposal was suggested by a task force in the Johnson administration in 1967.[47]

Programs for the elderly, the blind, and the disabled were nationalized during the Nixon administration, but it is not likely that the program of aid to families with dependent children (AFDC) will be. No administration wants to add $5 to $10 billion to its budget, and politicians do not want to increase the benefits of women receiving this aid, half of whom are from minorities and many of whom are having children out of wedlock. Many states are just as happy to provide low benefits and encourage recipients to migrate elsewhere (preferably to northern cities). Their representatives in Congress would oppose a standardized payment.

The Reagan administration has gone in the other direction. Its welfare reform proposals of 1981 would have given the AFDC program (and the food stamp program) back to the states and required them to institute a mandatory "workfare" program to force able-bodied recipients off the rolls. If such a system were to go into effect, southern states would lose the most in federal funds (although a special federal trust fund would reimburse them until 1991). They would then feel the pressure to keep benefits low, which in turn might force northern states to keep their benefits down in order to discourage potential welfare recipients from migrating north.

Family assistance. Another approach to solving the welfare problem is to provide *family assistance*—for example, through the family assistance plan (FAP) proposed by President Nixon.[48] It would have given money to *families* with children, unlike the welfare approach, which views a family as capable of supporting its members and provides payments only when the family breaks up and the household is headed by a single mother. The FAP would have provided cash to families headed by a male who was earning an inadequate amount to support his family decently, adding 13 million persons to the list of those receiving federal payments. But the FAP would have given the working poor an incentive to keep working and try to earn higher wages. The FAP benefit would have been reduced by only 50 cents for each dollar the recipient earned, and so anyone receiving benefits under this plan would be better off working than not working. The FAP would have provided $1600 a year for a family of four (plus $800 in food stamps).

The program would have added $5 billion or more to federal costs, but in the early 1970s this was politically appealing to a moderate Republican president: it promised to maintain the stability of the family, which is always good politics; it was a radical departure from the "services" approach to poverty taken by the Democrats in the 1960s, since it offered a more direct way to alleviate the problems of the poor; and it involved less government regulation and less supervision of the poor and did not require a large services bureaucracy of "social work" types to run the program.

But the public, according to the polls, opposed the idea. Fiscal conservatives viewed it as a raid on the Treasury. Liberals thought that it offered too little. The National Welfare Rights Organization (representing welfare recipients), opposed it, favoring instead a guaranteed minimum income plan, which would have provided $5500 per recipient at a total estimated cost of more than $71 billion. There was significant opposition from southern legislators; many senators from the "deep south" opposed a plan that would add large numbers of the working poor to the welfare rolls. With liberals in the north responding to pressure from welfare recipients and with conservatives in the south responding to pressure from local business groups (the employers of the working poor), the bill was defeated.

Negative income tax. The simplest approach to helping the poor would be the **negative income tax.** The government receives money in the form of tax payments, and it could just as easily send checks out as take money in.[49] Since the system would work through the Internal Revenue Service rather than through welfare bureaucracies, it would eliminate caseworkers and the stigma of welfare. It would establish the principle that every citizen has the "right" to a minimum income. This extremely "radical" idea is supported by some leading conservatives, such as Professor Milton Friedman, the Nobel prizewinning economist at the University of Chicago, who first proposed such a plan in 1962. Because it would eliminate government supervision of citizens and substitute the private market, he argued, people could act as rational consumers of the things they need for their survival. A variation of the plan was suggested by George McGovern, the Democratic presidential candidate in 1972, who proposed a payment of $1000 to each family whose income was below a certain level. Still other proposals, made by people who believe that no one should receive such an income without working, would make the income payment either a supplement to wages for the working poor or a form of unemployment insurance for those out of work.

Critics wonder what effect such a negative income tax would have on work incentives.[50] If the payment level was set low, to discourage people from quitting their jobs so that they could get payments, then either the plan would keep people in poverty, or else a welfare supplement would be required for nonworking families. If the payment level was set high, could the Treasury afford the bill? If everyone was eligible for the payments, there would have to be an offset against earned income. People who earned nothing, for example, might be given a $5000 "negative tax payment" from the Treasury. But what about someone who earned $4000? You might say that this person should receive only $1000 from the Treasury so that both people would have $5000. But note that you would really be "taxing" the person who earned $4000 at a 100 percent rate, because he or she would not get anything at all beyond what would be gotten without working—that is, $5000 in total income. This would mean that those whose income was less than $5000 would not work, since they could get the same income just by waiting for the negative income payment.

To maintain work incentives among low-income people, they must keep some of what they earn. The person who earned $4000 might have 50 percent of that amount deducted from the government payment, thus keeping what was earned ($4000) plus half of the negative tax payment—putting that person ahead of one who does not work. But setting the offset against earned income at 50 percent would increase the costs of the minimum income program greatly. Why? Because now people earning all the way up to $10,000 would still be eligible for the negative tax payment. (At $10,000, the deduction of $5000 exactly equals the payment, and the cost to the government becomes nothing.) Someone earning $9500, for example, would still receive $250 from the Treasury. This means that some payments would have to go to people who are not considered poor in order to maintain work incentives among people who are poor. Thus the "trilemma": there is simply no way to have a plan that simultaneously provides adequate income to the poor, maintains work incentives among the poor and those just above the poverty line, and can be implemented at a low cost to the Treasury. The negative tax stands no chance of being accepted politically, because far too many middle-income people simply will not accept any program that allows working-class people to avoid paying taxes. The votes in Congress are simply not there for a program that has the upper half of the income group paying taxes and the lower half

receiving government checks—especially not when such a program might cost anywhere from $10 to $40 billion a year.

IN CONCLUSION

Historically, American society has been based on the notion of the rugged individual, whose temporary need for help can best be met by private charity. Yet the laissez-faire state has in practice given way to a vast social welfare system, part public and part private.

The system distinguishes between middle-class and working-class people (mostly voters), who are protected by social insurance systems, and the poor (mostly nonvoters), who receive certain limited forms of categorical assistance. The poor are tested for eligibility, supervised, and stigmatized.

Historically, the Democrats have tried to expand the number of programs and increase expenditures for social welfare, viewing this as effective coalition politics. The Republicans have alternated between supporting New Deal programs and trying to eliminate them. Eisenhower and Nixon scored major victories with the first approach, while Reagan won two terms in office with the second. At present the gap between the Democrats and the Republicans over social policy is the widest it has been since the New Deal.

Social welfare programs are not implemented effectively. They suffer from diffusion, lack of coordination, corruption, and bureaucratic incompetence. How best to rationalize the system, coordinate its many programs, economize sensibly, and help those in poverty to get out remains an open question in American politics, and one that will continue to be at the center of the differences between the Democrats and the Republicans and between liberals and conservatives.

NOTES

1. *Report of the Council of Economic Advisors, 1964*, GPO, Washington, D.C., 1964; Mollie Orshansky, "Counting the Poor," *Social Security Bulletin*, vol. 27, no. 1, January 1965, pp. 3–29; Helen LaMale, "Poverty: The Word and Reality," *Monthly Labor Review*, vol. 50, no. 7, July 1965; *HEW Indicators*, February 1964.
2. Robert Pear, "Middle Class Shrinking as More Families Sink into Poverty, Two Studies Find," *The New York Times*, Dec. 11, 1983.
3. Joseph Pechman, *Who Paid the Taxes, 1965–1985*, Brookings, Washington, D.C., 1985.
4. Lester Thurow, "The Disappearance of the Middle Class," *The New York Times*, Feb. 5, 1984; for a skeptical view of this theory, see Robert Z. Lawrence, "Sectoral Shifts and the Size of the Middle Class," *The Brookings Review*, fall 1984, pp. 3–11.
5. Richard Hofstadter, *Social Darwinism in American Thought*, rev. ed., Beacon Press, Boston, 1955.
6. James Bryce, *The American Commonwealth*, Macmillan, New York, 1909, vol. 2, p. 123.
7. Elizabeth Wickendon, "Unemployment Insurance and the War on Poverty," *Unemployment Insurance Review*, vol. 2, no. 8, August 1965, pp. 26–31.
8. Gunnar Myrdal, *Challenge to Affluence*, Pantheon, New York, 1963.
9. Yankelovich survey, October 1984.
10. Greg J. Duncan et al., *Years of Plenty, Years of Poverty*, University of Michigan, Institute for Social Research, Ann Arbor, 1984.
11. Alan Keith-Lucas, "The Political Theory Implicit in Social Casework Theory," *American Political Science Review*, vol. 47, no. 4, December 1953, pp. 1076–1091.
12. C. Wright Mills, "The Professional Ideology of Social Pathologists," *American Journal of Sociology*, vol. 49, September 1943, pp. 165–180.

13. Nathan E. Cohen, *Social Work*, Dryden Press, New York, pp. 3–6.

14. Jancis V. F. Long and George Vaillant, "Natural History of Male Psychological Health," *American Journal of Psychiatry*, vol. 141, March 1984, pp. 341–346, also *Changed Lives*, High/Scope Educational Research Foundation, Ypsilanti, Mich., 1984.

15. *Falling Behind: A Report on How Blacks Have Fared under Reagan Policies*, Center for Budget and Policy Priorities, Washington, D.C., 1983.

16. *Older Women: The Economics of Aging*, Congressional Caucus for Women's Issues, Washington, D.C., 1984.

17. *A Freedom Budget for All Americans*, A. Phillip Randolph Institute, New York, 1966.

18. Eli Ginzberg (ed.), *Employing the Unemployed*, Basic Books, New York, 1980; Bernard Anderson and Isabell Sawhill, (eds.), *Youth Employment and Public Policy*, Prentice-Hall, Englewood Cliffs, N.J., 1980; Sar Levitan, Martin Rein, and David Marwick, *Work and Welfare Go Together*, Johns Hopkins, Baltimore, 1972.

19. Marris and Rein, *Dilemmas of Social Reform*, Routledge, London, 1967.

20. Edgar Cahn and Jean Cahn, "The War on Poverty: A Civilian Perspective," *The Yale Law Journal*, July 1964.

21. Saul Alinsky, *Reveille for Radicals*, Vintage Books, New York, 1946; Frank Reisman, "Self-Help among the Poor," *Transaction*, vol. 3, no. 6, September–October 1965.

22. Daniel P. Moynihan, "The Professionalization of Reform," *The Public Interest*, no. 1, fall 1965, pp. 6–16; David Stockman, "The Social Pork Barrel," *The Public Interest*, no. 39, spring 1975, pp. 3–30; Bruce Biggs (ed.), *The New Class?* Transaction Books, New Brunswick, N.J., 1979.

23. This biography was researched by Joel Bloom of Columbia College.

24. *The New York Times*, Dec. 12, 1965.

25. Douglas Schoen, *Pat*, Harper and Row, New York, 1979, p. 111.

26. *The New York Times*, Mar. 1, 1970.

27. Peter Flora and Arnold J. Heidenheimer (eds.), *The Development of Welfare States in Europe and America*, Transaction Books, New Brunswick, N.J., 1981.

28. Richard M. Pious, "Policy and Administration: The Legal Services Program in the War on Poverty," *Politics and Society*, vol. 1, no. 2, May 1971, pp. 365–391.

29. Alice Rivlin, *Systematic Thinking for Social Action*, Brookings, Washington, D.C., 1971.

30. *The Washington Post National Weekly Edition*, Jan. 28, 1985, p. 37.

31. Nicholas Lehmann, "The Culture of Poverty," *The Atlantic*, vol. 255, no. 3, September, 1984.

32. Alan Gartner, Colin Greer, and Frank Reisman (eds.), *What Reagan Is Doing to Us*, Harper and Row, New York, 1982, p. 82.

33. *The Washington Post National Weekly Edition*, Sept. 3, 1984.

34. *The New York Times*, Dec. 16, 1983.

35. Martha Derthick, *The Influence of Federal Grants: Public Assistance in Massachusetts*, Harvard University Press, Cambridge, Mass., 1970.

36. Robert Pear, "Shift for Social Welfare," *The New York Times*, Oct. 27, 1982, p. A-22.

37. Jack Kemp, *An American Renaissance*, Harper and Row, New York, 1979.

38. *The New York Times*, Feb. 18, 1981.

39. *The Wall Street Journal*, Jan. 12, 1983.

40. *The New York Times*, Jan. 17, 1983.

41. Claude D. Pepper, "The Elderly May Dump Reagan," *The New York Times*, Sept. 21, 1984.

42. Data from the Urban Institute, 1985.

43. *The New York Times*, Sept. 13, 1982; *The Reagan Record: An Assessment of America's Changing Domestic Priorities*, Urban Institute, 1984; Richard Nathan et al., *Reductions in U.S. Domestic Spending*, Princeton University Press, Princeton, N.J., 1983.

44. *Jewish-Week American Examiner*, Apr. 18, 1982, p. 2.

45. *Poverty, Race, and Sex*, report of the National Advisory Council on Economic Opportunity, GPO, Washington, D.C., 1982.

46. *FY 1986 Budget Targets and Spending "Freeze Plus" Framework*, Office of Management and Budget, Washington, D.C., January 1985.
47. Richard M. Pious, "Nationalizing Welfare," *Current History*, vol. 65, no. 384, August 1973, pp. 66–70.
48. Robert F. McNown, "The Story of the Family Assistance Plan," *Current History*, vol. 65, no. 384, August 1973, pp. 37–61; Richard Nathan, "Family Assistance Plan: Workfare/Welfare," *The New Republic*, vol. 161, Feb. 24, 1973, pp. 19–21; Richard Zeckhauser and Peter Schuck, "An Alternative to the Nixon Income Maintenance Plan," *The Public Interest*, no. 19, spring 1970, pp. 120–130.
49. James Tobin, "The Case for an Income Guarantee," *The Public Interest*, no. 4, summer 1966, pp. 31–41.
50. Wilbur Cohen, "Welfare Reform: A Persistent Quest," *Current History*, vol. 61, no. 363, November 1971, p. 258.

FURTHER READING

Aaron, Henry: *Why Is Welfare So Hard to Reform?* Brookings, Washington, D.C., 1973. A study of the politics of welfare reform.

Duncan, Greg J., et al.: *Years of Poverty, Years of Plenty*, University of Michigan, Institute for Social Research, Ann Arbor, 1984. A ten-year study of welfare recipients and why some succeed and others fail in ending welfare dependency.

Edsall, Thomas: *The New Politics of Inequality*, Norton, New York, 1984. An account of government policies and their differential impact on the wealthy and the poor.

Fine, Sidney: *Laissez-Faire and the General Welfare State*, University of Michigan Press, Ann Arbor, 1956. A discussion of Americans' ideas about poverty and welfare programs throughout our history.

Gartner, Alan, Colin Greer, and Frank Reissman (eds.): *What Reagan Is Doing to Us*, Harper and Row, New York, 1982. Liberal social policy practitioners describe and critique the policies of the Reagan administration.

Gilder, George: *Wealth and Poverty*, Basic Books, New York, 1981. A supply-side critique of welfare programs, in which the author argues that economic growth and the entrepreneur will do more for the poor than antipoverty programs.

Greer, Thomas H.: *American Social Reform Movements*, Kennikat Press, Port Washington, N.Y., 1965. A history of social reformers and their causes.

Harrington, Michael: *The Other America*, New York, Macmillan, 1963. A study of how the poor fared in the 1960s. This book focused President Kennedy's attention on poverty and led him to order planning for an antipoverty program.

Lowi, Theodore: *The End of Liberalism*, 2nd ed., Norton, New York, 1979. An analysis of the failure of post-New Deal programs, focusing on their lack of explicit goals and standards. The author argues for programs based on juridical democracy.

Moynihan, Daniel P.: *Maximum Feasible Misunderstanding*, Free Press, New York, 1969. A former counselor to President Nixon and now a senator from New York explains why the community action program was doomed to controversy and failure.

Murray, Charles: *Losing Ground: American Social Policy, 1950–1980*, Basic Books, New York, 1984. An argument that social programs have failed, that some are responsible for increasing poverty, and that many should be scrapped.

Page, Benjamin: *Who Gets What from Government*, University of California Press, Berkeley, 1983. A study of the redistribution of wealth by governments, set in comparative perspective.

Piven, Francis Fox, and Richard A. Cloward: *Regulating the Poor*, Vintage Books, New York, 1971. An argument by two professors of social work that the welfare system is used to regulate the supply of labor for the benefit of industry and agriculture and should be completely revamped.

The Reagan Record: An Assessment of America's Changing Priorities, Urban Institute, 1984. A description of Reagan's policy of retrenchment.

Riis, Jacob: *How the Other Half Lives*, Hill and Wang, New York, 1957. A journalist's account of how the poor lived in New York City at the turn of the century.

Rivlin, Alice: *Systematic Thinking for Social Action*, Brookings, Washington, D.C., 1971. A call for systematic experimentation and innovation in the delivery of social services.

Steiner, Gilbert Y.: *The State of Welfare*, Brookings, Washington, D.C., 1971. A book about the welfare mess, including some sobering proposals for reform.

THE STUDY BREAK

Angelou, Maya: *I Know Why the Caged Bird Sings*, 1979. A movie about a black writer's recollections of growing up in the south during the depression.

Brown, Claude: *Manchild in the Promised Land* MacMillan, New York, 1965. A book about growing up poor in Harlem.

Sounder. A 1972 movie starring Cecily Tyson and Paul Winfield as sharecroppers in the south.

Steinbeck, John: *The Grapes of Wrath* (originally published in 1939). A novel about white rural poor people in the midst of the depression. Henry Fonda starred in the 1941 movie version.

USEFUL SOURCES

U.S. Department of Commerce, Bureau of the Census: *Population Reports and Survey of Income and Program Participation*. Reports on the characteristics of the population and on people who receive income, services, or benefits.

U.S. Department of Health and Human Services: *Social Security Bulletin*. A magazine which follows developments in the social security and medical insurance programs.

U.S. Department of Labor: *Monthly Labor Review*. A magazine with articles on social policy and programs.

U.S. Department of Labor: *Unemployment Insurance Review*. A magazine which deals with unemployment and national programs to alleviate it.

ORGANIZATIONS

American Enterprise Institute. 1150 17th St., N.W., Washington, D.C. 20036. Conservative research institute which makes policy recommendations and publishes studies on social programs. For more information telephone 202-862-5800.

Brookings Institution. 1775 Massachusetts Avenue, N.W., Washington, D.C. 20036. A research institute which publishes studies on social welfare policy, often written by former government officials. For more information telephone 202-797-6000.

Center on Budget and Policy Priorities. 236 Massachusetts Avenue, N.E., Suite 305, Washington, D.C. 20002. A research center which offers a liberal critique of governmental budgeting on domestic social programs. For more information telephone 202-544-0591.

Heritage Foundation. 214 Massachusetts Avenue, N.E., Washington, D.C. 20002. A research organization with a "new right" orientation, seeking to dismantle most of the positive state and institute free-market solutions to social problems. For more information telephone 202-546-4400.

Urban Institute. 2100 M St., N.W., Washington, D.C. 20037. A research institute which documents the effects of budget cutbacks on city budgets and services, especially to the poor. For more information telephone 202-223-1950.

University of Wisconsin, Institute on Poverty. Social Science Building, Room 3412, Madison, Wisconsin 53706. Research organization which analyzes the size and composition of the American population under the poverty line. For more information telephone 608-262-6358.

CHAPTER 17

CIVIL RIGHTS: EQUAL OPPORTUNITY OR AFFIRMATIVE ACTION?

President Johnson signed the Civil Rights Act of 1964 in the presence of civil rights leaders and members of Congress. On July 1, 1982, time ran out for ratification of the proposed Equal Rights Amendment. (*National Archives; Shephard Sherbell: Picture Group.*)

The Fourteenth Amendment to the Constitution guarantees all Americans equal protection of the law. But what does *equal protection* mean? Must all laws and government actions be *color-blind* and *sex-blind*, or may the government take race, sex, and other characteristics of individuals into account in order to remedy past discrimination? What should be the proper role of government: to ensure equality of opportunity or equality of results?

Today, the majority of Americans believe that racial discrimination and gender discrimination have no place in our nation. But they do not agree on how to remedy the effects of past discrimination or on the issue of equal opportunity versus equal results. In a national poll of college students taken in 1983, for example, 36 percent of the students questioned said that giving minorities some preference was a good idea, while 54 percent said that this would be unfair to whites.[1] But William Coleman, a prominent black Republican and a former secretary of transportation, argues:

> The consequences of centuries of slavery and second-class citizenship cannot be overcome by simply pretending that those consequences do not exist. It is nothing but a sham to allocate jobs, university admissions, government contracts, and other scarce opportunities and resources on the basis of so-called "neutral" criteria that in fact perpetuate the legacy of slavery and discrimination.[2]

Opponents of affirmative action, such as Thomas Sowell, a black economist at Stanford, argue that it does not work, that it rests on the false premise that most differences between groups are based on discrimination, and that it is unconstitutional. Sowell holds that "what the masses of blacks get from affirmative action (and busing) is mainly the resentment of the rest of society."[3]

How to reconcile the competing demands of those who want equality of opportunity and those who emphasize equality of results through affirmative action is the central problem in making civil rights policies today.

EQUAL PROTECTION OF THE LAW

The Fourteenth Amendment, passed in 1868 in the aftermath of the Civil War, provides that no state may "deny to any person within its jurisdiction the equal protection of the laws." The courts have applied equal protection guarantees to the national government as well.[4]

The meaning of equal protection

In 1875, as part of the post–Civil War Reconstruction, Congress passed an "Act to Protect All Citizens in Their Civil and Legal Rights." It ended racial discrimination in public accommodations and transportation and provided blacks with access to the federal courts and the right to sue for damages if they could prove discrimination. But the first definitions of *equal protection* actually set back the blacks' quest for equality. In the *Slaughterhouse Cases* the Supreme Court ruled that it was "not the purpose of the Fourteenth Amendment . . . to transfer the security and protection of . . . civil rights . . . from the States to the federal government."[5] In the *Civil Rights Cases* of 1883 the Court struck down

584

most of the provisions of the Civil Rights Acts of 1866 and 1875.[6] Other cases denied blacks protection against discrimination by individuals.

By the 1890s race relations had taken an ugly turn. Blacks were disenfranchised throughout the south. Laws and ordinances separated the races in schools, transportation, hospitals, jails, cemeteries, recreational facilities, and other public accommodations—the so-called Jim Crow policy. All over the United States, blacks, Asians, and non-Christians were denied access to "social clubs, fraternities and sororities, private schools, colleges and universities, churches, cemeteries, hospitals, hotels, dwellings, restaurants, movies, bowling alleys, swimming pools, bath houses, sporting events, comfort stations, drinking fountains, barber and beauty shops, employment agencies, and employment itself."[7]

The Jim Crow laws were challenged in the federal courts. In 1895 a black man, Homer Adolph Plessy, bought a ticket from the East Louisiana Railroad Company and seated himself in a "whites only" coach. The conductor told him that he was violating an 1890 state law which required him to sit in the "colored only" coach. Plessy refused to leave and was arrested. Acting on behalf of a group of eighteen prominent blacks, known as the Committee to Test the Constitutionality of the Separate Car Law, Plessy then sued in federal court, arguing that the state law impaired his right to make a contract with the railroad company to sit in any car, thus violating the Civil Rights Act of 1866 and the Constitution. He also argued that the segregated seating was a "badge of servitude" akin to slavery, which is forbidden by the Thirteenth Amendment.

Louisiana and the railroad company claimed that there was no impairment of contract, since Plessy bought his ticket and the company was prepared to deliver him to his destination, provided that he sit in the "colored only" coach. The state argued that it had a police power to regulate seating on the basis of race to protect passengers and provide for their safety and comfort. If the races could mingle in the same coaches, it argued, violence might break out: the law was designed as much to enforce Plessy's contract and deliver him safely to his destination as it was to benefit any white.

The Supreme Court upheld this police power of the state. If Plessy believed that the seating arrangements constituted a badge of servitude, the Court said, that was all in his mind, not something the courts could do anything about. Ironically, the only southerner on the Supreme Court, Justice Harlan, registered a vigorous dissent. He urged the idea of the *color-blind Constitution*, arguing:

> In view of the Constitution, in the eye of the law, there is in this country no superior, dominant, ruling class of citizens. There is no caste here. Our Constitution is color-blind. . . . The law regards man as man, and takes no account of his surroundings or of his color when his civil rights as guaranteed by the supreme law of the land are involved.[8]

But the majority remained unconvinced, arguing that even if the races were legally segregated, equal protection of the law was possible. After all, they said, Plessy would arrive at his destination at exactly the same time as any white passenger.

Following this reasoning, the lower federal courts created the *separate-but-equal doctrine*, which allowed the states and localities to use their police pow-

A year before passage of the Civil Rights Act of 1964, a deputy attorney general, Nicholas Katzenbach, still had to chart the progress of integration of public facilities such as lunchrooms and hotels. (*National Archives.*)

ers to separate the races, claiming that if facilities were approximately equal, there would be no violation of the Fourteenth Amendment. But in fact, the states provided blacks with inferior facilities. Black schools, for example, were poorly financed and dilapidated, and often they had fewer school days and shorter hours. Public expenditures for parks, recreation, comfort stations, and the like were far less per capita for blacks than for whites.

Equal protection: The case of education

During and after the Second World War the climate of public opinion regarding the Jim Crow laws changed, especially in the north and west: the United States fought in World War II on the basis of the "four freedoms" of the Atlantic Charter, against racist Nazi and fascist dictatorships. The extermination of 6 million Jews and 6 million gentiles in Nazi concentration camps brought home the terrible consequences of doctrines of racial and religious bigotry. During the war, blacks worked in defense industries, and in response to their request President Franklin Roosevelt issued executive orders banning discrimination in defense plants and establishing a Fair Employment Commission. Later, President Harry Truman issued an order banning racial segregation in the armed forces. Other executive orders banned discrimination in companies doing business with the federal government.

By the late 1940s black organizations such as the National Association for the Advancement of Colored People (NAACP) and the Urban League forged alliances with labor and liberal organizations and became increasingly influential in national politics. The courts soon responded to the disintegration of the national consensus about the Jim Crow laws with a series of decisions, primarily involving education, that chipped away at the doctrine and finally overturned it.

Dismantling Jim Crow: Professional schools. *Jim Crow* practices were vulnerable where separate facilities were clearly unequal. As early as 1938

Lloyd Gaines, a black from Missouri, was denied entrance to the all-white law school at the University of Missouri, which had a program to give scholarships to blacks to attend law schools in other states. Gaines argued that the contacts he could make by attending law school in his home state would be invaluable in advancing his career and that attending an out-of-state school would handicap him in learning Missouri state laws and passing the bar examination. The Supreme Court ruled that Gaines had the right to attend law school in Missouri, but it interpreted "separate but equal" to mean that Missouri could create a separate law school for blacks.[9]

But could any segregated graduate or professional school provide an equal education? Herman Sweatt, a black from Texas, sued to attend the all-white University of Texas Law School, instead of the black school which the state created after the *Gaines* decision. He argued that since most of the lawyers and judges in Texas were white, a black student who was not admitted to the all-white school would be denied the opportunity to interact with the better faculty members, with classmates who would be lawyers (and therefore business contacts), and with the numerous alumni of the law school. Chief Justice Vinson agreed, observing that there are "qualities which are incapable of objective measurement but which make for greatness in a law school," including "reputation of the faculty, experience of the administration, position and influence of the alumni, standing in the community, tradition and prestige."[10]

Oklahoma, following the *Sweatt* decision, agreed that blacks could attend its graduate and professional schools, but it tried to segregate a student named McLaurin. He was required to sit

> . . . at a designated desk in what was variously described as a "hallway," or an "anteroom adjoining the classroom," where he and the instructor could see and hear each other. . . . In the library he was assigned a special desk . . . in the school cafeteria he was directed to eat at a specifically designated table and to do so at a different time than his fellow white students.[11]

The Supreme Court ruled this segregation unconstitutional.[12]

Brown v. Board of Education of Topeka: Striking down Jim Crow. The Jim Crow system was shaken to its foundations by the Supreme Court in the 1954 landmark decision in *Brown v. Board of Education of Topeka*. Nominally involving Linda Brown, a black girl whose parents wanted her to go to the Sumner School a block away (reserved for whites) because they did not want her to cross a dangerous railroad track (Linda's interest in the case was "to go to school with Mona and Guinivere, because that's who I played with every day"), the case was actually prepared by the NAACP's Legal Defense Fund, which had sponsored social-psychological research on the effects of racial segregation on black children. Linda Brown's lawyers argued that segregation caused psychological damage and therefore violated the equal protection clause because it was a badge of servitude which made black children feel inferior to white children, harming both races by creating feelings of inferiority and resentment in one and feelings of superiority and contempt in the other. They offered the testimony of a psychologist, Dr. Kenneth Clark, whose studies indicated that the stigma of such segregation could affect children's performance in school and their behavior in other settings. Because of such damage, a segregated school system, no matter how well funded, could never be equal.

Damages were borne by blacks which made equal education impossible (unlike the situation in *Plessy*).

The lawyers for the school district argued that the Fourteenth Amendment did not deal directly with public education (because there were few public schools at the time it was drafted). They pointed to a long line of federal court cases upholding separate-but-equal facilities, suggesting that these precedents should settle this case. They argued that children of both races were being educated in publicly funded schools and thus were being treated equally (along the lines of the argument in *Plessy*). If blacks chose to view segregation as a badge of inferiority, or if it damaged them, that was not the fault of the state.

The Supreme Court, in a unanimous opinion written by Chief Justice Earl Warren, agreed with Dr. Clark and other social scientists, holding that "segregation of white and colored children in public schools has a detrimental effect upon the colored children" and concluding that it "generates a feeling of inferiority as to their status in the community that may affect their hearts and minds in a way unlikely ever to be undone."[13] The Court also went beyond this reasoning to accept Harlan's view in *Plessy* that the Constitution is color-blind. Separation of the races was unconstitutional, not simply because children were psychologically damaged by it, but because "separate educational facilities are inherently unequal."[14] By 1954, equal protection of the law meant an end to racial classifications. It seemed as if the courts had accepted the doctrine of the color-blind Constitution.

The need to be color-conscious. Paradoxically, the decision in *Brown* required the courts to become *color-conscious* in order to get school districts to become color-blind. In *Brown II*, decided in 1955, the Supreme Court ruled that segregated school districts would have to desegregate with "all deliberate speed." The federal courts, however, did not require full and immediate desegregation, but allowed local boards to develop and implement plans on a timetable rather than act immediately. The hope was to minimize violence or disruption by those who opposed the ruling.

Southern states adopted a strategy of "massive resistance," and local politicians adopted as their slogan "segregation now, segregation tomorrow, and segregation forever." Most southerners in Congress signed a manifesto pledging to use "all lawful means" to reverse the decision. Moderates urging compliance were voted out of office. School administrators refused to comply with the federal court orders. In 1957 President Eisenhower had to order federal troops to desegregate the high school in Little Rock, Arkansas, and in 1961 President Kennedy had to use troops to desegregate the University of Mississippi. Prince Edward County in Virginia closed down its entire public school system rather than desegregate, and so federal judges ordered it to remain open.[15] Some districts adopted "freedom-of-choice" enrollment plans which permitted a few token blacks to enroll in "white" schools. Others assumed that they could comply with *Brown* if they established a unitary system that did not mention race at all—housing patterns and discriminatory districting would maintain segregated schools. In 1958 there was still not a single black child in a "white" public school in Virginia, Alabama, Mississippi, Georgia, Florida, or South Carolina.

The federal courts, dealing with suits brought by civil rights organizations

Nicholas Katzenbach, the deputy attorney general (right), hands a federal court order to Governor George Wallace of Alabama ordering the admission of black applicants to the University of Alabama. Wallace defied the order; federal troops enforced it. (*UPI; Bettmann Newsphotos.*)

on behalf of black parents, were forced to consider the actual racial composition of the schools and the actions of their administrators. They had to act in situations in which the revised laws and regulations seemed color-blind but were designed to maintain racial segregation. The federal courts in the 1960s began to strike down freedom-of-choice plans and require unitary systems to actually desegregate the schools.[16]

The courts distinguish between school districts with a past history of discriminatory action and those in which racial imbalance may have been due to other factors (such as residential patterns). The former were involved in de jure segregation based on state action; the latter had de facto segregation, without discrimination by the state. The courts fashioned remedies only for de jure segregation, and only where an intent to segregate could be demonstrated.[17] Even a northern school system that had never used explicit racial classifications might have tried to segregate by its location of schools or its drawing of district lines, in which case the courts would assume de jure segregation.[18]

In such districts, in both the north and the south, the courts fashioned color-conscious remedies. They would assign students to particular schools, on the basis of their race, to overcome existing racial imbalances.[19] They would order any or all of the following: pupil assignments based on race; school busing; redrawing of district lines; consolidation of schools; pairing of formerly all-white with all-black schools in larger districts; "educational parks" and larger school districts; conversion of schools to all lower or all upper grades; and closing of schools and reassignment of pupils. The courts were cautious about extending these remedies across city or county school district lines. In a case in Detroit it held that if the suburban systems had not discriminated, they could not be involved in the desegregation of the Detroit system.[20] But in cases in Indianapolis and Louisville, the courts found that the suburban systems had discriminated and therefore could be included in the desegregation plans.[21]

Equity powers of the federal courts. The federal courts may use color-conscious means to obtain color-blind ends, for as Justice Harry Blackmun noted,

---

CIVIL RIGHTS: SOME OF THE LEGAL PROTECTIONS

Civil Rights Act of 1964. This act prohibits discrimination in public accommodations, such as hotels, restaurants, and movie theaters; prohibits discrimination based on race, color, or national origin in any program or activity receiving federal financial aid; and prohibits discrimination in employment based on race, color, or national origin.

Age Discrimination in Employment Act of 1967. This act prohibits employers, employment agencies, and labor organizations from discriminating against individuals on the basis of age.

Civil Rights Act of 1968. This act prohibits discrimination in the sale or rental of residential property.

Education Amendments of 1972 (Title IX). This act prohibits discrimination on the basis of sex by any educational program or activity receiving federal financial assistance.

State and Local Fiscal Assistance Act of 1972. This act prohibits discrimination by state and local governments in programs utilizing revenue sharing funds.

Rehabilitation Act of 1973. This act forbids discrimination on the basis of physical or mental handicaps.

"In order to get beyond racism, we must first take account of race. There is no other way. And in order to treat some persons equally, we must first treat them differently."[22] The courts use their *equity powers:* powers to fashion remedies which offer an equitable (that is, fair and just) solution to a conflict. These equity powers allow the courts to go beyond remedies which Congress may provide. *The courts can even adopt means which Congress has prohibited as ends.* For example, Congress has passed laws prohibiting school busing to overcome racial imbalance as an *end* of governmental policy. But the courts can order such busing as an interim *means* to desegregate a formerly segregated school system.

In a landmark case in 1971, the Supreme Court ruled that the Charlotte-Mecklenburg school district had long practiced segregation and for fifteen years had not complied with the *Brown* decision. The justices' goal remained a color-blind school system. But to achieve it, they would allow lower federal courts to do the following: (1) take into account the race of children attending schools in the district, (2) use a special educational consultant to prepare desegregation plans, and (3) order pupil assignments based on race to achieve the maximum feasible racial balance among the district's schools.[23]

In its decision the Court noted that Congress had specifically provided that the Justice Department could not institute lawsuits to promote racial balance, that the federal courts were not empowered by the Civil Rights Act of 1964 to "issue any order seeking to achieve a racial balance in any school," and that the term *desegregation* would "not mean the assignment of students to public schools in order to overcome racial imbalance."[24] The Court decided that in this law Congress had simply not authorized the use of busing to overcome racial imbalance. But it also held that Congress did not and could not prohibit the courts from using their own judicial powers to fashion remedies.

Administering school desegregation. After passage of the Elementary and Secondary Education Act of 1965, federal funds were used to help disadvantaged students. The Department of Health, Education and Welfare (HEW) de-

veloped guidelines which were color-conscious: they specified the percentages of minority students that had to be enrolled in previously all-white schools in order for them to remain eligible for funding. Enforcement of these target enrollments proved to be the most effective instrument in obtaining compliance with *Brown*. By 1967, funding for 122 districts had been cut off, and the lesson had been learned by the remainder. By 1968, of 4588 districts in 17 southern and border states, 3013 had complied with the HEW guidelines, 1225 were operating under voluntary plans approved by the HEW, and 350 were under court orders to desegregate.[25]

THE POLITICS OF BUSING. But a backlash developed against this desegregation. By 1969, conservatives in Congress had gained passage of legislation providing that no federal funds could "force busing" or force attendance at particular schools. The following year they blocked passage of Nixon's $1.5 billion proposal to provide funds for school districts that made *voluntary* efforts to overcome racial imbalance (Nixon himself was opposed to involuntary court-ordered busing). In 1974 the conservative coalition amended the aid to education bill to prohibit federal funds from being used to bus children beyond the school "next closest" to their homes and when busing posed a risk to their health. Nothing in the act diminished the authority of the courts to order busing, however.

A large majority of the public oppose busing as a tool for ending racial segregation in schools. But in cities like Charlotte-Mecklenburg, court-ordered busing was successful; students' achievement scores rose, and the actual bus-riding for most students was reduced (since they did not have to attend more distant segregated schools). Atlanta, Austin (Texas), and Seattle have also reported that black students' achievement scores have risen in stable school settings where busing has worked.[26] But in cities like Boston, busing failed, achievement scores did not rise, and the flight of white students from the public school system left it more segregated than when busing was started. Overall, there was more racial segregation in the 1980s than in the late 1960s, according to a report issued by the Joint Center for Political Studies, a black research organization. The report indicated that in 1980 two-thirds of the students in the ten largest school districts were from minority groups and that the percentages were increasing.

EQUAL EDUCATION IN THE 1980S. The Supreme Court has ruled that if "white flight" made desegregation unworkable, then the federal courts could order remedial programs to upgrade education in predominantly black schools.[27] Such court orders to increase funding for black schools could supersede budgets prepared by city councils, state legislatures, and local school boards. By the 1980s, with the support of the Justice Department and the approval of the federal courts, civil rights groups and local school officials in many communities were hammering out agreements which would reduce the amount of busing, reestablish neighborhood schools, attempt to attract white students to "magnet" schools (those with enriched programs), and improve the quality of education in predominantly black schools. Cities such as Memphis, Atlanta, Little Rock, Norfolk, Jacksonville, and Augusta were experimenting with such plans.[28] (In Memphis, it helped that 3 of the 9 board members and the superintendent were themselves black.)

These plans had the full support of the Reagan administration. In various court cases the Justice Department dropped busing as a potential remedy and

instead proposed detailed plans for desegregation using other methods, such as its magnet-school plan for East Baton Rouge, Louisiana, and Bakersfield, California. As William Reynolds, the head of the Justice Department's Civil Rights Division, put it, "Involuntary busing has largely failed in two major respects: it has failed to elicit public support, and it has failed to advance the overriding goal of equal educational opportunity. Adherence to an experiment that has not withstood the test of experience obviously makes little sense."[29]

Opponents, such as Julian Bond, Georgia's leading black legislator, argued that this was simply a return to the separate-but-equal approach, and they charged that the Reagan administration was acting in bad faith by abandoning desegregation cases prepared by the previous Carter administration, refusing to appeal cases which went against civil rights groups, and filing no new desegregation cases during Reagan's first twenty months in office.

REFERENDUMS AND BUSING. Local groups opposed to busing have used referendums in attempts to defeat plans developed by school authorities. In California, Proposition 1, which restricts the power of the state courts to order busing, was passed in 1980. The Supreme Court upheld the referendum, claiming that the state could establish its own busing policies, provided that these did not interfere with the powers of the federal courts or the other two branches of the national government. In 1978 voters in the state of Washington passed a referendum preventing school busing for desegregation. Seattle, which had its own voluntary busing plan, sued the state, arguing that the referendum infringed on its own local powers. The Supreme Court declared the state's referendum unconstitutional and upheld Seattle's power to bus students as it saw fit.[30]

The constitutional interest in equal protection of the law overrides the democratic principle of majority rule under certain circumstances. A city or a state may not use a referendum or an initiative to decide on policies which perpetuate discrimination. The Fourteenth Amendment bars not only state action which fosters discrimination but also state action which would prevent a reversal of past discrimination.

The issue arises when a referendum passes which forbids a local or state government from taking remedial actions or which requires that such actions be submitted to voters. The courts have decided that these referendums or initiatives are subject to the Fourteenth Amendment.[31] The results of referendums are struck down if the courts conclude that voters wished to deny a minority equal protection of the laws. Thus referendums stating that homeowners could sell to anyone they wished and that children could attend any school in a city—which seemed on their face to involve freedom of choice—were actually designed to prevent desegregation of housing and schools and were struck down. A law requiring that any fair housing ordinance be submitted to voters in a referendum was also held unconstitutional.[32]

DESEGREGATION AND THE BLACK COMMUNITY. Substantial segments of the black community remain skeptical about students' performance in schools that have been desegregated under judicial supervision. Jesse Jackson argues that "blacks sometimes are against busing because all decisions about desegregation are being made for them, not with and by them."[33] Some desegregation plans mean that blacks lose teaching and administrative jobs and that black children lose their identification with black authority figures. Students who attend formerly all-white schools may not identify with the teams, bands, and

social clubs. They may encounter hostility from white students and their parents and even from teachers, who view them as "invaders" into their community. Black students are likely to receive harsher punishment than white students and are more likely to be suspended or expelled. They may be "tracked" into remedial classes or classes for non-college-bound students because teachers and guidance counselors do not recognize their intelligence.[34]

But the situation is not hopeless. In some cities where leaders of both races have made good-faith efforts to desegregate, the schools function effectively. A large proportion of inner-city parochial schools, especially in the south, are effectively integrated. Some of the best private schools in the east and midwest take minority students and place them in good colleges. By 1975 the proportion of blacks enrolled in college equaled the proportion of blacks in the total population (though not the proportion of 18- to 21-year old blacks, which was considerably higher).

With or without substantial integration, the gap between black and white children has narrowed in achievement tests. The National Assessment of Educational Progress reported the gap between the races to be 18 percent in 1970, but only 13 percent in 1980. According to Dr. Lyle Jones, the data indicate that "if an area goes down, blacks go down less," while "if an area's getting better, blacks go up more."[35] It seemed that improvements in educational techniques, additional funding, and a renewed emphasis on the "basics" would further narrow the gap in achievement tests between blacks and whites.

CLOSE-UP

DR. MARTIN LUTHER KING, JR. On August 28, 1963, people came from all across the nation, a quarter of a million strong, to join in a "march on Washington" for civil rights. Endorsed by President Kennedy as "a peaceful assembly calling for the redress of grievances," it brought trade unionists, church congregations, students, and summer congressional interns (like the author of this textbook) marching down the mall, from the Washington Monument to the Lincoln Memorial, to hear one speaker after another denounce segregation and demand racial justice.

And then the most charismatic leader in the nation, Dr. Martin Luther King, Jr., addressed the crowd: "I have a dream," he told the nation, that one day "my

The march on Washington, 1963. Reverend Dr. Martin Luther King, Jr., made his "I have a dream" address to 200,000 marchers at the Lincoln Memorial. (*Bob Adelman: Magnum.*)

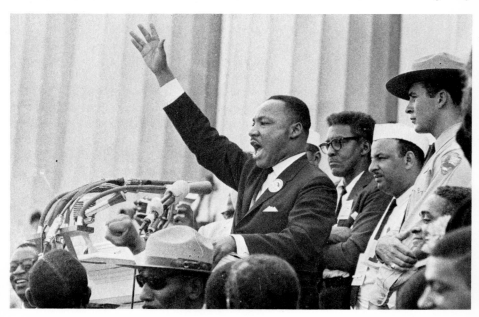

children will no longer be judged by the color of their skin, but by the content of their character." He described the realities of segregation, the harm it did to blacks and whites alike—poisoning the spirit of Americans. And then he concluded:

> When we let freedom ring, when we let it ring from every village and every hamlet, from every state and every city, we will be able to speed up that day when all God's children, black men and white men, Jews and Gentiles, Protestants and Catholics, will be able to join hands and sing in the words of that old Negro spiritual, "Free at last! Free at last! Thank God almighty, we are free at last!"

King's magnificent address marked the start of a breakthrough in civil rights which some historians have aptly termed the *second reconstruction*. It culminated almost a decade of nonviolent demonstrations organized by King and his movement, the Southern Christian Leadership Conference (SCLC), and designed to topple the Jim Crow laws segregating the races.

The son of an influential Atlanta minister, "Daddy" King, Martin Luther King, Jr., began his struggle in 1956. As a young Baptist minister in Montgomery in 1956, he led demonstrations seeking to desegregate the local bus line. In 1960 King participated in a sit-in at Rich's department store in Atlanta, where he was arrested. He was sentenced by a county judge to four months of hard labor. He was taken to a rural prison farm, and his wife believed that he was in danger from the local guards. That evening John Kennedy, then running for president, called Coretta King to express his concern (King was released two days later). "I'll vote for him, even though I don't want a Catholic," Daddy King announced. Kennedy later remarked that it was "a hell of a bigoted thing to say, wasn't it?" But the endorsement helped Kennedy with black voters.

King continued working with black students in sit-in campaigns to desegregate lunch counters and local city libraries and parks. In 1963 he organized an Easter season boycott of stores in Birmingham, Alabama. Arrested along with thousands of his supporters, King wrote "Letter from a Birmingham Jail," in response to eight clergymen of the community who condemned him as an outsider who was raising racial tensions. King pointed out that no one can be an outsider when there is a question of justice, that he had been invited to Birmingham by local civil rights groups, and that his movement was purely nonviolent. True, he agreed, his followers had broken segregation ordinances and had refused to disperse when the police demanded that they do so; but these laws were themselves unjust, he said, since they discriminated against one group of citizens and had been passed by unrepresentative local and state governments which did not allow most black citizens to vote.

The local sheriff, Eugene "Bull" Connor, tried to stop the demonstrations with police brutality. His police dogs bit at demonstrators, his fire hoses swept them off their feet, and his officers beat marchers with clubs. When King's coleader, the Reverend Fred Shuttlesworth, was beaten by the police, Connor's response was "I wish they'd carried him away in a hearse." Yet the demonstrators kept coming and kept getting arrested, and the downtown area remained (nonviolently) chaotic. Eventually the leading white businesspeople of Birmingham—the Senior Citizens Council—capitulated and agreed to negotiate on ending segregation of some facilities in the city, though not before the Birmingham home of King's brother was bombed. The negative worldwide publicity over the brutality in Birmingham led the Kennedy administration to propose a civil rights bill which would make it

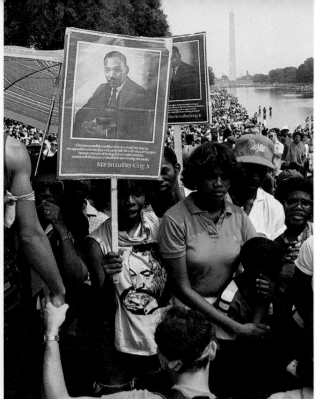

The march from Selma to Montgomery, Alabama, in March 1965 dramatized the case of the Voting Rights Act, passed later the same year. (*Dan Budnik: Woodfin Camp.*)

A rally commemorating Dr. King petitioned Congress for a federal holiday in his name. The holiday begins on January 15, 1986. (*Charles Steiner: Picture Group.*)

a federal offense to segregate public accommodations, and Congress passed it into law in 1964.

A similar campaign in 1965 to register blacks to vote in Selma, Alabama, pitted King and his followers against Sheriff Clark. Again, police dogs, fire hoses, and brutal beatings were used against King and his followers on a march from Selma to the state capital. Again, the worldwide publicity about these actions caused national revulsion. Capitalizing on the mood of the public, Congress passed the Voting Rights Act.

For his nonviolent efforts to change race relations, King was awarded the Nobel peace prize in 1968. In June of that year he was killed in Memphis by James Earl Ray, who is currently serving a life sentence for the crime. In the aftermath of King's death, Congress passed the Fair Housing Act of 1968, a bill which King had fought for vigorously but which, until the assassination, seemed stalled in Congress. His birthday, along with Washington's and Lincoln's, has been made a national holiday by an act of Congress.

Equal protection in public accommodations, housing, and employment

The equal protection clause and various civil rights laws prohibit discrimination in public accommodations, housing, and employment.

Public accommodations. The Civil Rights Act of 1964 makes racial discrimination illegal in public accommodations involved in interstate commerce. These include hotels and motels, restaurants, movie theaters, and bowling alleys. The act was upheld by the Supreme Court.[36] Today, most of the Jim

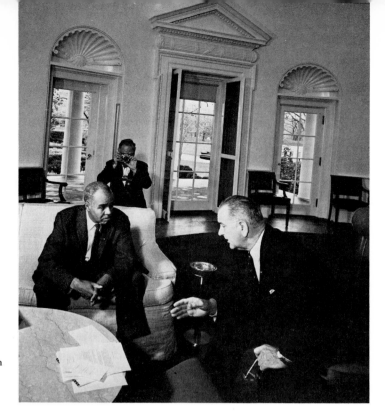

President Johnson consulted with Roy Wilkins, then chairman of the NAACP, before passage of 1964 Civil Rights Act. (*National Archives.*)

Crow barriers requiring separate public facilities and accommodations for blacks have been removed, although in some smaller communities blacks may be subjected to harassment and even violence if they attempt to exercise these rights. Ironically, businesses, hotels, and restaurants in the downtown business districts and suburban malls have gained minority customers, while black businesses have often lost them, once facilities were desegregated.

Housing. As early as 1917 the Supreme Court ruled that no state law or city ordinance could exclude people from a neighborhood on the basis of race.[37] But the decision did not forbid private homeowners from putting restrictive covenants in their deeds prohibiting any owner of the property to sell to racial or religious minorities. Such deeds were enforced by the courts until 1948, when the Supreme Court, in *Shelley v. Kraemer*, ruled that the state and federal courts could not enforce such convenants, because to do so would be state action in violation of the equal protection clause.[38] In 1968, in *Jones v. Mayer*, the Supreme Court barred all racial discrimination in the sale and rental of housing.[39] In that same year Congress passed the Fair Housing Act to end discrimination by brokers, realty companies, and housing developers in the sale and rental of owner-occupied homes consisting of more than four units. It gave the Department of Housing and Urban Development the power to seek voluntary compliance with the law—including agreements with developers to rent or sell a specified percentage of housing units to minorities. The Justice Department could sue in the federal courts for orders to desegregate housing.

In spite of these measures, most residential neighborhoods remain segregated. This is due in part to discriminatory practices by realtors and banks and in part to "white flight"—the selling of homes by panicked whites when blacks move into a neighborhood, aided by realtors who "turn" a neighborhood (that

---

CIVIL RIGHTS: EXECUTIVE ENFORCEMENT OF THE LAWS

United States Commission on Civil Rights. This is an independent, bipartisan agency, appointed by the president. It investigates complaints about voting rights, studies and collects information about discrimination in public accommodations, appraises federal civil rights laws, serves as a national clearinghouse for research and information about civil rights, and reports and submits recommendations to Congress.

Department of Education, Office of Civil Rights. This office oversees and ensures compliance with laws prohibiting discrimination in education, receives and investigates complaints, and conducts reviews involving compliance by local school districts.

Equal Employment Opportunity Commission. This agency's purpose is to end discrimination based on race, color, religion, sex, national origin, or age in hiring, promotions, firings, wages, testing, training, and apprenticeships. It promotes voluntary action programs, investigates complaints, conducts negotiations, and, if necessary, litigates against offenders.

Department of Housing and Urban Development, Office of Fair Housing and Equal Opportunity. This office investigates and processes complaints about discrimination in housing, holds hearings, conducts studies, litigates, and provides training and technical assistance.

Department of Labor, Office of Federal Contract Compliance Programs. This office ensures that contractors and subcontractors who apply for jobs are protected against discrimination. It receives and investigates complaints, litigates, conducts compliance reviews, and provides training and technical assistance.

Department of Justice, Civil Rights Division. The division enforces the civil rights laws through criminal and civil litigation. The Community Relations Service aids communities in resolving civil rights disputes in employment, education, housing, and the administration of justice through conciliation and public education.

---

is, they buy homes from whites cheaply and then sell them at high prices to blacks).

To prevent white flight, some suburbs and housing developers have used "benign quotas." The management of the 6000-unit Starret City in Brooklyn, for example, maintains a 65-35 balance between blacks and whites in apartment rentals. This reassures whites that the complex will not become entirely black, prevents white flight, and maintains an integrated community. The Justice Department, however, opposes such quotas, arguing that the housing laws require color-blind tenant selection, even if a community would become resegregated as a result.

Employment. Between 1948 and 1961 the federal government issued executive orders ending racial discrimination in its own employment practices and requiring government contractors to hire and treat workers without regard to race, color, or national origin. Title VII of the Civil Rights Act of 1964 provided that other private employers could not discriminate on the basis of race.

The enforcement of laws banning discrimination in employment involves several different agencies. Complaints may be filed with the Office of Federal Contract Compliance Programs if federal funds are involved. Other complaints may be filed with the Equal Employment Opportunity Commission (EEOC), which tries conciliation. If a settlement with a company cannot be reached, individuals may sue in the state or federal courts for back pay or damages and for changes in hiring and promotion practices.

Can a public pool become a private club? Whites in Cairo, Illinois, tried to declare the town pool a private association, but the courts found the attempt to be a thinly disguised conspiracy at racial discrimination. (*Danny Lyon: Magnum.*)

Privacy and discrimination

Not all private activities are subject to antidiscrimination injunctions by the government. The Ninth Amendment provides a *zone of privacy* into which the national government and the state government may not intrude. People may choose their friends, issue invitations to social functions, and admit or refuse to admit people into their homes for any reason. Private clubs and religious organizations are free to discriminate if they so choose.

Sometimes it is hard to distinguish between public and private spheres and to determine what the zone of privacy should include. Clubs, churches, and private schools often accept government funds or provide public services to the community. The courts recognize that "conduct that is formally 'private' may become so entwined with governmental policies or so impregnated with a governmental character" as to become a form of state action requiring equal protection of the law. Public facilities, such as parks and swimming pools, may not be turned over to "private clubs" just to keep them segregated, nor may they be leased to private schools. Where the purchase of a home involves the right to join a beach or a pool club, it must be open to people of all races.[40]

The right to associate freely yields to the state interest in guaranteeing equal protection of the laws in education. The parents of some black children who were denied admission to two all-white private schools in Virginia sued in federal court, citing a provision of the Civil Rights Act of 1866 that gives blacks the same rights as whites to make and enforce contracts. They argued that their right to contract for private education for their children was impaired by racial discrimination, and the Supreme Court, in *Runyon v. McCrary,* agreed— although it left open the question of admission based on religion or sex.[41]

AFFIRMATIVE ACTION

How can Americans have racial justice when past discrimination leaves some people who are competing for schooling and employment at a substantial disadvantage? Justice Thurgood Marshall argued that "because of a legacy of unequal treatment we now must permit the institutions of this society to give consideration to race in making decisions about who will hold the positions of influence, affluence, and prestige in America."[42] Such consideration, referred to as *affirmative action,* may take several forms:

- Making minorities aware of opportunities previously denied to them

- Reevaluating admissions, hiring, training, and promotion practices to end discrimination
- Setting goals in schooling, training, and hiring to overcome racial imbalance
- Instituting numerical quotas with timetables for implementation to overcome racial imbalance
- Paying damages to groups which have been discriminated against

Implications of affirmative action

Conflicts. There is little controversy about the first two approaches listed above. But the other three are controversial. Proponents argue that they provide tangible equality of results for groups (such as blacks, Hispanics, Asians, and women) who in the past have been subject to discrimination. They say that instituting goals, quotas, or timetables and making companies or government agencies abide by them is the only practical way to overcome institutional and individual discrimination. They point to the rise in college enrollments of minorities and to the increased numbers of minority managers and administrators as evidence that affirmative action works. As William Coleman argues, timetables and goals are not ends in themselves but only means:

> The ultimate goal of affirmative action . . . is not to set up a permanent system of proportional representation for all racial and ethnic groups. Rather, it is to break the cycle of discrimination and to achieve equality of opportunity which is not illusory.[43]

Opponents argue that treating people as members of groups ignores the fact that many are not disadvantaged and have not suffered discrimination. The child of a wealthy third-generation Hispanic or Asian family who has all the educational and cultural advantages might be given preference over a white child whose family just immigrated and who lives in poverty. The black child of an upper-class professional family who attended private schools might be given preference in college admissions over the child of a white tenant farmer.

Affirmative action programs include or exclude groups on an arbitrary basis. All blacks are included, although blacks from the West Indies have not suffered from the past history of American racial discrimination, and their education and income put them above the median for the American population. All Hispanic-surnamed people are included—wealthy Cuban refugees and Spaniards, for example. Other groups that are included are American Indians, Asian-Pacific Americans, and Asian-Indian Americans (from India, Pakistan, or Bangladesh). But Jews, Irish, Italians, Germans, Poles, and Scandinavians are excluded, though all these groups could claim that they suffered prejudice during the nineteenth century. If affirmative action is meant to help the disadvantaged, then why are Asian Americans included, a group with the highest educational and occupational attainments of any group of Americans?[44] And why are Cuban Americans, with similar accomplishments, included?

Treating people according to their ancestry means that someone has to classify American citizens. This is not always easy: anyone can claim some Hispanic or black ancestry. The government must make a decision, by means of either visual inspection (as directed by the Office of Personnel Management for federal employees) or the inspection of genealogical records. Is a person who has one Hispanic great-great grandparent, for example, a member of that ancestor's group? The government opens a Pandora's box when it attempts to classify people by race and ethnicity. To some people, such identifications

smack of practices in Nazi Germany, South Africa, and the Soviet Union. Quotas have been used in the past to discriminate against minorities, which accounts for the strong opposition to them among Jews, who remember how quotas were used to keep down their admissions to universities until the 1960s.

Ironically, the more Americans have accepted equality of opportunity and the concept of the color-blind society, the less they have been willing to accept equality of results through a system of affirmative action. In the late 1970s Gallup polls indicated that 64 percent of blacks and 80 percent of women rejected the notion that they should be given preferential treatment in employment or college admissions, and white males were opposed to affirmative action by a similar margin.[45]

Implementation. An affirmative action plan is implemented in the following manner. First, a school or an organization estimates the number of women and minorities who are qualified for admission or employment. Then it estimates the total number of persons who are qualified and divides that number by the first figure to get the *percentage* of women and minorities who are qualified. Then it determines what percentage of its existing students, trainees, or employees are minorities or women. If that percentage is much less than the percentage of qualified women and minorities, the school or organization looks for ways to increase its admissions or hirings of women and minorities so that its work force will mirror the percentage that are qualified.

Problems occur when there are too few openings for all qualified applicants. Should a position be offered to the person who is best qualified, or should it be offered to a qualified minority or woman in order to meet the affirmative action goal? There are no easy answers. A white male might argue that he is not to blame for past discrimination and that if he has higher grades or more experience, he should be admitted to the better school or get the better job. He may believe that if he is passed over, this is a form of *reverse discrimination*. Proponents of affirmative action argue that the interest of society in ending discrimination takes precedence over the individual.

Group tensions. Affirmative action programs raise tensions between groups. "Are there now so many protected groups that none are protected?" asks Dr. Kenneth Clark, on behalf of blacks who resent the inclusion of other groups in affirmative action programs.[46] Women (51 percent of the population), blacks (12 percent), Hispanics (8 percent), American Indians (1 percent), and Asians (3 percent) are all covered, and so close to two-thirds of the entire population is now qualified for preference. Blacks argue that affirmative action, originally intended as a redress for slavery and later segregation by the states, is now used to benefit groups who have not suffered nearly as much as they have.

Affirmative action for minorities: Education and employment

Education. In the 1970s college and university officials changed their admissions policies to increase enrollments of minorities. They gave less weight to scores on standardized examinations, which might not adequately reflect the potential of minority students. They responded to a growing belief that enrollments should better reflect the racial composition of the entire population. But these new policies became controversial when some minority applicants were accepted, while whites who had higher test scores and better grades were rejected.

Allan Bakke, a white, won a court order admitting him to the University of California–Davis medical school, after the Supreme Court struck down the school's plan to reserve a specific number of places for minorities. (*AP/Wide World.*)

The issue reached the courts when the medical school at the University of California at Davis set aside sixteen places in its entering class for qualified minorities. Alan Bakke, a white applicant, was rejected in 1973 and 1974, although his grades and his scores on the medical school entrance examination were higher than those of some of the minority applicants who were admitted. Bakke sued the university, claiming that the equal protection clause and laws passed by Congress forbade the medical school to consider the minority status of candidates. He demanded that admissions be made on a color-blind basis. The California Supreme Court ordered that Bakke be admitted, and the university appealed the decision to the United States Supreme Court.

The Court's landmark decision in *Regents of the University of California v. Bakke* is as important for what it did not decide as for what it did. A majority of the justices could not agree on any aspect of the case. Four justices held that Title VI of the Civil Rights Act of 1964 prohibited the university from making racial distinctions in admissions. Four other justices, in opposition, argued that both Title VI and the Fourteenth Amendment permitted a state to institute race-conscious programs to "remove the disparate racial impact its actions might otherwise have and if there is reason to believe that the disparate impact is itself the product of past discrimination, whether its own or that of the society at large."[47]

Justice Lewis Powell held the crucial swing vote. He disagreed with the color-conscious bloc because he did not believe that the Constitution permitted racial distinctions to advantage a group or to make up for prior discrimination. But he also thought that racial distinctions could be made by a state if they benefited the society at large. Here the Fourteenth Amendment could be read to permit colleges and universities to use many criteria—including race and ethnicity—to maintain academic freedom, provide for diversity among the student body, and benefit the public at large. Powell combined with the color-conscious bloc to uphold an affirmative action program of admissions. But he also joined the color-blind bloc to strike down the quota of sixteen places for minorities in the Davis plan.

As a result of *Bakke*, numerical quotas were held unconstitutional, but affirmative action programs which took minority status into account in accepting students were upheld. Bakke, incidentally, was admitted to the medical school as a result of this decision and is now a doctor.

Employment. The Civil Rights Act of 1964 on its face seems to ban affirmative action. It provides that nothing in the law requires an employer to grant preferential treatment to any individual on account of any imbalance in the work force, compared with the pool of qualified workers. It also makes it clear that employers are liable only for intentional discrimination against individuals, not for any imbalance in the work force that is due to societal or inadvertent discrimination. Congress took a color-blind rather than a color-conscious approach.

The executive and judicial branches approached employment rights differently. An executive order issued by President Johnson in May 1968 required the Labor Department's Office of Federal Contract Compliance Programs to issue affirmative action guidelines to employers. The guidelines issued by the Labor Department included numerical quotas and timetables for implementation. Then in 1970 the Nixon administration shifted to "results-oriented" procedures designed to put a significant number of minorities into jobs in federally funded construction projects. By 1971 the Labor Department was using numerical quotas to end the underutilization of minorities. It required contractors to submit affirmative action plans, known as *conciliation agreements*, or "letters of commitment," promising increased hiring of minorities—the so-called Philadelphia plan. During the Carter administration the Labor Department started awarding back pay to workers who had been discriminated against in promotions; not only individuals, but also classes of people (such as all women employed in a company), might receive payments.

The Reagan administration broke with these affirmative action policies. "We no longer will insist upon or in any respect support the use of quotas or any other numerical or statistical formula designed to provide to nonvictims of discrimination preferential treatment based on race, sex, national origin or religion," the Justice Department announced.[48] Instead, the department restricted its efforts to filing suits protecting individuals in discrimination cases.

GOVERNMENT EMPLOYMENT. Some of the most important affirmative action cases have involved the federal government and local and state governments. Minority police officers and fire fighters in Houston won $320,000 in back pay and a court order requiring revised hiring procedures. An affirmative action plan for the police department in Detroit was challenged by a sergeants' organization but was upheld by a federal court. Discriminatory hiring practices by the city of Louisville were ended by a district court which required the police department to appoint at least one black for every two whites between 1981 and 1986. The Justice Department in the Reagan administration attacked these arguments when they were appealed to higher courts, arguing in amicus curiae ("friend of the court") briefs that government action based on race was a violation of the Fourteenth Amendment guarantee of equal protection of the law.[49]

The federal government has changed some of its own practices as a result of court cases. The Professional and Administrative Career Examination, a test for 100 management positions, was phased out by the federal government after civil rights groups charged that it was culturally biased and not predictive of management ability. Instead, an affirmative action plan for hiring in the federal civil service was scheduled to be implemented in 1985.

SENIORITY SYSTEMS. Training, promotions, pay increases, and job security are often based on accumulated seniority (continuous employment with a

company). Seniority rules are written into contracts negotiated by unions; usually they provide that the last workers hired are the first fired if layoffs take place. Civil rights groups argue that seniority rules protect white workers at the expense of the more recently hired minorities. But the Supreme Court ruled that seniority systems negotiated between labor and management are constitutional, regardless of their *impact* on minorities or women, provided they were not adopted for a discriminatory *purpose.* Similarly, the Court upheld the city of Memphis when it laid off some fire fighters, even though the majority were black, because it did so according to seniority rules which were color-blind.[50]

TRAINING PROGRAMS. Some corporations have instituted training and promotion programs to increase the number of minorities and women in skilled jobs. The Kaiser Aluminum and Chemical Corporation's plan for a plant in Gramercy, Louisiana, called for half the openings in skilled jobs to be filled by blacks, until the percentage of blacks in the work force—then 2 percent—increased to 39 percent, commensurate with the percentage of blacks in the local labor pool. When black workers with little seniority were hired, a white worker with more seniority, Brian Weber, sued the company in federal court alleging discrimination. He argued that Section 703(a) of the Civil Rights Act of 1964 made it unlawful for employees to discriminate on the basis of race, while Section 703(d) made it unlawful for them to discriminate in apprenticeship or training programs. The union and the company that negotiated the agreement both defended it in court.

The Supreme Court decided, in *United Steelworkers of America v. Weber,* that the Civil Rights Act of 1964 neither required nor forbade companies to institute voluntary affirmative action training programs.[51] Such efforts were purely management's prerogative and might result from its decision to improve labor or community relations. Justice Brennan held that the law did not bar "temporary, voluntary, affirmative action measures undertaken to elimi-

The Supreme Court ruled that Kaiser Aluminum's voluntary affirmative action policy did not violate the civil rights of Brian Weber, a white laboratory technician who was not accepted for the company's training program. (*AP Laserphoto.*)

nate manifest racial imbalance in traditionally segregated job categories."[52] Justice Rehnquist, taking the color-blind position, argued that the law did prohibit color-conscious affirmative action efforts, and he viewed Brennan's attempt to put a different construction on the law as "a tour de force reminiscent of escape artists such as Houdini."[53]

MINORITY CONTRACTING. In its 1977 amendments to the Public Works Employment Act, Congress provided that at least 10 percent of the $4 billion authorized for public works had to be contracted to minority business enterprises (MBEs). For the first time in American history, Congress had passed a law with racial classifications. In theory the provision would channel $400 million to MBEs, compared with the $753 million that 21,000 such contractors had grossed in all their business activities the preceding year—it would increase their gross income by more than half. Yet this $400 million represented less than one-fourth of 1 percent of all construction business, and so the losses to white contractors were insignificant.

The law was challenged in the federal courts by some white contractors. The Supreme Court upheld it in *Fullilove v. Klutznick*, with Chief Justice Warren Burger arguing that Congress need *not* "act in a wholly 'color-blind' fashion" when attempting to ensure that government expenditures not perpetuate past discrimination.[54] For the first time the Court accepted the notion of strict quotas and upheld the authority of Congress to legislate such remedies. However, the provisions of the law were often evaded; white contractors created dummy corporations (nominally headed by blacks, but controlled by whites) for the purpose of bidding on federal contracts.

IMPACT OF AFFIRMATIVE ACTION ON EMPLOYMENT. The Labor Department's Office of Federal Contract Compliance Programs has concluded that affirmative action programs have been highly effective in increasing employment among blacks, Hispanics, and other minorities. Companies that do business with the federal government, for example, "have posted significantly greater gains" than other companies, according to the report, because of "the good-faith efforts of Federal contractors to comply with their contractual obligations of affirmative action."[55] The rate of employment of minorities rose 20 percent among the 30,000 federal contractors (with a total of 14.1 million workers) but only 12 percent among companies not covered by affirmative action requirements. Minorities also did better in promotion and training in such companies.

Equal protection, affirmative action, and gender discrimination

In the past American women had constitutional and legislative *protected status*, which in practice discriminated against them and prevented them from gaining control of their own lives and property. In 1873, in a landmark decision, the Supreme Court ruled that Myra Bradwell was not constitutionally entitled to practice law if a state refused to admit her to the bar. "The natural and proper timidity and delicacy which belongs to the female sex evidently unfits it for many of the occupations of civil life," held Justice Bradley, adding: "The paramount destiny and mission of women are to fulfill the noble and benign office of wife and mother."[56]

Throughout most of the nineteenth century and the early twentieth century, women supported gender-based distinctions in law, believing that these provisions would protect them from exploitation as workers. Women's rights groups joined with the Women's Bureau of the Labor Department to sponsor *protective legislation:* laws which gave women a shorter workday and work-

week, prohibited heavy manual labor, and provided better safety and sanitation facilities than employers offered to men.

Responding to a coalition of women's organizations, the progressive movement, and some industrial and trade associations (which promoted the legislation in order to make it easier to bring women into the industrial labor force), the Supreme Court generally ruled that the Fourteenth Amendment did not apply to gender-based classifications. In *Muller v. Oregon*, a state law limiting the workday for women to ten hours was upheld by the Court in 1908 as a valid exercise of state police power.[57] In 1948 laws preventing women from practicing many professions were upheld in *Goesaert v. Cleary.*[58] Laws discriminating against women in choosing jurors were upheld in *Hoyt v. Florida* as late as 1961.[59] Other measures prevented women from disposing of property without the consent of their spouses or legal guardians and from making wills, entering contracts, and owning businesses.

Combating discrimination in employment. WOMEN IN THE WORK FORCE. Today, 53 percent of American women are in the work force (up from 34 percent in 1950); more than 47 million strong, they constitute more than 41 percent of the entire work force. Yet women have been (and still are being) paid less money for the same work than men. Their median average earnings are just 59 percent of those of their male counterparts—a drop from 63 percent in 1955, which indicates that the situation has been getting worse as more women have entered the work force.

These results cannot be explained by lower educational levels: as women have narrowed the educational gap, the earnings gap has widened. Since the mid-1970s, more women than men have graduated from high school and college; *yet women college graduates, on the average, earn $400 less each year than men who have had no education beyond elementary school!* Men who have a college degree can expect to earn about $329,000 more than men with only a high-school education, while the figure for women is only $142,000 according to the Census Bureau (calculated in 1981 dollars). The Labor Department reported in 1982 that the median weekly earnings of women were lower than those of men in the same occupation. In 1981 the National Research Council of the National Academy of Sciences concluded that "the work women do is paid

Despite the public perception of great changes in women's employment patterns, women have really made little headway in construction and industrial jobs. (*Michael Heron.*)

Women are entering business in ever greater numbers. A "Women in Business" conference in New York in 1984 drew an enthusiastic audience. (*Mario Ruiz: Picture Group.*)

less, and the more an occupation is dominated by women the less it pays." Less than half the gender gap in earnings is due to more training or more seniority. The rest is due to discrimination.

Four-fifths of women workers are concentrated in low-paying service, clerical, sales, domestic, and machine-operator jobs. They constitute 70 percent of retail clerks and 87 percent of cashiers, but only a tiny percentage of store managers and owners. They are poorly represented in skilled trades and other blue-collar work; in 1982 only 1.4 percent of carpenters, 1.7 percent of electricians, 2.5 percent of highway construction workers, 3.9 percent of housepainters, and 3.6 percent of tinsmiths were women. Most were employed in nonunionized factories and offices where the pay was low and the working conditions were poor. Only about 5 percent of executives in the top fifty American corporations are women.[60] Women are concentrated at the low end of the corporate ladder: 97 percent of typists, 98.7 percent of receptionists, 99 percent of secretaries, and 86 percent of file clerks are women.

Professional women have made major gains in recent years in finance and banking, real estate, pharmacy, medicine (1 doctor in 7), law (1 lawyer in 7), and college teaching (1 instructor in 4). They now constitute the majority of insurance adjusters, examiners, and investigators; bill collectors; real estate agents; brokers—and bartenders. Between 1966 and 1979, white women increased their share of professional jobs from 13 to 31 percent, and black women increased their share from 0.6 to 2.2 percent. In the high-paying professional positions, women entering their fields make close to or equal to what men are paid.

EQUAL PAY. President Kennedy proposed, and Congress enacted, the Equal Pay Act of 1963, which requires federal contractors to pay female workers the same wages they pay males. In 1971 the act was extended to cover executive, administrative, and professional employees. Under a 1971 regulation, companies with fifty employees doing $50,000 or more in federal business are required to develop affirmative action plans to move women into jobs where they are underrepresented relative to the qualified pool of workers. Since the mid-1970s this has been interpreted to mean that women can fill 6.9 percent of skilled jobs. (The Reagan administration revised the rule to mean that women can fill 6.9 percent of all jobs, whether skilled or not.) Kennedy also issued an

executive order, revised and extended by Johnson and Nixon, barring gender discrimination in federal employment.

The most important tool barring gender discrimination in other companies is the Civil Rights Act of 1964. Women cannot be discriminated against with regard to employment, pay, promotion, training, or benefits. The law is enforced by the EEOC.

COMPARABLE WORTH. Because so-called women's work is undervalued, women's groups have argued for *comparable worth:* jobs which require similar education and training and which entail similar responsibility should pay the same. This would end the practice of paying female "cleaning women" less than male "custodians," even though the two jobs are comparable, and of paying female teachers, librarians, and nurses less than male ambulance drivers and window cleaners. Most of the male-dominated uniformed services (the police, fire fighters, and sanitation workers) oppose this idea, while teachers, social workers, librarians, and nurses are in favor of it. The Democratic Party's leadership in Congress has endorsed it, as did its 1984 presidential ticket. The Reagan administration, on the other hand, opposes it strongly. William Niskanen, a White House economist, called it "a truly crazy proposal," and the chairman of the Civil Rights Commission, Clarence Pendleton, said that it was "the looniest idea since looney tunes."[61] In 1985 the Equal Employment Opportunity Commission ruled that federal law does not require equal pay for jobs of comparable worth.

In *Washington County, Oregon, v. Gunther*, the Supreme Court ruled that women may sue under the Civil Rights Act of 1964 if there was discrimination when their pay scales were set, without showing that men in exactly the same jobs were paid more for identical work.[62] Some lower federal courts have ruled in favor of pay comparability and have required some cities and counties to institute new pay scales that will add greatly to their budgets. One such case, if upheld by the Supreme Court, would require the state of Washington to give women employees $642 million in back pay and $195 million in pay raises; this gives some idea of the stakes involved in the issue.

DISCRIMINATORY TESTING. Women are sometimes excluded from some jobs which have strength or endurance requirements. Tests may be discriminatory because the requirements are not really necessary for the job, are set too high, or are not properly measured. In a 1982 case a federal judge in New York City ordered changes in the test for fire fighters to measure more accurately the skills needed to fight fires, rather than brute strength. And he ordered that up to forty-five women be accepted as trainees.

MATERNITY POLICY. Until recently, many companies refused to hire women because they might become pregnant and quit their jobs. Some companies required women to remain single and fired them if they married. These policies have not been in effect since the 1950s, but vestiges of the attitudes behind them remain. Until recently, on some airlines female flight attendants who became pregnant lost their seniority or their jobs. The Supreme Court has ruled that such policies violate the Civil Rights Act of 1964 and has ordered reinstatement and back pay for these women.[63]

Combating discrimination in education. The key to the strides that women have made in the professional work force has been their access to higher education. Title IX of the Education Amendments of 1971 provides that "no

person in the United States shall, on the basis of sex, be excluded from participation in, be denied the benefits of, or be subjected to discrimination under any education program or activity receiving federal financial assistance." The law does not, however, apply to admission to private single-sex colleges or schools or to preschool programs. It does not cover such organizations as the Girl Scouts or Boy Scouts. It does not cover fraternities or sororities and similar social organizations. And it does not cover various "father-son" and "mother-daughter" activities sponsored by schools.

Partly as a result of this law, barriers to women in higher education fell in the 1970s. Between 1972 and 1979 the proportion of degrees awarded to women increased dramatically: in engineering, from 1 to 8 percent; in business, from 10 to 31 percent; in law, from 7 to 40 percent; in medicine, from 9 to 23 percent; in veterinary medicine, from 12 to 39 percent; and in the arts and sciences from 16 to 30 percent. Intercollegiate sports were opened to women, and more than 10,000 women now attend college on athletic scholarships.

In the 1970s education officials applied the law to *all* activities of schools receiving federal funds (other than the exceptions mentioned above), not just to activities financed by federal funds. The laws were also applied to schools which received money for student aid, but no other federal funds, and schools could not practice discrimination against faculty or staff members.

Opponents of these policies argued for a *pinpoint* theory: only those programs which were federally funded would be covered by antidiscrimination provisions, and schools that received only scholarship and financial aid funds would not be covered by the law. In *Grove City v. Bell*, decided by the Supreme Court by a 6–3 vote in 1984, the pinpoint theory was upheld; the Court decided that Title IX coverage was "program-specific" and applied only to federally funded activities.[64] Justice Sandra Day O'Connor, the only women on the Court, concurred in Justice Powell's observation that the case presented an "unedifying example of overzealousness on the part of the Federal Government" in its broad interpretation of Title IX. Yet Congress itself intended a broad view. The Court acted in spite of a resolution, passed by a 414–8 vote by the House of Representatives in November 1983, which expressed the sense of the House that Title IX should be given broad scope, and in spite of a brief given to it by forty-nine senators stating that the purpose of Title IX was to "prohibit gender discrimination in all aspects of the American educational system."

As a result of the cases upholding the pinpoint theory, some liberal Democrats in Congress sponsored bills which would restore the status quo ante and extend the antidiscrimination coverage to all activities in all schools that accept any federal funds. Some conservative Republicans sponsored opposing measures, which would enact the pinpoint theory into law, eliminate coverage of college and university faculty members and employees, and exempt schools that receive only financial aid, loans, and scholarship funds. It would also remove from coverage all student clubs, athletic programs, claims of sexual harassment, health insurance and services, housing, financial aid, and dormitory hours, unless these involved federal funds.

Gender, race, and suspect classification. Since the *Brown* decision the federal courts have developed the concept of ***suspect classification:*** racial classifications put into a law or administrative regulation will be struck down as

---

WOMEN AND THE DRAFT

Women have never been subject to draft registration. As volunteers they are explicitly barred by law from certain military occupations and from combat. These provisions have been defended as beneficial examples of "protective legislation." But women's rights groups have opposed all gender-based laws—not just those which burden them, but those which "protect" them as well.

The Military Selective Service Act provides that only men are to register for the draft on their eighteenth birthday. When President Carter asked Congress in 1980 to revive his authority to order registration, he requested it to amend the law to provide for registration of women. Congress refused to do so, and only men were covered under the law.

The resumption of registration requirements revived a long-dormant court case, *Rostker v. Goldberg*, 101 S. Ct. 2646 (1984), which had been initiated by men challenging the "men only" draft law. The Supreme Court decided that in military matters it must pay special deference to the competence of the political branches. In this case it would defer to Congress, which, under Article I of the Constitution, raises the armed forces. Justice Rehnquist, writing for the majority, argued that such deference took precedence over the ordinary standards which the Court otherwise used in equal protection cases.

Justices Thurgood Marshall, William Brennan, and Byron White argued in dissent that many groups not used in combat are still required to register, such as the handicapped and conscientious objectors. If a draft were to be instituted, women would have many noncombat roles to fill. Since no rational basis had been shown for the exclusion of women, the Court should have struck the classification down.

---

suspect on their face, unless the government shows a compelling rationale for the law, a burden of proof which is usually impossible to meet. This rule is the opposite of *presumptive rationality*, which places the burden of proof on the plaintiff to show that the state had no rational reason for its classification.

CASE-BY-CASE LITIGATION. The courts do not view gender as a suspect classification in the same way they view race. They do not automatically strike down such classifications. Provisions are examined on a case-by-case basis, and the courts uphold some and strike down others. In 1971, in *Reed v. Reed*, the Supreme Court decided that an Idaho law which gave men preference over women in administering the estates of deceased relatives was unconstitutional.[65] In 1975, *Frontiero v. Richardson*, it decided that a federal law which gave the wives of servicemen certain benefits automatically but which provided that the husbands of servicewomen would have to pass a "needs" test was unconstitutional.[66] The federal courts have ruled that widows and widowers should receive equal social security benefits, that men and women in private retirement plans who make equal contributions should receive the same benefits and have the same rights to sue for alimony, that the drinking age must be the same for both sexes, that men must be admitted to state-supported nursing schools, and that unwed fathers have the same rights as unwed mothers in adoption proceedings.

But the Supreme Court has sustained state laws which grant certain tax benefits to widows but not to widowers, which permit men but not women to serve as guards in maximum-security prisons, and which allow single-sex schools. It has upheld laws permitting women who have retired to calculate their earning years for social security benefits differently from the way men do.

THE RULE OF STRICT SCRUTINY. The courts apply the rule of *strict scrutiny* in deciding gender classification cases—a middle ground which places the burden of proof on the government to demonstrate that gender classifications serve important government objectives. The Supreme Court has held that gender classifications are constitutional only when they are "substantially related" to the achievement of "important governmental objectives," making it more difficult for a state to win its case.[67] The Court has warned that protective laws would be reviewed and would not be saved if they simply reflected the "baggage of sexual stereotypes" about the "weaker sex."[68]

The courts often deal with laws that are *facially neutral*: laws which make no mention of gender and do not classify by sex but which have a different impact on men and women. For example, Massachusetts provides that veterans of the Vietnamese war be given preference for state jobs. Since most of these veterans are men, this has a gender impact. The Supreme Court upheld the provision, however, arguing that it was not intended to discriminate against women. The Court held that *discriminatory intention* and not mere *differential impact* was necessary for a provision of state law to be held unconstitutional in such cases.

ISSUE AND DEBATE

THE EQUAL RIGHTS AMENDMENT.   ***The background.*** In 1972 Congress passed a proposed Equal Rights Amendment to the Constitution (known as the *ERA*), which would provide that "equality for rights under the law shall not be denied or abridged by the United States or by any State on account of sex." If the amendment were approved, Congress could enforce it by appropriate legislation, and the courts could apply their judicial and equitable powers to it, just as they do with the Fourteenth Amendment. The purpose of the ERA is to make gender a suspect classification, much as the Fourteenth Amendment does for race. It would end case-by-case litigation and substitute a rule by which laws that make distinctions based on gender could be held unconstitutional.

The ERA has been favored by both political parties (although the Republicans turned against it in their 1980 and 1984 platforms), by most Democrats in Congress and many moderate and liberal Republicans, by the Women's Political Caucus, and by a coalition of women's rights groups, minorities' rights groups, labor groups, and liberal organizations. Opponents of the ERA consist of conservative women's organizations, right-wing political groups, some business lobbyists, and the fundamentalist religious groups, organized in the Stop ERA coalition. Opponents favored some of the protective laws, such as the provisions which would keep women out of the military draft and out of combat. Many of the groups fighting against abortion, pornography, and school busing and for prayer in schools opposed the ERA as part of an overall "profamily" orientation. The anti-ERA coalition defeated the first attempt at ratification. Thirty-eight states were required to ratify the amendment by 1982, and only thirty-five did so; of these, six later rescinded their actions, leaving the whole issue of state ratification under a constitutional cloud (it was not clear whether a state could rescind its actions).

The pros and cons. Opponents of the ERA favored some of the protective legislation, which they claimed encouraged women to stay at home and raise families. Some opponents charged that it would break up family life, force women to work, legalize homosexual marriages, and require single-sex dormito-

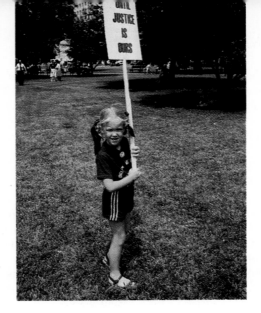

The civil rights agenda still has unfinished business. (*Shepard Sherbell: Picture Group.*)

ries, athletic teams, and bathrooms—even though supporters argued that it would do nothing of the kind. Opponents said that women were already protected by state and federal laws in the workplace and did not need the amendment.

Supporters pointed to the experience of sixteen states which already had provisions comparable to those of the ERA in their own state constitutions. Such provisions do not affect any law, practice, or action that is protected by the Ninth Amendment zone of privacy. These involve bathrooms, changing rooms, dormitory facilities, and the like. The ERA *would* affect state and national laws containing gender classifications, including those which provide opportunities or benefits for only one sex, place restrictions or regulations on only one sex, or base age differentials (such as for drinking or driving) on sex. States which had passed legislation resembling the ERA, for example, had repealed laws providing scholarships for men only at state colleges (Massachusetts), laws preventing young women from attending prestigious high schools (such as Central High School in Philadelphia), and laws assigning ownership of all household goods to the husband in a divorce proceeding (Virginia). A two-year transition period between ratification by the states and the effective date of the amendment would minimize any disruptions. Approximately 500 federal and countless state laws would have to be rewritten, should the amendment pass, according to its supporters, who claimed that these laws showed the need for sweeping constitutional change.

Public opinion versus state legislative action. Supporters of the ERA won the battle for public opinion, with a large majority of the public in favor of the proposed amendment and with support increasing between 1975 and 1981. At the time of its defeat, a July 1981 Gallup poll showed that 63 percent of the people, men and women equally, favored the ERA and only 32 percent opposed it. It won majority support from Republicans as well as from Democrats and from those who identified themselves as conservatives as well as from self-identified liberals. States in which the overwhelming majority of the population live had ratified the amendment, but slightly more than one-fourth of the states, representing a tiny fraction of the population, were able to block it.

Other activities. Whether the ERA becomes part of the Constitution or not, the fight for its passage has already had an important effect on women's rights. Pro-ERA groups have concentrated on putting similar provisions into state constitu-

tions, electing women to state office, suing in state courts corporations which have discriminated, and taking advantage of the activism in state courts in eliminating gender-based laws. At both the national and state levels, greater efforts have been made to identify gender-based laws and work for their repeal. Republicans who came out against the ERA in order to avoid antagonizing the conservative coalition found that they could build a women's rights record for their constituents by working to repeal specific gender-based laws. In 1976 a review of federal laws indicated that as many as 3000 sections of the United States Code contain some form of gender bias, but by 1983 there were only an estimated 175 gender-based provisions in federal laws, according to an internal memorandum prepared by the Reagan administration. Nevertheless, the struggle to incorporate the ERA into the Constitution was not yet over, as supporters vowed to win passage of the amendment again in Congress.

IN CONCLUSION

American society has moved away from racial segregation and gender discrimination and toward a color-blind national Constitution. Racial segregation has been outlawed in education, public accommodations, and housing. Racial and gender discrimination in education and employment have also become illegal.

Nevertheless, our legal and judicial protections have not yet put an end to discrimination. Women, for example—even women whose education and job qualifications are the same as, or better than, those of men—earn less than men in comparable or less important positions. It is still difficult for blacks to find adequate housing in integrated neighborhoods without triggering white flight.

Civil rights battles have moved from an emphasis on ending legal discrimination to an emphasis on encouraging schools and employers to make affirmative action efforts. Nevertheless, the concept of affirmative action remains controversial, with a large majority of whites and the top officials in the Reagan Justice Department opposed to it. The women's movement has concentrated on ratification of the Equal Rights Amendment, which failed to pass the necessary three-fourths of the state legislatures in 1981, and on comparable-worth programs, which are opposed by most trade and craft unions, private employers, state and local government officials, and the Justice Department because of the high costs involved in raising women's salaries. Given the current conservative lineup on the Supreme Court and in the lower federal courts, it is not likely that comparable worth will survive judicial scrutiny.

There seems to be a consensus that discrimination is an evil that must be uprooted from American life, but no consensus has yet formed on how best to achieve this goal.

NOTES

1. *Newsweek on Campus*, March 1983, p. 6.
2. William Coleman, "Statement," Subcommittee on Constitutional Rights, Senate Committee on the Judiciary, June 11, 1982, p. 21.
3. Thomas Sowell, "Weber and Bakke and the Presuppositions of 'Affirmative Action,'" *Wayne Law Review*, vol. 26, no. 4, 1980, p. 1336; "The Civil Rights Industry's Misguided Ideas about Blacks," The *Washington Post National Weekly Edition*, Aug. 20, 1984, p. 24.
4. *Bolling v. Sharpe*, 347 U.S. 497 (1954).
5. *The Slaughterhouse Cases*, 16 Wallace 36 (1873).
6. *The Civil Rights Cases*, 109 U.S. 3 (1883).

7. Henry J. Abraham, *Freedom and the Court*, Oxford University Press, New York, 1970, p. 551.
8. *Plessy v. Ferguson*, 163 U.S. 537 (1896), p. 559.
9. *Missouri ex. rel. Gaines v. Canada*, 305 U.S. 337 (1938).
10. *Sweatt v. Painter*, 339 U.S. 629 (1950), p. 634.
11. Abraham, op. cit., p. 367.
12. *McLaurin v. Oklahoma State Regents*, 339 U.S. 637 (1950).
13. *Brown v. Board of Education of Topeka*, 347 U.S. 483 (1954), p. 494.
14. Ibid., p. 495.
15. *Griffin v. Prince Edward County School Board*, 377 U.S. 218 (1964).
16. *Green v. County School Board of New Kent County*, 391 U.S. 430 (1968).
17. *Washington v. Davis*, 426 U.S. 229 (1976); *Keyes v. School District No. 1, Denver*, 413 U.S. 921 (1975).
18. *Dayton Board of Education v. Brickman*, 443 U.S. 526 (1979).
19. *Columbus Board of Education v. Pernick*, 443 U.S. 449 (1979).
20. *Milliken v. Bradley*, 418 U.S. 717 (1974).
21. *Evans v. Buchanan*, 423 U.S. 963 (1975).
22. *Regents of the University of California v. Bakke*, 438 U.S. 265 (1978).
23. *Swann v. Charlotte Mecklenburg*, 402 U.S. 1 (1971).
24. 42 U.S.C. sec. 2000c-B.
25. *Congressional Quarterly Almanac*, Congressional Quarterly Press, Washington, D.C., 1967, p. 802.
26. *The New York Times*, May 19, 1982; *Three Cities That Are Making Desegregation Work*, National Education Association, Washington, D.C., 1984.
27. *Milliken v. Bradley*, 418 U.S. 717 (1975).
28. Reginald Stewart, "Schools Try to Attract Whites by Easing Integration Efforts," *The New York Times*, June 21, 1982.
29. Milton Coleman, "Race Relations: Uncle Sam Has Stopped Running Interference for Blacks," *The Washington Post National Weekly Edition*, Dec. 19, 1983.
30. *Crawford v. Board of Education*, 458 U.S. 527 (1982); *Washington v. Seattle*, 458 U.S. 457 (1982).
31. *Reitman v. Mulkay*, 387 U.S. 369 (1967).
32. *Hunter v. Erickson*, 393 U.S. 385 (1969).
33. Jesse Jackson, "It's Not the Bus, It's Us!" *The New York Times*, Mar. 8, 1982.
34. Ibid., citing research conducted by Nancy L. Arnez, chairman of the Department of Community Services, Howard University, Washington, D.C.
35. *Educational Researcher*, April 1982.
36. *Atlanta Motel v. United States*, 379 U.S. 241 (1964).
37. *Buchanan v. Warley*, 245 U.S. 60 (1917).
38. *Shelley v. Kraemer*, 334 U.S. 1 (1948).
39. *Jones v. Mayer*, 392 U.S. 409 (1968).
40. *Daniel v. Paul*, 395 U.S. 298 (1969); *Shape Spa for Health and Beauty, Inc. v. Rousseve*, 44 L.W. 3359 (1976).
41. *Runyon V. McCrary*, 44 L.W. 5034 (1976).
42. *Regents of the University of California v. Bakke*, 438 U.S. 265 (1978).
43. Coleman, op. cit., p. 25.
44. Sowell, op. cit.
45. *Gallup Opinion Index*, report 143, June 1977, p. 23.
46. *The New York Times*, Aug. 12, 1980, p. B-6.
47. *Regents of the University of California v. Bakke*, 438 U.S. 265 (1978).
48. *The New York Times*, Nov. 16, 1981.
49. U.S. Commission on Civil Rights, Annual Report, 1984, GPO, Washington, D.C., 1985.
50. *American Tobacco v. Patterson*, 456 U.S. 63 (1982); *Firefighters v. Stotts*, no. 82-206, June 12, 1984.
51. *United Steelworkers of America v. Weber*, 443 U.S. 193 (1979).

52. *Ibid.*, p. 207.
53. *Ibid.*, p. 222.
54. *Fullilove v. Klutznick*, 100 S. Ct. 2758 (1980).
55. *The New York Times*, June 18, 1983.
56. *Bradwell v. Illinois*, 83 U.S. 130 (1872).
57. *Muller v. Oregon*, 208 U.S. 412 (1908).
58. *Goesaert v. Cleary, U.S. (1948).*
59. *Hoyt v. Florida*, 368 U.S. 57 (1961).
60. *Time*, July 12, 1982.
61. *The New York Times*, Nov. 17, 1984, p. 15.
62. *Washington County, Oregon v. Gunther*, 452 U.S. 161 (1981).
63. *Zipes v. TWA*, 455 U.S. 385 (1982).
64. *Grove City v. Bell*, 104 S. Ct. 1211 (1984).
65. *Reed v. Reed*, 404 U.S. 71 (1971).
66. *Frontiero v. Richardson*, 411 U.S. 677 (1973).
67. *Craig v. Boren*, 429 U.S. 190 (1976), p. 197.
68. *Orr v. Orr*, 99 S. Ct. 1102 (1979); *Califano v. Westcott*, 99 S. Ct. 2655 (1979).

FURTHER READING

Dunbar, Leslie (ed.): *Minority Report*, Random House, New York, 1984. A book about the way government policies have affected minority groups in the last five years.

Dworkin, Ronald: *Taking Rights Seriously*, Harvard University Press, Cambridge, Mass., 1977. The case for affirmative action.

Flexner, Eleanor: *Century of Struggle*, Harvard University Press, Cambridge, Mass., 1959. An account of women's attempt to gain suffrage and the 100 years it took them to do so in the United States.

Glazer, Nathan: *Affirmative Discrimination*, Basic Books, New York, 1975. The case against affirmative action.

Hamilton, Charles V., and Stokely Carmichael: *Black Power*, Random House, New York, 1967. A treatment of the theoretical underpinnings of the black movement in the late 1960s.

Hufstedler, Shirley M.: *Women and the Law*, Aspen Institute, New York, 1977. A study of women's constitutional and legal rights.

King, Donald B., and Charles W. Quick: *Legal Aspects of the Civil Rights Movement*, Wayne State University Press, Detroit, 1965. A collection of articles about the constitutional law of civil rights.

King, Martin Luther: *Why We Can't Wait*, Signet Books, New York, 1964. The Nobel prizewinning civil rights leader discusses the reasons why he led marches of blacks in the south against segregated facilities.

Logan, Rayford: *The Betrayal of the Negro*, Collier, New York, 1954. A historian's account of the legal and constitutional subjugation of blacks in the aftermath of the Civil War.

Mill, Harriet Taylor, and John Stuart Mill: *Essays on Sex Equality*, University of Chicago Press, Chicago, 1970. Nineteenth-century arguments for the emancipation of women.

Miller, Loren: *The Petitioners*, World Publishing, Cleveland, 1966. A history of civil rights cases brought before the federal courts.

President's Advisory Committee for Women: *Voices for Women*, GPO, Washington, D.C., 1980. A report by the committee on the status of women, together with recommendations.

Sowell, Thomas: *Civil Rights: Rhetoric or Reality?* Morrow, New York, 1984. A study of the case against affirmative action by a black conservative economist.

Tanner, Leslie B.: *Voices from Women's Liberation*, New American Library, New York, 1970. Articles on the woman's movement in the 1960s.

Vose, Clement: *Caucasians Only*, University of California Press, Berkeley, 1967. A study of the NAACP Legal Defense Fund and the case that ended racial convenants in housing.

Warren, Robert Penn: *Segregation*, Vintage Books, New York, 1956. Conversations about segregation with southerners of all viewpoints, in the aftermath of the *Brown* case.

Woodward, C. Vann: *The Strange Career of Jim Crow*, 2d rev. ed., Oxford University Press, New York, 1966. An account of the southern segregation ordinances and the reasons why they were instituted.

THE STUDY BREAK

Baldwin, James: *Another Country*, Dial Press, New York, 1962. A fictional but harrowingly realistic account of the lives of blacks in New York City.

Malcolm X: *The Autobiography of Malcolm X*, Grove Press, New York, 1965. The autobiography of an important black nationalist leader.

USEFUL SOURCES

Civil Rights Directory, 1981, U.S. Commission on Civil Rights, Washington, D.C., 1981. The last of a set of volumes listing the most important civil rights organizations at the national and state levels.

Civil Rights Quarterly, U.S. Commission on Civil Rights. Federal government policies are described.

Civil Rights Research Review, Center for National Policy Review. Articles, often critical of government policies.

Nelson, Barbara J.: *American Women and Politics: A Selected Bibliography and Resource Guide*, Garland Publishing, New York, 1983. A useful bibliography.

Ploski, Harry A., and James Williams (eds.): *The Negro Almanac: A Reference Work on the Afro-American*, Wiley, New York, 1983. Articles and statistical information.

U.S. Bureau of the Census: *American Women: Three Decades of Change*, Special Demographic Analysis CDS-80-8, August 1983, Washington, D.C. Social and economic data.

Williams, James D. (ed.): *The State of Black America*, National Urban League, New York, annually. A compendium of articles containing economic and social statistics.

ORGANIZATIONS

Citizen's Commission on Civil Rights. Catholic University Law School, 620 Michigan Avenue, N.E., 20064. Washington, D.C. For more information phone 202-832-8525.

Department of Education, Office for Civil Rights. 400 Maryland Avenue, S.W., Washington, D.C. 20202. For more information phone 202-245-3192.

Department of Housing and Urban Development, Office of Fair Housing and Equal Opportunity. 451 Seventh Street, S.W., Washington, D.C. 20410. For more information phone 202-655-4000.

Department of Justice, Civil Rights Division. Tenth Street and Pennsylvania Avenue, N.W., Washington, D.C. 20530. For more information phone 202-633-4224.

Department of Labor, Office of Federal Contracts Compliance Programs. 200 Constitution Avenue, N.W., Washington, D.C. 20210. For more information phone 202-523-9475.

Equal Employment Opportunity Commission. 2401 E Street, N.W., Washington, D.C. 20506. For more information phone 202-655-4000.

Joint Center for Political Studies. 1426 H Street, N.W., Suite 926, Washington, D.C. 20005. For more information phone 202-638-4477.

Mexican American Legal Defense Fund, Inc. 28 Geary Street, 6th Floor, San Francisco, Calif. For more information phone 415-981-5800.

NAACP Legal Defense Fund, Inc., 99 Hudson Street, New York, N.Y. 10013. For more information telephone 212-219-1900.

National Organization of Women, NOW National Action Center. 425 Thirteenth Street, N.W., Suite 1048, Washington, D.C. 20004. For more information phone 202-347-2279.

NOW Legal Defense Education Fund. 132 West 43 Street, New York, N.Y. 10036. For more information phone 212-354-1225.

U.S. Commission on Civil Rights. 1121 Vermont Avenue, N.W., Washington, D.C. 20425. For more information phone 202-376-8177.

Women's Equity Action League, Educational and Legal Defense Fund. 805 Fifteenth Street, N.W., Suite 822, Washington, D.C. 20005. For more information phone 202-638-1961.

THE WORLD'S CONSTABLE.

CHAPTER 18

FOREIGN AFFAIRS: THE MAKING OF AMERICAN DIPLOMACY

From Theodore Roosevelt's Nobel Peace Prize for his mediation of the 1905 Russo-Japanese War to Jimmy Carter's delight at the success of his Camp David talks between Israel and Egypt, presidents have long been shapers of American diplomacy. (*Granger Collection; AP Laserphoto.*)

The United States is a military and economic superpower. For what ends, and by what means, should we use our power? This chapter examines ideas about the means and ends of foreign policy, as well as the competition between the diplomatic, the military, and the intelligence communities to control foreign policy. We will consider presidential-congressional relations, focusing on the most important decision that any nation can make—whether to go to war.

WHAT ARE FOREIGN AFFAIRS?

Foreign affairs involve all our relations with other nations: diplomatic, economic, cultural, scientific, and military. Modern advances in transportation and communications have made us a "global village," with no neat division between domestic policy and foreign policy. The latter involves more than the diplomacy of the State Department—it consists of the impact on other nations of all our programs, whether run by the Agriculture Department, the Commerce Department, or the Treasury Department. Much of our foreign policy involves bilateral or multilateral agreements between American and foreign scientific, educational, cultural, and economic agencies.

People-to-people relations

The right of foreigners to visit the United States—to study, work, lecture, receive medical care, or immigrate here—is controlled by American consular authorities located in foreign nations. Our right to travel abroad (and restrictions on our travel, such as those involving Cuba), is regulated by the State Department as well as by the consular authorities of other nations. The Commerce Department and other agencies handle export licensing and other business regulations.

Economic relations

Our corporations do business around the world. Exports now account for almost one-fifth of the gross national product, and each additional $1 billion in exports creates 40,000 jobs. We want open access to foreign markets in exchange for foreign companies' access to our domestic markets. We may also want high tariffs or voluntary "orderly marketing" agreements to restrict imports of meat, shoes, steel, radios, televisions, and automobiles, for example. Our steel, aerospace, arms, and chemical industries must compete with companies owned by foreign governments, some of which sell at below-market prices to maintain high employment. Our companies want protection from unfair trade practices.[1]

We want a favorable investment climate so that our companies can invest in other nations, and we oppose regimes which nationalize investments. We try to protect the patents and copyrights of our companies. For national security reasons we may wish to restrict the export of some of our advanced technology, which puts us in conflict with western European allies who use such items as our semiconductor chips, advanced computers, and telecommunications equipment in their products. We try to convince Belgium not to sell a

nuclear power plant to Libya or computer-controlled lathes to the Soviet Union, for example, and we ask West Germany to provide adequate safeguards in the nuclear plants that it sells in Latin America.

Diplomatic alliances

We enter into collective security alliances such as NATO (which links western Europe with the United States and Canada), the Rio Pact (a nonaggression pact between nations in the western hemisphere), and ANZUS (which links us to Australia and New Zealand). We sign bilateral pacts with other nations, such as the Philippines and Japan. These provide our military with bases, monitoring posts, and refueling stations. (See Figure 18-1.)

Covert actions

We may try to overthrow unfriendly governments (Iran in 1953 and Guatemala in 1954), assassinate their leaders (Cuba's Fidel Castro in the 1960s), bribe their politicians or subsidize political parties in their elections (Italy, Chile, South Vietnam, and El Salvador), or influence the climate of opinion by indirectly financing newspapers and other media.[2] We may employ mercenaries, aid one side in a civil war (Afghanistan), or sabotage facilities and mine harbors (Nicaragua).

Decisions about peace and war

The ultimate foreign policy decision is whether to go to war. When other nations are at war, should we join in or declare our neutrality? These were important issues in the 1790s (leading to a naval war with France); in 1812, when we went to war against Great Britain to preserve freedom of the seas (and

Figure 18-1. The cornerstone of American foreign policy is the Atlantic alliance (NATO) which provides collective security against aggression for the United States, Canada, Iceland, Norway, the United Kingdom, the Netherlands, Belgium, Luxembourg, West Germany, Italy, Portugal, Spain, and Turkey. France is a member of the alliance but has withdrawn its forces from the NATO military structure. Greece is also a member but does not participate in certain NATO military exercises involving Turkey. The United States participates with Latin American nations in the Rio collective security pact and with Australia and New Zealand in the ANZUS Pact; it maintains bilateral defense agreements with several other nations, including the Philippines, Japan, and South Korea.

tried to take Canada); in the two world wars, when we joined the Allies against Germany; and in the undeclared wars in Korea and Vietnam. If we do not go to war, we may decide to "tilt" on the side of one of the belligerents, as we did in 1967 and 1973, when Israel fought Arab nations; in 1971, when we supported Pakistan against India; and in 1982, when we supported Great Britain against Argentina in the Falklands war. We may attempt to mediate foreign disputes, as Theodore Roosevelt did between Russia and Japan (for which he won the Nobel peace prize), or even guarantee accords between other nations, as Jimmy Carter did with the Camp David peace accords between Israel and Egypt.

PERSPECTIVES ON FOREIGN POLICY

Our diplomacy is inconsistent. We sometimes export democracy or act as a police officer for the world. We sign collective security pacts, but sometimes we act like the Lone Ranger—free to do anything without consulting our allies. We see ourselves as the richest nation in the world, an economic superpower that can show other nations how to manage their economies, and yet we behave like a local merchant, fearful of the competition. Our strategic allies may be our economic adversaries, as when we compete with Japan or western Europe, while our strategic adversaries are sometimes our business clients, as when we invest in eastern Europe and finance Soviet grain deals and factories or conclude oil deals with Libya and Angola. Sometimes we intervene in the affairs of other nations for noble principles—to uphold international law and strengthen democratic regimes or repel aggression—and at other times we intervene to maintain special advantages for United States corporations, toppling regimes which would deny these favors or propping up those which grant them. We shift in ways which leave our allies and adversaries puzzled over our intentions and skeptical about the strength of our commitments. Often our leadership lacks authority in international affairs.

Don Wright, The Miami News, Tribune Company Syndicate. Reprinted by permission: Tribune Media Services, Inc.

The Food for Peace program moved supplies and personnel into Marxist Ethiopia in 1985 to alleviate a famine affecting millions. (*M. Phillipot: Sygma.*)

Idealism versus realism

Historically, we have believed that ours was an "exceptional" nation, part of a "new world" free from the power politics of Europe. Our nation is a democracy. We believe in progress, in the perfectibility of humankind, and in the possibility of ending hunger, disease, and poverty. Our *idealism* has led us to try to export our political practices and beliefs to other countries. We act in foreign affairs, according to President Wilson, "to make the world safe for democracy." In World War II we fought for the "four freedoms" of the Atlantic Charter proclaimed by President Roosevelt and Prime Minister Churchill. Today we prod the dictators who rule other countries to hold elections, and we insist that they improve their human rights records.

Realism downplays the notion that the United States is unique and therefore can become a standard by which to judge other nations or a model that can be exported to help other people rule themselves. Every nation must find its own way on the basis of its own traditions. We must take the world for what it is, rather than try to make it over into our image. Instead of trying to make the world safe for democracy, we should concentrate on trying to make it safe— period! We must "see the world as it really is and not as we would like it to be," says the deputy secretary of state, Kenneth Dam; we have "to recognize that not everyone plays by our rules; to accept that defense of the national interests can require unpleasant choices."[3] This may mean allying with a repressive and dictatorial regime, however much this offends our ideals, if it adds to our national security.

Idealism suggests that allying with repressive regimes is a shortsighted, unrealistic policy. After all, consider what happened when the Greek colonels, the Libyan king, the shah of Iran, and the Somoza family in Nicaragua were overthrown; the regimes that took over were anti-American. In the long run, an approach based on democratic values may be more likely to win allies and ensure our security.

In practice, American diplomacy is often a blend of realism and idealism. Ronald Reagan portrays Soviet leaders as evil, arguing that "they reserve unto themselves the right to commit any crime, to lie, to cheat . . . and [they believe] that is moral, not immoral, and we operate on a different set of standards."[4]

621

But in spite of this idealistic comparison between us and the Soviets, the president sends Vice President Bush to Moscow to work for détente after the death of Andropov, knowing that is good election-year politics, and he meets with Gromyko, the former Soviet foreign minister. Grain embargoes are lifted. The president calls for new arms negotiations with the Soviets. The State Department promotes a policy of "differentiation" in eastern Europe, maintaining cordial ties with Romania and Hungary and improving relations with East Germany.

Isolationism versus interventionism

The attack on Pearl Harbor in 1941 led the United States after the war to enter into a global network of collective security alliances to ward off future aggression and extend American influence in Europe, Latin America, the middle east, and Asia. (*Department of Defense.*)

George Washington, in his farewell address to the nation, urged Americans to avoid "entangling alliances" by remaining friendly with all nations but allied with none. We would influence other nations by example rather than by alliance.[5]

Isolationism was the dominant mood in the aftermath of the First World War. The United States Senate defeated the Treaty of Versailles, which would have enabled the US to join the League of Nations. We also refused to join the World Court. Congress passed neutrality laws so that we would never again enter a European war. While Congress remained paralyzed and fearful of reprisals from isolationists, President Roosevelt, even before Pearl Harbor, prepared for war and made his own commitments to the Allies fighting against the Nazis. Because in hindsight (after Pearl Harbor) war with the Axis powers seemed to have been inevitable, the isolationists were completely discredited. Congress agreed that the United States could no longer stand apart from the world. Then an era of American *interventionism* began. As Harry Truman put it at the end of the war, the United States would have to "take the lead in running the world the way that the world ought to be run."

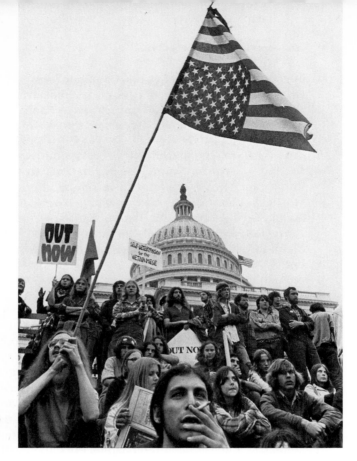

The failure of the Vietnamese war left many Americans reluctant to use military force to accomplish diplomatic ends. (*Roland Freeman: Magnum.*)

The Pearl Harbor paradigm. Postwar American policy was based on the Pearl Harbor paradigm (a *paradigm* is the way professionals in any field think the world works; it involves their assumptions about reality).[6] This paradigm involved the following assumptions: Totalitarian nations are bent on expansion, even if it means war; the only way to deter aggression is by a show of strength; appeasing dictators only encourages them; and containment may induce them to change their behavior.[7] "We shall pay any price, bear any burden, meet any hardship, support any friend, oppose any foe," President Kennedy pledged in his inaugural address in 1961, "in order to assure the survival and the success of liberty."[8] But the costly Korean and Vietnamese wars proved that we would have to make hard choices as to what prices we would pay and what burdens we would bear.

The post-Vietnam paradigm. By the late 1960s critics of the Vietnamese war had developed a paradigm which emphasized the limits of American military and economic power and the need to conserve that power for vital interests. Walter Lippman argued that the essence of wise statecraft was to keep commitments and power in balance, with a reserve left over for emergencies. The new paradigm saw communism as divided internally and split into many different and often warring camps: we should not attempt to police the world, and we should not use military force to prevent other nations from going communist. Many of these critics were pragmatists: the Vietnamese war cost more than $200 billion, left the economy a shambles and with runaway inflation, left 50,000 dead and more than 200,000 wounded, and in the end resulted

623

in communist regimes in Laos, Cambodia, and Vietnam. Such interventions in areas remote from our vital national interests were simply not worth the price. They diverted the United States from its more important defense interests, delayed modernization of our armed forces, and convulsed American society.

Nationalism versus internationalism

Nationalism is the principle that one's nation comes first. It sees foreign relations as a zero-sum game between nations: to the extent that we win something, others must lose, and conversely, if others win something, then we lose. The goal of our foreign policy must be to outmaneuver other nations or to use our power in such a way that we win more than we lose.

Internationalism involves the idea that we can make agreements in which everyone gains something (efficiency negotiations) or which involve constructive exchanges (in which a nation that gets something is willing to compensate the nation that gave it up). When the nations of the Common Market dropped their tariffs, they all gained because the volume of trade increased and the prices of consumer goods were lowered. Similarly, as the United States lowered its tariffs on a reciprocal basis from 30 percent to an average of 6 percent between 1930 and 1980, its economy grew enormously—and so did the economies of its trading partners.

But with an annual trade deficit approaching $150 billion, it is hard for members of Congress to explain to their constituents, some of whom have lost manufacturing jobs, why they should vote for foreign aid that might create new industrial jobs in other nations. Nationalists argue that the funds should be spent on job-training and public works programs in the United States. They argue that international tariff agreements just mean trouble for us, since they allow other nations to send their cheap imports to this country and since American workers and American manufacturers cannot compete with foreign labor and with products that are subsidized by foreign governments. They want high tariffs, import quotas, antidumping laws, and laws requiring foreign manufacturers to build plants in the United States, hire American workers, or put a specified "domestic content" in their products.

Internationalists argue that every country should use capital and labor most efficiently. More capital will be available for modernizing and competing on world markets. Thus internationalists believe that there should be no (or low) tariffs among nations or any other artificial barriers against trade or investment. Our tariff and marketing policies should be designed to open up other nations on a reciprocal basis, rather than protect our own inefficient industries.

But nationalists remain unconvinced. What happens if some nations do not play by the rules—if they do not import goods that would compete with goods produced by their own industries, while taking advantage of other countries that impose no barriers? The response of the internationalists is that a nation which cheats is only hurting itself: it protects its inefficient and noncompetitive industries, makes it difficult for its more efficient industries to obtain needed capital and labor, and therefore raises the prices in its own markets, which hurts its own consumers.

AMERICAN FOREIGN POLICY

The struggle over foreign policy goals is paralleled by what Edward Corwin once described as the constitutional "invitation to struggle for the privilege of directing American foreign policy."[9]

The constitutional dimensions

Presidential powers. "Politically, the President is the leader of the nation," argued Dean Acheson, Truman's secretary of state, adding: "Constitutionally he is the director of American foreign policy."[10] Acheson's argument rests on few specific provisions of the Constitution. Article II gives the president the duty to receive representatives of foreign nations, a function which might be considered purely ceremonial, although presidents combine it with their power to appoint ambassadors (with the advice and consent of the Senate) in order to create a recognition power. Because presidents appoint ambassadors and receive foreign ambassadors, they claim that they are the "sole organ of the federal government in the field of international relations." As the Supreme Court put it in *United States v. Curtiss Wright*, "The President alone has the power to speak or listen as a representative of the nation."[11]

CHIEF DIPLOMAT. Presidents take this claim one step further, arguing that the clauses of Article II—especially those involving the executive power, the oath of office, the title of commander in chief, and the duty to faithfully execute the laws (including treaties made under the authority of the United States)—can be taken, in the aggregate, to give them all the powers of the nation in foreign affairs except those specifically assigned to Congress. They may do in foreign affairs anything that the general welfare of the nation requires, subject only to express constitutional limits. Presidents argue that one branch must make policy and that it is up to Congress to legitimize what they do.

TREATY POWERS. Presidents may negotiate and conclude treaties—agreements by which states commit themselves to take certain actions or assume certain obligations—with one or more foreign nations for the purpose of collective security or international cooperation. They may ask members of Congress to participate in a delegation or allow influential senators to "nominate" or "veto" negotiators. Treaties are submitted by presidents to the Senate for its advice and consent. If presidents refuse to submit the draft of a treaty,

American presidents participate annually in an "economic summit" of the heads of the seven most industrialized nations of the west, such as this London meeting in 1984, chaired by the British prime minister, Margaret Thatcher. (*J. L. Atlan: Sygma.*)

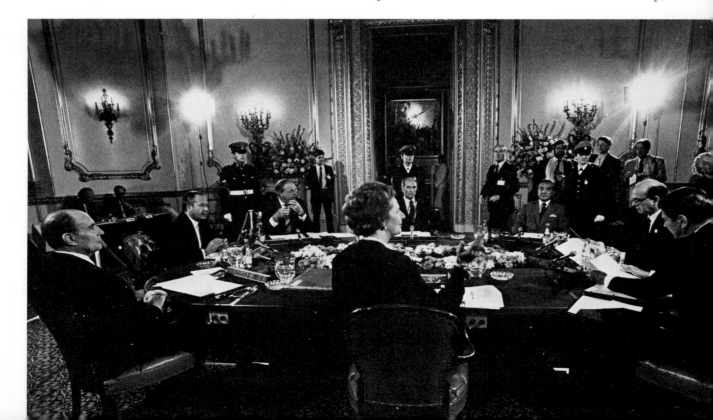

the Senate may pass a nonbinding resolution requesting them to do so, as it did in 1982 when it asked President Reagan to submit two arms control treaties negotiated with the Soviet Union which had never been ratified. The Senate approves treaties by a two-thirds vote of the members present. This is no formality; important treaties—such as the arbitration treaties of the early 1900s, the Treaty of Versailles in 1919, the genocide convention of 1950, and the SALT II treaty in 1979—have been either defeated or stalled. Secretary of State John Hay once remarked that "a treaty entering the Senate is like a bull going into the arena; no one can say just how or when the blow will fall—but one thing is certain—it will never leave the arena alive."[12] Alternatively, the Senate may *amend* a draft, changing its wording, which means that it must be resubmitted to other parties for approval; it may write *reservations*, whereby the United States limits its obligations; and it may state its *understandings*, which interpret provisions. Although the House does not have a role in the approval of a treaty itself, it usually must pass legislation that implements or funds some of the treaty's provisions. Important legislators are often consulted by the United States government and foreign governments while the negotiations are going on to see what they will accept.

Once the Senate approves a treaty, it is the president who decides whether to put it into force by ratifying it (that is, exchanging the signed treaty document with the other nation).

COMMITMENT POWERS. Presidents often negotiate executive agreements with foreign heads of government; these need not be sent to the Senate for approval. Theodore Roosevelt once negotiated a treaty with Santo Domingo which the Senate refused to approve; he then put it into effect as an executive agreement, informing the outraged senators that if they ever consented to the treaty, he would ratify it and put the same provisions into effect as a treaty! Franklin Roosevelt concluded an agreement in 1940 to swap naval bases for fifty destroyers that Britain needed, a deal which cemented an alliance against Nazi Germany. Several arms control agreements with the Soviet Union have involved executive agreements, as did the resolution of the Iranian hostage crisis.

Congress has not challenged the right of the president to conclude such agreements, and several times it has defeated bills that would require the president to obtain congressional approval for them. The Case Amendment of 1972 provides that all such agreements must be submitted by the president to Congress within sixty days (except in the case of a secret agreement, which can be submitted to the House Foreign Affairs Committee and the Senate Foreign Relations Committee under an injunction of secrecy). About 200 such agreements are submitted each year.

Presidents can make other commitments. They may exchange letters with the heads of other governments, giving them assurances of our backing. They may issue, along with the heads of other governments, a simultaneous declaration of their intent to take certain action—known as a *parallel unilateral policy declaration* (PUPD)—which commits them to actions in the absence of a treaty or an executive agreement. Such declarations have been used by the United States and the Soviet Union for the SALT II arms control agreement, never consented to by the United States Senate.

Congressional powers. Congressional foreign affairs powers involve the reg-

ulation of foreign commerce, tariffs, immigration, and naturalization. Congress raises military forces, regulates their conduct, and declares war. It creates and funds the departments that deal with military, diplomatic, and intelligence matters. The Senate advises on, and consents to, presidential appointments. By a two-thirds vote the Senate advises on, and consents to, treaties made by the president.

LIMITING PRESIDENTIAL COMMITMENT POWERS. Congress need not honor national commitments that it has had no hand in making. In 1967 it amended the foreign aid bill to state that economic or military aid to another nation "shall not be construed as creating a new commitment . . . to use Armed Forces of the United States for the defense of any foreign country." In 1969 the Senate passed the national commitments resolution, which specified that only treaties or commitments made pursuant to legislation would be considered *national* commitments. As part of the 1975 Sinai disengagement agreement, the United States promised to consult with Israel if the Soviet Union threatened it, using language similar to that used in treaty commitments. But when it appropriated the funds for an American observer force to monitor the pullback, Congress stated that it did not regard this administration promise as a national commitment.

Congress is most powerful when it is most obstructive—when it limits presidential commitments rather than making its own. It ended American warmaking in Indochina by passing the Eagleton Amendment in 1973, ended funding for covert actions in the Angolan civil war by passing the Clark Amendment in 1975, and, with the Symington Amendment of 1976, prohibited shipment of nuclear fuel to nations that detonate nuclear weapons. The Boland Amendment of 1982 makes it illegal for the American government to fund covert activities designed to overthrow the Sandinista government in Nicaragua, and Congress has voted four times to cut off funding for the "Contra" faction in the Nicaraguan civil war, inhibiting the administration's policy.

CONGRESSIONAL COMMITMENT POWERS. Congress often collaborates with the president in making foreign commitments. It passes laws to implement treaties. It provides foreign aid, such as aid to Greece and Turkey in 1947, which was instrumental in preventing the Soviets from destabilizing regimes in the eastern Mediterranean, and the Marshall Plan, which was the key to western Europe's economic recovery after World War II. It funds peacekeeping missions, such as that of the 1200 American soldiers in the Sinai police force who monitor the treaty between Israel and Egypt. By joint resolution Congress often supports the president, especially in crises. Such resolutions backed Truman when the Soviets blockaded West Berlin in 1949; Eisenhower in 1955, during a confrontation between the nationalist Chinese government on Taiwan and the communist Chinese government on the mainland, and in 1958, when he sent 20,000 marines to Lebanon to ensure the stability of a pro-western government; and Johnson in 1964, when the government claimed that North Vietnamese gunboats had attacked American ships in the Gulf of Tonkin.

Congress sometimes makes its own commitments to foreign nations. By providing foreign economic and military aid at levels above those suggested by the president, it can create a de facto alliance with another nation, such as Israel. The government on Taiwan, although no longer recognized by the United States, is still "recognized" by Congress, which in laws refers to that regime as the "Republic of China." Congress can "tilt" toward one side in a

dispute, even if the president wishes to remain neutral or tilt the other way. After Turkey invaded Cyprus and established its military government on one-third of the island, Congress cut off all aid to Turkey in spite of White House opposition. (Eventually the aid was resumed.)

Members of Congress can unofficially negotiate with leaders of foreign governments. They have sometimes gained concessions from the Soviet Union on Jewish emigration. They have won pledges from other governments to crack down on drug growers and smugglers and to improve the living conditions of Americans held in their prisons.

The foreign policy communities

Within the executive branch there are fundamental differences about the means as well as the ends of foreign policy. Faced with an unfriendly action by another nation, the instinct of the diplomat is to talk, the instinct of the military officer is to threaten to use force; and the instinct of the intelligence agent is to use covert action.

The president and the National Security Council. The president may use the *National Security Council* (NSC), which was established in 1947, to make foreign policy. The statutory members of the council are the president, who chairs its meetings; the vice president; the secretary of state; and the secretary of defense. Meetings are also usually attended by invitees, including the president's adviser for national security affairs (who also directs the council staff), the chair of the Joint Chiefs of Staff, and the director of central intelligence.

The council has no powers of its own. When presidents make decisions, they do so under their constitutional authority or under the authority delegated to them by Congress. The council takes no votes and makes no decisions. Most presidents use the council in the same way they use the Cabinet. With the exception of President Eisenhower, who took the meetings seriously, NSC sessions are convened for the purpose of symbolism (for example, a White House announcement that the president is meeting with the council to discuss a crucial situation).

Presidents rely on their informal groups. John Kennedy used the "ex com," a small group of important officials and former government servants whom he trusted to deliberate in crises. Lyndon Johnson relied on the "Tuesday lunch" group. Richard Nixon held private meetings with the national security adviser, Henry Kissinger; sometimes they were referred to as the "two-man band." Ronald Reagan uses the National Security Planning Group, consisting of the members of the NSC, the director of central intelligence, the national security adviser, and (in his first term) three top White House political aides.

The national security assistant. The assistant to the president for national security affairs briefs the president on issues and options, prepares the staff work for NSC meetings, manages the flow of paperwork and briefing papers, communicates presidential decisions to officials and oversees their implementation, and acts as an "honest broker" when different agencies get into turf disputes. The more powerful assistants dominate policy-making by advocating their own policies, conducting crucial negotiations (such as in arms control and the middle east), organizing NSC committees to formulate options for the president, and implementing the president's decisions.

President Ford consults with his national security adviser, Henry Kissinger. (*Henri Bureau: Sygma.*)

Other presidential advisers. Presidents may also assign lower-level officials to serve as their personal envoys in dealing with foreign governments, the so-called back channels. They may even use private citizens as go-betweens to communicate unofficially with foreign leaders. They may rely on the "wise men," officials in previous administrations, to brief them on issues, as Reagan did when he called in Ford, Nixon, and Kissinger before meeting with Gromyko, the Soviet foreign minister.

The Department of State and the diplomatic community. The diplomatic community consists of the Department of State (the oldest government department and one of the smallest), presidential envoys and emmissaries, delegations to international arms talks and other talks, and agencies nominally affiliated with the Department of State, such as the Arms Control and Disarmament Agency, the Agency for International Development (which administers our foreign aid program), and the International Communications Agency (which sends American cultural programs abroad and broadcasts foreign news on the Voice of America). The State Department runs the embassies, staffed by its Foreign Service officers, who are responsible for routine negotiations with other nations and who coordinate negotiations between other United States departments and foreign governments.

The State Department is organized partly by geography and partly by function. Handling diplomatic affairs and proposing new policies are officials at the 150 or so country desks, which in turn are grouped by region (western Europe and southern Africa, for example) under the supervision of assistant secretaries. There are also bureaus for policy planning, intelligence, military assistance programs, and political-military affairs.

These agencies do not always coordinate their policies or their programs, either with one another or with the Treasury Department, the Commerce Department, or the Agriculture Department, each of which also has important

foreign policy interests, such as the Agriculture Department's food for peace program. The State Department is only nominally in charge of the "country team" of United States officials in other lands, and rarely can it control what they do in their negotiations; this is especially true of officials in the Defense Department and the Central Intelligence Agency.

Presidents seem to like it this way; they often prefer to see agencies clash with the State Department, and they help the process along by putting in people who are White House loyalists rather than subordinates to the secretary of state. The secretary of state serves as the spokesperson for American foreign policy, but becomes a trusted adviser in the White House only by gaining the confidence of the president. That way the White House can always choose between policies proposed by the State Department and those proposed by other departments or the national security advisor.

The CIA and the intelligence community. The Central Intelligence Agency (CIA) is responsible for coordinating the work of all agencies in the intelligence community, since its director is also the director of central intelligence, briefs the president, and prepares the national intelligence estimates for the government. CIA research analysts estimate the military intentions and capabilities of other nations. The CIA also sends agents abroad to obtain information from foreign informants. More important than any cloak-and-dagger operations are the data gathered from our spy satellites and the "elints" (electronic intelligence) gathered by the National Security Agency (NSA), which can eavesdrop on telephone, telex, cable, radio, and television communications anywhere on earth. The Federal Bureau of Investigation (FBI) is responsible for counterintelligence operations. The State Department has its own Bureau of Intelligence, and the Defense Department relies on the Defense Intelligence Agency, plus military intelligence units in each service, for its assessments. Differing estimates are produced by these agencies, and it is up to the director of central intelligence to present summaries of these estimates, plus the director's own recommendations, to the president.

Even covert operations can be publicly scrutinized. William Casey, director of the CIA, goes to Capitol Hill to deny CIA authorship of an assassination manual distributed in Nicaragua. (*AP Laserphoto.*)

The intelligence community conducts covert operations against unfriendly governments and their leaders. The CIA makes its recommendations for particular actions to the National Security Council, and they require presidential approval. In 1974 Congress passed the Hughes-Ryan Amendment, which provided that no covert actions could be initiated until the president reported to eight congressional committees, with the understanding that operations would not take place if the committees objected. In 1980 Congress amended the law, and at present the CIA reports only to the House and Senate intelligence committees.

The CIA is usually not a "rogue elephant," operating outside presidential and congressional controls. Since the new systems were instituted in the 1970s, the CIA has usually mounted covert operations only after fully briefing the president and important members of Congress, who at one point stopped a plan to overthrow the leftist government in Suriname. But in 1984 members of the Senate committee claimed that they had not been briefed on the CIA's mining of Nicaraguan harbors, and the House committee said that it had not been given information on the CIA's interference in the elections in El Salvador. The Senate overwhelmingly passed a resolution demanding that the mining be stopped (which the administration complied with), and later in the year Congress passed an intelligence budget containing no money for the "Contras." On the other hand, these committees have fully supported the CIA's aid to rebels in Afghanistan, at times proposing more funding than the administration recommended.

The armed forces and the defense community. The United States uses the military to make foreign policy: there were twenty-five military interventions in Central America between 1900 and 1930, and there were 215 uses of force for political purposes between 1946 and 1975 alone![13] Such uses of the military include holding maneuvers offshore with a large fleet (as we do periodically in the Gulf of Sidra near Libya, the eastern Mediterranean near Syria, the Persian Gulf near Iran, and the Caribbean near Nicaragua); flying reconnaissance mis-

Drawing by Lorenz; © 1981 The New Yorker Magazine, Inc.

"As I see it, our commitment to the peace process is only credible if our commitment to the war process is credible."

Much of the improvement in relations between the United States and the People's Republic of China has been predicated on the perception of a common Soviet military threat. Defense Secretary Weinberger observes Chinese military exercises. (*Wide World.*)

sions and sending military units or airplanes to neighboring nations (which we did as a signal to Libya after it invaded Chad in 1983); and quarantining another nation with our fleet (as we did in Cuba in 1962 to force the Soviet Union to remove the offensive missiles that it had placed there). We can use force to weaken or topple a foreign government or to protect our allies from attack. Our counterterrorist forces, supervised by the Pentagon's Joint Special Operations Agency, conduct hostage rescues and protect facilities and diplomats against state-sponsored terrorists.

Our military delegations negotiate with allies (even communist regimes such as Yugoslavia and China) and offer them military aid, including training and technical assistance, and credits for arms purchases (El Salvador and Honduras). We share bases with them and repair their facilities and hospitals (Oman). We conduct joint maneuvers with their forces (Egypt and Jordan), fly reconnaissance missions for them (Saudi Arabia), and even airlift their forces into battle (Zaire). We station United States forces in other countries as a "trip wire" to deter aggression (West Germany). Our military officials conclude agreements with their counterparts in foreign countries, as Secretary of Defense Weinberger did in 1982 with a memorandum of strategic cooperation between United States and Israeli forces and in 1984 with an agreement to help the Israelis produce the Lavie fighter, and as our Navy has done with Venezuela and Colombia in patrolling the Caribbean.

"Military diplomacy" is conducted by the secretary of defense, the deputy and assistant secretaries in the Pentagon, the service secretaries, and the Joint Chiefs of Staff. By and large, the military community has been cautious in recommending use of American combat forces. Many officials counseled against sending United States troops to Vietnam because they did not want to fight a limited Korea-style war in Asia a second time. The military initially opposed the invasion of Grenada in 1983. It was reluctant to intervene in Lebanon in 1983 and pressured the administration to take the Marines out. It has been cautious in its recommendations for Central America. It opposed the State Department's proposals in 1984 for immediate retaliation against middle eastern terrorists. "Hell no, we won't go" seems to be the chiefs' motto. They

are adamantly opposed to sending United States forces into dangerous situations as a "signal" or "presence" to bolster our diplomacy, fearing high casualties in a no-win situation. Nevertheless, presidents have often used the armed forces to send signals in crises. During the 1985 hostage crisis in Lebanon (when a TWA flight was hijacked to Beirut), naval warships, tactical air wings, and combat brigades were sent to the eastern Mediterranean as a warning to the Shiites and their Syrian protectors that the Reagan administration would take reprisals unless the hostages were released.

Interest groups and issue networks. The debates over the means and ends of foreign policy are spurred on by the think tanks in Washington, such as the Institute for Policy Studies, the Brookings Institution, the American Enterprise Institute, and the Heritage Foundation. Just as with domestic policies, the "in-and-outers" who move from academic, media, or research positions often come back into government when party control of the White House changes.

Foreign governments also have access to American public officials and to issue networks that are developing new policies. Their embassies and missions in the United Nations are in frequent contact with officials, and their prime ministers and foreign ministers may come to Washington for consultation. Foreign governments may hire their own lobbyists (who must register with the government as "foreign agents" if they try to get changes in laws). These organizations include many public relations and communications concerns (such as Gray and Company for Canada, Argentina, Japan, Haiti, Turkey, and Korea), law firms (such as Arnold and Porter for Israel and Dutton and Dutton for Saudi Arabia), and even former representatives, senators, and White House officials (such as former senator Richard Stone for China and the former White House aide John Sears for South Africa).[14]

American interest groups and PACs traditionally have been concerned more with domestic affairs than with foreign affairs, but as the two have become fused, they have stepped up their attempts to influence foreign policy. Trade associations and corporate lobbyists pressure Congress for subsidies for exports, protection against imports, and favorable tax treatment of foreign profits. Religious and ethnic groups try to "tilt" American foreign policy: blacks with regard to apartheid in South Africa and the famines in sub-Saharan Africa, American Jews and Arabs with regard to the Arab-Israeli conflicts, and Greek Americans with regard to the disputes over Cyprus. The activities of interest groups involve making campaign contributions, testifying before congressional committees, trying to influence presidential agencies and the departments, and attempting to influence public opinion. They ally themselves with the issue networks whose policy proposals are most favorable.

CLOSE-UP

JEANE KIRKPATRICK. Jeane Kirkpatrick, a former American ambassador to the United Nations, is part of a neoconservative issue network that has great influence on American foreign policy. Born in 1926 in Oklahoma, the daughter of an oil wildcatter, she graduated from Barnard College in 1948, received a master's and a doctorate in political science from Columbia University, and became a professor at Georgetown University. Kirkpatrick is part of a "new consensus," which she says "stands above all for a restoration of American military strength and the legitimacy of America playing an active role in foreign affairs."[15] Kirkpatrick used

Jeane Kirkpatrick. (*Charles Steiner: Picture Group.*)

to describe herself as a "Hubert Humphrey–Henry Jackson Democrat," adding: "I am a Democrat because I have been a Democrat all my life, but that doesn't mean that I always agree with my party."[16] In 1972 she helped found the Coalition for a Democratic Majority, which was made up of Democrats who were opposed to the antiwar, dovish platform of their party in that election year. Kirkpatrick's outspoken criticism of Carter's foreign policy culminated in an article published in 1979 in *Commentary* (a neoconservative magazine published by the American Jewish Committee), in which she criticized the "very odd" policies of that administration. She argued that Carter behaved "not like a man who abhors autocrats, but like one who abhors only right-wing autocrats."[17] She believed that the lesson of the Vietnamese war was that we could not impose our democratic standards on other nations and that "it should also have taught us the dangers of trying to be world's midwife to democracy when the birth is scheduled to take place under the conditions of guerilla war."[18] She denounced the Carter administration's acceptance of the Sandinista regime in Nicaragua.

As a result of this article and her subsequent meeting with President Reagan, she was appointed United States ambasador to the United Nations. Her hard line and tough style led her into many confrontations with third world nations at the United Nations. "A posture of continuous self-abasement and apology vis-à-vis the Third World is neither morally necessary nor politically appropriate," she says.[19] Critics have charged that her academic style is better suited to a classroom than to a political forum and that she has a tendency to lecture representatives of other nations rather than discuss differences with them. Nevertheless, she was an effective promoter of the administration's policies, until her resignation in 1985. In 1985 she switched to the Republican party, fueling speculation that she might become a presidential or (more likely) vice presidential contender in 1988.[20]

Managing foreign policy

The president must decide among policy options and then must choose the organizations to carry them out. The struggle over the content of foreign policy is therefore paralleled by bureaucratic conflicts.

Turf wars. The president presides over agencies with competing missions and overlapping jurisdictions. Who, for example, should handle arms negotiations—the president's adviser for national security affairs or the secretary of state? Who should supervise arms sales—the State Department or the Defense Department? Should foreign trade be handled by the Commerce Department, the State Department, or the president's special representative for trade negotiations? Should food aid be handled by the Agriculture Department, the State Department, or the Agency for International Development? Almost every facet of our foreign policy involves more than one agency and more than one policy option.

The State Department versus the NSC. "The real organization of government at higher echelons is not what you find in textbooks or organization charts," says Dean Rusk, the secretary of state in the Kennedy and Johnson administrations; "it is how confidence flows down from the President."[21] Often presidents have more confidence in their advisers than in the secretary of state. They may choose the secretary to handle the routine affairs of the department while they make the policy. The crucial turf war involves the secre-

tary of state versus the national security adviser: Kissinger versus Secretary of State Rogers in the Nixon administration, Brzezinski versus secretaries Vance and Muskie in the Carter administration, and Allen versus Secretary of State Haig in the first term of the Reagan administration. Who develops the policy options for the president—State Department planning staff or the NSC staff? Who communicates with foreign governments—State Department officials or the adviser? Can the adviser remain an advocate of specific positions and still perform the important role of briefing the president, and, if so, can the secretary see the president to press a case? Who coordinates and oversees policies which are made by the president?

According to Brzezinski, the best system would be if "the definition of the strategic direction would originate from [the] assistant for National Security Affairs, who would then tightly coordinate and control the Secretary of State, the Secretary of Defense, the Chairman of the Joint Chiefs, and the Director of Central Intelligence as a team, with them knowing that he was doing so on the President's behalf."[22] When officials—including Secretary of State Cyrus Vance—have been sent on diplomatic missions, sometimes their instructions have been written in the White House, and their speeches cleared and their cable traffic reviewed by the White House. Reagan's secretary of state Alexander Haig, in contrast, argued that the president's advisers should be "those officials who have undergone the confirmation process with the legislature," not NSC or White House staffers.[23] Even before he took office, he argued in a secret memorandum to Reagan that "the secretary of state [should] be your vicar to the community of departments having an interest in the several dimensions of foreign policy," adding that he should become the "single manager to present views and choices."[24]

Presidents may set up either a *State-centered* or an *NSC-centered* system. The former makes the secretary of state the key adviser and spokesperson and the negotiator with foreign governments, and it puts most operations under the State Department's control, as occurred when Harry Truman allowed Secretary of State George Marshall great latitude in developing policies for the postwar reconstruction of Europe in the 1940s. The latter approach is best exemplified by Henry Kissinger's activities during the Nixon administration. His NSC committees controlled the arms talks negotiations with the Soviets and intelligence briefings to the president. He negotiated the Paris peace accords, which ended American military combat in the Vietnamese war, and he was the presidential emissary to the People's Republic of China, laying the groundwork for Nixon's diplomacy. Crucial negotiations with the Soviets were carried on not by the State Department but through a ***back channel*** between Kissinger and the Soviet ambassador to the United States.

Presidents can set up a *White House-centered* system. Like Kennedy, Carter, and to some extent Reagan, they can parcel out assignments and make foreign policy officials de facto presidential assistants. Reagan sometimes plays off his NSC director against the State Department, and both of them against his secretary of defense and vice president. His political advisers balance off his national security advisers. He has different interdepartmental coordinating groups chaired by officials in the State Department and the Department of Defense and by the director of central intelligence; this divides responsibility, but provides him with multiple options. Reagan established the Kissinger Commission to recommend policy on Central America and the Scowcroft

President Reagan confers with Secretary of State George Schultz (left) and Vice President Bush. (*Wide World Photos.*)

Commission to do the same for MX missile basing, and he appointed a special presidential envoy to Central America and a succession of such envoys to the middle east.

The White House keeps control of crisis situations. Secretary of State Haig asked Reagan in 1981 for jurisdiction over crisis operations, but Reagan named Vice President George Bush to head his "crisis management team" in the absence of the president. Had Reagan wanted an NSC-centered operation, he could have resurrected the Washington Special Action Group established during the Nixon administration under Kissinger, or he could have allowed the State Department to handle matters.

Control of information. Information is power. At the heart of the conflict between the foreign policy communities, and between the president and Congress as well, is the struggle to control the flow of sensitive information about foreign policy.

EXECUTIVE BRANCH SECRECY. Congress has created some secrecy systems; these include military plans and nuclear secrets. Presidents, on their own authority (after consultation with the National Security Council), set up classification systems and restrict access to classified information to those officials who have security clearances. Approximately 7,000 officials have authority to classify documents, and their work is supervised by the Information Security Oversight Office, created in 1978 as part of the National Archives. More than 1.4 million documents are classified as "top secret," but more than 1 million officials have clearances. When even the White House menu is classified as "top secret," the result is a silly system that fails to guard any real secrets but simply creates impediments for officials, Congress, and the public in discussing foreign policy.

Presidents create "limited distribution" (LimDis) systems, which restrict information on a "need to know" basis to only a handful of top officials on any foreign policy issue on which a presidential decision is pending. Reagan's system is called *sensitive compartmentalized information* (SCI). The purpose of these systems is to keep other officials in the dark about pending policy: the president can freeze the Joint Chiefs of Staff out of deliberations for the next arms control proposals. The White House and the Defense Department might use a channel to keep the State Department from knowing about its next pro-

posal to sell arms abroad. The president might use the national security adviser to negotiate with the Soviets, establishing a back channel that bypasses the State Department.

Members of Congress may be given top-secret classifications (along with staffers), but this does not give them any access to SCI or LimDis systems. They may be given closed-door briefings based on such information by officials, but the ground rules then may keep them from disclosing this information.

EXECUTIVE AND DEPARTMENT PRIVILEGE. Presidents can keep information from Congress by invoking executive privilege: a claim that they need not disclose conversations or release material involving the confidential advice they receive from officials in the executive branch. The Supreme Court, in *United States v. Nixon*, limited this privilege to national security matters and has refused to require presidents to furnish such information to Congress. Corresponding to executive privilege is ***departmental privilege:*** sometimes officials in the State Department or the Defense Department simply disregard congressional requests for testimony or information, or committees are given summaries of sensitive documents instead of the originals. Data and documents may be delayed for months before being supplied to committees. Congress cannot require presidents or department officials to testify. About all it can do is negotiate with the important officials and establish some ground rules, which usually favor the administration.

MEDIA LEAKS. Issue networks and foreign policy communities can use copying machines and telephones to set forth their version of events to the media or to members of Congress. There is no way physically to stop information from being leaked. The White House tries to keep hostile leaks from getting out of hand. It may *wiretap* officials without their knowledge or put them under surveillance. Aides may be warned to break off conversations with certain reporters. *Lie detectors* may be used with all officials who have access to classified information. In 1983 President Reagan signed National Security Decision Directive 84, which gave top officials in all agencies the right to institute random testing of subordinates to ferret out those who were leaking information. But lie detectors can be beaten, while honest officials who are afraid of the test may show up as liars.[25] In 1984, just as Congress was about to pass a law prohibiting such tests, the administration withdrew its polygraph program.

CENSORSHIP. Officials may be required to sign lifetime agreements stating that they will submit all their future writings—including academic articles, books, op-ed articles, and even letters to editors—to government censors. This system was ordered in a national security decision directive issued by Reagan in March 1983. It covers more than 112,000 employees and another 15,000 contracted employees, including the president, the secretary of state, and all the important presidential aides. It also covers officials in the Defense Department, the CIA, the FBI, the NSA, the State Department, and the United States Information Agency. In 1983 more than 15,000 books, articles, and other writings by officials and former officials of the Defense Department were subject to clearance. This provision may prevent officials who resigned because of disagreements with foreign policy decisions from discussing their differences if they were based on classified information. Such prepublication clearance agreements have been used routinely for employees in the intelligence community for years and were upheld by the Supreme Court in *United States v. Snepp.*[26]

It is not clear whether the courts will enforce sweeping procedures which go well beyond CIA and NSA agreements that they have upheld in the past. George Ball, a former undersecretary of state, calls the Reagan order an "appalling document" which would "require the establishment of a censorship bureaucracy far larger than anything known in our national experience."[27]

NEWS MANAGEMENT. Presidents have always tried to manage the news. They "stroke" favored journalists with exclusive interviews. They call up network news executives after unfavorable stories appear and ask them for "balanced" coverage. During the Nixon administration an Office of Telecommunications Policy even made threats to television executives concerning license renewals. Officials in the Reagan administration have tried novel techniques of managing news coverage of foreign policy crises. During the invasion of Grenada they kept all reporters off the island for two days and removed the few who managed to sneak ashore. They distributed their own films and videotapes to the networks; these showed battle victories for the United States but no pictures of killed or wounded Americans. After the fighting ended, they escorted reporters on carefully supervised tours. The United States International Communications Agency did the same for foreign journalists. The columnist Hodding Carter said that "we were deliberately and systematically excluded from direct contact with what was happening, fed grossly distorted information and, if not lied to in the simplest meaning, regularly kept from the truth."[28] The media uproar caused the Pentagon to appoint a commission to draft new guidelines. Eventually the Pentagon named a panel of reporters who would cover future conflicts and "pool" their reports with those of their colleagues.

Presidents versus Congress

Presidential prerogatives. Presidents make and execute foreign policy. "I took the Canal Zone and let Congress debate," Theodore Roosevelt boasted at the turn of the century, and presidents have been acting in the same fashion ever since. Not only can they act on their own authority, but they also can interpret laws passed by Congress as they see fit. They have the widest possible latitude in faithfully executing the laws, because in a number of cases, such as in the Iranian hostage agreement, the Supreme Court has ruled that in foreign affairs presidents must retain great flexibility.[29] Presidents sometimes even dispense with the execution of the laws if they believe that it would harm relations with other nations (though when they do so, they always cite other laws or treaties as a justification). They may interpret treaties and execute them in ways not contemplated by the Senate when it gave its consent. They may unilaterally abrogate treaties, as Carter did with a mutual defense pact with Taiwan when he wished to establish diplomatic relations with communist China.

The role of Congress. Congress influences foreign policy through laws and appropriations. But it is at an extreme disadvantage because the legislative process is so cumbersome, a point first argued by John Jay in *The Federalist*, when he assigned most diplomatic powers to the executive because it was the only branch capable of "unity, secrecy, and dispatch." Congress is divided by party and decentralized through its committee and subcommittee structure. It has lots of chiefs, all with their own power base, and precious few Indians who are prepared to follow them. It is subject to pressure by interest groups who care about their own concerns, not about the "big picture." It cannot keep

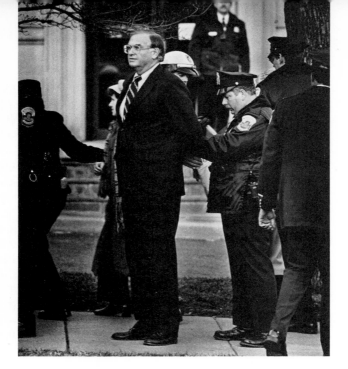

Senator Lowell Weicker of Connecticut makes a personal foreign policy statement about human rights by getting arrested at the South African Embassy in 1984. (*Harry Naltchayan: Washington Post.*)

secrets and is not trusted with vital information by the executive branch. Its laws and appropriations are subject to presidential veto, which means that unless it can rally support from an overwhelming majority of members, the president can usually defeat its challenges.

Yet in spite of all these disadvantages, Congress plays an important role in foreign policy-making. It sometimes negates the president's initiatives, as Woodrow Wilson found out when he was unable to get the Senate to consent to the Treaty of Versailles, as Carter found out when he was unable to get the SALT II treaties approved, and as Reagan found out when Congress pressured him to take the marines out of Lebanon. Congress often modifies White House initiatives, as when it reoriented the foreign aid program away from huge industrial projects and toward rural reconstruction and development. It attempts to set priorities or establish standards by which our foreign relations are to be conducted (for example, concern for human rights). Members may try to negotiate directly with foreign leaders and sometimes can "toughen up" our negotiations with other countries, as occurred with the negotiations over the Panama Canal treaty in 1978.

Congress may also legitimize the president's foreign policy initiatives. It sets goals, creates and funds organizations, and oversees programs. It serves as a barometer of public satisfaction or dissatisfaction with presidential policies. Presidents are well-advised either to persuade or to pressure Congress to back them, because if they do not, it means that they do not have public support, which in the long run is a prescription for disaster.

Presidential leadership of Congress. In domestic affairs presidents have difficulty leading Congress, but in foreign policy, as Aaron Wildavsky put it in the 1960s, "there has not been a single major issue on which Presidents, when they were serious and determined, have failed."[30] In recent years this "two-presidency" thesis has not held up completely. Not only did Congress put an end to American combat activities in Indochina in 1973, but in that same year

639

it passed, over President Nixon's veto, the war powers resolution, which was designed to regulate presidential warmaking. Congress put new curbs on the CIA's operations, reoriented the foreign aid program, and interfered with presidential trade negotiations. By the middle of the 1970s it seemed that presidential leadership of foreign policy was no more effective than presidential leadership of domestic policy.

But by the 1980s the two-presidency thesis seemed valid once again. The congressional embargo against Turkey was lifted, seeming to validate the president's criticisms. Covert operations have been approved by congressional committees as the president has wished. Initiatives in Lebanon, the Caribbean, and Central America have been funded in spite of doubts on the part of Congress. Presidents have controlled trade policy and fended off attempts in Congress to increase protections for American industry. The levels of military assistance and sales have jumped enormously.

PARTY POLITICS IN CONGRESS. Presidents try to create a bipartisan coalition of supporters. These are based on shifting coalitions: in defense matters, Reagan must put conservative Republicans and southern Democrats together with centrist Democrats; in trade matters, moderate Republicans may be combined with liberal Democrats; and in the case of foreign assistance bills, Reagan tries to keep Republicans in line by making it an issue of "supporting your president," while he relies on the Democratic leadership to come up with an equivalent number of supporters. Curiously, presidents often have the greatest difficulty with leaders of their own party. During Reagan's first term, for example, his failure to pursue arms negotiations with the Soviets was challenged by Charles Percy, then the chairman of the Senate Foreign Relations Committee; Percy and Howard Baker, then the majority leader, rounded up Republicans to support the invocation of the war powers resolution in the aftermath of the invasion of Grenada, a move that the White House opposed; and Senator Goldwater attacked the CIA for failing to brief Congress on covert operations in Nicaragua. Similarly, Carter found that important Democratic leaders, such as senators Henry Jackson and Sam Nunn, opposed his arms control policies. His Panama Canal treaties were modified by the Senate, with Robert Byrd, the majority leader, playing an important role. Johnson was opposed on his Vietnamese war policy in 1968 by the chairman of the Senate Foreign Relations Committee, William Fulbright.

Throughout American history the pattern has been the same: Adams was opposed by Federalist leaders in Congress who forced him into war with France; Jefferson's neutrality policy was opposed by his party's leaders; Madison was required to go to war with England because of party pressure; McKinley was unable to restrain the "imperial" faction within the Republican party; and Wilson was opposed by his party's leaders when he "tilted" toward the British before the United States entered the First World War.

PRESIDENTS, CONGRESS, AND THE PUBLIC. Presidents can make national agenda issues out of foreign policy. They can deliver major televised addresses or go before a joint session of Congress, as Reagan did the day before Congress was to vote on aid for El Salvador. They can announce doctrines, such as the Truman doctrine (the United States will give aid to nations to prevent them from being taken over by communists), the Nixon doctrine (the United States will help other nations help themselves in stopping aggression), and the Carter doctrine (the Persian Gulf is an area vital to our national interest). Presidents

President Kennedy hoped that committing American advisers would pressure the Soviet Union to halt communist advances in Laos and thus make American intervention elsewhere in Indochina unnecessary. (*Cornell Capa: Magnum.*)

can influence the "international agenda" by speaking at the United Nations or participating in economic or security summits. They can even influence the international agenda by using the Worldnet and Euronet communications systems, which were created by our government between 1984 and 1986 and which link Washington to most of our embassies; thus presidents (or more often the secretary of state) can hold two-way press conferences with reporters around the world.

Presidents often benefit from a "rally round the flag" effect; during a major national crisis, presidents' popularity and job approval ratings tends to climb—irrespective of how they are handling the crisis. After the Japanese attack on Pearl Harbor, Roosevelt's popularity rating rose 12 percent. In the midst of the Berlin blockade, Truman's job approval rating began a 25-point climb that culminated in his reelection. After Kennedy ordered the Bay of Pigs invasion in Cuba, his popularity rating increased by close to 10 points, even though the exiles failed in their efforts. When the American embassy in Iran was taken over in November 1979, Carter's job approval rating stood at 30 percent; thereafter it climbed sharply, and by December it stood at almost 60 percent. But presidential popularity ratings can decline sharply over foreign policy. Both Truman and Johnson slipped badly as casualties mounted in the second and third years of the Korean and Vietnamese wars. Some studies have also shown a sharp correlation between casualties in congressional districts and lessened support for a war by the representatives. The more hawkish the foreign policy, the more likely men and women are to split in their attitudes, with women providing less support. (See Figure 18-2, page 642.)

Codetermining foreign policy. Congress wants its interests in foreign policy accommodated. It seeks, not operational control, but rather consultation, collaboration, and cooperation. "Let us in on the takeoffs if you want us in on

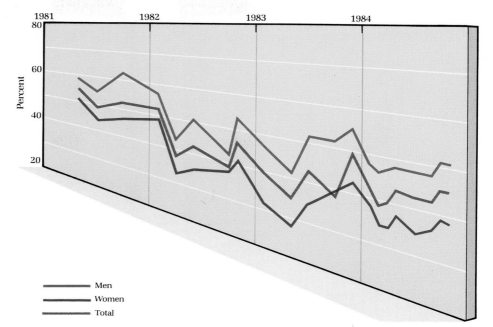

Figure 18-2. The foreign policy gender gap. Many public opinion polls have shown significant differences between men and women on foreign policy. Women are more likely to approve steps to negotiate, less likely to approve military actions, and less likely to approve of President Reagan's foreign policy. (Source: *The New York Times*, October 21, 1984.)

the crash landings," Senator Vandenberg advised Truman.[31] Every president and every secretary of state promise just such a relationship. "By partnership I do not mean occasional, retrospective reporting," Alexander Haig said at his confirmation hearings in 1981. "I mean active consultation, exchange of ideas and proposals in a timely manner, in an atmosphere of mutual trust and confidence."[32] But it does not work out that way. Presidents and their advisers put a curtain of secrecy around their plans. They give briefings on plans and decisions already made rather than consulting freely beforehand. They make crucial decisions by *faits accomplis*, and then allow Congress to play around with the lesser aspects: the exact amount of funding and the bureaucratic details.

COLLABORATION. For a collaborative relationship to exist, it would be necessary to reconstitute the process by which the government makes decisions. Information would have to be shared with Congress on a timely basis. Members of Congress and their staffs would have to have access to intelligence reports, military assessments, and cable traffic from agencies abroad. There would be real exchanges of views before decisions were made, instead of mere briefings or nominal and manipulative "consultation," with no weight given to the opinions of members of Congress.

Perhaps the most successful venture in collaborative decision making occurred in 1954, when President Eisenhower was under strong pressure within his administration to accede to a request by the French that we intervene militarily in Indochina. He called in congressional leaders to advise him, and they insisted that we not use military power unless we had the agreement of our other allies. Eisenhower decided to follow their recommendation, and this collaboration kept us out of war.[33]

CONGRESSIONAL OVERSIGHT. Congress focuses on the White House; on the top levels of the State Department, the Defense Department, and the CIA; and on the workings of the NSC staff. Committee staffers, outside consultants and

experts, and the Congressional Budget Office prepare detailed options on defense and foreign aid spending; the General Accounting Office also develops foreign aid and military assistance options and criticizes existing programs; the Office of Technology Assessment deals with the transfer of technology and scientific cooperation; and the Congressional Research Service prepares bills that develop new procedures for ensuring collaboration between committees and bureaucracies.

Congress has established several legal mechanisms, the purpose of which is to get presidents to consult with it before making final decisions. These include:

- *Restriction and certification.* Presidents may not take a particular action unless they certify to Congress that certain conditions exist. Presidents must certify that a nation is making progress in human rights in order for it to receive military aid from the United States.
- *Restriction and waiver.* Presidents may not act unless certain conditions exist, in which case they are permitted to waive the restriction. President Carter used a waiver to send military aid to southern Yemen, and President Reagan did the same for Saudi Arabia.
- *Report and wait.* Presidents must report to Congress and wait (usually thirty days) before acting. This gives Congress time to persuade presidents to change their course or to pass a law preventing them from implementing their decision.
- *Periodic reporting.* Presidents must report every six months or every year on an issue such as violations of human rights in nations that are receiving aid from the United States.

Until recently, Congress could also use the *legislative veto* to prevent presidents from implementing decisions in areas such as arms sales, the transfer of nuclear technology and fuel, foreign military assistance, construction of military bases overseas, famine relief, the stationing of American observers in the Sinai, tariffs, and contributions by the United States to international lending agencies. Although such vetoes were never actually employed, they did lead the administration to make substantial concessions to its critics in Congress. Consider the issue of arms sales, for example. Under the Nelson Amendment of 1976, sales over $25 million (this figure was later reduced to $7 million) were subject to the veto of both chambers. No arms deal was ever killed, but many were modified: a Hawk missile sale to Jordan in 1975 went through only after the missiles were designed for fixed rather than mobile sites (making them easier for Israel to destroy); the number of Maverick missiles sold to Saudi Arabia was cut from 1500 to 650; an AWACs sale to Iran was delayed and then canceled by the administration after the fall of the shah (luckily none of these planes ever wound up in the hands of the ayatollah); and a sale of jet planes to Israel, Egypt, and Saudi Arabia went through only after assurances that the Saudis would base them far away from Israel and after the Saudi planes were modified to pose less of an offensive threat. In 1983 the Supreme Court ruled these vetoes unconstitutional, greatly weakening the powers of Congress in foreign policy.

FOCUS

THE DECISION TO MAKE WAR. The Constitution grants Congress the power to declare war. Barring foreign aggression or invasion, which presidents may

repel on their own authority, the framers expected that the decisions about peace or war would be made by Congress. It has not worked out that way.

How we go to war. Of the more than 200 cases in which the armed forces have been used (half of them involving fighting for more than thirty days), only eight have involved declarations of war: the War of 1812, the Mexican-American War, the Spanish-American War, World War I, and World War II (with four declarations against various Axis nations). In other cases presidents have used the armed forces on their own authority: actions against pirates or bandits threatening commerce or against drug traffickers and smugglers; rescue missions involving the lives and property of Americans or of other nationals; the protection of our diplomats and other officials; the acquisition of territory (for example, the acquisitions of Florida, the southwest and California, Hawaii, the Philippines, and Puerto Rico); and intervention into the affairs of other nations, including temporarily running their affairs (the major incidents involved Haiti from 1915 to 1934, Nicaragua from 1912 to 1925, and Cuba from 1906 to 1909). We use force to occupy foreign territory at the invitation of the regime or a regional organization (Grenada in 1983), to support a regime against civil insurrection (military advisers in El Salvador in the 1980s and invasion of the Dominican Republic in 1965), and to support a regime against external aggression (Korea between 1950 and 1953 and South Vietnam from 1964 through 1973).

Presidential warmaking powers. Presidents claim that they can make war on their own authority. They argue that their power to see that the laws are faithfully executed gives them an "international police power" to see that other nations pay their debts, protect lives and property, and even (in the case of Grenada) abide by democratic rules of the game. The president is the executor of United States treaty commitments (which are part of the law of the land), and certain treaties require the United States to use the armed forces as part of guarantees of collective security. Presidents argue that they can unilaterally use the military to honor treaties and executive agreements and other presidential commitments. They argue that the oath of office, the duty to uphold the laws, the executive power in foreign relations, and the commander-in-chief clause, when fused together, result in the authority to make any decision for peace or war. In the age of nuclear warfare, when the credibility of our deterrent power and our ability to strike against an enemy with nuclear weapons are crucial factors in maintaining the "nuclear balance of terror," presidents argue that they must have the power to retaliate without waiting for Congress to act.

Controversies over presidential warmaking. Presidential warmaking may be opposed if it leads to protracted commitments, involves large expenditures and many casualties, and is unsuccessful. Presidents split their own party, which loses heavily in the midterm elections, and they run the risk of losing reelection. During both the Korean and the Vietnamese wars the incumbents decided not to run again because mounting casualties were associated with steep declines in their job approval ratings in the polls.

The legitimacy of presidential warmaking becomes an issue. "The President is usurping his power as commander-in-chief," warned Senator Robert Taft, a Republican, during the Korean war, adding: "If the President can intervene in Korea without congressional approval, he can go to war in Malaya or Indonesia or Iran or South America."[34]

If Congress wishes to oppose the president, it can do so in several ways. It can

revoke a joint resolution supporting the president's use of force, as it did in 1970 with the Tonkin Gulf Resolution. Congress did so in that instance because President Johnson had deceived it in 1964 when he asked Congress for a resolution backing his use of force in Vietnam, claiming that United States ships were in international waters and had been fired on without provocation. Subsequent Senate hearings revealed that the ships were in waters claimed by the North Vietnamese, close to a major South Vietnamese naval operation being mounted that day against North Vietnam, and that they were mistaken by the North Vietnamese for ships involved in that operation. Some of the "attacks" may not even have taken place; the sonar operator might have mistaken the sound of his own ship's propeller for the sound of an enemy torpedo![35]

Congress can also cut off appropriations for presidential warmaking. During the Vietnamese war, it barred troops from engaging in operations in Thailand and Laos with the Cooper Amendment (1969) and from taking action in Cambodia (after the 1970 invasion); finally, the 1973 Eagleton Amendment cut off funding for military operations anywhere in Indochina (and ended the bombing of Cambodia). But Congress took this action only after the Paris peace accords of January 1973 had already ended American combat in Vietnam. Usually Congress votes for appropriations requested by the president during a period of hostilities. It does so, in spite of any doubts, because most members do not want to be vulnerable to charges in an election year that they voted to deny "our boys on the front line" the funding needed to supply them with ammunition.

The war powers resolution of 1973. In 1973 Congress passed the war powers resolution over President Nixon's veto. The purpose of the resolution is to "insure that the collective judgment of both the Congress and the President will apply to the introduction of United States Armed Forces into hostilities" or situations in which "hostilities might be imminent." Presidential warmaking is to be restricted to situations in which Congress has declared war or has given specific statutory authorization or in the event of an attack on the United States, its territories or possessions, or its armed forces.[36]

In deciding to use the armed forces, the president "in every possible instance shall consult with Congress before introducing United States Armed Forces in hostilities." And after every such introduction, the president is to "consult regularly with the Congress until United States Armed Forces are no longer engaged in hostilities or have been removed from such situations."

The resolution requires the president to report to Congress if forces are introduced into hostilities or into situations in which hostilities are imminent. The first report is due within forty-eight hours of such introduction and is to indicate the circumstances in which the troops found themselves in the hostilities, the constitutional and statutory basis on which the president acted, and the estimated scope and duration of the involvement. Every six months the President is to submit a new report.

The report requirement triggers a *sixty-day clock:* at the end of sixty days the president must remove troops unless a declaration of war, a specific statutory authorization to continue, or an extension of the clock is obtained. Congress must go on record if it wishes to continue the war, but if it does not, it can sit on its hands, and after sixty days the president will have to withdraw. The onus is on the president and the president's supporters in Congress to get a positive action. Any time the president uses forces without a declaration of war or a specific statutory

authorization, the resolution states that Congress, by concurrent resolution (not subject to presidential veto), can order the president to withdraw the forces. The president then has thirty days to complete the withdrawal.

The war powers resolution is poorly drafted. The consultation provisions do not specify with whom the president should consult or when. Consultation is required not in all cases, but only if the president thinks that it is feasible, which is unlikely. Nor does the language define *consult*. Presidents have assumed that it means that they can brief members after the fact, not while a decision was pending on an issue. Although the president is required to submit a report within forty-eight hours, Congress cannot compel the president to do so. It is not clear whether Congress can start the sixty-day clock itself.

The resolution gives the president sixty days to obtain a declaration of war or some other form of congressional approval. "I cannot imagine a situation," argued Senator Frank Church, one of the leading critics of the Vietnamese war, "where the President would take us into a foreign war of major proportions under circumstances that would not cause both the public and Congress to rally around the flag for at least 60 days."[36]

But suppose that Congress backed the president by resolution in the early stages of the fighting. Could it later pass a concurrent resolution directing the president to withdraw forces? The way the law is drawn makes it seem that if Congress initially supports the president and authorizes hostilities, it loses its chance to veto the war later.

The resolution provides that Congress can direct a withdrawal by a concurrent resolution, not subject to the president's veto. In the aftermath of the Supreme Court decision in *Chadha v. INS,* which invalidated legislative vetoes, such a concurrent resolution might well be held unconstitutional by the Supreme Court.

The war over the war powers resolution. Presidents claim that the entire resolution is unconstitutional. They argue that it weakens the certainty of collective security arrangements; that it fails to cover important uses of force, such as the evacuation or protection of United States citizens in foreign countries; and that it poses the danger that an enemy might miscalculate what the United States would do in a crisis.

Presidents have no incentive to make the act work. On the contrary, they have every incentive to reduce its scope. President Ford ignored the resolution when he had to evacuate Americans, South Vietnamese, and citizens of other nations from Vietnam in 1975. American ships were sent into Vietnamese waters, troops were sent ashore, and some fighting occurred. Although United States forces were involved in hostilities or were in situations in which hostilities were imminent, Ford did not start the sixty-day clock. Instead, he sent Congress several short letters describing the introduction of forces, arguing that they had been sent for a peaceful evacuation, not combat.

The wisdom of ignoring the resolution can be challenged by examining the *Mayaguez* crisis. Just after Indochina fell to communist forces, the new government in Cambodia seized an American merchant ship, the *Mayaguez,* in international waters. It was taken to the island of Kho Tang. Ford demanded that the ship be released, but the message, relayed through Peking, was slow in getting to the new Cambodian rulers. Two days later, without consulting members of Congress in advance, Ford ordered United States planes to attack Cambodian patrol boats. The next day, again without advance consultation, the president ordered Marines

to rescue the crew on Kho Tang. The Marines stormed onto the wrong island, ran into an ambush, and suffered heavy casualties. Yet shortly before the operation was launched, the Cambodians had released the crew and had sent them across the border into Thailand! Had Ford taken the extra time to consult with members of Congress, the operation would have been delayed, the news of the crew's release would have reached Washington, and forty-one Marines might not have died or fifty have been wounded.

Carter did not use the war powers resolution as Congress had intended. He made no report when he sent four AWAC planes and ninety-six airmen to Saudi Arabia at the start of the Iran-Iraq war. When surveillance planes were sent over north Yemen, an action which might have draw hostile fire, the administration argued that the resolution did not apply because the planes were unarmed, a clear misreading of the law. When United States planes airlifted troops of other nations into Shaba province of Zaire in order to put down a rebellion against the central government, the administration said that no report was necessary because the planes did not land at the front lines—in spite of language in the law that clearly covers the transport of foreign troops into battle.

Before the attempted rescue of American hostages in Iran, the Senate Foreign Relations Committee sent President Carter a letter asking him to consult with Congress before an attempt was made. Secretary of State Vance had already pledged (at his confirmation hearing) that the administration would consult with Congress before committing United States forces to hostilities. Carter decided to take the military action without the consultation that Vance had promised, and Vance promptly resigned as a matter of honor.

Reagan and the war powers resolution. Reagan has ignored important provisions of the law, has delayed complying with others, and has narrowed the reach of the act.

Reagan sent fifty military advisers to assist in El Salvador. They were to be unarmed and were not to engage in combat. But advisers did accompany troops in the field, were seen by reporters carrying weapons, and entered areas that had recently been cleared of guerrillas. The administration refused to invoke the war powers resolution, claiming that it would apply only if the advisers had been *authorized* to accompany foreign troops in the field or enter a combat zone. This disregarded the approach taken in 1973 by the House Foreign Affairs Committee, which in passing the act defined *imminent hostilities* as situations in which "there is a reasonable expectation that American military personnel will be subjected to hostile fire."

The Reagan administration sent 6000 Marines and airborne troops into Grenada in 1983 with instructions to evacuate American medical students, eliminate all armed resistance to United States occupation, and prepare the way for the establishment of a new civilian government. The administration also claimed to be acting at the invitation of the Organization of Eastern Caribbean States, a regional security organization (though Grenada itself was not a member).

Reagan did not consult with Congress or obtain its approval beforehand. Two days after the invasion began, Reagan sent a letter to Congress, just meeting the forty-eight hour reporting deadline, but he did not even cite the resolution; he said merely that he was reporting in order to keep Congress informed. Moreover, Reagan did not start the sixty-day clock, although United States forces were involved in combat and there had been deaths and casualties.

In justifying the invasion overthrowing the Marxist government of Grenada, the United States stressed the invitation by a federation of eastern Caribbean island states. *(Woodfin Camp.)*

Congress then decided to invoke the resolution itself. The House voted 403–23, and the Senate 64–20, to start the clock. The majorities included senior Republican Party and committee leaders with responsibilities in foreign affairs. Reagan responded to this pressure by speeding up the timetable for the removal of troops to meet the sixty-day deadline, thus avoiding the necessity for a vote in Congress on the operation.

In September 1982 Reagan ordered 1200 Marines to Beirut at the invitation of the Lebanese government as part of a multinational force (British, French, Italian, and American) that was to help police the country. The Marines became a symbol of United States backing for the government, which soon embroiled them in internal Lebanese politics, because the government was opposed by a coalition of Muslim, Palestinian, and Druse forces, which were backed by the Syrians. The Marines were now a symbol of occupation and a target for those opposed to the Beirut government.

The Reagan administration did not make use of the consultation provisions of the war powers resolution. Its first report to Congress when the Marines arrived in Lebanon as part of the multinational force did not specify that they were in combat or in a situation involving imminent hostilities, because, as the administration argued, there was no intention that they would be involved in hostilities. For a year, while the Marines were subjected to snipings, bombings, land minings, and other attacks, Reagan made no further report. In August 1983, after the Marines came under intensive shelling from Druse forces, Reagan issued a report but made no effort to start the sixty-day clock. Congress decided to start the clock itself.

When Congress passed the Beirut resolution of 1983, invoking the war powers resolution, it gave the president the authority to keep the Marines in Lebanon for eighteen months, which would take Congress past the next election without the need for further action. Moreover, it did so in the form of a joint resolution,

648

subject to presidential veto. The precedent had been established that in the future, any time Congress wished to invoke the war powers resolution, it could do so only in a form subject to the president's veto power—which meant that the president could always act without reference to that resolution unless two-thirds of Congress (enough to override a presidential veto) were opposed. The Beirut resolution of 1983 also specified that Congress could direct a removal of troops in the future only by a joint resolution, again subject to a presidential veto—significantly weakening the war powers resolution as a check on presidential warmaking.

Reagan won a great public relations victory. He signed the Beirut resolution in a White House ceremony. He released a statement which said that Congress could not set any time limits on the president's use of forces or limit their deployment. He argued that "the initiation of isolated or infrequent acts of violence against United States Armed Forces does not necessarily constitute actual or imminent involvement in hostilities, even if casualties to those forces result." (This meant that attacks such as the bombing of the marine barracks at the Beirut airport, which resulted in the deaths of 240 Americans, would not be taken as a situation triggering the sixty-day clock.) Finally, Reagan insisted that by signing the resolution, with its provisions that Congress can direct the president to withdraw, he was not giving up any of his powers and that the resolution could not "be interpreted to revise the President's constitutional authority to deploy United States Armed Forces."[37] The president clearly signaled that he would regard the war powers resolution as a dead letter and would continue to take full responsibility for making decisions about war.

Because of the destruction of the American embassy in Beirut and the subsequent massacre at the Marine barracks there, President Reagan decided to end the American military presence in Lebanon. (*Bill Pierce: Sygma.*)

IN CONCLUSION

American foreign policy lacks a consensus about both the means and the ends of foreign policy. Idealism versus realism, isolationism versus interventionism, and nationalism versus internationalism—these disputes over ends remain. The diplomatic, intelligence, and military communities each have their own ways of influencing foreign affairs, and each seeks to manage events. The president must choose not only from among policies but also from among the organizations which carry out policies, which results in considerable jockeying for position among administration officials. The winners are those who gain and retain the confidence of the president.

The management of foreign affairs is complicated by a constitutional environment that invites the president and Congress to compete for power. Both the president and Congress have their own set of powers, and the powers of one often overlap or check those of the other. Presidents can dominate Congress by playing national agenda politics or horse trading for votes, but their efforts are often hampered by legislative leaders of their own party. They are least likely to retain public and party support when they engage in an unpopular war, though in times of other crises the public often "rallies round the flag." Congressional efforts to develop collaborative systems of policy-making have failed: the legislative veto systems have been ruled unconstitutional by the courts, and the war powers resolution has become almost a dead letter.

NOTES

1. Joseph Monson and Kenneth Waters, *Nationalized Companies*, McGraw-Hill, New York, 1983.
2. Christopher C. Pyle and Richard M. Pious, *Presidents, Congress and the Constitution*, Free Press, New York, 1984, chap. 7, pp. 378–379. Acts of assassination are contrary to the express policies of the United States government, according to Executive Order 12333 (1981), which states: "No person employed by or acting on behalf of the United States Government shall engage in, or conspire to engage in, assassination." The order also forbids our intelligence agencies from requesting outside groups to commit assassinations.
3. Kenneth Dam, speech to the American Jewish Committee, Stephen Wise dinner, Nov. 21, 1983.
4. *The New York Times*, Jan. 30, 1981, p. A-10.
5. Albert K. Weinberg, "The Historical Meaning of the American Doctrine of Isolation," *American Political Science Review*, vol. 34, no. 2, April 1940, p. 539.
6. Michael Roskin, "From Pearl Harbor to Vietnam: Shifting Generational Paradigms and Foreign Policy," *Political Science Quarterly*, vol. 89, no. 3, fall 1974, pp. 563–588.
7. George Kennen ("Mr. X"), "The Sources of Soviet Conduct," *Foreign Affairs*, vol. 25, no. 7, July 1947, pp. 556–583.
8. John F. Kennedy, inaugural address, 1961, reprinted in *The Inaugural Addresses of the Presidents of the United States*, GPO, Washington, D.C., 1965
9. Edward Corwin, *The Presidency: Office and Powers*, New York University Press, New York, 1940, p. 200.
10. Quoted in Ronald J. Stupak, *The Shaping of Foreign Policy*, Oddyssey, New York; 1969, p. 84.
11. *U.S. v. Curtiss Wright*, 299 U.S. 304 (1936).
12. Quoted in Thomas Franck and Edward Weisband, *Foreign Policymaking by Congress*, Oxford University Press, New York; 1979, p. 137.
13. Barry M. Blechman and Stephen S. Kaplan, "U.S. Military Forces as a Political Instrument since World War II," *Political Science Quarterly*, vol. 94, no. 2, summer 1979, p. 195.

14. Barbara Gamerakian, "Foreign Image-Making: It's a Job for the Experts," *The New York Times*, Oct. 14, 1984.

15. *The New York Times*, June 24, 1981, p. 11.

16. *The New York Times*, Dec. 23, 1980, p. 13.

17. Jeane Kirkpatrick, "Dictatorships and Double Standards," *Commentary*, 1979, p. 49.

18. Ibid., p. 34.

19. Ibid., p. 52.

20. Prepared with the assistance of Bernard Yee, Columbia College.

21. Quoted in Morton Halperin, *Bureaucratic Politics and Foreign Policy*, Brookings, Washington, D.C.; 1974, p. 219.

22. *The New York Times*, Jan. 6, 1982.

23. *The New York Times*, Mar. 25, 1981.

24. Memorandum of Jan. 6, 1981.

25. Chris Pyle, "Managing by Intimidation," *First Principles*, vol. 8, March—April 1983, p. 10.

26. *United States v. Snepp.* 444 U.S. 507 (1980).

27. *The Washington Post National Weekly Edition*, Nov. 7, 1983, p. 37.

28. *The Wall Street Journal*, Nov. 3, 1983, p. 31.

29. *United States v. Curtiss Wright*, 299 U.S. 304 (1936); *Dames and Moore v. Regan*, 452 U.S. 654 (1981).

30. Aaron Wildavsky, "The Two Presidencies," *Transaction*, vol. 4, no. 12, December 1966, pp. 7–14.

31. Quoted in James Sundquist, *The Decline and Resurgence of Congress*, Brookings, Washington, D.C., 1982, p. 300.

32. *The New York Times*, Mar. 4, 1983.

33. Chalmers Roberts, "The Day We Didn't Go to War," in Marvin E. Gettleman (ed.), *Vietnam: History, Documents and Opinions in a World Crisis*, Fawcett, New York, 1965, pp. 96–104.

34. *The Congressional Record*, June 28, 1950, pp. 9320–9323.

35. U.S. Senate, Foreign Relations Committee, *The Gulf of Tonkin: The 1964 Incidents*, GPO, Washington, D.C., 1968.

36. U.S. Senate, Committee on Foreign Relations, *War Powers Resolution*, GPO, Washington, D.C., 1977, pp. 172–173.

37. *The New York Times*, Oct. 13, 1983.

FURTHER READING

Allison, Graham T.: *Essence of Decision*, Little, Brown, Boston; 1971. Three theories of foreign policy-making are tested against the Cuban missile crisis of 1962.

Brzezinski, Zbigniew: *Power and Principle*, Farrar, Straus and Giroux, New York, 1983. A former presidential assistant for national security describes his problems in trying to manage foreign policy in the Carter administration.

Destler, I.M.: *Presidents, Bureaucrats and Foreign Policy*, Princeton University Press, Princeton, N.J., 1974. A book about the way presidents cope with the foreign policy communities.

————, Leslie H. Gelb, and Anthony Lake: *Our Own Worst Enemy: The Unmaking of American Foreign Policy*, Simon and Schuster, New York, 1984. A critical assessment of the think tanks and the policy professionals who form issue networks and shape foreign policy.

Franck, Thomas, and Edward Weisband: *Foreign Policymaking by Congress*, Oxford University Press, New York; 1979. An insightful study of how Congress tries to influence or control foreign policy, including a trenchant critique of how the decentralized structure of power affects its performance.

Gaddis, John Lewis: *Strategies of Containment*, Oxford University Press, New York, 1982. A study of postwar American foreign policy, emphasizing strategies to deal with the Soviet Union.

Hilsman, Roger: *To Move a Nation*, Doubleday, New York; 1964. A study of how foreign policy was made during the Kennedy administration, together with a theory of bureaucratic politics and coalition building.

Hoffman, Stanley: *Primacy or World Order*, McGraw-Hill, New York, 1978. An incisive analysis of current problems in international politics and a call for new internationalist approaches to United States foreign policy.

Powers, Thomas: *The Man Who Kept the Secrets*, Knopf, New York, 1979. A study of the intelligence community in the form of a biography of a CIA director.

Richelson, Jeffrey T.: *The United States Intelligence Community*, Ballinger, Cambridge; Mass., 1984. A systematic overview of the thirty intelligence agencies of the United States government.

Turner, Stansfield: *Secrecy and Democracy*, Houghton Mifflin, Boston, 1985. A former CIA director discusses his reform of the agency during the Carter administration.

THE STUDY BREAK

Advise and Consent. A movie, made in 1962 and starring Henry Fonda and Charles Laughton, about the struggle to confirm a presidential nominee for secretary of state.

Fail-Safe. In this 1964 movie, a United States plane is mistakenly ordered to bomb the Soviet Union, leading to high-level diplomatic maneuvering.

The Missiles of October. A television documentary produced in 1974, about the Cuban missile crisis of 1962, starring William Devane and Martin Sheen.

Missing. A 1982 movie in which Jack Lemmon plays the father of an American who is missing in a Latin nation; the father is frustrated by the complicity of the American embassy in covering up his son's whereabouts.

The Ugly American. A 1963 movie about the doings of American diplomats in southeast Asia.

USEFUL SOURCES

Burns, Richard D. (ed).: *Guide to American Foreign Relations since 1700*, ABC-CLIO, Santa Barbara; Calif., 1983. Comprehensive bibliography.

Declassified Documents Quarterly Catalog (and accompanying microfiche set). Documents from the CIA, the NSC, the FBI, and the White House, as well as from the State Department and the Defense Department.

The Department of State Bulletin. A monthly journal published by the State Department containing speeches, texts of international agreements, new summaries, and articles of foreign policy.

Foreign Affairs. A monthly journal with articles written by heads of state, diplomats, and academics.

The Foreign Relations of the United States: Diplomatic Papers, Department of State, Washington, D.C. A series containing the texts of the important government documents involving American diplomacy.

The Foreign Service Journal. A monthly journal containing articles by and about members of the Foreign Service.

Plano, Jack C., and Roy Olton: *The International Relations Dictionary*, ABC-CLIO, Santa Barbara; Calif., 1982. Defines key terms.

United States Treaties and Other International Agreements, Department of State, Washington, D.C. A series containing the texts of important American international agreements.

Young, Harry F., and Colleen Sussman: *Atlas of United States Foreign Relations*, Department of State, Washington, D.C., 1983. Information on American diplomacy and alliances.

ORGANIZATIONS

Carnegie Endowment for Peace. 11 Dupont Circle, N.W., Washington, D.C. 20036. For more information phone 202-797-6400.

Coalition for a New Foreign and Military Policy. 120 Maryland Avenue, N.E., Washington, D.C. 20002. For more information phone 202-546-8400.

Committee on the Present Danger. 1800 Massachusetts Avenue, N.W., Washington, D.C. 20036. For more information phone 202-466-7444.

The Council on Foreign Relations. 58 East 68th Street, New York, N.Y. 10021. For more information telephone 212-734-0400.

The Foreign Policy Association. 205 Lexington Avenue, New York, N.Y. 10016. For more information telephone 212-481-8450.

Institute for Policy Studies. 1901 Q Street, N. W., Washington, D.C. 20009. For more information phone 202-234-9382.

CHAPTER 19
THE DEFENSE ESTABLISHMENT: PROCUREMENT, BUDGETS, AND STRATEGIES

When Theodore Roosevelt sent the "great white fleet" steaming out of Hampton Roads, Virginia, on a round-the-world voyage, the United States was showing the flag as a newly emerging power. The Strategic Air Command bunker in Omaha, Nebraska, is a stark demonstration of the responsibility of a superpower. (*Naval Historical Center; Department of the Army.*)

One of the most important functions of government, according to the Constitution, is "to provide for the common defense," and military matters involve one-third of the government's express powers. Since World War II there have been more than 150 armed conflicts between nations and more than 25 million combat-related deaths. The world spends more than $1 trillion annually on armaments. The United States has maintained a large and costly military establishment, has been involved in two limited wars and several other military interventions, and since 1945 has fired more weapons, dropped more bombs, and inflicted more combat fatalities than any other nation in the world.

Critics of our defense policies claim that our use of force has been a disaster. We could not rescue the hostages in Iran, defeat terrorists in the middle east, or win police actions in Korea and Vietnam. Our military force has not enabled us to influence events in Central America decisively. Defenders of the military claim that it has achieved major successes: collective security has kept peace in Europe and has protected other allies.

Defense policy-making involves important questions: What is the role of the military in American life, and how do we maintain civilian control over the military while giving military officers an appropriate role in making defense policy? How do we promote economic growth while competing with allies that spend far less on defense than we do? Are we procuring effective weapons at a reasonable cost? Have we matched our diplomatic objectives with our military strategy and matched both with our weapons procurement?

THE ARMED FORCES

Structure and command

The armed forces are constitutionally subordinate to the president and Congress. The president is commander in chief of the armed forces and may set strategy and issue orders to field commanders. Congress declares war, raises and organizes the services, and funds weapons procurement. Officers are nominated for their positions by the president and are appointed with the advice and consent of the Senate. The president assigns, reassigns, or removes them from command.

The national command authority. The president, presiding over the National Security Council (NSC), establishes national security policies, which are incorporated into presidential decision memorandums. The military strategy is then implemented through the secretary of defense and the secretary's civilian subordinates, as well as through military officers represented by the Joint Chiefs of Staff and the military commanders.

CIVILIAN POLICY-MAKING. The president, as commander in chief, works with the NSC and the secretary of defense to develop overall strategic and budgetary policies. Below the secretary are the other presidential appointees in the Defense Department, who work on the budget, strategic plans, weapons procurement, and research and development, but who do not issue orders to military forces. These political executives come and go so often that few develop the expertise needed to understand military issues. Most do not have extensive military backgrounds. They average fewer than three years in office.

In some administrations, such as Nixon's and Ford's, many of the deputy assistant secretaries are active-duty or retired generals or admirals; they provide expertise but weaken the principle of civilian control of the military.

The Army, the Navy, and the Air Force are departments, not at the Cabinet level, located within the Defense Department. (The Marine Corps is not a department.) They are headed by civilian secretaries, who are responsible for induction, training, assignment of personnel, and other support functions. These officials also do not issue orders to combat units.

THE MILITARY CHAIN OF COMMAND. The president issues orders to the secretary of defense, who transmits them (through the Joint Chiefs of Staff if the secretary chooses) to the *military commands*, which are responsible for territorial land, sea, and air defense of the United States, as well as for operations in various theaters (such as the Pacific, the Indian Ocean, Europe, the Persian Gulf, and Central America). The commands operate under the supervision of CINCs—commanders in chief of operational forces. Each CINC reports back to the Joint Chiefs of Staff, who plan military operations, and they in turn report back to the secretary of defense and to the president.

The president makes decisions regarding the use of *strategic* nuclear weapons, but there are 7000 or so *tactical* nuclear weapons in special depots in Germany, Britain, and Turkey, and many are assigned to NATO forces under programs of cooperation. Combat units must request release of these weapons; such a request goes up the chain of command to the secretary of defense and the president.[1] It is not clear whether this system can work in the event of war: it is possible that decisions to "go nuclear" could be made at much lower levels.

The Joint Chiefs of Staff. The Joint Chiefs of Staff (JCS) consists of the top military commanders of the services: the chief of staff of the Army, the chief of staff of the Air Force, the chief of naval operations, and, since 1979, the commandant of the Marine Corps. The chiefs are the principal military advisers to the president and Congress. The chair of the JCS, or the chief designated by the chair, sits as a nonvoting adviser to the NSC and also participates in high-level crisis management teams, such as the Washington Special Situations Committee, chaired by Vice President Bush in the Reagan administration. The chair of the JCS is also a member of the administration group that advises the president on arms limitations negotiations. No chief may, in peacetime, serve more than two four-year terms on the JCS; this ensures that no military officer will gain undue influence. The JCS does not have the authority to command troops, unless it is delegated that power from the civilian secretary of defense.[2]

The JCS now has more than 1300 officers and enlistees assigned to it, as well as some civilians in the Pentagon, and it has become the "organization of the JCS," a Pentagon bureaucracy. The majors, lieutenant colonels, and lieutenant commanders on the staff draw up war plans, military budgets, and strategy. Their work goes to operational commands for comment, then up the ladder to the director of the joint staff for revision, and finally to the chiefs themselves in their meeting room, known as the "tank." If approved, it is "red-striped" (that is, sent to the secretary of defense) for final approval by civilian officials.

The JCS originated as an informal body to advise President Roosevelt during World War II.[3] It was formally established in 1947 as part of a congressional reorganization of the military, also with a guaranteed role in advising Con-

The Joint Chiefs of Staff are the chiefs of staff of the Army, Air Force, Navy, and Marine Corps. The chair serves as the president's principal military adviser. (*Department of Defense.*)

gress. As Army Chief Earl Wheeler interpreted the law, "In answer to direct questions, the military leader has no moral alternative to giving Congress the same candid professional judgments that he had previously stated within the JCS, to the Secretary of Defense, or the President." Thus the Air Force chief of staff has testified before Congress against the high-altitude antisatellite weapons proposed by the Reagan administration, and the chiefs have slowed down the administration's proposals to expand special military forces for guerrilla and commando operations.

The chiefs are the president's principal military advisers. Sometimes they meet with the president regularly (as they do with Reagan), or they advise the president through the secretary of defense. Members of the JSC always profess their loyalty to the administration's defense program, but their loyalty must usually be won. They first try to reach a consensus in the "tank," and then they bargain with the president and the secretary of defense. Their arguments convinced Eisenhower to exceed the Pentagon's personnel recommendations by 65,000. They got Kennedy to expand procurement of the B-52 bomber, and when he proposed a test ban treaty with the Soviets, their price was his promise to continue underground testing and research and development on other weapons. Carter promised the chiefs greater funding for conventional forces to get their support for the Panama Canal treaties.

The president usually shields the chiefs from criticism when military missions fail. Kennedy refused to use the Air Force during the abortive Bay of Pigs invasion launched against Cuba in 1961, and he took the blame for the failure of the mission. But in private he fumed that the chiefs and the CIA had given him overly optimistic assessments. He lost confidence in the chiefs and turned to his own military adviser. Johnson took the blame for setbacks in Vietnam after the Tet offensive of 1968, but he refused the chiefs' demand for more troops. He complained that his "generals know only two words—spend and bomb."[4] After the Tet offensive, they got a free hand with neither spending nor

bombing. Carter took the responsibility for the abortive mission to rescue the American hostages in Iran. But he also ordered an inquiry into preparations for the mission, and major shortcomings were revealed: inadequate training, interservice rivalries, poor contingency planning, loss of vital documents, and flawed procedures.

Sometimes the protective relationship breaks down. Truman had conflicts with all the chiefs and threatened to fire several of them. Army chiefs Taylor and Ridgeway accused their old comrade-in-arms, Eisenhower, of undermining the Army with budget cuts. Defense Secretary McNamara feuded with every chief, and with Kennedy's approval he fired them all. When their replacements turned against him during the Johnson administration, it was McNamara who left, to head the World Bank. In the 1984 presidential debates Reagan shifted the blame onto the military commanders for moving the marines into the barracks in Lebanon, where 240 were killed in a terrorist attack.

The officer corps. There are approximately 285,000 officers in the armed forces, of whom approximately 1200 are generals and admirals. All officers receive their commissions from the president, subject to the advice and consent of the Senate, though of course this consent is given routinely. Actual promotions are made by service committees, consisting of high-ranking officers who review the records of subordinates and make recommendations to the secretary of defense.

To attract and train candidates for the officer corps, Congress has created military academies: West Point for the Army, Annapolis for the Navy, and the Air Force Academy. Men and women are appointed on the basis of competitive examinations or by the president on the recommendation of members of Congress. Officer candidate schools run by the services allow enlistees to obtain commissions. Universities and colleges also offer Reserve Officers' Training Corps (ROTC) programs and give scholarships to 30,000 students (tuition, fees, books, and $100 a month) and $100 monthly payments to nonscholarship students. From a low of 60,000 in 1973, enrollment had soared to 120,000 by 1984. More than 200,000 high school students receive an introduction to military science through the junior ROTC program.

Pay and benefits for officers are supposed to be comparable to those offered in the private sector, but they are lower, and as a result, there is considerable turnover in the officer corps. But generous half-pay pensions after twenty years, indexed to inflation, allow many officers to take civilian jobs while they are in their forties and still receive large pensions, a practice known as *double-dipping* if they also get a civilian pension later. These pension costs are enormous: future liabilities to taxpayers for officer corps pensions amount to almost $600 billion, and the annual cost to taxpayers is the equivalent of the salaries of current officers.

The military and civilian politics

There is an ebb and flow of military influence in civilian politics. At the end of a successful war, military officers assume high-level civilian posts. After World War I they took part in the reconstruction of Europe and staffed the newly formed Bureau of the Budget. After World War II they supervised the occupations of Japan, Germany, and South Korea. The official in the Truman administration who was most influential in shaping foreign policy was Secretary of State George Marshall, a former five-star general in the Army. "It is very hard to

define where the military begins and the civilians leave off in our form of government," according to Earl Wheeler, a former Army chief.[5]

After successful wars, victorious commanders sometimes enter the Cabinet or run for president. But in every case their political careers were advanced by civilians and supported by the public. Washington, Grant, and Eisenhower were pressured by party leaders to run for office, and there has never been a case in which the officer corps put pressure on a party to nominate an officer. While about half the members of Congress are veterans, few made the military their career, and there are hardly any career officers in state and local politics.

The officer corps has little influence on civilian politics (other than on the budget process). The curriculums in the service academies stress the concept of the professional soldier who is subordinate to civilian authorities and would not disobey a valid order transmitted through the chain of command. Officers are educated primarily in engineering, managerial, and military subjects; public affairs and the social sciences are given only limited attention. Officers look inward, to military problems, rather than outward, to civilian politics. They generally do not debate or make pronouncements on issues in civilian politics, and they are careful to steer clear of election politics. When they do not follow this rule, they are usually reprimanded or forced to retire. "The military is at no time more powerful than the President of the United States is prepared to allow it to be," concludes Adam Yarmolinsky, a former assistant secretary of defense.[6]

Military procurement

The military does get involved in civilian politics to protect its own interests: bigger defense budgets and the acquisition of larger forces equipped with more advanced weapons. President Eisenhower, a five-star general in the Army, warned the nation in his farewell address that it must be on guard "against this acquisition of unwarranted influence, whether sought or unsought, by the military-industrial complex," adding that "the potential for the disastrous rise of misplaced power exists and will persist."

Interservice rivalries and issue networks. It would be misleading to state that procurement policies involve military officers on one side and civilian officials on the other. Although President Eisenhower argued that "separate ground, sea, and air warfare is gone forever," the services and their chiefs do not agree. General Westmoreland once described himself as "the Army's Representative on the Joint Chiefs of Staff," and a naval chief admitted, "I am a naval officer first." The issue networks involved in defense policy-making cross the military-civilian boundary. They consist of competing alliances of military and civilian officials. The comptroller and office of systems analysis in the Pentagon, plus the OMB and a committee of the NSC, may square off against the JCS, several weapons manufacturers, and the Pentagon officials involved in technology and procurement. Think tanks, such as the Brookings Institution, the Council on Economic Priorities, and the Institute for Defense Information, get involved in these debates and try to influence the Democrats and Republicans on important congressional committees.

In the 1950s the Air Force argued that aircraft carriers were obsolete, while the Navy claimed that a long-range bomber could never penetrate the Soviets' air defenses. The Army and the Navy fought over control of the early space satellite programs, and the Army and the Air Force fought over control of

NATO forces on annual maneuvers in West Germany. (*Wally McNamee: Woodfin Camp.*)

intercontinental ballistic missiles. The Army and the Marine Corps competed for new divisions. In the 1980s the Army and the Marine Corps have continued their battles, now over which branch should control the rapid deployment force (with Army "light divisions" proposed instead of another Marine division) and which should handle special forces used in antiterrorist or antiguerrilla operations.

Even within the services there are conflicts. Army officers identified with European commands are rivals of those whose careers involve combat in the Pacific. Navy submariners clash with surface ship officers (so-called brown shoes versus black shoes). In the Air Force rivalries involve missile versus bomber commands. Officers in charge of recruitment and training want to spend money on facilities, pay, and bonuses. Field officers care more about the readiness, maintenance, and sustainability of their forces. Higher-level commanders worry about base facilities, transport, resupply, modernization of weaponry, and logistics. Even the National Guard and reserve units ask for more modern weapons and better training, since they constitute 51 percent of what they refer to as the "total Army."

These conflicts spill over into civilian politics. The State Department wants NATO units modernized to pressure allies into upgrading their own forces. NATO allies demand that we increase our forces to meet the Soviet buildup, which now involves a 2–1 personnel, a 3–1 airplane, and a 3–1 tank advantage to the Warsaw Pact. We want them to pay more for our forces stationed in their countries. Allies want to coproduce our weapons and want us to buy theirs, but Congress may insist on a "buy American" policy.

Public opinion and procurement. Public opinion can affect preparedness and procurement (Figure 19-1). Between 1947 and 1968, approximately 30 percent of the public favored increased defense expenditures, while almost everyone else supported the existing levels. During the subsequent period of détente with the Soviet Union, from 1968 to 1979, most Americans preferred lower defense spending and fewer overseas commitments to allies.[7] Consequently, presidents Nixon and Ford presided over major *reductions* in force levels, and

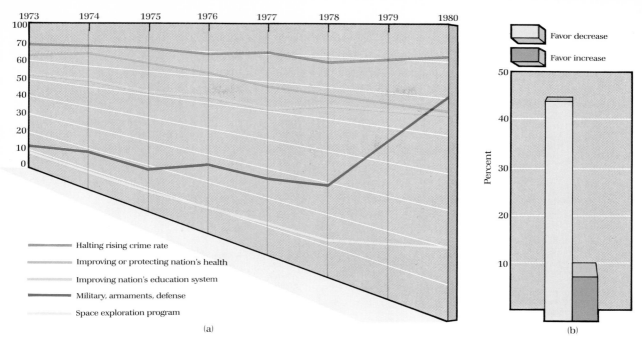

1973 1974 1975 1976 1977 1978 1979 1980

Favor decrease
Favor increase

Halting rising crime rate

Improving or protecting nation's health

Improving nation's education system

Military, armaments, defense

Space exploration program

(a)

(b)

Figure 19-1. Public attitudes toward a defense buildup. (a) During the Vietnamese war there was little support for an increase in defense expenditures. In 1978 public opinion shifted, and support rocketed to 60 percent range by 1980, permitting Carter and Reagan to call for a massive buildup. (Source: *Public Opinion,* October-November 1980.) (b) After five years of higher expenditures, however, another poll showed that those favoring decreased spending outnumbered those favoring increased spending by over four to one. (Source: Gallup poll, January 25–28, 1985.)

President Carter made a campaign pledge to cut the Pentagon budget by at least $5 billion and get United States forces out of South Korea.

Then public opinion turned hawkish, especially after the Iranian hostage crisis, the Soviet invasion of Afghanistan, and the pressure on Poland. The majority of Americans believed that the nation would be involved in war in the 1980s and favored defending the Persian Gulf, western Europe, and Japan.[8] Yet by the third year of that buildup, public opinion once again had shifted, with majorities now saying that it had gone too far and should be scaled back, as the total price tag began to sink in. In 1982 Harris polls showed that only 17 percent favored more military spending, and in 1983 only 14 percent favored it.

Public opinion is influenced by the Pentagon's own public relations machinery. Over 100,000 defense contractors around the country support the Pentagon's call for a military buildup. Press releases, documentary films, and other materials are prepared by the department's assistant secretary for public affairs, and the 200 Defense Department, the 1500 Army, the 1800 Navy, and the 1300 Air Force personnel. The military wines and dines influential opinion leaders and provides guided tours of military facilities. It also runs the government's transportation for members of Congress and high-level civilian officials out of Andrews Air Force Base, near the capital.[9]

Strategy and procurement: Defense systems. The President and the Defense Department formulate strategies for the use of military forces. These are based on national security objectives, which, according to the Defense Department, include deterring nuclear attacks on the United States and its allies; deterring conventional war in Europe; protecting the oil lifeline from the middle east; forestalling nuclear blackmail by other nations; and maintaining the ability to retaliate after a nuclear strike.[10]

Rational procurement would directly relate these national security objectives to weaponry purchased. Commanders in each theater would then develop specific tactics on the basis of local conditions. Weapons which were most useful in each theater would be procured, while those which did not

work well in simulated battle conditions would be retired. The overall defense budget would match objectives, strategies, doctrines, and tactics. In practice, things do not work out so neatly. Weapons procured do not always match strategic doctrines. Procurement may reflect pressure by defense contractors and congressional delegations.[11]

Instead of strategy determining doctrine and doctrine determining procurement, the reverse is sometimes the case: a decision to procure a weapon is followed by an attempt to justify its acquisition. As David Jones, a former chair of the JCS, put it, we have a defense establishment "that is derived primarily from the disparate desires of the individual services rather than from a well-integrated plan based on serious examination of alternatives."[12]

Decisions to acquire major new weapons systems are made in the Pentagon by the Defense Systems Acquisition Review Council (DSARC). On it sit the highest-ranking civilian officials in the Pentagon, the service secretaries, and the chair of the Joint Chiefs. They have established a procedure for the services to follow in procuring weapons:

- *Mission need.* The service must determine a mission for which no weapon currently exists.
- *Demonstration and validation.* The service must decide what the weapon will do to advance the mission.
- *Full-scale development.* Contractors build and test prototype weapons with the approval of the DSARC.
- *Production and deployment.* Contractors produce the weapon in quantity, as well as the support equipment and spare parts, with the approval of the DSARC and congressional authorization.[13]

THE PROCUREMENT PROCESS. The Pentagon's director of design, research, and engineering consults with defense contractors on the specifications for a new weapon. Often company officials draft initial proposals and "sell" these ideas to the Pentagon, and then they help defense officials draft the formal proposals and mission requirements. The contractor designs and builds a prototype model of the weapon, which is tested by the military service. The company

The east-west standoff leads to continual investment in new military hardware. This assembly line in Marietta, Georgia, turns out a Starfighter jet cargo aircraft with one-third more cargo capacity and greater range than its predecessor, the Lockheed C-141. (*Department of Defense.*)

and sympathetic military officials then try to "market" the weapon to the Pentagon and Congress. The administration must decide whether to request funds for the weapon in the procurement authorization and appropriations bills submitted to Congress. Congress then approves, modifies, or rejects the proposal. If funding is approved, the Pentagon must open up the process to competitive bidding on cost, specifications, and performance, before eventually approving production.

THE PLAYERS IN THE PROCUREMENT GAME. Defense contractors compete for weapons contracts. Lockheed, Boeing, and McDonnel-Douglas fought over cargo planes; Pratt and Whitney confront General Electric on engines for fighters; Northrop, with its "stealth" bomber, competes with Lockheed and its B-1B. Each company develops close working relationships with some Pentagon scientists, engineers, and procurement officers. The companies try to create an iron triangle: contractors, legislators, and bureaucrats, who control procurement for mutual benefit.[14] The contractors win business for their companies, the legislators get defense plants in their districts (see Figure 19-2), and the defense officials not only get promotions if the weapons are successful but also may retire from the service and go to work in the defense industry, often for companies with which they have worked.

The presidential perspective.

Electoral politics influences procurement. In 1961 Kennedy realized that the United States would have more missiles than the Soviet Union for the foreseeable future, but his campaign rhetoric about a "missile gap" in favor of the Russians led him to approve an increase in missile production. In that same election, outgoing president Eisenhower had increased funding for a proposed new bomber (later canceled) to carry California for the Republicans.

THE PRODEFENSE POSTURE. Presidents cancel weapons only with promises to procure something else. Kennedy scrapped the B-70 bomber and the Skybolt missile but had to acquire ballistic missiles. Carter dropped the B-1 bomber

Figure 19-2. The defense dollar: where it goes. Regions which do well in the competition for defense contracts include the west coast and the east coast. California obtains the largest per capita share, followed by New England. The heavily industrialized states of the east north central region, in contrast, have not done well in gaining contracts, and in consequence their members of Congress have formed a caucus devoted to increasing their share.

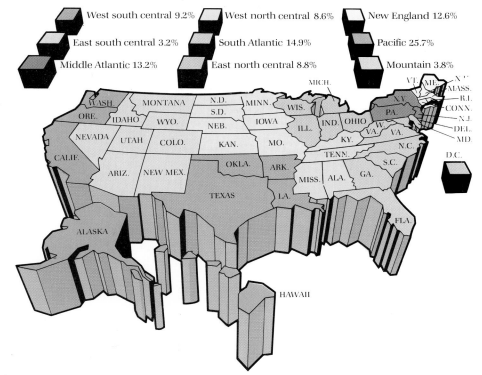

but stepped up development of a stealth bomber and a cruise missile. Each protected himself from criticism that he was weakening our defense. No president wants to be in the position that Eisenhower found himself in during the 1950s, when the Soviets tested a missile that was larger and more advanced than anything the United States had. By 1958, Premier Khruschev was boasting that he would soon have hundreds of missiles deployed. The Democrats charged that the president had permitted a missile gap. In the 1958 congressional elections and the 1960 presidential elections, the Republicans were on the defensive. Once in the White House, Kennedy admitted that no missile gap existed, since the Russians at that time produced fewer missiles than we did.[15]

Johnson had to deal with the Army's proposal for an antiballistic missile system (ABM). He was reluctant to confront the Joint Chiefs of Staff, military contractors, and legislators who wanted such a system. He needed their support for the Vietnamese war, and he did not want the Republicans to claim that there was an "ABM gap." Therefore, Johnson ordered a "light deployment" of a scaled-down ABM system to defend American cities against an attack by communist China—even though no one assumed that the Chinese had any capability, let alone any intention, of launching such an attack. Yet the decision kept the defense contractors happy and mollified the Army and the legislators allied with the contractors. Since the decision was not directed against the Soviet Union, it would not complicate arms control talks. Best of all from Johnson's viewpoint, the Republicans could not use the issue in the elections.[16]

ARMING TO PARLEY. Presidents procure arms as a "bargaining chip" in negotiations with the Soviet Union. In the early 1970s, the United States had a force of forty-one submarines, thirty-one of which were equipped with Poseidon missiles. In 1972 Nixon overruled the Defense Department, which wanted to expand this program, while continuing research on a much more advanced submarine. Instead he ordered procurement of the slightly advanced Trident submarine, which would become operational by 1978. Each of these ships would be larger, faster, quieter, and equipped with more powerful and more accurate missiles. But going ahead with this program would eclipse development of a completely new submarine force in the 1980s, based on even more advanced technology. Nixon decided on the Trident rather than the next generation of ships so that he could negotiate with the Soviets.[17]

Similar reasoning was behind Nixon's decision to develop multiple warheads for ballistic missiles (multiple independently targeted reentry vehicles, or MIRVs). His defense secretary, the service secretaries, the Joint Chiefs, and the director of engineering all favored deployment. The only opposition came from the arms control advocates, who argued that MIRVs would complicate negotiations. In spite of intense opposition from some Republican senators allied with this group, Nixon decided to go ahead with development. At the arms talks he offered the Soviets a choice: a "MIRV race" or a ban that would include on-site inspection of missile warheads. The Soviets rejected the offer, thus beginning a new and dangerous phase in the arms race.

The Reagan administration has also embraced the "arm to parley" approach, in spite of the fact that it has never resulted in the giving up of a weapon by either side. Its deployments of neutron bombs, cruise missiles, and Pershing II missiles in Europe (which can hit targets in the Soviet Union within 100 yards and within six minutes) were designed to influence the outcome of

As land-based weapons systems are developed, the United States more and more often has to convince its NATO allies to deploy them. Pershing missiles were installed in West Germany only after considerable resistance. (*Department of the Army.*)

European arms limitation talks. These weapons were bargaining chips against the Soviet SS-20 missiles aimed at European targets. Similarly, deployments of the MX missile, the development of the B-1 bomber, and the production of 8500 new nuclear warheads in the 1980s were also designed to put the United States in a better bargaining position. The Soviets responded by increasing their own procurement of new strategic weapons, deploying a new generation of submarines off the coasts of the United States, and temporarily breaking off participation in strategic arms talks—another indication of the failure of the "arm to parley" approach.

The congressional impact on procurement. The administration takes legislative politics into consideration in awarding defense contracts. PACs run by aerospace defense contractors make contributions to members of Congress that are greater than those made by any other sector of the economy. Corpo-

S. Kelley © 1983
San Diego Union.

666

Dan Wasserman, Los Angeles Times Syndicate. Reprinted by permission: Los Angeles Times Syndicate.

rate lobbyists work closely with hundreds of Pentagon officers and with associations of retired officers and veterans associations to put pressure on members to vote for funds for particular systems. Contractors have hired thousands of former military officers and civilian Defense Department employees to give them access to the Pentagon. They hire former legislators and staffers to grease their way on Capitol Hill. Sometimes such lobbying works. Kennedy's decision to give General Dynamics the TFX fighter-bomber contract may have had something to do with its location in Texas, the home of his vice-president and of important members of the armed services and appropriations committees. Army bases, home ports for the Navy, and defense plants are often located in districts represented by legislators on these committees.[18] Sometimes a powerful member can push a project against the wishes of the Pentagon or the services. "So help me God, we are going to have a follow-on bomber if it kills everyone in the Department of Defense, and I die in the process," vowed L. Mendell Rivers, chair of the House Armed Services Committee.[19] He got what he wanted. The Speaker of the House, Tip O'Neill, has won defense contracts for favored firms in Massachusetts, and Representative Joseph Adabbo, the chair of an important armed services subcommittee, won a contract for Grumman Corporation on Long Island.[20]

But in spite of such pressures, the ***military-industrial complex*** does not get everything it wants. Consider what happened to strategic weapons systems between 1964 and 1974. The number of long-range bomber squadrons declined from seventy-eight to twenty-eight. The number of aircraft carriers was reduced from twenty-four to fourteen. Most new weapons systems were either delayed or canceled. A president who is committed to arms negotiations and control of strategic weapons can delay procurement, as Nixon did in the period of détente, to give arms talks a chance.

There is little evidence to suggest that the way contracts are distributed or the way lobbyists operate has much effect on Congress's voting for the defense budget. More important are members' attitudes toward defense spending, and these can change with public opinion. There is some evidence that in highly competitive districts members who are vulnerable to defeat will vote for increased defense spending.[21]

Members of Congress have differing opinions about procurement, and Congress rarely speaks with one voice. Thus its role is somewhat contradictory. Sometimes it wants to cut, and at other times it emphasizes preparedness; it views procurement partly as a pork barrel, and yet it also sponsors investigations of rip-offs by contractors. Legislators have forced the Pentagon to produce the A-7 fighter for the National Guard, expand the size of the reserves, produce upgraded A-6 and F-14 fighters, upgrade Harrier jets and C-130 air transports, keep unneeded military bases and shipyards open, and distribute subcontracting for the B-1 bomber to forty-eight states. "It primarily keeps things alive that ought to die," says Jacques Gansler, a former assistant secretary of defense.[22] Defense secretaries have charged that Congress adds $2 to $3 billion of unnecessary contracting annually.

The pork is distributed by the House and Senate armed services committees and the two subcommittees of the appropriations committees that deal with military budgets. Their approach has been to emphasize hardware and capital construction rather than strategy or tactics. "God help the American people if Congress ever starts legislating military strategy," Senator Richard Russell said in the 1950s.[23] The House committee has more than thirty professionals on its staff, many of whom are retired military officers. The members of the House committees are generally from "promilitary" districts with many defense plants and bases. They use their influence to increase the payrolls of military and defense contractors in their districts.[24]

In contrast, critical attitudes toward the military emerge from the House and Senate foreign relations committees, which are concerned about the militarization of our foreign policy; from the House and Senate budget committees, which deal with the fiscal implications of military buildups; and from the congressional Military Reform Caucus, which consists of fifty representatives and senators who are critical of existing doctrines and procurement policies.

The influence of Congress was at a high point at the end of the Eisenhower administration and again two decades later, at the end of the Vietnamese war. Between 1957 and 1960, Congress speeded up the Polaris submarine program and the Atlas ICBM program and provided more funds for air defense, antisubmarine warfare, and military transport. About 5 percent of the procurement and the research and development budgets were modified, or priorities were rearranged.[25] In the 1970s, as Congress reorganized and added staff resources, members began to rely on the Defense Division of the General Accounting Office, on the Congressional Reference Service, and on the Congressional Budget Office. No longer was Congress dependent on Pentagon officers who were "on loan" to committees. Its increased expertise meant that it would not be "taken in" by the Pentagon.[26] Congress influenced more specific procurement decisions.

Some observers argue that the Pentagon has won all the big weapons fights. "The Pentagon generally comes away with everything it wants," claims Representative Les Aspin, "and sometimes more besides."[27] The ABM system that

Nixon proposed passed by one vote in the Senate, although later it was abandoned with the concurrence of the administration. The B-1 bomber, the F-14 fighter, MIRV warheads, and the Trident submarine all were approved. In the 1970s Congress made marginal changes: it provided more funds for shipbuilding and repairs, cut back on C-5A transport planes, and procured fewer F-111 fighters. Pressure from liberals led Carter to drop the B-1 bomber in 1977, and pressure from conservatives led Reagan to restore it in 1981.

But Congress can make significant changes in the president's program. It cut the number of MX missiles to forty, and the Senate, emboldened by the Joint Chiefs of Staff's testimony against the "densepack" plan, rejected the administration's proposal (calling it "duncepack") to place MX missiles in "hardened" silos. Congress limited the testing of antisatellite weapons as long as the Soviets abided by their agreement not to test. It delayed deployment of sea-launched cruise missiles armed with nuclear weapons in order to encourage further arms negotiations.

But Congress cannot always bring military procurement under control. The Pentagon can *reprogram* funds from other weapons acquisitions programs; *relabel* a new weapon and "disguise" its purchase; *lease* equipment (for example, cargo ships) from private investors, who receive tax breaks for building them, thus transferring the cost from the Pentagon budget to the Treasury (which forgoes the taxes); *borrow and lend* from the off-budget Federal Financing Bank so that it can make military sales to other nations at subsidized rates of interest; and *spend* money already obligated by Congress. By 1984 Congress had funded $128 billion which the Pentagon had contracted but had not yet spent, and $43 billion which the Pentagon had not yet even contracted.

Problems with weapons procurement. Business wants to sell, and the Pentagon wants to buy. Companies are interested in profits, and the Pentagon wants to keep a strong industrial base for future procurement. Neither partner has much incentive to keep costs down.

UNDERESTIMATING COSTS. Contractors collude with the Pentagon on low cost estimates and high performance claims to convince the administration and Congress to "buy into" a weapon. The General Accounting Office (GAO) claims that the Reagan administration may have underestimated the cost of its procurement plans by as much as $324 billion, in part because of low bids. When an inferior weapon has been produced, the contractors and the Pentagon pressure Congress to pay up to repair, redesign and upgrade it. Barry Goldwater (a conservative Republican) and Howard Metzenbaum (a liberal Democrat) argue, "Runaway costs characterize our entire defense procurement program. These vast expenses have nothing to do with maintaining the strength of our military forces."[28]

COST OVERRUNS. Lawrence Korb, an assistant secretary of defense, has shown that cost overruns are enormous: forty-seven weapons were produced for double their original estimates. The C-5A transport went from $23 to $60 million per plane, and it had a smaller payload and a shorter flying time than its specifications called for. Its wings had to be strengthened later at great extra cost. The F-111 fighter-bomber went from $2.8 to $14.7 million per plane, and its design configuration was so unstable that the Navy refused to accept its version and ordered other planes, while the Air Force tried to phase it out as

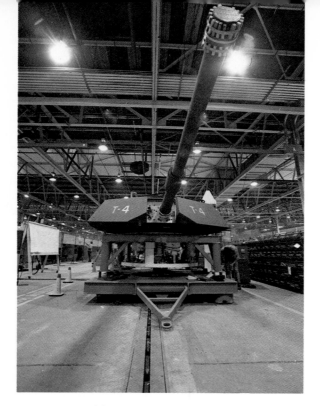

Defense contracting is a nationwide major industry. M-1 tanks are manufactured in Lima, Ohio. *(Department of the Army.)*

soon as possible. According to the conservative Heritage Foundation, the practice of underpricing weapons has continued in the Reagan administration, and "budget plans are as unrealistic today as they have been in the past."[29]

ESCALATING COSTS. Even without overruns, costs are astronomical. In 1960 each Polaris submarine cost $330 million, while in the 1980s each Trident submarine costs $2 billion. In the 1960s a B-52 bomber could be had for $8 million, while the B-1 bomber today may cost as much as $21 million per plane. Each MX missile will cost 10 times as much as its predecessor, Minuteman II. Each XM-1 battle tank will cost 3 times as much as the M-60 tank. Every F-15 fighter costs at least $18 million; they are replacing the F-4 phantom jets, which cost $2.6 million. (All these figures are in 1980 dollars to hold inflation constant.)

The Pentagon buys new weapons but then skimps on training; thus vital flying time for pilots is reduced, and troops may be trained on simulators rather than on real weapons. A House committee reported in 1984 that "shortages in aircraft and equipment spare parts, personnel, fuel storage capacity, casualty care, communications and munitions continue as severe limitations in the capability to sustain war against Soviet forces."[30]

The most sophisticated weapons are often in the repair shop. But there are shortages of mechanics. "We have started a budget with readiness items high on the list," Secretary of Defense Harold Brown admitted in 1981, "but as the budget evolved and the resource limitations took their toll, one by one readiness items were squeezed out by the new weapons programs for other more glamorous proposals."[31]

INFLATED CHARGES. Contractors may bill the Pentagon for research or facilities used in the production of civilian equipment. An Air Force study showed that some contractors billed the Pentagon for as much as 20 times their hourly labor costs, compared with a standard of 3 times in nonmilitary industries.[32]

670

Joint Chiefs have proposed that there be twenty-three Army divisions by 1989, while Reagan has proposed sixteen. The chiefs wanted twenty-four Navy carrier groups to Reagan's fifteen, forty-four Air Force fighter wings to the administration's twenty-seven, and 1308 air transports to Reagan's proposed 348.

Clearly, buildups of this size raised fundamental questions about American defense policy. Was all this armament necessary for American security? Could the nation afford such a buildup without fundamentally damaging the economy? Would the buildup further militarize our foreign policy, or would it better enable us to keep the peace?

Pentagon budgeting

Since World War II presidents have set spending ceilings for the Pentagon. Under Truman the military received one-third of the national budget (more once the war began in Korea). Under Eisenhower the figure was set at 10 percent of the GNP. Meanwhile, the Joint Chiefs would submit their own recommendations, which ranged from 5 to 15 percent higher than the president's. The services tried to reach an agreement among themselves. They compromised on a "fair share" for each, which between 1955 and 1961 averaged out to 25 percent for the Army, 30 percent for the Navy, and 45 percent for the Air Force. The Defense Department would then reduce the chiefs' requests in compliance with the president's wishes. Truman precipitated the "revolt of the admirals" when he canceled some of their pet aircraft carriers and fought the Air Force over the number of bomber wings; Eisenhower, a former general, denied the Army extra divisions and new equipment and took away its role in developing ballistic missiles.

Critics argued that there was no rational relationship between the size and composition of the armed forces and military strategy. The secretary of defense mediated between the military and the president and did not formulate strategy or budgets. Decisions maintained the existing military structure and did not advance combat goals. The budget was a tool by which existing services and commands could survive without changing force requirements. Presidents did not combine economic constraints, national security goals, and strategic doctrines into a coherent defense policy.

CLOSE-UP

SECRETARY MCNAMARA OVERHAULS PENTAGON BUDGETING. President Kennedy's secretary of defense, Robert McNamara, revolutionized Pentagon budgeting. A graduate of Harvard Business School, McNamara did logistical and financial analyses of the B-17 and B-29 bomber programs during World War II and became an assistant professor at Harvard. He then worked at Ford Motor Company, pioneering new forms of statistical analyses and managerial theory, and eventually he became president of the company. Shortly thereafter, President Kennedy asked him to take over the Pentagon, even though he was a Republican. Kennedy did not start with an arbitrary limit on defense spending, but told him to "develop the force structure necessary to our military requirements without regard to arbitrary or predetermined budget ceilings . . . and produce it at the lowest possible cost." The secretary was to act not as a judge of budget recommendations brought to him by the military services, but rather as the architect of defense strategy, military organization, and expenditures. To do this, the new secretary brought in systems analysts, the so-called whiz kids who had worked with him at Ford Motor Company (where he had been president). He created the

used to face the enemy with a succession of dangerous and unexpected situations more rapidly than he can react to them." The new weaponry and the organization of American forces into brigade-size units of 6000 troops (instead of larger divisions) will allow our forces to engage the enemy as we choose and to confuse and disrupt its advance. Battlefield tanks, artillery, howitzers, and antitank missiles, all with expensive computerized sensing and aiming devices, will apply massive firepower. Technology will act as a *force multiplier*, which, together with our superiority in communication, transportation, and leadership, will defeat the enemy.[39]

The new weapons may be easier to operate than less advanced weapons. As computers become more "user-friendly," they will perform some of the complex calculations and aiming now done by humans. Precision-guided munitions require fewer shots and give more direct hits, and planes or squads of soldiers are in less danger from retaliatory fire. With the 200,000 TOW missiles and other defensive weaponry, our forces can defend NATO territory at less cost than the Warsaw Pact forces must expend in an advance, which should act as a deterrent. Once crews are trained to maintain and repair the weapons, performance will improve and downtime will be lowered. Upgrading training, rather than downgrading weaponry, is the solution the Pentagon prefers.

DEFENSE BUDGETS

How much defense do we want to buy? This is the "great equation," the trade-off between guns and butter (see Figure 19-3). The defense buildup proposed by the Carter and Reagan administrations dwarfed any previous buildup since World War II, including the expenditures for the Vietnamese war. While total nondefense outlays fell (adjusted for inflation), Pentagon expenditures rose massively: $264 billion in FY 1984 and $292 billion in FY 1985, with plans for $333.7 billion by FY 1986 and increases to $464.7 billion by FY 1989. And these totals do not include the $8 billion spent annually by the Department of Energy for nuclear warheads and other defense activities, the funds spent by other agencies (such as NASA) on defense, or the more than $26 billion spent by the Veterans Administration for former military personnel. Even so, the

Figure 19-3. Defense buildups: guns and butter. In the past three decades the defense share of the national budget has declined sharply. In 1958 it constituted the largest budget category; since then domestic transfer payments have assumed first place, while the defense proportion has been halved. (Source: *Budget of the United States Government, FY 1986*, p. B-6.)

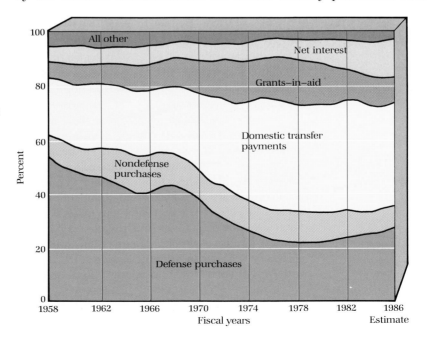

Defending the procurement system. Those who defend the Pentagon's procurement policies argue that it is impossible to prevent waste when the military procures more than $100 billion worth of weapons each year and deals with 150,000 contractors and subcontractors. They point out that as a weapon is produced, the military may order changes in specifications or quantities, which can raise costs. And they claim that the Pentagon itself has tried to curb overruns through new bidding and cost controls. The Pentagon has instituted "fly before you buy" contracting: it pays only for prototypes from companies which compete with one another before the Pentagon decides which weapon to procure. Typically it awards three-fourths of a contract to the winner, and the remainder to the loser as a form of "insurance" and as an incentive for the loser to keep up with the weapons technology for the next round. It has refused to pay for shoddy products and has sometimes renegotiated contracts to lower costs, even in the middle of production runs.

The Defense Department claims that its attempts to root out fraud and corruption between 1981 and 1984 resulted in more than 1300 convictions and the suspension of 1110 companies from contracting. "I keep turning over rocks," the Pentagon inspector general reported, "and [under] each one I turn over I keep finding things."[38] The Defense Contract Audit Agency, which inspects all Pentagon contracts, claims to have saved $24 billion in its reviews of procurement.

What appears to be gold-plating, the military argues, is actually a response to the fact that Soviet and Warsaw Pact forces outnumber American and NATO forces. Army field manual FM-105 warns the Army that it "must prepare its units to fight outnumbered." The military doctrine embodied in the Army's study of warfare in the future, *Airland Battle 2000*, emphasizes highly maneuverable units equipped with weapons employing the latest technology and observes that "agility, deception, maneuver, and all other tools of combat are

The modern military utilizes all aspects of technology. Army Rangers now use computers in field training. (*Department of the Army.*)

Procurement officers have paid up to $7622 for a coffee pot for flight crews, $400 for a hammer, $7417 for an alignment pin that costs 3 cents in a hardware store, $2043 for a nut that costs 13 cents, $2543 for a circuit breaker that costs $3.64, and $10,186 for a tool kit that can be bought for $92.44. Even the inspector general of the Pentagon has admitted that its auditing of most subcontracting is "minimal or non-existent."[33] A Pentagon study of spare parts indicated that at least one-third had been overpriced.[34]

GOLD-PLATING. Some weapons are needlessly sophisticated. Companies push the state of the art to the limit, and engineers who are eager to advance their careers are encouraged to make weapons more complex in order to boost costs, a system known as ***gold-plating.*** Yet some Air Force competitions have shown that under many circumstances larger numbers of low-performance aircraft can defeat a smaller number of high-performance planes, a position argued by many Air National Guard officers who want "austere" fighters, and lots of them.

THE BLOAT FACTOR. The weight and size of United States ground force equipment increase at a 4 percent rate annually, This makes for cumbersome forces, which are slow in the field and need more supplies to maintain and advance. The "bloat factor" also makes it difficult to transport them to crisis spots.[35] Battlefield dependability may be sacrificed if weapons are too advanced for military personnel to handle in combat conditions. In 1978 more than three-fourths of the personnel operating computers and automated weapons failed their skills qualification tests.[36] In combat the new rifles jam, and the gas-turbine tank engine for the XM-1 Abrams tank is susceptible to dust, wears out too soon, and requires too much gas. Some computer systems on weapons are unforgiving or break down if there is a single flaw in a microchip of the software. The Pentagon now requires redundancy and several levels of operability so that if one part fails, the weapon can still operate, even though performance is reduced.

DEGRADED PERFORMANCE. Performance is low for several reasons. Quality control in the manufacture is poor, according to John Wickam, a former Army chief of staff.[37] A former deputy secretary of defense, Paul Thayer, admitted that shoddy workmanship may add as much as 30 percent to procurement costs each year. There is not enough testing before full field deployment, and at times equipment which is faulty or not effective is deployed.

OUTMODED PROCUREMENT. The military procures and trains for the last war rather than the next. Once it was cavalry officers versus artillery and tanks, and later it was battleships versus aircraft carriers. Today, it is "things people can ride on"—like ships, planes, and tanks—although they can be destroyed by the unmanned, precision-guided munitions of the "electronic battlefield," whose kinetic-energy projectiles may make massed formations of tanks and motorized infantry extremely vulnerable.

MUZZLING THE CRITICS. Critics argue that the Pentagon has demonstrated neither the will nor the way to reform procurement. When lower-level officers complain about weapons, they are warned that they risk not being promoted. The military tries to deny the GAO access to performance records so that it cannot make procurement evaluations. Pentagon officials at lower levels who "blow the whistle" on cost overruns may find themselves in the predicament of Ernest Fitzgerald, an Air Force auditor who was transferred to Thailand, where he was assigned to audit military bowling alleys.

President Kennedy's defense secretary, Robert McNamara, on an inspection tour of Vietnam. (*Rene Burri: Magnum.*)

Office of Systems Analysis (OSA) and made its director an assistant secretary.

McNamara centralized budget decisions. The OSA prepared draft presidential memorandums (DPMs) for the secretary. The DPMs became the basic working documents on national security goals, and budget allocations were to be made around them. About three-fourths of the military's recommendations would be rejected in a typical DPM in favor of the policies of the secretary.[40]

The system provided a closer mesh between strategy and budgets, but it did not reduce conflict between the secretary and the military. The budget recommendations of the chiefs ran about 20 percent higher than the Defense Department's recommendations to Congress. McNamara argued that "a nation can reach the point at which it does not buy more security for itself simply by buying more military hardware."[41] He fired two chiefs and gave another one a different job when they protested his decisions to Congress. But during the Vietnamese war the chiefs were able to take their arguments directly to the president, who needed their support for his war policies and who followed their advice on missile production, ABMs, and new military facilities.

McNamara established the secretary as the direct link between the military and the president. He cut waste by promoting interservice combined procurement. He created unified commands, such as the United States Strike Command (Air Force tactical air and Army strategic corps). He created the Defense Communications Agency to handle all field and logistical information for field commanders, the Defense Intelligence Agency, and the Defense Supply Agency for all nonweapons procurement.

Although McNamara was a strong supporter of the Vietnamese war at the beginning, he gradually came to believe that the war could not be won. He opposed the bombing of North Vietnam but was overridden by Johnson. He left the Pentagon in 1967 when Johnson nominated him for the presidency of the World Bank, where he served for fourteen years and made a major contribution in reorienting the organization toward agricultural development in third world nations.[42]

Budgeting Under Nixon, Ford, and Carter

In the Nixon administration Defense Secretary Melvin Laird decentralized budget decisions to the undersecretary and the director of research and engineering.[43] He relied on the Research and Engineering Office, with its bias toward gold-plating. Cuts in service budget requests dropped to 4.3 percent during the Nixon years, far below cuts in the Kennedy-Johnson period. The president kept peace among the services by allowing them to allocate the budget pie by consensus.[44]

But Nixon cut the military. The strategic doctrine reduced preparedness from 2.5 to 1.5 wars (that is, simultaneous operations in one large theater and one small one), which allowed reductions in ships, planes, and divisions. Nixon created a Defense Program Review Committee, chaired by the national security adviser, Henry Kissinger, to review the defense budget. Aided by the programs analysis staff of the NSC, it reviewed weapons systems, formulated five-year strategic plans, and set the budget ceilings for the Pentagon.[45] The chiefs tried to outmaneuver Kissinger: they submitted budget requests late and tried to make decisions without clearing them, but the NSC staff killed off the Air Force's manned orbital laboratory and the Navy's antisubmarine carrier program.

President Ford kept Nixon's system, but friction developed between him and Defense Secretary James Schlesinger. Ford had served on the Appropriations Committee and on its subcommittee on military affairs and believed himself an expert on defense budgeting. Schlesinger, a former college professor, had a habit of lecturing the president. Ford and Secretary of State Kissinger wanted to limit strategic forces and negotiate a new arms agreement with the Soviets. After Schlesinger threatened to resign if Congress did not restore at least $2.6 billion in budget cuts, Ford fired him.

Contrary to popular belief, the defense burden decreased substantially between the end of the Korean war and the late 1970s. Pentagon outlays accounted for 57 percent of the budget in FY 1953, at the end of the Korean war, but for only 23.8 percent by FY 1981, when Carter began a new buildup. In that same period of time the Pentagon's share of the GNP dropped from 12.1 to 5.5 percent.[45] Although defense spending increased during the Vietnamese war, most of the money went for the war itself, while spending for force modernization and strategic arms was lower than in the 1950s. In running for president, Carter pledged to cut defense expenditures by $5 to $7 billion each year. But once in office, he reversed his course and increased the annual budget by 3 percent annually. At the end of his term Carter and Defense Secretary Harold Brown submitted a defense budget calling for an increase in outlays of 4.7 percent between FY 1981 and FY 1986, for a total increase of 26 percent.

Reagan's defense buildup

The Reagan budget process involves four steps. First, the secretary of defense issues the *Defense Guidance*, a document which is intended to guide service staffs in their planning. Second, the services prepare their own weapons and force-level recommendations in their budget plans. Third, the secretary of defense modifies these proposals and prepares a budget request which goes to the president. Finally, the president (with assistance from the OMB) reconciles this document with his overall fiscal planning and submits the United States budget to Congress.

The Reagan administration used this process to fund the most expensive arms buildup since the Second World War, a six-year, $1.6 trillion defense plan

Figure 19-4. (*a*) The Carter administration's defense buildup was (*b*) increased by the Reagan administration. Starting in 1977 the Carter administration proposed a large increase in the budget authority and outlays for the military. The Reagan administration accelerated the rate and amount of increased spending, reaching Carter's targets three years ahead of the original schedule and exceeding its budget authority by more than $60 billion by the end of 1985. (Source: *Department of Defense Annual Report to Congress, FY 1985*, chart IIA.4, p. 67.)

(see Figure 19-4)—3 times the comparable Vietnamese war buildup from 1965 to 1970. By 1985 we were spending more than we had spent during either the Korean or the Vietnamese war. Reagan proposed to increase the defense budget's share of the GNP from 5.8 percent in FY 1982 to more than 7 percent in FY 1986, an increase of more than 1 percent over the GNP allocation planned by Carter.

The major emphasis would be on the strategic weapons already developed and in production. These included MX missiles, B-1 bombers, a stealth bomber (which could elude enemy radar), and cruise missiles; deployment of the Pershing II missiles in Europe; deployment of new Trident submarines equipped with new missiles; deployment of the neutron bomb and the production of new nuclear warheads; and a strategic defense initiative to shoot down enemy missiles, promptly dubbed "star wars" by the media.

Conventional forces would also be improved. The Navy would receive eighteen new ships each year, including three battleships taken out of mothballs and refitted as launching platforms for artillery and cruise missiles. The Army would receive 960 new tanks. More spare parts would be stockpiled.

But the defense budget ran into opposition within the administration. Although the services and the chiefs supported the budget, the Treasury Department and the OMB were lukewarm at best and hinted to Congress that cuts could be made. In 1981 and 1985 David Stockman, then director of the OMB, tried to cut Pentagon increases against the strong opposition of Defense Secretary Caspar Weinberger, who mounted a national agenda campaign to defend his budget.

Congress and the defense budget

In the 1950s and the 1960s Congress rarely cut much from the overall defense budgets proposed by the administration. It cut an average of 3.7 percent from Truman's budget, 0.7 percent from Eisenhower's, and 1.6 percent from Kennedy's and Johnson's. In these same years Congress cut an average of 8.2 percent from the domestic budget requests of these presidents. (See Figure 19-5.)

In the 1970s things changed when Republican presidents Nixon and Ford faced Democratic majorities in Congress. Defense cuts averaged 6 percent while domestic spending was increased 4.7 percent over these administrations' requests. During the first three years of the Carter administration, Congress cut back on defense spending only 2.2 percent, while in 1980 it actually added $5.9 billion to the defense budget.[46]

While Reagan's defense budget was cut by less than 2 percent in 1981, many legislators questioned its size. Senator Robert Dole warned the Pentagon that it "must accept some share of the cuts" proposed to reduce the deficit. And Peter Domenici, chair of the Senate Budget Committee, called for cuts of at least $26 billion between FY 1982 and FY 1985. Buildups like the one proposed by President Reagan in 1983 prompted six former Cabinet members—three

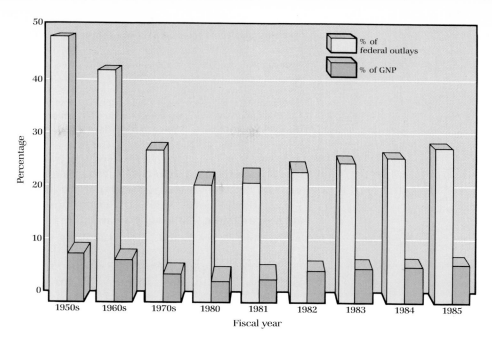

Figure 19-5. The defense budget as a percent of gross national product, 1950–1985. Defense spending has consumed between 5.2 and 9.2 percent of the gross national product in the past three decades, rising almost 2 percentage points in the last five years as a result of Reagan's defense buildups. (Source: *Federal Budget Trends, Department of Defense Annual Report to Congress, FY 1985,* table 3, p. 280.)

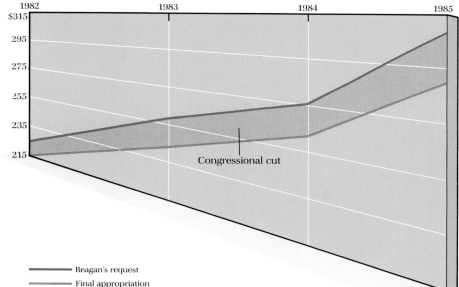

Figure 19-6. How Congress cut Reagan's defense budget. Congressional budget authority for the Pentagon and the nuclear weapons programs run by the Department of Energy increased greatly during Reagan's first term, but not as much as the presidential budget requested. (Source: Congressional Budget Office.)

Democrats and three Republicans—to form the Bi-Partisan Appeal to Resolve the Budget Crisis and seek $25 billion in cuts. "There is no reason to believe that throwing money at defense now will achieve more satisfactory results than throwing money at social problems in the 1960s," according to this group.[47] Meanwhile, some members of Congress also were gearing up to make major cuts. "When I began to dig into it, I was quite appalled," Senator Mark Andrews, a Republican from North Dakota, commented about the 1982 defense requests, "and I say that as a fairly consistent hawk."[48] In 1983 Congress cut administration funding increases from the 11 percent requested to 5 percent. By 1984, with deficits soaring, the Republicans in Congress decided to

include approximately $16 billion in defense cuts as part of the three-year package to trim the deficit.

That same year Congress virtually dismissed the Pentagon's request for a 17 percent increase to $321.4 billion for FY 1985 as a fantasy. The Democrats, with some support from the Republicans, required the administration to agree that military spending was "negotiable" as a price for participating in efforts to reduce the deficit—an effort supported on the administration's side by David Stockman, then director of the OMB, and Treasury Secretary Regan. The result was another round of major cuts. In 1985, as the deficit soared and as domestic programs were being cut by $30 billion, the Republicans in Congress insisted that the Pentagon also take its share of cuts. (See Figure 19-6.)

ISSUE AND DEBATE

GUNS VERSUS BUTTER. The great equation between military and civilian spending is in part, as the first secretary of defense put it, a matter of "securing the proper balance between military necessities and national solvency."[49] So-called *military Keynesians* argue that military spending can stimulate a lagging economy, since there is unused capacity and an unemployed work force which can be devoted to military production. Military spending may reduce unemployment: the Pentagon claims that each $1 billion in defense spending creates 50,000 to 60,000 jobs.

But critics believe that excessive spending by the Pentagon may damage the economy. The capital needs of defense contractors may clash with the need to invest in enterprises to rebuild our industrial base and make it competitive in world markets, especially as capital spending by the Pentagon goes from 35 to 51 percent of its budget. As the Pentagon orders more goods than industry can supply, bottlenecks develop, higher prices result, and there is a need to import raw and finished products from abroad, which hurts our balance of payments.[50] If our industrial base concentrates on military goods, it lags behind in technology and becomes less competitive.[51] Jim Thompson of Illinois, chair of the Republican Governors Conference, argued that a sound economy and a rebuilt industrial base would contribute more to national security than the diversion of scarce resources to a defense buildup.[52] (See Figure 19-7.)

Figure 19-7. The military burden and economic productivity. Critics of excessive military spending argue that the more funds a nation invests in military production, the less it has left to invest in productive manufacturing facilities. The greater the military burden, they say, the lower the annual rate of growth in manufacturing productivity. (Source: Ruth Sivard, *World Military and Social Expenditures, 1977,* copyright by World Priorities, Box 25140, Washington, D.C. 20007.)

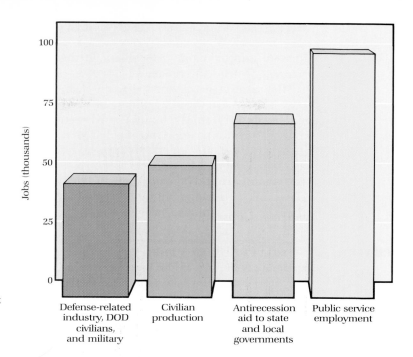

Figure 19-8. Civilian spending creates more jobs than military spending. Defenders of military spending argue that it creates jobs. This is true, but critics argue that even more jobs would be created if the money were diverted to nonmilitary purposes. The Center for Defense Information prepared data to illustrate its point, by calculating the effects on employment of each $1 billion of additional spending. (Source: Center for Defense Information; based on data from Department of Defense, Congressional Budget Office, and Bureau of Labor Statistics.)

Critics argue that increases in a nation's military spending correlate closely with declining investment in civilian enterprises. There is an inverse relationship between military expenditures and economic growth.[53] In the 1970s, while the domestic economy flagged, our yearly investment in nonmilitary and nonresidential enterprises ranged from 17 to 19 percent of the GNP. In contrast, West Germany invested between 20.6 and 26.7 percent of its GNP, and Japan invested between 31 and 36.6 percent. Our per capita military spending was twice that of Germany and more than 10 times that of Japan. "When you spend money for defense, you don't spend it on education or health or other services or goods," President Carter pointed out, adding that "the shift away from weapons toward peaceful goods and services in the long run is favorable for world peace, and also you get more jobs per dollar spent."[54] The money spent on every 50,000 defense jobs can create 76,000 jobs building sewer systems, 76,000 jobs building new housing, 77,000 jobs if we hire new nurses, and 100,000 jobs if we hire teachers, according to Representative Les Aspin, chair of the House Armed Services Committee. (See Figure 19-8.)

Defenders of the buildup argue that in the past conventional wars have lasted long enough for the United States to mobilize its forces and equip them once war had broken out. Today the nation must be completely armed before hostilities begin. Even small wars consume large amounts of armaments, and we must be ready to resupply our own or allied forces from existing stockpiles. (In the 1973 conflict between Israel and two Arab nations, 130 Israeli tanks and 90 planes were knocked out in less than two days; in two weeks, Egypt and Syria lost 450 planes, 1200 tanks, and 1000 armored personnel carriers.) The size of our defense budget is itself taken by our allies as a sign of our commitment to their defense, and it is taken by our adversaries as a sign of our resolve to defend our interests. If we insist that our NATO allies spend more on their own defense, we must do likewise. Yet critics say that in doing so, we weaken our competitiveness in the world economy.

NUCLEAR STRATEGY

As of 1985 the United States had over 9500 nuclear warheads carried in 1897 launchers (bombers or missiles), with a total force of 3448 megatons. The Soviets had about 8000 warheads carried in 2612 launchers, with a total force of 4535 megatons. Some scientists believe that the dust clouds that would be raised by a 5000-megaton nuclear exchange would rise through the atmosphere and create a layer that would block out sunlight for months, lowering the temperature 75 degrees and eliminating most plant and animal life.[55] Others say that even a 100-megaton exchange would do it. The Defense Nuclear Agency has funded several studies of the problem; the first, published by the National Research Council, concludes that there is a "clear possibility" that a **nuclear winter** could occur.[56] Perhaps a nuclear winter is cause for optimism: as the Nobel laureate Herbert Simon put it, "If the analysis is correct, then no nation can make a major nuclear attack even against an unarmed opponent without committing suicide."[57]

Formulating nuclear strategy

The president and the secretary of defense formulate American nuclear strategy on the basis of *flexible response:* the president is given a range of options, from conventional warfare to first use of tactical nuclear weapons, and from a limited escalation involving a response to enemy use of strategic weapons all the way to full-scale nuclear war. Each year, after reviewing the Strategic Integrated Options Plan (SIOP), prepared by the Joint Chiefs, the secretary of defense responds with a memorandum which indicates the strategic assumptions under which the services and the commands are to prepare their operations. The secretary also prepares a draft presidential memorandum, which outlines the relationship between the strategic doctrine and force levels and capabilities. When the president approves this document, the nuclear strategy is authorized—although the actual decision to use the weapons remains the president's. War plans are then prepared by the Pentagon and are

Nagasaki, 1945. Some modern scientists predict a "nuclear winter"—nuclear radiation clouds blocking all sunlight—in the event of a nuclear war. (*U.S. Air Force.*)

**THE DANGER OF ALL-OUT NUCLEAR WAR:
THE ASSESSMENT OF THE PENTAGON**

An all-out nuclear war between the United States and the Soviet Union would involve the use of most of the approximately 16,000 strategic nuclear warheads and bombs that the two countries possess. Because the damage done by such an exchange would be unprecedented in scale—indeed indescribable—it is perhaps easier to begin to appreciate the destructive potential of nuclear weapons by looking first at the effects of the use of one typical nuclear weapon—a 1-megaton warhead, the equivalent of 1 million tons of TNT. As a recent study by the Congressional Office of Technology Assessment points out, if one such warhead were detonated on a major American city, the effects would include the following:

  All reinforced concrete structures within a radius of 0.8 miles would be completely destroyed, as would all small wood-frame and brick residences within 3 miles and all lightly constructed commercial buildings and typical residences within 4.4 miles.

  Virtually everyone within a radius of 1.7 miles would be killed instantly, as would more than half of those within 2.7 miles—a total of about a quarter of a million immediate fatalities.

  Anywhere up to 200,000 additional people would eventually die from severe burns.

  Several hundred thousand others would be injured, including tens of thousands who would suffer serious burns.

For massive nuclear exchanges involving military and economic targets in the United States and the Soviet Union, fatality estimates range from a low of 20 to 55 million up to a high of 155 to 165 million in the United States, and from a low of 23 to 34 million up to a high of 64 to 100 million in the Soviet Union.

Source: Department of Defense, *Annual Report, FY 1982*.

---

integrated into the SIOP, which would go into effect in the event of nuclear war.

Nuclear deterrence. Deterrence assumes that the best way to prevent adversaries from using nuclear weapons is to threaten them with retaliation and that the purpose of acquiring our own strategic weapons is to dissuade opponents from employing theirs. Although the Pentagon draws up plans for "prevailing in a protracted nuclear war" and the Soviet military believes that it too can win in a nuclear exchange, all sane world leaders recognize that a nuclear war is unwinnable, no matter what their defense chiefs claim. "No meaningful victory is even conceivable in a third unlimited world war," argued Robert McNamara, then secretary of defense; "no nation can possibly win a full-scale thermonuclear exchange."[58] Therefore, proponents of the deterrence doctrine believe that the forces should be organized to inhibit other nations from using their atomic weapons against us by enabling us to retaliate after a first strike.

Counterforce. In 1963 the *counterforce* strategy was developed: after an enemy attack, we retaliate against their remaining missiles. With their forces destroyed and ours still capable of hitting Soviet cities, the plan was to force the Soviets to surrender, even if they attacked first, which in turn would be the best way to deter such an attack. In 1964 the policy was modified to include a variety of military targets after a Soviet first strike.

Mutual assured destruction. In 1968 the ***mutual assured destruction*** (MAD) doctrine took hold. Each side could now destroy the other even if it had been attacked. The Pentagon assumed that the Soviets could inflict between 100 and 140 million fatalities on the United States, while we could inflict between 100 and 120 million on them.[59] As few as 400 warheads could destroy one-fourth of their population, 70 percent of their industrial capacity, and all their military forces. Each side could wait until the other had struck, knowing that its remaining missiles could still destroy the enemy. Thus neither side would have any incentive to attack the other.

Countervailing targeting. By the end of the Carter administration, Presidential Directive 59 had established the strategy of ***countervailing targeting,*** which relied on the delivery of more than 11,000 nuclear warheads which would strike not only at enemy missiles and other military targets but also at targets necessary for the "preservation of the regime and . . . the survival and continued effectiveness of the instruments of state power and control."[60] The targets included the Soviets' industrial base, cities, and facilities used for political control; this would convince their leaders that they could not maintain political power in the aftermath of a nuclear exchange.[61]

Problems of nuclear strategy

First use? Because the United States and NATO forces are outnumbered and outgunned by the Soviet and Warsaw Pact conventional forces, the United States plans for ***first use*** of tactical nuclear weapons in Europe (something the Soviets claim to have renounced). Presidents claim the right of first use of the 10,800 medium- and short-range tactical nuclear weapons as their own prerogative, although recently it has been suggested that the president be required to obtain the approval of a joint congressional "nuclear planning committee" before taking such a drastic step. Theater nuclear weapons such as the intermediate-range missiles and cruise missiles deployed in Europe, as well as tactical nuclear weapons, would be used to stem an advance by Warsaw Pact forces into Germany. Some planners believe that such weapons could be used without triggering an all-out nuclear war and would serve as a deterrent to Soviet conventional forces. Others believe that we must match the Soviets in such forces, because our reliance on first use of nuclear weapons would lead to an all-out nuclear war.

Winnable nuclear wars? Defense Secretary Weinberger's goal, in his defense guidance paper issued in 1982, was to use nuclear weapons "to force the Soviet Union to seek earliest termination of the hostilities on terms favorable to the United States." Some critics have taken this to mean that the administration believes that it is possible to fight a protracted war with nuclear weapons and win a meaningful victory. Pentagon planners argue that they are simply trying to find ways to contain nuclear exchanges at lower thresholds and induce the other side to "cease fire" as early as possible.

Strategic sufficiency? Through the 1960s the United States' doctrines relied on our strategic superiority and our ability to destroy thousands of targets in the Soviet Union even after a ***first strike.*** Under Nixon, Ford, and Carter the United States pursued an approach which involved *essential equivalence* of United States and Soviet nuclear forces, based on arms limitation agreements. As long as we kept enough missiles after a Soviet first strike to inflict unaccept-

able damage on them, we would be able to deter them. But the real problem was to convince the other side that our forces were adequate for a second strike, without scaring them into thinking that we intended to strike first and destroy most of their missiles. If a nation can launch its missiles first and destroy all the enemy's strategic forces, it has a first-strike capability. Alternatively, if it has a defense system that can destroy all the enemy's missiles once they are launched, it also has a first-strike capability, since it is invulnerable to retaliation.

First-strike capability? What happens when one side believes that the other side has a first-strike capability—the ability to destroy its opponent's missiles? It assumes that the other side *would* strike first, especially in a crisis. Therefore, it has an incentive to develop its own first-strike capability. Each side may believe that the other side could strike first and win; each may have an incentive to preempt the enemy and strike first itself ("use it or lose it"). If both sides start thinking that way, the situation will become so unstable that a first strike will be inevitable. Moreover, if a mishap on a radarscope leads to a false report that the other side has launched its missiles, it becomes necessary to "launch on warning" in order to have any chance of hurting the enemy. Such radarscope and computer malfunctions happen frequently.

Second-strike stability? The only stable nuclear system is one in which neither side could destroy all the other side's missiles in a first strike, but in which each side could retaliate and destroy the other side with its second strike. Under such circumstances neither side has an incentive to launch a surprise attack, and each side has every incentive to wait and make sure that it has been attacked before launching its own missiles to retaliate.

In the 1980s missiles have become more accurate, they contain many warheads, and they can destroy even heavily fortified missiles on the other side. Simultaneously, their payloads have become smaller and less destructive: the 20-megaton warheads of the 1960s have given way to 1-megaton warheads—less powerful but militarily much more useful. Ironically, the new generation of missiles has left each side more vulnerable to a first strike by the other side. Accurate missiles could destroy the enemy force; small payloads would leave enough of the other country's resources intact so that it would be a prize worthy of conquest.

United States and Soviet perceptions. The stable second-strike possibilities of the 1960s and 1970s have evolved into unstable first-strike possibilities in the 1980s. Each side has developed weapons which have led the other side to assume that it might try for a first strike. The Soviets—viewing Reagan's plans for the MX missiles; the B-1 and stealth bombers; military uses of the space shuttle; the deployment in Europe of Pershing II missiles, which can hit Soviet missiles in six minutes; and the planned deployment of 4000 warheads for air-launched cruise missiles and 1000 warheads for sea-launched missiles (all with hard-target capability)—charged that "the Pentagon plans for building up strategic offensive armaments and deploying anti-missile and space defense systems is timed to complete the development of a so-called first strike potential in the 1980s."[62]

Most of the Soviet force is land-based. If we deployed the new Mark 12

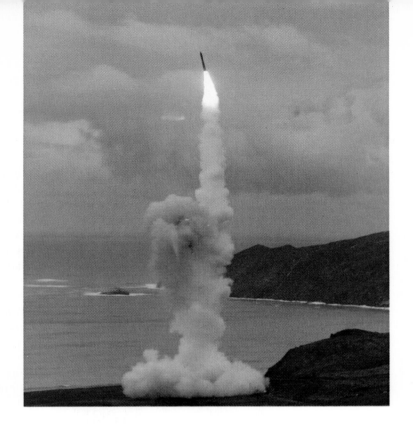

A Minuteman III missile takes off on a test launching in the Pacific in 1983. (*Department of Defense.*)

warheads, their accuracy would make the Soviet missiles vulnerable. If we attacked first, we would have 6 times the number of warheads remaining in our arsenal after our strike than the Soviets would have to retaliate with. From their perspective, it would make sense for us to attack, destroy their missiles, and then threaten them with further destruction unless they surrendered.

Pentagon officials—looking at the new generation of long- and short-range missiles deployed by the Soviets, their new bombers, their efforts to develop an anti-ballistic missile system, and their placement of submarines armed with cruise missiles off our coastal waters—have claimed that the Soviets were developing a first-strike capability. The Pentagon booklet *Soviet Military Power* pointed out that the Soviets had placed 6000 new MIRV warheads on a new generation of SS-18 missiles and could destroy our missiles in hardened silos. Therefore, American analysts argued that a dangerous "window of vulnerability" had opened in 1982 and would remain open until 1987, when enough of our Trident submarines, cruise missiles, and MX missiles would be operational to restore our second-strike capability.

The "star wars" defense. An issue network consisting of engineers from Boeing, United Technologies, McDonnell-Douglas, the think tank High Frontier project, and the Citizen's Advisory Council on Space Policy is pushing for a high-tech antiballistic missile defense. It is possible to use "swarmjet" weapons, lasers mounted in space, and electrically charged particle guns to destroy the guidance system of enemy missiles or satellites armed with heat-seeking missiles. Combinations of these systems deployed in space and in the United States—the "layer defense"—might destroy a large percentage of enemy missiles. In 1983 President Reagan decided to accelerate research on these systems, holding out the promise that if they succeeded, "we could intercept and

destroy strategic ballistic missiles before they reached our own soil." During the presidential debates he even offered to share such a system with the Soviet Union so that each side could defend itself against the other, thus restoring strategic stability. The initial plans called for spending $2 billion in 1985 and as much as $26 billion through 1990, although within the Pentagon opinion was divided as to whether we should try for an intermediate technology system that could be operational in the late 1980s or for a much more advanced system that could be operational by the late 1990s.[63]

Proponents of the "star wars" type of defense argue that it will contribute to stability. They claim that it will enable us to shoot down missiles launched by terrorists or fanatical leaders of small nations. It will also make the Soviets pause before launching a first strike because they will not know how many of their missiles can get through. The only period of instability would occur when one side was deploying such a system, because very briefly the other side might be tempted to strike before the system was operational. But if both sides deployed at the same time, this would enhance rather than diminish stability. At the very least, proponents argue, having the ability to deploy such a system at the same time the Russians do creates a bargaining chip for arms negotiations.

Opponents, such as a panel of scientists from the Union of Concerned Scientists, who were instrumental in building many of our weapons systems, argue that the development of such systems would make war more likely and cause an escalation of the arms race and that the systems are technically unfeasible. Even if only 5 percent of the enemy warheads got through, they have concluded, it would cost the lives of 60 million Americans. A workable system would require the equivalent of the existing United States power grid and oil consumption just to boost enough satellites with lasers into orbit to provide adequate global coverage, they argue, and the costs might exceed $300 billion.

Strategic arms negotiations

The process. Arms negotiations are conducted as much within the United States government as between it and the Soviet Union. The secretary of state formulates a position with the help of the assistant secretary of state for European affairs (who deals with NATO allies), the Bureau of Politico-Military Affairs, and the director of the Arms Control and Disarmament Agency. The secretary of defense relies on the assistant secretary of defense for international security policy, while the JCS takes its own position. The CIA is in charge of preparing estimates of the Soviets' military buildup and intentions, but may be challenged by the Defense Intelligence Agency and the State Department.

Before arms negotiations begin, these officials thrash out their differences in intraagency forums, such as the Political Military Interdepartmental Group. Sometimes the NSC director takes control of the process or even ignores these agencies and formulates a different set of proposals (as Kissinger did for Nixon). The Reagan administration used the Senior Arms Control Policy Group (SACPG), a unit of the NSC (referred to disparagingly as "Sackpig" by its critics). The Arms Control Verification Committee, another offshoot of the NSC, deals with issues involving the Soviets' compliance with existing agreements.

Ultimately it is up to the president to choose from among the various options and to instruct negotiators at the strategic arms limitation and talks and the negotiations for intermediate-range nuclear weapons in Europe. Some-

times these negotiators may modify the positions developed in Washington in an attempt to break a deadlock; if so, they may take back tentative agreements and try to sell the president and the NSC on them, as Paul Nitze and his Soviet counterpart unsuccessfully attempted to do in 1983, when the ideas they developed were rejected by both governments.[64] The president may work through the official delegation or may use the national security adviser or other special emissaries to open up presidential channels for negotiation.

Arms negotiations: The outcomes. Presidents from Eisenhower through Reagan have all negotiated with the Soviet Union about nuclear weapons. Eisenhower proposed an "open skies" plan, which would have allowed aerial surveillance and inspection; the Soviets rejected the proposal, asking instead that each nation simply agree not to produce nuclear weapons—a completely unrealistic and unverifiable proposal. But the two powers did agree on a 1959 treaty to ban nuclear weapons in the Antarctic. President Kennedy successfully negotiated the hotline agreement in 1962 establishing communication links between the White House and the Kremlin in order to reduce the possibility of future nuclear confrontation. He also negotiated the Limited Test Ban Treaty (1963), which banned atmospheric testing of atomic weapons. Underground testing, however, has continued on a variety of nuclear weapons.

President Johnson negotiated the Outer Space Treaty (1967), banning nuclear weapons in space; the Latin American Nuclear Free Zone (1967); and the Non-Proliferation Treaty (1968), under which nuclear powers agreed not to give bombs or bomb-making technology to other nations and under which other signatories agreed not to produce atomic weapons. President Nixon, with his policy of détente, achieved the most in the way of arms agreements. The Sea-bed Arms Control Treaty (1971) banned nuclear weapons near continental shelves. The Anti-Ballistic Missile Treaty (1972) and later protocol (1974) banned the destabilizing defensive missiles. The Salt I interim agreement put numerical limits on the offensive arms which the United States and the Soviet Union could build.

President Carter continued these negotiations. His Salt II treaty would have further limited the buildup of offensive missiles. It ran into stiff opposition in the Senate, however, because some senators did not like the terms and others thought that the Soviets had cheated on other agreements. Carter withdrew it from consideration after the Soviets invaded Afghanistan, but both governments have agreed to abide by its terms, and the United States Senate in 1984 voted 82-17 to support continuing adherence.

Although three-fourths of the public in 1984 supported a mutual and verifiable agreement to freeze deployment of nuclear weapons (including a majority of the delegates to the Republican convention), the Reagan administration has not yet concluded a single agreement. Its talks on strategic weapons floundered after the United States introduced Pershing missiles into Europe—the Russians walked out in 1983, only to return in late 1984. Similar negotiations on the reduction of intermediate-range missiles in Europe have also been deadlocked.

As of 1985 it appeared that both sides might be ready to resume serious negotiations. The Soviets accepted the principle of on-site inspection and monitoring—this had been a problem in reaching agreements with them in

the past. They indicated that they would stop work on their antisatellite weapon system in return for a ban. They proposed a nuclear freeze and a reduction in strategic nuclear weapons under the Salt II accord. The Reagan administration showed similar flexibility in the procedural arrangements for the 1985 talks. But its decision to go ahead with research and testing for its "star wars" initiative, strongly opposed by the Soviet Union, left little prospect for an arms control agreement during the Reagan presidency.

Reagan's strategy was to build up American strategic forces, to increase a first-strike capability in Europe, and to threaten the Soviets with even more weapons. He believed that this would bring the Russians to a more accommodating posture in arms talks; then the United States could use some of its weapons as bargaining chips to induce the Soviets to agree to real cuts in strategic weapons. Meanwhile, the unstable system of deterrence became even more unstable, as each side deployed additional first-strike weapons in a deadly game of "nuclear chicken."

IN CONCLUSION

The political role of the military in American life usually turns inward, toward the acquisition of funding and new weapons, rather than outward, toward influencing civilian politics. Unlike the military in many other nations, the military in the United States does not play an important role in determining who gains political power and who retains it.

The procurement of weapons for the defense establishment is characterized by interservice rivalries, alliances between Pentagon officials and defense contractors, and abuses which inflate costs and degrade performance. Congress has contributed to these abuses by allowing favoritism to influence the awarding of contracts and the location of facilities.

In recent years the gradual decline in defense expenditures (as a percentage of the GNP) has been reversed by the Carter and Reagan administrations. At present a massive buildup, especially in strategic weapons systems, is under way, in spite of public opinion polls which show little support for such spending increases. At times Congress has slowed down the acquisition of weapons systems, but the high point of its influence seems to have passed, and the administration usually gets what it wants.

Most American presidents since Eisenhower have reached agreements with the Soviet Union on limiting the testing and deployment of nuclear weapons. The Reagan administration, however, has used the "arm to parley" strategy. Since then, both sides have moved to deploy a new generation of nuclear weapons, with first-strike capabilities that decrease the stability of the existing balance of terror.

NOTES

1. U.S. Army, *Operations*, FM 100-5, pp. 10–19.
2. Blue Ribbon Defense Panel, *Report to the President and the Secretary of Defense on the Department of Defense*, GPO, Washington, D.C., 1970. Although in 1958 Congress by law removed the chiefs from the formal chain of command, which runs from the president through the secretary of defense to the military commands, the secretary of defense that same year assigned the JCS the function of serving as the military staff in the chain of command.
3. Demetrios Caraley, *The Politics of Military Unification*, Columbia University Press, New York, 1966.
4. Evans and Novak, *Lyndon Johnson*, New American Library, New York, 1969, p. 539.

5. *Department of Defense Appropriations for 1964*, Hearings before the House Committee on Appropriations, 88th Cong., 1st Sess., GPO, Washington, D.C., 1963, pt. 2, p. 131.

6. Adam Yarmolinsky, *The Military Establishment*, Harper and Row, New York, 1971, p. 25.

7. Bruce Russett and William DeLuca, "Don't Tread on Me," *Political Science Quarterly*, vol. 96, no. 3, fall 1981, pp. 38–50.

8. Ibid.

9. J. W. Fulbright, *The Pentagon Propaganda Machine*, Liveright, New York, 1970.

10. Caspar Weinberger, *Annual Report of the Secretary of Defense, FY 1984*, GPO, Washington, D.C., 1983.

11. Samuel Huntington, *The Common Defense*, Columbia University Press, New York, 1960.

12. Mark Kovner, *Defense Dollars and Sense*, Common Cause, Washington, D.C., 1984, p. 2.

13. Ibid., p. 23.

14. Gordon Adams, *The Iron Triangle*, Council on Economic Priorities, New York, 1981.

15. Edgar Bottome, *The Missile Gap*, Fairleigh Dickinson University Press, Rutherford, N.J., 1971.

16. Morton Halperin, "The Decision to Deploy the ABM," *World Politics*, vol. 25, no. 1, October 1972, pp. 62–95.

17. John Steinbruner and Barry Carter, "Organizational and Political Dimensions of the Strategic Balance," *Daedalus*, vol. 104, no. 3, summer 1975, pp. 131–154.

18. Yarmolinsky, op. cit., pp. 38–53, Les Aspin, "The Defense Budget and Foreign Policy: The Role of Congress," *Daedalus*, vol. 104, no. 3, summer 1975, pp. 155–174.

19. Kantor, p. 43.

20. James R. Anderson, "Bankrupting America: The Tax Burden and Expenditures of the Pentagon by Congressional District," Employment Research Associates, Lansing, Mich., 1984.

21. Wayne Moyer, "House Voting on Defense: An Ideological Explanation," in Russett and Stepan (eds.), *Military Force and American Society*, Harper and Row, New York, 1973; Stephen Cobb, "Defense Spending and Foreign Policy in the House of Representatives," *Journal of Conflict Resolution*, vol. 13, no. 3, September 1969, pp. 358–369; Charles Gray and Glenn Gregory, "Military Spending and Senate voting," *Journal of Peace Research*, vol. 5, no. 145, 1969, pp. 44–54.

22. *The National Journal*, Aug. 11, 1981, p. 1233.

23. *The New York Times*, Mar. 15, 1953.

24. Bruce A. Ray, "Defense Department Spending and Hawkish Voting in the House of Representatives," *Western Political Quarterly*, vol. 34, no. 3, September 1981, pp. 438–446.

25. Edward Kolodjiez, *The Uncommon Defense and Congress: 1945–1963*, Ohio State University Press, Columbus; 1966.

26. Ralph Sanders, *The Politics of Defense Analysis*, Dunellen, New York, 1973, pp. 169–204.

27. Aspin, op cit., p. 153.

28. *The Sun-Times*, June 24, 1981.

29. *The Wall Street Journal*, Jan. 10, 1983.

30. *The New York Times*, June 22, 1984.

31. *Department of Defense Annual Report, FY 1982*, GPO, Washington, D.C., 1982, p. viii.

32. *The New York Times*, Oct. 11, 1984.

33. *The New York Times*, Feb. 23, 1984.

34. *The New York Times*, Sept. 27, 1984.

35. Lieutenant Colonel David Evans, "Technological Bloat Plagues the Pentagon," *The Wall Street Journal*, Aug. 15, 1983.

36. Thomas H. Etzold, *Defense or Delusion?* Harper and Row, New York, 1982, p. 102.

37. *The New York Times*, Aug. 8, 1983.

38. *The New York Times*, Sept. 27, 1984.

39. Deborah Shapley, "The Army's New Fighting Doctrine," *The New York Times Magazine*, Nov. 28, 1982, p. 37.

40. Robert A. Bender, "The Defense Budget and Civil-Military Relations," in Charles Cochran (ed.), *Civil-Military Relations*, Free Press, New York, 1974; Sanders, op. cit., pp. 3–132.

41. Robert S. McNamara, *The Essence of Security: Reflections in Office*, Harper and Row, New York, 1968, p. 144.

42. Prepared with the assistance of Jerry Filippatos of Columbia University.

43. James Roherty, "The Office of the Secretary of Defense: The Laird and McNamara Styles," in John P. Lovell and Philip S. Kronenberg (eds.), *New Civil-Military Relations*, Transaction Books, New Brunswick, N.J., 1974.

44. Robert A. Bender, "The Defense Budget and Civil-Military Relations," in Cochran, op. cit.

45. Sanders, op. cit.

46. *Department of Defense Annual Report, FY 1982*, GPO, Washington, D.C., 1982, table C-9.

47. *The New York Times*, Mar. 26, 1983.

48. *The New York Times*, Dec. 5, 1982.

49. *Department of Defense Annual Report, FY 1948*, GPO, Washington, D.C., 1948.

50. *The Defense Buildup and the Economy*, JEC staff study, Washington, D.C., February, 1982.

51. Simon Ramo, *America's Technology Slip*, Wiley, New York, 1980.

52. *The New York Times*, Nov. 25, 1981.

53. Bruce Russet, *What Price Vigilance?* Yale University Press, New Haven, Conn., 1970.

54. *U.S. Military Force—1980*, Center for Defense Information, Washington, D.C., p. 86.

55. Thomas Powers, "Is Nuclear War Impossible?" *The Atlantic*, vol. 254, no. 5, November 1984, pp. 53–64.

56. The National Academy of Science, *The Effects on the Atmosphere of a Major Nuclear Exchange*, National Academy Press, Washington, D.C., 1984.

57. *The New York Times*, Aug. 5, 1984.

58. *Nuclear War: A Handbook*, Common Cause, Washington, D.C., 1983, p. 37.

59. Warner Schilling, "U.S. Strategic Nuclear Concepts in the 1970s: The Search for Sufficiently Equivalent Countervailing Parity," *International Security*, vol. 6, no. 2, fall 1981, pp. 49–79.

60. *Department of Defense Annual Report, FY 1982*.

61. Robert Jervis, *The Illogic of American Nuclear Strategy*, Cornell University Press, Ithaca, N.Y., 1984.

62. Ministry of Defense, U.S.S.R., *Whence the Threat to Peace?* translated in *The New York Times*, Jan. 18, 1982.

63. Ashton B. Carter and David N. Schwartz, *Ballistic Missile Defense*, Brookings, Washington, D.C., 1984.

64. Strobe Talbott, *Deadly Gambits*, Knopf, New York, 1984.

FURTHER READING

Adams, Gordon: *The Iron Triangle*, Council on Economic Priorities, New York, 1981. A discussion of how procurement decisions are made when Pentagon officers, legislators, and contractors team up.

Allison, Graham, et al.: *Hawks, Doves and Owls*, Norton, New York, 1985. Proposals to reduce the risks of nuclear war.

Bracken, Paul: *The Command and Control of Nuclear Forces*, Yale University Press, New Haven, Conn., 1983. A description of the chain of command for the use of nuclear weapons.

deGrasse, Robert, Jr., et al.: *The Costs and Consequences of Reagan's Military Buildup*, Council on Economic Priorities, New York, 1982. The case for the reallocation of defense funding to civilian use.

Erlich, Paul R., et al.: *The Cold and the Dark: The World after Nuclear War*, Norton, New York, 1985. A report of the Conference on the Long Term Worldwide Biological Consequences of Nuclear War.

Etzold, Thomas H.: *Defense or Delusion?* Harper and Row, New York, 1982. A trenchant critique of our present defense posture by a professor at the Naval War College.

Fallows, James: *The National Defense*, Random House, New York, 1983. A journalistic account of corruption in the Pentagon.

Ford, Daniel: *The Button*, Simon and Schuster, New York, 1985. The Pentagon's command and control of nuclear weapons.

Freedman, Lawrence: *The Evolution of Nuclear Strategy*, St. Martin's, New York, 1981. A narrative and analytical account of theories on fighting a nuclear war.

Gansler, Jacques: *The Defense Industry*, M.I.T., Cambridge, Mass., 1981. A former Pentagon official discusses inefficiencies in the defense industry and how to improve its performance.

Huntingon, Samuel: *The Soldier and the State*, Harvard University Press, Cambridge, Mass. 1957. A study of soldiers and politicians throughout history, in Europe, Asia, and the United States.

Jordan, Amos, and William Taylor: *American National Security*, Johns Hopkins, Baltimore, 1981. A discussion by two instructors at West Point of the issues, organizations, and players in defense politics.

Kovner, Mark: *Defense Dollars and Sense*, Common Cause, Washington, D.C., 1983. An overview of the defense budget process.

Powers, Thomas: *Thinking about Nuclear War*, Knopf, New York, 1982. A discussion of nuclear doctrines and their consequences.

Reichart, John F., and Steven R. Sturm (eds.): *American Defense Policy*, 5th ed., Johns Hopkins, Baltimore, 1982. A compendium, edited by professors at the Air Force Academy, of articles on national security, nuclear strategy, arms control, and civil-military relations.

Sedacca, Sandra: *Up in Arms*, Common Cause, Washington, D.C., 1984. An introduction to nuclear strategy and arms control efforts, along with chilling descriptions of the consequences of nuclear war.

U.S. Congress, Office of Technology Assessment: *The Effects of Nuclear War*, GPO, Washington, D.C., 1979.

THE STUDY BREAK

All My Sons. A 1948 movie, based on a play by Arthur Miller, about a corrupt defense contractor in World War II. Edward G. Robinson and Burt Lancaster star.

The Anderson Platoon. An award-winning French documentary, produced in 1967, about American soldiers in Vietnam.

The Atomic Cafe. A compendium of United States government film clips, made in 1982, designed to prepare Americans for atomic war.

The Day After. An ABC television special, produced in 1983, depicting the effects of a nuclear attack on Lawrence, Kansas.

Dr. Strangelove, Or How I Learned To Stop Worrying and Love the Bomb. A 1964 comic satire about generals, presidents, and nuclear strategists, starring Peter Sellers.

MASH. A movie and a television series presenting a tragicomic view of war from the perspective of surgeons in an army field hospital.

On the Beach. A 1959 movie, starring Anthony Perkins, Gregory Peck, and Ava Gardner about what happens when nuclear fallout reaches Australia after World War III.

Patton. A 1970 movie starring George C. Scott. Old-fashioned entertainment about what went on in the front lines during the Second World War.

Seven Days in May. A 1964 thriller about a plot by the United States military to overthrow the government, starring Ava Gardner, Burt Lancaster, and Kirk Douglas.

Testament. A public television drama, produced in 1983, about the way small-town people cope with the aftereffects of an atomic attack on a nearby city. Jane Alexander stars.

USEFUL SOURCES

Aerospace and Aviation Week. Developments in the design and procurement of high tech weaponry.

Arms Control: Journal of Arms Control and Disarmament. Articles on arms control policies and alternatives.

The Bulletin of Atomic Scientists. Articles by nuclear scientists and others on arms control and weaponry.

Cochran, Thomas, William M. Arkin, and Milton M. Hoenig: *Nuclear Weapons Databook,* vol. 1, *U.S. Nuclear Forces and Capabilities,* Ballinger, Cambridge, Mass., 1984. The first of eight projected volumes, sponsored by the Natural Resources Defense Council, describing nuclear weapons and carriers, capabilities, range, destructive power, and accuracy.

Collins, John M.: *U.S./Soviet Military Balance: Statistical Trends: 1970–1982,* Congressional Research Service, Washington, D.C., 1983. An account of what the other side is doing, periodically updated.

Congressional Budget Office: *Modernizing U.S. Strategic Offensive Forces: The Administration's Program and Alternatives,* GPO, Washington, D.C., 1983. A critique of the Reagan administration's arms buildup.

Fine, Melinda, and Peter M. Steven (eds.): *American Peace Directory, 1984,* Ballinger, Cambridge, Mass., 1984. The names and addresses of grass-roots peace and détente organizations.

The International Institute for Strategic Studies: *The Military Balance,* Institute for Strategic Studies, London, annually. A study of east-west force postures.

————: *Strategic Survey,* Institute for Strategic Studies, London, annually. A discussion of what force postures mean in terms of national strategy and balance of power.

Keegan, John (ed.): *World Armies,* 2d ed., Gale Research Company, Detroit; 1983. A study of the military forces of each nation.

Leontief, Wassily, and Faye Duchin: *Military Spending: Facts and Figures, Worldwide Implications and Future Outlook,* Oxford University Press, New York, 1983. A report on the military budgets of each nation.

Office of the Secretary of Defense: *Annual Report of the Secretary of Defense,* GPO, Washington, D.C., annually. Doctrines, force postures, and budgets of the military.

Setting National Priorities, Brookings, Washington, D.C., annually. A volume usually containing a chapter offering a critique of the current budgets and military doctrines.

Sivard, Ruth L.: *World Military and Social Expenditures, 1985,* World Priorities, Washington, D.C., 1985. Annual breakdowns of military budgets, by country.

ORGANIZATIONS

The American Security Council. 499 South Capitol Street, S.W., Washington, D.C. 20003. For more information phone 202-484-1676.

Center for Defense Information. 600 Maryland Avenue, S.W., Suite 303 West, Washington, D.C. 20024. For more information phone 202-484-9490.

Center on Budget and Policy Priorities. 236 Massachusetts Avenue, N.E., Suite 505, Washington, D.C. 20002. For more information phone 202-546-9737.

Coalition for a New Foreign and Military Policy. 120 Maryland Avenue, N.E., Washington, D.C. 20002. For more information phone 202-546-8400.

Committee on the Present Danger. 1800 Massachusetts Avenue, N.W., Washington, D.C. 20036. For more information phone 202-466-7444.

Council on Economic Priorities. 84 Fifth Avenue, New York, N.Y. For more information phone 212-691-8550.

GLOSSARY

Action-forcing process. A sequence of events which requires advance planning to meet a deadline.

Administration. A small unit of government (for example, the Welfare Administration) or the top officials appointed by the president (for example, the Reagan administration).

Affirmative action. Efforts to take into consideration characteristics such as race to improve the employment and educational opportunities of people who have been discriminated against in the past.

Agency. A unit of government (for example, the Agency for International Development).

Amendments. Proposed changes to a bill or constitution.

Amicus curiae brief. A legal argument filed by a group that is not itself a party to a case.

Anarchy. A society without government or law, based on the theory that government does more harm than good.

Anti-Federalists. The faction which opposed ratification of the Constitution. Also, the politicians in the 1790s who favored a weak central government. *See also* Federalists.

Appellate jurisdiction. The jurisdiction of the higher courts in reviewing cases from lower courts.

Appropriations. Funds requested in a bill which is reported by an appropriations committee and which provides budget authority. *See also* Budget authority.

Aristocracy. In theory, rule by the most talented. In practice, a term used by rulers to legitimize their power.

Articles of Confederation. The political compact of American states created by the Continental Congress in 1777 and ratified in 1781.

Authoritarian. Relating to nondemocratic rule by leaders who claim to know what is best for the people and who usually threaten or use force to maintain themselves in power.

Authority. The degree to which people accept a ruler's competence to govern.

Authorizing legislation. Laws which empower the government to act or set limits on governmental action.

Back channel. A person who channels communication between officials by bypassing normal procedures, especially in matters of diplomacy.

Ballot. A record of a voter's choice in an election. *Open* ballots involve a voice vote, a show of hands, or congregating in a location; *closed* or *secret* ballots involve a ballot box or voting machine; *party* ballot is a list of all the nominees for office of a single party which may be put in a *ballot box* (if one is used) by a voter to vote a straight ticket. A *party-column* ballot makes it easy to vote a straight ticket; an *office-column* ballot encourages voters to think about the candidate, not the party.

Bicameral. Consisting of two legislature chambers, which must pass identical bills in order for a measure to become law.

Bill of Rights. The first Ten Amendments to the national Constitution. Also, the provisions of state constitutions guaranteeing civil rights and liberties.

Bipartisan. Relating to or involving support by the two major parties.

Block grant. Funds distributed by one unit of government to another for a general purpose, such as law enforcement or housing.

Bond. A promise by a unit of government (or a corporation) to repay a loan at a specified rate of interest.

Borrowing authority. The authority of the government, established by law, to borrow money and incur obligations, usually by selling bonds.

Brandeis brief. A legal argument submitted to a court, consisting of facts that show the impact of laws or previous court cases on society.

Budget authority. The authority of government officials, established by laws passed by Congress, to spend money. *See also* Appropriations, Borrowing authority, and Contract authority.

Budget debt. The cumulative amount owed by the government in the form of Treasury bonds, bills, and notes.

Budget deficit. The amount in a fiscal year by which government spending exceeds budget receipts. A *stimulative* deficit is designed to boost the economy out of a recession or depression; a *structural* deficit is designed to run the economy at full employment.

Budget receipts. Money collected by the government in a fiscal year, including taxes, tariffs, fees, fines, sales of assets, and gifts.

Budget resolution. A congressional concurrent resolution (not subject to presidential veto) which sets targets or binding totals for budget authority and outlays.

Budget surplus. The amount by which budget receipts exceed outlays in a fiscal year.

Bureau. A small unit of government. *See also* Administration and Agency.

Bureau chief. The official who heads an administration, agency, bureau, or other small unit of government.

Business cycle. The period of time during which the performance of the economy goes from recession to recovery through boom and downturn.

Cabinet. A body consisting of the twelve secretaries and the attorney

general, who run the executive departments; the vice president of the United States; and other officials with Cabinet status who meet as a group with the president.

Cabinet councils. Committees which consist of Cabinet secretaries and other top officials and which focus on government activities that cross departmental lines (for example, natural resources).

Candidate. A person who is running for an elective office.

Capital gains tax. The tax levied on the increase in value of an asset at the time of sale. Capital gains are usually taxed at a lower rate than income.

Casework. The help given by congressional staffers to people in their districts.

Categorical grant. Funds transferred from one level of government to another for a specified program (for example, highway construction).

Caucus. A meeting of the members of a political party at which they nominate candidates, discuss issues, and plan strategy. Until 1824 the congressional caucus was used to nominate candidates for president. Today, *precinct* caucuses in half the states choose delegates to district or state conventions, which send delegates to a national convention. At conventions delegates may caucus by geographic area, ideology, or issues. The Democrats and Republicans in the House and Senate meet in four separate *legislative party* caucuses.

Censorship. The suppression of information by the government.

Censure. A resolution condemning an official for a specific action or pattern of conduct.

Certification. A legal provision which requires officials to indicate that a specified circumstance exists before they act.

Certiorari (writ of). A petition to a higher court to review the decision of a lower court.

Chain of command. The channels through which orders are transmitted from superiors to subordinates.

Chamber seniority. Uninterrupted years of service in a legislative chamber.

Charismatic. Relating to the attributes of a ruler which lead people to believe that he or she has exceptional leadership qualities.

Checks and balances. The constitutional grants of power to the three branches of government enabling them to interfere with one another so as to prevent any one branch from accumulating all power or going beyond the bounds of the Constitution.

Chilling effect. The effect of a governmental action which leads people to believe that they will suffer adverse consequences if they exercise their civil liberties.

Civil liberties. The individual freedoms of speech, expression, assembly, religion, conscience, privacy, and due process of law, guaranteed by the national constitution and the state constitutions.

Civil service. The administrative service of the government consisting of permanently employed nonmilitary government workers. *See also* Political executives and Senior Executive Service.

Class. In politics, a large aggregate of people with similar social and economic characteristics.

Class action. A lawsuit which is filed by an individual but which seeks damages or relief for "all persons similarly situated."

Class polarization. Polarization that occurs when different classes support different candidates in elections or have different attitudes toward public policies.

Clear and present danger. The basis of a test advanced by Supreme Court Justice Oliver Wendell Holmes, Jr., specifying that the government may not abridge freedom of speech unless an illegal act is about to be committed because of a speech.

Clientele policy. A policy providing for costs to be widely shared, while benefits go to a clearly defined clientele group.

Closed rule. A rule permitting no amendments to a bill.

Cloture. A motion to end debate, usually requiring more than a simple majority to pass.

Coalition building. Bringing people into a temporary agreement until

the number necessary for action to be taken on an issue has been reached (usually a majority). A *partisan* coalition consists primarily of members of a single party; a *bipartisan* coalition brings in some members of the other party; a *conservative,* coalition combines most Republicans in Congress with many southern Democrats; a *liberal-labor* coalition combines liberal and moderate Democrats with urban or suburban Republicans from the northeast and the mid-Atlantic states.

Coattail effect. The positive or negative impact that a candidate running for a high office can have on candidates running for lower offices on the same party ticket. The *reverse* coattail effect is the impact of a candidate running for a lower office on candidates running for high offices.

Codetermination. Policy development and implementation by more than one branch of government.

Collective security. An agreement according to which each nation involved agrees to defend its allies against attack in return for similar pledges from them.

Committee hearing. A meeting of a committee to consider testimony on a bill by government officials and interested parties.

Committee leaders. The chair of a committee, the ranking majority member (next in line to be the chair), and the ranking minority member (who would be chair if his or her party had a majority).

Committee report. A document describing a bill that a committee wants Congress to pass. A *minority* report may urge defeat or amendments.

Committee seniority. Years of uninterrupted service on a congressional committee.

Concurrent power. Power that exists when more than one branch of government claims or has a constitutional power, such as the power to decide to go to war or conclude agreements with another nation.

Conditional delegation. The legislative authority to take action if certain conditions are met.

Confederation. A government in

which the constituent units retain their sovereignty and cede limited powers to national institutions.

Conference committee. A meeting of legislators from both chambers at which they reconcile their versions of a bill before final passage.

Conference report. The version of a bill returned to both chambers for final passage by the conference committee.

Congressional caucus. *See* Caucus.

Congressional coalitions. *See* Coalition building.

Congressional party. The members of a political party in Congress and the party committees which help them campaign.

Congressional roles. The routine ways in which legislators act. A *delegate* tries to "vote the district" and represent the wishes of the voters; a *trustee* "votes conscience" and tries to do what is in the best interest of the voters; a *politico* trades votes and tries to win influence.

Connecticut Compromise. An agreement consisting of compromises between the small and the large states at the Constitutional Convention involving equal representation of the states in the Senate.

Conscience rule. The proposal that delegates to national presidential nominating conventions be allowed to vote as they see fit, even if they are pledged to vote for a particular candidate.

Consensus. An agreement on what is to be done.

Conservative. In American politics, someone who believes in limiting the role of the national government in domestic affairs and in giving the states or the market more scope in allocating resources or solving problems. *See also* Liberal.

Constitution. The fundamental governing principles of a nation. It may be an unwritten collection of laws, customs, and usages (as in Great Britain) or a written document, like the American Constitution.

Constitutional Convention of 1787. The convention held in Philadelphia at which the Constitution was drafted.

Constitutional courts. The federal courts that deal with constitutional

and statutory issues. Federal court judges are appointed for life. *See* Statutory courts.

Constitutional law. Decisions based on an interpretation of the Constitution in court cases. Commentary on constitutional law is found in law reviews.

Contempt of court. Failure to obey a judicial order. Persons found in contempt of court may be imprisoned or fined.

Continental Congress. The congress of representatives from the states which declared independence in 1776.

Contingency elections. Elections that are held when normal procedures fail. If the electoral college system fails to work, the House elects the president, and the Senate elects the vice president.

Continuing resolution. A law which provides budget authority to keep ongoing activities at their present level when one or more bills providing new budget authority have not been enacted.

Contract authority. The authority of government officials, established by law, to enter into contracts or incur other obligations in advance of congressional appropriations.

Convention. A meeting of delegates representing different territorial units at a single place. A *constitutional* convention creates or revises a state constitution or the national Constitution; a *nominating* convention (district, state, or national) selects party candidates for office.

Convention delegates. The representatives of a party's organization or primary and caucus voters. *Personalists* attend to nominate a candidate to whom they are pledged; *purists* are committed to particular issues or ideologies; *professionals* seek benefits for their state and local parties.

Corruption. The misuse of public office for personal gain.

Council of Economic Advisors (CEA). A presidential advisory unit which prepares the annual economic report of the president.

Counterforce. The targeting of an enemy's nuclear launchers.

Counterstrike. A retaliatory nuclear strike on enemy targets.

Countervailing targeting. The tar-

geting of an enemy's political institutions.

County courthouse ring. A corrupt local party organization which controlled county judges, prosecutors, and sheriffs.

Covert action. An action involving the use of force against another nation without official acknowledgment or responsibility.

Critical election. An election in which the majority party retains office but loses support from part of its coalition.

Current services estimates. Estimates of receipts, outlays, and budget authority for coming fiscal years which assume no change in activities.

Dealignment. The detachment of electoral constituencies from traditional party identifications.

Debt. *See* Budget debt.

Deferral. An action or a lack of action by government officials that delays outlays to future fiscal years. Deferrals may be overturned by Congress.

Deficit. *See* Budget deficit.

Delegation of power. The designation of a unit of government by the executive, legislative, or judicial branch to implement policy.

Democracy. Government of, by, and for the people, who retain the right to choose their rulers and policies.

Demonstration grant. Funds provided by the government to try out new programs.

Department. A large unit of government, whose secretary sits in the Cabinet.

Departmental privilege. The claim that departmental business involving the White House may be kept from Congress and the courts.

Department secretary. *See* Cabinet and Department.

Depression. A period of economic decline, stock market collapse, and high unemployment.

Deregulation. The reduction or elimination of government economic controls.

Deviating election. An election in which the minority party wins but the majority party retains its advantage in terms of party identification.

Direct democracy. Government in which the people vote directly on the issues, as in a New England town meeting.

Distributive policy. A policy providing for costs to be broadly shared, while benefits are distributed to specific groups, usually those which have influence among decision makers in the bureaucracy.

Dual federalism. A constitutional interpretation which assigns powers strictly to either the states or the national government.

Due process of law. The requirement that the government not interfere with people's lives, liberty, or property without adhering to constitutional procedures and impartial administration of the laws. Due process of law is guaranteed by the Fifth and Fourteenth Amendments.

Dynamic factors. The influences on elections which change between one contest and the next, such as personalities and issues. *See also* Stable factors.

Elastic clause. Article I, Section 8, paragraph 18 of the Constitution, which states that Congress may make laws which are "necessary and proper" for carrying out the duties of all branches of government.

Election district. *See* Precinct.

Electoral college. A body consisting of the state electors who choose the president and the vice president of the United States.

Electors. The individuals chosen by the voters for the purpose of selecting one or more government officials. *See also* Electoral college.

Entitlements. Goods and services which government officials must provide to individuals who meet certain criteria set by law (for example, social security payments, welfare, and food stamps).

Equal protection clause. The Fourteenth Amendment to the Constitution, which provides that the states must guarantee all citizens equal protection under the laws. The courts use this clause to strike down laws which discriminate against people on the basis of race.

Equal Rights Amendment. A proposed amendment to the Constitution that would prohibit gender discrimination.

Equity power. The judicial power to effect a civil remedy which does not involve a monetary award to an injured party.

Establishment clause. The First Amendment prohibition of an official religion and of government funding of, and participation in, religious practices.

Exclusionary rule. A rule that makes evidence which was knowingly obtained by the government in violation of the Constitution or the legal rights of the accused inadmissible in judicial proceedings.

Exclusive power. Power assigned to a single branch of government. *See also* Concurrent power.

Executive branch. The president, the vice president, and the principal heads of the departments and other agencies accountable to the president. The term does not appear in the Constitution.

Executive Office of the President (EOP). The agencies which provide information, advice, and staff services to the executive branch. *See also* Council of Economic Advisors, National Security Council, and Office of Management and Budget.

Executive power. The power of the president, set forth in Article II of the Constitution, to make policy for the executive branch.

Executive privilege. The claim that the president's conversations with aides and departmental officials and the president's documents may be kept from Congress and the judiciary.

Executive supremacy. The claim that the president heads the government and that the other branches should cooperate with the president's policy initiatives.

Exploratory committee. A committee established by a contender for elective office before the official announcement of the candidacy.

Family assistance program. A proposed program that would have replaced the welfare system with grants to all families with children.

Favor. Patronage given by a politician in return for support of policies.

Favorite son. A home-state candidate who is put in nomination by a delegation to keep it uncommitted until it decides which contender to support.

Federalism. The division of powers between a national government (with sovereignty) and subordinate geographic units (such as states or provinces) which are guaranteed their powers by the constitution. *See also* Confederation.

The Federalist. A series of essays written in 1788 by Alexander Hamilton, John Jay, and James Madison. They were intended to persuade the New York convention to ratify the Constitution.

Federalists. The groups which favored ratification of the Constitution in 1788 and 1789. Also, the political party which formed in the 1790s around Alexander Hamilton and John Adams and which favored a strong national government and a national bank. *See also* Anti-Federalists.

Federal Reserve Board. The agency established by Congress to regulate the national banking system and currency.

Federation. A federal system. *See also* Federalism.

Filibuster. A prolonged debate in a legislative assembly, the purpose of which is to prevent a vote on a bill.

First strike. A surprise attack on an enemy's strategic nuclear forces, designed to eliminate its retaliatory capability.

First use. The use of tactical nuclear weapons to neutralize a conventional attack launched by a larger military force.

Fiscal equalization. The use of the national government's taxing and spending powers to redistribute national wealth from richer to poorer areas.

Fiscal federalism. The impact of the taxing and spending policies of the states on the national economy.

Fiscal policy. A policy of using taxing and spending powers to influence economic performance. *A compen-*

satory policy attempts to moderate the business cycle; a *propulsive* policy tries to achieve high rates of growth; a *corrective* policy is designed to alleviate a specific problem, such as high inflation.

Fiscal year. A twelve-month period used by the government to measure receipts and outlays. The calendar year begins on January 1, while the fiscal year for the national government starts on October 1 of the previous year.

Flexible response. The multiple targeting options and levels of retaliation in response to an enemy's use of strategic or tactical nuclear weapons.

Foreign Service. The career officials in American embassies, consulates, and the State Department.

Free market. An economic market in which the pricing and allocating mechanism for goods and services is based on supply and demand and in which neither sellers nor buyers combine to influence prices.

Gaffe. An inaccurate, offensive, or vulgar remark.

General revenue sharing. A program established by the national government to provide the states with funds for general government services.

Gerrymander. To draw district lines in such a way as to favor one party. Also, a district drawn as a result of gerrymandering.

Gold-plating. Providing features on military equipment that are unnecessary to carry out a mission.

Government. The institutions established by a society to make policies and enforce the laws. A government possesses a monopoly on the legitimate use of force. *See also* Legitimacy.

Grandfather clause. A legal provision stating that individuals who have rights or claims against the government do not lose them as a result of changes in the law. Grandfather clauses were used to guarantee whites the right to vote in southern states after literacy tests were introduced in the 1890s.

Grant-in-aid. Funds allocated by one level of government for programs carried out by another.

Habeas corpus, writ of. A constitutional provision requiring officials to bring anyone whom they arrest or detain before a magistrate and to state their reasons for the arrest. A writ of habeas corpus may be suspended in times of emergency.

Hearing. *See* Committee hearing.

Honeymoon effect. The tendency of legislators to cooperate with a newly elected executive official for a few months.

Impeachment. The constitutional method of charging presidents or judicial officials with high crimes or misdemeanors and of trying them for their misconduct in office. If convicted, they are removed from office. The House votes for impeachment, and the Senate conducts the trial.

Imperial presidency. A presidency such as those of post-World War II presidents who made war without congressional declaration and who vastly expanded their other powers. *See also* Executive supremacy, Prerogative powers, and Presidential powers.

Impoundment. An action or a lack of action by an official that precludes expenditures provided for by Congress. *See also* Deferral and Rescission act.

Incorporation. The judicial doctrine that extends some or all of the first Ten Amendments to the Constitution to state actions.

Incumbency effect. The tendency of voters to support the incumbent of the other party in an election.

Incumbent. A person who holds an office that is being contested in an election.

Independent agencies. Units of government that are not under the direct supervision of the president and whose officials are usually not subject to the president's removal powers, except for misconduct. These include independent *regulatory* agencies, *public corporations*, and many *authorities* and *boards*. *See also* Federal Reserve Board.

Independent expenditures. Funds spent on behalf of a candidate by a political action committee (PAC) which are not coordinated with the candidate's campaign and are not subject to federal limitations on contributions.

Indirect democracy. Government in which voters elect the representatives who make policies and the officials who carry them out. *See also* Direct democracy.

Industrial policy. A government tax, spending, and regulatory policy designed to influence investment in industrial enterprises.

Inflation. A general rise in prices.

Influence. The power to get others to do something of their own volition by convincing them that it is in their own best interest.

Initiative. A petition which puts a proposal on a ballot for decision by voters, bypassing the legislature. *See also* Direct democracy and Referendum.

Institutionalized presidency. A presidency in which the agencies and staff assistants help the president and the staff officials to whom the president delegates responsibility. *See also* Executive Office of the President and White House Office.

Interactive media. Media involving two-way communication, which allows viewers to transmit information back to a broadcasting studio or a central computer.

Interest group. An organization whose members have common goals and which attempts to influence government policy by helping candidates run for office, testifying before elected officials, and participating in the administration of programs. *See also* Pluralism.

Intergovernmental system. The system of administrative relationships between the national government, the state governments, and local units of government.

Internationalism. A government's participation in international

agreements and organizations to promote national security and prosperity.

Interstate compacts. Agreements between two or more states. Most such compacts require the assent of Congress.

Interventionism. A government's protection of its national interests through involvement in the internal affairs of other nations.

Iron triangles. Alliances formed between bureau chiefs, lobbyists, and committee leaders.

Isolationism. A policy of defending the national interest by keeping foreign involvement and commitments to a minimum.

Issue networks. Groups of policy experts who communicate, leading to coalitions that attempt to influence policy. Issue networks have a broader range of participants than iron triangles.

Jim Crow. Laws and ordinances in southern states which segregated the races in the 1890s. Many were not overturned until passage of the Civil Rights Act of 1964.

Judicial activism. The tendency of some judges to use their understanding of the original constitutional principles to fashion judicial remedies for today's problems and to give less weight to previous judicial decisions. *See also* Judicial restraint and Stare decisis.

Judicial administration. The power of the judiciary to supervise state and national agencies in order to effect compliance with court orders, such as those ending racial discrimination.

Judicial branch. The federal district courts, the courts of appeals, the federal legislative courts, and the Supreme Court of the United States. The term does not appear in the Constitution.

Judicial orders. Orders requiring government officials or private parties to take or to refrain from taking specified actions.

Judicial restraint. The tendency of some judges to follow past precedents and defer to the policies of the other two branches. *See also* Judicial activism and Stare decisis.

Judicial review. The power of the courts to determine the constitutionality of the actions of the other two branches of government and to hold unconstitutional actions null and void.

Judicial supremacy. The doctrine that the judiciary is the final arbiter of what the Constitution means.

Laissez-faire. The doctrine that the government should not interfere with the allocation of resources by the marketplace.

Lame duck. An incumbent who is ineligible to run for reelection. A lame-duck Congress is an outgoing Congress that meets after the November elections.

Landmark decision. A Supreme Court decision that establishes important principles of constitutional law.

Legislative branch. The House of Representatives, Senate, and various congressional agencies, such as the Congressional Budget Office. The term does not appear in the Constitution.

Legislative courts. The federal courts (such as tax courts) established by Congress to try specialized cases involving specific statutes. Judges serve fixed terms. *See also* Constitutional courts.

Legislative party caucus. *See* Caucus.

Legislative party leaders. The Speaker of the House, the majority and minority leaders, and other legislators selected by the House and Senate party caucuses to hold important posts.

Legislative supremacy. The doctrine that Congress embodies national sovereignty and should set policy through its laws and appropriations.

Legislative veto. The provision of a law that allows a committee, a chamber, or the entire Congress to veto executive decisions or actions before or after implementation. The legislative veto was ruled unconstitutional in 1983 by the Supreme Court in *Chadha v. INS.*

Legitimacy. In politics, the perceived attribute of having a right to rule and of doing so justly.

Libel. A false written or recorded statement made knowingly and maliciously to damage someone. A spoken statement of this kind is called *slander*.

Liberal. In American politics, a person who believes that the national government should increase its role in domestic affairs, regulate the marketplace, and try to solve the country's economic and social problems. In European politics, the term refers to a person who relies more on the market than on the government. *See also* Conservative.

Literacy tests. Tests of a prospective voter's ability to read at a certain grade level or to interpret a section of the state constitution in order to register to vote.

Living Constitution. The Constitution as a set of principles guiding the solution of modern problems.

Lobbyist. A representative of an interest group who tries to influence government officials.

Lockean prerogative. The power claimed by executive officials to ignore or even violate the Constitution and laws if necessary to preserve the nation in times of extreme crisis.

Maintaining election. An election which is won by the majority party and in which the stable factors remain unchanged.

Majority. More than half. A *simple* majority is half plus 1; an *extraordinary* majority is anything greater than that.

Mandamus, writ of. A judicial order requiring officials to perform their duties.

Media politics. Campaigning which relies primarily on reaching voters through advertising rather than through the efforts of party workers.

Merit system. A system of appointment to office based on expertise and competence rather than political connections, quotas, wealth, or family background. The merit system is used for many appointments in the civil service.

Midterm convention. A convention held by a political party for the

purpose of discussing issues rather than nominating a candidate.

Military-industrial complex. The close association that exists between the Pentagon, defense contractors, and congressional committees.

Military Keynesians. People who believe that military spending promotes employment and business prosperity.

Monetarists. People who believe that the most important economic factor is the supply of money and credit.

Monetary policy. A policy that attempts to influence economic conditions by influencing the supply of money and its cost.

Multiple advocacy. The presentation of different viewpoints on issues to decision makers by officials at the top levels of government.

Mutual assured destruction (MAD). The theory that if each superpower can retaliate against the other's first strike, a system of stable deterrence will be created.

National agenda politics. Politics aimed at influencing the outcome of a policy controversy by winning public support.

National command authority. The authority of the highest-level civilian officials who supervise the military chain of command.

Nationalism. The doctrine that a people should govern themselves. Also, the doctrine that the principal responsibility of a nation is to safeguard its own interests, even at the expense of other nations. *See also* Internationalism.

National Security Council (NSC). The advisory board that debates national security policies. The NSC consists of the president, the vice president, the secretary of state, the secretary of defense, and the chair of the Joint Chiefs of Staff (plus other officials invited to attend meetings). Its staff is supervised by the *national security assistant* to the president, one of the president's most important foreign policy advisers.

Necessary and proper clause. *See* Elastic clause.

Negative campaigns. Campaigns in which candidates attack the patriotism, character, or personal life of other candidates. Negative campaigns are often conducted by ideological and single-issue PACs. *See also* Independent expenditures and Political action committee.

Negative income tax. A proposed system that would give low-income people income from the government's tax agencies.

Negotiations. The processes by which parties try to resolve their differences on an issue. A *logroll* is a promise by each party to support a proposal of the other; a *package deal* puts all proposals in one bill; a *side payment* is something which is given to one or more of the parties but which has nothing to do with the issue; a *compromise* is an agreement according to which all parties modify their goals.

Neoconservatives. Democrats who remain liberal in domestic matters but who want strong national action in foreign affairs, including a military buildup.

Neoliberals. Democrats who have become skeptical about the ability of the national government to solve social problems and who believe that the size and scope of the bureaucracy should be reduced.

New Jersey Plan. Proposals put forward by the small states at the Constitutional Convention, calling for a weak executive and a Congress in which the states would have equal representation.

New patronage. Consulting contracts and professional retainers given to politically connected firms whose personnel have helped elect candidates to office.

New right. An alliance of conservatives who believe that a party can win elections only if it appeals to the broad mass of Americans on tax and social issues and of religious fundamentalists who believe that the government's policies should follow their interpretation of biblical precepts and prophecy.

Nightwatchman state. A government that restricts itself to maintaining domestic peace and providing for the national security. *See also* Positive state.

Nomination. The selection by a party of a candidate to run for office in the general elections, by *designation* of a party committee, by a *convention* representing party organizations, or by a *primary* that is open to the party voters and sometimes to independents.

Noncoordinated campaigns. Campaigns which are made without any communication with the candidate's organization and which are therefore exempt from the limits on campaign financing. *See also* Independent expenditures, Negative campaigns, and Political action committee.

Normal vote. The vote in an election if only party identification and the turnout rates of different groups determine the results. The normal vote is never the actual election results.

Nuclear winter. The condition that would exist (in the view of some scientists) after nuclear explosions produced enough smoke and dust to block out sunlight for a year or more, thus eliminating most life on earth.

Nullification. The doctrine that in a federal system a state may refuse to allow the enforcement of national laws which its legislature rules violate the national Constitution.

Obligations. Orders placed, contracts awarded, and other legally binding commitments made by government officials during a fiscal year. *See also* Outlays.

Office of Management and Budget (OMB). The presidential agency which prepares the budget and the budget message, determines whether departmental legislative proposals are in accord with the presidential program, and briefs the president on bills which contain provisions that the president might wish to veto.

Open rule. A legislative rule permitting a proposal to be amended.

Open seat. A seat in Congress for which no incumbent is running.

Original jurisdiction. Jurisdiction involving cases brought before a court for trial on the basis of both facts and law.

Outlays. Checks issued or cash disbursed to discharge obligations. Outlays also include interest on the public debt, even if not disbursed, such as interest credited to United States savings bonds.

Oversight. Legislative review of executive actions. Also known as *legislative, administrative,* and *congressional* oversight.

Parliamentary system. A system in which the majority party in the legislature chooses from its ranks the ministers, who run the principal departments, as well as the prime minister, who presides over the cabinet.

Party committees. Organizations that are responsible for the conduct of party business. These include the *national* committees, which represent the state parties; the *congressional campaign* and *senatorial campaign* committees, which assist candidates for Congress in fund-raising and advertising campaigns; and *state* and *local* committees.

Party government. The officials in government who act in concert to implement the program which their party presented to the voters in the preceding election.

Party identification. Voters' predisposition to consider themselves members of a party and to vote for the candidates of that party.

Patronage. Government employment or business received as a result of political connections.

Per curiam decision. An unsigned decision representing the opinion of a court.

Persuasion. *See* Influence.

Plebiscite. An election held to decide an issue. *See also* Direct democracy.

Pledge rule. A rule for a nominating convention that the delegates must vote for the candidates whom they pledged to support in the primary and caucus contests.

Pluralism. The decentralization of power and influence to autonomous public and private organizations, which can form temporary coalitions to influence public policy.

Plurality. The largest number of votes for a candidate or for a position in an election. A majority is always a plurality, but in a multichoice contest a plurality may be less than a majority.

Plutocracy. Rule by the wealthy.

Pocket veto. Presidents' power to veto a bill presented to them within ten days of the adjournment of Congress. Such a veto cannot be overridden by Congress. *See also* Veto.

Policies. *See* Clientele policy, Distributive policy, Redistributive policy, and Regulatory policy.

Political action committee (PAC). A nonparty organization which may legally raise and spend funds to influence elections by running noncoordinated campaigns and which may donate limited amounts directly to candidates' campaign organizations.

Political culture. The core beliefs about how politics is and should be conducted.

Political executives. The presidential appointees to the top positions in the government. They may be removed at the president's discretion. *See also* Administration.

Political party. A group of people who organize to control the government by electing public officials. A political party consists of the *party organization,* which recruits and elects candidates; the *party-in-government,* which consists of party members who hold office; and the *party-in-the-electorate,* which is made up of voters who identify with the party and usually vote for its candidates.

Political question. An issue designated by the judiciary for resolution by the president and Congress.

Political socialization. Education about politics gained in school or in the political arena.

Politics. The art of using power and influence to form coalitions or create a consensus, to manage problems, to allocate resources, and to resolve conflicts without resort to force.

Poll tax. A small fee charged by local officials for the right to vote. Poll taxes are now unconstitutional as a result of the Twenty-Fourth Amendment, which was ratified in 1964.

Positive state. A government that deals with and solves economic and social problems. *See also* Nightwatchman state.

Poverty line. A measurement of income used by the Census Bureau. Families whose incomes are below the poverty line are classified as poor.

Power. The ability to get others to do things that they would not otherwise do. *See also* Influence.

Power elite. A permanent group which exercises the most power in society. A society with a power elite is the opposite of a pluralist society, in which many alliances form, all are temporary, and no group resolves all issues. Whether the United States has a power elite or is a pluralist society is a question on which political scientists are divided.

Power stakes. The factors in a situation that affect the power and influence of politicians.

Precinct. The smallest geographic unit in which votes are recorded by election officials. Also known as an *election district.*

Precinct captain. A local party official who mobilizes votes from supporters in a precinct.

Preferred freedoms doctrine. A judicial doctrine that emphasizes protection of the First Amendment guarantees against legislative action without due process.

Prerogative powers. Presidential powers exercised by virtue of the Constitution, sovereignty, international commitments and treaties, or the nature of an emergency. *See also* Lockean prerogative.

Presidential party. The party identifiers and committees which are oriented toward winning presidential (as opposed to congressional) elections. It includes the administration and most of the party's national committee.

Presidential powers. Powers that are assigned to the president by the Constitution, delegated by law, or established by custom and precedent. *Express* powers are mentioned in the Constitution; *inherent*

powers are those which are exercised pursuant to the responsibilities of the office (that is, the president's responsibilities as the chief executive, the chief diplomat, and the commander in chief); *implied* powers are those which enable the president to perform the express and inherent duties of the office and which are not prohibited by the Constitution.

Presidential Republicans. Registered Democrats, located mainly in the south, who vote Republican in many presidential elections.

President pro tempore. The presiding officer of the Senate in the absence of the vice president of the United States, usually the most senior member of the majority party.

Primaries. Contests for party nominations that are decided by the party-in-the-electorate.

Prior restraint. The power to prevent a speech or a publication from reaching its intended audience.

Professionalization of reform. The initiation of social and economic reform by experts in issue networks.

Proportional representation. The apportioning of seats in presidential primaries or legislative elections on the basis of the percentage of votes received by a candidate or a party. *See also* Winner-take-all elections.

Protective legislation. Regulatory laws which single out women and children for special treatment.

Proxy. The power to act in the absence of another. The proxy rule permitted party leaders at nominating conventions to cast the votes of delegates from their states.

Pseudo event. An event staged solely so that it will be covered by the news media.

Realigning election. An election in which the minority party wins and gains the advantage in terms of party identification.

Recession. A downturn in business activity, corporate profits, and employment.

Reconciliation act. A law passed by Congress which brings budget and

tax legislation into line with a congressional budget resolution.

Redistributive policy. A policy according to which costs are borne by all taxpayers to provide funds for cash payments or in-kind benefits to many people.

Redistricting. Changing legislative district lines.

Redundancy. In reference to weapons systems, the capability of completing a task in different ways; as a guard against a system malfunction.

Referendum. A popular vote on a proposal submitted to a state legislature. *See also* Direct democracy and Initiative.

Registrars. The public officials who register voters.

Registration. The process of legally qualifying to vote.

Regulatory policy. A government law or order designed to modify behavior by imposing costs or allocating benefits.

Reinforcing election. An election which is won by the majority party and which increases its advantage in party identification.

Reinstating election. An election, following a deviating election, which is won by the majority party.

Republic. A government in which the representatives of the people hold office and determine most public policies. *See also* Indirect democracy.

Reputation. A public official's overall character, as judged by the electorate. It may influence the official's calculations and conduct.

Reregulation. The restoration of regulations previously eliminated by Congress. *See also* Deregulation.

Rescission act. A law passed by Congress reducing or eliminating budget authority.

Responsible party. *See* Party government.

Responsible party system. A system of party competition in which each party takes a distinct position on important issues.

Retirement slump. The drop in electoral support of a party in a legislative district after its incumbent vacates a seat.

Retrospective voting. Voting based on a candidate's past performance.

Ripeness doctrine. The judicial rule specifying that a case should not be accepted for decision until the issues have fully evolved.

Runoff primary. A second primary held between the top two vote-getters if neither received a majority in the first primary.

Sedition. An attempt to overthrow the government by force. Seditious *speech* advocates the forceful overthrow of the government.

Self-regulation. The exercise of regulatory powers by private interest groups, without the interference of the government.

Senatorial courtesy. Presidents' practice of consulting senators from their party before nominating federal officials to positions in their states; soliciting the names of prospective nominees from these senators; and withdrawing the name of a nominee who a senator from the nominee's state says is "personally objectionable."

Senior Executive Service. The top-level managers of government programs who work under the political executives.

Seniority rule. A congressional rule which assigns members to committees partly on the basis of their *chamber seniority* and which determines their ranking on committees primarily on the basis of their *committee seniority*.

Separation of powers. The principle that legislative, executive, and judicial powers should be exercised by different institutions.

Shays's rebellion. A protest by farmers and former Revolutionary War soldiers in western Massachusetts in 1786 and 1787. It helped convince conservatives to organize the Constitutional Convention.

Social Darwinism. The theory that poverty and starvation improve the human species by eliminating the weak and promoting the "survival of the fittest."

Social insurance. Programs which spread the risk of unemployment or illness. Workers pay insurance premiums in the form of payroll taxes and receive benefits if they are ill or out of work.

Social issues. Issues such as busing to overcome racial segregation, prayer in schools, pornography, censorship in school libraries and textbooks, abortion, gun control, and other primarily non-economic issues.

Socialize risk. To implement programs by which the national government insures people or companies against risk (for example, flood insurance for individuals, export insurance, and insured loans for businesses).

Socioeconomic status (SES). A measurement of income, education, occupational prestige, and other social and economic characteristics for the purpose of ranking people and correlating these rankings with political behavior. *See also* Class.

Soft money. Funds used for voter registration and party building which are not subject to federal limitations on campaign financing.

Sophomore surge. The increased support that many incumbents receive from voters in their first bid for reelection.

Sovereignty. The condition that exists when a people are free to organize politically as they wish and are not subject to the will of any other political organization outside their territory.

Speaker of the House. The presiding officer of the House of Representatives. Formally chosen by the whole House, the Speaker is actually chosen by the majority party caucus. The Speaker is third in line for succession to the presidency.

Stable factors. Party identification, turnout rates among different electoral groups, and the tendency of groups to support one party or the other. These factors usually change slowly between one election and the next.

Stagflation. High inflation accompanied by low or negative economic growth and high unemployment.

Standing. The right to sue in court.

Standing legislative committees. Committees which may report legislation and which do not expire at the end of a session. There are approximately sixteen in the Senate and twenty in the House.

Stare decisis. The doctrine that judges should follow the reasoning and conclusions in previous cases and that they should be bound by previous rules of law when a case presents the same issue.

State. In European politics, a term that means considerably more than the term *government*. The state is the embodiment of the sovereignty of a nation, and its rights precede and are superior to those of the individual. The Constitution of 1787 did not create a state in this sense.

State action. Activities undertaken by private groups which are so regulated or supported by the government, or which perform such an important governmental function, that they may be considered the equivalent of actions taken by government officials. Party primaries are an example.

States' rights. The doctrine that all powers not specifically assigned to the national government are to be exercised by the states and that the powers of the national government should be strictly construed.

Statutory authority. The authority granted by laws passed by a legislature for public officials to act.

Statutory interpretation. A judicial or executive interpretation of the meaning of a law.

Subcommittees. Units which take initial action, including hearings, on legislation referred to the full committee.

Subsidy. A political allocation of funds from the government to private individuals or corporations.

Sunshine legislation. Laws requiring officials to allow the public access to administrative proceedings or files.

Super-PAC A political party which uses some of the fund-raising and campaign techniques developed by PACs.

Supply-side economics. An approach to economic problems that emphasizes stimulating the economy by cutting personal, corporate, and capital gains taxes; providing increased tax credits and depreciation for businesses; and deregulation.

Supremacy clause. Article VI of the Constitution, providing that national and state officials must enforce the Constitution, treaties, and laws of the United States over conflicting state constitutions or laws.

Suspect classification. A classification put into law based on race, religion, or ethnicity. Such classifications are considered "suspect" and are struck down by the courts unless there is compelling evidence that they achieve governmental purposes that cannot be achieved in any other way. Gender is not suspect classification.

Symbolic speech. Actions which are intended to communicate ideas but do not involve speech (such as wearing armbands) and which are therefore protected under the First Amendment.

Tariff. A tax levied by the government on goods imported from foreign nations. Tariffs are used to raise revenue or protect domestic companies.

Tax credits. Reductions in taxes owed due to an offsetting expenditure for a designated purpose.

Tax expenditures. The tax revenues lost to the government as a result of tax credits, deductions, income exclusions, exemptions, preferential rates, and deferrals of payments.

Totalitarianism. The concentration of all power, influence, and authority in the state. *See also* State.

Town meeting. An assembly of all the citizens of a community for the purpose of voting for candidates for office and deciding issues of local concern.

Trade association. An interest group consisting of companies engaged in the same kind of business.

Transformational leadership. Leadership that elevates the aspirations of the public and promotes the longer-term interests of the people, including their ability to act politically.

Treaty reservations. Stipulations accompanying the Senate's consent to a treaty, specifying the limits that the Senate puts on the terms of the treaty.

Turnout rate. The percentage of people who voted in an election. It is calculated by dividing the number of those who voted by the number of adults who are eligible to vote.

Tyranny. A system of government based largely on the concentrated power and influence of a small political elite, with no autonomous centers of countervailing power. Tyrannical rule may *usurp* power by displacing those who have a legitimate claim to rule, or it may *abuse* power by exercising it outside the rule of law.

Unanimous consent agreement. An agreement between party leaders in the Senate to facilitate the consideration of proposed legislation.

Uncoordinated expenditures. *See* Independent expenditures.

Unit rule. A rule providing that the majority of a state's delegation can determine how the entire delegation will vote at a national nominating convention.

Urban machine. A party organization in large cities which relied on patronage to gain control of city hall and which engaged in systematic graft and corruption.

Veto override. A two-thirds vote by both chambers of Congress by which measures previously vetoed by the president are enacted into law.

Veto power. The presidential power to prevent bills passed by Congress from being enacted into law.

Virginia Plan. A proposal made by the large states at the Constitution Convention for a strong national government and Congress. The states would be represented according to the size of their population. *See also* New Jersey Plan.

Waiver. A decision to exempt someone from the provision of a law.

Warrant. Judicial permission for the police or prosecutors to conduct a search, seize evidence, or make an arrest.

Watergate. The name given to the legal and constitutional violations that occurred during the Nixon administration. These included attempts to burglarize and wiretap the Democratic National Committee headquarters, seize confidential patient files of a psychiatrist, use the Federal Bureau of Investigation and other government agencies to harass "enemies" of the administration and conduct illegal surveillance of groups, play "dirty tricks" on the Democrats in the 1972 primary campaigns, raise illegal corporate funds for the presidential election, and reduce President Nixon's income tax liability. Several of Nixon's advisers went to jail because of their participation in these events, and Nixon himself resigned because of his attempts to cover up these crimes.

Welfare. Cash payments made by the government to categories of people (such as unmarried mothers) whose income is below a specified level.

White House Office (WHO). The collective name given to the staff assistants who perform personal and political tasks for the president, including scheduling, traveling, speech writing, planning political strategy, maintaining liaison with Congress and interest groups, and dealing with the media.

Winner-take-all elections. Contests in which the candidate who receives the plurality wins everything and in which the loser receives nothing. *See also* Proportional representation.

Wolfpack journalism. Journalism that focuses on candidates' gaffes and on scandals rather than on issues.

The Constitution, signed in 1787, is housed today in the National Archives. (*Howard Chandler Christy, "Signing of the United States Constitution," Granger Collection; Fred J. Maroon.*)

The Constitution of the United States

We the people of the United States, in Order to form a more perfect Union, establish Justice, insure domestic Tranquility, provide for the common defence, promote the general Welfare, and secure the Blessings of Liberty to ourselves and our Posterity, do ordain and establish this CONSTITUTION for the United States of America.

ARTICLE I

Section 1. All legislative Powers herein granted shall be vested in a Congress of the United States, which shall consist of a Senate and House of Representatives.

Section 2. The House of Representatives shall be composed of Members chosen every second Year by the People of the several States, and the Electors in each State shall have the Qualifications requisite for Electors of the most numerous Branch of the State Legislature.

No Person shall be a Representative who shall not have attained to the Age of twenty-five Years, and been seven Years a Citizen of the United States, and who shall not when elected, be an Inhabitant of that State in which he shall be chosen.

Representatives and direct Taxes shall be apportioned among the several States which may be included within this Union, according to their respective Numbers, which shall be determined by adding to the whole Number of free Persons, including those bound to Service for a Term of Years, and excluding Indians not taxed, three fifths of all other Persons. The actual Enumeration shall be made within three Years after the first Meeting of the Congress of the United States, and within every subsequent Term of ten Years, in such Manner as they shall by Law direct. The Number of Represent-atives shall not exceed one for every thirty Thousand, but each State shall have at Least one Representative; and until such enumeration shall be made, the State of New Hampshire shall be entitled to chuse three, Massachusetts eight, Rhode-Island and Providence Plantations one, Connecti-cut five, New-York six, New Jersey four, Pennsylvania eight, Delaware one, Maryland six, Virginia ten, North Carolina five, South Carolina five, and Georgia three.

When vacancies happen in the Representation from any State, the Executive Authority thereof shall issue Writs of Election to fill such Vacancies.

The House of Representatives shall chuse their Speaker and other Officers; and shall have the sole Power of Impeachment.

Section 3. The Senate of the United States shall be composed of two Senators from each State, chosen by the Legislature thereof, for six Years; and each Senator shall have one Vote.

Immediately after they shall be assembled in Consequence of the first Election, they shall be divided as equally as may be into three Classes. The Seats of the Senators of the first Class shall be vacated at the Expiration of the second Year, of the second Class at the Expiration of the fourth Year, and of the third Class at the Expiration of the sixth Year, so that one-third may be chosen every second Year; and if Vacancies happen by Resignation, or otherwise, during the Recess of the Legislature of any State, the Executive thereof may make temporary Appointments until the next Meeting of the Legislature, which shall then fill such Vacancies.

No Person shall be a Senator who shall not have attained to the Age of thirty Years, and been nine Years a Citizen of the United States, and who shall not, when elected, be an Inhabitant of that State in which he shall be chosen.

The Vice President of the United States shall be President of the Senate, but shall have no vote, unless they be equally divided.

The Senate shall chuse their other Officers, and also a President pro tempore, in the absence of the Vice President, or when he shall exercise the Office of the President of the United States.

The Senate shall have the sole Power to try all Impeachments. When sitting for that purpose, they shall be on Oath or Affirmation. When the President of the United States is tried, the Chief Justice shall preside: And no person shall be convicted without the Concurrence of two thirds of the Members present.

Judgment in Cases of Impeachment shall not extend further than to removal from Office, and disqualification to hold and enjoy any Office of honor, Trust, or Profit under the United States: but the Party convicted shall nevertheless be liable and subject to Indictment, Trial, Judgment, and Punishment, according to Law.

A Congress elected in November did not meet until thirteen months later, the following December, unless called into session after March 4 by the president. This provision has been superseded by the Twentieth Amendment.

Section 4. The Times, Places and Manner of holding Elections for Senators and Representatives, shall be prescribed in each state by the Legislature thereof; but the Congress may at any time by Law make or alter such Regulations except as to the Places of Chusing Senators.

The Congress shall assemble at least once in every Year, and such Meeting shall be on the first Monday in December, unless they shall by Law appoint a different Day.

Members of Congress may be expelled without impeachment or trial. Contrast this with the impeachment provisions regarding the executive and judicial branches.

Section 5. Each House shall be the Judge of the Elections, Returns and Qualifications of its own Members, and a Majority of each shall constitute a Quorum to do Business; but a smaller number may adjourn from day to day, and may be authorized to compel the Attendance of absent Members, in such Manner, and under such Penalties, as each House may provide.

Each House may determine the Rules of its Proceedings, punish its Members for disorderly Behaviour, and, with the Concurrence of two thirds, expel a Member.

Each House shall keep a Journal of its Proceedings, and from time to time publish the same, excepting such Parts as may in their Judgment require Secrecy; and the Yeas and Nays of the Members of either House on any question shall, at the Desire of one fifth of those Present, be entered on the Journal.

Neither House, during the Session of Congress, shall, without the Consent of the other, adjourn for more than three days, nor to any other Place than that in which the two Houses shall be sitting.

The separation clause prohibits members of Congress from being appointed department secretaries, thus preventing the possibility of a parliamentary government.

Section 6. The Senators and Representatives shall receive a Compensation for their Services, to be ascertained by Law, and paid out of the Treasury of the United States. They shall in all Cases, except Treason, Felony, and Breach of the Peace, be privileged from Arrest during their Attendance at the Session of their respective Houses, and in going to and returning from the same; and for any Speech or Debate in either House, they shall not be questioned in any other Place.

No Senator or Representative shall, during the Time for which he was elected, be appointed to any civil Office under the Authority of the United States, which shall have been created, or the Emoluments whereof shall have been increased, during such time; and no Person holding any Office under the United States shall be a Member of either House during his continuance in Office.

The Senate initiates its own tax bills in spite of this provision. Bills providing budget authority may be initiated in either chamber.

Section 7. All Bills for raising Revenue shall originate in the House of Representatives; but the Senate may propose or concur with Amendments as on other Bills.

Every Bill which shall have passed the House of Representatives and the Senate, shall, before it become a Law, be presented to the President of the United States; If he approve he shall sign it, but if not he shall return it, with his Objections, to that House in which it shall have originated, who

Bills become law if the president does not return them to Congress with a veto message within ten days. If Congress adjourns within ten days after presenting a bill to the president, it is pocket-vetoed if the president does not sign it.

shall enter the Objections at large on their Journal, and proceed to reconsider it. If after such Reconsideration two thirds of that House shall agree to pass the Bill, it shall be sent, together with the Objections, to the other House, by which it shall likewise be reconsidered, and if approved by two thirds of that House, it shall become a Law. But in all such Cases the Votes of both Houses shall be determined by Yeas and Nays, and the Names of the Persons voting for and against the Bill shall be entered on the Journal of each House respectively. If any Bill shall not be returned by the President within ten Days (Sundays excepted) after it shall have been presented to him, the Same shall be a Law, in like Manner as if he had signed it, unless the Congress by their Adjournment prevent its Return, in which Case it shall not be a Law.

Concurrent resolutions need not be presented to the president.

The two-thirds vote refers to a quorum, not the entire membership.

Every Order, Resolution, or Vote to which the Concurrence of the Senate and House of Representatives may be necessary (except on a question of Adjournment) shall be presented to the President of the United States; and before the Same shall take Effect, shall be approved by him, or being disapproved by him, shall be repassed by two thirds of the Senate and House of Representatives, according to the Rules and Limitations prescribed in the Case of a Bill.

Section 8 contains seventeen enumerations of legislative power, which permit social programs, taxation, the regulation of currency, and interstate and foreign commerce (including manufacturing and service industries) and which enable the national government to manage the economy.

Section 8. The Congress shall have Power To lay and collect Taxes, Duties, Imposts and Excises, to pay the Debts and provide for the common Defence and general Welfare of the United States; but all Duties, Imposts and Excises shall be uniform throughout the United States;

To borrow money on the credit of the United States;

To regulate Commerce with foreign Nations, and among the several States, and with the Indian Tribes;

To establish an uniform Rule of Naturalization, and uniform Laws on the subject of Bankruptcies throughout the United States;

To coin Money, regulate the Value thereof, and of foreign Coin, and fix the Standard of Weights and Measures;

To provide for the Punishment of counterfeiting the Securities and current Coin of the United States;

To establish Post Offices and post Roads;

To promote the Progress of Science and useful Arts, by securing for limited Times to Authors and Inventors the exclusive Right to their respective Writings and Discoveries;

To constitute Tribunals inferior to the Supreme Court;

To define and punish Piracies and Felonies committed on the high Seas, and Offenses against the Law of Nations;

To declare War, grant Letters of Marque and Reprisal, and make Rules concerning Captures on Land and Water;

To raise and support Armies, but no Appropriation of Money to that Use shall be for a longer Term than two Years;

To provide and maintain a Navy;

To make Rules for the Government and Regulation of the land and naval forces;

To provide for calling forth the Militia to execute the Laws of the Union, suppress Insurrections and repel Invasions;

To provide for organizing, arming, and disciplining the Militia, and for governing such Part of them as may be employed in the Service of the United States, reserving to the States respectively, the Appointment of the Officers, and the Authority of training the Militia according to the discipline prescribed by Congress;

The elastic clause adds a second dimension to the enumerated powers by broadening their scope. The clause allows Congress to legislate on the powers of all three branches.

To exercise exclusive Legislation in all Cases whatsoever, over such District (not exceeding ten Miles square) as may, by Cession of particular States, and the acceptance of Congress, become the Seat of Government of the United States, and to exercise like Authority over all Places purchased by the Consent of the Legislature of the State in which the Same shall be, for the Erection of Forts, Magazines, Arsenals, dock-Yards, and other needful Buildings;—And

To make all Laws which shall be necessary and proper for carrying into Execution the foregoing

These are limitations on congressional powers.

Slave trade was protected until 1808.

Habeas corpus requires officials to bring a suspect before a magistrate and give reasons for the arrest.

This prohibits acts of Congress that would result in punishment without a trial and also prohibits acts that would impose penalties retroactively.

These are limitations on the states' powers. Those dealing with currency, credit, and contracts were directed against radicals and debtors in the aftermath of Shays's rebellion.

The national government controls trade and diplomacy with foreign nations.

Most interstate compacts are subject to congressional approval.

It is not clear what executive power means. Is it a title, referring to enumerated powers, or is it a separate grant of power?

Presidential electors need not be popularly elected.

This part of the Constitution was superseded by the Twelfth Amendment to avoid a recurrence of what happened in

Powers, and all other Powers vested by this Constitution in the Government of the United States, or in any Department or Officer thereof.

Section 9. The Migration or Importation of such Persons as any of the States now existing shall think proper to admit, shall not be prohibited by the Congress prior to the Year one thousand eight hundred and eight, but a tax or duty may be imposed on such Importation, not exceeding ten dollars for each Person.

The privilege of the Writ of Habeas Corpus shall not be suspended, unless when in Cases of Rebellion or Invasion the public Safety may require it.

No Bill of Attainder or ex post facto Law shall be passed.

No Capitation, or other direct, Tax shall be laid unless in Proportion to the Census or Enumeration herein before directed to be taken.

No Tax or Duty shall be laid on Articles exported from any State.

No Preference shall be given by any Regulation of Revenue to the Ports of one State over those of another: nor shall Vessels bound to, or from, one State, be obliged to enter, clear, or pay Duties in another.

No Money shall be drawn from the Treasury, but in Consequence of Appropriations made by Law; and a regular Statement and Account of the Receipts and Expenditures of all public Money shall be published from time to time.

No Title of Nobility shall be granted by the United States: And no Person holding any Office of Profit or Trust under them, shall, without the Consent of the Congress, accept of any present, Emolument, Office, or Title, of any kind whatever, from any King, Prince, or foreign State.

Section 10. No State shall enter into any Treaty, Alliance, or Confederation; grant Letters of Marque and Reprisal; coin Money; emit Bills of Credit; make any Thing but gold and silver Coin a Tender in Payment of Debts; pass any Bill of Attainder, ex post facto Law, or Law impairing the Obligation of Contracts, or grant any Title of Nobility.

No state shall, without the Consent of the Congress, lay any Imposts or Duties on Imports or Exports, except what may be absolutely necessary for executing its inspection Laws: and the net Produce of all Duties and Imposts, laid by any State on Imports or Exports, shall be for the Use of the Treasury of the United States; and all such Laws shall be subject to the Revision and Control of the Congress.

No State shall, without the Consent of Congress, lay any duty of Tonnage, keep Troops, or Ships of War in time of Peace, enter into any Agreement or Compact with another State, or with a foreign Power, or engage in War, unless actually invaded, or in such imminent Danger as will not admit of delay.

ARTICLE II

Section 1. The executive Power shall be vested in a President of the United States of America. He shall hold his Office during the Term of four Years, and, together with the Vice President, chosen for the same Term, be elected, as follows:

Each State shall appoint, in such Manner as the Legislature thereof may direct, a Number of Electors, equal to the whole Number of Senators and Representatives to which the State may be entitled in the Congress: but no Senator or Representative, or Person holding an Office of Trust or Profit under the United States, shall be appointed an Elector.

The Electors shall meet in their respective States, and vote by Ballot for two Persons, of whom one at least shall not be an Inhabitant of the same State with themselves. And they shall make a List of all the Persons voted for, and of the Number of Votes for each; which List they shall sign and certify,

and transmit sealed to the Seat of the Government of the United States, directed to the President of the Senate. The President of the Senate shall, in the Presence of the Senate and House of Representatives, open all the Certificates, and the Votes shall then be counted. The Person having the greatest Number of Votes shall be the President, if such Number be a Majority of the whole Number of Electors appointed; and if there be more than one who have such Majority, and have an equal Number of Votes, then the House of Representatives shall immediately chuse by Ballot one of them for President; and if no Person have a Majority, then from the five highest on the List the said House shall in like Manner chuse the President. But in chusing the President, the Votes shall be taken by States, the Representation from each State having one Vote; a quorum for this Purpose shall consist of a Member or Members from two-thirds of the States, and a Majority of all the States shall be necessary to a Choice. In every Case, after the Choice of the President, the Person having the greatest Number of Votes of the Electors shall be the Vice President. But if there should remain two or more who have equal votes, the Senate shall chuse from them by Ballot the Vice President.

The Congress may determine the Time of chusing the Electors, and the Day on which they shall give their Votes; which Day shall be the same throughout the United States.

No person except a natural-born Citizen, or a Citizen of the United States, at the time of the Adoption of this Constitution, shall be eligible to the Office of President; neither shall any Person be eligible to that Office who shall not have attained to the Age of thirty-five Years, and been fourteen Years a Resident within the United States.

In Case of the Removal of the President from Office, or of his Death, resignation, or Inability to discharge the Powers and Duties of the said Office, the same shall devolve on the Vice President, and the Congress may by Law provide for the Case of Removal, Death, Resignation, or Inability, both of the President and Vice President, declaring what Officer shall then act as President, and such Officer shall act accordingly, until the Disability be removed, or a President shall be elected.

The President shall, at stated Times, receive for his Services a Compensation, which shall neither be increased nor diminished during the Period for which he shall have been elected, and he shall not receive within that Period any other Emolument from the United States, or any of them.

Before he enter on the Execution of his Office, he shall take the following Oath or Affirmation:— ''I do solemnly swear (or affirm) that I will faithfully execute the Office of President of the United States, and will, to the best of my Ability, preserve, protect, and defend the Constitution of the United States.''

Section 2. The President shall be Commander in Chief of the Army and Navy of the United States, and of the Militia of the several States, when called into the actual Service of the United States; he may require the Opinion, in writing, of the principal Officer in each of the executive Departments, upon any subject relating to the Duties of their respective Offices, and he shall have Power to Grant Reprieves and Pardons for Offences against the United States, except in Cases of Impeachment.

He shall have Power, by and with the Advice and Consent of the Senate, to make Treaties, provided two thirds of the Senators present concur; and he shall nominate, and by and with the Advice and Consent of the Senate, shall appoint Ambassadors, other public Ministers and Consuls, Judges of the Supreme Court, and all other Officers of the United States, whose Appointments are not herein otherwise provided for, and which shall be established by Law: but the Congress may by Law vest the Appointment of such inferior Officers, as they think proper, in the President alone, in the Courts of Law, or in the Heads of Departments.

The President shall have Power to fill up all Vacancies that may happen during the Recess of the Senate, by granting Commissions which shall expire at the End of their next Session.

Section 3. He shall from time to time give to the Congress Information of the State of the Union, and recommend to their Consideration such Measures as he shall judge necessary and expedient; he may, on extraordinary occasions, convene both Houses, or either of them, and in Case of Disagreement

the 1800 election, in which Jefferson, the presidential candidate, and Burr, the vice presidential candidate, received the same number of electoral votes from their supporters, which forced a contingency election in the House of Representatives.

This allows Congress to set a particular day on which presidential and midterm congressional elections are held.

This part of the Constitution was superseded by the Twenty-Fifth Amendment.

The oath does not specifically require the president to execute the laws; in a crisis the president may decide to dispense with their execution temporarily if it would interfere with higher constitutional obligations.

Section 2 enumerates the powers of the president. Contrast these few general terms with the many specific powers granted to Congress. The president is not given full executive powers. There is no removal power and no provision for issuing orders to heads of executive departments.

The Senate consents to nominations by a majority vote and to treaties by a two-thirds vote of those present.

Congress can give the power to appoint inferior officers to the president or the courts, but it cannot make appointments.

The president does not execute the national laws, but rather oversees government officials; this justifies the president's claims to administrative powers.

The Constitution does not specify whether high crimes and misdemeanors involve offenses under federal laws or include a general pattern of abuse of power.

The judicial power extends to cases involving the Constitution, treaties, and federal statutory law.

The Supreme Court is the only court mentioned in the Constitution. The structure and jurisdiction of the federal court system are determined by Congress. *Good behavior* means life tenure for judges of federal constitutional courts. Judges of federal legislative courts serve fixed terms.

Section 2 specifies the jurisdiction of the federal courts. The original jurisdiction of the Supreme Court cannot be expanded by Congress.

The Seventh Amendment guarantees a trial by jury in most civil cases.

The Constitution limits the definition of *treason* and requires a judicial proceeding. This provision, along with prohibitions against ex post facto laws and bills of attainder, protects minority parties and factions.

Judgments in one state are enforceable in another state only by judicial decree obtained in the second state.

Fugitives are returned at the governor's discretion.

between them, with respect to the Time of Adjournment, he may adjourn them to such Time as he shall think proper; he shall receive Ambassadors and other public Ministers; he shall take Care that the Laws be faithfully executed, and shall Commission all the Officers of the United States.

Section 4. The President, Vice President and all civil Officers of the United States, shall be removed from Office on Impeachment for, and Conviction of, Treason, Bribery, or other high Crimes and Misdemeanors.

ARTICLE III

Section 1. The judicial Power of the United States, shall be vested in one supreme Court, and in such inferior Courts as the Congress may from time to time ordain and establish. The Judges, both of the supreme and inferior Courts, shall hold their Offices during good Behaviour, and shall, at stated Times, receive for their Services, a Compensation, which shall not be diminished during their Continuance in Office.

Section 2. The judicial Power shall extend to all Cases, in Law and Equity, arising under this Constitution, the Laws of the United States, and Treaties made, or which shall be made, under their Authority;—to all Cases affecting Ambassadors, other public Ministers and Consuls;—to all Cases of admiralty and maritime Jurisdiction;—to Controversies to which the United States shall be a Party;—to Controversies between two or more States;—between a State and Citizens of another State;—between Citizens of the same State claiming Lands under Grants of different States, and between a State, or the Citizens thereof, and foreign States, Citizens or Subjects.

In all Cases affecting Ambassadors, other public Ministers and Consuls, and those in which a State shall be Party, the supreme Court shall have original Jurisdiction. In all the other Cases before mentioned, the supreme Court shall have appellate Jurisdiction, both as to Law and Fact, with such Exceptions, and under such Regulations as the Congress shall make.

The trial of all Crimes, except in Cases of Impeachment, shall be by Jury; and such Trial shall be held in the State where the said Crimes shall have been committed; but when not committed within any State, the Trial shall be at such Place or Places as the Congress may be Law have directed.

Section 3. Treason against the United States, shall consist only in levying War against them, or in adhering to their Enemies, giving them Aid and Comfort. No Person shall be convicted of Treason unless on the Testimony of two Witnesses to the same overt Act, or on Confession in open Court.

The Congress shall have power to declare the Punishment of Treason, but no Attainder of Treason shall work Corruption of Blood, or Forfeiture except during the Life of the Person attainted.

ARTICLE IV

Section 1. Full Faith and Credit shall be given in each State to the public Acts, Records, and judicial Proceedings of every other State. And the Congress may by general Laws prescribe the Manner in which such Acts, Records and Proceedings shall be proved, and the Effect thereof.

Section 2. The Citizens of each State shall be entitled to all Privileges and Immunities of Citizens in the several States.

A Person charged in any State with Treason, Felony, or other Crime, who shall flee from Justice, and be found in another State, shall on demand of the executive Authority of the State from which he fled, be delivered up, to be removed to the State having Jurisdiction of the crime.

No Person held to Service or Labour in one State, under the Laws thereof, escaping into another, shall, in Consequence of any Law or Regulation therein, be discharged from such Service or Labour, but shall be delivered up on Claim of the Party to whom such Service or Labour may be due.

Section 3. New States may be admitted by the Congress into this Union; but no new State shall be formed or erected within the Jurisdiction of any other State; nor any State be formed by the Junction of two or more States, or parts of States, without the Consent of the Legislatures of the States concerned as well as of the Congress.

The Congress shall have Power to dispose of and make all needful Rules and Regulations respecting the Territory or other Property belonging to the United States; and nothing in this Constitution shall be so construed as to Prejudice any Claims of the United States, or of any particular State.

Section 4. The United States shall guarantee to every State in this Union a Republican Form of Government, and shall protect each of them against Invasion; and on Application of the Legislature, or of the Executive (when the Legislature cannot be convened) against domestic Violence.

ARTICLE V

The Congress, whenever two thirds of both Houses shall deem it necessary, shall propose Amendments to this Constitution, or, on the Application of the Legislatures of two thirds of the several States, shall call a Convention for proposing Amendments, which, in either Case, shall be valid to all Intents and Purposes, as part of this Constitution, when ratified by the Legislatures of three fourths of the several States, or by Conventions in three fourths thereof, as the one or the other Mode of Ratification may be proposed by the Congress; Provided that no Amendment which may be made prior to the Year One thousand eight hundred and eight shall in any Manner affect the first and fourth Clauses in the Ninth Section of the first Article; and that no State, without its Consent, shall be deprived of its equal Suffrage in the Senate.

ARTICLE VI

All Debts contracted and Engagements entered into, before the Adoption of this Constitution, shall be as valid against the United States under this Constitution, as under the Confederation.

This Constitution, and the Laws of the United States which shall be made in Pursuance thereof; and all Treaties made, or which shall be made, under the Authority of the United States, shall be the supreme Law of the Land; and the Judges in every State shall be bound thereby, any Thing in the Constitution or Laws of any State to the Contrary notwithstanding.

The Senators and Representatives before mentioned, and the Members of the several State Legislatures, and all executive and judicial Officers, both of the United States and of the several States, shall be bound by Oath or Affirmation to support this Constitution; but no religious Test shall ever be required as a qualification to any Office or public Trust under the United States.

ARTICLE VII

The Ratification of the Conventions of nine States shall be sufficient for the Establishment of this Constitution between the States so ratifying the same.

Done in Convention by the Unanimous Consent of the States present the Seventeenth Day of September in the Year of our Lord one thousand seven hundred and Eighty seven, and of the Indepen-

---

This is the fugitive slave provision, now an anachronism.

The Constitution does not refer to or forbid the acquisition of new territory. New states are admitted to the union on an equal footing with the existing states. Congress regulates the public lands of the United States within the territory of a state.

The president may use the armed forces or call a state militia into national service to maintain a state government or oust one that is not republican in form. This power has never been used against states that denied suffrage to a part of their citizenry.

Congress acts by a two-thirds vote of those present. It has never called a convention to propose amendments. It is not clear whether such a convention would be limited to subjects specified by Congress.

A state which has turned down an amendment may later ratify it, but a state which has ratified an amendment may not rescind its action.

The linchpin of the Constitution, the supremacy clause establishes the Constitution, the laws of Congress, and treaties as the supreme law of the land, which state as well as national officials must enforce.

State and local officials must take oaths to support the national Constitution.

Requiring that a person believe in a supreme being in order to quality to hold public office is unconstitutional.

The ratification provision is inconsistent with the requirement under the Articles of Confederation that it be amended by unanimous vote of the state delegations to Congress.

712 THE CONSTITUTION OF THE UNITED STATES

dence of the United States of America the Twelfth. In Witness whereof We have hereunto subscribed our Names.

George Washington, President and Deputy from Virginia
New Hampshire—John Langdon, Nicholas Gilman
Massachusetts—Nathanial Gorham, Rufus King
Connecticut—William Samuel Johnson, Roger Sherman
New York—Alexander Hamilton
New Jersey—William Livingston, David Brearly, William Paterson, Jonathan Dayton
Pennsylvania—Benjamin Franklin, Thomas Mifflin, Robert Morris, George Clymer, Thomas Fitzsimons, Jared Ingersoll, James Wilson, Gouverneur Morris
Delaware—George Read, Gunning Bedford, Jr., John Dickinson, Richard Bassett, Jacob Broom
Maryland—James McHenry, Daniel of St. Thomas Jenifer, Daniel Carroll
Virginia—John Blair, James Madison, Jr.
North Carolina—William Blount, Richard Dobbs Spaight, Hugh Williamson
south Carolina—John Rutledge, Charles Cotesworth Pinckney, Charles Pinckney, Pierce Butler
Georgia—William Few, Abraham Baldwin
Attest: William Jackson, Secretary

Articles in Addition to, and Amendment of, the Constitution of the United States of America, Proposed by Congress, and Ratified by the Legislatures of the Several States, Pursuant to the Fifth Article of the Original Constitution.

AMENDMENT I [1791]

These prohibitions apply to all branches of the national government, and by the due process clause of the Fourteenth Amendment they apply to state officials as well.

Congress shall make no law respecting an establishment of religion, or prohibiting the free exercise thereof; or abridging the freedom of speech, or of the press; or the right of the people peaceably to assemble, and to petition the Government for a redress of grievances.

AMENDMENT II [1791]

This amendment guarantees the right to bear arms to the militias of the states but not necessarily to individuals.

A well regulated Militia, being necessary to the security of a free State, the right of the people to keep and bear Arms, shall not be infringed.

AMENDMENT III [1791]

This amendment provides protection against abuses like those committed by British troops before the Revolutionary War.

No Soldier shall, in time of peace, be quartered in any house, without the consent of the Owner, nor in time of war, but in a manner to be prescribed by law.

AMENDMENT IV [1791]

This amendment forbids the general warrant, which allows the police to go on a "fishing expedition" for evidence of crimes. It has been interpreted to require a judicial warrant for wiretapping and surveillance.

The right of the people to be secure in their persons, houses, papers, and effects, against unreasonable searches and seizures, shall not be violated, and no Warrants shall issue, but upon probable cause, supported by Oath or affirmation, and particularly describing the place to be searched, and the persons or things to be seized.

AMENDMENT V [1791]

This amendment guarantees due process in criminal and civil proceedings.

No person shall be held to answer for a capital otherwise infamous crime, unless on a presentment or indictment of a Grand Jury, except in cases arising in the land or naval forces, or in the Militia, when in actual service in time of War or public danger; nor shall any person be subject for the same offence to be twice put in jeopardy of life or limb; nor shall be compelled in any criminal case to be a witness against himself, nor be deprived of life, liberty, or property, without due process of law; nor shall private property be taken for public use, without just compensation.

AMENDMENT VI [1791]

Due process includes the right to knowledge of charges, free counsel for indigents, the right to effective legal representation, the right to a speedy and fair trail, the right to present witnesses and cross-examine hostile witnesses, and the right of appeal.

In all criminal prosecutions, the accused shall enjoy the right to a speedy and public trial, by an impartial jury of the State and district wherein the crime shall have been committed, which district shall have been previously ascertained by law, and to be informed of the nature and cause of the accusation; to be confronted with the witnesses against him; to have compulsory process for obtaining witnesses in his favor, and to have the Assistance of Counsel for his defence.

AMENDMENT VII [1791]

This amendment guarantees the right to a jury trial in civil cases unless waived by the parties.

In Suits at common law, where the value in controversy shall exceed twenty dollars, the right of trial by jury shall be preserved, and no fact tried by a jury, shall be otherwise re-examined in any Court of the United States, than according to the rules of the common law.

AMENDMENT VIII [1791]

For certain offenses specified by Congress, bail may be denied, and the accused detained before trial.

Excessive bail shall not be required, nor excessive fines imposed, nor cruel and unusual punishments inflicted.

AMENDMENT IX [1791]

In some judicial cases this amendment has been taken to create a "zone of privacy" for individuals into which the government may not intrude.

The enumeration in the Constitution, of certain rights, shall not be construed to deny or disparage others retained by the people.

AMENDMENT X [1791]

This amendment is rarely invoked today to prevent national action.

The powers not delegated to the United States by the Constitution, nor prohibited by it to the States, are reserved to the States respectively, or to the people.

AMENDMENT XI [1798]

This amendment limits the jurisdiction of the federal courts.

The Judicial power of the United States shall not be construed to extend to any suit in law or equity, commenced or prosecuted against one of the United States by Citizens of another State, or by Citizens or Subjects of any Foreign State.

AMENDMENT XII [1804]

The Electors shall meet in their respective States and vote by ballot for President and Vice-President, one of whom, at least, shall not be an inhabitant of the same States with themselves; they shall name in their ballots the person voted for as President, and in distinct ballots the person voted for as Vice-President, and they shall make distinct lists of all persons voted for as President, and of all persons voted for as Vice-President, and of the number of votes for each, which lists they shall sign and certify, and transmit sealed to the seat of the government of the United States, directed to the President of the Senate;—The President of the Senate shall, in the presence of the Senate and House of Representatives, open all the certificates and the votes shall then be counted;—The person having the greatest number of votes for President, shall be the President, if such number be a majority of the whole number of Electors appointed; and if no person have such majority, then from the persons having the highest numbers not exceeding three on the list of those voted for as President, the House of Representatives shall choose immediately, by ballot, the President. But in choosing the President, the votes shall be taken by states, the representation from each state having one vote; a quorum for this purpose shall consist of a member or members from two-thirds of the states, and a majority of all the states shall be necessary to a choice. And if the House of Representatives shall not choose a President whenever the right of choice shall devolve upon them, before the fourth day of March next following, then the Vice-President shall act as President, as in the case of the death or other constitutional disability of the President—The person having the greatest number of votes as Vice-President, shall be the Vice-President, if such number be a majority of the whole number of Electors appointed, and if no person have a majority, then from the two highest numbers on the list, the Senate shall choose the Vice-President; a quorum for the purpose shall consist of two-thirds of the whole number of Senators, and a majority of the whole number shall be necessary to a choice. But no person constitutionally ineligible to the office of President shall be eligible to that of Vice-President of the United States.

The House chooses from among the top three candidates for president, and the Senate from among the top two candidates for vice president. The date of March 4 was changed by the Twentieth Amendment.

AMENDMENT XIII [1865]

This amendment supersedes Lincoln's Emancipation Proclamation.

Section 1. Neither slavery nor involuntary servitude, except as a punishment for crime whereof the party shall have been duly convicted, shall exist within the United States, or any place subject to their jurisdiction.

Section 2. Congress shall have power to enforce this article by appropriate legislation.

AMENDMENT XIV [1868]

This is the first time the Constitution defines *national citizenship*. This section converted former slaves into citizens. All persons have the right to due process and equal protection of the law against state action.

The reduction in congressional representation mentioned in this section was never implemented, even after southern states disenfranchised blacks.

Section 1. All persons born or naturalized in the United States, and subject to the jurisdiction thereof, are citizens of the United States and of the State wherein they reside. No State shall make or enforce any law which shall abridge the privileges or immunities of citizens of the United States; nor shall any State deprive any person of life, liberty, or property, without due process of law; nor deny to any person within its jurisdiction the equal protection of the laws.

Section 2. Representatives shall be apportioned among the several States according to their respective numbers, counting the whole number of persons in each State, excluding Indians not taxed. But when the right to vote at any election for the choice of electors for President and Vice President of the United States, Representatives in Congress, the Executive and Judicial officers of a State, or the members of the Legislature thereof, is denied to any of the male inhabitants of such State, being twenty-one years

of age, and citizens of the United States, or in any way abridged, except for participation in rebellion, or other crime, the basis of representation therein shall be reduced in the proportion which the number of such male citizens shall bear to the whole number of male citizens twenty-one years of age in such State.

The provision in this section barring secessionists from holding office was widely ignored.

Section 3. No person shall be a Senator or Representative in Congress, or elector of President and Vice President, or hold any office, civil or military, under the United States, or under any State, who, having previously taken an oath, as a member of Congress, or as an officer of the United States, or as a member of any State legislature, or as an executive or judicial officer of any State, to support the Constitution of the United States, shall have engaged in insurrection or rebellion against the same, or given aid or comfort to the enemies thereof. But Congress may by a vote of two-thirds of each House, remove such disability.

This section voids claims made by slaveholders and secessionists against the state governments and the national government.

Section 4. The validity of the public debt of the United States, authorized by law, including debts incurred for payment of pensions and bounties for services in suppressing insurrection or rebellion, shall not be questioned. But neither the United States nor any State shall assume or pay any debt or obligation incurred in aid of insurrection or rebellion against the United States, or any claim for the loss or emancipation of any slave; but all such debts, obligations, and claims shall be held illegal and void.

Section 5. The Congress shall have the power to enforce, by appropriate legislation, the provisions of this article.

AMENDMENT XV [1870]

This section did not prevent states in the 1890s from introducing literacy tests, levying poll taxes, or imposing other restrictions on blacks which did not explicitly mention race.

Section 1. The right of citizens of the United States to vote shall not be denied or abridged by the United States or by any State on account of race, color, or previous condition of servitude—

Section 2. The Congress shall have power to enforce this article by appropriate legislation.

AMENDMENT XVI [1913]

This amendment overturned an 1895 Supreme Court decision voiding an income tax.

The Congress shall have power to lay and collect taxes on incomes, from whatever source derived, without apportionment among the several States, and without regard to any census or enumeration.

AMENDMENT XVII [1913]

This amendment replaced legislative election of senators with popular election.

The Senate of the United States shall be composed of two Senators from each State, elected by the people thereof, for six years; and each Senator shall have one vote. The electors in each State shall have the qualifications requisite for electors of the most numerous branch of the State legislatures.

When vacancies happen in the representation of any State in the Senate, the executive authority of such State shall issue writs of election to fill such vacancies: *Provided,* That the legislature of any State may empower the executive thereof to make temporary appointments until the people fill the vacancies by election as the legislature may direct.

This amendment shall not be so construed as to affect the election or term of any Senator chosen before it becomes valid as part of the Constitution.

AMENDMENT XVIII [1919]

This amendment, which legislated Prohibition, represents the only attempt that has ever been made to put a "social issue" into the Constitution.

Section 1. After one year from the ratification of this article the manufacture, sale, or transportation of intoxicating liquors within, the importation thereof into, or the exportation thereof from the United States and all territory subject to the jurisdiction thereof for beverage purposes is hereby prohibited.

Section 2. The Congress and the several States shall have concurrent power to enforce this article by appropriate legislation.

Section 3. This article shall be inoperative unless it shall have been ratified as an amendment to the Constitution by the legislatures of the several States, as provided in the Constitution, within seven years from the date of the submission hereof to the States by the Congress.

AMENDMENT XIX [1920]

This amendment guarantees the right to vote in federal and state elections. Many states had already granted women suffrage.

The right of citizens of the United States to vote shall not be denied or abridged by the United States or by any State on account of sex.

Congress shall have power to enforce this article by appropriate legislation.

AMENDMENT XX [1933]

As a result of this amendment, the president is inaugurated on January 20 rather than March 4. This amendment put an end to the situation in which a lame-duck president and Congress ran the government from November until the following March and in which the newly elected Congress did not convene for thirteen months. The new Congress now convenes on January 3, two months after the elections.

Section 1. The terms of the President and Vice President shall end at noon on the 20th day of January, and the terms of Senators and Representatives at noon on the 3rd day of January, of the years in which such terms would have ended if this article had not been ratified; and the terms of their successors shall then begin.

Section 2. The Congress shall assemble at least once in every year, and such meeting shall begin at noon on the 3rd day of January, unless they shall by law appoint a different day.

Section 3. If, at the time fixed for the beginning of the term of the President, the President elect shall have died, the Vice President elect shall become President. If a President shall not have been chosen before the time fixed for the beginning of his term, or if the President elect shall have failed to qualify, then the Vice President elect shall act as President until a President shall have qualified; and the Congress may by law provide for the case wherein neither a President elect nor a Vice President elect shall have qualified, declaring who shall then act as President, or the manner in which one who is to act shall be selected, and such person shall act accordingly until a President or Vice President shall have qualified.

Section 4. The Congress may by law provide for the case of the death of any of the persons from whom the House of Representatives may choose a President whenever the right of choice shall have devolved upon them, and for the case of the death of any of the persons from whom the Senate may choose a Vice President whenever the right of choice shall have devolved upon them.

Section 5. Sections 1 and 2 shall take effect on the 15th day of October following the ratification of this article.

Section 6. This article shall be inoperative unless it shall have been ratified as an amendment to the

Constitution by the legislatures of three-fourths of the several States within seven years from the date of its submission.

AMENDMENT XXI [1933]

As a result of this amendment, the experiment with Prohibition ended.

Section 1. The eighteenth article of amendment to the Constitution of the United States is hereby repealed.

Section 2. The transportation or importation into any State, Territory, or possession of the United States for delivery or use therein of intoxicating liquors, in violation of the laws thereof, is hereby prohibited.

This is the only amendment to be ratified by state conventions rather than by state legislatures.

Section 3. This article shall be inoperative unless it shall have been ratified as an amendment to the Constitution by conventions in the several States, as provided in the Constitution, within seven years from the date of the submission hereof to the States by the Congress.

AMENDMENT XXII [1951]

This amendment, which limits presidents to two terms in office (a proposal made by Republicans), first affected a Republican president, Dwight D. Eisenhower.

No person shall be elected to the office of the President more than twice, and no person who has held the office of President, or acted as President, for more than two years of a term to which some other person was elected President shall be elected to the office of the President more than once.

But this Article shall not apply to any person holding the office of President when this Article was proposed by the Congress, and shall not prevent any person who may be holding the office of President, or acting as President, during the term within which this Article becomes operative from holding the office of President or acting as President during the remainder of such term.

AMENDMENT XXIII [1961]

This amendment gives the District of Columbia representation in presidential elections equivalent to that of the least populous state.

Section 1. The District constituting the seat of Government of the United States shall appoint in such manner as the Congress may direct:

A number of electors of President and Vice President equal to the whole number of Senators and Representatives in Congress to which the District would be entitled if it were a State, but in no event more than the least populous State; they shall be in addition to those appointed by the States, but they shall be considered, for the purposes of the election of President and Vice President, to be electors appointed by a State; and they shall meet in the District and perform such duties as provided by the twelfth article of amendment.

Section 2. The Congress shall have power to enforce this article by appropriate legislation.

AMENDMENT XXIV [1964]

This amendment ended state poll taxes in federal elections.

Section 1. The right of citizens of the United States to vote in any primary or other election for President or Vice President, for electors for President or Vice President, or for Senator or Representative in Congress, shall not be denied or abridged by the United States or any State by reason of failure to pay any poll tax or other tax.

Section 2. The Congress shall have the power to enforce this article by appropriate legislation.

AMENDMENT XXV [1967]

Section 1. In case of the removal of the President from office or his death or resignation, the Vice President shall become President.

Section 2. Whenever there is a vacancy in the office of the Vice President, the President shall nominate a Vice President who shall take the office upon confirmation by a majority vote of both houses of Congress.

Section 3. Whenever the President transmits to the President pro tempore of the Senate and the Speaker of the House of Representatives his written declaration that he is unable to discharge the powers and duties of his office, and until he transmits to them a written declaration to the contrary, such powers and duties shall be discharged by the Vice President as Acting President.

Thereafter, when the President transmits to the President pro tempore of the Senate and the Speaker of the House of Representatives his written declaration that no inability exists, he shall resume the powers and duties of his office unless the Vice President and a majority of either the principal officers of the executive departments, or of such other body as Congress may by law provide, transmit within four days to the President pro tempore of the Senate and the Speaker of the House of Representatives their written declaration that the President is unable to discharge the powers and duties of his office. Thereupon Congress shall decide the issue, assembling within 48 hours for that purpose if not in session. If the Congress, within 21 days after receipt of the latter written declaration, or, if Congress is not in session, within 21 days after Congress is required to assemble, determines by two-thirds vote of both houses that the President is unable to discharge the powers and duties of his office, the Vice President shall continue to discharge the same as Acting President, otherwise, the President shall resume the powers and duties of his office.

AMENDMENT XXVI [1971]

Section 1. The right of citizens of the United States, who are 18 years of age or older, to vote shall not be denied or abridged by the United States or any state on account of age.

Section 2. The Congress shall have the power to enforce this article by appropriate legislation.

This amendment supersedes informal arrangements about disability between presidents and vice presidents, such as those negotiated between Dwight Eisenhower and Richard Nixon. Filling a vacancy for vice president makes it unlikely that a double vacancy can occur. Gerald Ford, who was elected vice president by Congress and succeeded to the presidency upon the resignation of Richard Nixon, is the only American president ever to have come to office under this amendment.

This amendment lowered the voting age in most states from 21 to 18.

The Declaration of Independence

In Congress, July 4, 1776: The Unanimous Declaration of the Thirteen United States of America

When, in the course of human events, it becomes necessary for one people to dissolve the political bands which have connected them with another, and to assume, among the powers of the earth, the separate and equal station to which the laws of nature and of nature's God entitle them, a decent respect to the opinions of mankind requires that they should declare the causes which impel them to the separation.

We hold these truths to be self-evident: That all men are created equal; that they are endowed by their Creator with certain unalienable rights; that among these are life, liberty, and the pursuit of happiness; that, to secure these rights, governments are instituted among men, deriving their just powers from the consent of the governed; that whenever any form of government becomes destructive of these ends, it is the right of the people to alter or to abolish it, and to institute new government, laying its foundation on such principles, and organizing its powers in such form, as to them shall seem most likely to effect their safety and happiness. Prudence, indeed, will dictate that governments long established should not be changed for light and transient causes; and accordingly all experience hath shown that mankind are more disposed to suffer, while evils are sufferable, than to right themselves by abolishing the forms to which they are accustomed. But when a long train of abuses and usurpations, pursuing invariably the same object, evinces a design to reduce them under absolute despotism, it is their right, it is their duty, to throw off such government, and to provide new guards for their future security. Such has been the patient sufferance of these colonies; and such is now the necessity which constrains them to alter their former systems of government. The history of the present King of Great Britain is a history of repeated injuries and usurpations, all having in direct object the establishment of an absolute tyranny over these states. To prove this, let facts be submitted to a candid world.

He has refused to assent to laws, the most wholesome and necessary for the public good.

He has forbidden his governors to pass laws of immediate and pressing importance, unless suspended in their operation till his assent should be obtained; and, when so suspended, he has utterly neglected to attend to them.

He has refused to pass other laws for the accommodation of large districts of people, unless those people would relinquish the right of representation in the legislature, a right inestimable to them, and formidable to tyrants only.

He has called together legislative bodies at places unusual, uncomfortable, and distant from the depository of their public records, for the sole purpose of fatiguing them into compliance with his measures.

He has dissolved representative houses repeatedly, for opposing, with manly firmness, his invasions on the rights of the people.

He has refused for a long time, after such dissolutions, to cause others to be elected; whereby the legislative powers, incapable of annihilation, have returned to the people at large for their exercise; the state remaining, in the mean time, exposed to all the dangers of invasions from without and convulsions within.

He has endeavored to prevent the population of these states; for that purpose obstructing the laws for naturalization of foreigners; refusing to pass others to encourage their migration hither, and raising the conditions of new appropriations of lands.

He has obstructed the administration of justice, by refusing his assent to laws for establishing judiciary powers.

He has made judges dependent on his will alone, for the tenure of their offices, and the amount and payment of their salaries.

He has erected a multitude of new offices, and set hither swarms of officers to harass our people and eat out their substance.

He has kept among us, in times of peace, standing armies, without the consent of our legislatures.

He has affected to render the military independent of, and superior to, the civil power.

He has combined with others to subject us to a jurisdiction foreign to our constitution and unacknowledged by our laws, giving his assent to their acts of pretended legislation:

For quartering large bodies of armed troops among us;

For protecting them, by a mock trial, from punishment for any murders which they should commit on the inhabitants of these states;

For cutting off trade with all parts of the world;

For imposing taxes on us without our consent;

For depriving us, in many cases, of the benefits of trial by jury;

For transporting us beyond seas, to be tried for pretended offenses;

For abolishing the free system of English laws in a neighboring province, establishing therein an arbitrary government, and enlarging its boundaries, so as to render it at once an example and fit instrument for introducing the same absolute rule into these colonies;

For taking away our charters, abolishing our most valuable laws, and altering fundamentally the forms of our governments;

For suspending our own legislatures, and declaring themselves invested with power to legislate for us in all cases whatsoever.

He has abdicated government here, by declaring us out of his protection and waging war against us.

He has plundered our seas, ravaged our coasts, burned our towns, and destroyed the lives of our people.

He is at this time transporting large armies of foreign mercenaries to complete the works of death, desolation, and tyranny already begun with circumstances of cruelty and perfidy scarcely paralleled in the most barbarous ages, and totally unworthy the head of a civilized nation.

He has constrained our fellow-citizens, taken captive on the high seas, to bear arms against their country, to become the executioners of their friends and brethren, or to fall themselves by their hands.

He has excited domestic insurrections among us, and has endeavored to bring on the inhabitants of our frontiers the merciless Indian savages, whose known rule of warfare is undistinguished destruction of all ages, sexes, and conditions.

In every stage of these oppressions we have petitioned for redress in the most humble terms; our repeated petitions have been answered only by repeated injury. A prince, whose character is thus marked by every act which may define a tyrant, is unfit to be the ruler of a free people.

Nor have we been wanting in our attentions to our British brethren. We have warned them, from time to time, of attempts by their legislature to extend an unwarrantable jurisdiction over us. We have reminded them of the circumstances of our emigration and settlement here. We have appealed to their native justice and magnanimity; and we have conjured them, by the ties of our common kindred, to disavow these usurpations, which would inevitably interrupt our connections and correspondence. They, too, have been deaf to the voice of justice and of consanguinity. We must, therefore, acquiesce in the necessity which denounces our separation, and hold them, as we hold the rest of mankind, enemies in war, in peace friends.

We, therefore, the representatives of the United States of America, in General Congress assembled, appealing to the Supreme Judge of the world for the rectitude of our intentions, do, in the name and by the authority of the good people of these colonies, solemnly publish and declare, that these United Colonies are, and of right ought to be, FREE AND INDEPENDENT STATES; that they are absolved from all allegiance to the British crown, and that all political connection between them and the state of Great Britain is, and ought to be, totally dissolved; and that, as free and independent states, they have full power to levy war, conclude peace, contract alliances, establish commerce, and do all other acts and things which independent states may of right do. And for the support of this declaration, with a firm reliance on the protection of Divine Providence, we mutually pledge to each other our lives, our fortunes, and our sacred honor.

John Hancock [*President*]
[*and fifty-five others*]

INDEX